ACCA

Strategic Professional

Advanced Audit and Assurance – UK (AAA – UK)

Practice & Revision Kit

For exams in September 2023, December 2023, March 2024 and June 2024

BPP

Seventeenth edition 2023 (v1.1)

ISBN 9781 0355 0127 4

(Previous ISBN 9781 5097 4414 5)

eISBN 9781 0355 0080 2

Cataloguing-in-Publication Data

A catalogue record for this book is available from the British Library

Published by

BPP Learning Media Ltd

BPP House, Aldine Place

London W12 8AA

learningmedia.bpp.com

Printed in the United Kingdom

We are grateful to the Association of Chartered Certified Accountants for permission to reproduce past examination questions. The suggested solutions in the practice answer bank have been prepared by BPP Learning Media Ltd, except where otherwise stated.

BPP Learning Media is grateful to the IASB for permission to reproduce extracts from IFRS® Standards, IAS® Standards, SIC and IFRIC. This publication contains copyright © material and trademarks of the IFRS Foundation®. All rights reserved. Used under license from the IFRS Foundation®. Reproduction and use rights are strictly limited. For more information about the IFRS Foundation and rights to use its material please visit www.IFRS.org.

A note about copyright

Dear Customer

What does the little © mean and why does it matter?

Your market-leading BPP books, course materials and e-learning materials do not write and update themselves. People write them on their own behalf or as employees of an organisation that invests in this activity. Copyright law protects their livelihoods. It does so by creating rights over the use of the content.

Breach of copyright is a form of theft – as well as being a criminal offence in some jurisdictions, it is potentially a serious breach of professional ethics.

With current technology, things might seem a bit hazy but, basically, without the express permission of BPP Learning Media:

- Photocopying our materials is a breach of copyright
- Printing our digital materials in order to share them with or forward them to a third party or use them in any way other than in connection with your BPP studies is a breach of copyright

You can, of course, sell your books, in the form in which you have bought them – once you have finished with them. (Is this fair to your fellow students? We update for a reason.) Please note the e-products are sold on a single user licence basis: we do not supply 'unlock' codes to people who have bought them secondhand.

And what about outside the UK? BPP Learning Media strives to make our materials available at prices students can afford by local printing arrangements, pricing policies and partnerships which are clearly listed on our website. A tiny minority ignore this and indulge in criminal activity by illegally photocopying our material or supporting organisations that do. If they act illegally and unethically in one area, can you really trust them?

IFRS

Contents

Question index

The headings in this checklist/index indicate the main topics of questions, but questions are expected to cover several different topics.

Questions set under the previous syllabus, P7, are included because their style and content are very similar to that of the current AAA exam. The questions have been amended to reflect the current exam.

Since September 2015 there have been four exam sittings per year, but ACCA only publish two exams' worth of questions per year. These releases are compiled from questions selected from the preceding sessions. These compilation exams are denoted as 'Mar/Jun' and 'Sept/Dec' in the index below.

	Marks	Time allocation (mins)	Page number	
			Questions	Answers
22 Adder (P7 June 2015 amended)	25	49	34	259
23 Beth & Co (Mar/Jun 2021 amended)	25	49	35	265
24 York (P7 Mar/Jun 2016 amended)	25	49	36	272
25 Mondrian (P7 Sep/Dec 2015 amended)	50	98	37	276
26 Zed (P7 Sep/Dec 2016 amended)	50	98	39	285
27 Redback (December 2018 amended)	50	98	42	294
28 Margot (Mar/Jun 2019 amended)	50	98	47	305
29 Pale Ltd (Mar/Jun 2021 amended)	50	98	51	315
30 Grohl (P7 December 2012 amended)	50	98	55	324
31 Eagle (September 18 amended)	50	98	58	333
32 Ryder (Sep/Dec 2019 amended)	50	98	63	344
33 Sunshine (P7 Sep/Dec 2017 amended)	50	98	67	356
34 Laurel (P7 Mar/Jun 2017 amended)	50	98	69	365
35 McClane & Co (Sep/Dec 2021)	50	98	72	376
36 Awdry (Mar/Jun 2019 amended)	25	49	75	388
37 Willow (P7 December 2011 amended)	25	49	77	395
38 Jovi (P7 December 2012 amended)	25	49	79	398
39 Jolie (P7 December 2010 amended)	50	98	82	401
40 Vancouver (P7 Mar/Jun 16 amended)	50	98	85	410
41 Adams (ACCA 2018 Specimen amended)	50	98	88	418
42 Robster (P7 June 2009 amended)	25	49	92	429
43 Connolly (P7 December 2014 amended)	50	98	93	434
44 Osier (P7 Mar/Jun 2017 amended)	25	49	95	444
45 Macau (P7 Mar/Jun 2016 amended)	25	49	96	451
46 Northwest (P7 Sep/Dec 2016 amended)	25	49	98	456
Part E: Completion, review and reporting				
47 Rope (P7 Sep/Dec 2016 amended)	25	49	100	461
48 Kandinsky (P7 Sep/Dec 15 amended)	25	49	101	466
49 Kelly & Co (Sep/Dec 2021)	25	49	103	470
50 Yew (P7 December 2011 amended)	25	49	105	478
51 Fern (P7 Mar/Jun 2017 amended)	25	49	106	482
52 Boston (P7 Mar/Jun 2016 amended)	25	49	107	486
53 Coram (September 2018 amended)	25	49	109	493

Topic index

Listed below are the key AAA syllabus topics and the numbers of the questions in this Kit covering those topics. We have also included a reference to the relevant Chapter of the BPP AAA Workbook, the companion to the BPP AAA Practice and Revision Kit, in case you wish to revise the information on the topic you have covered.

If you need to concentrate your practice and revision on certain topics or if you want to attempt all available questions that refer to a particular subject, you will find this index useful.

Syllabus topic		Question numbers	Workbook chapter
A1:	International regulatory frameworks for audit and assurance services	26	1
A2:	Money laundering	1(a), 4(c), 7(a), 11(a)	1
A3:	Laws and regulations	22(b), 28(d)	1
B1:	Code of Ethics and Conduct	1(b), 2(b), 3, 4(b), 5, 6, 7(a), 8(b), 9, 10(a), 11(b), 12(b), 15(a)–(b), 21(d), 26(d), 27(d), 29(d), 30(a), 31(d), 32(d), 33(d), 35(d), 39(d), 40(d), 43(e), 46(b)–(c), 47(b), 51(a), 53(b), 60(b), 61(d), 63(a)-(b), 69(c)	2
B2:	Fraud and error	24(a), 25(a), 27(e), 69(b)	3
B3:	Professional liability	13(a)	4
C1:	Quality management (firm-wide)	9, 10(b), 12(a), 23(a), 45(a), 54	4
C2:	Advertising, tendering and obtaining professional work and fees	7(a), 17(a), 39(d), 66(a)	5
C3:	Professional appointments	2(a)–(b), 15(a)–(b), 34(d), 49(a)	5
D1:	Planning, materiality and assessing the risk of material misstatement	7(a), 17(b)–(c), 21(b), 25(a), 26(a)–(b), 27(a)–(b), 28(a), 29(a)-(b), 30(a), 31(a)&(c), 32(a), 34(a)–(c), 35(a)-(b), 39(a)–(b), 40(b), 41(a), 43(a)–(c)	6
D2:	Evidence and testing considerations	26(c), 34(a), 40(a), 60(a)	7
D3:	Audit procedures and obtaining evidence	7(b), 13(b), 17(b)&(d), 19, 21(a), 22(a), 25(b), 27(c), 28(b), 29(c), 30(b), 31(b), 32(b)-(c), 33(d), 34(e), 35(c), 36(b), 37(a), 39(c), 41(b), 42(a), 43(d), 44(a), 51(b), 53(a), 60(b), 64(b)–(c)	8
D4:	Using the work of others	20(a), 28(c)	7
D5:	Group audits	18, 21(a), 32(b), 34(c), 40(c), 47, 54, 61(b)	9
E1:	Subsequent events and going concern	18(b), 47(b), 48(a), 50(a), 52(a), 58(a), 59, 65(c)	10
E2:	Completion and final review	12(b), 21(c), 23(a), 24(b), 37,	10

Syllabus topic		Question numbers	Workbook chapter
		38(a), 45, 46(c), 50(b)–(c), 53(a), 58, 61(c), 70(b)	
E3:	Auditor's reports	1(c), 14(c), 23(b), 47(c), 51(c), 52(c), 53(a), 55(b), 56(c), 57(a), 58(b), 59(c), 60(c), 61(a)–(c), 62(a), 63(c), 64(b)	11
E4:	Reports to those charged with governance and management	37(b), 52(b), 62(b)	11
F1:	Audit-related and assurance services	7(b), 8(a)	12
F2:	Specific assignments	35(d), 49, 65, 66, 67, 68(a)–(b), 69, 71(a)	12, 13, 14
F3:	The audit of social, environmental and integrated reporting	6(c), 20(c), 29(d), 41(c), 44(b), 56(a)–(b)	15
F4:	Auditing aspects of insolvency (and similar procedures)	48(b), 70, 71(b)	15
F5:	Reporting on other assignments	64(a), 68(c)	12
G1:	Professional and ethical developments	4(a), 36(a), 50(a)	1, 2
G2:	Other current issues	38(b), 57(b)	16

The exam

Computer-based exams

Strategic Professional exams are all computer-based exams (CBE).

CBE practice platform

Practising as many exam-style questions as possible in the ACCA CBE practice platform will be the key to passing this exam. You must do questions under timed conditions and ensure you produce full answers to the discussion parts as well as doing the calculations.

Also ensure that you attempt all mock exams under exam conditions.

ACCA have launched a free on-demand resource designed to mirror the live exam experience helping you to become more familiar with the exam format. You can access the platform via the Study Support Resources section of the ACCA website navigating to the CBE question practice section and logging in with your myACCA credentials.

Approach to examining the syllabus

If you are preparing to sit AAA you should pay particular attention to the following in order to maximise your chances of success. The following is taken from a recent AAA examining team's report.

> 'In order to pass this exam, candidates are required to **apply the principles and rules** from their earlier studies to more complex scenarios and demonstrate their ability to handle different situations which may arise in audit and related services. In addition, candidates are expected to develop **a broader knowledge of audit services** and practice management. Candidates should also keep abreast of **current developments** and challenges in the field of both auditing and financial reporting to allow them to demonstrate the ability to handle these challenges in the context of auditing financial statements and as areas they may need to brief clients on.

'This **combination of learned knowledge and its application** to complex situations requires candidates to be able to go beyond the topics as covered in text books and be able to react to the scenarios described in the requirement. Study through question practice and following developments in the field through the media, and through IFAC and IAASB will be crucial in taking the learned knowledge from earlier parts of the qualification and converting it into a demonstrable ability to provide audit and advisory services to clients.

'AAA also tests candidates' **ability to tailor their answer to the context in which the requirement is written.** Often the audience of the requirement will dictate the pitch and depth of the answer along with its focus. Failure to take into account such matters will often lead to **time pressures** in the exam as candidates lose time by detailing knowledge that is not relevant to the requirement. This is particularly noticeable in question 1 which is set at the planning stage of an audit and is addressed to the senior members of the audit team, meaning an explanation of the audit risk model is not appropriate. Candidates should allow themselves time to focus on the requirement that is set before they begin their answers. **It would be useful for candidates to visualise delivering the requirement verbally to the report recipient and therefore imagining how a partner in a firm, already qualified and experienced, would react to listening to the answer.'**

Format of the exam

		Number of marks
Section A	One compulsory question	50
Section B	Two compulsory questions (25 marks each)	50
		100

The **time allowed** for this exam is 3 hours and 15 minutes. The pass mark is 50%.

The examination is constructed in two sections. Questions in both sections will be largely discursive. However, candidates will be expected, for example, to be able to assess materiality and calculate relevant ratios where appropriate.

Question format

The format of questions in AAA is slightly different between Section A and Section B. Section A questions will feature scenarios, with simple requirements such as 'Respond to the partner's request', or 'Draft the briefing notes as requested'. You will have to work out for yourself what you need to include in your answer. Section B questions will feature requirements akin to those in your previous ACCA exams.

AAA UK stream papers will from September 2019 onwards feature the same split of marks in Question 1 as the International steam. (In the past the UK exams did not show the split of marks between each part.)

For sittings from September 2019 onwards, all questions have been set as at the fictitious date of 1 July 20X5.

As AAA is a Strategic Professional exam, **10 professional level marks** will be awarded in Question One, and **5** each in Questions Two and Three. Some of these should be easy to obtain. The examining team has stated that marks may be available for presenting your answer in the form of a letter, presentation, email, report or briefing notes. You may also be able to obtain marks for the style and layout of your answer.

Reports should always have an appropriate title. They should be **formally written**, with an **introductory paragraph** setting out the aims of the report. You should use **short paragraphs** and **appropriate headings**, with a summary of findings as a **conclusion**.

Memoranda and **Briefing notes** should have the following four things at the beginning:

From: Name of author

To: Name of recipient

Date: 1 July 20X5

Subject: ....

Letters should be addressed appropriately to the correct person and be dated. They should have a short introductory paragraph, a conclusion and should be in a formal writing style. Letters beginning with 'Dear Sir/Madam' should end with 'Yours faithfully'.

Remote invigilated exams

In certain geographical areas it may be possible for you to take your exam remotely. This option, which is subject to strict conditions, can offer increased flexibility and convenience under certain circumstances. Further guidance, including the detailed requirements and conditions for taking the exam by this method, is contained on ACCA's website at https://www.accaglobal.com/an/en/student/exam-entry-and-administration/about-our-exams/remote-exams/remote-session-exams.html.

Analysis of past exams

The table below provides details of when each element of the syllabus has been examined in the ten most recent sittings and the question number and section in which each element was examined. We have also included a reference to the relevant Chapter of the BPP AAA Workbook, the companion to the BPP AAA Practice and Revision Kit, in case you need to revise the information on the topic covered.

Since September 2015, ACCA has been issuing two exams each year, after the December and June exam sessions. These exams are compiled from questions selected from the two preceding sessions eg in December 2019, the sample questions were compiled from September 2019 and December 2019 exams. The ACCA also released individual exams for September and December 2018.

A specimen exam was also issued for the change in question format for 2018/19, but this has not been included in the analysis below.

Workbook chapter		Sept 2022	Mar/Jun 2022	Sep/Dec 2021	Mar/Jun 2021	Sep/Dec 2020	March 2020	Sep/Dec 2019	Mar/Jun 2019	Dec 2018	Sept 2018
	REGULATORY ENVIRONMENT										
1	International regulatory frameworks for audit and assurance services										
1	Money laundering		1(c)							3(a)	
1	Laws and regulations	1(d)									
	PROFESSIONAL AND ETHICAL CONSIDERATIONS										
2	Code of Ethics and Conduct		2(b)	1(d)	1(d)	1(c)	3(b)		1(d)	3(b)	1(d), 2(b), 3(a)
3	Fraud and error						2(a)			1	

Workbook chapter		Sept 2022	Mar/Jun 2022	Sep/Dec 2021	Mar/Jun 2021	Sep/Dec 2020	March 2020	Sep/Dec 2019	Mar/Jun 2019	Dec 2018	Sept 2018
3	Professional liability										
	QUALITY MANAGEMENT AND PRACTICE MANAGEMENT										
4	Quality management	2			2, 3(a)	2(a)					
5	Advertising, tendering and obtaining professional work and fees					2(b)					
5	Professional appointments		1(d)				3(a)			1	
	ASSIGNMENTS										
6, 7, 8	The audit of historical financial information including: Planning, materiality and assessing the risk of misstatement Evidence	1(a), 1(b), 1(c)	1, 2	1	1	1	1, 2		1, 3	1	1
9	Group audits						1				
	COMPLETION, REVIEW AND REPORTING										
10	Completion		3(a)	3	3(a)	3				2(a)-(b)	2(a)
11	Auditor's reports	3(c)	3(b)	3(b)	3(b)	3	2(b)		2(a)	2(c)	2(a)
11	Communications to management								2(b)		
11	Other reports										
	OTHER ASSIGNMENTS										
12	Audit-related services									1(e)	
12	Assurance services										
13	Prospective financial information	3(a), 3(b)		2			3(a)				3(a)
14	Forensic audits							3(a) –(b)			
15	Social and environmental					1(c)					

Workbook chapter		Sept 2022	Mar/Jun 2022	Sep/Dec 2021	Mar/Jun 2021	Sep/Dec 2020	March 2020	Sep/Dec 2019	Mar/Jun 2019	Dec 2018	Sept 2018
	auditing										
15	Insolvency						3(b)				3(b)
	CURRENT ISSUES AND DEVELOPMENTS										
1, 2, 3	Professional and ethical developments						1(c)				
16	Other current issues					1(d)			3(a)		

IMPORTANT!

The table above gives a broad idea of how frequently major topics in the syllabus are examined. It should **not be used to question spot** and predict for example that Topic X will not be examined because it came up two sittings ago. The examining team's reports indicate that the examining team is well aware some students try to question spot. The examining team avoids predictable patterns and may, for example, examine the same topic two sittings in a row.

Syllabus and Study Guide

The complete AAA syllabus and study guide can be found by visiting the exam resource finder on the ACCA website.

Examinable documents

Knowledge of new examinable regulations issued by 31 August will be examinable in examination sessions being held in the following exam year. Documents may be examinable even if the effective date is in the future. This means that all regulations issued by 31 August 2022 will be examinable in the September 2023 to June 2024 examinations.

Accounting Standards

The accounting knowledge that is assumed for AAA is the same as that examined in Strategic Business Reporting (SBR). Therefore, candidates studying for AAA should refer to the Accounting Standards listed under SBR.

Note. AAA will only expect knowledge of accounting standards and financial reporting standards from SBR. Knowledge of exposure drafts and discussion papers will not be expected.

	International Standards on Auditing (ISAs) (UK)
	Glossary of terms (ethics and auditing) December 2019
	Scope and Authority of Audit and Assurance pronouncements
ISA 200	Overall Objectives of the Independent Auditor and the Conduct of an Audit in Accordance with ISAs (UK) (Updated January 2020)
ISA 210	Agreeing the Terms of Audit Engagements (Revised June 2016) (Updated July 2017)
ISA 220	Quality Management for an Audit of Financial Statements (Revised July

	International Standards on Auditing (ISAs) (UK)
	2021)
ISA 230	Audit Documentation (Updated January 2020)
ISA 240	The Auditor's Responsibilities Relating to Fraud in an Audit of Financial Statements (Revised May 2021)
ISA 250A	Consideration of Laws and Regulations in an Audit of Financial Statements (Revised November 2019)
ISA 260	Communication With Those Charged With Governance (Updated January 2020)
ISA 265	Communicating Deficiencies in Internal Control to Those Charged With Governance and Management
ISA 300	Planning an Audit of Financial Statements (Revised June 2016)
ISA 315	Identifying and Assessing the Risks of Material Misstatement (Revised July 2020)
ISA 320	Materiality in Planning and Performing an Audit (Revised June 2016)
ISA 330	The Auditor's Responses to Assessed Risks (Revised July 2017)
ISA 402	Audit Considerations Relating to an Entity Using a Service Organisation
ISA 450	Evaluation of Misstatements Identified During the Audit (Revised June 2016) (Updated July 2017)
ISA 500	Audit Evidence (Updated January 2020)
ISA 501	Audit Evidence – Specific Considerations for Selected Items
ISA 505	External Confirmations (Updated July 2017)
ISA 510	Initial Audit Engagements – Opening Balances (Revised June 2016)
ISA 520	Analytical Procedures
ISA 530	Audit Sampling
ISA 540	Auditing Accounting Estimates and Related Disclosures (Revised December 2018)
ISA 550	Related Parties
ISA 560	Subsequent Events
ISA 570	Going Concern (Revised September 2019)
ISA 580	Written Representations (Updated January 2020)
ISA 600 (Revised September 2022)	Special Considerations - Audits of Group Financial Statements (Including the Work of Component Auditors)
ISA 610	Using the Work of Internal Auditors (Revised June 2013)
ISA 620	Using the Work of an Auditor's Expert (Revised November 2019)
ISA 700	Forming an Opinion and Reporting on Financial Statements (Revised

	International Standards on Auditing (ISAs) (UK)
	January 2020)
ISA 701	Communicating Key Audit Matters in the Independent Auditors Report (Revised January 2020)
ISA 705	Modifications to the Opinion in the Independent Auditor's Report (Revised June 2016)
ISA 706	Emphasis of Matter Paragraphs and Other Matter Paragraphs in the Independent Auditor's Report (Revised June 2016)
ISA 710	Comparative Information – Corresponding Figures and Comparative Financial Statements
ISA 720	The Auditor's Responsibilities Relating to Other Information (Revised November 2019)

	International Standards on Quality Management (ISQM)
ISQM (UK) 1	Quality Management for Firms that Perform Audits or Reviews of Financial Statements, or Other Assurance or Related Services Engagements (Revised July 2021)
ISQM (UK) 2	Engagement quality reviews (Revised July 2021)
	Conforming and consequential amendments to the IAASB's other standards as a result of the new and revised quality management standards (January 2022)

	International Standards on Assurance Engagements (ISAEs)
ISAE (UK) 3000	Assurance Engagements other than Audits or Reviews of Historical Financial Information (July 2020)
	IAASB Non-authoritative guidance on applying ISAE 3000 (Revised) to extended external reporting assurance engagements (April 2021)
ISAE 3400	IAASB: the Examination of Prospective Financial Information

	Practice Notes (PNs)
PN 23	Special considerations in Auditing Financial Instruments

	Ethical Standards (ESs)
ES	Revised Ethical Standard December 2019

	Bulletins
2009/4	Developments in corporate governance affecting the responsibilities of auditors of UK companies
2010/1	XBRL tagging of information in audited financial statements – guidance for auditors
Bulletin	Illustrative Auditor's Reports on United Kingdom Private Sector Financial Statements (August 2021)

	Statement of Standards for Reporting Accountants (SSRAs)
ISRE (UK) 2410	Review of Interim Financial Information Performed by the Independent Auditor of the Entity (Revised May 2021)

	Exposure Drafts (EDs)
	FRC – Proposed International Standard on Auditing (ISA) (UK) 600 (Revised), Special Considerations – Audits of Group Financial Statements (Including the Work of Component Auditors)

	Other Documents – Ethical guidelines
	ACCA's Code of Ethics and Conduct (January 2022)
	IESBA's International Code of Ethics for Professional Accountants (Revised 2021)

	Other Documents – Ethical guidelines
	IESBA – Quality Management Related Conforming Amendments to the Code (April 2022)
	IESBA – Revisions to the definitions of listed entity and public interest entity in the Code (April 2022)

	Other Documents – ACCA
	ACCA's Anti-money Laundering Guidance for the Accountancy Profession

	Other Documents – FRC
	The UK Corporate Governance Code (Revised July 2018)
	FRC Guidance on Audit Committees (Revised April 2016)
	FRC Audit Quality – Practice aid for audit committees (December 2019)
	Audit Quality Thematic Review – The Use of Technology on the Audit of Financial Statements (March 2020)
	Audit Quality Thematic Review – Other Information in the Annual Report (December 2018)
	FRC Staff Guidance: Auditor responsibilities under ISA (UK) 720 in respect of climate related reporting by companies required by the Financial Conduct Authority (2022)
	FRC Climate Thematic: Audit (November 2020)
	Extended auditor's reports – a further review of experience (January 2016)
	FRC Professional Judgement Guidance (June 2022)

	Other Documents – IAASB
	IAASB Discussion Paper: Fraud and Going Concern in an Audit of Financial Statements (October 2020)
	IAASB Towards Enhanced Professional Skepticism (August 2017)

	Other Documents – IAASB
	IAASB Frequently Asked Questions: Reporting Going Concern Matters in the Auditors Report (August 2022)
	IAASB Auditor Considerations Regarding Significant Unusual or Highly Complex Transactions (September 2010)
	IAASB The consideration of climate-related risks in an audit of Financial Statements (October 2020)
	Integrated Reporting Working Group: Supporting Credibility and Trust in Emerging Forms of External Reporting: Ten Key Challenges for Assurance Engagements (January 2018)

	Other Documents – Technology
	IAASB Exploring the Increasing Use of Technology in the Audit with a Focus on Data Analytics (September 2016)
	IAASB Feedback Statement – Exploring the Growing Use of Technology in the Audit with a Focus on Data Analytics (January 2018)
	IAASB Support Material: Using Automated Tools and Techniques when Identifying Risks of Material Misstatement in Accordance with ISA 315 (Revised) (November 2020)
	IAASB Support Material: Using Automated Tools and Techniques in Performing Audit Procedures (September 2020)
	IAASB Addressing risk of overreliance on technology arising from the use of automated tools and techniques and from information produced by an entity's system (March 2021)
	IAASB Feedback Statement – Exploring the Growing Use of Technology in the Audit of with a Focus on Data Analytics
	IAASB Support Material Related to Technology: Audit Documentation when using Automated Tools and Techniques (April 2020)

Note. Topics of exposure drafts are examinable to the extent that relevant articles about them are published in *Student Accountant.*

Helping you with your revision

BPP Learning Media – ACCA Approved Content Provider

As an ACCA **Approved Content Provider**, BPP Learning Media gives you the **opportunity** to use revision materials reviewed by the ACCA examining team. By incorporating the ACCA examining team's comments and suggestions regarding the depth and breadth of syllabus coverage, the BPP Learning Media Practice & Revision Kit provides excellent, **ACCA-approved** support for your revision.

These materials are reviewed by the ACCA examining team. The objective of the review is to ensure that the material properly covers the syllabus and study guide outcomes, used by the examining team in setting the exams, in the appropriate breadth and depth. The review does not ensure that every eventuality, combination or application of examinable topics is addressed by the ACCA Approved Content. Nor does the review comprise a detailed technical check of the content as the Approved Content Provider has its own quality assurance processes in place in this respect.

BPP Learning Media do everything possible to ensure the material is accurate and up to date when sending to print. In the event that any errors are found after the print date, they are uploaded to the following website: https://learningmedia.bpp.com/catalog?pagename=Errata.

The structure of this Practice & Revision Kit

This Practice & Revision Kit is divided into sections which correspond to the different parts of the AAA syllabus. There are also four mock exams which provide sufficient **opportunity to refine your knowledge and skills as part of your final exam preparations.**

Question practice

This is the most important thing to do if you want to get through. Many of the most up-to-date exam questions are in this Kit. Practice doing them under timed conditions, then go through the answers and go back to the Workbook for any topic you are really having trouble with. Come back to a question a week later and try it again – you will be surprised at how much better you are getting. Be very ruthless with yourself at this stage – you have to do the question in the time, without looking at the answer. This will really sharpen your wits and make the exam experience less worrying. Just keep doing this and you will get better at doing questions and you will really find out what you know and what you don't know.

Sitting this exam as a computer-based exam and practicing as many exam-style questions as possible in the ACCA CBE practice platform will be the key to passing this exam. You should attempt questions under timed conditions and ensure you produce full answers to the discussion parts as well as doing the calculations. Also ensure that you attempt all mock exams under exam conditions.

ACCA have launched a free on-demand resource designed to mirror the live exam experience helping you to become more familiar with the exam format. You can access the platform via the Study Support Resources section of the ACCA website navigating to the CBE question practice section and logging in with your myACCA credentials.

Selecting questions

To help you plan your revision, we have provided a full **topic index** which maps the questions to topics in the syllabus (see p viii).

Making the most of question practice

At BPP Learning Media we realise that you need more than just questions and model answers to get the most from your question practice.

- Our **Top tips**, included for certain questions, provide essential advice on tackling questions, presenting answers and the key points that answers need to include.
- We show you how you can pick up **Easy marks** on some questions, as we know that picking up all readily available marks often can make the difference between passing and failing.
- We include **marking guides** to show you what the examining team rewards.
- We include comments from the examining team to show you where students struggled or performed well in the actual exam.
- We refer to the 2023 BPP Workbook (for exams in September 2023, December 2023, March 2024 and June 2024) for detailed coverage of the topics covered in questions.

Attempting mock exams

This Kit has four mock exams, including the ACCA Specimen Exam, which provide practice at coping with the pressures of the exam day. We strongly recommend that you attempt them under exam conditions. All the mock exams reflect the question styles and syllabus coverage of the exam.

Topics to revise

The examination is constructed in two sections. Questions in both sections will be largely discursive. However, candidates will be expected, for example, to be able to assess materiality and calculate relevant ratios where appropriate.

Section A will comprise a Case Study, worth 50 marks, set at the planning stage of the audit, for a single company, a group of companies or potentially several audit clients. Candidates will be provided with detailed information, which will vary between examinations, but is likely to include extracts of financial information, strategic, operational and other relevant financial information for a client business, as well as extracts from audit working papers, including results of analytical procedures. The 50 marks will comprise of 40 technical marks and 10 professionals skills marks. All professional skills with be examined in Section A.

Candidates will be required to address a range of requirements, predominantly from syllabus sections A, B, C and D, thereby tackling a real-world situation where candidates may have to address a range of issues simultaneously in relation to planning, risk assessment, evidence gathering and ethical and professional considerations. Please note that other syllabus areas, excluding E, may also be drawn on as part of the Case Study. Section B will contain two compulsory 25-mark questions, with each being predominately based around a short scenario which may relate to more than one client. The 25 marks will comprise of 20 technical marks and 5 professional skills marks. Section B questions will examine a combination of professional skills appropriate to the question. Each question will examine a minimum to two professional skills from analysis and evaluation, professional scepticism and judgement and commerical acumen.

One question will always predominantly come from syllabus section E, and consequently candidates should be prepared to answer a question relating to completion, review and reporting. There are a number of formats this question could adopt, including, but not limited to, requiring candidates to assess going concern, the impact of subsequent events, evaluating identified misstatements and the corresponding effect on the auditor's report. Candidates may also be asked to critique an auditor's report or evaluate the matters to be included in a report which is to be provided to management or those charged with governance.

The other Section B question can be drawn from any other syllabus section, including A, B, C, D and F.

Quality management and ethics. The auditor's assessment of effective quality management procedures and consideration of ethical issues are fundamental to all stages of the audit and therefore these concepts could be examined in any section of the exam.

Current issues. Syllabus Section G on current issues may be examined in Section A or B as appropriate. Current issues is unlikely to form the basis of any question on its own but instead will be incorporated into the Case Study or either of the Section B questions dependent on question content and the topical issues affecting the profession at the time of writing.

We **strongly advise** that you do not selectively revise certain topics – there are no optional questions for AAA, so there is nowhere to hide if a difficult topic is examined. Selective revision will limit the number of questions you can answer and hence reduce your chances of passing.

Essential skills areas

There are three areas you should develop in order to achieve exam success in Advanced Audit and Assurance (AAA). These are:

(a) Knowledge application

(b) Professional skills

(c) Exam success skills

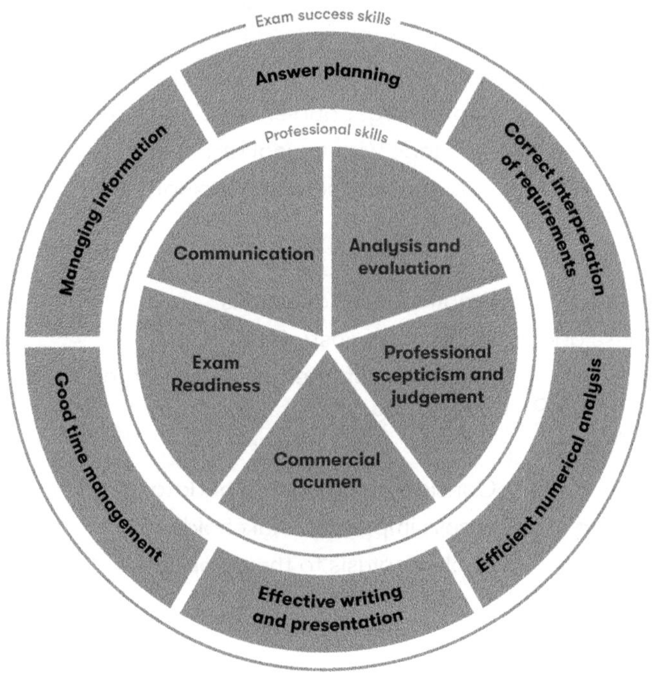

Professional skills

From the September 2022 exam onwards, 20 marks will be available for demonstrating 'professional skills' that would be expected from a proficient senior financial professional.

There are four professional skills, which are introduced gradually in a series of skills checkpoints. The fifth skills checkpoint will bring these professional and exam success skills together and consider them in the context of the CBE where you can also demonstrate employability and technology skills.

The four professional skills are:

(a) Analysis and evaluation

(b) Communication

(c) Professional scepticism and judgement

(d) Commercial acumen

In section A of the exam, which is a single 50-mark case study, 10 of the 50 marks will be allocated to demonstrating professional skills. All of the professional skills will be examined in Section A.

Section B will consist of two compulsory scenario-based 25-mark questions. Each section B question will allocate five marks to professional skills, so 10 marks in total will be available for professional skills marks in Section B.

Each question will contain a minimum of two professional skills: Analysis and evaluation plus Professional scepticism and judgement and/or Commercial acumen. Professional skills will apply to the whole question and not any of the individual requirements. Just like the technical marks available for each question, you can also expect a certain amount of headroom in the marking scheme for the demonstration of professional skills. In Section A, Question 1 will include 10 professional skills marks, but the mark scheme will have up to 14 marks available for demonstrating professional skill in all four categories, although the weighting of marks across each skill will not always be the same. Each Section B question worth 25 marks will have up to seven professional skills marks available, this time split across two or three of the professional skills, depending on the question, and will be capped at five marks in line with the requirement.

The following table introduces these skills briefly with some examples of each:

ACCA professional skill: Definition	Three aspects of each professional skill
Communication To express yourself clearly, concisely and convincingly through an appropriate medium, while being sensitive to the needs of the intended audience.	Inform target audience using clear format Persuade with logical argument Appropriate use of technology
Commercial acumen To show awareness of the wider business and external factors affecting business and use commercially sound judgement and insight to resolve issues and exploit opportunities.	Practical considerations Recognise constraints Awareness of alternative opportunities to those suggested
Analysis and evaluation To appraise information objectively and to draw logical conclusions from both quantitative and qualitative information, recognising the impact on relevant stakeholders and prioritising issues appropriately.	Consider the meaning of data Assess impact on stakeholders Apply analysis to the company in the question
Professional scepticism and judgement To probe, question and challenge information and views presented to you, in order to fully understand business issues, establish facts objectively and reach appropriate conclusions, based on ethical values and professional standards.	Question the validity of approaches Challenge opinions Make informed decisions in the context of the engagement

Exam success skills

Passing the AAA exam requires more than applying syllabus knowledge and demonstrating the specific AAA skills; it also requires the development of excellent exam technique through question practice.

We consider the following six skills to be vital for exam success. These skills were introduced in the BPP Workbook, and you can revisit the Skills Checkpoints in the BPP Workbook for tutorial guidance of how to apply each of the six Exam success skills in your question practice and in the exam.

Aim to consider your performance in all six Exam success skills during your revision stage question practice and reflect on your particular strengths and weaker areas which you can then work on.

Exam success skill 1

Managing information

Questions in the exam will present you with a lot of information. The skill is how you handle this information to make the best use of your time. The key is determining how you will approach the exam and then actively reading the questions.

Advice on developing managing information

Approach

The exam is 3 hours 15 minutes long. There is no designated 'reading' time at the start of the exam, however, one approach that can work well is to start the exam by spending 10–15 minutes carefully reading through all of the questions to familiarise yourself with the exam.

Once you feel familiar with the exam consider the order in which you will attempt the questions; always attempt them in your order of preference. For example, you may want to leave to last the question you consider to be the most difficult.

If you do take this approach, remember to adjust the time available for each question appropriately – see Exam success skill 6: Good time management.

If you find that this approach doesn't work for you, don't worry – you can develop your own technique.

Active reading

You must take an active approach to reading each question. Focus on the requirement first, underlining key verbs such as 'prepare', 'comment', 'explain', 'discuss', to ensure you answer the question properly. Then read the rest of the question, underlining and annotating important and relevant information, and making notes of any relevant technical information you think you will need.

The CBE

At first glance, the CBE is quite daunting as the screenshot of the workspace below illustrates:

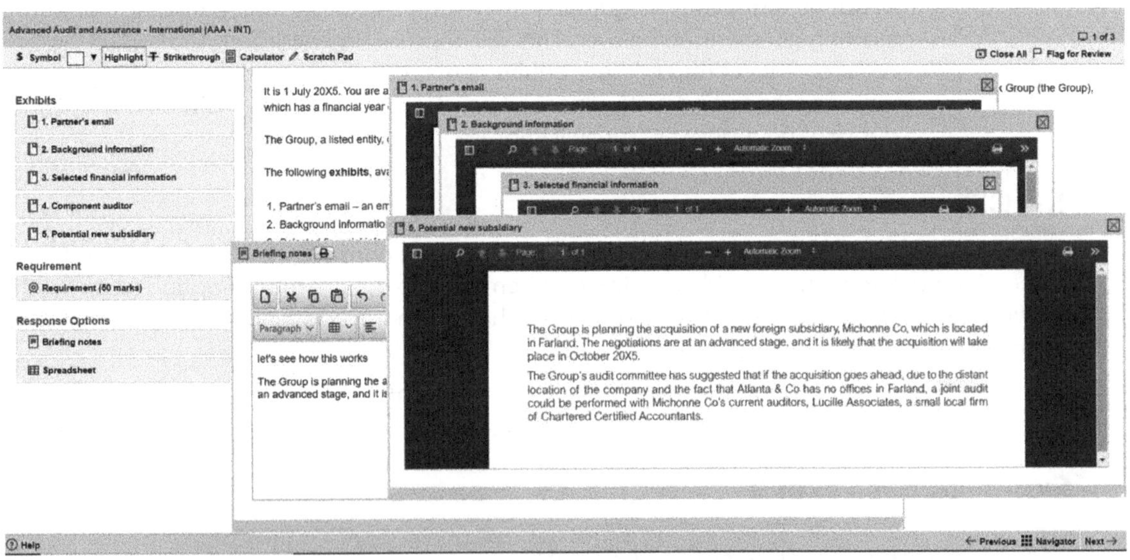

Managing this information is quite a challenge – however, on the left-hand side of the screen is all the information you need:

- The exhibits (for Question 1 of the AAA exam, the partner's email will usually outline the requirements, so is a good place to start)
- The requirement (for other questions, you will find the requirements here)
- The response options (in most cases you will just need the word processing document but if presented with more complex financial statements extracts, the spreadsheet option may be of use)

You will also note that the various windows can be re-sized and moved around the screen to help you navigate each of the exhibits as you make sense of the question.

Exam success skill 2

Correct interpretation of the requirements
The active verb used often dictates the approach that written answers should take (eg 'explain', 'discuss', 'evaluate'). It is important you identify and use the verb to define your approach. The **correct interpretation of the requirements** skill means correctly producing only what is being asked for by a requirement. Anything not required will not earn marks.

Advice on developing correct interpretation of the requirements

This skill can be developed by analysing question requirements and applying this process:

Step 1 **Read the requirement**

Firstly, read the requirement a couple of times slowly and carefully and highlight the active verbs. Use the active verbs to define what you plan to do. Make sure you identify any sub-requirements.

Step 2 **Read the rest of the question**

By reading the requirement first, you will have an idea of what you are looking out for as you read through the case overview and exhibits. This is a great time saver and means you don't end up having to read the whole question in full twice. You should do this in an active way – see Exam success skill 1: Managing Information.

Step 3 **Read the requirement again**

Read the requirement again to remind yourself of the exact wording before starting your written answer. This will capture any misinterpretation of the requirements or any missed requirements entirely. This should become a habit in your approach and, with repeated practice, you will find the focus, relevance and depth of your answer plan will improve.

The CBE

The workspace allows you to copy and paste as you would normally do within any word processing package – you could copy the requirement into your response option (such as the briefing note shown in the screenshot) and it will then be there to remind you what the question is asking for.

There is a 'flag for review' function within the CBE which can be used to highlight areas that you may wish to revisit later in the exam.

Exam success skill 3

Answer planning: Priorities, structure and logic
This skill requires the planning of the key aspects of an answer which accurately and completely responds to the requirement.

Advice on developing answer planning: priorities, structure and logic

Everyone will have a preferred style for an answer plan. For example, it may be a mind map, bullet-pointed lists or simply annotating the question. Choose the approach that you feel most comfortable with, or, if you are not sure, try out different approaches for different questions until you have found your preferred style.

For a discussion question, annotating the question is likely to be insufficient. It would be better to draw up a separate answer plan in the format of your choosing (eg a mind map or bullet-pointed lists). For a risk question, you should annotate the scenario noting which areas present the type of risk being examined and explain why.

The CBE

In the screenshot below, you can see that some of the text has been highlighted:

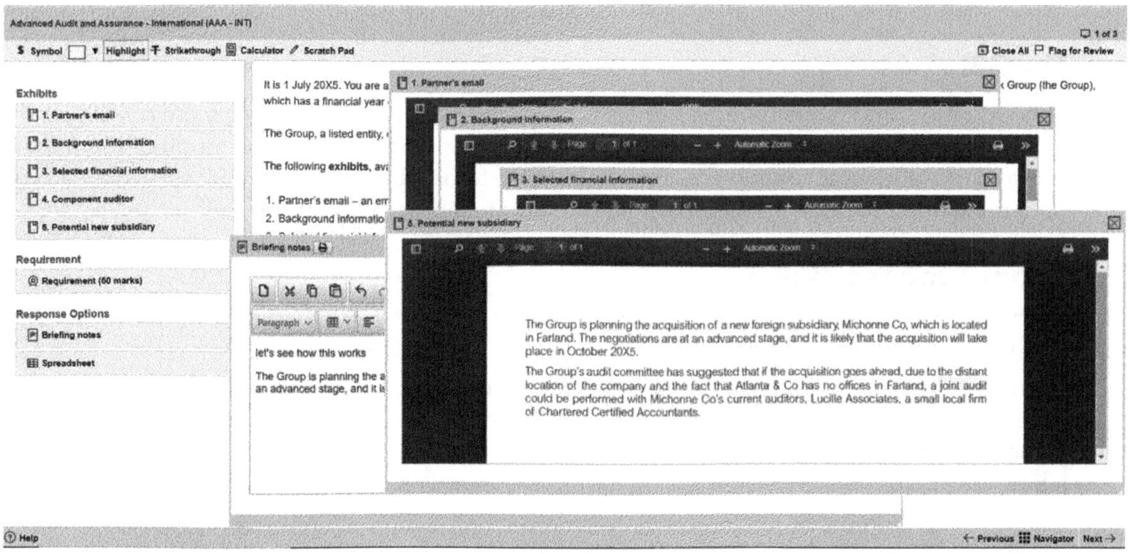

You can use a variety of colours to highlight different parts of the exhibits to address separate aspects of the requirements.

There is a 'scratch pad' that you can also use to organise your thoughts and make rough workings. You can copy and paste content from the scratch pad into your response option, but the scratch pad itself is not submitted for marking at the end of the exam. The answer space can also be used for rough workings.

Exam success skill 4

Efficient numerical analysis

This skill aims to maximise the marks awarded by making clear to the marker the process of arriving at your answer. This is achieved by laying out an answer such that, even if you make a few errors, you can still get some credit for your calculations. It is vital that you do not lose marks purely because the marker cannot follow what you have done.

Advice on developing efficient numerical analysis

This skill can be developed by applying the following process:

Step 1 **Explain your workings where relevant**

Materiality calculations or other forms of analytical procedure should have a brief explanation of their purpose so the examining team can understand what your calculations are trying to tell them. Remember, for AAA, calculations are just a way of quantifying a part of your answer (such as a form of risk assessment or when considering going concern indicators).

Step 2 **Show your workings**

Keep your workings as clear and simple as possible and ensure they are cross-referenced to the main part of your answer. Where it helps, provide brief narrative explanations to help the marker understand the steps in the calculation. This means that if a mistake is made you should not lose any subsequent marks for follow-on calculations.

Step 3 **Keep moving!**

It is important to remember that, in an exam situation, it is difficult to get every number 100% correct. The key is therefore ensuring you do not spend too long on any single calculation. If you are struggling with a solution then make a sensible assumption, state it and move on. It's also important to remember that for AAA, you will not be expected to generate a large number of calculations: usually, only key ratios or calculations will be required.

The CBE

Although the spreadsheet function exists to help you perform calculations more quickly and efficiently than using the onscreen calculator, there may not always be enough of them to merit using the spreadsheet function. It is probably best to practise using the CBE software as part of your revision so you can settle on a style that you feel comfortable with.

Exam success skill 5

Effective writing and presentation

Written answers should be presented so that the marker can clearly see the points you are making, presented in the format specified in the question. The skill is to provide efficient written answers with sufficient breadth of points that answer the question, in the right depth, in the time available.

Advice on developing Effective writing and presentation

Step 1 **Use headings**

Using the headings and sub-headings from your answer plan will give your answer structure, order and logic. This will ensure your answer links back to the requirement and is clearly signposted, making it easier for the marker to understand the different points you are making. Underlining your headings will also help the marker.

Step 2 **Write your answer in short, but full, sentences**

Use short, punchy sentences with the aim that every sentence should say something different and generate marks. Write in full sentences, ensuring your style is professional.

Step 3 **Do your calculations first and explanation second**

Questions often ask for an explanation with suitable calculations, such as materiality. The best approach is to prepare the calculation first and then add the explanation. It is important that your calculation is incorporated into your answer points, as they will earn no marks if they stand alone. Performing the calculation first should enable you to then explain what you have done.

The CBE

Within the workspace, the response option does allow you to format your answer as you would in any word processing package: eg **bold**, <u>underline</u> or *italics*. These will help you provide emphasis on different parts of your answer (and in the case of Question 1, will help you earn the professional marks by use of sub-headings etc).

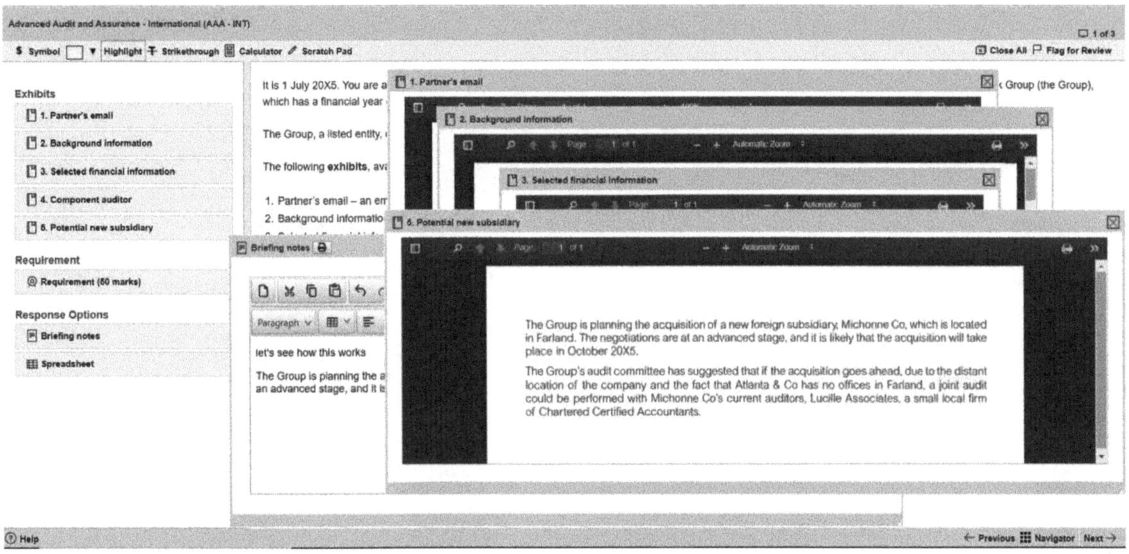

Tables and bullets can also be introduced into your response (although you should only be using these if you feel it still helps you to address the requirement fully).

Exam success skill 6

Good time management

This skill means planning your time across all the requirements so that all tasks have been attempted at the end of the 3 hours 15 minutes available and actively checking on time during your exam. This is so that you can flex your approach and prioritise requirements which, in your judgement, will generate the maximum marks in the available time remaining.

Advice on developing good time management

The exam is 3 hours 15 minutes long, which translates to 1.95 minutes per mark. Therefore a 10-mark requirement should be allocated a maximum of 20 minutes to complete your answer before you move on to the next task. At the beginning of a question, work out the amount of time you should be spending on each requirement and note the finishing time next to each requirement on your exam. If you take the approach of spending 10–15 minutes reading and planning at the start of the exam, adjust the time allocated to each question accordingly – eg if you allocate 15 minutes to reading, then you will have 3 hours remaining, which is 1.8 minutes per mark.

Keep an eye on the clock

Aim to attempt all requirements but be ready to be ruthless and move on if your answer is not going as planned. The challenge for many is sticking to planned timings. Be aware this is difficult to achieve in the early stages of your studies and be ready to let this skill develop over time.

If you find yourself running short on time and know that a full answer is not possible in the time you have, consider recreating your plan in overview form and then add key terms and details as time allows. Remember, some marks may be available, for example, simply stating a conclusion which you don't have time to justify in full.

The CBE

ACCA has made a number of resources available to you that will help you get familiar with the CBE software, including the specimen exam and other recent exam sittings. Central to this is the practice platform where you will find all the questions and exams as CBEs. It is essential that you attempt questions using the CBE software under timed conditions so that you are prepared for how to use it effectively and efficiently on the day of the CBE. You can access the practice platform via the Study Support Resources section of the ACCA website then navigating to the CBE question practice section and logging in with your myACCA credentials.

Questions

Parts A and B: Regulatory environment and professional and ethical considerations

Questions 1 to 8 cover Regulatory Environment and Professional and Ethical considerations, the subjects of Parts A and B of the BPP Workbook for AAA.

1 Lark (P7 June 2012 amended) (49 mins)

(a) It is 1 July 20X5. You are a manager in Lark & Co, responsible for the audit of Heron Ltd, an owner-managed business which operates a chain of bars and restaurants. This is your firm's first year auditing the client and the audit for the year ended 31 March 20X5 is underway.

The following **exhibit**, available on the left-hand side of the screen, provides information relevant to the question:

1 Audit senior's a note for your attention.

This information should be used to answer the question **requirements** within the **response option** provided.

Exhibit 1

'When I was auditing revenue, I noticed something strange. Heron Ltd's revenue, which is almost entirely cash-based, is recognised at £5.5 million in the draft financial statements. However, the accounting system shows that till receipts for cash paid by customers amount to only £3.5 million. This seemed odd, so I questioned Ava Gull, the financial controller about this. She said that Jack Heron, the company's owner, deals with cash receipts and posts journals dealing with cash and revenue. Ava asked Jack the reason for these journals, but he refused to give an explanation.

'While auditing cash, I noticed a payment of £2 million made by electronic transfer from the company's bank account to an overseas financial institution. The bank statement showed that the transfer was authorised by Jack Heron, but no other documentation regarding the transfer was available.

'Alarmed by the size of this transaction and the lack of evidence to support it, I questioned Jack Heron, asking him about the source of cash receipts and the reason for electronic transfer. He would not give any answers and became quite aggressive.'

Required

Using the information contained in Exhibit 1:

Discuss the implications of the circumstances described in the audit senior's note. **(5 marks)**

(b) You are also responsible for the audit of Coot Ltd, and you are currently reviewing the working papers of the audit for the year ended 28 February 20X5. In the working papers dealing with payroll, the audit junior has made several comments.

The following **exhibit**, available on the left-hand side of the screen, provides information relevant to the question:

2 Audit junior's comments in payroll working papers.

This information should be used to answer the question **requirement** within the **response option** provided.

Exhibit 2

'Several new employees have been added to the company's payroll during the year, with combined payments of £125,000 being made to them. There does not appear to be any authorisation for these additions. When I questioned the payroll supervisor who made the amendments, she said that no authorisation was needed because the new employees are only working for the company on a temporary basis. However, when discussing staffing levels with management, it was stated that no new employees have been taken on this year. Other than the tests of controls planned, no other audit work has been performed.'

Required

Using the information contained in Exhibit 2:

In relation to the audit of Coot Ltd's payroll, explain the meaning of the term 'professional scepticism', and recommend any further actions that should be taken by the auditor.

(5 marks)

(c) You are the manager responsible for the audit of the Nassau Group, which comprises a parent company and six subsidiaries. The audit of all individual companies' financial statements is almost complete, and you are currently carrying out the audit of the consolidated financial statements. One of the subsidiaries, Exuma Ltd, is audited by another firm, Jalousie & Co. Your firm has fulfilled the necessary requirements of ISA (UK) 600 (Revised) *Special Considerations – Audits of Group Financial Statements (Including the Work of Component Auditors)* and is satisfied as to the competence and independence of Jalousie & Co.

The following **exhibit**, available on the left-hand side of the screen, provides information relevant to the question:

3 Extract of Jalousie & Co's draft auditor's report on Exuma Ltd's financial statements.

This information should be used to answer the question **requirement** within the **response option** provided.

Exhibit 3

You have received from Jalousie & Co the draft auditor's report on Exuma Ltd's financial statements, an extract from which is shown below.

Qualified Opinion (extract)

'In our opinion, except for effects of the matter described in the Basis for Qualified Opinion paragraph, the financial statements give a true and fair view of the financial position of Exuma Ltd as at 31 March 20X5...'

Basis for Qualified Opinion (extract)

'The company is facing financial damages of £2 million in respect of an ongoing court case, more fully explained in Note 12 to the financial statements. Management has not recognised a provision but has disclosed the situation as a contingent liability. Under International Financial Reporting Standards, a provision should be made if there is an obligation as a result of a past event, a probable outflow of economic benefit, and a reliable estimate can be made. Audit evidence concludes that these criteria have been met, and it is our opinion that a provision of £2 million should be recognised. Accordingly, net profit and shareholders' equity would have been reduced by £2 million if the provision had been recognised.'

An extract of Note 12 to Exuma Ltd's financial statements is shown below.

'Note 12 (extract)

The company is the subject of a court case concerning an alleged breach of planning regulations. The plaintiff is claiming compensation of £2 million. The management of Exuma Ltd, after seeking legal advice, believe that there is only a 20% chance of a successful claim being made against the company.'

Figures extracted from the draft financial statements for the year ending 31 March 20X5 are as follows.

	Nassau Group	*Exuma Ltd*
	£m	£m
Profit before tax	20	4
Total assets	85	20

Required

Using the information contained in Exhibit 3:

Identify and explain the matters that should be considered, and actions that should be taken by the group audit engagement team, in forming an opinion on the consolidated financial statements of the Nassau Group. **(10 marks)**

Professional marks will be awarded for the demonstration of skill in analysis and evaluation, and professional scepticism and judgement in your answer. **(5 marks)**

(Total = 25 marks)

2 Plant (P7 December 2012 amended) (49 mins)

(a) It is 1 July 20X5. You are an audit manager in Weller & Co, an audit firm which operates as part of an international network of firms. This morning you received a note from a partner regarding a potential new audit client.

The following **exhibit**, available on the left-hand side of the screen, provides information relevant to the question:

1 Audit partner's note regarding potential new audit client.

This information should be used to answer the question **requirements** within the **response option** provided.

Exhibit 1

'I have been approached by the audit committee of the Plant Group, which operates in the mobile telecommunications sector. Our firm has been invited to tender for the audit of the individual and group financial statements for the year ending 31 December 20X5, and I would like your help in preparing the tender document. This would be a major new client for our firm's telecoms audit department.

'The Plant Group comprises a parent company and six subsidiaries, one of which is located overseas. The audit committee is looking for a cost-effective audit and hopes that the strength of the Plant Group's governance and internal control mean that the audit can be conducted quickly, with a proposed deadline of 28 February 20X6. The Plant Group has expanded rapidly in the last few years and significant finance was raised in April 20X5 through a stock exchange listing.'

Required

Using the information contained in Exhibit 1:

Evaluate the specific matters to be included in the tender document for the audit of the Plant Group. **(10 marks)**

(b) Weller & Co is facing competition from other audit firms, and the partners have been considering how the firm's revenue could be increased. A proposal has been made that all audit managers should suggest to their audit clients that, as well as providing the external audit service, Weller & Co can provide its clients with an 'extended audit' service in which it would offer firms advice on their financial and operational controls, and on any related performance information.

Required

Comment on the ethical and professional issues raised by the proposal to increase the firm's revenue. **(10 marks)**

Professional marks will be awarded for the demonstration of skill in analysis and evaluation, and professional scepticism and judgement in your answer. **(5 marks)**

(Total = 25 marks)

3 Monet (P7 Sep/Dec 2016 amended) (49 mins)

You are a manager in Monet & Co, a firm of accountants which has 12 offices and 30 partners, 10 of whom are members of ACCA. As an expert in ethics and professional conduct, you have been asked to advise the partners on a number of issues that were raised at a recent meeting. An advertisement has been drafted as part of the firm's drive to increase the number of clients. It is suggested that it should be placed in a number of quality national as well as local newspapers. Issues have been discovered in relation to two of the firm's audit clients.

The following **exhibits**, available on the left-hand side of the screen, provide information relevant to the question:

(1) Draft advertisement for Monet & Co firm of accountants

(2) Account of the audit of Renoir Ltd

(3) Account of the audit of Juliet Ltd

This information should be used to answer the question **requirements** within the **response options** provided.

(a) **Exhibit 1**

> Have you had enough of your accountant charging you too much for poor quality services?
>
> Does your business need a kick-start?
>
> Look no further; Monet & Co provides the most comprehensive range of finance and accountancy services in the UK as well as having the UK's leading tax team who are just waiting to save you money.
>
> Still not sure? We guarantee to be cheaper than your existing service provider and, for the month of January, we are offering free business advice to all new audit clients.
>
> Drop in and see us at your local office for a free consultation.
>
> Monet & Co, Chartered Certified Accountants.

Required

Using the information contained in Exhibit 1:

Comment on the ethical and professional issues raised and recommend any actions necessary in response to the issues identified. **(6 marks)**

(b) **Exhibit 2**

The planning for the audit of Renoir Ltd's financial statements for the year ending 31 March 20X6 will commence shortly. In preparation, the audit partner telephoned Renoir Ltd's finance director, Jim Cassatt, to set up a planning meeting and to remind him that fees relating to a tax engagement from the previous year were still outstanding. Mr Cassatt raised concerns about the conduct of the previous audit, stating numerous examples of when he and his staff had been interrupted when they were busy. He stated that he wanted guarantees that this year's audit will be more efficient, less intrusive and cheaper, otherwise he will seek an alternative auditor.

Required

Using the information contained in Exhibit 2:

Comment on the ethical and professional issues raised and recommend any actions necessary in response to the issues identified. **(4 marks)**

(c) **Exhibit 3**

You are also the manager responsible for the audit of Juliet Ltd, and you are planning the final audit of the financial statements for the year ending 30 June 20X6. Juliet Ltd is a supplier of components used in the manufacture of vehicle engines. Due to a downturn in the economy, and in the automotive industry particularly, the company has suffered a decline in sales and profitability over the last two years, mainly due to the loss of several key customer contracts. Many of Juliet Ltd's non-current assets are impaired in value, and a significant number of receivables balances have been written off in the last six months.

In response to the deteriorating market conditions, the management of Juliet Ltd decided to restructure the business. The main manufacturing facility will be reduced in size by two-thirds, and investment will be made in new technology to make the remaining operations more efficient and to enable the manufacture of a wider variety of components for use in different types of engines and machinery. In order to fund this restructuring, the management of Juliet Ltd approached the company's bank with a request for a significant loan. You are aware that without the loan, Juliet Ltd is unlikely to be able to restructure successfully, which will raise significant doubt over its ability to continue as a going concern.

Your firm has been asked to advise on the necessary forecasts and projections that the bank will need to see in order to make a decision regarding the finance requested. Management has also requested that your firm attend a meeting with the bank at which the forecasts will be discussed.

Required

Using the information contained in Exhibit 3:

(i) Identify and explain the matters that should be considered, and the principal audit procedures to be performed, in respect of the additional funding being sought. **(5 marks)**

(ii) Comment on the ethical and other implications of the request for your firm to provide advice on the forecasts and projections, and to attend the meeting with the bank. **(5 marks)**

Professional marks will be awarded for the demonstration of skill in analysis and evaluation, and professional scepticism and judgement in your answer. **(5 marks)**

(Total = 25 marks)

4 Peaches (P7 December 2009 amended) (49 mins)

(a) Recent surveys of the quality of audits being performed have noted that auditors too often treat the requirements of the IESBA *Code of Ethics* and of ISAs as though they were prescriptive (rules-based) requirements, when in fact they are intended to be principles-based.

Required

(i) Contrast the prescriptive and the principles-based approaches to auditing; and

(ii) Outline the arguments for and against a prescriptive (rules-based) approach to auditing.

Note. You should address both parts in order to score the marks available. **(5 marks)**

(b) You are a manager in the audit department of Peaches & Co, a firm of Chartered Certified Accountants. One of your responsibilities is to act as a mentor to new recruits into the department. A new junior auditor, Glen Rambaran, has asked you to answer some questions which relate to issues encountered in his first few weeks working at Peaches & Co. The questions are shown below.

Intimidation threat

When I was on my initial training course, there was a session on ethics in which the presenter talked about being intimidated by a client. I assume this does not mean physical intimidation, so what is an intimidation threat?

Advertising

I know that Peaches & Co is facing competition from a new audit firm, and that our firm is advertising its services in a national newspaper. What are the rules on advertising for new clients?

Required

For each of the questions raised, provide a response to the audit junior, in which you identify and explain the ethical or professional issue raised.

Note. The marks will be shared equally between these two questions. **(8 marks)**

(c) You are also responsible for the audit of Adderley Ltd, which operates a chain of cinemas across the country. Currently its cinemas are out of date, and management is planning to invest in all of its cinemas. The company has sufficient cash to fund half of the necessary capital expenditure but has approached its bank with a loan application of £8 million for the remainder of the funds required.

The audit strategy for this audit concludes that the company has a relatively high risk associated with money laundering, largely due to the cash-based nature of its activities. The majority of customers purchase their cinema tickets and refreshments in cash, and the company transfers its cash to overseas bank accounts on a regular basis.

Required

(i) Evaluate why Adderley Co has been identified as high risk in relation to money laundering. **(3 marks)**

(ii) Recommend the elements of an anti-money laundering programme which audit firms such as Peaches & Co should have in place. **(4 marks)**

Professional marks will be awarded for the demonstration of skill in analysis and evaluation, and professional scepticism and judgement in your answer. **(5 marks)**

(Total = 25 marks)

5 Cobra (P7 Sep/Dec 2017 amended) (49 mins)

It is 1 July 20X5. You are a senior manager at Cobra & Co, a firm of Chartered Certified Accountants. You are responsible for reviewing quality management and ethical matters which arise with the firm's portfolio of clients. During recent investigations you identified the following matters:

Asp Ltd

Asp Ltd currently qualifies as a small company. The company has revenue of £7.5 million (20X4 – £5.3 million) and meets the audit exemption criteria. The company is therefore not required to have an audit. Until recently, your firm has provided a range of non-audit services to Asp Ltd including bookkeeping, payroll and tax computation and advice. The company recently obtained an offer for a significant amount of finance to help the company grow. The management of Asp Ltd has ambitious plans for growth which they believe will result in revenue doubling within one year and then continuing to grow at a similar rate for at least the next five years. In order to secure the funding, the directors have decided to have the financial statements audited and have asked if Cobra & Co will become the company's auditors, as well as continuing to provide the existing services. This will include auditing the financial statements for the year ended 31 December 20X5 at the request of the new financers.

Viper Ltd

You have been approached by Viper Ltd, a retail company, to provide audit and tax services. In response you have written to the outgoing auditor to ask if there are any matters which you should be made aware of which might prevent you from accepting the assignment. Despite a number of follow up phone calls, you have not been able to obtain a response from the outgoing audit firm. On discussing this with the management team of Viper Ltd, you are made aware that the company is suing the outgoing auditor for damages due to the detrimental effect on their reputation following the auditor issuing a modified opinion, which the directors of Viper Ltd felt was inappropriate. The reason for the modified opinion was the application of an accounting treatment, which the outgoing auditor considered to be inappropriate and a material misstatement.

Adder plc

Adder plc is a listed audit client of your firm. The management team of Adder plc has asked you to perform a valuation of the shares of another audit client, Slowworm Ltd, with a view to buying the entire shareholding. Slowworm Ltd is a private company whose shares are owned entirely by the original founder, Mr Jim Slow.

Required

Comment on the ethical and other professional issues raised, and recommend any actions which should be taken in respect of:

(a) Asp Ltd **(7 marks)**

(b) Viper Ltd **(7 marks)**

(c) Adder plc **(6 marks)**

Professional marks will be awarded for the demonstration of skill in analysis and evaluation, and professional scepticism and judgement in your answer. **(5 marks)**

(Total = 25 marks)

6 Smith & Co (P7 June 2008 amended) (49 mins)

It is 1 July 20X5. You are an audit manager in Smith & Co, a firm of Chartered Certified Accountants. You have recently been made responsible for reviewing invoices raised to clients and for monitoring your firm's credit control procedures. Several matters came to light during your most recent review of client invoice files.

In addition, some issues have arisen in relation an assurance client of the firm, Sci-Tech Ltd.

The following **exhibits**, available on the left-hand side of the screen, provides information relevant to the question:

(1) Details of client invoice review of Norman Ltd

(2) Details of client invoice review of Wallace Ltd

(3) Details of assurance client, Sci-Tech Ltd

This information should be used to answer the question **requirements** within the **response options** provided.

Exhibit 1

Norman Ltd, a large company, has not paid an invoice from Smith & Co dated 5 June 20X4 for work in respect of the financial statement audit for the year ended 28 February 20X4. A file note dated 30 November 20X4 states that Norman Ltd is suffering poor cash flows and is unable to pay the balance. This is the only piece of information in the file you are reviewing relating to the invoice. You are aware that the final audit work for the year ended 28 February 20X5, which has not yet been invoiced, is nearly complete and the auditor's report is due to be issued imminently.

Exhibit 2

Wallace Ltd, whose business is the manufacture of industrial machinery, has paid all invoices relating to the recently completed audit planning for the year ended 31 July 20X5. However, in the invoice file you notice an invoice received by your firm from Wallace Ltd. The invoice is addressed to Valerie Hobson, the manager responsible for the audit of Wallace Ltd. The invoice relates to the rental of an area in Wallace Ltd's empty warehouse, with the following comment handwritten on the invoice: 'Rental space being used for storage of Ms Hobson's speedboat for six months – she is our auditor, so only charge a nominal sum of £100.' When asked about the invoice, Valerie Hobson said that the invoice should have been sent to her private address. You are aware that Wallace Ltd sometimes uses the empty warehouse for rental income, though this is not the main trading income of the company.

Required

Using the information contained in Exhibits 1 and 2:

Identify and discuss the ethical and other professional issues raised by the invoice file review, and recommend what action, if any, Smith & Co should now take in respect of:

(a) Norman Ltd **(7 marks)**

(b) Wallace Ltd **(5 marks)**

(c) **Exhibit 3**

Another client, Sci-Tech Ltd, is a pharmaceutical research company. Your firm is engaged to provide an assurance conclusion on some KPIs that it discloses in its operating and financial review. Sci-Tech Ltd receives funding from governmental health departments, as well as several large charitable donations, the amount of which depends on whether three key performance indicator (KPI) targets are met annually. All three of the targets must be met in order to secure the government funding.

KPI target	Draft KPI 20X5	Actual KPI 20X4
Pharmaceutical products donated free of charge to health care charities: 1% revenue	1% revenue	1.2% revenue
Donations to, and cost of involvement with, local community charities: 0.5% revenue	0.6% revenue	0.8% revenue
Accidents in the work place: Fewer than 5 serious accidents per year	4 serious accidents	2 serious accidents

Required

Using the information contained in Exhibit 3:

(i) Discuss why it may not be possible to provide a high level of assurance over the stated key performance indicators. **(4 marks)**

(ii) Describe the procedures to verify the number of serious accidents in the year ended 30 June 20X5. **(4 marks)**

Professional marks will be awarded for the demonstration of skill in analysis and evaluation, professional scepticism and judgement, and commercial acumen in your answer. **(5 marks)**

(Total = 25 marks)

7 Vizsla (P7 Mar/Jun 2018 amended) (49 mins)

It is 1 July 20X5. You are an audit manager in Pointer & Co, a firm of Chartered Certified Accountants which offers a range of assurance services. You are responsible for the audit of Vizsla Ltd, a company which provides approximately 10% of your firm's practice income each year.

The following **exhibits** provide information relevant to the question:

(1) An extract of an email from finance director of Vizsla Ltd

(2) Information regarding a review of prospective financial information for Vizsla Ltd

This information should be used to answer the question **requirements** within the response option provided.

Exhibit 1

The finance director of Vizsla Ltd has recently contacted you to provide information about another company, Setter Co, which is looking to appoint a provider of assurance services. An extract from the email which the finance director of Vizsla Ltd has sent to you is shown below:

'One of my friends, Gordon Potts, is the managing director of Setter Ltd, a small company, with annual revenue of around £8 million, which is looking to expand in the next few years. I know that Gordon has approached the company's bank for finance of £6 million to fund the expansion. To support this loan application, Gordon needs to appoint a firm to provide a limited assurance review on the company's financial statements. He would also want the appointed firm to provide tax planning advice and to prepare both the company's and his personal tax computations for submission to HMRC. I have asked Gordon to contact you, and I hope that Pointer & Co will be able to provide these services to Setter Ltd for a low fee. If the fee you suggest is too high, and unacceptable to Gordon, then I will recommend that Gordon approaches Griffon & Co instead, and I would also consider appointing Griffon & Co to provide the audit of Vizsla Ltd.'

Griffon & Co is a firm of Chartered Certified Accountants which has an office in the same town as Pointer & Co.

You have done some research on both Setter Ltd and Gordon Potts and have confirmed that the company is owner-managed, with the Potts family owning 90% of the share capital. Gordon Potts is a director and majority shareholder of three other companies. An article in a newspaper from several years ago about Gordon Potts indicated that one of his companies was once fined for breach of employment law and that he had used money from one of the company's pension plans to set up a business abroad, appointing his son as the managing director of that business.

Exhibit 2

Pointer & Co has agreed to perform an assurance engagement for Vizsla Ltd; the engagement will be a review of prospective financial information which is needed to support the company's overdraft facilities. Vizsla Ltd had a financial year ended 30 September 20X4, and an unmodified opinion was issued on these financial statements. Pointer & Co's partner responsible for ethics has agreed that any threats to objectivity will be reduced to an acceptable level through the use of a team separate from the audit team to perform the work.

The operating profit forecast for the two years to 31 March 20X7 prepared by a member of the accounting team of Vizsla Ltd is shown below, along with some accompanying notes.

	Note	*Six months to 30 September 20X5*	*Six months to 31 March 20X6*	*Six months to 30 September 20X6*	*Six months to 31 March 20X7*
		£'000	£'000	£'000	£'000
Revenue	1	12,800	16,900	13,700	18,900
Gross profit %		34%	45%	36%	46%
Operating costs:					
Staff costs		(2,800)	(2,900)	(2,800)	(2,900)
Design costs	2	(1,200)	(1,200)	(1,250)	(1,250)
Marketing		(900)	(1,000)	(1,100)	(1,100)
Interest on overdraft	3	(25)	(10)	–	–
Other expenses	4	(3,840)	(5,070)	(4,110)	(5,670)
Operating profit		4,035	6,720	4,440	7,980

Notes.

1 Vizsla Ltd is a producer of greetings cards and giftware, the demand for which is seasonal in nature.

2 Design costs are mostly payroll costs of the staff working in the company's design team, and the costs relate to the design and development of new product ranges.

3 Vizsla Ltd has agreed with its bank to clear its overdraft by 1 September 20X6, and the management team is confident that after that point the company will not need an overdraft facility.

4 The total 'Other expenses' is calculated based on 30% of the projected revenue for the six-month period.

Required

Using the information contained in Exhibits 1 and 2:

(a) In relation to Pointer & Co's potential acceptance of Setter Ltd as a client of the firm:

(i) Explain the ethical issues and other matters which should be considered; and **(7 marks)**

(ii) Explain the importance of obtaining customer due diligence and recommend the information which should be obtained. **(6 marks)**

(b) Design the examination procedures which should be used in the review of the profit forecast. **(7 marks)**

Professional marks will be awarded for the demonstration of skill in analysis and evaluation, and professional scepticism and judgement in your answer. **(5 marks)**

(Total = 25 marks)

8 Chennai (P7 Mar/Jun 2016 amended) (49 mins)

It is 1 July 20X5. You are a manager at Chennai & Co, a firm of Chartered Certified Accountants. One of the partners has asked you to investigate and respond to a number of issues which have arisen with two different companies.

(a) **Exhibit 1**

Delhi Ltd is a potential new client. It is a privately owned and rapidly expanding company. The company's management is currently considering having either a full audit or a limited assurance review of the financial statements.

The audit partner would like you to write a response to Delhi Ltd's management in which you:

(1) Explain the difference between an audit of historical financial statements and a limited assurance review; and

(2) Discuss the relative advantages and disadvantages to Delhi Ltd of having an audit of their historical financial statements as opposed to a limited assurance review.

The financial statements for the year ended 31 March 20X5 recognise revenue of £5.4 million (20X5 – £4.3 million) and total assets of £2.7 million (20X5 – £2.1 million).

Delhi Ltd was incorporated in 20W5, with founder and chief executive Mr Nimesh Dattani as the sole shareholder. After a period of rapid growth, Delhi Ltd took out a ten-year bank loan facility in June 20W7 to finance Mr Dattani's ambitious expansion plans. This was supported by a further injection of financial capital in 20X4 through a new issue of shares in the company. The shares were sold to Mr Robert Hyland, an ex-business partner of Mr Dattani. The sale gave Mr Hyland a 40% shareholding in Delhi Ltd. He has no involvement in the management of the company.

Until recently Delhi Ltd operated with a small accounting department, comprising one full-time member of staff and one part-time employee. Due to the expansion of the company and Mr Dattani's plans to expand the customer base outside the UK, it has been necessary to increase the size of the accounting function to include two new full-time members of staff.

Both of the new recruits are part-qualified accountants and Mr Dattani has committed to sponsoring them through their remaining training and ACCA examinations.

Required

Using the information contained in Exhibit 1:

Prepare the response to the management of Delhi Ltd as requested by the partner.

(12 marks)

(b) **Exhibit 2**

The audit committee of another client, Mumbai plc, has contacted you to ask whether Chennai & Co can perform a review of the company's internal control system. A number of recent incidents have raised concerns amongst the management team that controls have deteriorated and that this has increased the risk of fraud, as well as inefficient commercial practices. The auditor's report for the audit of the financial statements of Mumbai plc for the year ended 31 March 20X5 was signed two weeks ago.

Required

Using the information contained in Exhibit 2:

In respect of the request for Chennai & Co to review Mumbai plc's internal control systems:

Identify and discuss the relevant ethical and professional issues raised, and recommend any actions necessary.

(8 marks)

Professional marks will be awarded for the demonstration of skill in analysis and evaluation, professional scepticism and judgement, and commercial acumen in your answer. **(5 marks)**

(Total = 25 marks)

A) Legal Requirement
Scope
Assurance

Advantage
- Expanding business
- Credibility/Assurance to Shareholders
- Struggling Accounting

Dis
Costs
Time/effort for Acc Team

B) Ethical threats
- Self-Review
- Management
- Listed- Prohibited

Part C: Quality management and practice management

Questions 9 to 15 cover Quality management and practice management, the subject of Part C of the BPP Workbook for AAA.

9 Bunk (P7 June 2015 amended) (49 mins)

It is 1 July 20X5. You are a senior manager in Bunk & Co, a global audit firm with offices in more than 30 countries. You are responsible for monitoring audit quality and ethical situations which arise in relation to audit clients. Wire Ltd is an audit client whose operations involve haulage and distribution. The auditor's report for the financial statements of Wire Ltd for the year ended 31 December 20X4 was issued last week. You are conducting a review of the quality of that audit, and of any ethical issues which arose in relation to it. Relevant information obtained from a discussion with Lester Freeman, the audit engagement partner, is given below. The financial statements recognised revenue of £8.7 million, assets of £15.2 million and profit before tax of £1.8 million.

The following **exhibit** provides information relevant to the question:

(1) Information obtained from a discussion with Lester Freeman, the audit engagement partner

This information should be used to answer the question **requirements** within the response options provided.

Required

Using the information contained in the Exhibit:

Comment on the quality management, ethical and professional issues raised in respect of the audit of Wire Ltd and the firm-wide policies of Bunk & Co, and recommend any actions to be taken by the audit firm.

Note. The split of the mark allocation is shown against each of the issues below. **(20 marks)**

Professional marks will be awarded for the demonstration of skill in analysis and evaluation, professional scepticism and judgement, and commercial acumen in your answer. **(5 marks)**

(Total = 25 marks)

Exhibit: Discussion with Lester Freeman, audit engagement partner

(a) Wire Ltd's audit committee refused to agree to an increase in audit fees despite the company's operations expanding into new locations. In response to this, the materiality level was increased during the audit, and some review procedures were not carried out. To reduce sample sizes used in tests of detail, the samples were selected based on judgement rather than statistical methods. In addition, only parts of the population being tested were sampled, for example, certain locations were not included in the sample of non-current assets selected for physical verification. **(6 marks)**

(b) Some of the audit work was performed by an overseas office of Bunk & Co in an 'off-shoring' arrangement. This practice is encouraged by Bunk & Co, whose managing partners see it as a way of improving audit efficiency. The overseas office performs the work at a lower cost, and it was largely low-risk, non-judgemental work included in this arrangement for the audit of Wire Ltd, for example, numerical checks on documentation. In addition, the overseas office read the minutes of board meetings to identify issues relevant to the audit. **(5 marks)**

(c) In July 20X4, Russell Bell, Wire Ltd's former finance director, joined Bunk & Co as an audit partner, working in the same office as Lester Freeman. Although Russell was not a member of the audit team, he did update Lester on some business developments which had taken place at the company during the period before he left. Russell held a number of equity shares in Wire Ltd, which he sold in January 20X5. Since joining Bunk & Co, Russell has been developing initiatives to increase the firm's income. One initiative is that audit team members should be encouraged to cross-sell non-audit services and references to targets for the cross-selling of non-audit services to audit clients is now included in partner and employee appraisal documentation. **(9 marks)**

10 Grape (P7 December 2009 amended) (49 mins)

It is 1 July 20X5. You are a manager in Grape & Co, a firm of Chartered Certified Accountants. You have been temporarily assigned as audit manager to the audit of Banana Ltd, because the engagement manager has been taken ill. The final audit of Banana Ltd for the year ended 28 February 20X5 is nearing completion, and you are now reviewing the audit files and discussing the audit with the junior members of the audit team.

The following **exhibits** provide information relevant to the question:

(1) Background information on Banana Ltd

(2) Information arising from your review of the audit files

(3) Concerns raised by audit junior in relation to the management of the audit

This information should be used to answer the question **requirements** within the response options provided.

Exhibit 1

Banana Ltd designs and manufactures equipment such as cranes and scaffolding, which is used in the construction industry. The equipment usually follows a standard design, but sometimes Banana Ltd designs specific items for customers according to contractually agreed specifications. The draft financial statements show revenue of £12.5 million, net profit of £400,000, and total assets of £78 million.

Exhibit 2

The following information has come to your attention during your review of the audit files.

During the year, a new range of manufacturing plant was introduced to the factories operated by Banana Ltd. All factory employees received training from an external training firm on how to safely operate the machinery, at a total cost of £150,000. The training costs have been capitalised into the cost of the new machinery, as the finance director argues that the training is necessary in order for the machinery to generate an economic benefit. After the year end, Cherry Ltd, a major customer with whom Banana Ltd has several significant contracts, announced its insolvency and that procedures to shut down the company had commenced. The administrators of Cherry Ltd have suggested that the company may be able to pay approximately 25% of the amounts owed to its trade payables. A trade receivable of £120,000 is recognised on Banana Ltd's statement of financial position in respect of this customer.

Exhibit 3

One of the junior members of the audit team voiced concerns over how the audit had been managed. The junior said the following:

'I have only worked on two audits prior to being assigned to the audit team of Banana Ltd. I was expecting to attend a meeting at the start of the audit, in which the partner and other senior members of the audit team would discuss the audit, but no meeting was held. In addition, the audit manager has been away on holiday for three weeks and left a senior in charge. However, the senior was busy with other assignments, so was not always available.

'I was given the task of auditing the goodwill which arose on an acquisition made during the year. I also worked on the audit of inventory and attended the inventory count, which was quite complicated as Banana Ltd has a lot of work in progress. I tried to be as useful as possible during the count and helped the client's staff count some of the raw materials. As I had been to the inventory count, I was asked by the audit senior to challenge the finance director regarding the adequacy of the provision against inventory, which the senior felt was significantly understated.

'Lastly, we found that we were running out of time to complete our audit procedures. The audit senior advised that we should reduce the sample sizes used in our tests as a way of saving time. He also suggested that if we picked an item as part of our sample for which it would be time consuming to find the relevant evidence, then we should pick a different item which would be quicker to audit.'

Required

Using the information provided in Exhibits 1 and 2:

(a) Comment on the matters to be considered, and explain the audit evidence you should expect to find during your file review in respect of:

(i) The training costs that have been capitalised into the cost of the new machinery; and **(6 marks)**

(ii) The trade receivable recognised in relation to Cherry Ltd. **(6 marks)**

(b) Using the information provided in Exhibit 3:

Evaluate the audit junior's concerns regarding the management of the audit of Banana Ltd. **(8 marks)**

Professional marks will be awarded for the demonstration of skill in analysis and evaluation, and professional scepticism and judgement in your answer. **(5 marks)**

(Total = 25 marks)

11 Clean (December 2018 amended) (49 mins)

It is 1 July 20X5. You are an audit manager in Thomasson & Co, a firm of Chartered Certified Accountants. You have recently been assigned to the audit of Clean Ltd for the year ended 31 March 20X5. Clean Ltd is an unlisted company and has been an audit client of your firm for a number of years.

The following **exhibits** provide information relevant to the question:

(1) Background information on Clean Ltd

(2) Review of audit working papers

This information should be used to answer the question **requirements** within the response options provided.

Exhibit 1

Clean Ltd is a national distributor of cleaning products. The company buys the cleaning products from wholesalers and employs a team of approximately 750 sales staff across the UK who sell the company's products door to door to both domestic households and small- to medium-sized businesses. Around 75% of Clean Ltd's sales transactions are cash-based and each of the company's sales staff prepares a cash sales report on a monthly basis. According to Clean Ltd's chief executive, Simon Blackers, and in order to foster 'an entrepreneurial spirit' amongst his staff, each staff member (including the senior management team) is encouraged to make cash sales and is paid on a commission basis to sell the company's products to friends and family. Mr Blackers leads the way with this scheme and recently sold cleaning products with a value of £33,000 to a business associate of his. He has transferred these funds directly into an off-shore bank account in the company's name on which he is the sole signatory.

Exhibit 2

Your initial review of the audit working papers and an initial meeting with Mr Blackers have identified the following potential issues:

Following your review of the audit engagement letter and the working papers of the taxation section of the audit file, you have established that Thomasson & Co performed the taxation computation for Clean Ltd and completed the tax returns for both the company and Mr Blackers personally. All of the taxation services have been invoiced to Clean Ltd as part of the total fee for the audit and professional services. Mr Blackers' personal tax return includes a significant number of transactions involving the purchase and sale of properties in various international locations.

The taxation working papers include a detailed review of a number of offshore bank accounts in Mr Blackers' name which identified the property transactions.

During your initial meeting with Mr Blackers, he informed you that Clean Ltd is planning to develop a new website in order to offer online sales to its customers. He has asked Thomasson & Co to provide assistance with the design and implementation of the website and online sales system.

As a result of your audit review visit at the client's premises, you have learned that the audit team was invited to and subsequently attended Clean Ltd's annual office party. The client provided each member of the audit team with a free voucher worth £30 which could be redeemed at the venue during the party. The audit senior, Paula Metcalfe, who has worked on the audit for the last three years has informed you that the audit team has always been encouraged to attend the party in order to develop good client relations.

Required

Using the information provided in Exhibits 1 and 2:

(a) (i) Discuss the policies and procedures which Thomasson & Co should have in place in relation to an anti-money laundering programme; and **(3 marks)**

(ii) Evaluate whether there are any indicators of money laundering activities by either Clean Ltd or its staff. **(5 marks)**

(b) Comment on the ethical and professional issues arising from your review of the audit working papers and recommend any actions which should now be taken by Thomasson & Co. **(12 marks)**

Professional marks will be awarded for the demonstration of skill in analysis and evaluation, and professional scepticism and judgement in your answer. **(5 marks)**

(Total = 25 marks)

12 Bradley (ACCA 2018 Specimen amended) (49 mins)

The audit of Bradley Ltd's financial statements for the year ended 31 August 20X4 is nearly complete, and the auditor's report is due to be issued next week. Bradley Ltd operates steel processing plants at 20 locations and sells its output to manufacturers and engineering companies. You are performing an engagement quality review on the audit of Bradley Ltd, as it is a significant new client of your firm. The financial statements recognise revenue of £2.5 million, and total assets of £35 million.

The following **exhibits** provide information relevant to the question:

(1) Audit assistant's comments on audit of Bradley Ltd

(2) Audit working paper schedule of uncorrected misstatements

This information should be used to answer the question **requirements** within the response options provided.

Required

(a) Using the information provided in Exhibit 1:

Explain the quality management and other professional issues raised by the audit assistant's comments, discussing any implications for the completion of the audit. **(10 marks)**

(b) Using the information provided in Exhibit 2:

Explain the matters which should be discussed with management in relation to each of the uncorrected misstatements. **(10 marks)**

Professional marks will be awarded for the demonstration of skill in analysis and evaluation, and professional scepticism and judgement in your answer. **(5 marks)**

(Total = 25 marks)

Exhibit 1:

One of the audit assistants who has been working on the audit of Bradley Ltd made the following comments when discussing the completion of the audit with you:

'I was assigned to the audit of provisions. One of the provisions, amounting to £10,000, relates to a legal claim made against the company after an employee was injured in an accident at one of the steel processing plants. I read all of the correspondence relating to this, and tried to speak to Bradley Ltd's legal advisers, but was told by the finance director that I must not approach them and should only speak to him about the matter. He said that he is confident that only £10,000 needs to be recognised and that the legal advisers had confirmed this amount to him in a discussion of the matter. I noted in the audit working papers that I could not perform all of the planned audit procedures because I could not speak to the legal advisers. The audit manager told me to conclude that provisions are correctly recognised in the financial statements based on the evidence obtained, and to move on to my next piece of work. He said it didn't matter that I hadn't spoken to the legal advisers because the matter is immaterial to the financial statements.

'We received the final version of the financial statements and the chairman's statement to be published with the financial statements yesterday. I have quickly looked at the financial statements, but the audit manager said we need not perform a final detailed analytical review on the financial statements as the audit was relatively low risk. The manager also said that he had discussed the chairman's statement with the finance director, so no further work on it is needed. The audit has been quite time-pressured, and I know that the client wants the auditor's report to be issued as soon as possible.'

Exhibit 2:

The schedule of uncorrected misstatements included in Bradley Ltd's audit working papers is shown below, including notes to explain each matter included in the schedule. The audit engagement partner is holding a meeting with management tomorrow, at which the uncorrected misstatements will be discussed.

	Statement of profit or loss		*Statement of financial position*	
	Debit	*Credit*	*Debit*	*Credit*
	£	£	£	£
1. Share-based payment scheme	300,000			300,000
2. Restructuring provision		50,000	50,000	
3. Estimate of additional allowance required for slow-moving inventory	10,000			10,000
Totals	310,000	50,000	50,000	310,000

Notes.

1 A share-based payment scheme was established in January 20X4. Management has not recognised any amount in the financial statements in relation to the scheme, arguing that due to the decline in Bradley Ltd's share price, the share options granted are unlikely to be exercised. The audit conclusion is that an expense and related equity figure should be included in the financial statements.

2 A provision has been recognised in respect of a restructuring involving the closure of one of the steel processing plants. Management approved the closure at a board meeting in August 20X4, but only announced the closure to employees in September 20X4. The audit conclusion is that the provision should not be recognised.

3 The allowance relates to slow-moving inventory in respect of a particular type of steel alloy for which demand has fallen. Management has already recognised an allowance of £35,000, which is considered insufficient by the audit team.

13 Groom (P7 June 2013 amended) (49 mins)

(a) It is 1 July 20X5. You are a manager in Groom & Co, a firm of Chartered Certified Accountants. You have just attended a monthly meeting of audit partners and managers at which the audit of Spaniel Ltd was discussed.

The auditor's report on the financial statements of Spaniel Ltd, a long-standing audit client, for the year ended 31 December 20X4 was issued in April 20X5, and was unmodified. In May 20X5, Spaniel Ltd's audit committee contacted the audit engagement partner to discuss a fraud that had been discovered. The company's internal auditors estimate that £4.5 million has been stolen in a payroll fraud, which has been operating since May 20X4.

The audit engagement partner commented that neither tests of controls nor substantive audit procedures were conducted on payroll in the audit of the latest financial statements as in previous years' audits there were no deficiencies found in controls over payroll. The total assets recognised in Spaniel Ltd's financial statements at 31 December 20X4 were £80 million. Spaniel Ltd is considering suing Groom & Co for the total amount of cash stolen from the company, claiming that the audit firm was negligent in conducting the audit.

Required

Explain the matters that should be considered in determining whether Groom & Co is liable to Spaniel Ltd in respect of the fraud. **(12 marks)**

(b) You are also responsible for the audit of Clooney Ltd, the final audit of which is nearing completion. The following points have been noted for your attention by the audit senior:

Clooney Ltd is one of the world's leading leisure travel providers, operating under several brand names to sell package holidays. The company catered for more than 10 million customers in the last 12 months. Draft figures for the year ended 31 March 20X5 show revenue of £3,200 million, profit before tax of £150 million, and total assets of £4,100 million. Clooney Ltd's executives earn a bonus based on the profit before tax of the company.

You are the manager responsible for the audit of Clooney Ltd. The final audit is nearing completion, and the following points have been noted by the audit senior for your attention:

In January 20X5, thousands of holidaymakers were left stranded abroad after the company operating the main airline chartered by Clooney Ltd went into liquidation. The holidaymakers were forced to wait an average of two weeks before they could be returned home using an alternative airline. They have formed a group which is claiming compensation for the time they were forced to spend abroad, with the total claim amounting to £20 million. The items which the group is claiming compensation for include accommodation and subsistence costs, lost income and distress caused by the situation. The claim has not been recognised or disclosed in the draft financial statements, as management argues that the full amount payable will be covered by Clooney Ltd's insurance.

Required

Comment on the matters that you should consider, and explain the audit evidence you should expect to find in your review of the audit working papers for the year ended March 20X5 in respect of the compensation claim. **(8 marks)**

Professional marks will be awarded for the demonstration of skill in analysis and evaluation, and professional scepticism and judgement in your answer. **(5 marks)**

(Total = 25 marks)

14 Raven (P7 June 2012 amended) (49 mins)

It is 1 July 20X5. You are a senior manager in the audit department of Raven & Co. You are reviewing three situations which have arisen in respect of audit clients, which were recently discussed at the monthly audit managers' meeting

The following exhibits, available on the left-hand side of the screen, provide information relevant to the question:

(1) Proposal for development work with Grouse Co

(2) Information about a subsequent event at Plover Co

(3) Note from audit senior regarding a computer virus attack at Hendrix Co

This information should be used to answer the question requirements within the response options provided.

Exhibit 1

Grouse Ltd is a significant audit client which develops software packages. Its managing director, Max Partridge, has contacted one of your firm's partners regarding a potential business opportunity. The proposal is that Grouse Ltd and Raven & Co could jointly develop accounting and tax calculation software, and that revenue from sales of the software would be equally split between the two firms. Max thinks that Raven & Co's audit clients would be a good customer base for the product.

Exhibit 2

Plover Ltd is a private hospital which provides elective medical services, such as laser eye surgery to improve eyesight. The audit of its financial statements for the year ended 31 March 20X5 is currently taking place. The audit senior overheard one of the surgeons who performs laser surgery saying to his colleague that he is hoping to finish his medical qualification soon, and that he was glad that Plover Ltd did not check his references before employing him. While completing the subsequent events audit procedures, the audit senior found a letter from a patient's solicitor claiming compensation from Plover Ltd in relation to alleged medical negligence resulting in injury to the patient.

Exhibit 3

Dylan plc is a listed client of the firm and the audit for the year ended 31 March 20X5 is in progress. Dylan plc outsources its entire payroll, invoicing and credit control functions to Hendrix Ltd. In February 20X5, Hendrix Ltd suffered a computer virus attack on its operating system, resulting in the destruction of its accounting records, including those relating to Dylan plc. We have therefore been unable to perform the planned audit procedures on payroll, revenue and receivables, all of which are material to the financial statements. Hendrix Ltd has manually reconstructed the relevant figures as far as possible and has supplied a written statement to confirm that they are as accurate as possible, given the loss of accounting records.

Required

Using information contained in Exhibits 1 and 2:

Evaluate the ethical, commercial and other professional issues raised, and recommend any actions that should be taken in respect of:

(a) Grouse Ltd **(7 marks)**

(b) Plover Ltd **(7 marks)**

(c) Using information contained in Exhibit 3:

Comment on the actions that should be taken by the auditor and the implications for the auditor's report. **(6 marks)**

Professional marks will be awarded for the demonstration of skill in analysis and evaluation, professional scepticism and judgement, and commercial acumen in your answer. **(5 marks)**

(Total = 25 marks)

15 Dragon Group (P7 June 2009 amended) (49 mins)

The Dragon Group is a large group of companies operating in the furniture retail trade. The group has expanded rapidly in the last three years, by acquiring several subsidiaries each year. The management of the parent company, Dragon plc, has decided to put the audit of the group and all subsidiaries out to tender, as the current audit firm is not seeking re-election. The financial year end of the Dragon Group is 30 September 20X9.

You are a senior manager in Unicorn & Co, a global firm of Chartered Certified Accountants, with offices in over 150 countries across the world. Unicorn & Co has been invited to tender for the Dragon Group audit (including the audit of all subsidiaries). You manage a department within the firm which specialises in the audit of retail companies, and you have been assigned the task of drafting the tender document. You recently held a meeting with Edmund Jalousie, the group finance director, in which you discussed the current group structure, recent acquisitions, and the group's plans for future expansion.

The following **exhibit** provides information relevant to the question:

(1) Meeting with Edmund Jalousie

This information should be used to answer the question **requirements** within the response options provided

Exhibit 1

Meeting notes – Dragon Group

Group structure

The parent company owns 20 subsidiaries, all of which are wholly owned. Half of the subsidiaries are located in this country, and half overseas. Most of the foreign subsidiaries report under the same financial reporting framework as Dragon plc, but several prepare financial statements using local accounting rules.

Acquisitions during the year

Two companies were purchased in March 20X9, both located in this country:

- Mermaid Ltd, a company which operates 20 furniture retail outlets. The audit opinion expressed by the incumbent auditors on the financial statements for the year ended 30 September 20X8 was modified by a material misstatement in relation to the non-disclosure of a contingent liability. The contingent liability relates to a court case which is still ongoing.
- Minotaur Ltd, a large company, whose operations are distribution and warehousing. This represents a diversification away from retail, and it is hoped that the Dragon Group will benefit from significant economies of scale as a result of the acquisition.

Other matters

The acquisitive strategy of the group over the last few years has led to significant growth. Group revenue has increased by 25% in the last three years, and it is predicted to increase by a further 35% in the next four years as the acquisition of more subsidiaries is planned. The Dragon Group has raised finance for the acquisitions in the past by becoming listed on the stock exchanges of three different countries. A new listing on a foreign stock exchange is planned for January 20Y0. For this reason, management would like the group audit completed by 31 December 20X9.

Required

(a) Recommend and describe the principal matters to be included in your firm's tender document to provide the audit service to the Dragon Group: **(9 marks)**

(b) Evaluate the matters that should be considered before accepting the audit engagement, in the event of your firm being successful in the tender; and **(8 marks)**

(c) Define 'transnational audit', and discuss the features of a transnational audit that may contribute to a high level of audit risk in such an engagement. **(3 marks)**

Professional marks will be awarded for the demonstration of skill in analysis and evaluation, and professional scepticism and judgement and commercial acumen in your answer. **(5 marks)**

(Total = 25 marks)

Part D: Planning and conducting an audit of historical financial information

Questions 16 to 46 cover Planning and conducting an audit of historical financial information, the subject of Part D of the BPP Workbook for AAA.

16 Goldfinch (P7 Sep/Dec 2017 amended) (49 mins)

You are a manager in the audit department of Pigeon & Co, a firm of Chartered Certified Accountants. You are responsible for the audit of Goldfinch Gas plc, a company which is the main supplier of gas to business and residential customers across the country.

The audit fieldwork for the year ended 30 June 20W7 is nearing completion. The draft financial statements recognise profit before tax of £130 million (20W6 – £110 million), and total assets of £1,900 million (20W6 – £1,878 million).

You are reviewing the audit files and the following matters have been noted for your attention by the audit senior:

(1) File review points for Goldfinch

Required

Using the information contained in the Exhibit:

Comment on the matters to be considered, and explain the audit evidence you should expect to find during your file review in respect of each of the issues described below.

You are **NOT** required to explain the potential impact of the matters on the auditor's opinion or report.

Note. The split of the mark allocation is shown against each of the issues below. **(20 marks)**

Professional marks will be awarded for the demonstration of skill in analysis and evaluation, and professional scepticism and judgement in your answer. **(5 marks)**

(Total = 25 marks)

Exhibit: File review points for Goldfinch

(a) **Decommissioning provision**

A provision of £430 million (20W6 – £488 million) is recognised as a long-term liability. The provision is in respect of decommissioning a number of gas production and storage facilities when they are at the end of their useful lives. The estimate of the decommissioning costs has been based on price levels and technology at the reporting date and discounted to present value using an interest rate of 8% (20W6 – 6%). The timing of decommissioning payments is dependent on the estimated useful lives of the facilities but is expected to occur by 20Z6, with the majority of the provision being utilised between 20X5 and 20Z0.

The accounting policy note discusses the methodology used by management for determining the value of the decommissioning provision and states that this is an area of critical accounting judgements including key areas of estimation uncertainty. The estimate has been made by management. In previous years, a management expert was engaged to provide the estimate but as this was expensive, management decided to produce their own estimate for the year ended 30 June 20W7. **(8 marks)**

(b) **Depreciation**

The draft statement of financial position includes plant and equipment, unrelated to gas production and storage facilities, at a carrying amount of £65 million. There was a change in the estimation technique used to determine the depreciation in respect of these assets during the year. Depreciation was previously calculated on a straight-line basis over a 10-year useful life, but from 1 July 20W6, the useful life has been amended to 15 years. The finance director explained to the audit team that the review of estimated useful life has been made on the basis that the assets are lasting longer than originally anticipated.

The change in depreciation policy has been accounted for as a prior year adjustment, resulting in an increase of £20 million to property, plant and equipment and to retained earnings. The depreciation expense recognised in draft profit for the year to 30 June 20W7 is £12 million (20W6 – £15 million). **(6 marks)**

(c) **Trade receivables**

The draft statement of financial position recognises total trade receivables of £450 million (20W6 – £390 million).

The audit team has performed substantive analytical procedures on trade receivables with the following results:

Receivables collection period:	*20W7*	*20W6*
Residential customers	65 days	58 days
Business customers	50 days	55 days

The notes to the financial statements contain the following information relating to trade receivables:

Trade receivables:	*20W7*	*20W6*
	£ million	£ million
Residential customers	158	145
Business customers	356	289
Less allowance for credit losses	(64)	(44)
Net trade receivables	450	390

Receivables from business customers are generally reviewed for impairment on an individual basis when a customer changes their gas supplier, discontinuing their relationship with the Group. Receivables from residential customers are reviewed for impairment where they are more than 90 days late in paying their bill, or where customers have a history of late payment. Since a new customer billing system was introduced in September 20W6, management has exercised additional judgement regarding the appropriate level of allowance for these trade receivables. **(6 marks)**

17 Ted (P7 June 2015 amended) (98 mins)

It is 1 July 20X5. You are a senior audit manager in Craggy & Co, which is an international firm of Chartered Certified Accountants with branches in many countries, and which offers a range of audit and assurance services to its clients. Your responsibilities include, in addition to audit work, reviewing ethical matters which arise with audit clients, and dealing with approaches from prospective audit clients.

The following exhibits provide information relevant to the question:

(1) Partner's email: an email which you have received from Jack Hackett, the audit engagement partner.

(2) Information regarding a request received to submit an audit proposal.

(3) Notes from a meeting between Jack Hackett and Len Brennan, Ted plc's finance director.

(4) Extracts from the draft financial statements and results of preliminary analytical review.

This information should be used to answer the question requirement within your chosen response option(s).

Required

Respond to the instructions in the email from the audit engagement partner.

Note. The split of the mark allocation is shown in Exhibit 1 – Partner's email. **(40 marks)**

Professional marks will be awarded for the demonstration of skill in communication, analysis and evaluation, professional scepticism and judgement, and commercial acumen in your answer. **(10 marks)**

(Total = 50 marks)

Exhibit 1:

To: Audit manager

From: Jack Hackett

Subject: Ted plc audit planning

Hello

Our firm has been invited to submit an audit proposal to the management of Ted plc. If we are successful in gaining the work, I will need you to begin planning the audit of Ted plc.

I have already gathered some information about Ted plc and also had an initial meeting with the company's finance director, Len Brennan, and have provided you with that information. In addition, I have asked one of the audit seniors to begin to carry out preliminary analytical review procedures on Ted plc's draft financial statements, and the results of the review performed so far are also provided to you.

For the purpose of providing some practical training to some of our audit supervisors, please can you use the information in Exhibit 2 to:

(a) (i) Explain the specific matters to be included in the audit proposal (tender document), other than those relating to the audit fee; and **(8 marks)**

(ii) Discuss the issues to be considered by the audit firm in determining a fee for the audit including any ethical matters raised assuming that Craggy & Co is appointed auditor of Ted plc. **(6 marks)**

Then, using the remaining information, I need you to prepare briefing notes for my use in which you:

(b) Discuss the matters specific to the planning of an initial audit engagement which should be considered in developing the audit strategy. **(5 marks)**

(c) Evaluate and prioritise the significant audit risks to be considered in planning the audit of Ted plc. **(17 marks)**

(d) Design the principal audit procedures to be performed in the audit of the portfolio of short-term investments. **(4 marks)**

Thank you.

Exhibit 2:

The management of Ted plc has invited Craggy & Co to submit an audit proposal (tender document) for their consideration. Ted plc has grown rapidly in the last few years, and has recently achieved a stock exchange listing. The previous auditors of Ted plc, a small and unrelated firm called Crilly & Co, resigned in September 20X4 as the firm's resources were no longer sufficient to meet the demands of the audit of a listed company. The audit opinion on the financial statements for the year ended 31 May 20X4 was unmodified.

The company designs, develops and publishes computer games, and some of its start-up funding was raised from a venture capital company. The software used in the computer games is developed in this country, but the manufacture of the physical product takes place overseas. Ted plc has two full-time accountants who use an off-the-shelf accounting package to record transactions and to prepare financial information. The company has a financial year ending 31 May 20X5.

The following comment was made by Dougal Doyle, the company's founder and managing director, in relation to the audit proposal and potential audit fee:

'I am looking for a firm of auditors who will give me a competitive audit fee. I am hoping that the fee will be quite low, as I am willing to pay more for services that I consider more beneficial to the business, such as strategic advice. I would like the audit fee to be linked to Ted plc's success in expanding overseas as a result of the audit firm's advice. Hopefully the audit will not be too disruptive and I would like it completed within four months of the year end.'

Exhibit 3:

Ted plc was formed ten years ago by Dougal Doyle, a graduate in multimedia computing. The has published many highly successful games which have won industry awards. In the last two years the company invested £100 million in creating games designed to appeal to a broad, global audience and sales are now made in over 60 countries, with demand being particularly strong in North America and Europe.

Computer games are largely sold through retail outlets, but approximately 25% of Ted plc's revenue is generated through sales made on the company's website. In some countries Ted plc's products are distributed under licences which give the licence holder the exclusive right to sell the products in that country. The cost of each licence to the distributor depends on the estimated sales in the country to which it relates, and licences last for an average of five years. The income which Ted plc receives from the sale of a licence is deferred over the period of the licence. At 31 May 20X5 the total amount of deferred income recognised in Ted plc's statement of financial position is £18 million.

As part of a five-year strategic plan, Ted plc obtained a stock market listing in December 20X4. The listing and related share issue raised a significant amount of finance, and many shares are held by institutional investors. Dougal Doyle retains a 20% equity shareholding, and a further 10% of the company's shares are held by his family members.

Despite being listed, the company does not have an internal audit department, and there is only one non-executive director on the board. These issues are explained in the company's annual report.

Recently, a small treasury management function was established to manage the company's foreign currency transactions, which include forward exchange currency contracts. The treasury management function also deals with short-term investments. In January 20X5, cash of £8 million was invested in a portfolio of equity shares held in listed companies, which is to be held in the short term as a speculative investment. The shares are recognised as a financial asset at cost of £8 million in the draft statement of financial position. The fair value of the shares at 31 May 20X5 is £6 million.

As a listed company, Ted plc is required to disclose its earnings per share figure. Dougal Doyle would like this to be based on an adjusted earnings figure which does not include depreciation or amortisation expenses.

Exhibit 4:

STATEMENT OF PROFIT OR LOSS (EXTRACT)

	Year to 31 May 20X5	*Year to 31 May 20X4*	*% change*
	Draft	*Actual*	
	£'000	£'000	
Revenue	98,000	67,000	46.3% increase
Gross profit	65,000	40,000	62.5% increase
Operating profit	12,000	9,200	30.4% increase
Finance charge	4,000	3,800	5.3% increase
Profit before tax	8,000	5,400	48.1% increase

	Year to 31 May 20X5	Year to 31 May 20X4	% change
	Draft	Actual	
	£'000	£'000	
Earnings per share	89.6 pence per share	–	

Note. Earnings per share has been calculated as follows:

	£'000
Profit before tax	8,000
Add depreciation	1,100
Amortisation	6,000
Adjusted profit before tax	15,100
Adjusted profit before tax	15,100,000
Number of equity shares at 31 May 20X5	16,850,000 = 89.6 pence per share

STATEMENT OF FINANCIAL POSITION (EXTRACT)

	31 May 20X5	31 May 20X4	% change
	Draft	Actual	
	£'000	£'000	
Non-current assets			
Intangible assets – development costs	58,000	35,000	65.7% increase
Total assets	134,000	105,000	27.6% increase

18 Francis (P7 December 2014 amended) (49 mins)

You are a manager in the audit department of Williams & Co and you are reviewing the audit working papers in relation to the Francis Group (the Group), whose financial year ended on 31 July 20X4. Your firm audits all components of the Group, which consists of a parent company and three subsidiaries – Marks Ltd, Roberts Ltd and Teapot Ltd.

The Group manufactures engines which are then supplied to the car industry. The draft consolidated financial statements recognise profit for the year to 31 July 20X4 of £23 million (20X3 – £33 million) and total assets of £450 million (20X3 – £455 million).

Information in respect of two issues has been highlighted for your attention during the file review:

Required

Using the information contained in the Exhibit:

Comment on the matters to be considered, and explain the audit evidence you should expect to find during your review of the audit working papers in respect of each of the issues described below.

Note. The split of the mark allocation is shown against each of the issues below. Assume it is 10 December 20X4. **(20 marks)**

Professional marks will be awarded for the demonstration of skill in analysis and evaluation, and professional scepticism and judgement in your answer. **(5 marks)**

(Total = 25 marks)

Exhibit:

(a) An 80% equity shareholding in Teapot Ltd was acquired on 1 August 20X3. Goodwill on the acquisition of £27 million was calculated at that date and remains recognised as an intangible asset at that value at the year end. The goodwill calculation performed by the Group's management is shown below:

	£'000
Purchase consideration	75,000
Fair value of 20% non-controlling interest	13,000
	88,000
Less fair value of Teapot Ltd's identifiable net assets at acquisition	(61,000)
Goodwill	27,000

In determining the fair value of identifiable net assets at acquisition, an upwards fair value adjustment of £300,000 was made to the book value of a property recognised in Teapot Ltd's financial statements at a carrying value of £600,000.

A loan of £60 million was taken out on 1 August 20X3 to help finance the acquisition. The loan carries an annual interest rate of 6%, with interest payments made annually in arrears. The loan will be repaid in 20 years at a premium of £5 million. **(12 marks)**

(b) In September 20X4 a natural disaster caused severe damage to the property complex housing the Group's head office and main manufacturing site. For health and safety reasons, a decision was made to demolish the property complex. The demolition took place three weeks after the damage was caused. The property had a carrying value of £16 million at 31 July 20X4.

A contingent asset of £18 million has been recognised as a current asset and as deferred income in the Group statement of financial position at 31 July 20X4, representing the amount claimed under the Group's insurance policy in respect of the disaster. **(8 marks)**

19 Thurman (P7 Sep/Dec 2016 amended) (49 mins)

It is 1 July 20X5. You are the manager responsible for the audit of Thurman Ltd, a manufacturing company which supplies stainless steel components to a wide range of industries. The company's financial year ended on 31 March 20X5 and you are reviewing the audit work which has been completed on a number of material balances and transactions: assets held for sale, capital expenditure and payroll expenses. A summary of the work which has been performed is given below and in each case the description of the audit work indicates the full extent of the audit procedures carried out by the audit team.

Required

In respect of each of the three matters described below:

(i) Comment on the sufficiency and appropriateness of the audit evidence obtained; and

(ii) Design further audit procedures to be performed by the audit team.

Note. The split of the mark allocation is shown against each of the matters below. **(20 marks)**

Professional marks will be awarded for the demonstration of skill in analysis and evaluation, and professional scepticism and judgement in your answer. **(5 marks)**

(Total = 25 marks)

Exhibit:

(a) **Assets held for sale**

Due to the planned disposal of one of Thurman Ltd's factory sites, the property and associated assets have been classified as held for sale in the financial statements. A manual journal has been posted by the finance director to reclassify the assets as current assets and to adjust the value of the assets for impairment and reversal of depreciation charged from the date at which the assets met the criteria to be classified as held for sale. The finance director asked the audit senior to check the journal before it was posted on the basis of there being no one with the relevant knowledge to do this at Thurman Ltd.

The planned disposal was discussed with management. A brief note has been put into the audit working papers stating that in management's opinion the accounting treatment to classify the factory as held for sale is correct. The manual journal has been arithmetically checked by a different member of the audit team and the amounts agreed back to the non-current asset register. **(7 marks)**

(b) **Capital expenditure**

When auditing the company's capital expenditure, the audit team selected a material transaction to test and found that key internal controls over capital expenditure were not operating effectively. Authorisation had not been obtained for an order placed for several vehicles, and appropriate segregation of duties over initiating and processing the transaction was not maintained.

The audit team noted details of the internal control deficiencies and updated the systems notes on the permanent audit file to reflect the deficiencies. The audit work completed on this order was to agree the purchase of the vehicles to purchase invoices and to the cash book and bank statement. The rest of the audit work on capital expenditure was completed in accordance with the audit programme. **(6 marks)**

(c) **Payroll expenses**

The payroll function is outsourced to Jackson Ltd, a service organisation which processes all of Thurman Ltd's salary expenses. The payroll expenses recognised in the financial statements have been traced back to year-end reports issued by Jackson Ltd. The audit team has had no direct contact with Jackson Ltd as the year-end reports were sent to Thurman Ltd's finance director who then passed them to the audit team. **(7 marks)**

20 Faster Jets (P7 December 2014 amended) (49 mins)

Faster Jets Ltd is an airline company, and is a new audit client of Brown & Co. You are responsible for the audit of the financial statements for the year ended 30 November 20X4. The draft financial statements recognise revenue of £150 million and total assets of £250 million.

The following **exhibits** provide information relevant to the question:

(1) Information about Faster Jets Ltd purchase of land

(2) Faster Jets Ltd CSR report

This information should be used to answer the question **requirements** within the response options provided.

Exhibit 1

During the year, Faster Jets Ltd purchased several large plots of land located near major airports at a cost of £12.5 million. The land is currently rented out and is classified as investment property, which is recognised in the draft financial statements at a fair value of £14.5 million. The audit partner has suggested the use of an auditor's expert to obtain evidence in respect of the fair value of the land.

Exhibit 2

Your firm has also been engaged to perform a separate assurance engagement on Faster Jets Ltd's corporate social responsibility (CSR) report. This engagement will be performed by Brown & Co's specialist social and environmental assurance department and there are no ethical threats created by the provision of this service in addition to the audit. An extract from the draft CSR report is shown below.

CSR objective	CSR target	Performance in 20X4
Continue to invest in local communities and contribute to charitable causes	Make direct charitable cash donations to local charities	Donations of £550,000 were made to local charities
	Build relationships with global charities and offer free flights to charitable organisations	800 free flights with a value of £560,000 were provided to charities
	Develop our Local Learning Initiative and offer free one-day education programmes to schools	£750,000 was spent on the Local Learning Initiative and 2,250 children attended education days
Reduce environmental impact of operations	Reduce the amount of vehicle fuel used on business travel by our employees	The number of miles travelled in vehicles reduced by 5%, and the amount spent on vehicle fuel reduced by 7%

Required

(a) Using the information provided in Exhibit 1:

(i) Explain the additional information which you require to plan the audit of the land; and **(5 marks)**

(ii) Explain the matters to be considered in assessing the reliance which can be placed on the work of an auditor's expert. **(5 marks)**

(b) Using the information provided in Exhibit 2:

(i) Discuss the difficulties in measuring and reporting on social and environmental performance; and **(4 marks)**

(ii) Design the procedures to be used to gain assurance on the validity of the performance information in Faster Jets Ltd's CSR report. **(6 marks)**

Professional marks will be awarded for the demonstration of skill in analysis and evaluation, and professional scepticism and judgement in your answer. **(5 marks)**

(Total = 25 marks)

21 Magpie (P7 June 2012 amended) (98 mins)

It is 1 July 20X5. You are a manager in Magpie & Co, responsible for the audit of the CS Group.

The following exhibits provide information relevant to the question:

(1) An email which you have received from Jo Daw, the audit engagement partner.

(2) Extracts from the permanent file on the audit of the CS Group.

(3) Notes from a meeting between Jo Daw and Steve Eagle, the finance director of the CS Group.

This information should be used to answer the question requirement within your chosen response option(s).

Required

Respond to the instructions in the email from the audit engagement partner.

Note. The split of the mark allocation is shown in the partner's email (Exhibit 1). **(40 marks)**

Professional marks will be awarded for the demonstration of skill in communication, analysis and evaluation, professional scepticism and judgement, and commercial acumen in your answer. **(10 marks)**

(Total = 50 marks)

Exhibit 1: Email from the audit engagement partner

To: Audit manager

From: Jo Daw

Subject: CS Group audit planning

Hello

I have just been to a meeting with Steve Eagle, the finance director of the CS Group. We were discussing recent events which will have a bearing on our forthcoming audit, and my notes from the meeting are attached to this email. One of the issues discussed is the change in group structure due to the acquisition of Canary Ltd earlier this year. Our firm has been appointed as auditor of Canary Ltd, which has a year ending 31 August 20X5, and the terms of the engagement have been agreed with the client. We need to start planning the audits of the three components of the Group, and of the consolidated financial statements.

(a) Using the information provided, I require you to prepare briefing notes for my use, in which you:

(i) Evaluate the implications of the acquisition of Canary Ltd for the audit planning of the individual and consolidated financial statements of the CS Group. **(7 marks)**

(ii) Evaluate and prioritise the significant risks of material misstatement to be considered in the audit planning of the individual and consolidated financial statements of the CS Group, identifying any matters that are not relevant to the audit planning. **(22 marks)**

(iii) Design the principal audit procedures to be performed in respect of the goodwill initially recognised on the acquisition of Canary Ltd **(5 marks)**

(b) During the discussion, Steve Eagle said that he would like me to attend the CS Group's board meetings on a monthly basis so that our firm can be made aware of any issues relating to the audit as soon as possible. Also, Steve asked if one of our audit managers could be seconded to Starling Co in temporary replacement of its finance director who recently left, and he asked for our help in recruiting a permanent replacement.

Please provide me with a response to Steve in which you:

Evaluate the ethical implications of these three requests.

Thank you. **(6 marks)**

Exhibit 2: Permanent file (extract)

An extract from the permanent audit file describing the CS Group's history and operations is shown below.

Crow Ltd was incorporated 100 years ago. It was founded by Joseph Crow, who established a small pottery making tableware such as dishes, plates and cups. The products quickly grew popular, with one range of products becoming highly sought after when it was used at a royal wedding. The company's products have retained their popularity over the decades, and the Crow brand enjoys a strong identity and good market share.

Ten years ago, Crow Ltd made its first acquisition by purchasing 100% of the share capital of Starling Ltd. Both companies benefited from the newly formed CS Group, as Starling Ltd itself had a strong brand name in the pottery market. The CS Group has a history of steady profitability and stable management.

Crow Ltd and Starling Ltd have a financial year ending 30 September 20X5, and your firm has audited both companies for several years.

Exhibit 3: Notes from meeting with Steve Eagle, finance director of the CS Group

Acquisition of Canary Ltd

The most significant event for the CS Group this year was the acquisition of Canary Ltd, which took place on 1 April 20X5. Crow Ltd purchased all of Canary Ltd's equity shares for cash consideration of £125 million, and further contingent consideration of £30 million will be paid on the third anniversary of the acquisition, if the Group's revenue grows by at least 8% per year. Crow Ltd engaged an external provider to perform due diligence on Canary Ltd, whose report indicated that the fair value of Canary Ltd's net assets was estimated to be £110 million at the date of acquisition. Goodwill arising on the acquisition has been calculated as follows.

	£m
Fair value of consideration:	
Cash consideration	125
Contingent consideration	30
	155
Less fair value of identifiable net assets acquired	(110)
Goodwill	45

To help finance the acquisition, Crow Ltd issued loan stock at par on 31 March 20X5, raising cash of £100 million. The loan has a five-year term and will be repaid at a premium of £20 million. 5% interest is payable annually in arrears. It is Group accounting policy to recognise financial liabilities at amortised cost.

Canary Ltd manufactures pottery figurines and ornaments. The company is considered a good strategic fit to the Group, as its products are luxury items like those of Crow Ltd and Starling Ltd, and its acquisition will enable the Group to diversify into a different market. Approximately 30% of its sales are made online, and it is hoped that online sales can soon be introduced for the rest of the Group's products. Canary Ltd has only ever operated as a single company, so this is the first year that it is part of a group of companies.

Financial performance and position

The Group has performed well this year, with forecast consolidated revenue for the year to 30 September 20X5 of £135 million (20X4 – £125 million), and profit before tax of £8.5 million (20X4 – £8.4 million). A breakdown of the Group's forecast revenue and profit is shown below.

	Crow Ltd	*Starling Ltd*	*Canary Ltd*	*CS Group*
	£m	£m	£m	£m
Revenue	69	50	16	135
Profit before tax	3.5	3	2	8.5

Note. Canary Ltd's results have been included from 1 April 20X5 (date of acquisition) and forecast up to 30 September 20X5, the CS Group's financial year end.

The forecast consolidated statement of financial position at 30 September 20X5 recognises total assets of £550 million.

Other matters

Starling Ltd received a grant of £35 million on 1 May 20X5 in relation to redevelopment of its main manufacturing site. The government is providing grants to companies for capital expenditure on environmentally friendly assets. Starling Ltd has spent £25 million of the amount received on solar panels which generate electricity, and it intends to spend the remaining £10 million on upgrading its production and packaging lines.

During the year to 30 September 20X5 it was discovered that an error had been made by a member of Crow Ltd's finance department which had resulted in the overstatement of deferred revenue by £10,000 in the prior period. A thorough investigation of the causes of the error was conducted, which concluded that the error was isolated.

On 1 March 20X5, a new IT system was introduced to Crow Ltd and Starling Ltd, with the aim of improving financial reporting controls and to standardise processes across the two companies. Unfortunately, Starling Ltd's finance director left the company last week.

Share options

Crow Ltd granted 150 of its employees 600 share options each on 1 October 20X4. The options vest on 30 September 20X6. Only those employees working for Crow Ltd at the vesting date will actually vest.

The fair value of the options at various dates has been estimated as follows:

1 October 20X4	£6
30 September 20X5	£8
30 September 20X6	£9

During 20X5, five employees left the company, and Crow Ltd anticipates that a total of 10% of the current employees will leave in the course of the vesting period.

Crow Ltd has recognised £720,000 (150 × 600 × 8) as an expense, and a non-current liability of the same amount.

22 Adder (P7 June 2015 amended) (49 mins)

It is 1 July 20X5. The Adder Group (the Group) has been an audit client of your firm for several years. You have recently been assigned to act as audit manager, replacing a manager who has fallen ill, and the audit of the Group financial statements for the year ended 31 March 20X5 is underway. The Group's activities include property management and the provision of large storage facilities in warehouses owned by the Group. The draft consolidated financial statements recognise total assets of £150 million, and profit before tax of £20 million.

The following **exhibits** provide information relevant to the question:

(1) Details of audit working paper review points arising from the Group audit

(2) Note from audit senior on the Group audit.

This information should be used to answer the question **requirements** within the response option provided.

Exhibit 1

The audit engagement partner, Edmund Black, has asked you to review the audit working papers in relation to two audit issues which have been highlighted by the audit senior. Information on each of these issues is given below:

(1) In December 20X4, a leisure centre complex was sold for proceeds equivalent to its fair value of £35 million, the related assets have been derecognised from the Group statement of financial position, and a profit on disposal of £8 million is included in the Group statement of profit or loss for the year. The sale qualifies as a sale in line with IFRS 15 Revenue from Contracts with Customers.

At the date of the sale the fair value of the complex was £33 million. According to the Group's website, it continues to operate services from this leisure centre and a lease liability of £22 million has been created on the 20X5 draft financial statements in relation to the complex.

(2) In January 20X5, the Group acquired 52% of the equity shares of Baldrick Ltd. This company has not been consolidated into the Group as a subsidiary, and it is instead accounted for as an associate. The Group finance director's reason for this accounting treatment is that Baldrick Ltd's operations have not yet been integrated with those of the rest of the Group. Baldrick Ltd's financial statements recognise total assets of £18 million and a loss for the year to 31 March 20X5 of £5 million.

Exhibit 2

The audit senior also left the following note for your attention:

'I have been working on the audit of properties, including the Group's storage facility warehouses. Customers rent individual self-contained storage areas of a warehouse, for which they are given keys allowing access by the customer at any time. The Group's employees rarely enter the customers' storage areas.

'It seems the Group's policy for storage contracts, which generate revenue of less than £10,000, is that very little documentation is required, and the nature of the items being stored is not always known. While visiting one of the Group's warehouses, the door to one of the customers' storage areas was open, so I looked in and saw what appeared to be potentially hazardous chemicals stored in large metal drums marked with warning signs. I asked the warehouse manager about the items being stored, and he became very aggressive, refusing to allow me to ask other employees about the matter and threatening me if I alerted management to the storage of these items. I did not mention the matter to anyone else at the client.'

Required

(a) Using the information provided in Exhibit 1, comment on the matters to be considered, and explain the audit evidence you should expect to find in your review of the audit working papers. **(13 marks)**

(b) Discuss the implications of the information provided in Exhibit 2 for the completion of the audit, commenting on the auditor's responsibilities in relation to laws and regulations, and on any ethical matters arising. **(7 marks)**

Professional marks will be awarded for the demonstration of skill in analysis and evaluation, and professional scepticism and judgement in your answer. **(5 marks)**

(Total = 25 marks)

23 Beth & Co (Mar/Jun 2021 amended) (49 mins)

It is 1 July 20X5. You are a manager in Beth & Co, a firm of Chartered Certified Accountants, responsible for the audit of Matty plc for the year ended 31 March 20X5.

You have been provided with the following exhibits:

(1) Audit completion review – provides details of matters which have been brought to your attention by the audit supervisor.

(2) Update and draft auditor's report – provides an update on the outcome of initial discussions with the client and details of the auditor's report which has now been drafted by the audit supervisor.

Required

(a) Using the information in Exhibit 1, comment on the matters to be considered and explain the audit evidence you would expect to find during your review of the audit working papers on 1 July 20X5, in relation to the issues identified.

Note. The following mark allocation is provided as guidance for this requirement:

(i) Railway operating licence and going concern **(7 marks)**

(ii) Purchased customer list **(8 marks)**

(b) With reference to Exhibit 2, and assuming that no further adjustments will be made to the financial statements in relation to the railway operating licence, evaluate the appropriateness of the draft auditor's report produced by the audit supervisor. **(5 marks)**

Professional marks will be awarded for the demonstration of skill in analysis and evaluation, professional scepticism and judgment, and commercial acumen in your answer **(5 marks)**

(Total = 25 marks)

Exhibit 1: Audit completion review

Matty plc is a listed transport company which provides train and bus services for the public on a national basis. The audit of Matty plc for the year ended 31 March 20X5 is nearly complete and you are reviewing the audit working papers. Matty plc is a new audit client for Beth & Co this year. The previous auditors issued an unmodified opinion on the financial statements for the year ended 31 March 20X4.

Matty plc's draft financial statements recognise revenue of £60.1 million (20X4 – £94.3 million), profit before tax of £10.5 million (20X4 – £22.1 million) and total assets of £28.4 million (20X4 – £31.1 million). Materiality has been set by the audit engagement partner at £1.05million.

The audit supervisor has brought the following matters to your attention:

Railway operating licence and going concern

Matty plc has operated a national railway service for the last 19 years. Matty plc's national railway operations have been the subject of adverse publicity over the last 12 months in relation to the unreliability of its services including the late running of its trains.

The licence to operate the national railway is put out to tender by the national government every five years. Matty plc's existing licence is due for renewal on 28 February 20X6. The current tendering process is approaching completion and despite the recent operational problems, Matty plc was informed on 30 June 20X5 that the company was the government's preferred option. This was on the understanding that the company would address the recent criticisms of its poor service levels. The company was also informed that the tender would still be subject to a detailed review in one month's time prior to its being awarded. The national railway generated £40.2 million of revenue in 20X5 (£47.2 million in 20X4) and contributed pre-tax profit of £11.2 million this year (£13.3 million in 20X4).

Purchased customer list

On 1 April 20X4, Matty plc paid £6.9 million to acquire the customer list of Jess Coaches, a business which was terminating its operations. Jess Coaches hires out coaches and drivers to private and public sector customers. Its customer list includes many highly reputable listed companies and government bodies with a customer relationship and trading history going back more than 30 years.

On the basis of this trading history and the associated customer loyalty, the management of Matty plc assessed the useful life of the customer list as indefinite. The draft statement of financial position as at 31 March 20X5 recognises the customer list as an intangible asset at a total carrying amount of £6.9 million.

In the second half of the reporting period, however, two of Jess Coaches' largest clients moved to a new competitor. The management of Matty plc believe that while it would be difficult to identify a sales value for the customer list at the reporting date, they estimate the value in use of the customer list to be £7.2 million.

Exhibit 2: Update and draft auditor's report

It is now 22 July 20X5 and all matters, in relation to the purchased customer list have now been satisfactory resolved.

Following the submission of a customer petition to the government complaining about the company's poor service levels, on 19 July 20X5 the government released a statement announcing that it had withdrawn Matty plc's preferred bidder status and was reopening the tender process for the national railway licence.

The company's finance director has provided details of a short disclosure note he plans to include in the financial statements which refers to the uncertainties in relation to the current status of the tender and possible going concern issues which might arise for the company as a result. The disclosure note concludes with a statement that the management of Matty plc is very confident that the company will be successful in the tender process and that it will retain the national railway licence for at least a further five years.

The draft auditor's report includes an unmodified audit opinion and a key audit matters section which refers to the disclosure note described above and to related uncertainties in relation to Matty plc's going concern status.

24 York (P7 Mar/Jun 2016 amended) (49 mins)

(a) According to ISA (UK) 240 *The Auditor's Responsibilities Relating to Fraud in an Audit of Financial Statements*:

> 'When identifying and assessing the risks of material misstatement due to fraud, the auditor shall, based on a presumption that there are risks of fraud in revenue recognition, evaluate which types of revenue, revenue transactions or assertions give rise to such risks.'

Required

Discuss why the auditor should presume that there are risks of fraud in revenue recognition and why ISA (UK) 240 requires specific auditor responses in relation to the risks identified.

(7 marks)

(b) It is 1 July 20X5. You are the manager responsible for the audit of York Ltd, a chain of health and leisure clubs owned and managed by entrepreneur Phil Smith. The audit for the year ended 31 March 20X5 is nearing completion and the draft financial statements recognise total assets of £27 million and profit before tax of £2.2 million. The audit senior has left the following file notes for your consideration during your review of the audit working papers:

Cash transfers

During a review of the cash book, a receipt of £350,000 was identified which was accompanied by the description 'BD'. Bank statements showed that the following day a nearly identical amount was transferred into a bank account held in a foreign country. When I asked the financial controller about this, she requested that I speak to Mr Smith, as he has sole responsibility for cash management. According to Mr Smith, an old friend of his, Brian Davies, has loaned the money to the company to fund further expansion and the money has been invested until it is needed. Documentary evidence concerning the transaction has been requested from Mr Smith but has not yet been received.

Required

Evaluate the implications for the completion of the audit, recommending any further actions which should be taken by your audit firm. **(7 marks)**

(c) It is still 1 July 20X5. You are also responsible for the audit of Squire plc, and you are completing the review of its interim financial statements for the six months ended 31 March 20X5. Squire plc is a car manufacturer and historically has offered a three-year warranty on cars sold. The financial statements for the year ended 30 September 20X4 included a warranty provision of £1.5 million and recognised total assets of £27.5 million. You are aware that on 1 December 20X4, due to cost cutting measures, Squire plc stopped offering warranties on cars sold. The interim financial statements for the six months ended 31 March 20X5 do not recognise any warranty provision. Total assets are £30 million at 31 March 20X5.

Required

Assess the matters that should be considered in forming a conclusion on Squire plc's interim financial statements, and the implications for the review report. **(6 marks)**

Professional marks will be awarded for the demonstration of skill in analysis and evaluation and professional scepticism and judgement in your answer. **(5 marks)**

(Total = 25 marks)

25 Mondrian (P7 Sep/Dec 2015 amended) (98 mins)

It is 1 July 20X5. You are a manager in the audit department of Mondrian & Co, a firm of Chartered Certified Accountants. You are responsible for the audit of Dali plc, a longstanding client of your firm and a listed company specialising in the design and manufacture of equipment and machinery used in the quarrying industry. You are planning the audit of the financial statements for the year ending 30 September 20X5. The projected financial statements for the 20X5 year end recognise revenue of £138 million (20X4 – £135 million), profit before tax of £9.8 million (20X4 – £9.2 million) and total assets of £90 million (20X4 – £85 million). Dali plc became listed on an alternative stock exchange in the UK on 1 December 20X4 and is hoping to achieve a listing on a foreign stock exchange in March 20X6.

You have been provided with the following exhibits:

(1) An email which you have received from Sam Hockney, the audit engagement partner.

(2) Information about Dali plc's general background and activities.

(3) Notes from a meeting held between Sam Hockney and Dali plc's audit committee.

(4) Results of preliminary analytical review procedures performed on Dali plc's projected financial statements and other financial information.

Required

Respond to the instructions in the email from the audit engagement partner.

Note. The split of the mark allocation is shown in the partner's email (Exhibit 1). **(40 marks)**

Professional marks will be awarded for the demonstration of skill in communication, analysis and evaluation, professional scepticism and judgement, and commercial acumen in your answer.

(10 marks)

(Total = 50 marks)

Exhibit 1:

To: Audit manager

From: Audit engagement partner, Sam Hockney

Subject: Audit planning – Dali plc

Hello

I need you to start planning the audit of Dali plc. I know you are new to this audit client, so I have provided you with some background information, the results of some preliminary analytical review performed by one of the audit team members, and notes from a discussion I had with the company's audit committee yesterday. I require you to prepare briefing notes for use in the audit planning meeting which will be held next week. More junior members of the audit team will be present at the meeting, and I would like to give them an explanation of the term 'fraudulent financial reporting' so that they know what to look out for.

In these notes you are required to:

(a) (i) Evaluate and prioritise the significant audit risks to be considered in planning the audit of Dali plc; and **(24 marks)**

(ii) Recommend the additional information which would be relevant in the evaluation of audit risk. **(6 marks)**

(b) Explain the principal audit procedures to be performed in respect of:

(i) The valuation of work in progress; and **(5 marks)**

(ii) The recognition and measurement of the government grant. **(5 marks)**

Thank you.

Exhibit 2:

Dali plc was established 20 years ago and has become known as a leading supplier of machinery used in the quarrying industry, with its customers operating quarries which extract stone used mainly for construction. Its customer base is located solely in the UK but most of the components used in Dali plc's manufacturing process are imported from foreign suppliers.

The company operates several manufacturing sites where the machinery is designed and manufactured. Some of the sites provide employment in economically deprived areas, and Dali plc is keen to promote its success in community engagement and to demonstrate the positive social impact of its activities in these areas.

The machines and equipment made by Dali plc are mostly made to order in the company's manufacturing sites. Customers approach Dali plc to design and develop a machine or piece of equipment specific to their needs. Where management considers that the design work will be significant, the customer is required to pay a 30% payment in advance, which is used to fund the design work. The remaining 70% is paid on delivery of the machine to the customer. Typically, a machine takes three months to build, and a smaller piece of equipment takes on average six weeks. The design and manufacture of bespoke machinery involving payments in advance has increased during the year. Dali plc also manufactures a range of generic products which are offered for sale to all customers, including drills, conveyors and crushing equipment.

Exhibit 3:

This year has been successful from a strategic point of view in that Dali plc achieved its stock exchange listing in December 20X4, and in doing so raised a significant amount of equity finance.

The company's corporate governance was reviewed as part of the flotation process, resulting in the recruitment of three new non-executive directors and a new finance director. The company already had an internal audit department in place prior to the flotation, and the department's reports indicate that no significant issues have arisen in relation to systems and controls over financial reporting during this financial year.

In December 20X4, a cash-settled share-based payment plan was introduced for senior executives, who will receive a bonus on 30 September 20X7. The amount of the bonus will be based on the increase in Dali plc's share price from the date of the flotation, when it was £2.90, to the share price at 30 September 20X7. On the advice of the newly appointed finance director, no accounting entries have been made in respect of the plan, but the details relating to it will be disclosed in the notes to the financial statements.

The finance director recommended that the company's manufacturing sites should be revalued. An external valuation was performed in March 20X5, resulting in a revaluation surplus of £3.5 million being recognised in equity. The finance director has informed the audit committee that no deferred tax needs to be provided in respect of the valuation because the property is part of continuing operations and there is no plan for disposal.

In April 20X5, a government grant of £10 million was received as part of a government scheme to subsidise companies which operate in economically deprived areas. Specifically £2 million of the grant compensates the company for wages and salaries incurred in the year to 30 September 20X5. The remaining grant relates to the continued operations in the deprived area, with a condition of the grant being that the manufacturing site in that area will remain operational until April 20Y0.

In September 20X5 Dali plc entered into a new contract for the lease of several portable cleaning machines. The present value of the lease payments is £850,000. The contract is for five years, and the supplier has a substantive right to substitute alternative machines.

All of the company's engineering sites will be closed at the year end to allow the inventory counts to take place. According to the most recent management accounts which are available, at 31 August 20X5 work in progress is valued at £12 million (20X4 – £9.5 million) and the majority of these orders will not be complete until after the yearend. In recent weeks several customers have returned equipment due to faults, and Dali plc offers a warranty to guarantee that defective items will be replaced free of charge.

Dali plc's newly established audit committee has asked Mondrian & Co to perform an actuarial valuation on the company's defined benefit pension plan. One of the audit partners is a qualified actuary and has the necessary skills and expertise to perform the service. The pension liability in the 20X4 financial statements was £255,000.

Exhibit 4:

	Based on projected figures to 30 September 20X5	*Based on audited figures to 30 September20X4*
Operating margin	15%	13%
Inventory days	175 days	150 days
Receivables collection period	90 days	70 days
Trade payables payment period	60 days	55 days
Earnings share	75 pence per share	-
Share price	£3.50	-

26 Zed (P7 Sep/Dec 2016 amended) (98 mins)

It is 1 July 20X5. The Zed Communications Group (ZCG) is an audit client of your firm, Tarantino & Co, with a financial year ending 30 September 20X5. You are the manager assigned to the forthcoming audit. ZCG is a listed entity, one of the largest telecommunications providers in the UK and is seeking to expand internationally. ZCG also provides broadband and fixed telephone line services.

The following **exhibits** provide information relevant to the question:

(1) An email which you have received from Vincent Vega, the audit engagement partner.

(2) Notes from a meeting held between ZCG's finance director and Vincent Vega.

(3) Background information on ZCG's internal audit function and an extract of a report.

(4) Gull Ltd information.

This information should be used to answer the question **requirements** within the response option provided.

Required

Respond to the instructions in the email from the audit engagement partner.

Note. The split of the mark allocation is shown in the partner's email (Exhibit 1). **(40 marks)**

Professional marks will be awarded for the demonstration of skill in communication, analysis and evaluation, professional scepticism and judgement, and commercial acumen in your answer. **(10 marks)**

(Total = 50 marks)

Exhibit 1: Email from audit engagement partner

To: Audit engagement manager

From: Vincent Vega, audit engagement partner

Subject: ZCG audit planning, plus Gull Ltd

Hello

We need to begin planning the final audit of ZCG, which as you know is one of our largest audit clients. I met with the Group's finance director yesterday and I have provided you with notes from this meeting along with extracts from the latest management accounts. We also discussed the possibility of using the work of the Group's internal audit team, as this should improve audit efficiency. I have provided you with an extract from the latest report of the internal audit department.

Using all the information provided, you are required to prepare briefing notes for my use in which you:

(a) Evaluate and prioritise the significant audit risks relevant to planning the final audit of ZCG; **(17 marks)**

(b) Discuss the matters to be considered in determining the assistance which could be provided by, and the amount of reliance, if any, which can be placed on the work of ZCG's internal audit department; and **(7 marks)**

(c) Design the principal audit procedures to be performed on:

- The classification of the 50% equity shareholding in WTC as a joint venture; and
- The measurement of the intangible asset recognised in respect of the licence to operate in Farland.

Marks will be allocated equally between each area. **(10 marks)**

(d) Separately from this work on the ZCG audit, a matter has arisen in relation to another client of ours, Gull Ltd. The details are provided in Exhibit 4; I would like you to provide me with your comments on:

The ethical and professional matters in relation to the recruitment requests made by Gull Ltd **(6 marks)**

Your comments on the final situation – with Gull Ltd – should be presented separately from the briefing notes.

Thank you.

Exhibit 2: Notes from meeting with finance director

One of ZCG's strategic aims is to expand internationally, either by acquiring existing telecommunications providers in foreign countries, or by purchasing licences to operate in other countries.

In December 20X4, ZCG purchased a 50% equity shareholding in Wallace Tele Coms Ltd (WTC), a company operating in several countries where ZCG previously had no interests. The other 50% is held by Wolf Communications Ltd. The cost of the 50% equity shareholding was £45 million. ZCG is planning to account for its investment in WTC as a joint venture in the Group financial statements.

On 1 October 20X3, ZCG purchased a licence to operate in Farland, a rapidly expanding economy, at a cost of £65 million. The licence lasts for 10 years from the date that it was purchased. Since purchasing the licence, ZCG has established its network coverage in Farland and the network became operational on 1 April 20X5. The licence was recognised as an intangible asset at cost in the Group statement of financial position at 30 September 20X4. Since the network became operational, customer demand has been less than anticipated due to a competitor offering a special deal to its existing customers to encourage them not to change providers.

Most of ZCG's mobile phone customers sign a contract under which they pay a fixed amount each month to use ZCG's mobile network, paying extra if they exceed the agreed data usage and airtime limits. The contract also allows connection to a fixed landline and internet access using broadband and most contracts run for two or three years.

In order to extend its broadband services, ZCG has started to purchase network capacity from third-party companies. ZCG enters a fixed-term contract to use a specified amount of the seller's network capacity, with the seller determining which of its network assets are used by ZCG in supplying network services to its customers. Between October 20X4 and March 20X5 (the first six months of the year ended 30 September 20X5), ZCG purchased £17.8 million of network capacity from a range of suppliers, with the contract periods varying from twelve months to three years. The cost has been capitalised as an intangible asset.

ZCG makes substantial use of Equimal, a credit rating firm which holds the personal information of all of ZCG's customers for the purpose of providing ZCG with credit ratings for them. During June 20X5 it was reported in the national media that Equimal was the subject of a large-scale hacking attack, and that many of its customers' data may have been lost. It is not known at this stage precisely which data were stolen, but it is certain that at least some of ZCG's customers' data were among them.

In June 20X5, an employment tribunal found that for six months ZCG had not been paying the legal minimum wage to some of the new workers in its customer services call centre. Whenever a worker had been late for work, even by just one minute, ZCG had refused to pay them for the entire shift. This is contrary to the relevant regulations. It is likely that a fine will be levied against ZCG, but the tribunal is yet to determine its amount. In ZCG's jurisdiction, the maximum fine for breaching this legislation is £20,000. In addition to this, the wages that would need to be paid to the workers in question total around £210,000.

Exhibit 3: Internal audit background and report

ZCG has a well-established internal audit department which is tasked with a range of activities including providing assurance to management over internal controls and assisting the Group's risk management team. The internal audit department is managed by Jules Winfield, a qualified accountant with many years' experience. An extract from the executive summary of the latest internal audit report to the Group finance director is shown below:

'We are pleased to report that ZCG's internal controls are working well and there have been no significant changes to systems and controls during the year. As a result of our testing of controls we uncovered only two financial irregularities which related to:

- Failure to obtain appropriate authorisation and approval of senior management expense claims, such as travel and other reimbursements; the unsubstantiated expense claims amounted to £575,000.
- Inadequate access controls over the Group's IT systems; this resulted in a payroll fraud amounting to £750,000.'

FINANCIAL INFORMATION – EXTRACTS FROM LATEST MANAGEMENT ACCOUNTS

	8 months to 31 May 20X5	*Audited financial statements to 30 September 20X4*
	£m	£m
Revenue		
Europe	106	102
Americas	30	68
Southeast Asia	33	30
India	29	20
Total	198	220
	At 31 May 20X5	At 30 September 20X4
	£m	£m
Total assets	598	565

Exhibit 4: Gull Ltd information

Gull Ltd is a large company that is currently owned by the Brenner family, who own the majority of the company's shares. Following the completion of the audit this year, the finance director, Jim Brenner, contacted our firm and informed us that the family is now hoping to list the company on the UK stock exchange. They would like to recruit one of our audit partners for a six-month period to help prepare for the listing. As the board is concerned that the necessary skills and personnel to support the listing are not currently present within the company, Jim Brenner has also requested that our firm assist them in identifying and recruiting new members to the board.

Currently, most of the executive director roles are performed by family members, except for the directors of operations and human resources, who are both long-serving employees. The board operates no audit committee and there is only one non-executive director, who works elsewhere as an IT consultant. Other than the recruitment of new board members, Gull Ltd is not planning on making any changes to its governance structure prior to or subsequent to listing.

Gull Ltd has a financial year ending 31 December 20X5, and audit planning is scheduled to take place in October 20X5.

27 Redback (December 2018 amended) (98 mins)

It is 1 July 20X5. You are a manager in the audit department of Huntsman & Co, a firm of Chartered Certified Accountants, responsible for the audit of several companies and for evaluating the acceptance decisions in respect of potential new audit clients.

One of your audit clients is Redback Sports Ltd, which operates a chain of sport and leisure centres across the UK. The company has a financial year ending 30 September 20X5, and you are about to start planning the audit. Stella Cross, the audit engagement partner, met with the company's finance director last week to discuss business developments in the year and recent financial performance.

In addition, Stella has been approached by Mick Emu, the managing director of Emu Gyms Ltd. Mick has enquired regarding whether Huntsman & Co can provide the company with an audit or limited assurance review, and Stella would like you to evaluate this request. Huntsman & Co already provides a payroll service to Emu Gyms Ltd and has assisted Mick with his personal tax planning in the past. Mick also has a suspicion that several employees are carrying out a fraud at the company, and he has asked whether an audit or limited assurance review would have alerted him earlier to the situation.

You are provided with the following exhibits:

(1) An email you have received from Stella Cross, in respect of both Redback Sports Ltd and Emu Gyms Ltd.

(2) Notes of a meeting which Stella held recently with the finance director of Redback Sports Ltd.

(3) Extracts from the latest management accounts of Redback Sports Ltd.

(4) Notes of a telephone conversation which Stella had yesterday with Mick Emu, managing director of Emu Gyms Ltd.

Required

Respond to the instructions in the email from the audit engagement partner.

Note. The split of the mark allocation is shown in the partner's email (Exhibit 1). **(40 marks)**

Professional marks will be awarded for the demonstration of skill in communication, analysis and evaluation, professional scepticism and judgement, and commercial acumen in your answer. **(10 marks)**

(Total = 50 marks)

Exhibit 1: Email from audit engagement partner

To: Audit manager

From: Stella Cross, Audit engagement partner for Redback Sports Ltd

Subject: Audit planning for Redback Sports Ltd, and evaluation of accepting Emu Gyms Ltd as a potential audit client

Hello

I have provided you with some information in the form of a number of exhibits which you should use to help you with planning the audit of Redback Sports Ltd for the financial year ending 30 September 20X5.

Using the information provided in Exhibits 2 and 3, I require you to prepare briefing notes for my own use, in which you:

(a) Evaluate the significant business risks to be considered in planning the company's audit. **(7 marks)**

(b) Evaluate and prioritise the significant risks of material misstatement to be considered in developing the audit strategy and audit plan. **(16 marks)**

(c) Design the principal audit procedures to be used in the audit of the grant received from the government in April 20X5. **(5 marks)**

(d) In Exhibit 4, I have provided you with some information relating to Emu Gyms Ltd. In respect of this, in your briefing notes you should also:

Evaluate the matters to be considered in deciding whether to accept an engagement to provide Emu Gyms Co with an audit or limited assurance review. **(7 marks)**

(e) In relation to the suspicion of fraud being carried out at Emu Gyms Ltd:

Discuss whether an audit or limited assurance review of financial statements in previous years could have uncovered the fraud. **(5 marks)**

Thank you.

Exhibit 2: Notes of a meeting held yesterday

Meeting attendees:

Stella Cross, audit engagement partner, Huntsman & Co

Aneta Bay, finance director, Redback Sports Ltd.

Business background

Redback Sports Ltd operates 20 sport and leisure centres across the UK. Each centre has a large gym and a swimming pool, and many also have tennis and badminton courts. Given the nature of the company's operations, it has to comply with health and safety regulations set by the UK government, and its facilities are inspected regularly to ensure that all regulations are being followed, and for the company to retain its operating licence.

The company is not listed and therefore does not need to comply with the UK *Corporate Governance Code*. However, the company's chief operating officer and chairman consider it good practice to have independent input to the board, and there are two non-executive directors. One of the non-executive directors is a leisure industry expert who was chairman of a rival company, Lyre Leisure Ltd, for ten years. The second non-executive director is an academic who specialises in organisational behaviour and who has written several books on performance management in the sport and leisure industry.

The company's board has approved a plan to expand through acquiring other leisure and sport facility providers. The strategy is not likely to be implemented for another two years, when the board would like the first acquisition to take place. However, potential target companies will be identified in the next 12 to 18 months. Ultimately, the board would like to seek a flotation of the company within five years, and they consider that expanding the company would improve profits and make a stock exchange listing more feasible.

Redback Sports Ltd has a small internal audit department with two staff who report to the finance director, as the board does not have an audit committee.

The company offers a membership scheme whereby, for an annual subscription, members can use the facilities at any of the centres. Customers who are not members can pay to access a centre for a day under the company's 'pay as you go' plan. The membership scheme accounts for approximately 85% of the company's revenue, with the remaining revenue resulting from 'pay as you go' sales.

Business developments in the year

The industry is competitive, and the company's strategy is to encourage customers to renew their membership and to attract new members by offering a range of new activities. According to the finance director, a successful initiative which started in October 20X4 is the 'Healthy Kids' campaign; this offers children two hours coaching per week in a range of sports including swimming and tennis. This coaching is provided free as part of their parents' membership, and it has proved to be very successful – the finance director estimates that it has led to 3,000 new members since it was launched.

In January 20X5, the company opened a new sport and leisure centre in Cornwall which, as well as offering the usual facilities, also has a scuba diving centre and offers other water sports facilities. An investment of £12 million was also made in new gym equipment across all centres, to ensure that the company offers the most modern facilities to its customers.

An advertising campaign has been launched, to promote the company brand generally, and to make customers aware of the investments in the facilities which have been made.

Redback Sports Ltd is also involved with a UK government initiative to help unemployed people have access to sport facilities. The company received a grant of £2 million in April 20X5, under the terms of which it allows unemployed people three hours of free access to its facilities per month. By the end of June, it is forecast that 33,900 free hours of facility use will have been provided under this scheme. The government intends the initiative to run for three years, to promote long-term health of participants.

Exhibit 3: Extracts from management accounts of Redback Sports Ltd

	Note	*Based on projected figures to* 30 September 20X5	*Based on audited figures to* 30 September 20X4
Revenue	1	£53 million	£45 million
Income from government grant	2	£2 million	-
Operating margin	3	15%	10.7%
Profit before tax		£6.9 million	£4.6 million
Capital expenditure and associated borrowings	4	£32 million	£20 million
Cash		£1.4 million	£5.6 million
Total assets		£130 million	£110 million
Number of sport and leisure centres	5	20	18
Number of members	6	38,000	33,800
Number of 'pay as you go' entry tickets sold		108,000	102,600

Notes.

1 Revenue is forecast to increase significantly this year. This is largely due to the success of the advertising campaign and the 'Healthy Kids' programme (referred to in Exhibit 2).

2 The grant received of £2 million, the details of which are explained in Exhibit 2, has been recognised in full as income for the year.

3 The company's operating expenses includes the following items:

	20X5	*20X4*
	£'000	£'000
Staff costs	15,300	14,300
Marketing	8,500	8,500
Maintenance and repairs of facilities	5,500	5,300

4 Capital expenditure was mostly financed through borrowings. On 1 October 20X4, a ten-year, £30 million loan was received from the company's bank. The loan does not bear interest and is repayable at par value of £34 million.

5 Two new sport and leisure centres were opened this year. As well as the sport and leisure centre in Cornwall (referred to in Exhibit 2), a new centre was opened in an affluent area of London.

6 The management information system shows that members visit a sport and leisure centre on average three times per week.

Exhibit 4: Notes of a telephone conversation between Stella Cross and Mick Emu, managing director of Emu Gyms Ltd

Notes taken by Stella Cross

Mick Emu phoned me this morning to discuss developments at Emu Gyms Ltd and to enquire whether our firm could carry out either an audit of the company' financial statements, or a limited assurance review of them. This would be the first time that the financial statements have been subject to audit or limited assurance review.

Business background

The company was founded by Mick in 20X2, and since that time our firm has provided a payroll service for the company's staff, which now number 35 employees working in the company's four gyms, which are all in London. We have also provided Mick with advice on his personal tax position and financial planning in respect of his retirement, as he wants to sell the company in a few years' time. Mick runs the company with his son, Steve, who is a qualified personal trainer, and with his daughter, Siobhan, who is the marketing director. The company employs one accountant who prepares the management and financial accountants and who deals with customer memberships.

The company has grown quite rapidly in the last year, with revenue of £8 million for the financial year to 31 March 20X5, and with total assets of approximately £5.5 million. The comparative figures for 20X4 were revenue of £6.5 million and total assets of £4.8 million.

Loan application

Mick thinks that it will be difficult to attract more members for his gyms in existing locations and would like the company to expand by constructing a new gym in Oxford. He has discussed a loan of £4 million with the company's bank to fund the necessary capital expenditure. The bank manager has asked for the company's financial statements for the year to 31 March 20X5 and comparative information and has also requested a cash flow and profit forecast for the next three years in order to make a lending decision within the next two months.

Mick has asked whether a representative of the firm can attend a meeting with Mick and the company's bank manager, to support the loan application and answer questions from the bank manager, assuming that we are engaged to perform either an audit or a limited assurance review on the financial statements.

Suspected fraud

Mick mentioned that one of the reasons he would like an audit or limited assurance review of the financial statements is because he has noticed some unusual trends in the company's financial information. This has led him to suspect that several employees are carrying out a fraud. Each gym has a small shop selling gym wear and a café, where customers can buy light meals, drinks and snacks. Mick has noticed that the cash receipts from sales in the shops and cafés have reduced significantly in the last year, however, there has been no reduction in purchases from suppliers. As a consequence, the gross margin for these sales as reported in the management accounts has fallen from 32% to 26%. This indicated to him that staff members could be giving away items for free to customers, or they could be taking inventories from the shops and cafés for their personal use or to sell.

The shops and cafés keep a relatively small amount of inventory which is replenished on a regular basis. Until this year, sales in the shops represented approximately 5%, and café sales represented approximately 8% of the company's revenue. The figures for this year are 3% and 6% respectively.

Mick wonders whether the potential fraud would have been uncovered earlier, had the financial statements been subject to audit or limited assurance review in previous years.

28 Margot (Mar/Jun 2019 amended) (98 mins)

It is 1 July 20X5. You are a manager in the audit department of Snow & Co, a firm of Chartered Certified Accountants, and you are responsible for the audit of Margot Ltd. The company has a financial year ending 30 September 20X5, and you are about to start planning the audit.

Margot Ltd produces fruit-based food products using agricultural produce grown on its farms. Ben Duval, the audit engagement partner, met with the company's finance director last week to discuss business developments in the year and recent financial performance.

The following **exhibits** provide information relevant to the question:

(1) An email you have received from Ben Duval, in respect of the audit of Margot Ltd.

(2) Notes of a meeting which Ben held recently with the finance director of Margot Ltd.

(3) A reference document prepared by Snow & Co containing an overview of the accounting requirements applied in the agriculture sector.

(4) Extracts from the latest management accounts of Margot Ltd and accompanying notes, including the results of preliminary analytical procedures, which have been performed by a member of the audit team.

(5) An email which the audit engagement partner received from Len Larch, a production manager working at one of the company's orchards and soft fruit farms.

Required

Respond to the instructions in the email from the audit engagement partner.

Note. The split of the mark allocation is shown in the partner's email (Exhibit 1). **(40 marks)**

Professional marks will be awarded for the demonstration of skill in communication, analysis and evaluation, professional scepticism and judgement, and commercial acumen in your answer. **(10 marks)**

(Total = 50 marks)

Exhibit 1: Email from Ben Duval

To: Audit manager

From: Ben Duval, Audit engagement partner for Margot Ltd

Subject: Audit planning for Margot Ltd

Hello

I have provided you with some information in the form of a number of exhibits which you should use to help you with planning the audit of Margot Ltd for the financial year ending 30 September 20X5.

Using the information provided, I require you to prepare briefing notes for my own use, in which you:

(a) Evaluate and prioritise the significant risks of material misstatement to be considered in planning the company's audit. You **should not** include risks of material misstatement relating to the valuation of the company's bearer plants or biological assets, which will be evaluated separately. **(19 marks)**

(b) Design the principal audit procedures to be used in the audit of the impairment of the factory. **(5 marks)**

(c) Discuss the matters to be considered in planning to use an auditor's expert in the audit of the fruit, which are recognised as biological assets of the company. **(6 marks)**

(d) In Exhibit 5, I have provided you with an email I received from Len Larch, one of the company's production managers.

In respect of this, in your briefing notes you should also:

Discuss the audit implications of the email from Len Larch, recommending any further action to be taken by our firm. **(10 marks)**

Thank you.

Exhibit 2: Notes of a meeting held on 30 May 20X5

Meeting attendees:

Ben Duval, audit engagement partner, Snow & Co

Ayana Easton, finance director, Margot Ltd

Business background

Margot Ltd was established 30 years ago by Jim Margot, who began processing the fruit grown on his family farm to make a small range of food products including canned fruit and fruit juice. The farm includes apple and cherry orchards and fields in which soft fruit including strawberries and blueberries are grown. The business was relatively small until ten years ago, when the company began to expand by acquiring more farmland with different crops and building new production facilities. This extended the range of food products which could be processed, which now includes dried fruit and frozen fruit. The company sells its products under the 'Fructus Gold' brand name, and the goods are sold in major supermarkets and online on the company's website.

The company is not listed, and the Margot family members are the company's majority shareholders. Jim Margot retired several years ago, his daughter, Mia Margot, is the company's chief executive officer, and other family members hold positions in senior management.

Business developments in the year

Online sales

In the last year, sales made through the company's website grew significantly. The finance director believes that this was in response to an advertising campaign costing £225,000, which promoted the 'Fructus Gold' brand and coincided with the launch of a new online sales portal on the company website designed to make online ordering easier. To encourage online sales, the company has regular special offers, with discounts periodically offered on a selection of product lines and offers such as 'Buy One Get One Free' for a limited time on some products.

Research and development

Recently, concern over the level of plastic used in packaging has encouraged food producers to investigate the use of plastic-free packaging for their products. In October 20X4, the board approved a budget of £400,000 to be spent on research and development into new packaging for its products. By 30 May 20X5, £220,000 has been spent, with this amount being paid to ProPack, a firm of packaging specialists, to design and develop a range of plastic-free bottles, bags and containers. It is anticipated that the packaging will be ready for use in two years' time at which point the company will introduce it for use across its product range. ProPack is currently testing prototypes of items which have been developed, with encouraging results.

Loan

A loan of £375,000 was taken out during the year to support the company's research and development plans.

Factory damage

One of the company's several factories, used to process fruit and produce fruit juice, was damaged in November 20X4 when a severe storm occurred. High winds destroyed part of the factory roof, and heavy rain led to flooding and damage to machinery and processing equipment. The factory has not operated since the storm, and the finance director has performed an impairment review on the building and plant and equipment; details of the impairment review are given in the extract from the management accounts (Exhibit 4).

Use of an auditor's expert

The fruit growing on trees and the harvested agricultural produce are biological assets which were recognised at fair value of £3.1 million in the 20X4 audited financial statements. Due to the specialised nature of these assets, an auditor's expert will be used to provide evidence relating to their valuation. A resource document containing an overview of the accounting requirements in relation to the company's activities is provided in Exhibit 3.

Exhibit 3: Reference document Extract from Snow & Co's internal technical guidance for audit staff working with clients in the agriculture sector

IAS 16 *Property, Plant and Equipment* Bearer plants

Definition: A bearer plant is defined under IAS 16 as 'a living plant that:

- is used in the production or supply of agricultural produce;
- is expected to bear produce for more than one period; and
- has a remote likelihood of being sold as agricultural produce, except for incidental scrap sales.'

In line with the requirements of IAS 16, bearer plants are recorded at accumulated cost until they reach maturity and then they are depreciated over their useful life.

IAS 41 *Agriculture* Biological assets

Produce growing on bearer plants, and harvested agricultural produce are biological assets and should be accounted for under IAS 41. Biological assets are measured on initial recognition and at subsequent reporting dates at fair value less estimated costs to sell, unless fair value cannot be reliably measured. A gain or loss arising on initial recognition of agricultural produce at fair value less costs to sell shall be included in the statement of profit or loss for the period in which it arises.

IAS 2 *Inventories* Agricultural produce

When agricultural produce enters the production process, it should be accounted for under IAS 2.

Production process:

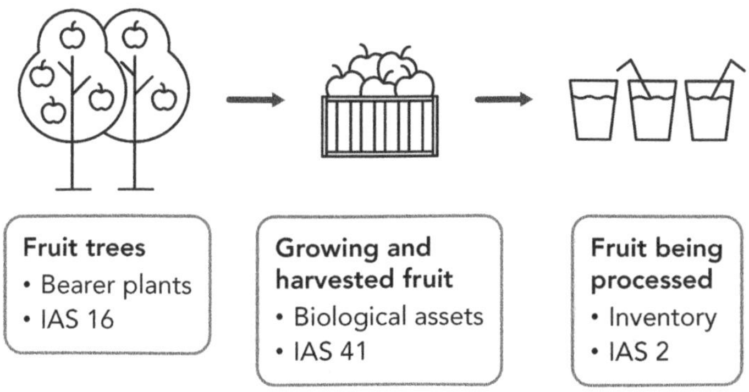

Exhibit 4: Extract from management accounts and results of preliminary analytical procedures

Extract from statement of financial position:

	Note	*As at 30 September*	*As at 30 September*
		20X5	*20X4*
		Projected	*Actual*
		£'000	£'000
Total assets		12,500	11,900
Included in total assets:			
Intangible assets	1	525	50
Property, plant and equipment	2	6,150	6,470
Total current assets		3,350	2,190

	Note	As at 30 September 20X5 Projected £'000	As at 30 September 20X4 Actual £'000
Cash included in current assets		760	750
Current ratio		6	1.4
Gearing ratio		28%	32%
Extract from statement of profit or loss:			
Total revenue		35,600	32,750
Online sales included in total revenue		2,495	1,310
Operating margin		28%	26%
Return on capital employed		5%	4.5%
Profit before tax		2,100	1,900
Extract from statement of changes in equity:			
Dividend payments		1,200	1,000

Notes.

1 Intangible assets include the following items:

	20X5 £'000	20X4 £'000
Software development costs	80	50
Advertising costs relating to 'Fructus Gold' brand	225	0
Development costs in respect of new packaging	220	0
Total	525	50

Software development costs of £30,000 were capitalised during the year, which relate to development of the online sales portal. The finance director suggests that both the software development costs and the advertising costs should be capitalised because the increased sales in the year are a direct result of the advertising campaign and improvements in the online sales portal.

The 'Fructus Gold' brand name is not recognised in the statement of financial position, as it is an internally generated asset. This accounting treatment has been confirmed as correct and in accordance with IAS 38

Intangible Assets. The notes to the 20X5 financial statements disclosed that the estimated fair value of the brand name is £18 million.

2 Property, plant and equipment

The carrying amount of £6.15 million includes £880,250 relating to the storm-damaged factory (referred to in Exhibit 2) and its fixtures and fittings. The factory is a cash-generating unit for the purpose of impairment testing. The finance director has provided a summary calculation, detailing the following impairment review which indicates that an impairment loss of £210,250 needs to be recognised:

	£
Carrying amount at 30 November 20X4	880,250
Recoverable amount	
Higher of: Fair value less costs to sell	135,000
Value in use	670,000
Impairment loss (880,250 – 670,000)	210,250

The fair value less costs to sell has been estimated based on the sales proceeds which could be generated from selling the damaged machinery. The value in use is estimated based on the future sales which could be generated if the damage to the building is repaired and new machinery is put into the factory. The company is planning on carrying out the restoration and buying new machinery, at a total estimated cost of £450,000. This amount has been provided for within current liabilities, with a corresponding entry accounted for as a prepayment.

Exhibit 5: Email sent from Len Larch, employee of Margot Ltd, to Ben Duval, audit engagement partner

To: Ben Duval

From: Len Larch

Subject: Business practices

Hello Ben

I obtained your contact details from your firm's website. I hope you don't mind me approaching you directly. I am emailing to voice some concerns over recent business practices at Margot Ltd.

In my role as production manager in one of the company's factories, I inspect samples of the fruit which comes into the factory from the company's farms and speak to the farmers on a regular basis. Recently, several farmers told me that they have been instructed to use certain chemicals to spray the fruit trees, which should increase the fruit yield. However, some of these chemicals are prohibited for use in the UK because they can be toxic to humans.

While talking to one of my friends who is a production manager from another factory, it transpired that he had also become suspicious that banned chemicals are being used in the farms. He raised the issue with one of the company directors, who allegedly gave him £10,000 and asked him not to discuss it with anyone. My friend said that I should ask for the same sum of money, but I felt uncomfortable and thought I should tell someone from outside the company about what is going on.

Please do not mention my name if you decide to investigate this further.

Thank you, Len.

29 Pale Ltd (Mar/Jun 2021 amended) (98 mins)

It is 1 July 20X5. You are a manager in the audit department of Chief & Co, a firm of Chartered Certified Accountants. You are assigned to the audit of Pale Ltd which has a financial year ending 30 September 20X5.

Pale Ltd manages timber plantations, its core business being the management of timber plantations and the production and sale of a range of timber products. It is not currently a listed entity.

The following **exhibits** provide information relevant to the question:

(1) Partner's email – an email which you have received from Harvey Rebus, the audit engagement partner.

(2) Background information – information relevant to audit planning.

(3) Notes from meeting – summary of business developments discussed at a recent meeting between the chief finance officer (CFO) and the audit engagement partner.

(4) Key performance indicators – a summary of financial and non-financial information.

(5) Notes from phone call – a summary of issues raised by the CFO during a discussion with the audit engagement partner

Required

Respond to the instructions in the email from the audit engagement partner.

Note. The split of the mark allocation is shown in Exhibit 1 – Partner's email. **(40 marks)**

Professional marks will be awarded for the demonstration of skill in communication, analysis and evaluation, professional scepticism and judgement, and commercial acumen in your answer. **(10 marks)**

(Total = 50 marks)

Exhibit 1:

Partner's email

To: Audit manager

From: Harvey Rebus, Audit engagement partner

Subject: Audit planning for Pale Ltd

Date: 1 July 20X5

Hello

I have provided you with some information which you should use to help you in planning the audit of Pale Ltd for the financial year ending 30 September 20X5.

As you know, Pale Ltd is a new audit client of our firm. I hope you are looking forward to working on this interesting new client which is the first timber company we have secured as an audit client. You should also be aware that the management team is planning for Pale Ltd to achieve a stock market listing within the next two years.

Based on the analysis I have done on this industry, it is appropriate for overall materiality to be based on profit before tax as this is a key focus for investors and providers of finance.

I require you to prepare briefing notes for my own use, in which you:

(a) Evaluate the significant business risks to be considered in planning the audit of Pale Ltd. **(10 marks)**

(b) Evaluate and prioritise the significant audit risks to be considered in planning the audit of Pale Ltd for the financial year ending 30 September 20X5.

Note

In relation to the company's timber plantation asset (referred to in Exhibit 4) **you are only required to consider audit risks relating to changes in fair value**. Any other relevant audit risks relating to the timber plantation asset will be dealt with separately, later in the planning stage of the audit. **(16 marks)**

(c) Design the audit procedures to be performed in relation to the change in fair value of the timber plantation asset caused by the recent storms. Your procedures should include those relating to the evaluation of the expert appointed by management and the work they have performed. **(6 marks)**

(d) Using Exhibit 5, explain the ethical issues and other audit planning implications which arise in relation to the phone call from the company's chief finance officer, Mark York. **(8 marks)**

Thank you

Exhibit 2: Background information

Pale Ltd Owns and manages several large timber plantations. Approximately 5% of the trees are harvested each year. The company immediately processes the timber which is harvested from felled trees in its own sawmills (a facility where trees are processed into logs and other timber products). The processed timber, which is mainly logs and planks of wood, is then sold to a range of customers including construction companies and furniture manufacturers. Approximately 30% of the timber is exported.

Your firm was appointed as auditor to Pale Ltd in March 20X5 following the resignation of the previous auditor, Hare Associates. As part of your firm's client acceptance procedures, communication was received from Hare Associates indicating that their reason for resignation was due to retirement of the partner responsible for the audit and that they had no issues to bring your attention regarding the audit.

Pale Ltd has a small internal audit department with two staff who report to the company's CFO, as the company does not have an audit committee.

Exhibit 3:

Notes from meeting

Meeting date: 10 June 20X5

Attendees: Harvey Rebus, audit engagement partner

Mark York, chief finance officer (CFO)

Accounting policies

Mark York confirms that Pale Ltd applies the requirements of IAS® 41 Agriculture as follows:

- Standing timber, which means trees which are growing in the timber plantation prior to being felled, are biological assets, measured at fair value less costs to sell. The change in fair value less costs to sell is included in profit or loss for the period in which it arises.
- Felled trees are agricultural produce which are measured at fair value less costs to sell at the point of harvest. Immediately after felling, trees are processed, so that the value of felled trees awaiting processing is minimal at any point in time.
- Processed timber such as logs are measured in accordance with IAS 2 *Inventories*.

A technical expert from the audit firm has confirmed that the accounting policies outlined above appear appropriate in the context of Pale Ltd's activities.

International expansion

Pale Ltd's operations are currently all based in its home jurisdiction. However, the board has recently approved the acquisition of several large areas of tropical rainforest in Farland, a remote developing country. The expansion will allow the company to process new types of timber for which there is significant demand from luxury furniture manufacturers. The acquisition of the areas of the rainforest will cost £25 million and the purchase is due to take place in August 20X5. The cost of £25 million is equivalent to the fair value of the rainforest. Farland uses the same currency as Pale Ltd so the expansion is not creating any foreign exchange risk exposure to the company.

The purchase is being funded through a share issue to existing and new shareholders, who are mainly family members of the Pale family, who established the company 20 years ago. A share issue was the only option for funding the international expansion as the company is at the limit of its bank borrowing agreement.

An international development agency has agreed to provide a grant of £20 million to assist Pale Ltd in its Farland expansion, on condition that the expansion represents sustainable and ethical business practice. The grant is provided specifically for training the local workforce and building accommodation for the workforce in a town near to the rainforest.

The grant is due to be received in September 20X5 and relevant expenditure will commence in November 20X5. Mark York is planning to recognise half of the amount received as income in this year's financial statements, on the basis that it "will cover some of management's expenses in planning the international expansion".

Gold Standard

The company is proud to have recently been awarded an industry 'Gold Standard' accreditation for its sustainable timber management. To achieve the Gold Standard, which denotes the highest possible level of sustainable timber management and ethical business practice, the company must adhere to a number of strict standards. This includes maintaining the biodiversity of the timber plantation, ensuring that rare species of tree are not harvested, and that animal habitats within the timber plantation are preserved. To maintain the Gold Standard accreditation, one condition is that at least 80% of timber sold must be harvested according to the strict standards set by industry regulators. The Gold Standard applies to all of the company's activities, including the Farland expansion.

Contract with Royal Ltd

The company's revenue has increased this year, largely due to it signing a significant contract with a new customer, Royal Ltd. The contract was signed on the basis of Pale Ltd receiving the Gold Standard accreditation for its timber.

Legal case

A group of employees has recently commenced legal action against the company, claiming that breaches of health and safety guidelines regularly take place. The company has made some redundancies this year, which has put pressure on the remaining staff to work harder in order to maintain productivity; the employees are alleging that this has caused an increase in the number of accidents at work, some of which have resulted in fatalities. The company's management and legal advisors believe that the legal claim, which amounts to £19 million, is unjustified and will not be successful. Mark York does not intend to recognise a provision for the claim or make any disclosure in the financial statements in relation to this issue as it is at such an early stage in the legal proceedings.

News report

Mark informed us that a news report has emerged in Farland, alleging that Pale Ltd paid a government official a sum of £15,000 in order to secure the purchase of tropical rainforest which is taking place next month. Mark wanted to make us aware of the story, which is spreading quickly on social media, and to inform us that these incentive payments are routine business practice in Farland.

Use of expert – change in fair value due to recent storms

In the last month, several storms caused damage to some areas of timber plantation. An independent expert has been appointment by management to determine the extent of damage caused and to quantify any financial implications, including determination of the change in fair value of the standing trees which have been damaged by the storm. The expert's report indicates a large number of trees have been completely destroyed, and many have been badly damaged. Based on the expert's report, management has determined that a reduction in fair value of £7.5 million should be recognised in respect of the timber plantation asset recognised in the statement of financial position.

Exhibit 4:

Key performance indicators

The information in the table below will be published as part of the Annual Report, in a section titled 'Key results for the year', which forms part of management's commentary on the company's performance. The financial information is before recognising the change in fair value of the timber plantation caused by the recent storm, and also before accounting for the government grant.

	Projected 30 September 20X5	*Actual 30 September 20X4*	*% Change*
Financial key performance indicators:	*£ million*	*£ million*	
Revenue	42·5	40·3	+5·5%
Operating profit	22·0	21·0	+4·8%
Profit before tax	**16·5**	**12.5**	**+32%**
Social and environmental key performance indicators:			
% timber harvested in line with 'Gold Standard'	82%	85%	
Number of employees	1,300	1,420	
Total staff days lost due to accidents at work	78	65	

You are also provided with the following information relating to balances which are extracted from management accounts as at 30 June 20X5:

Total assets – £550 million (20X4 – £540.5 million)

Timber plantation – £500 million (20X4 – £490 million) – this amount, relating to standing timber, is before accounting for any change in value caused by the recent storms referred to in Exhibit 3.

Cash – £4·5 million (20X4 – £6·8 million) – cash levels are depleted this year due to inflationary pressures and demands for higher wages from our employees, which we have met.

Exhibit 5:

Notes from phone call

Notes from a phone call yesterday between Harvey Rebus, audit engagement partner and Mark York.

Request from Mark York

Pale Ltd publishes a wide range of non-financial social and environmental Key Performance Indicators (KPIs) as part of the Annual Report, including the three shown as part of Exhibit 4. Mark has asked if our firm can provide assurance on these KPIs as part of performing the annual audit. Mark has suggested that in order to pay for this extra work, the agreed audit fee will be increased by 20%, assuming that the assurance provided on the KPIs is favourable.

30 Grohl (P7 December 2012 amended) (98 mins)

It is 1 July 20X5. You are a manager in Foo & Co, responsible for the audit of Grohl Ltd, a company which produces circuit boards which are sold to manufacturers of electrical equipment such as computers and mobile phones. It is the first time that you have managed this audit client, taking over from the previous audit manager, Bob Halen, last month.

The audit planning for the year ending 30 September 20X5 is about to commence.

The following **exhibits** provide information relevant to the question:

(1) An email which you have received from Mia Vai, the audit engagement partner.

(2) Notes from your meeting with Mo Satriani, the finance director of Grohl Ltd.

(3) Financial information provided by Mo Satriani.

(4) Phone call from Mo Satriani.

This information should be used to answer the question **requirements** within the response option provided.

(a) Using the information contained in Exhibits 1, 2 and 3:

Required

Respond to the instructions in the email from the audit engagement partner.

Note. The split of the mark allocation is shown in the partner's email (Exhibit 1). **(32 marks)**

(b) Using the information contained in Exhibit 4:

Required

Comment on the matters that should be considered, and design the audit procedures to be performed, in respect of the insurance claim. **(8 marks)**

Professional marks will be awarded for the demonstration of skill in communication, analysis and evaluation, professional scepticism and judgement, and commercial acumen in your answer. **(10 marks)**

(Total = 50 marks)

Exhibit 1: Email from the audit engagement partner

To: Audit manager
From: Mia Vai, Audit partner, Foo & Co
Subject: Grohl Ltd – audit planning

Hello,

I am meeting with the other audit partners tomorrow to discuss forthcoming audits and related issues. I understand that you recently had a meeting with Mo Satriani, the finance director of Grohl Ltd.

(a) Using the information from your meeting together with the financial information that I understand Mo has sent you, I would like you to prepare briefing notes for my use in which you:

(i) Evaluate the significant business risks faced by Grohl Ltd. **(8 marks)**

(ii) Evaluate and prioritise the significant risks of material misstatement to be considered in planning the audit. **(17 marks)**

(iii) Discuss any ethical issues raised and recommend the relevant actions to be taken by our firm. **(7 marks)**

Thank you.

Exhibit 2: Notes from the meeting with Mo Satriani

Business overview

Grohl Ltd's principal business activity remains the production of circuit boards. One of the key materials used in production is copper wiring, all of which is imported. As a cost cutting measure, in February 20X5 a contract with a new overseas supplier was signed, and all of the company's copper wiring is now supplied under this contract. Purchases are denominated in a foreign currency, but the company does not use forward exchange contracts in relation to its imports of copper wiring.

Grohl Ltd has two production facilities, one of which produces goods for the export market, and the other produces goods for the domestic market. About half of its goods are exported, but the export market is suffering due to competition from cheaper producers overseas. Most domestic sales are made under contract with approximately 20 customers.

Recent developments

In early June 20X5, production was halted for a week at the production facility that supplies the domestic market. A number of customers had returned goods, claiming faults in the circuit boards supplied. On inspection, it was found that the copper used in the circuit boards was corroded and therefore unsuitable for use. The corrosion is difficult to spot, as it cannot be identified by eye, and relies on electrical testing. All customers were contacted immediately and, where necessary, products recalled and replaced. The corroded copper remaining in inventory has been identified and separated from the rest of the copper.

Work has recently started on a new production line which will ensure that Grohl Ltd meets new regulatory requirements prohibiting the use of certain chemicals, which come into force in January 20X6. In May 20X5, a loan of £30 million with an interest rate of 4% was negotiated with Grohl Ltd's bank, the main purpose of the loan being to fund the capital expenditure necessary for the new production line. £2.5 million of the loan represents an overdraft which was converted into long-term finance.

Website sales

Grohl Ltd started to develop a website for sales on 1 October 20X4, which was completed and available for use by 31 March 20X5. The website has facilities for customers to design their own circuit boards, to choose the products they need and to make a payment. The total cost of website development in the year ending 30 September 20X5 was £200,000. This was capitalised and is to be written off over five years.

After initial development, the operation of the website, including collection of payments from customers, was outsourced to a specialist provider, Khalifa Co. Khalifa Co pays Grohl Ltd each month, after deducting its fee. Grohl Ltd's prices have been reduced by roughly 10% for online sales, which by the end of the year is expected to make up about a quarter of Grohl Ltd's total revenue.

The website initiates the fulfilment process automatically once payment has been made by the customer, working on the basis of the information entered by the customer. Grohl Ltd has also outsourced the final delivery of goods to a courier company.

Grohl Ltd has experienced some difficulties with the website, including relatively high rates of returns from customers. There have also been errors in goods delivered arising from customers' misunderstanding of the website.

Other matters

Several of Grohl Ltd's executive directors and the financial controller left in May 20X5, to set up a company specialising in the recycling of old electronic equipment. This new company is not considered to be in competition with Grohl Ltd's operations. The directors left on good terms and replacements for the directors have been recruited. One of Foo & Co's audit managers, Bob Halen, is being interviewed for the role of financial controller at Grohl Ltd. Bob is a good candidate for the position, as he developed good knowledge of Grohl Ltd's business when he was managing the audit.

At Grohl Ltd's most recent board meeting, the audit fee was discussed. The board members expressed concern over the size of the audit fee, given the company's loss for the year. The board members would like to know whether the audit can be performed on a contingent fee basis.

Exhibit 3: Financial information provided by Mo Satriani

EXTRACT FROM FORECAST STATEMENT OF PROFIT OR LOSS AND OTHER COMPREHENSIVE INCOME FOR THE YEAR ENDING 30 SEPTEMBER 20X5

	20X5	*20X4*
	Draft	*Actual*
	£'000	£'000
Revenue	12,500	13,800
Operating costs	(12,000)	(12,800)
Operating profit	500	1,000
Finance costs	(800)	(800)

	20X5 Draft £'000	20X4 Actual £'000
Profit/(loss) before tax	(300)	200

The forecast statement of financial position has not yet been prepared, but Mo states that the total assets of Grohl Ltd at 30 September 20X2 are expected to be £180 million, and cash at bank £130,000. Based on these forecast figures, the company's current ratio is expected to be 1.1, and the quick ratio 0.8.

Exhibit 4: Phone call from Mo Satriani

After having completed your briefing notes for Mia Vai, you received a phone call from Mo Satriani, Grohl Ltd's finance director, in which he made the following comments:

'There is something I forgot to mention in our meeting. Our business insurance covers us for specific occasions when business is interrupted. I put in a claim on 28 June 20X5 for £5 million which I have estimated to cover the period when our production was halted due to the problem with the corroded copper. This is not yet recognised in the financial statements, but I want to make an adjustment to recognise the £5 million as a receivable as at 30 September.'

31 Eagle (September 18 amended) (98 mins)

It is 1 July 20X5. You are a manager in the audit department of Bison & Co, a firm of Chartered Certified Accountants, responsible for the audit of the Eagle Group (the Group), which has a financial year ending 30 September 20X5. Your firm is appointed to audit the parent company, Eagle plc, and all of its subsidiaries, with the exception of Lynx Co, a newly acquired subsidiary located in a foreign country which is audited by a local firm of auditors, Vulture Associates.

All companies in the Group report using IFRS Standards as the applicable financial reporting framework and have the same financial year end.

The following **exhibits** provide information relevant to the question:

(1) An email which you have received from Maya Crag, the audit engagement partner.

(2) Background information about the Group including a request from the Group finance director in respect of a non-audit engagement.

(3) Extracts from the Group financial statements projected to 30 September 20X5 and comparatives, extracted from the management accounts, and accompanying explanatory notes.

(4) Management's determination of the goodwill arising on the acquisition of Lynx Co.

(5) An extract from the audit strategy document prepared by Vulture Associates relating to Lynx Co.

Required

Respond to the instructions in the email from the audit engagement partner.

Note. The split of the mark allocation is shown in the partner's email (Exhibit 1). **(40 marks)**

Professional marks will be awarded for the demonstration of skill in communication, analysis and evaluation, professional scepticism and judgement, and commercial acumen in your answer. **(10 marks)**

(Total = 50 marks)

Exhibit 1: Email from audit engagement partner

To: Audit manager

From: Maya Crag, Audit engagement partner

Subject: Audit planning for the Eagle Group

Hello

I have provided you with some information in the form of a number of exhibits which you should use in planning the audit of the Eagle Group (the Group). I held a meeting yesterday with the Group finance director and representatives from the Group audit committee, and we discussed a number of issues which will impact on the audit planning.

Using the information provided, I require you to prepare briefing notes for my use in which you:

(a) Evaluate and prioritise the audit risks to be considered in planning the Group audit. You should use analytical procedures to assist in identifying audit risks. You are not required to consider audit risks relating to disclosure, as these will be planned for later in the audit process. **(21 marks)**

(b) Design the principal audit procedures to be used in the audit of the goodwill arising on the acquisition of Lynx Ltd. Management's calculation of the goodwill is shown in Exhibit 4. You do not need to consider the procedures relating to impairment testing, or to foreign currency retranslation, as these will be planned later in the audit. **(5 marks)**

(c) Using the information provided in Exhibit 5, evaluate the extract of the audit strategy prepared by Vulture Associates in respect of their audit of Lynx Ltd and discuss any implications for the Group audit. **(8 marks)**

(d) After considering the request in Exhibit 2 from the Group finance director in respect of our firm providing advice on the Group's integrated report, discuss the ethical and professional implications of this request, recommending any further actions which should be taken by our firm. **(6 marks)**

Thank you.

Exhibit 2: Background information about the Group and request from Group finance director

Group operational activities

The Group, which is FTSE 350 listed, operates in distribution, supply chain and logistics management. Its headquarters are in Leeds, and its operations are worldwide, spanning more than 200 countries. The Group's strategy is to strengthen its market share and grow revenue in a sustainable manner by expansion into emerging markets. There are over 50 subsidiaries in the Group, many of which are international. There are three main business divisions: post and parcel delivery, commercial freight and supply chain management, each of which historically has provided approximately one-third of the Group's revenue.

A fourth business division which focuses purely on providing distribution channels for the oil and coal sector was established two years ago, and in the year ended 20X5 began to grow quite rapidly. It is forecast to provide 12% of the Group's revenue this year, growing to 15% in the year ended 20X6. This division is performing particularly well in developing economies. In recent years, revenue has grown steadily, based mainly on growth in some locations where e-commerce is rapidly developing. This year, revenue is projected to decline slightly, which the Group attributes to increased competition, as a new distribution company has taken some of the Group's market share in a number of countries. However, the Group management team is confident that this is a short-term drop in revenue, and it forecasts a return to growth in 20X6.

Innovation

The Group has invested in automating its warehousing facilities, and while it still employs more than 250,000 staff, many manual warehouse jobs are now performed by robots. Approximately 5,000 staff were made redundant early in this financial year due to automation of their work. Other innovations include increased use of automated loading and unloading of vehicles, and improvements in the technology used to monitor and manage inventory levels.

Integrated reporting

The Group is proud of this innovation and is keen to highlight these technological developments in its integrated report. The Group finance director has been asked to lead a project tasked with producing the Group's first integrated report. The finance director has sent the following request to the audit engagement partner:

'We would like your firm to assist us in developing our integrated report, and to provide assurance on it, as we believe this will enhance the credibility of the information it contains. Specifically, we would like your input into the choice of key performance indicators which should be presented, how to present them, and how they should be reconciled, where relevant, to financial information from the audited financial statements.'

The publication of an integrated report is not a requirement in the UK, but there is a growing pressure from stakeholders for the Group to publish an integrated report.

If Bison & Co accepts the engagement in relation to the Group's integrated report, the work would be performed by a team separate from the audit team.

Exhibit 3: Extracts from consolidated financial statements

STATEMENT OF FINANCIAL POSITION

	Note	*As at 30 September 20X5*	*As at 30 September 20X4*
		Projected	*Actual*
		£m	£m
Non-current assets			
Goodwill	1	1,100	970
Other intangible assets	2	200	170
Property, plant and equipment		657	600
Other investments		85	100
Total non-current assets		2,042	1,840
Current assets		1,450	1,420
Total assets		3,492	3,260
Equity and liabilities			
Equity			
Share capital	3	1,250	1,150
Retained earnings		840	780
Other components of equity		130	140
Non-controlling interests		25	23
Total equity		2,245	2,093
Non-current liabilities	4	650	620
Current liabilities		597	547
Total equity and liabilities		3,492	3,260

STATEMENT OF PROFIT OR LOSS

	Note	*Year to 30 September 20X5*	*Year to 30 September 20X4*
		Projected	*Actual*
		£m	£m
Revenue	5	5,770	5,990
Other operating income	6	120	80
Operating expenses	7	(5,540)	(5,800)
Operating profit		350	270
Finance charges		(28)	(30)
Profit before tax		322	240
Tax expense		(64)	(60)
Profit for the year		258	180

Notes.

1 **Goodwill**

Goodwill relates to the Group's subsidiaries and is tested for impairment on an annual basis. Management will conduct the annual impairment review in September 20X5, but it is anticipated that no impairment will need to be recognised this year due to anticipated growth in revenue which is forecast for the next two years.

In December 20X4, the Group acquired an 80% controlling shareholding in Lynx Co, a listed company located in a foreign country, for consideration of £351 million. Management's determination of the goodwill arising on this acquisition is shown in Exhibit 4.

2 **Other intangible assets**

Other intangible assets relate mostly to software and other technological development costs. During the year £35 million was spent on developing a new IT system for dealing with customer enquiries and processing customer orders. A further £20 million was spent on research and development into robots being used in warehouses, and £5 million on developing new accounting software. These costs have been capitalised as intangible assets and are all being amortised over a 15-year useful life.

3 **Equity and non-current liabilities**

A share issue in April 20X5 raised cash of £100 million, which was used to fund capital expenditure.

4 Non-current liabilities includes borrowings of £539 million (20X4 – £500 million), pension plan deficit, which relates only to the acquired subsidiary Lynx Co, of £11 million (20X4 – no comparative as acquired in the year), and provisions of £100 million (20X4 – £120 million). Changes in financing during the year have impacted on the Group's weighted average cost of capital. Information from the Group's treasury management team suggests that the weighted average cost of capital is currently 10%.

5 **Financial performance**

Revenue has decreased by 3.7% over the year, due to a new competitor in the market taking some of the Group's market share.

6 Other operating income comprises the following items:

	20X5	*20X4*
	£m	£m
Reversal of provisions	60	40

	20X5	20X4
	£m	£m
Reversal of impairment losses on receivables and other assets	30	20
Foreign currency gains	28	23
Profit/(loss) on disposal of non-current assets	2	(3)
Total	120	80

7 Operating expenses includes the following items:

	20X5	20X4
	£m	£m
Staff costs	3,650	3,610
Cost of raw materials, consumables and supplies	1,725	1,780
Depreciation, amortisation and impairment	145	140
Other operating expenses	20	270
Total	5,540	5,800

Exhibit 4: Determination of goodwill on the acquisition of Lynx Co

	Note	£m
Cash consideration – paid 1 December 20X4		80
Contingent consideration	1	271
Total consideration		351
Fair value of non-controlling interest	2	49
		400
Less: Fair value of identifiable net assets	3	(300)
Goodwill		100

Notes.

1 The contingent consideration will be payable four years after the initial acquisition date and is calculated based on a payment of £525 million, only payable if Lynx Co reaches revenue and profit targets outlined in the purchase documentation. The amount included in the goodwill calculation has been discounted to present value using a discount factor based on an 18% interest rate.

2 The non-controlling interest is measured at fair value, the amount being based on Lynx Co's share price on 1 December 20X4.

3 The assets and liabilities acquired and their fair values were determined by an independent firm of Chartered Certified Accountants, Sidewinder & Co, who was engaged by the Group to perform due diligence on Lynx Co's prior to the acquisition taking place. A fair value uplift of £12 million was made in relation to property, plant and equipment.

Exhibit 5: Extract from audit strategy – prepared by Vulture Associates in respect of the audit of Lynx Co

The two points below are an extract from the audit strategy. Other sections of the audit strategy, including the audit risk assessment, have been reviewed by the Group audit team and are considered to be satisfactory. Lynx Co is projected to be loss making this year, and the Group audit team is confident that sufficient procedures on going concern have been planned for.

Controls effectiveness

We will place reliance on internal controls, which will reduce the amount of substantive testing which needs to be performed. This is justified on the grounds that in the previous year's audit, controls were tested and found to be highly effective. We do not plan to re-test the controls, as according to management there have been no changes in systems or the control environment during the year.

Valuation of pension plan

Lynx Co has a defined benefit pension plan in place for its employees. The draft financial statements recognise a net non-current liability of £11 million in relation to plan assets with a value of £38 million, and plan liabilities valued at £49 million. In previous years the pension plan has been valued by an external valuer, and in 20X4 a net deficit of £3 million was recognised in non-current liabilities. However, this year the valuation has been performed by one of Vulture Associates' partners, who is a qualified actuary. The fee for providing this valuation was £35,000. It is expected that the audit fee will be £600,000 and fees for other audit-related services will be in the region of £100,000.

32 Ryder (Sep/Dec 2019 amended) (98 mins)

It is 1 July 20X5. You are a manager in the audit department of Squire & Co, a firm of Chartered Certified Accountants, responsible for the audit of the Ryder Group (the Group), which has a financial year ending 30 September 20X5. The Group, a listed entity, operates in the hospitality sector, running restaurants, coffee shops and hotels.

Squire & Co audits the Group consolidated financial statements, and the individual financial statements of each Group company. All companies in the Group use IFRS Standards as their financial reporting framework.

The following **exhibits** provide information relevant to the question:

(1) An email which you have received from Mo Iqbal, the Group audit engagement partner.

(2) Background information about the Group's current structure and business activities.

(3) Notes taken at a recent meeting between Mo Iqbal and the Group finance director.

(4) Selected financial projections to 30 September 20X5 and comparative financial information.

(5) Notes taken by Mo Iqbal during a phone call with a representative of the audit committee.

This information should be used to answer the question **requirements** within the response option provided.

Required

Respond to the instructions in the email from the audit engagement partner.

Note. The split of the mark allocation is shown in the partner's email (Exhibit 1). **(40 marks)**

Professional marks will be awarded for the demonstration of skill in communication, analysis and evaluation, professional scepticism and judgement, and commercial acumen in your answer. **(10 marks)**

(Total = 50 marks)

Exhibit 1: Email from audit engagement partner

To:	Audit manager
From:	Mo Iqbal, Group audit engagement partner
Subject:	Ryder Group audit planning
Date:	1 July 20X5

Hello

You need to start planning the Ryder Group (the Group) audit, and to help with this I have provided you with some relevant information. I met with the Group finance director yesterday to discuss a number of matters including some recent business developments. I also spoke with a representative from the Group audit committee regarding several issues.

Using all the information provided, I require you to prepare briefing notes for my own use, in which you:

(a) Evaluate and prioritise the significant audit risks to be considered in planning the Group audit for the financial year ending 30 September 20X5. Given the planned Group restructuring, you should evaluate audit risks relating to disclosure issues at this stage in the audit planning. **(22 marks)**

(b) Identify the additional information which should be requested from management in order to effectively audit the disposal of Primal Burgers Ltd, and explain why this information is required. **(4 marks)**

(c) Design the principal audit procedures to be performed in respect of:

- The classification of the £48 million investment in Peppers Ltd, and
- The government grant of £20 million received in January 20X5.

(8 marks)

(d) Using the notes from the audit committee phone call in Exhibit 5, discuss any ethical issues relevant to the Group audit, and recommend appropriate actions to be taken by our firm. **(6 marks)**

Thank you.

Exhibit 2: Background information about the Group

The Ryder Group is one of the UK's leading hospitality providers. Over the last 15 years, the Group has grown steadily and has a range of successful hospitality brands, each brand being operated by a separate, wholly owned, subsidiary of the Group.

The Group is planning some restructuring, which is discussed in the notes from the client meeting (Exhibit 3). The Group structure shown below is the Group's existing structure, before any restructuring takes place.

Existing Group structure:

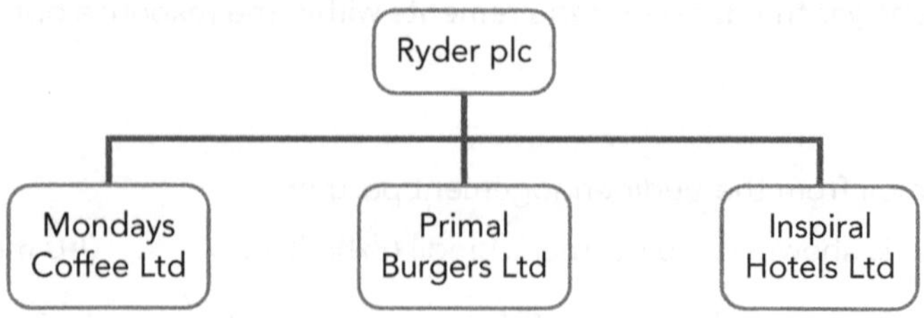

Information about each of the Group companies is given below:

Ryder plc is the parent company of the group, a listed company, which does not trade, and holds the shares in each subsidiary company.

Mondays Coffee Ltd operates one of the leading coffee shop chains in the country under the 'Mondays Coffee' brand. It enjoys a strong market share and operates more than 1,200 coffee shops across the UK.

Primal Burgers Ltd operates over 150 fast food restaurants. In recent years, revenue from Primal Burgers Ltd has declined, but it still provides approximately 30% of Group revenue.

Inspiral Hotels Ltd is a successful hotel business, with over 75 hotels across the UK. The Group acquired Inspiral Hotels Ltd three years ago, as part of a growth strategy based on diversification.

Exhibit 3: Notes from client meeting

Group restructuring

The Group is restructuring, as part of a strategy for continued growth in revenue and profitability. As part of this strategy, the Group is investing £48 million in a newly formed company, Peppers Ltd, representing 50% of the share capital of the company. The remaining 50% shareholding is owned by Smiths Ltd, a property development company. The contract behind this investment states that the Group and Smiths Ltd will work together to develop six new hotels, all based at major UK airports. The investment in Peppers Ltd is likely to take place in August 20X5.

Partly to provide some of the finance needed for the restructuring, and partly because of its declining revenue, the Group is planning to dispose of Primal Burgers Ltd. The board approved this disposal in March 20X5. Vendor's due diligence has been carried out by Usami & Co, a firm of Chartered Certified Accountants. Usami & Co conducted an independent review of the company's financial position and future prospects and produced a report on their findings, which is made available to potential buyers. At today's date, several potential buyers have expressed an interest and the Group expects that the disposal will take place just after the financial year end.

Due to the success of the Inspiral Hotels brand, the Group plans to expand its hotel offering, and a target company for acquisition has been identified. The Group aims to acquire Valentine Ltd, which operates the successful Valentine Hotel chain. Negotiations are underway, and it is likely that the acquisition will go ahead in the first quarter of the next financial year. The purchase price has yet to be agreed but is likely to be around £100 million. Due diligence performed on Valentine Ltd indicates that the fair value of its identifiable net assets is £85 million.

Mondays Coffee drive-through

The Group has previously trialled 20 drive-through coffee shops situated on busy roads, which offer customers the convenience of purchasing coffee without leaving their cars. This year the Group opened 50 new drive-through coffee shops, open 24 hours a day, seven days a week, which have proven to be extremely popular with customers. The associated capital expenditure recognised in property, plant and equipment was £43 million, which, according to the Group finance director, includes the cost of constructing the coffee shops amounting to £28 million, and the cost of acquiring three-year licences to allow 24-hour trading, at a cost of £15 million. The Group's accounting policy is to depreciate property over 20 years, and a full year's worth of depreciation will be charged in the year to 30 September 20X5 in respect of the £43 million capitalised.

According to the Group finance director, the new drive-through coffee shops are projected to account for almost all of the increase in revenue generated from the Mondays Coffee brand in the year. His comment is based on data produced from the management information system which separately records revenue generated from the drive-through coffee shops so that management can assess its performance and determine the return on the £43 million of capital expenditure.

Government grant

The UK government provides grants to organisations which commit to investing in properties to reduce carbon emissions and energy consumption. Grants are also available to organisations to promote the benefits of recycling to their customers.

In January 20X5, Ryder plc received a grant of £20 million. The only condition attached to the grant is that half of the amount must be used to upgrade existing assets to make them more environmentally friendly. None of the amount received has yet been spent, but it is planned that it will be used to finance capital expenditure across the Group's property portfolio. The other half of the grant will be used to fund an advertising campaign.

According to the Group finance director, the full £20 million is included within operating profit in the projected Group statement of profit or loss for the year (Exhibit 4)

Exhibit 4: Selected financial projections

	Projected to 30 September 20X5	*Projected to 30 September 20X5*	*Actual to 30 September 20X4*	*Actual to 30 September 20X4*
	£ million	£ million	£ million	£ million
Subsidiary	**Revenue**	**Assets**	**Revenue**	**Assets**
Mondays Coffee Ltd	155	200	110	160
Primal Burgers Ltd	99	110	103	113
Inspiral Hotels Ltd	66	140	62	125
Total	320	450	275	398

The table above is based on management information which forms the basis of the segmental reporting disclosed in the notes to the financial statements.

Other financial information for the Group as a whole is given below:

	Projected to 30 September 20X5	*Actual to 30 September 20X4*
	£ million	£ million
Operating profit	76	75
Profit before tax	20	18
Total assets	475	450

Exhibit 5: Notes from audit committee call

The Group currently has three non-executive directors, who form the Group audit committee. Until January 20X5, there was a fourth non-executive director who was also the financial reporting expert of the Group audit committee. The Group is looking to find a replacement but is finding it difficult to recruit for this position and has requested that a senior partner from Squire & Co become a member of the Group audit committee while a replacement is being sought.

In addition, the Group audit committee is looking to appoint a firm of professional accountants to perform corporate finance work in relation to the planned Group restructuring. The audit committee understands that Squire & Co cannot provide this non-audit service as it would create a significant threat to auditor objectivity. However, the audit committee has asked if our firm can recommend another firm to perform the work.

Following the call, the managing partner of Squire & Co has suggested that the firm recommend Ranger Associates, an unconnected firm, to carry out the work. If Ranger Associates is appointed, Squire & Co will charge Ranger Associates a referral fee equivalent to 10% of the fee for the corporate finance engagement.

In addition, the audit committee has asked Squire & Co to work with the Group internal audit team to design internal controls over the part of the accounting system which deals with revenue, and also evaluate the operating effectiveness of the internal controls.

33 Sunshine (P7 Sep/Dec 2017 amended) (98 mins)

You are a manager in the audit department of Dove & Co, responsible for the audit of the Sunshine Hotel Group (the Group), which has a financial year ending 31 December 20X7. The Group operates a chain of luxury hotels and it is planning to expand its operations over the next three years by opening hotels in countries with increasingly popular tourist destinations.

The following **exhibits** provide information relevant to the question:

(1) An email which you have received from John Starling, the audit engagement partner.

(2) Information about the Group's general background and activities.

(3) Notes from a meeting held between John Starling, the Group's finance director and a representative of the Group audit committee

(4) Extract of an email from the Group finance director to John Starling, audit engagement partner

This information should be used to answer the question **requirements** within the response option provided.

Required

Respond to the instructions in the email from the audit engagement partner.

Note. The split of the mark allocation is shown in the partner's email (Exhibit 1). **(40 marks)**

Professional marks will be awarded for the demonstration of skill in communication, analysis and evaluation, professional scepticism and judgement, and commercial acumen in your answer. **(10 marks)**

(Total = 50 marks)

Exhibit 1: Email from John Starling, audit engagement partner

To: Audit manager

From: John Starling, audit engagement partner

Subject: Audit planning, the Sunshine Hotel Group

Hello,

I need you to begin planning the audit of the Sunshine Hotel Group for the year ended 31 December 20X7. I have provided you with several pieces of information in relation to this audit.

Using the information provided you are required to prepare briefing notes for my use in which you:

(a) Evaluate the significant business risks facing the Group. **(11 marks)**

(b) Evaluate and prioritise the significant risks of material misstatement which should be evaluated as part of our audit planning. **(12 marks)**

(c) In respect of the email received from the finance director:

(i) Discuss the additional implications for planning the Group audit and explain any relevant actions to be taken by the firm; and **(5 marks)**

(ii) Design the planned audit procedures to be performed on the claim of £10 million, assuming that the audit team is given access to all relevant sources of audit evidence. **(5 marks)**

(d) Identify and discuss the ethical and other professional issues raised, and recommend any actions that should be taken, in relation to the request to tender for taxation services for the Group. **(7 marks)**

Thank you.

Exhibit 2: Background information

The Group owns 20 hotels, all located in popular beachside holiday resorts. The hotels operate on an 'all-inclusive' basis, whereby guests can consume unlimited food and drink, and take part in a variety of water sports including scuba diving as part of the price of their holiday. Each hotel has at least four restaurants and a number of bars. The 'Sunshine Hotel' brand is a market leader, with significant amounts spent each year on marketing to support the brand. The hotels are luxurious and maintained to a very high standard and are marketed as exclusive adult-only luxury holiday destinations.

When customers book to stay in the hotel, they are charged a deposit equivalent to 20% of the total cost of their stay, and a further 20% is payable eight weeks before arrival. The remaining 60% is settled on departure. If a booking is cancelled prior to a week before a guest's stay commences, then a full refund is given, but no refunds are given for cancellations within the week leading up to a guest's stay.

Exhibit 3: Notes from meeting with finance director and representative of Group audit committee

The Group has seen continued growth, with revenue for the year to 31 December 20X7 projected to be £125 million (20X6 – £110 million), and profit before tax projected to be £10 million (20X6 – £9 million).

According to the latest management accounts, the Group's total assets are currently £350 million. The 'Sunshine Hotel' brand is not recognised as an asset in the financial statements because it has been internally generated. The Group has cash of £20 million at today's date. Most of this cash is held on short-term deposit in a number of different currencies. Based on the latest management accounts, the Group's gearing ratio is 25%.

In January 20X7, the Group entered into an agreement with an internationally acclaimed restaurant chain, Moulin Blanche, to open new restaurants in its five most popular hotels. The agreement cost £5 million, lasts for 10 years, and allows the Group to use the restaurant name, adopt the menus and decorate the restaurants in the style of Moulin Blanche. The cost of £5 million has been recognised within marketing expenses for the year. After a period of refurbishment, the new restaurants opened in all five hotels on 1 July 20X7. Unfortunately there were some problems with the quality of some of the seafood served in the restaurants' opening week, which led to several customers being taken ill, and a report in a small newspaper local to one of the hotels.

Part of the Group strategy is to expand into new countries, and in July 20X7 the Group purchased land in three new locations in Farland at a cost of £75 million. There are currently no specific plans for the development of these locations due to political instability in the country. In addition to the Farland acquisitions, an existing hotel complex was purchased from a competitor for £23 million. The hotel complex is located in a country where local legislation prohibits the private ownership and use of beaches, so the Group's hotel guests cannot enjoy the private and exclusive use of a beach which is one of the Group's key selling points. For this reason, the Group has not yet developed the hotel complex and is currently being used as a location for staff training. All of these assets are recognised at cost as property, plant and equipment in the Group statement of financial position.

Due to the problems with these recent acquisitions, the Group is planning to invest in alternative locations, with capital expenditure on sites in new locations of £45 million budgeted for 20X8. This will be funded entirely from an undrawn borrowing facility with the Group's bank which has a fixed interest rate of 3.5% per year.

The Group's management is considering further overseas expansion in the coming year and intends to obtain professional tax planning advice in relation to a planned acquisition. Dove & Co has been invited to submit a tender for these services, with the finance director commenting that it should be able to leverage its existing knowledge of the Group and thus be able to give a competitive price.

Improvements in technology have resulted in efficiency savings in the Group's central catering facilities, which supply the hotel restaurants. This has meant that the Group has been able to bring catering functions in its domestic country together into one building. One building thus became surplus to the Group's requirements, and on 30 September 20X7, the Group contracted to sell this building for £5.5 million. The building had last been revalued in September 20X4 and had a carrying amount of £4.2 million at the date of sale. The gain on disposal has been credited to revenue and the balance of the revaluation surplus relating to the building, £1.7 million, has been credited against other operating charges in the statement of profit or loss.

Two of the Group's hotels are located in an area prone to hurricanes, and unfortunately only last week, a hurricane caused severe damage to both of these hotels. Under the Group's 'hurricane guarantee scheme', customers who were staying at the hotels at the time of the hurricane were transferred to other Group hotels, at no cost to the customer. Customers with bookings to stay at the closed hotels have been offered a refund of their deposits, or to transfer their reservation to a different Group hotel, under the terms of the scheme. The hotels are closed while the necessary repair work, which will take two months, is carried out at an estimated cost of £25 million. The repair work will be covered by the Group's insurance policy, which typically pays half of the estimated cost of repair work in advance, with the balance paid when the repair work is completed. No accounting entries have been made as yet in relation to the hurricane.

Exhibit 4: Extract of email from the Group finance director to John Starling, audit engagement partner

John

The Group's lawyer has received a letter from Ocean Protection, a multi-national pressure group which aims to safeguard marine environments. Ocean Protection is claiming that our hotel guests are causing environmental damage to delicate coral reefs when scuba diving under the supervision of the Group's scuba diving instructors.

Ocean Protection is pressing charges against the Group and alleges that our activities are in breach of international environmental protection legislation which is ratified by all of the countries in which the Group operates. Damages of £10 million are being sought, Ocean Protection suggesting that this amount would be used to protect the coral reefs from further damage.

The Group is keen to avoid any media attention, so I am hoping to negotiate a lower level of payment and an agreement from Ocean Protection that they will not make the issue public knowledge.

From an accounting point of view, we do not want to recognise a liability, as the disclosures will draw attention to the matter. We will account for any necessary payment when it is made, which is likely to be next year.

I understand that your audit team will need to look at this issue, but I ask that you only speak to me about it, and do not speak to any other employees. Also, I do not want you to contact Ocean Protection as this could impact on our negotiation.

34 Laurel (P7 Mar/Jun 2017 amended) (98 mins)

It is 1 July 20X5. You are a manager in Holly & Co, a firm of Chartered Certified Accountants, and you are responsible for the audit of the Laurel Group (the Group), with a financial year ending 30 September 20X5. The Group produces cosmetics and beauty products sold under various brand names which are globally recognised and which are sold in more than 100 countries.

The following **exhibits** provide information relevant to the question:

(1) An email which you have received from Brigitte Sanders, the audit engagement partner.

(2) Extracts of the permanent file for the audit of the Group.

(3) Extracts of the Group's projected and actual financial statements, together with associated notes from meeting with Group finance director.

(4) Notes on the planned acquisition of Azalea Ltd by the Group.

(5) Notes on the audit of Bulldog Ltd.

This information should be used to answer the question **requirements** within the response option provided.

Required

Respond to the instructions in the email from the audit engagement partner.

Note. The split of the mark allocation is shown in the partner's email (Exhibit 1). **(40 marks)**

Professional marks will be awarded for the demonstration of skill in communication, analysis and evaluation, professional scepticism and judgement, and commercial acumen in your answer. **(10 marks)**

(Total = 50 marks)

Exhibit 1: Email from audit engagement partner

To: Audit manager

From: Brigitte Sanders, Audit Engagement Partner

Subject: Audit planning – the Laurel Group

Hello

It is time for you to begin planning the audit of the Laurel Group. I have provided you with some information – a summary of relevant points from the permanent audit file, notes from a meeting with the Group finance director and some extracts from the latest forecast financial statements with comparative figures.

Using this information, I require you to prepare briefing notes for my use, in which you:

(a) Evaluate and prioritise the significant risks of material misstatement to be considered in planning the Group audit. Your evaluation should utilise analytical procedures as a method for identifying relevant risks. **(17 marks)**

(b) Recommend any additional information which should be requested from the Group which would allow a more detailed preliminary analytical review to be performed. **(5 marks)**

(c) Design the principal audit procedures to be performed on:

(i) The impairment of the Chico brand; and **(4 marks)**

(ii) The planned acquisition of Azalea Ltd. **(4 marks)**

(d) In addition to these briefing notes, there is one further matter I require your assistance with. I have provided you with some information that relates to the audit of another, separate audit client, Bulldog Ltd (Exhibit 5), whose audit is about to commence. Using this information, please can you:

Explain the matters Holly & Co should have considered before continuing with the engagement to audit Bulldog Ltd. **(3 marks)**

(e) Discuss why the audit of financial instruments is particularly challenging, and explain the matters to be considered in planning the audit of Bulldog Ltd's forward exchange contracts. **(7 marks)**

Your response to these final two requirements need not be in the form of briefing notes.

Thank you.

Exhibit 2: Points from the permanent audit file

Holly & Co was appointed as Group auditor three years ago, and the firm audits all components of the Group, which is a listed entity.

The Group sells its products under well-known brand names, most of which have been acquired with subsidiary companies. The Group is highly acquisitive, and there are more than 40 subsidiaries and 15 associates within the Group.

Products include cosmetics, hair care products and perfumes for men and women. Research into new products is a significant activity, and the Group aims to bring new products to market on a regular basis.

Exhibit 3: Extract from projected and actual financial statements and associated notes from meeting with Group finance director

CONSOLIDATED STATEMENT OF FINANCIAL POSITION

	Notes	*Projected 30 September 20X5*	*Actual 30 September 20X4*
		£m	£m
Assets			
Non-current assets			
Property, plant and equipment	1	92	78
Intangible assets – goodwill		18	18
Intangible assets – acquired brand names	2	80	115
Intangible assets – development costs		25	10
Total non-current assets		215	221
Current assets		143	107
Total assets		358	328
Equity and liabilities			
Equity			
Equity share capital		100	100
Retained earnings		106	98
Non-controlling interest		23	23
Total equity		229	221
Non-current liabilities			
Debenture loans	3	100	80
Deferred tax	4	10	2
Total non-current liabilities		110	82
Current liabilities		19	25
Total liabilities		129	107
Total equity and liabilities		358	328

CONSOLIDATED STATEMENT OF PROFIT OR LOSS FOR THE YEAR TO 30 SEPTEMBER

	Notes	*Projected 20X5*	*Actual 20X4*
		£m	£m
Revenue		220	195
Operating expenses	5	(185)	(158)
Operating profit		35	37

	Notes	Projected 20X5	Actual 20X4
		£m	£m
Finance costs		(7)	(7)
Profit before tax		28	30
Tax expense		(3)	(3)
Profit for the year		25	27

Notes.

1 Capital expenditure of £20 million has been recorded so far during the year. The Group's accounting policy is to recognise assets at cost less depreciation. During the year, a review of assets' estimated useful lives concluded that many were too short, and as a result, the projected depreciation charge for the year is £5 million less than the comparative figure.

2 Acquired brand names are held at cost and not amortised on the grounds that the assets have an indefinite life. Annual impairment reviews are conducted on all brand names. In April 20X5, the Chico brand name was determined to be impaired by £30 million due to allegations made in the press and by customers that some ingredients used in the Chico perfume range can cause skin irritations and more serious health problems. The Chico products have been withdrawn from sale.

3 A £20 million loan was taken out in May 20X5, the cash being used to finance a specific new product development project.

4 The deferred tax liability relates to timing differences in respect of accelerated tax depreciation (capital allowances) on the Group's property, plant and equipment. The liability has increased following changes to the estimated useful lives of assets discussed in note 1.

5 Contracts were signed in June 20X5 for the hire of five new machines for use in production. Contract payments of £1 million have been charged to operating expenses as they were made, on the basis that the machines are of low value.

Exhibit 4: Details of planned acquisition of Azalea Ltd

Group management is currently negotiating the acquisition of Azalea Ltd, a large company which develops and sells a range of fine fragrances. It is planned that the acquisition will take place in early October 20X5, and the Group is hopeful that Azalea Ltd's products will replace the revenue stream lost from the withdrawal of its Chico perfume range. Due diligence is taking place currently, and Group management is hopeful that this will support the consideration of £130 million offered for 100% of Azalea Ltd's share capital. The Group's bank has agreed to provide a loan for this amount.

Exhibit 5: Bulldog Ltd audit

You are also responsible for the audit of another audit client, Bulldog Ltd, a clothing manufacturer that has been a client of Holly & Co for many years, but which has recently expanded its operations overseas. To manage exposure to cash flows denominated in foreign currencies, the company has set up a treasury management function, which is responsible for entering into hedge transactions such as forward exchange contracts. These transactions are likely to be material to the financial statements.

35 McClane & Co (Sep/Dec 2021) (98 mins)

It is July 20X5. You are a manager in the audit department of McClane & Co, a firm of Chartered Certified Accountants. You are assigned to the audit of Gruber Ltd which has a financial year ending 30 September 20X5.

Gruber Ltd is a new audit client of McClane & Co, the audit firm having been appointed in January 20X5. The audit was previously performed by Ellis Associates.

Gruber Ltd is owned and managed by the Gruber family, its principal operations being the design and construction of bespoke machinery used in the oil industry.

The following **exhibits**, available on the left-hand side of the screen, provide information relevant to the question:

(1) Partner's email – an email which you have received from Al Powell, the audit engagement partner.

(2) Business and governance – information and matters relevant to audit planning.

(3) Financial information – Gruber Ltd most recent management accounts.

(4) Business developments – information relating to an investment property and customer contracts.

(5) Meeting notes – extracts from meeting notes taken at a recent meeting with the board of directors of Gruber Ltd.

This information should be used to answer the question **requirement** within your chosen **response option(s)**.

Required

Respond to the instructions in the email from the audit engagement partner.

Note. The split of the mark allocation is shown in the partner's email (Exhibit 1). **(40 marks)**

Professional marks will be awarded for the demonstration of skill in communication, analysis and evaluation, professional scepticism and judgement, and commercial acumen in your answer. **(10 marks)**

(Total = 50 marks)

Exhibit 1:

To: Audit manager

From: Al Powell, Audit engagement partner

Subject: Audit planning for Gruber Ltd

Date: 1 July 20X5

Hello

I have provided you with some information which you should use to help you with planning the audit of Gruber Ltd for the financial year ending 30 September 20X5. As you know, Gruber Ltd is a new client and the firm's client due diligence (know your client) and acceptance procedures were all successfully completed.

I require you to prepare briefing notes for my own use in which you:

(a) Discuss the matters specific to the planning of an initial audit engagement which should be considered in developing the audit strategy for Gruber Ltd.

Note

As above, you do NOT need to discuss matters relating to whether it was appropriate for McClane & Co to accept Gruber Ltd as an audit client, as the acceptance is confirmed. **(5 marks)**

(b) Using the information in **Exhibits 1, 2, 3 and 4**, evaluate and prioritise the significant audit risks to be considered in planning the company audit. **(21 marks)**

(c) Design the principal audit procedures to be performed in respect of the Nakatomi building, including those relating to the use of an expert to provide the fair value. **(7 marks)**

(d) Using the information in Exhibit 5:

Discuss the ethical issues raised and recommend actions to be taken by our firm.

(7 marks)

Thank you.

Exhibit 2:

The company was established 15 years ago by Martin Gruber, an engineer who had patented a new type of machine used in the oil industry. Martin, who is the company's chief executive officer, owns 60% of the shares in the company, with the remainder split equally between his brother and sister, Craig and Iris Gruber.

The company's board of directors includes Craig Gruber as chief finance officer (CFO), Iris Gruber as marketing director, and a non-family member, Kali Hayes, who is director of operations. Gruber Ltd has 300 employees, most of whom are mechanical engineers.

Martin is planning to sell his shares and retire from the business. Craig and Iris, who are younger than Martin, will retain their shares and their board positions. Initial discussion with a potential acquirer for Martin's shares began last month.

The company owns a head office and leases a production facility where machines are designed and assembled under contract with individual customers. Typically, an order takes 14 months to complete, from the initial design through to installation at the customer's premises. This is due to the large size of the machinery being produced to customer order and the very specific requirements of customers.

Exhibit 3:

Key information extracted from the management accounts

	Notes	*Projected to 30 September 20X5*	*Actual to 30 September 20X4*
		£ million	£ million
Revenue	1	75	65
Operating profit	2	18	10
Profit before tax	3	**14**	**9**
Total assets		**120**	**88**
Included in total assets:			
Intangible assets	4	19	10

Notes.

1 Revenue is derived from contracts involving the design, manufacture and installation of machinery to customer order. Currently, the company establishes all of its customer contracts to contain only one performance obligation – the successful installation of the machine at the customer's premises.

However, around a quarter of the contracts also include a three-year support service for the machinery installed.

2 Operating profit includes a profit of £2.2 million relating to the Argyle contract, details of which are given in Exhibit 4. This is the full amount of profit estimated to be made on the contract. The company's CFO suggests that while the company's accounting policy is to use the output method to determine the completion stage of a contract at the year end, it is appropriate to recognise the full amount of profit on this contract because the customer has paid in advance.

Operating profit also includes a loss of £700,000 relating to the Johnson contract, details of which are given in Exhibit 4. The loss is determined based on the estimated loss of £840,000 pro-rata over the number of months completed on the contract by 30 September 20X5.

3 Profit before tax includes an estimated increase in the fair value of the Nakatomi building investment property of £2 million. Details are provided about this investment in Exhibit 4.

4 The change in value of intangible assets represents a transaction which took place in March 20X5, whereby Gruber Ltd purchased some designs from Martin Gruber for £9 million. The value of this transaction was determined by Martin Gruber. The audit engagement partner has asked for information to support this value, but nothing has yet been received from Martin.

Exhibit 4:

Argyle contract

In October 20X4, Gruber Ltd entered into a significant contract to design, construct and install a large piece of machinery for a new customer, Argyle Ltd. In October 20X4, it was estimated that the design and construction of the machine would take 15 months, with installation estimated to take place in January 20X6. The agreed price of the machine is £6 million and Gruber Ltd will have incurred costs of £2.6 million in relation to this contract by 30 September 20X5. Based on the project plans, the estimated value of the work certified at 30 September 20X5 is £4 million and the estimated cost to complete is £1.2 million. As noted in Exhibit 3, operating profit includes a profit of £2.2 million relating to the Argyle contract.

Johnson contract

On 1 December 20X4, Gruber Ltd entered into a contract with Johnson Ltd, to design, construct and install a machine. The contract, which will take 12 months to complete, was initially projected to make a profit of £2.8 million. However, due to cost inflation and errors made in the initial project budget, the contract is now estimated to make a loss of £840,000.

Investment property

In October 20X4, following the completion of a significant contract, the company purchased an investment property, the Nakatomi building, for £15 million. The property is a retail development in the country's capital city. The company is going to appoint an expert to provide a valuation of the property and an initial estimate of the increase in fair value of £2 million has been included in the company's financial projections to 30 September 20X5.

Exhibit 5:

A meeting took place yesterday in which the audit engagement partner discussed the potential sale of Martin Gruber's shares with the company directors.

The company directors revealed that Willis Ltd is the company with whom negotiations have started in relation to the sale of Martin Gruber's shares. Willis Ltd is an existing audit client of McClane & Co.

The directors have requested that McClane & Co assist them with the sale by performing a vendor's due diligence service, in which they would conduct an independent review of Gruber Co's financial position and future prospects and produce a report on their findings to be provided to Willis Ltd.

36 Awdry (Mar/Jun 2019 amended) (49 mins)

The following exhibit provides information relevant to the question:

(1) Audit of Awdry plc

This information should be used to answer the question requirements within the response option provided.

Exhibit 1: Audit of Awdry plc

It is 1 July 20X5. You are the manager responsible for the audit of Awdry plc, a listed entity whose principal activity is the operation of a regional railway network. The audit for the year ended 31 May 20X5 is the first year your firm has audited Awdry plc. The draft financial statements recognise total assets of £58 million and profit before tax of £7.4 million. The detailed audit fieldwork has started, and the audit supervisor has brought the following matters to your attention in relation to the testing of key accounting estimates:

Cash-settled share-based payment scheme

On 1 June 20X4, Awdry plc granted 550,000 share appreciation rights to 55 executives and senior employees of the company with each eligible member of staff receiving 10,000 of the rights. The fair value of the rights was estimated on 31 May 20X5 by an external expert using an options pricing model at £4.50 each. Awdry plc prides itself on good employee relations and the senior management team has estimated that all 55 staff will qualify for the rights when they vest three years after the granting of the rights on 1 June 20X4. The company has recognised a straight-line expense in this year's draft accounts of £825,000.

Regulatory penalties

Awdry plc has been subject to a review by the national railways regulator following a complaint from a member of staff with safety concerns. The regulator identified breaches in safety regulations and issued a penalty notice on 31 December 20X4. Awdry plc has appealed against the initial penalty payable. Negotiations with the regulator are still ongoing and the amount payable has not yet been finalised. Awdry plc currently estimates that the total penalty payable as a result of the breach will be £1.3 million, which it expects to repay in equal annual instalments over the next ten years with the first payment falling due on 1 June 20X5. The company's draft statement of profit or loss for the current year recognises an expense of £1.3 million and the draft statement of financial position includes a liability for the same amount.

Property development

Awdry plc owns an industrial property which it has historically used as a maintenance depot for its engines and carriages. The company has an accounting policy of revaluing its properties to fair value and at the interim audit it was noted that the depot was recorded at a carrying amount of £2.5 million in the non-current asset register. During the first week of the audit fieldwork, the audit supervisor identified a year-end journal which uplifted the depot to a fair value of £4.9 million in this year's statement of financial position as at 31 May 20X5. Management has advised that this represents the estimated sales value of the building following Awdry plc's plan to develop the building as a residential property. The client has confirmed that the property is suitable for conversion into residential apartments at an estimated cost of £1.2 million and has negotiated secured finance for the development with its bank. The development will be subject to the payment of fees to the local council's building regulator of £173,000.

(a) The IAASB has recently issued three new quality management standards which have been adopted by the FRC as follows:

- ISQM (UK) 1 *Quality Management for Firms that Perform Audits or Reviews of Financial Statements, or Other Assurance or Related Services Engagements*
- ISQM (UK) 2 *Engagement Quality Reviews*
- ISA (UK) 220 (Revised) *Quality Management for an Audit of Financial Statements*

The new standards replaced older guidance, which focused on quality control, with a new proactive risk-based approach to the management of quality.

Required

Explain why quality management is important to the profession, commenting on the likely effect of the FRC's new standards on audits conducted under them. **(5 marks)**

(b) Using the information provided in Exhibit 1:

(1) Evaluate the client's accounting treatments and the difficulties which you might encounter when auditing each of the accounting estimates described above; and

(2) Design the audit procedures which should now be performed to gather sufficient and appropriate audit evidence.

Note. The marks will be split equally between the issues within the Exhibit. **(15 marks)**

Professional marks will be awarded for the demonstration of skill in analysis and evaluation, professional scepticism and judgement and commercial acumen in your answer. **(5 marks)**

(Total = 25 marks)

37 Willow (P7 December 2011 amended) (49 mins)

It is 1 July 20X5. Willow Ltd is a print supplier to businesses, printing catalogues, leaflets, training manuals and stationery to order. It specialises in using 100% recycled paper in its printing, a fact which is promoted heavily in its advertising.

You are a senior audit manager in Bark & Co, and you have just been placed in charge of the audit of Willow Ltd after the manager previously assigned to the audit was moved to another urgent assignment. The audit for the year ended 31 March 20X5 is nearing completion, and the auditor's report is due to be issued in two weeks' time. You are currently reviewing a summary of matters for your considering, prepared by the audit senior.

Summary of issues for manager's attention

Materiality has been determined as follows.

- £800,000 for assets and liabilities
- £250,000 for income and expenses

Issues related to audit work performed:

(1) **Audit work on inventory**

Audit procedures performed at the inventory count indicated that printed inventory items with a value of £130,000 were potentially obsolete. These items were mainly out of date training manuals. The finance director, Cherry Laurel, has not written off this inventory as she argues that the paper on which the items are printed can be recycled and used again in future printing orders. However, the items appear not to be recyclable as they are coated in plastic. The junior who performed the audit work on inventory has requested a written representation from management to confirm that the items can be recycled and no further procedures relevant to these items have been performed.

(2) **Audit work on provisions**

Willow Ltd is involved in a court case with a competitor, Aspen Ltd, which alleges that a design used in Willow Ltd's printed material copies one of Aspen Ltd's designs which are protected under copyright. Our evidence obtained is a verbal confirmation from Willow Ltd's lawyers that a claim of £125,000 has been made against Willow Ltd, which is probable to be paid. Cherry Laurel has not made a provision, arguing that it is immaterial. Cherry refused our request to ask the lawyers to confirm their opinion on the matter in writing, saying it is not worth bothering the lawyers again on such a trivial matter.

Other issues for your attention:

Property revaluations

Willow Ltd currently adopts an accounting policy of recognising properties at cost. During the audit of non-current assets Willow Ltd's property manager said that the company is considering a change of accounting policy so that properties would be recognised at fair value from 1 August 20X5.

Non-current asset register

The audit of non-current assets was delayed by a week. We had asked for the non-current asset register reconciliation to be completed by the client prior to commencement of our audit procedures on non-current assets, but it seems that the person responsible for the reconciliation went on holiday having forgotten to prepare the reconciliation. This happened on last year's audit as well, and the issue was discussed with the audit committee at that time.

Procurement procedures

We found during our testing of trade payables that an approved supplier list is not maintained, and invoices received are not always matched back to goods received notes. This was mentioned to the procurement manager, who said that suppliers are switched fairly often, depending on which supplier is the cheapest, so it would be difficult to maintain an up-to-date approved supplier list.

Required

(a) Assess the audit implications of the issues related to audit work performed, that have been raised by the audit senior. Your assessment should consider the sufficiency of evidence obtained, explain any adjustments that may be necessary to the financial statements, and describe the impact on the auditor's report if these adjustments are not made. You should also recommend any further audit procedures necessary. **(13 marks)**

(b) Explain the matters, arising from the 'Other issues for your attention', which should be brought to the attention of the audit committee of Willow Co. **(7 marks)**

Professional marks will be awarded for the demonstration of skill in analysis and evaluation, and professional scepticism and judgement in your answer. **(5 marks)**

(Total = 25 marks)

38 Jovi (P7 December 2012 amended) (49 mins)

You are a manager in Sambora & Co, responsible for the audit of the Jovi Group (the Group), which is listed. The Group's main activity is steel manufacturing and it comprises a parent company and five subsidiaries. Sambora & Co currently audits all components of the Group.

You are working on the audit of the Group's financial statements for the year ended 30 June 20X2.

The following exhibit provides information relevant to the question:

(1) Notes from audit engagement partner

Required

(a) Using the information provided in Exhibit 1:

Respond to the note from the audit engagement partner. **(15 marks)**

(b) The audit engagement partner now sends a further note regarding the Jovi Group:

'The Group finance director has just informed me that last week the Group purchased 100% of the share capital of May Co, a company located overseas in Farland. The Group audit committee has suggested that due to the distant location of May Co, a joint audit could be performed, starting with the next financial statements for the year ending 30 June 20X3. May Co's current auditors are a small local firm called Moore & Co who operate only in Farland.'

Required

Discuss the advantages and disadvantages of a joint audit being performed on the financial statements of May Co. **(5 marks)**

Professional marks will be awarded for the demonstration of skill in analysis and evaluation, and professional scepticism and judgement in your answer. **(5 marks)**

(Total = 25 marks)

Exhibit: Notes from audit engagement partner

Hello,

The audit senior has provided you with the draft consolidated financial statements and accompanying notes which summarise the key audit findings and some background information.

At the planning stage, materiality was initially determined to be £900,000 and was calculated based on the assumption that the Jovi Group is a high-risk client due to its listed status. During the audit, a number of issues arose which meant that we needed to revise the materiality level for the financial statements as a whole. The revised level of materiality is now determined to be £700,000.

I would like you to help me with the following matter:

Assess the implications of the key audit findings for the completion of the audit. Your assessment must consider whether the key audit findings indicate a risk of material misstatement. Where the key audit findings refer to audit evidence, you must also consider the adequacy of the audit evidence obtained, but you do not need to recommend further specific procedures.

The Group's draft consolidated financial statements, with notes referenced to key audit findings, are shown below:

DRAFT CONSOLIDATED STATEMENT OF PROFIT OR LOSS AND OTHER COMPREHENSIVE INCOME

	Notes	30 June 20X2 Draft	30 June 20X1 Actual
		£'000	£'000
Revenue	1	98,795	103,100
Cost of sales		(75,250)	(74,560)
Gross profit		23,545	28,540
Operating expenses	2	(14,900)	(17,500)
Operating profit		8,645	11,040
Share of profit of associate		1,010	900
Finance costs		(380)	(340)
Profit before tax		9,275	11,600
Taxation		(3,200)	(3,500)
Profit for the year		6,075	8,100
Other comprehensive income/expense for the year, net of tax:			
Gains on property revaluation	3	800	–
Actuarial losses on defined benefit plan	4	(1,100)	(200)
Other comprehensive income/expense		(300)	(200)
Total comprehensive income for the year		5,775	7,900

Notes.

1 Revenue has been stable for all components of the Group with the exception of one subsidiary, Copeland Ltd, which has recognised a 25% decrease in revenue.

2 Operating expenses for the year to June 20X2 is shown net of a profit on a property disposal of £2 million.

Our evidence includes agreeing the cash receipts to bank statement and sale documentation, and we have confirmed that the property has been removed from the non-current asset register. The audit junior noted, when reviewing the sale document, that there is an option to repurchase the property in five years' time but did not discuss the matter with the management.

3 The property revaluation relates to the Group's head office. The audit team have not obtained evidence on the revaluation, as the gain was immaterial based on the initial calculation of materiality.

4 The actuarial loss is attributed to an unexpected stock market crash. The Group's pension plan is managed by Axle Ltd – a firm of independent fund managers who maintain the necessary accounting records relating to the plan. Axle Ltd has supplied written representation as to the value of the defined benefit plan's assets and liabilities at 30 June 20X2. No audit work has been performed other than to agree the figure from the financial statements to supporting documentation supplied by Axle Ltd.

DRAFT CONSOLIDATED STATEMENT OF FINANCIAL POSITION

	Notes	30 June 20X2 Draft £'000	30 June 20X1 Actual £'000
Assets			
Non-current assets			
Property, plant and equipment		81,800	76,300
Goodwill	5	5,350	5,350
Investment in associate	6	4,230	4,230
Assets classified as held for sale	7	7,800	–
		99,180	85,880
Current assets			
Inventory		8,600	8,000
Receivables		8,540	7,800
Cash and cash equivalents		2,100	2,420
		19,240	18,220
Total assets		118,420	104,100
Equity and Liabilities			
Equity			
Share capital		12,500	12,500
Revaluation reserve		3,300	2,500
Retained earnings		33,600	29,400
Non-controlling interest	8	4,350	4,000
Total equity		53,750	48,400
Non-current liabilities			
Defined benefit pension plan		10,820	9,250
Long-term borrowings	9	43,000	35,000
Deferred tax		1,950	1,350
Total non-current liabilities		55,770	45,600
Current liabilities			
Trade and other payables		6,200	7,300
Provisions		2,700	2,800
Total current liabilities		8,900	10,100
Total liabilities		64,670	55,700
Total equity and liabilities		118,420	104,100

5 The goodwill relates to each of the subsidiaries in the Group. The management has confirmed in writing that the goodwill is stated correctly, and our other audit procedure was to arithmetically check the impairment review conducted by the management.

6 The associate is a 30% holding in James Ltd, purchased to provide investment income. The audit team have not obtained evidence regarding the associate as there is no movement in the amount recognised in the statement of financial position.

7 The assets held for sale relate to a trading division of one of the subsidiaries, which represents one third of that subsidiary's net assets. The sale of the division was announced in May 20X2, and is expected to be complete by 31 December 20X2. Audit evidence obtained includes a review of the sales agreement and confirmation from the buyer, obtained in July 20X2, that the sale will take place.

8 Two of the Group's subsidiaries are partly owned by shareholders external to the Group.

9 A loan of £8 million was taken out in October 20X1, carrying an interest rate of 2%, payable annually in arrears. The terms of the loan have been confirmed to documentation provided by the bank.

39 Jolie (P7 December 2010 amended) (98 mins)

It is 1 July 20X5. You are a manager in Jen & Co, a firm with three offices and 12 partners. About one third of the firm's clients are audit clients, the remainder are clients for whom Jen & Co performs tax, accounting and business advisory services.

You are responsible for the audit of Jolie Ltd, a large company operating in the retail industry, which has a year ended 30 September 20X5. As this is the first year that your firm will be acting as auditor for Jolie Ltd, you need to gain an understanding of the business risks facing the new client.

The following **exhibits** provide information relevant to the question:

(1) An email which you have received from the audit engagement partner.

(2) Notes from meeting held between the audit engagement partner and Mo Pitt the finance director of Jolie Ltd.

(3) Extract from financial and non-financial information of Jolie Ltd.

(4) Revenue-raising suggestions for Jen & Co.

This information should be used to answer the question **requirements** within the response option provided.

Required

Respond to the instructions in the email from the audit engagement partner.

Note. The split of the mark allocation is shown in the partner's email (Exhibit 1). **(40 marks)**

Professional marks will be awarded for the demonstration of skill in communication, analysis and evaluation, professional scepticism and judgement and commercial acumen in your answer. **(10 marks)**

(Total = 50 marks)

Exhibit 1: Email from audit engagement partner

To: Audit Manager

From: Audit Partner

Re: Jolie Ltd audit planning

Hello

I need you to begin planning the audit of Jolie Ltd for the year ended 30 September 20X5. I have just attended a planning meeting with Mo Pitt, the finance director of the company, and have provided you with notes.

Using the information contained in Exhibits 2 and 3, you are required to prepare briefing notes to be used at a planning meeting with your audit team, in which you:

(a) Prepare briefing notes to use used at a planning meeting with your audit team, in which you evaluate the significant business risks facing Jolie Ltd to be considered when planning the final audit for the year ended 30 September 20X5. **(12 marks)**

(b) Using the information provided, evaluate and prioritise the significant risks of material misstatement. **(17 marks)**

(c) Design the principal audit procedures to be performed in respect of the valuation of the JLC brand name. **(5 marks)**

(d) Our firm has been considering how, in general terms, it might improve its revenue figures going forward. Our firm's business development manager has made some suggestions of how we might do this, and I have provided you with a summary of these.

Using the information contained in Exhibit 4, please:

Evaluate each of the revenue-raising suggestions made in Exhibit 4, commenting on the ethical and professional issues raised. **(6 marks)**

Thank you.

Exhibit 2: Notes from meeting with Mo Pitt

Jolie Ltd sells clothing, with a strategy of selling high fashion items under the JLC brand name. New ranges of clothes are introduced to stores every eight weeks. The company relies on a team of highly skilled designers to develop new fashion ranges. The designers must be able to anticipate and quickly respond to changes in consumer preferences. There is a high staff turnover in the design team.

Most sales are made in-store, but there is also a very popular catalogue, from which customers can place an order online, or over the phone. The company has recently upgraded the computer system and improved the website, at significant cost, in order to integrate the website sales directly into the general ledger, and to provide an easier interface for customers to use when ordering and entering their credit card details. The new on-line sales system has allowed overseas sales for the first time.

The system for phone ordering has recently been outsourced. The contract for outsourcing went out to tender and Jolie Ltd awarded the contract to the company offering the least cost. The company providing the service uses an overseas call centre where staff costs are very low.

A new inventory system was introduced in April 20X5, with the aim of keeping better track of the movement of inventory within and across Jolie Ltd's sites, including factories, stores and online distribution centres. The system keeps track of all cost inputs as inventory is produced, allowing management to keep close control over these processes.

Jolie Ltd has recently joined the Ethical Trading Initiative. This is a 'fair-trade' initiative, which means that any products bearing the JLC brand name must have been produced in a manner which is clean and safe for employees and minimises the environmental impact of the manufacturing process. A significant advertising campaign promoting Jolie Ltd's involvement with this initiative has recently taken place. The JLC brand name was purchased a number of years ago and is recognised at cost as an intangible asset, which is not amortised. The brand represents 12% of the total assets recognised on the statement of financial position.

The company owns numerous distribution centres, some of which operate close to residential areas. A licence to operate the distribution centres is issued by each local government authority in which a centre is located. One of the conditions of the licence is that deliveries must only take place between 8 am and 6 pm. The authority also monitors the noise level of each centre and can revoke the operating licence if a certain noise limit is breached. Two licences were revoked for a period of three months during the year.

During the course of the year, Jolie Ltd's finance function began to make use of an off-the-shelf data analysis package, which provided the finance director with a number of metrics that related to the risk of fraud taking place within the company. The director noted that a new purchase ledger assistant had posted a number of journals out of office hours. Upon investigation, the finance director discovered that the assistant had perpetrated a fraud. The assistant was dismissed, and an exercise was undertaken to correct any errors in the purchase ledger.

In April 20X5 Jolie Ltd began to pilot a new policy (in one retail outlet) whereby all new staff recruited were placed on casual agreements rather than employment contracts. The aim of this initiative is to reduce the company's fixed operating costs as well as staff costs in absolute terms.

Jolie Ltd owns a manufacturing division which is located in Nearland, and comprises a small factory and office, together with various items of plant and equipment. This division processes raw materials such as fabrics and dyes, which are then transported to Jolie Ltd's own jurisdiction, where they are worked into finished products. Jolie Ltd decided to sell some of this division's assets during the year, on the grounds that it is now possible to purchase processed materials which are of equivalent or better quality more cheaply from elsewhere. The factory and office belonging to the division were advertised for sale in May 20X5; offers have been received and the sale is expected to be completed within six months. The factory and office were therefore classified as 'held for sale' in the financial statements, and they are carried at revalued amounts of £14 million and £8 million respectively.

Exhibit 3: Extract from financial and non-financial information

Year ending 30 September	*20X5 Draft* £m	*20X4 Actual* £m
Revenue:		
Retail outlets	1,030	1,140
Phone and online sales orders	425	395
Total revenue	1,455	1,535
Operating profit	245	275
Finance costs	(25)	(22)
Profit before tax	220	253
Additional information:		
Total assets	£1,675m	£1,625m
Number of stores	210	208
Average revenue per store	£4.905m	£5.48m
Number of phone orders	680,000	790,000
Number of online orders	1,020,000	526,667
Average spend per order	£250	£300

Exhibit 4: Revenue-raising suggestions for Jen & Co

Jen & Co is considering how to generate more revenue, and the following suggestion has been made by the firm's business development manager.

An advertisement could be placed in national newspapers to attract new clients. The draft advertisement has been given to you for review:

Jen & Co is the largest and most professional accountancy and audit provider in the country. We offer a range of services in addition to audit, which are guaranteed to improve your business efficiency and save you tax.

If you are unhappy with your auditors, we can offer a second opinion on the report that has been given.

Introductory offer: for all new clients we offer a 25% discount when both audit and tax services are provided. Our rates are approved by ACCA.

40 Vancouver (P7 Mar/Jun 16 amended) (98 mins)

It is 1 July 20X5. You are an audit manager in Montreal & Co, a firm of Chartered Certified Accountants, and you are responsible for the audit of the Vancouver Group (the Group). The Group operates in the supply chain management sector, offering distribution, warehousing and container handling services. Its operations are wholly in the UK. The Group comprises a parent company, Vancouver Ltd, and two subsidiaries, Toronto Ltd and Calgary Ltd. Both of the subsidiaries were acquired as wholly owned subsidiaries many years ago. Montreal & Co audits all of the individual company financial statements as well as the Group consolidated financial statements.

The following **exhibits** provide information relevant to the question:

(1) An email which you have received from Albert Franks, the audit engagement partner.

(2) Notes from a meeting held between Albert Franks, the Group's finance director and a representative of its audit committee.

(3) Financial information on the Group, provided by the Group finance director.

This information should be used to answer the question **requirements** within the response option provided.

Required

Respond to the instructions in the email from the audit engagement partner.

Note. The split of the mark allocation is shown in the partner's email (Exhibit 1). **(40 marks)**

Professional marks will be awarded for the demonstration of skill in communication, analysis and evaluation, professional scepticism and judgement and commercial acumen in your answer. **(10 marks)**

(Total = 50 marks)

Exhibit 1: Email from audit engagement partner

To: Audit manager

From: Albert Franks, audit engagement partner

Subject: The Vancouver Group – audit planning, year ended 30 September 20X5

Hello

I would like you to begin to plan the Group audit for the financial year ending 30 September 20X5.

I held a meeting yesterday with Hannah Peters, the Group finance director. A representative of the Group audit committee was also at the meeting to discuss two issues raised for our attention by the committee. Hannah gave me some projected financial information for the Group's forthcoming year end, along with comparatives and explanatory notes, and we discussed some matters relevant to the Group this year. I am preparing for the audit team briefing next week at which there will be a number of recent recruits into the audit department whose first assignment will be the Vancouver Group.

I have attached some notes from my meeting as well as the financial information provided by Hannah. Using the information provided you are required to prepare briefing notes for use in the audit team briefing in which you:

(a) Evaluate and prioritise the significant audit risks which should be considered in planning the Group audit. You should ensure that you consider all of the information provided as well as utilising analytical procedures, where relevant, to identify the audit risks. **(24 marks)**

(b) Design the principal audit procedures that should be performed on the consolidation process. **(8 marks)**

(c) Discuss the ethical issues relevant to Montreal & Co, and recommend any actions which should be taken by our firm. **(8 marks)**

Thank you.

Exhibit 2: Notes from meeting with the Group finance director and audit committee representative

The Group has not changed its operations significantly this year. However, it has completed a modernisation programme of its warehousing facilities at a cost of £25 million. The programme was financed with cash raised from two sources: £5 million was raised from a debenture issue, and £20 million from the sale of 5% of the share capital of Calgary Ltd, with the shares being purchased by an institutional investor.

The Group fell victim during the year to a significant cyberattack, which fortunately did not adversely affect its operations. It did, however, result in the loss of files containing the contact details of many of the Group's employees.

An investigation by HMRC into the Group's tax affairs started in March 20X5, focusing on the possible underpayment of corporation taxes by each of the companies in the Group. The Group's tax planning was performed by another firm of accountants, Victoria & Co, but the Group's audit committee has asked if our firm will support the Group by looking into its tax position and liaising with HMRC in respect of the tax investigation on its behalf. Victoria & Co has resigned from their engagement to provide tax advice to the Group. The matter is to be resolved by a tribunal which is scheduled to take place in November 20X5.

The Group is not listed but aims to apply the provisions of the UK Corporate Governance Code as best practice. The Group audit committee has asked whether one of Montreal & Co's audit partners can be appointed as a non-executive director and serve on the audit committee. The audit committee lacks a financial reporting expert, and the appointment of an audit partner would bring much needed knowledge and experience.

Exhibit 3: Financial information provided by the Group finance director

CONSOLIDATED STATEMENT OF FINANCIAL POSITION

	Notes	*Projected* 30 September 20X5	*Actual* 30 September 20X4
		£m	£m
Assets			
Non-current assets			
Property, plant and equipment	1	230	187
Intangible assets – goodwill		30	30
Deferred tax asset	2	10	15
Total non-current assets		270	232

	Notes	Projected 30 September 20X5	Actual 30 September 20X4
		£m	£m
Current assets			
Inventories		35	28
Trade and other receivables		62	45
Cash and cash equivalents		–	10
Total current assets		97	83
Total assets		367	315
Equity and Liabilities			
Equity			
Equity share capital		50	50
Retained earnings		126	103
Non-controlling interest	3	5	–
Total equity		181	153
Non-current liabilities			
Debenture		60	55
Provisions	4	6	12
Total non-current liabilities		66	67
Current liabilities			
Trade and other payables		105	95
Overdraft		15	–
Total current liabilities		120	95
Total liabilities		186	162
Total equity and liabilities		367	315

CONSOLIDATED STATEMENT OF PROFIT OR LOSS FOR THE YEAR TO 30 SEPTEMBER

	Notes	*Projected* 20X5	*Actual* 20X4
		£m	£m
Revenue	5	375	315
Operating expenses		(348)	(277)
Operating profit		27	38
Profit on disposal of shares in Calgary Co		10	–
Finance costs		(4)	(3)
Profit before tax		33	35
Tax expense		(10)	(15)
Profit for the year		23	20

Notes.

1 Several old warehouses were modernised during the year. The modernisation involved the redesign of the layout of each warehouse, the installation of new computer systems, and the replacement of electrical systems.

2 The deferred tax asset is in respect of unused tax losses (tax credits) which accumulated when Toronto Ltd was loss making for a period of three years from 20W8 to 20X1.

3 The non-controlling interest has arisen on the disposal of shares in Calgary Ltd. On 1 March 20X5, a 5% equity shareholding in Calgary Ltd was sold, raising cash of £20 million. The profit made on the disposal is separately recognised in the Group statement of profit or loss.

4 The provisions relate to onerous leases in respect of vacant properties which are surplus to the Group's requirements.

5 The Group has always recognised distribution revenue when a shipment leaves its distribution centre.

41 Adams (ACCA 2018 Specimen amended) (98 mins)

It is 1 July 20X5. You are a manager in Dando & Co, a firm of Chartered Certified Accountants responsible for the audit of the Adams Group, a listed entity, for the year ended 31 May 20X5. The Group operates in the textile industry, buying cotton, silk and other raw materials to manufacture a range of goods including clothing, linen and soft furnishings. Goods are sold under the Adams brand name, which was acquired by the Group many years ago. Your firm was appointed as auditor in January 20X5.

The following **exhibits** provide information relevant to the question:

(1) An email which you have received from Joss Dylan, the audit engagement partner.

(2) Information about the Group's general background and activities.

(3) Extracts from the draft Group financial statements for the year ending 31 May 20X5.

(4) Notes from a meeting held between Joss Dylan and the Group's finance director and representatives from its audit committee.

This information should be used to answer the question requirements within the response option provided.

Required

Respond to the instructions in the email from the audit engagement partner.

Note. The split of the mark allocation is shown in the partner's email (Exhibit 1). **(40 marks)**

Professional marks will be awarded for the demonstration of skill in communication, analysis and evaluation, professional scepticism and judgement and commercial acumen in your answer. **(10 marks)**

(Total = 50 marks)

Exhibit 1: Email from audit engagement partner

To: Audit manager

From: Joss Dylan

Subject: Adams Group audit planning

Hello

I need you to begin planning the audit of the Adams Group (the Group) for the year ended 31 May 20X5. As you know, we have been appointed to audit the Group financial statements, and we have also been appointed to audit the financial statements of the parent company and of all subsidiaries of the Group except for a foreign subsidiary, Lynott Co, which is audited by a local firm, Clapton & Co. All components of the Group have the same year end of 31 May, report under IFRS Standards and in the same currency.

Using the information provided, I require you to prepare briefing notes for my use, in which you:

(a) Evaluate and prioritise the significant audit risks to be considered in planning the audit of the Group. Your evaluation should utilise analytical procedures for identifying relevant audit risks. **(19 marks)**

(b) Explain the matters to be considered, and the procedures to be performed, in respect of planning to use the work of Clapton & Co. **(8 marks)**

(c) Design the principal audit procedures to be performed in respect of the £12 million investment in associate recognised as a non-current asset in the Group statement of financial position. **(5 marks)**

(d) Using the information provided in Exhibit 4, identify and evaluate any ethical threats and other professional issues which arise from the requests made by the Group audit committee. **(8 marks)**

Thank you.

Exhibit 2: Background and structure of the Adams Group

The Group structure and information about each of the components of the Group is shown below.

Group structure:

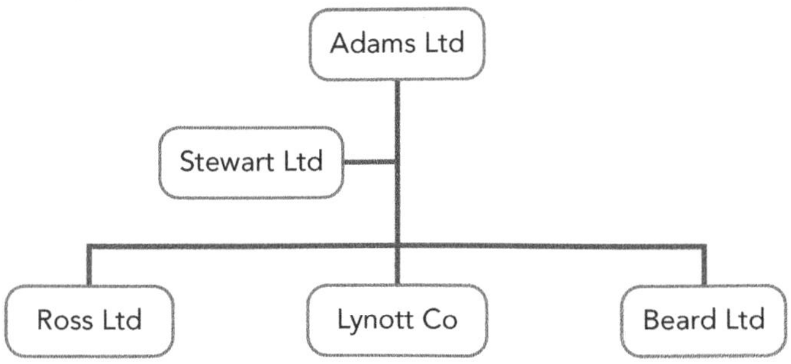

Ross Ltd, Lynott Co and Beard Ltd are all wholly owned, acquired subsidiaries which manufacture different textiles. Adams plc also owns 25% of Stewart Ltd, a company which is classified as an associate in the Group statement of financial position at a value of £12 million at 31 May 20X5. The shares in Stewart Ltd were acquired in January 20X6 for a consideration of £11.5 million. Other than this recent investment in Stewart Ltd, the Group structure has remained unchanged for many years.

Information relevant to each of the group companies

Adams plc is the parent company in the group and its main activities relate to holding the investments in its subsidiaries and also the brand name which was purchased many years ago. Adams plc imposes an annual management charge of £800,000 on each of its subsidiaries, with the charge for each financial year payable in the subsequent August.

Ross Ltd manufactures luxury silk clothing, with almost all of its output sold through approximately 200 department stores across the UK. Ross Ltd's draft statement of financial position recognises assets of £21.5 million at 31 May 20X5. Any silk clothing which has not been sold within 12 months is transferred to Lynott Co, where the silk material is recycled in its manufacturing process.

Lynott Co is located in Farland, where it can benefit from low-cost labour in its factories. It produces low price fashion clothing for the mass market. A new inventory system was introduced in December 20X4 in order to introduce stronger controls over the movement of inventory between factories and stores. Lynott Co is audited by Clapton & Co, and its auditor's reports in all previous years have been unmodified. Clapton & Co is a small accounting and audit firm but is a member of an international network of firms. Lynott Co's draft statement of financial position recognises assets of £24 million at 31 May 20X5.

Beard Ltd manufactures soft furnishings which it sells through an extensive network of retailers. The company is cash-rich, and surplus cash is invested in a large portfolio of investment properties primarily in London and Manchester, which generate rental income. The Group's accounting policy is to measure investment properties at fair value. Beard Ltd's draft statement of financial position recognises assets of £28 million at 31 May 20X5, of which investment properties represent £10 million.

Exhibit 3: Extracts from draft Group consolidated financial statements

DRAFT CONSOLIDATED STATEMENT OF PROFIT OR LOSS AND OTHER COMPREHENSIVE INCOME

	Year ended 31 May 20X5	*Year ended* 31 May 20X4
	£'000	£'000
	Draft	*Actual*
Revenue	725,000	650,000
Cost of sales	(463,000)	(417,500)
Gross profit	262,000	232,500
Other income – rental income	200	150
Operating expenses	(250,000)	(225,000)
Operating profit	12,200	7,650
Net finance cost	(1,000)	(1,000)
Profit before tax	11,200	6,650
Income tax expense	(1,500)	(1,000)
Profit for the year	9,700	5,650
Other comprehensive income:		
Gain on investment property revaluation	1,000	3,000
Total comprehensive income	10,700	8,650

DRAFT CONSOLIDATED STATEMENT OF FINANCIAL POSITION

	31 May 20X5	*31 May 20X4*
	£'000	£'000
	Draft	*Actual*
Non-current assets		
Property, plant and equipment	45,000	45,000
Investment property (recognised at fair value)	10,000	7,500
Intangible asset – brand name (recognised at cost)	8,000	8,000
Investment in associate	12,000	–
	75,000	60,500
Current assets		
Inventory	12,000	6,000

	31 May 20X5	31 May 20X4
	£'000	£'000
	Draft	*Actual*
Receivables	10,500	6,600
Cash	10,000	22,000
	32,500	34,600
Total assets	107,500	95,100
Equity and liabilities		
Share capital	35,000	35,000
Retained earnings	34,000	24,600
	69,000	59,600
Non-current liabilities		
Bank loan	20,000	20,000
Current liabilities		
Trade payables	16,000	13,500
Tax payable	2,500	2,000
	18,500	15,500
Total equity and liabilities	107,500	95,100

Exhibit 4: Notes from discussion with Group audit committee and finance director

Recent publicity

During the year, the Group attracted negative publicity when an investigation by a well-known journalist alleged that child-labour was being used by several suppliers of raw materials to Lynott Co. The Group refuted the allegations, claiming that the suppliers in question had no contract to supply Lynott Co, and that the Group always uses raw materials from ethically responsible suppliers. The media coverage of the issue has now ended. The Group finance director is confident that the negative publicity has not affected sales of the Group's products, saying that in fact sales are buoyant, as indicated by the increase in Group revenue in the year.

Systems and accounting policies

The Group has a policy of non-amortisation of the Adams brand name. The brand name was acquired many years ago and is recognised at its original cost. The previous audit firm accepted the policy due to the strength of the brand name and the fact that the Group spends a significant amount each year on product development and marketing aimed at supporting the brand. The Group has maintained a good market share in the last few years and management is confident that this will continue to be the case.

As part of management's strategy to increase market share, a bonus scheme has been put in place across the Group under which senior managers will receive a bonus based on an increase in revenue.

The Group's accounting and management information systems are out of date, and the Group would like to develop and implement new systems next year. The audit committee would like to obtain advice from Dando & Co on the new systems as they have little specialist in-house knowledge in this area.

Financing

In addition, the audit committee requests that the Group audit engagement partner attends a meeting with the Group's bank, which is planned to be held the week after the auditor's report is issued. The purpose of the meeting is for the Group to renegotiate its existing lending facility and to extend its loan, and will be attended by the Group finance director, a representative of the audit committee, as well as the bank manager. The Group is hoping that the audit partner will be able to confirm the Group's strong financial position at the meeting, and also confirm that the audit included procedures on going concern, specifically the audit of the Group's cash flow forecast for the next two years, which the bank has requested as part of their lending decision.

42 Robster (P7 June 2009 amended) (49 mins)

It is 1 July 20X5. Robster Ltd is a company which designs and creates high-value items of jewellery. You are the manager responsible for the audit of Robster Ltd, and you are reviewing the audit working papers for the year ended 28 February 20X5. The draft financial statements show profit before tax of £3.2 million, and total assets of £45 million.

The audit senior has left you the following note on the audit file, relating to assets recognised in the statement of financial position for the first time this year, and a consignment inventory arrangement.

Leases

In July 20X4, Robster Ltd entered into five new rental contracts for land and buildings. The contracts have been recognised as leases, and the statement of financial position includes right-of-use assets presented as tangible non-current assets at a value of £3.6 million, and a total lease liability of £3.2 million.

Financial assets

Non-current assets include financial assets recognised at £1.26 million. A note to the financial statements describes these financial assets as investments classified as at fair value, and the investments are described in the note as 'held for trading'. The investments are all shares in listed companies. A gain of £350,000 has been recognised in net profit in respect of the revaluation of these investments.

Consignment inventory

Approximately half of Robster's jewellery is sold from its own retail outlets. The other half is sold by external vendors under a consignment inventory arrangement, the terms of which specify that Robster Ltd retains the ability to change the selling price of the jewellery, and that the vendor is required to return any unsold jewellery after a period of nine months. When the vendor sells an item of jewellery to a customer, legal title passes from Robster Ltd to the customer.

On delivery of the jewellery to the external vendors, Robster Ltd recognises revenue and derecognises inventory. At 28 February 20X5, jewellery at cost price of £1 million is held at external vendors. Revenue of £1.25 million has been recognised in respect of this jewellery.

Required

In your review of the audit working papers, comment on the matters you should consider, and state the audit evidence you should expect to find in respect of:

(a) The lease **(7 marks)**

(b) The financial assets **(6 marks)**

(c) The consignment inventory **(7 marks)**

Professional marks will be awarded for the demonstration of skill in analysis and evaluation, and professional scepticism and judgement in your answer. **(5 marks)**

(Total = 25 marks)

43 Connolly (P7 December 2014 amended) (98 mins)

It is 1 July 20X5. You are an audit manager in Davies & Co, responsible for the audit of Connolly plc, a listed company operating in the pharmaceutical industry. You have managed the audit of Connolly plc for the last two years and you are planning the audit of the financial statements for the year ending 30 September 20X5. The audit partner, Ali Stone, has sent you an email (shown in the Exhibit below) with a number of attachments. Within the partner's email, there are a number of instructions.

Required

Respond to the instructions in the email from the audit engagement partner.

Note. The split of the mark allocation is shown in the partner's email. **(40 marks)**

Professional marks will be awarded for the demonstration of skill in communication, analysis and evaluation, professional scepticism and judgement and commercial acumen in your answer. **(10 marks)**

(Total = 50 marks)

Exhibit: Email and attachments from audit engagement partner

To: Audit manager

From: Ali Stone, Audit engagement partner

Subject: Audit planning – Connolly plc

Hello

I would like you to start planning the audit of Connolly plc. The company's finance director, Maggie Ram, has sent to me this morning some key financial information discussed at the latest board meeting.

I have also provided you with the minutes of a meeting I had with Maggie last week and some background information about the company. Using this information I would like you to prepare briefing notes for my use in which you:

(a) Explain why analytical procedures are performed as a fundamental part of our risk assessment at the planning stage of the audit. **(5 marks)**

(b) Evaluate the business risks faced by Connolly plc. **(8 marks)**

(c) Evaluate and prioritise the significant risks of material misstatement to be considered in planning the audit. **(10 marks)**

(d) Design the principal audit procedures to be performed in respect of:

(i) the acquired 'Cold Comforts' brand name; and **(5 marks)**

(ii) the research and development costs spent on the new GreenPack packaging **(5 marks)**

(e) Discuss the ethical issues relevant to the audit firm, and recommend appropriate actions to be taken. **(7 marks)**

Thank you.

Background information

Connolly plc is a pharmaceutical company, developing drugs to be licensed for use around the world, with sales made in over 30 countries. Its head office and main research facility is located in the Midlands where the majority of its staff are employed. The company obtained a stock exchange listing five years ago after being operated as a large privately owned company for several decades.

Products include medicines such as tablets and medical gels and creams. Some drugs are sold over the counter at pharmacy stores, while others can only be prescribed for use by a doctor.

Products are heavily advertised to support the company's brand names. In some countries television advertising is not allowed for prescription drugs.

The market is very competitive, encouraging rapid product innovation. New products are continually in development and improvements are made to existing formulations. Four new drugs are in the research and development phase. Drugs have to meet very stringent regulatory requirements prior to being licensed for production and sale. Research and development involves human clinical trials, the results of which are scrutinised by the licensing authorities.

It is common in the industry for patents to be acquired for new drugs, and patent rights are rigorously defended, sometimes resulting in legal action against potential infringement. Connolly plc was successful in bringing a legal action against a competitor two years ago when the competitor was found to be in breach of a patent held by Connolly plc.

Minutes from Ali Stone's meeting with Maggie Ram

Connolly plc has approached its bank to extend its borrowing facilities. An extension of £10 million is being sought to its existing loan to support the on-going development of new drugs. Our firm has been asked by the bank to provide a guarantee in respect of this loan extension.

In addition, the company has asked the bank to make cash of £3 million available in the event that an existing court case against the company is successful. The court case is being brought by an individual who suffered severe and debilitating side effects when participating in a clinical trial in 20X3.

In October 20X4, Connolly plc began to sell into a new market – that of animal health. This has been very successful, and the sales of veterinary pharmaceuticals and grooming products for livestock and pets amount to approximately 15% of total revenue during the year ended 30 September 20X5.

Another success during the year ended 30 September 20X5 was the acquisition of the 'Cold Comforts' brand from a rival company. Products to alleviate the symptoms of coughs and colds are sold under this brand. The brand cost £5 million and is being amortised over an estimated useful life of 15 years.

Included within receivables on the statement of financial position is a balance of £25,000. This amount is owed to Connolly plc by Billy Ltd, a company which is controlled by Maggie Ram. Maggie has provided me with a note to the effect that the amount is due to be repaid within the next 12 months, but we have no further information about this transaction.

In the context of the climate crisis, Connolly plc has begun looking into using plastic-free packaging for its products sold directly to customers. The board has approved a research and development budget of £0.5m for the new packaging, and by the end of the year, £0.2m has been spent, with this amount being paid to GreenPack, a firm of packaging specialists, to design and develop a new range of plastic-free packaging specifically for Connolly plc's products. It is anticipated that the packaging will be ready for use in three years' time. GreenPack is currently testing prototypes of the proposed packaging.

Connolly plc's accounting and management information systems are out of date. This is not considered to create any significant control deficiencies, but the company would like to develop and implement new systems next year. Management has asked our firm to give advice on the new systems as they have little specialist in-house knowledge in this area.

KEY FINANCIAL INFORMATION

	30 September 20X5 – *Projected unaudited*	30 September 20X4 – *Actual audited*
	£'000	£'000
Revenue	40,000	38,000

	30 September 20X5 – *Projected unaudited*	30 September 20X4 – *Actual audited*
	£'000	£'000
Operating profit	8,100	9,085
Operating margin	20%	24%
Earnings per share	25p	29p
Net cash flow	(1,200)	6,000
Research and development cash outflow in the year	(3,000)	(2,800)
Total development intangible asset recognised at the year end	50,000	48,000
Total assets	200,000	195,000
Gearing ratio (debt/equity)	0.8	0.9

44 Osier (P7 Mar/Jun 2017 amended) (49 mins)

You work for a professional firm that offers audit and assurance services to a variety of clients. The following exhibits provide information relevant to the question:

(1) Osier Ltd

(2) Moosewood Hospital

This information should be used to answer the question requirements below.

Required

(a) Using the information provided in Exhibit 1, comment on the matters to be considered, and explain the audit evidence you should expect to find during your file review in respect of each of the issues described below.

Note. The split of the mark allocation is shown against each of the issues within Exhibit 1. You are not required to discuss any potential implications for the auditor's report. **(11 marks)**

(b) Discuss the benefits of independent assurance being provided on the key performance indicators included in the integrated report of Moosewood Hospital Ltd to the company's management and to external users of the report. **(3 marks)**

(c) Using the information provided in Exhibit 2, design the examination procedures which should be used in obtaining assurance relating to the key performance indicators of Moosewood Hospital Ltd. **(6 marks)**

Professional marks will be awarded for the demonstration of skill in analysis and evaluation, and professional scepticism and judgement in your answer. **(5 marks)**

(Total = 25 marks)

Exhibit 1: Osier Ltd

You are the manager responsible for the audit of Osier Ltd, a jewellery manufacturer and retailer. The final audit for the year ended 31 March 20X7 is nearing completion and you are reviewing the audit working papers. The draft financial statements recognise total assets of £1,919 million (20X6 – £1,889 million), revenue of £1,052 million (20X6 – £997 million) and profit before tax of £107 million (20X6 – £110 million). Two issues from the audit working papers are summarised below:

(a) (i) **Cost of inventory**

Inventory costs include all purchase costs and the costs of conversion of raw materials into finished goods. Conversion costs include direct labour costs and an allocation of production overheads. Direct labour costs are calculated based on the average production time per unit of inventory, which is estimated by the production manager, multiplied by the estimated labour cost per hour, which is calculated using the forecast annual wages of production staff divided by the annual scheduled hours of production. Production overheads are all fixed and are allocated based upon the forecast annual units of production. At the year end, inventory was valued at £21 million (20X6 – £20 million). **(6 marks)**

(ii) **Impairment**

At the year end, management performed an impairment review on its retail outlets, which are a cash generating unit for the purpose of conducting an impairment review. While internet sales grew rapidly during the year, sales from retail outlets declined, prompting the review. At 31 March 20X7 the carrying amount of the assets directly attributable to the retail outlets totalled £137 million, this includes both tangible assets and goodwill.

During the year management received a number of offers from parties interested in purchasing the retail outlets for an average of £125 million. They also estimated the disposal costs to be £1.5 million, based upon their experience of corporate acquisitions and disposals. Management estimated the value in use to be £128 million. This was based upon the historic cash flows attributable to retail outlets inflated at a general rate of 1% per year. This, they argued, reflects the poor performance of the retail outlets.

Consequently the retail outlets were impaired by £9 million to restate them to their estimated recoverable amount of £128 million. The impairment was allocated against the tangible assets of the outlets on a pro rata basis, based upon the original carrying amount of each asset in the unit. **(5 marks)**

Exhibit 2: Moosewood Hospital

Fern & Co is also engaged to produce an assurance report on the performance information of Moosewood Hospital Ltd which is included in the company's integrated report. The integrated report will be published on the company's website later in the year and is not part of the information published with the financial statements.

Fern & Co has a specialist team, independent from the audit department, which provides assurance on key performance indicators. Under the terms of the engagement, this team is required to provide assurance with regard to both the accuracy and completeness of the key performance indicators which are used to monitor the hospital's efficiency and effectiveness.

Several of the key performance indicators included in the draft integrated report, all of which the Hospital claims to have met, are shown below:

(1) To maintain an average patient to nurse ratio of no more than 6:1.

(2) To achieve a minimum 75% annual usage of surgical rooms.

(3) To ensure that the rate of admissions within 28 days for previously treated conditions does not exceed 3%.

45 Macau (P7 Mar/Jun 2016 amended) (49 mins)

You are a senior manager in Macau & Co, a firm of Chartered Certified Accountants. In your capacity as engagement quality reviewer, you have been asked to review the audit files of Stanley Ltd and Kowloon Ltd, both of which have a financial year ended 31 December 20X5, and the audits of both companies are nearing completion.

(a) Stanley Ltd is a company that processes frozen food, selling its products to wholesalers and supermarkets. From your review of the audit working papers, you have noted that the level of materiality was determined to be £1.5 million at the planning stage, and this materiality threshold has been used throughout the audit. There is no evidence on the audit file that this threshold has been reviewed during the course of the audit.

From your review of the audit planning, you know that a new packing machine with a cost of £1.6 million was acquired by Stanley Ltd in March 20X5 and is recognised in the draft statement of financial position at a carrying amount of £1.4 million at 31 December 20X5. The packing machine is located at the premises of Aberdeen Ltd, a distribution company which is used to pack and distribute a significant proportion of Stanley Ltd's products. The machine has not been physically verified by a member of the audit team. The audit working papers conclude that 'we have obtained the purchase invoice and order in relation to the machine, and therefore can conclude that the asset is appropriately valued and that it exists. In addition, the managing director of Aberdeen Ltd has confirmed in writing that the machine is located at their premises and is in working order. No further work is needed in respect of this item.'

Inventory is recognised at £2 million in the draft statement of financial position. You have reviewed the results of audit procedures performed at the inventory count, where the test counts performed by the audit team indicated that the count of some items performed by the company's staff was not correct. The working papers state that 'the inventory count was not well organised' and conclude that 'however, the discrepancies were immaterial, so no further action is considered necessary'.

The audit senior spoke to you yesterday, voicing some concerns about the performance of the audit. A summary of his comments is shown below:

'The audit manager and audit engagement partner came to review the audit working papers on the same day towards the completion of the audit fieldwork. The audit partner asked me if there had been any issues on the sections of the audit which I had worked on, and when I said there had been no problems, he signed off the working papers after a quick look through them.

When reading the company's board minutes, I found several references to the audit engagement partner, Joe Lantau. It appears that Joe recommended that the company use the services of his brother, Mick Lantau, for advice on business development, as Mick is a management consultant. Based on that recommendation, Mick has provided a consultancy service to Stanley Ltd since September 20X5. I mentioned this to Joe, and he told me not to record it in the audit working papers or to discuss it with anyone.'

Required

Comment on the quality of the audit performed discussing the quality management, ethical and other professional issues raised. **(13 marks)**

(b) Kowloon Ltd works on contracts to design and manufacture large items of medical equipment such as radiotherapy and X-ray machines. The company specialises in the design, production and installation of bespoke machines under contract with individual customers, which are usually private medical companies. The draft financial statements recognise profit before tax of £950,000 and total assets of £7.5 million.

The audit senior has left the following note for your attention:

'One of Kowloon Ltd's major customers is the Bay Medical Centre (BMC), a private hospital. In June 20X5 a contract was entered into, under the terms of which Kowloon Ltd would design a new radiotherapy machine for BMC. The machine is based on a new innovation and is being developed for the specific requirements of BMC. It was estimated that the design and production of the machine would take 18 months with estimated installation in December 20X6. As at 31 December 20X5, Kowloon Ltd had invested heavily in the contract, and design costs totalling £350,000 have been recognised as work in progress in the draft statement of financial position. Deferred income of £200,000 is also recognised as a current liability, representing a payment made by BMC to finance part of the design costs. No other accounting entries have been made in respect of the contract with BMC.

'As part of our subsequent events review, inspection of correspondence between Kowloon Ltd and BMC indicates that the contract has been cancelled by BMC as it is unable to pay for its completion. It appears that BMC lost a significant amount of funding towards the end of 20X5, impacting significantly on the financial position of the company. The manager responsible for the BMC contract confirms that BMC contacted him about the company's financial difficulties in December 20X5.

'The matter has been discussed with Kowloon Ltd's finance director, who has stated that he is satisfied with the current accounting treatment and is not proposing to make any adjustments in light of the cancellation of the contract by BMC. The finance director also advised that the loss of BMC as a customer will not be mentioned in the company's integrated report, as the finance director does not consider it significant enough to warrant discussion.

'Kowloon Ltd is currently working on six contracts for customers other than BMC. Our audit evidence concludes that Kowloon Ltd does not face a threat to its going concern status.'

Your review of the audit work performed on going concern supports this conclusion.

Required

Comment on the matters to be considered, and recommend the actions to be taken by the auditor.

(7 marks)

Professional marks will be awarded for the demonstration of skill in analysis and evaluation, and professional scepticism and judgement in your answer. **(5 marks)**

(Total = 25 marks)

46 Northwest (P7 Sep/Dec 2016 amended) (49 mins)

It is 1 July 20X5. You are an audit manager at Thornhill & Co responsible for the audit of Northwest Ltd, a subsidiary of Valerian Ltd. A different audit firm is responsible for the audit of Valerian Ltd and the Valerian Group financial statements.

The audit of the financial statements of Northwest Ltd for the year ended 31 March 20X5 is nearing completion, but the following issues require your attention before the auditor's report is signed and your final communication is made to the group auditor in response to their request for information. The draft financial statements of Northwest Ltd recognise a loss before tax of £50,000.

Northwest Ltd has been loss making for several years and it generates insufficient cash to meet its significant debt obligations. The company relies on support from Valerian Ltd in order to continue trading. The management of Valerian Ltd has confirmed verbally that it will continue to support Northwest Ltd, but it has not provided a formal letter of support despite a number of requests.

You are aware that Valerian Ltd is the subject of a major lawsuit following an industrial accident which led to significant pollution of local agricultural land and, most seriously, loss of life. You attempted to discuss the matter with the directors of Valerian Ltd, but they refused, saying that it had already been investigated by the group auditor. The group auditor informed you that the case is ongoing and that they have obtained satisfactory representations from both management and legal advisers stating that they were confident of successfully defending the claim. When you asked for copies of the representations, the group auditor refused, saying it was a matter relevant to the parent company and that it was not relevant to the audit of Northwest Ltd.

Shortly after making your enquiries, you received a phone call from the group engagement partner who said that the board of Valerian Ltd was concerned that you might modify the auditor's report of Northwest Ltd. The group engagement partner also said that, as the only person with full oversight of audit matters relating to the Valerian Group, they did not think that it would be necessary to modify the auditor's report of Northwest Ltd and that they would oppose any attempt to do so. The group engagement partner suggested that if the debt in the financial statements of Northwest Ltd was the reason for seeking parental support, they would transfer it to the Group and the letter of support would no longer be necessary.

Required

(a) Discuss how professional scepticism should be applied to the statements made by the management and auditors of Valerian Ltd regarding the outstanding legal case. **(6 marks)**

(b) Comment on the ethical and professional issues raised, considering any implications for the completion of the audit, in respect of:

(1) The evidence obtained in relation to the support offered by Valerian Ltd

(2) The request not to modify the auditor's report Northwest Ltd

Note: The total marks will be split equally between each part. **(14 marks)**

Professional marks will be awarded for the demonstration of skill in analysis and evaluation, and professional scepticism and judgement in your answer. **(5 marks)**

(Total = 25 marks)

Questions 47 to 64 cover Completion, review and reporting, the subject of Part E of the BPP Workbook for AAA.

47 Rope (P7 Sep/Dec 2016 amended) (49 mins)

You are the manager responsible for the audit of Rope Ltd for the year ended 30 September 20X6. During a visit to the team performing the fieldwork, the audit senior shows you a cash flow forecast covering six-month periods to 30 September 20X8 as prepared by management as part of their assessment of the going concern status of the company. The audit senior asks whether any of the forecast cash flows disclosed require any further investigation during the audit fieldwork.

THE ACTUAL AND FORECAST SIX-MONTHLY CASH FLOWS FOR ROPE LTD FOR THE PERIODS ENDED:

			Actual			*Forecast*
	31 March 20X6	*30 Sept 20X6*	*31 March 20X7*	*30 Sept 20X7*	*31 March 20X8*	*30 Sept 20X8*
	£'000	£'000	£'000	£'000	£'000	£'000
Operating cash flows						
Receipts from customers	13,935	14,050	14,300	14,700	14,950	15,400
Payments to suppliers	(10,725)	(10,850)	(11,050)	(11,400)	(11,600)	(12,000)
Salaries	(1,250)	(1,300)	(1,275)	(1,326)	(1,301)	(1,353)
Other operating cash payments	(1,875)	(1,850)	(1,913)	(1,887)	(1,951)	(1,925)
Other cash flows						
Sale of investments	–	–	–	–	–	500
Repayment of J Stewart loan	–	–	–	–	–	(500)
Repayment of bank loan	–	–	–	–	(1,500)	–
Receipt of bank loan	–	–	–	–	1,500	–
Cash flow for the period	85	50	62	87	98	122
Opening cash	(275)	(190)	(140)	(78)	9	107
Closing cash	(190)	(140)	(78)	9	107	229

The following additional information has been provided in support of the forecasts:

- Receipts from customers and payments to suppliers have been estimated based on detailed sales forecasts prepared by the sales director.
- Salaries and overheads have been estimated as the prior year cost plus general inflation of 2%.

- The bank loan expires on 5 January 20X8. The finance director expects to take out a matching facility with the current lender to pay off the existing debt.
- On 1 October 20X5, the chief executive, Mr J Stewart, gave the company a three-year, interest-free loan secured by a fixed charge over the operational assets of Rope Ltd. The audit team was unaware of this loan prior to obtaining the cash flow forecast.
- The directors plan to sell some investments in listed shares to fund the repayment of the chief executive's loan. At 30 September 20X6, the investments were carried in the statement of financial position at their fair value of £350,000.

Required

(a) Evaluate the appropriateness of the cash flow forecast prepared by Rope Ltd and design the further audit procedures which should be performed. **(12 marks)**

(b) The finance director of Rope Ltd, Uma Thorton, has requested that your firm present the draft financial statements into a format appropriate for publication at the forthcoming company general meeting. Uma has also commented that the previous auditors did not use a liability disclaimer in their auditor's report, and would like more information about the use of liability disclaimer paragraphs.

Required

Discuss the ethical issues raised by the request for your firm to prepare the financial statements of Rope Ltd. **(3 marks)**

(c) In the context of a standard unmodified auditor's report, describe the content of a liability disclaimer paragraph, and discuss whether its use should be considered appropriate. **(5 marks)**

Professional marks will be awarded for the demonstration of skill in analysis and evaluation, and professional scepticism and judgement in your answer. **(5 marks)**

(Total = 25 marks)

48 Kandinsky (P7 Sep/Dec 15 amended) (49 mins)

Malevich & Co is a firm of Chartered Certified Accountants offering audit and assurance services to a large portfolio of clients. You are a manager in the audit department responsible for the audit of two clients, Kandinsky Ltd and Viola Ltd.

(a) Kandinsky Ltd is a manufacturer of luxury food items including chocolate and other confectionery which are often sold as gift items individually or in hampers containing a selection of expensive items from the range of products. The company has a financial year ended 31 July 20X5, much of the planned audit work has been completed, and you are reviewing issues which have been raised by the audit senior. Due to an economic recession, sales of products have fallen sharply this year and measures have been implemented to support the company's cash flow. You are aware that the company only has £150,000 in cash at the year end.

Extracts from the draft financial statements and other relevant information are given below.

	Notes	*July 20X5 (Draft)*	*July 20X4 (Actual)*
		£'000	£'000
Revenue		2,440	3,950
Operating expenses		(2,100)	(2,800)
Finance charge		(520)	(500)
(Loss)/profit before tax		(180)	(650)

	Notes	July 20X5 (Draft)	July 20X4 (Actual)
		£'000	£'000
Total assets		10,400	13,500
Long-term liabilities – bank loan	1	3,500	3,000
Short-term liabilities – trade payables	2	900	650
Disclosed in notes to financial statements:			
Undrawn borrowing facilities	3	500	1,000
Contingent liability	4	120	–

Notes.

1 The bank loan was extended in March 20X5 by drawing on the borrowing facilities offered by the bank. The loan carries a fixed interest rate and is secured on the company's property including the head office and manufacturing site. The first repayment of loan capital is due on 30 June 20X6 when £350,000 is due to be paid.

2 Kandinsky Ltd renegotiated its terms of trade with its main supplier of cocoa beans, and extended payment terms from 50 days to 80 days in order to improve working capital.

3 The borrowing facilities are due to be reviewed by the bank in April 20X6 and contain covenants including that interest cover is maintained at 2, and the ratio of bank loan to operating profit does not exceed 4:1.

4 The contingent liability relates to a letter of support which Kandinsky Ltd has provided to its main supplier of cane sugar which is facing difficult trading conditions.

Required

In respect of the audit of Kandinsky Ltd:

Identify and explain the matters which may cast significant doubt on Kandinsky Ltd's ability to continue as a going concern. **(9 marks)**

(b) You are also responsible for the audit of Viola Ltd, a small engineering company located in the Midlands with a financial year ended 31 March 20X5. The auditor's report for the financial year then ended, which was issued in September 20X5, contained a 'Material Uncertainty Related to Going Concern' section outlining the going concern issues facing the company. The auditor's report was otherwise unmodified.

The finance director of Viola Ltd phoned you yesterday to discuss some recent developments at the company. His comments are shown in the following note:

'I am getting in touch to update you on our situation and to ask for your firm's advice.

As you know, in the last financial year the company lost several contracts and we had to make a number of staff redundant. In recent months further contracts have been lost and Viola Ltd has faced severe working capital problems, resulting in the sale of some of our plant in order to meet liabilities as they fall due. We are restricted on the assets which can be sold as the company's bank loan is secured by a floating charge over non-current assets. In November 20X5 the accounts recognised net liabilities of £500,000 and without securing further finance, the future of the company does not look good.

We are tendering for three new contracts to supply components to local car manufacturers. However, our bank is reluctant to extend our borrowing facilities until the contracts are secured, which may not be for another few months.

My fellow directors are becoming concerned about the possibility of our creditors applying for compulsory liquidation of the company, which we want to avoid if possible. We also wish to avoid a creditor's voluntary liquidation. Can you please advise me on the alternatives which are available given the company's precarious financial situation? I need you to explain the procedures involved with any alternatives which you can recommend, and describe the impact on the employees and directors of the company.'

Required

Respond to the instructions in the note from the finance director. **(11 marks)**

Professional marks will be awarded for the demonstration of skill in analysis and evaluation, and professional scepticism and judgement in your answer. **(5 marks)**

(Total = 25 marks)

49 Kelly & Co (Sep/Dec 2021) (49 mins)

It is 1 July 20X5. You are a manager in Kelly & Co, a firm of Chartered Certified Accountants which offers a range of assurance services.

The managing director of Flynn Ltd, which is not currently a client of Kelly & Co, has contracted you regarding a review engagement which he would like your firm to provide. Kelly & Co has already conducted specific client identification procedures in line with money laundering regulations with satisfactory results.

Flynn Ltd operates in the food processing industry, and the company is planning to build a new food processing facility in a foreign country. This will cost approximately £15 million to build, and Flynn Ltd has approached its lenders to provide the necessary finance.

The following **exhibits**, available on the left-hand side of the screen, provide information relevant to the question:

(1) Flynn Ltd – information regarding Flynn Ltd and the review engagement your firm is invited to provide.

(2) Cash flow forecast – a cast flow forecast and supporting notes and assumptions to be used in support of a loan application.

This information should be used to answer the question **requirements** within your chosen **response option(s)**.

(a) Using the information in Exhibit 1 – Flynn Ltd:

Required

Evaluate the matters to be considered by Kelly & Co in deciding whether to accept Flynn Ltd as a client of the firm and whether to perform the review engagement to report on the business plan.

Note. You do NOT need to include matters relating specifically to client due diligence (Know Your Client) procedures. **(8 marks)**

(b) Using the information in Exhibit 2 and assuming that Kelly & Co accepts the engagement to review Flynn Ltd's cash flow forecast:

Required

(i) Evaluate the assumptions used by management and the completeness of the cash flow forecast prepared, explaining why particular assumptions should be challenged and approached with professional scepticism; and **(5 marks)**

(ii) Design the examination procedures which should be performed in the review of Flynn Ltd's cash flow forecast. **(7 marks)**

Professional marks will be awarded for the demonstration of skill in analysis and evaluation, professional scepticism and judgement and commercial acumen in your answer. **(5 marks)**

(Total = 25 marks)

Exhibit 1: Flynn Ltd

Flynn Ltd is an unlisted company whose main activity involves processing frozen food. The company has several processing plants in its home country and one located in a foreign country, Nearland. In order to expand its product range, the company is planning to build a new facility and begin processing in another foreign country, Farland. Flynn Ltd has approached its provider of finance, Mortons Bank, to provide a £15 million loan which will cover the necessary capital expenditure. Nearland and Farland both have a different currency than that used by Flynn Ltd.

Mortons Bank has asked Flynn Ltd to provide a business plan for the next three years in support of the loan application. The business plan includes forecast statements of profit or loss and cash flow. The bank has requested that the forecasts be subject to an independent review and that a review report should be included with the loan application.

Flynn Ltd is expecting to submit the business plan and review report to the bank on 5 August 20X5.

Flynn Ltd is audited by Roxie Associates. A new audit manager, Mary Sunshine, has recently been recruited to your firm from Flynn Ltd where she worked in the internal audit department, and she told you the following:

'I know that Flynn Ltd's auditor, Roxie Associates, has performed review engagements for the company in the past. I am aware that the latest external auditor's report, for the year ended 31 March 20X5, included a Material Uncertainty Related to Going Concern section due to the company's liquidity problems.'

In his communication with Kelly & Co, the managing director of Flynn Ltd has suggested that should Kelly & Co provide the report to the bank, and assuming that the finance is provided to the company, he will be willing to remove Roxie Associates as the company's auditor and appoint Kelly & Co to provide the audit service. The managing director has also requested that Mary Sunshine is part of the review team and the audit team, given her past experience with the company.

Exhibit 2: Cash flow forecast

Cash Flow Forecast for the three years to 30 June 20X8

Six-month periods to:

	Note	*31 December 20X5*	*30 June 20X6*	*31 December 20X6*	*30 June 20X7*	*31 December 20X7*	*30 June 20X8*
		£'000	£'000	£'000	£'000	£'000	£'000
Average monthly sales	1	200	234	265	288	308	318
Revenue		1,200.00	1,404.00	1,589.33	1,727.60	1,846.80	1,909.60
Cash inflow from customers	2	1,050.00	1,201.00	1,399.50	1,578.00	1,723.50	1,836.00
Operating expenses	3	(920.00)	(940.00)	(1,080.00)	(1,150.00)	(1,280.00)	(1,340.00)
Marketing for new product ranges		-	(100.00)	-	-	-	-
Interest payments and other finance costs		(30.00)	(30.00)	(30.00)	(30.00)	(30.00)	(30.00)
Dividends		(100.00)	-	(100.00)	-	(100.00)	-
Loan receipt		15,000.00	-	-	-	-	-
Capital expenditure	4	(7,500.00)	(7,500.00)	-	-	-	-

	Note	31 December 20X5	30 June 20X6	31 December 20X6	30 June 20X7	31 December 20X7	30 June 20X8
		Six-month periods to:					
		£'000	£'000	£'000	£'000	£'000	£'000
Net cash flow		**7,500.00**	**(7,369.00)**	**189.50**	**398.00**	**313.50**	**466.00**
Opening cash		50.00	7,550.00	181.00	370.50	768.50	1,082.00
Closing cash		**7,550.00**	**181.00**	**370.50**	**768.50**	**1,082.00**	**1,548.00**

Notes and key assumptions:

Notes.

1 Monthly sales are based on management's forecasts with predicted sales growth as follows:

Six months to 31 December 20X5	0%
Six months to 30 June 20X6	17.00%
Six months to 31 December 20X6	13.20%
Six months to 30 June 20X7	8.70%
Six months to 31 December 20X7	6.90%
Six months to 30 June 20X8	3.40%

Sales are expected to increase in 20X6 when the new processing facility opens in Farland. The new product ranges are expected to be very popular, and the product launch will be supported by an advertising campaign. In addition to output from the new processing facility, production levels at existing facilities are planned to increase by at least 10%.

2 On average, cash is received from customers in the following pattern:

25% in month of sale

50% following month of sale

25% two months after sale

3 Operating expenses are forecast to increase over the three-year period as production increases. The company is expecting to benefit from economies of scale as production increases at each processing facility.

4 The new processing facility is planned to commence production on 31 March 20X6.

50 Yew (P7 December 2011 amended) (49 mins)

(a) Auditors should accept some of the blame when a company on which they have expressed an unmodified audit opinion subsequently fails, and they should also do more to highlight going concern problems being faced by a company.

Required

Discuss this statement. **(6 marks)**

(b) You are the manager responsible for the audit of Yew Ltd, a company which designs and develops aircraft engines. The audit for the year ended 31 July 20X1 is nearing completion and the audit senior has left the following file note for your attention:

'I have just returned from a meeting with the management of Yew Ltd, and there is a matter I want to bring to your attention. Yew Ltd's statement of financial position recognises an intangible asset of £12.5 million in respect of capitalised research and development costs relating to new aircraft engine designs. However, market research conducted by Yew Ltd in relation to these new designs indicated that there would be little demand in the near future for such designs. Management has provided written representation that they agree with the results of the market research.

'Currently, Yew Ltd has a cash balance of only £125,000 and members of the management team have expressed concerns that the company is finding it difficult to raise additional finance.

'The new aircraft designs have been discussed in the chairman's statement which is to be published with the financial statements. The discussion states that 'developments of new engine designs are underway, and we believe that these new designs will become a significant source of income for Yew Ltd in the next 12 months.

'Yew Ltd's draft financial statements include profit before tax of £23 million, and total assets of £210 million.

'Yew Ltd is due to publish its annual report next week, so we need to consider the impact of this matter urgently.'

Required

Discuss the implications of the audit senior's file note on the completion of the audit and on the auditor's report, recommending any further actions that should be taken by the auditor. **(11 marks)**

(c) You are responsible for answering technical queries from other managers and partners of your firm. An audit partner left the following note on your desk this morning.

'We are auditing Sycamore Ltd for the first time. The prior period financial statements were audited by another firm. We are aware that the auditor's report on the prior period was qualified due to a material misstatement of trade receivables. We have obtained sufficient appropriate evidence that the matter giving rise to the misstatement has been resolved and I am happy to issue an unmodified opinion. But should I refer to the prior year modification in this year's auditor's report?'

Required

Respond to the audit partner's comments. **(3 marks)**

Professional marks will be awarded for the demonstration of skill in analysis and evaluation, and professional scepticism and judgement in your answer. **(5 marks)**

(Total = 25 marks)

51 Fern (P7 Mar/Jun 2017 amended) (49 mins)

(a) You are the manager responsible for the audit of Fieldwood Hospital Ltd, for the year ended 31 March 20X7, working in the audit department of Fern & Co. You have recently visited the audit team, who are currently on site performing the fieldwork, to review the work performed to date and to discuss their progress. During your visit the audit senior informed you of the following matter:

During a review of the valuation of medical inventories, including medicines used in a variety of treatments at the hospital, it was noted that a number of items had passed their recommended use by dates. These were recorded on an inventory spreadsheet maintained by the financial controller and were easy to spot because they were highlighted in red. One of the audit team inspected a sample of the inventories in question and confirmed that their use by dates had expired. When asked about this, the financial controller stated that the audit team must be mistaken. The audit team requested to look at the spreadsheet again, but the financial controller refused. The next day the finance director confronted the audit team accusing them of extending their investigations 'beyond their remit'. The finance director also threatened to remove them from the premises if they continued to ask questions which were not relevant to the audit of the hospital's financial statements. Since then the audit team have been unable to complete their audit of medical inventories. They have also noted that the room where the inventories were previously kept has been emptied.

Required

Identify and explain the ethical and professional issues raised and recommend any actions which should be taken in respect of the matter described by the audit senior. **(9 marks)**

(b) You are also currently involved in the completion stage of the audit of Rocket plc, which is a listed client operating in the engineering industry. The company manufactures machinery for use in the aircraft, defence and marine sectors. The audit for the year ended 30 April 20X7 is almost complete. The revenue and profit before tax figures recognised in the draft financial statements are £1,437 million and £139 million, respectively (20X6 – £1,489 million and £175 million respectively).

Audit procedures identified two sales transactions in the final quarter of the year that related to two different customers but where the goods were delivered to the same location. Further investigations revealed that the goods were delivered to a third party, who agreed to store them until the customers were ready to receive delivery. The goods have yet to be delivered to the customers because they are both building new facilities and neither is sufficiently progressed to receive the new machinery. The contract terms explicitly state that Rocket plc is obliged to deliver the goods to the customers for final inspection and acceptance and the client has not agreed to any consequent amendments to these terms. The sales invoices were raised, and the revenue recognised upon despatch of the goods to the storage facility. During discussions with the audit team, the finance director stated that the company had fulfilled its contractual obligations to provide the goods by a specified date. The revenue attributable to the two transactions totalled £17 million.

Required

(i) Comment upon the matter described above and explain the further actions necessary before the auditor's report can be signed; and **(6 marks)**

(ii) Discuss the implications for the auditor's report if no adjustments are made to the financial statements **(5 marks)**

Professional marks will be awarded for the demonstration of skill in analysis and evaluation, and professional scepticism and judgement in your answer. **(5 marks)**

(Total = 25 marks)

52 Boston (P7 Mar/Jun 2016 amended) (49 mins)

You are the manager responsible for the audit of Boston Ltd, a producer of chocolate and confectionery. The audit of the financial statements for the year ended 31 December 20X5 is nearly complete and you are reviewing the audit working papers. The financial statements recognise revenue of £76 million, profit before tax for the year of £6.4 million and total assets of £104 million.

The summary of uncorrected misstatements included in Boston Ltd's audit working papers, including notes, is shown below. The audit engagement partner is holding a meeting with the management team of Boston Ltd next week, at which the uncorrected misstatements will be discussed.

		Statement of profit or loss		*Statement of financial position*	
Summary of uncorrected misstatements:	**Notes**	*Debit*	*Credit*	*Debit*	*Credit*
		£	£	£	£
Impairment	1	400,000			400,000
Borrowing costs	2		75,000	75,000	
Irrecoverable debt	3	65,000	–	–	65,000

	Statement of profit or loss		Statement of financial position	
Totals	465,000	75,000	75,000	465,000

Notes.

1 During the year Boston Ltd impaired one of its factories. The carrying value of the assets attributable to the factory as a single, cash-generating unit totalled £3.6 million at the year end. The fair value less costs of disposal and the value in use were estimated to be £3 million and £3.5 million respectively and accordingly the asset was written down by £100,000 to reflect the impairment. Audit procedures revealed that management used growth rates attributable to the company as a whole to estimate value in use. Using growth rates attributable to the factory specifically, the audit team calculated the value in use to be £3.1 million.

2 Interest charges of £75,000 relating to a loan taken out during the year to finance the construction of a new manufacturing plant were included in finance charges recognised in profit for the year. The manufacturing plant is due for completion in November 20X6.

3 One of Boston Ltd's largest customers, Cleveland Ltd, is experiencing financial difficulties. At the year end, Cleveland Ltd owed Boston Ltd £100,000, against which Boston Ltd made a 5% specific allowance. Shortly after the year end Cleveland Ltd paid £30,000 of the outstanding amount due but has since experienced further problems, leading to their primary lender presenting a formal request that Cleveland Ltd be liquidated. If successful, only secured creditors are likely to receive any reimbursement.

Required

(a) Explain the matters which should be discussed with management in relation to each of the uncorrected misstatements, including an assessment of their individual impact on the financial statements. **(10 marks)**

(b) Assuming that management does not adjust any of the misstatements, discuss the effect on the audit opinion and auditor's report. **(5 marks)**

(c) As a result of the audit engagement partner's meeting with management, all uncorrected misstatements were corrected, and an auditor's report was issued with an unmodified opinion.

Three days after the auditor's report was issued, management informed the audit engagement partner that it had discovered that significant errors had been made in the processing of the company's payroll. The overall effect of these errors is not yet clear, but they appear to have been ongoing for several months and are likely to be significant.

Required

Explain the auditor's responsibilities in relation to this matter, and the actions that should be taken by the auditor. **(5 marks)**

Professional marks will be awarded for the demonstration of skill in analysis and evaluation, and professional scepticism and judgement in your answer. **(5 marks)**

(Total = 25 marks)

53 Coram (September 2018 amended) (49 mins)

You are an audit manager in Coram & Co, a firm of Chartered Certified Accountants. The audit of one of your clients, Clark Ltd, for the year enFded 31 May 20X8 is nearly complete and the auditor's report is due to be issued next week. Clark Ltd is an unlisted, family-owned business which specialises in the service and repair of both commercial and privately owned motor vehicles. The company operates from seven geographically distinct sites, each of which is considered a separate cash generating unit for impairment review purposes. The draft financial statements recognise profit before taxation for the year of £2.3 million and total assets of £22 million.

The schedule of uncorrected misstatements plus other information prepared by the audit supervisor included in Clark Ltd's audit working papers are shown in the exhibits below. You are due to attend a meeting with the finance director of Clark Ltd tomorrow, at which the uncorrected misstatements will be discussed.

You have been provided with the following exhibits:

Exhibit 1

Schedule of uncorrected misstatements

	Statement of profit or loss		*Statement of financial position*	
Schedule of uncorrected misstatements	*Debit*	*Credit*	*Debit*	*Credit*
	£	£	£	£
(i) Lease of testing equipment				
• lease assets			475,000	
• lease liabilities				475,000
(ii) Asset impairment				
• assets				85,000
• expenses	85,000			
Total	85,000	–	475,000	560,000

Exhibit 2

Lease of testing equipment

According to UK legislation, all motor vehicles over three years old are required to undergo an annual test of vehicle safety and roadworthiness. The annual test requires specialist testing equipment which is inspected by government officials on a regular basis. Following inspection visits in May 20X8, the government inspection report required Clark Ltd to replace the testing equipment at three of its sites. In order to comply with this requirement, Clark Ltd has agreed to lease new testing equipment from a leasing company on six-month leases. Under the terms of the leases, the company has no option to purchase the equipment. The testing equipment was made available for use by Clark Ltd at each of the three sites on 31 May 20X8. The client has capitalised leases with a total carrying amount of £625,000 at two of the sites but has elected to take advantage of the IFRS 16 *Leases* exemption not to capitalise short-term leases at the largest of the three sites. As a result, the present value of the lease payments of £475,000 relating to this site has not been recognised on the company's statement of financial position.

Exhibit 3

Asset impairment

During the year, a significant new competitor entered the market place at one of Clark Ltd's seven sites. As a result, the site has experienced a decline in market share and revenue. The company has therefore conducted an impairment test on the site's assets. The company's working papers for the impairment test have been audited and the following figures have been agreed by the audit team:

	Site assets
	£
Carrying amount on statement of financial position as at 31 May 20X8	3.6 million
Value in use	2.9 million
Fair value	3.9 million

Related costs of selling the assets:

• legal costs	126,000
• transaction taxes	174,000
• costs of removing the assets	85,000
• costs of reorganising the business following the asset disposals	96,000

On the basis of the results of these figures, the client has calculated the recoverable amount of the assets as £3.6 million and concluded that the site has not suffered an impairment. No adjustments have therefore been made to the financial statements in this regard.

Required

(a) Using the information in Exhibits 1, 2 and 3:

Recommend and explain the matters which should be discussed with management in relation to each of the proposed adjustments, including an assessment of their individual impact on the financial statements and on the auditor's opinion if management does not make the proposed adjustments. You should structure your answer as follows:

(i) Lease of testing equipment **(7 marks)**

(ii) Asset impairment **(5 marks)**

(b) Your portfolio as an audit manager at Coram & Co includes the following two clients. Turner Ltd is a financial institution offering loans and credit facilities to both commercial and retail customers. You have received an email from the audit supervisor who is currently supervising interim testing on systems and controls in relation to the audit for the year ending 31 October 20X8. The email gives the following details for your consideration:

One of the audit team members, Janette Stott, has provisionally agreed to take out a loan with Turner Ltd to finance the purchase of a domestic residence. The loan will be secured on the property and the client's business manager has promised Janette that he will ensure that she gets 'the very best deal which the bank can offer.'

A second audit client for which you are responsible is Taverner Ltd. Taverner Ltd is a property developer which often enters into financial contracts with the aim of protecting the value of its overseas investments. An asset manager at Taverner Ltd, Mischa Lee, has said that she would appreciate some expert help from Coram & Co in relation to the actuarial valuation of certain of the firm's financial assets. Taverner Ltd has asked whether Coram & Co would be able to provide such a service, since it has actuarial department which is capable of performing such a valuation.

Required

Comment on the ethical and professional issues raised in respect of the audits of Turner Ltd and Taverner Ltd, and recommend any actions to be taken by the audit firm. **(8 marks)**

Professional marks will be awarded for the demonstration of skill in analysis and evaluation, and professional scepticism and judgement in your answer. **(5 marks)**

(Total = 25 marks)

54 James & Co (Mar/Jun 2021) (49 mins)

It is 1 July 20X5. You are an audit manager in James & Co, a firm of Chartered Certified Accountants. Your role includes performing post-issuance audit quality reviews, and you are currently reviewing the audit of the Bond Group (the Group), which had a financial year ended 31 January 20X5, and in respect of which an unmodified audit opinion was issued last month. The Group supplies computer components, specialising in graphics cards.

You are reviewing the Group audit file as well as the audit files for three of the Group's subsidiaries. All three of these components are material to the Group and have a financial year end of 31 January 20X5. Each subsidiary's audit opinion was also unmodified.

You have been provided with the following **exhibits**, which provide information about the Bond Group and the points you have identified for each subsidiary in the group:

(1) Cameron Co – points you have identified from your review of the information provided by the component auditor.

(2) Dean Ltd – points you have identified during your audit quality review.

(3) Horner Ltd – points you have identified during your audit quality review.

Required

In relation to the matters described in Exhibits 1, 2 and 3, comment on the quality of the planning and performance of the Group audit and the audit of the components of the Group, discussing the quality management and other professional issues raised in respect of:

(a) **Cameron Co** **(8 marks)**

(b) **Dean Ltd** **(5 marks)**

(c) **Horner Ltd** **(7 marks)**

Professional marks will be awarded for the demonstration of skill in analysis and evaluation, professional scepticism and judgment, and commercial acumen in your answer **(5 marks)**

(Total = 25 marks)

Exhibit 1: Cameron Co

Your firm audits all Group companies with the exception of Cameron Co, a subsidiary which was acquired during the last financial year.

Cameron Co was acquired by the Group in April 20X4, and is audited by Carrey Associates, a small local firm. Cameron Co also outsources its internal audit function to Carrey Associates. The section of the external audit working papers provided by Carrey Associates and relevant to internal controls contains very little documentation other than a cross reference to the files maintained by the internal audit team, and a statement that 'we can rely on the internal controls as they were tested by our firm in May 20X4'.

In respect of Carrey Associates, the Group audit working papers contain the following statement: 'our firm can rely on the work of Carrey Associates, as one of James & Co's audit partners left the firm to become an audit partner at Carrey Associates, and he was involved with the audit of Cameron Co'. Other than some background about Carrey Associates which had been printed off from the firm's website to provide background information, there is nothing else on file in relation to the firm.

The Group audit working papers also include a note relating to the consolidation of Cameron Co into the Group financial statements. Cameron Co prepares its individual financial statements using local accounting rules, which is allowed under national regulation; it does not use IFRS® Standards which is applied by the rest of the Group. The Group audit partner commented in the working papers that 'local accounting rules are very similar to IFRS Standards so there is no need to perform any additional audit work in relation to the consolidation of Cameron Co due to it using different accounting policies to the rest of the Group'.

Exhibit 2: Dean Ltd

Dean Ltd owns a small number of shares in Corden Ltd, amounting to a 2% shareholding. The investment is accounted for as a financial asset at fair value through profit or loss, as required by IFRS® 9 Financial Instruments. Corden Ltd's shares are not traded in an active market, and the value of £68,000 which is recognized in Dean Ltd's financial statements is management's estimate of fair value, based on an offer received for the shareholding in April 20X4.

The audit team checked the arithmetic of management's computation but did not obtain further audit evidence, because according to the audit conclusion 'the value of the shareholding is below the Group materiality level'. The latest financial statements of Corden Ltd, prepared to 31 January 20X5, are included in the audit file to provide 'background information', and show that the company has net assets of £550,000.

Materiality for the Group consolidated financial statements was determined to be £350,000.

Exhibit 3: Horner Ltd

During the audit of Horner Ltd, the audit team became aware of a breach of data protection regulation, whereby an employee of the company had made its customer database available to a third party. This disclosure is in contravention of the regulation.

The audit working papers refer briefly to this situation and conclude that 'it has little to do with the audit, as no one outside of the company is aware'. No further investigations were made by the audit team, and the audit manager noted in the working papers that the 'matter does not need to be discussed any further with Horner Ltd's or the Group's management teams as I have received assurance that the person responsible for the breach of regulation has been dismissed'.

55 Lifeson (Sep/Dec 2019 amended) (49 mins)

It is 1 July 20X5. You are a manager in the audit department of Peart & Co, a firm of Chartered Certified Accountants, responsible for the audit of Lifeson Ltd for the year ended 31 March 20X5. Lifeson Ltd is an unlisted retail company which is a new audit client of your firm this year. The company's draft financial statements recognise profit before tax of £2.15 million (20X4 – £1.95 million) and total assets of £13.8 million (20X4 – £12.7 million).

The audit is nearly complete and you are reviewing the audit working papers. The audit supervisor has brought the following matters to your attention:

Exhibit 1

Sale and leaseback transaction

On 31 March 20X5, Lifeson Ltd sold a property to a leasing company, Clive Ltd, for its fair value at this date.

The property is situated in a sought-after area with a high demand for rental properties for retail purposes.

Clive Ltd has assessed the remaining life of the property to be in excess of 50 years, and under the terms of the sales agreement, Lifeson Ltd will lease the property back from Clive Ltd for a period of ten years. Lifeson Ltd has treated the transaction as a sale and leaseback transaction in accordance with IFRS 16 *Leases*, and it derecognised the property in its financial statements and recorded a sale in accordance with IFRS 15 *Revenue from Contracts with Customers*.

Exhibit 2

Shopping mall

Lifeson Ltd purchased a shopping mall on 1 April 20X3 for £9.5 million. At the date of purchase, the mall was estimated to have a remaining useful life of 20 years and a nil residual value. On 31 March 20X4 following an impairment review, the property was written down to its recoverable amount based on value in use of £8.25 million and an impairment loss of £775,000 was recognised in the statement of profit or loss for the year ended 31 March 20X4.

Lifeson Ltd conducted a further impairment review as at 31 March 20X5 which indicated that the property's recoverable amount, based on value in use, was now £8.85 million. As a result, Lifeson Ltd has recognized an impairment reversal of £1.034 million in its profit before tax for the current year. The impairment reversal of £1.034 million has been calculated as its new recoverable amount of £8.85 million less its carrying amount of £7.816 million. The audit supervisor has prepared the following working paper which summarises the accounting transactions in relation to the shopping mall:

Summary of transactions

Date		£ million	*Accounting treatment by management*
1 April 20X3	**Cost of asset**	**9.500**	
	Depreciation (9.5m/20 years)	(0.475)	Depreciation charge for the year to 31 March 20X4
	Impairment	(0.775)	Impairment loss charged to profit for the year to 31 March 20X4
31 March 20X4	**Year-end carrying amount**	**8.250**	
	Depreciation (8.25m/19 years)	(0.434)	Depreciation charge for the year to 31 March 20X5
		7.816	Carrying amount prior to impairment review
	Reversal of impairment	1.034	Reversal of impairment credited to profit for the year to 31 March 20X5
31 March 20X5	**Year-end carrying amount**	**8.850**	

Required

(a) Using information from Exhibits 1 and 2:

Comment on the matters to be considered and explain the audit evidence you would expect to find during your review of the audit working papers in respect of the issues described above. You should structure your answer as follows:

(i) **Sale and leaseback transaction** **(8 marks)**

(ii) **Shopping mall** **(7 marks)**

(b) It is now 1 September 20X5 and the auditor's report on Lifeson Ltd's financial statements for the year ended 31 March 20X5 is due to be issued in the next few days.

Following discussions with management, you are satisfied that the sale and leaseback transaction has been treated correctly and that you have gathered sufficient and appropriate audit evidence to support this treatment.

However, management has indicated that they are not willing to make any further adjustments to the financial statements in relation to the shopping mall and you are now considering the form and content of the auditor's report in relation to this matter.

Required

Discuss the implications for the auditor's report on the basis that no further adjustments have been made to the financial statements in relation to the shopping mall. **(5 marks)**

Professional marks will be awarded for the demonstration of skill in analysis and evaluation, and professional scepticism and judgement in your answer. **(5 marks)**

(Total = 25 marks)

56 Newman (P7 December 2010 amended) (49 mins)

You are a manager in Newman & Co, a global firm of Chartered Certified Accountants. You are responsible for evaluating proposed engagements and for recommending to a team of partners whether or not an engagement should be accepted by your firm.

Eastwood Ltd is an existing audit client and is an international mail services operator, with a global network including more than 180 countries and 300,000 employees. The company offers mail and freight services to individual and corporate customers, as well as storage and logistical services.

Eastwood Ltd takes its corporate social responsibility seriously and publishes social and environmental key performance indicators (KPIs) in an Integrated Report, which is published with the financial statements in the annual report. Partly in response to requests from shareholders and pressure groups, Eastwood Ltd's management has decided that in the forthcoming annual report, the KPIs should be accompanied by an independent assurance report. An approach has been made to your firm to provide this report in addition to the audit.

To help in your evaluation of this potential engagement, you have been given an extract from the draft Sustainability Report, containing some of the KPIs published by Eastwood Ltd. In total, 25 environmental KPIs, and 50 social KPIs are disclosed.

EXTRACT FROM INTEGRATED REPORT

	Year ended 31 October 20Y0	Year ended 31 October 20X9
	Draft	*Actual*
CO_2 emissions (million tonnes)	26.8	28.3
Energy use (million kilowatt hours)	4,895	5,250
Charitable donations (£m)	10.5	8.2
Number of serious accidents in the workplace	60	68
Average annual spend on training per employee	£180	£175

You have also had a meeting with Ali Monroe, the manager responsible for the audit of Eastwood Co, and notes of the meeting are given below.

Notes from meeting with audit manager, Ali Monroe

Newman & Co has audited Eastwood Ltd for three years, and it is a major audit client of our firm, due to its global presence and recent listing on two major stock exchanges. The audit is managed from our office in Oldtown, which is also the location of the global headquarters of Eastwood Ltd.

We have not done any work on the KPIs, other than review them for consistency, as we would with any 'other information' issued with the financial statements. The KPIs are produced by Eastwood Ltd's Sustainability Department, located in Fartown. We have not visited Eastwood Ltd's offices in Fartown as it is in a remote location overseas, and the departments based there are not relevant to the audit.

We have performed audit procedures on the charitable donations, as this is disclosed in a note to the financial statements, and our evidence indicates that there have been donations of £9 million this year, which is the amount disclosed in the note. However, the draft KPI is a different figure – £10.5 million, and this is the figure highlighted in the draft Chairman's Statement as well as the draft Sustainability Report. £9 million is material to the financial statements.

The audit work is nearly complete, and the annual report is to be published in about four weeks, in time for the company meeting, scheduled for 31 January 20Y1.

Your firm has recently established a sustainability reporting assurance team based in Oldtown, and if the engagement to report on the Sustainability Report is accepted, it would be performed by members of that team, who would not be involved with the audit.

Required

Using the information above:

(a) Identify and explain the matters that should be considered in evaluating the invitation to perform an assurance engagement on the Sustainability Report of Eastwood Ltd. **(11 marks)**

(b) Design procedures that could be used to verify the following draft KPIs.

(i) The number of serious accidents in the workplace **(3 marks)**

(ii) The average annual spend on training per employee **(3 marks)**

(c) You have a trainee accountant assigned to you, who has read the notes taken at your meeting with Ali Monroe. She is unsure of the implications of the charitable donations being disclosed as a different figure in the financial statements compared with the other information published in the annual report.

Required

Prepare briefing notes to be used in a discussion with the trainee accountant, in which you:

Recommend the action to be taken by Newman & Co if the figure relating to charitable donations in the other information is not amended **(3 marks)**

Professional marks will be awarded for the demonstration of skill in analysis and evaluation, and professional scepticism and judgement in your answer. **(5 marks)**

(Total = 25 marks)

57 Marr (P7 June 2014 amended) (49 mins)

(a) Your firm is responsible for the audit of Marr plc, a listed company with a year ended 28 February 20X4. The draft financial statements recognise profit for the year of £11 million. The audit for the year end is nearing completion, and several matters have been highlighted for your attention by another audit senior, Xi Smith. The matters have been discussed with management and will not be adjusted in the financial statements:

(1) In January 20X4 a major customer went into administration. There was a balance of £2.5 million owing to Marr plc from this customer at 28 February 20X4, which is still included in trade receivables.

(2) A court case began in December 20X3 involving an ex-employee who is suing Marr plc for unfair dismissal. Lawyers estimate that damages of £50,000 are probable to be paid. The financial statements include a note describing the court case and quantifying the potential damages, but no adjustment has been made to include it in the statement of financial position or the statement of profit or loss.

Xi Smith has produced a draft auditor's report for your review, an extract of which is shown below:

Basis for opinion and disclaimer of opinion

We have performed our audit based on a materiality level of £1.5 million. Our audit procedures have proven conclusively that trade receivables are materially misstated. The finance director of Marr plc, Rita Gilmour, has refused to make an adjustment to write off a significant trade receivables balance. Therefore in our opinion the financial statements of

Marr plc are materially misstated, and we therefore express a disclaimer of opinion because we do not think they show a true and fair view.

Key audit matters

The audit team spent considerable time working on Marr plc's revenue recognition policies, which are highly complicated. We were concerned that Marr plc might recognise revenue too early but, in our opinion, revenue is presented fairly in accordance with IFRSs.

Emphasis of matter paragraph

Marr plc is facing a legal claim for an amount of £50,000 from an ex-employee. In our opinion this amount should be recognised as a provision, but it is not included in the statement of financial position. We draw your attention to this breach of the relevant IFRS.

We also draw your attention to the absence of any TCFD compliance disclosure in the annual report of Marr plc.

Required

Critically appraise the proposed auditor's report of Marr plc for the year ended 28 February 20X4.

Note. You are **NOT** required to redraft the extracts from the auditor's report. **(15 marks)**

(b) Having been appointed as the new audit engagement partner to Marr plc, Afzal Siddiqui has stated that he would like to use 'data analytics' on the next audit engagement. He has heard that many large audit firms now make use of these techniques, but he does not know what the term means.

Required

Explain what the term 'data analytics' means, and discuss current thinking about their anticipated impact on the auditing profession. **(5 marks)**

Professional marks will be awarded for the demonstration of skill in analysis and evaluation, professional scepticism and judgement, and commercial acumen in your answer. **(5 marks)**

(Total = 25 marks)

58 Sol & Co (Sep/Dec 2021) (49 mins)

It is 1 July 20X5. You are an audit manager in Sol & Co, a firm of Chartered Certified Accountants. You are currently working on two existing clients.

Arjan Ltd and Barnaby Ltd are both manufacturing companies with a financial year end of 31 March 20X5. Both audits are in the completion phase, and you are in the process of reviewing the audit files.

The following **exhibits**, available on the left-hand side of the screen, provide information relevant to the question:

(1) Arjan Ltd – selected results of the subsequent events and final analytical procedures which have been performed by the audit team.

(2) Barnaby Ltd – a copy of the schedule of uncorrected misstatements which have been recorded during the audit.

This information should be used to answer the question **requirements** within the **response option** provided.

Required

(a) Using information contained in Exhibit 1 – Arjan Ltd:

Evaluate the results of the subsequent events and final analytical procedures, commenting on any inconsistencies in relation to the audit evidence gathered. **(12 marks)**

(b) Using information contained in Exhibit 2 – Barnaby Ltd:

Recommend and explain the matters which should be discussed with management in relation to each of the uncorrected misstatements, including an assessment of the individual impact on the auditor's opinion if management does not make any changes.

Note. The following mark allocation is provided as guidance for this question: (i) Grant (5 marks); (ii) Machine sale (3 marks) **(8 marks)**

Professional marks will be awarded for the demonstration of skill in analysis and evaluation, professional scepticism and judgement and commercial acumen in your answer. **(5 marks)**

(Total = 25 marks)

Exhibit 1:

Arjan Ltd's draft financial statements show revenue of £120 million (20X4: £114 million), profit before tax of £11 million (20X4: £10.4 million) and total assets of £56 million (20X4: £74 million).

As part of your review of the audit file, you are considering the following results of the subsequent events procedures and final analytical procedures.

Subsequent events procedures

Newspaper reports in June 20X5 revealed that Cami Ltd, a significant customer of Arjan Ltd, entered liquidation and creditors are unlikely to receive more than 20% of amounts outstanding. The amount outstanding from Cami Ltd at 31 March 20X5 was £0.8 million. None of the amount outstanding has been received to date. No further work has been performed as a result of these procedures.

An extract of the final analytical procedures prepared by the audit assistant

Ratio	20X5	20X4	Auditor expectation	Comment	Corroborating evidence
Inventory value	£4 million	£25 million	Inventory has fallen by 84% in the year. This is in line with expectations as in November 20X4 management moved to a just-in-time (JIT) system for managing inventory.	The significant fall in inventory levels is consistent with a reduction in holding period.	Auditor attendance at year-end inventory count, sample counts performed, and count controls observed. No inaccuracies were identified. No further work over the completeness, accuracy and existence of inventory required.
Inventory holding period	15 days	94 days	Movement to JIT will reduce inventory holdings, so movement is in line with expectations. Per management lead times with suppliers average 20	Inventory holding of 15 days appears to be shorter than expected. Management states that holdings are less than 20 days as customer orders are	A sample of customer contract terms was reviewed and confirmed that they state that orders are expected to be manufactured within five working days with fulfilment

Ratio	20X5	20X4	Auditor expectation	Comment	Corroborating evidence
			days, hence inventory holding period is expected to be 20 days.	manufactured one week after an order is placed.	within 10 working days of order. This is consistent with the company's advertised terms and therefore supports the reduction in inventory holding period.
Write down for obsolete inventory as % of inventory held	10%	5%	The move to a JIT system should eliminate obsolete inventory and the need for a write down, so the expectation would be that write downs would be lower or close to 0.	Management has advised that they do not currently have sufficient experience with the new system to ensure only required inventory has been ordered. As a result, they have taken a cautious approach to the write down.	Total write down for obsolete inventory of £0.4 million in 20X5 is lower than the 20X4 amount of £1.25 million. This is less than 5% of profit before tax and therefore immaterial, so no further work performed.
Receivables collection period	53 days	49 days	No changes in credit period have been enacted in the year, hence the collection period is expected to remain in line with prior years.	The increase in the receivables collection period relates to the slow payment of invoices by Cami Ltd, a major customer. The financial controller is confident that payment will be made.	Outstanding invoice agreed to trade receivables ledger and a sample of customer confirmations of the balance owed were obtained in writing.
Allowance for irrecoverable receivables as % of total receivables	3%	5%	No changes have been made to controls over receivables during the year, so the allowance is expected to be in line with prior years.	The financial controller reviewed all trade receivables at the year end and concluded that fewer defaults were expected than in the prior year, hence the	Total fall in allowance of £0.5 million is below 5% of profit before tax and is therefore immaterial. No further work was performed.

Ratio	20X5	20X4	Auditor expectation	Comment	Corroborating evidence
				reduction in the allowance.	

Exhibit 2:

You are preparing for a discussion with the management of Barnaby Ltd about misstatements identified in the financial statements during the audit for the year ended 31 March 20X5. The audit working papers contain the following schedule of uncorrected misstatements prepared by the audit team. Barnaby Ltd's financial statements, prior to any adjustment for the items below, show profit before tax of £43 million (20X4: £45 million) and total assets of £105 million (20X4: £120 million).

Schedule of uncorrected misstatements

	Statement of profit or loss		*Statement of financial position*	
	Debit	*Credit*	*Debit*	*Credit*
	£million	£million	£million	£million
(1) Government grant	5	–	–	5
(2) Machine sale	1	–	–	1
Total	6	–	–	6

(1) **Government grant**

Barnaby Ltd received a government grant on 31 December 20X4 to invest in new machinery. A condition of the grant requires the funds to be invested within 12 months of the grant date or it becomes repayable. The grant has been recognised in full in the statement of profit or loss for the year, however, the machinery has not yet been purchased. The finance director of Barnaby Ltd assured the audit team that the money will be invested by 30 September 20X5.

(2) **Machine sale**

On 31 March 20X5, Barnaby Ltd sold a machine which was no longer in use. Under the terms of the sale agreement, the total sales price of the machine of £10 million would be paid on 31 March 20X6. The company has recognised the full sales value of £10 million when calculating profit on disposal for the asset and for the value of the receivable in the current year financial statements. The audit team has calculated that the net present value of the receivable at the reporting date of 31 March 20X5 is £9 million and therefore the profit on disposal and the receivable are overstated at the reporting date by £1 million. This is based on the company's cost of capital of 10% which has been calculated by the client. Sufficient and appropriate evidence has been obtained in relation to this calculation to conclude that 10% is an appropriate cost of capital.

59 Daley (December 2018 amended) (49 mins)

It is 1 July 20X5. Daley Ltd is a family owned, unlisted company which imports motor cars. The company buys cars from a variety of car manufacturers in Europe and Asia for sale to car dealerships and vehicle leasing companies within its own domestic market. Daley Ltd has been a client of your firm for the last three years and you are the newly appointed audit manager on the audit for the year ended 28 February 20X5. The audit for the current reporting period is nearing completion and you are reviewing the working papers of the going concern section of the audit file.

Extracts from the draft financial statements and other relevant information are given below.

STATEMENT OF FINANCIAL POSITION

	28 February 20X5 Draft	*28 February 20X4 Actual*
	£m	£m
Assets		
Non-current assets		
Property, plant and equipment	13.5	14.6
	13.5	14.6
Current assets		
Inventory	5.8	3.7
Trade receivables	3.7	2.6
Cash at bank and in hand	–	0.6
	9.5	6.9
Total assets	23.0	21.5
Equity and liabilities		
Equity		
Share capital	1.0	1.0
Retained earnings	1.3	4.7
	2.3	5.7
Non-current liabilities		
Long-term borrowings	11.2	12.4
Provisions	3.5	0.5
	14.7	12.9
Current liabilities		
Trade payables	4.2	2.9
Bank overdraft	1.8	–
	6.0	2.9
Total equity and liabilities	23.0	21.5

STATEMENT OF PROFIT OR LOSS FOR THE YEAR

	28 February 20X5 *Draft*	*28 February 20X4* *Actual*
	£m	£m
Revenue	11.3	8.8
Cost of sales	(4.4)	(2.9)
Gross profit	6.9	5.9
Other operating expenses	(9.1)	(1.3)
Operating (loss)/profit	(2.2)	4.6
Finance costs	(1.5)	(0.7)
Profit/(loss) before taxation	(3.7)	3.9
Taxation	0.3	(1.3)
Net (loss)/profit for year	(3.4)	2.6

You have also ascertained the following information during your review:

(1) Daley Ltd has undergone a period of rapid expansion in recent years and is intending to buy new warehousing facilities in July 20X5 at a cost of £4.3 million.

(2) In order to finance the new warehousing facilities, the company is in the process of negotiating new finance from its bankers. The loan application is for an amount of £5 million and is to be repaid over a period of four years.

(3) The provision of £3.5 million in this year's statement of financial position relates to legal actions from five of Daley Ltd's largest customers. The actions relate to the claim that the company has sold cars which did not comply with domestic regulations.

(4) A major new competitor has moved into Daley Ltd's market in April 20X5.

(5) The going concern working papers include a cash flow forecast for the 12 months ending 28 February 20X6. The cash flow forecast assumes that Daley Ltd's revenue will increase by 25% next year and that following the reorganisation of its credit control facility, its customers will pay on average after 60 days. The forecast also assumes that the bank will provide the new finance in July 20X5and that the company will have a positive cash balance of £1.7 million by 28 February 20X6.

(6) The financial statements have been prepared on a going concern basis and make no reference to any significant uncertainties in relation to going concern.

Required

(a) Using analytical review where appropriate, evaluate the matters which may cast doubt on Daley Ltd's ability to continue as a going concern. **(9 marks)**

(b) Explain the audit evidence in respect of the cash flow forecast which you would expect to find in your review of the audit working papers on going concern. **(6 marks)**

(c) You have established through discussions with Daley Ltd's directors that they do not wish to disclose uncertainties over the going concern status of the company in the notes to the financial statements.

Required

Explain the possible reasons why the directors may wish to exclude these disclosures and evaluate the possible implications for the auditor's report. **(5 marks)**

Professional marks will be awarded for the demonstration of skill in analysis and evaluation, professional scepticism and judgement, and commercial acumen in your answer. **(5 marks)**

(Total = 25 marks)

60 Basking (P7 Sep/Dec 2017 amended) (49 mins)

(a) Discuss the three types of misstatement identified in ISA (UK) 450 *Evaluation of Misstatements Identified during the Audit* and comment on why it is important for the auditor to consider the type of misstatement when evaluating their effect on the financial statements and determining the further actions to be taken. **(5 marks)**

(b) You are responsible for the audit of Basking plc, a large, listed package delivery company. The audit of the financial statements for the year ended 31 July 20X7 is nearly complete and you are reviewing the audit working papers. The financial statements recognise revenue of £56,360 million (20X6 – £56,245 million), profit for the year of £2,550 million (20X6 – £2,630 million) and total assets of £37,546 million (20X6 – £38,765 million).

The uncorrected misstatements identified during the audit of Basking plc are described below. The audit engagement partner is holding a meeting with the management team of Basking plc next week, at which the uncorrected misstatements will be discussed.

Depreciation

The accuracy of the depreciation charge was investigated for a sample of motor vehicles with a carrying value of £4.5 million. The investigation revealed that the accounting system had failed to correctly depreciate vehicles acquired during the year. Consequently, depreciation in the sample had been understated, and the carrying value of the vehicles overstated, by £350,000. The total value of all motor vehicles at the year end was £125 million (20X6 – £131 million).

Loan

In January 20X7, the board of Basking plc approved a loan to Mrs C Angel, who is a key member of the senior management team of the company. The total amount of the loan was £75,000. Following a review of the board minutes, it was discovered that the directors agreed that the amount was clearly trivial and have, therefore, not disclosed the loan in the notes to the financial statements.

Provision

During the year Basking plc reduced the value of their provision for customer refunds which is recognised in the financial statements. For the past five years the value of the provision has been calculated based on 7% of one month's sales, using an average monthly sales value. Management argued that due to improved internal processing systems, such a high rate of provision was no longer necessary and reduced it to 4%.

Audit procedures found that refund levels were similar to previous years and there was insufficient evidence at this early stage to confirm whether the new system was more effective or not.

Required

For each of the matters described above:

(1) Explain the matters which should be discussed with management in relation to each of the uncorrected misstatements; and

(2) Assuming that management does not adjust the misstatements identified, evaluate the effect of each on the audit opinion.

Note. The total marks will be split equally between each matter. **(15 marks)**

Professional marks will be awarded for the demonstration of skill in analysis and evaluation, and professional scepticism and judgement in your answer. **(5 marks)**

(Total = 25 marks)

61 Hopper (P7 Sep/Dec 2015 amended) (49 mins)

You are an audit manager at Rockwell & Co, a firm of Chartered Certified Accountants. You are responsible for the audit of the Hopper Group, a listed audit client which supplies ingredients to the food and beverage industry worldwide.

The audit work for the year ended 30 June 20X5 is nearly complete, and you are reviewing the draft auditor's report which has been prepared by the audit senior. During the year the Hopper Group purchased a new subsidiary company, Seurat Sweeteners Ltd, which has expertise in the research and design of sugar alternatives. The draft financial statements of the Hopper Group for the year ended 30 June 20X5 recognise profit before tax of £495 million (20X4 – £462 million) and total assets of £4,617 million (20X4 – £4,751 million).

An extract from the draft auditor's report, which has been prepared by the audit senior, is shown below:

Basis of modified opinion (extract)

In their calculation of goodwill on the acquisition of the new subsidiary, the directors have failed to recognise consideration which is contingent upon meeting certain development targets. The directors believe that it is unlikely that these targets will be met by the subsidiary company and, therefore, have not recorded the contingent consideration in the cost of the acquisition. They have disclosed this contingent liability fully in the notes to the financial statements. We do not feel that the directors' treatment of the contingent consideration is correct and, therefore, do not believe that the criteria of the relevant standard have been met. If this is the case, it would be appropriate to adjust the goodwill balance in the statement of financial position.

We believe that any required adjustment may materially affect the financial statements. Therefore, in our opinion, the financial statements do not give a true and fair view of the financial position of the Hopper Group and of the Hopper Group's financial performance and cash flows for the year then ended in accordance with International Financial Reporting Standards.

Emphasis of Matter Paragraph

We draw attention to the note to the financial statements which describes the uncertainty relating to the contingent consideration described above. The note provides further information necessary to understand the potential implications of the contingency.

Required

(a) Critically appraise the draft auditor's report of the Hopper Group for the year ended 30 June 20X5, prepared by the audit senior.

Note. You are **NOT** required to re-draft the extracts from the auditor's report. **(10 marks)**

(b) The audit of the new subsidiary, Seurat Sweeteners Ltd, was performed by a different firm of auditors, Fish Associates. During your review of the communication from Fish Associates, you note that they were unable to obtain sufficient appropriate evidence with regard to the breakdown of research expenses. The total of research costs expensed by Seurat Sweeteners Ltd during the year was £1.2 million. Fish Associates has issued a qualified audit opinion on the financial statements of Seurat Sweeteners Ltd due to the inability to obtain sufficient appropriate evidence.

Required

Comment on the actions which Rockwell & Co should take as the auditor of the Hopper Group, and the implications for the auditor's report on the Hopper Group financial statements. **(6 marks)**

(c) Discuss the quality management procedures which should be carried out by Rockwell & Co prior to the auditor's report on the Hopper Group being issued. **(4 marks)**

Professional marks will be awarded for the demonstration of skill in analysis and evaluation, and professional scepticism and judgement in your answer. **(5 marks)**

(Total = 25 marks)

62 Kilmister (Mar/Jun 2019 amended) (49 mins)

(a) You are the manager responsible for the audit of Kilmister plc, a listed company specialising in the manufacture and installation of sound-proof partitions for domestic and industrial buildings. You are currently reviewing the draft auditor's report on the company's financial statements for the year ended 31 March 20X5. Extracts from the draft auditor's report are shown below:

Independent auditor's report to the shareholders and directors of Kilmister plc

Basis for opinion

We conducted our audit of Kilmister plc (the Company) in accordance with International Standards on Auditing (UK) (ISAs (UK)). Our responsibilities under those standards are further described in the auditor's responsibilities for the audit of the financial statements section of our report. We are independent of the Company in accordance with the ethical requirements which are relevant to our audit of the financial statements in the jurisdiction in which the Company operates, and we have fulfilled our other ethical responsibilities in accordance with these requirements. We believe that the audit evidence we have obtained is sufficient and appropriate to provide a basis for our opinion.

Opinion

We have audited the financial statements of Kilmister plc (the Company), which comprise the statement of financial position as at 31 March 20X5, and the statement of comprehensive income, statement of changes in equity and statement of cash flows for the year then ended, and notes to the financial statements, including a summary of significant accounting policies. In our opinion, the accompanying financial statements present fairly, in all material respects, the financial position of the Company as at 31 March 20X5, and of its financial performance and its cash flows for the year then ended in accordance with IFRS Standards.

Material uncertainty regarding going concern

The Company is financed by a long-term loan from its bankers which is due for redemption in August 20X5. At the date of this auditor's report, the Company is in the process of renegotiating the loan but has not yet reached a final agreement with its bankers. It is our view that the loan finance is essential to the continued survival of the Company and that at the time of reporting, therefore, the absence of a finalised agreement represents a material uncertainty regarding going concern. The financial statements have been prepared on a going concern basis but do not make any reference to the loan redemption or the ongoing negotiations with the bank. As the external auditor, therefore, we are fulfilling our duty by bringing the matter to the attention of users of the financial statements.

Other information

The Company's principal activity is the manufacture and installation of sound-proof partitions for domestic and industrial buildings. The Company therefore engages in long-term contracts which are incomplete at the reporting date and which are material to its revenue figure. The installation process is complex and significant judgement is applied in assessing the percentage of completeness which is applied to calculate the revenue for the year. The significance of this judgement requires us to disclose the issue as other information which is relevant to the users of the financial statements.

Required

Critically appraise the extract from the draft auditor's report for the year ended 31 March 20X5.

Note. You are **NOT** required to re-draft the extracts from the auditor's report. **(8 marks)**

(b) Your firm, Eddie & Co, has asked you to perform an engagement quality review of the working papers of Taylor plc, which is a listed entity and has been an audit client of your firm for the last eight years. The audit fieldwork is almost complete and as part of your review, you have been asked to advise the audit team on the drafting of their report to those charged with governance. Taylor plc is a discount food retailer which operates 85 stores nationally. The financial statements for the year ended 30 April 20X5 recognise revenue of £247 million

(20X4–£242 million), profit before tax of £14.6 million (20X4–£14.1 million) and total assets of £535 million (20X4–£321 million).

After a period of rapid expansion, 20X5 has been a year in which Taylor plc has strengthened its existing position within the market and has not acquired any additional stores or businesses. The company's draft statement of financial position for 20X5 includes a property portfolio of £315 million, all of which are legally owned by the entity. In the current year, the company has chosen to adopt a policy of revaluing its property portfolio for the first time and this is reflected in the draft figures for 20X5. The audit work on property, plant and equipment included testing a sample of the revaluations. Eddie & Co requested at the planning stage that independent, external valuation reports should be made available to the audit team at the start of the final audit visit. A number of these documents were not available when requested and it took three weeks for them to be received by the audit team. The audit working papers also identify that on review of the non-current asset register, there were four properties with a total carrying amount of £11.1 million which had not yet been revalued and were still recorded at depreciated historic cost.

The audit supervisor's review of Taylor plc's board minutes identified that the company has renovated car parking facilities at 17 of its stores which has resulted in a significant increase in customer numbers and revenue at each of these locations. The total cost of the renovation work was £13.2 million and has been included in operating expenses for the current year. The audit file includes a working paper recording discussions with management which confirms that capital expenditure authorisation forms had not been completed for this expenditure.

You are aware that your firm had intended to replace the current engagement partner, Bryony Robertson, with Philip Campbell who is Eddie & Co's other specialist in food retail. Unfortunately, Mr Campbell was taken ill earlier in the year and will not now be available until next year's audit engagement. As a result, 20X5 is the sixth consecutive year in which Bryony Robertson has acted as engagement partner.

Required

From the information provided above, recommend the matters which should be included in Eddie & Co's report to those charged with governance, and explain the reason for their inclusion. **(12 marks)**

Professional marks will be awarded for the demonstration of skill in analysis and evaluation, and professional scepticism and judgement in your answer. **(5 marks)**

(Total = 25 marks)

63 Chester & Co (P7 December 2013 amended) (49 mins)

You are an audit manager in Chester & Co, a firm of Chartered Certified Accountants, and you are reviewing two situations which have recently arisen with respect to potential and existing audit clients of your firm.

Tetbury Ltd's managing director, Juan Stanton, has approached Chester & Co to invite the firm to tender for its audit. Tetbury Ltd is a small, owner-managed company providing financial services such as arranging mortgages and advising on pension plans. The company's previous auditors recently resigned. Juan Stanton states that this was due to 'a disagreement on the accounting treatment of commission earned, and because they thought our controls were not very good'. You are aware that Tetbury Ltd has been investigated by the Financial Conduct Authority for alleged non-compliance with its regulations. As well as performing the audit, Juan would like Chester & Co to give business development advice.

The audit of Stratford Ltd's financial statements for the year ended 30 November 20X3 will commence shortly. You are aware that the company is in financial difficulties. Stratford Ltd's managing director, Colin Charlecote, has requested that the audit engagement partner accompanies him to a meeting with the bank where a new loan will be discussed, and the draft financial statements reviewed. Colin has hinted that if the partner does not accompany him to the meeting, he will put the audit out to tender. In addition, an invoice relating to interim audit work performed in August 20X3 has not yet been paid.

Required

Identify and discuss the ethical and other professional issues raised, and recommend any actions that should be taken in respect of:

(a) Tetbury Ltd **(7 marks)**

(b) Stratford Ltd **(5 marks)**

(c) The audit of Crow Ltd, a designer and manufacturer of mobile information technologies, for the year ended 30 June 20X6 is nearly complete and the auditor's report is to be signed imminently. The following outstanding matters still require your consideration. The draft reported profit before tax and total assets for the year are £65 million (20X5 – £111 million) and £650 million (20X5 – £910 million) respectively.

Military research project

During the year expenses totalling £7 million, relating to a new military research project, were recorded in the statement of profit or loss. The audit team was given brief summaries of the costs incurred but when asked for further corroborating evidence, management stated that they had signed a confidentiality agreement with the military and were unable to provide any further details. The only additional information provided was that they anticipated the project to last for three years and that it may lead to a highly lucrative contract.

Fire

During the year a major catastrophe took place when a fire caused significant damage to the operations of the company, leading to production ceasing for several months. While operations have resumed, repairs are ongoing and it is anticipated that full production will not resume for at least another six months. Audit procedures revealed that the matter has been fully and satisfactorily reflected and disclosed in the financial statements and that it does not pose a significant risk to the going concern status of Crow Ltd.

Required

In respect of each of the matters described above, discuss the implications for the auditor's report and recommend any further actions necessary.

Note. The total marks will be split equally between each matter. **(8 marks)**

Professional marks will be awarded for the demonstration of skill in analysis and evaluation, and professional scepticism and judgement in your answer. **(5 marks)**

(Total = 25 marks)

64 Gillan (P7 Mar/Jun 2018 amended) (49 mins)

You are an audit manager in Gillan & Co and are responsible for several audit clients.

The following **exhibits** provide information relevant to answering the question:

(1) Details about the audit of the Blackmore Group

(2) Details about the audit of the Hughes Group

This information should be used to answer the question **requirements** within the response option provided.

Exhibit 1: Blackmore Group

One of these clients is the Blackmore Group (the Group), a listed manufacturer of high-quality musical instruments, for the year ended 31 March 20X8. The draft financial statements of the Group recognise a loss before tax of £2.2 million (20X7 – loss of £1.5 million) and total assets of £14.1 million (20X7 – £18.3 million). The audit is nearing completion and the audit senior has drafted the auditor's report which contains the following extract:

Key audit matters

(1) **Customer liquidation**

Included in receivables shown on the consolidated statement of financial position is an amount of £287,253 from a customer which has ceased trading. On the basis that the Group has no security for this debt, we believe that the Group should make a full provision for impairment of £287,253 thereby reducing profit before taxation for the year and total assets as at 31 March 20X8 by that amount.

(2) **Qualified opinion arising from disagreement about accounting treatment**

In our opinion, except for the effect on the financial statements of the matter described above, the financial statements have been properly prepared in all material respects in accordance with IFRS Standards.

(3) **Emphasis of matter**

We draw attention to the loss before tax of £2.2 million for the year ended 31 March 20X8 and that the Group is in breach of loan covenants with its key finance providers. A material uncertainty therefore exists which may cast doubt on the Group's ability to continue as a going concern. Our opinion is not modified in respect of this matter.

Exhibit 2: Hughes Group

You are also responsible for the audit of the Hughes Group (the Group). You are reviewing the audit working papers for the consolidated financial statements relating to the year ended 31 March 20X8. The Group specialises in the wholesale supply of steel plate and sheet metals. The draft consolidated financial statements recognise revenue of £7,670 million (20X7 – £7,235 million), profit before taxation of £55 million (20X7 – £80 million) and total assets of £1,560 million (20X7 – £1,275 million). Gillan & Co audits all of the individual company financial statements as well as the Group consolidated financial statements. The audit senior has brought the following matters, regarding two of the Group's companies, to your attention:

Willis Ltd

Willis Ltd is a foreign subsidiary whose functional and presentational currency is the same as Hughes plc and the remainder of the Group. The subsidiary specialises in the production of stainless steel and holds a significant portfolio of forward commodity options to hedge against fluctuations in raw material prices. The local jurisdiction does not mandate the use of IFRS Standards and the audit senior has noted that Willis Ltd follows local GAAP, whereby derivatives are disclosed in the notes to the financial statements but are not recognised as assets or liabilities in the statement of financial position. The disclosure note includes details of the maturity and exercise terms of the options and a directors' valuation stating that they have a total fair value of £6.1 million as at 31 March 20X8. The disclosure note states that all of the derivative contracts were entered into in the last three months of the reporting period and that they required no initial net investment.

Knott Ltd

Knott Ltd is a long-standing subsidiary in which the Group parent has a direct holding of 80% of the equity and voting rights. Audit work on revenue and receivables at Knott Ltd has identified sales of aluminium to its parent company in March 20X8 with a total sales value of £77 million which have been recorded in the subsidiary's financial statements. Audit procedures have identified, however, that the receipt of aluminium was not recorded by the parent company until 2 April 20X8. The group has made no adjustment for this transaction in the draft consolidated financial statements. Knott Ltd makes a 10% profit margin on all of its sales of aluminium.

Required

(a) Using the information provided in Exhibit 1, critically appraise the extract from the auditor's report on the consolidated financial statements of the Blackmore Group for the year ended 31 March 20X8.

Note. You are **NOT** required to re-draft the extract from the auditor's report. **(8 marks)**

(b) Using the information provided in Exhibit 2, comment on the matters to be considered and explain the audit evidence you should expect to find during your review of the Hughes Group audit working papers.

Note. The total marks will be split equally between the two companies discussed in Exhibit 2. **(12 marks)**

Professional marks will be awarded for the demonstration of skill in analysis and evaluation, and professional scepticism and judgement in your answer. **(5 marks)**

(Total = 25 marks)

Part F: Other assignments

Questions 65 to 71 cover Other assignments, the subject of Part F of the BPP Workbook for AAA.

65 Leopard (P7 Sep/Dec 2017 amended) (49 mins)

(a) You are a manager in one of the assurance departments of Leopard & Co, a large firm of Chartered Certified Accountants. You are currently assigned to a due diligence engagement for one of your firm's audit clients, Cheetah Ltd, a manufacturer of bespoke furniture. The audit of Cheetah Ltd is conducted by a team from a different department; you have never been involved in the audit of this client.

The engagement is to conduct a financial and operational due diligence review of Zebra Ltd, a company which has been identified as a potential acquisition target by Cheetah Ltd, due to the synergies offered and the potential to expand the existing production facilities. As part of the due diligence review, you have been asked to provide a valuation of Zebra Ltd's assets and liabilities and an analysis of the company's operating profit forecasts. This will assist Cheetah Ltd in determining an appropriate purchase price for Zebra Ltd.

During the engagement fieldwork your team identified two matters, which require your further consideration, as follows:

(1) While reviewing correspondence with customers in relation to outstanding receivables, one of the team found a letter from a large retailer, for which Zebra Ltd produces a number of unique products, providing advanced notice that they are not renewing their purchasing agreement when the current one expires. The customer advised that they are switching to a new entrant to the market who is substantially cheaper than Zebra Ltd. A brief analysis identified that the customer provides, on average, almost 5% of Zebra Ltd's annual revenues.

(2) Zebra Ltd owns a piece of land which was given to it as a gift by the local authorities ten years ago. The land surrounds the entrance to the main production premises and is designated as a nature reserve. Restrictions were imposed on the usage of the land which also limits who the owner is able to sell the land to in the future. The land has zero carrying value in the financial statements.

No additional matters have arisen for your consideration. You are also aware that the financial statements for the last ten years have been audited and no modifications have been made to the auditor's opinion during this period.

Required

In respect of the two matters identified above:

(i) Explain why each matter requires further investigation as part of the due diligence review; and **(6 marks)**

(ii) Design the investigation procedures to be performed. **(6 marks)**

(b) The management team of Cheetah Ltd has also approached Leopard & Co to ask whether representatives of the firm would be available to attend a meeting with the company's bankers, who they are hoping will finance the acquisition of Zebra Ltd, to support the management team in conveying the suitability of the acquisition of Zebra Ltd. For the meeting the bank requires the most up-to-date interim accounts of Cheetah Ltd with the accompanying auditor's independent interim review report. Your firm is due to complete the interim review shortly and the management team of Cheetah Ltd has requested that the interim review is completed quickly so that it does not hold up negotiations with the bank, stating that if it does, it may affect the outcome of the next audit tender, which is due to take place after the completion of this year's audit.

Required

Comment on the ethical and professional issues raised, and recommend any actions which should be taken in respect of the request from the management team of Cheetah Ltd. **(8 marks)**

Professional marks will be awarded for the demonstration of skill in analysis and evaluation, and professional scepticism and judgement in your answer. **(5 marks)**

(Total = 25 marks)

66 Beyer (Sep/Dec 2019 amended) (49 mins)

(a) You are a manager in the forensic department of your firm, Kaffe & Co. You have received a request from Beyer Ltd about an inventory fraud which was brought to the attention of the company's audit committee by a whistle-blower. Beyer Ltd is not currently a client of your firm.

Beyer Ltd manufactures and sells parts used in the automotive industry to both car manufacturers and to garages specialising in the repair and servicing of cars. The audit committee would like Kaffe & Co to perform a forensic investigation to quantify the loss suffered as a result of the inventory fraud, and to recommend improvements in the company's internal controls to avoid similar issues in the future. In addition, the audit committee has mentioned that although the quantification of the loss is to form the basis of an insurance claim, the matter has been reported to the police who will be investigating the matter further.

Required

Evaluate the matters which should be considered before your firm accepts the invitation to perform a forensic investigation for Beyer Ltd. **(8 marks)**

(b) Having accepted the engagement, the operations director provides you with the following summary of the allegations of the whistle-blower:

'The warehouse manager has been working with one of the sales representatives to dispatch goods to a fictitious customer which the warehouse manager has created on the dispatch system. The sales orders are input by the sales representative into the dispatch system which is not directly linked to the invoicing and accounting system. After the goods dispatch note is issued by the warehouse manager and the goods leave the warehouse for delivery to the fictitious customer, the sales representative cancels the original order. The warehouse manager reverses the dispatch immediately so that the daily report on inventory movement used to generate invoices in the sales system does not reflect movement of the goods. The sales representative takes delivery of the goods at the address of the fictitious customer and then sells the parts on the internet, splitting the proceeds with the warehouse manager. The warehouse manager supervises and participates in all inventory counts, and this way ensures he is able to adjust the records of inventory to disguise the missing items.'

The operations director has informed you that no authorisation is required for either the cancellation of orders or the reversal of dispatch notes.

Required

(i) Recommend the procedures which should be performed in order to quantify the inventory loss; and **(6 marks)**

(ii) Evaluate the deficiencies in Beyer Ltd's internal control system, and explain how they contributed to the fraud, together with recommendations to prevent such a fraud reoccurring. **(6 marks)**

Professional marks will be awarded for the demonstration of skill in analysis and evaluation, and professional scepticism and judgement and commercial acumen in your answer. **(5 marks)**

(Total = 25 marks)

67 Mizzen (P7 December 2013 amended) (49 mins)

You are a manager in the business advisory department of Goleen & Co. Your firm has been approached to provide assurance to Baltimore Ltd, a company which is not an audit client of your firm, on a potential acquisition.

The following **exhibits** provide information relevant to the question:

(1) Conversation with Mark Clear

(2) Company background

(3) Extracts from audited financial statements

Required

Using the information in Exhibits 1, 2 and 3, respond to the request from Mark Clear.

Note. The mark allocation is shown against the instruction given in Exhibit 1. **(20 marks)**

Professional marks will be awarded for the demonstration of skill in analysis and evaluation, and professional scepticism and judgement and commercial acumen in your answer. **(5 marks)**

(Total = 25 marks)

Exhibit 1: Conversation with Mark Clear

You have just had a conversation with Mark Clear, Baltimore Ltd's managing director, who made the following comments:

'Baltimore Ltd is a book publisher specialising in publishing textbooks and academic journals. In the last few years the market has changed significantly, with the majority of customers purchasing books from online sellers. This has led to a reduction in profits, and we recognise that we need to diversify our product range in order to survive. As a result of this, we decided to offer a subscription-based website to customers, which would provide the customer with access to our full range of textbooks and journals online.

'On investigating how to set up this website, we found that we lack sufficient knowledge and resources to develop it ourselves and began to look for another company which has the necessary skills, with a view to acquiring the company. We have identified Mizzen Ltd as a potential acquisition, and we have approached the bank for a loan which will be used to finance the acquisition if it goes ahead.

'Baltimore Ltd has not previously acquired another company. We would like to engage your firm to provide guidance regarding the acquisition. I understand that a due diligence review would be advisable prior to deciding on whether to go ahead with the acquisition, but the other directors are not sure that this is required, and they don't understand what the review would involve. They are also unsure about the type of conclusion that would be issued and whether it would be similar to the opinion in an auditor's report.

'To help me brief the other directors and using the information I have provided, I would like you to:

(a) 'Discuss the benefits to Baltimore Ltd of a due diligence review being performed on Mizzen Ltd **(6 marks)**

(b) 'Identify and explain the matters which you would focus on in your due diligence review and recommend the additional information which you will need to perform your work.' **(14 marks)**

Mark Clear has sent you the following information about Mizzen Ltd:

Exhibit 2: Company background

Mizzen Ltd was established four years ago by two university graduates, Vic Sandhu and Lou Lien, who secured funds from a venture capitalist company, BizGrow, to set up the company. Vic and Lou created a new type of website interface which has proven extremely popular, and which led to the company growing rapidly and building a good reputation. They continue to innovate and have won awards for website design. Vic and Lou have a minority shareholding in Mizzen Ltd.

Mizzen Ltd employs 50 people and operates from premises owned by BizGrow, for which a nominal rent of £1,000 is paid annually. The company uses few assets other than computer equipment and fixtures and fittings. The biggest expense is wages and salaries and due to increased demand for website development, freelance specialists have been used in the last six months. According to the most recent audited financial statements, Mizzen Ltd has a bank balance of £500,000.

The company has three revenue streams:

(1) Developing and maintaining websites for corporate customers. Mizzen Ltd charges a one-off fee to its customers for the initial development of a website and for maintaining the website for two years. The amount of this fee depends on the size and complexity of the website and averages at £10,000 per website. The customer can then choose to pay another one-off fee, averaging £2,000, for Mizzen Ltd to provide maintenance for a further five years.

(2) Mizzen Ltd has also developed a subscription-based website on which it provides access to technical material for computer specialists. Customers pay an annual fee of £250 which gives them unlimited access to the website. This accounts for approximately 30% of Mizzen Ltd's total revenue.

(3) The company has built up several customer databases which are made available, for a fee, to other companies for marketing purposes. This is the smallest revenue stream, accounting for approximately 20% of Mizzen Ltd's total revenue.

Exhibit 3: Extracts from audited financial statements

STATEMENT OF PROFIT OR LOSS AND OTHER COMPREHENSIVE INCOME

	Year ended 30 September 20X3	*Year ended 30 September 20X2*	*Year ended 30 September 20X1*	*Year ended 30 September 20X0*
	£'000	£'000	£'000	£'000
Revenue	4,268	3,450	2,150	500
Operating expenses	(2,118)	(2,010)	(1,290)	(1,000)
Operating profit/(loss)	2,150	1,440	860	(500)
Finance costs	(250)	(250)	(250)	–
Profit/(loss) before tax	1,900	1,190	610	(500)
Tax expense	(475)	(300)	(140)	–
Profit/(loss) for the year	1,425	890	470	(500)

There were no items of other comprehensive income recognised in any year.

68 Jacob (P7 June 2011 amended) (49 mins)

You are a manager at Thyme & Co, a firm of Chartered Certified Accountants. Jacob Ltd, an audit client of your firm, is a large privately owned company whose operations involve a repair and maintenance service for domestic customers. The company offers a range of services, such as plumbing and electrical repairs and maintenance, and the repair of domestic appliances such as washing machines and cookers, as well as dealing with emergencies such as damage caused by flooding. All work is covered by a two-year warranty.

The directors of Jacob Ltd have been seeking to acquire expertise in the repair and maintenance of swimming pools and hot tubs as this is a service increasingly requested, but not offered by the company. They have recently identified Locke Ltd as a potential acquisition. Preliminary discussions have been held between the directors of the two companies with a view to the acquisition of Locke Ltd by Jacob Ltd. This will be the first acquisition performed by the current management team of Jacob Ltd. Your firm has been asked to perform a due diligence review on

Locke Ltd prior to further discussions taking place. You have been provided with the following information regarding Locke Ltd.

(1) Locke Ltd is owner-managed, with three of the five board members being the original founders of the company, which was incorporated 30 years ago. The head office is located in a prestigious building, which is owned by the founders' family estate. The company recently acquired a separate piece of land on which a new head office is to be built.

(2) The company has grown rapidly in the last three years as more affluent customers can afford the cost of installing and maintaining swimming pools and hot tubs. The expansion was funded by a significant bank loan. The company relies on an overdraft facility in the winter months when smaller operating cash inflows arise from maintenance work.

(3) Locke Ltd enjoys a good reputation, though this was tarnished last year by a complaint by a famous actor who claimed that, following maintenance of his swimming pool by Locke Ltd's employees, the water contained a chemical which damaged his skin. A court case is on-going and is attracting media attention.

(4) The company's financial year end is 31 August 20X1. Its accounting function is outsourced to Austin Ltd, a local provider of accounting and tax services.

Required

(a) Explain the potential benefits of an externally provided due diligence review to Jacob Ltd. **(5 marks)**

(b) Recommend additional information which should be made available for your firm's due diligence review, and explain the need for the information.

Note. Assume it is 7 June 20X1. **(9 marks)**

(c) Tulip Ltd is another client of your firm, for which you are currently reviewing the draft assurance report in relation to the examination of a forecast. The forecast is included in a proposal due to be sent to Tulip Ltd's lenders as part of an effort to secure a new loan. Audit procedures concluded that there is no reason to believe that the forecast is unrealistic or that it has not been properly prepared. You are currently reviewing the draft assurance report, which is provided below.

> **Independent auditor's report on the forecast of Tulip Ltd to the shareholders of Tulip Ltd**
>
> We have examined the forecast information of Tulip Ltd contained in the loan proposal in accordance with the relevant standards on assurance engagements applicable to the examination of prospective financial information. Thyme & Co is not responsible for the forecast, including the assumptions on which it is based.
>
> Based on our examination of the evidence supporting the assumptions, we believe that these assumptions provide a reasonable basis for the forecast. Further, in our opinion the forecast is properly prepared on the basis of the assumptions and is presented in accordance with IFRS.
>
> Actual results are likely to be different from the forecast since the assumptions on which the forecast is based are unlikely to be accurate.
>
> Signed by assurance engagement partner, Thyme & Co

Required

Critically appraise the proposed assurance report extract of Tulip Ltd.

Note. Note. You are **NOT** required to redraft the assurance report. **(6 marks)**

Professional marks will be awarded for the demonstration of skill in analysis and evaluation, and professional scepticism and judgement and commercial acumen in your answer. **(5 marks)**

(Total = 25 marks)

69 Crocus (P7 December 2008 amended) (49 mins)

You are a manager in the forensic investigation department of your audit firm. The directors of a local manufacturing company, Crocus Ltd, have contacted your department regarding a suspected fraud, which has recently been discovered operating in the company, and you have been asked to look into the matter further. You have held a preliminary discussion with Gita Thrales, the finance director of Crocus Ltd, the notes of this conversation are shown below.

Notes of discussion with Gita Thrales

Four months ago Crocus Ltd shut down one of its five factories, in response to deteriorating market conditions, with all staff employed at the factory made redundant on the date of closure.

While monitoring the monthly management accounts, Gita performs analytical procedures on salary expenses. She found that the monthly total payroll expense had reduced by 3% in the months following the factory closure – not as much as expected, given that 20% of the total staff of the company had been made redundant. Initial investigations performed last week by Gita revealed that many of the employees who had been made redundant had actually remained on the payroll records, and salary payments in respect of these individuals were still being made every month, with all payments going into the same bank account. As soon as she realised that there may be a fraud being conducted within the company, Gita stopped any further payments in respect of the redundant employees. She contacted our firm as she is unsure how to proceed and would like our firm's specialist department to conduct an investigation.

Gita says that the senior accountant, Miles Rutland, has been absent from work since she conducted her initial investigation last week, and it has been impossible to contact him. Gita believes that he may have been involved with the suspected fraud.

Gita has asked whether your department would be able to provide a forensic investigation but is unsure what this would involve. Crocus Ltd is not an audit client of your firm.

Required

(a) Identify and explain the matters that should be considered before accepting the engagement to perform a forensic investigation at Crocus Ltd. **(4 marks)**

(b) Prepare a report to be sent to Gita Thrales (the finance director), in which you describe the objectives of a forensic investigation and explain the steps involved in a forensic investigation into the payroll fraud, including examples of procedures that could be used to gather evidence. **(11 marks)**

(c) Assess how the fundamental ethical principles of the IESBA's *International Code of ethics for professional accountants* should be applied to the provision of a forensic investigation service. **(5 marks)**

Professional marks will be awarded for the demonstration of skill in analysis and evaluation, professional scepticism and judgement, and commercial acumen in your answer. **(5 marks)**

(Total = 25 marks)

70 Prosperitas (49 mins)

You are Khalid Huq, an audit senior at Veritas & Co, a medium-sized audit firm based in the UK.

You have just received an email from Sue Dixon, a partner at Veritas.

Required

Using the information contained in the Exhibit, respond to the partner's request.

Note. The split of marks is shown in the partner's email. **(20 marks)**

Professional marks will be awarded for the demonstration of skill in analysis and evaluation, professional scepticism and judgement and commercial acumen in your answer. **(5 marks)**

(Total = 25 marks)

Exhibit: Email from partner

To:	Khalid Huq
From:	Sue Dixon
Date:	15 June 20X1
Subject:	New audit client – Prosperitas Ltd

Khalid,

As you know, the auditor's report for Prosperitas Ltd contained a 'Material Uncertainty relating to Going Concern' section. Well, since then Prosperitas' situation has gotten worse, and the directors have asked me to meet with them to discuss insolvency proceedings with them. I'd like you to prepare some briefing notes for me, in which you:

(a) Identify and explain the two main grounds under which a company may be wound up by the court; **(5 marks)**

(b) Identify and explain the distinguishing characteristics of a creditors' voluntary winding up; and **(6 marks)**

(c) Explain the immediate legal effect of an order of the court for the compulsory winding up of a company. **(9 marks)**

Regards,

Sue

71 Jansen (September 2018 amended) (49 mins)

You are an audit manager in Jansen & Co which offers a range of audit and other assurance services to its clients. One of your audit clients is Narley Ltd, which operates a commercial haulage company. Narley Ltd has been an audit client for the last five years. The company is UK-based but is currently planning a significant expansion of its operations into Europe. In order to finance the planned expansion, Narley Ltd needs funds to purchase additional heavy goods vehicles, expand its warehousing facilities and recruit more drivers. The company is also planning a major advertising and marketing campaign targeted at potential customers in Europe.

Narley Ltd's finance director, Suzanne Seddon, has approached you to ask if your firm will provide a report on the prospective financial information which has been prepared in support of a loan application. The application is for a new long-term loan of £22 million from the company's current lender which it intends to use exclusively to finance the planned expansion. The company currently has an existing long-term loan of £31 million from the same bank which is redeemable in five years' time.

Suzanne Seddon has provided you with the following extract from the prospective financial information which will form part of the company's loan application:

FORECAST STATEMENTS OF PROFIT OR LOSS

	Note	*Year ended 31 August 20X8 Unaudited £'000*	*Year ending 31 August 20X9 Forecast £'000*	*Year ended 31 August 20Y0 Forecast £'000*
Revenue	1	138,861	174,965	225,705
Cost of sales	2	(104,862)	(124,786)	(157,230)
Administrative expenses	3	(22,936)	(21,984)	(20,743)
Operating profit		11,063	28,195	47,732
Finance costs	4	(1,450)	(1,638)	(1,597)
Profit before tax		9,613	26,557	46,135

Notes.

1 Revenue represents the amounts derived from the provision of haulage services to commercial customers operating principally in the retail sector. Narley Ltd's board of directors believes that trade in both its existing and new markets will experience significant growth over the next two years.

2 Cost of sales comprises the costs of warehousing and distribution including relevant staff costs, maintenance and repair of vehicles and depreciation of property, equipment and vehicles.

3 Administrative expenses are mainly the costs of running Narley Ltd's central head office facility.

4 Finance costs represent the cost of servicing long-term finance from Narley Ltd's bankers.

Required

(a) (i) Explain the matters which should be considered by Jansen & Co before accepting the engagement to review and report on Narley Ltd's prospective financial information. **(5 marks)**

(ii) Assuming Jansen & Co accepts the engagement, recommend the examination procedures to be performed in respect of Narley Ltd's forecast statements of profit or loss. **(7 marks)**

(b) Krupt Ltd is a family-owned business which has been an audit client of Jansen & Co for many years and on which you have been the audit manager for the last two years. The audit for the year ended 30 June 20X8 is approaching completion and the audit supervisor has asked for your advice in relation to recent developments at the client.

Krupt Ltd is a wholesaler of electronic goods and is owned by Mr and Mrs Krupt who are both 50% shareholders and directors of the company. The company's principal source of finance is a loan from Hongclays Bank of £1.2 million which is secured by a floating charge over the company's inventory. The bank has also taken out personal guarantees on the domestic residence owned jointly by Mr and Mrs Krupt under the terms of which the bank has the right to take possession of the property in the event that it cannot recover its debts from the company.

As part of the going concern review, the audit supervisor, Jemma Jones, has scrutinised the management accounts for the first four months of the current reporting period and has identified that the company is making significant losses which she believes to be unsustainable. She has also inspected correspondence between the company and Hongclays Bank which indicates that the company has already breached key loan covenants.

Jemma has been informed by the company's procurement manager that Krupt Ltd has recently taken delivery of a large quantity of a new inventory line with a value of £0.75 million which it has purchased on credit from one of its suppliers. At present the company also has other inventory with a total value of approximately £0.5 million. Based on a review of the company's bank statements and cash flow forecasts, Jemma does not believe that there is any realistic prospect that the company will be able to pay this supplier for the foreseeable future and is concerned about the possible implications of this transaction for the directors of the company. Jemma has not come across these issues before. She has a clear sense that something is wrong and she has asked you to:

(1) explain the concepts of fraudulent and wrongful trading; and

(2) evaluate the possible implications of the circumstances and transactions noted during the going concern review for the directors of Krupt Ltd.

Required

Respond to Jemma's request. **(8 marks)**

Professional marks will be awarded for the demonstration of skill in analysis and evaluation, professional scepticism and judgement, and commercial acumen in your answer. **(5 marks)**

(Total = 25 marks)

Answers

Parts A and B: Regulatory environment and professional and ethical considerations

1 Lark

Workbook references

Chapters 1, 2 and 11.

Top tips

This question examined two connected issues: money laundering and professional scepticism. In part (a), you needed to spot that money laundering was taking place. This was mainly a matter of explaining what is going on in the scenario. You should be aware of the three stages of a money laundering regime (placement, layering and integration), and could have scored well by simply applying them to the scenario. But even if you had forgotten what the stages were, you could still have done well by just explaining how each bit of the scenario might be evidence of a money laundering regime.

Part (b) should have been straightforward, as this was a topical area that you should have been aware of – given that there was an IAASB Q&A paper on this area.

Part (c) of this question was deceptively difficult. At first sight it may appear to be a standard question on group audits, but delve into it more deeply and you will find that it is actually relatively tricky. The key issue is making sense of what has already happened: the component auditor has sent you a draft report.

This report contains a qualified opinion which appears to be drafted correctly – you need to draw on your knowledge of ISA (UK) 705 Modifications to the Opinion in the Independent Auditor's Report to make this assessment. If you didn't know ISA (UK) 705 well enough to do this correctly, then you might have struggled with this question.

The auditor says in the report that a provision should have been made, but in Note 12 to the financial statements, management says that the probability of an outflow is only 20%, so no provision is necessary. The question for the group auditor (which is you!) is: who is right? In order to decide this, the auditor must review the audit evidence that the component auditor based its conclusion on. If the evidence is sufficient and appropriate, then the draft auditor's report is OK; if the evidence is not sufficient and appropriate, then either further evidence must be obtained, or the draft auditor's report is wrong.

You then have to think about the matter practically: what would happen from here? If Exuma is right, then the draft auditor's report is wrong. If the auditor is right, then Exuma may change the financial statements.

If this does not happen, then the group financial statements may or may not need changing, all of which will have an impact on the group auditor's report.

This is quite a lot of work for the ten marks on offer, and you should make sure that you do not go over time on this part of the question. The important thing is to be scoring marks with each point you make.

Easy marks

The point about 'tipping off' is always an easy mark in a question on money laundering. It's one of the more important things to be aware of in the real world, so markers tend to like it when you mention it.

Also calculating materiality in part (c) was easy – but don't just do the figures, make sure you say what you are doing and conclude on whether or not the matter is material to the group, and on whether the component is significant or not.

ACCA examining team's comments

In part (a), most candidates covered a range of points and the majority correctly discussed fraud and/or money laundering. Weaker answers tended to focus on the materiality of the cash transferred to overseas and seemed not to notice the client's suspicious behaviour. Candidates are reminded that they will often be expected to identify a key issue in a question scenario and that in a question of this type it is important to stop and think about what is happening in the scenario before rushing to start to write an answer.

Answers to part (b) were reasonably good, with most candidates able to attempt an explanation of the term, and most identifying poor controls leading to a possible fraud involving the payroll supervisor.

Requirement (c), for ten marks, asked candidates to identify and explain the matters that should be considered and the actions that should be taken by the group audit engagement team in forming an opinion on the consolidated financial statements. Most candidates gained marks by calculating the materiality of the provision to the group and to the individual financial statements of the subsidiary. However, few determined the materiality of the component itself to the group.

Candidates are usually happy to be critical of auditors in question scenarios, but in this case when it was actually appropriate to raise concerns over the evidence (or lack of it) obtained to support the qualified opinion, very few answers tackled this issue. However, some candidates did waste time criticising the extract auditor's report that had been provided – this was not asked for – and implied that candidates had not read the question requirement at all.

Marking guide	Marks
(a) **Implications of the audit senior's note**	
Generally 1 mark for each matter discussed relevant to money laundering:	
• Definition of money laundering	
• Placement – cash-based business	
• Owner posting transactions	
• Layering – electronic transfer to overseas	
• Secrecy and aggressive attitude	
• Audit to be considered very high risk	
• Senior may have tipped off the client	
• Firm may consider withdrawal from audit	
• But this may have tipping off consequences	
	5
(b) **Professional scepticism**	
Generally 1 mark for each comment:	
• Definition of professional scepticism	
• Explain – alert to contradictory evidence/unusual events/fraud indicator (up to 2 marks)	
• Part of ethical codes	
• Reference to FRC discussion paper on auditor scepticism	
• Coot Ltd – evidence is unreliable and contradictory	
• Absence of authorisation is fraud indicator	
• Additional substantive procedures needed	
• Management's comments should be corroborated	
• Control deficiency to be reported to management/those charged with governance	

- Audit junior needs better supervision/training on how to deal with deficiencies identified

Maximum 5

(c) **Matters/actions**

Up to 2 marks for each matter/action identified and explained (max 3 marks for identification):

- Consideration of aggregation risk relating to Exuma Ltd
- Matter is material to individual and group financial statements
- Accounting treatment/qualification for Exuma Ltd's financial statements
- Review of audit work performed
- Consideration of further audit work
- Discuss with group management and those charged with governance
- Request that Exuma Ltd's management adjust financial statements
- Adjustment could be made on consolidation
- Impact on group opinion if no adjustment made

Maximum 10

Professional marks

Analysis and evaluation

Appropriate assessment of the ethical and professional issues raised, using examples where relevant to support overall comments

Effective appraisal of the information to make suitable recommendations for appropriate courses of action (for example in relation to Coot's payroll)

Professional scepticism and judgement

Effective challenge and critical assessment of the evidence supplied in relation to Heron and Coot, with appropriate conclusions

Demonstration of the ability to probe into the reasons for the client's responses at Coot, and for the money laundering issues at Heron

Explanation of the meaning of professional scepticism in relation to Coot

Maximum 5

Total 25

(a) The implication of the circumstances described is that there may be money laundering going on at Heron Ltd, involving its owner-manager Jack Heron.

Money laundering is a process by which criminals may attempt to conceal the origins of the proceeds of criminal activity. The aim is to transform 'dirty' money, which can be tied to its criminal origin, into 'clean' money which can be spent.

The fact that Heron Ltd's revenue is almost entirely cash makes it an ideal 'front' business for a money laundering regime. The aim here would be to transform the 'dirty' money into revenue from the legitimate business. What appears to be happening here is that the legitimate cash receipts of £3.5m are being topped up with £2m 'dirty' money. This is the placement stage of the money laundering regime. The idea is that the £5.5m revenue will eventually appear legitimate if it can be said to all come from a legitimate business (Heron Ltd).

The £2m electronic transfer is then part of the layering process, which aims to maximise the distance between the placement of the 'dirty' money and its eventual 'integration' into the financial system as 'clean' money. The fact that this is an overseas transfer only heightens its suspiciousness, as money launderers often move money across national boundaries to make it harder to trace.

The fact that Jack Heron has sole responsibility for cash receipts and postings gives him the opportunity to launder money in this way. The fact that no documentation was available to support the transfer means it is possible that it was done to launder money. The fact that Jack did not answer the senior's questions and became aggressive seems to confirm his desire for secrecy here.

There is a risk that the senior has 'tipped off' Jack Heron by questioning him about the transfer. This is itself an offence, although it may be argued here that the senior was not aware that the disclosure could prejudice any future money laundering investigation.

From the point of view of the audit, the amount is clearly highly material. It is possible that Lark & Co may seek to withdraw from the engagement, however, there is a risk that this could be construed as 'tipping off' if Jack Heron thinks it is because the audit firm has suspicions over money laundering. The firm should obtain advice from its legal counsel.

(b) **Professional scepticism**

Professional scepticism is an attitude that includes a questioning mind, being alert to conditions which may indicate possible misstatement due to error or fraud, and a critical assessment of audit evidence (ISA (UK) 200: para. 13).

This means being alert to the actual circumstances of the engagement and the work being done, and to the possibility that things may not be as they appear to be on first sight, eg that evidence obtained is unreliable, or may point to fraud. If an auditor is not sceptical in this way, then they may not realise that something is unusual; they may not tailor audit procedures to the actual risk at hand; or they may jump to hasty conclusions.

Professional scepticism lies at the heart of auditing, both in the sense that it is part of being a competent auditor, and that it is an important part of being ethically independent.

Further actions

The evidence obtained already may not be reliable.

The payroll supervisor's assertion that no authorisation is needed for temporary workers must be corroborated. Evidence should also be gathered about the claim that the employees are temporary.

If the supervisor is correct that no authorisation is required for new employees, then this is a major deficiency of internal controls that should have been identified as part of controls testing. It may be a point to include in the report to management.

There is a contradiction between the supervisor's claim that there were new temporary staff, and management's claim that there are no new staff. It should be clarified that when management said there were no new employees, this included temporary staff.

It is possible that there is a fraud taking place here, possibly by the payroll supervisor. The new employees could be 'ghost employees' to whom money is paid via payroll but who do not exist. The money is then taken criminally, eg by the payroll supervisor or an associate of his.

The audit junior should be made aware that when he comes across issues like this, she must raise them with her supervisor.

(c) **Materiality to group**

ISA (UK) 600 (Revised) *Special Considerations – Audits of Group Financial Statements (Including the Work of Component Auditors)* states that the group auditor should assess aggregation risk. This is the probability that the aggregate of uncorrected and undetected misstatements exceed the materiality for the financial statements for the group as a whole.

Exuma Ltd's profit before tax is 20% of group profit before tax (PBT), and total assets is 23.5%. It is therefore likely that an uncorrected misstatement in Exuma's financial statements could be material to the group financial statements as a whole.

Materiality of issue

The £2m legal claim represents 50% of Exuma's PBT, and 10% of total assets and so is material to Exuma as an individual entity.

The claim is also material to the group, at 10% of PBT and 2.4% of total assets.

Qualified opinion – Exuma

Jalousie & Co have expressed a qualified opinion on Exuma in relation to IAS 37 *Provisions, Contingent Liabilities and Contingent Assets*. Audit evidence was obtained that led the auditor to conclude that the Note 12 to the financial statements of Exuma materially misstates the probability of the claim against the company being successful. Presumably Jalousie & Co must have obtained audit evidence that the claim's chance of success was not 20% as stated but was 50% or more. This would mean that a liability should have been recognised in accordance with IAS 37.

This misstatement is material but is unlikely to be deemed pervasive, so the qualified opinion is correct provided that the audit evidence obtained is sufficient and appropriate.

Audit evidence

Exuma Ltd is material to the group, as is this specific issue. The group auditor should therefore review Jalousie & Co's audit evidence in relation to it.

The key question is the assessment of the probability of the court-case being lost, and the consequent future outflow of £2m. The group auditor should discuss the matter with Jalousie & Co's audit engagement partner. Audit evidence should include copies of all legal correspondence, as well as written representations from Exuma's management regarding their accounting treatment of the matter.

Depending on the strength of this evidence, it may have been appropriate for Jalousie & Co to have used an auditor's expert to provide a separate legal opinion on the matter.

Further evidence

The group auditor may determine that further audit evidence needs to be obtained, such as the opinion of an auditor's expert if this has not been sought. This can be done either by collaboration with the component auditor, or by the group auditor alone.

It is possible that there is not sufficient appropriate evidence to qualify the opinion on this matter, and that Exuma Ltd's management is correct. In this case, Jalousie & Co would have to redraft its auditor's report to show an unmodified opinion.

Impact on group – discussion with group management

The matter should be discussed with group management in order to ascertain what the impact will be on the group financial statements and auditor's report. There are a number of possible outcomes, examined below.

Exuma's financial statements changed

The group auditor should request that Nassau Group's management ask Exuma to adjust its financial statements and recognise a provision. This would mean that Jalousie & Co's auditor's report, which has not yet been issued, could potentially be issued with an unmodified opinion if the adjusted financial statements are not materially misstated.

Only group accounts changed

If Exuma's financial statements are not adjusted, then the group financial statements themselves could still be adjusted to rectify the material misstatement. The auditor's opinion on Exuma would still be qualified, but the group auditor's opinion would not be modified in relation to this matter.

No adjustment made at all

If no adjustment is made to Exuma's or the Nassau Group's financial statements, then the group audit opinion is qualified due to a material misstatement. The work of the component auditor would not be referred to in the group auditor's report.

2 Plant

Workbook references

Chapters 2 and 5.

Top tips

Part (a) should not have posed you many difficulties. The contents of the audit tender document are basic knowledge at this level, but here you really need to apply your knowledge to the situation of the Plant Group. You can use the basic contents of the tender as a starting point, and then bring in points from the scenario where they are relevant. For example, the tender must assess 'the needs of the prospective client'; here, the tender must clarify that all of the subsidiaries will require audits.

There are also points that come out of the scenario itself. These are likely to be practical points; here, the proposed deadline was very close to the year end and should be discussed in the tender document as a practical issue.

In part (b), it is crucial that you are aware not only of the content of the latest guidance in this area, but the reasons behind it. This is an example of a requirement that, although it does not use the word 'discuss', could be considered to require a discursive approach from candidates.

Easy marks

There were easy marks in part (a) for noting that the tight deadline would cause problems – this came straight from the scenario and should stand out prominently.

ACCA examining team's comments

Requirement (a) was generally well-attempted, with a significant minority of answers achieving close to full marks. The best answers went through each of the typical contents of a tender document and related them specifically to the Group in the question, resulting in focused and well-explained answer points. Interestingly, these answers were often relatively brief, but still managed to attract a high mark through application of knowledge to the question scenario.

Some answers tended to either be much too brief – sometimes little more than a list of bullet points - or did not answer the question requirement, and instead of explaining matters to be included in a tender document, discussed the matters that may impact client acceptance, such as whether the audit firm has sufficient resources, and whether a fee dependency would be created. Candidates are advised to read question requirements carefully and not to make assumptions about what is being asked for.

Note. This question has been adapted since it was originally set so there are no ACCA examining team comments available for part (b).

Marking guide | **Marks**

(a) **Matters to be included in tender document**

Up to 1.5 marks for each matter identified and explained with relevance to the Plant Group (up to a maximum of 2 marks in total for matters identified only):

- Outline of the audit firm including international network
- Audit firm specialism in telecoms
- Client audit requirements
- Outline of audit firm's audit methodology
- Deadlines
- Discuss provision of audit-related services
- Quality management and ethics
- Fees

Marking guide | **Marks**

- Discuss provision of non-audit services

Maximum | 10

(b) **Ethical matters**

Up to 1.5 marks for each relevant comment:

- Self-review threat if Weller & Co seeks to rely on controls in audit
- Self-review threat possible safeguards
- Threat of management responsibility
- Public interest entity rules per IESBA *Code of Ethics*
- If advice relates to IT systems important to accounting system, cannot provide
- FRC ES requirements: ban on providing internal audit service
- FRC ES: permitted to provide advice that is a by-product of the audit
- Current proposals unlikely to be acceptable due to revenue-raising intention
- FRC ES: providing advice on controls is a specifically named non-audit service

Maximum | 10

Professional marks

Analysis and evaluation

- Appropriate assessment of the ethical and professional issues raised, using examples where relevant to support overall comments
- Effective appraisal of the information to make suitable recommendations for matters to include in the tender document for the Plant Group audit

Professional scepticism and judgement

- Effective challenge and critical assessment of the revenue-raising suggestions
- Demonstration of the ability to probe into the possible effects of the suggestions and their impact on the audit work
- Appropriate application of professional judgement to the audit tender and the matters that are specific to the client in question

Commercial acumen

- Assessment of resources and profitability of audit tender
- Appropriate recognition of the wider implications on the engagement, the audit firm and the company.

Maximum | 5

Total | 25

(a) **Matters to include in tender**

Overview of Weller & Co

A brief overview of the firm's structure. This should state that the firm is part of an international network of firms, and that it therefore has access to a considerable depth of audit expertise.

This could be particularly relevant to the audit of the Plant Group's overseas subsidiary.

Areas of expertise and key staff

The firm has a telecoms audit department, and therefore already has staff with expertise in the Plant Group's specific industry. This may make it particularly well placed to audit the

Plant Group. Details should also be provided of the approximate size and makeup of the audit team, as well as of the expected audit engagement partner together with details of his or her relevant experience.

It is possible that the addition of a significant new telecoms audit client could create conflicts with existing clients in this industry. It should be possible to manage these, however, by applying safeguards to reduce the risk of independence being threated.

Assessment of Plant Group's needs

The Plant Group is composed of a parent and six subsidiaries, and it should be clarified that the tender includes the audit of each of the subsidiaries as single companies, together with the parent company and the group as a whole.

Audit approach

A brief description of Weller & Co's audit approach. In the case of the Plant Group, this is likely to include reliance on the internal controls, which are described as strong. The tender document should point out that controls would be tested before they were relied upon, but that if they did prove reliable then the audit should indeed be cost-effective.

Deadline

The proposed deadline is just two months after the year end. It would be very difficult to meet such a deadline while still maintaining audit quality. It might make it difficult to obtain evidence in specific areas, such as receivables recoverability or going concern. There is also a risk of putting significant pressure on the audit team to do work quickly rather than thoroughly, which could result in things being missed.

The tender should therefore propose a later deadline for audit completion.

Fees

The tender should state the proposed audit fee, together with a breakdown of the fee. The fee proposed should be sufficient to ensure that a high-quality audit could be conducted.

Non-audit services

The firm may wish to outline any relevant non-audit services that it could provide to the Plant Group. These will be curtailed by the fact that the Plant Group is now listed and thus a public interest entity, but there may still be some areas in which Weller & Co could provide help.

Quality management & ethics

Weller & Co should state its adherence to the IESBA's *Code of Ethics for Professional Accountants*, and to International Standards on Quality Management. This will give the Plant Group confidence in the auditor's report that would be issued.

(b) A number of issues arise with the proposal to provide advice on financial and operational controls. The principal threats that would arise to Weller & Co's independence would be: a self-review threat, and the threat of taking on a management responsibility.

Self-review threat

If Weller & Co seeks to rely on work performed on financial or operational controls as part of its external audit, then there will be a self-review threat if it has itself provided advice in relation to those controls. The risk is that the systems work relied upon is not treated with enough objectivity. It may be possible to surmount this problem by using a team or department that is separate from the external audit team, to provide the advice on the controls.

Management responsibility

If firm personnel assume a management responsibility as part of the engagement to provide advice, then either the service must not be provided or else the firm must withdraw from the external audit.

A management responsibility would be assumed where, for example, the auditor performs internal control procedures, or takes responsibility for designing, implementing and maintaining internal controls.

Public interest entities

If the audit client is a public interest entity (PIE), then advice cannot be provided where it relates to the following areas:

- A significant part of controls over financial reporting
- Accounting systems that generate information significant to the client's accounting records or financial statements
- Amounts or disclosures that are material to the financial statements (IESBA *Code of Ethics*)

Where the advice provided covers IT systems, and those systems are 'important to any significant part of the accounting or financial management system' (FRC ES: para. 5.50), then this cannot be provided to an audit client.

FRC *Ethical Standard* (ES)

One important area in which the guidance contained in the FRC ES goes further than that of the IESBA *Code of Ethics* is the provision of internal audit services to audit clients. The IESBA *Code* permits the provision of these services subject to the assessment of threats and the application of safeguards (to reduce the risk to an acceptable level). The FRC ES however contains an outright ban on the provision of internal audit services to audit clients.

This is relevant here because there is a risk that the advisory service being proposed could be construed as an internal audit service, and it may therefore fall outside the scope of what is allowed in line with the FRC ES. Weller & Co will therefore need to take great care not to offer its clients an internal audit service as it would thereby be in breach of the FRC ES.

Further, the guidance provided by the FRC ES distinguishes sharply between audit clients that are public interest entities and those which are not.

Where the firm is not a PIE then it may be permissible to provide the advice subject to the caveat above regarding internal audit. The FRC ES states that where auditors 'provide management with observations on matters that have come to their attention' such as control deficiencies and suggested improvements – then this 'is a by-product of the engagement rather than an internal audit service' (FRC ES: para. 5.45). Such a service is therefore acceptable. In the case of the proposals being made at Weller & Co, in view of the fact that the stated aim is to generate revenue, it seems unlikely that significant revenue could be generated from non-PIE clients on the basis of what could only be a re-packaging of information obtained as part of the audit itself.

When it comes to PIE clients, the FRC ES only permits the provision of non-audit services that are specifically named in the ES. With regard to the engagement in question, therefore, the situation is broadly similar, since the provision of advice regarding financial or operational controls is indeed included in the FRC ES's list of services which may be provided.

3 Monet

Workbook references

Chapters 2, 3, 5 and 10.

Top tips

Part (a) basically meant criticising an advert from an ethical and professional perspective. There are only 6 marks available but there is quite a lot to criticise here, so it was important not to go over your time allowance.

When you were reading through the scenario, you would hopefully have noticed that the opening paragraph gives details of the accounting firm. If you didn't notice this or skipped past it then the lesson is that these opening bits are not just waffle – they contain information that can get you marks. In this case, the firm is a fairly small firm, which does not fit well with the advert's claim that it has 'the most comprehensive range of services in the country'.

The requirement asks you to 'recommend any actions necessary', and it's important that you do not overlook this. Actions often get more marks than other comments, so (i) make sure you include some in your answer, and (ii) make it clear to your marker that you're giving an action, eg by using the phrase 'the action would be [...]'.

Part (b) was a normal AAA ethics question and should not have been unduly difficult. Try to identify the kind of threats that are present, as there are usually half-marks available for correctly stating the type of threat (eg 'self-review threat'). Once you have done this, try to think of some appropriate safeguards, and then evaluate whether the threat will be reduced to an acceptable level (this is one place where the verb 'evaluate' comes in from the requirement).

Part (c) asked for audit procedures on funding that was being sought. It was important here to stick to the requirement, which focuses on additional funding, rather than simply following the points from the scenario. This question part is a good test of your ability to strike a balance between allowing your points to come naturally out of the question, and that of actively filtering the information so as to read it only from the perspective of the requirement.

Easy marks

Part (c)(ii) was probably the easiest part of the question, as most of the ethical implications should come out of the scenario.

ACCA examining team's comments

Performance on parts (a) and (b) of this question was generally strong and most candidates were able to identify and discuss the relevant issues. These parts of the question focused on ethics and practice management, and candidates were required to critique the appropriateness of advertising being utilised by the firm. The majority of students were well prepared to answer this question with a format that has been used before and were able to confidently identify and evaluate the ethical issues associated with the proposed advertisement.

Part (b) combined overdue fees with an intimidation threat and again was well answered. The final part dealt with a conflict of interest between two competing clients arising after an acquisition of another firm and candidates attempting this question tended to score well.

Candidates were asked in requirement (c)(i), for five marks, to identify and explain the matters that should be considered, and the principal audit procedures that should be performed in respect of the funding being sought. The main problem with answers were that they did not focus as required on the additional funding being sought, but instead discussed more generally the plight of the company.

Requirement (c)(ii) was well answered. Most candidates correctly identified and went on to explain the self-review, management and advocacy threats created by the situation, and many discussed the potential liability issue caused by attending the meeting.

Marking guide	Marks
(a) In general up to 1.5 marks for each point of evaluation and up to 1 mark for each response recommended.	
Advertisement	
• Advert reflects adversely on other professional accountants	
• Misleading with regards to size of firm	
• Misleading comments regarding expertise of tax team	
• Threat to professional behaviour by guaranteeing to save tax	
• Lowballing – self-interest threat and threat to professional competence and due care	
• Potential threats to objectivity from business advice	
• Free consultations permitted	
• Remove misleading claims from advert	
• Separate teams for audit and other services advertised	
Maximum	6

(b) In general up to 1.5 marks for each point of evaluation and up to 1 mark for each response recommended.

Renoir Ltd

- Intimidation threat to objectivity
- Meet senior management and explain the terms of the audit
- Consider integrity of Jim Cassatt and possible implications for audit
- Thorough performance and review of planning
- Early notice of audit requirements and logistics
- Self-interest threat created by overdue fees
- Delay audit until fees paid (1 max)
- Consider resignation where level of outstanding fees is not trivial

Maximum 4

(c) (i) **Matters and procedures on funding**

Up to 1 mark each point:

Matters

- Area of critical importance to the audit
- Bank reluctant to confirm arrangements
- Assets impaired
- Have alternative providers been discussed?
- Potential impact on FS and auditor's report if significant doubt remains over going concern

Procedures

- Review assumptions used in forecasts and projections
- Written representation on reasonableness of assumptions used
- Review potential finance for adequacy
- Consider if any previous defaults
- Consider terms of finance – can the company meet repayment terms?
- Written confirmation from bank
- Discuss with bank
- Discuss with management

Maximum 5

(ii) **Ethical and other implications** – Up to 1 mark each point explained:

- Advice is a non-audit service
- Self-review threat
- Advocacy threat
- Management threat
- Safeguards should be used to reduce threats
- Firm may decide that no safeguards can reduce threats to an acceptable level
- Attending meeting could create legal proximity

Maximum 5

ANSWERS

Professional marks

Analysis and evaluation

- Appropriate use of the information to determine matters to consider and audit procedures to be performed in relation to additional funding being sought by Juliet
- Identification of difficulties with advertisement presented
- Balanced understanding of the implications of the conversation with Renoir's finance director

Professional scepticism and judgement

- Effective challenge of draft advertisement to support key facts and/or decisions regarding ethical acceptability
- Appropriate professional judgements regarding the proposed attendance of the meeting with the bank
- Appropriate application of professional judgement to draw conclusions and make informed decisions about the actions which are appropriate in the context and stage of the engagement. 5

Total 25

(a) **Advertisement**

Accountants are permitted to advertise subject to the requirements set out in the ACCA *Code of Ethics and Conduct* that the advert should 'not reflect adversely on the professional accountant, ACCA or the accounting profession' (ACCA *Rulebook*: para. R115.2 and s B13). The advert does not appear to be in keeping with this principle; it suggests that other firms of accountants charge inappropriately high fees and that the quality of their services is questionable. This discredits the services offered by other professional accountants as well as implying that the services offered by Monet & Co are far superior.

The advert states that the firm offers 'the most comprehensive range of finance and accountancy services in the UK'. This is misleading; with 12 offices and only 30 partners Monet & Co is unlikely to be one of the largest accountancy firms in the UK and is therefore unlikely to offer the most comprehensive range of services. If it is misleading, this statement must be withdrawn from the advertisement.

The advert also implies that the firm has the UK's leading tax team; it is not possible to substantiate this claim as it is not possible to measure the effectiveness of tax teams and even if it were, no such measure currently exists. This is, therefore, also potentially misleading and should be withdrawn from the advert.

The suggestion that the tax experts are waiting to save the client money is inappropriate; no such guarantees can be made because tax professionals must apply relevant tax legislation in an objective manner. This may lead to a reduction in a client's current tax expense or it may not. Any failure to apply these regulations appropriately could raise questions about the professional behaviour of the practitioner.

Guaranteeing to be cheaper than other service providers is often referred to as 'lowballing'. This could create a potential self-interest threat to objectivity and could also threaten professional competence and due care if the practitioner is unable to apply the appropriate professional standards for that level of fee. Where a low fee is charged for an audit, the firm may cut corners or allocate inexperienced staff to the audit team in an attempt to recover the costs incurred. The FRC's *Ethical Standard* states that the audit engagement partner shall be satisfied and able to demonstrate that the audit engagement has assigned to it sufficient partners and staff with appropriate time and skill to perform the audit in accordance with all applicable Auditing and Ethical Standards, irrespective of the audit fee to be charged.

According to the FRC *Ethical Standard*, offering a non-audit service such as business advice to audit clients potentially creates self-interest, self-review, management and advocacy threats to objectivity. It depends on the sort of advice offered but it is possible that the auditor in subsequent years may have to audit aspects of the business affected by the advice given. This would be particularly relevant if the practitioner provided advice with regard to systems design. It would be possible to offer both services if Monet & Co can use different teams to provide each service, assuming the systems concerned would not be significant to the accounting system or production of financial statements. Given that they have 12 offices, it may be possible to keep these services completely separate and they may be able to offer both. The audit engagement partner should determine whether safeguards are available to reduce such threats to an acceptable level for each audit engagement.

Monet & Co will also need to be very careful when it comes to clients which are public interest entities. The FRC *Ethical Standard* allows only a very restricted set of non-audit services to be provided to these entities – only those which are explicitly mentioned in the standard. It is important that Monet & Co does not fall foul of this rule. At 30 partners in 12 offices, it seems unlikely that the firm would have many (if any) listed clients, but it needs to take care nonetheless.

Offering services for free as part of a promotion is not prohibited but, similar to lowballing, this increases the threat to competence and due care if sufficient time and resources are not allocated to the task. This may also devalue the services offered by Monet & Co as they may be perceived as being a promotional tool as opposed to a professional service.

Firms of accountants are permitted to offer free consultations, so this does not create any specific threats. The phrase 'drop in and see us' may cause a problem with potential clients though as it may not always be possible to expect to see senior staff members without an appointment. To avoid damaging the professional profile of the firm, Monet & Co would need to make sure they had a dedicated member of staff available to meet potential customers who is available without prior notice.

Finally, Monet & Co is not permitted to use the term 'Chartered Certified Accountants' because less than 50% of the partners of the firm are ACCA members (ACCA *Code of Ethics*: B4. Para. 15). This reference should be removed.

(b) **Renoir Ltd**

Mr Cassatt's threat that he will seek an alternative auditor unless the audit is cheaper and less intrusive than the prior year constitutes an intimidation threat to objectivity. This has arisen because Mr Cassatt is trying to unduly influence the conduct of the audit of Renoir Ltd.

The audit manager or partner should arrange a meeting with the senior management of Renoir Ltd and the audit committee, if one exists, and they should explain how the audit has to be performed and how the fee is calculated. They should take care to explain the professional standards which they have to comply with and the terms of the engagement which the client agreed to, specifically that management should provide all necessary documents and explanations deemed necessary by the auditor to collect sufficient appropriate evidence. It should be explained that due to the need to comply with these standards, they cannot guarantee to reduce either the volume of procedures or the audit fee.

Monet & Co should also consider the integrity of Mr Cassatt. If the audit firm considers any threat created too significant, then they may wish to resign from the engagement. If not, it may be necessary to use more senior, experienced staff on the assignment who are less likely to be intimidated by Mr Cassatt while performing audit fieldwork.

If the audit proceeds, the planning should be performed by an appropriately experienced member of the audit team. This should be reviewed thoroughly by the audit manager and the partner to ensure that the procedures recommended are appropriate to the risk assessment performed. In this way Monet & Co can ensure that any unnecessary, and potential time wasting, procedures are avoided.

The audit manager should then make sure that Mr Cassatt is given adequate notice of the timing of the audit and provide him with a list of documentation which will be required during the course of the audit so that Renoir Ltd may prepare for the visit by the audit team. The manager could also recommend that Mr Cassatt and his team make specific time available to meet with the audit team and then request that the audit team use that time to ask all the necessary enquiries of the client. This should minimise any disruption experienced by the client during fieldwork.

The overdue fees create a self-interest threat. IESBA's *Code of Ethics for Professional Accountants* states that a self-interest threat may be created if fees due from an audit client remain unpaid for a long time, especially if not paid before the issue of the auditor's report for the following year. The audit firm should determine the amount of fee, which is unpaid, and whether it could be perceived to be a loan made to the client. It may be a relatively insignificant amount, and it may not be long overdue, in which case the threat to objectivity is not significant. The FRC *Ethical Standard* (section 4) states that ordinarily, any outstanding fees for the previous audit period are paid before the audit firm commences any new audit work. Where they are not, it is important for the audit engagement partner to understand the nature of any disagreement or other issue.

If the self-interest threat is significant, then no audit work should be performed until the fees are paid. This decision, and the reason for it, should be communicated to the management of Renoir Ltd or their audit committee, if possible. Where the level of outstanding fees cannot be considered trivial, the audit firm may consider resignation.

(c) (i) The central issue here is going concern; there are a number of indications that Juliet Ltd may not be a going concern. For instance: declining sales and profitability over two years; the loss of key customers; the impairment of assets; debts going bad. Most significant of all is the question of whether the loan will be obtained.

If Juliet Ltd does not obtain the loan, then the financial statements must contain disclosures regarding the material uncertainty over going concern. The auditor's report should contain a section headed 'Material uncertainty related to going concern', in which the auditor would draw attention to the disclosures, and state that they cast doubt over going concern but that the auditor's opinion is not modified in relation to them. If the financial statements do not contain these disclosures, then the auditor's opinion would need to be either qualified or adverse.

Procedures in respect of the loan include:

- Obtain and review the forecasts and projections prepared by management and consider if the assumptions used are in line with business understanding.
- Obtain a written representation confirming that the assumptions used in the forecasts and projections are considered achievable in light of the economic recession and state of the automotive industry.
- Obtain and review the terms of the loan that has been requested to see if Juliet Ltd can make the repayments required.
- Consider the sufficiency of the loan requested to cover the costs of the intended restructuring.
- Review the repayment history of any current loans and overdrafts with the bank, to form an opinion as to whether Juliet Ltd has any history of defaulting on payments. (Any previous defaults or breach of loan conditions makes it less likely that the new loan would be advanced).
- Discuss the loan request with the company's bankers and attempt to receive confirmation of their intention to provide the finance, and the terms of the finance.
- Discuss the situation with management and those charged with governance, to ascertain if any alternative providers of finance have been considered, and if not, whether any alternative strategies for the company have been discussed.
- Obtain a written representation from management stating management's opinion as to whether the necessary finance is likely to be obtained.

(ii) **Ethical**

These forecasts are crucial for the assessment of whether the company is a going concern. There is a self-review threat if the auditor is both advising on the preparation of the forecasts and auditing them as part of its work on going concern under ISA (UK) 570 (Revised) *Going Concern*.

The issue is given added weight by ISA (UK) 570 (Revised)'s insistence that where cash flow is important for the assessment of going concern, particular consideration should be given not only to what the forecasts say, but to their reliability. This exacerbates the potential impact of the self-review threat.

There is potentially an advocacy and management threat, as the auditor is advising on a matter significant to the company's operational existence and promoting the company's position to the potential provider of finance.

The auditor must consider whether safeguards can be put in place to reduce these threats to an acceptable level. For instance, a separate team could review the forecasts, and management could be asked to provide representations to the effect that they alone are responsible for the forecasts.

If the firm decides that the threat is still not reduced to an acceptable level, then either, or both, of the services should not be provided.

Other

A further issue is that if the auditor does attend the meeting with the bank, it must be careful not to create the impression that it is responsible for the forecasts or is in any way guaranteeing the future existence of the company. In legal terms, attending the meeting and promoting the interests of the client could create legal 'proximity', which increases the risk of legal action against the auditor in the event of Juliet Ltd defaulting on the loan.

4 Peaches

Workbook references

Chapters 1, 2 and 5.

Top tips

Part (a) tested around the edge of the syllabus, but you should have been able to score very well, as you should already be familiar with the arguments in favour of principles- and rules-based approaches from your earlier studies. In addition to this, the examining team did discuss this issue in an article in *Student Accountant* shortly before the exam. This underlines again the advantage that you can gain just by carefully reading the examining team's articles there!

There is a possibility you might have been put off by the question text on recent surveys of the audit market, but if you read the requirement, you'll see that all you need to do is talk about the different approaches to auditing in general. Take care in part (ii), though, only to talk about the pros and cons of a prescriptive approach – the question is not asking you to talk about a principles-based approach at all (although the advantages of one and pretty much the same as the disadvantages of the other).

Part (b) was a standard question on ethics. You should have scored well here, as was mainly a test of factual knowledge but in the guise of a scenario.

Part (c) on money laundering was quite a nice requirement in this area. Part (i), on the stages of money laundering, was partly pre-learned knowledge in an area that is quite interesting by AAA standards, and partly application to Adderley Ltd. If you explained each stage well, then you only needed to say two further things in relation to Adderley Ltd to get maximum marks – and there were two strong hints in the scenario (tickets purchased in cash, and the regular overseas bank transfers). Part (ii) was knowledge-based and in a key area of the syllabus, so it's important that you get a good number of these marks.

Easy marks

Part (a)(i) should have been very easy, as should the elements of an anti-money laundering programme in (c)(ii).

ACCA examining team's comments

This question focused on ethical and professional issues. The topic should not have been a surprise to candidates given the importance of this current issue, and the examining team's recent article covering the subject.

Requirement (a) tested candidates' knowledge and understanding of prescriptive and principles-based approaches to auditing. Generally, this requirement was answered well.

Requirement (b) contained two sub-requirements, testing candidates understanding of the terms 'intimidation threat' and also including a section on the advertising rules which auditors should abide by. Most candidates could demonstrate that they knew the basic facts about each, but generally did not explain their points in sufficient detail to score a high mark on requirement (b) as a whole. It was pleasing that the requirement on advertising rules was well answered, given that this is a relatively peripheral area of the syllabus. Unusually for the ethics question, at this sitting it tended to be the optional question in which candidates scored the highest mark.

Requirement (c) of the question focused on money laundering, and in contrast to previous sittings where this subject has been examined, the answers were generally of a reasonable standard. Most answers were reasonably well attempted, and most candidates demonstrated knowledge of both the stages of money laundering, and the elements of an anti-money laundering programme. The weaker answers tended to simply be too short, limiting the marks that could be awarded. Some answers failed to comment on why Adderley Ltd had been assessed as having a high risk of money laundering, even though the reasons were fairly obvious from the information provided.

Marking guide — **Marks**

(a) (i) **Prescriptive and principles-based approach to auditing**

- 1 mark per point up to a maximum of 2

(ii) **Arguments for and against prescriptive approach**

- 1 mark for each advantage – clarity, increase in quality, uniformity, easy to monitor
- 1 mark for each disadvantage – lack of tailoring, over-auditing, no use of skill/judgement, process becomes mundane/routine
- Additional marks may be given for relevant comments on practical issues related to adoption of ISAs, eg additional costs, increase in audit fee, training needs

5

(b) **Intimidation threat**

1 mark per comment explained:

- Independence/objectivity threat
- Example – aggressive individual
- Example – fear of dismissal
- Link to familiarity (or other) threat
- Safeguards needed

Advertising

1 mark per comment explained:

- Must abide by professional
- Must not make false/exaggerated claims
- Must not make disparaging remarks about other firms
- Must abide by local rules on advertising generally

Maximum 8

(c) (i) **Stages of money laundering**

Up to 1 mark for each stage explained specifically with relevance to Adderley Ltd:

Marking guide | **Marks**

- Placement – cash-based business and mixing of illegal and legitimate sources of cash
- Layering – complex transactions to hamper tracing the cash such as transfer overseas
- Integration – investing or spending cash to place it into the legitimate economy

Maximum — 3

(ii) **Elements of an anti-money laundering programme**

Up to 1 mark for each element recommended:

- MLCP and MLRO – senior person, responsibilities
- Firm-wide training programme
- Know your client procedures
- Record keeping

Maximum — 4

Professional marks

Analysis and evaluation

- Appropriate assessment of the ethical and professional issues raised, using examples where relevant to support overall comments
- Effective appraisal of the information to make suitable recommendations for appropriate courses of action

Professional scepticism and judgement

- Effective challenge and critical assessment of the evidence supplied with appropriate conclusions
- Demonstration of the ability to probe into the stages of money laundering and the complexity of its presentation
- Understanding of the principle of professional judgement in relation to the principles-based approach
- Application of professional scepticism and judgement to the two ethical issues presented

Maximum — 5

Total — 25

(a) (i) Rules-based (prescriptive) auditing is where the auditor follows prescribed rules on how to audit a particular area but does not use any judgement about how to apply the rules.

Principles-based auditing is where no detailed rules are prescribed, but where the auditor must apply more general, guiding principles to the particular area being audited.

(ii) **Arguments for**

Improved clarity and understandability. Prescriptive auditing standards leave the auditor in no doubt as to what he needs to do to audit a particular area. He just needs to follow the rules precisely and to the letter. As long as he has done this, he will be able to say that he has audited in accordance with the standards.

It can be argued that prescriptive standards lead to an improvement in the quality of audits because they leave less scope for the auditor to choose how to audit each area, which reduces the risk that the auditor might make the wrong choice or might make a poor judgement. This also makes it much easier for the regulatory authorities to monitor audit quality, as it is much clearer what the auditor needs to do in accordance with the standards.

Arguments against

The key disadvantage is that it reduces the auditor's ability to take into account the individual circumstances of the entity that is actually being audited. There is a danger of just applying the rules irrespective of whether the audit procedures are appropriate in this particular case. Worse than this, there may not even be a rule for the particular situation being audited, leaving the auditor in a very difficult position. This would lead to audit procedures being done that may not be adequate to gather sufficient appropriate audit evidence.

Prescriptive approaches diminish the extent to which auditors need to use their own judgement. This may not be too much of a problem in the case of a simple entity that is straightforward to audit, but it can be problematic in the case of a complex entity that is difficult to audit.

There is therefore a danger that a prescriptive approach might actually reduce the quality of audits.

(b) **Intimidation threat**

An intimidation threat is a threat to compliance with the fundamental principle of an auditor's objectivity, which is a crucial part of his independence.

An example of an intimidation threat would be a client threatening to replace the auditor if the auditor intends to modify the audit opinion (IESBA *Code of Ethics*).

When an auditor identifies that there is a threat to his independence, he should apply safeguards to reduce the threat to an acceptably low level. There may, for instance, be a specific mode of recourse available through the individual regulatory framework that the auditor is operating in.

Advertising

The ACCA's general rule on advertising is that the medium used should not reflect adversely on the member, ACCA or the accountancy profession (ACCA *Rulebook*).

In particular, adverts should not discredit the services offered by others, whether by claiming superiority for the member's or firm's own services or otherwise. They should also not be misleading, either directly or by implication – they must not make false claims.

It is important that short adverts do not include information about fees. It is possible to mention fees in longer adverts, but these must include information about the basis on which fees would be calculated, such as hourly rates, etc.

(c) (i) There are three stages in money laundering: placement, layering and integration. Each of these may be seen in the case of Adderley, with their presence suggesting a heightened risk of money laundering.

Placement

This is the initial placing of ill-gotten cash into the financial system. Cash-based business provide good cover for this, as it is easier for criminals to disguise dirty money as clean, eg by mixing it in with cash receipts.

For Adderley, it might be possible to place dirty money into the system in the guise of till receipts, after which it could be mixed with the clean money and subsequently treated as such.

Layering

This is the creation of 'layers' of transactions which seek to disguise the original origin of the placed cash. In practice this can be so complex that the cash is almost impossible to trace.

For Adderley, the regular transfer of cash into overseas bank accounts could be a way of introducing complexity to the layering process.

Integration

This is the integration of the money back into the legitimate economy, so that the criminals can use it to make purchases or investments.

For Adderley, the use of £8 million of its own cash could be a way of integrating laundered money back into a legitimate activity for the purpose of investment.

(ii) **MLCP and MLRO**

Peaches & Co should appoint a Money Laundering Compliance Principal (MLCP) and a Money Laundering Reporting Officer (MLRO), who should occupy a senior position in the firm. Suspicions of money laundering are reported to the MLRO, who then considers whether to pass them on to the National Crime Agency.

Firm-wide

Firm-wide elements include a training programme for staff, so that they are aware of relevant legislation and what they must do if they suspect or encounter money laundering. Training should include money laundering risk factors, so that individuals are better able to spot money laundering and respond appropriately.

Customer due diligence

Customer due diligence (know your client) procedures involve an audit firm establishing the identity of clients, eg through passports, and understanding the sources of clients' income and the rationale for business transactions.

Records

Peaches & Co must maintain records of client identification procedures and of any transactions, eg the receipt of payment of the audit fee. This helps ensure that the auditor does not inadvertently become involved in laundering money for its clients.

5 Cobra

Workbook references

Chapters 2 and 5.

Top tips

This was a typical ethics question and was a fair test. The requirement asks for comments on the issues raised, but also actions which should be taken. These are sometimes slightly easier marks to get, although to get them you must say both **what** the auditor should do, and **why** they should do it.

Part (a) was about a small but growing company that was choosing to have an audit. Most candidates would have realised that providing these non-audit services would threaten Cobra & Co's independence as auditor, however the question tested candidates' knowledge of the Code of Ethics: it is permissible to provide these services to a non-listed audit client, provided that any threats are reduced to an acceptable level.

When answering part (b), don't overlook the first point, which is about an auditor providing tax services to an audit client. This is not the core of this question part but nevertheless, there are marks available. The central issue in part (b) is the conflict between the client and the outgoing auditor. The issue is relatively clear-cut and should have provided you with ample opportunity to score marks.

Part (c) contained plenty of possible marks too, as it is clear that there is a conflict of interest between the two clients, irrespective of their ownership.

Easy marks

There were marks available for simply stating the types of threats that were present, as well as for explaining why these are threats. Note, however, that the examining team does not like it when candidates simply list out all of the categories of threat – this is not likely to score any marks.

Marking guide	Marks
(a) **Asp Ltd**	
• Self-review threat due to financial statements impact of other services	
• Not prohibited because Asp Ltd is not listed	
• Use different teams and make sure that this is possible and acceptable to client (max 1 mark)	
• Potential management threat	
• Discussion of informed management at a small company	
• No safeguards available for management threat relating to an audit client	
• Communicate management threat issues with management and potentially obtain new engagement letter (max 1 mark)	
• Second partner review of audit for 31 December 20X5 (max 1 mark)	
Maximum	7
(b) **Viper Ltd**	
• Self-review threat to objectivity	
• Inadequate acceptance procedures	
• Preconditions for accepting audit	
• Question over integrity of management	
• Possible that previous auditor is at fault, not management	
• Obtain further information relating to financial reporting dispute (max 1 mark)	
• Investigate matter independently (max 1 mark)	
• Decision based on outcome of further investigations (max 1 mark)	
Maximum	7
(c) **Adder plc**	
• Conflict of interest with competing audit clients	
• Potentially private information held by Cobra & Co in relation to Slowworm Ltd	
• Self-review threat caused by valuation service	
• Possible use of separate teams (max 1 mark)	
• Not permitted to conduct valuation for audit client (max 1 mark)	
Maximum	6
Professional marks	
Analysis and evaluation	
• Appropriate assessment of the ethical and professional issues raised, using examples where relevant to support overall comments	
• Effective appraisal of the information to make suitable recommendations for appropriate courses of action	
Professional scepticism and judgement	
• Effective challenge and critical assessment of the evidence supplied with appropriate conclusions	
• Understanding of the principle of professional judgement in relation to the principles-based approach	
• Application of professional scepticism and judgement to the two ethical issues presented	
Maximum	5
Total	25

(a) **Asp Ltd**

Self-review threat

If Cobra & Co accepts the audit of Asp Ltd and continues to provide the other services, this would create a self-review threat to objectivity. This would arise because all of the other services would have an impact on the financial statements which Cobra & Co would then be responsible for forming an opinion on. Given the nature of the services, the impact on the financial statements would most likely be material.

The FRC *Ethical Standard* does not prohibit firms from providing bookkeeping and tax services to non-listed audit clients but requires that sufficient safeguards are implemented to reduce any threat to an acceptable level. The response should, however, be considered in light of the complexity of the other services and amount of judgement required in providing the other services, particularly in relation to the application of tax regulations.

Management responsibility

Undertaking bookkeeping and taxation services on behalf of a client may require the service provider to make decisions on behalf of the client or may create the perception that the service provider is acting in a managerial capacity. If Cobra & Co were to assume such responsibility for an audit client, this would create a threat to their objectivity.

This is particularly an issue for a small company such as Asp Ltd, where there may not be 'informed management', meaning that management relies on Cobra & Co for advice. This increases the management threat to objectivity significantly. The FRC *Ethical Standard* requires that in determining whether a non-audit service does or does not give rise to a management threat, the persons conducting the engagement should consider whether there is informed management by evaluating whether:

- A member of management (or senior employee of the entity) has been designated by the entity to receive the results of the non-audit service and has been given the authority to make any judgements and decisions;
- That member of management has the capability to make independent management judgements and decisions on the basis of the information provided; and
- The results of the non-audit service are communicated to the entity and, where judgements or decisions are to be made by management, they are supported by an objective analysis of the issues to be considered and the entity is given the opportunity to decide between reasonable alternatives.

If all the services currently provided to Asp Ltd are administrative and routine, then the threat will be minimal. However, in the absence of informed management, it is unlikely that any other safeguards can eliminate a management threat or reduce it to a level where independence is not compromised.

Audit of financial statements for 31 December 20X5

Cobra & Co has already had significant involvement in the preparation of amounts which have been included in the financial statements for this year end and they may have already applied significant judgement in determining those figures, particularly in relation to any tax amounts or liabilities. Given this heightened risk, as well as using a separate team to do the audit, it would be prudent to ensure that an engagement quality review is carried out prior to signing the auditor's report.

Actions

Assuming that Cobra & Co takes up the audit of Asp Ltd, before also accepting to continue to provide non-audit services, the FRC *Ethical Standard* requires that the firm must:

- Identify and assess the significance of any related threats to the integrity or objectivity of the firm including whether independence would be compromised;
- Identify and assess the effectiveness of the available safeguards to eliminate the threats or reduce them to a level where independence would not be compromised; and
- Consider whether it is probable that an objective, reasonable and informed third party, having regard to the threats and safeguards, would conclude that the proposed non-audit

service would not impair integrity or objectivity and compromise the independence of the firm.

These assessments must be fully documented and discussed with those charged with governance at Asp Ltd.

If Cobra & Co accepts the audit engagement, they will need to use different staff to undertake the audit to those involved in the other services. Cobra & Co must ensure that they have sufficient staff with the necessary competence within the firm to enact such segregation of duties and they must ensure that the client understands that different teams will be used for the various services provided.

If Cobra & Co has been responsible for any managerial decisions, they must cease this if they accept the audit engagement. However, it is likely that the firm would have to wait a period of time before they would be able to audit the financial statements as, even if they cease to assume management responsibility in the current year, the firm will have influenced the financial statements for the year ended 31 December 20X5. They should communicate this to the management of Asp Ltd and obtain written confirmations from the client that they understand and accept this. This will help the firm to evaluate whether 'informed management' exists and that this has been acknowledged by the client. If this requires any change in the nature of the engagements provided, new engagement letters must be issued and signed before the services can be continued.

Tutorial note. Credit will be awarded where candidates answer with reference to the IESBA *Code of Ethics for Professional Accountants*.

(b) **Viper Ltd**

Self-review threat

Once again, providing both audit and tax services creates a self-review threat to objectivity. The tax service also gives rise to a management threat, but as Viper Ltd is a non-listed client, Cobra & Co may accept the assignment provided sufficient safeguards are implemented. However, the issue identified in relation to the outgoing auditor does raise concern as to whether these engagements should be accepted.

Acceptance procedures

ISA (UK) 220 (Revised) *Quality Management for an Audit of Financial Statements* requires that the engagement partner ensures Cobra & Co's quality objectives addressing acceptance of client engagements have been followed. One of the matters is considering the integrity and ethical values of the owners and management of the client. One such procedure to obtain this information is to communicate with the outgoing auditor. If the engagement partner is not satisfied that they have obtained sufficient information to conclude acceptance of the engagement is appropriate, they should not accept the engagement.

Previously modified opinion

It appears that the management of Viper Ltd has had a significant disagreement with their outgoing auditor over a certain accounting treatment. This raises a number of separate issues:

- If management is applying an incorrect accounting treatment and the effect on the financial statements is material, it will lead to a modification in future periods. If management does not accept their responsibility to apply appropriate accounting treatments, then the preconditions for accepting the audit, as prescribed in ISA (UK) 210 *Agreeing the Terms of Audit Engagements*, will not have been met. In these circumstances Cobra & Co must not accept the engagement.
- There is a doubt over the integrity of management as they appear to have disagreed with the auditor, an expert in the application of financial reporting standards, over an accounting treatment. This may indicate an unwillingness to accept financial reporting requirements or a conscious effort to distort the financial statements. Either way, if Cobra & Co is not satisfied as to the integrity of management, they should not accept the engagement.

- The lawsuit indicates that Viper Ltd believes that it is correct and that the auditor is incorrect in the matter disputed. This may indicate that, contrary to the previous point, management is not at fault. If this is the case and the auditor is indeed negligent, then there is no reason for Cobra & Co to refuse the engagement.

Actions

Cobra & Co should try to obtain further information from management relating to the lawsuit. It is likely that in these circumstances additional expertise has been sought to determine if the auditor has acted negligently or not. If this is the case, Cobra & Co should request to see any communications with the experts, if permitted.

If not, Cobra & Co should request to review information relating to the matter under dispute. Cobra & Co should be able to use their own expertise to determine an appropriate accounting treatment.

If, following these procedures, Cobra & Co decides that it can proceed with the engagement, it should first of all consult with its own legal team, or at least with senior partners responsible for executive decisions, before accepting given the potentially litigious nature of Viper Ltd.

If Cobra & Co determines that Viper Ltd is incorrect or that there is insufficient information to enable a satisfactory conclusion, then it would be prudent in the circumstances to politely decline the engagement.

(c) **Adder plc**

Conflict of interest

The FRC *Ethical Standard* does not address conflict of interest in any detail. However, the IESBA *Code of Ethics for Professional Accountants* (the *Code*) defines a conflict of interest as arising when a firm provides a service in relation to two or more clients whose interests in respect of the matter are in conflict.

In this case, the interests of Adder plc and Slowworm Ltd will be conflicting; Adder plc will want to purchase the shares for the lowest possible amount and the owner of Slowworm Ltd will want to sell them for the highest possible amount. This creates, therefore, a significant threat to the objectivity of Cobra & Co, who may be seen to be acting in the interest of one party at the expense of the other.

The problem is exacerbated by the nature of the engagement; Adder plc will use information about the company, including operational information, to bargain over the price. Cobra & Co may be privy to private information gained during their time as auditor of Slowworm Ltd which Adder plc might not have become aware of during normal due diligence procedures. If Cobra & Co were to divulge this to Adder plc, it would give them a potentially unfair advantage over the other client and would be a breach of confidentiality.

Self-review threat

Performing the valuation service for Adder plc would also create a self-review threat because Cobra & Co would have a significant influence over the valuation of Slowworm Ltd, which would consequently be used to consolidate their accounts into the new, enlarged group which Cobra & Co would be responsible for auditing in the future.

Actions

It is possible to reduce both the conflict of interest and self-review threats by using different teams to conduct the various services provided.

The *Code* stipulates, however, that a firm should not provide valuation services for a listed client. The FRC *Ethical Standard* prohibits the provision of almost all non-audit services for listed clients.

Therefore, before accepting the assignment, Cobra & Co should consider the potential impact of the transaction and, if they believe it will be material, they should politely decline the engagement.

6 Smith & Co

Workbook references

Chapters 2 and 15.

Top tips

In this type of question it is important to pay attention to the mark allocation and make sure you allocate your time accordingly.

Part (c) would appear difficult as there is no specific technical material on which to base an answer. What was needed here was a common-sense approach, thinking about factors that affect the levels of assurance, and the natures of information that would be likely to exist about the particular performance indicators given in the question.

Easy marks

By suggesting some sensible action points – such as reviewing credit control procedures – you should be able to score some easy marks in this question. Norman Ltd is worth seven marks and so you need to spend more time on this than the other two.

Examining team's comments

It is crucial that in ethics questions, the reason **why** something is a threat to independence is fully explained. The answers given to requirements (a) and (b) were usually the same length, despite there being more marks available for (a). Again, candidates are reminded to be careful with time allocation within each question that they attempt.

In answering part (c), which invited candidates to suggest procedures used to verify the number of serious accidents reported, the marks awarded to scripts were polarised. Many candidates seemed to think that the auditor has access to absolutely any kind of evidence that they could wish for. Common sources of evidence referred to included the private medical records of employees, police reports on 'dangerous' incidents, hospital admissions data, interviews with ambulance drivers/paramedics/doctors and death certificates.

Candidates need to appreciate that although the auditor will have access to books and records held by their client, they will not be able to access external and possibly highly confidential information as a means to gather evidence. The above examples show of a lack of commercial, or even, common sense.

Marking guide	Marks
(a) **Norman Ltd**	
Generally 1 mark each per comment and action point:	
• Poor credit control	
• FRC ES Part B4 – Independence threat – free audit/loan	
• FRC ES Part B4 – Independence threat – self-interest in 20X5 report	
• Financial distress leads to going concern threat for the company	
• Non-payment due to financial distress does not necessitate resignation	
• Discuss with client – ethical problem/payment arrangements	
• Ethics partner notification	
• Assess significance of amount outstanding	
• Policy to check prior invoices paid	
• Continue to improve credit control	
• Second partner review	
• Review of audit work performed on going concern	
Maximum	7

(b) **Wallace Ltd**

Generally 1 mark each per comment and action point:

- FRC ES Part B2 – Non arm's length commercial transaction
- Material to audit manager
- Self-interest/intimidation threat
- Question audit manager's integrity
- Potential disciplinary action
- Remove Valerie from audit team
- Review all work performed on Wallace Ltd
- Consider Valerie's relationship with and likelihood of bias towards her other clients
- Disclosure of ethical threat to those charged with governance
- Provide clear communication to all staff regarding transactions with clients

Maximum 5

(c) (i) **KPI assurance difficulties**

- Discussion of problems in defining KPI terms (max 2 marks)
- Discussion of difficulty in gathering evidence (max 2 marks)

4

(ii) **Procedures on number of accidents**

Generally 1 mark per procedure:

Ideas list:

- Review log book
- Discuss and clarify criteria
- HR/payroll records
- Employee correspondence
- Board minute review
- Legal letter review
- Discuss with employees

4

Professional marks

Analysis and evaluation

- Appropriate assessment of the ethical and professional issues raised, using examples where relevant to support overall comments
- Effective appraisal of the information to make suitable recommendations for appropriate courses of action

Professional scepticism and judgement

- Effective challenge and critical assessment of the evidence supplied with appropriate conclusions
- Application of professional scepticism and judgement to the two ethical issues presented

Commercial acumen

- Inclusion of appropriate recommendations regarding overdue fees in relation to Norman
- Appropriate recognition of the wider implications on the engagement and the firm

Maximum 5

Total 25

ANSWERS

(a) **Norman Ltd**

Credit control

The fees for the 20X4 audit have been outstanding for over 12 months and it seems that little has been done to collect them. Since the file note states that Norman Ltd is suffering poor cash flows, the balance may no longer be recoverable. Credit control has been poorly managed at Smith & Co regarding this client and the debt should not have remained outstanding for so long.

Action

Credit control procedures at the firm need to be reviewed to prevent this situation reoccurring. It appears that some improvements have already been made with the audit manager now being responsible for reviewing client invoices raised and monitoring credit control procedures.

Independence

The overdue fees for the 20X4 audit may make it appear the audit has been performed for free or could effectively be seen as a loan from Smith & Co to Norman Ltd. The ACCA *Code of Ethics and Conduct* specifically states that an audit firm should not enter into a loan arrangement with a client that is not a bank or similar institution. It highlights overdue fees as an area where a self-interest threat could arise and independence is threatened. Smith & Co should not have allowed outstanding fees to build up as their independence is now compromised.

Action

Smith & Co should discuss the recoverability of the 20X4 audit fee with the audit committee (if one exists) or those charged with governance. A payment plan should be put into place.

If the overdue fees are not paid, the firm should consider resigning as auditors per the FRC's *Ethical Standard* (FRC ES), Part B4 *Fees, remuneration and evaluation policies, litigation, gifts and hospitality*. In this case a valid commercial reason appears to exist as to why the fees remain unpaid. Smith & Co can remain as auditors provided that adequate safeguards are in place and the amount outstanding is not significant. If the overdue fees are significant, it may be that no safeguards could eliminate the threat to objectivity or independence or reduce them to an acceptable level.

The ethics partner at Smith & Co should be informed of the situation. The ethics partner should evaluate the ethical threat and document the conclusions including the significance of the overdue fees.

FRC ES Part B4

Under the FRC ES, the 20X4 audit fee and arrangements for payment should have been agreed before Smith & Co formally accepted appointment as auditor for the 20X5 audit. Since the 20X5 audit has now almost been completed, it appears this could not have happened.

Action

The ethics partner at Smith & Co should take steps to ensure that there are no outstanding audit fees before commencing new client work. This could involve a new firm-wide policy that audit managers check payment of previous invoices.

Self-interest in 20X5 report

The 20X5 auditor's report has not yet been signed. This creates a self-interest threat to Smith & Co's objectivity and independence because the issue of an unmodified auditor's report may enhance their prospects of securing payment of the overdue 20X4 audit fees.

Action

The working papers for the 20X5 audit of Norman Ltd should undergo an independent review by the engagement quality reviewer.

Going concern

Norman Ltd is known to be having cash flow problems and so there is an issue of whether the company is a going concern for the 20X5 auditor's report.

Action

Smith & Co should carry out a review of the 20X5 audit working papers on going concern. It may be necessary to carry out further audit procedures to ensure that sufficient evidence has been gathered to support the audit opinion.

(b) **Wallace Ltd**

Terms of FRC ES

Under the FRC ES (Part B2 *Financial, business, employment and personal relationships*), persons in a position to influence the conduct and outcome of the audit should not enter into business relationships with a client except where they involve the purchase of goods and services from the client in the ordinary course of business, are on an arm's length basis and are clearly inconsequential to each party.

As audit manager of Wallace Ltd, Valerie Hobson has influence over the audit outcome and should only rent the warehouse space if the conditions prescribed by the FRC *ES* are met. Since the warehouse space is already known to be used for rental income, this transaction is in the ordinary course of business. However, the note on the invoice about only charging a nominal sum indicates that the transaction is not on an arm's length basis. The criteria in the FRC *ES* have therefore been breached. It is also worth noting that the transaction may represent a material discount for Valerie Hobson.

Action

Valerie Hobson should not retain the position of audit manager at Wallace Ltd and a new manager should be assigned. All planning work for the 20X5 audit should be independently reviewed as planning decisions may have been influenced by the transaction. The situation should be disclosed to those charged with governance at Wallace Ltd and the audit committee, if one exists.

Self-interest threat

Valerie Hobson has created a self-interest threat, by renting the warehouse space at a reduced rate. Valerie's objectivity could be biased by her desire to please Wallace Ltd so that she can benefit financially.

Action

Valerie Hobson may need to be disciplined for her actions by Smith & Co who could also send her for ethics training. Smith & Co should investigate for evidence of bias in other audits where Valerie Hobson has had influence.

(c) **Key performance indicators**

(i) **Level of assurance over meeting KPIs**

There are two main reasons why the level of assurance given in relation to the KPIs cannot be a high level of assurance:

- Lack of precision in the description of the KPIs
- Likely lack of appropriate audit evidence

Lack of precision

The KPIs are defined imprecisely and are also subjective. For example:

- Donated product should be 1% of revenue, but what price will be free products be valued at – cost or retail price?
- Similarly, how will 'donations' to local charities be valued if these donations are more than just financial donations, such as the use of Sci-Tech's expert employees or products?
- 'Serious' accidents should be fewer than five, but what constitutes 'serious'?

Audit evidence

Some of these matters may be well documented, such as cash donations or accidents, because of health and safety procedures, but others, such as time spent by employees at local charities, may not be so well documented.

(ii) **Evidence in relation to serious accidents**

- Obtain and review health and safety accident logbooks for all Sci-Tech's premises and review the number of accidents.
- Discuss the definition of 'serious' with the directors and obtain written verification of this definition.
- Select a number of accidents designated serious and not serious, and review associated correspondence, payroll records and compensation payments to determine whether the accidents have been properly designated serious or not.
- Review correspondence with legal advisors to ascertain if any action has been taken in relation to accidents not designated serious by the directors.
- Review board minutes to obtain directors' opinions on the increase in serious accidents in 20X5.
- Review correspondence and reports from regulatory bodies to ensure that controls over health and safety reporting are considered to be strong.
- Discuss health and safety controls with health and safety officer to ensure that all accidents are reported.

7 Vizsla

Workbook references

Chapters 1, 2, 4 and 13.

Top tips

The scenario in part (a) was slightly different from the norm in that it involved two clients. It would therefore have been important to keep your head and trust your knowledge. In reality part (a)(i) was not impossible, and you should have been able to pass it. The model answer spends some time on ISQM (UK) 1, which is justified because the requirement asks for 'other matters' as well as ethics. If your knowledge of ISQM (UK) 1 is patchy then this is an opportunity to make sure you're able to apply it where the requirement allows it.

Part (a)(ii), on CDD/KYC, was fairly topical (being related to money laundering), and this was a good test in this area. There is quite a lot of pre-learned knowledge here, which underscores how difficult AAA can be as there are so many areas of the syllabus that you will need to be able to draw on. That being said, however, there were marks available here for application. If you had approached the scenario with penetrating questions such as 'who', 'why', 'how' in mind, then you can use these to generate the 'information which should be obtained'.

Part (b), on examination procedures for prospective financial information, tests an area that has come up fairly frequently in recent AAA exams. This part of the question should have been within your reach.

Easy marks

There were no standout easy marks in this question. In this case it is important that you stuck to your timings, as the first few marks in each question part will usually be the easiest to get (so if you spend too long on a question part, you will necessarily only be getting the difficult marks).

ACCA examining team's comments

Part (a) related to the ethical issues and other matters which should be considered in respect of the acceptance of a potential new client. The introduction was made through an existing client who sought to intimidate the auditor into taking on the new client of doubtful reputation.

A number of candidates had obviously studied an article on the ACCA website on how to answer ethics questions and were able to earn good marks. Candidates are reminded that they need to identify the indicator in the scenario, what the relevant ethical threat is, to describe why this is the case and further explain the implication to the auditor if relevant safeguards aren't then put in place.

The potential new client had a questionable history and not enough candidates explored this in sufficient detail.

The importance of new customer due diligence was also a requirement of this question, and this was poorly answered as many confused this with a due diligence review. Many candidates talked about initial acceptance procedures such as reviewing accounts and contacting the previous auditor rather than concentrating on the main Customer Due Diligence (CDD) procedures such as money laundering, sources of client funds, the identity of the beneficial owner, any shadow directors and other companies owned by the prospective client. Other candidates incorrectly discussed procedures, which would be undertaken when performing audit planning. Most, however, did pick up on needing photographic identification, Companies House searches and Certificates of Incorporation as proof of identification as well as wanting to understand the previous issues of alleged pension fund misappropriation & breach of employment laws.

Part (b) required candidates to recommend examination procedures to be used when reviewing a profit forecast and was generally well answered with all of the main areas covered. Candidates were able to include the need to identify who prepared the forecast and their competence, unusual trends in revenue, revenues growing quicker than costs and the risk of management bias while the objective of the forecast was to procure a bank loan. Marks were also available for calculating relevant trends and good candidates were able to earn extra credit here.

Marking guide

	Marks
(a) (i) **Ethical and other matters to be considered before accepting Setter Ltd as a client of the firm**	
Up to 0.5 marks for each ethical or other professional issue explained:	
• General requirements of ISQM (UK) 1	
• Competence to perform the work – this should not be a problem	
• Verify that a limited assurance review is appropriate, ie the company meets the audit exemption criteria	
• Intimidation and self-interest threat from Vizsla Ltd	
• Level of fees from Visla Ltd needs to be discussed with ethics partner and the client	
• Low fees potentially impair quality of work	
• Pressure on fees from Setter Ltd indicates lack of integrity	
• Self-review, self-interest, advocacy and management threats from performing tax planning for the company	
• Issue of whether there is informed management at the client, if not the threats are more severe	
• Safeguards should be used to reduce threats to an acceptable level, if this is not possible the tax planning should not be performed	
• Providing personal tax advice not ethically wrong but may not want to accept work due to integrity issues	
• Breach of employment law and taking money from pension plan indicates lack of integrity/criminal activity/poor reputation	
	7
(ii) **Know your customer – procedures and recommended information**	

Up to 0,5 marks for each point explained/recommended:

- Part of anti-money laundering regulations (up to 3 marks for detailed explanation of regulations)
- Identity of Gordon Potts – passport, recent utility bills or bank statements
- Identity of other shareholders including the other family members and other 10% shareholders
- Setter Ltd – the company certificate of incorporation, to confirm legal status, date and place of incorporation
- A Companies House search (or equivalent) on Setter Ltd – confirm the existence of the company, the shareholders and directors, beneficial owners
- Other companies controlled by Gordon Potts – confirm their existence and the nature of the relationship with Setter Ltd
- Review of the latest financial statements of Setter Ltd, and the other companies in which Gordon Potts has an interest should be reviewed
- Identify the source of funding, when funding is repayable and the existence of any security provided by the company or by personal guarantee of owners
- Facts surrounding the breach of employment law as reported by the newspaper

6

(b) **Examination procedures**

Up to 1 mark for each procedure explained. In addition, 0.5 mark for relevant calculations, eg trend analysis, up to a maximum of 2 marks:

General procedures:

- Identify of the preparer of the operating profit forecast, and assess their competence
- Understanding the procedures/controls which have been followed in the preparation of the forecast
- Confirm the consistency of accounting policies applied
- Confirm that the assumptions underpinning the forecast are in line with knowledge of the business obtained from performing the company's audit
- Re-cast the forecast to ensure it is arithmetically correct

Specific procedures:

- Ask management to prepare a more detailed profit forecast in an appropriate format and to provide forecast statement of financial position and statement of cash flows
- Recalculate the gross profit margins and compare with gross profit margins from audited financial statements
- Obtain a break down showing the components of cost of sales and other expenses; perform analytical review and discuss results
- Assess whether there are any missing categories of expenditure
- For revenue, consider whether the forecast appears overly optimistic – allow credit for calculation of appropriate trends from the forecast
- Compare revenue forecast with revenue from prior years' audited financial statements. Investigate any unusual trends through discussion with management

Marking guide **Marks**

- Review any marketing plans and discuss with an appropriate senior member of staff, for example, the sales director
- Review design costs, discuss with management and assess if such an increase in revenue can be achieved with such a small increase in design costs
- Confirm costs to appropriate supporting documentation, eg staff costs to human resources projected costs, marketing costs to advertising budgets
- Obtain and review the cash flow forecast prepared for the same period as the operating profit forecast
- Discuss with management the rationale for using 30% of revenue as a basis for determining the amount of other expenses

7

Professional marks

Analysis and evaluation

- Appropriate assessment of the ethical and professional issues raised in relation to the proposed acceptance of Setter as a client
- Effective appraisal of the information given about the proposed client to determine the issues involved in the decision about acceptance
- Relevant explanation of importance of obtaining customer due diligence information, and of the information that is required

Professional scepticism and judgement

- Effective challenge and critical assessment of the details given of the client
- Demonstration of the ability to probe into what might lie behind the issues that the client (Setter) presents with
- Appropriate application of professional judgement to determine the procedures to perform on Setter's profit forecast

Maximum	5
Total	25

(a) (i) **Ethical and other matters to be considered before accepting Setter Ltd as a client of the firm**

Requirements and guidance relevant to accepting and continuing client relationships is contained in ISQM (UK) 1 *Quality Management for Firms that Perform Audits or Reviews of Financial Statements or Other Assurance or Related Services Engagements*. The fundamental requirements are that a firm must consider:

- Its competence to perform the engagement and whether the firm has the capabilities, including time and resources to do so,
- Whether the relevant ethical requirements can be complied with, and
- The integrity of the client, and whether there is information which would lead it to conclude that the client lacks integrity.

Competence and resources

Looking at each consideration in turn, there seems no reason why Pointer & Co would not have the competence to carry out the assignment, which is a limited assurance review of historical financial statements. Being a firm of Chartered Certified Accountants and performing assurance services such as the audit of Vizsla Ltd means that the firm has the relevant knowledge and experience to perform a high-quality limited assurance review.

ANSWERS

It should be confirmed that a limited assurance review of the financial statements is appropriate. The company's revenue is stated as £8 million, which is below the audit exemption threshold of £10.2 million. However, according to the Companies Act 2006, to be exempt from audit, two out of three of the following criteria must be met:

- Annual turnover of no more than £10.2 million
- Assets worth no more than £5.1 million
- 50 or fewer employees on average

It is possible, though perhaps unlikely, that the company's assets and number of employees exceed the criteria, in which case a full audit would be necessary. In addition, the £8 million stated revenue should be confirmed, in case the actual amount of revenue is higher.

However, the pressure to perform the audit for a low fee could impact on Pointer & Co's ability to perform a high-quality limited assurance review if insufficient resources are made available, given the potential restriction on the fee which can be charged to provide the service. ISQMISQM 1 also mentions that where the client is aggressively concerned with maintaining the firm's fees as low as possible, this can indicate a lack of integrity of the client.

Ethical issues

In terms of ethics there are several matters to consider. First, it appears that Vizsla Ltd is putting pressure on Pointer & Co to accept the engagement. Vizsla Ltd is a relatively significant client of Pointer & Co, providing 10% of the firm's annual practice income, and there is an intimidation threat in that Vizsla Ltd has threatened to move to another audit provider if Pointer & Co does not accept Setter Ltd as a client and perform the work for a low fee. This could also be perceived as a self-interest threat in that Pointer & Co has a financial interest in maintaining a good relationship with Vizsla Ltd.

In relation to the self-interest threat created by potential fee dependency, the FRC *Ethical Standard* requires that where it is expected that the total fees for services receivable from a non-listed audit client will regularly exceed 10% of the annual fee income of the firm but will not regularly exceed 15%, the engagement partner shall disclose that expectation to the firm's ethics partner and to those charged with governance of the audited entity and the firm shall arrange an external independent quality review of the engagement to be undertaken before the firm's report is finalised.

A further ethical issue arises from the suggestion that Pointer & Co should provide tax planning advice to Setter Ltd and prepare its tax submissions. The FRC *Ethical Standard* suggests that this type of work could give rise to a range of threats to independence including management, advocacy, self-interest. A self-review threat could also rise if the tax figures are material to the financial statements because Pointer & Co would have some input to the tax figures which form part of the financial statements which would then be subject to the limited assurance review. Providing the tax planning advice could also be seen as acting on behalf of management, further impairing the objectivity of the limited assurance provided on the financial statements. An advocacy threat may arise should the firm represent the client's interests, for example, when presenting the tax submissions to HMRC.

However, the firm may be able to provide such services, provided that there is informed management and appropriate safeguards are applied to reduce the self-review threat to a level where independence is not compromised, for example, through the use of separate teams to provide the limited assurance review and the tax services and by having an independent second partner to review the work performed. If safeguards do not reduce the threats to an acceptable level, then the tax service should not be carried out in addition to the limited assurance review.

Client integrity

Preparing the personal tax computations of Gordon Potts is less of an ethical issue in terms of objectivity as his personal tax is a separate issue and not reflected in the company's financial statements, but there may be other issues with providing this advice, linked to integrity, which will be discussed next.

The integrity of Gordon Potts will need to be carefully evaluated. There is nothing wrong with him having business interests in several companies, though information about each of these will need to be obtained. The key issues with integrity relate to the breach of employment law and his taking money from a company pension plan to set up a business which is managed by his son. The breach of employment law indicates that Gordon Potts has a questionable reputation and possibly that he has been involved in criminal activity, depending on what laws have been breached, and the seriousness of the non-compliance. The information comes from a newspaper article, so it may not be very credible and may not even be true, and more information will need to be sought on this issue.

Taking money from the company pension plan is likely to be a breach of the relevant regulations, and it would seem that this was done for the benefit of his son. The fact that this business is located in a foreign country makes the business arrangements complicated, and while it could be completely innocent, it could also mean that there is something more sinister behind the connections between the companies, for example, it could be an arrangement to facilitate money laundering.

Pointer & Co must obtain sufficient information to carefully evaluate the appropriateness of accepting Setter Ltd as a client, and they must document the acceptance decision in accordance with ISQM (UK) 1.

(ii) **The importance of performing know your client procedures and the information which should be obtained**

Know your client (KYC) procedures are performed as part of anti-money laundering regulations, which all audit firms should have in place when accepting new clients. It refers to the firm obtaining information to be able to identify who the prospective client is and verify identity by reference to independent and reliable source material. This is a crucial part of risk assessment when taking on a new client and allows the firm to understand not only the identity of the prospective client, but also the nature of the business and its source of funds.

Specifically, the firm should perform the following procedures:

- Identify the customer and verify their identity using documents, data or information obtained from a reliable and independent source.
- Confirm the identities of all shareholders, including the specific family members who collectively own 90% of the company's share capital, and the other shareholder(s) who own the remaining 10%.
- Identify any beneficial owner who is not the client. This is the individual (or individuals) behind the client who ultimately own or control the client or on whose behalf a transaction or activity is being conducted.
- Where a business relationship is established, understand the purpose and intended nature of the relationship, for example, details of the customer's business or the source of the funds.

Businesses must also conduct ongoing monitoring to identify large, unusual or suspicious transactions as part of KYC. All of the documents obtained for the purpose of carrying out KYC checks must be retained for a minimum of five years from the end of the business relationship.

In this scenario, the information which should be obtained includes:

- Confirm the identity of Gordon Potts; photographic evidence, for example his passport, should be seen and a copy taken, along with other means of identification showing his address, for example, recent utility bills or bank statements.
- In relation to Setter Ltd, the company certificate of incorporation should be seen, to confirm its legal status and the date and place of incorporation.

- A Companies House search on Setter Ltd should take place, this will confirm the existence of the company, the shareholders and directors and will provide some financial information. This will confirm that Gordon Potts is the 'beneficial owner' of the entity – ie that he is the person who owns or controls, directly or indirectly, more than 25% of the shares or voting rights or who otherwise exercises control over the directors.
- The identity of the other companies controlled by Gordon Potts should also be found, and searches on them conducted, to confirm their existence and the nature of the relationship with Setter Ltd.
- The latest financial statements of Setter Ltd, and the other companies in which Gordon Potts has an interest should be reviewed. This will help Pointer & Co to understand the businesses and their relationship with each other, identify the sources of income and whether there are significant transactions between the companies.
- Identify the source of funding for the company, whether there are bank loans or other providers of finance, and the nature of the finance provided in terms of when it is repayable, whether any company assets are provided as collateral for the debt, and whether Gordon Potts or other shareholders have made personal guarantees in respect of any sources of company finance.
- While not strictly part of confirming the identity of Gordon or his companies, Pointer & Co would clearly need to obtain further information about the breach of employment law and confirm the facts surrounding the situation. Currently the only information available is from a newspaper article and this may not be a credible source.

(b) **Examination procedures on the operating profit forecast of Vizsla Ltd**

General procedures:

- Enquire as to the identity of the preparer of the operating profit forecast, and assess their competence, especially given that interest costs have been included as part of operating profit which is incorrect.
- Obtain an understanding as to the procedures and controls which have been followed in the preparation of the forecast, for example, has the forecast been approved by a senior member of the company's accounting team.
- Confirm that the accounting policies applied in Vizsla Ltd's financial statements have been consistently applied in the preparation of the operating profit forecast, for example, that design costs are expensed rather than capitalised as a development cost.
- Confirm that the assumptions underpinning the forecast are in line with knowledge of the business obtained from performing the company's audit, for example, the seasonality of the sales can be confirmed by looking at the audit evidence obtained in the audit of revenue.
- Re-cast the forecast to ensure it is arithmetically correct.

Specific procedures:

- Enquire whether a more detailed profit forecast is available, or ask management to prepare one, for example, detailing out cost of sales and other expenses. In addition, request a forecast statement of financial position and statement of cash flows.

> **Tutorial note.** There could be matters which make the profit forecast unachievable revealed through assessment of the statement of financial position and statement of cash flows, eg the timing of the working capital cycle may make achieving the profit forecast unachievable if funds are not available at certain points of time especially given the seasonal nature of the business.

- Request that management prepare a profit forecast in the same format as audited financial statements and in accordance with IFRS Standards, ie the interest cost should be shown below the operating profit line.

- Having obtained the cost of sales figure for each six-month period, recalculate the gross profit figures given in the forecast. Compare this to gross profit margins in the prior year audited financial statements and investigate any anomalies.
- Having obtained a break down showing the components of cost of sales and other expenses, for each significant category of expense, perform analytical review to confirm that the forecast costs appear to be in line with expectations, and discuss any unusually high or low forecast costs with management.
- Based on the above, assess whether there are any missing categories of expenditure which have not been included in the forecast, eg there is no depreciation included in the forecast.
- For revenue, which is forecast to increase by a significant amount (eg 11.8% increase comparing the six months ending 31 March 20X6 and 31 March 20X7), consider whether the forecast appears overly optimistic. For instance, there is not a corresponding increase in marketing costs to support the forecast increase in revenue.
- Compare revenue in the year forecast to 30 September 20X6 with revenue from prior years' audited financial statements. Investigate any unusual trends through discussion with management.
- Review any marketing plans and discuss with an appropriate senior member of staff, for example, the sales director, to establish the rationale for forecasting a significant increase in revenue, for example, there may be plans to introduce new product lines. Consider this in light of the fact that design costs and marketing are not forecast to increase by a significant amount.
- Review the design costs as they appear to be fairly static with just a small increase to achieve a much bigger % increase in revenue. Discuss with management and assess if such an increase in revenue can be achieved with such a small increase in design costs.
- Confirm costs to appropriate supporting documentation, eg staff costs to human resources projected costs, marketing costs to advertising budgets.
- Assess whether the overdraft is likely to be repaid in September 20X6, for example, by obtaining and reviewing the cash flow forecast prepared for the same period as the operating profit forecast.
- Discuss with management the rationale for using 30% of revenue as a basis for determining the amount of other expenses. In addition, compare this to the results of audit procedures performed on expenses to gauge whether 30% appears to be a reasonable basis.

8 Chennai

Workbook references

Chapters 2 and 12.

Top tips

Part (a)(i) was a real bread-and-butter question for AAA – this material should be very familiar to you indeed. The main issue here should have been keeping to a reasonable time limit for this question part. If you did find this requirement tricky then you will need to make sure you know this material well for your exam.

Part (a)(ii) followed on from (i). The key was that the requirement asked for 'advantages and disadvantages **to Delhi**', ie you had to apply yourself to the scenario. In many respects this makes the question easier, as all you need to do is to read the scenario and think about how an audit might help in this situation. As usual, each part of the scenario is there to tell you something, so try to think about what bearing it might have on whether an audit is needed.

Don't forget that it's about disadvantages as well; some are implied by the scenario, eg the part about staff studying for their ACCA exams hints at staff being less experienced at dealing with auditors, and also perhaps having less time available.

Part (b) should have been a reasonable ethics question. The self-review threat is fairly clear. You should have been able to spot that designing internal controls is management's responsibility – not the auditor's – and therefore should not be undertaken.

In a way the question was a little tricky, because the existence of internal control problems hints at the audit process – how can the auditor rely on these controls? – but the requirement asks only for the ethical and professional issues. If your answer focuses on the audit process then presumably there will be no marks for this, but there are marks available for the effect on governance (communication with the audit committee), and for whether the audit was conducted properly. In any case, you only need four marks to pass this part of the question.

It should be noted that the solutions given for this question in particular are significantly longer than anything a student could produce in an exam, so you should not be aiming to write this much in your answer.

Easy marks

Part (a)(i) was easy and was probably why many people chose this question in their real exam.

ACCA examining team's comments

This question required candidates to provide advice to two clients around the difference between an audit and a limited assurance review, and providing non-audit services.

In relation to the differences between audit and limited review, most candidates demonstrated a sound understanding of both and were able to succinctly explain the differences between them, including the different audiences for each.

Strong answers were tailored based on the specifics of the scenario and therefore provided relevant advice to the client in question. For example, strong answers highlighted that a full audit would be beneficial to the fast-growing client as it would give more credibility to the company, especially as it may be seeking bank finance. Candidates are reminded that at this level answers need to be responsive to the question requirements and should not simply be an exercise in reproducing everything that they know about a topic.

Candidates were also asked to advise a listed audit client, asking for a review of their control systems due to concerns about weaknesses in controls shortly after your firm had signed off the most recent auditor's report.

Few candidates recognised the potential implications on the accuracy of the auditor's report which had been recently issued and that these potential weaknesses could undermine that opinion. Clearly further details were needed to establish if the deficiencies in control would have had any significant impact on those financial statements.

Many candidates simply provided a discussion of the advantages to the client of having a review of the internal control system but failed to appreciate that undertaking such a review for a listed client would be prohibited by the *Code*, and this again demonstrated that many candidates did not have a good enough understanding of the requirement of the ethical guidelines. In such circumstances, opting for a separate team is not an effective safeguard and the review should not be done.

Marking guide

Marks

(a) Generally 1 mark available for each well explained point:

Audit v limited review

- Regulatory requirements – audit exemption limit
- Determination of scope
- Nature of procedures
- Reasonable v moderate levels of assurance
- Audit **opinion**

'The financial statements are true and fair...'

- Review engagement conclusion

'Based on our review nothing has coming to our attention...'

- Negative v positive wording

Advantages and disadvantages of audit

- Accountability to external shareholder
- Renegotiation of loan facility
- Reliability of information for internal decisions
- Potential mandatory audit if company grows
- Overseas trading relationships
- Review of internal controls
- Risk of misstatement due to changes in accounting staff
- Cost of full audit
- Potentially no need for high level of assurance
- More invasive nature of audit

Maximum 12

(b) **Mumbai plc**

Generally 1 mark for each well explained ethical and professional threat; 0.5 mark available for each recommended safeguard:

- Self-review threat
- Management threat
- Engagement quality reviewer considers significance of threats
- Discussion on provision of internal audit service to client
- Possible safeguards to avoid management threat
- Restriction on internal audit services for listed clients
- Competence if review is not related to financial controls
- Responsibilities of auditor in relation to internal controls
- Possible deficiency in external audit procedures
- Nature/severity of deficiencies not clear

Maximum 8

Professional marks

Analysis and evaluation

- Apposite discussion of the differences between an audit and a review
- Effective appraisal of the information given about Delhi to determine the relative advantages and disadvantages to it of having a full audit

Professional scepticism and judgement

- Effective challenge and critical assessment of the details given of the client
- Awareness of the risks that could arise when providing services to a listed client
- Appropriate application of professional judgement to the request to review Mumbai's internal control system

Commercial acumen

- Appropriate consideration of the commercial context of the audit and the balance between its costs and benefits for audit clients

Maximum 5

Total 25

(a) **Difference between an audit and a limited assurance review**

The Companies Act 2006 exempts small companies from the requirement to have an audit where revenue is not more than £10.2 million, aggregate gross assets are not more than £5.1 million and the number of employees is not more than 50. The company must satisfy two out of three of these criteria for two years to be considered small and therefore audit exempt. From the information given in respect of Delhi Ltd, it would seem that it is indeed exempt from the statutory audit requirement. The company can, however, choose to have an audit of its financial statements.

The scope of and procedures performed during an audit are determined by the audit firm in accordance with ISA (UK) requirements. The scope of a limited assurance review is agreed by the firm providing the services and the client. In the UK, there are no specific regulatory requirements relevant to review engagements for financial statements (other than guidance on the review of interim financial statements) and the firm may use guidance contained in documents such as International Standards on Review Engagements issued by the IAASB in determining the scope.

An audit involves a wide range of procedures used to obtain evidence, including both tests of controls and substantive procedures. An audit involves inspection of documents, recalculation, observation, enquiry and analytical procedures, amongst other procedures. Limited reviews use a narrower range of procedures, focusing primarily on enquiry and analytical procedures.

Overall, the level of assurance provided by an audit is much higher than that provided by a limited review. In an audit, the practitioner gives a reasonable level of assurance, whereas in a review engagement the practitioner gives a moderate level of assurance.

This has a significant impact on the wording of the respective reports. In an auditor's report, the practitioner expresses an opinion on the fair presentation of the financial statements. An example of this would be:

'In our opinion the financial statements give a true and fair view, in all material respects, of the financial position of the company, its financial performance and its cash flows for the year ended in accordance with International Financial Reporting Standards (IFRSs).'
(ISA (UK) 700)

A review engagement report does not express any opinion on the fair presentation of the financial statements reviewed, instead the report expresses a conclusion based only upon the work performed. For example:

'Based on the review performed, nothing has come to our attention which causes us to believe that the financial statements do not present fairly, in all material respects, ... in accordance with International Financial Reporting Standards.' (ISRE 2400)

The review engagement report is often referred to as a negative form of opinion, whereas the auditor's report is referred to a positive statement regarding the fair presentation of the financial statements.

Advantages and disadvantages to Delhi Ltd of having an audit

Advantages

One of the key differences between an audit and a review engagement is that an audit provides a reasonable level of assurance, whereas a review only provides limited assurance. This means that an audit provides stronger assurances to users of the financial statements regarding their accuracy and credibility.

This would be significant for Delhi Ltd for a number of reasons. The first is that the company now has an external shareholder, Robert Hyland, who is not part of the executive management team. With this separation of ownership and control comes an increased need to hold the management of the company accountable to the external shareholders and having a full audit will provide a much stronger form of accountability.

Second, Delhi Ltd has a bank loan facility which is due to expire in 20X7. Given the ambitious expansion plans of Delhi Ltd, it is likely that the company will want to renew this facility and they may even seek to obtain more loan finance. If this is the case, it is very likely that the bank will seek a reasonable level of assurance over the financial statements. By electing to have an annual audit now, it may avoid delays in 20X7 when the company comes to renegotiate terms with the bank.

Finally, the internal management team needs good quality information on which to base their operational and strategic decisions. As the business grows and the significance of those decisions increases, it becomes more important that the management team has information which they can rely on. Having fully audited financial statements, as opposed to a limited review, will increase the confidence of management in the accuracy of the information used.

Another benefit of having a full audit now is that, whilst the business is currently under the audit exemption threshold, it is rapidly expanding and may soon exceed the threshold and be subject to mandatory audit. One of the key problems of auditing a business for the first time is that there is no existing assurance over the opening balances and comparative figures. In this case the first audit is much more time consuming, and therefore expensive, as the audit team has to invest more time investigating prior year figures. The requirement to review the prior year would be much less onerous if the company began to have their financial statements audited now while they were still relatively small, and this would lead to a more efficient audit in the future.

Delhi Ltd also plans to expand its customer base. Trading internationally usually adds extra complications due to the added complexity in the supply chain, foreign exchange and simple lack of familiarity with the company. Customers may want assurances that any company they sign a trading agreement with has the resources to satisfy their contractual obligations. For this reason, having fully audited accounts, as opposed to accounts which have had a limited review, may give potential customers increased confidence in the financial position of Delhi Ltd and may improve their chances of forming new trade partnerships.

There has also been a recent change in the accounting department of Delhi Ltd. This is normal in a rapidly expanding business but it creates new challenges. Often the accounting systems of small companies are unsophisticated but as the company grows the systems soon become outdated and less effective. An audit incorporates a review of effectiveness of the internal control systems relevant to the production of the financial statements and any deficiencies identified by the auditor would be reported to management. Given the changes Delhi Ltd has experienced, a full audit may help them assess the effectiveness of their internal systems and make changes where necessary. The systems would not be assessed with a limited review.

The change in staff in the accounts department also increases the risk of misstatement of the financial statements due to their lack of familiarity with the company and the accounting systems. The fact that the new recruits are both part-qualified further increases the risk of misstatement of the financial statements because the trainees may not be fully able to process all of the transactions and events relevant to the business. An audit is a more thorough investigation of the financial statements than a review and would be much more likely to identify misstatements, providing management with more reliable figures upon which to base their decisions.

Disadvantages

While an audit is a more thorough investigation, it is also more expensive than a review. For a small company an audit may be prohibitively expensive, whereas a review may be more affordable.

If the company is exempt, an audit may also be an unnecessary cost. Delhi Ltd already managed to raise a loan without the need for audited accounts. The external shareholder is also an ex-business partner of Mr Dattani and it is likely that they have a good working relationship. If Mr Hyland needs assurances, it is possible that Mr Dattani could satisfy this on an informal basis without the need to incur the costs of an audit. Mr Hyland also decided to invest knowing that the company was not subject to audit, so it may not be a concern of his.

An audit is also more invasive than a limited review and would require the staff of Delhi Ltd to provide more information to the auditor and give up more of their time than would be the case with a limited review. Given the relative inexperience of the accounts team, Mr Dattani may prefer to choose the less invasive limited review now and perform a full audit in the future when the team is more knowledgeable of the business.

(b) **Mumbai plc**

Review of internal controls

Reviewing the internal controls of an audit client would fall under the definition of an audit related service according to the FRC *Ethical Standard* if the review was being conducted as part of the audit. However, in this case the audit is complete, and the review would therefore be a separate engagement to provide a non-audit service.

There are several ethical threats which arise when an audit firm reviews the internal controls of an audited entity, especially if that review relates to controls relevant to the financial reporting of the company. First, a self-review threat is created as the auditor would consequently assess the effectiveness of the control system during the next external audit.

Second, the design, implementation and maintenance of internal controls are management responsibilities. If the auditor were to assist in this process, it may be considered that they were assuming these management responsibilities and making management decisions regarding the company's control environment and control activities. The FRC's *Ethical Standard* states that a management threat arises where the audit firm becomes closely aligned with the views and interests of management and the auditor's objectivity and independence may be impaired or may be perceived to be impaired.

There is a risk that the engagement could stray into an internal audit service. The FRC's *Ethical Standard* is clear in stating that the audit firm shall not undertake an engagement to provide internal audit services to an audited entity under any circumstances. It is therefore crucial that the scope of the engagement be clarified to ensure that it is limited to the provision of information that is a by-product of the audit, rather than an internal audit service.

The FRC's *Ethical Standard* states that for listed entities such as Mumbai plc, only the non-audit services that are specifically listed in the *Ethical Standard* may be provided. The *Ethical Standard* includes an entry for a service to review operational controls, so it may be possible in principle for the service to be accepted.

The consequences of any threats to objectivity are heightened due to Mumbai plc being a listed entity. The FRC's *Ethical Standard* requires that for listed entities the engagement quality reviewer must consider ethical threats and compliance with Ethical Standards, form an independent opinion as to the appropriateness and adequacy of the safeguards applied, and consider the adequacy of the documentation of the audit engagement partner's consideration of the auditor's objectivity and independence.

It would be prudent for the firm to turn down the non-audit work, as the threats appear too significant to be reduced to an acceptable level by the use of safeguards, unless it can be clearly demonstrated that the controls subject to review form an insignificant part of the financial reporting process, that management acknowledges all responsibility in relation to any changes which will be made to the systems and controls, and it is clear that the service does not constitute an internal audit service.

If the audit firm were ethically able to accept the appointment, the competence of the firm to provide the non-audit work would need to be considered. The review of internal controls is part of routine audit work, and therefore the audit firm should possess the necessary competencies.

Concerns regarding deterioration in controls

One of the responsibilities of the auditor is to evaluate the design and implementation of the client's controls relevant to the audit in order to assist with the identification of risks of material misstatement. This includes the specific requirement to consider the risk of material misstatement due to fraud.

If deficiencies of internal controls are identified, the auditor has to assess the potential impact on the financial statements and design a suitable response in order to reduce audit risk to an acceptable level. The auditor is also responsible for communicating significant deficiencies in internal control to those charged with governance on a timely basis.

The audit committee has suggested that a number of internal control deficiencies have recently been identified which they were not previously aware of. This suggests that these were not issues identified or reported to those charged with governance by the auditor.

If these internal control deficiencies relate to systems relevant to the audit, it may suggest that the audit firm's consideration of the internal control system failed to detect these potential problems, which may indicate ineffective audit planning. If so, this increases the risk that the audit procedures designed were inappropriate and that there is a heightened risk that the audit team failed to detect material misstatements during the audit. In the worst-case scenario this could mean that Chennai & Co issued an inappropriate audit opinion.

The circumstances are not clear though; the audit committee of Mumbai plc has not specified which controls appear to have deteriorated and whether these were relevant to the audit. There is also no indication of the potential scale of any fraud or inefficient commercial practice. It is possible that the risks resulting from the deficiencies are so small that they did not lead to a risk of material misstatement. In these circumstances, the audit team may have identified the deficiencies as not being significant and reported them to an appropriate level of operating management.

In order to assess this further, the manager should examine the audit file and review the documentation in relation to the evaluation of the internal controls of Mumbai plc and assess any subsequent communications to management and those charged with governance. The concerns raised by the audit committee should be noted as points to take forward into next year's audit, when they should be reviewed and evaluated as part of planning the audit for the 20X6 year end.

Additionally, Chennai & Co should contact the audit committee of Mumbai plc to seek further clarification on the nature and extent of the deficiencies identified and whether this has resulted in any actual or suspected acts of fraud.

9 Bunk

Workbook references

Chapters 2 and 4.

Top tips

The requirement for this question contained several different elements, so you had a lot to bear in mind when reading the scenarios and constructing your answer. There are at least four elements that you had to think of: ethics, quality management, firm-wide policies, and actions for the firm to take. The marking scheme contains quite a few marks for actions, and it would have been difficult to score well if you had not included any.

Part (a) was a nice mini scenario on fee pressure and a related drop in audit quality. You needed to respond to the issues in the scenario and connect them up with your book-knowledge. For example, the scenario contains the issue of the audit committee refusing to increase the fee – you needed to note this, and state that it is an intimidation threat. Likewise, you should note that materiality was increased in order to reduce the amount of audit work done, and then connect this to your book knowledge of quality management.

Part (b) should not have been difficult, provided that you read the scenario carefully. This may have been more difficult, however, if you do not have experience of working in an audit firm (and thus of off-shoring). In some ways there was not that much to say for the 5 marks available. Essentially, it is OK to off-shore non-judgemental work, but it is not OK to off-shore work that requires judgement and in particular knowledge of the client (which those working off-shore are unlikely to have). It's fairly clear in the scenario that the numerical checks on documentation are OK, but that reviewing board minutes is not OK. This then raises quality management issues, which connect to the 'firm-wide policies' asked for by the requirement because the scenario states that Bunk & Co encourages this practice, ie this is a firm-wide policy that may have implications for quality management.

Part (c) featured a slightly tricky situation in that the finance director was not the audit engagement partner, but merely another audit partner in the firm. This means that the issue is not quite cut-and-dried, but it is clear that this partner had an influence on the audit of the company he had just left, and that ethical threats arose from this. This was a good place to suggest actions for the auditor, such as discussing the issue with the ethics partner and the audit committee.

Easy marks

Part (a) contained some easy marks for identifying the intimidation threat, and the quality management issues there were fairly clear-cut.

ACCA examining team's comments

Part (a) described how the audit committee of Wire Ltd had refused to agree to an increase in audit fees despite an increase in the company's operations. Consequently the audit firm increased the materiality level used during the audit, reduced sample sizes used when obtaining audit evidence and cut out some review procedures. Many candidates attempted this part of the question well. **Effective answers** explained the intimidation threat to objectivity caused by fee pressure and went on to discuss the impact of each of the issues raised in the scenario on the quality of the audit that had been performed. It was pleasing to see many candidates discuss matters such as sampling risk and the need for review procedures to assure the quality of audit work and to reduce the audit firm's detection risk. **Weaker answers** tended to be repetitive, and for each of the issues simply say that 'not enough evidence could be obtained' resulting in material misstatements and an inappropriate audit opinion.

Part (b) focused on the issue of off-shoring audit work. Answers ranged in quality, with some good attempts which identified that while off-shoring can bring efficiencies to an audit, care must be taken in deciding the type of work that is performed by the overseas office. From this scenario it should have been identified that off-shoring procedures such as the reading of board minutes to identify audit issues was not appropriate, but relatively few answers mentioned this point. Weaker answers tended to suggest that overseas offices would be incompetent and unable to perform even the simplest of audit procedures. Some candidates misinterpreted the information provided and assumed that the scenario was about using component auditors in a group situation, which was not the case.

In part (c) most candidates realised that the former finance director could have influenced the partner and had motivation to do so given that he held shares in Wire Ltd for a period of time after joining the audit firm. **Stronger candidates** were able to clearly explain the specific ethical threats that arose from the scenario, provided sensible recommendations, and also commented on the audit firm needing stronger firm-wide policies in the event of recruiting new audit partners from audit clients.

The scenario also stated that audit team members were being encouraged to cross-sell non-audit services to audit clients and that they would be appraised on this. The answers here tended not to focus on the problems caused by appraising staff on their success in selling services to audit clients but instead discussed generally the ethical problems of providing non-audit services to audit clients. While not irrelevant, these discussions tended to be very general and not applied to the information in the scenario, resulting in answers that lacked focus.

It was also clear that **many candidates were not guided by the mark allocation for the various parts of the question**, and a significant number of answers to part (c) were the same length as the answer to part (a). As mentioned earlier, candidates should bear the mark allocation in mind, and use it to determine how long to spend in answering each part of the question.

Marking guide	**Marks**
(a) Generally up to 1.5 marks for each relevant point explained, to include 1 mark for each action recommended and 0.5 mark for identification of ethical threats.	
Fee pressure and sampling risk	
• Intimidation threat identified and explained	
• Fee should not remain the same when the scope of audit is increased	
• Discuss with audit committee and communicate with those charged with governance	
• Increased materiality level reduces audit work and increases detection risk	
• Audit work to be reviewed for completeness and sufficiency (1 mark)	
• Use of judgement increases sampling risk	
• Some items excluded from sample, so sample cannot be representative of population	
Maximum	6
(b) Generally up to 1.5 marks for each relevant point explained, to include 1 mark for each action recommended and 0.5 mark for identification of ethical threats.	
Off-shoring audit work	
• No regulation to prohibit off-shoring arrangements	
• Increasingly common way to improve audit efficiency	
• Problem is those performing audit work lack knowledge and experience of the client	
• Off-shoring should focus on low-risk and low-judgement areas of the audit	
• Strong controls and monitoring should be in place	
Maximum	5

ANSWERS

Marking guide	**Marks**

(c) Generally up to 1.5 marks for each relevant point explained, to include 1 mark for each action recommended and 0.5 mark for identification of ethical threats.

Recent service with audit client, financial self-interest and cross-selling services

- Recent service with client creates self-interest, self-review and familiarity threats
- Persons joining audit firm from a client should not be part of that client's audit team
- Russell seems to have acted as if he were a member of the audit team
- A review of quality management procedures should be performed
- Russell's shareholding creates a self-interest threat
- The shareholding should have been disposed of immediately
- Consider why this did not happen – firm's policies should be reviewed
- Cross-selling creates a self-interest threat
- According to the Code key audit partners should not be evaluated based on cross-selling
- According to ES 4 no audit team members should be involved with cross-selling
- The initiative should be withdrawn as soon as possible

Maximum 9

Professional marks

Analysis and evaluation

- Analysis of the ethical issues present in a range of scenarios
- Effective appraisal of the information to make suitable recommendations for appropriate courses of action

Professional scepticism and judgement

- Effective identification of potential threats from complex scenario information
- Awareness of the risks that could arise from different situations

Commercial acumen

- Appropriate consideration of the commercial determinants of audit fees and their interaction with ethical issues
- Discuss of the interaction between commercial and quality management issues in relation to the proposed off-shoring of audit work

Maximum 5

Total 25

(a) **Intimidation threat**

When the audit client imposes fee pressure on the audit firm, an intimidation threat to objectivity arises. IESBA's *Code of Ethics* defines the intimidation threat as the threat that a professional accountant will be deterred from acting objectively because of actual or perceived pressures, and gives an example of an intimidation threat where the audit firm is being pressured to reduce inappropriately the extent of work performed in order to match the fee they can obtain to the work performed.

Action

The matter should have been discussed with Wire Ltd's audit committee, with the audit firm stressing that the new locations would lead to an increased scope of the audit, and therefore the fee should increase rather than remain the same. It should also be brought to the attention of Bunk & Co's partner responsible for ethics.

Materiality – quality management

The fee pressure has resulted in the materiality level being increased, presumably in order to reduce the level of audit procedures performed and thus the cost of the audit. This leads to a risk that insufficient audit evidence may have been obtained to support the audit opinion, with the risk heightened by the fact that some review procedures were not carried out. This in itself indicates that appropriate quality management procedures have not been applied to the audit.

ISA (UK) 220 (Revised) *Quality Management for an Audit of Financial Statements* requires the audit engagement partner to review the audit documentation to be satisfied that audit work is complete and that sufficient appropriate audit evidence has been obtained to support the conclusions reached and for the auditor's report to be issued.

Sample sizes

There are also quality management issues with the selection of samples to be used in tests of detail. First, the use of judgemental sampling may result in sample sizes which are smaller than would have been selected using statistical sampling methods, or in the selection of items which are not representative of the whole population. ISA (UK) 530 *Audit sampling* requires the auditor to determine a sample size sufficient to reduce sampling risk to an acceptably low level, and to select items for the sample in such a way that each sampling unit in the population has an equal chance of selection. The risk is that the use of judgement has led to inappropriate audit conclusions being made.

Second, it seems that some items in the populations were completely excluded from the sample. There is a high risk that these items have not been subject to sufficient audit procedures and that the relevant assertions have not been covered by audit testing. For example, if the non-current assets have not been physically verified, and no other procedures relevant to their existence have been performed, then assets recognised in the financial statements may be overstated.

Conclusion

Given the pressure on fees which seems to be affecting the quality of audit work performed, Bunk & Co may wish to consider whether it is appropriate to continue with the audit engagement. The audit firm's concerns should be communicated to those charged with governance of Wire Ltd, and the audit committee should be made aware of the implications of the fee pressure on the audit.

(b) **Off-shoring of audit work**

The off-shoring of audit work has become increasingly common in the audit profession in the last few years, with global audit firms using low-cost overseas audit offices or service centres to perform some audit procedures. There is no regulation to prohibit this practice, but quality management implications have been brought into question.

If the overseas office is performing only low-risk and non-judgemental work, the risk to audit quality is relatively low. However, it seems in the case of Wire Ltd's audit other more subjective tasks were included in the off-shoring arrangement, such as the review of board minutes. In order to properly assess the contents of the board minutes for audit implications, the work should be performed by an auditor with sufficient knowledge and understanding of the audit client to be able to identify matters which are significant in the context of that audit. It is unlikely that an auditor in an overseas office with no direct understanding or experience of Wire Ltd would be able to identify relevant matters for the attention of the rest of the audit team.

If Bunk & Co wishes to continue the off-shoring of audit procedures, then controls must be put in place to ensure that only appropriate tasks are included in the arrangement, and that monitoring and review procedures are performed to give comfort on the quality of the work performed. The audit firm must ensure that its firm-wide policies adhere to the requirements of ISQM (UK) 1 *Quality Management for Firms that Perform Audits or Reviews of Financial Statements, or Other Assurance or Related Services Engagements*, and that commercial considerations do not take priority over the performance of high-quality audits.

Tutorial note. Credit will be awarded for other relevant comments on the issue of off-shoring audit work.

(c) **Finance director becoming audit partner**

Russell Bell moving from Wire Ltd to Bunk & Co to take up the position of audit partner creates potential threats to objectivity.

The IESBA *Code* states that self-interest, self-review or familiarity threats may be created if a member of the audit team has recently served as a director, officer, or employee of the audit client. Though the threats may be mitigated somewhat by him not being a formal member of the audit team of Wire Ltd, the fact that Russell helped the audit team (by providing information about the audited entity) means that the threats described above apply in this situation. There is a perception that the audit team is not independent.

The IESBA *Code* requires that if, during the period covered by the auditor's report, a member of the audit team served as a director or officer of the audit client (or was an employee in a position to exert significant influence over the preparation of the client's accounting records or the financial statements on which the firm will express an opinion), that person may not be included in the audit team. Clearly Russell's former position as finance director of Wire Ltd means that this requirement should have been applied to him.

The FRC's *Ethical Standard* (section B2) contains similar guidance and a more specific requirement, stating that where a former director or a former employee of an audited entity, who was in a position to exert significant influence over the preparation of the financial statements, joins the audit firm, that individual shall not be assigned to a position in which he or she is able to influence the conduct and outcome of the audit for that entity or its affiliates for a period of two years following the date of leaving the audited entity.

Action

The matter should be discussed with Bunk & Co's partner responsible for ethics, and it should also be discussed with Wire Ltd's audit committee, who are responsible for oversight of auditor independence.

Shareholding in client

The second issue is that Russell retained a shareholding in Wire Ltd for six months after his appointment as an audit partner in Bunk & Co. This gives rise to a self-interest threat to objectivity, as it would have been in Russell's interests to act in such a way as to maximise his financial interest in Wire Ltd until the point when he sold his shares. There is a general prohibition on auditors holding a financial interest in an audit client. The IESBA *Code* states that when a financial interest arises, it should be disposed of immediately in the case of an audit team member, or as soon as possible in the case of an individual who is not a member of the audit team. Given Russell's seniority, and the fact that he seems to have closely advised the audit team on matters relating to Wire Ltd, he should have made the disposal immediately. The FRC *Ethical Standard* (Part B2) contains similar guidance and requirements.

Concerns may arise over Bunk & Co's procedures in relation to staff and partner disclosure of financial interests in audited entities. Six months is a long period for the shares to have been held, and the firm should have procedures in place to ensure that such matters are monitored and quickly resolved.

Action

A review of the firm's procedures should take place, and Russell should be asked why he did not dispose of the shares more quickly.

Cross-selling

Finally, the audit firm's policy on cross-selling non-audit services raises ethical issues. The IESBA Code states that a self-interest threat is created when a member of the audit team is evaluated on or compensated for selling non-assurance services to that audit client. This is because the audit team member clearly has a financial interest in successful cross-selling, which may result in the selling of services which are inappropriate to the client, or which give rise to other independence threats which exist when non-audit services are provided to audited entities, or when fees from non-audit services are dependent on the audit service.

The significance of the self-interest threat depends on:

- The proportion of the individual's compensation or performance evaluation which is based on the sale of such services;
- The role of the individual on the audit team; and
- Whether promotion decisions are influenced by the sale of such services. (IESBA *Code*)

The IESBA *Code* states that a key audit partner shall not be evaluated on or compensated based on that partner's success in selling non-assurance services to the partner's audit client. Under the *Code*, it is not prohibited for other audit team members to cross-sell, but safeguards must be in place to reduce the potential threat to an acceptable level, such as a review of audit work performed.

However, the FRC *Ethical Standard* (section 4) *Fees, Remuneration and Evaluation Policies, Gifts and Hospitality, Litigation* contains more restrictive requirements. Under the FRC ES, it is not permissible for the performance evaluation of engagement team members to include elements relating to the cross-selling of goods and services to audited entities, and remuneration should not include elements based on such activity.

The audit firm's initiative therefore appears to contravene the requirements of the FRC ES, and the initiative should be removed as soon as possible. The firm must find other ways to generate income which are compliant with ethical standards and other relevant regulation.

10 Grape

Workbook references

Chapters 4, 8 and 0.

Top tips

The scenario gives you the figures to calculate materiality in a fairly obvious way (by stating that the 'draft financial statements show revenue of £12.5m, net profit of £400,000, and total assets of £78m'). This is almost always a hint that you're going to have to calculate materiality at some point in your answer, and the opportunity to do so comes up straight away in part (a)(i)'s requirement for 'matters to consider' in relation to audit evidence. These are easy marks, so to make sure you get them: calculate materiality, and then apply it to the scenario by stating whether the matter in question is actually material.

Part (a)(i) was a tricky requirement. If you read the question carefully, you could have noticed that it is asking for the 'audit evidence you should expect to find ***during* your file review**' in relation to the 'training costs **that have been capitalised**'. In other words, you're being asked for the evidence that you would find for the training costs as non-current asset additions in the year, **given that the audit team have not yet realised that the accounting treatment is wrong**. This is tricky, but these questions do come up. When they do, it's important not to panic. Read the requirement very carefully – as long as you answer the requirement, you should get marks for every (correct) thing that you say. Once you've understood the requirement correctly, it's actually a very straightforward question on audit evidence.

Part (b) should have been straightforward, as there were plenty of points in the scenario that you should have picked up on. You should have been looking to pass this part of question well – but without exceeding the time allocation for it!

Easy marks

There is one mark for just writing a conclusion to your answer to part (b), indicated by the word 'evaluate' in the requirement. As a general point, the examining team does like candidates to write introductions and conclusions to their answers, so get into the habit of writing something, no matter how short.

ACCA examining team's comments

This question was the best answered on the exam. It was pleasing to see that many candidates appeared to have read and understood the examining team's article on audit evidence and matters to be considered, as the quality of answers was undoubtedly better than previous sittings. Most candidates could discuss the relevant accounting treatments with a degree of confidence, most determined materiality, and most could come up with several specific pieces of audit evidence.

Approximately 10% of answers agreed with the accounting treatment for the capitalised training costs, which is not allowed. A further disappointment was how few candidates considered any inventory held by Banana Ltd in relation to its insolvent customer, which would need to be considered in terms of obsolescence.

For requirement (b), the vast majority of answers were sound, with almost all candidates able to identify some, if not all, of the quality management issues in the scenario. The lack of a planning meeting, inappropriate delegation of work, poor direction and supervision were identified by most. Some candidates considered not only the most obvious issues from the scenario, but also the overall impact on the audit, and went beyond simply repeating points from the scenario. However, some candidates failed to really evaluate the quality management issues and did little more than copy out sentences from the question, providing little explanation and development of the issue identified.

Marking guide	**Marks**

(a) (i) **Training costs**

Generally 1 mark per matter/evidence point:

Matters

- Correct calculation and assessment of materiality (max 1 mark)
- Cannot capitalise training costs
- Expenditure does not create an asset which the entity controls
- Potential qualification re material misstatement

Evidence

- Schedule of costs (0.5 mark only)
- Agree costs to supporting documentation
- Agree costs to cash book/bank statement (0.5 mark only)
- Cut-off procedure
- Compare to budgeted cost
- Confirm cost to approved plan/budget

Maximum — 6

(ii) **Trade receivable**

Generally 1 mark per matter/evidence point:

Matters

- Correct calculation and assessment of materiality (max 1 mark)
- Receivable impaired
- Consider any inventory in relation to Cherry Ltd

Marking guide	Marks
• Potential qualification re material misstatement	
• Impact of the two issues together on the audit opinion	
Evidence	
• Initial correspondence with administrators of Cherry Ltd	
• Confirmation with the administrators	
• Agreement to receivables ledger	
• Recalculations of impairment losses	
• Review of inventory schedules	
Maximum	6
(b) **Quality management matters**	
Up to 1.5 marks for each point evaluated from ideas list, plus 1 mark for overall conclusion:	
• No audit planning meeting – lack of direction	
• Absence of manager and senior – lack of supervision	
• Junior assigned difficult audit work (goodwill and WIP)	
• Junior helped out with inventory count – lack of understanding/supervision	
• Junior asked to challenge FD – inappropriate delegation	
• Audit running out of time – poor planning?	
• Changed sample size – inappropriate response to time pressure	
• Changed item selected in sample – inappropriate response to time pressure	
Maximum	8
Professional marks	
Analysis and evaluation	
• Appropriate use of the information given to determine the matters that require further investigation	
• Analysis of the areas of risk in relation to the scenario in order to determine the audit evidence that should be obtained	
Professional scepticism and judgement	
• Effective challenge of information, such as that given by the audit junior, evidence and assumptions supplied and, techniques carried out to support key facts and/or decisions	
• Appropriate application of professional judgement to draw conclusions and make informed decisions about the actions which are appropriate in the context and stage of the engagement.	
• Identification of faults in the degree of scepticism applied in the scenario described by the audit junior	
Maximum	5
Total	25

(a) (i) **Matters to consider**

Materiality

Materiality on revenue: (£150,000 ÷ £12.5m) = 1.2%

Materiality on net profit: (£150,000 ÷ £400,000) = 37.5%

Materiality on total assets: (£150,000 ÷ £78m) = <0.1%

The training costs are not material to the statement of financial position. They would, however, be material to profit.

Accounting treatment

The training costs are currently recognised as non-current assets. This is not in accordance with IAS 16 *Property, Plant and Equipment*, which states that the costs of training staff should always be treated as an expense, as they do not meet the definition of an asset, which requires that the entity has control of the asset (IAS 16: para. 19). This is very unlikely to be the case with training costs, as the staff will probably have the right to leave the company, meaning that Banana Ltd would not receive any subsequent economic benefit from having trained them.

The training costs should be treated as an expense in the statement of profit or loss.

Evidence

The file should contain:

- A review of the nature of the expenses themselves to verify that they are classified correctly and that they are in fact training costs
- Testing of entries selected according to sampling procedures detailed in the audit plan to supporting documentation, such as purchase invoices, and agreement of payment of related payables to the cashbook and to bank statements
- Evidence that a sample (selected according to audit plan) of entries are included in the accounts in the correct period
- Testing for completeness and that all invoices that should have been accrued for were in fact accrued for.

(ii) **Matters to consider**

Materiality for whole receivable

Materiality on revenue: (£120,000 ÷ £12.5m) = 1%

Materiality on net profit: (£120,000 ÷ £400,000) = 30%

Materiality on total assets: (£120,000 ÷ £78m) = <0.1%

The receivable is not material to the statement of financial position. It would, however, be material to the statement of profit or loss and other comprehensive income if an impairment loss were recognised in relation to it.

Accounting treatment

IFRS 9 *Financial Instruments* requires receivables to be recognised at fair value. The fair value of the Cherry Ltd receivable is the 25% that the administrators suggest it may be able to pay, ie £30,000. £90,000 (= £120,000 – £30,000) should therefore be recognised as an impairment loss in the statement of profit or loss.

Calculating materiality for the impairment loss:

Materiality on revenue: (£90,000 ÷ £12.5m) = 0.72%

Materiality on net profit: (£90,000 ÷ £400,000) = 22.5%

This is likely to be material to profit for the year.

Inventory

As Cherry Ltd is a customer, it is possible that Banana Ltd is holding inventory or work in progress that was ordered by Cherry Ltd. Grape & Co needs to ascertain whether this is the case, and if so whether the inventory can in fact be sold. If it cannot be, then it may be impaired and should be written down, recognising the loss in profit for the year.

Audit evidence

- External documentation confirming the insolvency of Cherry Ltd and the possible repayment of only 25% of the receivable
- Confirmation from the administrator of the 25% to be paid, including an indication of when this is likely to happen

- Agreement of the amount owed from the receivables listing to the ledger
- Review of inventory documentation, and evidence of enquiries made of management, regarding the value and the potential recoverability of any inventory relating to contracts with Cherry Ltd
- Calculations regarding the amount to be recognised as an impairment loss

(b) **Selection of engagement staff**

The fact that the junior had only worked on two audits before this is not a problem. However, it is important that they be given work appropriate to their level of skill and experience. This does not appear to have happened here, as detailed below.

No audit planning meeting

The audit planning meeting, led by the engagement partner, is a crucial part of the audit. It is the best way of giving the team an understanding of the client and should discuss both the overall strategy and the detailed audit plan, perhaps going into difficulties that have been experienced in previous years and which could come up again. The discussion should focus on what individual members of the team need to do. This is particularly important for less experienced and junior members of the team. Under ISA (UK) 220 (Revised) *Quality Management for an Audit of Financial Statements* the engagement partner must take overall responsibility for the audit, so this is a failure that starts and ends with them.

Audit manager away

The manager should not have given the senior responsibility for the audit while they were away on holiday for three weeks. It is important that an audit is properly supervised, and it may have been more appropriate for another manager to take responsibility for the audit.

Senior busy

Not only is there a question mark over whether they have the experience to manage the audit, but the senior is also busy with other assignments and thus unable to devote sufficient time to this one. It is very important that someone is available to supervise junior members of the audit team. This is not happening here.

It is also possible that the lack of attention paid by both the manager and the senior has led to the misstatements in respect of the trading costs and trade receivables not being picked up by the audit team.

Junior auditing goodwill and inventory

Goodwill is a complex accounting area to audit and should not be given to a junior to do. The same can be said of inventory and in particular work-in-progress. A junior is very unlikely to have developed the judgement needed to audit these areas. This seems to be the case here, as shown by the junior's error at the inventory count (see below).

Inventory count

The junior helped the client's staff to count raw materials at the inventory count, when they should instead have been observing that the client's staff were counting them correctly and in accordance with the count procedures. This would seem to imply that the junior had not been properly briefed on their responsibilities at the inventory count, as this is a relatively basic error.

It is likely that more audit evidence will be needed to be collected on inventory as a result of this error.

Junior asked to challenge FD

It is not appropriate for a junior to be asked to challenge a client's finance director regarding an accounting issue that they are unlikely to understand fully. This should have been done by either the audit manager or the partner, as they would be in a position to understand the technical issues involved and would carry sufficient authority with the client to make the challenge effective.

Running out of time to complete procedures

Pressure of time is an important contributor to audit risk. Audit time budgets should allow staff enough time to complete the audit to the required quality. It is also possible that the lack of supervision of the audit team's work has led to the audit being conducted inefficiently, with inadequate monitoring of progress and discussion of issues as they arise.

Reduction of sample sizes

It is clearly unacceptable to reduce sample sizes as a way of saving time. The sample sizes detailed in the audit plan should have been designed to gather sufficient appropriate audit evidence. Reducing the sample size beneath this point increases detection risk, and the risk of the auditor giving the wrong opinion.

Basis of sample selection

Selecting a sample on the basis of the ease of finding evidence for an item, is not an appropriate basis. Indeed, this might actively increase detection risk as it means by definition that those items for which evidence is not readily available, or might not even exist, are not tested.

Conclusion

The litany of failures above suggests that this engagement has not been adequately supervised, and that the audit work performed is inadequate in some areas. A detailed review should be performed so that any other shortcomings can be addressed.

Doubt is also cast over the sufficiency of the firm's quality management procedures. This matter should be referred to the relevant partner for consideration.

11 Clean

Workbook references

Chapters 1 and 2.

Top tips

Part (a) covered money laundering. This is another topical area, and one that is required to be on the AAA syllabus. Part (a)(i) is straight knowledge, so you should be looking to score at least two out of these three marks (but of course knowledge is a double-edged sword – if you don't know the material then you are in a difficult position).

Part (a)(ii) is trying to get you to think about how money laundering might appear in the real world, although the fact that you are told in the requirement that there may be indicators of money laundering makes it easier to pick them up post hoc.

Part (b) was the second appearance of ethics in this exam, and should again have been reasonable if you had been familiar with the material from Chapter 2 of the workbook.

Easy marks

The marks for stating anti-money laundering policies, in part (a), were among the easiest on the exam.

ACCA examining team's comments

This was a 25-mark question centred on money laundering and ethics at an existing audit client.

Requirement (a)(i) asked for a discussion of policies and procedures a firm should have in place in relation to an anti-money laundering programme. Most candidates were able to score full marks here. Candidates who did not score well either simply listed points with no discussion or confused the audit firm with the client and discussed controls over cash sales or places where the client could implement policies.

The second requirement (a)(ii) asked candidates to evaluate whether there were indicators of money laundering by the client or its staff. The majority of answers to this requirement were disappointing. Most candidates were able to correctly identify the indicators at the client which might suggest money laundering activities but made no attempt at explaining or evaluating those indicators. Simply stating sales are cash based or there is an off-shore bank account does not demonstrate an understanding of why these things are an indicator.

Candidates would do well to add the word **because** at the end of such sentences to force them to explain why something is a red flag. An example would be: 'The company sales are 75% cash based. This is a potential indicator of money laundering **because** cash-based sales are harder to trace.' An even stronger answer would then relate this back to the stages of money laundering, giving a 'So What?' to their answer: 'This means that additional cash can be introduced alongside genuine sales. This would represent the placement stage of money laundering.' Another mistake candidates often made in this part of the question was to discuss the risk of employee fraud/theft of the cash which was not required.

[BPP Note: the examiner's comments are based on the INT exam, which split part (a) into (i) and (ii). The comments are also applicable to the UK exam.]

Part (b) was a requirement to discuss the ethical and professional issues arising at the client. Candidates tended to perform poorly in this requirement. This was partly down to candidates not leaving enough time to properly address the requirement and partly because candidates are still not demonstrating the understanding of ethical issues or how to describe them sufficiently to attain marks. Candidates here also often showed a lack of detailed knowledge of the ethical guidance that would help them to properly analyse the issues in the question. In addition to the points on describing ethics made above in relation to question one, common mistakes made by candidates were to assume that invoicing the company for the tax work done on behalf of the directors was disallowed (rather than identifying that if the company was paying for his tax work, this should be considered director's remuneration and not part of the audit fee for disclosure and possible personal tax reasons) or stating that a trivial benefit provided to the auditors was not permitted which again is not the case, trivial hospitality benefits are permitted but should be approved by the firm. One of the most concerning points that was made in many answers was to correctly tie in the risk of money laundering at the client and the need to report this to the firm's money laundering reporting officer while avoiding tipping off but then to follow that with the suggestion that the firm resign from the client immediately and inform TCWG of the money laundering – so effectively then tipping off the client.

Marking guide | **Marks**

(a) (i) **Money laundering**

Generally up to 1 mark for each well-explained point of explanation, for example:

Reporting duties and procedures:

- Suspicions should be reported to nominated person within audit firm (MLRO); MLRO should possess suitable level of experience/seniority
- Audit firm should have established internal reporting lines which should be followed to report any suspicions
- Any individual in audit firm who has suspicions of money laundering activities must disclose them to MLRO; non-disclosure/failure to report constitutes an offence
- MLRO must consider all circumstances, document the process and decide whether to report to appropriate authorities; legal duty to report even though this may conflict with auditor's duty of confidentiality

3

(ii) Generally up to 2 marks for each well-explained point of explanation, for example:

Cash-intensive business:

- High level of cash sales and high volume of individual sales reports; risk illicit cash funds are being passed off as legitimate sales
- Mr Blackers' sale to business associate for £33,000 may be example of placement of illegal funds in order to legitimise them as genuine sales.

ANSWERS

International property transactions:

- May be example of real estate laundering by Mr Blackers in his personal affairs; may be purchasing international property with illegal funds (placement) and then selling them in order to make funds appear legitimate (integration)
- High volume of transactions and off-shore bank accounts in Mr Blackers' name may be indicative of layering of transactions in attempt to make original source of funds difficult to trace

5

(b) **Ethical and professional issues**

Generally 1 mark for each point identified and explained.

Taxation services

- Company tax computation is self-review threat as tax calculation forms basis of tax payable and tax charge in financial statements
- Advocacy threat re acting on client's behalf with tax authorities
- Management threat if the tax work involves making management judgements
- Firm should consider the use of safeguards, eg using professionals not members of audit team or independent senior/partner review
- Preparation of Mr Blackers' personal tax return may be taxable benefit which should be included in tax return and fee should be reflected in his director's loan account with the company
- Preparation of personal tax return may result in auditor being associated with criminal activities (ie money laundering as above)

Website and online sales system

- Self-review threat as auditor will audit sales figures generated by system
- Management threat from taking on responsibility of management in relation to designing systems and controls
- New system appears to be significant to client's financial statements and records
- The significance must be evaluated, and it is likely that the work on systems should not be performed

Office party

- Client hospitality (attendance at party) may create familiarity risks as audit staff may be getting too close to client especially given that this happens every year
- Gifts may create self-interest risk as audit staff receiving direct financial benefit from client
- Unless value is trivial and inconsequential, threats would be too significant to mitigate with safeguards and should not be accepted
- Auditor should have internal authorisation procedures to establish whether value is trivial and inconsequential
- In this case, value appears trivial but auditor should consider declining given possible criminal activities by client staff
- Implications of the Bribery Act (2010)

Maximum 12

Professional marks

Analysis and evaluation

- Appropriate use of the information to support discussion, draw appropriate conclusions and design appropriate responses

Marking guide	Marks
• Identification of omissions from the analysis or further analysis which could be carried out, particularly in relation to money laundering	
• Balanced assessment of the information to determine the appropriate ethical actions in the circumstances	
Professional scepticism and judgement	
• Effective challenge of information, evidence and assumptions supplied and, techniques carried out to support key facts and/or decisions	
• Appropriate application of professional judgement to draw conclusions and make informed decisions about the actions which are appropriate in the context and stage of the engagement.	
Maximum	5
Total	25

(a) **Money laundering**

(i) **Policies and procedures**

Thomasson & Co should have established an anti-money laundering programme within the firm. As part of this programme, the firm should have appointed a money laundering reporting officer (MLRO) with an appropriate level of experience and seniority. The audit firm should also have established internal reporting lines which should be followed to report any suspicions. Thomasson & Co will probably have a standard form which should be used to report suspicions of money laundering to the MLRO. Staff should receive appropriate training on compliance with the anti-money laundering requirements and how to report issues to the MLRO.

The typical content of an internal report on suspected money laundering may include the name of the suspect, the amounts potentially involved, and the reasons for the suspicions with supporting evidence if possible, and the whereabouts of the criminal property such as laundered cash. The firm's internal policies should have been set up to ensure that all pertinent information is captured in this standardised report.

Any individual in the audit firm who has suspicions of money laundering activities is then required to disclose these suspicions to the MLRO. The report must be done as soon as possible as any non-disclosure or failure to report such suspicions will constitute an offence under the money laundering regulations.

On receipt of the internal report, the MLRO must consider all of the circumstances surrounding the suspicions of money laundering activities, document this process and decide whether to report the suspicions to the National Crime Agency. The audit firm has a legal duty to report even though this may conflict with the auditor's duty of confidentiality.

> **Tutorial note.** Credit will be awarded for other relevant answer points in relation to a firm's anti-money laundering programme such as client due diligence, further staff training and maintaining adequate records.

(ii) **Evaluation of possible indicators of money laundering activities**

Money laundering is the process by which criminals attempt to conceal the true origin and ownership of the proceeds of criminal activity, allowing them to maintain control over the proceeds, and ultimately providing a legitimate cover for their sources of income.

In the case of Clean Ltd, the circumstances which may be indicative of money laundering activities include the following:

ANSWERS

Cash-intensive business

Clean Ltd has a high level of cash-based sales (75%) and a high volume of individual sales reports. The nature of its business therefore creates a significant risk that illicit cash funds are being passed off as legitimate sales. More specifically, Mr Blackers' sale to a business associate for £33,000 may be an example of the placement of illegal funds in order to legitimise them as genuine sales. The size of the transaction in a business selling cleaning products and the round sum amount may be additional grounds for suspicion in relation to this transaction.

International property transactions

The performance of Mr Blackers' personal taxation computation has identified a significant number of transactions involving the purchase and sale of properties in international locations. These transactions may be examples of real estate laundering by Mr Blackers in his personal affairs. It is possible that he may be purchasing these properties with illegal funds ('placement') and then selling them in order to make funds appear legitimate ('integration'). A high volume of such transactions may also be indicative of the 'layering' of transactions in an attempt to make the original source of the funds more difficult to trace.

(b) **Ethical and professional issues**

Taxation services

Company tax computation

According to the *FRC Ethical Standard*, performing tax services for an audit client can give rise to a number of ethical threats to objectivity including self-interest, self-review, advocacy and management threats. The natures of the threat created depends on the nature of the tax service which is being performed.

In this case, the performance of the company tax computation creates a self-review threat. A self-review threat arises when an auditor reviews work which they themselves have previously performed – for example, if the external auditor is involved in the process of preparing the financial statements and then audits them. As a result, there is a risk that the auditor will not be sufficiently objective in performing the audit and may fail to identify any shortcomings in their own work. In this case, therefore, a self-review threat to auditor independence arises because the tax calculation forms the basis of the tax payable and the tax charge in the financial statements and as such the audit team may be more likely to accept the tax calculations without adequate testing. There is also a potential advocacy threat. An advocacy threat arises when the auditor is asked to promote or represent their client in some way. In this situation, there is a risk of the auditor being seen to promote the interests of Clean Ltd with a third party such as the tax authorities and therefore that the auditor will be biased in favour of the client and cannot be fully objective.

Completing tax returns does not generally create a threat of management involvement by the auditor, as completing the tax return may not involve the auditor making any judgements. Provided management takes responsibility for the returns, including any judgements which have been made, the threat to objectivity is not likely to be significant.

The FRC *Ethical Standard* requires that safeguards must be used to reduce any threat, for example, self-review, to an acceptable level. Appropriate safeguards may include the following:

- The tax services are provided by partners and staff who have no involvement in the engagement
- The tax services are reviewed by an independent tax partner, or other senior tax employee
- External independent advice is obtained on the tax work
- Tax computations prepared by the engagement team are reviewed by a partner or senior staff member with relevant expertise who is not a member of the audit team
- A partner with relevant expertise not involved in the audit reviews whether the tax work has been properly and effectively addressed in the context of the audit.

Mr Blackers' personal tax computation

From an ethical perspective, there is no prohibition in the FRC *Ethical Standard* on the preparation of personal tax returns for the directors of an audit client such as Clean Ltd. However, in this case the auditor should consider whether the preparation of Mr Blackers' personal tax return may result in the auditor being associated with criminal activities if the suspicions of money laundering activities noted above prove to be well-founded.

The auditor should also consider the appropriateness of personal taxation services being billed to the company. Indeed, the preparation of Mr Blackers' personal tax return may be a taxable benefit which should be included in his tax return and the fee for this service may need to be reflected in his director's loan account with the company.

Website and online sales system

According to the FRC *Ethical Standard*, providing information technology services can create management and self-review threats to independence. The management threat arises because the design and implementation of information systems is the responsibility of management. If the auditor becomes involved in making management decisions with regard to the website and online sales system, the perception that the auditor is independent of management would be impaired.

The self-review threat arises as the new systems will produce data which will be used directly in the preparation of the financial statements. The audit process will therefore include reviewing and testing of financial data and systems which Thomasson & Co has helped to design and implement. As a result, there is a clear risk that the audit team may too readily place reliance on these systems.

With reference to Clean Ltd, therefore, it is clear that providing assistance with the design and implementation of the website and online sales system will constitute a self-review threat as the auditor will audit sales figures which are generated by the system. In the case of revenue, this self-review threat may be heightened further by the auditor's reliance on controls testing and on analytical review of the data summaries generated by the new system.

The new online sales system is likely to be significant to the client's financial statements and records. The FRC *Ethical Standard* states that the audit firm shall not design, provide or implement information technology systems where the systems concerned would be important to any significant part of the accounting system or to the production of the financial statements.

The FRC *Ethical Standard* also states that the design, provision or implementation of information technology systems which are not important to any significant part of the accounting or financial management system or to the production of the financial statements audited by the firm and do not have significant reliance placed on them by the persons conducting the audit may be undertaken, provided that there is informed management and appropriate safeguards are applied to reduce the self-review threat to a level where independence is not compromised.

Therefore, before making any decision, the audit firm must evaluate the significance of the systems to financial reporting, and if they are significant, which is likely to be the case as the systems deal with revenue, then the service should not be provided.

Office party

The FRC *Ethical Standard* states that client hospitality (in this case, the attendance of the office party by the audit team) may create a familiarity threat. A familiarity threat occurs when the auditor is too sympathetic or trusting of the client because of a close relationship with them. There is a risk therefore that as a result of attending the client office party, the audit staff may be getting too close to the client staff especially given that according to the audit senior, this practice has occurred every year. This close relationship may result in the audit team becoming less objective and less able to challenge explanations provided by the client.

The FRC *Ethical Standard* also states that gifts from a client to a member of the audit team may create a self-interest threat. A self-interest threat arises when the auditor derives a potential personal benefit from an audit client which may motivate them to behave in a manner which aims to protect that benefit. With reference to the office party, therefore, the audit staff are receiving a direct financial benefit from the client (in this case, in the form of vouchers).

The FRC *Ethical Standard* states that auditors shall not provide or accept gifts and hospitality in relation to an audit unless it is probable that an objective, reasonable and informed third party would consider the value thereof to be trivial or inconsequential. Therefore, unless the value of such gifts is trivial and inconsequential, the self-interest threat would be too significant to mitigate with safeguards and the gifts should not be accepted. The audit firm should consider introducing internal authorisation procedures in order to ensure transparency and to establish whether the value is trivial and inconsequential. In this case, the value of £30 per head does appear to be trivial but the auditor might still consider declining the gifts in order to maintain a visible professional distance from a client which may be involved in criminal activities.

Finally, there may be implications from the Bribery Act (2010). Under the Bribery Act, it is an offence to bribe another person or to be bribed yourself. This offence is widely defined and covers all bribes which are given or received to 'improperly perform' a function which is expected to be carried out in good faith, impartially, and where the person involved is in a position of trust. To ensure that there is no actual or perceived breach of the Bribery Act, the auditor might consider it prudent to decline the gifts and hospitality which has been offered by the client, even if it is trivial in monetary value.

12 Bradley

Workbook references

Chapters 4, 10 and 11.

Top tips

This question focused on the review stage of the audit, encompassing the review of the financial statements and the auditor's report.

Part (a) should have been full of potential marks for you to pluck from the mark tree like low-hanging fruit. You need to work through the scenario and point out the issues.

Part (b) was very practical, and on the whole much more difficult. However, even if you weren't certain of the accounting treatments, marks were available for discussing the audit issues around them. These were not particularly technical accounting points, so you should really have been comfortable with them.

Easy marks

Calculating materiality in part (b) gets you plenty of marks.

ACCA examining team's comments

Requirement (a) provided some information in the form of a comment made by the audit senior, who indicated that there may have been some problems with the performance of the audit. The concerns raised included the lack of a detailed review of the final version of the financial statements and the chairman's statement had been discussed with the finance director, but no further work had been conducted. The justification for not carrying out these tasks was the conclusion by the audit manager that the audit was relatively low risk. The requirement was for 10 marks, and asked candidates to explain the quality management and other professional issues raised by the audit senior's comments.

Candidates did not perform well on this requirement, which was somewhat surprising as in the past questions on quality management issues have been well attempted. Only a minority of candidates were able to identify that the audit of a significant new client could not be classified as low risk, and that a final review would be needed on the financial statements at the completion stage of the audit. Very few candidates however mentioned that final analytical review is a requirement of ISA (UK) 520 *Analytical Procedures* and even fewer could explain why the final review is so important prior to the issuance of the auditor's report. In respect of the work performed on the chairman's statement, few candidates identified that there was a lack of documentation of the work performed, but most at least understood the auditor's responsibilities in relation to the chairman's statement.

Generally the answers to this requirement were not made relevant to the information given in the scenario and instead mentioned general features of quality management such as the need for supervision and review. This will earn minimal credit, as marks are severely limited when answer points are not related to the scenario. Many answers discussed at length the auditor's report implications of uncorrected inconsistencies in the chairman's statement, but discussing this in a lot of detail was not answering the question requirement.

Requirement (b) dealt with the evaluation of misstatements. The information was presented as a schedule of proposed adjustments to uncorrected misstatements in relation to three issues – a share-based payment scheme, a restructuring provision, and slow-moving inventory. In each case the auditor's proposed correcting journal was presented, along with an explanation of the audit findings and audit conclusion on the matter.

Requirement (b) **was not well attempted**. Answers were much too brief for the marks available and unfortunately many candidates could not competently demonstrate that they understand the topic of auditor's reports. Firstly in relation to the share-based payment, the required financial reporting requirements were not well understood, with most candidates suggesting that a provision should be created rather than an adjustment made to equity, which was disappointing as this detail was actually given in the question. In relation to the restructuring provision, many candidates did not consider the specific requirements of IAS 37 *Provisions, Contingent Liabilities and Contingent Assets* in relation to restructuring provisions, and instead applied the general recognition criteria for provisions to the scenario. The slow-moving inventory was better dealt with, as most candidates could explain that inventory should be measured at lower of cost and net realisable value. On the whole, the only marks that many candidates were awarded in this requirement were for materiality calculations. There seems to be very little knowledge or understanding of ISA (UK) 450 *Evaluation of Misstatements Identified During the Audit* with almost no candidates differentiating between judgemental misstatements and misstatements caused by a breach of IFRS requirement.

Marking guide **Marks**

(a) **Explanation of quality management and other professional issues**

Generally up to 1 mark for each point explained:

- Insufficient audit evidence obtained in relation to legal provision
- Possible limitation on scope imposed by management and intimidation threat
- Matter is immaterial but the issue is potential understatement of provisions
- Further procedures should be performed, necessary to exercise professional scepticism
- Audit manager's instructions are not appropriate and increase detection risk
- Analytical review mandatory at the final review stage
- Objective to ensure that financial statements consistent with auditor's understanding
- A quick look unlikely to be sufficient especially as this is a new audit client
- The fact that it is deemed low risk does not negate the need for analytical review
- Lack of analytical review increases audit risk especially for a new client
- Other information must be read with objective of identifying material inconsistencies
- Manager to be questioned to see what work has been done and what documentation exists
- Likely that chairman's statement needs to be properly read and audit conclusion documented

Marking guide	Marks
• Audit manager lacks understanding of ISA (UK) requirements or taking short-cuts	
• Audit manager may need further training	
• Time pressure increased detection risk and impacts on the quality of the audit performed	
Maximum	10
(b) **Explain matters to be considered in forming audit opinion**	
Generally 1 mark for each point explained:	
• ISAs (UK) require auditor to understand management's reason for not adjusting misstatements	
• ISAs (UK) require auditor to communicate impact of unadjusted misstatement on opinion	
Share-based payment:	
• Materiality assessment including appropriate calculation	
• Fall in share price not valid reason for not recognising expense and credit to equity	
• Material misstatement due to breach of financial reporting standards, encourage management to make necessary adjustment	
Provision:	
• Materiality assessment including appropriate calculation	
• Provision recognised too early, obligating event when closure announced	
• Material misstatement due to breach of financial reporting standards, encourage management to make necessary adjustment	
• Consider if any additional information to explain recognition of provision, eg an announcement before the year end which auditor unaware of	
• In the absence of further information, material misstatement exists due to breach of financial reporting standards, encourage management to make necessary adjustment	
Inventory provision	
• Materiality assessment including appropriate calculation	
• Discussion of difference between clearly trivial, immaterial and material items	
• Misstatement is a matter of judgement rather than a matter of fact	
• Management should still be encouraged to make adjustment but no impact on audit opinion if not done	
Impact on auditor's report	
Generally up to 1 mark per point explained:	
• Determination of aggregate impact of adjustments and combined materiality	
• Material misstatement and modified opinion necessary	
• Discussion and conclusion as to whether opinion should be qualified or adverse	
• Basis for qualified opinion paragraph to include a description and quantification of the financial effects of the misstatement	
Maximum	10

Professional marks

Analysis and evaluation

- Appropriate use of the information to support discussion, draw appropriate conclusions and design appropriate responses
- Identification of omissions from the analysis or further analysis which could be carried out
- Balanced assessment of the information to determine the appropriate audit opinion in the circumstances

Professional scepticism and judgement

- Effective challenge of information, evidence and assumptions supplied, particularly in relation to the quality management and other issues present on the Bradley Ltd audit.
- Appropriate application of professional judgement to draw conclusions and make informed decisions about the actions which are appropriate in the context of the completion stage of the Bradley Ltd audit.

Maximum	5
Total	25

(a) **Quality management, ethical and other issues**

The first comment made by the audit assistant shows that the audit of the provision in relation to the legal claim has not been properly carried out, and it would seem that there is not sufficient, appropriate audit evidence to conclude that provisions are fairly stated. First, the finance director telling the audit assistant not to approach the company's legal advisers would appear to be placing a limitation on the evidence which can be obtained. Also, the finance director could have used his seniority to intimidate the audit assistant.

The situation indicates that the finance director may be trying to hide something, and professional scepticism should be exercised. Possibly the finance director knows that the amount which should be provided is much larger than the £10,000, and he is reluctant to recognise a larger liability in the financial statements or that the legal advisers are aware of other provisions which should be included with the financial statements which are currently not being recognised. As the key risk for provisions is understatement, the audit team should not so readily accept the finance director's assessment that the amount included is complete. The audit team should challenge his statement regarding the adequacy of the provision and ask for written evidence, for example, confirmation from the legal advisers.

It is also concerning that the audit manager told the audit assistant to conclude on the audit work when the planned procedures had not been performed. This does not provide good direction to the audit team and increases audit risk. There could be a material misstatement if the provision is significantly understated, and there is not sufficient evidence on the audit file to currently support the conclusions drawn.

Regarding the second comment made by the audit assistant, it is a requirement of ISA (UK) 520 *Analytical Procedures* that analytical procedures are performed at the overall review stage of the audit. An objective of ISA (UK) 520 is that the auditor should design and perform analytical procedures near the end of the audit which assist the auditor when forming their opinion as to whether the financial statements are consistent with the auditor's understanding of the entity.

It is unlikely that the audit senior's 'quick look' at Bradley Ltd's financial statements is adequate to meet the requirements of ISA (UK) 520 and audit documentation would seem to be inadequate. Therefore if the audit manager, or another auditor, does not perform a detailed analytical review on Bradley Ltd's financial statements as part of the completion of the audit, there is a breach of ISA (UK) 520. Failing to perform the final analytical review could mean that further errors are not found, and the auditor will not be able to check that the presentation of the financial statements conforms to the requirements of the applicable financial reporting framework. It is also doubtful whether a full check on the presentation and disclosure in the financial statements has been made. The firm should evidence this through the use of a disclosure checklist.

The lack of final analytical review increases audit risk. Because Bradley Ltd is a new audit client, it is particularly important that the analytical review is performed as detection risk is higher than for longer-standing audit engagements where the auditor has developed a cumulative knowledge of the audit client.

The fact that the audit manager suggested that a detailed review was not necessary shows a lack of knowledge and understanding of ISA (UK) requirements. An audit client being assessed as low risk does not negate the need for analytical review to be performed, which the audit manager should know. Alternatively, the audit manager may have known that analytical review should have been performed, but regardless of this still instructed the audit assistant not to perform the review, maybe due to time pressure. The audit manager should be asked about the reason for his instruction and given further training if necessary.

The manager is not providing proper direction and supervision of the audit assistant, which goes against the principles of ISA (UK) 220 (Revised) *Quality Management for an Audit of Financial Statements*, and ISQM1 (UK) *Quality Management for Firms that Perform Audits or Reviews of Financial Statements or Other Assurance or Related Services Engagements*. Both of these discuss the importance of the audit team having proper direction and supervision as part of ensuring a good quality of audit engagement performance.

The final issue relates to the chairman's statement. ISA (UK) 720 *The auditor's Responsibilities Relating to Other Information* requires that the auditor shall read the other information to identify material inconsistencies, if any, with the audited financial statements.

The audit manager has discussed the chairman's statement, but this does not necessarily mean that the manager has read it for the purpose of identifying potential misstatements, and it might not have been read at all. Even if the manager has read the chairman's statement, there may not be any audit documentation to show that this has been done or the conclusion of the work. The manager needs to be asked exactly what work has been done, and what documentation exists. As the work performed does not comply with the ISA (UK) 720 requirements, then the necessary procedures must be performed before the auditor's report is issued. This is especially important as the necessary paragraphs will need to be included within the auditor's report setting out that the other information has been obtained, the responsibility that the auditor has for the other information explained and whether anything needs to be reported in relation to any inconsistencies.

Again, the situation could indicate the audit manager's lack of knowledge of ISA (UK) requirements, or that a short-cut is being taken, probably as a result of time pressure. In either case, the quality of the audit is in jeopardy.

(b) **Evaluation of uncorrected misstatements**

During the completion stage of the audit, the effect of uncorrected misstatements must be evaluated by the auditor, as required by ISA (UK) 450 *Evaluation of Misstatements Identified During the Audit*. In the event that management refuses to correct some or all of the misstatements communicated by the auditor, ISA (UK) 450 requires that the auditor shall obtain an understanding of management's reasons for not making the corrections and shall take that understanding into account when evaluating whether the financial statements as a whole are free from material misstatement. Therefore a discussion with management is essential in helping the auditor to form an audit opinion.

ISA (UK) 450 also requires that the auditor shall communicate with those charged with governance about uncorrected misstatements and the effect that they, individually or in aggregate, may have on the opinion in the auditor's report.

Each of the matters included in the schedule of uncorrected misstatements will be discussed below and the impact on the auditor's report considered individually and in aggregate.

Share-based payment scheme

The adjustment in relation to the share-based payment scheme is material individually to profit, representing 12% of revenue. It represents less than 1% of total assets and is not material to the statement of financial position.

IFRS 2 *Share-based Payment* requires an expense and a corresponding entry to equity to be recognised over the vesting period of a share-based payment scheme, with the amount recognised based on the fair value of equity instruments granted. Management's argument that no expense should be recognised because the options are unlikely to be exercised is not correct. IFRS 2 would classify the fall in Bradley Ltd's share price as a market condition, and these are not relevant to determining whether an expense is recognised or the amount of it. Therefore management should be requested to make the necessary adjustment to recognise the expense and entry to equity of £300,000. If this is not recognised, the financial statements will contain a material misstatement, with consequences for the auditor's opinion.

Restructuring provision

The adjustment in relation to the provision is material to profit, representing 2% of revenue. It represents less than 1% of total assets so is not material to the statement of financial position.

The provision appears to have been recognised too early. IAS 37 *Provisions, Contingent Liabilities and Contingent Assets* requires that for a restructuring provision to be recognised, there must be a present obligation as a result of a past event, and that is only when a detailed formal plan is in place and the entity has started to implement the plan or announced its main features to those affected. A board decision is insufficient to create a present obligation as a result of a past event. The provision should be recognised in September 20X5 when the announcement to employees was made.

Management should be asked to explain why they have included the provision in the financial statements, for example, there may have been an earlier announcement before 31 August 20X5 of which the auditor is unaware.

In the absence of any such further information, management should be informed that the accounting treatment of the provision is a material misstatement, which if it remains unadjusted will have implications for the auditor's opinion.

Inventory provision

The additional slow-moving inventory allowance which the auditor considers necessary is not material on an individual basis to either profit or to the statement of profit or loss or the statement of financial position, as it represents only 0.4% of revenue and less than 1% of total assets.

Despite the amount being immaterial, it should not be disregarded, as the auditor should consider the aggregate effect of misstatements on the financial statements. ISA (UK) 450 does state that the auditor need not accumulate balances which are 'clearly trivial', by which it means that the accumulation of such amounts clearly would not have a material effect on the financial statements. However, at 0.4% of revenue the additional provision is not trivial, so should be discussed with management.

This misstatement is a judgemental misstatement as it arises from the judgements of management concerning an accounting estimate over which the auditor has reached a different conclusion. This is not a breach of financial reporting standards, but a difference in how management and the auditor have estimated an uncertain amount. Management should be asked to confirm the basis on which their estimate was made, and whether they have any reason why the provision should not be increased by the amount recommended by the auditor.

If this amount remains unadjusted by management, it will not on an individual basis impact the auditor's report.

13 Groom

Workbook references

Chapters 3, 4 and 8.

Top tips

Part (a) represented a little bit of a twist on this issue. Usually one might expect questions on auditors and fraud to require candidates to state that the auditor is not responsible for preventing and detecting fraud. While you should have done this here, there was also the twist that the auditor appears to have been negligent in performing the audit.

As you are reading through the information for part (b), jot down the accounting standards you believe are relevant and note down the matters to consider that arise from them. Think if any ISAs are relevant as well (this is particularly important as your examining team has recently commented that candidates tend to show too little knowledge of the requirements of ISAs). Always comment on the materiality of matters.

Easy marks

Calculating materiality in parts (a) and (b) was easy, as was listing out the three things to prove in order to prove negligence (a duty of care existed; this duty was breached; financial loss resulted from this breach).

ACCA examining team's comments

There were some excellent answers to requirement (a). The best ones clearly outlined the factors that have to be proven to determine negligence and applied them methodically to the scenario. Some answers tended to only provide a rote-learnt description of responsibilities in relation to fraud, and usually failed to reach an appropriate conclusion. With little application to the scenario there is limited scope for marks to be awarded.

For requirement (b), almost all candidates were able to generate marks by calculating the materiality of the amount and describing the basic accounting treatment for provisions. Fewer went on to discuss the potential impact of the insurance cover, and some answers drifted into a discussion of going concern and other business risks. Audit procedures were often inadequately focused, with no regard to the scale of the issue. Although most suggested looking at legal documents, candidates rarely mentioned looking at the group claim document. Some candidates proposed lots of very detailed tests on the validity of individual claims, such as checking hotel bills and airline tickets.

Marking guide

	Marks
(a) **Fraud and auditor's liability**	
Generally up to 2 marks for each point explained:	
• Not auditor's primary responsibility to detect fraud unless it is material in impact on FS	
• Determine that the payroll fraud would have been material (include calculation)	
• Reasons why fraud is hard to detect	
• Audit firm may not have been sufficiently sceptical	
• Non-adherence to ISAs on controls assessment and evidence obtained	
• Discuss whether duty of care owed to client	
• Discuss breach of duty of care	
• Identify financial loss suffered and firm likely to have been negligent	
Maximum	12
(b) **Compensation claim**	
1 mark per matter, 1 mark per specific procedure	
Matters	
• Materiality	
• Provision/contingent liability	

Marking guide	Marks
• Recoverability under insurance	
• Management reluctant to provide	
Evidence	
• Copy of legal claim	
• Legal correspondence	
• Press releases/news stories to establish constructive obligation	
• Booking conditions to verify legal obligation	
• Advice given by the company at the time of the incident	
• Copy of insurance contract	
• Copy of claim made on insurance	
• Written representation on outcome	
Maximum	8
Professional marks	
Analysis and evaluation	
• Appropriate use of the information to support discussion, draw appropriate conclusions and design appropriate responses	
• Identification of omissions from the analysis or further analysis which could be carried out	
• Balanced assessment of the information to determine the materiality and significance of an issue in the context of an engagement	
Professional scepticism and judgement	
• Effective challenge of information, evidence and assumptions supplied and, techniques carried out to support key facts and/or decisions	
• Appropriate discussion of the factors which make fraud difficult to detect, and of the special need to apply professional scepticism in connection with this	
Maximum	5
Total	25

(a) **Responsibilities**

Detecting fraud is the primary responsibility of management, not the auditor. However, the matter is complicated because the auditor is required to give reasonable assurance that the financial statements are not materially misstated as a result of fraud (or error). Moreover, auditors are required by ISA (UK) 240 *The Auditor's Responsibilities Relating to Fraud in an Audit of Financial Statements* to identify and assess the risks of material misstatement due to fraud. This means that an audit conducted in line with ISAs should obtain evidence specifically in relation to fraud.

The audit process is, however, subject to inherent limitations which are particularly pertinent to the problem of fraud. Fraud may involve sophisticated attempts at concealment, which can make it difficult to detect. Furthermore, there may be collusion by management which makes the auditor's task even more difficult. It is therefore quite possible for the auditor to have conducted an audit in accordance with ISAs, but still have failed to detect a material misstatement resulting from fraud.

Materiality

The total amount stolen is 5.6% of total assets. Not all of this took place within the year, so the amount could be pro-rated as follows: if the theft was at a constant rate, then 8 out of 12 months fell within the year in question, which is £3m or 3.75% of total assets. This is material and appears to have result in an incorrect auditor's opinion having been expressed.

Conduct of audit

Professional scepticism is a key weapon in the auditor's attempt to detect misstatements resulting from fraud. The audit of Spaniel does not appear to have been conducted with an attitude of professional scepticism, possibly as a result of it being a long-standing audit client.

However, irrespective of the auditor's specific duties in relation to fraud, sufficient appropriate evidence does not in any case seem to have been obtained in relation to payroll. ISAs (UK) require the auditor to design and perform tests of controls in each period under audit. Substantive evidence should have been obtained in relation to payroll. This is particularly important given that payroll is likely to be a material area.

On this basis it is apparent that the audit was not conducted in accordance with ISAs. The audit partner may therefore find it very difficult to defend the conduct of the audit.

Negligence?

Three things must be proved for the auditor to be found to have been negligent:

- A duty of care existed
- The duty of care was breached
- A financial loss resulted from the negligence

As there is a contract between Groom & Co and Spaniel, a duty of care can be shown to have existed (in this case, to the shareholders as a body).

The financial loss here would be the value of the theft, although it is not clear whether the auditor could be held responsible for the full amount of the theft.

It is likely that Groom & Co were negligent, and that Spaniel would be able to prove this in court.

(b) **Matters to consider**

The claim is material to profit at 13.3% of profit before tax (20/150 × 100%). It is not material to the statement of financial position at only 0.49% of total assets (20/4,100 × 100%).

Management has an incentive to manipulate the financial statements through fraudulent financial reporting, as its bonus is based on profit before tax. There is a risk that profit may be overstated. It may not want to provide for the claim because this would reduce profit.

IAS 37 *Provisions, Contingent Liabilities and Contingent Assets* requires a provision to be recognised where, as a result of a past event, an outflow of economic benefits is probable, the amount of which can be estimated reliably. If such an outflow is only possible but not probable, then it is a contingent liability and should be disclosed in a note to the financial statements. Further evidence is required to determine whether the compensation claim should be provided for or not.

If Clooney can make a claim on its insurance policy in respect of the legal case, then per IAS 37 this is treated as a separate event, in accordance with IAS 37's requirements on contingent assets. For an asset to be recognised, IAS 37 states that it should be certain to be received. As in this case receipt of an insurance payment is only probable, no asset should be recognised. The insurance claim should be disclosed by way of a note.

In addition to the provision that must be created, it may be necessary for Clooney to provide for any legal costs associated with defending the claim, which would further reduce its profit for the year.

Evidence

- Copy of claim made by the group of holiday makers, detailing the £20 million claimed and the basis of the claim
- Review of correspondence between 'claim group' and the company
- Correspondence from Clooney's legal counsel, showing their opinion on the likely outcome
- Copy of any press releases made by Clooney, which could help establish there is a constructive obligation

- Review of press coverage of the situation, to assess any comments made in public by company representatives regarding the claim
- Review of the standard terms and conditions that holidaymakers agree to on booking a holiday – this could help to establish any legal obligation, eg to cover the cost of accommodation before being returned home
- Details of any helpline or other means by which the stranded holidaymakers were given advice at the time of the incident (eg if the company advised them to book alternative accommodation this may imply that the company is liable for the cost)
- Copy of insurance contract detailing level of cover, if any, provided for this situation, and any amount that will not be covered (eg an excess on the policy)
- Correspondence between insurance company and Clooney to establish whether an insurance claim has been made
- Written management representation stating management's opinion on the outcome of the court case, and the likelihood of reimbursement from the insurance cover
- Review of invoices received pre and post year end in respect of legal costs, to ensure adequately included in expenses and accrued for if necessary

14 Raven

Workbook references

Chapters 1, 2 and 11.

Top tips

The main difficulty that many students will have faced with part (a) is that seven marks are available for what seems like quite a clear-cut issue. However, if you read the requirement carefully you will have seen that it is not only about ethics, but the 'commercial and other professional issues' raised by the scenario. This question is typical of the current examining team's approach to AAA in that it mixes together different areas – here, ethics and commercial matters. To answer this part well, you needed to know the main categories of ethical threat and then think whether any circumstances in the scenario fell into any of these categories.

Part (b) may have been a bit easier, with a further seven marks for an issue that is clear-cut and that there is quite a lot to write about. The main thing here is to be sceptical and question the information in the scenario – eg whether there really is a connection between the surgeon's comments and the solicitor's letter. The best approach here is often to break the scenario down into parts and take each one in turn.

Part (c) on auditor's reports was a fairly difficult question in this area. You should have known that either a qualified opinion or a disclaimer of opinion would be issued, but the difficulty comes from the fact that you cannot be entirely sure from the information given in the question.

Notice that there are marks available here for actions such as communicating with those charged with governance before issuing a report with a modified opinion. The examining team likes this kind of point because it shows that you are thinking practically about what would happen, rather than simply reciting your knowledge about the different kinds of audit opinions. There are also usually marks available for the format of any modified report, eg stating that there should be a 'basis for modification paragraph', what the paragraph should say, and that it should be immediately after the opinion paragraph.

Easy marks

Part (b) contains easy marks for just recognising that there may be a breach of law and regulations in respect of the possibly unqualified surgeon.

ACCA examining team's comments

Sound answers to part (a) used a logical approach, being prompted by the question requirement to discuss in turn the ethical issues, then commercial issues, then professional issues and leading to a set of recommended actions. Weaker answers tended to just list in bullet point format all of the possible threats to objectivity without any real discussion or development of the threats specific to the scenario. Candidates are reminded that the IESBA's *Code of Ethics for Professional Accountants* provides a framework for the evaluation of threats to objectivity, including the identification of threats, the evaluation of the significance of threats identified, and the use of professional judgement in deciding whether the application of safeguards can reduce threats identified to an acceptable level.

In part (b), most candidates identified that the main issues for the audit firm to consider related to a potential breach of law and regulations by the hospital, and that the audit firm should consider disclosure in the public interest. Most answers identified that confidentiality was in issue, and that the matter should be firstly discussed with those charged with governance.

Some candidates focused on disciplinary action to be taken against the employee of the hospital, and on the possibility that the hospital's management were somehow colluding with the employee to deliberately breach law and regulations and commit some type of fraud, which missed the point. Weaker answers also failed to consider the financial statement and therefore audit implications of a letter claiming negligence, which could lead to the recognition of a provision or disclosure of a contingent liability, and could potentially have going concern implications. These matters were relevant as the audit was ongoing.

In requirement (c), most candidates correctly discussed that fact that the auditor was unable to obtain sufficient, appropriate audit evidence based on the reconstructed records, leading them to explain that the audit opinion should be disclaimed. Fewer candidates suggested that alternative procedures could be used to obtain evidence, and fewer still recognised that as the accounting records were available for eleven months of the year, the auditor's report may not necessarily be subject to a disclaimer of opinion, or even qualified at all if alternative procedures could take place.

Marking guide	Marks
(a) **Grouse Ltd**	
Generally 1 mark for each matter discussed:	
• Situation is a close business arrangement giving rise to threat to objectivity	
• Explain self-interest threat	
• Explain intimidation threat	
• Only acceptable if financial interest immaterial and relationship insignificant	
• Sale of software to audit clients would require full disclosure of financial benefit	
• Sale of software to audit clients creates self-review threat	
• Sale of software perceived as providing non-audit service	
• Risks heightened for listed/public interest entities	
• If enter business arrangement must withdraw from audit of Grouse Ltd	
• Commercial consideration – demand for product	
• Commercial consideration – experience of partners	
Maximum	7
(b) **Plover Ltd**	
Generally 1 mark for each matter discussed:	
• Potential breach of law and regulations	
• Further understanding to be obtained	

Marking guide	Marks
• Consider potential impact on financial statements	
• Discuss with those charged with governance	
• Management should disclose to relevant regulatory body	
• Auditor could disclose in public interest	
• Issues with confidentiality	
• Take legal advice	
• Extend audit work in relation to the legal claim	
• Risk of material misstatement	
• Consider integrity of audit client	
Maximum	7
(c) **Actions and implications in respect of the auditor's report on Dylan plc**	
Up to 1.5 marks for each action/implication:	
• Insufficient appropriate audit evidence so far obtained	
• Possible to extend audit procedures on reconstructed figures/other procedures	
• Majority of transactions during the year likely to have sufficient evidence	
• If no further evidence available, consider modification to opinion	
• Discuss whether material or pervasive	
• Description of auditor's report contents if opinion modified	
• Communicate with those charged with governance	
• Report by exception on inadequate accounting records	
Maximum	6
Professional marks	
Analysis and evaluation	
• Appropriate assessment of the ethical and professional issues raised, using examples where relevant to support overall comments	
• Effective appraisal of the information to make suitable recommendations for appropriate courses of action	
Professional scepticism and judgement	
• Effective challenge and critical assessment of the evidence supplied with appropriate conclusions	
• Demonstration of the ability to consider whether the evidence obtained in relation to Dylan is of the required standard	
Commercial acumen	
• Inclusion of appropriate recommendations regarding the proposal of Grouse	
• Appropriate recognition of the wider implications on the engagement, the audit firm and the company	
Maximum	5
Total	25

(a) **Close business relationship**

Grouse Ltd's proposal would create very significant threats to Raven's independence.

This would be a 'close business relationship' per the IESBA *Code of Ethics* and may give rise to a self-interest threat. The *Code* states that unless the financial interest is immaterial, and the business relationship insignificant, then no safeguards can reduce the threat to an acceptable level. Therefore Raven should not enter into this relationship if it still wants to be Grouse's auditor.

It should be remembered that independence includes independence in appearance (IESBA *Code of Ethics*). A joint venture with an audit client would probably have a severe effect on how Raven appeared, so even if it had been acceptable on ethical grounds, the fact that it looks so bad may well have ruled it out anyway.

Selling to clients

In addition to the close business relationship, Grouse is also proposing that the software be sold to Raven's audit clients. There are several issues here.

Firstly, there is a self-interest threat to Raven's independence if its joint venture is selling to its clients. It may be possible to reduce this to an acceptable level by using the safeguard of disclosing the relationship to clients, along with the benefit that Raven would receive from any sales.

Secondly, there would be a self-review threat if any of the audit clients used the accounting and tax software to prepare its financial statements. It may be possible to use an auditor's expert here; however, accounting software is usually pervasive to the internal controls over financial reporting, so it may be that the expert would have to be used to conduct most of the audit. This would be extremely expensive and impracticable.

Thirdly, the use of the firm's accounting and tax software could be seen as a non-audit service. This could create a perception of taking on management's responsibilities. The risk would be greater still for clients that are public interest entities, and the firm should not be involved in any tax calculations for these clients.

Taking into account these factors, Raven must choose between selling the software to its clients and continuing to act as their auditor. It would not be possible to sell this software to clients and continue to audit them. Raven must therefore make a business decision to choose between the potential income from the software, and the loss of audit fees from every client to whom the software is sold. Raven should also take into account the loss of the audit fee from Grouse itself.

The software joint venture therefore represents a major diversification from audit to the preparation of accounting and tax software. This is a major decision that must be considered very carefully, taking into account the firm's long-term interests, where its expertise really lies, and the potential risks from diversifying into such an unknown area.

(b) **Unqualified surgeon?**

The audit senior has heard that one of the surgeons has not finished his medical qualification. This appears to be connected to the solicitor's letter that was later found which alleged medical negligence. As an auditor, we need to deal with each issue separately.

ISA (UK) 250 Section A *Consideration of Laws and Regulations in an Audit of Financial Statements* states that compliance with laws and regulations is management's responsibility, and that it is not the auditor's responsibility to either prevent or detect it. However, if – as here – we become aware of any NOCLAR (Non-Compliance with Laws and Regulations) then we must consider its effect on the financial statements. This breach could have an indirect but material effect on the financial statements.

As auditors we have no expert knowledge of medicine, and it is possible that we may be jumping to conclusions about whether the surgeon is qualified to do his work. It may be, for example, that he is a qualified doctor, and the 'medical qualification' he is hoping to finish is merely a further qualification that is not a requirement for his work as a surgeon. Although he was glad that Plover did not check his references, this could be a separate issue from whether or not he is qualified.

We must therefore obtain further evidence about this surgeon's qualifications, and whether they meet the requirements for his job. This could entail simply reviewing the personnel file, which may contain evidence about his qualifications.

Effect of unqualified surgeon

If we find that the surgeon is not qualified to do his job, then we must consider the effect on the financial statements. There are two main risks:

(1) Risk of litigation resulting from errors made by the surgeon

(2) Risk of action by regulatory bodies

In relation to 1, this is potentially a very serious problem. If the surgeon has made many errors, then this could result in multiple patients suing the company. The potential cost of these actions is not known but could be very considerable indeed. It is even possible that Plover's ability to continue as a going concern could be affected. Further evidence must be obtained about the extent of further errors and possible legal actions. It may be necessary to obtain advice from our legal counsel.

In relation to 2, the medical profession is highly regulated, and it is possible that Plover will be fined by any relevant regulatory authorities. There is a legal question about whether Plover's management could be found guilty of possible negligence as a result of breaking its duty of care to patients. It may be necessary to obtain legal advice here.

It is even possible that any licences which Plover requires to operate will be removed, and that its ability to continue as a going concern will be in doubt. It may be necessary to use an auditor's expert here to provide advice about the possible regulatory consequences, and/or to obtain legal advice.

Control failure?

The surgeon's comment that his references were not checked raises questions about the effectiveness of Plover's internal controls over recruitment. It will be necessary to obtain evidence about whether or not there are other employees in this position – the main issue being that there could be other employees (eg surgeons) who are not qualified to do their work. Uncovering these could lead to the discovery of further liabilities.

Public interest?

If the surgeon is not qualified, then it is possible that management will not disclose this to the relevant authorities. They should be encouraged to do so by the auditor, but if they do not then it may be necessary to make this disclosure in the public interest. This is a difficult issue to decide, as the auditor must balance the duty of confidentiality that is owed to Plover, with the duty to the public. Matters to consider here include the gravity of the situation, whether members of the public may be affected, and the likelihood of further non-compliance. This will all depend on whether the surgeon was in fact unqualified, and on what impact this may have had on patients.

Disclosure in the public interest would require careful consideration, and it may be necessary to obtain legal advice before doing so.

Legal claim

The letter that was found in the subsequent events review may be evidence of a liability under IAS 37 *Provisions, Contingent Liabilities and Contingent Assets*. The key question is whether the event in question took place before or after the year end. The crucial date here is likely to be the date on which the medical service was provided.

If the surgery was after the year end, then this is a non-adjusting event and no provision is necessary. If the surgery was before the year end, then a provision may be required. This will depend on how probable it is that Plover will have to pay to settle the claim, with a provision being necessary if it is probable that a payment will be made. If the matter is material and Plover's management refuse to make any necessary provisions or disclosures, then it may be necessary to express a qualified auditor's opinion.

(c) **Actions**

We have not performed audit procedures on payroll, revenue and receivables, and have not obtained sufficient appropriate audit evidence as yet.

Hendrix Ltd has reconstructed the figures 'as far as possible', which means that they could still be materially and pervasively misstated. In any event, their representation is not sufficient audit evidence.

It may be possible to perform additional procedures on the information that Hendrix Ltd has reconstructed. This could obtain evidence about revenue and payroll. Receivables could still be tested by a circularisation.

It is not clear, however, what records may still be in existence: Hendrix Ltd may have sent information to Dylan plc during the year. As the virus attack only happened in February, Dylan plc could have 10 or 11 months' information on which it might be possible to perform audit procedures.

As a listed company, Dylan plc may have issued interim financial statements, which could provide accounting information for part of the year that could be audited.

Practically, it may be necessary to request an extension to any deadlines for completion of the audit.

Auditor's report

It is possible that additional procedures may obtain sufficient appropriate evidence, in which case an unmodified report could be issued.

If this evidence is not obtained, then either a qualified opinion will be expressed, or the auditor will disclaim an opinion.

A qualified opinion would be expressed if the auditor judges that the inability to obtain sufficient appropriate audit evidence is material but not pervasive. The auditor would then state that the financial statements give a true and fair view except for the areas where there is insufficient evidence – payroll, revenue and/or receivables.

A disclaimer of opinion would be made if the problem is both material and pervasive.

Further actions

The details of any potential modification should be communicated in advance to those charged with governance, who should be given a chance to provide further explanations.

15 Dragon Group

Workbook references

Chapters 5 and 9.

Top tips

Part (a) was probably the hardest part of this question. You should try to strike a balance between making general remarks about what a tender document should include, and sticking to the specific information given in the scenario.

Part (b) offered a lot of marks in this area and was a good test of your knowledge.

Part (c) should have been straightforward provided that you knew what a transnational audit was. In our answer we have provided three features, but only two were required to gain full marks.

Easy marks

Part (c) was a standalone, knowledge-based requirement that you should have scored well on.

ACCA examining team's comments

In part (a), sound answers appreciated that the point of the tender document is to sell your audit firm's services to the client. Those candidates who tailored their answer to the question scenario tended to do well. However, candidates who provided a list of points to be included in **any** tender scored inadequately. Weak answers simply stated vague comments: 'we should discuss fees', 'we should set a deadline', etc. Answers to part (b), which asked for matters to consider re: acceptance, were weak, despite this being a regularly examined syllabus area. Most answers were not tailored to the question, and just provided a list of questions or actions. Requirement (c) was the worst answered on the exam. Clearly, very few candidates had studied the issue of transnational audits, and answers displayed a lack of knowledge.

Marking guide	Marks
(a) **Contents of tender document**	
Up to 1.5 marks per matter described:	
• Outline of firm	
• Specialisms	
• Audit requirement of Dragon Group	
• Outline audit approach (max 3 marks if detailed description)	
• Communication with management	
• Timing	
• Key staff/resources	
• Fees	
• Extra services	
Maximum	9
(b) **Matters to consider re acceptance**	
Generally 0.5 mark for identification – cap at max 3, 1 further mark for explanation, from ideas list:	
• Large and expanding group – availability of staff now and in the future	
• Use of overseas offices	
• Visits to overseas audit teams	
• Skills/experience in retail/foreign subsidiaries consolidation	
• Timing – tight deadline	
• Mermaid Ltd – implication of prior year qualification	
• Minotaur Ltd – implication of different business activity	
• Highly regulated – risk/additional reporting requirements	
• Reason for previous auditors leaving office	
Maximum	8
(c) **Define transnational audit**	
1 mark for definition	
Audit risk factors in a transnational audit	
2 marks per difference explained:	
• Auditing standards	
• Regulation of auditors	
• Financial reporting standards	
• Corporate governance/control risk	
Maximum	3

Professional marks

Analysis and evaluation

- Appropriate assessment of the ethical and professional issues that should be consider before accepting the audit engagement
- Effective appraisal of the information to make to determine the matters that should be included in the audit tender document
- Discussion of the issues involved in transnational audits

Marking guide	Marks
Professional scepticism and judgement	
• Effective challenge and critical assessment of the evidence supplied with appropriate conclusions	
• Demonstration of the ability to consider whether the evidence obtained in relation to Dragon is of the required standard	
Commercial acumen	
• Appropriate consideration of fees in the context of the audit tender for Dragon Group	
• Demonstration of ability to set commercial needs alongside ethical and quality issues in providing the required level of audit service	
Maximum	5
Total	25

(a) **Fees**

The proposed fee should be included, along with an explanation of how it is calculated. This would include details of the charge-out rates of the staff likely to be used on the audit, along with estimates of the amount of time the audit would be likely to take.

Dragon Group's needs and how Unicorn & Co could meet them

(1) An explanation of the need for each subsidiary (as well as Dragon Co) to have its own individual audit, and for the consolidated financial statements then to be audited too.
That Unicorn & Co is a large firm and would be capable of auditing a large group such as this.

(2) The Dragon Group may also need some non-audit services (see below).
That Unicorn & Co can provide a variety of non-audit services, should they be required.

(3) Several subsidiaries prepare accounts under local accounting rules, so the auditor of these would need to audit under different financial reporting frameworks.
That Unicorn & Co is a global firm with offices in over 150 countries. It would be well-placed to conduct an audit under local accounting rules, and to audit their consolidation into the group accounts.

(4) The Dragon Group operates in the furniture retail trade.
That Unicorn & Co has a specialist retail department and therefore has the experience to audit the group efficiently.

Proposed audit approach

This section should include a description of the methodology to be used in the audit. For instance:

(1) How the firm would acquire knowledge of the business

(2) Methods used in planning and risk assessment

(3) Procedures used to gather audit evidence

Brief outline of Unicorn & Co

A short history of the firm, including a description of its organisational structure, the services it can offer and the locations in which it operates.

Other services

A description of any other services Unicorn & Co can offer, such as offering advice in relation to the proposed stock exchange listing. Careful consideration should be given to ethical requirements relating to independence when offering other services to a potential audit client.

Key staff

Details of the proposed engagement partner and of his experience that is relevant to this audit. Details should also be given of the approximate size and composition of the audit team, together with a description of the relevant experience of key members of that team.

Communication with management

An outline of the various communications that will be made to management over the course of the audit. This may include information on the way in which these reports could add value to the Dragon Group's business, for instance the production of a written report on the effectiveness of internal control procedures.

Timing

Details should be provided of the timeframe envisaged for the various aspects of the audit. This might include details of when the subsidiaries would be audited, when the consolidation process would be audited, and an estimate of by when the group audit opinion could be completed.

Conclusion

This is a large, transnational group, carrying a high level of risk. Unicorn & Co should take on the audit only once it is sure that it is able to do so, and it is assured of a fee that adequately compensates it for the level of risk involved in undertaking the audit.

(b) **Matters to consider if tender is successful**

Size of Dragon Group

The Dragon Group is large and expanding group of companies and would therefore require a high level of resources to audit. Unicorn & Co must consider whether it has sufficient staff available to audit a growing group of this size.

Overseas subsidiaries

Half of the subsidiaries are located overseas. Unicorn & Co has a large number of overseas offices which could perform some or all of the overseas audits. However, these offices may not all have specialist retail audit departments, so consideration needs to be given to whether there is enough experienced staff to carry out the audit.

If some of the overseas audit work needs to be done by auditors outside of Unicorn & Co, then this work would need to be evaluated in order to express an opinion on the group financial statements.

Relevant expertise

As Unicorn & Co has a department specialising in retail audits, it is likely that it will have sufficient expertise in this country.

As a large auditing firm, it is also likely that Unicorn & Co will have staff sufficiently experienced in auditing the consolidation process to audit the consolidation of the Dragon Group's results.

Time pressure

The group's year end is 30 September 20X9, and management wants the audit completed by 31 December 20X9. This represents a tight deadline, given that the audit involves a large number of subsidiaries located in several different countries and reporting under a number of different accounting rules. The fact that this would be the first year that Unicorn & Co would have audited the group also makes the deadline tight. There is also a possibility that management does not fully understand what is required for an audit.

Planned listing

Management is planning a new listing on a foreign stock exchange. This will increase the risk of management manipulation of the accounts, as management may be under pressure to report favourable results. Audit risk is also increased by the fact that as a result of the listing, the financial statements will be subject to heavy scrutiny by regulators.

Previous auditor

Unicorn & Co should consider the reason for the group seeking to change its auditor, as this might affect the decision to accept the engagement. On the face of it, it appears likely that the quickly growing group has outgrown its previous auditors, but Unicorn & Co should still seek to obtain the reason for the change from the previous auditors.

Mermaid Ltd

Mermaid Ltd's previous auditors expressed a qualified audit opinion. Unicorn & Co should gather information about the related contingent liability, part of which would involve contacting the previous auditors. Management's refusal to disclose the contingent liability may indicate a lack of integrity on their part, which would increase audit risk. Consideration then needs to be given to whether any future non-disclosure would be material to the group financial statements.

Minotaur Ltd

Minotaur Ltd operates in a different business area from the rest of the group, so Unicorn & Co must consider whether it has staff available with the appropriate level of expertise. This difficulty should be straightforward for a firm of Unicorn & Co's size to overcome.

(c) **Transnational audits**

A transnational audit means an audit of financial statements which are or may be relied upon outside the audited entity's home jurisdiction for purposes of significant lending, investment or regulatory decisions (*TAC*, 2010).

Regulation and oversight of auditors differs from country to country

In some countries audits are self-regulated, whereas in others a legislative approach is used. There is a risk that auditors of transnational groups may not be sufficiently aware of the requirements in all of the relevant countries.

Differences in auditing standards from country to country

Although ISAs are now in operation in many countries, these standards are frequently modified by individual countries. Moreover, not all countries have adopted the standards.

There is a risk that auditors may not have the required understanding of the relevant auditing standards in each country.

Variability in audit quality in different countries

It may be the case that the quality of auditing required may differ between relevant countries. There is a risk either that the auditor does not perform an audit that is up to the required standard in some countries, or that the audits performed on some overseas subsidiaries are not up to the standard required to express an opinion on the group financial statements.

16 Goldfinch

Workbook references

Chapters 7 and 8.

Top tips

This was a reasonable question in a format that should be familiar to AAA students.

Part (a) featured a decommissioning provision. In a way this was an easy question part, because the only hard pieces of information you are given tell the story of the provision going down. If you had thought about it, you could have worked out that the provision should be going up; however, even if you didn't get this point, you could have spotted the change in the discount rate used, which signals what is going on. The audit points themselves should be straightforward.

Part (b) gave us another suspicious-looking adjustment by management, this time a change in how depreciation is estimated. This should not have posed you significant problems, as the scenario was clear and the points coming out of it were not too complex – the main things being the change in the useful lives themselves, and then accounting for it retrospectively instead of prospectively.

One thing to bear in mind with questions like this is that the examining team tends not to like it when students go too far in criticising management, or do not use professional language when doing so. Notice that the answer here is quite restrained in its language, and that the key response is to apply professional scepticism.

Part (c) may have seemed more difficult as it is full of inconsistencies. You might have been thrown off by the existence of two different types of trade receivable, by the unexplained differences in collection periods between the types of receivable, or by the unexplained change in the allowance for credit losses. The question does not actually give you a great deal to go on here, so it is reasonable to feel unsure of how to answer it. The model answer keeps things simple – more information is needed. Two of the evidence points are for 'notes of a discussion with management' – this is a type of evidence that is very useful in questions like this one.

Easy marks

The marks for calculating materiality are the easiest on the question.

Marking guide | **Marks**

(a) Generally up to 1 mark for each relevant matter considered, and 1 mark for each well explained point on audit evidence.

Decommissioning provision

Matters

- Materiality of the provision
- Requirements of ISA (UK) 540 (Revised) regarding obtaining appropriate evidence
- Unusual that a decommissioning provision has reduced in value but there could be valid reasons
- Provision should be measured at best estimate and discounted to present value
- The reason for the change in interest rate needs to be fully understood

- Whether it is appropriate that management has not used an expert to determine the estimateConsideration of accounting entries and whether they indicate an attempt to boost profit for the year

Evidence

- A copy of management's calculation of the £430 million provision, with all components agreed to underlying documentation, and arithmetically checked
- Notes of a meeting with management, at which the reasons for the reduction in the provision were discussed
- Copies of the source data used to produce management's estimate
- A comparison of the calculation for this year's provision with previous years, confirming consistency in the overall approach used by management
- Copies of the underlying information relating to the expected costs of the decommissioning
- An evaluation of all key assumptions, considering consistency with the auditor's knowledge of the business, and a conclusion on their validity
- An independent estimate prepared by the audit team, compared to management's estimate, and with significant variances discussed with management
- Alternatively, an estimate prepared by an auditor's expert, with all workings and assumptions evaluated by the audit team
- A schedule of the movement in the provision, checked for arithmetical accuracy, opening and closing figures agreed to the draft financial statements and general ledger
- Evaluation, and a conclusion on the appropriateness of the accounting entries used, especially in relation to the profit impact of the entries
- A copy of the notes to the financial statements which describe the decommissioning provision, reviewed for completeness and accuracy

Maximum 8

(b) **Depreciation**

Matters

- Materiality
- Annual review of estimated useful life is required
- Amendment has a significant impact on profit and could be an attempt to inflate profit
- Professional scepticism should be applied
- Incorrectly accounted for as a prior year adjustment, should be a prospective adjustment
- Retained earnings and PPE are overstated

Evidence

- Notes of a meeting with management on incorrect accounting treatment
- Confirmation from management that a correction will be made to account for it prospectively rather than retrospectively
- Agreement of the carrying value of the plant and equipment to the non-current asset register
- Documentation supporting the extension of the useful lives of the assets
- A written representation from management explaining the justification for the amendment to the estimated life of the assets

- A copy of management's calculation of the amended depreciation charge, checked for arithmetical accuracy, and each element of the calculation agreed to supporting documentation 6

(c) **Trade receivables**

Matters

- Materiality
- Trend in receivables collection periods is inconsistent
- New billing system could explain the change in trends
- Management using more judgement in determining allowance, the increase is significant and not adequately explained by management

Evidence

- Notes of a discussion with management on the results of the analytical procedures
- A copy of the aged receivables analysis, reviewed for significant changes in year
- Documentation on the new billing system, to confirm our understanding of the system and relevant controls
- Further analytical procedures performed on the allowance for credit losses
- Notes of a discussion with management which include the assumptions used by management in determining the amount of the allowance, and the method by which it was calculated

6

Professional marks

Analysis and evaluation

- Appropriate assessment of the matters to consider, using examples where relevant to support overall comments
- Effective appraisal of the information to make accurate determinations of the audit evidence required in relation to each matter

Professional scepticism and judgement

- Effective challenge and critical assessment of the information supplied with appropriate conclusions
- Appropriate consideration of the risk of management bias in relation to the issues raised.
- Demonstration of the ability to probe into the reasons for quality issues including the identification of missing information or additional information which would be required
- Appropriate application of professional judgement to draw conclusions and make informed comments regarding the quality of the work carried out.

Maximum	5
Total	25

(a) **Decommissioning provision**

Matters

The provision is material as it amounts to 22.6% of total assets. The provision has changed in value over the year, declining by £58 million, which is a significant reduction of 11.9%.

According to ISA (UK) 540 (Revised) *Auditing Accounting Estimates and Related Disclosures*, the audit team should have considered estimation uncertainty, including the complexity and subjectivity of this provision. It should have tested how management made the accounting estimate, and the data on which it is based, due to the risk that there may be management bias which could lead to an incorrect amount being recognised. The audit team should also have tested the operating effectiveness of any relevant controls and developed their own point estimate or range in order to evaluate management's estimate.

The value of a decommissioning provision would normally be expected to increase, as the date of the anticipated settlement of the liability draws closer, so the audit team must fully understand the reasons for the reduction in the provision. There could be valid reasons – for example, the estimated costs of dismantling the assets have reduced, or the estimated date of decommissioning is later – but the change in value should have been fully investigated by the audit team.

IAS 37 *Provisions, Contingent Liabilities and Contingent Assets* requires that the amount recognised as a provision should be the best estimate of the expenditure required to settle the present obligation at the reporting date, and that provisions are measured at present value. For the decommissioning provision recognised by Goldfinch Gas Co, where the obligation will not be settled for many years, the method used to discount the liability to present value will have a significant impact on the measurement of the provision. For example, the use of 8% to determine the discount factor, rather than 6%, will have reduced the value of the provision and the reasons for the change in interest rate should have been an important consideration for the audit team.

Consideration should be given to the accounting entries which have been made to effect the change in the value of the provision. When a decommissioning provision is first recognised, there is no profit impact, because the cost is capitalised as part of the relevant non-current asset. Subsequent adjustments to the value of the provision could be charged or credited to profit, or recognised as an adjustment to the asset value, depending on the reason for the adjustment. The audit work should conclude on the appropriateness of how the change to the provision of £58 million has been recognised in the current year financial statements. In particular, the validity of any credit entries made to profit should be scrutinised, as this could indicate creative accounting, specifically earnings management.

In previous years management has engaged an expert to provide the estimate, but this year the estimate has been prepared by management. There are therefore increased risks of both error and management bias in the estimation techniques and methodology which have been used. The audit team should approach this issue with professional scepticism and consider whether the expense of engaging an expert is the real reason as to why a management estimate has been used this year.

Evidence

- A copy of management's calculation of the £430 million provision, with all components agreed to underlying documentation, and arithmetically checked.
- Notes of a meeting with management, at which the reasons for the reduction in the provision were discussed, including the key assumptions used by management. In particular, management should provide justification of the change in interest rate used in their estimation from 6% to 8%.
- Copies of the source data used to produce management's estimate, including information on the relevant assets' estimated useful lives and expected date of their decommissioning, which may be part of a licence agreement to operate gas production and storage facilities.
- A comparison of the calculation of this year's provision with previous years, confirming consistency in the overall approach and methodology applied in creating the estimate.
- Copies of the underlying information relating to the expected costs of the decommissioning, evaluated for reasonableness by the audit team, for example, by comparison to the cost of any current decommissioning which is taking place.
- An evaluation of all key assumptions, considering consistency with the auditor's knowledge of the business, and a conclusion on their validity.
- An independent point estimate prepared by the audit team, compared to management's point estimate, and with significant variances discussed with management.

- As an alternative to the above, if the audit team does not have the necessary skill to prepare the estimate, an estimate prepared by an auditor's expert should be included in the audit file, with all workings and assumptions evaluated by the audit team.
- A schedule obtained from management showing the movement in the decommissioning provision in the accounting period, checked for arithmetic accuracy, and with opening and closing figures agreed to the draft financial statements and general ledger.
- Evaluation by the audit team, and a conclusion on the appropriateness of the accounting entries used, especially in relation to the profit impact of the entries.
- A copy of the notes to the financial statements which describe the decommissioning provision, reviewed for completeness and accuracy.

(b) **Depreciation**

The plant and equipment is recognised at £65 million; this is material to the financial statements as it represents 3.4% of total assets. The depreciation which has been recognised in profit for the year represents 9.2% of profit before tax and is also material.

There are two main issues to be considered regarding the accounting treatment of the depreciation. First, the reason for the change in the estimated useful life needs to be properly justified. There is nothing wrong in amending the estimated useful life of non-current assets – indeed it is a requirement of IAS 16 *Property, Plant and Equipment* that the useful life of an asset should be reviewed at least at each financial year end.

However, the adjustment to the estimated useful life appears to be fairly significant, resulting in a £3 million reduction in the annual depreciation charge, equivalent to a reduction of 20% of the expense recognised in the previous year, and increasing profit before tax in 20W7 by 2.3%. Management could have changed the estimated useful life with the intention of boosting profit, and the audit team should be sceptical of the reasons used to justify the change in estimated useful life. The need to be sceptical is augmented by the boost to profit which may have been achieved through the reduction in the decommissioning provision.

Second, the change in estimate has been accounted for incorrectly. According to IAS 16, when a change in estimated useful life is recognised, this is accounted for prospectively as a change in estimate under IAS 8 *Accounting Policies, Changes in Accounting Estimates and Errors*. In this case, it has been incorrectly accounted for as a prior year adjustment, effectively being treated as an error rather than a change in estimation technique.

Based on the information provided, both non-current assets and retained earnings are overstated by £20 million. This represents 1.1% of total assets and is borderline in terms of its materiality to the financial statements, though given the possibility of earnings management techniques being used to boost profit, the audit team should consider revising its risk assessment for the audit as a whole and reducing the level of materiality applied when evaluating the risk of material misstatement. Further, this is effectively the misapplication of an accounting policy and is therefore likely to be considered material by nature.

Evidence

- Notes of a meeting with management where the incorrect accounting treatment of the change in estimate has been discussed, along with confirmation from management that a correction will be made to account for it prospectively rather than retrospectively.
- Confirmation that the carrying value of the plant and equipment and the retained earnings have been adjusted to remove the £20 million incorrectly recognised as a prior year adjustment.
- Agreement of the carrying value of the plant and equipment to the non-current asset register and physical verification of a sample of assets where the asset life has been extended to confirm condition and operation of the asset.
- Documentation supporting the extension of the useful lives of the assets concerned, for example, maintenance reports indicating continued efficiency of the assets, and engineers reports showing that there are no major operational problems with the assets.

- A written representation from management explaining the justification for the amendment to the estimated life of the assets.
- A copy of management's calculation of the amended depreciation charge, checked for arithmetical accuracy by the audit team, and each element of the calculation agreed to supporting documentation.

(c) **Trade receivables**

The total trade receivables is material to the financial statements, representing 23.7% of total assets.

The analytical procedures performed by the audit team reveal an unusual trend in that the trade receivables collection period for residential customers has increased from 58 to 65 days, whereas the collection period for business customers has reduced from 55 to 50 days. The reasons for this inconsistent trend should be fully explored with management. Net trade receivables in total have increased by 15.4%. The use of additional judgement could increase the risk of material misstatement, particularly in relation to the residential customers who are deemed to be historically late in paying their bills.

The changes in collection period could be related to the new customer billing system which has been introduced during the year, and management should confirm whether this relates to both residential and business customers, or to just one of them.

The allowance for credit losses has increased significantly, by 45.5%. The allowance is material to the financial statements as it represents 3.4% of total assets and the movement in the allowance in the year represents 15.3% of profit. The note to the financial statements indicates that the introduction of the new billing system has impacted on how management estimates the allowance for credit losses, and the reasons for this should be discussed with management. It would seem unusual that the introduction of a new billing system would have such a significant effect on the level of bad or doubtful debts, so possibly there is another reason to explain why the allowance has increased by such a large amount.

The audit team should have documented and evaluated the new system, using walk through tests to confirm understanding of how the system works, and controls should also have been evaluated for effectiveness in their design and operation. This is particularly important given that there are significant changes in the collection periods for both residential and business customers since last year end, which could indicate that customers are not being billed in the same way or that there is some misallocation between residential and business customers' accounts.

Evidence

- Notes of a discussion with management on the change in the trade receivables collection period, including management's reasons for the increase in the residential customers' collection period, and reduction in the business customers' collection period.
- A copy of the aged receivables analysis, reviewed for significant changes in the year, for example, an increase in the age profile of the receivables could justify the increase in allowance against old receivables balances.
- Documentation on the new billing system, to confirm understanding of the system and the results of the evaluation of the controls which operate over the system.
- Further analytical procedures performed on the allowance for credit losses, for example, procedures which show a breakdown of the allocation of the allowance against residential and business customers.
- Notes of a discussion with management which include the assumptions used by management in determining the amount of the allowance, and the method by which it was calculated, for example as a % of receivables balances or specific allocation to individual customers' balances, and how the introduction of the new billing system has impacted on the determination of the allowance.

Tutorial note. Credit will be awarded for audit evidence on the collectability and existence of trade receivables including after date cash tests, relevant enquiries with credit controllers and receivables confirmations and reconciliations.

17 Ted

Workbook references

Chapters 2, 5, 6, and 8.

Top tips

As ever you needed to stick closely to the scenario to do well – including reading it carefully.

Part (a) was a good question on audit tendering and ethics, which provided you with a fair test. Audit tendering is a slightly peripheral but still important part of the syllabus. You can approach questions like part (a)(i) by using a standard set of issues to include in the tender (eg taken from the Workbook), which you must then adapt to the scenario. The easy marks here come from the scenario, and you do not need to know very much about tendering to get those marks.

One obvious point to bear in mind when answering part (a)(i) is that there are no marks for mentioning fees in this part of your answer! Also it was possible to mention ethics in both part (i) and part (ii), but your answer needed to be focused on the requirement in each part, so do not discuss detailed ethical issues in part (i), but only the coverage of ethical matters in the tender.

Part (a)(ii) was again fair, and most candidates would have been able to muster up enough comments about how fees are determined and the necessity of maintaining quality. This part of the requirement breaks down into two elements – the issues to consider in determining a fee, and the ethical matters – so you need to cover both of these.

The first part of the embedded requirement was almost standalone, and although it is better if you can bring bits of the scenario into your answer you do not strictly have to do so to answer the requirement. It is important to stick to your allotted time here – it may have been a temptation to go over the 10 minutes available (5 marks × 1.95 minutes).

The wording of the requirement itself was quite complicated, containing several subordinate clauses – to discuss planning matters, specific to an initial audit engagement, which should be considered in developing the audit strategy. Yet in the end most planning matters would affect the audit strategy, so your focus should have been mainly on planning matters for initial audit engagements, provided that the points you come up with are not so detailed as to be irrelevant to the strategy.

Note that it is assumed the audit has already now been accepted, so matters related to obtaining professional clearance from the predecessor auditor were not relevant to this part of the question. The predecessor auditor would only be contacted as part of our planning process. (This is one way in which you needed to bear the scenario in mind in order to answer this question part.)

Although the client is a new client, it has previously been audited so the matters to consider here do not include matters where the prior year financial statements are unaudited.

The second part of the embedded requirement was a typical AAA question on audit risk. Your approach here should be to work through the scenario, noting and thinking about audit risks as you spot them.

There were marks available for calculating an item's materiality, and for saying whether or not it was material. These are easy marks and you should make sure you get them, although there is likely to be a cap on the number of marks you can get here.

Although a preliminary analytical review has already been performed, there are still marks available for calculating a few extra figures – for example, profit margins. These are easy marks, but to get them you need to calculate the comparative as well (ie both this year's margin and last year's margin). Again, these marks are likely to be capped so don't spend all of your time doing calculations!

The requirement is on audit risk – rather than the risk of material misstatement – so this includes detection risk, as well as any more practical issues that could affect the audit planning.

The final requirement of the question may have looked harder than it was. You can get quite a few marks for saying simple things like: the need to vouch the payment for purchasing the investments to the cashbook and bank statement; to review board minutes for evidence of authorisation; and to review the disclosure note to ensure that disclosure is accurate and complete. Once you have these points you only need to think of a few more in order to pass this question part. It should go without saying that you need to make your procedures as specific as possible, eg do not just say 'vouch to documentation', but rather state which piece of documentation you would use.

Easy marks

The marks for calculating and assessing materiality in the second part of the question are simple. Not to mention the professional marks: notice that the professional marks are for presentation (among other things), something which will also help to get your marker on your side.

ACCA examining team's comments

The first part of the question focused on practice management and client acceptance issues. The scenario described a potential new audit client, Ted plc, a small but rapidly growing company. The audit firm had been approached to tender for the audit of Ted plc, and this would be the first year that the company required an audit.

Requirement (a)(i) for eight marks asked candidates to explain the specific matters to be included in the audit proposal document, other than those relating to the audit fee. This was **quite well attempted by many**, with almost all candidates understanding the main components of an audit proposal document such as a background of the audit firm, discussion of audit methodology, an outline of the firm's resources and timings and deadlines. Where **candidates did not score well** on this requirement was where the answer provided was very generic and was not made specific to the requirements of Ted plc.

Requirement (a)(ii) for six marks went on to ask candidates to discuss the issues relating to determining the audit fee to be considered by the audit firm, assuming its appointment as auditor of Ted plc. Unfortunately many answers to this requirement did not identify the relevant matters in the question scenario, including the issue of contingent fees, intimidation on fees and lowballing that were implied by the comments made by the owner-manager of Ted plc. **Better candidates** were able to make the very valid point that the potential client needed a better understanding of the purpose of an audit and why it needs to be seen to be independent and tied this back to the content of the proposal document.

Where these matters were not discussed, answers tended to be generic, and simply focused on the fact that audit fees should be determined by time, resources and charge-out rates. Many of the weaker answers did not focus on the specific nature of the question requirement, and instead discussed matters that had little to do with the audit fee, such as self-review threats and other irrelevant acceptance procedures such as customer due diligence.

Answers to the **first embedded requirement** were very mixed in quality, with the best answers concentrating on practical matters such as reviewing the previous audit firm's working papers, planning procedures to obtain evidence on opening balances, and ensuring that the audit team developed a thorough understanding of the business.

Unfortunately the majority of candidates provided generic answers discussing whether or not the firm could take on the audit, engagement letters, fees, customer due diligence and checking to see if the previous auditors had been correctly removed from office. It was not relevant to discuss whether the audit firm should take on the client and associated acceptance issues as it was clearly expressed in the scenario that this decision had already been taken and consequently answers of this nature scored limited credit.

Other weaker answers discussed general audit planning matters such as the need to determine a materiality level. This was not tailored to the specifics of this scenario as this would be relevant for any audit. **Candidates are reminded to answer the specific question that has been set**, which in this case should have meant answers focusing on matters relevant to planning an initial audit engagement after the engagement has been accepted.

Some candidates wrote a lot for what was only a five-mark requirement. Candidates are reminded that the marks for each requirement are a guide as to how long should be spent on answering the question. In some cases the answers to this question part ran to several pages, leading to time pressure on subsequent answers.

There were some excellent answers to the second embedded part of the question, with many responses covering a range of audit risks, all well explained, and all relevant to the scenario. The best answers demonstrated that a methodical approach had been applied to the information in the scenario, and the better candidates had clearly worked through the information logically, identifying the risk factors, then going on to explain them fully and specifically.

The audit risks that were generally dealt with well included those relating to the foreign currency transactions and to the portfolio of short-term investments. The risk relating to whether research and development costs could be capitalised was also identified by the majority of candidates, but the issue of amortisation was not often discussed.

To achieve a good mark for this type of requirement, candidates should look for a range of audit risks, some of which are risks of material misstatement and some are detection risks. **Candidates** however **do not need to categorise the risks they are discussing** or to spend time explaining the components of the audit risk model.

When discussing audit risks relating to a specific accounting treatment, well explained answers will include an evaluation of the potential impact of the risk factor on the financial statements, for example, in this scenario there was a risk that the short-term investments were overstated in value and that profit also was overstated. Materiality should be calculated when possible, as this allows prioritisation of the risks identified. **Strong candidates**, as well as providing detailed analysis and explanation of the risks, also **attempted to prioritise the various risks identified**, thus demonstrating appropriate judgement and an understanding that the audit partner would want to know about the most significant risks first. Candidates are reminded that it is those risks that could result in a material misstatement in the financial statements, which need to be identified and addressed.

Weak answers included answer points that were too vague to be awarded credit. Comments such as 'there is a risk this has not been accounted for properly', 'there is risk that this is not properly disclosed' and 'there is a risk that the accounting standard has not been followed' are unfortunately too common and will not earn marks due to the lack of specificity. It would be beneficial for candidates to review their answers and to consider whether what they have written would provide the audit engagement partner with the necessary knowledge to understand the risk profile of the client in question.

Regarding the third embedded part of the question, some candidates proved able to provide a good list of recommendations, but this was the minority. Answers here were good, with many candidates appreciating that determining the short-term nature of the investments was an important issue and that the fair value of the shares at the year end could be agreed to stock market listings. However, most candidates could only provide vague suggestions such as 'discuss with the board' or 'agree to supporting documentation', and in relation to the fair value of the share many candidates could only suggest to 'rely on an expert' which was not necessary given that the investment relates to the shares of listed companies. Some candidates tried to make the recommended procedures much too complicated, not fully appreciating that traded equity shares can be easily valued and documented.

Marking guide — **Marks**

(a) (i) **Matters to be included in the audit proposal**

Generally up to 2 marks for each matter explained:

- Outline of the audit firm
- Audit requirement of Ted plc
- Audit approach (allow up to 3 marks for well-explained points made relevant to scenario)
- Deadlines
- Quality management and ethics
- Additional non-audit and assurance services

Maximum 8

(ii) **Matters to be considered in determining audit fee**

Generally up to 2 marks for each point discussed:

- Fee to be based on staffing levels and chargeable hours
- Low fees can result in poor-quality audit work and increase audit risk
- Lowballing and client expectation issues
- Contingent fees not allowed

Maximum 6

(b) **Initial audit engagement**

Generally up to 1.5 marks for each point discussed, including:

- Communicate with the previous auditor, review their working papers
- Consider whether any previous auditor reports were modified
- Consider any matters which were raised when professional clearance was obtained
- Consider matters discussed with management during our firm's appointment
- Need to develop thorough business understanding
- Risk of misstatement in opening balances/previously applied accounting policies
- Firm's quality management procedures for new audit clients
- Need to use experienced audit team to reduce detection risk

Maximum 5

(c) **Evaluation and prioritisation of audit risks**

Generally up to 1.5 marks for each point discussed, and 1 mark for each calculation of materiality:

- Management bias due to recent stock market listing – pressure on results
- Management bias due to owner's shareholding – incentive to overstate profit
- Management lacks knowledge and experience of the reporting requirements for listed entities
- Weak corporate governance, potential for Dougal to dominate the board
- Revenue recognition – should the revenue be deferred
- Revenue recognition – whether deferred income recognised over an appropriate period
- E-commerce (allow up to 3 marks for discussion of several risks factors)
- Foreign exchange transactions – risk of using incorrect exchange rate
- Forward currency contracts – risk derivatives not recognised or measured incorrectly
- Portfolio of investments – risk fair value accounting not applied
- New team dealing with complex issues of treasury management
- EPS – incorrectly calculated (allow 3 marks for detailed discussion)

- EPS – risk of incomplete disclosure
- Rapid growth – control risk due to volume of transactions
- Profit margins – risk expenses misclassified (also allow 1 mark for each margin correctly calculated with comparative)
- Development costs – risk of over-capitalisation of development costs
- Inventory – year-end counts already taken place, difficulties in attending future inventory counts
- Opening balances (give mark here if not given in (a) above)

Maximum 17

(d) **Procedures on portfolio of investments**

Generally 1 mark for each procedure explained:

- Agree the fair value of the shares held as investments to stock market share price listings
- Confirm the original cost of the investment to cash book and bank statements
- Discuss the accounting treatment with management and confirm that an adjustment will be made to recognise the shares at fair value
- Review the notes to the financial statements to ensure that disclosure is sufficient to comply with the requirements of IFRS 9
- Enquire with the treasury management function regarding disposals and reinvestment
- Review board minutes to confirm the authorisation and approval of the amount invested
- Confirm the number of shares held to supporting documentation such as dividend received vouchers
- Review documentation relating to the scope and procedures of the new treasury management function

Maximum 4

Professional marks

Communication

- Briefing notes format and structure - use of headings/sub-headings and an introduction
- Style, language and clarity - appropriate layout and tone of briefing notes, presentation of materiality and relevant calculations, appropriate use of the CBE tools, easy to follow and understand
- Effectiveness and clarity of communication - answer is relevant and tailored to the scenario
- Adherence to the specific requests made by the audit engagement partner

Analysis and evaluation

- Appropriate use of the information to determine suitable calculations
- Appropriate use of the information to support discussions and draw appropriate conclusions
- Assimilation of all relevant information to ensure that the risk evaluation performed considers the impact of contradictory or unusual movements
- Effective prioritisation of the results of the risk evaluation to demonstrate the likelihood and magnitude of risks and to facilitate the allocation of appropriate responses
- Balanced discussion of the information to objectively make a recommendation or decision

Professional scepticism and judgement

- Effective challenge of information supplied, and techniques carried out to support key facts and/or decisions
- Determination and justification of a suitable materiality level, appropriately and consistently applied

- Appropriate application of professional judgement to draw conclusions and make informed decisions about the courses of action which are appropriate in the context of the audit engagement

Commercial acumen

- Audit procedures are practical and plausible in the context of Ted.
- Use of effective examples and/or calculations from the scenario to illustrate points or recommendations.
- Recognition of the appropriate commercial considerations of the audit firm — 10

Total — 50

(a) (i) **Outline of audit firm**

An outline of Craggy & Co (Craggy) should be provided, perhaps including a brief history and a summary of key information about the firm (eg the number of partners and offices).

Any specialisms of Craggy should be mentioned, particularly if it has expertise in auditing software development companies. It should also be stated that Craggy has branches in many countries, as this may prove useful if any audit work needs to be performed overseas.

Client requirements

The statutory audit requirements in Ted plc ('Ted')'s jurisdiction should be stated, to confirm that an audit is needed. It should be stated that the audit must conform to ISAs. Any additional reporting requirements that result from Ted's listing should be stated.

Audit approach

The tender should outline the stages of an audit. This should include the possibility that Craggy will need to test Ted's opening balances, which were audited by a predecessor auditor. It should be stated that this will depend on whether Craggy is able to review the predecessor auditor's working papers and is satisfied with the evidence obtained.

Craggy should describe the proposed audit approach, including the firm's audit methodology, and should explain that audit is risk-based, involving an assessment of the company's accounting systems and internal controls. It is possible that Ted's controls may not be reliable, given the accounting function's limited resources (there are only two full-time accountants), which would affect the audit approach.

Client expectations

Dougal Doyle hopes that the audit will not be disruptive. Craggy may attempt to manage his expectations here, as a certain degree of disruption is unavoidable. It will be necessary, for example, to receive explanations from employees, including the accountant, which will take time.

Communications

The tender should outline the various communications which will be made to management and those charged with governance, including the value which Ted may derive from them, particularly in relation to any control deficiencies identified.

Deadlines

The tender should seek to clarify the timeframe for the audit. The proposed deadline of four months may be reasonable, although Ted is a recently listed company so the audit is likely to be a large one (and potentially time-consuming). If there are problems with the audit, eg Ted's internal controls are less reliable than expected, then the audit may take longer. Ted needs to be prepared for this possibility.

Quality management and ethics

Craggy should state its adherence to the IESBA's *Code of Ethics for Professional Accountants*, and to International Standards on Quality Management. This will give Ted and its venture capitalist investor confidence in the auditor's report that would be issued.

Predecessor auditor

Crilly & Co, the predecessor auditor, resigned and it is crucial that professional clearance is obtained before proceeding with the audit. Crilly & Co resigned because it did have sufficient resources to perform a listed company audit, so Craggy & Co should ensure that it does.

Additional services

The tender should make mention of any other non-audit services which Craggy is in a position to provide. These are particularly relevant to Ted in light of Dougal Doyle's comments. It should be stated that these services can only be provided subject to meeting the ethical requirements by which Craggy is bound.

(ii) **Issues in determining fee level**

Commercial factors

The audit firm has a commercial desire to make a profit, which it does by offering a fee which is high enough to be profitable but low enough to attract business. It must do this without compromising its professional independence or its standards of quality.

Costs

The fee should be linked to costs incurred. The main cost is the time spent by the audit team, so this component of the fee is calculated using a charge-out rate which is multiplied by the time spent. Basing the fee on the costs incurred is both commercially sound (it ensures that costs and normal profits are covered), and ethically relevant because it ensures that the fee is sufficient to pay for the work that needs to be done.

Additional costs included in the audit fee are the fees of any auditor's experts, and the costs of any travel that is needed for the audit team. The cost of auditing Ted may be increased by its stock exchange listing, which will impose more extensive reporting requirements on it and thus more audit work.

Low fees

There is a suggestion that the fee for the Ted audit may be set below market rate in order to win the audit. This is known as lowballing, and while this is not prohibited as such, it does carry the ethical risk that the fees may not be sufficient to pay for the work required. Craggy must not, therefore, reduce the amount of audit work done because the fee is insufficient, but must do whatever work is necessary to reduce audit risk to an acceptable level.

Contingent fee

To link the audit fee to the success of the company is to charge a contingent fee. This creates a self-interest threat.

The threat is so significant that no safeguards could reduce it to an acceptable level, so such an arrangement should not be entered into.

Intimidation

Taken together, Dougal Doyle's two suggestions in relation to fees (low and contingent fees) and his hope for a fixed deadline may amount to an intimidation threat. If this is the case, then Craggy must consider not continuing with the tender.

(b) **Briefing notes**

To: Jack Hackett

From: Manager

Subject: Audit of Ted plc, y/e 31 May 20X5

Introduction

These briefing notes will discuss planning matters to consider in relation to the audit strategy of an initial audit engagement, evaluate the audit risks relevant to planning the Ted audit, and recommend the principal audit procedures for the portfolio of investments.

Although professional clearance should already have been obtained, we should consider the effect on our strategy of any matters that the predecessor auditor may have brought to our attention. The reason for the predecessor auditor's resignation should be established, as this may have a bearing on our assessment of risk and planning of resources for the audit.

ISA (UK) 300 *Planning an Audit of Financial Statements* suggests contacting the predecessor auditor in order to review their working papers (as long as this is not prohibited by laws or regulation). This would help Craggy to plan its audit if there are any matters which would still be relevant to the current year, such as accounting policies. It is possible, however, that the predecessor auditor may refuse access to their working papers.

Although last year's auditor's opinion was unmodified, if any previous years' auditors' reports were modified then the reason for the modification(s) should be sought, as the matter(s) may continue to be relevant in the current year.

It is possible that, during the appointment process, matters were discussed which might have a bearing on the audit, eg there might have been a discussion of accounting policies. This may affect the audit strategy.

Craggy must obtain evidence on opening balances. Procedures should be performed on whether they have been brought forward correctly, and whether accounting policies are consistent.

Understanding the entity is crucial with an initial audit engagement, and this understanding would clearly have an impact on the audit strategy. It would help Craggy to decide on the areas of audit risk, would facilitate analytical review, and would help to plan practical matters such as the use of auditor's experts.

(c) **Development costs**

Development costs capitalised are 43% of total assets. This is highly material and should be considered a high priority risk for the audit.

The 65.7% increase over last year is significant, so there is a risk of misstatement. Given that £100m was invested, however, capitalising 58% may be reasonable; this can only be known once audit evidence has been obtained in this area. Professional scepticism will be important, given the highly material nature of the asset but also the risk of management bias (see below).

Development costs are capitalised only when they meet the IAS 38 *Intangible Assets* criteria, such as whether it is probable that future economic benefits will flow to the entity, whether the cost can be measured reliably, whether the asset is technically and commercially feasible, or whether Ted has the resources to complete the development (IAS 38: para. 57). Costs not meeting these criteria are expensed in profit or loss.

Overseas manufacturing

Overseas manufacture of physical product brings a detection risk in relation to inventory. For example, it may be difficult for the firm to attend inventory counts overseas at the year end if inventory is held overseas, in which case alternative sources of evidence should be consulted.

Website sales

25% of revenue is generated through the website. This is material.

There is a control risk here, and this is particularly acute given the company's rapid expansion – there is a danger that the website cannot cope with a large increase in sales, which could affect the figures reported in the financial statements.

There is a detection risk, because the website may not leave a significant audit trail.

There is a cut-off risk, because it may be difficult to determine the exact time when performance obligations are satisfied in line with IFRS 15 *Revenue from Contracts with Customers*, ie when control is passed from Ted to the customer.

License income

Deferred income from licences is 13.4% of total assets. This is material.

This income should be accounted for in line with IFRS 15, and again it may be difficult to determine exactly when performance obligations are satisfied. This depends on whether the promise to grant a licence includes any other promised goods or services, for example whether the software will be updated during the period of the licence. If no such goods or services are included, then it may be that performance obligations are satisfied at that point in time, ie when the licence is sold. In this case no licence income should be deferred at all and there is a material misstatement, understating revenue and overstating assets. The audit plan should ensure that sufficient resources are devoted to this technical area.

Listing

Ted obtained a listing during the year, which brings a risk of manipulation. This is an inherent risk at the financial statement level. Management will want to present good results for the new (and potential) shareholders, so there is an incentive to overstate profit and assets. Profit before tax is up 48.1%, and there is a risk that this is overstated.

The listing may bring further reporting responsibilities (eg in relation to earnings per share), so there is a risk of misstatement here which is heightened given that it is probably the first time this has been reported.

Many shares are held by institutional investors, bringing an increased level of scrutiny to the financial statements and the audit process. This increases the risk of litigation to the auditor.

This is a high priority risk for the audit, because of the potential impact that new reporting and regulatory requirements may have on the auditor's reporting responsibilities.

Corporate governance

Corporate governance structures do not appear to be strong: there are too few non-executive directors, and there is no internal audit department. There is a risk of Dougal Doyle dominating the board and influencing the preparation of the financial statements. This is amplified by the incentive for management bias in relation to the listing.

Foreign exchange

Ted must have significant foreign currency transactions, as it sells in over 60 countries and manufactures products overseas. The risk is that IAS 21 *The Effects of Changes in Foreign Exchange Rates* is not followed. IAS 21 requires all items to be translated into Ted's functional currency (£) when the transactions occur (historical rate) (IAS 21: paras. 21–22). All monetary balances at the year end must then be retranslated at the closing rate (IAS 21: para. 23). Misstatements may occur in either of these processes, leading to over- or under-statement of assets, liabilities, income, expenses, and exchange gains or losses.

The establishment of a treasury management function may help reduce this risk by improving controls. However, the fact that the team is new may mean it takes time to become effective, and there is a risk of mistakes being made while it gains experience.

The use of forward contracts to try to manage business risk represents an audit risk. First, unless they are managed properly these contracts may not have the desired effect (the team is new), which could result in an audit risk if problems occur. Second, they are derivative financial instruments and are accounted for in line with IFRS 9 *Financial Instruments*. This is complex, and there is a risk that not all contracts may be identified. Further, the contracts should be measured at fair value, which may be difficult and judgemental to determine. Hedge accounting rules must be followed, which are complex in nature. Taken together, there is a significant control risk in this area.

Investment portfolio

The cost of the shares of £8m is 6% of total assets. This is material.

The fall in value of £2m is 25% of profit before tax. This is material.

In line with IFRS 9, shares held in the short term as a speculative investment should be held at fair value through profit or loss (they are not being held to collect contractual cash flows) (IFRS). They are currently held at cost, which is therefore incorrect. They should be remeasured to fair value; if this is not done, then both profit and total assets are overstated by £2m.

The fact that such a large sum of money was lost on speculative investments raises a number of questions. This seems an ill-advised venture, and it is not clear why Ted has established a new treasury function which has spent (and lost) such sums speculating in shares, outside the company's principal activity. This may be further evidence of poor governance, and a lack of internal control which could affect the assessment of audit risk.

Rapid growth

Ted has grown rapidly in recent years, which often results in control risk as systems and people struggle to keep up with both greater volumes and new types of transactions. This may be the case here, as a lack of proper governance and control structures appears evident in several places.

Earnings per share (EPS)

IAS 33 *Earnings per Share* requires Ted to present both EPS and diluted EPS on the face of the statement of profit or loss.

The EPS calculation must be based on profit (or loss) attributable to ordinary shareholders, from the statement of profit or loss (IAS 33: para. 66). To calculate it otherwise is a material misstatement. It is possible to present an alternative figure in the notes to the financial statements, however.

There are two further errors in the EPS calculation. Profit before tax should not be used, and the number of shares used should be a weighted average for the year – not just the number at the year end, as here.

This is a significant given the new listing during the year which will expose Ted to significant scrutiny in this area.

Profit margins

	20X5	*20X4*
Gross margin	65,000 / 98,000 = 66.3%	40,000 / 67,000 = 59.7%
Operating margin	12,000 / 98,000 = 12.2%	9,200 / 67,000 = 13.7%

There is a risk that the coincidence of a rising gross margin with a falling operating margin is a result of the misclassification of expenses between cost of sales and operating expenses. This could also indicate an understatement of cost of sales. Alternatively, it could be that Ted has simply incurred more operating expenses as it has grown – for example backroom and administrative functions (such as treasury management). In any case, explanations need to be obtained of the reasons for this discrepancy.

Conclusion

A number of risks have been identified as significant risks for the audit. The highest priority risks are likely to be those arising from the highly material development costs, and in relation to the company's stock exchange listing (which connects to its corporate governance structure, and to the EPS figure). The company's operations are becoming increasingly complex, which is likely to bring with it higher levels of risk for the auditor.

(d) **Procedures on investment portfolio**

- Agree fair value of shares to stock market listings at 31 May 20X5.
- Confirm original cost of investment to cash book and bank statements.
- Discuss accounting treatment with management and confirm that an adjustment will be made to recognise the shares at fair value.
- Review notes to the financial statements to ensure that disclosure is sufficient.
- Enquire with treasury management function whether there have been any disposals of the original shares and reinvestment of proceeds into the portfolio.
- Review board minutes to confirm authorisation and approval of the investment.

- Review documentation relating to the scope and procedures of the new treasury management function, for example, to understand how the performance of investments is monitored.
- For investments from which dividends have been received, confirm the number of shares held to supporting documentation, eg dividend certificates.

Conclusion

These briefing notes depict a high level of audit risk for this engagement, which is due to the possibility of management bias and a number of indicators of poor internal controls.

18 Francis

Workbook references

Chapter 8, 9 and 10.

Top tips

This question may have been deceptively simple; it really was a question about goodwill, and a non-adjusting event. It was therefore quite possible to score well.

Throughout the question, your evidence points need to be as specific as possible, stating the evidence that you would want to see (eg the particular document – purchase documentation, say), and then why you want to see it. A simple list of pieces of evidence is unlikely to score well if it does not also say why the evidence is needed.

In the part (a) (on goodwill), you need to go through the various pieces of information thinking of what might go wrong in relation to each of them. Some housekeeping points in relation to FR: goodwill is not amortised; assets are revalued to fair value on acquisition, which does not involve a revaluation reserve; loans are held at amortised cost using an effective interest rate.

In part (b), it should be clear that this event is non-adjusting. Always try to think of when the obligating event happened – in this case it was after the year end, so it is never going to require adjustment to the financial statements. Mentioning IAS 37 in relation to the contingent asset is OK, but not strictly relevant because it's a non-adjusting event, so the fact that it may not be virtually certain to be received does not really matter. With this part of the question, there were so many marks available for calculating materiality that if you got them, you could still pass this part of the question even if you were wrong about the non-adjusting event.

Note that throughout this question, the evidence points in particular are far more comprehensive in our answer than any candidate would be able to include in their exam answer.

Easy marks

There are plentiful marks just for calculating materiality in each section, and for saying whether or not an item is material.

ACCA examining team's comments

This type of requirement is common in AAA, and it was encouraging to see that many candidates had obviously practised past exam questions containing similar requirements. Most candidates approached each of the issues in a sensible manner by firstly determining the materiality of the matters involved, considering the appropriate financial reporting treatment and risk of misstatement, and then providing some examples of appropriate audit evidence relevant to the matters discussed. However, the question was not well attempted by all, and it was usually a lack of knowledge of financial reporting requirements, and / or an inability to explain the relevant audit evidence that let some candidates down.

The first part of the question related to an acquisition of a subsidiary that had taken place during the year. A goodwill calculation had been provided, along with information regarding a fair value adjustment relevant to the net assets of the subsidiary at acquisition. In addition, a loan had been taken out to finance the acquisition and information relating to the interest rate and loan premium was given in the scenario.

Candidates were able to achieve a good mark here if they tackled each component of the information provided in turn and used that approach to deliver a structured answer. In relation to the goodwill calculation, many candidates identified that no impairment had been recognised, and therefore that the goodwill balance may be overvalued. Only the strongest candidates mentioned that a significant drop in the Group's profit for the year meant that it would be very likely that an impairment loss should be recognised. It was worrying to see how many candidates referred to the need for goodwill to be amortised over a useful life – a practice that has not been allowed under IFRS 3 *Business Combinations* for many years. Fewer candidates touched on the measurement issues in relation to the non-controlling interest component of goodwill, which was usually ignored in answers. Looking at the fair value adjustment to net assets, most candidates recognised that this would be a subjective issue and that ideally an independent valuer's report or due diligence report would be required as audit evidence to justify the adjustment. Weaker candidates thought that the accounting treatment of goodwill was incorrect and set about correcting the perceived errors.

The loan element tended to be well dealt with – most candidates seemed to be aware of the principles of IFRS 9 *Financial Instruments* in discussing the financial reporting implications of the loan taken out to finance the acquisition, and the need to measure the loan at amortised cost including the premium was frequently identified. It was encouraging to see many candidates also refer to the extensive disclosure requirements that would be necessary in relation to the acquisition itself, as well as the loan, and that a significant risk would be insufficient disclosure in the notes to the financial statements.

Some incorrect accounting treatments frequently discussed included:

- Goodwill should be amortised over an estimated useful life (discussed above)
- Goodwill only needs to be tested for impairment when indicators of impairment exist
- Non-controlling interest should not be part of the goodwill calculation
- Borrowing costs should be capitalised into the cost of investment/goodwill figures
- Fair value adjustments are not required and are an indication of fraudulent financial reporting

The evidence points provided by candidates for this requirement tended to revolve around recalculations of the various balances and confirming figures to supporting documentation such as the loan agreement, purchase documentation and due diligence reports. These were all valid evidence points but it would benefit candidates to consider a wider range of evidence that may be available especially in relation to the more subjective and therefore higher risk elements, for example a discussion with management regarding the need for an impairment review of goodwill or a review and assessment of the methods used to determine the fair value of the non-controlling interest.

The second part of the question related to a natural disaster that had taken place two months after the year end, resulting in the demolition of the Group's head office and main manufacturing site. The Group had claimed under its insurance an amount in excess of the value of the demolished property, and the whole amount of the claim was recognised in the statement of financial position as a current asset and deferred income. **This requirement was generally well answered**, with almost all candidates correctly determining the materiality of the property complex and the contingent asset. Most candidates also appreciated that the auditor should consider the event to be a non-adjusting event after the reporting date, requiring disclosure in the notes to the financial statements, in line with the requirements of IAS 10 *Events after the Reporting Period*. The audit evidence suggested was usually relevant and sensible, tending to focus on the insurance claim, discussing the need for demolition with management, and evidence from documents such as health and safety reports on the necessity for the demolition. Many answers identified that a key part of the audit evidence would be in the form of a review of the sufficiency of the required notes to the financial statements describing and quantifying the financial implications of the non-adjusting event. In a minority of scripts candidates suggested that the event was actually an adjusting event and that impairment of the property complex should be recognised in this financial year.

Weaker answers to this requirement suggested that the event should be recognised by impairing the property complex and recognising the contingent asset. However, encouragingly even where candidates had discussed the incorrect accounting treatment, the evidence points provided were generally appropriate to the scenario.

In summary, the second part was well attempted by many candidates, with the matters to consider element of the requirements usually better attempted than the audit evidence points. As in the first part, it was clear that many candidates had practised past questions of this type and were well prepared for the style of question requirement.

In the UK and IRL adapted variant exams it was much more common to see references to incorrect financial reporting requirements, specifically that goodwill must be amortised over an estimated useful life. Candidates are reminded that if they choose to attempt the UK or IRL adapted variant, the financial reporting requirements are still based on IFRS, as in the INT variant, and therefore discussing financial reporting requirements of UK and Irish GAAP will not score credit.

Marking guide **Marks**

(a) Generally 1 mark for each matter considered/evidence point explained:

Teapot Ltd

Matters

- Materiality of the goodwill
- Purchase price/consideration to be at fair value
- Risk of understatement if components of consideration not included
- Non-controlling interest at fair value – determination of fair value if Teapot Ltd is listed
- Non-controlling interest at fair value – determination of fair value if Teapot Ltd is not listed
- Use of fair value hierarchy to determine fair value
- Risk that not all acquired assets and liabilities have been separately identified
- Risk in the measurement of acquired assets and liabilities – judgemental
- Additional depreciation to be charged on fair value uplift
- Group accounting policies to be applied to net assets acquired on consolidation
- Impairment indicator exists – fall in revenue
- Impairment review required regardless for goodwill
- Risk goodwill and Group profit overstated if necessary impairment not recognised
- Loan – initial measurement at fair value
- Loan – subsequent measurement at amortised cost
- Risk effective interest not properly applied – understated finance cost and liability
- Risk of inadequate disclosure in relation to financial liability

Evidence

- Agreement of the purchase consideration to the legal documentation, and a review of the documents
- Agreement of the £75 million to the bank statement and cash book
- Review of board minutes for discussions relating to the acquisition, and for board approval
- A review of the purchase documentation and a register of significant shareholders of Teapot Ltd to confirm the 20% non-controlling interest

- If Teapot Ltd's shares are not listed, a discussion with management as to how the fair value of the non-controlling interest has been determined and evaluation of the appropriateness of the method used
- If Teapot Ltd's shares are listed, confirmation that the fair value of the non-controlling interest has been calculated based on an externally available share price at the date of acquisition
- A copy of any due diligence report relevant to the acquisition, reviewed for confirmation of acquired assets and liabilities and their fair values
- An evaluation of the methods used to determine the fair value of acquired assets, including the property, and liabilities to confirm compliance with IFRS 3 and IFRS 13
- Review of depreciation calculations, and recalculation, to confirm that additional depreciation is being charged on the fair value uplift
- A review of the calculation of net assets acquired to confirm that Group accounting policies have been applied
- Discussion with management regarding the potential impairment of Group assets and confirmation as to whether an impairment review has been performed
- A copy of any impairment review performed by management, with scrutiny of the assumptions used, and reperformance of calculations
- Reperformance of management's calculation of the finance charge in relation to the loan, to ensure that effective interest has been correctly applied
- Agreement of the loan receipt and interest payment to bank statement and cash book
- Review of board minutes for approval of the loan to be taken out
- A copy of the loan agreement, reviewed to confirm terms including the maturity date, premium to be paid on maturity and annual interest payments
- A copy of the note to the financial statements which discusses the loan to ensure all requirements of IFRS 7 have been met

Maximum 12

(b) **Subsequent event**

Matters

- Materiality of the asset (calculation) and significance to profit
- Identify event as non-adjusting
- Describe content of note to financial statements
- Consider other costs, eg inventories to be written off
- Contingent asset/deferred income should not be recognised

Evidence

- A copy of any press release/media reports
- Photographic evidence of the site after the natural disaster and of the demolished site
- A copy of the note to the financial statements describing the event
- A schedule of the costs of the demolition, with a sample agreed to supporting documentation
- A schedule showing the value of inventories and items such as fixtures and fittings
- A copy of the insurance claim

Marking guide	Marks
• Confirmation of the removal of the contingent asset from the financial statements	
Maximum	8
Professional marks	
Analysis and evaluation	
• Appropriate assessment of the matters to consider, using examples where relevant to support overall comments	
• Effective appraisal of the information to make accurate determinations of the audit evidence required in relation to each matter. Audit evidence should be relevant to each of the situations and should serve a clear purpose	
Professional scepticism and judgement	
• Effective challenge and critical assessment of the information supplied with appropriate conclusions, in relation to both the acquisition and the subsequent event	
• Appropriate consideration of the risk of management bias in relation to the issues raised, in particular in relation to the contingent asset	
• Appropriate application of professional judgement to draw conclusions and make informed comments	
Maximum	5
Total	25

(a) **Goodwill**

Goodwill is 6% of total assets and is therefore material.

Impairment

Management should review goodwill for impairment at the end of the year. No impairment loss has been recognised, and there is a risk that this is because no impairment review was conducted.

Group profit has declined by 30.3% (£10m/£33m) and assets have declined by 1.1% (£5m/£455m). These are both impairment indicators, although it is possible that the downward trends do not relate to Teapot Ltd's ('Teapot') activities. In any case there is a risk that assets and profit are both overstated.

Consideration

Consideration should be measured at its fair value. There is a risk that the calculation is incomplete, eg if there is any deferred or contingent consideration not included.

Non-controlling interest (NCI)

IFRS 3 *Business Combinations* permits NCI to be measured at fair value, so this is acceptable (IFRS 3). However there is a risk in relation to the estimation of fair value. If Teapot is listed then this is just the market price of the shares and is reliable; however, if it is not listed then the estimation must be done in line with IFRS 13 *Fair value measurement*. This involves an element of judgement, the basis of which must be clearly understood by the auditor.

Net assets

There is a risk that not all net assets will be identified, or that the estimation of their fair values is not reliable. Some form of due diligence should have been performed as part of the acquisition, which may have valued the business and identified its assets and liabilities.

Fair value adjustment

The adjustment of £300,000 is not material, at less than 1% of total assets. However, additional depreciation should be charged at group level on these assets (also not material).

Loan

The loan is 13.3% of total assets and is material.

Under IFRS 9 *Financial Instruments* it is measured at its fair value when initially recognised, and then subsequently at amortised cost as it is not held for trading (although there is a fair value option) (IFRS 9).

An effective interest rate should thus be used to allocate the premium over the 20-year life of the loan. There is a risk that the finance charge is not calculated using the effective rate, or that the premium is recognised incorrectly (for example, it may be recognised as a liability at its present value, which is incorrect).

IFRS 7 *Financial Instruments: Disclosure* contains extensive disclosure requirements, and there is a risk of misstatement in respect of inadequate disclosures in relation to the loan (eg of its significance for Teapot Co's financial position and performance).

Evidence

- Agreement of consideration to legal documentation, reviewing to ensure that the figures included in the goodwill calculation are complete.
- Agreement of £75 million to bank statement.
- Review of board minutes for discussions of acquisition, and for approval of the acquisition.
- Review of purchase documentation, and a register of significant shareholders of Teapot, to confirm 20% NCI.
- If Teapots shares are not listed, a discussion with management of how the fair value of the NCI was determined and evaluation of the appropriateness of the method used.
- If Teapot's shares are listed, confirmation that the fair value of NCI was calculated based on an externally available share price at the date of acquisition.
- Copy of due diligence report, reviewed for details of assets and liabilities and their fair values.
- Evaluation of methods used to determine fair value of assets and liabilities to confirm compliance with IFRS 3 and IFRS 13.
- Review of depreciation calculations, and recalculation, to confirm that additional depreciation is being charged on fair value uplift.
- Review of the calculation of net assets acquired to confirm that Group accounting policies have been applied.
- Discussion with management regarding the potential impairment of Group assets and confirmation of whether an impairment review has been performed.
- Copy of any impairment review performed by management, with scrutiny of the assumptions used, and reperformance of calculations.
- Reperformance of management's calculation of the finance charge on the loan, to ensure that the loan premium has been correctly accrued.
- Agreement of the loan receipt and interest payment to bank statement.
- Review of board minutes for approval of the loan to be taken out.
- Copy of the loan agreement, reviewed to confirm terms including the maturity date, premium to be paid on maturity and annual interest payments.
- Copy of the note to the financial statements which discusses the loan to ensure all requirements of IFRSs 7 and 13 have been met.

(b) **Property**

The carrying value is material, at 3.6% of total assets (= £16m / £450m).

Under IAS 10 *Events after the Reporting Period*, the natural disaster is a non-adjusting event because it relates to conditions which did not exist until two months after the year end (IAS

10: para. 3). Therefore, the value of the property complex should not be written off in the 20X4 financial statements.

The event should be disclosed in a note describing its impact and quantifying its anticipated effect on next year's financial statements. Consideration should be given to any other effects, eg other damage sustained in the disaster, and the costs of the demolition itself.

Contingent asset

The contingent asset is material, at 4.0% of total assets (= £18m / £450m).

This should not have been recognised, as it also relates to a non-adjusting event deriving from conditions which did not exist at the end of the reporting period. This fact is saliently admitted by the recognition as 'deferred income', which is itself incorrect because the amount has not yet been received.

Evidence

- Copy of any press release made by the Group after the natural disaster, and relevant media reports of the natural disaster, in particular focusing on its impact on the property complex.
- Photographic evidence of the site after the natural disaster, and of the demolished site.
- Copy of the note to the financial statements describing the event, reviewed for completeness and accuracy.
- Schedule of the costs of the demolition, with a sample agreed to supporting documentation, eg invoices for work performed.
- Schedule showing the value of inventories and items such as fixtures and fittings at the time of the disaster, and confirmation that this is included in the costs described in the note to the financial statements.
- Copy of the insurance claim and correspondence with the Group's insurers to confirm that the property is insured.
- Confirmation that an adjustment has been made to reverse out the contingent asset and deferred income which has been recognised.

19 Thurman

Workbook references

Chapters 9 and 16.

Top tips

This was quite a practical auditing question that you should have been able to pass well, particularly if you have experience of working in audit.

The format of the question and the requirement almost suggests a tabular format for your answer, but this is unlikely to be appropriate at this level (it would lead you away from writing full sentences, which you need to do in AAA). Instead, you should lay your answer out in the same way as the model answer, ie part (a) has (i) and (ii), and so on.

Regarding **timings**, one of the difficulties with this question was knowing how much to write for each sub-part (i and ii). There are different amounts that can be said in relation to each sub-part, so if you had divided your time equally between them then you might have struggled. The best method here would be to work out your time for each part (a, b, c), and then make sure you answer each sub-part within it.

Part (a) was typical of the things that can happen to an auditor in the real world. Much of the audit work that has been done is OK, but it is not enough. You should be able to pick some holes in it by asking yourself questions about how much more could have been done, eg not just checking that the journal is arithmetically correct, but that all the figures in it are included in line with IFRS 5 – and that there are no other adjustments that should have been made. Try to think about what other requirements the standard might have.

There were a few little distractors in this scenario that it's worth noting – the phrase 'manual journal' might have made you think of some kind of manual override of controls, suggesting that there was something amiss when in fact there was not (how else would this adjustment be made?). There is a hint that the audit senior is taking on a management role, but remember, the requirement does not ask for ethical issues so you should not write about them.

It is important to note that the requirement really focuses on the auditor's response to these issues, so that in eg part (a) the problem is not necessarily the accounting treatment per se, but rather whether the auditor has sufficient evidence for its reasonableness.

Make sure you spend enough time writing further audit procedures – they're worth a mark if explained properly, and these are relatively easy marks. State **what** should be done, and then say **why**.

Almost every statement in the scenario for part (a) that related to audit evidence contained an issue. Your task was simply to draw this out of the question and then, state some procedures that should now be performed. Parts (b) and (c) were similar in this respect.

Easy marks

The marks for audit procedures are easy. It is key to passing this question that you address each part of the requirement (i and ii) so that you picked up the easiest marks available in each.

ACCA examining team's comments

This question was set in the completion stage of the audit and as is generally the case with completion questions, it was focused on the accounting treatment and audit evidence obtained on three issues. Candidates generally demonstrated a good knowledge of the financial reporting implications of the areas and were often able to identify that the evidence obtained was insufficient and suggest further procedures.

Marking guide	Marks

(a) Generally 1 mark for each relevant point of discussion and well explained audit procedure:

Asset held for sale

(i) **Audit evidence**

- Discussion is relevant but management's assertions must be corroborated
- Discussion alone is not sufficient to reach an audit conclusion
- Evidence not obtained on whether IFRS 5 classification criteria have been met
- Evidence not obtained on whether disclosure of discontinued operations is necessary

(ii) **Further audit procedures**

- Review board minutes to confirm the sale approval and date
- Correspondence with estate agents to confirm that the factory is being actively marketed
- Confirmation, for example, by a review of production schedules, inventory movement records and payroll records that production at the factory has stopped
- Auditor's expert to confirm the fair value of the property and agree that this figure has been used in the impairment calculation
- Using management accounts, determine whether the factory is a separate major line of business in which case its results should be disclosed as a discontinued operation

Maximum	7

(b) **Capital expenditure**

(i) **Audit evidence**

- Testing should have been extended after the control deficiency was identified
- Reason for the controls not operating effectively should be investigated
- Increases the fraud risk in relation to capital expenditure
- Not all assertions have been covered by audit testing in respect of the vehicles purchased

(ii) **Further audit procedures**

- Obtain the insurance documents to confirm that Thurman Ltd is paying the relevant insurance for the vehicles
- Physically verify the vehicles and confirm that they are being used by employees on company business
- Obtain the log book and other relevant ownership documents such as those issued by the DVLA, to confirm the right of Thurman Ltd to recognise the vehicles
- Trace the vehicles to the company's fixed asset register
- Recompute the depreciation which should have been charged on the vehicles and agree to the statement of profit or loss for the year.

Maximum 6

(c) **Payroll**

(i) **Audit evidence**

- Agreeing payroll to the service organisation's report does not provide sufficient evidence on completeness, accuracy or validity of the amounts
- The controls at the service organisation must be assessed for their adequacy

(ii) **Further audit procedures**

- Review the service agreement between Thurman Ltd and Jackson Ltd to understand the exact work which is conducted by Jackson Ltd as a service organisation
- Read all reports made by Jackson Ltd during the year to identify any risks of misstatement in the payroll figure
- If necessary, obtain a type 1 or type 2 report from Jackson Ltd to obtain further assurance on the controls which the service organisation has in place
- Perform a substantive analytical review on payroll, preparing an auditor's expectation of the payroll figures and comparing it to that recognised in the financial statements and discussing any variance with management
- Perform test of detail by selecting a sample from the payroll records and agreeing the amounts to payslips and HR records

Maximum 7

Professional marks

Analysis and evaluation

- Appropriate use of the information to support discussion, draw appropriate conclusions and design appropriate responses
- Effective design of audit procedures to obtain evidence in the areas where it is needed

Professional scepticism and judgement

- Effective challenge and critical assessment of the information supplied with appropriate conclusions. This is relevant throughout the Thurman audit, but examples include the need to *corroborate* management's assertions in (a), or to consider the implications of having control deficiencies in (b)

Marking guide	Marks
• Application of professional scepticism to see beyond the evidence already obtained and to consider what further evidence is in fact required	
• Appropriate application of professional judgement to draw conclusions and make informed comments	
Maximum	5
Total	25

(a) **Assets held for sale**

(i) **Audit evidence**

The evidence does not appear to be sufficient to draw a conclusion on the appropriateness of classifying the property and any other related assets and liabilities as held for sale. A discussion with management regarding the accounting treatment is relevant, as the audit team will need to understand management's rationale. However, management's explanation should not be accepted at face value and should be corroborated through further audit procedures. It is not sufficient to simply put management's justification for the accounting treatment on the audit file and conclude that it is correct. For example, the factory can only be classified as held for sale if it is available for immediate sale in its current condition, which may not be the case.

In terms of the manual journal, checking that it is arithmetically correct, while relevant, is not sufficient evidence. Further evidence should be obtained in order to conclude that the basis of the calculation is in accordance with IFRS 5 *Non-current Assets Held for Sale and Discontinued Operations*and there should be consideration as to whether other requirements of the standard other than those related to the reclassification and measurement of the asset have been complied with. For example, the results specific to the factory may need to be disclosed as a discontinued operation in the statement of profit or loss and the statement of cash flows. No audit evidence appears to have been obtained in respect of these issues.

(ii) **Further audit procedures**

- Review board minutes to confirm that the sale of the factory has been approved and to agree the date of the approval to the board minutes and relevant staff announcements.
- Obtain correspondence with estate agents to confirm that the factory is being actively marketed.
- Obtain confirmation, for example, by a review of production schedules, inventory movement records and payroll records, that production at the factory has stopped and thus it is available for immediate sale.
- Use an auditor's expert to confirm the fair value of the property and agree that this figure has been used in the impairment calculation.
- Using management accounts, determine whether the factory is a separate major line of business in which case its results should be disclosed as a discontinued operation.

(b) **Capital expenditure**

(i) **Audit evidence**

The audit work has revealed that internal controls have not been operating and this should have led to more extensive testing of capital expenditure, rather than the audit programme being completed as planned. Generally, the audit team should extend audit testing on capital expenditure, for example, by extending sample testing and reducing the level of materiality applied in audit tests.

The audit team should also investigate why the controls are not operating, considering whether they are being deliberately ignored or overridden, whether time pressure or lack of resources is making the controls difficult to operate, or if there is a suspicion of collusion and possible fraud.

The procedures on the purchase of the vehicles do not appear to cover all relevant assertions, for example, there is nothing to confirm that Thurman Ltd has correctly depreciated the vehicles or that they are actually owned and being used by the company, or even that they exist.

(ii) **Further audit procedures**

- Obtain the insurance documents to confirm that Thurman Ltd is paying the relevant insurance for the vehicles.
- Physically verify the vehicles and confirm that they are being used by employees on company business.
- Obtain the log book and other relevant ownership documents such as those issued by the DVLA, to confirm the right of Thurman Ltd to recognise the vehicles.
- Trace the vehicles to the company's non-current asset register.
- Recalculate the depreciation which should have been charged on the vehicles and agree to the statement of profit or loss for the year.

(c) **Payroll**

(i) **Audit evidence**

The audit work in respect of the payroll needs to be much more thorough; simply agreeing the amounts to the reports issued by Jackson Ltd provides no evidence on the completeness, accuracy or validity of the payroll figures recognised in the financial statements. The audit team seems to have relied on Jackson Ltd's year-end reports as being accurate and the requirements of ISA (UK) 402 *Audit Considerations Relating to an Entity Using a Service Organisation* do not appear to have been followed.

The audit team needs to obtain assurance on the controls which Jackson Ltd has implemented in order to assess the risk of material misstatement in the payroll figures and to respond to the risk with appropriate audit procedures. The controls which Thurman Ltd uses to verify the information received from Jackson Ltd also need to be understood. With the permission of Thurman Ltd, the audit team should contact Jackson Ltd with the objective of obtaining more information which can be used to assess how the payroll has been processed, and the controls which are in place. The controls in place at Thurman Ltd should be documented and tested.

It is recommended that further substantive procedures should be carried out to provide a wider range of evidence on the payroll expense recognised in the financial statements.

(ii) **Further audit procedures**

- Review the service agreement between Thurman Ltd and Jackson Ltd to understand the exact work which is conducted by Jackson Ltd as a service organisation.
- Read all reports made by Jackson Ltd during the year to identify any risks of misstatement in the payroll figure.
- If necessary, obtain a type 1 or type 2 report from Jackson Ltd to obtain further assurance on the controls which the service organisation has in place.
- Perform a substantive analytical review on payroll, preparing an auditor's expectation of the payroll figures and comparing it to that recognised in the financial statements and discussing any variance with management.
- Perform test of detail by selecting a sample from the payroll records and agreeing the amounts to payslips and HR records.

20 Faster Jets

Workbook references

Chapters 6, 7 and 15.

Top tips

In part (a)(i), it is important that you stick to stating additional information that is needed rather than audit procedures that should be performed. Also the ACCA examining team's answer uses questions in places (presumably addressed to the client), however you are on safer ground if you phrase your answer as factual pieces of information that are needed. Writing questions could be construed as informal language. For each piece of information needed, try to state why you need it.

Part (b) was perhaps more difficult. In part (b)(i), you only needed to make a few simple points (but in sufficient detail) to pass the question – for example, the difficulty of attaching quantities to KPIs, of making comparisons between companies, and the lack of information systems relevant to social and environmental performance.

In part (b)(ii), many of the procedures were just like other audit procedures – for example, agreeing payments to the cashbook. There are four performance measures given in Faster Jets Ltd's report in the scenario, so if you tried to think of one or two procedures for each measure then you could have scored well.

Easy marks

Many of the points in part (a) are straightforward.

ACCA examining team's comments

In part (a), which was for ten marks spilt evenly over two requirements, focused on planning the audit work relating to several large plots of land that had been purchased by the company during the year and were being accounted for as investment property in the company's financial statements. The first requirement asked candidates to explain the additional information that would be required to plan the audit of the land. This type of requirement is often seen in audit planning questions and again, as in previous sittings, disappointingly candidates tended to provide specific audit procedures rather than considering information that would be helpful in determining the type of procedures that would be relevant. Candidates for future examinations should bear in mind that answer points for this type of requirement can be phrased as questions, eg 'what is management's future plans for the land?', as this helps to determine its classification as investment property. Many candidates may find this type of requirement difficult if they have limited practical audit experience, in which case it is especially important to use past questions to practise how to answer these questions.

The next requirement asked candidates to explain the matters to be considered in assessing the reliance to be placed on the work of an auditor's expert being used in the audit of the land. This was much better answered than the first requirement, with almost all answers identifying that the auditor's expert must be independent and competent. However most answers went little further than explaining those two matters, indicating little knowledge of the requirements of ISA 620 *Using the Work of an Auditor's Expert* in relation to agreeing the scope of the expert's work, and evaluating the relevance of their conclusions. The answers to this requirement were also often very brief, amounting to little more than a few sentences or bullet points. Candidates are reminded that the number of marks available should be used as a guide for the number of points and depth required. A couple of bullet points or brief sentences are unlikely to be sufficient to score the five marks that were available here.

The next part of the question focused on measuring and reporting on social and environmental information. The audit firm in the scenario had been asked to perform an assurance engagement on Faster Jets Ltd's corporate social responsibility (CSR) report, and a number of CSR objectives and targets were provided along with the performance indicators for 20X4 to be included in the CSR report. The first requirement asked for a discussion of the difficulties in measuring and reporting on social and environmental performance for which there was four marks available. This short requirement was well attempted by many candidates, with most identifying that it can be difficult to define and quantify CSR measures, that systems are often not in place to capture the relevant information and that comparisons are difficult due to the lack of a regulatory framework. This again indicates that many candidates had practised past exam questions, as this type of requirement has featured in a AAA exam on several previous occasions.

Candidates found the final requirement of this question more difficult, as they were asked to design of procedures that could be used to gain assurance on the validity of the performance information included in the CSR report for six marks.

The main weakness in responses was that candidates simply repeated the same procedures for each of the performance measures given, even if they weren't appropriate. For example, one of the performance measures related to free flights that had been donated to charities, and many candidates recommended that this should be agreed to bank statements or cash book even though it is not a cash transaction. Candidates are encouraged to think about whether the procedures they are recommending are sensible in the context of the scenario. As is often the case when presented with a requirement to detail procedures, many candidates provided procedures that were not well explained, and in many cases weren't procedures at all, eg 'review the free flights', 'inspect the education days', 'confirm the vehicle fuel'. This type of comment cannot be given credit as it is too vague and does not answer the question requirement.

Marking guide

Marks

(a) (i) **Further information requirements**

1 mark for each further information point explained:

- The reason for the purchase, to understand the business rationale
- Any specific plans for how Faster Jets Ltd may make use of the land in the future
- The date of purchase
- Whether the land was purchased for cash or if finance was taken out
- Who is leasing the land? This could establish whether the arrangement is with a related party
- Whether the arrangement is a lease
- What is the land being used for?
- The location of the purchased land – this is necessary to plan the logistics of the audit
- Does the company hold any other investment property, and if so, is that also held at fair value?
- What is management's rationale for the accounting policy choice to measure the land at fair value?

5

(ii) **Matters to consider regarding the use of the auditor's expert**

Up to 1.5 marks for each of the following explained:

- Objectivity
- Competence
- Scope of work
- Relevance and reasonableness of conclusions

5

(b) (i) **Difficulties in measuring and reporting on social and environmental performance**

Up to 1.5 marks for each point discussed:

- Measures are difficult to define
- Measures are difficult to quantify
- Systems not set up to capture data
- Hard to make comparisons

Maximum 4

(ii) **Procedures on Faster Jets Ltd's performance measures**

Generally 1 mark for a well explained procedure:

- Obtain a summary of all amounts donated to charitable causes and agree to cash book
- For large donation confirm that authorisation for the payment has been made
- Review correspondence with charities for confirmation of the amounts paid
- Review relevant press releases and publicity campaigns
- For the £750,000 spent on the local education scheme, obtain a breakdown of the amounts spent and scrutinise to ensure all relate to the scheme, eg payments to educators
- Obtain a sample of registers to confirm attendance of children on certain days
- For the free flights donated to charity perform analytical review to confirm that the average value of a flight seems reasonable – the average being £700
- For a sample of the 800 free flights, obtain confirmation that the passenger was a guest of Faster Jets Ltd
- Agree a sample of business miles travelled in vehicles and fuel costs to employee expenses claims forms

Maximum 6

Professional marks

Analysis and evaluation

- Appropriate use of the information to support discussion, draw appropriate conclusions and design appropriate responses
- Identification of omissions from the analysis or further analysis which could be carried out

Professional scepticism and judgement

- Effective challenge and critical assessment of the information supplied with appropriate conclusions
- Application of professional scepticism to see beyond the information already available to consider what has not been provided and is therefore needed.
- Appropriate application of professional judgement to draw conclusions and make informed comments

Maximum 5

Total 25

(a) (i) Additional information includes:

- Details of the reason for the purchase, to understand the business purpose, eg whether the land held for capital appreciation. This will help determine whether it is classified correctly as investment property.

- Whether management has any specific plans for how Faster Jets Ltd may make use of the land in the future, eg to construct buildings and if so, what their purpose will be.
- The date of purchase, to ascertain how long it has taken for the land to increase in value by £2 million and whether this is in line with the auditor's understanding of the entity and its environment.
- Whether the land was purchased for cash, or if finance was taken out to raise the £12.5 million paid.
- Details of who is renting the land, in order to establish whether the arrangement is with a related party.
- The type of rental arrangement, to determine whether it embodies a lease.
- What the land is being used for. As the legal owner, Faster Jets Ltd should be aware of its use and any associated risks, eg activities close to airports may convey security risks, eg terrorism.
- The location of the purchased land, in order to plan the logistics of the audit.
- Whether the company holds any other investment property, and if so, whether it is also held at fair value. This will help determine whether the accounting treatment is consistent for all investment property.
- Information on management's reasoning behind the accounting policy choice to measure the land at fair value. It will result in profit for the year including the £2 million fair value increase.
- Details of who holds the title deeds to the land as this may need to be inspected.

(ii) **Relying on an auditor's expert**

Independence

The auditor must evaluate whether the expert is independent of the client, and so should enquire into whether they have any interests or relationships which may threaten their independence.

For example, the expert must not be connected to Faster Jets Ltd and must not be a related party of anyone having influence over its financial statements. Less reliance will be placed on their work if they are not independent.

Competence

The expert's competence must be evaluated, eg by considering whether they are members of any relevant professional bodies. The expert's relevant experience should also be considered. An expert with extensive experience of valuing land and investment properties will be more reliable than a newly qualified one with relatively little experience.

In this case, an expert valuer may be a Chartered Surveyor, which would give the auditor confidence in the reliability of their work.

Scope of work

The auditor agrees the scope of the work with the expert, include its objectives, how it will be used (in relation to the audit), the methodology and any key assumptions to be used. These assumptions should agree with the auditor's understanding of the entity and its environment.

The scope should be agreed at the start of the engagement. If the expert deviates from it, then their work will be less useful to the auditor.

Conclusions

The auditor considers the source data used by the expert, focusing whether it is reliable and consistent with the auditor's understanding. The auditor then evaluates the conclusions drawn by expert, and whether they are warranted by the evidence obtained. Any inconsistencies should be investigated.

(b) (i) **Definition**

A company's social and environmental ('S&E') performance is a very wide subject area, as a company is likely to have multiple effects on a number of complex systems, so that any one measure is likely to present only a partial picture. In defining S&E performance in simple terms, there is a risk of distorting a complex reality. This diminishes the usefulness of any information produced.

Setting KPIs

Performance is defined by setting KPIs, but this process is not straightforward. If it is decided that S&E performance is to be considered in terms of the stakeholders affected by the company's operations, then there is the problem of deciding firstly which stakeholders are most important. and secondly which aspects of the company's operations are of interest to them.

Quantification

It can be difficult to quantify KPIs in monetary terms. As a result of the complexity of the underlying social and natural environments, a qualitative approach may be more faithful to the reality, but this foregoes the possibility of measurement. Assigning quantitative KPIs buys precision but at the risk of arbitrariness and distortion.

There are also difficulties deciding how to quantify performance. For example Faster Jets Ltd's provision of free flights can be quantified in monetary terms, but it is not clear what price should be used – cost price or market value?

Systems and controls

Companies are used to reporting on their financial performance and are required by law to have systems of internal control over financial reporting. This is not the case with S&E performance, so there may not be reliable systems and controls to process the relevant information.

Lack of standards

There is no single set of guidelines on reporting S&E performance that all companies have to apply, but rather a multiplicity of reporting practices based on the different situations of the different entities. This makes it very difficult to compare performance between different companies. Year on year comparisons for the same company may also be difficult if its targets change during the period.

(ii) **Procedures**

- Obtain a summary of all amounts donated to charitable causes and agree a sample to the cash book.
- For large donations above a certain limit (say £10,000) confirm that authorisation for the payment has been made, eg by agreeing to minutes of management meetings.
- Review correspondence with charities for confirmation of the amounts paid.
- Review relevant press releases and publicity campaigns, eg the free flight scheme and the local education schemes are likely to have been publicised.
- For the £750,000 spent on the local education scheme, obtain a breakdown of the amounts spent and scrutinise to ensure all relate to the scheme, eg payments to educators.
- Obtain a sample of classroom registers to confirm attendance of children on certain days.
- For the free flights donated to charity, perform analytical review to confirm that the average value of a flight seems reasonable – the average being £700 (£560,000/800).
- For a sample of the 800 free flights, obtain confirmation that the passenger was a guest of Faster Jets Ltd, eg through correspondence with the passenger and relevant charity.
- Agree a sample of business miles travelled in vehicles to a mileage log, and fuel costs to employee expenses claims forms and the general ledger.

21 Magpie

Workbook references

Chapters 2, 4, 6, 8 and 9.

Top tips

The first requirement was fair but was one that may have left you struggling for ideas to make up seven marks. The requirement divides itself naturally into two parts, with four marks each for the individual company and the consolidated financial statements. Make sure you noticed what point we were at in the audit process: it is audit planning, after the engagement has been accepted but before the audit work as such has begun. Comments relating to specific procedures will get no marks here, and neither will comments relating to eg audit acceptance procedures.

Next came the longest part of the question, and it was a fairly typical test of applying your knowledge to the scenario. The question did require perhaps a bit more financial reporting knowledge than in some previous sittings of AAA – IFRS 3, IFRS 9, IAS 20 and IFRS 2 came up – but you should not have struggled with any of it. Passing this part of the question is a matter of working steadily through the issues contained in the scenario. You can flag to your marker that you are answering the question by specifically stating for each issue something like 'the risk here is', and then using auditing terminology to pick out where there may be eg an understatement or an overstatement. It is also important that you make an effort to evaluate and prioritise risks; one of the main differences between candidates who pass and those who do not relates to the ability to consider the significance of risks, as this requires a deeper knowledge than simple identification of risks.

It should be possible to pass part (c) fairly easily, as there is one mark available per specific procedure. As with many questions asking for audit procedures in a specific area of financial reporting, a good approach is to think of each of the specific figures involved, and then think of what could go wrong with each of them and how you would test them. The question makes it easy for you here, as you have a goodwill calculation laid out for you. All you need to do is think of one or two good procedures for each figure in the calculation, and hey presto, you have passed the requirement!

It should be possible to pass the question part on procedures fairly easily, as there is one mark available per specific procedure. As with many questions asking for audit procedures in a specific area of financial reporting, a good approach is to think of each of the specific figures involved, and then think of what could go wrong with each of them and how you would test them. The question makes it easy for you here, as you have a goodwill calculation laid out for you. All you need to do is think of one or two good procedures for each figure in the calculation, and hey presto, you have passed the requirement!

The final part contained three tricky ethical issues. Even if you were not sure of the final answer in a given situation, you can try approaching questions like this by (1) working out what the issue is, perhaps using the general types of threats as a guide (self-interest, self-review, advocacy, familiarity and intimidation); then (2) trying to think of safeguards that might remove the issue; and then (3) if no safeguards would make the threat go away, recommending that the auditor doesn't do it.

As ever it is important that you stick to the scenario and do not offer too much theory. Your knowledge of ISAs should be applied rather than simply stated. Overall this was a requirement on which you should have looked to score well.

Easy marks

There were plenty of easy marks in part (b) for expanding on the risks you have identified.

ACCA examining team's comments

With respect to the first requirement, most answers identified the main planning implications, such as the determination of component and group materiality levels, the audit firm's need to obtain business understanding and assess the control environment in relation to the new subsidiary, and practical aspects such as the timings and resources needed for the group audit. Weaker answers tended to just list out financial reporting matters, eg that in the group financial statements related party transactions would have to be disclosed, and intra-group balances eliminated, but they failed to link these points sufficiently well to audit planning implications.

Answers to the next requirement tended to cover a wide range of points but very often did not discuss the points in much depth. For example, almost all candidates identified that accounting for goodwill can be complex, leading to risk of misstatement, but few candidates explained the specific issues that give rise to risk. Many answers also went into a lot of detail about how particular balances and transactions should be audited, recommending procedures to be performed by the auditor, which was not asked for. Weaker answers simply stated an issue, for example, that a grant had been received, and said the risk was that it would not be accounted for properly. Clearly this is not really an evaluation, as required, and will lead to minimal marks being awarded.

It was pleasing to see many candidates determining the materiality of the transactions and balances to the individual company concerned and to the group. However, candidates are reminded that materiality should be calculated appropriately, eg the materiality of an asset or liability should be based on total assets and not revenue.

Most answers to the final part of the question went through the issues in order and identified the ethical threats that arose. However, a lot of answers took a scattergun approach, and said that all of the issues would give rise to the same threats of familiarity, management, self-review and self-interest, but then did not go on to explain how, or why, the threats arose and whether it would be possible for safeguards to reduce the threats to an acceptable level.

Marking guide — **Marks**

(a) (i) **Audit implications of Canary Ltd acquisition**

Up to 1.5 marks for each implication explained (3 marks maximum for identification):

- Develop understanding of Canary Ltd business environment
- Document Canary Ltd accounting systems and controls
- Perform detailed analytical procedures on Canary Ltd
- Communicate with previous auditor
- Review prior year audit opinion for relevant matters
- Plan additional work on opening balances
- Consideration of aggregation risk relating to Canary Ltd
- Plan for audit of intra-group transactions
- Issues on auditing the one-month difference in financial year ends
- Impact of acquisition on analytical procedures at Group level
- Additional experienced staff may be needed, eg to audit complex goodwill

Maximum — 7

(ii) **Evaluation and prioritisation of risks of material misstatement**

Up to 2 marks for each risk (unless a different maximum is indicated below):

- General risks – diversification, change to group structure
- Goodwill – contingent consideration – estimation uncertainty (probability of payment)
- Goodwill – contingent consideration – estimation uncertainty (probability of payment) (discounting)
- Goodwill – fair value of net assets acquired

ANSWERS

- Goodwill – impairment
- Identify that the issues in relation to cost of investment apply also in Crow Ltd's individual financial statements (1 mark)
- Loan stock – premium on redemption
- Loan stock – accrued interest
- Loan stock – inadequate disclosure
- Identify that the issues in relation to loan stock apply to cost of investment in Crow Ltd's individual financial statements (1 mark)
- Online sales and risk relating to revenue recognition (additional 1 mark if calculation provided of online sales materiality to the Group)
- No group accounting policy for online sales
- Canary Ltd management have no experience regarding consolidation
- Financial performance of Crow Ltd and Starling Ltd deteriorating (up to 3 marks with calculations)
- Possible misstatement of Canary Ltd revenue and profit
- Grant received – capital expenditure
- Grant received – amount not yet spent
- Prior period error – clearly trivial
- New IT system
- Starling Ltd – no finance director in place at year end
- Share options – wrong FV used
- Share options – cost not spread over vesting period
- Share options – no adjustment for employees leaving
- Share options – recognised as liability instead of equity

Maximum 22

(iii) **Goodwill**

Generally 1 mark per specific procedure (examples shown below):

- Confirm acquisition date to legal documentation
- Confirm consideration details to legal documentation
- Agree 100% ownership, eg using Companies House search/register of significant shareholdings
- Vouch consideration paid to bank statements/cash book
- Review board minutes for discussion/approval of acquisition
- Obtain due diligence report and agree net assets valuation
- Discuss probability of paying contingent consideration
- Obtain written representation regarding contingency
- Recalculate goodwill including contingency on a discounted basis

Maximum 5

(b) **Ethical matters**

Generally 1 mark per comment:

- Reasonable for partner to attend board meetings
- But must avoid perception of management involvement
- Partner must not be appointed to the board

Marking guide	Marks
• Seconded manager would cause management and self-review threat	
• Prohibited by *Ethical Standard*	
• Some recruitment services may be provided – interviewing/CV selection	
• But avoid making management decision and put safeguards in place	
Maximum	6

Professional marks

Communication

- Briefing notes format and structure - use of headings/sub-headings and an introduction
- Style, language and clarity - appropriate layout and tone of briefing notes, presentation of materiality and relevant calculations, appropriate use of the CBE tools, easy to follow and understand
- Effectiveness and clarity of communication - answer is relevant and tailored to the scenario
- Adherence to the specific requests made by the audit engagement partner

Analysis and evaluation

- Appropriate use of the information to determine suitable calculations
- Appropriate use of the information to support discussions and draw appropriate conclusions
- Assimilation of all relevant information to ensure that the risk evaluation performed considers the impact of contradictory or unusual movements
- Effective prioritisation of the results of the risk evaluation to demonstrate the likelihood and magnitude of risks and to facilitate the allocation of appropriate responses
- Balanced discussion of the information to objectively make a recommendation or decision

Professional scepticism and judgement

- Effective challenge of information supplied, and techniques carried out to support key facts and/or decisions
- Determination and justification of a suitable materiality level, appropriately and consistently applied
- Appropriate application of professional judgement to draw conclusions and make informed decisions about the courses of action which are appropriate in the context of the audit engagement

Commercial acumen

- Audit procedures are practical and plausible in the context of the CS Group.
- Use of effective examples and/or calculations from the scenario to illustrate points or recommendations.
- Recognition of the appropriate commercial considerations of the audit firm

Maximum	10
Total	50

Briefing notes

For: Jo Daw

From: Audit manager

Subject: CS Group audit

Introduction

These notes identify and explain the implication of the Canary Ltd ('Canary') acquisition for planning the CS Group and individual companies' audits. The notes then evaluate and prioritise the significant risks of material misstatement for this audit.

(a) (i) **Planning implications of Canary Ltd acquisition**

Individual financial statements

ISA (UK) 315 (Revised) *Identifying and Assessing the Risks of Material Misstatement* requires us to understand the entity and its environment, and internal control.

To understand Canary and its environment, we must consider any relevant regulatory factors, eg whether it uses the same financial reporting ('FR') framework as the group; the nature of the entity's operations, ownership and governance, and the kinds of transactions and balances that should be expected in the financial statements; and its selection and application of accounting policies, and whether they are in line with its business and the FR framework.

To understand Canary's internal controls, we must consider its accounting systems as well as any other controls relevant to the audit. Our understanding of these controls must be documented. This is particularly important with a new audit client because we have not had time to build up knowledge of the entity, and so need to place special emphasis on this area now.

IT is likely to form a significant part of Canary's systems (since 30% of sales are online), and these will be different from the rest of the group. We should consider if we need to use an auditor's expert in this area.

It will be necessary to perform detailed analytical procedures on Canary at the planning stage. This will be necessary to determine planning materiality, and to help identify any significant events or transactions in the period.

ISA (UK) 300 *Planning an Audit of Financial Statements* requires us to communicate with Canary's predecessor auditor, asking if there is anything we should be aware of that may influence our plan. We should also review the prior period audit opinion and auditor's report.

Finally, we will need to perform additional procedures on Canary's opening balances, as these were audited by a predecessor auditor.

Consolidated financial statements

The first thing to consider is how the acquisition of Canary affects aggregation risk. ISA (UK) 600 (Revised) *Special Considerations – Audits of Group Financial Statements (Including the Work of Component Auditors)* states that aggregation risk is the probability that the aggregate of uncorrected and undetected misstatements exceed the materiality for the financial statements for the group as a whole. Aggregation risk should always be assessed, but the acquisition of a new subsidiary increases risk due to potential lack of familiarity with the entity. Canary's forecast revenue is 11.9% (16/135) of group revenue, and profit is 23.5% (2/8.5), and so it is likely that uncorrected misstatements in Canary's financial statements could be material to the group financial statements as a whole.

Although we are both the group auditors and Canary's individual auditors, we still need to (i) consider whether audit evidence obtained for the individual company is sufficient and appropriate for the group, and (ii) perform procedures on matters relevant to the consolidated financial statements. This includes procedures to determine whether intra-group balances have been eliminated, and whether IFRS 3 *Business Combinations* has been applied correctly in relation to the acquisition itself.

A particular issue is that Canary's 31 August year end is different from the rest of the group. In practice this will usually be changed soon after the company is acquired, so we need to obtain evidence to determine whether or not this has happened. This matter is absolutely crucial to the audit. If the year end has not been changed, then additional procedures must be performed on Canary's financial information so that its financial statements as at 30 September 20X5 can be consolidated.

Care must be taken when performing analytical review on at a group level, as Canary's figures are only included since the acquisition date and will not be comparable with the whole-year figures of the rest of the group.

Finally, the new acquisition introduces new complexities into the audit, so we must ensure that these aspects of the audit are done by staff with appropriate levels of experience, eg the goodwill asset and the contingent consideration.

(ii) **General**

There are several factors which together mean that this is a high-risk audit: there has been a significant acquisition, a move into a new line of business, and the introduction of new IT systems relating to financial reporting.

Goodwill

Goodwill is material to the financial statements, at 8.2% of total assets (45/550). This is therefore a significant risk that will be of high priority to the auditor.

The contingent consideration is a significant audit risk. It is currently recognised in full as an asset, which is in line with the IFRS 3 *Business Combinations* requirement to recognise it at its fair value at the acquisition date. However, this amount should be discounted to its present value, because in this the consideration is not payable until 1 April 20X8. As this has not been done, goodwill appears to be overstated.

A further risk relates to the valuation of identifiable net assets. This has been done by a management's expert in the context of a due diligence review. ISA (UK) 500 *Audit Evidence* requires the auditor to evaluate the expert's competence, capability and objectivity; to obtain an understanding of their work; and to evaluate the work's appropriateness as audit evidence. The auditor's evaluation of each of these issues should be documented.

IAS 36 *Impairment of Assets* requires goodwill to be tested for impairment annually, and there is no mention of this having been done at the year end. There is therefore a risk that goodwill may be overstated.

Loan stock

The loan stock issued is material, at 18.2% of total assets (100/550). Any risks arising in relation to this area are likely to be significant risks.

The premium of £20m should be recognised as a finance cost over the period of the loan using the amortised cost method, in line with IFRS 9 *Financial Instruments*. The risk is that this has not been done, and that finance costs are understated.

An interest cost of 5% is also payable in arrears, and there is a risk of further understatement of finance costs if this has not been accrued for.

These issues apply to both the group accounts and Crow Ltd's individual company financial statements.

Online sales

Canary's online sales represent 30% of its revenue, with approximately £4.8m (0.3 × 16) included in the group accounts, which is material at 3.55% of group revenue – a figure that should be even higher in future, when a full year's revenue will be included in the group accounts.

There is a risk that the requirements of IFRS 15 *Revenue from Contracts with Customers* on when revenue should be recognised are not met. This will be heavily dependent on the reliability of the IT system involved, its appropriateness for financial reporting, and its integration with the accounting system.

E-commerce can also represent a business risk as it may expose Canary to eg lost sales or reputational damage if its website does not operate effectively. With online sales at 30% of revenue, any significant problems in this area could affect Canary's status as a going concern.

Canary's management

Canary's management have no prior experience of the consolidation process at the CS Group, so it is possible that the process will operate inefficiently and that errors will be made. It is likely that more audit work will need to be done on the consolidation of Canary's results than on the rest of the group.

Financial performance

At first sight, the group's results are encouraging – revenue is up 8% and profit before tax is up 1.2%. However, this is not comparing like with like: the prior year figures do not include any of Canary's results, whereas the current year figures include Canary for six months.

If we include only Crow Ltd and Starling Ltd's results and compare them with the prior year, then a different picture emerges:

	20X5	*20X4*	
	Crow + Starling forecast	*Group actual*	*% change*
Revenue	119	125	(4.8%)
Profit before tax	6.5	8.4	(22.6%)

Instead of profit and revenue both growing, the picture these figures paint is of profit and revenue shrinking. This may be for operational reasons, but it is also possible that there has been a misstatement, with either costs being overstated or revenue understated.

Government grant

The grant is material, at 6.4% of total assets (35/550).

There are two issues in relation to the grant. The first is that in line with IAS 20 *Accounting for Government Grants and Disclosure of Government Assistance*, this is a grant related to assets. This may either be deducted from the cost of the related assets (in this case, solar panels), or recognised as deferred income that is released systematically into profit or loss. At the year end, only £25m of the £35m grant had been spent, so some of the grant should be deferred until the next year. There is a risk that this has not been done, and eg the £35m has simply been recognised in income during the year.

The second issue is that the grant is for capital expenditure on environmentally friendly assets, but Starling Ltd intends to spend the remaining £10m on upgrading its production and packing lines. This seems unlikely to meet the conditions of the grant, and it is possible that some of it will need to be repaid if it is spent in this way. The matter is likely to be material to the group, at 1.8% of total assets (10/550).

Prior period error not relevant

Deferred revenue in the prior period was overstated by £10,000. This is 0.014% of Crow Ltd's forecast revenue (=10,000/69,000,000), and 0.29% of profit. It is clearly immaterial and is not relevant to the audit planning.

New IT system

The new IT system, which is relevant to financial reporting, represents a risk of material misstatement per ISA (UK) 315 (Revised). There are two main issues: firstly, errors may have been made in transferring the data from the old to the new system; and secondly, the new system is likely to take time to bed in, and it is possible for teething problems to lead to a loss of data.

New FD

The fact that Starling Ltd's FD has recently left increases the risk of errors as it deprives the company of accounting skills it may need when producing its financial statements, and for the consolidation process. It may also make the audit more difficult to conduct, as it may not be possible to obtain explanations that are needed if there is no FD.

Finally, the reasons for the FD leaving should be ascertained, as it is possible that there has been a disagreement over accounting policies, or even a fraud.

Share options

An expense has been recognised of £720,000. This is 20.6% of profit before tax (= £720,000 / £3.5m) and is a material area of the statement of profit or loss. The options may also be material by nature if they have been granted to related parties, such as company directors.

In accordance with IFRS 2 *Share-based Payment*, Crow Ltd should recognise the remuneration expense as the employees' services are received, based on the fair value of the share options granted. The principal risk is that the accounting treatment will be inappropriate; there appear to be several misstatements in this regard.

The fair value at the grant date was £6. The calculation performed by the entity currently uses the fair value at the end of the reporting period of £8, which is incorrect.

Crow Ltd has recognised the full expense in profit or loss in the year of issue. This is incorrect; IFRS 2 requires the cost to be spread over the vesting period of 2 years.

Crow Ltd's calculation has not adjusted for the number of options expected to vest. IFRS 2 requires Crow Ltd to take into account estimates of the number of employees expected to leave.

Finally, a long-term liability has been recognised instead of equity.

Taking all of these points together, the expense should have been recognised as £243,000 (150 × 600 × 90% × £6 × ½ years), rather than £720,000. Profit is therefore understated by £477,000. This constitutes 13.6% of profit before tax (= 477 / 3,500), which is material.

Conclusion

These briefing notes have highlighted a number of significant risks of material misstatement which must now form the focus of audit procedures. Our priority should be the treatment of loan stock and goodwill and monitoring the group's ongoing financial performance.

(iii) **Audit procedures on goodwill**

- Obtain the legal purchase agreement and confirm the acquisition date
- Confirm (from the legal agreement) the consideration, and details of the contingent consideration
- Confirm that Canary is wholly owned by Crow Ltd through a review of its register of shareholders
- Agree cash payment of £125 million to cash book and bank statements
- Review board minutes for discussion regarding, and approval of, the purchase of Canary
- Obtain due diligence report on Canary and confirm estimate fair value of net assets

(b) **Partner at board meetings**

It is acceptable for the audit engagement partner to attend board meetings. There are even times when the partner should attend, eg to raise issues with management and/or those charged with governance.

The important thing is that the partner does not take on a management role, and that they are not involved in any discussions that are not relevant to the audit. If the partner served as a director of an audit client, then the self-review and self-interest threats created would be insurmountable.

Audit manager secondment

This is a temporary staff assignment and is entirely prohibited by the FRC *Ethical Standard* (FRC ES: para. s.2.36). This is because of the management and self-review threats that would be likely to exist. As a result, no member of staff should be seconded into this role.

Recruitment help

The FRC ES prohibits auditors from providing recruitment services to audit clients where this would involve the firm either taking responsibility for making an appointment or advising on it.

It may be therefore possible for help to be provided with recruitment, but only if the auditor does not make any management decisions. It would be possible to eg review a shortlist of candidates' CVs, but only against criteria set out by the CS Group itself.

If help is provided, then the final decision about recruitment must be left to the client. The firm would not be able to give advice regarding which candidate should be chosen. Safeguards should also be put in place, such as obtaining written acknowledgement from the client that they are responsible for the recruitment decision.

Conclusion

These briefing notes have addressed the issues around the Canary acquisition and the goodwill recognised thereon, around the share options scheme, and have highlighted a number of significant risks of material misstatement which must now form the focus of audit procedures.

22 Adder

Workbook references

Chapters 1, 2, 6, 8 and 9.

Top tips

In part (a), you must calculate materiality for each issue – the hint is that the question includes the figures for profit and total assets. This should be the first thing you write for each part of your answer. (Also note that marks are likely to be capped here, so don't go overboard and calculate it for every single number in the question if this is not needed.)

The question is on matters and evidence, which suggests the form for your answer to take.

Part (a) was a sale and leaseback arrangement which should be accounted for under IFRS 16 *Leases*. This standard features some complex calculations and so this question was a good test of your mettle in this area.

Part (b), on laws and regulations, is an area that is examined quite frequently. As ever, the auditor is in the tricky situation of discovering something and then finding themselves stuck in a dilemma about reporting vs confidentiality. The usual track is first to report to management, and then if management does not report it to the authorities, consider reporting it if eg there is a legal duty to do so, or if it's in the public interest. If in doubt, saying to 'obtain legal advice' allows you to sit on the fence in your exam!

Easy marks

The marks for calculating and assessing materiality in part (a) are simple.

ACCA examining team's comments

Answers to part (a) on the whole were good. In answers to part (a), candidates were able to identify that the accounting treatment seemed incorrect and could explain their reasoning. Fewer candidates appreciated that the loss-making status of Baldrick Ltd was the possible explanation for the Group's reluctance to consolidate it as a subsidiary and therefore that the Group's profits were overstated. Most candidates could provide some evidence points, with the most commonly cited being the board approval of the acquisition and agreeing the cash paid to bank statements. Fewer candidates could suggest how the audit firm should obtain evidence on the exercise of control by the parent company or on the mechanics of the consolidation that should have taken place.

In answers to part (b), most candidates identified the obvious issues, namely that this was likely to be a breach of laws and regulations, internal controls were poor, and that an intimidation threat existed. Beyond this, the quality of answers varied dramatically. The **best answers** used a methodical approach to explain the auditor's responsibilities in relation to a suspected breach of laws and regulations; including the need to obtain more evidence, the auditor's reporting responsibilities, and the need to consider client confidentiality as well as possibly reporting the matter in the public interest. It was pleasing to see many candidates deal well with these issues, as well as the ethical threat raised by the employee's behaviour.

Weaker answers focused solely on the potential money laundering implications, which while not irrelevant should not have been the only matter discussed. In addition, weaker answers simply stated facts without much attempt to apply the requirements of ISA (UK) 250A *Consideration of Laws and Regulations in an Audit of Financial Statements*, to the scenario. Some candidates suggested that the audit firm was responsible for ensuring that the Group was complying with relevant laws and regulations, saying that the audit firm should 'ensure compliance', and there were occasionally suggestions that the audit senior should be 'disciplined' for not taking further action when threatened by the employee of the Group. These comments, especially the latter, demonstrate a lack of judgement or real understanding of the role of the auditor in this regard.

This question was for many candidates the best attempted question on the exam.

Marking guide **Marks**

(a) **Audit matters and evidence**

Generally up to 1.5 marks for each matter discussed, and 1 mark for each well-explained procedure:

Sale and leaseback

Matters

- Correct determination of materiality
- Transaction is a lease with a right-of-use asset
- Appears to be a finance leaseback
- Assets and liabilities understated, profit overstated
- Adjustment recommended
- Implications for auditor's report if not adjusted

Evidence

- A copy of the lease, signed by the lessor, and a review of its major clauses to confirm that control has been transferred, and that the arrangement is a lease
- Review of forecasts and budgets to confirm that economic benefit is expected to be generated through the continued use of the property complex
- Physical inspection of the property complex to confirm it is being used by the Group
- Confirmation of the fair value of the property complex, possibly using an auditor's expert
- Evaluation of the expert's work including the appropriateness of assumptions and use of the correct financial reporting framework
- Agreement of the £35 million cash proceeds to bank statement and cash book
- Minutes of a discussion with management regarding the accounting treatment and including an auditor's request to amend the financial statements
- A copy of insurance documents stating that the Group is responsible for insuring the property complex

Baldrick Ltd

Matters

- Correct determination of materiality of Baldrick Ltd
- If Group exercises control, Baldrick Ltd is a subsidiary not an associate
- Need to determine nature of the Group's interest in Baldrick Ltd
- Impact on audit opinion is at least qualification due to material misstatement
- Discussion of impact on Group profit if Baldrick Ltd is treated as a subsidiary
- Presentation issues
- Impact could be pervasive in combination with the sale and leaseback

Evidence

- Agreement of the cash paid to acquire Baldrick Ltd to cash book and bank statements
- Review of board minutes for discussion of the change in Group structure and for authorisation of the acquisition and disposal
- Review of legal documentation pertaining to the acquisition of Baldrick Ltd, to confirm the number of equity shares acquired, and the rights attached to the shareholding, eg the ability to appoint board members

- Notes of discussion with management regarding the exercise of control over Baldrick Ltd, eg the planned level of participation in its operating and financial decisions
- Review of forecasts and budgets to assess the plans for integrating Baldrick Ltd into the Group
- Ensure that losses from the date of acquisition only are consolidated
- Evaluation and recalculation of amounts recognised in Group equity in respect of Baldrick Ltd, in particular the determination of pre- and post-acquisition results

Maximum 13

(b) **Completion issues and laws and regulations**

Generally up to 1.5 marks for each point discussed:

- Storage of hazardous chemicals likely to be a breach of law and regulations
- Auditor needs to understand law and regulations applicable to the Group
- Further evidence should be obtained about the storage of chemicals
- Implications for the financial statements to be considered, eg provisions for fines and penalties
- Matter to be reported as soon as possible to those charged with governance
- Auditor may have a legal duty to disclose, or consider disclosing in the public interest
- Disclosure in the public interest must be communicated to those charged with governance
- Deciding whether to disclose in the public interest requires the use of judgement
- Intimidation and threatening behaviour should be reported to those charged with governance
- Control deficiency and recommendation to be communicated to those charged with governance
- The audit firm may wish to seek legal advice regarding the situation

Maximum 7

Professional marks

Analysis and evaluation

- Appropriate use of the information to support discussion, draw appropriate conclusions and design appropriate responses
- Effective consideration of then evidence required in relation to the scenario information

Professional scepticism and judgement

- Effective challenge and critical assessment of the information supplied by Adder, with appropriate conclusions
- Application of professional scepticism to see beyond the evidence already obtained and to consider what further evidence is in fact required.
- Appropriate application of professional judgement to draw conclusions and make informed comments

Maximum 5

Total 25

(a) **Sale and leaseback**

The sale and leaseback transaction is material to the group statement of financial position. The proceeds received on the sale of the property, equivalent to the fair value of the assets, represents 23.3% of Group assets, and the carrying amount of the assets disposed of were £27 million (£35m – £8m), representing 18% of group assets. In addition, the profit recognised on the disposal represents 40% of the Group's profit for the year, so it is highly material to the statement of profit or loss.

The transaction is a sale and leaseback because part of the asset has been leased back after the sale.

The accounting treatment is not in line with IFRS 16 *Leases*. IFRS 16 would see this effectively as a part-disposal. Part of the right-of-use asset is retained, and a gain is recognised only in relation to the part that is sold/transferred.

First, we must work out the size of the gain. This is the difference between the selling price and the fair value on the date of the sale: £35m – £33m = £2m. Since the selling price is higher than the fair value, this is recognised as additional financing provided to the Group.

Next, we must work out the proportion of the asset that has been retained for use. We do this by comparing the present value (PV) of the lease liability (which is the value of the right-of-use asset retained), with the fair value. We must, however, adjust the PV of the liability for the additional financing, since this does not relate to the asset retained for use. In this case, the PV of the liability is £22m, from which we deduct the £2m gain ('additional financing') to give £20m.

The proportion of the asset that is retained for use is therefore £20m / £33m = 0.606.

IFRS 16 requires us to continue recognising the leased asset in terms of cost/carrying amount, so the asset is recognised at carrying amount × 0.606 = £27m × 0.606 = £16.4m. This asset must be recognised on the statement of financial position. The amount is material, at 11% of total assets.

There is a gain on the sale of the building, which is the difference between the fair value and the carrying amount, ie £35m – £27m = £8m. The Group can only recognise the part of the gain that relates to the part of the asset that was sold/transferred. Using the same proportion as before, we get £8m × 0.606 = £4.85m retained. This amount is material at 24% of profit. The rest relates to the part that was sold/transferred, ie the balancing amount of £8m – £4.85m = £3.15m.

Therefore, the Group's profit is materially overstated, and the total assets and liabilities are materially understated. An adjustment should be recommended to management, whereby the right-of-use asset would be reinstated, with a lease liability established.

If the adjustment is not made, the group financial statements will contain a material misstatement. The auditor's opinion would be modified due to a material misstatement following the misapplication of IFRS 16 to the sale and leaseback transaction.

Evidence:

- A copy of the lease, signed by the lessor, and a review of its major clauses to confirm that control has been transferred, and that the arrangement should be recognised as a lease in line with IFRS 16.
- Review of forecasts and budgets to confirm that economic benefit is expected to be generated through the continued use of the portion of the property complex now being leased.
- Physical inspection of the property complex to confirm that it is being used by the Group.
- Confirmation of the fair value of the property complex, possibly using an auditor's expert, in which case the expert's report should be included in the audit working papers.
- Where fair value has been established using an auditor's or management expert, evaluation of the expert's work including confirmation that the fair value is determined according to the applicable financial reporting framework, and that all assumptions are reasonable.
- Agreement of the £35 million cash proceeds to bank statement and cash book.

- Minutes of a discussion with management regarding the accounting treatment and including an auditor's request to amend the financial statements.
- A copy of insurance documents stating that the Group is responsible for insuring the property complex.
- Recalculation of finance charge and depreciation expense in relation to the leased asset.
- Review of the financial statements to confirm that appropriate adjustments have been made, and recalculation of right-of-use asset, lease liability and the gain on part-disposal.

Baldrick Ltd

The Group's interest in Baldrick Ltd is material, as the company's assets are equivalent to 12% of total Group assets, and its loss is equivalent to 25% of the Group's profit.

It is questionable whether Baldrick Ltd should have been accounted for as an associate. An associate arises where there is significant influence over an investee, according to IAS 28 *Investments in Associates and Joint Ventures*. Significant influence is typified by an equity shareholding of 20–50%, so the Group's shareholding of 52% would seem to indicate that the Group exercises control, rather than significant influence.

However, it may be that even with a 52% shareholding, the Group cannot exercise control, for example, if it is prevented from doing so due to agreements between other shareholders, or because it cannot appoint members to the board of Baldrick Ltd. This would be unusual though, so audit evidence must be sought on the nature of the shareholding in Baldrick Ltd and whether the Group actually exercises control or significant influence over the company. Baldrick Ltd not having been integrated into the Group's activities is not a valid reason for its non-consolidation as a subsidiary.

If the Group does have a controlling interest, and Baldrick Ltd remains recognised as an associate, the Group financial statements will be materially misstated, with implications for the auditor's opinion, which would be modified due to the application of an inappropriate accounting treatment.

If Baldrick Ltd should be treated as a subsidiary rather than an associate, then the company's loss for the year should be consolidated from the date of acquisition which was 1 January 20X5. Therefore, a loss of £1.25 million (£5 million × $^3/_{12}$) should be consolidated into Group profit. The loss which has already been recognised, assuming that equity accounting has been correctly applied, would be £650,000 (£5 million × $^3/_{12}$ × 52%), therefore an additional loss of £600,000 needs to be recognised.

In addition, there are presentation issues to consider. Equity accounting requires the investment in the associate to be recognised on one line in the statement of financial position, and the income from the associate to be disclosed on one line of the statement of profit or loss. Treating Baldrick Ltd as a subsidiary will require a line-by-line consolidation, which will have a significant impact on numerous balances within the financial statements.

The combination of adjustments in relation to the sale and leaseback transaction and the consolidation of Baldrick Ltd as a subsidiary may be considered pervasive to the Group financial statements, and if so, and the necessary adjustments are not made, then the audit opinion could be adverse.

Evidence:

- Agreement of the cash paid to acquire Baldrick Ltd to cash book and bank statements.
- Review of board minutes for discussion of the change in Group structure and for authorisation of the acquisition.
- Review of legal documentation pertaining to the acquisition of Baldrick Ltd, to confirm the number of equity shares acquired, and the rights attached to the shareholding, eg the ability to appoint board members.
- Inspection of other supporting documentation relating to the acquisition such as due diligence reports.
- Notes of discussion with management regarding the exercise of control over Baldrick Ltd, eg the planned level of participation in its operating and financial decisions.

- Review of forecasts and budgets to assess the plans for integrating Baldrick Ltd into the Group.
- Ensure that correct time apportionment has been applied in calculating the amount of losses recognised in the consolidation of Baldrick Ltd.
- Evaluation and recalculation of amounts recognised in Group equity in respect of Baldrick Ltd, in particular the determination of pre- and post-acquisition results.

(b) The storage of the potentially hazardous chemicals raises concerns that the Group may not be complying with regulations such as health and safety legislation. The auditor needs to consider the requirements of ISA (UK) 250A *Consideration of Laws and Regulations in an Audit of Financial Statements*, which states that while it is management's responsibility to ensure that the entity's operations are conducted in accordance with the provisions of laws and regulation, the auditor does have some responsibility in relation to compliance with laws and regulations, especially where a non-compliance has an effect on the financial statements.

The auditor is required by ISA (UK) 315 (Revised) *Identifying and Assessing the Risks of Material Misstatement* to obtain an understanding of the legal and regulatory framework in which the audited entity operates. This will help the auditor to identify non-compliance and to assess the implications of non-compliance. Therefore the auditor should ensure a full knowledge and understanding of the laws and regulations relevant to the storage of items in the Group's warehouses is obtained, focusing on health and safety issues and the implications of non-compliance.

ISA (UK) 250A requires that when non-compliance is identified or suspected, the auditor shall obtain an understanding of the nature of the act and the circumstances in which it has occurred, and further information to evaluate the possible effect on the financial statements. Therefore procedures should be performed to obtain evidence about the suspected non-compliance, for example, to identify any further instances of non-compliance in the Group's other warehouses.

Management may not be aware that the warehouse manager is allowing the storage of these potentially hazardous items. ISA (UK) 250A requires the matter to be discussed with management and where appropriate with those charged with governance. The IESBA *Code of ethics* requires that NOCLAR be communicated with the most appropriate level of management, ie at least one level above the person involved (IESBA *Code*: para. R360.11). The auditor must therefore ignore the warehouse manager's threats and communicate the suspected non-compliance as required by ISA (UK) 250A. Given the potential severity of the situation, and that the chemicals may not be safe, there is the risk of injury to the Group's employees or the general public, so the matter should be communicated as soon as possible.

The auditor needs to consider the potential implications for the financial statements. The non-compliance could lead to regulatory authorities imposing fines or penalties on the Group, which may need to be provided for directly in the financial statements. Audit procedures should be performed to determine the amount, materiality and probability of payment of any such fine or penalty imposed.

In terms of reporting non-compliance to the relevant regulatory authorities, ISA (UK) 250A requires the auditor to determine whether they have a responsibility to report the identified or suspected non-compliance to parties outside the entity. In the event that management or those charged with governance of the Group fail to make the necessary disclosures to the regulatory authorities, the auditor should consider whether they should make the disclosure. This will depend on matters including whether there is a legal duty to disclose or whether it is considered to be in the public interest to do so. Confidentiality is also an issue, and if disclosure were to be made by the auditor, it would be advisable to seek legal advice on the matter. This is very much a worst-case scenario, however, as the Group's management is likely to make the necessary disclosures, and should be encouraged by the auditor to do so.

ISA (UK) 250A states that if, having considered any views expressed on behalf of the entity and in the light of any legal advice obtained, the auditor concludes that the matter ought to be reported to an appropriate authority in the public interest, the auditor notifies those charged with governance in writing of the view and, if the entity does not voluntarily do so itself or is unable to provide evidence that the matter has been reported, the auditor reports it. The auditor must exercise judgement in deciding whether a matter should be disclosed in the public interest, and should consider matters such as:

- The extent to which the suspected or actual non-compliance with law or regulations is likely to affect members of the public;
- Whether those charged with governance have rectified the matter or are taking, or are likely to take, effective corrective action;
- The extent to which non-disclosure is likely to enable the suspected or actual non-compliance with law or regulations to recur with impunity;
- The gravity of the matter;
- Whether there is a general ethos within the company to disregard laws and regulations; and
- The weight of evidence and the degree of the auditor's suspicion that there has been non-compliance with laws and regulations.

There is also an ethical issue arising from the warehouse manager's aggressive attitude and threatening behaviour. It would seem that the manager has something to hide, and that he was the only person who knew about the storage of the chemicals. He may have been bribed to allow the storage of the dangerous chemicals. His behaviour amounts to intimidation of the auditor, which is not acceptable behaviour, and those charged with governance should be alerted to the situation which arose. ISA (UK) 260 *Communication with Those Charged with Governance* requires the auditor to communicate significant difficulties encountered during the audit, which may include examples of lack of co-operation with the auditor, and imposed limitations on auditors performing their work.

The final issue is that the Group should review its policy of requiring limited documentation for contracts less than £10,000. This would seem to be inappropriate because it may lead to other instances of unknown items being stored in the Group's warehouses. This would seem to be a significant control deficiency and should be reported to those charged with governance in accordance with both ISA (UK) 260 and ISA (UK) 265 *Communicating Deficiencies in Internal Control with Those Charged with Governance and Management*. The auditor could recommend improvements to the controls over the storage of items which should prevent any further non-compliance with laws and regulations from occurring.

23 Beth & Co

Workbook references

Chapters 8, 10 and 11.

Top tips

This question is set at the completion stage and asked for audit evidence in relation to two areas, and then moved on to consider the auditor's report.

The scenario for part (a) was fairly clear about the potential for the first issue to affect going concern. Notice how the model answer makes use of some carefully chosen numbers to investigate the issue.

Regarding the second issue, you are again given a little bit of a steer towards the relevant accounting issue (the application of IAS 38). If you were unsure of the accounting guidance in this area then you will need to spend some time making sure that you are comfortable with the material in the workbook, as this type of question could very easily come up in your exam.

In relation to the auditor's report in part (b), you needed to have a clear understanding of the relevant ISAs (UK). Thankfully many candidates find this to be a friendly area of the AAA syllabus, so this should have been one of the nicer requirements in the exam.

Easy marks

The were some fairly easy points to be made in relation to structure of the auditor's report in part (b).

ACCA examining team's comments

This was a two-part question set at the completion and reporting stage of the audit.

In (a)(i) a number of candidates incorrectly discussed accounting rules surrounding intangible assets and deemed the licence to be a purchased intangible and therefore that an impairment review was required. Similarly, a significant number of candidates failed to recognise the indicator of going concern and the requirement for management to disclose this material uncertainty in the notes to the financial statements. Responses by candidates for the matters to consider were generally poorly answered, also the evidence to consider was generally well answered.

Part (b) required candidates to evaluate the appropriateness of the draft auditor's report if no further adjustments were made regarding the railway operating licence.

Overall, the responses were poor, with candidates demonstrating a general lack of knowledge of reporting, in particular the contents of an auditor's report. Very few candidates that linked the details for part (a)(i) and the loss of the railway operating licence to the effect on the auditor's report based on whether the disclosure note for the material uncertainty regarding going concern was appropriate or not. Candidates demonstrated limited understanding of the use of the Material Uncertainty Related to Going Concern section and when it was appropriate, with many stating it would be used when the opinion is modified, showing a fundamental lack of understanding of the relevant ISAs.

It was also concerning to see candidates responding that an Emphasis of Matter paragraph should be used for listed clients, which was again fundamentally incorrect.

Candidates are once again reminded that they must ensure they know the difference between these sections of the auditor's report and the circumstances under which each apply.

Marking guide **Marks**

(a) **Matters and evidence**

Generally, up to 1 mark for each matter explained and each piece of evidence recommended.

(i) **Railway licence**

Matters

- Management should disclose material uncertainties and auditor should assess adequacy of this disclosure
- Significant uncertainty exists over renewal of licence
- Materiality of national railway licence contribution to revenue/profit
- Without national railway licence, company would be loss-making
- Company has deteriorating performance, declining revenue, profit and assets
- Company may be unable to renew capex and maintain liquidity

Evidence

- A review of the press reports in relation to the late running of Matty plc's trains and the quality of its service to assess the seriousness and significance of the issue.
- A review of any correspondence files between Matty plc and the government transport department in order to identify any developments in the licence renewal process and consider their impact on the likely

renewal of the licence.

- Notes of discussions held between the auditor and the management of Matty plc in relation to any contingency plans if the company fails to secure the national railway licence; for example, any other licences or opportunities which may exist in the market and any emergency sources of finance which might be available to the company.
- A review of the company's board minutes for evidence of management discussion of the status of the tender process and of any contingency plans.
- A review and analysis of budgets and cash flow forecasts by the auditor in order to assess the ability of the company to survive as a going concern for the foreseeable future.
- Copies of the company's bank facilities reviewed to assess the feasibility of the company's ability to operate within them should they be unsuccessful in winning the contract.
- Written representations from management in relation to the status of the tender process and management's expectations of its expected outcome.

Maximum 7

(ii) **Purchase of customer list**

Matters

- Materiality of customer list (0.5 mark)
- Accounting rules of intangible assets with indefinite life
- Assessment is matter of significant judgement and high audit risk
- Indefinite useful life must be substantiated
- Must test intangible with indefinite useful life annually for impairment
- Accounting rule for impairment review
- Possible manipulation by management to avoid impairment loss
- Loss of two major customers/new competitor- possible impairment indicators
- If recoverable amount is less than carrying amount, impairment loss should be recognised in P/L for year.

Evidence

- A copy of the purchase agreement to identify the details of the acquisition including the purchase consideration, the assets acquired, and the date of the acquisition agreed to the detail included in the accounting records.
- Agreement of the purchase consideration of £6.9 million to the company's cash book and bank statement to confirm purchase price.
- A review of Jess Coaches' trading history and any market research which has been performed on the ability of the purchased customer list for evidence of how it will generate future revenue for Matty plc.
- A copy of the client's schedule calculating the value in use of the purchased customer list as £7.2 million and a confirmation of the schedule's mathematical accuracy
- A review and assessment of the company's cash flow forecast which has been used to support the value in use of £7.2 million agreed to the value in use calculation.

- A discussion with management in relation to the basis of the calculation of value in use and an assessment by the auditor of the reasonableness of management's key assumptions
- A sensitivity analysis performed by the auditor varying these key assumptions and an assessment of the materiality of the potential impact of varying the assumptions on the calculation of the value in use of the customer list.
- A review of Matty plc's management accounts for the reporting period and for the post reporting date period to date in order to identify and quantify the cash flows generated by Jess Coaches customer list and any significant variances investigated.
- A comparison of the discount rate used in the value in use calculation to published market rates and notes of discussions with management in relation to the basis of any adjustments made by management, in order to ensure that an appropriate rate has been used
- Written representations from management confirming that to the best of its knowledge, the assumptions used in the calculation of value in use are reasonable, appropriate and that in its opinion, the purchased customer list is not impaired and its carrying amount is fairly stated.

Maximum 8

(b) **Appropriateness of draft auditor's report**

Generally, 1 mark for each reporting implication explained.

- Inappropriate disclosure - modified opinion due to material misstatement
- Opinion would be qualified or adverse based on auditor's judgement of pervasiveness.
- Discussion of pervasiveness - disclosure paragraph may lack detail/ be contradictory.
- If disclosures not adequate, matter should be detailed in 'Basis for Qualified/ Adverse Opinion' paragraph
- Disclosure adequate, uncertainties should be disclosed in separate section/ 'Material Uncertainties related to Going Concern /Not KAM
- KAM disclosures required for high-risk areas, significant judgements, materiality and the effect of significant events or transactions that occurred during the period
- Inclusion as KAM - carrying amount of customer list/ management's conclusion that intangibles not impaired

Maximum 5

Professional marks

Analysis and evaluation

- Identification of omissions from the analysis or further analysis which could be carried out in respect of the railway operating licence and the purchased customer list.
- Balanced assessment of the information to determine the appropriate audit opinion in the circumstances

Professional scepticism and judgement

- Effective challenge and critical assessment of information, evidence and assumptions supplied and demonstration of professional judgement in identifying appropriate evidence to support conclusions for the audit engagement team.
- Appropriate application of professional scepticism and judgement to draw conclusions and make informed decisions which are appropriate in the context of the engagement.

Marking guide	Marks
Commercial acumen	
• Appropriate recognition of the wider implications of the information obtained during the audit regarding the railway licence, and the potential impact for Matty plc.	
Maximum	5
Total	25

(a) **Matters and evidence**

(i) **Railway operating licence**

Matters

Uncertainties in relation to going concern

IAS 1 *Presentation of Financial Statements* requires management to disclose material uncertainties in relation to going concern and ISA (UK) 570 (Revised) *Going Concern* requires the auditor to assess the adequacy of this disclosure. Therefore, the principal matter raised by the unresolved status of the licence tender is the potential impact on Matty plc's financial performance and financial position if the company is unsuccessful in the tender process. This in turn creates uncertainties in relation to the going concern status of the company. The licence is due for renewal on 28 February 20X6 which is 11 months from the reporting date and therefore within the foreseeable future for the purpose of the going concern review. Although the company has been informed that it is the preferred bidder, there are still significant doubts as to whether the licence will be renewed given the government's requirement that the company addresses the recent criticisms and the pending review in one month's time.

The revenue generated from the national railway licence represents 66.9% of Matty plc's revenue for year and is highly material to the company's statement of profit or loss for the year and critical to its operations. It is also significant that the national railway licence contributed profit before tax of £11.2 million which is 106.7% of this year's profit; without this contribution to the company's profit this year, the company would be loss-making. In addition to these considerations, even with the inclusion of the national railway licence in this year's results, Matty plc's performance is deteriorating as evidenced by its declining revenue (down by 36.3%) and profit before tax (down by 52.5%). The company's assets are also down by 8.7% on the prior year which may be indicative of a business which is struggling to renew its capital expenditure and maintains its liquidity.

Evidence

- A review of the press reports in relation to the late running of Matty plc's trains and the quality of its service to assess the seriousness and significance of the issue.
- A review of any correspondence files between Matty plc and the government transport department in order to identify any developments in the licence renewal process and consider their impact on the likely renewal of the licence.
- Notes of discussions held between the auditor and the management of Matty plc in relation to any contingency plans if the company fails to secure the national railway licence; for example, any other licences or opportunities which may exist in the market and any emergency sources of finance which might be available to the company.
- A review of the company's board minutes for evidence of management discussion of the status of the tender process and of any contingency plans.
- A review and analysis of budgets and cash flow forecasts by the auditor in order to assess the ability of the company to survive as a going concern for the foreseeable future.

- Copies of the company's bank facilities reviewed to assess the feasibility of the company's ability to operate within them should they be unsuccessful in winning the contract.
- Written representations from management in relation to the status of the tender process and management's expectations of its expected outcome.

(ii) **Purchased customer list**

Matters

Assessment of useful life

The carrying amount of the customer list purchased from Jess Coaches is highly material to Matty plc's draft statement of financial position as it exceeds the materiality threshold set by the partner of £1.05 million. According to IAS 38 *Intangible Assets*, a reporting entity should recognise intangible assets initially at cost and should assess whether an intangible asset's useful life is finite or indefinite. An assessment of a useful life as indefinite is only appropriate if on an analysis of all of the relevant factors, there is no foreseeable limit to the period over which the intangible is expected to generate net cash inflows for the entity. This assessment requires a significant level of judgement to be exercised and the subjectivity of the carrying amount creates a high level of risk for the auditor. In this case, the trading history of Jess Coaches prior to its acquisition by Matty plc may provide some evidence that there is no foreseeable limit to the period over which the purchased customer list can be expected to generate cash flows. However, this assumption needs to be assessed carefully by the auditor. Intangible assets with an indefinite life should not be amortised according to IAS 38.

Impairment review

IAS 38 also requires a reporting entity to test intangibles with an indefinite useful life annually for impairment. This impairment review would involve a comparison of the carrying amount of the customer list to its recoverable amount which, given the difficulty in identifying a sales value for the customer list, is likely to be based on an assessment of its value in use. The assessment of value in use is a highly subjective exercise which involves an estimate of the future cash flows the entity expects to derive from the customer list, expectations about possible variations in the amount or timing of these future cash flows and the time value of money represented by the current market risk-free rate of interest. Management's assessment of value in use as £7.2 million appears to be very close to the asset's carrying amount of £6.9 million and it is possible that management may have manipulated its assumption to avoid the recognition of an impairment loss. The auditor will therefore need to carefully review and consider management's assessment of value in use and the assumptions implicit in its calculation.

In addition to these considerations, the emergence of a new competitor which is capable of taking major customers away from Jess Coaches and the loss of two key customers already, are indicators that the intangible asset may indeed be impaired. If the recoverable amount of the intangibles is therefore less than their total carrying amount of £6.9 million at the reporting date, an impairment loss should be recognised in the statement of profit or loss for the year and the intangibles should be written down accordingly.

Evidence

- A copy of the purchase agreement to identify the details of the acquisition including the purchase consideration, the assets acquired, and the date of the acquisition agreed to the detail included in the accounting records.
- Agreement of the purchase consideration of £6.9 million to the company's cash book and bank statement to confirm purchase price.
- A review of Jess Coaches' trading history and any market research which has been performed on the ability of the purchased customer list for evidence of how it will generate future revenue for Matty plc.
- A copy of the client's schedule calculating the value in use of the purchased customer list as £7.2 million and a confirmation of the schedule's mathematical accuracy.

- A review and assessment of the company's cash flow forecast which has been used to support the value in use of £7.2 million agreed to the value in use calculation.
- A discussion with management in relation to the basis of the calculation of value in use and an assessment by the auditor of the reasonableness of management's key assumptions.
- A sensitivity analysis performed by the auditor varying these key assumptions and an assessment of the materiality of the potential impact of varying the assumptions on the calculation of the value in use of the customer list.
- A review of Matty plc's management accounts for the reporting period and for the post reporting date period to date in order to identify and quantify the cash flows generated by Jess Coaches' customer list and any significant variances investigated.
- A comparison of the discount rate used in the value in use calculation to published market rates and notes of discussions with management in relation to the basis of any adjustments made by management, in order to ensure that an appropriate rate has been used.
- Written representations from management confirming that to the best of its knowledge, the assumptions used in the calculation of value in use are reasonable and appropriate and that in its opinion, the purchased customer list is not impaired and its carrying amount is fairly stated.

(b) **Appropriateness of the draft auditor's report**

The finance director has agreed to include a short note to the financial statements to disclose information relating to the material uncertainty relating to going concern. The note must be reviewed for completeness and if the auditor assesses that the client's disclosure is not adequate, a modified audit opinion would be appropriate in relation to a material misstatement as a result of the inadequate disclosure.

The form of the opinion would be qualified or adverse depending on the auditor's judgement of the matter's pervasiveness to the financial statements. In this case, adverse may be the appropriate form of audit opinion given that the disclosure note is described as 'short' and that management may appear to negate the significance of the uncertainties by stating that they are 'very confident' that they will be successful in the tender process. A full description of the status of the tender negotiations as at the date of the auditor's report and their potential impact on the financial statements should then be detailed in the 'Basis for Qualified or Adverse Opinion' paragraph.

However, if on the other hand, the outcome of the auditor's assessment is that the client's financial statement disclosures are considered by the auditor to be appropriate, the material uncertainty in relation to going concern should be disclosed in a separate section entitled 'Material Uncertainties related to Going Concern' which should appear immediately below the 'Basis for Opinion Paragraph' and not in the Key Audit Matters (KAM) section of the auditor's report. According to ISA (UK) 570, the Material Uncertainty Related to Going Concern section should:

- Draw attention to the note in the financial statements which discloses the going concern issue; and
- State that these events or conditions indicate that a material uncertainty exists which may cast significant doubt on the entity's ability to continue as a going concern and that the that auditor's opinion is not modified in respect of the matter.

Matty plc is a listed entity and according to ISA (UK) 701 *Communicating Key Audit Matters in the Independent Auditor's Report*, KAM disclosures are required in the auditor's report for high-risk areas, significant judgements and the effect of significant events or transactions which occurred during the period. The assessment of the useful life of the customer list as indefinite and management's conclusion that the intangibles are not impaired, are areas of both significant judgement and high risk given the materiality of the intangibles. The auditor should consider disclosing these matters in the KAM section of the auditor's report.

According to ISA (UK) 701, there should also be an explanation of how the scope of the audit addressed each key audit matter and was influenced by the auditor's application of materiality. The FRC Bulletin on illustrative auditor's reports in the UK would also require disclosure of the method used for calculating materiality.

24 York

Workbook references

Chapters 1, 3, 8 and 12.

Top tips

Although it's discussion-based, part (a) is not horribly difficult. It's really important here that you answer the requirement set, which asks why there is a risk of fraud in revenue recognition. Although it mentions fraud, the requirement is absolutely not about the responsibilities of management v auditors in relation to fraud. There are no marks available for this, so even if you're panicking, you're still better off using your time to do something else.

The matter is slightly confused by the fact that there is a second part of the requirement, about 'why ISA (UK) 240 requires specific auditor responses in relation to the risks identified' – but this is not really addressed by the examining team's answer. Anything you wrote in relation to this should, however, get credit from the marker as long as it is relevant and true.

You could probably have thought of the following points, and developed them just a bit, in order to pass the question:

- Performance targets for management lead to risk of manipulation
- Cut-off can be relatively easy to manipulate, particularly where judgement is needed to determine
- IFRS 15 is complex in some areas, eg how to account for warranties provided with products
- Cash sales can be manipulated relatively easily

If you developed these then you should have been able to get one mark each, and thus pass.

Part (b) was a bit nicer, so you could have made up for any shortfall in your marks from part (a). The first part was a sly little question on money laundering. The tell-tale signs here were:

- It's a cash deposit
- It's then transferred abroad
- It isn't part of the company's business activities
- No evidence is provided

Although it's possible that there's a reasonable explanation for all this – more information is needed – it's also quite possibly money laundering. You should have been able to spot this, so it's then a question of having the confidence to base your answer on this rather than anything else. From then on, it's fairly straightforward!

An approach to writing your answer would be to state the reasons why it might be money laundering, and then use a bit of terminology to describe it: this is 'layering'. The rest follows on from this – both anti-money laundering implications, but also audit implications (eg the need for increased scepticism).

Note that there are easy marks for calculating materiality in (b), so make sure you do this (and say if the issue is material).

Note that there are **no marks for auditor's report** implications here, even if it was something that seemed to follow on logically from the question. If you did write about this, then you need to be careful to only include it if it's asked for.

Part (c) was straightforward, as long as you were familiar with the reporting requirements for review engagements of this sort.

Easy marks

Calculating materiality gets you easy marks. You should also be aiming to score well in part (b) as it was quite a nice question. Stick to your time limit though for this part.

ACCA examining team's comments

The first part required candidates to discuss why auditors should presume that there is a risk of fraud in revenue recognition and this requirement was poorly answered with most candidates setting out lengthy explanations of the respective duties of the auditor and management for the identification and prevention of fraud and thereby not answering the question. Strong answers considered management bias and targets, judgements in complex business and cut-off errors.

The second part explored an unusual issue which had occurred in an entrepreneurial audit client. Many candidates were able to identify the potential money laundering transaction and identified the placement and layering stages which were involved. Most candidates answered this part of the question well and were able to identify; the need for proper evidence, the poor controls over payments, notification to the MLCP and avoiding tipping-off the client.

Most answers to requirement (c) were good at discussing the accounting treatment for the warranty provision, that the non-recognition was not appropriate, and the majority correctly assessed the materiality of the issue. Answers were inadequate in discussing the impact of this on the review report, being mostly unable to say much more than the auditor would need to mention it in the review report. There seemed to be a lack of knowledge on anything other than the standard wording for a review report, with many answers stating that the wording should be 'nothing has come to our attention' followed by a discussion that there actually was something to bring to shareholders' attention but with no recommendation as to how this should be done.

Marking guide	Marks
(a) **Fraud and revenue recognition**	
Generally 1 mark for each point of discussion:	
• Management targets/incentives	
• High volume of transactions	
• Use of judgement	
• Complexity of accounting	
• Cash sales	
• Common in recent accounting frauds	
• Not always complex/rebuttable permitted	
• Reporting responsibility for irregularity and fraud	–
Maximum	7
(b) **Implications for completion of audit**	
Generally 1 mark for each well explained implication for the audit or recommendation for further action:	
Cash transfers	
• Indication of money laundering	
• Layering	
• Weakness in controls over cash	
• Need to understand the accounting entries	
• Failure to provide evidence	
• Increased risk/need for scepticism	
• Need for independent review	
• Report to MLCP	
• Care in avoiding 'tipping off'	–
Maximum	7

Marking guide	Marks
(c) **Interim financial statement review**	
Up to 1.5 marks for each matter to be considered in forming conclusion/implication for report:	
• Interim financial information should use applicable financial reporting framework	
• Identify and explain unrecognised provision	
• Correct calculation of materiality (1 mark)	
• Communicate necessary adjustment to management/those charged with governance	
• If amount unadjusted, the conclusion will be qualified	
• Reason for qualified conclusion to be explained in the report	
• Consider withdrawing from engagement/resign from audit appointment	
Maximum	6
Professional marks	
Analysis and evaluation	
• Appropriate use of the information to support discussion, draw appropriate conclusions and design appropriate responses	
• Effective consideration of the matters to consider in relation to the scenario information	
Professional scepticism and judgement	
• Effective challenge and critical assessment of the information supplied with appropriate conclusions	
• Appropriate application of professional judgement to draw conclusions and make informed comments	
• Effective application of judgement to consider implications for review report	
Maximum	5
Total	25

(a) There are a number of reasons why there should be a presumption of risks of fraud in revenue recognition. One reason is that managers of companies are often under pressure, particularly in listed companies, to achieve certain performance targets. The achievement of those targets often affects their job security and their compensation. These performance targets often include measures of revenue growth, providing an incentive for management to use earnings management techniques.

In other companies there may be incentives to understate revenues, for example, to reduce reported profits and, therefore, company taxation charges. This may be more relevant to private limited companies where management may not be under such pressure to achieve revenue-based targets.

There is also usually a high volume of revenue transactions during a financial period. As the volume of transactions increases, the risk of failing to detect fraud and error using traditional, sample-based auditing techniques also increases. This means that it is potentially easier for management to successfully manipulate these balances than other balances which are subject to a lower volume of transactions. Material misstatement through the manipulation of revenue recognition can be readily achieved by recording revenue in an earlier or later accounting period than is proper or by creating fictitious revenues.

Revenue recognition can also be a judgemental area. Examples include the recognition of revenues on long-term contracts, such as the construction of buildings, and from the provision of services. These require the estimation of the percentage of completion at the period end, increasing the scope for management to manipulate reported results.

As well as requiring judgement, revenue recognition can also be a complex issue. For example, some sales have multiple elements, such as the sale of goods and the separate sale of related maintenance contracts and warranties. This added complexity increases the risk of manipulation.

In some companies, for example, those in the retail industry, a high proportion of revenue may be earned through cash sales. This increases the risk of the theft of cash and the consequent manipulation of recorded revenues to conceal this crime.

Methods of revenue manipulation have also featured prominently in cases of accounting fraud, such as Enron and WorldCom. The prevalence of these methods in modern accounting frauds and the failure of auditors to detect this in these cases suggests that it is one of the more common methods of earnings management and one which auditors should rightly consider as high risk.

While revenue recognition in general may be considered a high-risk area, it is not always the case; companies with simple revenue streams or a low volume of transactions may be considered at low risk of fraud through revenue manipulations. Accordingly ISA (UK) 240 *The Auditor's Responsibility Relating to Fraud in an Audit of Financial Statements* permits the rebuttal of the fraud risk presumption for revenue recognition. One example of simple revenue streams would be where a company leases properties for fixed annual amounts over a fixed period of time. If this is the case, the reasons for not treating revenue as a high fraud risk area must be fully documented by the auditor.

In line with the FRC Bulletin on illustrative auditor's reports in the UK, the auditor's responsibilities for an audit of financial statements should discuss the extent to which the firm's procedures are capable of detecting irregularities, including fraud, making this an issue that should be on the firm's radar regardless.

(b) **Cash transfers**

This unusual, unexplained cash transfer into a foreign bank account may indicate that Phil Smith is using York Ltd to carry out money laundering. Money laundering is defined as the process by which criminals attempt to conceal the origin and ownership of the proceeds of their criminal activity, allowing them to maintain control over the proceeds and, ultimately, providing a legitimate cover for the sources of their income.

It is possible that the proceeds of criminal activity have been placed into York Ltd's bank account to enable them to transfer the funds into a foreign account, thus providing them with the appearance of legitimacy and creating a trail which is difficult to trace to the original source. This process is known as 'layering'. According to ACCA's Technical factsheet 145 *Anti-money laundering guidance for the accountancy sector*, money laundering can result from just a single transaction such as the cash placed into York Ltd's bank account.

The fact that Mr Smith retains sole control over cash management and that the financial controller has no oversight or involvement in this indicates weak controls over cash, for example, there appears to be no segregation of duty which may be the intention of Mr Smith to facilitate illegal activity. That he has failed to provide any documentary evidence, despite the request to do so by the audit team, only arouses suspicion further. It is also possible that the company is being used as a vehicle for money laundering without Mr Smith's knowledge. It is possible that the money has been accepted in good faith without the source of the funding being adequately verified.

The amount which has been transferred represents 1.3% of total assets, which is material to the financial statements. The engagement, and particularly matters relating to cash transactions, should now be considered as high risk and approached with a high degree of professional scepticism. The audit files should now be subject to an independent second partner review. The firm may also wish to seek legal advice given the potential legal implications of dealing with a client involved in money laundering. The cash transfer and the activities underlying the transactions could be offences under either the Proceeds of Crime Act 2002 or the Money Laundering Regulations 2017.

To properly assess the impact of the transaction on the financial statements, the audit firm needs to understand the accounting entries which have been made. The debit side of the entry would be to cash, and the audit team should enquire as to where the credit side of the entry has been recognised. Possibly the credit has been recognised as revenue or possibly it has been contra'd against the cash payment which was made the next day.

The situation should be reported as soon as possible to the firm's Money Laundering Compliance Principal (MLCP). The MLCP is responsible for receiving and evaluating reports of suspected money laundering from colleagues within the firm. They will make a decision as to whether further enquiries are required and, if necessary, will make reports to the appropriate authorities such as the National Crime Agency.

Finally, care must now be taken during the remaining audit that no-one 'tips off' the client that their activity is being treated as suspicious and that a report will be made to the MLCP. 'Tipping off' the client could prejudice any consequent investigation and may itself be considered a criminal offence. According to Technical factsheet 145, a tipping-off disclosure may be made in writing or verbally, and either directly or indirectly so the audit team must ensure that when discussing the matter with Mr Smith, he is not alerted to the suspicions of money laundering.

(c) The review should be conducted in line with ISRE (UK) 2410 *Review of Interim Financial Information Performed by the Independent Auditor of the Entity*. The key elements of the review are enquiry and analytical procedures, which do not lead to reasonable assurance.

The applicable financial reporting framework should be the same as for the annual financial statements, so IFRSs apply.

In line with IAS 37 *Provisions, Contingent Liabilities and Contingent Assets*, a provision should be recognised for the warranty on the cars. Thus the treatment in the financial statements for the year ended 30 September 20X4 appears correct.

Squire plc has stopped offering warranties on cars sold from 1 December 20X4 onwards. However, it still has an obligation to honour warranties on cars already sold. Hence it should still provide for the cost of honouring those warranties. The interim financial statements therefore appear to understate liabilities and overstate profit.

If the same warranty provision needed to be recognised in the interim financial statements as at the year end, this would be £1.5m. This is 5% of total assets (= £1.5m/£30m) and is material.

The auditor should communicate this misstatement to management. If management does not respond appropriately, then the auditor must inform those charged with governance.

If appropriate adjustments are not made, then the report should contain a qualified or adverse conclusion. The report must include a 'Basis for qualified conclusion' paragraph immediately before the 'Qualified conclusion' paragraph.

25 Mondrian

Workbook references

Chapters 2, 6 and 8.

Top tips

First there was a typical question on audit risk that should not have carried too many surprises. Take note of the need to evaluate and prioritise significant audit risks, rather than just to list them.

There are marks available for calculating materiality, so you really should get these. With materiality, it is best not to calculate the general thresholds at the start of your answer because the marks are available in relation to each item. The best approach is that taken by the model answer, ie select the relevant figure (revenue, PBT or total assets), calculate the percentage and then state whether it is material.

Any extra trend calculations that you can do can be a source of easy marks, eg calculating that revenue has increased by 2.2%, which is not included in the analytical review given in the question. These will usually earn ½ a mark.

It should not need saying, but the question does not ask for business risks so you should not be mentioning these in your answer, no matter how tempting it is to do so!

It is also a bad idea to include any theoretical discussions of the nature of audit risk (ie inherent risk vs detection risk vs control risk). Further, it is not really necessary to classify risks as eg inherent risks or control risks; the best answers might do this and the ability to do so easily is certainly a sign of a strong answer, but there are no marks available for this, so it is unlikely to be a good use of your time to rack your brains over it.

The requirement to recommend additional information is a common one, and the five marks available are relatively easy ones (each well-explained piece of information should get a full mark, which is quite a good return given how little needs to be written). It's really important that you devote enough time to this part of the question, and it is probably a good idea to answer this separately from your audit risk evaluation, to make sure that you give it enough attention. You could do this by making a sheet of paper just for additional information and adding things to it as you write your answer to the requirement on audit risks, and then spending time at the end thinking of anything else that might get marks.

The question also asked for audit procedures on work in progress. The relevant parts of the scenario are towards the end, just before the preliminary analytical review. The paragraph on the government grant (for part (b)(ii)) contains a bit of a steer by stating that the grant comes with conditions – the audit procedures must surely test whether these conditions will be met. You should thus be able to get two relatively easy marks in this area just by thinking of procedures to verify that £2 million has been spent on wages, and that the manufacturing site is likely to operate until 20Y0.

Easy marks

The marks for additional information and for calculating materiality. The professional marks are absolutely basic and there is no reason not to get at least three of them.

ACCA examining team's comments

This question followed the pattern of previous examinations and was set at the planning stage of the audit/assurance cycle and covered risks, audit procedures and other information required.

Candidates were required to provide an analysis of audit risks for a manufacturer of bespoke and generic machines. Performance on this requirement was good with the majority of candidates correctly describing audit risks rather than business risks. This is an area that most candidates are well prepared on. However, stronger answers were able to develop and apply the relevant accounting treatment. Those able to identify specific areas of the financial statements which would be affected and to correctly identify whether the risk was over or understatement tended to score the strongest marks. A significant minority of candidates thought that the client was new to the firm as opposed to simply having a change in manager and spent time addressing opening balances and new client procedures which were not relevant to the question. Candidates are again reminded to read the question carefully and consider the context of the scenario both in terms of client history and timeframe before answering the question.

Candidates were further required to provide additional information needed to effectively plan the audit, and candidates showed a marked improvement over previous sittings where this requirement has been examined. This type of question requires candidates to identify information that would be available in advance of the audit that would assist in the planning of the audit. Such information would generally help in the identification or evaluation of risks rather than the information available at the year end for performing audit procedures. This is particularly relevant as the question was set almost a month prior to the year end, so financial statements and year-end balances would not yet be available.

Candidates were further required to provide audit procedures for the valuation of work in progress (WIP) and a government grant. With respect to the former, candidates often cited the need for an expert to value WIP rather than focusing on the components of cost and NRV in the machines. Similarly, there were a number of candidates who requested written representations from management on WIP despite the figure not being an issue where the knowledge was confined to management or one of management's intentions. Candidates are once again reminded that a written representation is not a suitable substitute for sufficient appropriate evidence. The audit procedures relevant to the grant were generally well described.

Marking guide			Marks
(a)	(i)	**Evaluation and prioritisation of audit risks**	
		Up to 3 marks for each audit risk evaluated (unless indicated otherwise below), and 1 mark for relevant calculations (eg trends) up to a maximum of 6 marks for calculations:	
		• Stock exchange listing and pressure on results (up to 2 marks)	
		• Foreign exchange transactions and potential derivatives	
		• Payment in advance and revenue recognition	
		• Potential for cancelled contracts and implication for valuation of work in progress	
		• New directors (up to 2 marks)	
		• Cash-settled share-based payment scheme	
		• Revaluation of property	
		• Deferred tax recognition	
		• Government grant recognition and potential for repayment if terms are breached	
		• Inventory valuation (up to 2 marks)	
		• Provision in respect of returned goods	
		• Working capital	
		• Materiality	
		Maximum	24
	(ii)	**Additional information**	
		1 mark for each relevant piece of relevant information recommended. The list below is indicative, and credit should be given for other relevant recommendations:	
		• Details of the stock exchange listing during the year	
		• Information on the specific listing rules relevant to the stock exchange	
		• Details on the planned foreign stock exchange listing	
		• Information on the background and experience of the new non-executive directors and the new finance director	
		• A full set of draft financial statements including a statement of cash flows	
		• Details on the valuation of properties such as date of valuation and name of the valuer	
		• Documentation on the cash-settled share-based payment scheme	
		Maximum	6
(b)	(i)	**Audit procedures on the valuation of work in progress**	
		1 mark for each well explained audit procedure:	
		• Obtain a schedule itemising the jobs included in work in progress at the year end, cast it and agree the total to the general ledger and draft financial statements	
		• Agree a sample of items from the schedule to the inventory count records	

- For a sample of jobs included on the schedule:
- Agree costs to supporting documentation such as supplier's invoice and payroll records
- For any overheads absorbed into the work in progress valuation, review the basis of the absorption and assess its reasonableness
- Assess how the degree of completion of the job has been determined at the year end and agree the stage of completion of the job to records taken at the inventory count
- Agree the details of the job specification to customer order and
- Confirm that net realisable value is greater than cost by agreeing the contract price and cash received from the customer post year end
- To assess the completeness of work in progress, select a sample of customer orders and trace through to the list of jobs included in work in progress

Maximum 5

(ii) **Audit procedures in respect of the government grant**

1 mark for each well explained audit procedure:

- Obtain the documentation relating to the grant to confirm the amount, the date the cash was received, and the terms on which the grant was awarded
- Review the documentation for any conditions attached to the grant, for example, is there a requirement that a certain number of people are employed at the manufacturing plant?
- Discuss with management the method of recognition of the amount received, in particular how much of the grant has been recognised in profit and the treatment of the amount deferred in the statement of financial position
- For the part of the grant relating to continued operation of the manufacturing plant, determine the basis on which this is being released into profit, assess its reasonableness and recalculate to confirm accuracy of management's calculations
- Review forecasts and budgets in relation to the manufacturing plant to assess the likelihood of its continued operations until 20Y0
- Using the draft financial statements, confirm the accounting treatment outlined by discussion with management has been applied and recalculate the amounts recognised
- Confirm the cash received to bank statement and cash book

Maximum 5

Professional marks

Communication

- Briefing notes format and structure - use of headings/sub-headings and an introduction
- Style, language and clarity - appropriate layout and tone of briefing notes, presentation of materiality and relevant calculations, appropriate use of the CBE tools, easy to follow and understand
- Effectiveness and clarity of communication - answer is relevant and tailored to the scenario
- Adherence to the specific requests made by the audit engagement partner

Analysis and evaluation

- Appropriate use of the information to determine suitable calculations

Marking guide	Marks

- Appropriate use of the information to support discussions and draw appropriate conclusions
- Assimilation of all relevant information to ensure that the risk evaluation performed considers the impact of contradictory or unusual movements
- Effective prioritisation of the results of the risk evaluation to demonstrate the likelihood and magnitude of risks and to facilitate the allocation of appropriate responses
- Balanced discussion of the information to objectively make a recommendation or decision

Professional scepticism and judgement

- Effective challenge of information supplied, and techniques carried out to support key facts and/or decisions (especially in the context of the risk of manipulation)
- Determination and justification of a suitable materiality level, appropriately and consistently applied
- Appropriate application of professional judgement to draw conclusions and make informed decisions about the courses of action which are appropriate in the context of the audit engagement

Commercial acumen

- Audit procedures are practical and plausible in the context of Dali.
- Use of effective examples and/or calculations from the scenario to illustrate points or recommendations.
- Recognition of the appropriate commercial considerations of both the audit firm and the client

Maximum	10
Total	50

Briefing notes

To: Audit engagement partner, Sam Hockney

From: Audit manager

Subject: Audit planning in respect of Dali plc

Introduction

These briefing notes are prepared to assist in the audit planning meeting for Dali plc, our manufacturing client supplying machinery and equipment to the quarrying industry. The notes contain an evaluation of audit risk along with recommendations of the additional information which is relevant to audit risk evaluation. The notes explain the principal audit procedures to be performed in respect of the valuation of work in progress, and the government grant received during the year. The notes also identify and discuss the ethical and other professional issues raised in respect of the client's request for a valuation service.

(a) (i) **Audit risk evaluation**

Stock exchange listing and pressure on results

The listing obtained during the year can create inherent risk at the financial statement level because management may feel under pressure to achieve good results in this financial year. The flotation raised equity capital, so there will be new shareholders who will want to see strong performance in the expectation of a dividend pay-out. In addition, the introduction of the cash-settled share-based payment plan motivates management to produce financial statements which show a favourable performance and position which is likely to lead to an increase in the company's share price. There is a risk that revenue and profits may be overstated. Revenue has increased by 2.2% and profit before tax by 6.5%, which may indicate overstatement.

Stock exchange regulation

Dali plc is listed on an alternative stock exchange. Such a listing is unlikely to carry with it the same degree of regulation as a premium listing would do (such as one on the London Stock Exchange), however there remains a risk that any further regulations will not be complied with. This could result in unrecognized liabilities for fines or penalties. It will also be important to take into account regulatory compliance when evaluating the company's going concern assessment, since non-compliance could affect the company's ability to raise capital in the future.

Foreign exchange transactions

Dali plc purchases many components from foreign suppliers and is therefore likely to be transacting and making payments in foreign currencies. According to IAS 21 *The Effects of Changes in Foreign Exchange Rates*, transactions should be initially recorded using the spot rate, and monetary items such as trade payables should be retranslated at the year end using the closing rate. Exchange gains and losses should be recognised within profit for the year. The risk is that the incorrect exchange rate is used for the translation and retranslation, or that the retranslation does not happen at the year end, in which case trade payables and profit could be over- or understated, depending on the movement in the exchange rate. The company may have entered into hedging arrangements as a way to reduce exposure to foreign exchange fluctuations. There is a risk that hedging arrangements are not identified and accounted for as derivatives according to IFRS 9 *Financial Instruments* which could mean incomplete recognition of derivative financial assets or liabilities and associated gains or losses.

Payment in advance and revenue recognition under contract with customers

For items where significant design work is needed, Dali plc receives a payment in advance. This gives rise to risk in terms of when that part of the revenue generated from a sale of goods is recognised. There is a risk that revenue is recognised too early, especially given the risk of management bias and the incentive to overstate revenue and profit as discussed above. According to IFRS 15 *Revenue from Contracts with Customers*, revenue should only be recognised as control is passed, either over time or at a point in time. The timing of revenue recognition will depend on the contractual terms with the customer, with factors which may indicate the point in time at which control passes including the transference of the physical asset, transference of legal title, and the customer accepting the significant risks and rewards related to the ownership of the asset. It is likely that the payments in advance should be treated as deferred revenue at the point when the payment is received as the conditions for recognition of revenue are unlikely to have been met at this point in time.

There is additional audit risk created if a customer were to cancel a contract part way through its completion, the bespoke work in progress may be worthless and would need to be written off according to IAS 2 *Inventories*. There is therefore a risk of overstated work in progress.

New directors

During the year several new non-executive directors were appointed, as well as a new finance director. While this may serve to strengthen the corporate governance structure including the control environment, equally the introduction of new personnel could mean inexperience and a control risk, particularly if the finance director is lacking in experience. Some of the suggestions and accounting treatments made by the finance director indicate that their knowledge of the applicable financial reporting framework is weak, signalling that errors may occur in the preparation of the financial statements.

Cash-settled share-based payment scheme

This falls under the scope of IFRS 2 *Share-based Payment* which states that the liability in respect of the plan should be measured at fair value at the year end. The increase in the share price from £2.90 at flotation to £3.50 (projected) at the year end indicates that a liability should be recognised at 30 September 20X5 based on the fair value of the liability which has accrued up to that date, with the expense recognised in the statement of profit or loss. This accounting treatment has not been followed, leading to understated liabilities and overstated profit, and the disclosure in respect of the plan may not be sufficient to meet the requirements of IFRS 2 which requires extensive disclosures including the effect of share-based payment transactions on the entity's profit or loss for the period and on its financial position.

Revaluation of property

The decision to revalue the company's manufacturing sites creates several risks. First, revaluation involves establishing a current market price or fair value for each property included in the revaluation, which can be a subjective exercise, leading to inherent risk that the valuations may not be appropriate. A risk also arises in that IAS 16 requires all assets in the same class to be revalued, so if any properties which are manufacturing sites have not been included in the revaluation exercise, the amounts recognised will not be correct. There is also a risk that depreciation has not been recalculated on the new, higher value of the properties, leading to overstatement of non-current assets and understatement of operating expenses. IAS 16 also requires a significant level of disclosure in relation to a policy of revaluation, so there is a risk that the necessary disclosures are incomplete. The revaluation gain recognised in equity represents 3.9% of total assets and is therefore material to the financial statements.

Deferred tax recognition

IAS 12 *Income Taxes* requires deferred tax to be recognised in respect of taxable temporary differences which arise between the carrying amount and tax base of assets and liabilities, including the differences which arise on the revaluation of non-current assets, regardless of whether the assets are likely to be disposed of in the foreseeable future. The finance director's suggestion that deferred tax should not be provided for is therefore incorrect, and at present liabilities are understated, representing an error in the statement of financial position. There is no profit impact, however, as the deferred tax would be recognised in equity. Depending on the rate of tax which would be used to determine the necessary provision, it may not be material to the financial statements.

Government grant recognition

The government grant represents 11.1% of total assets and is material to the financial statements. A risk arises in relation to the recognition of the grant. IAS 20 *Accounting for Government Grants and Disclosure of Government Assistance* requires that a grant is recognised as income over the period necessary to match the grant received with the related costs for which they are intended to compensate. Therefore, the £2 million relating to costs incurred this year should be recognised as income, but the remainder should be released to profit on a systematic basis; in this case it would seem appropriate to release on a straight-line basis until April 20Y0. The risk is that the grant has been recognised on an inappropriate basis leading to over or understated profit for the year. The part of the grant not recognised in profit should be recognised in the statement of financial position. IAS 20 allows classification as deferred income (a contract liability), or alternatively the amount can be netted against the assets to which the grant relates. There is therefore also a risk that the amount is recognised elsewhere in the statement of financial position, leading to incorrect presentation and disclosure.

If the terms of the grant have been breached, the grant or an element of it may need to be repaid. There is therefore a risk that if there is any breach, the associated provision for repayment is not recognised, understating liabilities.

Lease recognition

The present value of the contract represents 0.9% of total assets (= £850,000 / £90m) and is on the borderline of being material. Misstatements here could become material when aggregated with any other uncorrected misstatements.

IFRS 16 *Leases* states that a lease is a contract that gives control of the use of an identified asset for a period of time in exchange for consideration (IFRS 16). Although Dali plc may have the right to control the use of the cleaning machines, the supplier has substantive substitution rights, ie it could feasibly substitute other machines for the ones Dali plc is using. There is therefore no identified asset, so the lease should not be recognised. The risk is that Dali plc may have recognised a non-current asset and a lease liability, which would overstate both assets and liabilities. Dali plc should have recognised the lease payments in profit or loss as they occur.

Inventory valuation

Work in progress is material at 13.3% of total assets and has increased by 26.3% in the current year. The valuation of work in progress is likely to be complex as many different jobs for different customers are ongoing at the year end, and each will have a different stage of completion and cost base at the year end. There are also issues more generally with the valuation of inventory, due to the customer returns of items which have recently occurred showing that there are problems with the quality of the goods supplied. For items which have been returned, the net realisable value is likely to be less than the cost of the item indicating that a write-off may be necessary to reduce the value of the inventory according to IAS 2. The increase in the inventory holding period, as demonstrated by the increase in inventory days, shows that inventory has become more slow-moving during the year also indicating that inventory may be overstated.

Provision in respect of returned goods

A provision should be recognised where a reliable estimate can be made in relation to a probable outflow of economic resources and an obligating event has taken place. The fact that Dali plc replaces faulty products free of charge indicates that a provision should be recognised based on the best estimate of the future economic outflow. The risk is that no provision or an insufficient provision in relation to the warranty has been recognised, leading to understated liabilities and operating expenses.

Working capital

The preliminary analytical review reveals that Dali plc is struggling to manage its working capital. The liquidity ratios provided show that the operating cycle has increased from 165 days in 20X4 (150 + 70 – 55) to 205 days in 20X5 (175 + 90 – 60). The company may be finding it difficult to collect cash from customers, as the receivables period has increased by 20 days, and in turn the payment period to suppliers has increased by five days. If there is doubt over the collectability of receivables, then certain balances may need to be written off, and there is a risk of overstatement of receivables and understatement of operating expenses if bad debts are not recognised.

Conclusion

A number of risks have been identified as significant risks for the audit. The highest priority risks are likely to be those arising in relation to the company's stock exchange listing and the concomitant increase in complexity, and in the level of pressure on management. The company's operations are becoming increasingly complex, with the management of inventory and working capital being perhaps the most material single issue identified.

Tutorial note. Credit will be awarded for other relevant audit risks.

(ii) **Recommended additional information**

- Details of the stock exchange listing during the year including the terms of the flotation, number of equity shares issued and amount of equity capital raised
- Any information available in relation to the flotation – for example, investor prospectus, pre- and post-flotation press releases, communications with the stock exchange registrar
- Copies of the UK Corporate Governance code and any relevant listing rules, for disclosures in the company annual report and financial statements
- Details on the planned foreign stock exchange listing in March 20X6 including the jurisdiction, the strategic rationale for seeking the listing and proposed timescales
- Information on the background and experience of the new non-executive directors and the new finance director – for example, their professional qualifications and previous employment or directorships held
- A full set of forecast financial statements including a statement of cash flows to assess the working capital issues faced by the company

- Details on the valuation of properties including the date of the revaluation and information on the valuer such as their professional qualification and relationship with the company and a copy of the valuation report
- Documentation on the cash-settled share-based payment scheme to gauge the number of members of the scheme and its potential materiality to the financial statements

> **Tutorial note.** Credit will be awarded for other relevant information which would be available at this stage of the audit to help in the evaluation of audit risk.

(b) (i) **Audit procedures in respect of the valuation of work in progress**

- Obtain a schedule itemising the jobs included in work in progress at the year end, cast it and agree the total to the general ledger and draft financial statements.
- Agree a sample of items from the schedule to the inventory count records.
- For a sample of jobs included on the schedule:
  - Agree costs to supporting documentation such as supplier's invoice and payroll records
  - For any overheads absorbed into the work in progress valuation, review the basis of the absorption and assess its reasonableness
  - Assess how the degree of completion of the job has been determined at the year end and agree the stage of completion of the job to records taken at the inventory count
  - Agree the details of the job specification to customer order and
  - Confirm that net realisable value is greater than cost by agreeing the contract price and cash received from the customer post year end
- To assess the completeness of work in progress, select a sample of customer orders and trace through to the list of jobs included in work in progress.

(ii) **Audit procedures in respect of the recognition and measurement of the government grant**

- Obtain the documentation relating to the grant to confirm the amount, the date the cash was received, and the terms on which the grant was awarded.
- Review the documentation for any conditions attached to the grant, for example, is there a requirement that a certain number of people are employed at the manufacturing plant?
- Discuss with management the method of recognition of the amount received, in particular how much of the grant has been recognised in profit and the treatment of the amount deferred in the statement of financial position.
- For the part of the grant relating to wages and salaries, confirm that the grant criteria have been complied with by examining payroll records and timesheets to verify that £2m has been spent on wages in the deprived area.
- For the part of the grant relating to continued operation of the manufacturing site, determine the basis on which this is being released into profit and recalculate to confirm accuracy of management's calculations.
- Review forecasts and budgets in relation to the manufacturing site to assess the likelihood of its continued operations until 20Y0.
- Using the draft financial statements, confirm the accounting treatment outlined by discussion with management has been applied and recalculate the amounts recognised.
- Confirm the cash received to bank statement and cash book.

Conclusion

These briefing notes indicate that there are many areas of potential audit risk to be considered when developing the audit strategy for Dali plc, and that additional information should be requested from the client to be obtained as soon as possible to facilitate a more in-depth evaluation of certain audit risks identified. The audit procedures recommended in respect of work in progress will provide assurance on these significant issues.

26 Zed

Workbook references

Chapters 1, 2, 6, 7 and 8.

Top tips

This was a typical question that should not have contained too many nasty surprises.

The question asked you to evaluate audit risks, which is entirely to be expected in AAA. Most of the issues here should have been straightforward. The requirement asks you to 'prioritise' your risks, which you can demonstrate by including a simple conclusion that summarises the risks you consider to be the most important.

Since this question is set at the **planning stage**, you do not have to go into enormous detail about the kinds of evidence that should be obtained in relation to the revenue. Rather, you should simply discuss the areas of risk, ie the things that might go wrong. Furthermore, the key issue here is the **change** in financial reporting requirements, implementing a standard that is new to the client. Your answer should therefore have focused on the risks associated with this transition.

There was an audit risk in relation to **fraud**, but this was ever so slightly tricky because it was presented in the 'internal audit' part of the scenario. Although the examining team does generally try to help you with the way questions are set out, you do need to keep your wits about you (like here).

The following hopefully won't apply to many BPP students, but just in case: please do not write treatises on the audit risk model; we all know that it's made up of control risk, detection risk and inherent risk. There are no marks for this – the whole point of AAA is to apply your knowledge, not just to state it. (There are also unlikely to be any marks for categorising the risks you identify.) Also do not discuss business risks unless they're relevant to the question.

It's crucial that you **calculate materiality for each risk** that you discuss. This should be in the form of a % of the relevant benchmark, eg 'the payment of £17.8m is 3% of total assets and is material'. These are really easy marks, and don't take you long to calculate or to write.

Make sure you try for the communication element of the **professional marks** as well – introduction, conclusion, subheadings and clear language will get you most of them.

The question ended with a requirement on ethical matters in relation to a different company, and should have been a normal question on which you could score well.

Easy marks

The professional marks and the materiality marks are easy. The materiality marks in particular are often the difference between passing and failing the question – many good candidates don't score well because even though they aced the rest of the question, they didn't get these easy marks. It is important, of course that you select the most appropriate benchmark, and use the correct figures!

ACCA examining team's comments

This was a standard audit risk requirement and should have been an area where candidates were able to score strong marks for identifying audit risks from the scenario and describing the effects on the financial statements and elements of audit risk. This part of the question was disappointingly answered by many candidates. **There is a tendency for weaker candidates to**

produce long but irrelevant answers. There is no place in this requirement for describing the audit risk model or discussing ethical issues.

In this scenario the client was not a new client and had pre-existing international revenue streams, demonstrated by the prior year segmental revenue comparatives, therefore discussing detection risk due to a lack of auditor knowledge of the client or inability to audit international revenue was not relevant. The risks in this type of question are flagged up in the scenario and should be addressed using up to date knowledge of financial reporting standards to describe appropriate accounting treatment and highlighting the potential impact of errors on the financial statements. Generally, the direction of the error will be required to score well, simply stating that intangibles may be over or understated will not gain full credit as this does not demonstrate the level of knowledge which is required.

As in previous audit risk questions, there is credit available for calculating and concluding on the materiality of a balance in the financial statements. A majority of candidates are able to correctly select the appropriate benchmark for materiality (eg assessing an asset or liability in the context of total assets rather than on revenue or profits) but frequently answers were presented with materiality based on prior year rather than current year figures. Audit risk continues to be an area that candidates find difficult and particularly it continues to be noted that many candidates fail to engage with the information provided in enough depth, specifically when provided with extracts from financial statements. Candidates are again reminded that in order to provide a full answer in relation to audit risk they should utilise and analyse all the information that is provided.

Candidates were also required to discuss the considerations to be taken into account when assessing whether and how to use internal audit to assist the external auditor. The majority of candidates were able to list the criteria as per ISA (UK) 610 *Using the Work of Internal Auditors*, to assess against and relate that back to the scenario, which was an improvement on the last time this standard was examined.

In the final part of the briefing notes, candidates were required to provide the principal audit procedures to obtain audit evidence in relation to the classification of a joint venture and the measurement of an intangible asset. The majority of candidates performed satisfactorily in this requirement but again many had not read the requirement carefully enough and described tests covering other FS assertions than those required – for example assessing the cost of the joint venture which was not relevant to the classification risk, or failing to take into account that the intangible had been purchased in the prior year so the cost would have been audited at that point, so audit procedures should have focused on confirming the brought forward figure and any adjustments for amortisation or impairment.

Note. no comments are available for part (d), which covered Gull Ltd.

Marking guide **Marks**

(a) **Evaluation of audit risk**

Generally up to 3 marks for each well explained audit risk. In addition, 1 mark relating to each correct materiality calculation to a maximum of 2 marks, and 1 mark for each relevant calculation such as trends.

- Recognition of 50% equity shareholding in WTC
- Amortisation of licence to operate in Farland
- Possible impairment of licence
- Right to use network capacity
- Revenue recognition – max 5 marks if discuss a range of issues specific to IFRS 15 including multiple element contracts, timing of recognition, disclosure requirements, volume of transactions
- Minimum wage – NOCLAR, ISA (UK) 250A
- Cyberattack – use of expert, consideration of IAS 37

- Segmental reportingInternal controls and fraud risk – up to 4 marks for a detailed discussion of fraud risk

Maximum	17

(b) **Internal audit**

Generally up to 2 marks for discussion of each relevant matter:

- General introduction, identifying that direct assistance may not be provided
- Comment on the type of work which may be used by the external auditor
- Objectivity
- Competence
- Disciplined and systematic approach

Maximum	7

(c) **Audit procedures**

Generally 1 mark for each well explained audit procedure:

Investment in WTC

- Obtain the legal documentation supporting the investment and agree the details of the investment (max 2 marks for details of items to be verified)
- Read board minutes for approval of the investment and understanding of the business rationale for the investment
- Read minutes of relevant meetings between ZCG and Wolf Communications to confirm shared control and shared decision-making process
- Confirm that ZCG has successfully appointed members to the board of WTC and that board decisions are made equally

Amortisation of licence

- Obtain the licence agreement and confirm the length of the licence period
- Confirm whether the licence can be renewed at the end of the 10-year period
- Reperform management's calculation of the amortisation charged as an expense in the year ended 30 September 20X5
- Discuss with management the process for determining the method of amortisation
- Review management accounts to confirm that the Farland network became operational on 1 April 20X5 and that Farland is generating a revenue stream from that date
- Review customer contracts to confirm network operational from 1 April 20X5
- Enquire with management on the existence of factors indicating that a shorter useful life is appropriate
- Review management accounts and cash flow forecasts to confirm that Farland is generating an income stream and is predicted to continue to generate cash
- Obtain a management representation to confirm that there are no indications of impairment of the licence of which management is aware

Maximum	10

(d) **Ethical and professional matters**

In general up to 1.5 marks for each well explained point:

Temporary recruitment of audit partner

- Prohibited by FRC *Ethical Standard* (1 mark)

Recruitment services

- Potential management and familiarity threat

ANSWERS

- Management responsibility in appointing senior management
- As listed entity, service cannot be provided
- Decline engagement

6

Professional marks

Communication

- Briefing notes format and structure - use of headings/sub-headings and an introduction
- Style, language and clarity - appropriate layout and tone of briefing notes, presentation of materiality and relevant calculations, appropriate use of the CBE tools, easy to follow and understand
- Effectiveness and clarity of communication - answer is relevant and tailored to the scenario
- Adherence to the specific requests made by the audit engagement partner

Analysis and evaluation

- Appropriate use of the information to determine suitable calculations
- Appropriate use of the information to support discussions and draw appropriate conclusions
- Assimilation of all relevant information to ensure that the risk evaluation performed considers the impact of contradictory or unusual movements
- Effective prioritisation of the results of the risk evaluation to demonstrate the likelihood and magnitude of risks and to facilitate the allocation of appropriate responses
- Balanced discussion of the information to objectively make a recommendation or decision

Professional scepticism and judgement

- Effective challenge of information supplied, and techniques carried out to support key facts and/or decisions
- Determination and justification of a suitable materiality level, appropriately and consistently applied
- Appropriate application of professional judgement to draw conclusions and make informed decisions about the courses of action which are appropriate in the context of the audit engagement

Commercial acumen

- Audit procedures are practical and plausible in the context of ZCG.
- Use of effective examples and/or calculations from the scenario to illustrate points or recommendations.
- Recognition of the appropriate commercial considerations of the audit firm

Maximum	10
Total	50

Briefing notes

To: Vincent Vega, audit engagement partner

From: Audit engagement manager

Subject: Audit planning – ZCG Introduction

These briefing notes have been prepared to assist in the audit planning of ZCG and contain an evaluation of significant audit risks and a discussion of the matters to be considered in determining whether to place reliance on the Group's internal audit department. The notes also include the recommended audit procedures to be performed on the classification of the 50% shareholding in WTC as a joint venture and on the measurement of a licence acquired on 1 October 20X3.

(a) **Evaluation of audit risks**

Recognition of 50% equity shareholding in WTC

The 50% equity shareholding is likely to give rise to a joint venture under which control of WTC is shared between ZCG and Wolf Communications Ltd. IFRS 11 *Joint Arrangements* requires that an investor which has joint control over a joint venture should recognise its investment using the equity method of accounting. Audit risk arises in that despite owning 50% of the equity shares of WTC, ZCG may not actually share control with Wolf Communications, for example, if Wolf Communications Ltd retains a right to veto decisions or if ZCG cannot appoint an equal number of board members in order to make joint decisions with board members appointed by Wolf Communications Ltd. If ZCG does not have joint control, then WTC should not be treated as a joint venture.

Assuming that there is shared control, an audit risk arises in that ZCG may not have correctly applied equity accounting, thereby potentially over or understating ZCG's investment and resulting in incorrect presentation in the consolidated statement of financial position and statement of profit or loss. The cost of the investment in WTC represents 7.5% of ZCG's total assets at 31 May 20X5, thus the investment is material to the Group.

Amortisation of licence to operate in Farland

The licence acquired on 1 October 20X3 should be recognised as an intangible asset and amortised on a systematic basis over its useful life. According to IAS 38 *Intangible Assets*, the amortisation method should reflect the pattern of benefits, or if the pattern cannot be determined reliably, the straight-line method of amortisation should be used. Amortisation should begin when the asset is available for use, meaning when it is in the location and condition necessary for it to be capable of operating in the manner which management intends. ZCG therefore should begin to amortise the licence on 1 April 20X5 and amortise over the remaining licence period of eight and a half years. The audit risk is that amortisation did not commence at the right point in time or that it has been determined using an inappropriate useful life, leading to over or understatement of the amortisation charge to profit as well as the carrying value of the intangible asset.

Assuming that it is appropriate to use the straight-line method, amortisation for the year to 30 September 20X5 should be £3.8 million ($65/8.5 \times {}^{6}/_{12}$). This represents 1.3% of extrapolated revenue for the year of £297 million ($198 \times {}^{12}/_{8}$) and is therefore material, and the amortisation will be more material next year when a full year's charge to profit is made.

Impairment of the Farland licence

IAS 38 does not require an annual impairment review to be conducted for all intangible assets. However, management should consider whether there are indicators of impairment and if necessary perform an impairment review on the licence. The competitor's actions which appear to have reduced customer demand to a level below that anticipated is an indicator of potential impairment, so management must calculate the recoverable amount of the licence and compare to its carrying value in order to determine if the asset is impaired. Therefore there is a risk that the licence is overstated in value, and operating profit also overstated if any necessary impairment has not been recognised.

Revenue recognition

ZCG is supplying customers with a multiple-element contract and is providing access to a mobile phone network and a fixed landline and broadband service. The key audit risk arises in relation to whether ZCG accounts for the elements of the contract separately in accordance with IFRS 15 *Revenue from Contracts with Customers which* requires the revenue to be derived from the contract to be allocated to each component. ZCG should have robust systems in place to ensure that contracts can be 'unbundled', enabling the revenue from each part of the contract to be separately determined, otherwise there is a significant risk that the revenue element attributable to each component of the customer contracts will be over or understated.

There is also a risk that the timing of revenue recognition will not be in line with ZCG meeting its performance obligations, also a requirement of IFRS 15. Contracts vary in length, lasting two or three years, and there is an audit risk that the timing of revenue recognition is not appropriate. The fact that total revenue, when extrapolated for the 12-month period, is expected to increase by 35% could indicate that revenue is being recognised too early.

IFRS 15 contains significant disclosure requirements and there is a risk that ZCG fails to provide sufficient disclosure on a range of matters relevant to its contracts with customers, including the significant judgements made in applying IFRS 15 to those contracts and sufficient disaggregation of the necessary disclosures.

Given the significant volume of individual customer contracts and the complexity of the accounting treatment, revenue recognition is a significant audit risk.

Right to use network capacity

The payment of £17.8 million to acquire access to network capacity represents 3% of total assets and 6% of extrapolated revenue for the year, thus the amount is material.

It seems that risk and reward does not pass to ZCG in respect of the assets being used and the seller retains control over the use of its network assets. Therefore the network capacity should not be recognised as an intangible asset of ZCG and the Group is currently adopting an inappropriate accounting treatment which has resulted in intangible assets being overstated.

The accounting treatment for these rights should be discussed with ZCG as soon as possible. The most appropriate accounting treatment would seem to be for ZCG to record the cost of the right to use the network capacity as a prepayment and recognise the cost in profit or loss on a straight-line basis over the term of the agreements and this accounting treatment should be reflected in the financial statements as soon as possible. The audit team will need to be made aware of the risk that prepayments and operating expenses are over or understated if the cost has not been treated as a prepayment and/or is not released to profit or loss over an appropriate period.

A further risk is the payment to the network provider is for a specified amount of access to the network provider's network. There is a risk is that ZCG has exceeded the allocated allowance and that any necessary additional payment due for excess usage is not recognised in the financial statements.

Cyberattack

There is clearly a risk that data protection laws have been breached, so it is imperative that Tarantino & Co obtains an understanding of the relevant legislation in ZCG's jurisdiction – in the UK, this would likely include the Data Protection Act 1998. IAS 37 *Provisions, Contingent Liabilities and Contingent Assets* requires an entity to provide for a future liability where an outflow of resources embodying economic benefits is probable, and the amount can be measured reliably. Audit evidence will need to be obtained regarding whether ZCG is liable to its customers for the loss of their data, and further whether there is a possibility of winning a legal case against Equimal for losing ZCG's data.

It is likely that a legal expert would need to be consulted to help determine the likelihood of both of these outcomes. It should therefore be ascertained whether ZCG has engaged the services of a management's expert, and the significance of any work done by them for the purpose of the audit. Tarantino & Co would need to: evaluate the expert's competence and capabilities; obtain an understanding of the expert's work; and evaluate the appropriateness of their work as audit evidence (ISA (UK) 500 *Audit Evidence*: para. 8). It may be necessary Tarantino & Co to make use of an auditor's expert if there is no reliable management's expert.

ZCG does not appear to have provided for a possible outflow (or recognised any contingent assets), and this should be confirmed. A contingent asset should only be recognised when a future inflow is virtually certain, and that is not the case here (so no asset should be recognised). Whether a liability is recognised will depend on the outcome of any expert's work, but given that the details of the case are still not certain – it is not known whether all of ZCG's customers' data was stolen, for example – provision cannot be made because the amount of any future outflow cannot be measured reliably.

Minimum wage

This is a case of non-compliance with laws and regulations, or NOCLAR. ISA (UK) 250A *Consideration of Laws and Regulations in an Audit of Financial Statements* states that the auditor is not responsible for preventing non-compliance or detecting non-compliance with all laws and regulations (ISA (UK) 250A: para. 4). However, the auditor is responsible for obtaining reasonable assurance that the financial statements are not materially misstated.

In ISA (UK) 250A terms, the legislation that has been breached has a direct effect on the financial statements. Tarantino & Co should obtain an understanding of the non-compliance – together with further information if needed – so that it can evaluate the effect on the financial statements (ISA (UK) 250A: para. 19). Tarantino & Co should discuss the matter with the appropriate level of management (ISA (UK) 250A: para. 20) and determine the effect that the non-compliance will have on the financial statements. This is likely to include a fine of £20,000, in addition to any unpaid wages that will need to be paid to the employees in question. The fine is less than 0.1% of revenue, which is not material. The unpaid wages are estimated to be £210,000, which is 0.1% of revenue and is also not material.

The audit risk is that the fine has not been provided for in the financial statements, together with the effects of the unpaid wages. Tarantino & Co should also consider whether the issue indicates that ZCG's internal controls are not working effectively, which would increase control risk.

Internal controls and fraud risk

The internal audit department has reported that internal controls are 'working well'. This statement will need to be substantiated but gives the impression that control risk is likely to be low. The work of the internal audit department will be discussed in more detail in the next section of the briefing notes.

However, it is worth noting that two frauds have been found to be operating during the year, giving rise to audit risk. Although the total monetary amount attributable to the frauds is less than 1% of revenue, therefore immaterial, the fact that the frauds have occurred indicates that there are significant internal control deficiencies which could mean that other frauds are operating. We will need to carefully plan our audit approach to expenses and payroll in light of the increased fraud risk.

The lack of approval and authorisation of expenses discovered by internal audit is concerning as this appears to involve higher level management and may call into question management integrity. We should review the work of internal audit to establish if this is an area where controls have been overridden or if there are current gaps within the control framework. We should review and update our systems notes to identify where reliance can potentially be placed on controls and where there are deficiencies.

The issue uncovered by internal audit in relation to payroll suggests that there is inadequate control over the Group's IT system. Access controls, which form part of the Group's general IT controls, are weak which means that other areas of the system may be vulnerable. This significantly increases control risk and as a result presents a significant area of audit risk. We will need to ensure that we carefully plan our approach as this may mean that there are areas of the system where no reliance can be placed on internal controls and appropriate alternative procedures will need to be applied.

Segmental reporting

Being a listed entity, ZCG should provide segmental information in the notes to the financial statements in accordance with IFRS 8 *Operating Segments*. The audit risk is that the segmental information provided is not sufficiently detailed and/or not based on the information reported internally to the Group's chief operating decision maker. There are some unusual trends in the segmental revenue figures from the management accounts. For example, revenue from Southeast Asia appears to have increased significantly – if the 20X5 revenue figure is extrapolated to a 12-month period, the projected revenue from that segment is £49.5 million, an increase of 65% compared to 20X4. There is a risk that revenues have been misallocated between segments, especially as revenue from Americas has fallen so much as well, and that the disclosure is inaccurate.

Conclusion

The audit of ZCG brings with it a number of significant risks, chief among which are those arising from laws and regulations (cyberattack and minimum wage) and revenue recognition. It is important that Tarantino & Co prioritises these issues when planning the audit evidence it will need to obtain.

(b) **Matters to be considered in determining whether the work of ZCG's internal audit department can be used by the audit team**

According to ISA (UK) 610 (Revised) *Using the Work of Internal Auditors*, the external auditor may decide to use the work of the audit client's internal audit function to modify the nature or timing, or reduce the extent, of audit procedures to be performed directly by the external auditor. In the UK, ISA (UK) 610 prohibits the use of internal auditors in providing direct assistance to the external auditor; direct assistance is the use of internal auditors to perform audit procedures under the direction, supervision and review of the external auditor. However, the internal auditors can be used to provide non-direct assistance, for example, we may review their reports on risk management as a way of obtaining business understanding and identifying business risks and risks of material misstatement.

Tarantino & Co must evaluate the internal audit department to determine whether its work is suitable to rely on by evaluating:

- The extent to which the internal audit function's organisational status and relevant policies and procedures support the objectivity of the internal auditors
- The level of competence of the internal audit function, and
- Whether the internal audit function applies a systematic and disciplined approach, including quality management
- Under ISA (UK) 220 (Revised) *Quality management for an audit of financial statements*, the engagement partner is also required to determine whether internal audit has the capability and has been given sufficient time to perform their work

One of the key issues to be evaluated is objectivity – the internal audit department should be unbiased in their work and be able to report their findings without being subject to the influence of others. The fact that the latest internal audit report is addressed to ZCG's finance director could indicate that there is a conflict of interest, as according to the UK Corporate Governance Code, there should be an audit committee in place which has the responsibility to monitor the activities of the internal audit department who should report directly to the audit committee.

The internal audit team is managed by a qualified accountant who is presumably technically competent, though the nature and status of his qualification should be determined. Tarantino & Co should consider whether the rest of the internal audit department is staffed by professional accountants, whether ZCG has a training programme in place for the internal auditors, for example, to ensure that they are up to date with new IFRS requirements, and whether there are sufficient resources for the internal auditors to carry out their duties in a large multinational organisation.

When assessing competency, consideration must also be given to the overall findings which were reported regarding the deficiencies in the current internal control system. The internal audit department has concluded that controls are working well despite there being two instances of fraud in the year which may have more serious ramifications than first suggested. The scope of work carried out in this area and the resultant recommendations will need to be reviewed. This may further suggest that the internal audit department is not free to investigate or report their findings due to the current reporting chains.

If there are doubts over either the objectivity or the competence of the internal audit department, then Tarantino & Co should not rely on their work.

In order to determine whether the internal audit department works in a systematic and disciplined way, Tarantino & Co should consider matters including the nature of documentation which is produced by the department and whether effective quality management procedures are in place such as direction, supervision and review of work carried out.

(c) **Audit procedures on the classification of the 50% equity shareholding in WTC as a joint venture**

- Obtain the legal documentation supporting the investment and agree the details of the investment including:

- The date of the investment
- Amount paid
- Number of shares purchased
- The voting rights attached to the shares
- The nature of the profit-sharing arrangement between ZCG and Wolf Communications
- The nature of access to WTC's assets under the terms of the agreement
- Confirmation that there is no restriction of ZCG's shared control of WTC

- Read board minutes to confirm the approval of the investment and to understand the business rationale for the investment.
- Read minutes of relevant meetings between ZCG and Wolf Communications to confirm that control is shared between the two companies and to understand the nature of the relationship and the decision-making process.
- Obtain documentation such as WTC's organisational structure to confirm that ZCG has successfully appointed members to the board of WTC and that those members have equal power to the members appointed by Wolf Communications.

Audit procedures on the measurement of the operating licence to operate in Farland

- Agree the cost of the licence to the amount included within the opening balances, or the previous year's working papers.
- Obtain the licence agreement and confirm the length of the licence period to be 10 years from the date it was granted.
- Confirm whether the licence can be renewed at the end of the 10-year period, as this may impact on the estimated useful life and amortisation.
- Reperform management's calculation of the amortisation charged as an expense in the year ended 30 September 20X5.
- Discuss with management the process for identifying an appropriate amortisation method and where relevant, how the pattern of future economic benefits associated with the licence have been determined.
- Confirm with management that the Farland network became operational on 1 April 20X5.
- Review a sample of contracts with customers in Farland to verify that contracts commenced from the operational date of 1 April 20X5.
- Enquire with management on the existence of any factors indicating that a shorter useful life is appropriate, for example, the stability of market demand in Farland or possible restrictions on the network capacity in Farland.
- Review management accounts and cash flow forecasts to confirm that Farland is generating an income stream and is predicted to continue to generate cash.
- Obtain a written representation from management confirming that there are no indications of impairment of the licence of which management is aware.

Conclusion

These briefing notes highlight that there are a number of audit risks to be addressed, in particular revenue recognition, and fraud risks appear to be significant issues requiring a robust response from the audit team. We will need to carefully consider whether it is appropriate to receive direct assistance from the internal audit department.

(d) **Ethical and professional matters**

Temporary recruitment of audit partner

The FRC *Ethical Standard* section B2 *Financial, business, employment and personal relationships* expressly forbids auditors from entering into an arrangement to provide staff to work for a client for a temporary period. Gull Ltd's request must therefore be politely declined.

Recruitment services

In relation to the request for Tarantino & Co to provide assistance in recruiting new members of the board, the FRC *Ethical Standard* section B5 prohibits such activity, as the firm would essentially be advising on the recruitment of staff who will ultimately be in senior management positions and responsible for the running of and oversight of a listed company. Consequently, this could give rise to management or familiarity threats.

These new members of staff may also go on to be included in any audit committee which the company sets up and will be responsible for assessing the independence of the external auditors. Being involved in any decision on who should be appointed to such a senior position is also likely to involve the firm taking on a management responsibility, which is not appropriate.

Given that Gull Ltd is potentially going to be a listed company, Tarantino & Co should not be involved in any activity which involves providing recruitment services in relation to a key management position.

This request should be turned down by Tarantino & Co due to the potential management responsibility involved.

27 Redback

Workbook references

Chapters 2, 3, 4, 5, 6, 7, 8, 9 and 12.

Top tips

Your general approach should be to read the requirement carefully, and then to work through the question noting down issues (audit risks) as they occur to you.

Part (a) asks you to evaluate the business risks in planning the audit of Redback Sports Ltd. This may have been a slightly confusing form of words, as you could have understood the requirement to be about the business risk to the auditor; this was not the case. The requirement is trying to get you to consider business risk from the perspective of the auditor. If you had treated this as a standard requirement on business risk, then there was plenty of material to earn your marks from.

The question tells you to use the information provided in Exhibits 2 and 3. This is a way of helping you to avoid becoming lost in the long question scenario, and to focus on what you need to answer the question, so it is important that you heed this advice and restrict your answer to the material being focused on.

As ever it is important that you develop your points fully but with precision, and that you make use of the numbers available in Exhibit 3, as these help to tell the story of the company in question.

Part (b) was the expected AAA requirement to evaluate and prioritise the significant risks of material misstatement (ROMMs), and was worth more than twice the number of marks as the requirement on business risks. You will notice that you are not asked for 'audit risks', so detection risks are not directly relevant.

Materiality calculations are a key way of earning marks here – stating the relevant % and then whether it is material. These marks as likely to be capped, but this isn't something you should worry about.

Part (c) asked for audit procedures on a government grant, and was within reach. Your answers here should be as specific as possible, explaining why you would perform each procedure in addition to just saying what you would do. Both this and part (b) are still limited to Exhibits 2 and 3.

Parts (d) and (e) related to a different client and were really self-contained; this meant that Question 1 on this exam was almost like two questions rolled into one. Part (d) was similar to previous questions in this area and combined practical with ethical considerations.

Part (e) was an interesting twist on the theme of the auditor's responsibilities in relation to fraud, This was a fair test of a key area that you need to understand.

It is noteworthy that part (e) – and arguably (d) – was packed with easy marks but was at the end of the question. If you had not managed your time properly then you may have missed out on these marks. This can make the difference between passing and failing.

Easy marks

Easy marks were on offer for materiality in the second requirement, in addition to the professional marks.

ACCA examining team's comments

This question was a compulsory 50-mark case study style question comprising five parts.

Requirement (a) asked candidates to evaluate the business risks arising from the scenario in the question which focused on an existing audit client which operated a number of sports and leisure centres.

Although this requirement provided candidates with a strong start to the examination, there were a significant number of candidates who demonstrated a lack of understanding over the role of non-executive directors in relation to the scenario. Non-executive directors (NEDs) are typically brought onto a board for their knowledge and skill in a particular field. One such director in the question had previously been the chairman of a rival company. This director brought industry specific business experience to the board and this practice is typical in the business world, however many candidates appeared to think that he would leak information back to the company where he had previously held a non-executive position, out of loyalty. Very few candidates identified the real weaknesses in the board, such as a lack of financial expertise amongst the NEDs and a lack of an audit committee.

Part (b) required candidates to evaluate and prioritise the significant risks of material misstatements (RoMM) arising from the scenario. This was generally well attempted by the majority of candidates and covered financial reporting issues such as revenue recognition, the treatment of government grants and loan finance, alongside control risks such as the lack of independence of the internal audit department. Where RoMMs covered financial reporting issues, candidates who followed the process of calculating materiality, stating the relevant accounting rule and applying that to the scenario to show where the risk arose and the impact on the financial statements were able to score full marks on risks covered.

Requirement (c) required candidates to state principal audit procedures to be used in the audit of a grant received from the government. Two common mistakes were noted; the first was the inclusion of irrelevant or ineffective tests such as reviewing board minutes for approval of the grant and written representations from management that the company had received the grant. Candidates who followed the guidance on audit procedures provided in the recent technical article should have been well prepared for this type of requirement and it should be noted that for five marks candidates should expect to give five well-described procedures.

Part (d) introduced another client into the scenario and covered specific acceptance considerations and overall the marks here were disappointing. While many candidates were able to state some of the areas to be considered most did not apply these to the scenario at all and made generic comments that did not demonstrate the skills required to evaluate the situation. In this exam it is unlikely that simply stating learnt knowledge without application will be sufficient to pass any question.

Typical answers that candidates wrote which would not attain any credit included:

- *Providing other services gives rise to a self-review threat* – this statement shows no appreciation of which services give rise to this threat nor any implication
- *Providing personal tax services to the owner is a self-review threat* – this is incorrect, there is generally no financial statement/audit impact arising from the owner's personal tax
- *Providing payroll services gives rise to self-review* – this answer is better but still does not demonstrate that candidates know that the threat arises because the payroll figure is a material figure in the financial statements and would therefore be subject to audit by the firm

Finally, requirement (e) asked candidates to discuss whether an audit or limited assurance engagement would have identified a fraud in a minor revenue stream at the second client in previous years. Candidates who discussed materiality, sampling and the different level of testing that the two alternatives would provide tended to score well. A common mistake from candidates was to discuss forensic audits to investigate fraud which was not something asked for in the requirement.

Marking guide	Marks
(a) **Business risk evaluation**	
Up to 2 marks for each business risk identified and explained. Marks may be awarded for other, relevant business risks not included in the marking guide.	
In addition, allow 0.5 mark for relevant trends which form part of the business risk evaluation, eg % increase in revenue and profit before tax.	
• Deficiencies in corporate governance/internal audit arrangements	
• Health and safety regulations – risk of non-compliance	
• Capital expenditure and maintenance – drain on cash flow	
• Liquidity problems and possible overtrading	
• Capacity restraints – due to big increase in members and government initiative	
• Marketing expenses – drain on cash	
• Government initiative – may impact negatively on existing memberships	
• Expansion plans – could distract management	
Maximum	7
(b) **Risk of material misstatement evaluation and prioritisation**	
Up to 3 marks for each ROMM evaluated. Allow 1 mark per audit risk for relevant materiality calculations, to a maximum of 4 marks. In addition, 0.5 mark for relevant trends which form part of the audit risk evaluation (max 3 marks).	
• Management bias – risk revenue/profit overstated, expenses understated	
• Deficiencies in internal controls – possibly ineffective audit committee (max 2 marks)	
• Revenue recognition – members' subscriptions and multiple streams of revenue	
• Capital expenditure and maintenance costs – risk of misclassification	
• Government grant – risk income recognised too early and provisions not recognised	
• Staff costs and maintenance costs – risk of understatement (max 2 marks)	
• Bank loan – risk that deep discount not treated as finance cost	
Maximum	16
(c) **Audit procedures on the government grant**	
Up to 1 mark for each well described procedure:	
• Obtain the documentation relating to the grant, confirm the amount, the date the cash was transferred to the company, the period covered by the grant, and terms on which the grant was awarded	
• Review the terms to confirm whether they contain any conditions relating to potential repayment of part or all of the grant	
• Agree the amount of cash received to the bank statement and cash book	
• Perform tests of control on the system used to record the number of free hours of access which have been used by the unemployed	

- Review forecasts and budgets to evaluate the pattern of anticipated use of the initiative by the unemployed, and to confirm that repayment of the grant is not likely
- Discuss with management the accounting policy used, to confirm understanding, and to understand management's rationale
- Recalculate the amount which should have been recognised on the basis of recognising the grant over the three-year period of the government's initiative

Maximum 5

(d) **Evaluation of the matters to be considered in deciding whether to provide Emu Gyms Ltd with an audit or limited assurance review**

Up to 2 marks for each issue evaluated:

- Recognition that engagement evaluation is part of a quality management framework (1 mark)
- Competence – our firm should be competent but deadline is a problem
- More resources will be needed for an audit rather than limited assurance review
- Self-review threat due to providing payroll service
- Whether 'informed management' exists
- Advocacy/management involvement if attend meeting with bank
- Conflict of interest as act for Redback Sports Ltd
- Safeguards/actions re potential conflict of interest (1 mark each)
- No difficulty regarding personal tax work previously performed for Mick Emu

Maximum 7

(e) **Suspected fraud**

Up to 2 marks for each point of discussion:

- Audit has wider scope with tests of detail and tests of control being likely to have uncovered the fraud
- Limited assurance review only includes enquiry and analytical review – less likely to have uncovered the fraud
- Even with audit, fraud could have been concealed and may not have been detected

Maximum 5

Professional marks

Communication

- Briefing note format and structure - use of headings/sub-headings and an introduction
- Style, language and clarity - appropriate layout and tone of briefing notes, presentation of materiality and relevant calculations, appropriate use of the CBE tools, easy to follow and understand
- Effectiveness and clarity of communication - answer is relevant and tailored to the scenario
- Adherence to the specific requests made by the audit engagement partner

Analysis and Evaluation

- Appropriate use of the information to determine and apply suitable calculations
- Appropriate use of the information relating to the government grant to design appropriate audit procedures
- Balanced discussion of the issues connected to the auditor's responsibilities when considering non-audit engagements for an audit client.

Marking guide	Marks

Professional scepticism and professional judgement

- Appropriate application of professional judgement to draw conclusions and make informed decisions following recognition of unusual or unexpected movements, missing/incomplete information or challenging presented information as part of the risk evaluation
- Determination and justification of a suitable materiality level, appropriately and consistently applied
- Identification of possible management bias and consideration of the impact on the financial statements and the possible reasons for management's preference for certain accounting treatments
- Effective application of technical and ethical guidance to effectively challenge and critically assess the risk of management bias

Commercial acumen

- Use of effective examples and/or calculations from the scenario to illustrate points or recommendations
- Appropriate use of the industry information to evaluate business risks
- Recognition of the increased risks to the future competitiveness of the company given the information provided in the scenario

Maximum	10
Total	50

Briefing notes

To: Stella Cross, Audit engagement partner

From: Audit manager

Subject: Audit of Redback Sports Ltd and potential provision of an audit or limited assurance review to Emu Gyms Ltd

Introduction

The first part of these briefing notes has been prepared in relation to the audit of Redback Sports Ltd. The audit planning will commence shortly, and these notes evaluate the business risks and the significant risks of material misstatement to be considered in planning the audit. The notes then go on to recommend the principal audit procedures to be used in the audit of a government grant which the company received during the year.

The second part of the briefing notes focuses on Emu Gyms Ltd, in particular, the request from the company's managing director for our firm to provide an audit or a limited assurance review of the company's financial statements. The notes finish by discussing a question which has been raised by the company's managing director, in relation to a suspected fraud at the company.

(a) **Evaluation of business risks to be considered in planning the audit of Redback Sports Ltd**

Corporate governance

The company does not have to comply with the UK Corporate Governance Code as it is not a listed entity, and it is good to note that the board includes two non-executive directors who seem able to offer independent views on strategy and management. However, the company lacks an audit committee and the internal audit team is small and lacking in independence as they report directly to the finance director. This means that the scope of their work is likely to be quite limited due to insufficient resources, and any recommendations made could potentially be ignored by the finance director. Overall, this could lead to deficiencies in controls and inefficiencies in business operations. In addition, given that the company is looking to achieve a stock market listing in the next few years, it would be good practice to implement stronger governance procedures sooner rather than later. For example, the lack of an audit committee means that the company does not comply with the UK Corporate Governance Code.

Health and safety regulations

The company operates in a highly regulated industry, and the risk of non-compliance with various laws and regulations is high. The sport and leisure industry has strict health and safety regulations which must be complied with, and there are regular health and safety inspections to ensure that regulations are being adhered to. If the company is found not to be in compliance with the relevant regulations, its operating licence could be revoked, which would have reputational consequences, and, ultimately, could impact on the company's going concern status. In addition to the risk of non-compliance, it will be costly to reduce this risk to an acceptable level, for example, through regular staff training on health and safety, leading to cash flow and profit implications. This is particularly relevant to the more adventurous sporting activities such as scuba diving, which the company has recently started to offer.

Capital expenditure and maintenance requirements

The company's success relies on gyms being equipped with modern equipment, and the other facilities, such as tennis courts, being maintained to a high standard. This requires a high annual expenditure, for example, this year alone £5.5 million has been incurred on maintenance and repairs. Such high annual expenditure is a big drain on cash, and the company could face liquidity problems if cash inflows from customers are not maintained.

Liquidity and overtrading

The company's cash position is projected to deteriorate significantly, with the level of cash falling from £5.6 million to £1.4 million in the year. At the same time, revenue and profit before tax are both projected to increase, by 17.8% and 50% respectively. While there is some doubt over the integrity of the figures reported by management, which will be discussed in the next section of the briefing notes, the trends could indicate that the company is expanding too quickly and overtrading, focusing on generating revenue rather than on managing cash flows appropriately. This is particularly concerning given the company's plans for further expansion in the next few years.

Capacity

There could be problems facing the company in terms of the capacity of its facilities. Membership has increased significantly during the year, by 12.4%, and the number of pay as you go visits has increased by 5.3%. Although two new sport and leisure centres have opened this year, this may not be sufficient expansion, and there may be times when the facilities are overcrowded. This may deter members from renewing their membership, and pay as you go customers might prefer to use other sport and leisure providers if overcrowding becomes problematical. The 'Healthy Kids' programme, and the government initiative to provide free access to the unemployed will exacerbate this problem.

Competition and marketing expenses

The industry is competitive, which itself is a business risk, meaning there is pressure on the company to maintain its market share and customer base. There may be pressure to cut membership or pay as you go prices, which will impact on profit margins and cash flow. The company appears to spend a lot on marketing to support its brand. This year, £8.5 million has been spent on marketing, which equates to 16% of revenue. This is a huge drain on cash and will impact significantly on the company's liquidity position.

Government initiative

While the company's involvement with the government initiative to promote a healthy lifestyle to unemployed people is commendable, it may not prove popular with the existing sport and leisure centre members and pay as you go customers. The initiative will put pressure on the capacity of the gyms, and could lead to the facilities becoming crowded, especially at peak time if the figure of 33,900 free hours used by the end of June is correct. Overcrowding could lead to memberships not being renewed, and pay as you go customers moving to other providers. There is also an opportunity cost issue for the company, as the £2 million grant receipt does not appear to be particularly profitable in terms of the number of hours of free access to the gyms which have to be provided for the next three years.

Expansion plans

The expansion plans could take management's attention away from running the business, especially if identification of potential target companies becomes a time-consuming process over the next year. Management controls over existing operations could deteriorate while attention is focused on the planned expansion and possible future flotation. If there is pressure from existing shareholders for the expansion to be successful and flotation to take place, management could be pressured into making unwise decisions to increase the pace of development of the company's activities.

(b) **Risk of material misstatement evaluation**

Management bias

The company has ambitious expansion plans and is aiming to achieve a stock market listing within five years. This can create significant pressure on management to report strong financial performance, and the risk of earnings management is high. This can lead to a range of inappropriate accounting treatments including early recognition of revenue and other income and deferral of expenses. There is some indication that earnings management may have taken place this year, for example, revenue is projected to increase by 17.8%, whereas the number of members, who provide the majority of the company's revenue, has increased by only 12.4%. Profit before tax is projected to increase by 50%. These trends indicate that income could be overstated and expenses understated, the specific reasons for which are evaluated below.

Corporate governance and internal controls

As discussed in the previous section, the company lacks an audit committee and only has a small internal audit team who is not operating independently. This has implications for controls over financial reporting, which could be deficient, and increases control risk. There is a high scope for errors in financial reporting processes and for deliberate manipulation of balances and transactions, as the internal audit team does not have sufficient resources for thorough monitoring and reporting.

Revenue recognition

With 85% of revenue being from members' subscriptions, there is a risk that revenue is recognised incorrectly. There is a risk that the timing of revenue recognition is not appropriate, for example, if an annual membership is recognised in full when it is received by the company, rather than being recognised over the period of membership, thereby overstating revenue.

There are multiple revenue streams which complicates the financial reporting process and increases the risk. As well as members paying an annual subscription, customers can pay for access under the pay as you go scheme. In addition, the free access to the unemployed should not result in revenue recognition.

Capital expenditure and maintenance costs

The company has high levels of both capital expenditure and maintenance costs. There is a risk of material misstatement that capital expenditure and operating expenditure have not been appropriately separated for accounting purposes. For example, maintenance costs could be incorrectly capitalised into non-current assets, overstating assets and understating operating expenses. This could be indicated by maintenance costs representing 10.4% of revenue this year, compared to 11.7% in the previous year. Capital expenditure is recorded at £32 million this year compared to £20 million in the previous year; this significant increase can be at least partly explained by two new centres being opened in the year, but audit work will need to focus on the possible overstatement of the capital expenditure.

Government grant

The company has received a £2 million grant this year, which has been recognised as other operating income. The amount is material, representing 29% of projected profit before tax. The risk of material misstatement relates to whether this should all have been recognised as income in the current accounting period. IAS 20 *Accounting for Government Grants and*

Disclosure of Government Assistance requires that government grants are recognised in profit or loss on a systematic basis over the periods in which the entity recognises expenses for the related costs for which the grants are intended to compensate. Redback Sports Ltd has recognised all the income this year, however, the scheme is intended to run for three years. Therefore there is a risk that the company has recognised the income too early, and a proportion of it should remain as deferred income; this leads to overstated profit and understated liabilities.

There could be a further issue in that the terms of the grant may require complete or partial repayment if the required number of hours of free access to sport facilities is not met. If any such terms exist, the company should evaluate whether the terms are likely to be met, and if not, should consider whether it would be appropriate to recognise a provision or disclose a contingent liability in the notes to the financial statements. The risk is therefore that this has not been considered by management, leading possibly to understated liabilities or inadequate disclosure as required by IAS 37 *Provisions, Contingent Liabilities and Contingent Assets*.

Operating expenses

Operating expenses includes staff costs, which are projected to increase by 7%, marketing costs, which are projected to stay at the same amount compared with 20X4, and maintenance and repair costs which have increased by 3.8%. Given the increase in revenue of 17.8%, and the scale of operations increasing by the opening of two new centres, these categories of expenses would be expected to increase by a larger amount this year. It could be that expenses have been omitted in error, or have been deliberately excluded, thereby understating expenses and overstating profit. These trends should be discussed with management, especially the staff costs, as this alone is highly material, representing 28.9% of projected revenue.

Bank loan

During the year, the company took out a significant loan of £30 million; this is material as it represents 23.1% of total assets. The loan has been issued at a deep discount and there is a risk of material misstatement in that the finance costs associated with this loan may not be accounted for in accordance with IFRS 9 *Financial Instruments*. IFRS 9 requires that the finance cost associated with a deep discount – in this case, the £4 million difference between the amount received by Redback Sports Ltd of £30 million, and the amount repayable on maturity of the debt of £34 million – should be amortised over the term of the loan. The risk is that finance costs and non-current liabilities will be understated if the appropriate finance cost is not accrued in this financial year.

(c) **Principal audit procedures to be used on the government grant**

- Obtain the documentation relating to the grant, to confirm the amount, the date the cash was transferred to the company, the period covered by the grant, and terms on which the grant was awarded.
- Review the terms to confirm whether they contain any conditions relating to potential repayment of part or all of the grant if a required number of hours of free access is not met in the period covered by the grant.
- Agree the amount of cash received to the bank statement and cash book.
- Perform tests of control on the system used to record the number of free hours of access which have been used by the unemployed, focusing on how the access is recorded, to ensure that the recording is complete and accurate and that revenue is not recorded.
- Review forecasts and budgets to evaluate the pattern of anticipated use of the initiative by the unemployed, and to confirm that repayment of the grant is not likely.
- Discuss with management the accounting policy used for the receipt of cash, to confirm understanding that it has all been recognised in full this year, and to understand management's rationale for this accounting treatment.
- Recalculate the amount which should have been recognised on the basis of recognising the grant over the three-year period of the government's initiative.

(d) **Evaluation of the matters to be considered in deciding whether to accept an engagement to provide Emu Gyms Ltd with an audit or limited assurance review**

Requirements and guidance relevant to accepting and continuing client relationships is contained in ISQM (UK) 1 *Quality Management for Firms that Perform Audits or Reviews of Financial Statements or Other Assurance or Related Services Engagements*. The fundamental requirements are that a firm must consider:

- Whether it is competent to perform the engagement and has the capabilities, including time and resources, to do so;
- Whether the relevant ethical and professional requirements can be complied with; and
- The integrity of the client, and whether there is information which would lead it to conclude that the client lacks integrity.

ISQM (UK) 1 also reminds the auditor that acceptance and continuance decisions should not be unduly influenced by commercial factors.

Competence and resources

In terms of competence, our firm should be competent to perform the audit of a small company or to conduct a limited assurance review of the company's financial statements. As a firm of Chartered Certified Accountants and performing the audit of Redback Sports Ltd – a much larger company in the same industry – this means that the firm has the relevant knowledge and experience to perform a high-quality audit or limited assurance review.

The deadline by which the work needs to be completed should be confirmed with Mick Emu. The bank manager has suggested that the loan could be made available within the next two months, meaning that the audit or limited assurance review on the financial statements needs to be carried out as soon as possible. Our firm may not have enough staff available at short notice to perform the work required.

The other matter relevant is the scope of work which is required; this can have a significant impact on the resources needed. An audit will require more work and is therefore more resource-intensive, so it may be more difficult for our firm to carry out an audit at short notice compared to a limited assurance review. In addition, we should clarify whether the bank manager expects any work to be performed, and conclusions drawn, on the cash flow and profit forecasts, in which case more resources will need to be available to complete the engagement.

Ethics

Huntsman & Co provides the payroll service to Emu Gyms Ltd. If Huntsman & Co were to provide the audit or limited assurance review, the provision of the payroll service becomes a non-audit or additional service. This would give rise to a self-review threat because our firm has determined the payroll figures which form part of the financial statements which would then be subject to audit or limited assurance review and may result in over reliance on the payroll figures included in the financial statements.

Huntsman & Co should consider whether the payroll figure is material to the financial statements, and whether safeguards can be used to reduce any ethical threats to an acceptable level, for example, through the use of separate teams to provide the audit or limited assurance review and the payroll services and by having an independent second partner to review the work performed. If safeguards do not reduce the threats to an acceptable level, then the payroll service should not be carried out in addition to the audit or limited assurance review.

Providing the payroll service could also be seen as acting on behalf of management, further impairing the objectivity of the audit or limited assurance provided on the financial statements. However, if the payroll service is purely routine transaction processing in its nature, this is less of a threat.

According to the FRC *Ethical Standard*, in determining whether a non-audit or additional service does or does not give rise to a management threat, the persons conducting the audit firm must consider whether there is 'informed management'. In a small company like Emu Sports Ltd, there is a risk that informed management does not exist.

Informed management exists when a member of management (or senior employee) of the entity:

- Has been designated by the entity to receive the results of the non-audit or additional service and has been given the authority to make any necessary judgements and decisions;
- That member of management has the capability to make independent management judgements and decisions on the basis of the information provided; and
- The results of the non-audit or additional service are communicated to the entity and, where judgements or decisions are to be made by management, they are supported by an objective analysis of the issues to consider and the entity is given the opportunity to decide between reasonable alternatives.

In the absence of such informed management, it is unlikely that any other safeguards can eliminate a management threat or reduce it to a level where independence is not compromised.

There would also be ethical threats arising if our firm were to perform work on the prospective financial information and also attend the meeting at the bank – this could again be perceived as management involvement and creates an advocacy threat whereby the audit firm is promoting the interests of the client. There could also be a perception by the bank that by attending the meeting, our firm is not only supporting our client's loan application, but also confirming the ability of the client to repay the loan, which is not the case. A liability issue could arise for our firm, in the event of the client defaulting on the loan, unless our firm's position is made very clear to the bank. If a member of our firm does attend the meeting with the bank manager, it should be a representative of the firm who has not been involved with the audit or limited assurance review, and Mick should acknowledge his responsibility with regard to the preparation of the financial statements.

A further potential ethical issue arises in that our firm audits Redback Sports Ltd, which could be a competitor of Emu Gyms Ltd despite their difference in size. This situation can create a conflict of interest. The FRC *Ethical Standard* suggests that conflicts of interest may give rise to threats to the auditor's objectivity and independence. In addition, according to the IESBA *Code of Ethics* for *Professional Accountants*, before accepting a new client relationship or engagement, the audit firm should identify circumstances which could give rise to a conflict of interest and evaluate the significance of any ethical threats raised. In this case, Huntsman & Co should disclose to both Emu Gyms Ltd and Redback Sports Ltd that the firm acts for both companies and obtain consent from both companies. The firm should also use separate teams to carry out work for the two companies and establish appropriate review procedures by an independent member of the firm.

Huntsman & Co should also remain alert for changes in circumstances which may make the conflict of interest more of an issue, for example, if Redback Sports Ltd identified that Emu Gyms Ltd could be a potential target company to acquire as part of its planned growth strategy.

Integrity

Emu Gyms Ltd is already a client of our firm, as we provide the company with a payroll service, therefore all of the necessary client due diligence will have taken place. There is nothing in the note provided by Stella Cross to indicate that client integrity could be a problem.

Personal tax planning

It is stated that the firm has in the past performed personal tax planning work for Mick Emu. There is nothing inherently unethical about performing such work, as it would not have an effect on the financial statements and thus on the audit.

(e) **Suspected fraud**

An audit and a limited assurance review differ in their scope and in the nature of procedures which are performed. It is not the purpose of either an audit or a limited assurance review to detect or prevent fraud, this is the responsibility of management, but arguably the indicators of fraud may have been noticed earlier if either had been performed.

In an audit, there is a wide scope in the work performed. Audit procedures are comprehensive, including tests of detail and tests of control, and will cover all material aspects of the financial statements. Given that historically the revenue from shop and café sales represented 5% and 8% of the company's revenue, these would represent a material source of revenue, and there would have been audit testing of the revenue transactions, including tests of detail performed on a sample basis. Additionally, the change in gross margin from 32% to 26% would have alerted the auditor to an unusual trend, leading to additional audit procedures being performed.

Part of the audit process is documenting and evaluating internal controls, and this would have involved an assessment of the controls over sales in the shops and cafés and over inventory. It is likely that deficiencies in internal controls, which may be allowing fraud to be carried out unnoticed, would be detected by the audit process and then communicated to management.

However, it is possible that even with an audit being conducted, the fraud might not have been detected. This is because frauds are usually concealed, and particularly if the employees involved have been colluding to carry out the fraud, it would be difficult to detect, especially if there has been deliberate falsification of accounting records.

In addition, the amounts involved are not highly material, the amount of inventory held by the company is small, meaning that this may not have been classified as an area with a high risk of material misstatement if an audit had been conducted. The inventory held at the shops is not likely to be material, and the inventory count might not have been attended by the audit team. Also, the detailed testing of sales transactions may not have uncovered the fraud given that the fraud appears to be based on theft of inventory. It is possible that the fraud would only have been uncovered through detailed testing of the controls over movement of inventory.

If a limited assurance review had been carried out, again it may have uncovered the fraud, but it is less likely compared to an audit. This is because a limited assurance review has a narrower scope than an audit, and investigation procedures are usually limited to only enquiry and analytical review. Tests of controls and detailed tests of detail are not carried out and therefore control deficiencies would not be picked up or reported to management, and it is not likely that inventory in the shop and café would have been a priority for review.

In conclusion, Mick is correct in thinking that if the company's financial statements had been subject to audit or limited assurance review before now, the suspected fraud is likely to have been uncovered by audit and may have been uncovered by a limited assurance review. However, if the fraud was well concealed it is possible that even an audit would not have uncovered the activities of the fraudsters.

Conclusion

The evaluation in relation to Redback Sports Ltd indicates that the company faces a range of business risks, for instance, possible overtrading and problems with liquidity. There are also a number of significant audit risks which will impact on our audit planning. The highest priority of these would include the accounting treatment which has been applied to a government grant, and the possible understatement of expenses. There is also a significant risk of management bias given the company's plans for expansion.

In relation to Emu Gyms Ltd, our firm should be able to provide a limited assurance review or audit of the company, provided that safeguards are put in place to reduce ethical threats, in particular, self-review in relation to payroll costs, to an acceptable level. Finally, a discussion has been provided which considers whether an audit or limited assurance review would have uncovered the fraud which Mick suspects is taking place.

28 Margot

Workbook references

Chapters 1, 6, 7 and 8.

Top tips

Your general approach should be to read the requirement carefully, and then to work through the question noting down issues (risks of material misstatement) as they occur to you.

In general terms, when it comes to materiality, it is best not to calculate the general thresholds at the start of your answer as the marks are available in relation to each item. The best approach is that taken by the model answer, ie select the relevant figure (revenue, PBT or total assets), calculate the percentage and then state whether it is material.

It is also unwise to include any theoretical discussions of the nature of the risk of material misstatement (ie inherent risk & control risk). When writing your answers, it is not really necessary to classify risks as eg inherent risks or control risks, although the evaluation of where items are placed on the spectrum of inherent risk using factors from ISA (UK) 315 (Revised) (such as subjectivity, complexity and management bias) does help you prioritise those risks that are considered most significant. Although the ability to do so easily may characterise a strong answer, there are no marks available for this, so classifying risks is likely to be a poor use of your time.

Part (a) asks for risks of material misstatement (not audit risk so the difficulty of auditing something (detection risk) is not relevant here). This was not an unusual requirement for AAA and was similar in style and content to past exams. The question does not ask for business risks so take care not to bring these up in your answer, no matter how tempting it is to do so. Similarly, the requirement does not ask for procedures or ways to address the risks, but simply an evaluation of the significant risks themselves.

It is important that you heed the warning not to include risks related to bearer plants or biological assets, as there are no marks available for this here. This links into another pitfall here: panicking at the sight of biological assets and IAS 41 *Agriculture*. The accounting requirements do not actually make up a large number of marks in the marking scheme for part (c), and much of the work in part (c) had to do with ISA (UK) 620 *Using the Work of an Auditor's Expert*, not IAS 41.

Part (b) was a reasonable and expected requirement, in this case asking for procedures relating to impairment. These were standard requirements that you should be prepared for.

Part (c) has been touched on already, but one further point to note is that this question is set at the planning stage, not the fieldwork or review stage. This means that you should not strictly be writing about the expert's conclusions but observe how the model answer gets around this by stating 'the auditor should plan' to assess the expert's conclusions (and data).

Part (d) tested non-compliance with laws and regulations, which has been topical in recent years and could be tested again. The twist here is that it is being tested as part of audit planning, so in addition to the question of reporting the non-compliance you will need to consider the effect on the audit plan, ie ISA (UK) 315 (Revised) and the financial effects of the non-compliance.

Easy marks

The marks for materiality (usually ½ for calculation + ½ for assessment) are easy but note that they are capped at three marks. The 'professional marks' are probably fairly easy too, especially those in relation to communication.

ACCA examining team's comments

Requirement (a) asked candidates to evaluate the risks of material misstatement. Candidates are reminded to read the question requirements carefully and ensure they are answering the question set.

As in previous sittings, the examining team highlighted within the scenario that there was an internally generated brand which had been accounted for correctly and should not be recognised within the statement of financial position. A significant number of candidates still described this as a risk of material misstatement, clearly wasting time on an area that was not a risk.

A further area of weakness was noted with regards to the family-owned business having a lack of corporate governance, audit committee and lack of controls leading to a risk of material misstatement. A significant number of candidates discussed the risk in very general terms, not linking any risk of management bias to the specifics of the question and therefore failed to score what would be regarded as standard risk marks that are easily achievable.

Some other common issues noted in candidate answers for RoMM included:

- Discussing audit procedures to be performed which did not meet the question requirement and therefore no credit awarded.
- Including detailed definitions of audit risk or risks of material misstatement.
- Lack of basic knowledge of double entry and assumption that every double entry has one under and one overstatement eg if liabilities are understated, then expenses must be overstated.
- Lack of correct direction of risk or not being precise in terms of the financial statement impact, eg 'liabilities will be under/overstated'.

For requirement (b), answers were weaker than the previous sitting, with many candidates providing procedures which referred to a weak information source or poorly explained purpose and were often not detailed enough to score full marks.

Some common issues noted in candidate answers for this requirement included:

- Focusing on board meeting minutes where this was not an appropriate source for a procedure based on the requirement.
- Procedures which simply stated 'obtain relevant documents' which is not specific or detailed enough to score full marks.
- Requests to obtain written representations from management without being specific regarding what should be confirmed or were not relevant to the area for which procedures were being performed.

The final requirements required candidates to discuss considerations for the use of an auditor's expert and for candidates to discuss the audit implications and actions to be taken, regarding professional and ethical issues present in the scenario.

Weaker answers focussed on practical considerations, such as whether the expert had the time and resources to perform the work rather than the key areas of the standard such as objectivity, competence, scope of work and relevance of conclusions.

It is disappointing to note that answers to ethics requirements continue to be weak, with many candidates not sufficiently justifying how the threat has arisen in line with the specifics of the scenario or the implication that arises for the auditor. Candidates would benefit from reading the exam technique article published on ACCA's website for detailed guidance on how to discuss ethical threats.

Marking guide

Marks

(a) **Evaluation and prioritisation of significant risks of material misstatement**

Up to 3 marks for each significant risk of material misstatement evaluated unless otherwise indicated. Marks may be awarded for other, relevant risks not included in the marking guide.

In addition, 0.5 mark for each relevant trend or calculation which form part of analytical review (max 3 marks).

Materiality calculations should be awarded 1 mark each (max 3 marks).

- Gearing ratio – indicates that long-term liabilities could be understated
- Improvements in margin and ROCE – possible overstatement of profit given the discounts offered to customers
- Online sales – trend indicates possible overstatement of revenue
- Risk of management bias due to owner-management and desire for dividend payments
- Discounts offered on online sales
- Research and development risk that expenditure should not have been capitalised and that research and development costs have not been distinguished
- Impairment risk that the value in use and therefore impairment loss is not correct (max 4 marks for detailed discussion)
- Provision for restoration of the impaired property provision should not have been made
- Intangible assets – whether amounts should have been capitalised
- Bearer plants/biological assets/inventory potentially difficult to distinguish the assets, with implications for their valuation

Maximum 19

(b) **Audit procedures on impairment**

Up to 1 mark for each well described procedure:

- Obtain management's detailed calculations and discuss with management to gain understanding of the methodology and assumptions used
- From the non-current asset register, confirm the carrying amount of the cash generating unit prior to any impairment being recognised, and confirm the carrying amount of each component of the cash generating unit
- Obtain a copy of the company's insurance policy and review the terms and conditions to confirm whether the buildings and machinery are covered by insurance
- Develop an auditor's estimate of the fair value less cost to sell and value in use and compare to management's estimate, this will include performing the following procedures:
- Obtain and review the reports from the engineer to confirm the nature and extent of damage caused to the factory
- Obtain and review any external valuation report which the company has used as a basis of the fair value less cost to sell, and evaluate the reasonableness of any assumptions used in the valuation
- For the value in use, discuss with management to obtain their view as to whether the factory has any value in use at all in its current state
- Visit the factory to view the extent of damage caused by the storm and evaluate whether it can be used without any further capital expenditure
- Given the materiality of the figures, an auditor's expert could be used to provide evidence

Maximum 5

(c) **Use of an auditor's expert**

Up to 2 marks for each well explained point:

- Objectivity
- Competence
- Scope of work

- Relevance of conclusions

Maximum 6

(d) **Impact of email on audit**

Up to 1 mark for each well explained point:

- Use of chemicals likely to be a breach of laws and regulations
- Management's responsibility to ensure compliance with law and regulations
- Bribe indicates lack of integrity and that the activity is a non-compliance
- Auditor needs to understand laws and regulations applicable to the Group (2 marks for detailed discussion)
- Further evidence should be obtained and the matter discussed with management (1 mark for discussion and up to 2 marks for examples of further procedures)
- Issue of lack of 'higher authority' as Margot Ltd is family owned and need to take legal advice
- Provisions for fines and penalties
- Valuation of inventory and biological assets (up to 2 marks for detailed discussion)
- Potential going concern issue due to bad publicity and impact on reputation
- Auditor may have a legal duty to disclose, or consider disclosing in the public interest
- Disclosure in public interest is a matter of judgement and must be carefully considered
- No issues regarding breach of confidentiality if disclosure in public interest
- The audit firm may wish to seek legal advice regarding the situation

Maximum 10

Professional marks

Communication

- Briefing notes format and structure – use of headings/sub-headings and an introduction
- Style, language and clarity – appropriate layout and tone of briefing notes, presentation of materiality and relevant calculations, appropriate use of the CBE tools, easy to follow and understand
- Effectiveness and clarity of communication – answer is relevant and tailored to the scenario
- Adherence to the specific requests made by the audit engagement partner

Analysis and evaluation

- Appropriate use of the information to determine suitable calculations
- Appropriate use of the information to support discussions and draw appropriate conclusions
- Effective prioritisation of the results of the risk evaluation to demonstrate the likelihood and magnitude of risks and to facilitate the allocation of appropriate responses likelihood and magnitude of risks and to facilitate the allocation of appropriate responses
- Balanced discussion of the information to objectively make a recommendation or decision

Professional scepticism and judgement

- Effective challenge of information supplied, and techniques carried out to support key facts and/or decisions
- Determination and justification of a suitable materiality level, appropriately and consistently applied
- Appropriate application of professional judgement to draw conclusions and make informed decisions about the courses of action which are appropriate in the context of the audit engagement

Commercial acumen

- Audit procedures are practical and plausible in the context of Margot.
- Use of effective examples and/or calculations from the scenario to illustrate points or recommendations.
- Recognition of the appropriate commercial considerations of the audit firm 10

Total 50

Briefing notes

To: Ben Duval, Audit engagement partner

From: Audit manager

Subject: Audit planning for Margot Ltd

Introduction

These briefing notes are prepared in respect of audit planning for our client Margot Ltd, with a financial year ending 30 September 20X5. The notes begin with an evaluation and prioritisation of the significant risks of material misstatement which should be considered in planning the audit. The notes then contain the audit procedures which have been designed in relation to two matters the impairment of property, plant and equipment and capitalised development costs. A discussion is provided on the use of an auditor's expert in the audit of the company's biological assets. Finally, a member of the client's staff has alerted us to some suspicious behaviour, which could indicate a breach of law and regulations. The notes discuss this issue and recommend actions to be taken by our firm.

(a) **Evaluation of significant risks of material misstatement**

Results from preliminary analytical procedures

The limited analytical procedures which have been performed indicate several potential risks of material misstatement. First, the current ratio has increased significantly, from 1.4 in 20X4, to a projected figure of 2.6 in 20X5. Using the information provided, the current liabilities in 20X4 were £1.564 million (£2.19 million/1.4) and are projected to be £1.288 million in 20X5 (£3.35 million/2.6).

Current assets are projected to increase by 53% and current liabilities projected to reduce by 17.6%. Given that the management accounts show that the cash balance is relatively static, there is a risk that other current assets, presumably inventory and receivables, could be overstated. However, the increase in current assets can at least partly be explained by the inclusion of the £450,000 prepayment relating to restoring the damaged factory; this is discussed in more detail later in the briefing notes. There is also a risk that the current liabilities are understated; this risk is particularly significant given that according to the finance director, current liabilities includes a provision of £450,000 in relation to restoring the damaged factory.

The projected movement in the gearing ratio is small, from 32% to 28%. This fall in the gearing ratio is inconsistent with the fact that the company has taken a loan of £375,000 to finance the research and development. The expectation would be for the gearing ratio to increase, unless there has been a repayment of finance of which we are unaware.

Looking at the operating margin and return on capital employed, both ratios have improved by a small amount. This trend is worthy of scrutiny during the audit as the offers and discounts offered to customers by the company should act negatively on margins and profitability, so the improvements in ratios could indicate a potential overstatement of operating profit.

Another trend which is worth further investigation relates to online sales, which are projected to increase by 90.5% in the year. This is a significant increase, and while the finance director has asserted that the increase in sales is due to the success of the advertising campaign, this needs to be corroborated further. There is a risk of overstatement of revenue in relation to online sales which is explored in more detail below. There is also a risk that revenue from other

ANSWERS

sources is overstated. Excluding online sales, revenue from other sources is projected to increase by 5.3%, a significant increase, which could also indicate overstatement of revenue.

Management bias

This is a private company where a majority of shares are owned by the Margot family. This brings a risk of management bias, especially as one of the family members is the company's chief executive officer, who is in a position to influence the financial statements. The extract from the management accounts shows that a significant dividend payment is made each year, so there is an expectation from the family members that the company will make sufficient profit to be able to pay these dividends each year. There is therefore a significant inherent risk at the financial statement level that profit will be overstated. The risk that the financial statements are being deliberately manipulated is indicated by the accounting treatment applied to impairment which is discussed in more detail below.

Online sales

The online sales make up an increasing proportion of the company's revenue according to the management accounts online sales are projected to represent 7% of total revenue in 20X5 (4% – 20X4).

Online sales can bring a number of risks of material misstatement, for instance, cut off and timing of revenue recognition can be problematical. In the case of Margot Ltd, risks attach to the discounts which are offered on online sales as the discounts offered to customers appear to change frequently. This brings some complexity into the accounting, and the company should ensure that internal controls are operating effectively so that the accounting system is updated whenever the level and range of discounts and offers to customers are changed. Revenue could be over or understated if discounts are not accounted for appropriately, either because a discount is not recorded at all by the accounting system or is applied to the wrong products.

> **Tutorial note.** Credit will be awarded for other risks relating to online sales, where relevant to the question scenario, for example, related to the launch of the new online sales portal, which implies a change to the system used to record revenue, with related control risks.

Research and development

In this financial year, £220,000 of research and development costs have been capitalised as an intangible asset. This represents 1.8% of total assets and 10.5% of profit before tax and would be considered material to the financial statements.

This relates to research and development into new plastic-free packaging. According to IAS 38 *Intangible Assets*, a distinction has to be made between research costs, which must be expensed, and development costs, which should only be capitalised if certain criteria are met including that the technical and commercial feasibility of the asset has been established. It appears that the full amount paid to ProPack has been capitalised, which indicates that no distinction has been made between research costs and development costs. Only development costs can be capitalised, so there is a potential overstatement of the intangible asset if it includes research costs, which should be expensed. This means that the entity must intend and be able to complete the intangible asset and either use it or sell it and be able to demonstrate how the asset will generate future economic benefits.

There is a further risk of material misstatement because costs which are development costs may have been capitalised but the necessary criteria demonstrating that an asset has been created have not been met. Given that ProPack is only at the stage of testing prototypes, it appears that there is not yet demonstrable evidence that the new packaging is technically feasible or that Margot Ltd will be able to use the packaging. In addition, there may be problems in demonstrating that Margot Ltd has control of the development of new packaging, given that the development has been outsourced to another company. In this case, the IAS 38 criteria for capitalisation do not appear to have been met; this will result in overstatement of intangible assets and understatement of operating expenses.

Impaired factory

The carrying amount of the impaired factory is material to the statement of financial position, representing 7% of total assets. The damage to the factory has triggered an impairment review, as required by IAS 36 *Impairment of Assets*. However, the finance director has not prepared the impairment calculations in accordance with IAS 36, specifically the recoverable amount has not been correctly determined. The recoverable amount is the higher of value in use and fair value less costs to sell the asset. However, a review of the calculation provided indicates that the determination of value in use is not correct. According to IAS 36, the cash flow projections which are used to determine the value in use of the impaired asset should relate to the asset in its current condition expenditures to improve or enhance the asset's performance should not be anticipated. The finance director's estimate of value in use is based on the assumption that the building is repaired and new machinery purchased neither of these assumptions should be included in the determination of value in use.

It is likely that the value in use, when properly determined, is much lower than the finance director's estimate, meaning that the impairment loss to be recognised is greater than the £210,250 as per the finance director's calculations. There is also a risk that the fair value less cost to sell is overestimated if the factory is damaged and the machinery needs to be completely replaced, then a value of £135,000 included in management's calculation may be over optimistic. Therefore there is a risk that the impairment loss is understated, and the carrying amount of the asset is overstated.

Tutorial note. Credit will be awarded for further development of the impairment issue, for example, whether the impairment loss has been appropriately allocated over the assets of the cash generating unit.

Provision for restoring the damaged factory and acquiring new machinery

Related to the point above, the financial statements include a provision of £450,000 for repairing the factory and buying new machinery. The amount recognised represents 3.6% of total assets and is material to the statement of financial position, though it has no impact on profit.

A provision should only be recognised if it meets the criteria of IAS 37 *Provisions, Contingent Liabilities and Contingent Assets*, including that there is a present obligation as a result of a past event, and that a probable future outflow of economic benefit which can be reliably estimated exists. In this case, there does not seem to be a present obligation, the company is not contractually obliged to repair the damage and there is no evidence that a constructive obligation exists. Neither does it appear appropriate to recognise a prepayment for an expense which has not yet been incurred. Therefore, the provision and related prepayment should not be recognised, and unless an adjustment is made to the financial statements, both current assets and current liabilities are overstated.

Software and advertising costs capitalised

During the year, software development costs of £30,000 and advertising costs of £225,000 are capitalised as intangible assets. The advertising costs are material, representing 1.8% of total assets and 10.7% of profit for the year. The advertising costs have been incurred to support the 'Fructus Gold' brand name, and the finance director justifies the capitalisation on the grounds that the advertising expenditure has led to an increase in sales. However, IAS 38 specifically states that advertising and promotional costs must not be recognised as intangible assets and must be expensed. Therefore intangible assets are overstated and operating expenses understated by a material amount.

The software development costs represent less than 1% of total assets and only 1.4% of profit, so are not considered to be material to the financial statements, and therefore in isolation do not represent a significant risk of material misstatement in monetary terms, especially given that according to IAS 38, it is appropriate to capitalise internally developed software costs assuming that the costs incurred give rise to an asset. However, this matter is being highlighted because the finance director has used a similar justification for capitalising the advertising costs, which are likely to be materially misstated, as discussed above, and therefore this gives rise to a general concern over whether all costs relating to intangible assets are being treated appropriately.

Identification and potential misclassification of assets

There is a risk that the agricultural assets are not identified and/or classified appropriately, which will have an implication for the valuation of the assets. For example, it may be difficult to distinguish between bearer plants and fruit growing on the trees, and it might be hard to identify the stage of development of fruit on the trees. This potentially impacts on the valuation of the assets, because bearer plants are measured at cost and depreciated in accordance with IAS 16 *Property, Plant and Equipment*, whereas the fruit should be measured at fair value in accordance with IAS 41 *Agriculture*.

> **Tutorial note.** Credit will be awarded for other, relevant risks of material misstatement, for example, the risk that the storm may have damaged assets other than the factory, in particular the bearer plants, which may have suffered impairment, and the risk that inventory may be overstated due to the perishable nature of the goods.

(b) **Audit procedures on impaired factory**

- Obtain management's detailed calculations to gain understanding and allow evaluation of the methodology and assumptions used, eg the basis of determining the fair value and the future period over which value in use was determined and the discount rate used to calculate the present value of future cash flows.
- Discuss the methodology and assumptions with management to confirm their rationale.
- From the non-current asset register, confirm the carrying amount of the cash generating unit prior to any impairment being recognised, and confirm the carrying amount of each component of the cash generating unit.
- Obtain a copy of the company's insurance policy and review the terms and conditions to confirm whether the buildings and machinery are covered by insurance.
- Develop an auditor's estimate of the fair value less cost to sell and value in use, in accordance with the IAS 36 requirements (ie not including the restoration costs and replacement of machinery), and compare to management's estimate. Developing an auditor's estimate would involve the following procedures:
  - Obtain and review the reports from the engineer to confirm the nature and extent of damage caused to the factory.
  - Obtain and review any external valuation report which the company has used as a basis of the fair value less cost to sell, and evaluate the reasonableness of any assumptions used in the valuation.
  - For the value in use, discuss with management to obtain their view as to whether the factory has any value in use at all in its current state.
  - Visit the factory to view the extent of damage caused by the storm and evaluate whether it can be used without any further capital expenditure.
- Consider whether the use of an auditor's expert is necessary to provide sufficient and appropriate evidence given the materiality of the figures.

(c) **Matters to consider before placing reliance on the work of the auditor's expert**

ISA (UK) 620 *Using the Work of an Auditor's Expert* contains requirements relating to the objectivity, competence and capabilities of the auditor's expert, the scope and objectives of their work, and assessing their work.

Objectivity

According to ISA (UK) 620, the auditor shall evaluate whether the auditor's expert has the necessary objectivity, and this should include inquiry regarding interests and relationships which may create a threat to the expert's objectivity. The audit firm will need to ensure that the expert has no connection to Margot Ltd, for example, that they are not a related party of the company or any person in a position of influence over the financial statements. If the expert's objectivity is threatened, little or no reliance can be placed on their work, and the audit firm should not treat it as a reliable source of audit evidence.

Competence

ISA (UK) 620 also requires the competence of the expert to be considered; this should include considering the expert's membership of appropriate professional bodies. Any doubts over the competence of the expert will reduce the reliability of audit evidence obtained. The expert should in this case have experience in valuing the fruit which are the agricultural assets recognised in the statement of financial position, and be familiar with the framework for measuring fair value of these assets in accordance with IAS 41 *Agriculture* and IFRS 13 *Fair Value Measurement*.

Scope of work

ISA (UK) 620 requires the auditor to agree the scope of work with the expert. This may include agreement of the objectives of the work, how the expert's work will be used by the auditor and the methodology and key assumptions to be used. In assessing the work performed by the expert, the auditor should confirm that the scope of the work is as agreed at the start of the engagement. If the expert has deviated from the agreed scope of work, it is likely to be less relevant and reliable.

Relevance of conclusions

ISA (UK) 620 states that the auditor shall evaluate the relevance and adequacy of the expert's findings or conclusions. This will involve consideration of the source data that was used, the appropriateness of assumptions and the reasons for any changes in methodology or assumptions. The conclusion should be consistent with other relevant audit findings and with the auditor's general understanding of the business. If the work involves using source data which is significant to their workings, the audit team should plan to assess the relevance, completeness and accuracy of that data. Any inconsistencies should be investigated as they may indicate evidence which is not reliable.

> **Tutorial note.** Credit will be awarded for more specific comments in relation to evaluating the expert's work, for example, reperformance of calculations, and establishing that assumptions are in line with the auditor's understanding of the entity.

(d) **Audit implications of email from Len Larch**

The alleged use of prohibited chemicals raises concerns that the company may not be complying with relevant law and regulations. The auditor needs to consider the requirements of ISA (UK) 250 Section A *Consideration of Laws and Regulations in an Audit of Financial Statements*. ISA (UK) 250 A states that while it is management's responsibility to ensure that the entity's operations are conducted in accordance with the provisions of laws and regulation, the auditor does have some responsibility in relation to compliance with laws and regulations, especially where a non-compliance has an impact on the financial statements.

There is also an ethical issue in that one of the production managers may have been bribed by one of the company directors. Clearly, if this is true, it indicates a lack of integrity and would seem to confirm that the chemicals which are being used are prohibited. There is also a risk that the Bribery Act (2010) has been breached by the inducement offered by the production manager.

The auditor is required by ISA (UK) 315 (Revised) *Identifying and Assessing the Risks of Material Misstatement* to gain an understanding of the legal and regulatory framework in which the audited entity operates. This will help the auditor to identify non-compliance and to assess the implications of non-compliance. Therefore the auditor should ensure a full knowledge and understanding of the laws and regulations relevant to the use of chemicals in the company's farms, and the implications of non-compliance.

ISA (UK) 250 A requires that when non-compliance is identified or suspected, the auditor shall obtain an understanding of the nature of the act and the circumstances in which it has occurred, and further information to evaluate the possible effect on the financial statements. Therefore procedures should be performed to obtain evidence about the suspected non-compliance, for example, to speak to the company's farm managers to understand whether the allegations are founded in fact. In addition, the audit team could perform further procedures, for example, reviewing purchase invoices to establish if these chemicals are actually being purchased and used in the business, and if so, on whose authority.

ISA (UK) 250 A requires the matter to be discussed with management and where appropriate with those charged with governance. Given the potential severity of the situation, and that the chemicals may be toxic, there is the risk of poisoning the company's employees or customers, and the matter should be communicated as soon as possible.

ISA (UK) 250 A also states that if a non-compliance is intentional but not material, the auditor considers whether the nature and circumstances make it appropriate to communicate to those charged with governance as soon as practicable. In relation to the payment to the production manager, as the £10,000 bribe itself is not material, the auditor needs to reach a judgement as to whether the potential implications of the bribe are significant enough to warrant disclosure to those charged with governance. While the amount involved may not be material, it does lead us to question the integrity of management and therefore impacts on our overall risk assessment of this client and how we plan the audit.

The auditor should attempt to find out whether any member of management had issued instructions for these chemicals to be used, ie that there is a deliberate breach of law and regulations. ISA (UK) 250 A suggests that when the auditor suspects management or those charged with governance of being involved with the non-compliance, the matter should be communicated to the next level of 'higher authority' such as an audit committee or supervisory board. Given the family-managed nature of Margot Ltd, it may be that no higher authority exists, in which case the audit firm should take appropriate legal advice if they think that the matter may not be communicated by the entity.

The auditor needs to consider the potential implications for the financial statements. The non-compliance, if proven to have taken place, could lead to regulatory authorities imposing fines or penalties on Margot Ltd, which may need to be provided for in the financial statements. Audit procedures should be performed to determine the amount, materiality and probability of payment of any such fine or penalty imposed.

In addition, there is a risk that the use of chemicals means that inventory of harvested fruit and the fruit trees are contaminated with poisonous chemicals and possibly will need to be destroyed. The assets could therefore need to be written down in value. If any necessary impairment of the assets is not recognised, then non-current assets and current assets could be misstated. The audit team should therefore plan procedures to determine the value of the contaminated assets.

There may be a going concern issue once the non-compliance and its implications has been established and the facts get out into the media. There would be considerable impact on the reputation of the company and its brand; customers may stop purchasing the products for fear of a health risk and this could affect the going concern of the business.

In terms of reporting non-compliance to the relevant regulatory authorities, ISA (UK) 250 A requires the auditor to determine whether they have a responsibility to report the identified or suspected non-compliance to parties outside the entity. In the event that management or those charged with governance of the company fails to make the necessary disclosures to the regulatory authorities, the auditor should consider whether they should make the disclosure. This will depend on matters including whether there is a legal duty to disclose or whether it is considered to be in the public interest to do so.

Confidentiality is also an issue, and if disclosure were to be made by the auditor, it would be advisable to seek legal advice on the matter. ISA (UK) 250 A also provides further advice on whether disclosure in the public interest should be made. The standard states that in rare circumstances disclosure might be justified in the public interest, providing an example of where the health and safety of members of the public or the environment is being endangered. ISA (UK) 250 A states that the auditor should discuss this with those charged with governance and if the entity does not voluntarily report the matter itself or is unable to provide evidence that the matter has been reported, the auditor reports it.

According to ISA (UK) 250 A, determination of where the balance of public interest lies requires careful consideration. An auditor whose suspicions have been aroused uses professional judgement to determine whether the auditor's misgivings justify the auditor in carrying the matter further or are too insubstantial to deserve reporting. The auditor is protected from the risk of liability for breach of confidence or defamation provided that the disclosure is made in the public interest, and such disclosure is made to an appropriate body or person, and there is no malice motivating the disclosure.

Conclusion

These briefing notes have indicated that there are several significant risks of material misstatement to consider while planning the audit of Margot Ltd. More information is needed to perform a detailed analytical review, which may highlight further potential risks. A key source of risk is the possibility of management bias, which can have a pervasive effect on the financial statements. The factory building is an important material issue to which significant audit work will need to be devoted.

The briefing notes also recommend relevant audit procedures for the significant risks of material misstatement in relation to the impaired factory. We will plan to use the work of an expert, following the requirements of ISA (UK) 620. Finally, we need to consider carefully the issues raised by Len Larch, as it seems that the company is operating in breach of relevant laws and regulations, and that this is a deliberate act involving bribery of company employees. There are implications for our audit planning in that we must plan to obtain detailed information about the situation and consider our reporting responsibilities in light of the severity of the situation and its implications for public health.

29 Pale Ltd

Workbook reference

Chapters 6, 7 and 9.

Top tips

Your general approach should be to read the requirement carefully, and then to work through the question noting down issues (audit risks) as they occur to you.

Part (a) asked for you to evaluate business risks. This is a standard AAA requirement, but one that only tends to come up every few sittings. What is slightly unusual here is that you are asked for the business risks 'to be considered in planning the audit', which may appear to confuse matters slightly. In reality, though, the auditor should consider the business risks being faced by the company as part of their understanding of the entity, which is what you are being asked to do here.

Part (b) was the expected requirement to evaluate and prioritise the significant audit risks. This is a normal requirement and one that is trying to get you to think; you need to show that you have considered the risk from the point of view of the audit and how significant it would be to the thinking auditor. So, when you are evaluating a risk, you need to say why it is a risk, and then include some consideration of its relative importance to the audit as a whole.

It is very important that you notice the instruction to consider only the risks in relation to the fair value of the timber plantation asset, as risks relating to other aspects of this asset will not earn marks.

Part (c) asked for audit procedures. Here it is important that your procedures address the points asked for in the requirement - simply listing lots of irrelevant procedures will not score many marks in your exam.

Finally part (d) asked you to consider ethics and other planning issues. As usual, it is important that you answer both parts of the requirement here, although in reality the issues are connected as they all arise out of the exhibit you are asked to focus on.

Easy marks

There should be marks available for adopting the correct format for your briefing notes, and these are well worth the time it takes to get them.

ACCA examining team's comments

This was a typical Section A question set at the planning stage, with requirements covering business risk, audit risk, audit procedures and ethics, for 50 marks. Typically, candidates perform best in the Section A question and there have been progressively better and more focused answers in recent sessions.

Unless specified otherwise, all exhibits should be considered when identifying business risks and audit risks and candidates should ensure that they carefully read the partner's email for any specific guidance in relation to how the information should be used. It is recommended that candidates review all the exhibits while planning their answers to the question but as mentioned should ensure they take note of any guidance given by the examining team in terms of which exhibits are relevant to each requirement. This allows for more detailed analysis and focus on specific information where relevant.

It is often the case that there will be interactions between the exhibits which will impact on the analysis performed by candidates. Candidates are encouraged to spend adequate time planning and aim to obtain a holistic view and understanding of the issues present in the question.

Part (c) was well answered. Generally, answers to procedure-based requirements are handled well by candidates.

Part (d) required candidates to explain the ethical issues and other planning implications arising from the phone call from the CFO. Several candidates incorrectly discussed fee thresholds for a listed client when determining if the fee could be undertaken but failed to recognise this was a contingent fee and is prohibited by the IESBA International Code of Ethics for Professional Accountants (the Code) and unfortunately received no marks. There were few candidates that identified the fee for assurance work could be on a contingent basis, yet it is more prudent to not undertake the basis.

The ethical threats were generally well recognised, but candidates continue to score relatively low marks for ethics due to not sufficiently explaining the ethical threat linked to the scenario and the implication of the threat to the auditor and therefore lose what are potentially easy marks – especially as a large proportion of knowledge of ethics is assumed knowledge from other ACCA examinations. Overall responses were mixed, and candidates who answered the ethical issues sufficiently scored highly but candidates who merely identify the ethical threat with no linkage to the scenario and explanation tended to score low marks.

Marking guide

	Marks
(a) **Business risks**	
Up to 2 marks for each business risk evaluated. In addition, 0.5 mark for each relevant trend or calculation which form part of a relevant explanation of the risk (max 2 marks).	
• International expansion	
• Gold Standard accreditation	
• Legal case	
• Damage to assets caused by storm	
• Liquidity	
• Industrial action	
• Incentive payment	
Maximum	10
(b) **Audit risks**	
Up to 3 marks for each audit risk evaluated unless otherwise indicated. Marks may be awarded for other, relevant risks not included in the marking guide.	
Appropriate materiality calculations (max 2 marks) and justified materiality level should be awarded to a maximum of 1 mark.	
In addition, 0.5 mark for each relevant trend or calculation which form part of a relevant explanation of the risk (max 2 marks).	
• New client (up to 2 marks)	

- Going concern
- Government grant (up to 4 marks)
- Change in fair value of standing trees
- Legal case
- Pressure on results
- Corporate governance (up to 2 marks)

Maximum 16

(c) **Audit procedures**

1 mark for each well explained audit procedure, examples of which include:

- Obtain the expert's report on the value of the storm-damaged timber plantation to understand methodology and overall results.
- Discuss the expert's methodology and assumptions with management to confirm their rationale and compliance with accounting requirements.
- Obtain confirmation of the expert's qualifications and experience.
- Obtain confirmation that the expert is independent.
- Visit the site of the storm damage to form a view on the scale of the destruction.
- Discuss with management the actions which have been taken in response to the storm.
- Obtain any documentation relating to the potential sale of damaged trees.
- From the non-current asset register, confirm the carrying amount of the standing trees prior to any change in fair value being recognised.
- Consider whether the use of an auditor's expert is necessary to provide sufficient and appropriate evidence given the materiality of the figures.
- Develop an auditor's estimate of the change in fair value and compare to management's estimate.
- Obtain a copy of the company's insurance policy and review the terms and conditions to confirm whether the storm damage is covered by insurance.

Maximum 6

(d) **Ethical and audit planning implications**

1 mark for each point discussed:

- KPIs are 'other information' which the auditor must review for material inconsistencies
- Self-review threat to objectivity (additional credit to be awarded for other relevant threats to objectivity explained)
- Assurance can be provided on the KPIs if safeguards can reduce threat to an acceptable level
- Example of safeguard eg separate team to perform the work, separate partner review
- Fee for the assurance work must be separate from the audit fee
- Fee for audit cannot be on a contingent basis
- Fee for assurance work can be on a contingent basis but more prudent if not on that basis
- Competence issues due to specialist nature of the work
- Resource issues ie staff availability to perform the work

Maximum 8

Marking guide — Marks

Professional marks

Communication

- Briefing note format and structure - use of headings/sub-headings and an introduction
- Style, language and clarity - appropriate layout and tone of briefing notes, presentation of materiality and relevant calculations, appropriate use of the CBE tools, easy to follow and understand
- Effectiveness and clarity of communication - answer is relevant and tailored to the scenario
- Adherence to the specific requests made by the audit engagement partner

Analysis and Evaluation

- Appropriate use of the information to determine and apply suitable calculations
- Appropriate use of the information relating to the fair valuation exercise on the forest asset to design appropriate audit procedures
- Effective prioritisation of the results of the audit risk evaluation to demonstrate the likelihood and magnitude of risks and to facilitate the allocation of appropriate responses
- Balanced discussion of the issues connected to the auditor's responsibilities in relation to ethical decisions when considering non-assurance engagements for an audit client.

Professional scepticism and professional judgement

- Appropriate application of professional judgement to draw conclusions and make informed decisions following recognition of unusual or unexpected movements, missing/incomplete information or challenging presented information as part of the risk evaluation
- Determination and justification of a suitable materiality level, appropriately and consistently applied
- Identification of possible management bias and consideration of the impact on the financial statements and the possible reasons for management's preference for certain accounting treatments
- Effective application of technical and ethical guidance to effectively challenge and critically assess how management has responded to the legal claim and the adequacy of any provision or disclosure requirements.

Commercial acumen

- Use of effective examples and/or calculations from the scenario to illustrate points or recommendations
- Appropriate use of the industry information to evaluate business risks
- Recognition of the increased risks to the future competitiveness of the company given the information provided in the scenario and any impact on going concern.

Maximum	10
Total	50

Briefing notes

To: Harvey Rebus, audit engagement partner

From: Audit manager

Subject: Audit planning in relation to Pale Ltd

Date: 1 July 20X5

Introduction

These briefing notes have been prepared to assist in planning the audit of Pale Ltd. The notes begin with an evaluation of the business risks facing the company and continue by evaluating and prioritizing the significant audit risks which should be considered in planning the audit. The notes also include the recommended principal audit procedures which have been designed in respect of a change in fair value to the company's timber plantation following a recent storm. Finally, the notes discuss some ethical and other professional issues arising from a recent phone call with the company's chief finance officer (CFO) which impact on our audit planning.

(a) **Business risks**

International expansion

The expansion into Farland introduces a business risk in that the company will be managing operations in a foreign country for the first time. Farland is remote, so it may be difficult for Pale Ltd's management team to plan regular visits to the new operations, so establishing robust management oversight and controls could be difficult. In addition, Farland may have different laws and regulations compared to the company's home jurisdiction, so there is a heightened risk of non-compliance. Even the type of trees growing in the rainforest will be different, and management may not have experience in their harvesting, processing and the sale of timber products. All of these issues create a risk that the international expansion may not be successful, and at the same time will represent a drain on management's time and resources. Operations in the home country of Pale Ltd may suffer as a result.

Gold Standard accreditation

There is a risk that the Gold Standard accreditation may not be renewed, with implications for reputation, and more specifically for the new contract with Royal Ltd, which largely accounts for an increase of 5.5% in the company's revenue this year. Several of the Key Performance Indicators (KPIs) which need to be met to retain the Gold Standard seem to be in jeopardy, for example there has been a decline in the percentage of timber which is harvested in line with Gold Standard requirements, and the projected metric of 82% is only just above the required level of 80%. In addition, the Gold Standard is linked to ethical business practice, and there are some indications that the company's business ethics is questionable – for example the legal case being brought by employees and the incentive payment made to a government official. If the Gold Standard accreditation is lost, Royal Ltd, and other customers may cancel contracts, resulting in a loss of revenue and cash flow.

Legal case

The legal action against the company by its own employees is a significant risk. If the issue becomes public knowledge there will be reputational problems, and the amount that is being claimed, £19 million, exceeds the company's cash balance. If the legal claim were to go against the company, it would struggle to find the funds to pay the damages given that it is already at the limit of its borrowing arrangements. The situation could also indicate poor governance of the company, if decisions are being made which puts the lives of employees at risk and results in days lost due to accidents at work, and the matter seems to be dismissed as unimportant by the management team and legal advisors.

Damage to assets caused by storms

The recent storms have caused significant damage to the company's timber plantation asset. Unpredictable weather patterns could cause further harm or even totally destroy the company's timber plantations. Assuming that trees will be replanted to replace the damage caused by the storm, it can take many years for trees to grow to a harvestable size, so the company faces a significant depletion of its future cash inflows for years to come. This risk is very difficult to mitigate, perhaps the diversification into tropical rainforest is a way to reduce the risk exposure of the company's operations being concentrated in one geographical area.

Liquidity

The financial information provided indicates that the company's liquidity position has deteriorated over the year. The company has only £4.5 million of cash – a reduction of 33.8% compared to the end of the last financial year. While this has been explained as due to inflationary pressures, management should be doing more to maintain a reasonable level of cash in order to properly manage its working capital. The company may become unable to meet obligations as they fall due especially if the industrial action continues to restrict the possibility of export sales which account for 30% of the company's revenue.

Industrial action

The industrial action at the country's ports has already meant lost sales, and as explained above, there is a risk that revenue and cash inflows will continue to be negatively impacted. Export sales account for 30% of total revenue, approximately £12.75 million, making this a potentially very significant issue should the industrial action continue. Customers may begin to look elsewhere for their supply of timber, leading to cancelled future orders and contracts.

There is also an issue that the increased storage of timber which is awaiting export to foreign customers will incur additional storage costs.

Incentive payment

The fact that the payment is being reported in the media indicates that there is something unusual about the payment and in fact, the incentive payment could be a bribe. The reputational risk to the company is high, especially given that it should be adhering to a high standard of business ethics in accordance with its Gold Standard accreditation. Customers may not wish to associate themselves with a supplier which engages with unethical and possibly illegal payments. The company could face legal action if indeed the payment is a bribe, and aside from this exacerbating the reputational risk, it has very little cash available to pay any fine or penalty imposed.

If the incentive payment is a bribe, there could be implications for the government grant, which contains stipulations regarding ethical business practices. In the worst case the grant may need to be repaid if the terms and conditions are found not to have been complied with.

> **Tutorial note.** Credit will be awarded for discussion of other relevant business risks, for example, the solvency issue raised by it being at the limit of its borrowing agreement, the lack of cash other than relating to the government grant available for establishing operations in Farland, the lack of an audit committee and independent internal audit team, the reputational damage which may be caused by the legal case and incentive payment, and the inflationary pressures which will make costs hard to control.

(b) **Evaluation of audit risks**

Materiality

For the purposes of these briefing notes, the following overall materiality level will be used to assess the significance of identified risks and as requested this has been based on the profitability of the company.

Benchmarks

5 – 10% of profit before tax = range of £825,000 - £1,650,000

This benchmark is only a starting point for determining planning materiality and professional judgement will need to be applied in determining a final level to be applied during the course of the audit. This is the first year that Chief & Co has audited the company, which increases detection risk, together with the specialisms of auditing an agricultural business. Therefore, materiality has been based on 7.5% of profit before tax at £1,237,500 and has been set at £1,250,000.

Financial analysis

Revenue is projected to increase by 5.5%, and profit before tax by 32% which suggest that there is a significant decrease, and potential understatement, in expected costs, potentially due to the interpretation of accounting policies or judgments made by management in respect of the fair value of the forest and provisions regarding legal claims. There is a risk that expenses are understated and assets (namely the forest) are overstated.

New client

This is the first year that Chief & Co has audited the company, which increases detection risk, as our firm does not have experience with the client, making it more difficult to detect material misstatements.

In addition, there is a risk that opening balances and comparative information may not be correct. The prior year figures were not audited by Chief & Co, therefore we should plan to audit the opening balances carefully, in accordance with ISA (UK) 510 Initial Audit Engagements – *Opening Balances*, to ensure that opening balances and comparative information are both free from material misstatement.

> **Tutorial note.** Credit will also be awarded for discussion of Pale Ltd operating in a specialised industry, which could create a detection risk given the audit firm's lack of experience in auditing clients in this industry.

Going concern

There are several indicators that despite its projected increase in revenue and profit, the company faces going concern problems. These indicators include, but are not limited to, operational problems including the destroyed timber plantation and industrial action, reputational damage caused by the legal claim and possible illegal payment, financial problems caused by lack of cash and the fact that its results are likely to be much worse than that projected by management when the decrease in fair value of the destroyed timber plantation is taken into account.

IAS 1 *Presentation of Financial Statements* requires that management provide a note to the financial statements which discusses any material uncertainty over the company's ability to continue as a going concern. If management fails to disclose this note, or provides the note but with inadequate detail, then the requirements of IAS 1 may not have been followed, creating a significant audit risk.

Government grant

A government grant of £20 million has been awarded to Pale Ltd, this is significantly above the materiality threshold which has been determined at £1.25million. Mark York has suggested that he will recognise £10 million of the amount received in profit for the year – projected profit before tax (before any adjustments) is £16.5 million so increasing the profit by this amount would be highly material to the financial statements.

The audit risk relates to whether this should be recognised as income in the current accounting period. IAS® 20 *Accounting for Government Grants and Disclosure of Government Assistance* requires that government grants are recognised in profit or loss on a systematic basis over the periods in which the entity recognises expenses for the related costs for which the grants are intended to compensate. Mark York is planning to recognise half of the grant as income this year, however, this is not appropriately justified. The grant has not been awarded to compensate for management time in planning the international expansion so the appropriate accounting treatment would seem to be that the entire amount of the grant should be recognised as deferred income in this financial year, as the expenditure for which the grant is specifically provided has not yet been incurred. Therefore, there is a risk that the company will recognise the income too early, leading to overstated profit and understated liabilities.

> **Tutorial note.** Credit will also be awarded for discussion relating to the company's use of the grant for building accommodation for employees, and relevant audit risks e.g. the recognition of the accommodation as Property, Plant and Equipment and treatment of the part of the grant relating to the construction of assets.

There could be a further issue in that the terms of the grant may require complete or partial repayment if the conditions of the grant are not satisfied, for example if Pale Ltd does not retain its Gold Standard accreditation or if the circumstances of the employees' legal case are considered to be indicative of unethical business practice by the company. The company should evaluate whether the terms are likely to be met, and if not, should consider whether it would be appropriate to recognise a provision or disclose a contingent liability in the notes to the financial statements. According to IAS 37 *Provisions, Contingent Liabilities and Contingent Assets* a provision should be recognised where a present obligation exists as a result of a past event which can be reliably measured and is probable to result in an outflow of economic benefit.

The risk is therefore that this has not been considered by management, leading possibly to understated liabilities or inadequate disclosure as required by IAS 37.

Reduction in fair value of timber plantation

The company's timber plantation asset, prior to recognising any change in fair value, is highly material based on the threshold calculated of £1.25 million.

The company has correctly obtained an expert's opinion on the change in fair value of the destroyed and damaged trees caused by the storm. The expert's valuation has helped management to determine that a reduction in fair value of £7.5 million should be recognised in the financial statements within profit. This amount is material as it meets the threshold materiality rate. When the loss in value is recognised, it will reduce the projected profit from £16.5 million to £9 million. There is a risk that management will not recognise the fair value adjustment in full due to the impact it will have on profit. This is therefore a significant issue for the audit planning.

There is a risk that the expert's valuation is not appropriate, for example if the expert does not have appropriate expertise to perform this specialist valuation, which would lead to issues in whether the valuation can be relied upon. In addition, the expert has considered only the value of the destroyed and damaged trees and not considered any other impact of the storm, for example if other assets such as roads and buildings have been affected by the storm and should be tested for impairment.

Therefore, based on the issues discussed above, there is a risk that the loss is not fully recognised in profit for the year, and the carrying amount of non-current assets is overstated.

Legal case

The legal case could also give rise to a risk of understated liabilities or inadequate disclosure if the company fails to provide for the £19 million claimed by employees or to disclose the matter as a contingent liability. It will be a matter of significant judgement to decide whether the legal claim is likely to go against Pale Ltd or not at this early stage, however the matter is material and therefore warrants careful consideration. Due to its sensitive nature, the auditor may also consider the issue to be material by nature.

Pressure on results

The company is not a listed entity, but the existing and new shareholders will be looking for a return on their investment in the form of a dividend payment. In addition, in the run up to a potential stock market flotation there will be pressure for the company to show good financial performance. The company also has ambitious international expansion plans. Pressure to return a better performance creates an incentive for management bias which means that management may use earnings management techniques, or other methods of creative accounting, to create a healthier picture of financial performance than is actually the case. This creates an inherent risk of material misstatement, at the financial statement level.

The fact that the projected profit before tax is 32% higher than the previous year's figure could indicate that operating expenses are understated. Management bias could also have led to some of the accounting treatments suggested by Mark York, which work to improve the company's profit for the year.

Corporate governance

The company does not have to comply with corporate governance requirements as it is not a listed entity. However, it is good practice to have an established audit committee, especially for a large company like Pale Ltd which is seeking a stock market flotation in the relatively near future. The internal audit team is small and lacking in independence as they report directly to the CFO. This means that the scope of their work is likely to be quite limited due to insufficient resources, and any recommendations made could potentially be ignored by Mark York. This has implications for controls over financial reporting, which could be deficient, and increases control risk. There is a high scope for errors in financial reporting processes and for deliberate manipulation of balances and transactions, as the internal audit team does not have sufficient resources for thorough monitoring and reporting.

Impact of the audit risks on the engagement planning

The audit risks have been considered with regard to the estimated magnitude and likelihood of any misstatement, as well as taking into consideration any associated detection risk. Both the potential adjustments to the fair value of the forest asset (£7.5 million) and the adjustment to the proposed accounting treatment of the government grant (£10 million) clearly meet the threshold materiality of £1.25 million, and in aggregate, they would reduce the estimated profit to a loss of £1.5 million. Ensuring the appropriate disclosures and accounting treatment in respect of the legal claim (which may result, upon investigation, in a further increase in the loss by up to £19 million) is also a material item by amount of it exceeding the materiality threshold. Chief & Co will need to ensure that they have sufficient staff and resources available, including but not limited to, an assessment of the validity of the legal claim and a review of the valuation of the forest.

(c) **Change in fair value of the timber plantation asset**

- Obtain the expert's report on the value of the destroyed and damaged timber plantation to:
  - Gain understanding and allow evaluation of the methodology and assumptions used, e.g. the basis of determining the amount of any income which may be generated from the timber to be salvaged from damaged trees.
  - Confirm the geographical extent of damage by the storm.
  - Confirm the basis of determining whether trees have been completely destroyed or damaged.
- Discuss the expert's methodology and assumptions with management to confirm their rationale and compliance with the measurement requirements of IAS 41.
- Obtain confirmation of the expert's qualifications and experience in assessing storm damage to timber plantation assets and quantifying financial losses.
- Obtain confirmation that the expert is independent from Pale Ltd and its management team.
- If possible, visit the site of the storm damage to form a view on the scale of the destruction and to evaluate whether any assets other than the trees have been destroyed or damaged.
- Discuss with management the actions which have been taken in response to the storm, e.g. the extent of progress made to clear the destroyed trees and harvest the damaged trees.
- Obtain any documentation relating to any potential sale of damaged trees, e.g. customer orders, to confirm any realisable value of damaged trees.
- From the non-current asset register, confirm the carrying amount of the standing trees prior to any change in fair value being recognised.
- Consider whether the use of an auditor's expert is necessary to provide sufficient and appropriate evidence given the materiality of the figures.
- Develop an auditor's estimate of the fair value of the timber plantation, in accordance with the IAS 41 requirements, and compare to management's estimate of the change in fair value.
- Obtain a copy of the company's insurance policy and review the terms and conditions to confirm whether the storm damage is covered by insurance.

(d) **Ethical issues**

Assurance on Key Performance Indicators (KPIs)

There are several issues to consider with regard to providing this service. A significant issue relates to auditor objectivity. The KPIs include financial and non-financial metrics. The financial metrics, including revenue, operating profit and profit before tax will be extracted from, or reconciled to, the figures as shown in the audited financial statements.

While the KPIs will not form part of the audited financial statements, they will be published in the Annual Report and therefore form part of the 'other information' in relation to which the auditor has responsibilities under ISA (UK) 720 *The Auditor's Responsibilities Relating to Other*

Information. ISA (UK) 720 requires that auditors read other information in order to identify any material inconsistencies between the financial statements and the other information.

There is therefore a potential self-review threat to objectivity in that the audit firm has been asked to provide assurance on these KPIs which would be read by the audit team as part of their review of other information. The team performing the assurance work would be reluctant to raise queries or highlight errors which may have been made during the external audit when reading the other information.

> **Tutorial note.** Credit will be awarded for discussion of other relevant threats to objectivity created by providing an assurance service on the KPIs, including the advocacy threat and self-interest threats.

The IESBA *International Code of Ethics for Professional Accountants* (the Code) provides guidance when auditors provide additional services to an audit client. Chief & Co needs to evaluate the significance of the threat and consider whether any safeguards can reduce the threat to an acceptable level. For example, a partner who is independent should be involved in reviewing the audit work performed.

There is also an ethical issue in respect to the fee proposed by Pale Ltd for the assurance engagement. If the firm decides to take on the engagement, it should be treated as an engagement separate from the audit and with a separate fee charged for the work and confirmed in a separate engagement letter. The suggestion to simply amend and increase the audit fee and to determine it on a contingent basis, as in the fee is only payable if the assurance is favourable, is not appropriate. Contingent fees can give rise to a self-interest threat, as it is in the financial interest of the audit firm to give a favourable assurance opinion in order to secure the income. The Code prohibits the use of contingent fees for audit services, but they are allowed for other types of work, depending on factors such as the nature of the engagement and the range of possible fee outcomes. The most prudent course of action, should Chief & Co take on the engagement, would be to charge the fee on a non-contingent basis, separate from the audit fee, to remove any ethical issues relating to the fee.

Aside from ethical issues, Chief & Co must also consider whether they have the competence to perform the work. Providing assurance on non-financial KPIs is quite a specialist area, and it could be that the audit firm does not have the appropriate levels of expertise and experience to provide a quality service. In particular, the firm would need to ensure that it fully understands the Gold Standard accreditation. Given that this is a specialised industry, and this is the first client which Chief & Co has in the industry, it is questionable whether the firm has the competence to carry out the work.

Aside from competence, the firm should also consider whether it has resources in terms of staff availability to complete the work to the desired deadline and to perform appropriate reviews of the work which has been completed.

Conclusion

These briefing notes highlight that the company faces significant business risk, in particular in relation to its financial position and the recent storm damage. There are a number of significant audit risks which will need to be carefully considered during the planning of the audit, to ensure that an appropriate audit strategy is devised. Going concern should be a key focus of the audit. We need to perform detailed work on the highly material change in fair value of the timber plantation due to the recent storm, as detailed in the notes. Finally, there are several ethical matters to be discussed with management and incorporated into our audit planning. The assurance engagement on the company's KPIs should only go ahead once all ethical implications have been carefully evaluated and appropriate safeguards put in place.

30 Grohl

> **Workbook references**
>
> Chapters 2, 6 and 8.

Top tips

This was a fairly standard AAA question on audit planning and should have been within your capabilities. The first part required you to evaluate significant business risks. Your approach here should be to read the scenario closely, noting the risks as they occur. There were plenty of risks there for you to pass the question.

The next part was on the significant risks of material misstatement. One possible pitfall here might have been talking about risks to do with the auditors themselves (eg that the Board members leaving might make it difficult to obtain explanations), when these are **not** part of the 'risk of material misstatement'.

The next part covered ethics in the scenario. The parts of the scenario that were relevant here should have stood out, although you might have struggled to write seven marks' worth of material here. It is important, then, that you do not try to 'pad' your answer with irrelevant information, as this will not earn you marks. With a focused and systematic discussion, you should have been able to pass this part of the question.

Part (b) should not have been difficult. The issue was fairly clear-cut, and there were plenty of marks available for some relatively straightforward points. Most of the procedures are really common sense and come straight from the scenario itself.

Easy marks

There were easy marks for identifying various risks and for the matters to consider – the insurance claim was obviously implausible. Also, it is basic knowledge for ethics questions that a contingent fee is not appropriate for an audit engagement. Make sure you get some of the professional marks as well – being able to construct an answer in the right format should earn most if not all of the communication marks.

Examining team's comments

It was clear that the majority of candidates were familiar with audit planning questions and seemed comfortable with the style of the question and with the amount of information that had been given in the scenario. There was little evidence of time pressure despite the length of the question.

Within the partner's email request, part (i) was by far the best-answered requirement of the exam, with most candidates identifying and explaining a range of relevant business risks, which on the whole were developed in enough detail.

For candidates who achieved lower marks on this requirement, the problem was that they did not develop their discussion enough to achieve the maximum marks per point. Some of the answers just repeated the business issue as stated in the question without discussing any of the impact on the business at all. Most candidates discussed going concern, which was relevant, but instead of relating going concern to specific matters such as liquidity problems and the large loan, it was simply mentioned as a conclusion in relation to every business risk discussed, and therefore was not specific enough to earn credit. Many answers could have been improved in relation to business risk evaluation by including some simple analysis of the financial information made available, for example through the calculation of profit margins and trends. This would have been an easy way to develop the point that financial performance was suffering, as well as liquidity being poor.

Answers were very mixed for part (ii). Some candidates clearly understood the meaning of a risk of material misstatement, and could apply their knowledge to the question requirement, resulting in sound explanations. However, despite this being a regularly examined topic and the cornerstone of audit planning, the majority of answers were unsatisfactory.

First, many candidates included a discussion about this being a first-year audit which would result in a risk of material misstatement, but this was both incorrect and showed that the question had not been read carefully enough. Then, when attempting to explain a risk of material misstatement, many candidates could do little more than state a financial reporting rule, and then say the risk was that 'this would be incorrectly accounted for'. It was not clear if this type of vague statement was down to candidates being reluctant to come to a decision about whether a balance would be over or understated, or if they thought that their answer was specific enough. Very few answers were specific enough on the actual risk of misstatement to earn credit.

Answers to part (iii) were mixed, and generally the answers in relation to the contingent fee were better than those in relation to employment at a client company. On the contingent fee most candidates seemed confident in their knowledge and correctly identified that a contingent fee is not allowed, and they recommended sensible actions such as ensuring a discussion of the matter with those charged with governance. The majority of candidates had the correct knowledge here and could apply appropriately to the question. As usual, candidates appear reasonably comfortable with the ethics part of the syllabus but are reminded that to score well on ethical requirements in AAA, they must do more than just identify a threat.

With respect to requirement (b) on the insurance claim, the audit procedures that were recommended were mixed in quality. Most candidates suggested a review of the terms and conditions of the insurance policy to see if the situation was covered, and most also recommended reviewing the actual claim and contacting the insurance provider. All of these are valid and appropriate procedures and generally were well described. Some answers tended to state that the matter should be 'discussed with management' with no further explanation, or that 'an expert should be consulted' but with no description of what evidence the expert should be asked to provide, or even who the expert should be. Too many candidates seemed to want to rely on representations and discussions about the possible outcome of the insurance claim when there were other stronger sources of audit evidence available.

Marking guide

Marks

(a) (i) **Significant business risks**

Up to 2 marks for each significant business risk evaluated (up to a maximum of 3 marks in total if risks identified but not evaluated):

- Exchange rate risk
- Imports – transportation costs and potential for disrupted supply
- Reliance on one supplier
- Quality control issues
- High-tech/competitive industry
- Reliance on key customer contracts
- Regulatory issues
- Website sales
- Outsourcing
- Liquidity/solvency issues
- Poor profitability
- Change in key management

8

(ii) **Significant risks of material misstatement**

Up to 3 marks for each significant risk of material misstatement evaluated (capped at 1 mark if risks are identified with no evaluation):

Up to 3 marks for valid discussions about materiality

- Initial translation of foreign exchange transactions
- Retranslation and exchange gains and losses
- Obsolete inventory
- Refunds to customers
- Capitalisation of borrowing costs to new production line

- Impairment of old production line
- Loan classification, measurement and disclosure
- Inventory obsolescence
- Going concern
- Website development costs
- Website sales

17

(iii) **Ethical issues**

Generally 1 mark per comment:

- Explain why familiarity threat arises
- Explain why intimidation threat arises
- Significant connections should be evaluated
- If significant connections remain, firm should resign
- If continue with audit, consider modifying audit approach and change audit team
- Review any work recently performed on Grohl Ltd audit by Bob Halen
- Consider firm's policies and procedures
- Contingent fee not acceptable
- The basis for calculation of the audit fee must be agreed with client

7

(b) **Insurance claim**

Generally 1 mark per matter/procedure:

Matters

- Accounting treatment for contingent asset
- Claim may not be covered by insurance
- Amount of the claim seems unreasonable
- Materiality
- Potential risk of material misstatement and impact on report

Procedures

- Inspect claim and supporting documentation
- Inspect insurance terms and conditions
- Review correspondence
- Communicate with insurance provider
- Enquiry with lawyers

Maximum 8

Professional marks

Communication

- Briefing notes format and structure – use of headings/sub-headings and an introduction
- Style, language and clarity – appropriate layout and tone of briefing notes, presentation of materiality and relevant calculations, appropriate use of the CBE tools, easy to follow and understand
- Effectiveness and clarity of communication – answer is relevant and tailored to the scenario

- Adherence to the specific requests made by the audit engagement partner

Analysis and evaluation

- Appropriate use of the information to determine suitable calculations
- Appropriate use of the information to support discussions and draw appropriate conclusions
- Assimilation of all relevant information to ensure that the risk evaluation performed considers the impact of contradictory or unusual movements
- Effective prioritisation of the results of the risk evaluation to demonstrate the likelihood and magnitude of risks and to facilitate the allocation of appropriate responses
- Balanced discussion of the information to objectively make a recommendation or decision

Professional scepticism and judgement

- Effective challenge of information supplied, and techniques carried out to support key facts and/or decisions
- Determination and justification of a suitable materiality level, appropriately and consistently applied
- Appropriate application of professional judgement to draw conclusions and make informed decisions about the courses of action which are appropriate in the context of the audit engagement

Commercial acumen

- Use of effective examples and/or calculations from the scenario to illustrate points
- Appropriate use of the industry information to evaluate business risks
- Recognition of the increased risks to the future competitiveness of the company given the information provided in the scenario and any impact on going concern

Maximum	10
Total	50

Briefing notes

For: Mia Vai

By: Audit Manager

Date: 1 July 20X5

Subject: Grohl Ltd audit planning

Introduction

These notes will: evaluate the significant business risks faced by Grohl Ltd; evaluate and prioritise the significant risks of material misstatement to be considered in audit planning; and discuss relevant ethical issues and recommend actions to be taken by our firm.

(a) (i) **Evaluation of business risks**

Overseas supplier

Copper wiring is a key production material, and it is imported from overseas. There is therefore a risk of unstable supply as a result of it being transported over a long distance, across borders. Any of the following could pose problems:

- A rise in fuel prices could affect the cost of materials.
- Political instability could lead to difficulties transporting across borders.
- Goods may not be subject to the same regulatory standards as those in Grohl's own jurisdiction and could be of poor quality.

- Environmental disruption could affect eg shipping or aviation, and lead to disruption of the supply of materials.

If there were a stock-out of this key material then this would severely affect Grohl Ltd's production, and its ability to supply its customers. This could lead to a loss of revenue and of customer goodwill.

Exchange rate risk

Purchases are made in a foreign currency, and fluctuations are not hedged against. This leaves Grohl Ltd exposed to the risk of price rises, which could affect both its cash position and its short-term profitability. It may be advisable for the company to use forward contracts to help mitigate this risk.

Key supplier

Grohl Ltd is reliant on just one supplier for all its copper wiring. It is thus exposed to any risks resulting from problems with this supplier, eg price rises, problems with supply, quality control.

Grohl Ltd also moved all of its copper purchases to just one new supplier, before using the supplier for a trial period. It was therefore highly exposed to any problems with the new supplier.

Competitive pressure

Grohl Ltd operates in a competitive industry and is subject to price competition from overseas. There is a risk that Grohl will be unable to keep its prices low enough to compete on this basis. It may need to consider alternative strategies.

The industry is dynamic and subject to rapid change, so in order to remain competitive Grohl Ltd must adapt quickly to any changes. It may not have sufficient resources to do this.

Quality control

Quality problems with the new copper supply have led to goods being returned by customers. This seems likely to be related to the use of a new, cheaper supplier. There is a risk of losing customers as a result of poor-quality products, which may be particularly dangerous in this competitive market.

It may be necessary in future for Grohl Ltd to test the quality of copper purchased. This would incur costs, which would in turn put further pressure on Grohl Ltd's already tight operating margins.

New regulations

New regulations come into force after the year end. There is a risk that these may not be complied with, which could lead to significant penalties. These could be fines or could result in suspending production.

New loan

The new £30 million loan is significant at 1/6 (16.7%) of forecast total assets. It is not known what proportion of net assets this constitutes. Annual interest on the loan is 4% × £30 million = £1.2 million for a full year, which is a significant amount in the context of a forecast loss of £300,000 before tax and a cash balance of only £130,000.

The fact that Grohl Ltd has a £2.5 million overdraft may be indicative of a cash shortage, a view that is borne out by low current and quick ratios. There is a risk that Grohl Ltd may not be a going concern for the next year.

Management change

The loss of several executive directors means that key business expertise has been lost, which might have been especially important given Grohl Ltd's current financial position.

Website sales

The introduction of website sales brings with it several risks. These include the risk of non-compliance with taxation, legal and other regulatory issues. There is a risk of technological failure (crashes) resulting in business interruption and possible brand damage.

There is a significant security risk from virus attacks, which could result in loss of company or customer data. This may in turn have legal ramifications.

The high rate of returns from the website is a concern, as this may indicate a flaw in the design of the website.

On balance the website is likely to help improve Grohl Ltd's sales, but it is notable that prices have been reduced by 10%. There is a risk of lost revenue if this reduction has not been given adequate consideration.

Outsourcing

Grohl Ltd has outsourced both its new website and the delivery service from it, which brings a risk that the services provided may not be of sufficient quality. Grohl Ltd is now reliant on two external entities for key elements of its business, over which it has now relinquished control.

There is also a cost risk with outsourced services, as they may be more expensive than performing the service in-house.

Profitability

Forecast revenue is down by £1.3 million from 20X4, or 9.4%. Operating profit is expected to have fallen by £500,000, or 50%, and the operating margin to have fallen from 7.2% to 4%, a fall of 44%.

Grohl Ltd is expecting to make a pre-tax loss of £300,000, although this does not appear to include the finance costs from the new loan (finance costs for 20X5 are forecast to be the same as 20X4). If these were included, then the loss would be about £0.5 million higher, at £0.8 million. This is a large loss and may again indicate going concern problems.

(ii) **Significant risks of material misstatement**

Materiality

A forecast loss of £300,000 is given in Exhibit 3, so an alternative benchmark will be required for determining a suitable materiality threshold. We are told that total assets are expected to be £180 million, so applying the standard range of 1-2% for this amount would indicate a materiality threshold of between £1.8 million and £3.6 million. However, even the lower amount of £1.8 million is significantly higher than the company's forecast operating profit of £500,000. Revenue is anticipated to be £12.5 million, so applying the standard range of 0.5-1% to this amount, a benchmark of between £62,500 and £125,000 could be used. It would therefore appear that given the range of values discussed here, the planning materiality level for the Grohl audit will need to take both quantitative and qualitative factors into account.

Foreign exchange

There is a risk of non-compliance with IAS 21 *The Effects of Changes in Foreign Exchange Rates*. IAS 21 requires that non-monetary items are recognised at the historical rate, which is the rate at the date of the transaction. This would include income and expenses in the statement of profit or loss. There is a risk that non-monetary items are not recognised at the correct historical rate, leading to under- or over-statement of these items.

IAS 21 requires monetary items to be measured at the closing rate. Thus any foreign currency payables and receivables must be retranslated at the year end, with any exchange gain or loss being recognised in the statement of profit or loss. There is a risk that the wrong rate is used, or that items are translated using the wrong date. There is also a risk that no exchange gain or loss is recognised in relation to payables and receivables settled during the year.

Product recall

Grohl Ltd may be liable to customers in relation to faulty goods supplied. Although the issue appears to be resolved, it is possible that there may be further liabilities which should be recognised in line with IAS 37 *Provisions, Contingent Liabilities and Contingent Assets*. IAS 37 requires a liability to be recognised where a present obligation exists as a result of a past event, and the outflow of resources embodying economic benefits is probable. There is a risk that liabilities are understated if a provision is not recognised.

There is a further risk that the accounting treatment of the product recall was incorrect. Any revenue recognised on recalled items should be cancelled against the corresponding receivables balance. The risk is therefore that revenue and receivables may be overstated.

New production line

The construction of the new production line is likely to result in new non-current assets which should be recognised in line with IAS 16 *Property, Plant and Equipment*. There is a risk that this has not been done correctly, leading to either under- or over statement of assets. The value of the loan is 16.7% of forecast total assets, so it seems likely the production line would be considered material to the financial statements.

The production line is likely to be a qualifying asset in line with IAS 23 *Borrowing Costs*, so all directly attributable borrowing costs should be capitalised. It is not clear how much of the £1.2 million finance cost from the new loan would be capitalised, as the loan appears to have been used only 'mainly' for the new production line, but there is a significant risk of material misstatement if finance costs are inaccurate given the company's operating profits are only expected to be £500,000.

Old production line – impairment

The new regulations coming into force after the year end indicate that the existing production may be impaired. IAS 36 *Impairment of Assets* requires management to conduct an impairment review. If this is not done adequately, then non-current assets and profit may be overstated.

IAS 36 requires assets to be carried at the lower of their carrying amount and their recoverable amount. In conducting the impairment review, management determines the recoverable amount, which is the higher of the assets' value in use, and their fair value less costs of disposal. If the new regulations have made the existing production line assets obsolete, then their value in use may be as low as zero; in this case the assets would need to be carried at their fair value less costs of disposal. The company would then need to recognize an impairment loss for the difference between this and the assets' carrying amount which may be material.

Inventory obsolescence

There is a risk that some inventory may have been rendered un-useable by the use of corroded copper. The matter is complicated by the fact that testing is required to determine whether an item has been affected.

IAS 2 *Inventories* requires inventory to be carried at the lower of cost and net realisable value. There is a danger that obsolete inventory has been included in the financial statements without being reviewed for impairment, resulting in an overstatement of inventory. This overstatement would affect both profit and total assets.

Website development costs

Website development costs may be treated as an internally generated intangible asset according to IAS 38 *Intangible Assets*, provided that the appropriate conditions are satisfied: it must be probable that future economic benefits will flow from the website, and the costs of the website must be measured reliably.

IAS 38 requires the website to be feasible, which seems to be the case since it is operational. Similarly, the costs appear to be able to be measured reliably at £200,000 which represent 40% of the company's operating profit and exceeds the range calculated for materiality based on revenue. It is unlikely to be correct, however, to capitalise the total costs of £200,000, since some of these must relate to the planning stage and should therefore have been recognised in profit or loss as they were incurred.

There is a further risk that subsequent costs have been included within this figure instead of being recognised as expenses. This could result in assets being overstated and expenses understated.

Website sales

A key risk is the use of an outsourced service provider. ISA 402 *Audit Considerations Relating to an Entity Using a Service Organisation* provides guidance on how auditors should obtain sufficient appropriate audit evidence when the audit client, which is a 'user entity', relies on such services.

The website sales are likely to be highly material to Grohl Ltd as they make up around a quarter of revenue, even though they have only been launched for half a year. The outsourced service therefore constitutes a key element of Grohl Ltd's internal control systems, so it will need to be assessed carefully.

Going concern

As indicated in the evaluation of significant business risks, there may be going concern problems at Grohl Ltd. The risk is either that the financial statements are prepared on the going concern basis when they should not be, or that appropriate disclosures are not made regarding any material uncertainties giving rise to significant doubts over going concern. The shortage of cash, increased reliance on debt financing and poor financial ratios all indicate going concern as the most significant risk for Grohl Ltd.

Conclusion

A number of risks have been outlined here, but the most important single risk is likely to be going concern, as this is a matter of crucial importance to the users of the financial statements and auditor's report. Beyond this, the assets and liabilities associated with the new production line are significant in value and must also be considered high-priority risk areas. The degree of change at Grohl Ltd seems to be an underlying source of risk and is something the firm will need to get to the bottom of during the audit.

(iii) **Ethical issues**

Audit manager joining client

An audit manager from Foo & Co may leave to become a financial controller at Grohl Ltd. According to the IESBA *Code of Ethics*, this could create familiarity and intimidation threats. The FRC *Revised Ethical Standard* adds self-interest threat to this list.

The audit team may be so familiar with Bob Halen that they lose independence, for example they may not challenge him if this is necessary. They may fail to exercise enough professional scepticism. Bob is also likely to be familiar with Foo & Co's audit methodology, so would be well placed to think of ways of hiding things from the audit team if he were so inclined.

The IESBA *Code* states that if a 'significant connection' remains between the firm and the individual who joined the client, then no safeguard could mitigate the threat and the firm should withdraw from the engagement. This would be the case if:

- Bob is entitled to benefits or payments from Foo & Co, unless in line with fixed pre-determined arrangements
- Bob is owed an amount by the firm that is material to the firm
- Bob continues to participate in the firm's business or professional activities

Alternatively, if there is no significant connection then safeguards may be acceptable. The threat here is significant, as Bob was in charge of the Grohl Ltd audit only very recently and would have maintained contact with Grohl Ltd's management.

Safeguards might include reviewing any work that Bob has done on the audit, although there is not likely to be much of this as planning is only just starting.

Contingent fee audit

The IESBA *Code* clearly states that an audit firm may not enter into a contingent fee arrangement, as the self-interest threat would be too great for safeguards to reduce the threat to an acceptable level. This prohibition is also reflected in the FRC *Revised Ethical Standard*.

Conclusion

Grohl Ltd is facing some significant business risks, which may affect the going concern assertion. There are a number of significant risks of material misstatement in relation to which the audit plan should design procedures to obtain sufficient appropriate audit evidence. The ethical issue with Bob Halen requires that safeguards be put in place, and it should be communicated to Grohl Ltd's Board that the audit cannot be performed on a contingent fee basis.

(b) **Matters to consider**

At £5 million, the claim represents 40% of forecast revenue and would turn a loss of £0.3 million into a profit of £4.7 million. It is therefore highly material.

This is a contingent asset. IAS 37 requires that contingent assets are not recognised, unless it is virtually certain that the inflow of economic benefits will take place.

At the moment, it is not certain that the claim will even be paid, even if it is more likely to be paid than not. Whether or not it is paid will depend on the specific terms of the insurance policy, which would need to be considered in detail and light of any communications with the insurer and/or Grohl Ltd's legal counsel.

Regarding the value of the claim, production was halted for just one week so 40% of annual revenue is far too high. It is very unlikely that this amount will be received.

Procedures

- Obtain a copy of the insurance claim made and confirm that £5 million is claimed.
- Enquire into the basis of the £5 million claimed, and review any supporting documentation such as extracts of management accounts showing lost revenue for the period of halted production.
- Inspect the terms of the insurance policy, to determine whether production halted in these specific circumstances would be covered.
- Seek Grohl Ltd's permission to contact the insurer, to ask about the status of the claim, and request written confirmation of any payment that may be made.
- Review correspondence between Grohl Ltd and the insurance provider, looking for confirmation of any amounts to be paid.

31 Eagle

Workbook references

Chapters 2, 6, 7 and 9.

Top tips

Your general approach should be to read the requirement carefully, and then to work through the question noting down issues (audit risks) as they occur to you.

Part (a) asks you to use analytical procedures, and the eagle-eyed student might have noticed that it even suggests a way of gaining marks: by using the results of your analytical procedures to identify risks (Exhibit 1).

It is crucial that you perform these calculations if you are going to pass the question; even if you scored strongly throughout the rest of the question, this can be the difference between passing and failing it. Don't go too far, though, as the marks for analytical procedures will usually be capped (in this case they're capped at 5).

Notice also that you're asked for 'audit risks' and not 'risks of material misstatement', so you can include detection risks. When the examining team includes audit risks in the requirement then this is the result of a deliberate decision that has been made – you can therefore take this as a clue that there will be at least one detection risk in the question.

The requirement also asks you to 'prioritise' your risks, which you can demonstrate by including a simple conclusion that summarises the risks you consider to be the most important.

Finally, it is vital that you get the marks for materiality. There were up to 4 marks available here. Taken together with the marks on materiality, this makes 9 marks for what are fairly mechanical skills at this level.

The second requirement in Exhibit 1 asked for audit procedures on goodwill, and it was not excessively difficult. As ever, your answers here should be as specific as possible, explaining why you would perform each procedure in addition to just saying what you would do. The requirement refers to Exhibit 4, which is a good source of ideas and thus marks.

The third requirement was not in fact too difficult, but this was a new style of question that you may not have been ready for. Really all you needed to do was to think about how these areas *should* be audited, and then compare this with what has been done here. This can help you to keep an independent mind about what should be done, and not fall into the trap of struggling to find problems with the approach suggested in the question.

The final requirement tested ethics which is a topical area of the syllabus. This should not have posed you too stern a test.

Easy marks

Easy marks were on offer for analytical procedures and materiality in the first requirement, in addition to the professional marks.

ACCA examining team's comments

The first requirement was to produce an analysis of audit risks using analytical review of financials and other information provided on specific issues arising during the year. The format was the same as in the [then] specimen exam and the requirement was worth 21 marks. Of these, up to five marks were available for the calculations forming part of the analytical review and up to four marks could be obtained for relevant materiality calculations and conclusions. The majority of marks were available for the evaluation of significant audit risks, which is consistent with past requirements of this type.

This requirement was generally well attempted by the majority of candidates who calculated relevant ratios, discussed the risks arising from unexpected trends and relationships, and then analysed the risks arising from the specific issues described in the question. Using this approach and providing an evaluation containing the level of detail provided in the recent article, well prepared candidates were able to identify the specific risks from the information provided and score a clear pass on this part of the question. The model answers provided to recent past audit risk questions will illustrate how to structure answers to achieve maximum credit on this sort of requirement. It was pleasing to note that very few candidates spent time describing the theory of audit risk which is not required and should not be included in an answer unless the examining team has asked for it.

Common issues arising from the analytical review were:

- Calculating too many ratios and trends which were not then mentioned in the main body of the candidate's answer and were a waste of effort. Candidates should consider how many risks and calculations are likely to be needed to score full marks rather than calculate 30+ ratio/trends which they then do not have time to discuss.
- Calculating ratios and then not referring to them – an analytical review is not simply calculating ratios.
- Not calculating any ratios – ignoring the requirement to perform an analytical review will restrict the risks identified from the scenario and hence make scoring maximum credit very difficult

Another common mistake candidates made on this requirement was to spend a lot of time discussing speculative risks which generally do not obtain credit. The fact that a company is multinational with many subsidiaries does not automatically result in a key audit risk regarding the inability of the company to know how to perform a consolidation, or to account for foreign currency. The fact that this is not a new client, and the audit engagement partner did not raise any concerns in this regard past should be taken as a sign that these are things are not key issues. Candidates should instead focus on the details given in the scenario that the engagement partner thought relevant to highlight.

Other commonly seen technical errors arose in relation to provisions where candidates would assume that redundancies early in the financial year would give rise to a year-end redundancy provision. Post year-end redundancies are those which may give rise to a provision. Similarly, candidates often thought that, because automation was introduced during the year, it was likely that a similar strategy would exist in the future therefore provisions should be made for more redundancies "just in case".

In addition to these issues, otherwise capable candidates failed to attain a strong mark on this section of the examination by failing to address the requirement. Particularly common in the UK and Irish versions of the examination was candidates discussing issues in terms of business risk or audit procedures, which were not asked for, and not actually evaluating the audit risk.

Candidates should note that the communication marks are awarded for a suitable heading, a brief introduction, a structured answer and clarity of explanations. All candidates should be scoring a minimum of three professional marks on this skill alone and should note that in this examination a brief introduction need be no more than a single sentence and time should not be spent writing a full-page introduction.

Marking guide | **Marks**

(a) **Audit risk evaluation**

Up to 3 marks for each audit risk identified and explained. Marks may be awarded for other, relevant audit risks not included in the marking guide.

In addition, 1 mark for relevant ratios and 0.5 mark for relevant trends which form part of analytical review (max 5 marks).

Materiality calculations should be awarded 1 mark each (max 4 marks).

- Operating margin and ROCE changes – risk understated expenses/overstated revenue
- Trends within operating expenses and related audit risks, eg misclassification of expenses
- Other operating income – risk of overstatement
- Risk of management bias due to listed status (max 2 marks)
- Current ratio and gearing and related audit risks, eg understated finance costs
- Effective tax rate and risk of tax expense being understated (max 2 marks)
- Consolidation of foreign subsidiaries
- Recognition and measurement of foreign exchange gains and losses
- Goodwill – audit risk regarding measurement, specifically lack of impairment review
- Goodwill on acquisition of Lynx Co (max 4 marks for detailed discussion)
- Intangible assets – audit risks in relation to unexplained movement in year, whether amounts should have been capitalised and amortisation period (max 5 marks)
- Increased detection risk regarding Lynx Co due to being audited by a component auditor

Maximum | 21

(b) **Audit procedures on the goodwill recognised on acquisition of Lynx Co**

Up to 1 mark for each well described procedure:

- Obtain and review the legal documentation, in particular, confirm the targets to be used as the basis for payment of the contingent consideration

ANSWERS

- Confirm that the Group has obtained an 80% shareholding and that this conveys control
- Agree the £80 million cash paid to the bank statement and cash book of the acquiring company
- Review the board minutes for relevant discussions including the minute of board approval
- Obtain management's calculation of contingent consideration, and evaluate assumptions used
- Discuss the 18% interest rate used in determining the discount factor and evaluate the justification given by management
- Confirm that the fair value of the non-controlling interest has been calculated based on an externally available share price at the date of acquisition by agreeing to stock market records
- Obtain a copy of the due diligence report issued by Sidewinder & Co, review for confirmation of acquired assets and liabilities and their fair values
- Evaluation of the methods used to determine the fair value of acquired assets, including the property, and liabilities to confirm compliance with IFRS 3 and IFRS 13 *Fair Value Measurement*
- Review the calculation of net assets acquired to confirm that Group accounting policies have been applied

Maximum 5

(c) **Evaluation of Vulture Associate's audit strategy**

Up to 2 marks for each issue evaluated:

- Controls – evidence needs to be obtained to confirm that controls have not changed
- Controls should be tested in a three-year cycle in order to place continued reliance on them
- Group audit team may decide to perform additional tests of control of Vulture Associates do not amend their strategy
- Evaluate status, competence and quality management approach of the internal audit department
- Objectivity should be evaluated where direct assistance is provided
- Consider the type of work – work on inventories and receivables is not appropriate due to subjective nature
- Internal auditors have worked on inventories and receivables so not objective
- Conclusion on audit quality (1 mark)

Maximum 8

(d) **Ethical issues relating to request to assist management in preparing an integrated report**

Up to 2 marks for each relevant point explained, and 1 mark for relevant safeguard or action:

- Explain the threats to objectivity created – self-review, familiarity and management involvement (1 mark each if fully explained)
- Conclusion as to whether service can be provided, following on from justification
- Suggest appropriate safeguards if engagement accepted, eg independent review (1 mark each)
- Explain that audit committee would need to pre-approve the engagement

Marking guide	Marks
• Bison & Co to consider competence and resource availability	
• Discuss with audit committee (1 mark)	
Maximum	6

Professional marks

Communication

- Briefing notes format and structure - use of headings/sub-headings and an introduction
- Style, language and clarity - appropriate layout and tone of briefing notes, presentation of materiality and relevant calculations, appropriate use of the CBE tools, easy to follow and understand
- Effectiveness and clarity of communication - answer is relevant and tailored to the scenario
- Adherence to the specific requests made by the audit engagement partner

Analysis and evaluation

- Appropriate use of the information to determine suitable calculations
- Appropriate use of the information to support discussions and draw appropriate conclusions
- Assimilation of all relevant information to ensure that the risk evaluation performed considers the impact of contradictory or unusual movements
- Effective prioritisation of the results of the risk evaluation to demonstrate the likelihood and magnitude of risks and to facilitate the allocation of appropriate responses
- Balanced discussion of the information to objectively make a recommendation or decision

Professional scepticism and judgement

- Effective challenge of information supplied, and techniques carried out to support key facts and/or decisions
- Determination and justification of a suitable materiality level, appropriately and consistently applied
- Appropriate application of professional judgement to draw conclusions and make informed decisions about the courses of action which are appropriate in the context of the audit engagement

Commercial acumen

- Audit procedures are practical and plausible in the context of the Eagle Group
- Use of effective examples and/or calculations from the scenario to illustrate points or recommendations.
- Recognition of the appropriate practical and commercial considerations of the audit firm in relation to the proposed audit strategy for the Eagle Group

Maximum	10
Total	50

Briefing notes

To: Maya Crag, Audit engagement partner

From: Audit manager

Subject: Eagle Group – Audit planning

Introduction

These briefing notes are prepared to assist with planning the audit of the Eagle Group (the Group) for the financial year ending 30 September 20X5. The notes contain an evaluation of the audit risks which should be considered in planning the Group audit. The notes also recommend the principal audit procedures to be used in the audit of the goodwill which has arisen in respect of a newly acquired subsidiary. The notes then go on to evaluate an extract from the audit strategy which has been prepared by a component auditor. Finally, the Group finance director has requested our firm to provide a non-audit service in relation to the Group's integrated report, and the notes discuss the professional and ethical implications of this request.

(a) **Evaluation of audit risk**

Selected analytical procedures and associated audit risk evaluation

	20X5	*20X4*
Operating margin	350/5,770 = 6.1%	270/5,990 = 4.5%
Return on capital employed	350/2,245 + 650 = 12.1%	270/2,093 + 620 = 10%
Current ratio	1,450/597 = 2.4	1,420/547 = 2.6
Debt/equity	550/2,245 = 24.5%	500/2,093 = 23.9%
Interest cover	350/28 = 12.5	270/30 = 9
Effective tax rate	64/322 = 19.9%	60/240 = 25%

Operating margin and operating expenses

The Group's operating margin has increased from 4.5% to 6.1% despite a fall in revenue of 3.7%. This is due to a reduction in operating expenses of 4.5% and increase in other operating income of 50%. Return on capital employed shows a similar positive trend, despite the fall in revenue. There is an audit risk that expenses are understated, with the reduction in expenses being proportionately more than the reduction in revenue.

Within operating expenses the trends for each component are different – cost of raw materials consumables and supplies has decreased by 3.1%, which appears reasonable given the decline in revenue of 3.7%. However, staff costs have increased slightly by 1.1% which seems inconsistent with the revenue trend and with the increased automation of operations which has led to 5,000 staff being made redundant, which presumably means lower payroll costs this year. Expenses could have been misclassified into staff costs in error.

Depreciation, amortisation and impairment has increased by 3.6%, which is not a significant change, but will need to be investigated to consider how each element of the category has changed in the year. The most noticeable trend within operating expenses is that the other operating expenses category has reduced very significantly. The amount recognised this financial year is only 7.4% of the amount recognised the previous year; this appears totally inconsistent with the other trends noted. It could be that some costs, for example, accrued expenses, have not yet been accounted for, or that the 20X4 figure was unusually high.

Other operating income

There is also an audit risk that other operating income is overstated. According to the information in note 6, during the year a credit of £60 million has been recognised in profit for reversals of provisions, this is 50% greater than the amount recognised in the previous year. In addition, a credit of £30 million has been recognised for reversals of impairment losses. There is a risk that these figures have been manipulated in order to boost profits, as an earnings management technique, in reaction to the fall in revenue in the year.

The risk of management bias is high given the listed status of the Group, hence expectations from shareholders for a positive growth trend. The profit recognised on asset disposal and the increase in foreign currency gains could also be an indication of attempts to boost operating profit this year.

Current ratio and gearing

Looking at the other ratios, the current ratio and gearing ratio do not indicate audit risks; however, more detail is needed to fully conclude on the liquidity and solvency position of the Group, and whether there are any hidden trends which are obscured by the high-level analysis which has been performed with the information provided.

The interest cover has increased, due to both an increase in operating profit and a reduction in finance charges. This seems contradictory to the increase in borrowings of £50 million – as a result of this, an increase in finance charges would be expected. There is an audit risk that finance charges are understated.

Effective tax rate

The effective tax rate has fallen from 25% to 19.9%. An audit risk arises in that the tax expense and associated liability could be understated. This could indicate management bias as the financial statements suggest that accounting profit has increased, but the profit chargeable to tax used to determine the tax expense for the year appears to have decreased. There could be alternative explanations, for instance a fall in the rate of tax levied by the authorities, which will need to be investigated by the audit team.

Consolidation of foreign subsidiaries

Given that the Group has many foreign subsidiaries, including the recent investment in Lynx Co, audit risks relating to their consolidation are potentially significant. Lynx Co has net assets with a fair value of £300 million according to the goodwill calculation provided by management, representing 8.6% of the Group's total assets and 13.4% of Group net assets. This makes Lynx Co material to the Group and increases aggregation risk. Audit risks relevant to Lynx Co's status as a foreign subsidiary also attach to the Group's other foreign subsidiaries.

According to IAS 21 *The Effects of Changes in Foreign Exchange Rates*, the assets and liabilities of Lynx Co and other foreign subsidiaries should be retranslated using the closing exchange rate. Its income and expenses should be retranslated at the exchange rates at the dates of the transactions. The risk is that incorrect exchange rates are used for the retranslations. This could result in over/understatement of the assets, liabilities, income and expenses which are consolidated, including goodwill. It would also mean that the exchange gains and losses arising on retranslation and to be included in Group other comprehensive income are incorrectly determined.

In addition, Lynx Co was acquired on 1 December 20X4 and its income and expenses should have been consolidated from that date. There is a risk that the full year's income and expenses have been consolidated, leading to a risk of understatement of Group profit given that Lynx Co is forecast to be loss making this year, according to the audit strategy prepared by Vulture Associates.

Measurement and recognition of exchange gains and losses

The calculation of exchange gains and losses can be complex, and there is a risk that it is not calculated correctly, or that some elements are omitted, for example, the exchange gain or loss on goodwill may be missed out of the calculation. IAS 21 states that exchange gains and losses arising as a result of the retranslation of the subsidiary's balances are recognised in other comprehensive income. The risk is incorrect classification, for example, the gain or loss could be recognised incorrectly as part of profit for the year, for example, included in the £28 million foreign currency gains which form part of other operating income, which would be incorrect. The amount recognised within other operating income has increased, as only £23 million foreign currency gains were recognised the previous year, indicating a potential risk of overstatement.

Goodwill

The total goodwill recognised in the Group statement of financial position is £1,100 million, making it highly material at 31.5% of total assets.

Analytical review shows that the goodwill figure has increased by £130 million during the year. The goodwill relating to the acquisition of Lynx Co is £100 million according to management's calculations. Therefore there appears to be an unexplained increase in value of goodwill of £30 million during the year and there is an audit risk that the goodwill figure is overstated, unless justified by additional acquisitions or possibly by changes in value on the retranslation of goodwill relating to foreign subsidiaries, though this latter point would seem unlikely given the large size of the unexplained increase in value.

According to IFRS 3 *Business Combinations*, goodwill should be subject to an impairment review on an annual basis. Management has asserted that while they will test goodwill for impairment prior to the financial year end, they do not think that any impairment will be recognised. This view is based on what could be optimistic assumptions about further growth in revenue, and it is likely that the assumptions used in management's impairment review are similarly overoptimistic. Therefore there is a risk that goodwill will be overstated and Group operating expenses understated if impairment losses have not been correctly determined and recognised.

Initial measurement of goodwill arising on acquisition of Lynx Co

In order for goodwill to be calculated, the assets and liabilities of Lynx Co must have been identified and measured at fair value at the date of acquisition. Risks of material misstatement arise because the various components of goodwill each have specific risks attached. The goodwill of £100 million is material to the Group, representing 2.9% of Group assets.

A specific risk arises in relation to the fair value of net assets acquired. Not all assets and liabilities may have been identified, for example, contingent liabilities and contingent assets may be omitted.

A further risk relates to measurement at fair value, which is subjective and based on assumptions which may not be valid. The fair value of Lynx Co's net assets according to the goodwill calculation is £300 million, having been subject to a fair value uplift of £12 million. This was provided by an independent firm of accountants, which provides some comfort on the validity of the figure.

There is also a risk that the cost of investment is not stated correctly, for example, that the contingent consideration has not been determined on an appropriate basis. First, the interest rate used to determine the discount factor is 18% – this seems high given that the Group's weighted average cost of capital is stated to be 10%. Second, the contingent consideration is only payable if Lynx Co reaches certain profit targets. Given that the company, according to Vulture Associate's audit strategy, is projected to be loss making, it could be that the contingent consideration need not be recognised at all or determined to be a lower figure than that currently recognised, based on a lower probability of it having to be paid. The results of the analytical review have indicated that the other side of the journal entry for the contingent consideration is not described as a component of the non-current liabilities and the accounting for this will need to be clarified as there is a risk that it has been recorded incorrectly, perhaps as a component of equity.

Intangible assets

In relation to expenditure on intangible assets during the year, which totals £60 million, there are several audit risks. First, there is a question over whether all of this amount should have been capitalised as an intangible asset. Capitalisation is only appropriate where an asset has been created, and specifically in relation to development costs, the criteria from IAS 38 *Intangible Assets* must all be met. There is a risk that if any criteria have not been met, for example, if there is no probable future economic benefit from research into the new technology, then the amount should be expensed. There is a risk that intangible assets are overstated and operating expenses understated.

There is also an unexplained trend, in that intangible assets has only increased by £30 million, yet expenditure on intangible assets, according to management information, is £60 million. More information is needed to reconcile the expenditure as stated by management to the movement in intangible assets recognised in the Group statement of financial position.

Second, there is a risk that the amortisation period is not appropriate. It seems that the same useful life of 15 years has been applied to all of the different categories of intangible assets; this is not likely to be specific enough, for example, the useful life of an accounting system will not be the same as for development of robots. Fifteen years also seems to be a long period – usually technology-related assets are written off over a relatively short period to take account of rapid developments in technology. In respect of amortisation periods being too long, there is a risk that intangible assets are overstated and operating expenses understated.

Detection risk in relation to Lynx Co

Lynx Co is the only subsidiary which is not audited by Bison & Co. This gives rise to a risk that the quality of the audit of Lynx Co may not be to the same standard as Bison & Co, as

Vulture Associates may not be used to auditing companies which form part of a listed group and results in increased detection risk at the Group level. The risk is increased by the problems with the audit strategy prepared by Vulture Associates, which will be discussed in part (c) to these briefing notes, which indicate that the audit of Lynx Co has not been appropriately planned in accordance with ISA requirements. Since our firm has not worked with Vulture Associates previously, we are not familiar with their methods and may have issues with the quality of their work; therefore the detection risk is high in relation to Lynx Co's balances which will form part of the consolidated financial statements.

Conclusion

The most important risks on the Eagle audit are the accounting for the acquisition of Lynx Co, and the existing goodwill, which is highly material to the statement of financial position. Issues relating to overseas subsidiaries and foreign currency transactions are also likely to be significant to the audit.

(b) **Principal audit procedures on the goodwill arising on the acquisition of Lynx Co**

- Obtain the legal documentation pertaining to the acquisition, and review to confirm that the figures included in the goodwill calculation relating to consideration paid and payable are accurate and complete. In particular, confirm the targets to be used as the basis for payment of the contingent consideration in four years' time.
- Also confirm from the purchase documentation that the Group has obtained an 80% shareholding and that this conveys control, ie the shares carry voting rights and there is no restriction on the Group exercising their control over Lynx Co.
- Agree the £80 million cash paid to the bank statement and cash book of the acquiring company (presumably the parent company of the Group).
- Review the board minutes for discussions relating to the acquisition, and for the relevant minute of board approval.
- For the contingent consideration, obtain management's calculation of the present value of £271 million, and evaluate assumptions used in the calculation, in particular to consider the probability of payment by obtaining revenue and profit forecasts for Lynx Co for the next four years.
- Discuss with management the reason for using an 18% interest rate in the calculation, asking them to justify the use of this interest rate when the Group's weighted average cost of capital is stated at 10%.
- Evaluate management's rationale for using the 18% interest rate, concluding as to whether it is appropriate.
- Confirm that the fair value of the non-controlling interest has been calculated based on an externally available share price at the date of acquisition. Agree the share price used in management's calculation to stock market records showing the share price of Lynx Co at the date of acquisition.
- Obtain a copy of the due diligence report issued by Sidewinder & Co, review for confirmation of acquired assets and liabilities and their fair values.
- Evaluate the methods used to determine the fair value of acquired assets, including the property, and liabilities to confirm compliance with IFRS 3 and IFRS 13 *Fair Value Measurement*.
- Review the calculation of net assets acquired to confirm that Group accounting policies have been applied.

(c) **Evaluation of the extract of the audit strategy prepared by Vulture Associates in respect of their audit of Lynx Co**

The extract from the audit strategy covers two areas – reliance on internal controls, and the use of internal audit for external audit work. In each area it appears that ISA requirements have not been followed, meaning that the quality of the audit planned by Vulture Associates is in doubt.

Controls effectiveness

In relation to reliance on internal controls, ISA (UK) 330 *The Auditor's Responses to Assessed Risks* contains requirements in relation to relying on work performed during previous audits on internal controls. ISA (UK) 330 states that if the auditor plans to use audit evidence from a previous audit about the operating effectiveness of specific controls, the auditor shall establish the continuing relevance of that evidence by obtaining audit evidence about whether significant changes in those controls have occurred subsequent to the previous audit. The auditor shall obtain this evidence by performing inquiry combined with observation or inspection, to confirm the understanding of those specific controls, and if there have been changes which affect the continuing relevance of the audit evidence from the previous audit, the auditor shall test the controls in the current audit. If there have not been such changes, the auditor shall test the controls at least once in every third audit, and shall test some controls each audit to avoid the possibility of testing all the controls on which the auditor intends to rely on a single audit period with no testing of controls in the subsequent two audit periods.

Therefore, in order to comply with ISA (UK) 330, Vulture Associates needs to do more than simply accept management's assertion that there have been no changes to controls. There needs to be some observation or inspection of controls, to confirm that there have been no changes, and this work and an appropriate conclusion need to be documented in the audit working papers.

In addition, there should be some testing of internal controls each year, so Vulture Associates should plan to perform some tests of controls each year, so that over a three-year cycle, all controls are tested to confirm that controls are still operating effectively and therefore can continue to be relied upon.

The Group audit team should discuss this issue with Vulture Associates to ensure that adequate controls testing is performed. If, for some reason, Vulture Associates does not amend its audit strategy, then the Group audit team may decide to perform additional testing, given that Lynx Co is material to the Group.

Internal audit

According to ISA (UK) 610 (Revised) *Using the Work of Internal Auditors*, it is acceptable, in some circumstances, for the external audit firm to use the internal audit function of an audited entity to provide direct assistance to the external audit team. However, in some jurisdictions (such as the UK), due to local regulations, the external auditor is prohibited from using internal auditors to provide direct assistance, and therefore the Group auditor team will need to consider whether the prohibition also extends to component auditors and, if so, it would not be appropriate for Vulture Associates to use the internal audit function. Assuming that there is no local restriction, before deciding whether to use the internal audit function, the external auditor must evaluate a number of factors, including:

- The extent to which the internal audit function's organisational status and relevant policies and procedures support the objectivity of the internal auditors.
- The level of competence of the internal audit function.
- Whether the internal audit function applies a systematic and disciplined approach, including quality management.

Vulture Associates must therefore perform this evaluation before making any decision about whether they should instruct the internal audit team to perform audit procedures. For example, if they find that the internal audit function does not have a good quality management procedure, it would not be appropriate to use them in external audit work.

Using the internal audit function to perform audit procedures is direct assistance to the external auditor. ISA (UK) 610 (Revised) requires that where direct assistance is being provided, the external auditor shall evaluate the existence and significance of threats to objectivity and the level of competence of the internal auditors who will be providing such assistance. The external auditor shall not use an internal auditor to provide direct assistance if there are significant threats to the objectivity of the internal auditor or the internal auditor lacks sufficient competence to perform the proposed work. Vulture Associates therefore needs to document and conclude upon their assessment of the internal auditors' objectivity and competence.

There is also an issue with regard to the type of work they are given to perform. Vulture Associates is planning to ask the internal auditors to perform specific audit procedures in relation to trade receivables, but this is not likely to be appropriate. ISA (UK) 610 (Revised) states that the external auditor shall make all significant judgements in the audit engagement. Performing a trade receivables circularisation and reviewing the allowance against trade receivables both involve judgements, in relation to sample selection and also in relation to measurement of the receivables. The trade receivables is also likely to be a material balance in the financial statements. Therefore it would not be appropriate for the internal audit team to complete the audit, though they could be used for performing routine procedures not involving the use of judgement.

A further issue is that ISA (UK) 610 (Revised) specifically states that the external auditor shall not use internal auditors to provide direct assistance to perform procedures which relate to work with which the internal auditors have been involved and which has already been, or will be, reported to management or those charged with governance. From the audit strategy, it appears that the internal audit function has worked on trade receivables during the year, so it would not be appropriate for the internal auditors to provide direct assistance to the external audit firm in relation to this area due to the self-review threat which would be created.

It may be possible for the internal auditors to provide direct assistance on non-judgemental areas of the financial statements if they have not performed internal audit work relating to those areas during the year.

In conclusion, from the evaluation of this extract from the audit strategy, it seems that Vulture Associates is planning to carry out the audit of Lynx Co in a manner which does not comply with ISA requirements. This is a concern, given the materiality of the subsidiary to the Group, and our firm should liaise with Vulture Associates as soon as possible to discuss their audit planning.

(d) **Ethical and professional implications of the request to provide a non-audit service on the Group's integrated report**

There are several issues to consider with regard to providing this service.

A significant issue relates to auditor objectivity. The IESBA *Code of Ethics for Professional Accountants* (the *Code*) provides guidance on situations where the auditor is asked by the client to provide non-assurance services. Bison & Co needs to evaluate the significance of the threat and consider whether any safeguards can reduce the threat to an acceptable level. This approach is mirrored by the FRC *Revised Ethical Standard* which requires the engagement partner to evaluate any potential threats to integrity, objectivity and independence from undertaking non-audit services.

While the integrated report is not part of the audited financial statements, the report will contain financial key performance indicators (KPIs), and the Group has asked for input specifically relating to the reconciliations between these KPIs and financial information contained in the financial statements. There is therefore a potential self-review threat to objectivity in that the audit firm has been asked to provide assurance on these KPIs which are related to figures which have been subject to external audit by the firm. The team performing the work will be reluctant to raise queries or highlight errors which have been made during the external audit when assessing the reconciliations of KPIs to audited financial information.

It could also be perceived that Bison & Co is taking on management responsibility by helping to determine content to be included in the integrated report, which is a threat to objectivity. The *Code* states that the audit firm shall not assume management responsibility for an audit client and that the threats created are so significant that safeguards cannot reduce them to an acceptable level. While the *Code* does not specifically state that helping the client to determine the content of its integrated report is taking on management responsibility, certainly there could be that perception as the auditor will be involved in setting measurements which the company will benchmark itself against. Additionally, working with management on the integrated report could create a familiarity threat to objectivity whereby close working relationships are formed, and the auditor becomes closely aligned with the views of management and is unable to approach the work with an appropriate degree of professional scepticism.

There is a potential problem in terms of compliance with ISA (UK) 720 *The Auditor's Responsibilities Relating to Other Information*, should Bison & Co accept the engagement. ISA (UK) 720 requires that auditors read other information in order to identify any material inconsistencies between the financial statements and information in the other information. ISA (UK) 720 applies only to other information in the annual report, and it is not stated whether the Group's integrated report will be included in the annual report, or as a standalone document.

Based on the above, it would seem unlikely that Bison & Co can provide this service to the Group, due to the threats to objectivity created. However, should the firm decide to take on the engagement, safeguards should be used to minimise the threats. For example, a partner who is independent should be involved in reviewing the audit work performed.

Aside from ethical issues, Bison & Co must also consider whether they have the competence to perform the work. Advising on the production of an integrated report is quite a specialist area, and it could be that the audit firm does not have the appropriate levels of expertise and experience to provide a quality service to the Group. The fact that the Group wants to highlight its technological achievements, and presumably will select a range of non-financial KPIs and technological issues to discuss in the integrated report, makes the issue of competence more significant, as the audit firm may not have the necessary technical knowledge to provide advice in this area. Aside from competence, the firm should also consider whether it has resources in terms of staff availability to complete the work to the desired deadline and to perform appropriate reviews of the work which has been completed.

Finally, given that the Group is a listed entity, it should comply with relevant corporate governance requirements. This means that the audit firm may be prohibited from providing services in addition to providing the external audit to the Group. The audit committee should apply the Group's policy on the engagement of the external auditor to supply non-audit services, the objective of which should be to ensure that the provision of such services does not impair the external auditor's independence or objectivity. The Group's audit committee will need to pre-approve the provision of the service, and in making this decision they should consider a number of matters, for instance, the audit committee should consider whether the skills and experience of the audit firm make it the most suitable supplier of the non-audit service, whether there are safeguards in place to eliminate or reduce to an acceptable level any threat to objectivity and the level of fees to be incurred relative to the audit fee.

Conclusion

These briefing notes indicate that there are a large number of audit risks to be considered in planning the audit, and that management needs to supply the audit team with a range of additional information for more thorough audit planning to be carried out. The audit of goodwill, and in particular the goodwill arising on the acquisition of Lynx Co, is an area of significant audit risk, and the notes recommend the principal audit procedures which should be conducted. An evaluation of the audit strategy prepared by Vulture Associates indicates that their audit of Lynx Co might not be a high-quality audit. Finally, our firm needs to discuss the request to assist in preparing the Group's integrated report with the Group audit committee, and it seems unlikely given the threat of management involvement that we would be able to carry out this work for the Group.

32 Ryder

Workbook references

Chapters 1, 2, 6, 7 and 8.

Top tips

Your general approach should be to read the requirement carefully, and then to work through the question noting down issues (such as audit risks) as they occur to you.

Part (a) asked you to evaluate and prioritise the significant audit risks. In recent sittings the ACCA has changed the phrasing of requirements here, and this is typical of the current form of words. The requirement asks you to 'evaluate' the risks (not just 'explain' them, for example); it also asks you to focus on the 'significant' risks and to prioritise them. All of these elements are trying to steer you away from simply writing down every risk you can think of. You will score better if you focus on the main risks for the audit, drawing your consideration of the issues from the scenario back to the effect on the financial statements (over- or under-statement? Of which accounts?) and considering materiality. Composing your answer in this way will also help you to earn more of the professional marks that are on offer. You should also write a conclusion to your answer, irrespective of whether you are asked to write briefing notes.

Part (b) asks for additional information in relation to the disposal of a subsidiary. Points in this area tend to get a full mark where they are explained well, including not just the piece of information needed but a full explanation of why it is needed. For four marks you should aim to make four solid points here.

Part (c) asks, typically, for audit procedures in two areas. You need to make sure you cover both areas here, as mark caps may be in operation so that you cannot score, for example, full marks in one area but no marks in the other.

Part (d) features several ethical issues and is virtually a self-contained question. There are quite a lot of issues here for the marks available, so this part should have been within reach – provided you had left yourself with enough time by being strict with yourself in the earlier parts of the question. Candidates who left themselves with less than twelve minutes here would have found it difficult to score well on this question.

Easy marks

The marks for materiality are always easy, as are the presentation marks. Every candidate should be able to get at least three communication professional skills marks. If you don't get them then it is going to be much harder to pass this question.

ACCA examining team's comments

Part (a) – common issues arising on this requirement were:

Candidates giving rote-learnt risks with no application to the scenario, for example stating that this was a new client (it was an existing client) or that a significant risk to a listed company is management bias without referring to any specific bias drivers from the scenario (eg to prove the success of a restructuring strategy, to maximise the sales price for a subsidiary being disposed of) or demonstrating where the bias might impact on the financial statements (eg the incorrect recognition of the grant received in profit or the under amortisation of a three-year licence).

Candidates describing audit risks that were highly unlikely to be a genuine risk – for example many candidates thought there was an audit risk that an acquisition planned for next year might be included in this year's consolidation in error.

Candidates not fully understanding the basic concepts of control or influence in the context of group accounts, for example stating that a 50% shareholding means a company must be a subsidiary.

Part (b) was a four-mark requirement regarding additional information required to plan the audit of a disposal. This was well answered by candidates who appreciated that this did not relate to the final audit procedures but information that could be requested in advance.

Part (c) required audit procedures regarding a government grant and the classification of an investment in a joint venture. Generally, this requirement was well answered although common errors with the requirement regarding the joint venture were to cover a wider scope than classification or instead to give procedures for a totally different transaction from the scenario (eg a common incorrect answer was to list procedures relating to the audit of the PPE investment in a different group company). These errors arose from a lack of attention to the specific requirement.

Part (d) was a six-mark ethics requirement and candidates' answers tended to be weak here. Many candidates simply listed the names of ethical threats without any application to the specific scenario. This is disappointing given the specific guidance published on the ACCA website as to what is required in terms of description for credit to be awarded in this area. Here candidates demonstrated that they had learned a list of threats but failed to demonstrate that they understood them or knew how they applied to a question. This was particularly apparent with regard to the request that an audit partner take a temporary position on the audit committee. Many candidates said this was a self-interest threat however they described it as arising because the partner would be paid a fee rather than because the partner would then be involved in the choice of audit firm and setting of the audit fee.

Candidates also demonstrated insufficient detailed knowledge of the IESBA *Code of Ethics for Professional Accountants*. Candidates often incorrectly stated that referral fees are not permitted but recommended the use of a separate team to devise and test controls over revenue as an internal audit assignment which, for a listed company, is prohibited as revenues are a material component of the financial statements.

Marking guide	**Marks**
(a) **Evaluation and prioritisation of significant audit risks**	
Up to 3 marks for each audit risk evaluated unless otherwise indicated. Marks may be awarded for other, relevant risks not included in the marking guide. In addition, 0.5 mark for each relevant trend or calculation which forms part of the audit risk evaluation (max 3 marks).	
Materiality calculations should be awarded 1 mark each (max 4 marks).	
• Disclosure of events after the reporting period in respect of Group restructuring – risk of inadequate disclosure	
• Assets held for sale in respect of planned disposal of Primal Burgers Ltd – risk assets not measured or recognised appropriately as assets held for sale (up to 4 marks)	
• Discontinued operation – risk that Group statement of profit or loss does not reflect results of Primal Burgers Ltd as a discontinued operation	
• Disposal of Primal Burgers Ltd – incentive for manipulation (2 marks)	
• Joint arrangement in Peppers Ltd – risk that the investment is not equity accounted	
• Misclassification of operating licence in respect of Mondays Coffee Ltd drive-throughs as PPE, impact on measurement of PPE and intangible assets and associated expenses	
• Mondays Coffee Ltd drive-throughs likely to be a reportable segment – risk of incomplete disclosure of operating segments	
• Government grant – risk that conditions will not be met and a liability should be recognised for repayment of the grant	
• Audit committee – lack of financial reporting expert creates control risk (2 marks)	
Maximum	22
(b) **Additional information required to plan the audit of the planned disposal of Primal Burgers Ltd**	
Up to 1 mark for each piece of additional information recommended:	
• The financial statements of Primal Burgers Ltd, to ascertain the detail of the amounts recognised	
• A copy of the vendor's due diligence report to ascertain key findings, eg valuations of assets and liabilities	
• Information surrounding the reasons for disposal, from the Group board minutes at which approval was given for the disposal	

- Information regarding the potential acquirers of Primal Burgers Ltd and the stage of negotiations
- Any preliminary determination by management of the anticipated profit or loss on disposal and expectation of any impairment to the value of assets held in the disposal group
- Obtain a copy of management's assessment/workings of the impact on the Group's financial position on the sale of Primal Burgers Ltd and the overall impact of the restructure of the Group

Maximum 4

(c) **Principal audit procedures**

Up to 1 mark for each well-designed audit procedure.

1. **The 50% investment in Peppers Ltd**

- Obtain the legal documentation supporting the investment and agree the details of the investment including (max 2 marks):
- The date of the investment
- Amount paid
- Number of shares purchased
- The voting rights attached to the shares
- The nature of the profit-sharing arrangement between the Group and Smiths Ltd
- The nature of access to Peppers Ltd's assets under the terms of the agreement
- Confirmation that there is no restriction of the Group's shared control of Peppers Ltd
- Review board minutes to confirm the approval of the investment and to understand the business rationale for the investment
- Review minutes of relevant meetings between the Group and Smiths Ltd to confirm that control is shared between the two investors and to understand the nature of the relationship and the decision-making process
- Obtain documentation such as Peppers Ltd's organisational structure to confirm that the Group has successfully appointed members to the board of the company and that those members have equal power to the members appointed by Smiths Ltd

2. **The government grant**

- Obtain the documentation relating to the grant and review to obtain understanding of:
- The terms of the grant, in particular requirements relating to the specific use of the funds
- The date by which the funds must be used
- Any clauses relating to repayment of some or all of the grant should certain conditions arise
- Agree the amount received to bank statement and cash book of Ryder plc
- Obtain and review the Group's capital expenditure forecast to confirm the amount planned to be spent on capital expenditure relating to environmental matters
- Discuss the use of the grant to fund an advertising campaign with an appropriate person, eg Group marketing director, and review any plans to use the funds for promotional purposes to confirm that recycling features in

the campaign, as intended by the government

- Confirm, through agreement to marketing plans, whether any funds will be spent during this financial year
- Obtain a written representation from management that the grant received will be used for the specific purposes required by the government

Maximum 8

(d) **Ethical issues**

Up to 1 mark for each point explained:

- Audit firm partner serving on Group audit committee – self-review threat explained
- Audit firm partner serving on Group audit committee – self-interest threat explained
- Audit firm partner serving on Group audit committee – management threat explained
- Cannot provide partner to serve on audit committee
- Concerning that audit committee is requesting audit firm involvement – they should be aware of the ethical threats
- Referral fee – self-interest threat to objectivity and professional competence explained
- Can earn referral fee as long as safeguards used – disclose to client and obtain agreement (up to 2 marks)
- Internal audit assistance – prohibited by *FRC Ethical Standard*

Maximum 6

Professional marks

Communication

- Briefing notes format and structure - use of headings/sub-headings and an introduction
- Style, language and clarity - appropriate layout and tone of briefing notes, presentation of materiality and relevant calculations, appropriate use of the CBE tools, easy to follow and understand
- Effectiveness and clarity of communication - answer is relevant and tailored to the scenario
- Adherence to the specific requests made by the audit engagement partner

Analysis and evaluation

- Appropriate use of the information to determine suitable calculations
- Appropriate use of the information to support discussions and draw appropriate conclusions
- Assimilation of all relevant information to ensure that the risk evaluation performed considers the impact of contradictory or unusual movements
- Balanced discussion of the information to objectively make a recommendation or decision

Professional scepticism and judgement

- Effective challenge of information supplied, and techniques carried out to support key facts and/or decisions, such as in relation to the risk of manipulation of the disposal of Primal Burgers
- Determination and justification of a suitable materiality level, appropriately and consistently applied
- Appropriate application of professional judgement to draw conclusions and make informed decisions about the courses of action which are appropriate in the context of the audit engagement

Marking guide	Marks
Commercial acumen	
• Audit procedures are practical and plausible in the context of the Ryder Group.	
• Use of effective examples and/or calculations from the scenario to illustrate points or recommendations.	
• Recognition of the appropriate commercial considerations of the audit firm	
Maximum	10
Total	50

Briefing notes

To: Mo Iqbal, audit engagement partner

From: Audit manager

Subject: Audit planning in relation to the Ryder Group

Introduction

These briefing notes have been prepared to assist in planning the audit of the Ryder Group (the Group). The notes begin with an evaluation of the audit risks which should be considered in planning the audit. The notes then identify and explain the additional information required to plan the audit of a significant disposal which is expected to take place shortly after the financial year end. The notes also include the recommended principal audit procedures which have been designed in respect of an investment made in a joint arrangement and a government grant received in the year. Finally, the notes discuss several ethical matters arising from requests made by the Group audit committee.

(a)

Evaluation of significant audit risks

Planned disposal of Primal Burgers Ltd and acquisition of Valentine Ltd – events after the reporting date

The Group is planning a significant restructuring. The disposal of Primal Burgers Ltd is planned to take place shortly after the year end, and the disposal will have a material impact on the Group financial statements given that Primal Burgers Ltd accounts for 23.2% of projected Group total assets and 30.9% of projected Group revenue.

The acquisition of Valentine Ltd, which is planned to take place in the first quarter of the next financial year, will be material to the Group, with the anticipated cost of investment and the fair value of identifiable net assets of Valentine Ltd representing 21.1% and 17.9% of projected Group assets respectively.

Both events will fall under the scope of IAS 10 *Events after the Reporting Period*, meeting the definition of a non-adjusting event. IAS 10 requires that non-adjusting events should be disclosed if they are of such importance that non-disclosure would affect the ability of users to make proper evaluations and decisions. The required disclosure is the nature of the event and an estimate of its financial effect or a statement that a reasonable estimate of the effect cannot be made. The audit risk is that incomplete or inaccurate disclosure relating to the acquisition and disposal is provided in the notes to the financial statements.

Disposal of Primal Burgers Ltd – assets held for sale and discontinued operations

The planned disposal should be accounted for under IFRS 5 *Non-current Assets Held for Sale and Discontinued Operations*, which requires that once certain conditions are met, a disposal group of assets should be classified as held for sale. The conditions include:

- Management is committed to a plan to sell
- The asset is available for immediate sale
- An active programme to locate a buyer is initiated

- The sale is highly probable, within 12 months of classification as held for sale
- The asset is being actively marketed for sale at a sales price reasonable in relation to its fair value
- Actions required to complete the plan indicate that it is unlikely that plan will be significantly changed or withdrawn.

Assuming that the conditions are met, which seems likely given that the board approved the sale in March 20X5 and that potential purchasers have already expressed an interest, the assets held in the disposal group should be reclassified as assets held for sale and measured at the lower of carrying amount and fair value less costs to sell. The assets should not be depreciated after reclassification. IFRS 5 also requires that immediately prior to classifying an asset or disposal group as held for sale, impairment is measured and recognised in accordance with the applicable IFRS Standards, which in this case would be IAS 16 *Property, Plant and Equipment* and IAS 36 *Impairment of Assets.*

Several audit risks arise as a result of the disposal. First there is a risk that the assets are not treated as a disposal group for the purpose of IFRS 5 and have continued to be depreciated. Assets are possibly overvalued if an impairment review has not been performed or assets not measured at the lower of carrying amount and fair value less costs to sell. The fact that Primal Burgers Ltd's revenue is projected to fall by 3.9% indicates that impairment of assets could be an issue, increasing the risk of misstatement.

There is also a risk relating to disclosure, as assets and liabilities held for sale should be recognised separately from other assets and liabilities in the statement of financial position, and if they have not been appropriately reclassified, then non-current assets and liabilities will be overstated.

There is also an audit risk that Primal Burgers Ltd is not treated as a discontinued operation in accordance with IFRS 5. A discontinued operation is defined as a component of an entity which either has been disposed of or is classified as held for sale, and it represents a separate major line of business or a geographical area of operations and is part of a single co-ordinated plan to dispose of a separate major line of business or geographical area of operations. Given the materiality of Primal Burgers Ltd and its products being a separate line of business for the Group, it meets the definition of a discontinued operation. In accordance with IFRS 5, the post-tax profit or loss of the discontinued operation and the post-tax gain or loss recognised on the measurement to fair value less cost to sell or on the disposal of the disposal group should be presented as a single amount on the face of the statement of comprehensive income. In addition, detailed disclosure of revenue, expenses, pre-tax profit or loss and related income taxes is required either in the notes or in the statement of comprehensive income in a section distinct from continuing operations. The risk is that the necessary disclosures are not made, leading to incorrect presentation of Group profit or loss and incomplete information in the notes to the Group financial statements.

Disposal of Primal Burgers Ltd – potential for manipulation

A further audit risk relating to the disposal of Primal Burgers Ltd is that the results of the subsidiary could be manipulated to make it look more favourable to any potential purchaser. The financial information indicates that this subsidiary's revenue has declined and therefore it could be that management attempts to manipulate the financial statements to present a healthier financial performance to potential buyers. For example, costs could be suppressed or shifted to other Group companies to maintain the profit of Primal Burgers Ltd and make it more attractive to purchasers.

> **Tutorial note.** Credit will be awarded for the evaluation of other relevant audit risks relating to the disposal, for example, in relation to the presentation of information in the Group statement of cash flows.

Investment in Peppers Ltd

The Group will be investing £48 million in Peppers Ltd; this represents 10.1% of projected Group assets and therefore is material to the Group financial statements. From the information provided, it seems that the investment is a joint venture, with control of Peppers

Ltd shared between the Group and Smiths Ltd. IFRS 11 *Joint Arrangements* defines a joint venture as a joint arrangement whereby the parties who have joint control of the arrangement have rights to the net assets of the arrangement. IFRS 11 requires that a joint venturer recognises its interest in a joint venture as an investment and shall account for that investment using the equity method in accordance with IAS 28 *Investments in Associates and Joint Ventures*. Audit risk arises if the Group fails to apply equity accounting to the investment, which may lead to an under or overstated value of investment and incorrect presentation of income and expenses relating to the joint venture in the Group statement of profit or loss.

Mondays Coffee drive-through – capital expenditure

During the year, there has been significant capital expenditure relating to 50 new drive-through coffee shops. The total amount capitalised is £43 million, of which £15 million relates to acquiring operating licences. The audit risk relates to the classification of the licences within property, plant and equipment, they should instead be recognised as intangible assets. This error is material, with the £15 million cost of the licences representing 3.2% of projected Group assets. If the error is uncorrected, property, plant and equipment is overstated and intangible assets are understated.

A consequence of the misclassification is that the £15 million should be amortised over its specific useful life of three years, so assuming that a full year's worth of amortisation should have been expensed, this amounts to £5 million. Currently, the amount has been treated as property, plant and equipment and depreciated over a 20-year life, so £0.75 million has been expensed. Therefore expenses are understated by £4.25 million. This is material, representing 21.3% of Group profit before tax. There is therefore an audit risk that Group profit is significantly overstated.

Tutorial note. Credit will be awarded for the evaluation of other relevant audit risks, for example, including the risk that revenue and capital expenditure incurred in establishing the coffee shops is not appropriately recognised, and that a 20-year estimated life appears long given the nature and usage of the assets involved.

Mondays Coffee drive-through – reportable operating segment

According to the Group finance director, revenue from the new drive-through coffee shops accounts for almost all of the increase in revenue from Mondays Coffee Ltd. The financial information shows that Mondays Coffee Ltd revenue is projected to increase by £45 million this year. Total Group revenue is projected to be £320 million; £45 million is 14.1% of this total.

The revenue from the drive-through coffee shops could be a reportable operating segment under IFRS 8 *Operating Segments*. An operating segment is a component of an entity:

- Which engages in business activities from which it may earn revenues and incur expenses,
- Whose operating results are reviewed regularly by the entity's chief operating decision maker to make decisions about resources to be allocated to the segment and assess its performance, and
- For which discrete financial information is available.

IFRS 8 requires an entity to report financial and descriptive information about its reportable segments. Reportable segments are operating segments or aggregations of operating segments which meet specified criteria, including that its reported revenue is 10% or more of the combined revenue of all operating segments.

It seems that the drive-through coffee shops should be treated as a reportable segment given that discrete information is available through the Group's management information system, the results are reviewed, and it generates more than 10% of Group revenue. The audit risk is that disclosure is not provided at all in relation to this reportable segment, or that disclosure is incomplete in the final version of the financial statements.

> **Tutorial note.** Credit will also be awarded for evaluation of the significance of the increase in revenue from the new drive-through coffee shops, and whether this could indicate overstatement of revenue. Other relevant audit risks will be credited, for example, relating to possible system changes introduced to incorporate the drive-through coffee shops in the financial reporting system.

Government grant

The Group received a government grant of £20 million, representing 4.2% of projected Group assets and therefore material to the Group statement of financial position. In addition, if the £20 million grant receipt had not been recognised in full as income this financial year, the projected Group profit before tax would be £0. The recognition as income is therefore extremely significant to the Group financial statements.

The grant should be accounted for in accordance with IAS 20 *Accounting for Government Grants and Disclosure of Government Assistance* which requires government grants to be recognised in profit or loss on a systematic basis over the periods in which the entity recognises as expenses the related costs for which the grants are intended to compensate.

The two parts of the grant should be accounted for separately. The amount relating to capital expenditure should be deferred on the statement of financial position and assuming that the grant will be used to upgrade items of property, plant and equipment, the grant should then be recognised in profit or loss over the periods in which depreciation expense on the assets to which it relates is recognised. The part of the grant relating to promotional activity should be recognised in profit or loss in the same period as the relevant expenses – which may be this year, or could be the next financial year, depending on when the expenses relating to the advertising campaign are incurred.

It is likely that if funds are not used in the manner intended by the government, ie that half of it is used to make the assets more environmentally friendly, then some or all of the grant would be repayable. This would mean that a provision or contingent liability should be recognised, and there is an audit risk that liabilities are understated if any amount probable to be repaid is not accounted for as a provision, or that insufficient disclosure is made in the note to the financial statements if a contingent liability arises.

Therefore the audit risk is that Group profit is overstated by a maximum amount of £20 million, and liabilities understated by the same amount. The accounting treatment could be a deliberate attempt to enhance the appearance of the Group profit for the year, and this issue should be approached with a high degree of professional scepticism during the audit.

Audit committee lack of financial reporting expert

Since January 20X5, the Group audit committee does not have a financial reporting expert. It is a provision of the UK *Corporate Governance Code* that the board should satisfy itself that at least one member of the audit committee has recent and relevant financial experience and that the committee as a whole shall have competence relevant to the sector in which the Group operates. The Group is in breach of this principle, as there has not been a financial reporting expert member of the audit committee for a significant period during the financial year, and this represents a control risk. One of the roles of the audit committee is to monitor the integrity of the financial statements of the Group and, in particular, to review significant financial reporting judgements contained in them. Without a financial reporting expert on the audit committee to provide this oversight, there is a risk that inappropriate judgements are made and a higher risk that errors or deliberate manipulation of the financial statements are not addressed.

(b) **Additional information required to plan the audit of the disposal of Primal Burgers Ltd**

- The individual financial statements of Primal Burgers Ltd, to ascertain the detail of the amounts recognised – this will assist the audit team in planning to audit the compliance with measurement and disclosure requirements of IFRS 5 and to confirm materiality of the balances involved.

- A copy of the vendor's due diligence report produced by Usami & Co, to ascertain key findings, eg valuations of assets and liabilities; this will help in planning to audit the measurement of the disposal group and whether any impairment should be recognised.
- Further information surrounding the reasons for disposal, from the Group board minutes at which approval was given for the disposal, to enable the auditor to develop an understanding of management's rationale and how the disposal fits in with the Group restructuring as a whole.
- Information regarding the potential acquirers of Primal Burgers Ltd and the stage of negotiations, this will help the audit team develop an expectation as to whether the disposal is likely to take place after the year end and the potential sales price.
- Any preliminary determination by management of the anticipated profit or loss on disposal and expectation of any impairment to the value of assets held in the disposal group.
- Obtain a copy of management's assessment/workings of the impact on the Group's financial position on the sale of Primal Burgers Ltd and the overall impact of the restructure of the Group.

(c) **Principal audit procedures in respect of the classification of the investment in Peppers Ltd**

- Obtain the legal documentation supporting the investment and agree the details of the investment including:
  - The date of the investment
  - Amount paid
  - Number of shares purchased
  - The voting rights attached to the shares
  - The nature of the profit-sharing arrangement between the Group and Smiths Ltd
  - The nature of access to Peppers Ltd's assets under the terms of the agreement
  - Confirmation that there is no restriction of the Group's shared control of Peppers Ltd
- Review board minutes to confirm the approval of the investment and to understand the business rationale for the investment.
- Review minutes of relevant meetings between the Group and Smiths Ltd to confirm that control is shared between the two investors and to understand the nature of the relationship and the decision-making process.
- Obtain documentation such as Peppers Ltd's organisational structure to confirm that the Group has successfully appointed members to the board of the company and that those members have equal power to the members appointed by Smiths Ltd.

Principal audit procedures in respect of the government grant received

- Obtain the documentation relating to the grant and review to obtain an understanding of:
  - The terms of the grant including the amount received, and in particular requirements relating to the specific use of the funds
  - The date by which the funds must be used
  - Any clauses relating to repayment of some or all of the grant should certain conditions arise.
- Agree the amount received to bank statements and Ryder plc's cash book.
- Obtain and review the Group's capital expenditure forecast to confirm the amount planned to be spent on capital expenditure relating to environmental matters.
- Discuss the use of the grant to fund an advertising campaign with an appropriate person, eg Group marketing director, and review any plans to use the funds for promotional purposes to confirm that recycling features in the campaign, as intended by the government.

- Confirm, through agreement to marketing plans, whether any funds will be spent during this financial year.
- Obtain a written representation from management that the grant received will be used for the specific purposes required by the government.

(d) **Ethical issues**

Partner to serve on audit committee

The Group audit committee has requested that a senior partner from Squire & Co could assume a role on the Group audit committee while a replacement for the financial reporting expert committee member is being sought. Should a partner from Squire & Co take this appointment, a self-review threat to objectivity arises because an audit committee member is in a position to exert influence over the financial statements, and the audit team would be less likely to challenge issues during the audit, thereby losing their professional scepticism. A self-interest threat also arises because the audit firm's interests become closely aligned to the interests of the Group, impacting on auditor objectivity.

> **Tutorial note.** Credit will also be awarded for discussion of other relevant threats to objectivity including the familiarity threat, and threat of assuming management responsibility.

For these reasons, the FRC *Ethical Standard (Ethical Standard)* prohibits an audit partner from being appointed as a member of a client's audit committee. Therefore, Squire & Co cannot provide a senior partner, or any other member of staff, to serve on the Group's audit committee.

It is concerning that the Group audit committee considers it appropriate to invite Squire & Co to supply a senior partner to serve on the audit committee and to perform the work on internal controls. A provision of the UK *Corporate Governance Code* states that one of the roles and responsibilities of an audit committee is to develop and implement policy on the engagement of the external auditor to supply non-audit services. This involves ensuring there is prior approval of non-audit services, considering the impact this may have on independence, taking into account the relevant regulations and ethical guidance in this regard. The Group audit committee appears either to not be aware of the ethical issues caused by their requests, or to be ignoring them.

Referral fee

The Group audit committee understands that Squire & Co cannot provide a corporate finance service, but could recommend another firm, Ranger Associates, for this work, for which the firm would earn a referral fee. A self-interest threat to objectivity and to professional competence and due care may arise. The self-interest threat arises from the income generated from the referral, and this may result in the audit firm recommending another firm for the work without proper consideration of their competence to perform the engagement.

The ACCA *Code of Ethics and Conduct* does not prohibit referral fees, but the significance of the threats should be evaluated and safeguards applied to reduce the threats to an acceptable level. Safeguards may include:

- Disclosing to the Group in writing the arrangement for a referral fee to be received from Ranger Associates, and
- Obtaining advance agreement from the Group that the arrangement is acceptable.

Therefore the matter should be discussed again with the Group audit committee, and if the committee confirms agreement with the proposed referral fee, Squire & Co can recommend Ranger Associates to perform the corporate finance work for the Group.

Internal audit

A further threat to the auditor's objectivity arises from the audit committee's request for Squire & Co to work with the Group internal audit team to design and evaluate internal controls relating to revenue. The FRC *Ethical Standard* states that an audit firm may not also provide an internal audit service to an audit client. This is because the nature and extent of the threats to the audit firm's independence when undertaking internal audit services will vary depending on the nature of the services provided. Providing an audit client with an internal audit service might create self-review and management threats to integrity, objectivity and independence.

The *Ethical Standard* does, however, note that the audit team may provide management with comments regarding the effectiveness of controls, and that this is ethically acceptable where it is a by-product of the audit.

On this basis, Squire & Co should politely decline the request made by the audit committee. Reinforcing the point made above, it seems that the audit committee is not aware, or is choosing to ignore the ethical issues raised, and their responsibilities under the UK *Corporate Governance Code* by asking Squire & Co to perform this work.

Conclusion

These briefing notes indicate that there is a range of audit risks to be considered in planning the forthcoming Group audit, many of the more significant and high-priority risks relate to the Group's plans to restructure. The notes contain recommended audit procedures which have been designed in relation to two material audit issues, and finally three ethical issues have been identified and evaluated. Our firm should not provide internal audit assistance to the Group, nor allow a partner to serve on the Group audit committee. However, a referral fee from Ranger Associates is acceptable, provided the Group agrees to the arrangement.

33 Sunshine

Workbook references

Chapters 2, 6, 7, 8 and 9.

Top tips

This question tested both business risks and risks of material misstatement (RoMM), which made it slightly unusual as AAA questions tend not to focus on business risk. It is clearly important that you keep the two separate. One approach might have been to mark each risk you notice as either a business risk or a RoMM, so that you can then return to them when writing your answers for parts (a) and (b) respectively.

The first part on evaluating significant business risks, required you to think a bit differently from usual, and to be critical of the company's actions. As ever, almost everything in the scenario can be seen as either a business risk or an audit risk, even if it doesn't appear to be at first sight. For instance, the significant expenditure on marketing the Group's brand gives rise to a business risk of the brand being damaged – for example by the pressure group's charge that the Group is damaging the environment.

The second part was more familiar territory. A number of key risks should have stood out, eg revenue recognition, the effect of the hurricane, and the potential provision. Your discussion of each risk should focus on the three elements for which marks are awarded: the accounting treatment, the RoMM itself, and materiality. Calculating and judging materiality is probably the easiest part of this, but the marks for the RoMM can be easy too – once you have the correct accounting treatment, you need to say whether there is a risk of under-/over statement of a particular figure.

The third part of the question focused on the potential provision. There was an attempt to limit the scope of the audit, which you should be able to perceive and denounce (politely). Part of the question asked for procedures, and as with all requirements of this type it was important to be specific and to state **why** each procedure should be performed.

The final part covered ethics. Tax planning is an important area in the real world, so you should understand and be able to apply the ethical requirements in this area.

Easy marks

Make sure you get at least six of the professional marks. The marks for calculating materiality – and stating whether the issue is material – are easy.

Marking guide	Marks
(a) **Significant business risk evaluation**	
Generally up to 1.5 marks for each business risk evaluated, in addition allow 0.5 mark for each relevant calculation, eg profit margin:	
• Luxury product – sensitive to changes in consumer's disposable income	
• Rapid expansion and inappropriate business strategy	
• Financial implications of business expansion including impact on gearing, interest cover and cash flows	
• Profit margins and cash flows	
• International operations	
• Catering operations	
• Hurricanes	
• Claim relating to environmental damage – reputational issue, loss of customers	
Maximum	11

(b) **Significant risks of material misstatement**

- Revenue recognition
- Cash/foreign exchange
- Licence agreement
- Impairment of property, plant and equipment – political instability and regulatory issues
- Gain on disposal of property
- Impairment of assets – effect of hurricane
- Provision/contingent liability regarding legal claim
- Repairs to properties damaged by hurricane

Maximum 12

(c) (i) **Implications for audit planning**

Up to 1.5 marks for each point of discussion/appropriate action:

- Limitation in scope imposed by finance director, not in accordance with agreeing the terms of an audit engagement
- Discuss with audit committee, who should intervene to remove the limitation
- Finance director lacks integrity, increase application of professional scepticism and increased audit risk
- Consider required response when an instance of non-compliance is suspected and the reporting responsibilities of the auditor

Maximum 5

(ii) **Audit procedures**

Up to 1 mark for each well described audit procedure:

- Obtain the letter received from Ocean Protection, review to understand the basis of the claim
- Discuss the issue with the Group's legal adviser, to understand whether in their opinion, the Group could be liable for the damages
- Discuss with legal advisers to obtain understanding of the remit and scope of the legislation in relation to environmental protection
- Discuss with management the procedures which the Group utilises to ensure that it is identifying and ensuring compliance with relevant legislation
- Obtain an understanding, through enquiry with relevant employees, such as those responsible for scuba diving and other water sports, as to the nature of activities which take place
- Obtain and read all correspondence between the Group and Ocean Protection up to the date that the auditor's report is issued
- Obtain a written representation from management
- Discuss the issue with those charged with governance
- Review the disclosures, if any, provided in the notes to the financial statements
- Read the other information published with the financial statements for consistency with the financial statements

Maximum 5

(d) **Ethics of tax engagement**

Generally up to 1.5 marks for each well explained matter and 1 mark for each well explained and relevant action:

- Issue may only relate to next year's audit

- Self-review threat
- Factors affecting severity of threat
- Clarification of type of advice needed
- Audit firm's competence
- Safeguards
- Cannot use existing knowledge

Maximum	7

Professional marks

Communication

- Briefing note format and structure - use of headings/sub-headings and an introduction
- Style, language and clarity - appropriate layout and tone of briefing notes, presentation of materiality and relevant calculations, appropriate use of the CBE tools, easy to follow and understand
- Effectiveness and clarity of communication - answer is relevant and tailored to the scenario
- Adherence to the specific requests made by the audit engagement partner

Analysis and Evaluation

- Appropriate use of the information to determine and apply suitable calculations
- Appropriate use of the information relating to the legal claim of £10m to design appropriate audit procedures
- Effective prioritisation of the results of the audit risk evaluation to demonstrate the likelihood and magnitude of risks and to facilitate the allocation of appropriate responses
- Balanced discussion of the issues connected to the auditor's responsibilities in relation to ethical decisions when considering non-assurance engagements for an audit client.

Professional scepticism and professional judgement

- Appropriate application of professional judgement to draw conclusions and make informed decisions following recognition of unusual or unexpected movements, missing/incomplete information or challenging presented information as part of the risk evaluation
- Determination and justification of a suitable materiality level, appropriately and consistently applied
- Identification of possible management bias and consideration of the impact on the financial statements and the possible reasons for management's preference for certain accounting treatments
- Effective application of technical and ethical guidance to effectively challenge and critically assess how management has responded to the legal claim

Commercial acumen

- Use of effective examples and/or calculations from the scenario to illustrate points or recommendations
- Appropriate use of the industry information to evaluate business risks
- Recognition of the increased risks to the future competitiveness of the company given the information provided in the scenario

Maximum	10
Total	50

Briefing notes

To: John Starling, audit engagement partner

From: Audit manager

Subject: Sunshine Hotel Group – audit planning

Introduction

These briefing notes relate to the initial audit planning for the Sunshine Hotel Group (the Group), for the year ending 31 December 20X7. As requested, the notes contain an evaluation of the significant business risks facing our client, and the significant risks of material misstatement to be considered in our audit planning. Finally, the notes contain a discussion of the impact which an email received from the Group finance director relating to a claim for damages will have on our audit planning, as well as the recommended actions to be taken by Dove & Co and principal procedures which should be carried out in relation to this claim.

(a) **Evaluation of significant business risks**

Luxury product

The Group offers a luxury product aimed at an exclusive market. This in itself creates a business risk, as the Group's activities are not diversified, and any decline in demand will immediately impact on profitability and cash flows. The demand for luxury holidays will be sensitive to economic problems such as recession and travel to international destinations will be affected by events in the transportation industry, for example, if oil prices increase, there will be a knock-on effect on air fares, meaning less demand for the Group's hotels.

Business expansion – inappropriate strategy

It is questionable whether the Group has a sound policy on expansion, given the problems encountered with recent acquisitions which have involved expanding into locations with political instability and local regulations which seem incompatible with the Group's operations and strategic goals. The Group would appear to have invested £98 million, accounting for 28% of the Group's total assets, in these unsuitable locations, and it is doubtful whether an appropriate return on these investments will be possible. There is a risk that further unsuitable investments will be made as a result of poor strategic decisions on where to locate new hotels. The Group appears to have a strategy of fairly rapid expansion, acquiring new sites and a hotel complex without properly investigating their appropriateness and fit with the Group's business model. The intention to obtain tax planning advice in relation to the next planned investment may be a step in the right direction, but the existence of further plans for expansion may be too much too soon for the Group.

Business expansion – finance

The Group is planning further expansion with capital expenditure of £45 million planned for new sites in 20X8. This equates to 12.9% of the Group's total assets, which is a significant amount and will be financed by a bank loan. While the Group's gearing is currently low at 25%, the additional finance being taken out from the Group's lending facility will increase gearing and incur additional interest charges of £1.6 million per year, which is 16% of the projected profit before tax for the year. The increased debt and finance charges could impact on existing loan covenants and the additional interest payments will have cash flow as well as profit implications.

In addition, £5 million has been spent on the Moulin Blanche agreement. A further £25 million is needed for renovating the hotels which were damaged following a hurricane. Despite the fact that the repair work following the hurricane will ultimately be covered by insurance, the Group's capital expenditure at this time appears very high and needs to be underpinned by sound financial planning in order to maintain solvency, especially given that only half of the insurance claim in relation to repair work will be paid in advance and it may take some time to recover the full amount given the significant sums involved.

Customer illness

Customers being taken ill as a result of eating poor quality food in some hotel restaurants has exposed the Group to some bad publicity. However, this does appear to have been limited to a small local newspaper report, so this is unlikely to have a significant effect on the performance of the new Moulin Blanche brand.

There is a risk that legal claims could be made against the Group, and that more significant bad publicity could arise from these. Such claim may be difficult to prove, however, and are unlikely to be financially significant to the Group.

Profit margins and cash management

The nature of the business means that overheads will be high and profit margins likely to be low. Based on the projected profit before tax, the projected margin for 20X7 is 8%, and for 20X6 was 8.2%. Annual expenses on marketing and advertising are high, and given the focus on luxury, a lot will need to be spent on maintenance of the hotels, purchasing quality food and drink, and training staff to provide high levels of customer service. Offering all-inclusive holidays will also have implications for profit margins and for managing working capital as services, as well as food and drink, will have to be available whether guests use or consume them or not. The Group will need to maintain a high rate of room occupancy in order to maintain cash flows and profit margins. Cash management might be particularly problematic given that the majority of cash is received on departure, rather than when the guests book their stay. Refunds to customers following the recent hurricane will also impact on cash flows, as will the repairs needed to the damaged hotels.

International operations

The Group's international operations expose it to a number of risks. One which has already been mentioned relates to local regulations; with any international operation there is risk of non-compliance with local laws and regulations which could affect business operations. Additionally, political and economic instability introduces possible unpredictability into operations, making it difficult to plan and budget for the Group's activities, as seen with the recent investment in a politically unstable area which is not yet generating a return for the Group. There are also foreign exchange issues, which unless properly managed, for example, by using currency derivatives, can introduce volatility to profit and cash flows.

Catering operations

The Group has introduced improved technologies into its in-house catering operations. This appears to have brought efficiency savings, but there may be risks associated with such a change, eg it is possible that the quality of the catering will not be maintained, or that there could be difficulties around managing the associated organisational changes.

Hurricanes

The hurricane guarantee scheme exposes the Group to unforeseeable costs in the event of a hurricane disrupting operations. The costs of moving guests to another hotel could be high, as could be the costs of refunding customer deposits if they choose to cancel their booking rather than transfer to a different hotel. The cost of renovation in the case of hotels being damaged by hurricane is also high, and while this is covered by insurance, the Group will still need to fund the repair work before the full amount claimed on insurance is received which as discussed above will put significant pressure on the Group's cash flow. In addition, having two hotels which have been damaged by hurricanes closed for several months while repair work is carried out will result in lost revenue and cash inflows.

Claim relating to environmental damage

This is potentially a very serious matter, should it become public knowledge. The reputational damage could be significant, especially given that the Group markets itself as a luxury brand. Consumers are likely to react unfavourably to the allegations that the Group's activities are harming the environment; this could result in cancellation of existing bookings and lower demand in the future, impacting on revenue and cash flows. The email relating to the claim from Ocean Protection refers to international legislation and therefore this issue could impact in all of the countries in which the Group operates. The Group is hoping to negotiate with Ocean Protection to reduce the amount that is potentially payable and minimise media attention, but this may not be successful, Ocean Protection may not be willing to keep the issue out of the public eye or to settle for a smaller monetary amount.

(b) **Significant risks of material misstatement**

Revenue recognition

The Group's revenue could be over- or understated due to timing issues relating to the recognition of revenue. Customers pay 40% of the cost of their holiday in advance, and the Group has to refund any bookings which are cancelled a week or more before a guest is due to stay at a hotel. There is a risk that revenue is recognised when deposits are received, which would be against the requirements of IFRS 15 *Revenue from Contracts with Customers*, which states that revenue should be recognised when, or as, an entity satisfies a performance obligation. Therefore, the deposits should be recognised within current liabilities as deferred revenue until a week prior to a guest's stay, when they become non-refundable. There is the risk that revenue is overstated and deferred revenue and therefore current liabilities are understated if revenue is recognised in advance of the date the amount becomes non-refundable.

> **Tutorial note.** Credit will be awarded for discussion of further risk of misstatement relating to revenue recognition – for example, when the Group satisfies its performance obligations and whether the goods and services provided to hotel guests are separate revenue streams.

Foreign exchange

The Group holds £20 million in cash at the year end, most of which is held in foreign currencies. This represents 5.7% of Group assets, thus cash is material to the financial statements.

According to IAS 21 *The Effects of Changes in Foreign Exchange Rates*, at the reporting date foreign currency monetary amounts should be reported using the closing exchange rate, and the exchange difference should be reported as part of profit or loss. There is a risk that the cash holdings are not retranslated using an appropriate year-end exchange rate, causing assets and profit to be over- or understated.

Licence agreement

The cost of the agreement with Moulin Blanche is 1.4% of Group assets, and 50% of profit for the year. It is highly material to profit and is borderline in terms of materiality to the statement of financial position.

The agreement appears to be a licensing arrangement, and as such it should be recognised in accordance with IAS 38 *Intangible Assets*, which requires initial recognition at cost and subsequent amortisation over the life of the asset, if the life is finite. The current accounting treatment appears to be incorrect, because the cost has been treated as a marketing expense, leading to understatement of non-current assets and understatement of profit for the year by a significant amount. If the financial statements are not adjusted, they will contain a material misstatement, with implications for the auditor's report. As the restaurants were opened on 1 July 20X7, six months after the licence was agreed, it would seem appropriate to amortise the asset over the remaining term of the agreement of 9.5 years as this is the timeframe over which the licence will generate economic benefit. The annual amortisation expense would be £526,316, so if six months is recognised in this financial year, £263,158 should be charged to operating expenses, resulting in profit being closer to £14.74 million for the year.

It is possible that the incident in which a newspaper reported that some customers were taken sick as a result of eating in Moulin Blanche restaurants could have an effect on the brand's performance. The brand should be tested for impairment in line with IAS 36 *Impairment of Assets*.

Impairment of non-current assets due to political instability and regulatory issues

The sites acquired at a cost of £75 million represent 21.4% of total assets, and the hotel complex acquired at a cost of £23 million represents 6.6% of total assets; these assets are material to the Group financial statements.

There are risks associated with the measurement of the assets, which are recognised as property, plant and equipment, as the assets could be impaired. None of these assets is currently being used by the Group in line with their principal activities, and there are indications that their recoverable value may be less than their cost. Due to the political instability and the regulatory issues, it seems that the assets may never generate the value in use that was anticipated, and their fair value may also have fallen below cost. Therefore, in accordance with IAS 36 *Impairment of Assets*, management should conduct an impairment review, to determine the recoverable amount of the assets and whether any impairment loss should be recognised. The risk is that assets are overstated, and profit overstated, if any necessary impairment of assets is not recognised at the end of the reporting period.

Property sale

The gain on disposal is £1.3m (= £5.5m – £4.2m), which is 13% of profit before tax (= £1.3m / £10m). This is material to the statement of profit or loss.

The gain should not be included in revenue but should be disclosed separately in the statement of profit or loss. There is a risk that revenue will be overstated if the financial statements include this gain within revenue. This classification misstatement is material, as the gain on disposal is just over 1% of the revenue figure in which it has been included (= £1.3m / £125m).

The revaluation gain is also material at 17% of profit before tax (= £1.7m / £10m). This gain should not be credited against operating charges in the statement of profit or loss. This amount should originally have been recognised in other comprehensive income and then held within other components of equity; it should now be transferred to retained earnings.

The sale should only be recognised in the year if the contract to sell is binding. There is a risk of the sale being recognised incorrectly if this is not the case.

If the contract is not binding before the year end but is completed before the auditor's report is eventually signed, then it will be a non-adjusting event after the end of the reporting period requiring disclosure in the financial statements.

If the contract is binding but not completed at the year end, there will be a material receivable of £5.5m (1.5% of total assets).

As the asset that has been sold is a revalued asset, all the assets in the same class will also be revalued as required by IAS 16: para. 36.

IAS 16 requires that revalued assets are revalued with sufficient regularity that the carrying amount does not differ materially from that which would be determined using fair value at the date of the statement of financial position (IAS 16: para. 31). The valuation on the sold building appeared to be out of date, as it sold at 31% above the valuation, which is material. It will therefore be necessary to ensure that the valuations on the other buildings are correct, particularly if the increase in capacity has increased their value.

Effect of the hurricane

Two of the Group's hotels are closed due to extensive damage caused by a recent hurricane. It is anticipated that the Group's insurance policy will cover the damage of £25 million and the terms of the policy are that half will be paid in advance and the remainder on completion of the repairs, although this will need confirming during our audit testing. The accounting for these events will need to be carefully considered as there is a risk that assets and profit are overstated if the damage and subsequent claim have not been accounted for correctly.

The damage caused to the hotels and resultant loss of revenue are likely to represent an indicator of impairment which should be recorded in line with IAS 36. IAS 16 *Property, Plant and Equipment* requires the impairment and derecognition of PPE and any subsequent compensation claims to be treated as separate economic events and accounted for separately in the period they occur. The standard specifically states that it is not appropriate to net the events off and not record an impairment loss because there is an insurance claim in relation to the same assets. As such, this may mean that the Group has to account for the impairment loss in the current year but cannot recognise the compensation claim until the next financial reporting period as this can only be recognised when the compensation becomes receivable. If it is indeed the case that the insurance company will pay half of the claim in advance, then it is likely that £12.5m could be included in profit or loss in the current year.

Provision/contingent liability

The letter received from Ocean Protection indicates that it may be necessary to recognise a provision or disclose a contingent liability, in respect of the £10 million damages which have been claimed. The amount is material at 2.9% of total assets, and 67.9% of profit before tax (adjusted for the incorrect accounting treatment of the licence agreement).

According to IAS 37 *Provisions, Contingent Liabilities and Contingent Assets*, a provision should be recognised if there is a present obligation as a result of a past event, and that there is a probable outflow of future economic benefits for which a reliable estimate can be made.

It remains to be seen as to whether the Group can be held liable for the damage to the coral reefs. However, the finance director seems to be implying that the Group would like to reach a settlement, in which case a provision should be recognised.

A provision could therefore be necessary, but this depends on the negotiations between the Group and Ocean Protection, the outcome of which can only be confirmed following further investigation by the audit team during the final audit.

A contingent liability arises where there is either a possible obligation depending on whether some uncertain future event occurs, or a present obligation but payment is not probable or the amount cannot be measured reliably. There is a risk that adequate disclosure is not provided in the notes to the financial statements, especially given the finance director's reluctance to draw attention to the matter.

Conclusions regarding significant risks of material misstatement

It would seem that the priority areas of concern for our audit will be revenue recognition and the accounting treatment for the licence agreement, although should the hurricane damage have broader impacts on the business than initially thought, our audit approach would also need to prioritise this as well.

> **Tutorial note.** Credit would also be awarded for discussion of other relevant risks of material misstatement.

(c) (i) **Environmental claim – implications for audit planning**

The finance director's requests which restrict the audit team's ability to obtain audit evidence in relation to the environmental damage claim are inappropriate. In particular, the finance director should not dictate to the audit engagement partner that the audit team may not speak to Group employees. According to ISA (UK) 210 *Agreeing the Terms of Audit Engagements*, the management of a client should acknowledge their responsibility to provide the auditor with access to all information which is relevant to the preparation of the financial statements which includes unrestricted access to persons within the entity from whom the auditor determines it necessary to obtain audit evidence.

This would appear to be an imposed limitation on scope, and the audit engagement partner should raise this issue with the Group's audit committee. The audit committee should be involved at the planning stage to obtain comfort that a quality audit will be performed, in accordance with corporate governance best practice, and therefore the audit committee should be able to intervene with the finance director's demands and allow the audit team full access to the relevant information, including the ability to contact Ocean Protection and the Group's lawyers.

The finance director would appear to lack integrity as he is trying to keep the issue a secret, possibly from others within the Group as well as the public. The audit engagement partner should consider whether other representations made by the finance director should be treated with an added emphasis on professional scepticism, and the risk of management bias leading to a risk of material misstatement could be high. This should be discussed during the audit team briefing meeting.

There is also an issue arising in relation to ISA (UK) 250A *Consideration of Laws and Regulations in an Audit of Financial Statements*, which requires that if the auditor becomes aware of information concerning an instance of non-compliance or suspected non-compliance with laws and regulations (NOCLAR), the auditor shall obtain an understanding of the act and the circumstances in which it has occurred, and further information to evaluate the possible effect on the financial statements. Therefore, the audit plan should contain planned audit procedures which are sufficient for the audit team to conclude on the accounting treatment and on whether the auditor has any reporting responsibilities outside the Group, for example, to communicate a breach of international environmental protection legislation to the appropriate authorities.

(ii) **Planned audit procedures**

- Obtain the letter received from Ocean Protection and review to understand the basis of the claim, for example, to confirm if it refers to a specific incident when damage was caused to the coral reefs.
- Discuss the issue with the Group's legal adviser, to understand whether in their opinion, the Group could be liable for the damages, for example, to ascertain if there is any evidence that the damage to the coral reef was caused by activities of the Group or its customers.
- Discuss with the Group's legal adviser the remit and scope of the legislation in relation to environmental protection to ensure an appropriate level of understanding in relation to the regulatory framework within which the Group operates.
- Discuss with management and those charged with governance the procedures which the Group utilises to ensure that it is identifying and ensuring compliance with relevant legislation.
- Obtain an understanding, through enquiry with relevant employees, such as those responsible for scuba diving and other water sports, as to the nature of activities which take place, the locations and frequency of scuba diving trips, and the level of supervision which the Group provides to its guests involved in these activities.
- Obtain and read all correspondence between the Group and Ocean Protection, to track the progress of the legal claim up to the date that the auditor's report is issued, and to form an opinion on its treatment in the financial statements.
- Obtain a written representation from management, as required by ISA (UK) 250A, that all known instances of non-compliance, whether suspected or otherwise, have been made known to the auditor.
- Discuss the issue with those charged with governance, including discussion of whether the Group has taken any necessary steps to inform the relevant external authorities, if the Group has not complied with the international environmental protection legislation.
- Review the disclosures, if any, provided in the notes to the financial statements, to conclude as to whether the disclosure is sufficient for compliance with IAS 37.
- Read the other information published with the financial statements, including chairman's statement and directors' report, to assess whether any disclosure relating to the issue has been made, and if so, whether it is consistent with the financial statements.

(d) **Tax planning engagement**

The invitation to tender for a tax planning engagement raises several issues. It is not stated when the engagement would take place, but if it is after the current year's auditor's report has been signed then it should not pose a problem for this year. If this is not the case, however, or if we continue to serve as the Group's auditor next year, then the following considerations are relevant.

Tax planning services encompass a range of different services, from advising a client how to structure its affairs in a tax-efficient manner, to advising on the application of a new tax law (IESBA *Code of Ethics*: para. 604.11 A1). There is a self-review threat if the planning advice affects matters to be reflected in the financial statements.

The significance of the threat depends on factors such as:

- The degree of subjectivity involved, and whether advice is supported by existing law
- The extent to which the effect of any advice on the financial statements is material
- Whether the tax planning advice given will depend on a ruling or other decision taken by the tax authority

(IESBA *Code of Ethics*: para. 604.7 A3)

One factor that we are not able to comment on without further information is whether the Group is listed or not: should the Group be a listed entity, tax planning and advisory services shall not be provided by the firm if such services would create a self-review threat (IESBA *Code of Ethics*: para. R604.15).

Given that this appears to be the first time the Group has obtained tax planning advice, the advice it wants may be relatively basic in nature. Dove & Co should ask the Group for further information about the advice it needs; more complex advice may pose a greater threat than simpler advice.

The Group is planning to make another acquisition, but it is not known whether this would be material to the financial statements, or whether the effect of any advice would be material. This is, however, possible. For example, tax planning advice could determine whether an acquisition takes the form of acquiring an entity's assets and liabilities, or whether a new subsidiary is acquired. The latter would be more likely to be material.

Providing tax planning advice on an overseas acquisition may require knowledge of overseas tax legislation, which may fall outside of Dove & Co's competence. Before submitting any tender Dove & Co must find out where the acquisition is planned to take place so that it can determine whether it would be in a position to do the work.

Depending on these considerations and assuming the Group is not listed, it is likely that an engagement could only be accepted on the basis that safeguards could be applied to reduce the self-review threat to an acceptable level. Safeguards could include:

- Using separate teams to perform the tax service and the audit
- Having an independent tax professional advise the audit team on the service
- Obtaining clearance from HMRC

(IESBA *Code of Ethics*: para. 604.14 A1)

Alternatively, if the Group were listed, then it will not be possible to give tax planning advice, as such engagements are prohibited by the FRC *Ethical Standard*.

It has been suggested that Dove & Co would be able to make use of its existing knowledge of the Group. This is unlikely to be possible, as the tax engagement would be separate from the audit engagement.

Conclusion

These briefing notes highlight that the Group faces significant and varied business risk, in particular in relation to its expansion strategy which is possibly unsound. There are a number of significant risks of material misstatement which will need to be carefully considered during the planning of the Group audit, to ensure that an appropriate audit strategy is devised. Several issues are raised by the claim from Ocean Protection, and our audit programme should contain detailed and specific procedures to enable the audit team to form a conclusion on an appropriate accounting treatment. Finally, several matters should be clarified with the Group before tendering for a possible tax planning engagement.

34 Laurel

Workbook references

Chapters 4, 5, 6 and 8.

Top tips

This was a relatively straightforward Section A case study-style question, albeit one with a fairly numerical focus. When attempting long questions such as this, it is crucial that you stick to your timings for each question part – if you multiply the number of marks by two then you'll come close to the number of minutes available.

The first part asked for risks of material misstatement **and** analytical procedures. It is essential that you do calculate enough ratios if you are going to pass this question. There are five marks available for this, and they are easy marks that you should be banking on getting.

Although the model answer does not do this, it is a good idea to put your ratios in an appendix to your answer. This makes them easier to mark and allows you to run through your calculations before you identify risks. You should also ensure that you're calculating relevant ratios, such as those shown here.

The requirement asks you to use analytical procedures as a way of identifying risks. If you work in this way, then the question will actually be easier as this is the easiest way to discover some of the risks.

As you should be aware, question asking for 'risks of material misstatement' does not want detection risks, so these will get no marks. In addition, weaker candidates often spend time writing long theoretical discussions of how audit risk is made up. This is a nice early signal to the marker that they are likely to fail – so take heed and do not do this!

The next part as closely connected to the first. One way of approaching this would be to write down additional information needed as a separate part of your answer as you answer (a). Note that the model answer combines parts (a) and (b) to reinforce this message, although there was no requirement to present answers in this way and a separate section addressing this would have been equally acceptable.

The next part was a straightforward question part featuring issues that have come up on past exams and which should therefore have been familiar to you.

Part (d) was not difficult, and you could have made headway here using common sense alone.

Part (e) was difficult, but it was possible to pass this part of the question with some fairly generic remarks on the audit of financial instruments, mentioning things like the complexity of the accounting standards in this area and the difficulty in determining the correct treatment.

Easy marks

The marks for calculating ratios, and those for additional information, were among the easiest on the exam. The professional marks should not be missed.

Examining team's comments

This question presented the scenario of a large cosmetics group and candidates were presented with three requirements.

Part (a) required risks of material misstatement in the audit to be considered, including using analytical procedures, and a full statement of financial position and statement of profit or loss were provided. This was generally well answered as there were lots of potential risks to discuss. Candidates that did not score well often concentrated on explaining audit procedures rather than evaluating risks. Disappointingly, many candidates only calculated one or two ratios or trends even though the question asked for analytical procedures and contained a full page of numerical data to analyse. Candidates' inability to utilise all the information provided when evaluating risks continues to be an area of concern and continues to demonstrate that candidates must improve their exam technique in this regard.

Part (b) required candidates to highlight additional information to enable more detailed analytical review to be performed. Answers to this part were collectively disappointing with most candidates giving generic lists of additional items that may be required, such as board minutes or impairment reviews. These would be required as part of a wider audit plan but that was not what the question asked for. Very few candidates actually answered the question and highlighted what information was required for analytical review purposes, such as a breakdown of sales by product or market.

Part (c) was split into two sections, firstly the audit procedures related to the impairment of a brand. This was reasonably answered with some good procedures highlighted but many candidates erroneously digressed into seeking the original cost of the brand and discussing whether any claims were being made against the company which would have been better included in part (a).

In part (c)(ii) the audit procedures related to a planned acquisition and were generally well answered with sensible procedures such as reviewing the due diligence report, board minutes and discussions with management about the likelihood of success. Theorising about whether the acquisition would be a subsidiary or associate or suggesting audit procedures for the enlarged group did not answer the requirement.

There were **professional marks** available, including some communication marks. Candidates who presented their answers in a logical and reasoned manner with sub-headings and references scored well on these. Again candidates are advised to consider their exam technique in this area, for example only one concise paragraph is necessary as an introduction, not a whole page.

On requirement (e), answers here were extremely mixed in quality. Satisfactory answers focused on why financial instruments generally are difficult to audit, discussing their complex nature, the changing landscape of financial reporting requirements, the potential for both client and auditor to lack appropriate knowledge and skills, and the frequent need to rely on an expert.

Inadequate answers did not include much reference to audit at all, and simply listed out financial reporting rules, with no consideration of audit implications other than saying that financial instruments are complex and subjective. There were very few references to relevant ISA (UK) requirements, and little evidence that the audit of complex matters such as financial instruments had been studied at all, even though it is a topical current issue.

Marking guide **Marks**

(a) **Evaluation and prioritisation of significant risks of material misstatement**

Generally 1 mark for each ratio (including comparative) calculated, and 0.5 mark for relevant trends calculated, up to a maximum of 5 marks. In addition, up to 2 marks for discussion of risks in relation to the ratios calculated. Risks in relation to ratio analysis could include:

- Understatement of operating expenses excluding the impairment loss
- Understatement of finance costs
- Tax expense not in line with movement in deferred tax liability
- Overstatement of current assets/understatement of current liabilities
- Significant new loan liability to be taken on around the end of the reporting period – recognition, measurement and disclosure risks
- Unexplained/inconsistent movement in intangible assets/loan raised to finance development
- Unreconciled movement in retained earnings

Other risks of material misstatement – up to 2 marks for each risk identified and explained:

- Allow 1 mark for each correct calculation and comment on materiality up to a maximum of 2 marks
- New loan may breach existing loan covenants – risk that IFRS 7 disclosures not made
- Change to PPE useful lives may not be appropriate – overstated assets and profit
- Management bias risk due to new loan being taken out
- Impairment to Chico brand may be understated if full carrying value of brand not written off
- Impairment may need separate disclosure due to materiality – risk of inadequate disclosure
- Chico inventories will need to be written off – risk of overstated assets
- Risk that goodwill has not been tested for impairment
- A provision may be needed for customer claims – risk of understated liabilities
- Hire contracts appear to result in lease that has not been recognised

ANSWERS

- Deferred tax liability appears incorrect and likely to be overstated

Maximum 17

(b) **Additional information to assist with preliminary analytical review**

Generally up to 1 mark for each piece of information recommended:

- Disaggregation of revenue into major brands to identify significant trends by brand
- Monthly breakdown of revenue to assess date at which Chico products were withdrawn
- Disaggregation of operating expenses to determine main categories and inclusion of impairment expense
- Disaggregation of current assets to assess movements in inventories, receivables and cash
- Disaggregation of current liabilities to assess significant decrease
- Details of the £20m loan taken out to evaluate appropriateness of finance charge
- Details of the new £130m loan to build into projected gearing and other ratios
- Details of machine hire contracts to determine size of any assets not recognised
- Reconciliation of brought forward and carried forward intangible assets
- Statement of changes in equity

Maximum 5

(c) **Audit procedures**

Up to 1 mark for each well described procedure:

(i) **Impairment of brand name**

- Obtain management's calculations relevant to the impairment and review to understand methodology
- Evaluate the assumptions used by management in their impairment review and consider their reasonableness
- Confirm the carrying value of the Chico brand pre-impairment to prior year financial statements or management accounts
- From management accounts, obtain a breakdown of total revenue by brand, to evaluate the significance of the Chico brand
- If the brand is not fully written off, discuss with management the reasons for this treatment given that the brand is now discontinued
- Obtain a breakdown of operating expenses to confirm that the impairment is included
- Review the presentation of the income statement, considering whether separate disclosure of the impairment is necessary given its materiality

Maximum 4

(ii) **Acquisition of Azalea Co**

- Read board minutes to understand the rationale for the acquisition, and to see that the acquisition is approved
- Discuss with Group management the way that control will be exercised over Azalea Ltd, enquiring as to whether the Group can determine the board members of Azalea Co
- Review the minutes of relevant meetings held between management of the Group and Azalea Ltd to confirm matters such as:
- That the deal is likely to go ahead

- Obtain any due diligence reports which have been obtained by the Group and review for matters which may need to be disclosed in accordance with IAS 10 or IFRS 3The likely timescale
- The amount and nature of consideration to be paid
- The shareholding to be acquired and whether equity or non-equity shares
- The planned operational integration (if any) of Azalea Ltd into the Group
- After the reporting date, agree the cash consideration paid to bank records

Maximum	4

(d) **Matters re recurring audit**

Generally up to 1 mark for each point explained:

- Consider changes in circumstances
- Examples of changes in circumstances
- Bulldog's circumstances have not changed significantly
- No need to remind entity of terms

Maximum	3

(e) **Audit of financial instruments**

Generally up to 1.5 marks for each point explained:

Why is audit of financial instruments challenging?

- Financial reporting requirements complex
- Transactions themselves difficult to understand
- Lack of evidence and need to rely on management judgement
- Auditor may need to rely on expert
- May be hard to maintain attitude of scepticism
- Internal controls may be deficient

Planning implications

- Obtain understanding of accounting and disclosure requirements
- Obtain understanding of client's financial instruments
- Determine resources, ie skills needed and need for an auditor's expert
- Consider internal controls including internal audit
- Determine materiality of financial instruments
- Understand management's method for valuing financial instruments

Maximum	7

Professional skills marks

Communication

- Briefing notes format and structure - use of headings/sub-headings and an introduction
- Style, language and clarity - appropriate layout and tone of briefing notes, presentation of materiality and relevant calculations, appropriate use of the CBE tools, easy to follow and understand
- Effectiveness and clarity of communication - answer is relevant and tailored to the scenario
- Adherence to the specific requests made by the audit engagement partner

Analysis and evaluation

- Appropriate use of the information to determine suitable calculations

- Appropriate use of the information to support discussions and draw appropriate conclusions
- Assimilation of all relevant information to ensure that the risk evaluation performed considers the impact of contradictory or unusual movements
- Effective prioritisation of the results of the risk evaluation to demonstrate the likelihood and magnitude of risks and to facilitate the allocation of appropriate responses
- Balanced discussion of the information to objectively make a recommendation or decision

Professional scepticism and judgement

- Effective challenge of information supplied, and techniques carried out to support key facts and/or decisions
- Determination and justification of a suitable materiality level, appropriately and consistently applied
- Appropriate application of professional judgement to draw conclusions and make informed decisions about the courses of action which are appropriate in the context of the audit engagement

Commercial acumen

- Audit procedures are practical and plausible in the context of the Laurel Group.
- Use of effective examples and/or calculations from the scenario to illustrate points or recommendations.
- Recognition of the appropriate commercial considerations of the audit firm 10

Total 50

Briefing notes

To: Brigitte Sanders, audit engagement partner

From: Audit manager

Subject: Laurel Group audit planning Introduction

These briefing notes are intended for use in planning the audit of the Laurel Group (the Group). The notes contain an evaluation of risks of material misstatement, which have been identified using information provided by the client following a meeting with the Group finance director and performing selected analytical procedures. The notes also identify the additional information which should be requested from the Laurel Group to allow for a more detailed preliminary analytical review to be performed.

The notes also recommend the principal audit procedures to be performed in respect of an impaired brand and a planned acquisition which will take place after the reporting period.

I shall start by responding jointly to parts (a) and (b) of your email, linking the significant risks of material misstatement with any relevant additional information required.

(a) **Evaluation of risk of material misstatement**

(b) **Additional information to help in performing analytical review**

Selected analytical procedures and associated evaluation of risk of material misstatement

	20X5	20X4
Operating margin	35/220 × 100 = 15.9%	37/195 × 100 = 19%
Return on capital employed	(35/229 + 110) × 100 = 10.3%	(37/221 + 82) × 100 = 12.2%
Interest cover	35/7 = 5	37/7 = 5.3

	20X5	20X4
Effective tax rate	3/28 × 100 = 10.7%	3/30 × 100 = 10%
Current ratio	143/19 = 7.5	107/25 = 4.3
Gearing ratio	(100/100 + 229) × 100 = 30.4%	(80/80 +221) × 100 = 26.6%

Revenue is projected to increase by 12.8% in the year, whereas operating expenses increase by 17.1%, explaining the reduction in operating margin from 19% in 20X4 to 15.9% in 20X5. The trend in return on capital employed is consistent, with the return falling from 12.2% to 10.3%.

The notes from the meeting with the finance director state that an impairment loss of £30m has been recognised during the year. Assuming that this cost has been included in operating expenses, it would be expected that operating expenses should increase by at least £30m. However, operating expenses have increased by only £27m during the year. If the £30m impairment loss is excluded, it would seem that operating expenses have actually decreased by £3m, which is not in line with expectations given the substantial increase in revenue. There is therefore a risk that operating expenses are understated and consequently profit is overstated. Detailed audit procedures will need to be performed to investigate the possible omission of expenses from the statement of profit or loss.

Conversely, there is also the risk that revenue is overstated given the withdrawal of the Chico branded products, implying that revenue should decrease due to lost sales from this revenue stream.

To assist with the analytical review on operating profit, the following additional information should be obtained:

- A disaggregation of revenue to show the revenue associated with the key brands of the Group, in particular the level of sales and contribution from the withdrawn Chico brand.
- A breakdown of revenue month by month, to establish when sales of the Chico brand cease.
- A disaggregation of the main categories of expenses included in operating expenses, which would confirm that the impairment loss has been included.

The interest cover is stable and indeed the finance cost recognised is constant at £7m each year. Given that the Group took out a £20m loan in May 20X5, it would be expected that finance charges should increase to take account of interest accruing on the new element of the loan. There is therefore a risk that finance charges and the associated loan liability are understated.

Additional information to help the analytical review here would include:

- Details of the loan taken out, including a copy of the new loan agreement to establish the interest rate payable, repayment terms and whether any borrowing costs other than interest were incurred.

The Group's effective tax rate also appears stable, increasing from 10% to 10.7% in the year. However, given the significant movement in the deferred tax liability there should be a corresponding change in the tax expense, assuming that the additional deferred tax should be charged to profit or loss. Currently, it is unclear how this increase in the deferred tax liability has been recorded. The deferred tax liability itself creates a risk of material misstatement, which will be discussed separately, and the audit plan must contain detailed responses to ensure that sufficient and appropriate evidence is obtained in respect of both the current and deferred tax recognised.

The current ratio has increased sharply in the year from 4.3 to 7.5. This could indicate that current assets are overstated or current liabilities understated and the reasons for the significant change must be discussed with the client as part of audit planning, in order to identify any specific risks such as potential overstatement of inventory included in current assets, for example, if any Chico inventory is not yet written down in value.

Additional information to help with this analysis would be:

- A breakdown of current assets so the individual figures for inventories, receivables and cash (and any other current assets recognised in the statement of financial position) can be identified and trends established
- A breakdown of current liabilities to establish the reasons for the decrease of 24% on the prior year

Gearing has increased due to the £20m loan taken out. It is noted that the Group is going to take out another significant loan of £130m should the acquisition of Azalea Ltd go ahead as planned in early October. Recognition of this loan as a liability will result in the gearing ratio increasing significantly to 50.1% (230 / 230 + 229). Several risks arise in respect of this additional loan. First, the timing of its receipt is important. If the deal is to take place in early October, the finance would need to be in place in advance, and therefore it is likely that the loan is taken out just prior to the year end on 30 September. In this case it would need to be recognised and disclosed in accordance with IFRS 9 *Financial Instruments* and IFRS 7 *Financial Instruments: Disclosures*, and there is a risk that the liability is not measured appropriately or that disclosure is incomplete. Given the potential materiality of the loan, at 36.3% of existing total assets, this is a significant risk.

There is also a risk that the increase in gearing will breach any existing loan covenants. While this is a business risk rather than an audit risk, the matter may require disclosure in the financial statements, leading to a risk of material misstatement if necessary disclosures are not made.

Additional information which will help with the assessment of this risk includes:

- Copies of any agreements with the bank so that terms can be verified, in particular the anticipated date of the receipt of the funds, and the impact on the financial statements and on analytical review procedures confirmed

According to note 3 to the forecast financial statements, the £20m loan was used to finance a specific new product development project. However, development costs recognised as an intangible asset has increased by only £15m. The difference of £5m is not explained by analytical review on the draft financial statements, and there is a risk that not all the amount spent on development costs has been capitalised, meaning that the intangible asset could be understated. Conversely, it could be the case that that £5m of the amount spent was not eligible for capitalisation under the recognition rules of IAS 38 *Intangible Assets*, however, as discussed above the movement in operating expenses does not suggest that £5m of research costs has been expensed. It may also be that the company continues to hold the £5m in cash and this may be supported by the significant increase in current assets in the year.

Additional information is required to explain how the £20m raised from the loan has been utilised, whether it was all spent on research and development, and the nature of the development costs which were funded from the loan.

Finally, retained earnings has increased by £8m. Projected profit for the year is £25m, therefore there is an unexplained reconciling item between retained earnings brought forward and carried forward. The difference could be due to a dividend paid in the financial year, but additional information including a statement of changes in equity is required in order to plan an appropriate audit response.

Property, plant and equipment

The change to the estimated useful lives of property, plant and equipment has increased profit by £5m, which represents 17.9% of profit before tax and is therefore material to the financial statements. This change in accounting estimate is permitted, but the audit team should be sceptical and carefully consider whether the change is justified. If the change were found to be inappropriate it would need to be corrected, increasing operating expenses by £5m, reducing operating profit to £30m and the operating margin would fall to only 13.6%. This would be a significant reduction in profit and it could be that management bias is a risk factor, especially given the sizeable loan which is about to be agreed meaning that the projected financial statements may have already been scrutinised by the Group's bank.

Chico brand name and associated issues

The Group finance director states that the Chico brand name has been impaired by £30m. However, the brand name intangible asset has fallen by £35m in the year, so there is an unexplained reduction of £5m. This may have been caused by the impairment or sale of another brand, and additional information should be sought to explain the movement in the year.

The audit team will need to verify whether the £30m impairment recognised in relation to the Chico brand name is a full impairment of the amount recognised in relation to that specific brand within intangible assets. Given that the branded products have been withdrawn from sale, it should be fully written off, and if any amount remains recognised, then intangible assets and operating profit will be overstated. The amount written off amounts to 8.4% of Group assets and 107% of profit before tax. It is a highly material issue which may warrant separate disclosure under IAS 1 *Presentation of Financial Statements*. It is a risk that the necessary disclosures are not made in relation to the discontinuance and/or the impairment of assets.

There is also a risk that other brands could be impaired, for example, if the harmful ingredients used in the Chico brand are used in other perfume ranges. The impairment recognised in the financial statements could therefore be understated, if management has not considered the wider implications on other product ranges.

There is also a risk that inventories are overstated if there are any Chico items included in the amount recognised within current assets. Any Chico products should be written down to the lower of cost and net realisable value in accordance with IAS 2 *Inventories*, and presumably the net realisable value would be zero.

There is a possibility that some non-current assets used in the production of the Chico fragrance may need to be measured and disclosed in accordance with IAS 36 *Impairment of Assets* and/or IFRS 5 *Assets Held for Sale and Discontinued Operations*. This would depend on whether the assets are impaired or meet the criteria to be classified as held for sale, for example, whether they constitute a separate major line of business.

There may also be an issue relating to the health issues caused by use of the Chico products. It is likely that customers may have already brought legal claims against the Group if they have suffered skin problems after using the products. If claims have not yet arisen, they may occur in the future. There is a risk that necessary provisions have not been made, or that contingent liabilities have not been disclosed in the notes to the financial statements in accordance with IAS 37 *Provisions, Contingent Liabilities and Contingent Assets*. This would mean that potentially liabilities are potentially understated and operating profit is overstated, or that disclosures are incomplete.

Goodwill

Goodwill has not been impaired this year; we shall need to carry out a review of management's annual impairment test to assess its appropriateness and whether any of the goodwill has been impaired by the media coverage of the Chico product allegations. This means that goodwill and operating profit could be overstated if any necessary impairment has not been recognised.

Deferred tax liability

The finance director states that the change in the deferred tax liability relates to the changes in estimated useful lives of assets and associated accelerated tax depreciation (capital allowances). However, the impact on profit of the change to estimated useful lives amounts to £5m, so the £8m increase in deferred tax seems inappropriate and it is likely that the liability is overstated.

The deferred tax liability has increased by five times, and the £10m recognised in the year-end projection is material at 2.8% of total assets. The changes in deferred tax and the related property, plant and equipment therefore do not appear to be proportionate and the amount recognised could be incorrect.

Machine hire

The payments are 3.5% of profit before tax (= £1m/£28m) and are thus not material by themselves. They may of course become material once aggregated with any other misstatements.

The contracts may qualify as leases in line with IFRS 16 *Leases*, if the Group has the right to control the use of specific identified assets. If this is the case then the machines should be recognised as right-of-use assets within non-current assets, and a lease liability for the present value of lease payments. The assets should then be treated in line with IAS 16 *Property, Plant and Equipment*. Not recognising these leases may mean that both non-current assets and liabilities are understated.

IFRS 16 does allow an exemption from recognition for low-value assets that are held on short-term leases. If the machines met these criteria, then the Group could elect merely to recognise the lease payments as an expense on a straight-line basis over the lease term. This does not apply in this case, because payments of £200,000 per machine (= £1m ÷ 5) indicate that the machines are not low-value assets.

Additional information needed would be the contracts, so that the present value of any lease liability can be determined. This could have an effect on the preliminary analytical review. Although the payments recognised this year are not material, it is quite possible that any right-of-use assets (and lease liabilities) not recognised would be material.

Acquisition of Azalea Co

The acquisition is planned to take place in early October and assuming it takes place, it will be a significant event to be disclosed in accordance with IAS 10 *Events after the Reporting Period*. Details of the acquisition will also need to be disclosed to comply with IFRS 3 *Business Combinations* which requires disclosure of information about a business combination whose acquisition date is after the end of the reporting period but before the financial statements are authorised for issue. There is a risk that the necessary disclosures are not made which would be a significant risk of material misstatement given the materiality of the acquisition.

Conclusion

These briefing notes highlight that there are a number of significant risks of material misstatement which will need to be carefully considered during the planning of the audit, to ensure that an appropriate audit strategy is devised. The new loan that has been taken out is a key issue for the audit, as are the movements on the statement of profit or loss. The audit will need to examine each of the material areas of risk carefully in order to obtain evidence of possible misstatements.

> **Tutorial note.** Credit will be awarded for evaluation of other relevant risks of material misstatement including management bias due to the loan of £130m being provided, and the complex and acquisitive nature of the Group, which leads to inherent risk of misstatement in relation to business combinations.

(c) **Audit procedures**

(i) **Impairment of Chico brand**

- Obtain management's calculations relevant to the impairment and review to understand methodology – for example, whether the brand has been entirely or partly written off
- Evaluate the assumptions used by management in their impairment review and consider their reasonableness
- Confirm the carrying value of the Chico brand pre-impairment to prior year financial statements or management accounts
- From management accounts, obtain a breakdown of total revenue by brand, to evaluate the significance of the Chico brand to financial performance and whether it constitutes a separate line of business for disclosure as a discontinued operation
- If the brand is not fully written off, discuss with management the reasons for this treatment given that the brand is now discontinued
- Obtain a breakdown of operating expenses to confirm that the impairment is included

- Review the presentation of the statement of profit or loss, considering whether separate disclosure of the impairment is necessary given its materiality

(ii) **Acquisition of Azalea Ltd**

- Read board minutes to understand the rationale for the acquisition, and to see that the acquisition is approved.
- Discuss with Group management the way that control will be exercised over Azalea Ltd, enquiring as to whether the Group can determine the board members of Azalea Ltd.
- Review the minutes of relevant meetings held between management of the Group and Azalea Ltd to confirm matters such as:
  - That the deal is likely to go ahead
  - The likely timescale
  - The amount and nature of consideration to be paid
  - The shareholding to be acquired and whether equity or non-equity shares
  - The planned operational integration (if any) of Azalea Ltd into the Group
- Obtain any due diligence reports which have been obtained by the Group and review for matters which may need to be disclosed in accordance with IAS 10 or IFRS 3.
- Obtain copies of the finance agreement for the funds used to purchase Azalea Ltd.
- After the reporting date, agree the cash consideration paid to bank records.

Conclusion

These briefing notes indicate that there are many potentially significant risks of material misstatement to be considered in planning the Group audit. The Group should provide the additional information requested to enable a more thorough analytical review to be performed as part of our audit planning. A range of audit procedures has been recommended, which should reduce our detection risk in relation to the impaired brand and the planned acquisition of Azalea Ltd after the year end.

(d) In relation to a recurring audit engagement such as this, Holly & Co needs to assess whether there have been any changes in circumstances which could require the terms of the engagement to be revised (ISA (UK) 210: para. 13). This could include any significant changes in the nature or size of an entity's business, changes in legal requirements, or changes in the financial reporting framework adopted (ISA (UK) 210: para. A30).

Although Bulldog Ltd has recently expanded overseas (and has set up a treasury management function), this is unlikely to constitute a significant change in the nature of its business.

Holly & Co should also consider whether Bulldog Ltd needs to be reminded of the existing engagement terms (ISA (UK) 210: para. 13). This might be needed where there are indications that the entity misunderstands the objective and scope of the audit (ISA (UK) 210: para. A30), but there are no such indications here.

> **Tutorial note.** Credit will be awarded for answers that consider continuance issues from ISA (UK) 220 (Revised) *Quality management for an audit of financial statements*, such as the integrity of those charged with governance at Bulldog Ltd and any ethical or resourcing issues that have arisen during previous audits.

(e) **Audit of financial instruments**

Financial instruments themselves may be difficult to understand. Management themselves may fail to understand the risks involved with them, which may expose the entity to substantial risks.

Financial reporting requirements in this area can be complex, which increases the risk of misstatement. It is possible that neither management nor the auditor will properly understand how the instruments should be accounted for.

Accounting for financial instruments may also involve an element of subjectivity, eg in determining fair values. Fair values may be estimated with the use of models which will involve making assumptions. Therefore is therefore a risk that the assumptions made by management are not reasonable.

Given the presence of subjectivity, it is all the more important that the auditor is professionally sceptical in this area, although this is likely to be difficult.

Alternatively, some financial instruments may be fairly simple to audit, eg where there is an active market, it may be possible to agree fair values to a broker's report. This would of course be subject to the requirements of ISA (UK) 500 *Audit Evidence* in relation to the use of a management's expert.

It may be necessary to make use of an auditor's expert, in which case the auditor must ensure that the expert is independent and competent, and must evaluate the suitability of the expert's work as audit evidence. This may not be straightforward to do, given the complexity of the subject matter. Using an auditor's expert may also have the effect of increasing the audit fee, which should be explained to and discussed with the client.

Matters to consider

The company's treasury management function has only been set up recently, so it is possible that there may be teething problems in an area such as this. Internal controls may not be well established, so the auditor will need to spend time obtaining an understanding of them. This increases audit risk in this area.

Consideration should be given to the level of competence of staff in the new department. If they are skilled in this area then they may be new to the company, in which case there may be difficulties integrating the department with the rest of Bulldog's finance function. Alternatively, there is a risk that staff do not have adequate knowledge or experience in this area.

It will be necessary to obtain an understanding of the kinds of financial instruments Bulldog uses to hedge transactions, including Bulldog's reasons for entering into them and the kinds of risks it may be exposed to thereby.

The materiality of the instruments should be considered, bearing in mind especially the possibility that transactions with either no, or very little, initial value may turn out to have effects on the financial statements that are material. Some types of derivative financial instruments may fall into this category.

Management's method for valuing financial instruments should be considered, and the auditor must choose whether to audit management's valuation model, or whether to construct a model of its own. This would depend on the assessed reliability of internal controls in this area.

35 McClane & Co

Workbook references

Chapters 2, 6, 7 and 8.

Top tips

Your general approach should be to read the requirements carefully, and then to work through the question noting down issues (mainly audit risks) as they occur to you.

Part (a) was on the issues specific to an initial audit engagement and was very clear that you do not need to consider acceptance issues. This statement, given in Exhibit 1, is the examiner trying to steer you in the right direction; although you need to demonstrate professional scepticism in relation to the scenario itself, you do not need to be sceptical of this statement!

Much of the substantive material here is knowledge based and should not have been too difficult for you. Five marks are available, and since this is an easier requirement, you should be looking to score at least 3.5 marks here if you are going to pass the exam overall.

Part (b) asked for your prioritisation and evaluation of significant audit risks. The key to scoring well here is the quality of your analysis. Yes, you need to identify the risks, but you then need to be able to weight and measure them from different points of view. Materiality will usually give you a good starting point for the significance of a risk, but you may need to take into account qualitative factors too, eg if a risk relates to a related party transaction (there was one in this question) then it may be qualitatively material. Similarly, risks that point to control deficiencies may have wider effects than those that don't.

You will need to include an introduction and a conclusion to your answer, using the conclusion to pick out the main risks and thus to signal to the marker that you are 'evaluating and prioritising', and not just simply stating.

Part (c) required you to design audit procedures for a building and its valuation. This is a standard requirement, the trick to which is to get as many marks from your procedures as you can. This means thinking practically and making sure you focus on the purpose of the procedure. Requirements like this are not difficult by nature, and you should be able to score at least 4 or 5 marks here.

Finally part (d) asked you to consider ethics and other planning issues. As usual, it is important that you answer both parts of the requirement here, although in reality the issues are connected as they all arise out of exhibit 5.

Lots of professional marks are on offer in Question One. Scoring well here is bound to involve the marker's judgement, so it is more important than ever before that your answer is structured clearly, and that your reasoning is clear and coherent. Many of the communication marks will come from using the correct format when constructing your answer, so it is worth the effort of getting these.

Easy marks

There should be marks available for adopting the correct format for your briefing notes, and for writing a conclusion prioritising the most important audit risks. There are usually marks available for materiality, and for relevant calculations.

ACCA examining team's comments

This question was a typical Section A question set at the planning stage, with requirements focusing on matters specific to the planning stage of an initial audit engagement, an evaluation of the significant audit risks, recommending specific audit procedures in relation to an investment property and ethical issues. The Section A question is where candidates perform best and there have been more focused answers in recent sessions. It is pleasing to see that candidates appear to have taken note of the guidance provided by the examining team in this area.

The entity in this scenario was a new client to the audit firm, with the core business being the design and construction of bespoke machinery within the oil industry. Candidates should note that they are not expected to have detailed industry specific knowledge when answering questions in this examination and the scenario will always have enough information to enable sufficient specific risks to be identified and evaluated to achieve full marks.

Unless specified otherwise, all exhibits should be considered when carrying out risk evaluations and candidates should ensure that they carefully read the partner's email for any specific guidance in relation to how the information should be used.

It is recommended that candidates review all the exhibits while planning their answers to the question but as mentioned should ensure they take note of any guidance given by the examining team in terms of which exhibits are relevant to each requirement. Thus, allowing for more detailed analysis and focus on specific information where relevant.

It is often the case that there will be interactions between the exhibits which will impact on the analysis performed by candidates. Candidates are encouraged to spend adequate time planning and aim to obtain a holistic view and understanding of the issues present in the question.

Requirement (a) required candidates to consider matters which are relevant to the initial audit of a new client. Disappointingly, many candidates struggled to attempt the question or omitted it entirely.

Stronger candidates were able to discuss planning issues specific to first time audits such as the interaction with previous auditors with regard to working papers; for example, in assessing the appropriateness of the accounting policies used by the client, details of related parties and transactions etc.

Weaker candidates tended to either focus on acceptance, for example, requesting clearance from previous auditors, which has already been obtained, or discussed generic planning matters relevant to all audits such as assigning a team, understanding the business and agreeing deadlines.

Overall, this requirement appeared to distinguish those who approach audit from a practical stance from those who demonstrated knowledge of generic planning matters but were unable to apply them to a specific situation. In this examination, it was crucial for candidates to apply their knowledge of the planning and early stages of the audit process in order to gain credit in this exam.

Requirement (b) asked for an **evaluation, not simply a list** of risks, nor a strategy or procedures to address those risks. The examining team are testing whether candidates understand how and why a risk arises and the implications this has on the financial statements or the audit itself. They are looking for an assessment of materiality, a demonstration of knowledge of the underlying accounting rules and the application of that to the scenario to identify the potential impact on the financial statements. A well evaluated risk has in depth analysis. **Candidates writing only a sentence or two are unlikely to attain many of the marks available for each risk.** The requirement states that risks should also be **prioritised**, so risks which are likely to have a greater impact on the audit should be presented first. Alternatively, you can prioritise your key risks in a separate section within your answer.

Candidates should be aware of the published **marking guides** for risk questions and understand how marks are credited. Each risk generally has a minimum of three marks attached to it. More complex risks carry additional credit. Materiality and calculation marks are over and above the marks available for the discussion of a risk. The marking guide published for this question has nine areas of risks, two of which centre around revenue recognition and one arises from an analytical review.

The requirement asks only for **significant audit risks**, which mean risks that are either specific to the scenario, non-routine or judgemental and have the potential to give rise to a material misstatement or give rise to a specific detection risk. **Speculative risks**, arising from routine transactions generally will not obtain credit.

Requirement (c) was well answered by a majority of candidates with practical, well described procedures given. The model answer provides a list of procedures which are indicative of the areas the examining team credited. Where a candidate suggests a procedure not on the list in the model answer they will still obtain credit providing it is relevant and practicable.

In **Requirement (d)**, the conflict-of-interest risks were generally well identified by candidates, although not always well described. Candidates generally appreciated the safeguards available and the requirement for consent from both parties.

The self-review threat arising with respect to the vendors due diligence and the safeguards available were again well performed. Some candidates lost time discussing rules for listed clients which Gruber Ltd is not, so the answers were irrelevant.

The advocacy threat arising from the due diligence work was the most often missed threat in candidates' discussions.

Overall, the responses from candidates on this question were stronger than in previous sessions and some good specific responses were seen.

Marking guide | **Marks**

(a) **Initial audit**

Generally, up to 1 mark for each relevant point discussed, including:

- Communicate with the previous auditor, review their working papers for significant planning issues
- Consider whether any previous auditor's reports were modified
- Consider any matters which were raised when professional clearance was obtained
- Consider impact of any ethical issues, eg the need for independent partner review
- Consider matters discussed with management during our firm's appointment, eg accounting treatment of construction contracts
- Need to develop thorough business understanding including in relation to significant accounting policies
- Risk of misstatement in opening balances/previously applied accounting policies
- Firm's quality management procedures for new audit clients
- Need to use experienced audit team to reduce detection risk

Maximum 5

(b) **Audit risk evaluation and prioritisation**

Up to 3 marks for each audit risk evaluated (unless indicated otherwise). Marks may be awarded for other, relevant risks not included in the marking guide.

In addition, 0.5 mark for relevant trends or calculations which form part of the evaluation of audit risk (max 3 marks).

Materiality calculations should be awarded 1 mark each (max 4 marks).

- New audit client (max 2 marks)
- Management bias due to sale of shares (max 2 marks)
- Overstatement of revenue/profit – from analytical review (max 2 marks)
- Recognition of revenue – support service
- Recognition of revenue/profit – Argyle contract
- Johnson – onerous contract (max 4 marks)
- Investment property (max 4 marks)
- Sale of 'designs' (max 4 marks)
- Related party transaction

Maximum 21

(c) **Audit procedures in respect of the Nakatomi building**

Up to 1 mark for each relevant audit procedure. Examples are provided below, marks will be awarded for other relevant points.

- Review board minutes for details of the reason for the purchase, to understand the business rationale, and confirm board approval of the transaction
- Agree the amount paid to the company's cash book and bank statements
- Agree the carrying amount of the property to Gruber Ltd's non-current asset register to confirm the initial value of the property has been recorded appropriately
- Obtain proof of ownership, eg title deeds, legal documentation to confirm that the company owns the building
- Visit the building to obtain evidence of existence and occupancy of the building by retail establishments to confirm that the property has been appropriately classified as an investment property

- Enquire as to whether the company holds any other investment property, and if so, confirm it is also held at fair value to confirm that the accounting treatment is consistent for all investment property
- Discuss with management the rationale for the accounting policy choice to measure the property at fair value and confirm that the notes to the financial statements state that this is the company's accounting policy
- With regard to the expert appointed by management to provide the valuation for the building (up to 4 marks):
- Obtain information to confirm the experience and qualifications held by the expert, eg certificate of registration with a recognised professional body
- Obtain confirmation of the expert's independence from Gruber Ltd and its management team
- Review the instructions provided to the expert by management, and agree that the valuation method is in accordance with IFRS requirements
- Obtain the final report issued by the expert and assess that the assumptions and methods used and conclusions reached by the expert are in line with the auditor's understanding of the business
- Confirm that the valuation has been carried out at the reporting date and in accordance with the company's accounting policy
- If the valuation is at a different date to the reporting date, assess the reasonableness of the valuation reflected in the financial statements
- Re-perform any calculations contained in the expert's working papers

Maximum 7

(d) **Ethical issues**

Up to 1 mark for each relevant, explained answer point:

- Conflict of interest between Gruber Ltd and Willis Ltd
- Conflict of interest impact on auditor's objectivity
- Requirement that a professional accountant shall not allow a conflict of interest to compromise professional judgement
- Risk relates to the valuation of the Gruber shares
- Risk of breach of confidentiality
- Full disclosure to be made to both parties and consent obtained
- Safeguards may be used to reduce the threat to objectivity (max 2 marks)
- Advocacy threat in relation to Gruber Ltd
- Safeguards to reduce advocacy threat (max 2 marks)
- Management responsibilities in relation to Gruber Ltd
- Self-review threat re audit of investment in Willis Ltd
- Safeguards to reduce self-review threat (max 2 marks)
- Valuation should not be provided if material impact on financial statements and involves significant degree of subjective judgement

Maximum 7

Professional marks

Communication

- Briefing note format and structure - use of headings/sub-headings and an introduction
- Style, language and clarity - appropriate layout and tone of briefing notes, presentation of materiality and relevant calculations, appropriate use of the CBE tools, easy to follow and understand

- Effectiveness and clarity of communication - answer is relevant and tailored to the scenario
- Adherence to the specific requests made by the audit engagement partner, Al Powell

Analysis and Evaluation

- Appropriate use of the information to determine and apply suitable calculations
- Appropriate use of the information relating to the sale of the property to design appropriate audit procedures
- Effective prioritisation of the results of the audit risk evaluation to demonstrate the likelihood and magnitude of risks and to facilitate the allocation of appropriate responses

Professional scepticism and professional judgement

- Appropriate application of professional judgement to draw conclusions and make informed decisions following recognition of unusual or unexpected movements, missing/incomplete information or challenging presented information as part of the risk evaluation
- Determination and justification of a suitable materiality level, appropriately and consistently applied to each of the risks presented at Gruber Ltd
- Identification of possible management bias and consideration of the impact on the financial statements and the possible reasons for management's preference for certain accounting treatments
- Effective application of technical and ethical guidance to effectively challenge and critically assess how management has recognised the company's revenue in line with IFRS

Commercial acumen

- Use of effective examples and/or calculations from the scenario to illustrate points or recommendations 10

Total 50

Briefing notes

To: **Audit engagement partner**

From: **Audit manager**

Subject: **Gruber Ltd – audit planning**

Introduction

These briefing notes are prepared to assist with planning the audit of Gruber Ltd for the financial year ending 30 September 20X5. The notes begin by discussing the implications of this being an initial audit engagement and then move onto evaluate the audit risks which should be considered in planning the audit. The notes also recommend the audit procedures to be performed in relation to an investment property. Finally, the notes address the ethical issues arising from a meeting with the company's management team.

(a) **Initial audit engagement**

In an initial audit engagement, there are several factors which should be considered in addition to the planning procedures which are carried out for every audit. ISA (UK) 300 *Planning an Audit of Financial Statements* provides guidance in this area.

ISA (UK) 300 suggests that unless prohibited by laws or regulation, arrangements should be made with the predecessor auditor, for example, to review their working papers. Therefore, communication should be made with Ellis Associates to request access to their working papers for the financial year ended 30 September 20X4. The review of the previous year's working papers would help McClane & Co in planning the audit, for example, as it may highlight matters pertinent to the audit of opening balances or an assessment of the appropriateness of Gruber Ltd's accounting policies. For example, Ellis Associates may have information on file regarding previous transactions between Martin Gruber and the company, or other related party transactions.

It will also be important to consider whether any previous years' auditor's reports were modified, and if so, the reason for the modification.

As part of the client acceptance process, professional clearance should have been sought from Ellis Associates. Any matters which were brought to the attention of McClane & Co when professional clearance was obtained should be considered for their potential impact on the audit strategy.

In addition, any ethical issues raised during client acceptance should be considered in terms of their potential impact on the audit strategy, for example, the need for an independent partner review of the audit, especially given the recent meeting with the company's management and their request for a non-audit service to be performed.

There should also be consideration of the matters which were discussed with Gruber Ltd's management in connection with the appointment of McClane & Co as auditors. The audit team should also consider any major issues which have been discussed with management at initial meetings and how these matters impact on the overall audit strategy and audit plan. For example, the accounting treatment applied to construction contracts may have been discussed given that this is a significant accounting policy applied in the company's financial statements.

Particular care should be taken in planning the audit procedures necessary to obtain sufficient appropriate audit evidence regarding opening balances, and procedures should be planned in accordance with ISA (UK) 510 *Initial Audit Engagements – Opening Balances*. Procedures should be performed to determine whether the opening balances reflect the application of appropriate accounting policies and to determine whether the prior period's closing balances have been correctly brought forward into the current period.

With an initial audit engagement, it is particularly important to develop an understanding of the business, including the specific legal and regulatory framework applicable to the company. For the audit of Gruber Ltd, it will be important to gain an understanding of the legal and regulatory issues within the oil industry, such as strict health and safety regulations and environmental legislation. This understanding must be fully documented and will help the audit team to perform effective analytical procedures and to develop an appropriate audit strategy. Obtaining knowledge of the business will also help to identify whether it will be necessary to plan for the use of auditor's experts, for example, in relation to accounting for customer contracts. Further, given the bespoke nature of the orders placed by customers, this may also have an impact on assessing the valuation of inventory or work in progress. The inventory is industry specific, so it is highly probable that an expert will need to be engaged to assess the valuation of the inventory.

McClane & Co may have quality management procedures in place for use in the case of initial engagements, for example, the involvement of another partner or senior individual to review the overall audit strategy prior to commencing significant audit procedures. Compliance with any such procedures should be fully documented.

Given that this is a new audit client, and because of other risk factors to be discussed in the next part of these briefing notes, when developing the audit strategy consideration should be given to using an experienced audit team in order to reduce detection risk.

(b) **Audit risk evaluation and prioritisation**

New audit client

This is the first year in which McClane & Co has audited the company which increases detection risk as our firm does not have experience with the client, making it more difficult to detect material misstatements. However, this risk can be mitigated through rigorous audit planning, including obtaining a thorough understanding of the business of the company.

In addition, as discussed in part (a), there is a risk that opening balances and comparative information may not be correct as the prior year figures were not audited by McClane & Co and therefore, we should plan to audit the opening balances carefully, in accordance with ISA (UK) 510 to ensure that opening balances and comparative information are both free from material misstatement. McClane & Co will need to communicate with Ellis Associates to arrange to review their files to identify any potential issues with prior audits. In particular, McClane & Co will need to investigate in detail the reasons why the former auditors resigned from the assignment. Their resignation may, for example, have been the result of disagreements with client management and may have implications in relation to management's competence or integrity.

Management bias

The company's major shareholder, Martin Gruber, is planning to sell his shares in the company and initial discussions have already taken place with a potential purchaser. This situation means that there is a risk of management bias in that Martin will want to maximise the sale price and for this reason there is a risk that assets will be overstated and revenue and profitability maximised, as he will want the company's financial statements to reflect as good a financial position and performance as possible.

Given the owner-managed status of the company, it could be easy for Martin to override controls relating to financial reporting, and/or to put pressure on the chief finance officer (CFO), who is his brother, to manipulate the financial statements. Several of the risks discussed below indicate that management bias could have been applied in a number of accounting treatments, in particular the valuation of investment property and recognition and measurement of intangible assets.

Analytical procedures – overstatement of revenue/profit

Analytical procedures of the financial information provided shows that:

- Revenue is projected to increase by 15.4%
- Operating profit is projected to increase by 80%
- Profit before tax is projected to increase by 55.6%

While there may be relevant and appropriate explanations for these trends, the auditor should be alert to the possibility that revenue and profit could be deliberately overstated. The trend in operating profit is particularly concerning, and management will need to provide explanations and corroboratory evidence in support of these projections. Martin Gruber has incentive for the financial statements to show growth in revenue and profit given the potential sale of his shares, so there is a risk of aggressive earnings management.

Recognition of revenue – support service

The company sells around one quarter of its machines under a contract which includes a support service, but all contracts are currently being established with only one performance obligation. There is a risk that the revenue related to these contracts is not being separated into component parts as required by IFRS® 15 *Revenue from Contracts with Customers*. IFRS 15 requires that when accounting for revenue, the performance obligations in the contract are identified and where a contract has multiple performance obligations, revenue should be allocated to the performance obligations in the contract by reference to their relative standalone selling prices. There is an audit risk that Gruber Ltd is not disaggregating the contract revenue between the obligation relating to the supply and installation of the machine and the provision of the support service. This could result in revenue being overstated if the revenue relating to the support service is recognised at the same time as the rest of the revenue.

Recognition of revenue/profit – Argyle contract

The CFO's suggestion that the full amount of profit can be recognised this year in respect of this contract is incorrect. When performing long-term contracts, IFRS 15 states that appropriate methods of measuring progress towards the satisfaction of a performance obligation, i.e. the completion of the contract, include output methods and input methods which are based on determining the stage of completion of the performance obligation by reference to the value to the customer of the goods or services transferred to date relative to the remaining goods or services promised under the contract (output method) or on the basis of the entity's efforts or inputs to the satisfaction of a performance obligation (input method).

Based on the company's stated accounting policy, which is to use the output method, the stage of completion should be based on work certified, which is projected to be £4 million compared with the contract price of £6 million, giving a percentage completion of 66.7%. The company should therefore recognise 66.7% of the estimated £2.2 million profit on the contract, which is £1.47 million. Profit is therefore overstated by £730,000.

This is material, at 5.2% of profit before tax. The accounting treatment could be an indication of management bias, and the desire of Martin Gruber to overstate profit for the year.

The audit team should also consider whether the accounting treatment applied to other contracts deviates from the company's stated accounting policy and whether there are further material misstatements in this regard.

Johnson – onerous contract

The projected profit to 30 September 20X5 includes a loss relating to the Johnson contract. It is correct that losses should be recognised, however, the method applied of recognising the loss over time is not appropriate.

The total loss on the contract, estimated at £840,000, is material as it represents 6% of profit before tax.

Where contracts are expected to be loss-making, they should be accounted for as onerous contracts in accordance with IAS® 37 *Provisions, Contingent Liabilities and Contingent Assets*, which requires a provision to be recognised for an onerous contract. An onerous contract is a contract in which the unavoidable costs of meeting the obligations under the contract exceed the economic benefits expected to be received. IAS 37 states a provision should be measured based on the unavoidable costs of fulfilling the contractual obligations. From the information provided, it is not possible to determine the exact amount which should be provided, but recognising the loss over time is not an appropriate method of accounting and it is likely that the loss recognised and provision in the statement of financial position are understated.

This could be a signal of management bias – the accounting treatment applied reduces the loss recognised within profit for the year and could be an indication of earnings management applied in the preparation of the financial statements.

There is also a risk that the 'cost inflation' and budgeting errors which have allegedly caused the contract to become loss-making would also have implications for other contracts which the company is working on. This may mean that further onerous contracts exist, and more losses need to be recognised, providing further risk that profit for the year is overstated.

Investment property

The £15 million invested in the Nakatomi building is material, representing 12.5% of total assets. The change in fair value which is recognised within profit is also material at 14.3% of profit before tax.

It is appropriate that the property is measured at fair value and that the gain is recognised within profit. This is in accordance with IAS 40 *Investment Properties* which permits entities to choose between a fair value model, and a cost model for the measurement of investment properties. When the fair value model is used, gains or losses arising from changes in the fair value of investment property must be included in net profit or loss for the period in which it arises.

However, an audit risk arises from the size of the fair value gain which has been recognised. The property was only purchased at the start of financial year, and an increase in fair value of 13.3% in a 12-month period is significant. The valuation of the property by the expert has yet to be performed, so the fair value currently included in the financial statements could be an attempt by management to boost profit for the year, for the reasons discussed above. The level of subjectivity which may be involved in determining the fair value increases the risk of material misstatement. Risk is heightened as Gruber Ltd may hire an expert who is known to them in order to achieve a higher fair value which will manipulate the profits for the year and therefore the objectivity of the expert used is also a risk.

Tutorial note. Credit will also be awarded for discussion of whether the use of an auditor's expert is appropriate.

Intangible asset

The intangible asset recognised in the year at cost to the company of £9 million is material to the statement of financial position as it represents 7.5% of total assets. It is also material by nature as it is a transaction between the company and the majority shareholder and chief executive officer, making it a related party transaction, which will be discussed in more detail below.

There is a risk of management bias relating to this transaction. Given that Martin is planning to sell his shares, there is a significant risk that the transaction is an attempt to window-dress the financial statements in order to maximise the asset value, influence the business valuation and ultimately increase the amount which Martin receives on selling his shares. Martin may also have engineered the transaction as a way to remove funds from the company without having to pay a dividend.

It is questionable whether Martin has sold anything at all to the company. Robust audit procedures will need to be performed to determine the existence of an asset in relation to the 'designs' which have been sold to the company. They could possibly relate to assets such as patents or some kind of intellectual property, but both the existence and valuation of such assets need to be supported by documentation from Martin, which has not been provided to the audit team. The lack of corroboratory evidence increases the risk of this being a 'fake' transaction which needs to be approached with a very high degree of professional scepticism.

For these reasons, there is a significant risk that intangible assets are overstated by a material amount.

There is also a risk that the £10 million opening balance of intangible assets is overstated, especially given that this is a new audit client. Martin may have set up similar transactions in the past, resulting in the recognition of intangible assets which may not be appropriate.

> **Tutorial note.** Credit will also be awarded for discussion regarding the specific accounting treatment of intangible assets, eg whether IAS 38 *Intangible Assets* criteria for recognition have been met and whether non-amortisation of assets is appropriate as trends indicate that the recognised assets are not amortised.

Related party transaction

The sale of the designs by Martin to Gruber Ltd is a related party transaction according to the definition of IAS 24 *Related Party Disclosures*. A related party is a person who has control or joint control over the reporting entity, therefore Martin is a related party of Gruber Ltd and the sale of his designs is a related party transaction which is defined in IAS 24 as a transfer of resources, services, or obligations between related parties, regardless of whether a price is charged.

There is a risk that disclosure of the transaction is not made in accordance with IAS 24 which requires that if there have been transactions between related parties, there should be disclosure regarding the nature of the related party relationship as well as information about the transactions and outstanding balances where necessary.

Conclusions about significant audit risks

Revenue recognition and intangible assets are likely to be considered the most significant areas of audit risk for planning the engagement, but given its influence across the reporting process overall, the impact of management bias cannot be ignored.

(c) **Audit procedures in respect of the Nakatomi building**

- Review board minutes for details of the reason for the purchase, to understand the business rationale, and confirm board approval of the transaction.
- Agree the £15 million paid to the company's cash book and bank statements.
- Agree the carrying amount of the property to Gruber Ltd's non-current asset register to confirm the initial value of the property has been recorded appropriately.

- Obtain proof of ownership, eg title deeds, legal documentation to confirm that the company owns the building.
- Visit the building to obtain evidence of existence and occupancy of the building by retail establishments to confirm that the property has been appropriately classified as an investment property.
- Obtain and inspect rental agreements for the retailers who occupy the Nakatomi building, to confirm that the property is not owner-occupied and that it generates a rental income to verify classification.
- Enquire as to whether the company holds any other investment property, and if so, confirm it is also held at fair value to confirm that the accounting treatment is consistent for all investment property.
- Discuss with management the rationale for the accounting policy choice to measure the property at fair value and confirm that the notes to the financial statements state that this is the company's accounting policy.
- With regard to the expert appointed by management to provide the valuation for the building:
  - Obtain information to confirm the experience and qualifications held by the expert, e.g. certificate of registration with a recognised professional body.
  - Obtain confirmation of the expert's independence from Gruber Ltd and its management team.
  - Review the instructions provided to the expert by management and agree that the valuation method is in accordance with IFRS requirements and can be relied upon as appropriate audit evidence.
  - Obtain the final report issued by the expert and assess that the assumptions and methods used and conclusions reached by the expert are in line with the auditor's understanding of the business, confirm that the expert's valuation has been used as the valuation recognised in the financial statements, and investigate any discrepancies.
  - Confirm that the valuation has been carried out at the reporting date and in accordance with the company's accounting policy.
  - If the valuation is at a different date to the reporting date, assess the reasonableness of the valuation reflected in the financial statements.
  - Re-perform any calculations contained in the expert's working papers.

(d) **Ethical issues**

Potential sale of shares

The request for McClane & Co to perform a vendor due diligence service creates a conflict of interest. A conflict of interest arises when an audit firm provides a service in relation to two or more clients whose interests in respect of the matter are in conflict.

Conflict of interest is related to objectivity. The IESBA *International Code of Ethics for Accountants* (the *Code*) states that objectivity requires the professional accountant not to compromise professional judgement because of bias, conflict of interest or the undue influence of others. It is a requirement of the *Code* that a professional accountant shall not allow a conflict of interest to compromise professional judgement.

In this case, the interests of Gruber Ltd and Willis Ltd will be conflicting; Willis Ltd will want to purchase the shares for the lowest possible amount and Martin Gruber will want to sell them for the highest possible amount. This creates, therefore, a significant threat to the objectivity of McClane & Co, who may be seen to be acting in the interest of one party at the expense of the other.

The problem is exacerbated by the nature of the engagement. The audit firm may be privy to confidential information gained during their time as auditor of Gruber Ltd. If the audit firm were to divulge this to Willis Ltd, it would give them a potentially unfair advantage over the other client and would be a breach of confidentiality.

In all cases of conflict of interest, the audit firm should make full disclosure to both parties and ask them both to confirm that they give permission in writing for the service to be provided. It is likely that one of the parties will refuse permission, in which case the service should not be provided.

If consent by both parties were to be provided, McClane & Co could safeguard the threats created by the situation by:

- Having separate engagement teams who are provided with clear policies and procedures on maintaining confidentiality;
- Having an appropriate reviewer who is not involved in providing either service to the two clients, to review the work performed to assess whether key judgements and conclusions are appropriate;
- Using confidentiality agreements signed by the relevant personnel; and
- Establishing separation of confidential information physically and electronically.

The *Code* states that providing a valuation service can give rise to an advocacy threat, which means that McClane & Co would be promoting the interests of their client in relation to the sales price, thus impacting objectivity.

Safeguards such as the following could reduce the threat to an acceptable level:

- Use of separate teams to perform the valuation service and the audit of Gruber Ltd, and
- Having an independent second partner review the audit of Gruber Ltd.

There is also a risk that performing such a service would result in the firm assuming a management responsibility because if the audit firm performs the valuation service, they could be perceived to be performing a role of management, therefore not appearing to be objective from the audit client. Assuming a management responsibility for an audit client is prohibited in the *Code*.

If McClane & Co were to value the shares, there is also a threat in relation to subsequent audits of Willis Ltd and the new group which will be formed, as in performing the valuation of Martin Gruber's shares, they would subsequently be auditing their own valuation work when they audit the new Group's consolidated financial statements. The self-review threat leads to an objectivity threat as the audit team may lack professional scepticism in their audit of the investment in Willis Ltd's financial statements, and over-rely on the valuation performed by colleagues from McClane & Co.

The self-review threat can be reduced to an acceptable level by the use of appropriate safeguards including:

- Use of separate teams to perform the valuation service and the audit of Willis Ltd, and
- Having an independent second partner review the audit of Willis Ltd.

The *Code* suggests that if the valuation would involve both a significant degree of subjective judgement and have a material effect on the financial statements, then it is likely the valuation service should not be performed. McClane & Co should therefore carefully consider whether it is appropriate to perform the service, evaluating the potential materiality of the shares and the level of subjective judgement involved.

Conclusion

These briefing notes have evaluated the significant audit risks relating to the audit of Gruber Ltd and highlight the issues caused by this being an initial audit engagement. The many incentives for management bias make this a high-risk audit. Revenue is likely be a key audit risk, connected to the risk of management bias, and will need to be a significant focus for our audit procedures. The notes also recommend audit procedures in relation to a new investment property, and conclude that due to a significant conflict of interest and possible restrictions in line with the ethical code, it is unlikely that McClane & Co can provide a vendor due diligence service to Gruber Ltd.

36 Awdry

Workbook references

Chapters 4, 5, 8 and 10.

Top tips

This was a two-part question which included a requirement to discuss a current issue.

Part (a) might have put you off and demonstrates the importance of reading the ACCA technical articles for AAA in the months leading up to your sitting, as they give you important information about topics that could come up in your exam. Discussion requirements such as this can be hard, but it is not as difficult to score points as you might think. Each good point scores 1 mark here, so you only need to make three good points to pass this part of the question. Remember that the FRC adapts standards from the IAASB for specific legislative and regulatory factors, meaning that there is standardisation up to a point but the ISQMs (UK) and ISA (UK) also reflect current practice in the UK.

Part (b) was set at the fieldwork stage, which is slightly unusual (AAA questions have typically been set either at planning, review or completion stages). As such it provides a very relevant test of your knowledge. The accounting standards being tested here are not overly complex, so if you struggled then you will need to spend some time making sure that you know this material.

Easy marks

There were no clear easy marks here, but if you are confident in your subject knowledge then this question was not unfair.

ACCA examining team's comments

This question was a 25-mark question which focused on the evaluation of the accounting treatment for specific estimates given in the question scenario, along with the audit procedures to be performed.

[Requirement (a) not in question as originally set, so no comment available.]

Requirement (b) for a total of 15 marks, was split into three sections and required candidates to evaluate the accounting treatment of three estimates given in the scenario. A large number of candidates demonstrated a weak understanding of the SBR syllabus and scored very poor marks. It was disappointing to note a lack of understanding of provisions. Only a limited number of candidates correctly stated the rule under IAS 37 *Provisions, Contingent Liabilities and Contingent Assets*, in relation to where the effect of the time value of money is material the provision should be recognised at present value. There was a clear indication in the question that this was relevant, and it was disappointing that more candidates did not identify this.

The quality of answers for this question was generally of a weaker standard and candidates were not able to demonstrate application of their knowledge of SBR in an audit context to the scenario.

Marking guide	Marks

(a) **New IAASB Quality Management Standards**

Generally 1 mark per point.

Suggested points to include the following:

- Context – audit failure and need to raise audit quality
- Shift from quality control to quality management
- Active risk assessment required

- Need to assess whether client is appropriate, not just profitable
- New guidance on engagement quality reviews
- Effect on firms – more work, higher quality audit, may reduce profitability
- ISA 220 – responsibility of audit partner.
- ISA 220 – 'stand back' requirement

5

(b) **Difficulties and procedures**

Generally up to 1 mark for each difficulty evaluated and each relevant procedure designed.

Cash-settled share-based payments

- Material expense to profit and borderline material to assets (with calculation(s))
- Treatment complies with IFRS 2 rules for accounting for cash-settled share-based payments

Difficulties when performing audit:

- Management assumption of 100% staff retention may be unrealistic
- Predicted staff retention estimation is based on historic trends and future expectations; actual outcomes unlikely to correspond exactly
- Options pricing models are complex and challenging to audit
- Judgement involved in which option pricing model to use
- Option pricing models include judgemental inputs such as current risk-free interest rate and measures of share price volatility

Procedures:

- Obtain copy of share-based payments agreement and supporting file notes detailing principal terms (0.5 mark per term agreed)
- Perform assessment of appropriateness of model used to value rights/options
- Obtain details of external expert used including assessment of professional certification, experience, reputation and objectivity
- Critically review expert's valuation including assessment of assumptions used to determine fair value of the SARs
- Obtain details of historic staff turnover rates obtained from human resources/payroll department
- Review of forecast staffing levels through to end of vesting period, including assessment of reasonableness of assumptions based on auditor's knowledge and understanding of client
- Discuss basis of staff retention assumptions with management and challenge their appropriateness
- Perform sensitivity analyses on valuation model and staffing forecasts

Regulatory penalties

- Material expense to profit and assets (with calculation)
- Expense and provision should have been recognised at present value per IAS 37

Difficulties when performing audit:

- Difficult to estimate final amount payable as not yet finalised; amount currently recognised is based on management's judgement
- Difficulties are compounded by need to measure at PV and therefore also predict payment dates and identify appropriate pre-tax rate; both require significant level of management judgement

- Addressing completeness assertion here is challenging and also difficult to predict, as costs to be incurred in future and have not yet been determined

Procedures:

- Obtain copy of regulator's notice detailing date of issue and any quantification of amount of penalty payable by Awdry plc
- Obtain copy of any draft instalment agreement detailing the timing and amount of each repayment
- Review correspondence with regulator for evidence of amount payable and details of repayment schedule
- Confirm payment to bank statement
- Review correspondence with Awdry plc's lawyers to ascertain current status of negotiations and views of legal advisers
- Review of cash flow statements and forecasts to assess company's ability to pay instalments
- Discuss with management the current status of negotiations; accounting treatment and non-compliance with IAS 37 (failure to measure at PV)
- Review board minutes for evidence of discussion of penalty, remedial action to address safety issues, and any other possible safety issues
- Request client calculation of present value (including identification of appropriate discount rate)

Property development

- Material to assets (with calculation)
- Incorrect valuation (non-compliance with IFRS 13); FV should be adjusted for all costs associated with alternative use

Difficulties when performing audit:

- Conversion costs will be based on estimation and will be inherently uncertain – hence challenge to obtain sufficient appropriate audit evidence that all costs have been identified and accurately quantified
- Judgement required to identify property's highest and best use per IFRS 13
- Per IFRS 13, highest and best use must be:
  - Physically possible – requires assessment of construction industry expert
  - Legally permissible – requires confirmation from local planning authority
  - Financially feasible – requires assessment of whether Awdry plc will have sufficient funds to complete development
- Valuation must be compared to the property's fair value in its existing use and other potential uses
- May be other potential uses which have not been considered

Procedures:

- Physical inspection of building by auditor
- Agree carrying value to non-current asset register
- Obtain valuation of completed development by independent external expert
- Obtain details of external expert including assessment of professional certification, experience, reputation and objectivity
- Inspect quotation/contract with building contractor to confirm cost of £1.2 million
- Inspect planning permission from local authority in order to ensure alternative use of property has been approved
- Inspect correspondence with local council confirming fees of £173,000

- Review board minutes for evidence of discussion of development

	15

Professional skills marks

Analysis and evaluation

- Appropriate assessment of the ethical and professional issues raised, using examples where relevant to support overall comments
- Effective appraisal of the information to make suitable recommendations for appropriate courses of action

Professional scepticism and judgement

- Effective challenge and critical assessment of the evidence supplied with appropriate conclusions
- Appropriate application of professional judgement to draw conclusions and make informed comments regarding the accounting treatments of the client

Commercial acumen

- Inclusion of appropriate recommendations regarding the additional audit procedures required by the firm
- Appropriate recognition of the wider implications of the new quality management standards for the audit firm
- Consideration of the commercial and professional context of auditing standards

Maximum	5
Total	25

(a) **New FRC Quality Management standards**

Towards the end of 2020, the IAASB issued two new quality management standards (ISQM 1 and ISQM 2) and a revision of ISA 220. These were subsequently adapted by the FRC and issued for use in the UK during 2021.

The aim of this project was to 'raise the bar' for quality management across the profession. The project took place against the backdrop of high-profile audit failures, and the need to ensure that audits are conducted to the required standard of quality in order to restore public trust in the profession.

The shift from 'quality control' to 'quality management' denotes a move from an unstated assumption that audits will be of a standard quality which then merely needs to be controlled, rather as an automated factory might monitor the goods produced by its machines and discard any items that are faulty. This constitutes a passive approach, which the new standards seek to replace with one that is more active and based on risk assessment.

The risk-based approach, which is at the centre of ISQM (UK) 1, requires firms to establish their own quality objectives, identify and assess quality risks and design and implement responses that address the quality risks. As a principles-based standard, ISQM (UK) 1 does not give many examples of objectives, risks and responses, because it is for firms to determine what these should be in the context of their own organisations.

One of the key pressures on firms is the need to meet their corporate objectives, which may include objectives relating to revenue or to profitability. ISQM (UK) 1 specifically states that acceptance or continuance decisions for a client should not be based purely on 'financial or operational priorities', but should include consideration of the ethical and other values of the client. In this way, the IAASB (and by association, the FRC) is attempting to raise the status of the audit profession, which it considers necessary in the light of the visible audit failures of recent years.

ISQM (UK) 2 is a new standard which covers quality reviews for specific engagements. The engagement quality review is a key safeguard where engagement quality is under threat. The effect of ISQM (UK) 2 will be to help auditors to navigate this important process.

The central revisions of ISA (UK) 220 (Revised) were to underline that the audit engagement partner is ultimately responsible for the management of quality at the engagement level, and to introduce a 'stand back' requirement allowing regular reflection in relation to audit quality. This should have a clear impact on the work of the audit engagement partner.

The effect on firms is therefore likely to be the implementation of a thoroughgoing risk management process in relation to audit quality, which should in the end result in higher levels of audit quality. It is possible, too, that such a process could bring with it new costs for audit firms, both in terms of the costs of performing the new quality management procedures and the need sometimes to reject or discontinue engagements with clients who do not embody the required ethical values.

(b) **Difficulties in auditing accounting estimates and procedures**

Cash-settled share-based payment scheme

The expense recognised this year of £825,000 in respect of the cash-settled share-based payment scheme represents 11.1% of profit before tax and is therefore material to Awdry plc's statement of profit or loss for the year. The related liability of £825,000, which would be recognised on the statement of financial position, is on the borderline of materiality to assets at 1.4%.

IFRS 2 *Share-Based Payment* requires that for cash-settled share-based payment transactions, the entity should measure the services acquired and the liability incurred at the fair value of the liability. Moreover, it states that until the liability is settled, the entity should remeasure the fair value of the liability at the end of each reporting period and at the date of settlement, with any changes in fair value recognised in profit or loss for the period. In the case of Awdry plc, the expense and the associated liability has been calculated based on the fair value of the rights as at the reporting date, and the treatment therefore complies with the requirements of IFRS 2 (£4.50 × 550,000 × 1/3 = £825,000).

IFRS 2 also requires that the amount recognised as an expense for cash-settled share-based payments should be based on the best available estimate of the number of awards that are expected to vest. The entity must therefore estimate the number of awards which are expected to vest. In this case, management's estimate that all 55 staff will qualify for the rights appears to be based on a perception of good historic staff relations, which may be inaccurate, and the expectation that none of the eligible staff will leave over the three-year vesting period may prove to be unrealistic. The predictive nature of management's estimate in this regard represents a challenge to the auditor, as it is difficult to obtain reliable evidence.

The fair value estimate of £4.50 is based on an options-pricing model that is an example of a complex valuation model which, according to ISA (UK) 540 (Revised) *Auditing Accounting Estimates and Related Disclosures*, is built on significant estimates and assumptions and is therefore challenging to audit. The initial choice of which option pricing model to use is also a matter of judgement and whichever model is selected, it will incorporate judgemental inputs, such as the current risk-free interest rate and measures of share price volatility.

Procedures:

- Obtain a copy of the contractual documentation for the share-based payment scheme and supporting file notes detailing principal terms and confirm:
  - Grant date and vesting date
  - Number of executives and senior employees awarded share appreciation rights
  - Number of share appreciation rights awarded to each individual member of staff
  - Conditions attaching to the share appreciation rights
- Perform an assessment of the appropriateness of the model used to value the share appreciation rights and confirm it is in line with the requirements of IFRS 2.
- Obtain details of the external expert used and assess the appropriateness of their appointment by considering their professional certification, experience, reputation and objectivity.
- Perform a review of the expert's valuation, including an assessment of the assumptions used in order to determine the fair value of the share appreciation rights.

- Obtain details of historic staff turnover rates obtained from the human resources department, including actual data for the first year of the vesting period, and consider this in conjunction with the assumptions made by management.
- Perform a review of the forecast staffing levels through to the end of the vesting period, including an assessment of the reasonableness of the assumptions used and their consistency with other budgets and forecasts.
- Discuss the basis of staff retention assumptions with management and challenge their appropriateness.
- Perform sensitivity analyses on both the valuation model and the staffing forecasts.

Regulatory penalties

The expense recognised in this year's statement of profit or loss for the year of £1.3 million is material to both profit (17.6%) and assets (2.2%). According to IAS 37 *Provisions, Contingent Liabilities and Contingent Assets*, the fine should be measured at its present value at the reporting date. IAS 37 states that where the effect of the time value of money is material, the amount of a provision should be the present value of the expenditures expected to be required to settle the obligation and that the discount rate used in the calculation should be a pre-tax rate that reflects current market assessments of the time value of money and the risks specific to the liability. The cash flows for the repayment of the fine over the ten years should therefore be discounted at an appropriate rate to present value as at 31 May 20X5.

The audit of the provision represents a challenge for the auditor in a number of respects. First, it is difficult to estimate the amount payable, as it has not yet been finalised and the amount currently recognised is an estimate based on management's judgement. These difficulties are compounded by IAS 37 requirements to measure the provision at present value. The measurement process therefore also requires management to predict the payment dates and to identify an appropriate pre-tax rate to be applied as the discount factor. Both of these will require a significant level of management judgement, which will be a challenge for the auditor to obtain sufficient relevant and reliable evidence on. Moreover, there is also the possibility of other provisions being needed in relation to the costs of remedying the safety issues that the regulator has identified and in relation to other potentially unidentified safety problems. Here, addressing the completeness assertion will represent a key challenge to the auditor, as it is inherently difficult to predict all of the costs to be incurred in the future, especially when they have not yet been determined.

Procedures:

- Obtain a copy of the regulator's notice detailing the date of the issue and any indication of the amount of the penalty to be paid by Awdry plc.
- Obtain a copy of any draft instalment agreement detailing the timing and amount of each repayment.
- Review Awdry plc's correspondence with the regulator for evidence of the amount payable and details of the repayment schedule.
- Confirm to post year-end cash book and bank statements if any amounts have been paid after the year end.
- Inspect Awdry plc's correspondence with its lawyers in order to ascertain current status of negotiations and the views of its legal advisers.
- Review Awdry plc's cash flow statements and forecasts in order to assess the company's ability to pay the instalments.
- Enquire of management in relation to the current status of the negotiations – the need to measure the provision at present value and their non-compliance with IAS 37 (ie their failure to measure the provision at present value).
- Review the board minutes for evidence of management's discussion of the penalty, any planned remedial action to address safety issues, and any other possible safety issues.
- Discuss with management the need for the company to perform a calculation of the present value of the provision, including identification of an appropriate discount rate.

Property development

The proposed valuation of the property at £4.9 million represents 8.4% of assets and is material to Awdry plc's statement of financial position as at 31 May 20X5. According to IFRS 13, the fair value measurement of a non-financial asset should take into account a market participant's ability to generate economic benefits by using the asset in its highest and best use or by selling it to another market participant who would use the asset in its highest and best use.

The audit of the property development will be challenging for the auditor, first because judgement will be required in order to identify the property's highest and best use per IFRS 13. The auditor must ensure, for example, that the valuation is compared to the property's fair value in its existing use, as well as in any other potential uses. Indeed, there may be other potential uses which have not been considered.

IFRS 13 also states that the highest and best use of a non-financial asset such as a property must be:

- Physically possible – this will therefore require independent expert confirmation that the conversion can be successfully undertaken;
- Legally permissible – this will require obtaining confirmation of formal permission from the local planning authority; and
- Financially feasible – this will require a detailed assessment of whether Awdry plc will have sufficient cash flows in order to fund the development through to completion to complete development.

Overall, therefore, the auditor will need extensive audit evidence, much of it from third parties, in order to confirm management's judgement that conversion into residential apartments represents the highest and best use of its former maintenance depot.

According to IFRS 13, when considering alternative uses for non-financial assets, the valuation should include all costs associated with the alternative uses. Hence, if the proposed development does represent the highest and best use of the property, the valuation should be adjusted for all of its associated costs. The proposed valuation at £4.9 million is not therefore in compliance with IFRS 13 and on the basis of the information available, the valuation should be £3,527,000 (ie £4.9 million £1.2 million £173,000). If the additional costs are fairly stated therefore, the property is currently overstated by £1.373 million (£4.9 million £3,527,000). The auditor will, however, need external confirmation of the £173,000 in fees from the local building regulator and will also need to obtain sufficient appropriate audit evidence that the conversion costs of £1.2 million are fairly stated. The conversion costs will present a particular challenge to the auditor, as they will be based on the estimation of industry experts and the amounts will be inherently uncertain. There may be unforeseen additional costs payable to complete the conversion which will be difficult for the auditor to identify and quantify.

Procedures:

- Physically inspect the building to assess its condition and perform an initial assessment of whether it might be suitable for conversion into residential apartments.
- Agree the carrying amount of the property to Awdry plc's non-current asset register.
- Obtain a valuation of the completed development by an independent external expert and agree the basis of valuation is in line with the requirements of IFRS 13.
- Obtain details of the external expert and assess their expertise and objectivity through assessment of their professional certification, experience, reputation and connections with Awdry plc.
- Inspect the quotation or contract with the building contractor to confirm the expected cost of £1.2 million.
- Inspect the planning permission documentation from the local authority in order to ensure that the proposed alternative use of property has been approved.
- Inspect correspondence with the local building regulator confirming the fees of £173,000.
- Discuss with management alternative uses of the property, explaining IFRS 13's valuation principles and confirming that no additional fees or costs will be payable.
- Review board minutes for evidence of management's discussion of the development.

- Review Awdry plc's cash flow statements and forecasts to ensure the project is financially feasible.
- Obtain written representations from management confirming all details and costs concerning development have been disclosed to the auditor.

37 Willow

Workbook references

Chapters 8 and 11.

Top tips

The question gave you two situations. Make sure you read the requirement carefully here, as there were a number of things to consider – you might have missed, for example, the requirement to recommend any further procedures. The trick with each of these issues is to take on a sceptical frame of mind. The audit work on inventory, for instance, appears to be complete as long as a written representation is obtained. But even if you did not remember the detailed requirements of ISA (UK) 580, you should have been able to question whether such a representation would be reliable, and to point out that it needs to be backed up by evidence. The further procedures are then just ways of obtaining this evidence.

The four short issues for your attention were deceptively difficult to deal with. On the face of it there should be two easy marks for each of the four issues, but in reality, the first issue in particular was not easy. You should, however, have been able to gather together enough marks to pass the question.

Easy marks

There were some relatively easy marks in part (a) in relation to describing further audit procedures.

Marking guide	Marks
(a) **Audit implications**	
Generally up to 1.5 marks for each implication assessed, 1 mark for each impact on the financial statements identified, and 1 mark for each effect on auditor's report:	
Inventory	
• Comment on individual materiality	
• Value at lower of cost and NRV and impact on profit	
• Written representation not sufficient evidence	
• Recommend procedures (1 mark each)	
Legal claim	
• Immaterial individually but material to profit when combined with inventory adjustment	
• Financial statements materially misstated when two issues combined – implication for opinion	
• Suitability of verbal representation as source of evidence	
• Recommended procedures (1 mark each)	
Maximum	13
(b) **Issues for attention of audit committee**	
Generally up to 2 marks for each matter discussed:	

- Property revaluations
- Delay in receiving non-current asset register affects audit efficiency
- Weak controls in procurement department
- Lack of approved supplier list on integrity of supply chain

Maximum	7

Professional skills marks

Analysis and evaluation

- Appropriate use of the information to support discussion, draw appropriate conclusions and design appropriate responses
- Identification of omissions from the analysis or further analysis which could be carried out
- Balanced assessment of the information to determine the effect on the auditor's report in the circumstances

Professional scepticism and judgement

- Effective challenge of information, evidence and assumptions supplied and, techniques carried out to support key facts and/or decisions
- Appropriate application of professional judgement to draw conclusions and make informed decisions about the actions which are appropriate in the context and stage of the engagement.

Maximum	5
Total	25

(a) **Matters raised by senior**

Inventory

This area is not material to net assets or to income and expenses but could become so in combination with any other immaterial misstatements detected. Unless this is the case, there would be no effect on the auditor's report.

IAS 2 *Inventories* requires inventory to be measured at the lower of cost and net realisable value (NRV). If the NRV is zero, then an expense of £130,000 will be incurred, reducing both and assets by the same amount.

ISA (UK) 580 *Written Representations* states that a written representation is not of itself sufficient appropriate audit evidence. Therefore further evidence must be obtained.

The assertion that must be tested here is that NRV is not less than £130,000. The finance director's claim that the inventory can be recycled would therefore need to be supported by evidence that the NRV of this recycled inventory would not be less than £130,000.

Further procedures include:

- Making enquiries with the operations director to ascertain whether or not the materials could be recycled
- Obtaining documentary evidence of the costs of recycling together with the potential selling price of recycled materials
- Reviewing invoices raised after the period end for evidence that the materials have in fact been recycled and sold on

Provisions

This area is not material to net assets or to income and expenses, but it could become so in combination with any other immaterial misstatements detected.

IAS 37 *Provisions, Contingent Liabilities and Contingent Assets* requires that a provision be recognised where it is probable that there would be an outflow of resources embodying economic benefits, as is the case here. If this adjustment is not made, then liabilities and expenses are both understated. There is also unlikely to be adequate disclosure of the circumstances surrounding the case.

When combined with the inventory misstatement, the result is a total misstatement of £255,000, which is material to income and expenses. If neither adjustment is made, then the audit opinion should be qualified.

The verbal confirmation that the case will probably be paid is not sufficient, and written confirmation from the lawyers is required. The finance director's refusal to provide this evidence may constitute a limitation on the scope of the audit if the evidence cannot be obtained elsewhere, and this throws into question management's integrity. This should trigger a reassessment of any written representations from management relied on elsewhere in the audit, for example in relation to inventory. The auditor's report is also likely to include a Companies Act 2006 disclosure that information and explanations required for the audit have not been obtained.

Further procedures include:

- Review correspondence with lawyers for evidence regarding the outcome of the legal claim
- Review board minutes for evidence about the claim

(b) **Property**

A move from recognising properties at cost to at fair value would be acceptable in line with IAS 16 *Property, Plant and Equipment*, as long as it is applied across an entire class of assets. The Committee should be aware of the benefits and drawbacks of such a change. Benefits include more relevant information on the values of properties, and quicker recognition of fair value gains in the financial statements. But the drawbacks include the need to remeasure fair value at each period end. It may also be necessary to employ an external expert to estimate fair values, which could be costly.

Asset register

The delay in receiving the non-current asset register would have impaired audit efficiency, and potentially resulted in greater audit costs and therefore fees.

The fact that the issue was discussed with the committee last year but then recurred, suggests some sort of controls failure; either the last year's discussion was not acted upon by the committee, or at some other point. In both cases the reason for this needs to be ascertained.

The fact the financial controller has been on holiday at the start of the audit for two years running is not just unhelpful, but may be indicative of something deeper awry, such as fraud.

Procurement

No explanation is actually given for why invoices are not matched to goods received notes; there is no reason why this cannot be done if suppliers are changed frequently, for example. Without this control, it is possible that invoices are paid without goods ever being received. There is also a risk of fraud if this is done intentionally, either delivering goods to another address or using dummy invoices. The committee should seek to improve controls in this area as a matter of some urgency.

Frequently switching suppliers is not itself a problem, but again this would not seem to totally preclude maintaining a list of approved suppliers – it only means that such a list would be a long one. If totally new suppliers really are being used so frequently, then there may be issues with quality rather than price.

38 Jovi

Workbook references

Chapters 6, 7, 8, 9 and 10.

Top tips

Part (a) was not an easy requirement. Your approach should be to work through each issue in turn, trying to think of what the problem might be, and not forgetting to think about whether the audit evidence was adequate. Note the importance of reading the question here (and remembering the requirement as you are writing), as candidates who recommended specific audit procedures would have wasted their time.

Part (b) should not have been too difficult. To score five marks you should have looked to make two to three points both for and against. To score well here you need to apply your knowledge to the scenario. Although joint audits are a current issue, you are not being asked for your opinion on the issue generally; you are being asked about a joint audit of the financial statements of May Co. You therefore need to think about the specific scenario. The examining team tends to like students who make points like 'the small local firm will probably offer a cheaper audit service than Sambora & Co', as this is something that can only really be said about this specific situation.

Easy marks

There were easy marks in part (b) for some of the pros and cons of the joint audit, but all in all this was a difficult question.

ACCA examining team's comments

Requirement (a) is a good example of a question requirement where candidates were expected to think on their feet and not rely on rote learnt facts. The candidates that did as the question instructed and took time to think about the information in the scenario scored well, and there were some sound answers. However, the majority of candidates could not apply their knowledge to this scenario, leading to unfocused answers that did not actually answer the question requirement. Answers were on the whole unsatisfactory. Candidates tended to approach the key audit findings in a logical way, working through them in the order presented in the question. However, for each key audit finding most answers simply stated that audit evidence was not adequate without explaining why, and then gave a list of audit procedures, which was specifically not asked for.

On requirement (b), some answers seemed to confuse a joint audit with an audit involving component auditors, and some used the fact that the foreign audit firm was a small firm to argue that it could not possibly be competent enough to perform an audit or have a good ethical standing. Most answers identified the cost implications for the client, and the advantage of involving a local firm who would have knowledge of the local law and regulations.

Marking guide **Marks**

(a) **Audit completion issues**

Up to 2 marks for each audit completion issue assessed:

- Property disposal/sale and leaseback
- Property revaluation
- Actuarial loss
- Goodwill impairment
- Goodwill classification into assets held for sale
- Associate
- Presentation of assets held for sale (separate and not netted off)

Marking guide	Marks
• Measurement of assets held for sale	
• Lack of disclosure of discontinued operation	
• Non-controlling interest	
• Finance cost and loan	
Maximum	15
(b) **Joint audit**	
Up to 1 mark for each advantage/disadvantage discussed:	
• Retain local auditors' knowledge of May Co	
• Retain local auditors' knowledge of local regulations	
• Sambora & Co can provide additional skills and resources	
• Cost effective – reduce travel expenses, local firm likely to be cheaper	
• Enhanced audit quality	
• But employing two audit firms could be more expensive	
• Problems in allocating work – could increase audit risk	
Maximum	5
Professional marks	
Analysis and evaluation	
• Appropriate use of the information to support discussion, draw appropriate conclusions and design appropriate responses	
• Identification of omissions from the analysis or further analysis which could be carried out	
• Balanced assessment of the information to determine the effect on the completion phase of the audit in the circumstances	
Professional scepticism and judgement	
• Effective challenge of information, evidence and assumptions supplied and, techniques carried out to support key facts and/or decisions	
• Appropriate application of professional judgement to draw conclusions and make informed decisions about the actions which are appropriate in the context and stage of the engagement.	
Maximum	5
Total	25

(a) **Statement of profit or loss and other comprehensive income**

(1) **Copeland revenue**

Copeland's 25% drop in revenue indicates that goodwill relating to this subsidiary may be impaired. There is a risk that this goodwill was not impaired when it should have been.

(2) **Property disposal**

At £2m, the property disposal is material.

The option to repurchase the property in five-years' time points to the possibility that this could not be a genuine sale but a finance arrangement whose economic substance is that of a secured loan. In this case, the audit evidence obtained is inadequate and further evidence needs to be obtained to determine the substance of the transaction.

If this is indeed a secured loan (in substance), then the asset will be recognised in the statement of financial position and the cash receipt will be recognised as a loan (liability). Finance costs will be accrued over the period of the loan – five years.

If this is the case, then profit has been materially overstated and liabilities understated.

(3) **Property revaluation**

The gain of £800,000 was just below initial materiality of £900,000but above the current materiality level of £700,000. Audit procedures must now be performed in this area, as it is possible that there could be a material misstatement here.

(4) **Actuarial loss**

The actuarial losses are material, at £1.1m, as is the defined benefit liability of £10.82m.

Axle Ltd is a service organisation, and ISA (UK) 402 *Audit Considerations Relating to an Entity Using a Service Organisation* requires the auditor to obtain an understanding of this organisation. This can be obtained:

- From the Group itself, we should gain an understanding of how Axle Co arrives at its valuation, its systems and its controls
- By obtaining a report from the auditor of Axle Ltd (the service organisation's auditor), which contains an opinion on the description of Axle Ltd's systems and controls

This has not been done, and we have no information about how the plan assets and liabilities were valued or how reliable their valuation might be. The audit team must therefore obtain this information before the service organisation's representation can be relied upon.

(5) **Goodwill impairment**

There is an indicator that goodwill relating to the Copeland subsidiary is impaired, but this does not appear to have been considered by the audit team. Audit procedures must be performed on the assumptions used by management in conducting this review. The reasons why the 25% fall in revenue has not resulted in impairment must be specifically addressed.

(6) **Associate**

The statement of profit or loss includes £1.01m share of profit of associate. The figure in the statement of financial position should include (as a minimum) the amount brought forward, plus any profit attributable, less any dividends received. It is thus highly unlikely that this figure would not have changed since last year.

(7) **Trading division held for sale**

The division held for sale is part of a subsidiary. Therefore, some of the goodwill relating to this subsidiary may need to be reclassified as part of the disposal group of assets held for sale. Although it is possible that no goodwill will need to be reclassified, evidence needs to be obtained that this is the case.

The statement of financial position contains one line within non-current assets for 'assets classified as held for sale'. This presentation is incorrect: the assets held for sale should be a separate section in the statement of financial position.

It appears that this £7.8m could be a net figure, which again is incorrect – there should also be a separate section within 'liabilities' showing the liabilities from the disposal group. Audit procedures should be performed to ascertain whether this in fact a net figure, in order to get the classification right.

Although there are assets held for sale from a trading division, the statement or profit or loss shows no discontinued operations. IFRS 5 *Non-current Assets Held for Sale and Discontinued Operations* requires the post-tax profit or loss of discontinued operations to be shown as a single line. This appears to be a material misstatement, and audit procedures should be performed to determine whether it is or not and whether there are any discontinued operations.

(8) **Non-controlling interest**

There is no disclosure in relation to the non-controlling interest in the statement of profit or loss and other comprehensive income. Both profit for the year and total comprehensive income attributable to the non-controlling interest should be disclosed.

(9) **New loan**

Finance costs should be included of £8m × 2% × $^{9}/_{12}$ = £120,000. However, finance costs have only risen by £40,000. No loans appear to have been paid off during the year, as long-term borrowings have increased by exactly the £8m received for the new loan. Therefore, finance costs appear to be understated.

The amount is not material of itself but should be accumulated together with any other misstatements that are discovered, as they could become material in aggregate.

Work should be performed to understand the components of the finance charge recognised, as other finance costs may have ceased during the year. The notes to the financial statements should also be reviewed to ensure there is adequate disclosure of the loan taken out.

(b) **Advantages of joint audit**

In the case of May Co, Sambora & Co would not currently have much understanding of May Co's business. It would therefore make sense to continue to make use of Moore & Co's accumulated understanding of the client's business.

The fact that May Co is located in Farland means that it could be subject to accounting, legal and professional regulations that are different from those under which Sambora & Co are accustomed to operating. It makes sense to continue to use the local auditors' knowledge of this potentially very different regulatory framework.

There may be some cost savings in using Moore & Co, as a result of the fact that Sambora & Co would no longer need to send the whole audit team out of Farland to conduct the audit procedures. It is also possible that Moore & Co might charge lower fees than Sambora & Co, so using Moore & Co's staff to perform procedures could work out less expensive.

Audit quality should increase as a result of a joint audit. As new auditors, Sambora & Co will be approaching the audit with a fresh outlook, unprejudiced by previous events and may be able to spot new issues or offer different solutions from those previously identified by Moore & Co.

Disadvantages of joint audit

A key disadvantage is the uplift in costs that results from the unavoidable duplication of work between the two auditors.

Moore & Co may use a different audit approach and methodology from Sambora & Co, leading to disagreements throughout the audit about which is the correct way to proceed. This could result in a loss of efficiencies, as time is spent agreeing on the best audit approach rather than carrying out actual audit work. If either audit firm's approach is followed exclusively, some of the benefits of a joint audit will be lost.

39 Jolie

Workbook references

Chapters 2, 5, 6 and 7.

Top tips

This question on planning an audit is typical of the kind of question you should expect to have to tackle in Section A of this exam. The question is tough but fair, and if you were well-prepared and well-practised at identifying a variety of risks in scenarios, you should have been able to achieve reasonable marks on it. To tackle questions like this, you have to devise a strategy along these lines:

- Make sure you understand the requirement and answer it
- Look for key words and themes in the scenario that indicate audit risk
- Ensure you explain **why** things are risks and **why** you would use a particular strategy
- Do not spend too long on the question to the detriment of others

In this particular question there are a lot of possible points that you could make in relation to the requirement on business risks, so it is crucial that you stick to your timings for this question part and do not overrun, otherwise you may find it difficult to score the easy marks that will be available elsewhere in the exam.

The requirement part on ethics should have been relatively straightforward, provided that you were familiar with the technical content. But even if you were struggling technically, you could have picked up quite a few marks just by working through the material given in the question.

Easy marks

Be sure to get at least five of the professional marks.

Examining team's comments

On the whole, candidates seemed to like this question, especially the business risk evaluation. However, many candidates failed to answer the specific question requirements, thereby denying themselves marks.

Answers to the first part tended to display reasonable application skills, with some candidates prioritising the risks identified, and reaching an overall conclusion. There was much less evidence here of 'knowledge-dumping' than in answers to other requirements. However, common weaknesses included:

- Repeating large chunks of text from the scenario with no explanation provided
- Not actually explaining or evaluating a risk identified – just saying 'this is a risk'
- Providing detailed definitions of business risk, which was not asked for
- Providing audit procedures for risks, again not asked for
- Providing recommendations for mitigating the risk, not asked for

In addition, it is worth noting that very few candidates used the figures provided in the scenario to identify risk exposure. The client's revenue and profit had fallen from the previous year, and some simple financial analysis could have revealed falling profit margins and worsening interest cover. This type of analysis is not difficult or time consuming, and it is something that demonstrates mark-generating application skills.

Finally, some candidates simply failed to answer the question requirement. A minority of candidates took the opportunity to provide many pages of answer which just described how you would plan an audit in general. All of this was totally irrelevant and failed to generate any marks.

The quality of answers to the second part was unsatisfactory. Some answers, which were by far the majority, tended to just outline an accounting treatment with no mention of the actual risk itself. Another common weakness was to discuss the detection risk which may arise with a new audit client, which is not a risk of material misstatement.

The third part was better answered, and some candidates scored well, providing well written procedures specific to the valuation of an intangible asset. Many of those that did not score well had misread the scenario.

Candidates are reminded that audit procedures must be tailored to the facts of the scenario provided and must be sufficiently detailed to make sense. 'Get management rep', 'discuss with management' and 'review cost' are examples of meaningless 'procedures' which earn no credit without further development. In addition, there were many instances where candidates were obviously trying to generate procedures using a list of words as a prompt. For example, 'observe the asset' or 'inquire about the asset'. Candidates must think carefully and not just use words as a prompt if they make no sense. Candidates are encouraged to read the examining team's article on exam technique in answering questions on audit procedures available on ACCA's website.

The few unsatisfactory answers to the **ethics requirement** tended to simply repeat extracts from the advertisement and say, 'This is unprofessional.'

Marking guide	Marks
(a) **Evaluate significant business risks**	
0.5 mark for each risk identified (to max 4 marks) and up to 1.5 further marks for explanation.	
Up to 2 marks for calculation of margins, trends, etc:	
• High fashion items/high staff turnover in design team	
• Obsolete inventory and pressure on margins	
• Widespread geographical business model hard to control	
• Volume of e-commerce sales – ability of systems to cope	
• Security of e-commerce operations	
• Tax and regulatory issues on e-commerce	
• Foreign exchange risk on new overseas transactions	
• Outsourcing of phone operations – quality issues	
• Outsourcing of phone operations – unpopular with customers	
• Long-term sustainability of outsourced function	
• Ethical Trading Initiative – supply chain issues	
• Potential restrictions on operation of distribution centres	
• Industrial unrest leading to disruption of operations	
• Financial performance – general comments on revenue/profitability/margins	
Maximum	12
(b) **Evaluate significant risks of material misstatement**	
Up to 3 marks for discussion of each risk.	
• Inventory valuation (IAS 2)	
• Inventory existence (IAS 2)	
• New inventory system	
• Unrecorded revenue	
• Capitalisation of IT/website costs	
• Valuation of brand name (IAS 38)	
• Valuation of properties (IAS 36)	
• Fraud	
• Data analysis software	
• Casual staff	
• Recognition of provision/contingent liability (IAS 37)	
• Opening balances and comparatives (1 mark only)	
Maximum	17
(c) **Audit procedures: brand name**	
1 mark per specific procedure:	
• Agree cost to supporting documentation/prior year accounts	
• Review assumptions used in management impairment review	
• Perform independent impairment review	
• Review planned level of expenditure to support the brand	
• Review results of any marketing/customer satisfaction surveys	
• Consider whether non-amortisation is GAAP for this industry	

ANSWERS

- Discuss reasons for non-amortisation with management

Maximum 5

(d) **Evaluation of advertisement**

Generally 1 mark per comment:

- Advertising not prohibited but must follow ACCA guidelines
- Cannot be misleading/exaggerated claims
- Exaggerated claim re size
- Unprofessional claim re 'most professional'
- Cannot guarantee improvements/tax saving
- Second opinions
- Introductory fee
- Audit and non-audit services
- Fees not approved by ACCA
- Improper reference to ACCA

Maximum 6

Professional marks

Communication

- Briefing notes format and structure - use of headings/sub-headings and an introduction
- Style, language and clarity - appropriate layout and tone of briefing notes, presentation of materiality and relevant calculations, appropriate use of the CBE tools, easy to follow and understand
- Effectiveness and clarity of communication - answer is relevant and tailored to the scenario
- Adherence to the specific requests made by the audit engagement partner

Analysis and evaluation

- Appropriate use of the information to determine suitable calculations
- Appropriate use of the information to support discussions and draw appropriate conclusions
- Assimilation of all relevant information to ensure that the risk evaluation performed considers the impact of contradictory or unusual movements
- Effective prioritisation of the results of the risk evaluation to demonstrate the likelihood and magnitude of risks and to facilitate the allocation of appropriate responses
- Balanced discussion of the information to objectively make a recommendation or decision

Professional scepticism and judgement

- Effective challenge of information supplied, and techniques carried out to support key facts and/or decisions
- Determination and justification of a suitable materiality level, appropriately and consistently applied
- Appropriate application of professional judgement to draw conclusions and make informed decisions about the courses of action which are appropriate in the context of the audit engagement

Commercial acumen

- Audit procedures are practical and plausible in the context of Jolie
- Use of effective examples and/or calculations from the scenario to illustrate points or recommendations.
- Recognition of the appropriate commercial considerations of the audit firm

Maximum 10

Total 50

Briefing notes

To: Audit Manager

From: Audit Partner

Subject: Jolie Ltd audit planning

Introduction

These briefing notes evaluate the significant business risks facing the new client, Jolie Ltd, and address significant issues arising in relation to the planning of the audit for the year ended 30 September 20X5.

(a) **Business risks**

Continuing quality of product

Jolie operates in a dynamic and volatile business environment, with new ranges being introduced every eight weeks. There is a constant need for talented designers to develop product ranges and, given the high staff turnover, it may be difficult to retain talented staff. The risk is that if Jolie fails to recruit the right designers the quality of the product could be reduced, which could lead to a fall in revenue. Lower-quality products could potentially tarnish the JLC brand, which is so crucial to Jolie's success.

Obsolete inventory

New ranges are introduced every eight weeks, so there is a risk of inventory becoming obsolete if it is not sold during this short period. Any older inventory may be marked down, which would affect margins. Margins fell from 17.9% in 20X4 to 16.8% in 20X5, which could be related to this.

E-commerce – sales volume

Online sales now account for £255 million (£250 per order × 1,020,000 orders). In the previous year, online sales accounted for £158 million (£300 per order × 526,667 orders). This represents an increase of 61.4% ((255 – 158)/158 × 100%).

The risk is that the system may be overwhelmed by the increase in sales volume, which could lead to difficulties fulfilling orders and potential damage to the all-important JLC brand.

E-commerce – new systems

There is a risk of system failure associated with any new system, which could result in unfulfilled orders and hence brand damage.

E-commerce – security

There is a risk that customers' details held on the system are not kept sufficiently securely. There is a risk that data protection laws could be breached. If security were to be breached, then the brand would be very likely to suffer.

E-commerce – overseas sales

Making sales overseas exposes Jolie to several new risks. If sales are made in foreign currencies, then there is a risk that the computer system may not be able to handle these sales (eg it could miscalculate foreign currency prices).

Overseas sales expose Jolie to potential tax complications, eg extra VAT to be paid on exported goods, and additional documentation to comply with foreign regulations.

Jolie may also now be exposed to foreign exchange risks and may find its profit margins affected by currency fluctuations.

Outsourced phone ordering

Jolie outsourced its phone ordering system to the cheapest provider. If the phone ordering system is not of a good quality, then this may be incongruent with the differentiated, high-quality nature of Jolie's products. If many errors occur with orders, then this may lead to customer dissatisfaction and damage to the brand.

The location of the call centre overseas, which presumably reflects the low cost, may be a source of frustration to customers, and may ultimately lead to a fall in revenue.

However, the risks associated with phone ordering may to some extent be mitigated by the expansion of e-commerce, which customers may prefer to use.

Ethical trading initiative

The fact that Jolie has spent a significant amount of money advertising its fair-trade credentials leads to a risk of bad publicity if these credentials were to be undermined. Any ethical failings in the supply chain may be subjected to public scrutiny, which would again damage the JLC brand.

Distribution centres

There is a real risk of local authorities revoking distribution centres' licences if conditions are breached (eg in relation to noise levels). This could pose Jolie significant operational difficulties if any of the centres are closed, as with its short inventory turnover period Jolie is especially reliant on its ability to deliver inventory on time.

Casual staff

The shift from employment contracts and onto casual agreements for new staff may give rise to a business risk of industrial unrest. This could result in disruption to the operation of the locations affected. Staff are likely to be an important non-financial asset of the business, so it will be important the Jolie Ltd manages the transition properly.

Financial performance

Overall revenue has decreased by £80 million, or 5.2% (80/1,535 × 100). Operating profit has also fallen, by £30 million, or 10.9% (30/275 × 100). Average spend per order has fallen from £300 to £250, and average revenue per store has fallen by 10.5%.

This may give cause for concern, but operating expenses for 20X5 are likely to include one-off items, eg the costs of the new sales system. The fall in spend per customer could be a symptom of general economic difficulties. The company has increased the volume of online transactions significantly.

On balance the overall reduction in profit and margins is unlikely to be a significant risk at this year end, though if the trend were to continue it may become a more pressing issue.

Jolie Ltd's finance costs have increased by £3 million, contributing to a fall in profit before tax of 13%. The company has sufficient interest cover to mean that this is not an immediate concern, but the company should ensure that finance costs do not escalate.

Conclusion

Perhaps the most significant risk for Jolie is that it fails to produce products of sufficient quality, which relates to its ability to make use of talented designers. The risk of inventory obsolescence is also significant. The downward trend in Jolie's financial performance needs to be monitored carefully in the future.

(b) **Inventory valuation**

IAS 2 *Inventories* states that inventory must be valued at the lower of cost and net realisable value (NRV). The high rate of inventory turnover leads to a risk of inventory becoming obsolete and to a fall in its NRV, and if NRV falls below cost then it will need to be written down. This may be the case with any inventory that is being sold at a reduced price, or which is slow-moving and may not be sold at all. Jolie's declining overall revenue may indicate falling NRVs and hence that inventory is impaired.

Inventory completeness and existence

It will be difficult to count inventory accurately across all of Jolie's 210 stores, and there may be a large number of goods in transit to keep track of. All of this means that the auditor will find it difficult to obtain sufficient evidence over the existence of inventory. There is a risk of fraudulent financial reporting in this area as it is difficult to verify the levels of inventory actually held.

New systems

The existence of a new sales system poses the risk of teething problems if the system did not function properly at first. As a result sales could be recorded incorrectly in the nominal ledger, either as a result of the new system not providing correct information, or because of problems with the integration of the system and the nominal ledger.

There may also be a different system in place for the newly outsourced phone sales, and there is a risk of sales being misstated if the systems are not properly integrated.

Website costs

The expenditure on the new IT systems may have been capitalised in line with IAS 38 *Intangible Assets*, according to which only expenditure in the development phase may be capitalised, with costs before (eg planning) and after (eg operational) being expensed. The risk is the overstatement of intangible assets, and understatement of operating expenses if these have not been expensed.

New inventory system

The auditor is likely to be ambivalent about the introduction of a new inventory management system; the new system may introduce better controls, but as a result of the system being new, the controls around it may not yet be fully developed or understood. The new system allows management to keep track of cost inputs into inventory, but with this greater complexity comes a risk that a new, relatively untested system may be prone to error. This suggests a control risk, and a risk of error in relation to inventories.

Jolie's inventory management appears to be complex, being held at multiple sites. Controls will need to be very robust to track the movement of inventory accurately, and to ensure reliable inventory counting across all of Jolie's locations. There is a risk of under- or over-statement of inventory as a result of this.

Brand name

An intangible asset has been recognised in respect of the JLC brand name, as this was purchased and not internally generated. This appears to be in line with IAS 38. At 12% of total assets this amount is likely to material to the financial statements.

IAS 38 requires an impairment review to be conducted at the end of each reporting period. If this is not conducted, the asset could be overvalued. The decline in revenue could be an indicator of impairment.

The significant advertising expenditure during the year should be expensed, and there is a risk of overstatement of assets and non-occurrence of expenses if this expenditure has been capitalised.

Property valuation

Jolie owns numerous distribution centres (rather than leasing them), and there is a risk of these assets being impaired if their licences are revoked. Additionally, there has been a fall in revenue per store, which is an indicator of impairment per IAS 36 *Impairment of Assets*.

Fraud

The existence of a fraud during the year gives rise to a risk of misstatement in relation to it, in this case affecting the purchase ledger. The company has begun an investigation to correct any errors here, so the audit firm needs to obtain information regarding how this investigation was conducted, and what its findings were. It should also be considered whether the monies directly lost to the fraud have been accounted for correctly as expenses recognised in profit or loss.

It is unlikely that any monies that may be recoverable would meet the criteria for recognition as a contingent asset (since their recovery would need to be virtually certain), so the auditor would need to consider whether the company has recognised any such asset.

Data analysis software

The use of data analysis software by the finance department suggests an improvement in the entity's system of internal control and thus a possible reduction in control risk. The auditor should consider whether management is using the software appropriately, and they would need to understand whether it has had any effect on the existing controls in operation at the entity.

Casual staff

The introduction of casual staff rather than employees carries with it a risk that the taxation authorities could deem them to be employees, in which case Jolie may become liable for further taxation payments. There is thus a risk that both expenses and liabilities are understated in relation to this.

There is a risk of misstatement of staff costs in general terms, since the introduction of casual staff will mean operating payroll in a way that is different from what has gone before. Payroll staff may not be familiar with the differing requirements which gives rise to a risk of error.

There may also be a risk of misclassification of costs between expense categories. The auditor will need to ensure that the expenses are accounted for within the most appropriate section of the statement of profit or loss, although the issue is unlikely to affect the profit or loss figure itself.

Division assets held for sale

The factory represents 0.8% of total assets (=£14m / £1,675m) and the office represents 0.5% (=£8m/£1,675m) of total assets. Individually these are not material but taken together, they may be considered material at 1.3% of total assets (=£22m/£1,675m).

The Nearland division factory and office buildings have been treated as 'held for sale' in the financial statements, but no mention is made of how the items of plant and equipment have been treated. It is possible that they will be sold together with the factory, but this is by no means certain and would need to be confirmed. Another possibility is that the plant and equipment no longer has a value in use to Jolie Co (if the factory is sold), and should therefore be subject to an impairment review. In this case there is a risk that assets are overstated if a required impairment is not recognised.

The assets held for sale may be material, so it is important that evidence is obtained regarding their classification in line with IFRS 5 *Non-current Assets Held for Sale and Discontinued Operations*. The IFRS 5 criteria for this classification appear to have been met for the factory and office because offers have been received. It should be confirmed whether these offers have been accepted, whether contracts have been signed and when the sale is likely to be completed.

It should be ascertained how the values of the assets held for sale were arrived at. They should be held at the lower of their carrying amount, and their fair value less any costs to sell. There is a risk that the assets may be overstated if, for example, costs to sell are not taken into account.

The gain recognised on revaluation should be calculated as the difference between fair value less costs to sell, and their carrying amount. The gain should be recognised in other comprehensive income, and not in profit or loss. There is a risk that profit may be overstated if the gain is recognised directly in profit.

(c) **Audit procedures on JLC brand**

- Agree cost of brand to supporting documentation, eg purchase invoice (if still available).
- Agree cost of brand to prior year audited financial statements.
- Review monthly income streams generated by brand, for indication of any decline in sales.
- Review results of impairment reviews by management, establishing the validity of any assumptions used in the review (eg discount rate used to discount future cash flows; growth rates used to predict cash inflows).
- Perform independent impairment review on the brand, and compare with management's impairment review.
- Review level of planned expenditure on marketing and advertising to support the brand name, and consider its adequacy to maintain the image of the brand.
- Inquire as to the results of any customer satisfaction surveys, to gain an understanding of the public perception of JLC as a high-fashion brand.
- Consider whether non-amortisation of brand names is a generally accepted accounting practice in the fashion retail industry by reviewing the published financial statements of competitors.

- Discuss with management the reasons why they feel that non-amortisation is a justifiable accounting treatment.

Tutorial note. As this is a first-year audit, no marks will be awarded for procedures relating to prior year working papers of the audit firm.

(d) **Ethical issues**

Advertisement

Neither the ACCA *Code of Ethics and Conduct* nor the IESBA *Code of Ethics for Professional Accountants* prohibit advertising. However, a professional accountant must not bring the profession into disrepute, and adverts must be both honest and truthful. There are a number of question marks over whether this is the case with the draft advert here.

The advert claims that Jen & Co is the largest accountancy and audit firm in the country, yet the firm has only three offices and 12 partners. This is neither honest nor truthful. Moreover, the claim that the firm is the most professional cannot be proven, and could imply that other firms are not professional, bringing the profession into disrepute.

The advert claims that a range of services are guaranteed to improve efficiency, which is not something that can be guaranteed, particularly given that the advert does not specify which services would do this.

The advert guarantees that tax would be saved, but again this cannot be guaranteed as it depends on the application of tax law in the specific circumstances of each client. To guarantee savings in this way may create a self-interest threat to the objectivity of tax work done by the firm, as rules may not be properly applied in order to save tax.

There is a risk of future litigation from clients who do not see improved efficiency or tax savings as a result of Jen & Co's work.

It is possible for an audit firm to give a second opinion on another firm's report, but this is unusual. The advert may imply that Jen & Co's opinion would be superior to another firms, which brings the profession into disrepute. Moreover, it may compromise the firm's independence in such cases by creating an expectation that Jen & Co would not modify its auditor's report if it were necessary to do so.

The 25% 'introductory offer' is effectively lowballing, which is prohibited. If fees are too low, there is a risk that fees are not sufficient to allow staff to be assigned to audits who have appropriate levels of skill and experience.

A reduction is offered where both audit and tax services are provided. Non-audit services should only be provided to an audit client where any threats to auditor objectivity can be reduced to an acceptable level. Offering such a reduction may create self-review and advocacy threats. Moreover in the UK, the FRC's *Ethical Standard* Part B, section 4 *Fees, Remuneration and Evaluation Policies, Gifts and Hospitality, Litigation* requires that audit fees are not influenced by the provision of other services, as this may compromise the objectivity of the auditor.

Finally, the advert claims that rates are approved by the ACCA. This is false, because the ACCA does not approve specific firms' rates, and in view of the ethical concerns raised above over fees is disingenuous and dishonest in its intention too.

Conclusion

Perhaps the most significant risk for Jolie is that it fails to produce products of sufficient quality, which relates to its ability to make use of talented designers. The risk of inventory obsolescence is also significant. The downward trend in Jolie's financial performance needs to be monitored carefully in the future.

These notes have also discussed the principal risks of material misstatement, which will need to be addressed by audit procedures. The notes have given the principal procedures that should be performed in relation to the valuation of the JLC brand name. Finally, a number of significant ethical and professional issues exist with the revenue raising suggestion, which these notes have evaluated.

40 Vancouver

Workbook references

Chapters 2, 6 and 9.

Top tips

This was quite numerical as AAA questions go. In order to pass the question, you needed to spend some time using your calculator! There is a 0.5 mark for each correct trend (eg a % change), but these are capped at five marks. That means you should calculate five trends, for both the current year and the comparative. Alternatively, you could calculate some ratios instead of some of these trends, but try not to exceed six or seven in total otherwise you'll be using up too much of your time. Candidates who don't do any calculations at all are unlikely to pass this question – and on the flipside, candidates who struggle elsewhere will benefit from these easy marks.

The first part was a fairly normal audit risk question, for 24 marks. This part of the question hinges on your ability to spot risks, and to eek marks out of each risk (up to a maximum of 2 marks per risk). There was not a great deal of written information in this scenario – unlike other examples of Q1 – so your performance depended on your analytical procedures.

Your approach here is to read through both the question and the results of your analytical procedures, making a note of the risks. If a risk relates to an accounting treatment, you should **briefly** summarise the accounting requirement, and then say what could have gone wrong. There are marks available for stating whether an issue is material, and these are easy marks. Every risk you discuss should therefore begin with a calculation of the item as a % of the relevant figure (eg x% of total assets), and then either 'this is material' or 'this is not material'.

It should not need pointing out that there are no marks available for generic discussions of audit risk. If you do this, then you will not get any marks for it! Also there is no need to classify risks into inherent risks/control risks/detection risks. You simply need to explore what the risk itself is. Lastly, do not mention business risks unless they're asked for in the requirement, as this is something the examining team has written about again and again.

The next part should have been straightforward; if you had revised the audit procedures on the consolidation then most of this was just knowledge.

The next part, on ethics, you needed first to spot the two ethical issues in the scenario. It's important that you state the **ethical threat** that's present (eg 'this presents an advocacy threat'), together with any **safeguards** that might help reduce it. Finally, conclude on whether the threat can be reduced to an acceptable level (after safeguards are applied).

Finally, be sure to get at least 5–7 of the professional marks. Write a 'briefing notes' heading, an introduction and a conclusion, and use subheadings throughout your answer and the communication marks should be fairly safe.

Easy marks

The professional marks, the marks for assessing materiality for each issue, and the marks for analytical procedures. Most of part (b) was easy, if you knew it. If not, then there is a very easy mark available for suggesting checking the 'arithmetical accuracy' of the consolidation schedule.

ACCA examining team's comments

The question followed the pattern of previous examinations and was set at the planning stage of the audit and candidates were presented with several requirements, which covered identifying audit risks and ethics.

The **best answers** demonstrated that a methodical approach had been applied to the information in the scenario, and strong candidates had clearly worked through the information logically, calculating the key ratios and trends from the information provided, identifying the risk factors from the calculations and the remaining information, assessing materiality before going on to explain the risk fully and specifically in terms of how the risk could impact the financial statements. Candidates are reminded that **when discussing risk** relating to a specific accounting treatment, well explained answers will include an **evaluation of the potential impact** of the risk factor on the financial statements [BPP note. ie calculate materiality!].

A disappointing number of candidates failed to calculate any ratios or trends from the information supplied and thus provided weak answers and were unable to identify an appropriate number of audit risks for the marks available. Conversely some candidates calculated every trend or ratio possible, which was excessive and demonstrated poor time management; for example there was insufficient information in the question to calculate inventory or trade payable days, so these ratios did not add to their answer.

Audit risk continues to be an area that candidates find difficult and particularly it continues to be noted that many candidates fail to engage with the information provided in enough depth, specifically when provided with extracts from financial statements. Candidates are again reminded that in order to provide a full answer in relation to audit risk they should utilise and analyse all the information that is provided.

In relation to the next part, many candidates clearly knew the consolidation process very well, but had trouble expressing this knowledge in terms of audit procedures. Many answers simply described what should happen in a consolidation, and they thought that by including the words 'check' or 'ensure' every so often that would be enough eg 'check goodwill calculation', 'ensure all subsidiaries included' but didn't actually say how these things should be done. However, despite these problems most answers were satisfactory.

Finally, candidates were required to discuss the ethical issues relevant to the audit firm and to recommend any necessary actions. Performance in this area was mixed and it was clear that many candidates did not know the requirements of the IESBA *Code of Ethics*. For example a sizeable number of candidates advised that the audit engagement partner could simultaneously become a non-executive director on the audit committee of the entity under audit and failed to identify that the *Code* expressly prohibits this due to the extent of the self-review and self-interest threats which would be created. This demonstrates a lack of knowledge of the ethical requirements and a lack of professional judgement. Candidates are reminded that they must revise and be comfortable with the content of the *Code of Ethics*. Most candidates were, however, able to highlight that there was a potential advocacy and self-review risk from representing the client in a tax enquiry but did not condition this on either grounds of materiality or that the firm had not been previously involved in the client's tax affairs.

There were professional marks available, and most candidates were able to earn the presentation marks by providing a clear introduction and conclusion and using headings to create an appropriate structure for their answer. Many candidates did not articulate their points in a clear or logical order and therefore many missed out on the logical flow and clarity marks.

Marking guide

Marks

(a) **Audit risk evaluation and prioritisation**

Generally 1 mark for each ratio (including comparative) calculated, and 0.5 mark for relevant trends calculated, up to a maximum of 5 marks.

In addition, up to 2 marks for discussion of audit risks, including the assessment of materiality. Risks in relation to ratio analysis could include:

- Overstatement of operating expenses
- Overstatement of revenue due to finance director's comments
- Interest cover and risk relating to disclosure
- Change in effective tax rates and risk tax expense incorrect
- Ongoing investigation and risk of fines and penalties which need to be provided for
- Liquidity issues and risk relating to disclosure

ANSWERS

- Increase in receivables days and overstatement of trade receivables
- Onerous lease provision has halved in value, risk of understatement of liability

Other audit risks – up to 1.5 marks for each risk identified and explained:

- Allow 1 mark for each correct calculation and comment on materiality
- Whether capital and revenue expenditure appropriately accounted for in respect of the modernisation programme
- Whether assets have been accounted for using the concept of significant components
- Treatment of borrowing costs and whether eligible for capitalisation
- The gain on disposal of shares in Calgary Ltd is incorrectly recognised in profit for the year
- Non-controlling interest has not been disclosed in respect of profit for the year
- Risk of inadequate disclosure regarding the rationale for, and consequences of, the share disposal
- Management bias due to sale of shares to institutional investor
- Deferred tax – risk of overstatement if the amount is not a recoverable asset
- Lack of financial reporting expert on the Group audit committee increases the risk of incorrect accounting treatments

Maximum 24

(b) **Principal procedures on consolidation**

Generally 1 mark per procedure explained:

- Test controls
- Review group instructions
- Recalculate adjustments
- Reconcile intra-group balances
- Review fair values/consider need for expert
- Consider consistency of accounting policies
- Recalculate deferred tax implications
- Agreement to component financial statements
- Consider treatment of non-controlling interests
- Arithmetical accuracy of consolidation schedule

Maximum 8

(c) **Ethical issues**

Generally up to 2 marks for each relevant matter discussed:

- Assisting in the tax investigation creates advocacy threat (1 mark where risk is explained)
- Appointment of audit partner to audit committee creates objectivity threat
- FRC ES s2 prohibits appointment of audit firm member as director of audit client
- Appointment would be against principles of UK Corporate Governance Code
- Matters to be discussed with client's audit committee and the audit firm's ethical partner

Maximum 8

Professional marks

Communication

- Briefing notes format and structure - use of headings/sub-headings and an introduction
- Style, language and clarity - appropriate layout and tone of briefing notes, presentation of materiality and relevant calculations, appropriate use of the CBE tools, easy to follow and understand
- Effectiveness and clarity of communication - answer is relevant and tailored to the scenario
- Adherence to the specific requests made by the audit engagement partner

Analysis and evaluation

- Appropriate use of the information to determine suitable calculations
- Appropriate use of the information to support discussions and draw appropriate conclusions
- Assimilation of all relevant information to ensure that the risk evaluation performed considers the impact of contradictory or unusual movements
- Effective prioritisation of the results of the risk evaluation to demonstrate the likelihood and magnitude of risks and to facilitate the allocation of appropriate responses
- Balanced discussion of the information to objectively make a recommendation or decision

Professional scepticism and judgement

- Effective challenge of information supplied, and techniques carried out to support key facts and/or decisions
- Determination and justification of a suitable materiality level, appropriately and consistently applied
- Appropriate application of professional judgement to draw conclusions and make informed decisions about the courses of action which are appropriate in the context of the audit engagement

Commercial acumen

- Audit procedures are practical and plausible in the context of Vancouver
- Use of effective examples and/or calculations from the scenario to illustrate points or recommendations.
- Recognition of the appropriate commercial considerations of the audit firm 10

Total 50

Briefing notes

To: Albert Franks, audit engagement partner

From: Audit Partner

Subject: Vancouver Group audit planning

Introduction

These briefing notes are prepared for use in the audit team briefing for the Vancouver Group (The Group). Following a meeting between the audit partner and the Group finance director and a member of the Group audit committee, and using information provided, significant audit risks have been identified and explained. Analytical procedures have been used to identify several audit risks. A recommendation is made of the procedures which should be performed on the consolidation process. Finally, the briefing notes discuss the ethical implications of suggestions made by the Group audit committee.

ANSWERS

(a) **Audit risk evaluation**

SELECTED ANALYTICAL PROCEDURES AND ASSOCIATED AUDIT RISK EVALUATION

	20X5	*20X4*
Operating margin	27/375 × 100 = 7.2%	38/315 × 100 = 12.1%
Return on capital employed	27/66 + 181 = 10.9%	38/67 + 153 = 17.3%
Interest cover	27/4 = 6.8	38/3 = 12.7
Effective tax rate	10/33 × 100 = 30.3%	15/35 × 100 = 42.9%
Receivables days	62/375 × 365 = 60 days	45/315 × 365 = 52 days
Current ratio	97/120 = 0.8	83/95 = 0.9

Analytical procedures reveal that the Group's revenue has increased by 19%, but that operating expenses have disproportionately increased by 25.6%, resulting in the fall in operating margin from 12.1% in 20X4 to 7.2% in 20X5. This is a significant change, and while the higher costs incurred could be due to valid business reasons, the trend could indicate operating costs are overstated or sales are understated. There is a risk that some of the costs involved in modernising the Group's warehousing facilities have been incorrectly treated as expenses when this should have been capitalised. The trend in operating margin is consistent with the change in return on capital employed which has also fallen. The treatment of the costs involved in the modernisation of the Group's warehouse facilities will need detailed investigation to ensure that costs have been classified appropriately.

However, given the finance director's comment that operations have not changed significantly during the year, the increase in revenue of 19% seems surprising, given that this is a significant increase, and there is therefore also a risk that revenue could be overstated. The Group's revenue recognition policy is to recognise revenue at the point of shipping. This must be assessed in relation to the requirements of IFRS 15 *Revenue from Contracts with Customers*, which requires revenue to be recognised when control passes to the customer (IFRS 15). If, for example, it is Group policy to compensate customers for loss or damage during shipping then this could indicate that revenue should be recognised at the point of delivery instead. Alternatively, it could mean that part of the transaction price needs to be allocated to a separate service covering this performance obligation. Audit work will need to be concentrated in this area to determine whether revenue is appropriately stated and recorded in the correct period.

The Group's interest cover has declined sharply, and finance costs have increased by 33%. This could indicate that finance costs are overstated, however, given that the Group has taken out additional debenture finance during the year, and also now has an overdraft, an increase in finance costs is to be expected and is more likely to simply reflect the significant drop which the Group has experienced in its operating profit levels. The debenture may contain a covenant in relation to interest cover, and if so, there is a risk that the covenant may have been breached. While this is a business risk rather than an audit risk, the matter may require disclosure in the financial statements, leading to a risk of material misstatement if necessary disclosures are not made.

The comparison of effective tax rates shows that the effective tax rate is much lower in 20X5. This could be due to the utilisation of Toronto Ltd's tax losses which seems to have taken place due to the reduction in the Group's deferred tax asset this year. However, this is a complex issue and there is a risk that the tax expense is understated in comparison with the previous year. Given the ongoing tax investigation regarding potential underpayment of tax, this is a significant audit risk. Depending on the possible outcome of the tax investigation, there may be a need to provide for additional tax liabilities and any penalties which may be imposed by HMRC. Details of the investigation and its findings so far will need to be considered and the probability of HMRC finding against the Group should be considered as part of our detailed audit testing to verify that liabilities are complete or that disclosures for contingent liabilities are complete.

The Group appears to be experiencing cash flow problems in the current year with its cash reserves being eradicated during the year and the Group now relying on an overdraft. Its current ratio has fallen from 0.9 to 0.8, indicating that liquidity is a problem. The receivables days figure has increased from 52 days in 20X4 to 60 days in 20X5. This could be due to poor credit control, and if this is a significant risk to the Group the issues involved may need to be disclosed according to IFRS 7 *Financial instruments: disclosure*, hence there is a risk of inadequate disclosure. The increase in receivables days may also indicate an overstatement of receivables balances.

The provisions balance has halved in value from £12 million in 20X5 to £6 million in 20X5. This could indicate that the provisions balance is understated and operating profit overstated, if there is not a valid reason for the reduction in value of the liability. Possibly if the onerous lease contracts have now expired, then that could justify the change in value, but this will need to be confirmed. In addition, provisions may be required in respect of dilapidation costs for leased properties, and there is a risk of understated liabilities if any such provisions have not been recognised.

The results of the analytical review should be reconsidered once any necessary adjustments are made to the financial statements in light of potential misstatements identified below.

Modernisation of warehousing facilities

Overall, property, plant and equipment has increased by £43 million or 23% which is a significant movement, representing 11.7% of total assets. A total amount of £25 million has been spent on modernising the warehousing facilities which is material, representing 6.8% of total assets. The modernisation programme explains part of the increase in property, plant and equipment but given that depreciation would have been charged, the reasons for the large increase must be carefully considered. As part of our audit work we will need to ensure that we understand how all of this movement has occurred as there are several risks of material misstatement associated with the expenditure.

First, there is a risk that the amounts capitalised into non-current assets are not correct in that capital and revenue expenditure may not have been correctly identified and accounted for separately. According to IAS 16 *Property, Plant and Equipment*, modernisation costs which give rise to enhanced future economic benefit should be capitalised where the costs are directly attributable, whereas costs which do not create future economic benefit should be expensed. It would seem that costs such as replacing electrical systems should be capitalised, but other incidental costs which may have been incurred such as repairing items within the warehouses should be expensed.

In addition, there is a risk that the various components of each warehouse have not been treated as separate components and depreciated over a specific useful life. IAS 16 requires that each part of an item of property, plant and equipment with a cost which is significant in relation to the total cost of the item must be depreciated separately. Items such as computer systems are likely to be significant components of the warehouses and as such should be accounted for as discrete assets in their own right. Failure to correctly determine the significant components of the capital expenditure could lead to misstatement of the assets' carrying values and depreciation expenses.

There is also an issue with the finance costs in respect of the £5 million debenture taken out to finance the modernisation programme. If the criteria of IAS 23 *Borrowing Costs* are met, in particular if the modernisation of the warehouses meets the definition of a qualifying asset, then borrowing costs should be capitalised during the period of modernisation. A qualifying asset is an asset which takes a substantial period of time to get ready for its intended use or sale, so depending on the length of time that the modernisation programme has taken, it may meet the definition so borrowing costs would need to be capitalised. There is therefore a risk that borrowing costs have not been capitalised if the qualifying asset definition has been met, and equally a risk that borrowing costs may have been capitalised incorrectly if the definition has not been met. The borrowing costs, however, may not be material in isolation.

If any accounting errors have occurred in the amounts capitalised into property, plant and equipment, then non-current assets may be over or understated, as would be the depreciation charge calculated on the carrying value of those assets.

Disposal of shares in Calgary Ltd

A comparison of the statement of profit or loss for both years shows that the profit made on the disposal of shares in Calgary Ltd has been separately disclosed as part of profit in the year ending 30 September 20X5. The profit recognised is material at 30.3% of profit before tax. Several errors seem to have been made in accounting for the disposal and in respect of its disclosure.

First, it is not correct that this profit on disposal is recognised in the statement of profit or loss. According to IFRS 10 *Consolidated Financial Statements*, changes in a parent's ownership interest in a subsidiary which does not result in the parent losing control of the subsidiary are treated as equity transactions. Any difference between the amount by which the non-controlling interests are adjusted and the fair value of the consideration paid or received is recognised directly in equity and attributed to the owners of the parent; this appears to have been incorrectly accounted for as there should not be a profit on disposal within the statement of profit or loss. Therefore profit before tax is overstated by £10 million. The tax charge may be overstated if it has been calculated based on profit including the gain made on the share disposal.

Second, while the non-controlling interest has been recognised in equity, the Group's profit for the year has not been attributed and disclosed between the Group and the non-controlling interest. There is also a risk that the disclosure requirements of IFRS 12 *Disclosure of Interests in Other Entities* are not followed, in particular in relation to the change in group structure which has taken place during the year, as IFRS 12 specifically requires disclosure relating to the consequences of changes in a group's ownership interest in a subsidiary which does not result in a loss of control.

Management bias

The sale of shares to an institutional investor creates an inherent risk of management bias as management may feel under pressure to return favourable results. This could explain the positive trends in revenue shown by the analytical review and could also explain the incorrect presentation of the profit on disposal which has incorrectly inflated profit by £10m.

Deferred tax asset

There is a risk that the deferred tax asset is overstated. According to IAS 12 *Income Taxes*, a deferred tax asset is recognised for an unused tax loss carry-forward or unused tax credit if, and only if, it is considered probable that there will be sufficient future taxable profit against which the loss or credit carry-forward can be utilised. While it appears that some of the deferred tax asset has been utilised this year, as the Group has returned to profit, there remains a risk that if it is no longer recoverable, then the amount would need to be written off. Audit work should be planned to confirm the recoverability of the amount recognised.

Audit committee – lack of financial reporting expert

Guidance on the composition of audit committees suggests that a financial reporting expert should be included in the committee. This is to ensure that the functions of the audit committee in relation to financial reporting are carried out effectively, for example, in ensuring that accounting policies are appropriate. The lack of an expert increases the risk that incorrect accounting treatments will occur and is effectively a control risk.

Cyber attack

The attack did not adversely affect operations, but this appears to have been merely fortunate. The attack demonstrates the vulnerability of the Group's IT systems, and there is a risk that further information could have been lost, unbeknown to the Group. Procedures should be performed to determine whether this was the case, and what effect this may have had on the Group's accounting records.

The Group may be subject to jurisdictional laws concerning information privacy – the Data Protection Act 1998 in the UK. This Act gives individuals, including employees, the right to control information about themselves. If the Group has failed to take appropriate measures to protect this data, then it may be in breach of the Act.

In line with ISA (UK) 250A *Consideration of Laws and Regulations in an Audit of Financial Statements*, the auditor must obtain an understanding of any non-compliance. In this case, it is possible that there may be fines as a result of a breach, which should be reported in the financial statements The auditor should discuss the non-compliance with the appropriate level of management and should consider whether disclosure is needed in the public interest.

It is possible that the employees affected by the loss of data could bring legal proceedings against the Group for failing to protect their data. IAS 37 *Provisions, Contingent Liabilities and Contingent Assets* requires the Group to provide for any liabilities that are certain or probable, but not those that are remote. IAS 37 also requires the obligating event to have taken place in the past, which is the case here. There is a risk that any provisions that should be made have not been made.

(b) **Consolidation process – audit procedures**

The audited accounts of each subsidiary should be agreed to the schedules used in the consolidation process, as figures may not have been transposed correctly. Verify that all subsidiaries are included on the schedule, and that the consolidation schedule agrees to the group financial statements.

The consolidation schedule should be arithmetically checked by casting and cross-casting.

All consolidation adjustments should be reviewed and recalculated, for example pre-acquisition reserves and goodwill for subsidiaries, along with any fair value adjustments. It will be necessary to agree adjustments to underlying documents, eg some of the figures making up goodwill may be agreed to prior year financial statements.

All intra-group balances should be reconciled, and a schedule obtained of intra-group transactions to ensure that they are eliminated from profit or loss.

Procedures should be performed to verify that subsidiary items that should be carried in the group accounts at fair value have been, where they may be measured in the subsidiaries' financial statements on a different basis, eg properties which must be carried at fair value in the group, but which may be at depreciated cost in the subsidiary.

The auditor should verify that accounting policies have been applied consistently across the group, and that where adjustments need to be made for the group accounts these have been made correctly (eg because of foreign subsidiaries which operate under different financial reporting requirements).

The deferred tax consequences of consolidation and fair value adjustments should be reviewed for completeness, and calculations reperformed for accuracy.

(c) **Ethical matters to be considered by our firm**

Tax investigation

There are two key issues to be considered by Montreal & Co. The first relates to the tax investigation by HMRC, and the request for the audit firm to look into the Group's tax position and to liaise with HMRC on the Group's behalf. The FRC's *Ethical Standard* contains guidance on situations where an audited entity is involved in a tax dispute and has requested assistance from the audit firm.

According to the FRC ES, where tax services to be provided by the audit firm include representing the audited entity in any negotiations or proceedings involving the tax authorities, advocacy threats to the auditor's objectivity and independence may arise. The advocacy threat arises due to the audit firm representing the client and promoting the interests of the client to the relevant authority, in this case HMRC.

The FRC ES contains a specific section relevant in a case such as this, stating that the audit firm shall not undertake an engagement to provide tax services to an audited entity where this would involve acting as an advocate for the audited entity.

A management threat to objectivity may also arise where the audit firm becomes so closely identified with management's arguments regarding the tax issue that the auditor is inhibited from forming an impartial view of the treatment of the issue in the financial statements. In this case the threat is lessened by the fact that it was another firm of accountants, Victoria & Co, which provided the tax planning advice to the Group, but the significance of the threats and the materiality of the issues to the financial statements will need to be carefully considered by Montreal & Co before they agree to take on the engagement to provide the necessary support to the Group.

If the firm does consider it possible to provide the service, safeguards must be applied to eliminate the threats or reduce them to an acceptable level. Examples of such safeguards include:

- Using professionals who are not members of the audit team to perform the service
- Having a tax professional provide advice to the audit team on the Group's tax position, and review the financial statement treatment

However, of greatest importance in deciding whether the firm can act is the nature of the client: if the Vancouver Group is a listed entity (and although it is not stated in the scenario, the presence of a group audit committee suggests that it is) then this work would be prohibited if it creates a self-review threat (IESBA Code: para. R604.24).

Partner on audit committee

The second ethical issue relates to the request for one of Montreal & Co's audit partners to be appointed as a non-executive director of the Group and to serve on the Group's audit committee. This would seem inappropriate as one of the functions of the audit committee is to oversee the external audit function, and it would not be possible for an audit partner of the firm to remain objective when evaluating matters such as determining the audit fee or being involved with the approval of non-audit services.

The FRC's *Ethical Standard* specifically states that the audit firm or a partner or employee of the audit firm shall not accept appointment or perform a role as an officer or member of the board of directors of the audited entity or as a member of any subcommittee of that board. This is due to the threats to objectivity being so significant that no safeguards could reduce the threats to an acceptable level.

> **Tutorial note.** Credit will also be awarded where answer points are provided in the context of the requirements of the IESBA *Code of Ethics for Professional Accountants*.

The *UK Corporate Governance Code* and associated FRC guidance contains provisions relating to the role of non-executive directors, some of which relate to the responsibilities of the non-executives who serve on the audit committee. It would not be appropriate for an audit partner to serve on the audit committee because one of the functions of the audit committee is to liaise between the audit firm and the company, and to decide on matters such as the approval of the audit firm to provide non-audit services and the audit firm's remuneration for services provided. It clearly would not be appropriate for a partner from the audit firm to be involved in such decisions from the company's perspective.

Hence, Montreal & Co must explain to the Vancouver Group that unfortunately it will not be possible for an audit partner to be appointed to serve as a non-executive director of the Group. The provision of the tax investigation service should also be discussed, and the audit committee's approval for Montreal & Co to provide the service should be obtained, depending on the materiality of the matter to the financial statements and the deployment of safeguards to reduce threats to an acceptable level.

Conclusion

These briefing notes have provided an evaluation and prioritisation of the audit risks to be considered in planning the audit of the Vancouver Group, including analytical procedures. The notes have recommended the principal audit procedures that should be performed on the consolidation process. There are several significant threats to our firm's objectivity which need to be discussed with the client prior to the audit fieldwork commencing.

41 Adams

> **Workbook references**
>
> Chapters 2, 6, 7, 8 and 9.

Top tips

Your general approach should be to read the requirement carefully, and then to work through the question noting down issues (audit risks) as they occur to you.

The question includes a set of draft financial statements for the group. Clearly the examining team wants you to look at them, but it is important not to spend too long performing detailed analytical procedures when this is not what the requirement asks you to do. The objective here is to do enough work on the figures to be able to identify the most important risks. The terms you need to use when writing your answer here come from the requirement – you can say things like, 'this is a significant risk', or equally that 'this risk is unlikely to be significant to the audit'. It will be to your advantage if you can show the marker that you are trying to prioritise risks, sorting them into important and less important.

The first requirement asks for 'audit risks', not 'risks of material misstatement' as is often seen in AAA questions. The difference is that audit risk includes detection risk, so this requirement is specifically allowing you to discuss detection risk where this is relevant. As always, there are no marks available for theoretical discussions of the nature of audit risk.

Detection risk is immediately relevant because Adams is a new client, so there is a risk in relation to our relative lack of knowledge of it, and in respect of opening balances and comparatives. Notice, though, that the point about opening balances and comparatives is made quite briefly in our answer. Sometimes candidates like to recite pre-learned material about these two issues, and this is something that your examining team has said it does not like.

With part (b), the procedures should come from each matter to consider. Much of the material here on component auditors is generic, so the trick is in working out which bits of your knowledge are relevant to the scenario and which bits are not.

Part (c) asked for procedures in relation to one area in the scenario and was very representative of AAA questions. There shouldn't have been anything untoward here.

Part (d) was effectively a self-contained ethics question featuring a few mini situations. None of these was unusual and there were easy marks available for categorising the kind of threat (eg 'self-review'), stating **why** this was a threat, and then for saying what the auditor should do about it.

Easy marks

The communication marks here are valuable and are well worth the time it takes to get them.

ACCA examining team's comments

In terms of **exam technique**, a significant minority of candidates attempted Question One [this question] last. This almost invariably was a flawed exam strategy, as not enough time had been left to attempt the longest and most detailed question in the exam. Candidates are advised to attempt Section A first, to ensure that sufficient time is devoted to these longer scenario-based questions.

This question was based on planning the audit of a new client – the Adams Group. The first requirement asked candidates to evaluate the audit risks to be considered in planning the audit of the Group. **This is a very typical requirement for Question One** in the AAA exam, and while it was encouraging to see that many candidates had clearly revised this part of the syllabus, there were many whose answers were extremely disappointing. The best answers worked through the information provided in the question to identify the various audit risks and evaluated them by including an assessment of materiality and a discussion of the significance of the risks identified.

Only the better candidates identified the risks arising from the opening balances and comparative information (due to this being a new audit client for the firm), the lack of presentation of income from the associate in the Group statement of profit or loss, the incorrect treatment of the investment property revaluation gains (which should be recognised as part of profit for the year) and the change in the effective tax rate.

The best answers included in their evaluation of each audit risk an **identification of the risk factor** from the scenario (eg the measurement of the investment properties), a **determination**

of materiality where possible given the information in the question, a **clear comment** on the appropriateness of the **accounting treatment** where relevant, and the **impact on the financial statements** (eg not cancelling inter-company transactions would lead to overstated revenue, cost of sales, receivables and payables).

The **key weakness** present in many answers was the **poor quality of explanations**. Most candidates could identify a reasonable range of risks but could not develop their answer to demonstrate a **clear evaluation of that risk**, in a suitable structure, like the one discussed above. For example, having identified that the portfolio of investment properties would give rise to some kind of audit risk, many candidates would then attempt to expand their answer with vague comments such as 'there is risk this is not accounted for properly', 'there is risk in the accounting treatment' or 'there is risk that IAS 40 will not be followed'. This type of comment does not represent a detailed evaluation of audit risk and does not earn credit.

Other weaknesses seen in many answers included:

- Incorrect materiality calculations or stating that a balance is material without justification
- Incorrect analysis of the financial statements provided or incorrect trend calculations, the most common of which was stating that inventory had increased by 50% when it had doubled
- Too much emphasis on business risk with no development or discussion of the audit implications
- Not using the draft financial statements at all to identify audit risks
- Not identifying from the scenario that all Group members use IFRS as their financial reporting framework and report in the same currency, leading to sometimes lengthy discussion of irrelevant matters
- Long introductions including definitions of audit risk, showing a lack of appreciation of the fact that the notes are for an audit partner, and general discussions about audit planning
- Lack of understanding of certain accounting treatments such as equity accounting for associates and the correct treatment of investment properties
- Focusing on goodwill – despite the fact that no goodwill was recognised in the Group financial statements many answers discussed at length that it must be tested for impairment annually
- Suggesting that the bonus scheme would lead to manipulation of expenses, when the bonus was based on revenue

Requirement (b), for 8 marks, asked candidates to explain the matters to be considered, and the procedures to be performed, in respect of planning to use the work of the component auditor. **This requirement was relatively well attempted**, with the majority of answers covering a range of relevant matters and associated procedures. It was clear that many candidates had studied this part of the syllabus, and could apply their knowledge to the question scenario. Most candidates identified that the component audit firm was a small firm, so resourcing the audit could be an issue, and that due to its overseas location there may be differences in the ethical code and auditing standards used by the firm. **Weaker answers** incorrectly discussed the problem of the overseas subsidiary not reporting under IFRS (the question clearly stated that it did) and tended to focus on accounting issues rather than answering the question requirement.

Note. Examining team comments are not available for all parts of this question. The specimen exam is based on a past exam sitting, so only those parts of it that were in the past exam have comments – the question parts that are new to the specimen exam do not have examining team comments for them.

Marking guide **Marks**

(a) **Audit risk evaluation**

In relation to the matters listed below:

Up to 1 mark for each relevant calculation/trend and 0.5 mark for relevant materiality calculations:

- New audit client
- Analytical review:
- Increased revenue and profitability, risk of overstatement
- Increased current ratio, risk of overstatement of current assets
- Unusual trend in PPE, risk of over- or understatement
- Brand name – indefinite useful life and lack of amortisation
- Brand name – potential impairment and overstatement if not recognised
- Equity accounting – measurement of associate and possible impairment
- Disclosure of income from associate
- Classification as an associate
- Ross Ltd's inventory – control issues relating to multi-location of inventory
- Lynott Co's new inventory control system
- Beard Ltd's investment property – measurement of the gain
- Beard Ltd's investment property – incorrect classification as other comprehensive income
- Possible error in comparative information and need for scepticism
- Bonus scheme – inherent risk of overstating revenue (linked to analytical review)
- Elimination of management charges
- Inventories – movement in the year and potential overstatement
- Intra-group trading (inventories)
- Goodwill – none recognised
- Reliance on component auditor

Maximum	19

(b) **Using the work of a component auditor**

Up to 1.5 marks for each matter explained:

- Willingness of component auditor to perform work required
- Compliance with ethical requirements
- Professional competence and sufficient resources
- Existence of a regulated environment
- Assess level of risk in the subsidiary audited by the component auditor

1 mark for each relevant procedure:

- Review the local ethical code (if any) and compare with the IESBA Code
- Obtain confirmation from Clapton & Co of adherence to any local ethical code and the IESBA Code
- Establish whether Clapton & Co is a member of an auditing regulatory body, and the professional qualifications issued by that body
- Obtain confirmations from the professional body to which Clapton & Co belong, or the authorities by which it is licensed
- Discuss the audit methodology used by Clapton & Co in the audit of Lynott Co, and compare it to those used under ISAs
- A questionnaire or checklist could be used to provide a summary of audit procedures used

ANSWERS

- Request any results of monitoring or inspection visits conducted by the regulatory authority under which Clapton & Co operatesAscertain the quality management policies and procedures used by Clapton & Co, both firm-wide and those applied to individual audit engagements

Maximum 8

(c) **Procedures to be performed – Investment in associate**

Generally 1 mark for each well explained procedure:

- Obtain and review the legal documents for key information
- Agree the cost of investment of £11.5 million to the legal documentation and bank statement and cash book
- Review the minutes of Group management meetings for understanding of the rationale behind the investment and means of exercising significant influence
- Obtain and review management's calculation to determine the £12 million
- Obtain the financial statements of Stewart Ltd to confirm the amount of profit made in the year and confirm that the Group's share of that profit is included in the Group financial statements
- Enquire with management as to whether any impairment review of the investment in Stewart Ltd has taken place, and if so, obtain management's workings and review the assumptions used and the method of calculation

Maximum 5

(d) **Ethical threats**

Generally 1 mark for each relevant point of discussion/explanation:

- Consideration of management integrity under ISA (UK) 220 (Revised) and ISQM 1 due to use of child labour
- Advice on new systems is a non-assurance service to an audit client
- Gives rise to a self-review threat and risk of taking on management responsibility (1 mark for each threat explained)
- Advice on new systems should not be given where systems form significant part of internal control over financial reporting
- Risk increased because Group is listed entity, service should not be provided
- Attending meeting with bank is an advocacy threat
- Legal implication for the firm if partner 'confirms' work performed
- Partner should not attend meeting with bank
- Matters and reasons for declining services should be discussed with Group audit committee

Maximum 8

Professional skills marks

Communication

- Briefing notes format and structure - use of headings/sub-headings and an introduction
- Style, language and clarity - appropriate layout and tone of briefing notes, presentation of materiality and relevant calculations, appropriate use of the CBE tools, easy to follow and understand
- Effectiveness and clarity of communication - answer is relevant and tailored to the scenario
- Adherence to the specific requests made by the audit engagement partner

Analysis and evaluation

- Appropriate use of the information to determine suitable calculations

- MaximumAppropriate use of the information to support discussions and draw appropriate conclusions
- Assimilation of all relevant information to ensure that the risk evaluation performed considers the impact of contradictory or unusual movements
- Effective prioritisation of the results of the risk evaluation to demonstrate the likelihood and magnitude of risks and to facilitate the allocation of appropriate responses
- Balanced discussion of the information to objectively make a recommendation or decision

Professional scepticism and judgement

- Effective challenge of information supplied, and techniques carried out to support key facts and/or decisions
- Determination and justification of a suitable materiality level, appropriately and consistently applied
- Appropriate application of professional judgement to draw conclusions and make informed decisions about the courses of action which are appropriate in the context of the audit engagement

Commercial acumen

- Audit procedures are practical and plausible in the context of Adams
- Use of effective examples and/or calculations from the scenario to illustrate points or recommendations.
- Recognition of the appropriate commercial considerations of the audit firm 10

Total 50

Briefing notes

To: Joss Dylan, Audit engagement partner

From: Audit manager

Regarding: Audit planning for the Adams Group

Introduction

These briefing notes are prepared for use by the audit engagement partner of the Adams Group and relate to the planning of the audit of the Group for the year ended 31 May 20X5. The notes contain an evaluation and prioritisation of the significant audit risks, and the matters to be considered in respect of using the work of Clapton & Co, and the relevant procedures to be performed. The notes also detail the procedures to be conducted in relation to the investment in Stewart Ltd, an associate of the group. Finally, the notes discuss the ethical and professional issues which need to be addressed as a result of the requests made by the audit committee of the Adams Group.

(a) **Evaluation and prioritisation of the significant audit risks**

New audit client

The Group is a new client of our firm which may create detection risk as we have no previous experience with the client. However, thorough planning procedures which focus on obtaining a detailed knowledge and understanding of the Group and its activities will minimise this risk. We need to obtain a thorough understanding of each of the subsidiaries as they are all material components of the Group, with Ross Ltd, Lynott Co and Beard Ltd's assets representing respectively 20%, 22.3% and 26% of Group assets, leading to increased aggregation risk. There is also a significant risk that comparative information and opening balances are not correct.

Analytical review

Relevant trends and ratio calculations:

- Revenue increased by 11.5%
- Gross profit increased by 12.7%
- Operating profit increased by 59.5%
- Cash fallen by 54.5%
- Inventories increased by 100%
- Receivables increased by 59.1%

	20X5	*20X4*
Gross margin	36.1%	35.8%
Operating margin	1.7%	1.2%
Interest cover	12.2	7.7
Current ratio	1.8	2.2
Gearing	22.5%	25.1%

The analytical review indicates that the Group's revenue generation and profitability has improved during the year. There could be valid business reasons to explain the trends, however, the audit team should be alert for possible overstatement of revenue and understatement of expenses.

The risk is increased due to the bonus scheme which gives rise to a risk of material misstatement at the financial statement level. Management will be biased towards accounting treatments which lead to overstatement of revenue, for example, the early recognition of revenue.

There is also a risk of management manipulation of the financial statements due to the renegotiation of the Group's lending facilities, for example, it would be favourable to present a good interest cover to the bank as an analysis of interest cover is likely to feature in their lending decision.

The current ratio has fallen, largely due to the significant reduction in cash of 54.5%. Other changes within current assets could indicate audit risk, as both inventories and trade receivables have increased significantly, by 100% and 59.1% respectively. Given that revenue has increased by only 11.5% in the year, these increases appear very large and could indicate potential overstatement.

The analytical review also reveals that the amount recognised in respect of property, plant and equipment has not changed over the year. This seems unlikely to be reasonable, as the Group would presumably have incurred some capital expenditure in the year, disposed of some assets and charged depreciation. There are implications for operating profit, which, for example, is overstated if any necessary depreciation has not been charged.

Brand name

The brand is material at 7.4% of Group assets. It is recognised in the statement of financial position as an intangible asset which is appropriate given that the brand is a purchased intangible asset. However, the asset is recognised at its original cost and there is risk attached to the policy of non-amortisation of the brand. IAS 38 *Intangible Assets* states that an intangible asset with a finite useful life is amortised, and an intangible asset with an indefinite useful life is not. The risk is that the assumption that the brand has an indefinite life is not correct, and that the asset is overstated and operating expenses understated through the lack of an annual amortisation charge against the asset.

There is also a risk that the brand could be impaired given the bad publicity and allegations made by the journalist against the Group. IAS 36 *Impairment of Assets* requires an impairment review to be carried out when indicators of potential impairment exist. The allegations may have damaged the Group's reputation, with consequential impact on revenue and cash flows, though the increase of 11.5% in the Group's revenue could indicate that this is not the case, as claimed by the Group finance director. However, sales of certain products could be in decline, and the fact that inventories have doubled in value could indicate problems in selling some of the Group's products. The risk is that if any necessary impairment has not been recognised, the asset is overstated and operating expenses understated by the amount of the impairment loss.

Associate

A new associate has been acquired during the year, which gives rise to several risks, including aggregation risk as mentioned above. It is material at 11.2% of Group assets.

Because this is the first addition to the Group for many years, there is an inherent risk that the Group lacks accounting knowledge on the appropriate accounting treatment. Associates are accounted for under IAS 28 *Investments in Associates and Joint Ventures*, which states that an entity with joint control of, or significant influence over, an investee shall account for its investment in an associate or a joint venture using the equity method. There is a risk that the equity method has not been properly applied. The investment in the associate recognised in the statement of financial position has increased in value since acquisition by £0.5 million, presumably due to the inclusion of the Group's share of profit arising since investment. There is a risk that this has not been calculated correctly, for example, it is not based on the correct share of profit, and the investment may therefore be over- or understated.

Risk also arises in relation to any possible impairment of the investment, which may cause it to be overstated in both the individual financial statements of Adams Ltd, and the Group financial statements.

There is also a disclosure issue, as the Group's share of post-investment profit of Stewart Ltd should be recognised in profit or loss, and IAS 1 *Presentation of Financial Statements* requires that the profit or loss section of the statement of profit or loss shall include as a line item the share of the profit or loss of associates accounted for using the equity method. The draft statement of profit or loss and other comprehensive income does not show income from the associate as a separate line item; it may have been omitted or netted against operating expenses, and the risk is inappropriate presentation of the income from investment.

There is also a risk that the investment should not have been classified as an associate. According to IAS 28, if an entity holds, directly or indirectly, 20% or more of the voting power of the investee, it is presumed that the entity has significant influence, unless it can be clearly demonstrated that this is not the case. If the 25% holding does not give rise to significant influence, for example, if the shares do not convey voting rights, it should be classified as an investment rather than an associate. There is a risk of inappropriate classification, recognition and measurement of the investment in Stewart Ltd.

Ross Ltd's inventory in multiple locations

A risk arises in relation to inventory, which is held in each of the department stores. There is a risk that controls are not sufficiently strong in respect of the movement of inventory and counting procedures at the year end, as it will be hard for Ross Ltd to ensure that all locations are subject to robust inventory counting procedures. This control risk leads to potential over or understatement of inventory and cost of sales.

Systems and controls

The audit committee states that the Group's systems are out of date; this may give rise to control risk across the Group as a whole. In addition, Lynott Co has implemented a new inventory control system. A new system introduced during the year can create control risk. With any new system, there are risks that controls may take time to develop or be properly understood, and the risk of error in relation to inventories is relatively high.

Beard Ltd's investment properties

The investment properties are material to both Beard Ltd's individual financial statements, representing 35.7% of its total assets, and also to the Group's financial statements, representing 9.3% of Group assets.

According to IAS 40 *Investment Property*, an entity can use either the fair value model or the cost model to measure investment property. When the fair value model is used the gain is recognised in profit or loss. The draft consolidated statement of profit or loss and other comprehensive income includes the investment property revaluation gain as other comprehensive income rather than as profit or loss, and therefore the gain is not presented in accordance with IAS 40.

An accounting error may have been made in the adjustment made to increase the value of the investment property. The statement of financial position shows an increase in value of investment properties of £2.5 million, however, the gain in the statement of profit or loss and other comprehensive income is stated at £1 million. There is a risk that the gain is understated and part of the gain may have been classified elsewhere in profit or loss. The gain as stated in the statement of profit or loss and other comprehensive income is material at 9.3% of total comprehensive income.

It would be important to obtain information on the type of properties which have been invested in, and whether there have been any additions to the portfolio during the year, as part of the movement in the investment property balance during the year could be explained by acquisitions and disposals. Information should also be obtained on any disposals of investment properties during the year, and whether a profit or loss was made on such disposals.

The possible error discussed above in relation to the presentation of the investment property gain is also relevant to the comparative information, which may also be materially misstated. This increases the risk that other balances and transactions in prior years have been incorrectly accounted for. The use of professional scepticism should be stressed during the audit, and further procedures planned on opening balances and comparative information.

Further information should be sought from the previous auditor of the Group in relation to the accounting treatment for the investment properties, and whether it had been identified as an error, in which case the auditor's reports of both Beard Ltd and the Group should have been modified. A review of prior year auditor's reports is necessary, as well as a review of the previous audit firm's working papers, assuming permission is given for this to take place.

Bonus scheme

It is noticeable from the draft statement of financial position that there is no accrual recognised in respect of the bonus scheme, unless it has been included inappropriately in trade or tax payables. This indicates a potential understatement of liabilities and overstatement of profit if any necessary accrual has not been made for any bonus which is payable.

Management charges

The management charges imposed by the parent company on the subsidiaries represent inter-company transactions. In the individual financial statements of each subsidiary, there should be an accrual of £800,000 for the management charge payable in August 20X4, and Adams Ltd's individual financial statements should include £2.4 million as a receivable. There is a risk that these payables and the corresponding receivable have not been accrued in the individual financial statements.

At Group level, the inter-company balances should be eliminated on consolidation. If this has not happened, the liabilities and receivables in the Group financial statements will be overstated, though there would be no net effect on Group profit if the balances were not eliminated.

> **Tutorial note.** Credit will also be awarded for comments on relevant issues to do with transfer pricing and relevant tax implications which have not been considered and recognised appropriately in the financial statements.

Inventory

The draft consolidated statement of financial position shows that inventory has doubled in the year. Given that the Group is involved in retail, there could be issues to do with obsolescence of inventory, leading to potentially overstated inventory and overstatement of profit if any necessary write down is not recognised. This may be especially the case for the mass market fashion clothing made by Lynott Co. Inventory is material to the Group, representing 11.2% of Group assets.

Intra-group transfers

Ross Ltd transfers goods to Lynott Co for recycling when its goods are considered obsolete. There is a risk that at Group level the intra-group trading is not eliminated on consolidation, which would lead to overstated receivables and payables. In addition, if the inventory is transferred at a profit or loss, which is then not realised by the Group at the year end, the Group inventory figure and operating profit could be over- or understated if any necessary provision for unrealised profit or loss is not recognised.

Goodwill

The draft consolidated statement of financial position does not recognise goodwill, which is unusual for a Group with three subsidiaries. It may be that no goodwill arose on the acquisitions, or that the goodwill has been fully written off by impairment. However, there is a risk of understatement of intangible assets at the Group level.

Component auditor

Lynott Co is audited by an overseas firm of auditors. This may introduce audit risk in that Dando & Co will be relying to some extent on their work. Careful planning will be needed to reduce this risk to a minimum, and this is discussed in the next section of the briefing notes.

> **Tutorial note.** Credit will be awarded for relevant calculations which form part of relevant analytical review performed, such as calculations relating to profit margins, liquidity and gearing, and for discussion which is relevant to the evaluation of audit risk. Credit will also be awarded for discussion of other relevant audit risks, for example, risks associated with the lack of a deferred tax figure in the statement of financial position, and the change in effective tax rate.

(b) **Matters to be considered and procedures to be performed in respect of using the work of Clapton & Co**

ISA (UK) 600 (Revised) *Special Considerations – Audits of Group Financial Statements Including the Work of Component Auditors)* sets out the considerations the group auditor should make when planning to use the work of a component auditor. These include:

- Whether the component auditor will perform work requested by the group auditor (ISA (UK) 600: para. 24)
- Whether the component auditors understand and will comply with the relevant ethical requirements, including those related to independence, that apply to the group audit engagement (ISA (UK) 600: para. 25b). When performing work on the financial information of a component for a group audit, the component auditor is subject to ethical requirements which are relevant to the group audit. Given that Clapton & Co is based overseas, the ethical requirements in that location may be different, possibly less stringent, to those followed by the Group.
- Whether the component auditors have the appropriate competence and capabilities, including sufficient time, to perform the assigned audit procedures at the component (ISA (UK) 600: para. 26a). As far as competence and capabilities are concerned, Lynott Co reports under IFRS, and so there is less likelihood of Clapton & Co having a knowledge gap in terms of the Group's applicable financial reporting framework than if the company used local accounting rules. The fact that Clapton & Co is a member of an international network means it is likely to have access to regular training programmes and technical updates, which adds to the credibility of its audit work. Regarding sufficient resources, Joss Dylan should evaluate whether the Group engagement team will be able to be involved in the work of the component auditor to the extent it is necessary to obtain sufficient appropriate audit evidence.

Consideration should also be made as to whether the component auditor operates in a regulatory environment which actively oversees auditors. The Group audit team should ascertain whether independent oversight bodies have been established in the jurisdiction in which Clapton & Co operates, to oversee the auditing profession and monitor the quality of audit. This allows greater reliance to be placed on its work.

Finally, the risk of material misstatement in the subsidiary being audited by the component auditor must be fully assessed, as areas of high risk may require input from the Group audit team, and not be subject to audit solely by the component auditors. For areas of high risk, such as Lynott Co's inventories, the Group audit team may consider providing instructions to the component auditor on the audit procedures to be performed.

Procedures:

- Review the local ethical code (if any) followed by Clapton & Co, and compare with the IESBA *Code of Ethics for Professional Accountants* for any significant difference in requirements and principles.
- Obtain confirmation from Clapton & Co of adherence to any local ethical code and the IESBA *Code*. Establish through discussion or questionnaire whether Clapton & Co is a member of an auditing regulatory body, and the professional qualifications issued by that body.
- Obtain confirmations of membership from the professional body to which Clapton & Co belongs, or the authorities by which it is licensed.
- Discuss the audit methodology used by Clapton & Co in the audit of Lynott Co, and compare it to those used under ISAs (UK) (eg how the risk of material misstatement is assessed, how materiality is calculated, the type of sampling procedures used).
- A questionnaire or checklist could be used to provide a summary of audit procedures used.
- Ascertain the quality management policies and procedures used by Clapton & Co, both firm-wide and those applied to individual audit engagements.
- Request any results of monitoring or inspection visits conducted by the regulatory authority under which Clapton & Co operates.

(c) **Audit procedures to be performed**

Investment in associate

- Obtain the legal documents relating to the share acquisition, and review to confirm the terms and conditions including the number of shares purchased and the voting rights attached to each share.
- Agree the cost of investment of £11.5 million to the legal documentation and to Adams Ltd's bank statement and cash book.
- Review the minutes of Group management meetings to understand the business rationale for the investment, and to confirm that the Group intends to exercise significant influence over Stewart Ltd, for example, through appointment of board members.
- Obtain management's calculation to determine the £12 million recognised in the Group financial statements, review the method of the calculation for compliance with IAS 28.
- Obtain the financial statements of Stewart Ltd to confirm the amount of profit made in the year and confirm that the Group's share of that profit is included in the Group financial statements.
- Enquire with management as to whether any impairment review of the investment in Stewart Ltd has taken place, and if so, obtain management's workings and review the assumptions used and the method of calculation.

(d) **Ethical matters**

The first threat relates to the audit committee's request for our firm to provide advice on the new accounting and management information systems to be implemented next year. If the advice were given, it would constitute the provision of a non-assurance service to an audit client. The IESBA's *Code of Ethics for Professional Accountants* has detailed guidance in this area and specific requirements in the case of a public interest entity such as the Group which is a listed entity.

The *Code* states that services related to IT systems including the design or implementation of hardware or software systems may create a self-review threat. This is because when auditing the financial statements the auditor would assess the systems which they had recommended, and an objective assessment would be difficult to achieve. There is also a risk of assuming the responsibility of management, especially as the Group apparently has little experience in this area, so would rely on the auditor's suggestions and be less inclined to make their own decision.

In the case of an audit client which is a public interest entity, the *Code* states that an audit firm shall not provide services involving the design or implementation of IT systems if doing so would create a self-review threat (IESBA Code: para. R606.6).

Therefore the audit firm should not provide a service to give advice on the accounting systems. With further clarification on the nature of the management information systems and the update required to them, it may be possible for the audit firm to provide a service to the Group, as long as those systems are outside the financial reporting system. However, it may be prudent for the audit firm to decline offering any advice on systems to the client especially as Adams Group is a listed entity.

Second, the audit committee has asked the audit engagement partner to attend a meeting with the bank, the objective of the meeting being the renegotiation of the Group's lending facilities. This is an advocacy threat to objectivity, as the audit partner will be supporting the client in its renegotiation.

If the partner were to attend the meeting and confirm the strength of the Group's financial position, or confirm any work performed on the cash flow forecast, there could be legal implications. These actions would potentially expose Dando & Co to liability, it could be perceived that the audit firm is in some way guaranteeing the loan or guaranteeing that the Group is in a position to service the debt. The partner should not attend the meeting or be seen to be supporting the Group in its attempt to raise further finance.

These ethical issues should be discussed with those charged with governance of the Group, with an explanation provided as to why the audit firm cannot attend the meeting with the bank.

Tutorial note. Credit will be awarded for relevant comments about the evaluation of management integrity as part of quality management processes in place at Dando & Co. This is in response to the allegations of the use of child labour in the company's supply chain.

Conclusion

These briefing notes have shown that the audit risk of this engagement is relatively high. The highest priority risks for the audit are the potential existence for management bias, a change to the group structure in the year and a requirement to place reliance on the work of another audit firm. As this is our firm's first audit of the Adams Group, an audit strategy needs to be developed to focus on these areas, as well as dealing with the additional planning issues associated with relying on the component auditor.

42 Robster

Workbook references

Chapter 8.

Top tips

Part (a) was straightforward and you should have done enough to pass this part. The examining team has given you the figures to calculate materiality, so you should do this straight away. You can then use your knowledge of IFRS 16 to generate matters to consider, and then use this in turn to think of audit procedures. Eight marks are available for this part, so you might develop three matters to consider and three pieces of audit evidence in order to pass the question.

Part (b) was simple provided that you knew IFRS 9 well. This is an example of the importance of keeping a good grasp of your knowledge of accounting standards from SBR.

Part (c) was relatively straightforward. The accounting issue was clear, and you should have had no trouble determining that there was a misstatement here. The examining team gave you the figures to calculate materiality, so you should have done this and stated whether or not the issue was material.

Easy marks

The marks for calculating materiality in part (a), and for identifying the correct accounting standards.

ACCA examining team's comments.

In part (a), evidence points tended to be quite brief, and better answers provided specific pieces of evidence that should be sought.

Part (b) was generally unsatisfactorily answered, and the information given in the question was often misinterpreted. Candidates tended to know the number of the relevant financial reporting standard for financial assets, but not the technical content of that standard.

Part (c) was generally well-attempted, with most candidates discussing that the accounting treatment adopted for the consignment inventory arrangement was not compliant with IFRS 15 *Revenue from Contracts with Customers*, and correctly determining the impact on profit, and the overall materiality of the transactions to the financial statements. Candidates were less competent at explaining the audit evidence they would expect to find, and the answers here were usually limited to a review of the terms of the consignment inventory arrangement, and evidence of an inventory count.

Marking guide **Marks**

(a) **Leases**

Generally 1 mark per matter/evidence point:

Matters

- Correct calculation and assessment of materiality
- Classification of lease
- IFRS 16 indicators of lease
- Asset recognised at cost
- Depreciation
- Disclosure

Evidence

- Lease clauses re substantially all benefits, control of use
- Recalculate lease liability
- Recalculate depreciation and finance charge
- Cash book for payments
- Review of disclosures
- Split current/non-current payable

7

(b) **Financial assets**

Generally 1 mark per matter/evidence point:

Matters

- Correct calculation and assessment of materiality
- Classification as held for trading
- Assets shown at fair value – could be subjective
- Disclosure

Marking guide	Marks
Evidence	
• Agree purchase price	
• Agree fair value	
• Recalculate gain	
• Review of disclosures in notes	
• Review of disclosure in OFR/other information published with financial statements	-
	6
(c) **Consignment inventory**	
Generally 1 mark for each matter/evidence point:	
Matters	
• Control not transferred to external vendor	
• Robster Ltd retains managerial involvement	
• Revenue recognised too early	
• Materiality	
• Implication for auditor's opinion	
• Opening balances could be misstated	
Evidence	
• Confirm terms of arrangement by review of signed contract	
• Consider whether terms of contract mean that revenue should be recognised	
• Confirmation of inventories held by external vendors	
• Determine amount of returns normally made under the contract	
• Attendance at external vendors inventory count	-
	7
Professional skills marks	
Analysis and evaluation	
• Appropriate use of the information to support discussion, draw appropriate conclusions and design appropriate responses	
• Identification of omissions from the analysis or further analysis which could be carried out	
• Balanced assessment of the information to determine the appropriate audit evidence in the circumstances	
Professional scepticism and judgement	
• Effective challenge of information, evidence and assumptions supplied and, techniques carried out to support key facts and/or decisions	
• Appropriate application of professional judgement to draw conclusions and make informed decisions about the actions which are appropriate in the context and stage of the engagement	
Maximum	5
Total	25

(a) **Matters to consider**

Materiality

Both the non-current assets recognised and the total lease liability are material at 8% and 7.1% of total assets respectively (breaching the 2–5% threshold).

Accounting treatment

We need to consider whether the contracts have been classified correctly as leases in line with IFRS 16 *Leases*.

For a contract to give rise to a lease in line with IFRS 16, there must be an **identified asset**. This must be explicitly specified in the contract (IFRS 16). Robster Ltd ('Robster') must be able to control (direct) the use of the asset, eg it should be able to use the building in whatever way it chooses.

The right-of-use asset must give Robster 'substantially all' the economic benefits from use of the asset, for the whole period of use (IFRS 16).

The right-of-use asset is initially measured at cost, ie the same as the initial measurement of the lease liability. Robster, however, has recognised the two at differing amounts. This appears to be incorrect. Further information is needed regarding why Robster has done this, and where the other £0.4m has been accounted for.

The lease liability should be measured at the present value of the lease payments, discounted using the implicit interest rate. If this rate cannot be determined, then Robster can use its incremental borrowing rate instead.

This interest is accounted for as a finance cost against profit and loss.

The right-of-use asset is accounted for under the cost model of IAS 16 *Property, Plant and Equipment*, unless Robster uses the revaluation model for assets of the same class.

Audit evidence

- A copy of Robster Ltd's workings in relation to the lease liabilities, which the auditor should have recalculated
- Further information regarding the recognition of the asset and the liability at differing amounts.
- To verify that the contracts are classified correctly as leases, review the lease contracts for indicators that Robster has substantially all the economic benefits of the asset, and has the right to control the asset's use
- Recalculation of the finance charges charged against profit and loss
- Agreement of interest rates used in calculations to lease agreements
- Recalculation of depreciation charges applied to non-current assets

(b) **Matters to consider**

Materiality

The financial assets of £1.26m are material at 2.8% of total assets. The gain of £350,000 is material at 10.9% of profit before tax.

Accounting treatment

- IFRS 9 *Financial Instruments* sets out the categories that financial instruments must fall into, along with the appropriate accounting treatment for each. The initial classification of the financial assets as 'held for trading investments' is therefore a crucial area of judgement as it determines the accounting treatment – in this case, at fair value. This means measuring the fair value at the year end and recognising any gains or losses directly in profit or loss.
- The assets should therefore have been purchased in order to sell them in the short term and must be part of a whole portfolio of instruments that are managed together with a view to short-term profit.

Audit evidence

- A schedule showing all the investments held in this category and the fair values of each
- Agreement of the fair values to external evidence such as year-end market price (current bid price)

- Recalculation of the total gain or loss as the overall movement in fair value over the course of the year
- Review of the internal controls and procedures followed by the trading department. Testing to confirm that details (quantities, dates, etc) shown on the schedule can be relied upon
- Analytical procedures to confirm that there is a portfolio of investments that are traded frequently with a view to short-term profit. Corroboration by a review of events after the year end

(c) **Matters to consider**

- IFRS 15 requires that revenue be recognised when the performance obligations contained in the contract are met, as control of goods is transferred to the purchaser.
- Robster retains legal title to the goods while they are with the vendor, and when they are sold, this title passes straight to the customer. Thus Robster still legally owns the jewellery when it is with the vendor.
- Robster retains the ability to change the selling price of the jewellery when it is with the vendor. This constitutes managerial involvement. Robster is also exposed to the risk of inventory not being sold, as unsold inventory must be returned back to it after nine months. Hence in addition to retaining legal title, Robster also retains control.
- This would suggest that Robster should only recognise revenue once the vendor has sold an item on to a customer. However, Robster currently recognises revenue as soon as the item is delivered to the vendor. This appears to be incorrect.
- The required adjustments would derecognise revenue of £1.25m, recognise inventory of £1m, and reduce retained earnings by £0.25m. Profit before tax would be reduced by £0.25m or 7.8%, which is material. The understatement of inventory by £1m is also material at 2.2% of total assets. If these adjustments are not made, then the audit opinion should be a qualified opinion due to material misstatement.

Audit evidence

- Copies of sales contracts with key vendors and confirmation of their terms
- Review of contract terms to determine if Robster retains risks and rewards relating to, and managerial involvement with, the goods
- Enquiries into the proportion of goods usually returned from vendors, to form an understanding of potential levels of obsolete goods
- Results of auditor's test counts of inventory at a selection of vendors' premises to ensure the existence of goods held on consignment

43 Connolly

Workbook references

Chapters 2, 6 and 8.

Top tips

This was a challenging question which featured both business risks with risks of material misstatement. To score well you needed to keep the two separate. Any discussion of risks of material misstatement within your section on business risks will not get any marks.

Part (a) was unusually knowledge-based, but it was not easy; in order to pass you needed to score three good points. The key here is thinking about how analytical procedures are used at the planning stage. You could think about it like this: analytical procedures help the auditor to spot something that looks wrong. There are two possibilities: it may be correct but looks wrong to the auditor because the auditor doesn't understand something. In this case, the auditor needs to obtain an understanding of the issue – so analytical procedures have helped the auditor to obtain an understanding of the entity. Alternatively, it might be that the figure looks wrong because something is going on, ie there is an audit risk. There could be a misstatement, so audit work needs to be focused on that area to see if this is the case. Knowing which areas are risky helps the auditor to plan the audit work.

In the next part of the question (on business risks), try to be as specific as you can in what you write, avoiding repetition from the scenario and being as clear as possible about what the business risk is. Using the form of words, 'the business risk is' might help here.

Note that there are no marks given in the marking scheme for theoretical discussions of the nature of business risk in general, nor are there marks available for categorising business risks as operational, compliance or financial.

There is often a temptation to talk about going concern wherever there is a hint of it in the scenario. In this question the company's ability to trade in the future may possibly have been at risk, but this was not a major issue and the marks available for mentioning it were limited (there are not on the marking scheme). Going concern certainly was not enough of a problem for you to include it as a risk of material misstatement.

In the next part of the question (on risks of material misstatement), take care to limit yourself to four risks of material misstatement. Any more than that will probably not be marked. There are plenty of marks for calculating materiality (and saying that a balance is material), and for stating the main aspects of the accounting treatment of the item in question.

Note that the new loan (of £10m) has not yet been taken out, so risks related to this are not relevant to this question. In relation to the accounting and management information system, the question is very clear that 'this is not considered to create any significant control deficiencies' – this is a signal from the examining team that you should include this as a risk of material misstatement.

In the next part of the question (on the brand), try to say two things for each procedure: which specific procedure to perform, and why it should be performed. For example, 'Obtain the purchase agreement (½ mark) to confirm that Connolly plc has the right to operate the brand (½ mark).' Note that the brand has been acquired by itself, not as a subsidiary company, so any procedures here relating to groups or goodwill are not relevant.

In the final part of the question (on ethics), candidates sometimes misunderstand the question as referring to ethical issues that might come up as part of doing the audit, eg confidentiality. This will get no marks. The ethical issues are threats to the fundamental principles and should be reasonably clear in the scenario (the loan guarantee and the systems advice). Your approach should be to state type of threat (eg advocacy threat), explain why it is a threat, and then to recommend actions (eg accept with safeguards, or do not accept and communicate to management).

Easy marks

The marks for audit procedures in relation to the brand are relatively simple. Make sure you maximise your professional skills marks.

ACCA examining team's comments

The second requirement asked candidates to evaluate the business risks faced by Connolly plc. This requirement was generally well attempted, and in fact for many candidates this was the best attempted out of all of the question requirements. Most candidates proved able to identify and discuss many of the relevant business risks within their briefing notes and the risks surrounding non-compliance with stringent regulations, the risk of losing the licences necessary to produce pharmaceutical products, the lack of cash to support on-going product development, the risks attached to diversifying into a new market, and reputational risks associated with the court case against the company were generally well discussed.

The **best answers** made full use of the information provided and performed analysis of the financial information, allowing for identification of the less obvious but often pertinent risks, such as that without the revenue derived from the new market entered into during the year the company's total revenue would have fallen by a significant amount. Furthermore strong candidates, as well as providing detailed analysis and explanation of the risks, also attempted to prioritise the various risks identified thus demonstrating appropriate judgement and an understanding that the audit partner would want to know about the most significant risks first.

The **key weakness** present in many answers continues to be the poor quality of explanations. Weaker answers tended to just repeat facts given in the scenario with little attempt to discuss or evaluate them. Some answers began with a lengthy discussion of the definition of business risk and its components which was not necessary and demonstrates a lack of judgement when the briefing notes are being requested by an audit partner. Further many answers were very repetitive and did not consider the number of distinct business risks that would be required for the marks available. Many candidates discussed at length risks over going concern that were tenuous or lacked appropriate explanation. Many candidates also confused business risk and audit risk and therefore provided responses that were not relevant to the question.

The third requirement asked candidates to identify and explain four risks of material misstatement to be considered in planning the audit and performance in this area was very mixed. There were some excellent answers to this requirement, with many candidates achieving close to full marks. Most candidates were able to identify the risks surrounding inappropriate accounting treatment that could lead to material misstatements, and they were also able to quantify the materiality of the matters discussed. The risks that were most commonly discussed related to provisions, recognition of research and development costs, the valuation of potentially obsolete inventory, and the segmental reporting that would be likely required in relation to the new market entered into during the year.

The **best answers** were well structured in how they explained the potential misstatement and included in their evaluation of each risk an identification of the risk factor from the scenario (eg the court case ongoing against the company), a determination of materiality where possible given the information in the question, a clear comment on the appropriateness of the accounting treatment where relevant, and the impact on the financial statements (eg non-recognition of a provision in relation to the court case could lead to an understatement of liabilities and an overstatement of operating profit). Only the better candidates identified that requesting additional finance from the bank to cover the damages from the court case implied that the outcome was probable rather than possible and should be provided for.

Weaker answers failed to observe the number of risks of material misstatement that had been asked for, with a significant minority wasting valuable time and providing five or more risks even though credit could only be awarded for four risks. Many candidates discussed a risk of material misstatement relating to accounting for the loan that had been applied for but, given that this had not yet been received, it would not give rise to a risk of this nature in this reporting period. Other candidates discussed at length the issue of going concern and that the company's financial statements should be prepared on a break-up basis but there was certainly not enough evidence in the scenario to justify this as a risk of material misstatement.

The fourth requirement asked candidates to recommend the principal audit procedures to be performed in respect of a brand name that had been acquired during the year. Answers to this requirement were very mixed, as is typical for requirements relating to audit procedures. The **best answers** provided well explained procedures that clearly set out how the test would be performed and where appropriate the documentation that would be used. **Weaker answers** contained vague or very brief lists that were not specific enough to constitute an audit procedure and therefore did not earn marks. Examples of weaker answer points include 'assess value of the brand' (this is not an audit procedure – how should the assessment take place?), 'discuss accounting treatment with management' (what specifically should be discussed?), 'look at the purchase contract' (what information should the auditor be looking for within the contract?). Candidates should ensure that procedures contain an actual instruction describing an action to be performed to satisfy a specific objective.

A minority of candidates thought that rather than acquiring a specific asset, ie the brand, as stated in the question, a company had been purchased. This led to candidates providing irrelevant audit procedures and wrongly discussing the accounting treatment for goodwill. Candidates are reminded to read the question extremely carefully.

The final requirement asked candidates to discuss the ethical issues arising from the engagement and to recommend appropriate actions. There were two matters present in the scenario that were appropriate to discuss – the fact that Connolly plc's bank had asked the audit firm to guarantee the loan extension that had been requested, and that the audit firm had been asked to give advice on the new management information system planned to be introduced the following year.

This requirement was generally well attempted with the majority of candidates correctly identifying the two issues and providing some relevant discussion for each. Most candidates were able to explain the ethical threats associated with the issues and recognised that the significance of the threats would need to be determined. Many candidates appreciated that due to Connolly plc's listed status it qualified as a public interest entity, and therefore the threats to objectivity were heightened. Many candidates demonstrated sound judgement by concluding that the services should not be provided to the audit client as it would be unlikely that safeguards could reduce the threats to an acceptable level. However, credit was awarded where candidates mentioned the types of safeguards that could be considered.

Weaker answers for this requirement identified the wrong ethical threats or failed to identify the significance of the company's listed status, concluding that it would be acceptable to provide the services. Other answers digressed into discussions on the general ethical issues surrounding the testing of medicines on animals or humans, which was not relevant to the question requirement.

The UK and Ireland (IRL) adapted exams had a slightly different style in that the question requirements were not separated out and some extra information had been included in the question. The candidates attempting these adapted exams dealt well with the style of question requirements, and on the whole devoted an appropriate amount of time to the discussion of each of the requirements. It was pleasing to see that candidates attempting these exams were often able to directly link business risks to risks of material misstatement, providing focused answers.

Marking guide	Marks
(a) **Analytical procedures and risk assessment**	
Generally up to 1.5 marks for each point explained:	
• Definition/examples of analytical procedure	
• Helps to identify risk of material misstatement	
• Helps to develop business understanding	
• Helps in developing the audit strategy and audit plan	
Maximum	5

(b) **Evaluation of business risks**

- Regulatory risk – licensing of products
- Regulatory risk – patent infringement
- Regulatory risk – advertising
- Skilled workforce
- Risk of diversification
- Cash flow issues – negative trend/cash management issues
- Cash flow issues – reliance on further bank finance (allow up to 3 marks here if several points covered)
- Cash flow issues – timing of cash flows
- Risk of overtrading

Maximum 8

(c) **Risks of material misstatement**

Up to 2 marks for each risk identified and explained. Also allow up to 1 mark for appropriate and correct materiality calculations:

- Management bias
- Development costs – recognition
- Development costs – amortisation
- Patent costs
- Court case – provision or contingent liability
- Segmental reporting
- Receivable

Maximum 10

(d) (i) **Procedures in relation to purchased brand name**

Generally 1 mark for each relevant, well described audit procedure:

- Review board minutes for evidence of discussion of the purchase, and for its approval
- Agree the cost of £5m to the company's cash book and bank statement
- Obtain the purchase agreement and confirm the rights of Connolly plc
- Discuss with management the estimated useful life of the brand of 15 years and obtain an understanding of how 15 years has been determined as appropriate
- If the 15-year useful life is a period stipulated in the purchase document, confirm the terms of the agreement
- If the 15-year useful life is based on the life expectancy of the product, review a cash flow forecast of sales of the product
- Obtain any market research or customer satisfaction surveys
- Consider whether there are any indicators of potential impairment
- Recalculate the amortisation expense for the year and confirm adequacy of disclosure in notes to the financial statements

5

(ii) **Research and development costs**

- Discuss the project to develop new packaging with management, to develop an understanding of matters such as how the company intends to use the new packaging, the stage of development reached by the year end and whether the project may need additional funding

ANSWERS

- Obtain and review the contract with Greenpack to determine contractual terms and if the asset will be owned and controlled by Connolly plc and that Greenpack does not have any continuing interest in the development once it is completeObtain and review reports and correspondence from Greenpack which will indicate the progress made so far
- Discuss the project with Greenpack, to obtain further understanding on a range of matters including technical feasibility and the results of testing of the prototype
- Discuss with the company's production and marketing directors to obtain understanding of how the company will use the new packaging
- Obtain any financial budgets prepared in relation to the project, to confirm the amount of expenditure which has been approved, and that the costs are clearly distinguishable
- By reference to the company's cash position and available finance, evaluate whether Connolly plc has sufficient funds to complete the development
- Obtain samples of the prototype packaging from Greenpack, to confirm existence
- Agree the amount spent to date to invoices submitted by Greenpack, and to the company's cash records

5

(e) **Ethical matters**

Generally up to 1 mark for each point discussed:

- Loan guarantee is a financial self-interest threat
- The loan is material and guarantee should not be given
- The advice on systems would be a non-audit service
- Self-review threat created
- Threat of assuming management responsibility
- Service can only be provided if systems unrelated to financial reporting
- In this case the advice relating to accounting systems must not be given
- Advisable not to provide the advice on management information systems
- Discuss both matters with management/those charged with governance

Maximum 7

Professional skills marks

Communication

- Briefing notes format and structure - use of headings/sub-headings and an introduction
- Style, language and clarity - appropriate layout and tone of briefing notes, presentation of materiality and relevant calculations, appropriate use of the CBE tools, easy to follow and understand
- Effectiveness and clarity of communication - answer is relevant and tailored to the scenario
- Adherence to the specific requests made by the audit engagement partner

Analysis and evaluation

- Appropriate use of the information to determine suitable calculations
- Appropriate use of the information to support discussions and draw appropriate conclusions
- Assimilation of all relevant information to ensure that the risk evaluation performed considers the impact of contradictory or unusual movements

- Effective prioritisation of the results of the risk evaluation to demonstrate the likelihood and magnitude of risks and to facilitate the allocation of appropriate responses
- Balanced discussion of the information to objectively make a recommendation or decision

Professional scepticism and judgement

- Effective challenge of information supplied, and techniques carried out to support key facts and/or decisions
- Determination and justification of a suitable materiality level, appropriately and consistently applied
- Appropriate application of professional judgement to draw conclusions and make informed decisions about the courses of action which are appropriate in the context of the audit engagement

Commercial acumen

- Audit procedures are practical and plausible in the context of Connolly
- Discussion of risk of commercial effects of adverse publicity arising from the court case
- Recognition of the appropriate commercial considerations of the audit firm 10

Total 50

Briefing notes

To: Ali Stone, Audit engagement partner

From: Audit manager

Subject: Audit of Connolly plc, year ended 30 September 20X5

Introduction

These briefing notes will evaluate the business risks facing our client, identify and explain the significant risks of material misstatement, recommend audit procedures in relation to a new brand acquired during the year and in relation to research and development costs, and finally explain ethical threats to our firm.

(a) **Analytical procedures and risk assessment**

According to ISA (UK) 520 *Analytical Procedures*, analytical procedures are the evaluation of financial information through analysis of plausible relationships between both financial and non-financial data. Analytical procedures can involve comparisons of financial data including trend analysis and the calculation and comparison of ratios. Analytical procedures include comparisons of the Group's financial information with, for example:

- Comparable information for prior periods
- Anticipated results of the Group, such as budgets or forecasts
- Expectations of the auditor
- Comparable information from competitors (ISA (UK) 520)

Analytical procedures performed at the planning stage help the auditor to identify and respond appropriately to risk, and to assist the auditor in obtaining an understanding of the audited companies within the Group.

ISA (UK) 315 (Revised) *Identifying and Assessing the Risks of Material Misstatement* requires the auditor to perform analytical procedures as part of risk assessment procedures at the planning stage of the audit, to provide a basis for the identification and assessment of risks of material misstatement at the financial statement and assertion levels.

An example of how analytical procedures assist the auditor is that performing analytical procedures may alert the auditor to a transaction or event of which they were previously unaware, therefore prompting the auditor to investigate the matter, obtain understanding of the matter and plan appropriate audit procedures to obtain sufficient appropriate audit evidence. Therefore analytical procedures are an essential part of developing the audit strategy and audit plan.

Analytical procedures may also help the auditor to identify the existence of unusual transactions or events, such as significant one-off events. Unusual amounts, ratios, and trends might also indicate matters which indicate risk. Unusual or unexpected relationships which are identified by these procedures may assist the auditor in identifying risks of material misstatement, especially risks of material misstatement due to fraud.

Without performing analytical procedures, the auditor would be unable to identify risks of material misstatement and respond accordingly. This would increase detection risk, making it more likely that an inappropriate audit opinion could be issued.

(b) **Business risks**

(Calculations of some key trends are included in an appendix to part (b) below.)

Licensing

There is a risk that Connolly plc ('Connolly') 's products in development are not licensed. Any costs incurred developing such products will therefore be wasted.

Research and development costs are significant, with the research and development cash outflow representing 7.5% of revenue (£3m/£40m). Failure to obtain licences is a major threat to achieving business objectives.

Patent infringements

If Connolly breaches a competitor's patent, then it will incur legal costs in defending its position. Time must be spent on monitoring to ensure this does not happen, which is a drain on precious resources.

If a competitor breaches one of Connolly's patents, then the costs of bringing legal action may also be substantial.

Advertising

Inappropriate advertising campaigns may breach local regulations, for example in countries where television advertising is not allowed. This may result in fines and damage to Connolly's reputation.

Moreover the fact that television advertising is not allowed will reduce Connolly's ability to earn crucial revenue in those countries. Other forms of advertising may be used instead, but these may be more costly and less effective.

Court case

The court case against the company will result in an outflow of resources which the company can scarcely afford. Increased scrutiny of Connolly by regulators may follow this case, which brings with it the risk of further problems in future.

It may also result in bad publicity, which is particularly damaging to Connolly given the importance of advertising and branding to its operations.

Skilled staff

Connolly needs a skilled workforce to be able to develop new drugs. There is thus a risk of losing key personnel, perhaps to competitors. This could delay drug development.

It may also be difficult to attract talented staff if Connolly's reputation is damaged by the pending court case.

New products

The growth of the new animal products market is certainly a boon, but brings risks. Since this is a new area, management may not be familiar with regulations and may therefore incur fines or penalties. There could be brand confusion between human and animal products.

Revenue in this area may continue to grow as it has done, but management needs to manage risks here carefully.

Revenue

Connolly has a *prima facie* growth in revenue of 5.2% during the year ended 30 September 20X5. However, the new products contribute about £6 million revenue (15% × £40m), which is significant. Without them, Connolly's revenue for the year would have been £34m (= £40m – £6m). This is a reduction of 10.5% (= (£38m – £34m)/£38m).

Cash flow

The cash outflow of £1.2m may be a cause for concern, however we do not know what Connolly's cash position is. The outflow may be related to the acquisition of the 'Cold Comforts' brand, expenditure to launch the new animal products range, or expenditure on research and development (up 7.1%). Many of these are one-off expenditures, so the cash outflow may not be as concerning as it might first appear to be.

The falling core revenues, however, will have an effect on cash. Connolly has been able to offset this with its new product range, but 85% of its revenue still comes from its traditional business so it needs to continue investing cash in product development.

The fact Connolly has approached the bank for two new loans, which are very material at 6.5% of assets combined (= £13m/£200m), indicates that it is experiencing cash difficulties. If the bank refuses this, then it may be unable to develop the new products which it sorely needs.

If the loan is accepted then Connolly's gearing ratio will worsen, and it may struggle to make interest payments to service its debts. On the other hand, if the loan application is refused, then it will need to raise alternative finance for development. Given the fall in its EPS and its high gearing in the year ended 20 September 20X5, a share issue may not be successful.

If Connolly fails to raise finance, then it may struggle to fund product development in the short-term and thus to generate cash in the longer term. This could become a going concern risk in the future, but this risk does not appear to be pressing at this year end.

Appendix – key trends (figures in £000)

Revenue – up by 5.2% (£2,000/£38,000)

Operating profit – down by 10.8% (£985/£9,085)

Operating margin – down by 16.7% (4%/24%)

Net cash flow – down by 120% (£7,200/£6,000)

Research & development ('R&D') cash outflow – up by 7.1% (£200/£2,800)

(c) **Risks of material misstatement**

- **Management bias**

  Connolly is trying to raise finance, and the bank will use the financial statements as part of its lending decision. Management is therefore under pressure to present a favourable position, which may result in bias in relation to any judgemental balances and transactions.

  Management may use earnings management techniques to overstate revenue and understate expenses. Estimates included in the financial statements may also be at a higher risk of misstatement, since these by nature involve an element of management judgement.

- **R&D costs**

  IAS 38 *Intangible Assets* requires research costs to be expensed and development costs to be capitalised. Criteria for capitalisation include: the technical feasibility of the developed product; the intention to complete the product development; the ability to sell the asset; that resources are available to complete the development.

  The R&D cash outflow is material at 1.5% of total assets (= £3m/£200m).

  There is a risk that research costs have been capitalised inappropriately as development costs. This is exacerbated by the possible management bias (above).

Connolly's liquidity position means that resources may not be available to complete the development. There is a risk that costs have been capitalised in spite of this.

Overall, the risk is of overstatement of assets and understatement of expenses.

- **Court case**

  IAS 37 *Provisions, Contingent Liabilities and Contingent Assets* requires a provision to be recognised where there is a present obligation as a result of a past event, there is a probable outflow of economic benefits, and this can be measured reliably.

  The amount of £3m is material to total assets at 1.5% (= £3m/£200m).

  The clinical trial was in 20X4, so the event is in the past. The fact that Connolly is requesting funds from the bank indicates that the event may be probable, and it appears to be measurable at £3m. Hence provision should be made for these costs.

  There is a risk that provision is not made, and that liabilities and expenses are both understated.

- **Segment reporting**

  The new product area may require separate disclosure under IFRS 8 *Operating Segments*. This requires listed companies to disclose the performance of the company disaggregated over its operating or geographical segments, as the information is viewed by management. Since the new area contributes 15% of revenue, it could be seen as a reportable segment. Disclosure of its revenue, profit and other figures may be required. The risk is non-disclosure or incomplete disclosure of the necessary information.

- **Receivable**

  The receivable is 0.0125% of total assets (= £25,000 / £200m) and is 0.3% of operating profit (= £25,000 / £8.1m). It is therefore not quantitatively material, but a further consideration means that it would be qualitatively material – this is as follows.

  The amount is due from a company controlled by Maggie Ram, who is Connolly plc's finance director. Under IAS 24 *Related Party Disclosures* this would likely count as a related party transaction, which should be disclosed. This would usually be in the notes to the financial statements. The non-disclosure of a transaction such as this is a serious matter, so it is important that the auditor works to obtain evidence in this area. There is also a risk that there are further transactions like this, but which the auditor does not know about – which is to say that the completeness assertion is under threat. Related party transactions should be considered a significant risk for the audit.

  There is also a question about the valuation of the receivable in the financial statements. There is a risk that the value is overstated if there are any doubts about whether it is recoverable. Furthermore, the classification of the debt as a current asset needs to be thought about, if it is not likely that the amount will be paid within 12 months.

  Conclusions about significant risks of material misstatement

  The most significant risks of material misstatement relate to the potential for management bias due to the bank loan application (as this could impact all areas of the financial statements); the appropriateness of the recognition of development expenditure and the impact of the outcome of the court case on the financial statements (both require the exercise of significant judgement). Davies & Co should prioritise these issues when planning the audit evidence it will need to obtain.

(d) **Audit procedures**

(i) **'Cold Comforts' brand**

- Review board minutes for discussion of purchase, and to verify that purchase was authorised.
- Agree the cost of £5m to the bank statement.
- Obtain purchase agreement and confirm both the cost and the rights of Connolly plc in respect of the brand.
- Discuss with management the estimated useful life of the brand of 15 years.

- Obtain an understanding of how 15 years has been determined as appropriate.
- If useful life is stipulated in the purchase document, confirm the terms of the agreement.
- If useful life is based on the life expectancy of the product, obtain an understanding of the basis for this, eg by reviewing a cash flow forecast of sales of the product.
- Obtain any market research or customer satisfaction surveys to confirm existence of a revenue stream.
- Consider whether there are any indicators of potential impairment at the year end by obtaining pre year-end sales information and reviewing terms of contracts to supply the products to pharmacies.
- Recalculate the amortisation expense and agree to the financial statements.

(ii) **Research and development costs**

- Discuss the project to develop new packaging with management, to develop an understanding of matters such as how the company intends to use the new packaging, the stage of development reached by the year end and in particular whether the project is technically feasible (in connection with the testing), and whether the project may need additional funding.
- Obtain and review progress reports and correspondence from Greenpack which will indicate the progress made so far.
- Obtain and review the contract with Greenpack to determine contractual terms and if the asset will be owned and controlled by Connolly plc and that Greenpack does not have any continuing interest in the development once it is complete.
- After receiving client's permission, arrange to discuss the project with Greenpack, to obtain further understanding on a range of matters including technical feasibility and the results of the testing on the prototype.
- Discuss with the company's production and marketing directors to obtain understanding of how the company will use the new packaging.
- Obtain any financial budgets prepared in relation to the project, to confirm the amount of expenditure which has been approved, and that the costs are clearly distinguishable.
- By reference to the company's cash position and available finance, evaluate whether Connolly plc has sufficient funds to complete the development.
- Obtain samples of the prototype packaging from Greenpack, to confirm existence.
- Agree the amount spent to date to invoices submitted by Greenpack, and to the company's cash records.

Tutorial note. Credit will be awarded for other relevant audit procedures, for example, in relation to assessing whether there are any reasons to doubt whether Greenpack can continue the development.

(e) **Ethical issues**

Loan guarantee

Guaranteeing a loan creates a financial interest in Connolly. If Connolly defaults on loan payments, then Davies & Co may become liable for them. This is a self-interest threat because Davies & Co has an incentive to express a better audit opinion than it should do, in order to not become liable for the loan. It is also unlikely to be a sound commercial move, since its potential liability may outweigh the audit fee received from Connolly.

The IESBA *Code of Ethics for Professional Accountants* states that where the loan guaranteed is material, then no safeguards can reduce the threat to an acceptable level. The loan is 5% of total assets here and is therefore material.

There is also an advocacy threat here because the auditor may find itself acting on Connolly's behalf before the bank.

The auditor should therefore communicate to the bank that it cannot provide such a guarantee.

Systems advice

Advice on the systems would be a non-assurance service. As a listed company, Connolly is a public interest entity.

A self-review threat may arise here in future if the auditor relies on systems it has itself developed. There is a risk of taking on a management role.

Connolly is a public interest entity, so in line with the *Code* it cannot be involved with the design or implementation of systems relating to internal controls over financial reporting as a result of the possible self-review threat (IESBA Code: para. R606.6). If it relates to these systems, the request must be declined.

If the engagement does not relate to financial reporting systems, then it may be possible to accept it. Safeguards may be applied in order to reduce the threat to an acceptable level, such as the use of separate teams for the two engagements.

> **Tutorial note.** Credit will be awarded for any reference to the prohibition of non-audit services to public interest clients under the FRC *Revised Ethical Standard.* Acknowledgement of the unlikely nature of systems not being financial should also be recognised (why else would the firm have been approached if it was not for a financial reporting system?).

Conclusion

Connolly faces a variety of business risks. A number of risks of material misstatement have been discussed, and the audit planning must design procedures to mitigate these risks. Detailed tests will need to be performed in relation the acquired brand and the research and development costs. Two ethical matters have been identified, both of which create significant threats to independence and objectivity.

44 Osier

> **Workbook references**
>
> Chapters 8 and 15.
>
> **Top tips**
>
> Part (a) asked about audit evidence in a way that is typical of what you should expect from your exam. Financial reporting knowledge is at the core of questions like this, so you need to remember what you learned in SBR.
>
> Part (a)(i) was probably deceptively simple. If you were comfortable with IAS 2 *Inventories* then you would have recognised that what the entity is doing is essentially OK, and that you really needed to focus on how to audit it. The matters to consider then become some simple points about subjectivity, estimates and bias.
>
> Part (a)(ii) may have been easier. This is a core accounting standard and one that you should be comfortable with – you only really needed to know its outlines to answer this question well.
>
> The hard part throughout (a) would have been thinking of enough pieces of evidence. There are a few points here. Firstly, evidence can be the results of audit procedures – so if you describe the evidence that a completed procedure would give, then this is acceptable. Secondly, it's really important that you say **why** a piece of evidence is needed, as this can double your marks for each point. You don't necessarily have to identify which financial statement assertion you're testing; if you review the model answer with this in mind you'll see that it's good on this point.
>
> Part (b) was knowledge, but this was a slightly tricky point. If you didn't know the answer, then review the answer here as it's an important point. Areas where candidates do badly are often examined again, so you don't want to get caught out.

Part (c) should have been within your reach, as this aspect of auditing performance information is really not dissimilar from thinking of audit procedures.

Easy marks

The marks for calculating materiality and assessing it against a benchmark (in part (a)).

ACCA examining team's comments

In part (a) there were two scenarios where candidates were asked to describe the key matters and audit evidence that would be expected in each. Overall there appeared to be a poor understanding of the accounting issues raised by the scenarios. Part (a)(i) concerned the audit of manufactured inventory and the appropriate inclusion of overhead and labour costs. Most identified the need to check the components back to source documentation and review the reasonableness of the process, but many candidates concentrated on discussing auditing and accounting standards rather than detailing the evidence that should have been gathered. However this was the best answered of the two sections.

Part (a)(ii) related to a topical subject – an impairment review of a retailer's property portfolio caused by diminishing shop sales countered by growing internet sales. Many candidates simply discussed whether or not an impairment review should be carried out as there were indicators of impairment (falling retail sales) but this was a given from the question as the review had already been undertaken. Few questioned whether it was reasonable to base the value in use on the assumption that sales would grow by 1% a year when in reality they were falling. Candidates appeared unwilling to challenge this underlying assumption which actually lacked commercial justification.

The UK and Irish exam had an alternative part (b) about the benefits of independent assurance provided on key performance indicators for both management and external users. Candidates mostly correctly commented that this would provide greater credibility to the information and so would be relied on more by external users. Fewer candidates identified that this would also provide management with assurance that the systems and controls in place to produce the information was sufficient and operating satisfactorily.

In part (c) candidates were required to explain how to audit some performance KPIs, and although some good points were made a number of candidates stretched their imagination as to how these could be verified and were simply impractical in the nature of their procedures.

Marking guide **Marks**

(a) (i) **Osier Ltd**

Generally up to 1.5 marks for each well explained matter and 1 mark for each well explained piece of evidence recommended.

Note. Marks will be awarded for explanations of why calculations and balances are complex or subjective and how this affects their accuracy. Simple statements that calculations and balances are complex or subjective will be awarded a maximum of 0.5 mark each, where relevant.

Inventory

Matters

- Materiality
- Complexity of calculation
- Subjectivity in calculation

Evidence

- Documentation of systems and controls
- Summary of purchase costs and matching to purchase invoices
- Calculation of forecast wages matched to underlying HR and payroll records
- Confirmations of wage increments/rises

- Calculation of forecast overheads corroborated to new agreements

Maximum 6

(ii) **Impairment**

Matters

- Materiality
- Uncertainty relating to estimates
- Growth rate assumption in relation to value in use
- Allocation of impairment does not seem to be correct

Evidence

- Copies of offers for retail outlets
- Copy of forecast cash flows relating to retail outlets
- Recalculation of forecasts using management's predictions
- Analytical review by unit/geographical region to assess appropriateness of general growth rate
- Notes re discussion about retail prospects by area
- Schedule of goodwill analysed by division
- Recalculation of allocation of impairment
- Copies of previous forecasts

Maximum 5

(b) **Moosewood Hospital**

Generally up to 1.5 marks for each well explained point and 1 mark for each well explained procedure recommended.

Benefits of an assurance report on the KPIs included in the integrated report

- Assurance report enhances credibility of the integrated report generally and specifically the KPIs
- Integrated report outside scope of audit
- Important to gain assurance given regulated nature of the industry
- Management use KPIs to monitor performance so credibility enhances management decision making processes

Maximum 3

(c) **Procedures in relation to key performance indicators**

General

- Document systems and test controls
- Identify level of senior management scrutiny of KPIs
- Recalculate KPIs to confirm mathematical accuracy
- Analytical review to historic performance

Patient/nurse ratio

- Obtain definition of 'average' for patient/nurse ratio
- Identify which patients to include
- Confirm patient numbers to patient records
- Confirm staff numbers to HR records

Surgical rooms

- Discuss normal levels of room usage
- Obtain hospital plans to identify number of surgical rooms

- Recalculate number of surgical hours available
- Confirm surgical times to underlying surgery/treatment records

Admissions for previously treated conditions

- Enquire how a previously treated condition is identified
- Inspect patient admission records to identify readmissions within 28 days
- Inspect underlying patient records to identify if conditions match

Maximum	6

Professional marks

Analysis and evaluation

- Appropriate use of the information to support discussion, draw appropriate conclusions and design appropriate responses
- Identification of omissions from the analysis or further analysis which could be carried out
- Balanced assessment of the information to determine the appropriate audit evidence in the circumstances

Professional scepticism and judgement

- Effective challenge of information, evidence and assumptions supplied and, techniques carried out to support key facts and/or decisions
- Appropriate application of professional judgement to draw conclusions and make informed decisions about the actions which are appropriate in the context and stage of the engagement.

Maximum	5
Total	25

(a) **Osier Ltd**

(i) **Cost of inventory**

Matters

Materiality

Inventory costs represent 1.1% of total assets and 19.6% of profit. Inventory is therefore material to both the statement of financial position and the statement of profit or loss.

Risk of material misstatement

The calculation of the cost of inventory is complex. This complexity increases the risk of error in the calculation, which increases the risk of misstatement.

The calculation is also subject to a number of estimates; the average production time per unit, the forecast annual wage cost, the scheduled hours of production and the forecast units of production are all estimates. These estimates increase the risk of both error and manipulation of the calculation to suit management's bias.

Given both the complexity and subjectivity involved in the calculation, there is a significant risk that the inventory cost may be misstated.

Evidence expected to be on file:

- Documentation of the system for obtaining the data used in the costing exercise and calculating the final cost. This should identify the key controls which operate in this system and there should be evidence on file that these controls have been appropriately tested.
- A copy of the summary of inventory purchase costs. A sample of the purchase costs, including the additional costs of transport and handling, should have been confirmed through inspection of original purchase invoices, copies of which should also be on file.
- Documentation of the results of a discussion with the production manager to ascertain how they estimate the average production time per unit of inventory. Any calculations referred to

ANSWERS

by management should have been reperformed by the audit team to confirm their mathematical accuracy and agreed to corroborating documentation.

- A copy of the calculation of the forecast annual wage cost. The initial staffing levels should have been confirmed through inspection of current human resource records and for a sample of the staff their initial wages should have been confirmed through inspection of payroll records.
- Forecast wage increments should have been agreed to either post year end confirmation issued by human resources or minutes of board meetings approving pay rises.
- Documentation of the results of a discussion with management regarding how the forecast is made and who is ultimately responsible for reviewing and approving the forecast.
- A copy of the calculation of forecast units of production. This should have been analytically reviewed in comparison to the previous year's production levels. Where there are significant differences, explanations should have been sought from management.
- A copy of the calculation of forecast production overheads. This should have been analytically reviewed by category of overhead in relation to the previous year to identify any significant variances. Corroborating evidence, such as rental and utilities agreements, should have been obtained where possible.
- There should be evidence on all management's schedules that the figures have been recalculated by the audit team to confirm the mathematical accuracy of management's calculations.

(ii) **Impairment**

Matters

Materiality

The impairment of £9m represents 0.47% of total assets and 8.41% of profit. While it is not material to the statement of financial position, it is material to the statement of profit or loss.

Calculation of recoverable amount

The fair value of the retail outlets, the disposal costs and the value in use are all management estimates. This increases the risk of material misstatement through both error and management manipulation of the reported figures.

In particular, while the estimate for the fair value appears to have a reasonable basis, the estimate of value in use appears to be too basic. The assumption that the cash flows attributable to the whole of the retail division will grow at 1% per year is too simplistic and appears to lack commercial justification. It is likely that each retail outlet will be subject to regional variations in growth and growth rates will also be subject to annual fluctuations based upon economic variables. There is also no justification as to why 1% growth has been selected to represent 'poor performance'; at the very least this should be benchmarked to more widespread and reliable growth forecasts, eg national forecasts of economic growth.

Allocation of the impairment

The impairment has been allocated against the tangible assets in the cash generating unit. This is incorrect; as a cash-generating unit the impairment should first be allocated against any goodwill relating to the cash-generating unit in accordance with IAS 36 *Impairment of Assets*. It should then be allocated against the remaining assets on a pro rata basis bearing in mind that an asset should not be impaired below the highest of either its fair value less costs of disposal or its value in use.

Evidence expected to be on file:

- Copies of the offers received to purchase the retail outlets, confirming the amounts offered. These should have been used to recalculate the average used for the estimate of fair value.
- Documentation of enquiries with management with regard to how they estimated the disposal costs and what experience they have had with the sale of similar operations.

- A copy of the forecast cash flows attributable to the retail outlets. This should contain evidence of analytical review in comparison to the year ended 31 March 20X7 to confirm the accuracy of the base cash flows.
- There should then be evidence of a recalculation of the future cash flows using management's estimates of 1% growth to confirm the mathematical accuracy of management's calculation.
- There should be evidence of a recalculation of the value in use using a range of growth rates to assess the sensitivity of management's calculations to economic variables. The differences between these valuations and management's valuation should have been reviewed to assess the likelihood of a material under or overvaluation.
- Evidence of an analytical review of performance by retail outlet or geographical area of operations, referenced to sales and cash flow records where available, to confirm whether growth rates are consistent across the brand or whether there are variances.
- Documentation of enquiries with management relating to their expectations for specific retail outlets or areas of operations and whether there are any specific matters which they are aware of which may affect regional performance, eg the opening of new out-of-town shopping facilities or competitors setting up in the same location.
- A schedule of any goodwill included in the statement of financial position with analysis of its various components to assess whether any part is attributable to the retail outlets as a cash generating unit. This is specifically relevant to any acquired brands which may be sold through the retail stores or any retail brands acquired by Osier Ltd.
- A recalculation of the allocation of the impairment by the auditor, first against any goodwill determined to be attributable to the cash generating unit, then against the remaining assets pro rata.
- Copies of previous forecasts. Where the retail outlets forecast performance exceeds the 1% currently predicted by management, there should be evidence of discussion with management to ascertain the reasons for changing their outlook.

(b) **Benefits of independent assurance**

Obtaining an independent assurance report on the integrated report, and specifically on the key performance indicators (KPIs) contained within the report, is a way to enhance the credibility of the integrated report. Information provided by an organisation without any external assurance being obtained may not be perceived as trustworthy or accurate. The integrated report is outside the scope of the audit, other than being read as part of 'other information' if it is published alongside the audited financial statements, which is not the case for Moosehead Hospital Ltd, and therefore without any assurance report being obtained, the contents of the integrated report including the KPIs could be seen as lacking in credibility.

Therefore, for users of the integrated report, a review report by Fern & Co can provide some assurance that the KPIs are relevant, derived from reliable source information and accurate. It is important to note, however, that only a low level of assurance is provided, and that the nature of the assurance will depend on the terms of the engagement between Fern & Co and Moosehead Hospital Ltd, for example, the engagement may be restricted to certain agreed upon procedures on specific KPIs.

Operating in a regulated industry makes the assurance even more important, as the KPIs may need to be reported to the authorities.

For management, the assurance report will also help in providing some assurance on how the KPIs have been determined, including that the systems and controls are sufficient to produce the necessary information. Management will presumably be using the KPIs to monitor performance and therefore having assurance on the accuracy of the KPIs should provide comfort to management that appropriate decisions are being made.

(c) **Procedures**

General

- Document the systems which are in place for recording the information relevant to the performance measures, noting the key controls which should operate to ensure the accuracy of the information which is captured, recorded and reported. Evidence of the operating effectiveness of these controls throughout the period should be obtained.

- In particular, the auditor should obtain an understanding of the level of scrutiny of the performance measures by senior management, including: the frequency of their reviews; the level of detail which is provided; and their responses should the reported performance measures differ from their expectations.
- Each of the calculations of the performance measures should be obtained. Using the figures supplied by management, these should be recalculated by the audit team to ensure mathematical accuracy.
- The performance measures should be analytically reviewed against historic performance levels, on a monthly basis if such information is available, to identify any significant fluctuations in reported performance levels. Where fluctuations occur reasons should be sought through management enquiry, which should then be corroborated with evidence wherever possible.

> **Tutorial note.** Other, relevant general procedures will also be awarded credit but will only be awarded credit once, ie candidates will not be given credit for repeating the same general procedure for each performance measure.

Patient/nurse ratio

- Obtain copies of the original document in which the basis for calculating the performance measures were agreed; this may be in the form of a strategic document agreed with the National Health Service or it may even be the minutes of the executive board. From this identify whether any specific definition is provided of the term 'average' or whether a specific formula is provided. In particular, it is important to ascertain over what period the average must be calculated.
- From the same document ascertain which patients must be included in the calculation, ie should this include emergency patients or just patients admitted for treatment by appointment.
- Confirm the calculation of the number of patients treated through inspection of underlying treatment and appointment records.
- Confirm the calculation of the number of nurses through inspection of underlying staff rotas and records of hours worked supplied to human resources and payroll departments.

Surgical room usage

- Enquire of the manager responsible for planning and co-ordinating surgical operations what the 'normal' period of time (ie excluding emergencies) is during which surgical procedures may be performed, ie which hours during the day and whether there are any days where scheduled procedures would not be performed.
- Obtain and inspect the hospital plans to identify the total number of surgical rooms available.
- Using the information above, calculate the total number of surgical hours available to the hospital. Compare the figure calculated to the figure used in management's calculation to identify any significant variances.
- Obtain a schedule of the total hours of surgery performed during the year. Confirm a sample of the times recorded to underlying hospital records to confirm the accuracy of the figures used in this calculation.

Admissions for previously treated conditions

- Enquire of management how they define a 'previously treated condition'. For example, does this depend upon the underlying symptoms or the diagnosis of the medical practitioner.
- Obtain a copy of the patient admissions records. Use computer assisted audit techniques to identify patients admitted to the hospital within 28 days of a previous admission. If possible, inspect the underlying patient records to identify whether the patient was

treated for either the same or a similar condition. If not, enquire of the medical practitioners responsible for their care during their admission.

- Where the above procedure identifies patients admitted for the same condition, ensure that these patients are recorded in management's calculation of the performance measure to ensure the completeness of the information used in the calculation.

45 Macau

Workbook references

Chapters 4, 6, 8 and 10.

Top tips

Part (a) was quite a nice question on audit quality management. If you worked through the scenario you should have found plenty of problems to comment on. It was important here that you did not get too carried away and go over your timing – you should have allocated 25 minutes to this question part (13 ´ 1.95), so don't go over it.

One tip on these questions is not to repeat too much from the question. Spend as little time as you can repeating the question, and as much time as you can saying what was wrong and what should have been done.

Part (b) combined audit evidence with quality management. The audit evidence on the WIP was a little bit tricky, as the treatment involved considering the recoverability of costs as well as subsequent events. Even if you didn't get quite the right answer here, you could have scored marks if you identified the general issue and stated what the standards say, eg that IAS 10 distinguishes adjusting from non-adjusting events, or that IFRS 15 allows costs to be recognised as an asset only if they can be recovered.

Lastly, the bit at the end of the scenario – saying that going concern is not an issue – might look open to question, but really this is just the examining team's way of saying not to worry about going concern. It is important that you learn to identify things like this in scenarios, as you would have wasted a lot of time if your answer had focused on going concern.

Easy marks

The marks in part (b) for calculating materiality were very easy.

ACCA examining team's comments

In part (a), there was tendency to rewrite statements of fact from the question which scored no marks but stronger candidates discussed the issues and explained why the firm's actions were clearly inappropriate.

Very few candidates were able to discuss the need for materiality to be constantly reviewed throughout the audit in light of changing circumstances. However, most candidates picked up that a significant addition to property, plant and equipment sited at a supplier's premises needed to be physically verified and that reliance on third party evidence for existence was inappropriate in the circumstances. The inventory count had been poorly performed but few candidates developed this to consider where the real audit risks may lie and the need to inform management of the weakness in internal controls and for the auditors to investigate the discrepancies and extend their testing. Improper manager/partner review was highlighted by the majority of candidates, but the implications of the partner's cursory review were not always followed through to a logical conclusion.

In relation to the matters to consider, candidates were faced with a situation where the client had encountered a cancelled manufacturing contract. Most candidates scored the materiality marks for both the value of WIP and deferred income. A significant number of candidates discussed how WIP should have been calculated and its composition without realising that this was irrelevant as it needed to be recognised at nil unless a further use for it could be validly identified. Stronger candidates identified that the client may be able to levy a compensation claim for breach of contract.

A worrying number of candidates also believed that writing off a deferred income creditor was a cost rather than a credit to the statement of profit or loss which shows a more fundamental lack of accounting knowledge. Likewise, many candidates confused WIP with R&D contracts and raised irrelevancies such as depreciation.

The question stated that going concern was not an issue, yet many candidates discussed this in depth as part of their answer. Candidates must realise that if the question makes a statement of this nature, then marks will not be awarded for discussion, regardless of the quality of their answer and are again reminded to read the question scenario carefully.

Marking guide **Marks**

(a) **Quality management, ethical and other professional issues**

Generally up to 1 mark for each point explained:

- Materiality should be reviewed as the audit progresses
- Insufficient audit evidence obtained in relation to packing machine:
  - 1 mark for comment on materiality
  - 1 mark for comment on physical verification
  - 1 mark for comment on external confirmation
  - 1 mark for comment on whether the distribution company is a related party
  - 1 mark for comment on assertions/inappropriate audit conclusion
- Lack of organisation at inventory count should have been discussed with management
- Test count discrepancies should be extrapolated over the population
- Audit staff may need training on inventory count attendance
- Misstatements should be accumulated and discussed with management
- The inaccuracy of the client's test counts should be reported to management as a control deficiency
- Insufficient review performed by audit manager
- Review left too late and should be ongoing during the audit
- Potential self-interest threat regarding audit engagement partner's brother
- Matter should be investigated and notified to audit firm's ethical partner
- The audit partner lacks integrity, maybe has something to hide
- The partner may need to be removed from the audit and his work reviewed as it does not appear to support ISA 220 (Revised)

Maximum 13

(b) **Matters and actions to take**

Generally 1 mark per comment/recommended action explained:

- Calculation and determination of materiality (1 mark for each of the work in progress and the deferred income)
- Calculation and determination of materiality (1 mark for each of the work in progress and the deferred income)
- The work in progress should be written off and charged to profit unless it can be used on a different contract
- The deferred income may be repayable, if not it should be released to profit
- Auditor's report implications if necessary adjustments not made
- Integrated report and Director's Report may be inconsistent with financial statements or contain a misstatement of fact

Marking guide	Marks
• Auditor's responsibility to read the integrated report to identify inconsistencies/misstatements	
• Matters to be discussed with management/those charged with governance	-
Maximum	7
Professional marks	
Analysis and evaluation	
• Effective appraisal of the information to make suitable recommendations for appropriate courses of action	
• Appropriate assessment of the ethical and professional issues relating to the assignment, using examples where relevant to support overall comments	
Professional scepticism and judgement	
• Effective challenge and critical assessment of the conduct and extent of the audit work and evidence obtained with appropriate conclusions.	
• Demonstration of the ability to probe into the reasons for quality issues including the identification of missing information or additional information which would be required	
• Appropriate application of professional judgement to draw conclusions and make informed decisions about the actions which are appropriate in the context and stage of the engagement	
Maximum	5
Total	25

(a) **Quality management, ethical and professional matters**

The audit of Stanley Ltd does not seem to have been performed with a high regard for the quality of the audit and there appear to be several ways in which the ISA (UK) requirements have been breached.

Materiality

First, it is not appropriate that the materiality level was determined at the planning stage of the audit but has not been reviewed or adjusted since. ISA (UK) 320 *Materiality in Planning and Performing an Audit* requires the auditor to determine materiality for the financial statements as a whole at the planning stage of the audit, and to revise it as the audit progresses as necessary where new facts and information become available which impact on materiality. It may be the case that no revision to the materiality which was initially determined is necessary, but a review should have taken place, and this should be clearly documented in the audit working papers.

Audit of property, plant and equipment

The audit of the packing machine has not been properly carried out, and there seems to be a lack of sufficient, appropriate audit evidence to support the audit conclusion. The cost of the asset is material, based on the initial materiality, therefore there is a risk of material misstatement if sufficient and appropriate evidence is not obtained. By the year end the asset's carrying value is less than materiality, presumably due to depreciation being charged, but this does not negate the need for obtaining robust audit evidence for the cost and subsequent measurement of the asset.

The packing machine should have been physically verified. Obtaining the order and invoice does not confirm the existence of the machine, or that it is in working order. In addition, without a physical verification, the audit team would be unaware of problems such as physical damage to the machine or obsolescence, which could indicate impairment of the asset.

Relying on the distribution company to provide evidence on the existence and use of the asset is not appropriate. ISA (UK) 500 *Audit Evidence* states that audit evidence obtained directly by the auditor is more reliable than audit evidence obtained indirectly or by inference. External confirmations can be used to provide audit evidence but, in this case, the external confirmation should corroborate evidence obtained directly by the auditor, rather than be the only source of evidence. The relationship between Stanley Ltd and Aberdeen Ltd should also be understood by the auditor, and evidence should be obtained to confirm whether or not the two companies are related parties, as this would impact on the extent to which the external confirmation can be relied upon as a source of evidence.

Inventory count

In respect of the inventory count attendance, the audit team should have discussed the discrepancies with management as they could indicate more widespread problems with the inventory count. Given the comment that the inventory count appeared disorganised, it is possible that count instructions were not being followed or that some items had not been included in the count. One of the requirements of ISA (UK) 501 *Audit Evidence – Specific Considerations for Selected Items* is that while attending an inventory count, the auditor shall evaluate management's instructions and procedures for recording and controlling the results of the entity's physical inventory counting. It is not clear from the conclusion of the audit work whether the problems noted at the inventory count have been discussed with management. The auditor attending the inventory count should have raised the issues at the time and assessed whether a recount of all of the inventory was required. Training may need to be provided to audit staff to ensure that they understand the auditor's role at an inventory count and can deal with problems which may arise in the appropriate manner.

The discrepancies noted at the inventory count should be subject to further audit work. The results of the test counts should be extrapolated over the population in order to evaluate the potential misstatement of inventory as a whole. The results should then be evaluated in accordance with ISA (UK) 450 *Evaluation of Misstatements Identified During the Audit* which requires that the auditor shall accumulate misstatements identified during the audit, other than those which are clearly trivial, and that misstatements should be discussed with management. The issues raised by the way in which the inventory count was performed could represent a significant control deficiency and should be raised with those charged with governance in accordance with ISA (UK) 265 *Communicating Deficiencies in Internal Control to Those Charged with Governance and Management.*

Working paper review

The audit senior's comments in relation to the review by the manager and partner indicate that elements of ISA (UK) 220 (Revised) *Quality Management for an Audit of Financial Statements* have been breached. ISA (UK) 220 (Revised) requires that the engagement partner shall, through a review of the audit documentation and discussion with the engagement team, be satisfied that sufficient appropriate audit evidence has been obtained to support the conclusions reached and for the auditor's report to be issued. It appears that in this case the partner has not properly reviewed the working papers, instead relying on the audit senior's comment that there were no problems in the audit work. ISA (UK) 220 (Revised) does state that the audit partner need not review all audit documentation, but they are supposed to be the driving force behind the application of quality on the audit engagement, so taking only a 'quick look' at the working papers could indicate that areas of risk or critical judgement have not been reviewed in sufficient detail.

There is also an issue in that the manager and partner reviews took place at the same time and near the completion of the audit fieldwork. Reviews should happen on a timely basis throughout the audit to enable problems to be resolved at an appropriate time. Reviews should also be hierarchical, and it appears that the audit partner has not reviewed the work of the audit manager.

Ethical considerations

Finally, there appears to be a potential threat to objectivity due to the audit engagement partner's brother providing a management consultancy service to the audit client. This amounts to a self-interest threat in that the partner's brother receives income from the audit client. The audit partner's objectivity is therefore threatened, and this is a significant risk due to his position of influence over the audit. He may even receive an introducer's commission from his brother.

The matter should be investigated further, and a senior member of the audit firm or the firm's partner responsible for ethics should discuss the comments made in Stanley Ltd's board minutes with Joe Lantau in order to evaluate the ethical threat and determine any necessary actions. The amount which is being paid to Mick Lantau should be made known, as well as whether the amount is a market rate, and whether other providers of management advice were considered by the company.

The partner's comments to the audit junior indicate a lack of integrity and that the partner may have something to hide, which increases the threat to objectivity. The audit partner may need to be removed from the audit and his work reviewed.

(b) **Matters to consider and actions to take**

The work in progress represents 4.7% of total assets and is therefore material to the statement of financial position. The deferred income is also material at 2.7% of total assets.

Even though the correspondence with BMC is dated after the end of the reporting period, BMC was suffering from financial problems during the year ending 31 December 20X5 which was notified to Kowloon Ltd before the year end. Therefore the cancellation of the contract appears to meet the definition of an adjusting event under IAS 10 *Events after the Reporting Period* because it confirms conditions which existed at the year end.

Management must consider whether it is still appropriate to recognise the work in progress as an asset. According to IFRS 15 *Revenue from Contracts with Customers*, costs incurred to fulfil a contract are recognised as an asset if and only if all of the following criteria are met:

- The costs relate directly to a contract (or a specific anticipated contract).
- The costs generate or enhance resources of the entity which will be used in satisfying performance obligations in the future.
- The costs are expected to be recovered.

The cancellation of the contract indicates that the costs of the work in progress are not recoverable from BMC, in which case the balance should be written off. Management is not planning to amend the balances recognised at the year end, and the audit team should investigate the reasons for this. Possibly management is asserting that the machine design costs could be utilised for a different contract, despite the fact that the machine was developed specifically for BMC. Audit work should focus on the contractual arrangements between Kowloon Ltd and BMC, particularly in relation to the ownership of the rights to the design work which has taken place. If the design work has been based on an innovation by BMC, then it needs to be determined if this information can still be used.

If the design work which has been undertaken to date can be used by Kowloon and results in an ability to develop a new type of product for other customers, there is the possibility that the costs (excluding any research costs) could be capitalised in line with IAS 38 *Intangible Assets*. This should be discussed with the project manager and finance director to assess if this has been considered and if the capitalisation criteria of IAS 38 can be satisfied.

The accounting treatment of the deferred income also needs to be considered. Depending on the terms of the contract with BMC, the amount could be repayable, though this may not be the case given that it is BMC which has cancelled the contract. If part or all of the amount is repayable, it can remain recognised as a current liability. If it is not repayable, it should be released to the statement of profit or loss.

If the costs cannot be capitalised, then there is a loss which needs to be recognised. Assuming that the advance payment is non-refundable, the net position of the development cost and the deferred income balances result in a loss of £150,000. This represents 15.8% of profit for the year and is material. If any necessary adjustments are not made there will be implications for the auditor's report, which would require a modified opinion due to material misstatement.

Due to the significance of the matter to the financial statements, the contract cancellation and loss of BMC as a major customer should be discussed in the other information to be issued with the financial statements, in this case in the integrated report. The audit firm must consider its responsibilities in respect of ISA (UK) 720 *The auditor's Responsibilities Relating to Other Information*. ISA (UK) 720 requires the auditor to read the other information to identify material inconsistencies, if any, with the audited financial statements. Depending on the wording used in the integrated report when referring to the company's activities during the year and its financial performance, omitting to mention the cancellation of the contract could constitute a material misstatement or a material inconsistency. The issue may also need to be disclosed in the Director's Report for the year and the auditor should consider the completeness and adequacy of any disclosure made in light of the requirements of the Companies Act 2006.

The matter should be discussed with management, who should be encouraged not only to amend the financial statements but also to discuss the cancellation of the contract and the loss of BMC as a significant customer in the integrated report and Director's Report. If management refuses to make the necessary amendments and disclosures, the matter should be discussed with those charged with governance and/or the company's legal counsel.

46 Northwest

Workbook references

Chapters 2, 9, 10 and 11.

Top tips

This is a demanding question set in the context of a group audit which requires some thought and planning.

Part (a) might have frightened you by mentioning professional scepticism but, in reality, it was just a normal audit evidence question in disguise. Professional scepticism has been a topical issue for a while now, plus you will notice that there are professional skills marks testing your ability to display professional scepticism and judgement. Although this scenario is full of statements that you should be sceptical of, the whole thing is still a bit difficult, because it's all **inconclusive** – we don't have enough information to really find out what is happening. What we do know, however, is **what evidence we *should* be able to obtain** as auditors, even if it doesn't look like we'll be able to. The auditor has to think in the dark here a little bit, which is difficult. How well you deal with this difficulty is key to demonstrating the professional skill of professional scepticism.

Part (b) asked for ethical and professional issues impacting the audit of Northwest Ltd and any further audit procedures that should be performed. There were two issues to address: the lack of evidence demonstrating Valerian's financial support for Northwest and also the group auditor's request not to modify Northwest's audit opinion.

One thing to note is that the model answer states that 'transferring the debt to the parent' would not work, because it would simply leave a liability to the parent. This is a valid reading of the scenario, but the group auditor's offer might also be read as saying that the debt could be transferred by the lender, ie so that it did not refer to Northwest Ltd at all.

Easy marks

This was a tough question, but the easiest marks were probably the ones for applying professional scepticism in part (a), which also link in with the professional skills marks here.

ACCA examining team's comments

Part (a) of this question examined the concept of scepticism in the context of a group audit where the parent company was reluctant to provide more than verbal assurances that they would support the loss-making subsidiary. The parent company was facing a lawsuit that they may lose, and hence good candidates could explain and apply the concept of professional scepticism by questioning why the parent company would not put the support in writing and whether this might reflect uncertainty of the parent company's going concern status given the lawsuit.

Part (b) required the implications for the audit of the subsidiary in terms of evidence, reporting and pressure from the parent company auditor to refrain from modifying the audit opinion despite insufficient evidence being available.

The structure of the requirements led candidates to conclude the parent company might not be able to provide support; that a lack of evidence had been obtained in this regard; there was an ethical threat of intimidation; and then discuss the auditor's report and the modification required. Disappointingly candidates often stated correctly that there was inability to collect sufficient appropriate evidence but then incorrectly proposed an adverse opinion.

Marking guide	Marks
(a) **Professional scepticism**	
Generally 1 mark for each well-discussed point made:	
• Risk of misstatement in relation to a material matter	
• Reliability of confirmation of internally generated evidence	
• Judgement required in relation ability to provide support	
• Material uncertainty facing parent company	
• Unusual behaviour of group engagement partner	
• Need to remain alert for other factors affecting going concern	
• Need to remain sceptical of all other matters requiring management judgement	-
Maximum	6
(b) **Ethical and professional matters**	
Generally 1 mark for each well-explained point and recommendation made:	
Support offered by Valerian Ltd	
• Northwest Ltd would not be a going concern without support of parent	
• Verbal confirmation not sufficient evidence	
• Additional evidence that Valerian Ltd is capable of providing support	
• Examples of further evidence required (0.5 mark each, maximum of 2 marks)	
• Suspicious conduct of parent and group auditor	
• Need for professional due care and potential reappraisal of fraud risk	
• Communication with those charged with governance	
• Possible modification of auditor's report if additional evidence not received	
Request not to modify report	
• Intimidation threat	
• Responsibility for audit opinion remains with Thornhill & Co	
• Transfer of debt to Valerian Ltd would not resolve the problem	
• Possible suggestion of inappropriate accounting treatment	
• Potential lack of integrity of group audit partner and potential fraud	
• Matter should be discussed with senior audit staff	
• Possible resignation as auditor	
	14

Professional skills marks

Analysis and evaluation

- Effective appraisal of the information to make suitable recommendations for appropriate courses of action

ANSWERS

Marking guide	Marks
• Appropriate assessment of the ethical and professional issues relating to the lack of audit evidence regarding the financial support offered by Valerian Ltd, using examples where relevant to support overall comments	
• Appropriate assessment of the ethical and professional issues relating to the request not to modify Northwest Ltd's audit opinion, using examples where relevant to support overall comments	
Professional scepticism and judgement	
• Effective challenge and critical assessment of the conduct and extent of the audit work and evidence obtained with appropriate conclusions	
• Demonstration of the ability to probe into the reasons for issues, including the identification of information that is important to the conduct of the group audit	
• Appropriate application of professional scepticism to the outstanding legal case	
• Appropriate application of professional scepticism to other judgements made by management	
Maximum	5
Total	25

(a) **Application of professional scepticism**

Potential for material misstatement

Without support from the parent, it is unlikely that Northwest Ltd would be considered a going concern. There is therefore a risk in relation to the going concern status of Northwest Ltd and a risk of material misstatement in the financial statements if an incorrect basis of preparing the accounts is selected. Professional scepticism requires the auditor to remain alert for any circumstances which may cause the financial statements to be materially misstated especially in relation to going concern matters.

Internally generated evidence

In order to reach a satisfactory conclusion in this matter, it would be essential to receive formal confirmation of support from Valerian Ltd. The auditor must be sceptical of this form of evidence because it is prepared by management and this sort of internally generated evidence is, generally, not as reliable as other forms of externally generated evidence.

Use of judgement

The ability to provide support to Northwest Ltd is also a matter of judgement. The management of Valerian Ltd would need to forecast their own cash flows and make a judgement as to whether they will have sufficient capacity to meet Northwest Ltd's obligations in the event that the subsidiary cannot. Clearly, such forecasts are prone to uncertainty and management bias.

In this case Valerian Ltd is itself facing a material uncertainty regarding the outcome of the legal case. It is plausible that this could affect their ability to provide full support. The failure to supply a formal letter of support adds weight to this concern. The auditor must therefore remain sceptical when considering management's pledge of support to Northwest Ltd.

Suspicious behaviour

The group engagement partner's request not to modify the audit opinion should also promote scepticism. This is an unusual request and appears to be based on pressure by the directors of Valerian Ltd. This reinforces the suspicion that both the group auditor and the directors of Valerian Ltd may be trying to conceal some sort of problem. It is possible that the outcome of the legal case is less favourable than is currently suggested and this may require some form of modification to the group accounts. This may, in turn, trigger further repercussions which Valerian Ltd is seeking to avoid.

Heightened scepticism

Based upon these concerns, the auditor needs to remain sceptical and alert for other factors which raise concerns in relation to the going concern status of Northwest Ltd. They should also be sceptical of all judgements made by management, particularly in relation to the forecasts prepared to assist with the assessment of going concern. It is possible that they are being over-optimistic in their estimates in order to make forecasts appear better than is reasonable to expect.

(b) **Offer of support by Valerian Ltd**

Insufficient evidence

Without the financial support of its parent company, Northwest Ltd would not be considered a going concern. A verbal pledge of support from Valerian Ltd would not be considered sufficient reliable evidence in regard to this matter.

Ability to provide parental support

In addition to a letter of support, the auditor of Northwest Ltd would need to obtain sufficient appropriate evidence that Valerian Ltd can provide the support which it promises.

The statement by the group auditor that they have received adequate representations from the directors and legal advisers of the company does not constitute sufficient appropriate evidence. At the very least, the auditor of Northwest Ltd would need copies of those representations. While the representations from management would suffer from the same lack of reliability, representations from the legal advisers would represent third-party evidence and, as such, be more reliable.

Uncertainty surrounding legal case

Given the uncertainty surrounding the court case and the gravity of preparing the financial statements on an incorrect basis, Thornhill & Co may seek further documentary evidence before concluding on the going concern status of the company. This could include correspondence between Valerian Ltd and its legal advisers, minutes of board meetings, copies of Valerian Ltd's assessments of going concern, and its current statement of financial position.

Conduct of client and group auditor

The suspicious behaviour of both the directors and auditors of Valerian Ltd suggests that they are not being entirely honest with Thornhill & Co. If their statements regarding the likely outcome of the legal case are appropriate and there are no other concerns, then there is no reason why they would not be able to provide copies of the representations and a written letter of support to the auditor of Northwest Ltd.

This increases the need for professional due care during the audit process, particularly in relation to the reappraisal of fraud risk and the potential for material misstatement in relation to the going concern status of the company and associated disclosures in the financial statements.

Further procedures

The auditor should communicate with those charged with governance of Northwest Ltd and explain the requirements to obtain sufficient appropriate evidence in this matter. The auditor should also explain the consequences of not receiving this information in terms of the impact this will have on the going concern status of the company and the adjustments they would be required to make to the financial statements.

Finally, the auditor should explain that if the additional evidence is not received and the recommended adjustments are not made, then this will lead to a modification of the auditor's report. The fact that necessary audit evidence is being withheld would constitute a limitation in the scope of the audit, which may result in a qualified opinion or a disclaimer of opinion being issued.

The request not to modify the auditor's report

Intimidation

By trying to influence the decisions in relation to the audit of Northwest Ltd, the group auditor is creating an intimidation threat to objectivity. IESBA's *Code of Ethics for Professional Accountants* defines this as the threat that a professional accountant will be deterred from acting objectively because of actual or perceived pressures. The FRC's *Ethical Standard* section B1 *Integrity, objectivity and independence* defines intimidation simply as arising when the auditor's conduct is influenced by fear or threats.

Responsibility for the opinion

As the auditor of Northwest Ltd, the responsibility for determining the final audit opinion and wording of the auditor's report remains with Thornhill & Co. If, based upon the evidence obtained, the engagement partner believes that a modification to the auditor's report is necessary, then it should follow this through, regardless of the opinion of the group auditor and the board of the parent company. The group partner's 'oversight' of the whole audit is irrelevant to the audit of Northwest Ltd – as a company in its own right, it must be audited in accordance with ISAs (UK).

Transferring the debt to the parent

The suggestion to transfer the debts into the parent company would not resolve the problem. If the debt obligations were 'transferred' to the parent using an appropriate journal, they would be replaced by a matching liability to the parent company in the financial statements of Northwest Ltd, and the same problem would exist. While this would be eliminated in the consolidated accounts, this does not allow the auditor of Northwest Ltd to gather sufficient appropriate evidence in relation to the going concern status of the company.

Possible manipulation of the financial statements

It is possible that the group engagement partner is recommending some form of inappropriate accounting treatment to transfer the debt into the parent company without any matching liability in Northwest Ltd's accounts – for example, by transferring the debts and then consequently cancelling any obligations from Northwest Ltd due to Valerian Ltd. This form of accounting manipulation could be used to disguise the true financial position of the group and may constitute fraud. Any suggestion to pursue this line of action should be firmly refused.

Integrity of the group auditor

The overall integrity of the group engagement partner must be questioned. Their aggressive attitude towards the audit of Northwest Ltd and their reluctance to cooperate by providing evidence in relation to the lawsuit indicate some form of inappropriate conduct in the audit of the parent company and group accounts. This matter should be discussed with the audit engagement partner and possibly with other senior partners, possibly including the firm's designated ethics partner. Further, the suggestion that 'the group engagement partner' would transfer the debt from Northwest Ltd to the parent company suggests that the auditor is becoming involved in the accounting transactions included in the financial statements and may suggest that the firm's independence is compromised.

Position as auditor of Northwest Ltd

Given the intimidation threat and the potential concerns relating to the audit of the parent and the group, Thornhill & Co may consider resignation from the audit of Northwest Ltd, if permitted, or may not seek re-election as auditor for the following year.

Part E: Completion, review and reporting

47 Rope

Workbook references

Chapters 2, 3, 7, 8 and 10.

Top tips

Time management is critical in this question so work out how much time you can allocate to each part of the question and stick to this. If you miss out whole parts of questions you are at very high risk of failing.

A point of confusion when this area has been examined in the past has been whether the engagement is an audit, or an assurance engagement in relation to PFI. This question is clear on this point: it's an audit.

You might think that this is going to be totally different from normal audit work, which deals with historical information (the financial statements are about things that have already happened). Really it isn't so different – what you're looking into is basically whether management's figures (in the forecast) are reasonable and reliable, whether there is some proper basis for them, and whether they have been produced by a system of controls. You don't need to check that each figure is 100% correct (and in the case of a forecast, you can't). The figures can't be completely accurate, so the auditor only needs to look for as much objective evidence as it's possible for there to be.

Since the question contains lots of numbers, you'll need to be fairly detailed in your examination of them. It is sensible, for instance, to calculate by how much the receipts and payments go up in each period.

Spend time thinking of your audit procedures, as these will be a source of marks. As ever, state both what and why wherever you can.

Part (b) was brief. It is common in practice for auditors to produce the financial statements for small entities, but this is prohibited for public interest entities.

Part (c) is a longstanding issue that you should be aware of with auditor's reports.

Easy marks

Audit procedures.

ACCA examining team's comments

This question covered prospective financial information in the form of a cash flow forecast and a related party transaction.

Part (a) required candidates to appraise the forecast and suggest further procedures in assessing the use of the report as part of the going concern review during the audit. This was generally well answered by the majority of candidates attempting the question.

[Examining team comments not available for parts (b) and (c).]

Marking guide | **Marks**

(a) **Rope Ltd**

Generally up to 1.5 marks for each well explained matter and 1 mark for each well-explained procedure recommended:

Cash flow forecast

Matters

- Potential overestimation of cash receipts from customers

- Lower than forecast sales may lead to net overdraft
- Potential underestimation of salary and other operating payments
- Simplistic assumption of cost inflation
- Investments do not match management's forecast disposal valuation
- Assumption of growth in value of investments is very optimistic
- Ability to repay loans dependent upon other assumptions
- Lack of specific consideration of non-operating cash flows

Procedures

- Review latest interim financial statements
- Discuss forecast sales and customer receipts with management
- Inspect J Stewart loan agreement
- Inspect terms of bank loan
- Enquire of management whether they have begun renegotiations regarding bank loan facility
- Enquire with management about contingency plans
- Perform analytical review of payroll costs
- Perform analytical review of other operating costs
- Inspect non-current asset registers
- Inspect post year end cash book
- Review outcomes of previous management forecasts
- Obtain written representations from management (maximum 0.5 mark)

Maximum 12

(b) **Preparation of financial statements**

Generally 1 mark per comment:

- Formatting or typing service not prohibited
- But could be seen as part of preparation of financial statements
- For listed client, service is prohibited
- Refuse if listed, apply safeguards if unlisted

Maximum 3

(c) **Liability disclaimer paragraph**

1 mark for each point:

Content of disclaimer

- Report intended for use by company's members as a whole
- No responsibility accepted to third parties
- Commonly used but not required by standards

Advantages

- Potential to limit liability exposure
- Clarifies extent of auditor's responsibility
- Reduces expectation gap
- Manages audit firm's risk exposure

Disadvantages

- Each legal case assessed individually no evidence that a disclaimer would offer protection in all cases
- May lead to reduction in audit quality

Maximum 5

Professional skills marks

Analysis and evaluation

- Appropriate use of the information to support discussion, draw appropriate conclusions and design appropriate responses
- Identification of omissions from the analysis or further analysis which could be carried out
- Balanced assessment of the forecast information to determine the appropriate audit procedures in the circumstances

Professional scepticism and judgement

- Effective challenge of information, evidence and assumptions supplied and, techniques carried out to support key facts and/or decisions
- Appropriate application of professional judgement to draw conclusions and make informed decisions about the actions which are appropriate in the context and stage of the engagement.

Maximum	5
Total	25

(a) **The cash flow forecast of Rope Ltd**

When a company has prepared a cash flow forecast as part of their assessment of going concern, in accordance with ISA (UK) 570 *Going Concern* the auditor needs to evaluate the reliability of the underlying data used to prepare the forecast and to determine whether there is adequate support for the assumptions underlying the forecast. There are a number of issues relating to the forecast which raise concerns about the assessment of Rope Ltd's going concern status and therefore warrant further investigation.

Receipts from customers

There was little growth in cash receipts in the second half of the year ended 30 September 20X6 (0.8%), yet in each consequent six-month period management predicts a significant rise in receipts of between 1.7% and 3.0%.

This could be based on overly optimistic forecasts in relation to sales growth for the same period. If sales forecasts are too optimistic, this could eliminate the forecast small positive cash flows, which could leave the company in a net overdraft position for the entire two-year period.

The movement in relation to customer receipts is a key assumption underpinning the return to a positive cash position and needs to be scrutinised further.

Salaries and other payments

While annual receipts from customers and payments to suppliers are forecast to rise during the forecast period by 8.5% and 9.4%, respectively, the amounts attributable to salaries and other operating payments are only forecast to rise by 4.1%.

This is based on management's simple assumption of a general 2% annual inflation in these costs. This seems to be overly simplistic and will require further investigation. Salary costs could be forecast using a more sophisticated methodology based on required employee numbers and average wages/salaries.

The significant forecast increase in sales suggests that operating activities will increase over the next two years and it might be expected that staff requirements may increase in line with this. For similar reasons, it is likely that a larger increase in other operating costs would be required to match the increased administrative burden of producing and selling more goods and/or services.

Sale of investments

Management is planning to sell some investments in listed shareholdings for £500,000 to repay a loan to the chief executive. At 30 September 20X6, however, the fair value of the investments was only £350,000. As the fair value of these investments is revalued at the end of each year based upon the current share price, this is assumed to reflect the amount at which the shares were trading at the end of September. Management is therefore expecting the shares to increase in value by £150,000 in the space of two years, which represents a 43% rise. This is an extremely optimistic assumption in comparison to average rates of growth across most stock markets.

It therefore appears likely that there will be a shortfall in the amount raised to repay Mr Stewart. Rope Ltd will therefore have to supplement the amount received from selling investments with cash from other sources, which will lead to a reduction in the cash position in comparison to the forecasts.

Repayment of the bank loan

The bank loan is due for repayment 15 months after the year end. Management is assuming that they will be able to fund the repayment with a new loan facility from the same finance provider. Without any agreement in place from the provider, this represents a significant assumption.

Without a new facility Rope Ltd will have no means with which to repay their obligation, which could lead to the lender taking action to recover the loan amount. This could include seizing assets which were provided as security over the loan or commencing insolvency proceedings. In either case, this could have a significant impact on Rope Ltd's ability to trade into the foreseeable future and, therefore, the loan repayment event represents a material uncertainty which may need to be fully disclosed in the financial statements of Rope Ltd in accordance with IAS 1 *Presentation of Financial Statements*.

Missing cash flows

There seems to be a lack of consideration of a number of non-operating cash flows which one might expect to see in a two-year forecast. For example, most companies maintain a practice of regular replacement of old, inefficient tangible non-current assets as opposed to making larger, less regular replacements which may create a significant drain on cash resources in one particular year. The forecast currently has no allocation for capital investment. In a similar fashion, there are no cash flows related to tax and dividend payments. It is possible that such transactions have been overlooked in the preparation of the forecast.

Further audit procedures

- Obtain a copy of the latest interim financial statements and compare the actual post year end sales performance with the forecast sales upon which the cash flow forecast is based.
- Discuss with management the rationale for the expected increase in customer receipts and where possible confirm this to customer correspondence, orders or contracts.
- Inspect the documentation detailing the terms of the loan with Mr Stewart to confirm the amount outstanding and the agreed date of repayment.
- Inspect the terms of the bank loan to confirm the final amount due for repayment, the date of repayment and whether any assets have been accepted as security for the loan.
- Enquire of management whether they have entered into any negotiations with their bank, or any other financial institution, to provide a replacement loan in January 20X8. If so, request corroborating evidence such as signed agreements, agreements in principle or correspondence with the financial institutions.
- Enquire of management whether they have any contingency plans in place to repay both loans on time should they not be able to raise the required amount through selling investments and obtaining new loan agreements.
- Perform an analytical review of actual monthly payroll costs incurred obtained from the payroll department. Include any available payment periods after 30 September 20X6 to help ascertain whether management's assumptions regarding salaries are appropriate. Seek corroborating evidence for any fluctuations in cost such as HR records confirming pay awards and changes in staff.

- Perform an analytical review of actual other operational costs and consider the level of other costs as a percentage of sales. Compare this to the levels included in the forecast. Investigate any significant differences.
- Corroborate the lack of investment in new tangible non-current assets by performing an analytical review of the levels of additions and disposals over the last, say, five years to see if this supports the absence of any allocation for this in the short-term future and consider this in light of our understanding of the entity and its production process.
- Compare the cash flow forecasts to any capital expenditure forecasts prepared by Rope Ltd to ensure that the cash flow forecast is consistent with this. Ask management to explain any differences identified.
- Review the non-current asset register and identify any assets with a zero or negligible carrying value which could indicate that the assets have fulfilled their useful lives and are due for replacement.
- Inspect the cash book post-year end to see if there are any significant cash transactions which do not appear to have been included in the forecasts, in particular cash transactions relating to purchases or disposals of assets and dividend payments.
- Review the outcome of previous forecasts prepared by management to assess how effective management has been in the past at preparing accurate forecasts.
- Obtain written representations from management confirming that they have no intention to either purchase or dispose of non-current assets or to pay dividends over the next two years.

(b) **Preparation of financial statements**

Preparation of financial statements for some clients is acceptable under certain circumstances, however a **self-review threat** may be created where an audit firm prepares financial statements and then audits them. There is also a risk that the audit firm may undertake, or be perceived to undertake, a **management role**.

Safeguards should be in place to ensure the risk is reduced to an acceptable level for these clients in these situations. For example, staff members other than the audit team should be responsible for typing the financial statements.

The IESBA *Code of Ethics for Professional Accountants* and the FRC's *Ethical Standard* (section B5) prohibit the preparation of accounts or financial statements for clients that are public interest entities. It is not stated whether Rope Ltd is listed, but if it is then the audit firm should decline Uma Thorton's request to put the financial statements into a format for publication.

(c) **Liability disclaimer paragraph**

The paragraph would state that the report is intended to be used only by the company's members as a body. It would state that the report is not to be relied upon by any third party.

Such a paragraph is not required by any auditing standards, and therefore has no specifically prescribed content.

Appropriateness

The advantage of a liability disclaimer paragraph is that it may reduce the exposure of the audit firm to liability claims from anyone other than the company or the company's body of shareholders. It is not certain, however, that this will be use in all situations. Every legal case is unique, and although a disclaimer might protect the audit firm in one circumstance, it may not offer any protection in another.

The paragraph could be argued to help bridge the 'expectation gap' by clarifying that responsibility of the auditor is to obtain reasonable assurance that the financial statements give a fair presentation, rather than for example to check every transaction.

In an increasingly litigious environment, such paragraphs may help audit firms to manage their risk exposure. There is a danger, however, that the use of such a paragraph could encourage low quality audits if the auditor takes the disclaimer into account when assessing the audit risk. The auditor might consider that the use of a disclaimer means that detection risk can be higher and may not obtain sufficient appropriate audit evidence. This would be for the auditor to fail in their duty to conduct their audit in line with ISAs, which applies irrespective of any issue of liability. In contrast, there should be no need for a disclaimer if the audit is of a high enough quality.

In conclusion, the ACCA discourages the use of liability disclaimer paragraphs, as these could have the effect of devaluing the auditor's report in the eyes of many (ACCA Technical factsheet 84: para. 23).

48 Kandinsky

Workbook references

Chapters 8 and 15.

Top tips

Part (a), on going concern, should have been straightforward as the scenario was absolutely replete with indicators of going concern problems. Marks could be harvested simply by working through the scenario and explaining why virtually every point represented a risk.

Note 3 hints that you need to calculate interest cover and the ratio of the bank loan to operating profit. These should be easy marks (calculations usually score well in AAA), provided that you get it correct – don't forget to take the finance charge out of your profit figure when you're calculating interest cover. This is a bit tricky, but it is just the kind of thing that happens in real exams, so you need to pay attention to the small details as well as the big ones.

Part (b) was on insolvency, a topic which is specific to students of the UK stream of AAA. This was a typical question on insolvency and required a fair bit of application to the scenario. Scoring well depends on you successfully identifying that administration is an option here, if the company is to avoid a compulsory creditors' liquidation (as stated in the requirement-part of the finance director's note).

There are very few marks available here for discussing liquidation. Your focus should be on determining that the company is insolvent, and that administration is appropriate. Marks should then flow from your discussion of administration. The last part of the requirement – the impact on directors and employees – should not be overlooked, as it's quite simple and contains many easy marks.

Easy marks

Much of part (a) was easy, but the marks for calculating trends in revenue and operating profit were practically no-brainers.

Marking guide	**Marks**
(a) **Identify and explain going concern matters**	
Up to 2.5 marks for matter identified and explained, to include 1 mark for relevant calculations:	
• Revenue, operating margins and profitability	
• Bank loan	
• Trade payables	
• Borrowing facility	
• Contingent liability	
Maximum	9
(b) **Response to finance director's instructions**	
Generally up to 1.5 marks for each point explained:	
• Identify Viola Ltd as insolvent	

Marking guide	**Marks**
• Purpose of administration	
• Procedure – commencing administration without court order	
• Procedure – commencing administration with a court order	
• Moratorium over debts – advantage to the company	
• Statement of affairs to be produced	
• Administrator proposes rescue plan or liquidation	
• Proposals agreed by members and creditors	
• Impact on directors – lose control of the company	
• Impact on employees – depends on recommendation of administrator	
• Period of administration and cessation of administration	
• Members' voluntary liquidation is a possibility but depends on declaration of solvency being made	
Maximum	11
Professional skills marks	
Analysis and evaluation	
• Appropriate use of the information to support discussion, draw appropriate conclusions and design appropriate responses	
• Identification of omissions from the analysis or further analysis which could be carried out	
• Balanced assessment of the information to determine the appropriate audit procedures in the circumstances	
Professional scepticism and judgement	
• Effective challenge of information in the forecast, evidence and assumptions supplied and, techniques carried out to support key facts and/or decisions	
• Appropriate application of professional judgement to draw conclusions and make informed decisions about the actions which are appropriate in the context and stage of the engagement.	
Maximum	5
Total	25

(a) **Going concern matters**

Revenue and profitability

The extract financial statements show that revenue has fallen by 38.2%. Based on the information provided, operating profit was £1,150,000 in 20X4 but is only £340,000 in 20X5. Operating margins have fallen from 29.1% to 13.9% during the year and the fall in revenue and margin has caused the company to become loss-making this year.

These changes are highly significant and most likely due to the economic recession which will impact particularly on the sale of luxury, non-essential products such as those sold by Kandinsky Ltd. The loss-making position does not in itself mean that the company is not a going concern. However, the trend is extremely worrying and if the company does not return to profit in the 20X6 financial year, then this would be a major concern. Few companies can sustain many consecutive loss-making periods.

Bank loan

The bank loan is significant, amounting to 33.7% of total assets this year end, and it has increased by £500,000 during the year. The company appears to be supporting operations using long-term finance, which may be strategically unsound. The loan is secured on the company's properties, so if the company defaults on the payment due in June 20X6, the bank has the right to seize the assets in order to recoup their funds. If this were to happen, Kandinsky Ltd would be left without operational facilities and it is difficult to see how the company could survive. There is also a risk that there is insufficient cash to meet interest payments due on the loan.

Trade payables

The trade payables balance has increased by 38.5%, probably due in part to the change in terms of trade with its major supplier of raw materials. An extension to the payable payment period indicates that the company is struggling to manage its operating cycle, with the cash being generated from sales being insufficient to meet working capital requirements. Relations with suppliers could be damaged if Kandinsky Ltd cannot make payments to them within agreed credit terms, with the result that suppliers could stop supplying the company or withdraw credit which would severely damage the company's operations. There is also a risk that suppliers could bring legal action against the company in an attempt to recover the amounts owed.

Borrowing facility

Kandinsky Ltd has £500,000 available in an undrawn borrowing facility, which does provide a buffer as there is a source of cash which is available, somewhat easing the going concern pressures which the company is facing. However, the availability of the borrowing facility depends on certain covenants being maintained. The calculations below show that the covenants have now been breached, so the bank is within its right to withdraw the facility, leaving Kandinsky Ltd exposed to cash shortages and possibly unable to make payments as they fall due.

	Covenant	*20X5*	*20X4*
Interest cover	2	340/520 = 0.65	1,150/500 = 2.3
Borrowings to operating profit	4:1	3,500/340 = 10.3:1	3,000/1,150 = 2.6:1

Contingent liability

The letter of support offered to a supplier of raw materials exposes Kandinsky Ltd to a possible cash outflow of £120,000, the timing of which cannot be predicted. Given the company's precarious trading position and lack of cash, satisfying the terms of the letter would result in the company utilising 80% of their current cash reserve – providing such support seems unwise, though it may have been done for a strategic reason, ie to secure the supply of a particular ingredient. If the financial support is called upon, it is not certain that Kandinsky Ltd would have the means to make the cash available to its supplier, which may create going concern issues for that company and would affect the supply of cane sugar to Kandinsky Ltd. There may also be legal implications for Kandinsky Ltd if the cash could not be made available if or when requested by the supplier.

(b) The net liabilities position indicates that Viola Ltd is insolvent, meaning that if the company were to dispose of all of its assets, there would not be sufficient funds to pay off the company's liabilities. In a situation of insolvency coupled with operational difficulties like those being faced by Viola Ltd, if the company wishes to avoid liquidation the best option would be to place the company in administration.

The aim of administration is to save the company if possible. The directors seek the assistance of experts, and the company continues to operate. An insolvency practitioner is appointed to act as administrator and will effectively take control of the company in an attempt to rescue it as a going concern. Administration protects the company from the actions of creditors while a restructuring plan is prepared. This is important for Viola Ltd, which is struggling to manage its working capital, meaning that some creditors' balances may be long overdue, and the creditors may already be considering actions to recover the amounts owed.

Administration can commence without a court order. The directors themselves may be able to appoint an administrator, though this depends on the company's articles of association. Alternatively, the company (a majority of shareholders) or qualifying floating charge holders can apply for administration without going through the court. Given that Viola Ltd's bank loan is secured by a floating charge over the company's assets, the bank could have the right to appoint an administrator, depending on the terms of the floating charge. If the directors or the company commence appointment of an administrator, notice must be given to any qualifying floating charge holders who are entitled to appoint an administrator.

Alternatively, administration proceedings can involve a court order. The company (a majority of shareholders), the directors, one or more creditors or in rare cases the Justice and Chief Executive of the Magistrates' Court can apply to court for an administration order. The court will consider the application and will grant the administration order if it appears that the company is unable to pay its debts.

Whichever method of appointment of an administrator is employed, the advantage for the company is that a moratorium over the company's debts commences. This means that no creditor can enforce their debt against the company during the period of administration and no security over the company's assets can be enforced. For Viola Ltd this would allow much needed breathing space and time to resolve the working capital problems and lack of cash.

The impact on the directors is that they will lose control of the company and all operational decisions will be made by the administrator. The administrator has the power to remove or appoint directors.

The administrator is likely to request that the directors prepare a statement of affairs detailing all of the company's assets and liabilities, information on the company's creditors and any security over assets.

Using the statement of affairs and other information, the administrator will prepare a proposal regarding the future of the company, in which the administrator recommends either a rescue plan to save the company, or states that the company cannot be saved. The proposal must be sent to all shareholders and creditors, and a creditors' meeting will be held at which the proposal will be either accepted or rejected.

For Viola Ltd, the proposal is likely to focus on the probability of obtaining the new contracts which have been tendered for, and the availability of bank finance which depends on the contracts being secured. If the contracts are secured, then it may be possible to save the company. However, in the event that the contracts are not secured and there is limited demand from other customers, the administrator may well recommend liquidation of the company.

The employees will remain employed unless the administrator decides that redundancies are an appropriate measure, and this could be a feature of any proposal to save the company. It must be noted that if the administrator recommends the winding up of Viola Ltd, then the loss of jobs will be inevitable.

Administration can last for up to 12 months, but the administration period will end sooner if the administration has been successful, or where there is application to court by one or more creditors or by the administrator.

An alternative to administration is a voluntary liquidation, which can be initiated by creditors or by members. Liquidation means that the company will be wound up – the assets will be sold, proceeds used to pay the company's debts in a prescribed order, and any remaining funds would be distributed to the shareholders.

For a member's voluntary liquidation to take place, the shareholders must pass a resolution, which can be an ordinary or a special resolution depending on the articles of association. However, a member's voluntary liquidation can only take place if the directors make a declaration of solvency. This is a statutory declaration that the directors have made full enquiry into the affairs of the company, and their opinion is that it will be able to pay its debts. The declaration must also include a statement of the company's assets and liabilities. According to the information supplied, Viola Ltd is in a position of net liabilities and therefore it does not seem likely that the directors will be able to make this statement. Therefore a member's voluntary liquidation does not appear feasible.

The recommendation therefore is for the company to be placed into administration, as this will protect the company from the actions of creditors and allow the administrator to consider all relevant facts before making a proposal on the future of the company.

49 Kelly & Co

Workbook references

Chapters 2, 5 and 13.

Top tips

Part (a) asked you for matters in relation to the acceptance of the proposed engagement. Questions in this area will usually be focused on the ethical dilemmas that are present in the scenario, and it will help your answer to make reference to the *Code of Ethics* and/or the FRC *Ethical Standard*, where this is relevant. Try to categorise the threats that arise, although be careful not to just list every category of threat in the hope of striking on the right one, as your marker may not then give you the marks.

The examining team tends to like practical points, and acceptance question always offer you to chance to consider practical aspects of performing the engagement, eg whether the firm has the resources to actually do the engagement.

As should be clear by now, heed the question's warning about client identification procedures, as there will be no marks on offer for these. It is crucial that you read the requirements very carefully and follow them as closely as you can. The need to read the question carefully was emphasised in the ACCA examining team's comments that stated: 'Some candidates were failing to answer the requirement relevant to the given scenario, instead they were answering a generic acceptance question. In this question we are not the current or prospective auditor. This requirement is specific to the acceptance for this assurance engagement reviewing a cash flow forecast. Candidates who stated points around self-review when auditing the financial statements or the request for professional clearance for audit from the existing auditor did not attain credit.'

Part (b) moved the scenario onto the engagement itself. The first sub-part asked you to evaluate the assumptions, and it was not easy. With requirements such as this, it is important to do the best that you can within the time available. All of your points must be reasonable, but as a starting point you can try to look for things in the information given that you can be sceptical of. Also try to think about anything that has *not* been included in the forecast. Your time limit should be roughly 9-10 minutes for this sub-part.

The second sub-part here asked for procedures. As ever, your procedures need to be specific and you should try to say why you're recommending them.

Easy marks

There were plenty of professional marks on offer but getting these is likely to be a secondary effect of doing well on the question generally. There is a lot of information available in the scenario that you can use as a springboard for generating procedures in part (b)(ii).

ACCA examining team's comments

This 25-mark question covered the client acceptance and non-assurance services areas of the syllabus. Candidates generally produced a complete answer covering all requirements.

Part b(ii) was the strongest part of candidates' answers with many good procedures being given. In part (a), many answers lacked the depth of discussion required for an evaluation rather than a list of criteria.

Candidates should note that there are two elements covered by the requirement for part (a) – the decision to accept the client as a client of the firm in principle, and the second decision regarding whether it was appropriate to perform the review engagement.

In order to pass the requirement candidates will need to **apply the ethical guidance to the scenario.**

For example, when deciding whether to accept a client, many candidates will correctly state the key requirements of ISQM 1, but then fail to show how the information in the scenario is assessed against these criteria.

Consider the different responses seen by the examining team *[BPP Note: these examples are based on outdated technical guidance, and should not be used for their technical content as such but rather to understand the point being made about marking]*:

'Client integrity – the firm must assess the integrity of the potential client to determine whether they wish to be associated with the client' – this is unapplied, it can't obtain more than ½ mark credit and will be part of the cap of unapplied points.

'Client integrity – the firm must assess the integrity of the potential client. Mary has told us that the latest auditor's report is expected to be issued with a material uncertainty paragraph in relation to going concern. The fact that the potential client did not tell us this themselves suggests management may be hiding something.

This would suggest that there is a high risk to the engagement as the client may not have integrity and we may be unable to place reliance on information provided to us by the client.'

This answer is applied to the scenario – there would be a mark for the specific 'red flag' identified from the scenario for client integrity and a further mark for developing that point into how it would impact the risk for the firm.

This scenario had three different 'red flags' regarding client integrity and candidates would receive credit for each flag identified as well as the development into how this might impact the assignment and the risk to the firm.

Part (b) assumed the assurance assignment has been accepted and was broken into two sub-requirements to assist candidates in the process of determining the procedures to be performed.

The first part enabled candidates to focus on the forecast given and evaluate the assumptions of management and the completeness of the forecast. This allowed candidates to demonstrate professional scepticism and at the same time generate ideas for areas to address with relevant procedures. Scepticism is a key skill for auditors and candidates were able to score a full mark for each assumption challenged appropriately.

The second part of the requirement was to design examination procedures for use when reviewing the cashflow forecast. This area was generally well covered and is typically well answered by candidates who have practised past questions of this nature. Candidates should note however that as far as possible, procedures should be applied to the specific information in the forecast and information provided ... As such, **a pass mark is not possible unless specific procedures are also covered**. Candidates should note that giving an answer learnt for a past exam question will not demonstrate the application skills required for a pass in this examination.

Marking guide | **Marks**

(a) **Ethical and other matters to be considered before accepting Flynn Ltd as a client of the firm and performing the review engagement**

Up to 1 mark for each matter explained:

- General requirements of ISQM 1

Ethical matters:

- Self-interest threat from 'incentive' to secure the audit appointment
- Advocacy threat from promoting loan application
- Mary Sunshine – potential self-review and familiarity threats explained (1 mark each)
- Recommended safeguards to reduce threats to an acceptable level (1 mark each to max 2)

Integrity matters:

- Incentive offered to Kelly & Co could indicate a lack of integrity
- Reason for not appointing existing audit firm for the review engagement

ANSWERS

- Risk exposure for Kelly & Co given Flynn Ltd's going concern problems

Competence and resources:

- Competence to perform the work – a review engagement should not be a problem
- But due to higher risk, more experienced and senior staff should be assigned to the team
- Short deadline could impact on quality of the work performed
- The deadline should be negotiated and extended if possible

ISAE 3400 considerations:

0.5 mark each to max 2 marks:

- The intended use of the information
- Whether the information will be for general or limited distribution
- The nature of the assumptions, that is, whether they are best-estimate or hypothetical assumptions
- The elements to be included in the information
- The period covered by the information
- Engagement should not be performed if assumptions unrealistic or PFI not appropriate for use
- Level of assurance to be provided and expected users of the report – impacts on scale of work to be performed

Maximum 8

(b) (i) **Evaluation of assumptions**

Generally, up to 1 mark for each relevant point of evaluation:

- Monthly sales figures – popularity of products
- Monthly sale figures – speed at which sales can be generated
- New processing facility – date of starting production
- New processing facility – lack of start-up costs
- Increase in production capacity
- Reduction in operating expenses and economies of scale
- Tax expenses – missing expenses
- Foreign exchange – not included to mask potential volatility
- Finance costs – unlikely to be static
- Conclusion

Maximum 5

(ii) **Examination procedures and professional scepticism**

Up to 1 mark for each procedure explained. In addition, 0.5 mark for relevant calculations, eg trend analysis, up to a maximum of 2 marks.

See model answer for detail of examination procedures covering:

- General procedures (to a maximum of 2 marks)
- Revenue
- Operating expenses
- Inclusion of foreign exchange transactions
- Interest and finance costs
- Tax and dividend cash flows
- Planned capital expenditure

- Going concern issues highlighted by the auditor's report

Maximum | 7

Professional skills marks

Analysis and evaluation

- Effective appraisal of the information to make suitable recommendations for appropriate procedures for the review of Flynn Ltd's cash flow forecast
- Appropriate assessment of the ethical and professional issues relating to the assignment, using examples where relevant to support overall comments

Professional scepticism and professional judgment

- Critical assessment of the context of the engagement, and of management's integrity in relation to the incentive offered to Kelly & Co
- Application of professional scepticism to the Flynn Ltd's decision not to appoint existing auditor to perform proposed engagement
- Appropriate application of professional scepticism to the cash flow forecast prepared by Flynn Ltd's management

Commercial acumen

- Appropriate recognition of the commercial context of the proposed engagement, both for Flynn Ltd and Kelly & Co, and awareness of the need to set aside commercial considerations in favour of ethical ones
- Assessment of the reasonableness and viability of commercial assumptions underlying the forecast information

Maximum	5
Total	25

(a) **Matters to be considered before accepting Flynn Ltd as a client of the firm and performing the review engagement**

Requirements and guidance relevant to accepting and continuing client relationships is contained in ISQM (UK) 1 *Quality Management for Firms that Perform Audits or Reviews of Financial Statements or Other Assurance or Related Services Engagements.*

The fundamental requirements are that a firm must consider:

- Whether the relevant ethical, legal and regulatory and other professional requirements can be complied with;
- The integrity and ethical values of the client, and whether there is information which would lead it to conclude that the client lacks integrity; and
- Whether the firm has the appropriate competence and resources (the financial and operational priorities of the firm).

Ethical issues

In terms of ethics, there are several matters to consider. First, it appears from the communication with the company's managing director that Flynn Ltd is encouraging Kelly & Co to accept the review engagement by offering the audit appointment as a 'reward', assuming that the outcome of the loan application is successful. This creates a self-interest threat in that Kelly & Co has a financial interest in accepting Flynn Ltd as a client and performing the review engagement in order to secure appointment as the company's auditor.

An advocacy threat is also created because Kelly & Co has an incentive to promote Flynn Ltd to the bank to ensure that the loan will be provided, and this may impact the quality and objectivity of the review engagement.

Kelly & Co should consider whether any safeguards can be implemented to reduce any ethical threats to an acceptable level, for example, using an independent second partner to

ANSWERS

review the work performed for the review engagement. If safeguards do not reduce the threats to an acceptable level, then the review engagement should not be performed.

Finally, the fact that Mary Sunshine, an audit manager of Kelly & Co, has recently been recruited from Flynn Ltd raises ethical threats to objectivity. The IESBA *International Code of Ethics for Professional Accountants* (the *Code*) states that self-interest, self-review and familiarity threats may arise where an audit team member has recently served as director, officer or employee of the client. These threats could arise should Mary Sunshine be part of the audit team, as suggested by Flynn Ltd's managing director. The provisions of the *Code* apply to review engagements as well as audit engagements and therefore are applicable to the review of the cash flow forecast.

Given that Mary Sunshine had previously worked in internal audit at Flynn Ltd, the self-review threat could arise, should she be included in the review engagement team, as she may lack the necessary professional scepticism to challenge the forecasts prepared by Flynn Ltd. However, given that Mary was part of internal audit at Flynn Ltd, she would not have been in a position to exert influence over the financial statements, so the risk is reduced. However, she may also have close personal relationships with the staff at Flynn Ltd making it likely that she would want to secure a favourable outcome for the loan application, impacting on her objectivity.

These threats to objectivity may appear significant but they can be reduced to an acceptable level by ensuring that Mary is not included in the review team, and should Kelly & Co become audit provider to Flynn Ltd, ensuring that she is not involved with the audit this year.

Client integrity

One issue relating to client integrity is the incentive which has been offered for Kelly & Co to become audit provider should the loan application be successful. In relation to client integrity, ISQM 1 suggests that the firm should consider the reasons for the proposed appointment of the firm and non-reappointment of the previous firm as a matter relating to client integrity.

In this case, the fact that the latest auditor's report contained a Material Uncertainty Related to Going Concern section and the comments by Mary Sunshine indicates that Flynn Ltd has financial problems and in particular, it appears that liquidity issues are creating doubts over going concern. Therefore, management of Flynn Ltd may be reluctant to appoint their existing audit firm to provide the review service on the basis that the audit firm may not be likely to support the application.

Related to this, Kelly & Co should carefully consider the going concern issue, as it creates a higher risk for the review engagement. The firm could become exposed to liability issues, should the bank provide the loan, and Flynn Ltd not be able to repay the amount advanced. For this reason, it could be that the existing audit firm has been approached to provide the review engagement but has declined the assignment.

Competence and resources

There seems no reason why Kelly & Co would not have the competence to carry out the assignment to review the cash flow forecast. Being a firm of Chartered Certified Accountants and performing a range of assurance services means that the firm has the relevant knowledge and experience to perform a high-quality review of a cash flow forecast for a business which does not appear to be a very complex organisation.

However, as discussed above, this is a high-risk engagement due to the going concern problems of Flynn Ltd. Should the work be performed, it is likely that Kelly & Co would want to include experienced and senior staff in the review engagement team, in order to reduce risk exposure. It may be that such staff are not available at this time.

Resourcing could be a problem given that Flynn Ltd expects the loan application to be submitted on 5 August 20X5, which is just over a month from now. Kelly & Co may not have capacity to provide staff to carry out the review engagement and the tight deadline could impact the quality of the work performed. Kelly & Co should discuss with Flynn Ltd whether there is any flexibility regarding the deadline, with the objective of having longer to plan and carry out the work required.

Matters specific to ISAE 3400 *The Examination of Prospective Financial Information*

Kelly & Co should also consider the matters outlined in ISAE 3400, which suggests that before accepting an engagement to examine prospective financial information, the auditor would consider, amongst other things:

- The intended use of the information;
- Whether the information will be for general or limited distribution;
- The nature of the assumptions, that is, whether they are best-estimate or hypothetical assumptions;
- The elements to be included in the information; and
- The period covered by the information.

Review engagements can vary in terms of the level of work that is required, depending on the level of assurance which is required from the review. This level of assurance required will impact on the scale of the assignment. Kelly & Co should clarify the expected form and content and expected wording of the review report and who will be using the review report, so they understand the risk exposure for the firm.

ISAE 3400 also contains a requirement that the auditor should not accept, or should withdraw from, an engagement when the assumptions are clearly unrealistic or when the auditor believes that the prospective financial information will be inappropriate for its intended use.

The above matters should be discussed with Flynn Ltd as soon as possible, to help Kelly & Co to establish whether to proceed with the engagement.

(b) (i) **Evaluation of the assumptions used by management in preparing the cash flow forecast**

Monthly sales figures

The forecast of monthly sales figures appears overly optimistic, e.g. the expected revenue growth of 17% in the period to 30 June 20X6 appears optimistic given that the new production plant is only expected to open in March 20X6. Expectations of the popularity of the new product range in particular may be overly optimistic, the successful launch of a new product is not guaranteed, even if it is supported by an advertising campaign. The advertising costs are only included in one period, however, the sales figures increase throughout the forecast. It is possible that additional marketing costs have been omitted or the increase in sales may be overstated.

Even if the processing plant is ready for use from 31 March 20X6, as stated in the forecast assumptions, it only leaves three months for a very significant increase in sales resulting from new product ranges produced at the plant to be achieved. Management may be manipulating the forecast to accelerate the cash inflows in order to reduce the payback period of the capital expenditure.

New processing plant – commencement of operations

Assuming that the loan is advanced in August 20X5, this allows only seven months for the construction and fitting of the new processing plant, which seems a short timeframe for this to take place. Management may be being over optimistic in their assessment of how quickly the plant can be constructed and brought into use.

In addition, there is no cash flow specific to factory start-up costs, e.g. staff recruitment and training, included in the cash flow forecast. There is a possibility that these costs have been omitted in error or deliberately in order to show the total cost of the new processing plant as £15 million, i.e. the costs will all be covered by the loan which has been applied for, and that no further costs will be incurred.

Increase in production capacity

Management's assumption that production capacity can be increased without any need for capital expenditure at existing production facilities should be challenged by the audit team. This assumption relies on there being spare capacity in the existing facilities, which may not be the case.

Reduction in operating expenses

Management's claim that economies of scale are being achieved, therefore improving operating margins, may not be appropriate and is an attempt to overstate the cash position shown in the forecast. Opening a new production facility separately located from the company's other production plants in a foreign country is unlikely to achieve economies of scale, certainly not in the timescale suggested by management.

Tax expenses

There does not appear to be any cash flows relating to tax payments included in the forecast. If management is claiming that there will be no tax payments during the period covered by the forecast, this assertion needs to be approached with professional scepticism as it is unlikely that no tax payments at all will occur during this time. These payments may be deliberately omitted to improve the cash flow position as shown in the forecast.

Foreign exchange transactions

The cash flow forecast does not indicate how foreign exchange transactions have been dealt with. Transactions relating to the existing processing plant in Nearland, and more significantly, the capital expenditure and other transactions for the new plant in Farland, are in a foreign currency but the cash flows, e.g. exchange gains and losses specific to these transactions, are not shown in the forecast, though they may be included in 'interest payments and other finance costs'. Management could be ignoring these impacts relating to foreign exchange to reduce the volatility of cash flows as presented in the forecast.

Finance costs

It is unusual that interest costs and other finance costs are completely static, indicating that the amount has not been accurately calculated. The amount also appears very low – if the category includes interest costs only, these amount to only £60,000 per annum which equates to only 0.4% of the £15 million loan. It appears that management is underestimating the interest costs, especially if the company has existing debt on which interest is being paid. It could also be the case that the company has existing debt which needs to be repaid – there is no cash outflow relating to capital repayments within the forecast.

Conclusion

Given the material uncertainty over going concern highlighted in the recent auditor's report, there is a significant risk that the assumptions used in preparation of the cash flow forecast are not realistic and have been applied to make the cash flow forecast look more favourable in an attempt to secure the loan finance from the bank.

(ii) **Examination procedures on the cash flow forecast**

- Re-cast the forecast to ensure it is arithmetically correct.
- Agree the opening cash balance of £50,000 to bank statement and management accounts.
- Discuss with appropriate personnel, eg sales director and product development team, to obtain understanding of the new product ranges to be produced in Farland and the basis for management's assumption regarding the expected popularity of the new products leading to the forecast high levels of demand.
- Obtain supporting evidence for the projected increase in sales attributed to the new product range, e.g. correspondence with potential customers and any signed customer contracts, results of market research.
- Obtain and review the plans for marketing the new product ranges including analysis of the planned expenditure of £100,000 and confirm there are no additional planned expenses to confirm completeness.
- Discuss with the sales director why marketing costs are only included in the period to 30 June 20X6 and the justification for the continuing increase in sales when there is no planned marketing cost in future periods.

- Obtain and review supporting documentation for management's assertion that production levels in existing processing facilities will increase by 10%, eg review production budgets, orders placed with suppliers for inputs to the processing, which should help to corroborate the assertion.
- Compare the monthly sales figures in the cash flow forecast to those in the profit forecast to ensure consistency.
- For the pattern of cash inflows from sales, confirm that the timing of cash receipts from customers used in the forecast agrees with those evidenced from past records, eg management accounts, aged receivables listing. Discuss any discrepancy with management.
- Recalculate the patterns of cash flows based on management's historical analysis of credit sales to confirm that the forecast has been properly prepared on the basis of these assumptions.
- Obtain a breakdown showing the components of operating expenses; perform analytical procedures comparing the forecasts to the actual expenses included in the audited financial statements, in particular reviewing for completeness and classification, and discuss results with management.
- Analyse the trend in operating expenses, compare with the trend in sales, eg over the whole period of the forecast, sales increase by 60% over the period of the forecast, whereas operating expenses increase by much less, only 45% over the same period.
- Discuss the timing of cash flows relating to operating expenses with the preparer of the forecast to obtain understanding of how these figures have been determined.
- Compare the level of operating expenses with historical financial information and with the profit forecast and discuss any significant variances with management.
- Assess whether there are any missing categories of cash flow, eg there does not appear to be any cash flows relating to tax payments. Discuss any potentially omitted expense categories with management to understand why they have not been included in the forecast.
- Enquire with management how foreign exchange transactions have been dealt with in the forecast.
- Agree interest costs to existing and potential loan documents or other relevant supporting documentation.
- For the planned capital expenditure, obtain a detailed breakdown of the costs included in the £15 million planned expenditure and agree a sample of costs to supporting documentation, eg quotes for construction, cost of land acquisition, quotes from suppliers of plant and machinery, to verify the completeness of the estimated cost of the construction of the new facility.
- Confirm the exchange rate which has been used to determine the £ value of the anticipated capital expenditure which has been included in the forecast.
- Confirm by agreeing to historical financial statements that the level of dividend of £100,000 each year appears in line with previous payments. Given the company's going concern problems, it may be that dividends have not been paid in recent years, in which case the forecast level of dividend payable should be discussed with management.
- Review the planned capital expenditure for any missing expenses, eg does it include incidental costs such as installing health and safety equipment, testing of machinery prior to use.
- Enquire with management to understand whether or how start-up costs for the new processing facility which are not capital in nature have been included in the cash flow forecast, eg recruitment and training of staff.
- Obtain supporting evidence that the new processing facility will be ready for use on 31 March 20X6, as claimed by management, eg a project plan provided by the construction firm.

- Obtain the published financial statements and auditor's report of Flynn Ltd for the year ended 31 March 20X5 and review the content of the auditor's report to confirm the opinion issued and the Material Uncertainty Related to Going Concern section.
- Given the material uncertainty related to going concern highlighted in the auditor's report, request permission to communicate with the auditor to discuss the going concern issues, to obtain understanding and to assist in evaluating the assumptions underpinning the cash flow forecast.
- Assuming that permission is given to communicate with the auditor, discuss the specific nature of the liquidity issue as mentioned in their auditor's report, eg have previous applications for finance been rejected, are there any specific factors contributing to financial distress in this financial year.
- Confirm that the assumptions underpinning the cash flow forecast are consistent with those used in the rest of the business plan to be provided to Mortons Bank.
- Review the outcomes of previous management forecasts and assess their accuracy compared to actual data.
- Assess the competence and experience of the preparer of the forecast.
- Confirm the consistency of the accounting policies used in the preparation of the forecast financial statements with those used in the last audited financial statements.
- For a sample of operating expenses, review the supporting documentation such as invoices and utility bills and agree the amount paid each month to the cash book.
- Agree the predicted collection and payment periods to the most recent sales ledgers and purchase ledgers.
- Perform sensitivity analyses on the cash flow forecast by varying the key assumptions (in particular, in relation to growth rates and payment periods) and assessing the impact of these variations on the company's forecast cash position.
- Obtain written representations from management confirming the reasonableness of their assumptions and that all relevant information has been provided to Kelly & Co.
- Request confirmation from the bank of the potential terms of the additional finance being negotiated, to confirm the interest rate.
- Review board minutes for approval of the purchase, and approval that the finance will be raised from Morton's Bank.
- Enquire about any other potential sources of finance in case Mortons Bank fails to provide the full amount required, or in case the new premises cost more than the estimated amount.
- Inspect the cash book from 1 July 20X5 to see if there are any significant cash transactions which do not appear to have been included in the forecasts.

50 Yew

Workbook references

Chapters 8, 10, 11 and 16.

Top tips

The first part of this question was difficult, and doubtless many candidates would struggle to make up six marks here. It is important with discussion questions that you plan your answer before you write. If you don't plan, there is a danger that you will change your mind about what you want to say while you are already writing. This will only waste time and will be unlikely to score marks. You need to plan your answer and divide your discussion into clearly structured paragraphs. Within each paragraph, you should aim to have an introduction, a point, and a conclusion.

It is also important that you didn't go over time on this part of the question – perhaps through struggling to write clearly.

Part (b) was a typical question on auditor's reports, this time mixed in with IAS 38 and some issues around audit completion. You should have had plenty to say here; the main difficulty would have been staying within the time limit for this part of the question.

Part (c) contained just one short situation. The situation was fairly straightforward, so how you did came down to your knowledge.

Easy marks

A lot of part (b) was easy – for example, stating that the treatment of the development costs was not in line with IAS 38.

ACCA examining team's comments

Candidates were asked to discuss firstly whether auditors should accept some of the blame when a company on which they have expressed an unmodified opinion subsequently fails, and secondly whether auditors should do more to highlight going concern problems. Very few answers were worthy of more than a few marks, most answers simply listing the auditor's responsibilities from ISA (UK) 570 *Going Concern*, with no discussion at all of the statement provided in the question. Those who did refer to the statement provided tended to just state whether or not they agreed with it but provided no discussion at all. Answers were especially poor at discussing whether auditors should disclose more in relation to going concern, with most just describing the various ways that going concern issues may affect the audit opinion. It is inadequate that at this level of examination candidates seem simply unable to express an opinion of their own or base a reasoned discussion around a statement provided to them, especially around such a significant current issue facing the profession.

Marking guide — **Marks**

(a) **Discussion**

Up to 2 marks for comments discussed from ideas list:

- Management responsibility for risk assessment
- Auditor should be aware of going concern issues
- Auditor must not take on management role
- Misunderstanding of roles of management and auditor
- Auditor may be to blame if overlooked a fraud/other matter
- Financial statements contain disclosure on risk assessment
- Users may not be financially literate
- Auditors could make problems more visible and understandable

Maximum — 6

(b) **Yew Co**

Generally up to 1.5 marks for each matter discussed/recommended:

- Calculate and comment on materiality
- No probable economic benefit – IAS 38 recognition criteria not met
- Lack of finance – IAS 38 recognition criteria not met
- Consider whether sufficient appropriate evidence obtained
- Financial statements contain material misstatement and implication for auditor's report
- Could indicate fraudulent financial reporting
- Lack of cash may indicate going concern problems – extend audit procedures
- Audit work should be subject to second partner review

Marking guide	Marks
• Consider asking for a delay in issuing financial statements if necessary for further evidence to be sought	
• Discuss apparent inconsistency in chairman's statement wording	
• Discuss accounting treatment, potential qualification and chairman's statement wording with those charged with governance	
• Describe matter in Other Information section of auditor's report if material misstatement of other information persists	
Maximum	11
(c) **Prior year auditor's opinion**	
Generally 1 mark per point:	
• Generally auditors do not refer to third parties in their report	
• But optional to refer to predecessor auditor unless prohibited by law and regulations	
• If reference made, should be in *Other Matter* paragraph	
• Describe contents of reference made to predecessor auditor	
• If prior year modified, explain this in *Other Matter* paragraph	
Maximum	3
Professional skills marks	
Analysis and evaluation	
• Appropriate use of the information to support discussion, draw appropriate conclusions and design appropriate responses	
• Identification of omissions from the analysis or further analysis which could be carried out	
• Balanced assessment of the information to determine the effect on the auditor's report in the circumstances	
Professional scepticism and judgement	
• Effective challenge of information, evidence and assumptions supplied and, techniques carried out to support key facts and/or decisions	
• Appropriate application of professional judgement to draw conclusions and make informed decisions about the actions which are appropriate in the context and stage of the engagement.	
Maximum	5
Total	25

(a) The concept of an expectations gap between auditors and the public is a key lens through which assertions such as this one can be viewed. The first part of the statement would appear to assert that the auditor is in some way responsible for the failure of a company. This is not the case: those charged with governance are responsible for risk assessment and risk management. It is not the role of the auditor to become involved with the entity's risk management processes – indeed, this could be deemed to constitute a management role, which would compromise the auditor's independence.

However, it is true that the auditor should gain an understanding of the client's business; this is a crucial requirement of ISAs (UK). Amongst other things, it is necessary for an auditor to audit management's assessment of the appropriateness of the going concern assumption, for which a good understanding of the business risks faced by the client is necessary. The auditor must judge whether the going concern assumption used is appropriate. However, this is never a matter of cut-and-dried logic: it is a judgement, based on an assessment of risk. It is in the nature of risk for there to be uncertainties, and it is in the nature of judgement to contain elements of doubt.

It is therefore to be expected that there will be cases where the auditor has judged the going concern assumption to be appropriate, and yet the company fails within the year (such as Carillion plc). The question is not whether the assumption was proved correct by subsequent events, but whether the auditor's assessment was reasonable and in line with auditing standards.

There is more scope for discussion on the question of whether auditors should do more to highlight problems. This may be the responsibility of management; it would be possible for regulators and setters of accounting standards to require increased disclosure on going concern. For example, financial statements could be required to provide more narrative detail regarding the risks faced by an entity.

At present, auditors should disclose the presence of material uncertainties over going concern by way of a 'material uncertainties related to going concern' section in the auditor's report, and if they deem the assumption to be inappropriate then the opinion would be modified. It may be possible for these disclosures to be made clearer than they are, or for auditors to use their report to draw users' attention to any parts of the financial statements that are significant to the assessment of going concern.

In conclusion, it is unfair to require auditors to accept the blame for company failures which are the proper responsibility of management, although it may be argued that more could be done by auditors to highlight going concern problems where they exist.

(b) The intangible asset is material to profit (54% of profit before tax) and to the statement of financial position (6% of total assets).

IAS 38 *Intangible assets* states that for development costs to be capitalised, the existence of a market – or the entity's ability to use the asset itself – must be demonstrable. The audit team has obtained documentation and a written representation which confirms that this is not the case.

IAS 38 also requires the entity to have the financial resources to bring the asset to the market. As Yew Ltd is short of cash, this may not be the case.

As a result, the financial statements appear to be materially misstated, and that the £12.5m should be treated as expenses. The matter must be discussed with management, who should be asked to amend the financial statements.

The matter should also be discussed with the chairman, as it is possible that he has different information which could change our assessment of the situation. If this is not the case, and if the financial statements are not amended, then the audit opinion will be a qualified opinion due to material misstatement.

The fact that Yew Ltd is finding it difficult to raise finance casts doubt over going concern. Further work may need to be done in this area. If there is significant doubt then disclosures should be included in the financial statements, and a 'Material uncertainty relating to going concern' section in the auditor's report provided that the auditor feels the level of disclosure is adequate.

If a modified opinion is expected to be expressed, then it may be necessary to consult externally on the effects of doing this, or at a minimum subjecting the audit work to review by another partner.

Consideration needs to be given to whether the misstatement is an indication of fraudulent financial reporting, and a possible lack of management integrity. The fact the company is struggling to raise finance provides a motive for it to inflate its results and statement of financial position. If this is the case, then any written representations relied upon elsewhere in the audit must be reconsidered.

If the development costs should not be capitalised and the financial statements are amended, then there will be an inconsistency with the directors' report. First, the chairman should be asked to amend his statement. If this is not done, then ISA (UK) 720 *The auditor's Responsibilities Relating to Other Information* comes into play. ISA (UK) 720 states that in these circumstances, the auditor's report should state that the directors' report is materially inconsistent with the financial statements in the Other Information section of the auditor's report, and describe the nature of this inconsistency in the Other Information section of the auditor's report.

(c) It is not generally appropriate to refer to third parties in an auditor's report, as this may give the impression that someone other than the auditor is responsible for the report.

However, ISA (UK) 710 *Comparative Information – Corresponding Figures and Comparative Financial Statements* permits reference to be made to a predecessor auditor's report; this is the auditor's own choice.

This reference should be made in an Other Matter paragraph, included after the Key Audit Matters section (or if there are none, after the Basis for Opinion section). This would which state that the financial statements for the prior period were audited by a predecessor auditor, state the opinion they expressed, and the date of their report.

51 Fern

Workbook references

Chapters 1, 2, 8 and 11.

Top tips

This question covered several different areas and should have been within your capabilities. Part (a), on ethics, was a slightly out-of-the-ordinary AAA question and covered professional issues as much as ethics. Non-compliance with laws and regulations is a topical area, and this scenario combined it with intimidation that threatened to limit the scope of the audit. In order to pass this question it was important that your answer covered each of these issues – and that you kept to your time for part (a) as a whole, but also within it.

Part (b) covered auditor reporting, an area which is guaranteed to feature in every exam. The material on IFRS 15 *Revenue from Contracts with Customers* tested your knowledge of the standard but was a fair test. Part (ii) on the auditor's report should have been second nature to you.

Easy marks

Questions on the auditor's report almost always contain marks (as here) for stating that eg the 'Basis for Qualified Opinion' section is placed immediately below the 'Opinion' section. These are like money for nothing.

ACCA examining team's comments

Part (a) was generally **not well-answered**. Part (a) focused on a potential breach of laws and regulations through the potential use of out-of-date medicines and an intimidating client. Most candidates discussed the implication for inventory valuation reasonably and some suggested highlighting the issues and lack of co-operation from the Finance Director to those changed with governance and the potential for a limitation on the scope of the audit. Disappointingly only a minority of candidates identified that there was a wider issue that using out-of-date medication could have severe or fatal health consequences and were able to discuss the balance between the auditor's duty of confidentiality to the client compared with their wider ethical duty to notify the appropriate regulators and after seeking legal advice.

Part (b) concerned revenue recognition. Many candidates gave a good summary of the IFRS 15 conditions that revenue cannot be recognised until the goods have been delivered, control transferred, and all performance obligations have been met. However, some candidates demonstrated out-of-date financial reporting knowledge by referencing the superseded IAS 18 *Revenue*. For the most part candidates usually correctly identified that the sale had not actually occurred before year end and should be adjusted for. However, many candidates digressed into visiting and inspecting the goods in a third-party warehouse when it was clear that the performance obligations had not yet been met. Most highlighted that they should ask management to amend the accounts and that the matter should be referred to those charged with governance.

Marking guide | | **Marks**

(a) Generally up to 1.5 marks for each well-explained point and 1 mark for each well-explained action recommended.

Ethical and professional issues

- Compliance with laws and regulations/NOCLAR
- Attempt to obtain more evidence for discussion with management
- Confidentiality threat
- Report to those charged with governance/regulator
- Limitation on scope of audit
- Impact on the financial statements
- Intimidation threat
- Management Integrity
- Withdrawal from engagement

Maximum — 9

(b) (i) **Matters**

Materiality:

- IFRS 15 – Satisfaction of performance obligations
- Control not yet passed to client
- Revenue recognition and management bias
- Revenue recognised too early and, therefore, misstated

Actions:

- Request adjustment to financial statements
- If refused communicate with those charged with governance
- Obtain written representation

6

(ii) **Auditor's report**

- Financial statements materially misstated
- Matter is not pervasive
- Modified auditor's report
- Qualified opinion
- Basis for qualified opinion paragraph

5

Professional marks

Analysis and evaluation

- Appropriate use of the information to support discussion, draw appropriate conclusions and design appropriate responses
- Balanced assessment of the information to determine the implications for the auditor's report for Rocket plc
- Appropriate assessment of the ethical and professional issues relating to the assignment, using examples where relevant to support overall comments

ANSWERS

Marking guide	Marks
Professional scepticism and judgement	
• Effective challenge of information, evidence and assumptions supplied and, techniques carried out to support key facts and/or decisions	
• Appropriate application of professional judgement to draw conclusions and make informed decisions about the actions which are appropriate in the context and stage of the engagement.	
Maximum	5
Total	25

(a) **Ethical and professional issues**

Compliance with laws and regulations

It appears that Fieldwood Hospital is storing and maybe using medicines that have passed their recommended use by date. This may be illegal, and it may breach the terms of agreement with their suppliers and, most significantly, this may lead to patient harm or ineffective treatment.

ISA (UK) 250A *Consideration of Law and Regulations in an Audit of Financial Statements* requires that in the event of a suspected non-compliance with law and regulations (NOCLAR), the auditor should document the findings and discuss them with management. The audit team should attempt to obtain more information about the suspected NOCLAR, though this will be difficult given the actions of the financial controller, who is denying access to the relevant source of information and the attempt to intimidate the audit team by the finance director.

The audit team should seek appropriate legal advice in relation to the use of out-of-date medicines. If this is a breach of regulations, then the auditor may have a statutory duty to report this incident to the relevant regulator.

Reporting non-compliance to those charged with governance

If Fern & Co believes that non-compliance with relevant law and regulation is taking place, then according to ISA (UK) 250A, the matter should be reported to those charged with governance of Fieldwood Hospital. This communication should happen without delay given that it appears to be deliberate and owing to the potential seriousness of the use of expired medical inventory. At present it is unclear whether those charged with governance are aware of these practices. The auditor should request that those charged with governance make any necessary disclosure to the relevant authorities, clearly state the reasons why Fieldwood Hospital should make the disclosure and that if the board fails to comply, that Fern & Co will be compelled to make the disclosure themselves.

If the auditor suspects that members of senior management including the board of directors are involved with the non-compliance, then the auditor should report the matter to the next higher level of authority, such as the audit committee.

Confidentiality

Reporting the incident to a regulator would require the auditor to report information about a client to a third party, which is a breach of client confidentiality. In these circumstances, however, legal/regulatory responsibilities would be considered to outweigh the confidentiality requirement.

Given the potential conflict with the IESBA *International Code of Ethics for Professional Accountants*, Fern & Co should seek legal advice before they act to minimise the risk of legal dispute with their client or legal action from the regulator due to inaction.

If Fern & Co concludes that the matter should be reported to a regulator, they should first communicate this belief to the board of Fieldwood Hospital and request that they make a disclosure. At present it is unclear whether those charged with governance are aware of these practices. They should clearly state the reasons why Fieldwood Hospital should make the disclosure and that if the board fails to comply, that Fern & Co will be compelled to make the disclosure themselves.

Impact on the financial statements

It is not correct for management to assert that the issue with out-of-date inventory is not relevant to the audit, because if any of the inventory is obsolete, then it should be written off in the financial statements.

By restricting the audit team's ability to audit inventory, management has imposed a limitation on the scope of the audit. If the auditor is unable to obtain satisfactory evidence relating to inventories, then this may lead to a modification of the auditor's report.

Fern & Co should report this matter to those charged with governance and request that they provide access to the necessary evidence. They should also explain what repercussions this will have on the auditor's report if they fail to comply.

If Fieldwood Hospital has failed to comply with any legal, regulatory or contractual requirements they may incur fines or other financial penalties. The audit approach should now be modified to include additional procedures aimed at investigating the potential implications of the use of out-of-date medicines and the potential value of fines and penalties.

Intimidation threat

The aggressive actions of the finance director amount to an intimidation threat to objectivity. The finance director has tried to influence the conduct of the audit with threatening behaviour.

Fern & Co should inform those charged with governance, explaining the significance of the matter and that it cannot be tolerated. Fern & Co should explain the reasons for the enquiries made by the audit team and the significance of being allowed to complete these procedures.

Management integrity

While the intentions of management are not clear it does appear that they are trying to conceal a matter of some significance from the auditor.

The audit team must increase their scepticism of all evidence provided by management, particularly written representations obtained from management as they may be subject to bias and evidence which they could potentially manipulate, such as internal spreadsheets. In particular, if the audit team is given access to the inventory valuation spreadsheet, it must remain vigilant for any indication that this has been subsequently altered.

Withdrawal from engagement

If the audit team believes that management is complicit in any significant illegal activity and/or attempt to manipulate the financial statements, it may reconsider their position as auditor. If permitted by local regulations, it may wish to resign from the engagement to protect their reputation and to protect themselves from being implicated in any ensuing legal case.

Before taking any action, the matter should be discussed with the senior partners of the firm and an appropriate legal advisor.

(b)

(i) **Matters**

Materiality

The revenue of £17m recognised in relation to the highlighted transactions represents 1.2% of revenue and 12.2% of profit before tax. The sales are, therefore, material to the financial statements.

Bill and hold arrangement

IFRS 15 Revenue from Contracts with Customers specifies that an entity shall recognise revenue only when it has satisfied its performance obligations by transferring the goods (or services) to its customer.

Rocket plc believes that it has satisfied its performance obligations by having the goods available for the customers by the specified date. The situation, however, represents a 'bill and hold' arrangement, whereby Rocket plc has billed the customer but has yet to physically transfer the goods to them.

Transfer of control

IFRS 15 specifies that in these circumstances it should be determined when the customer obtains control of the goods. The contracts specify that the goods have to be delivered for inspection and 'acceptance', implying that the customer will not accept control until they have satisfactorily completed their inspections. Rocket plc has, therefore, not fulfilled their performance obligations and should not recognise the revenue in relation to these two contracts.

Revenue recognition

Given Rocket plc's listed status, management may be under pressure to report better results. Revenue has fallen by 3.5% based on the draft financial statements. If the £17m relating to the bill and hold arrangement is excluded from the 20X7 financial statements, then the reduction in revenue is greater, at 4.6%.

Further actions

Fern & Co should request that the client adjusts their financial statements to reverse the revenue recognised in relation to the goods being stored at the third-party facility.

If they refuse to adjust the financial statements, Fern & Co should communicate the misstatement to those charged with governance. They should repeat the request to adjust the financial statements and inform them of the modifications that will be made to the auditor's report if the adjustments are not made.

If the client still refuses to amend the financial statements, Fern & Co should request a written representation from the client confirming their intention to proceed without amending the financial statements and that they are aware of the potential repercussions.

(ii) **Auditor's report**

Material but not pervasive misstatement

If management refuses to reverse the £17 million of revenue recognised in relation to these transactions the auditor will conclude that the financial statements are materially misstated.

The matter is material to the statement of profit or loss, but it is unlikely to be considered pervasive; the required adjustment would not lead to a reported profit being restated as a loss and the only captions of the financial statements affected will be revenue and receivables.

Qualified opinion

In these circumstances the auditor would issue a qualified audit opinion stating that 'except for' these matters the financial statements are fairly presented.

The auditor should also include a Basis for Qualified Opinion section below the opinion section. This should describe and quantify the financial effects of the misstatement.

52 Boston

Workbook references

Chapters 10 and 11.

Top tips

In part (a), there are marks available for making the general point that uncorrected misstatements should be discussed with management, so that management can correct the accounting records. The auditor also tells management what effect misstatements may have on the audit opinion.

All of this seems obvious but it gets you marks! Talking about communication with management is something that markers almost always like to see.

With each issue it is crucial that you calculate materiality – these are really easy marks so you really must get them. If you calculate it correctly and state whether it's material to each financial statement, this is one mark – so four marks on this question. If you then aim for at least one solid point on each issue, then you should be able to pass this part of the question.

Issue (i) – impairment – was odd because the treatment in the question was correct once the auditor's findings are taken into account. This might have confused you. What is not in the question is a proper discussion of IAS 36. If you do this – as in the answer below – then you're confirming that you know the required treatment.

The requirement asks for 'matters that should be discussed with management', so you can get easy marks for asking why management has adopted the treatment it has adopted – you need to pick **something specific** from the scenario, so eg 'ask management why it has used the company's forecast growth rates' – and also for asking management to adjust the financial statements.

Issue (ii) – interest charges – should have been straightforward. The treatment is not line with IAS 23, so the costs must be capitalised.

Issue (iii) – irrecoverable debt – was another tricky one, because the auditor's change in the scenario gives the correct response. Your answer should confirm that this is correct, but also think about something that could be asked of management – eg 'has any further correspondence been received?'

Part (b) was a standard auditor's report requirement. The main nuance here was that the auditor would have to ask management to adjust for all of the issues but would also state that the factory impairment is material on its own. Since management is not going to make any changes, we only have to consider the aggregate effect on the auditor's report – qualified opinion due to material misstatement. (Although there are multiple misstatements, the effect is not pervasive.)

As ever, there are marks available for discussing whether the opinion should be adverse, and for talking about the precise format of the auditor's report – ie that the 'qualified opinion' section comes first, followed by a 'basis for qualified opinion' section, and so on.

Part (c) should have been straightforward, provided that you had a good grasp of the material. As usual, a good answer to this part would have a clear structure. The examining team is attuned to the fact that weaker students tend to only be able to make general statements, whereas stronger students make specific, accurate statements that are clear about what they are saying. Make sure that your comments are specific and avoid rambling!

Easy marks

Whenever a question asks for the effect on the auditor's report, the easiest marks will usually be those relating to the contents and structure of the report – eg what should be included in the 'Opinion' and 'Basis for' sections, and where each should be positioned in the report. Part (c) contained easy marks in relation to subsequent events, some of which is knowledge brought forward from your earlier studies.

Examining team's comments

Unfortunately, performance was on the whole unsatisfactory.

Part (a) set out three potential audit adjustments and candidates were required to discuss each, considering the individual and aggregate impact on the auditor's report. The values of each potential adjustment were given in the question, so there were materiality marks available and many candidates scored these but performed less well in discussing the associated issues. Most of the adjustments were relatively straightforward – such as the capitalisation of loan interest and the allowance for an irrecoverable debt and revaluation of investments – and the issues around these were reasonably answered. The issue of impairment was less well answered.

There was significant inconsistency in answers where candidates concluded that an issue was not material but concluded that the auditor's report required modification. Furthermore, candidates need to ensure that they understand what Emphasis of Matter and Other Matters paragraphs are. They are not a substitute for a modified opinion and should only be used where there are significant issues that the auditor wants to bring to the attention of the users of the accounts.

Requirement (ca) was a fairly factual requirement, asking for an explanation of the auditor's responsibility in relation to subsequent events. It was obvious that some candidates had studied ISA 560 Subsequent Events, and those that had done so performed well on this requirement. However, the majority of candidates clearly knew very little about ISA 560 (making it therefore surprising that they would pick to attempt this question), leading to answers which almost exclusively focused on the financial reporting requirements of IAS 10 Events After the Reporting Period, while other answers simply listed the various types of auditor's reports that could be issued in relation to a variety of subsequent events.

Marking guide	Marks
(a) **Summary of uncorrected misstatements**	
In general up to 1 mark for each point of explanation and up to 0.5 mark for each appropriate calculation:	
• Obtaining an understanding of management's reasons	
• Encourage management to amend all misstatements	
• Communicate effect of misstatements to those charged with governance	
Impairment	
• Explanation of original calculation	
• Inappropriate estimates used	
• Revised impairments	
• Justification of the proposed adjustment	
• Request further clarification at meeting	
• Matter is material individually	
Borrowing costs	
• Capitalisation rules	
• Qualifying asset	
• Identification of incorrect treatment of interest costs	
• Explanation of adjustment	
• Not material individually	
Cleveland	
• Liquidation is indication of further impairment	
• Adjusting event after the reporting period	
• Need to write off remainder of outstanding balance	
• Request evidence of any further correspondence	
• Not material individually	
Maximum	10
(b) **Auditor's report**	
• Aggregate impact on financial statements	
• Material to profit	
• Impairment individually material	

Marking guide	Marks
• Modification of opinion due to a material misstatement	
• Discussion of whether it is pervasive	
• Qualified opinion	
• Basis for qualified opinion paragraph	
Maximum	5
(c) **Subsequent event**	
Generally 1 mark per comment:	
• Definition of subsequent events	
• Adjusting event	
• Auditor's responsibility depends on whether financial statements issued	
• No active duty, but has been informed	
• Consider materiality	
• Perform extended procedures	
Maximum	5
Professional marks	
Analysis and evaluation	
• Appropriate use of the information to determine the misstatements that were present, and then to assess their significance to the auditor	
• Appropriate determination of the impact on the auditor's report in part (b)	
• Balanced assessment of the information to determine the matters to discuss with management in the circumstances	
Professional scepticism and judgement	
• Effective challenge of information, evidence and assumptions supplied and, techniques carried out to support key facts and/or decisions	
• Appropriate application of professional judgement to draw conclusions and make informed decisions about the actions which are appropriate given that this is the completion stage (and then subsequent events stage) of the Boston Ltd engagement.	
Maximum	5
Total	25

(a) **Matters to discuss at meeting**

During the completion stage of the audit, the effect of uncorrected misstatements must be evaluated by the auditor, as required by ISA (UK) 450 *Evaluation of Misstatements Identified During the Audit*. This requires that the auditor obtains an understanding of management's reasons for not making recommended adjustments to the financial statements and that they take this into account when evaluating whether the financial statements as a whole are free from material misstatement.

In order to maintain accurate accounting records, management should be encouraged to record all misstatements to ensure that the risk of material misstatements in future periods is reduced due to the cumulative effect of immaterial uncorrected misstatements.

ISA (UK) 450 also requires that the auditor communicates with those charged with governance about uncorrected misstatements and the effect that they, individually or in aggregate, may have on the opinion in the auditor's report. Each of the matters included in the summary of uncorrected misstatements will be discussed below and the impact on the auditor's report considered individually and in aggregate.

Impairment

When performing an impairment test, in accordance with IAS 36 *Impairment of Assets*, the carrying value of the asset (or cash generating unit) in question is compared to the recoverable amount of the asset. If the recoverable amount is lower than the carrying value an impairment loss should be recognised, reducing the asset down from its carrying value to the recoverable amount.

The recoverable amount is calculated as the higher of the fair value less costs to sell and value in use. In relation to the cash generating unit, Boston Ltd estimated that the greater of these two figures was the value in use at £3.5m. This was compared to the carrying value of £3.6m and the asset has been impaired by £100,000 accordingly.

The findings of audit procedures carried out suggest that an inappropriate estimate was used in the calculation of value in use. Boston Ltd applied the company's annual growth rates when estimating the cash flows attributable to the cash-generating unit. A more relevant estimate for the growth rates, specific to the cash-generating unit, was available and should have been used.

This would have generated a value in use of £3.1m which is still higher than fair value less cost to sell of £3m and should be used as the recoverable amount. As management already impaired the asset to £3.5m, a further impairment of £400,000 is required to value it appropriately at £3.1m.

At the meeting management should be asked why they used the company's forecast growth rates, rather than the factory's growth rates and whether any matters have arisen since the audit to suggest that the growth rates used by the audit team are now inappropriate.

The adjustment represents 6.25% of profit and 0.4% of total assets. While not material to the statement of financial position, it is material to profit. If management does not adjust for this or provide justifications as to why their valuation is more appropriate, then this will lead to a material misstatement of the financial statements.

Borrowing costs

Interest charges are borrowing costs. The borrowing costs relating to the construction of qualifying assets, such as property and plant, should be capitalised during the construction period, in accordance with IAS 23 *Borrowing Costs*.

As the manufacturing plant is not due for completion until November 20X6, it is still a qualifying asset and the interest should have been capitalised. Boston Ltd has incorrectly expensed the interest as part of the finance charges for the year.

The correcting adjustment is therefore to reduce finance charges and to add the interest to the cost of the asset on the statement of financial position.

The charges of £75,000 represent 1.2% of profit and 0.07% of assets so are not material to either profits or the statement of financial position.

Cleveland Ltd

At the year end, Boston Ltd would have recognised a net receivable of £95,000 as being due from their customer Cleveland Ltd. Although £30,000 has been received after the year end, the request to have the company liquidated indicates that any further payment is unlikely to be received. In accordance with IAS 10 *Events after the Reporting Period*, this is an adjusting event indicating that management's assessment of the recoverability of the balance is inaccurate and that the remainder of the outstanding balance should be written off as an irrecoverable debt.

As Boston Ltd has previously provided for £5,000, management should provide for the remaining £65,000 in the financial statements for the year ended 31 December 20X5. This will reduce trade receivables in the statement of financial position and profit before tax by £65,000.

At the meeting enquiries should be made as to whether any further correspondence has been received from either the management of Cleveland Ltd or the liquidators offering any form of reimbursement to Boston Ltd. If not, then the proposed adjustment should be encouraged.

The adjustment represents 1.0% of profit and 0.06% of total assets so is not material individually to either profit or the statement of financial position.

(b) **Impact on the audit opinion and auditor's report**

When considering their opinion, the auditor must conclude whether the financial statements as a whole are free from material misstatement. In order to do this, they must consider whether any remaining uncorrected misstatements are material, either on an individual basis or in aggregate.

The aggregate effect of the misstatements would be to overstate Boston Co's profit by £390,000 (= £400,00 – £75,000 + £65,000). Total assets on the statement of financial position would also be overstated by this amount.

This represents 6.1% of profit before tax (= £390,000 / £6.4m) and 0.4% of total assets (= £390,000 / £104m). The overstatement would therefore be material to the statement of profit or loss on an aggregate basis but not to the statement of financial position.

However, as the necessary adjustment regarding the impairment of the factory building is individually material, management should be informed that if the valuation calculated by the audit team is more appropriate then failure to incorporate this adjustment will result in the auditor concluding that the financial statements are materially misstated. Based upon this, a modification to the audit opinion in accordance with ISA 705 *Modifications to the Opinion in the Independent Auditor's Report* will be required.

The type of modification depends on the significance of the material misstatement. In this case, the misstatement regarding the impairment is material to the financial statements but is unlikely to be considered pervasive. This is supported by the fact that the adjustment is not material to the statement of financial position, and it is therefore unlikely that the auditor will conclude that the financial statements as a whole are misleading.

Therefore a qualified opinion should be expressed, with the auditor stating in the opinion that the financial statements show a true and fair view 'except for' the effects of the matters described in the basis for qualified opinion paragraph.

A basis for qualified opinion section should be placed immediately after the opinion section. This should include a description of the matter giving rise to the qualification, including quantification of the financial effects of the misstatement.

The remaining uncorrected misstatements are, individually and in aggregate, immaterial to the financial statements and it will be at the discretion of management to amend and will have no impact on the auditor's report. Although as previously mentioned because of the impact on future periods, management should be encouraged to amend for all misstatements. If management intends to leave these as uncorrected misstatements, written confirmation of their immaterial nature should be obtained via a written representation.

(c) **The discovery of an ongoing error in the company's payroll is a subsequent event.**

A subsequent event is any event occurring after the reporting period of the financial statements being audited. The first question for the auditor is whether these have been accounted for properly in accordance with IAS 10 *Events after the reporting period.*

Since the errors were made over a period of several months, it is likely that they were made during the reporting period. This would suggest that this is an adjusting event, and that the financial statements may be materially misstated.

The auditor's duty in relation to adjusting subsequent events depends on the point that has been reached when the event is discovered. It is not stated whether the financial statements have been issued, and it is upon this that the auditor's actions depend.

Financial statements not yet issued

If the financial statements have not yet been issued, then the auditor has no active duty to perform procedures (or make enquiries) during this period.

Facts have come to light, however, that suggest that the financial statements should be amended. In this case, the auditor should enquire how management intends to address the errors in the financial statements that are issued. The auditor should assess the materiality of the misstatements and should consider whether further audit procedures need to be performed as a result of discovering the misstatements.

If the financial statements are amended, then the auditor should perform extended procedures on the amendments and issue a new auditor's report on the amended financial statements.

Financial statements have been issued

Although the auditor has no active duty to perform procedures during this period, something has been discovered and the auditor should discuss with management how the misstatements are going to be addressed.

If management then amends the financial statements, then a revised auditor's report should be issued including an Emphasis of Matter paragraph discussing the amendment.

If management does not amend the financial statements but the auditor thinks that they should, then the auditor needs to take legal advice in the relevant national jurisdiction to prevent reliance on the auditor's opinion.

53 Coram

Workbook references

Chapters 2, 8, 10 and 11.

Top tips

The format used in part (a) has cropped up in several recent AAA exams and appears to be favoured by the examining team for AAA. This time the question did not simply deal with the auditor's report, however, but focused on communicating with management.

The first issue, leases, tested an accounting standard that is relatively new but that you should certainly have been familiar with. It did, however, focus on what might appear to be a finer point of the standard (that the short-term lease exemption must be applied to all assets in a class). If you had not been aware of this, then you will need to make sure your financial reporting knowledge is strong enough for this paper.

The second issue focused on impairment. This is an area that is popular with the AAA examining team, so you should review the financial reporting requirements carefully if you were not comfortable with it.

The auditor reporting aspect of this question was as expected for AAA. This is a core area of the syllabus in which you should have been able to score well.

Part (b) was an ethics requirement that effectively split itself into two sub-parts of four marks each. Neither issue should have been horribly unexpected to you. If you had managed to score, say, three marks on each de facto sub-part then you would have put yourself in a good position for the rest of the exam.

Easy marks

The two marks for assessing materiality in part (a) were very simple indeed. Not getting these would make it significantly harder to pass this question.

ACCA examining team's comments

This was a 25-mark question comprising two parts. Part (a) was worth 12 marks and was presented as a list of proposed audit adjustments and was very similar to the reporting requirement in the specimen exam. In this case, the requirement was more straightforward and asked for the matters to discuss with management and the impact on the audit opinion should management fail to adjust the errors. Candidates often did not remain focused on the requirement and detailed effects elsewhere in the auditor's report and the other actions they would take if management did not agree to amend the errors. In this question the correct accounting treatment was described for leases in addition to presenting the correctly calculated audit adjustments.

Candidates often scored well in this requirement if they explained why the proposed treatments by the directors were not compliant with accounting standards. Common mistakes made in this question arose where candidates determined the directors were right and the auditors wrong or where they proposed to include a qualified audit opinion for an immaterial misstatement. Candidates should not assume that every issue in a reporting question will lead to a qualified opinion.

Candidates should also note that when presenting audit opinions, it is not sufficient to say the opinion would be modified as this could mean any of four possibilities. Candidates should state the type of modification proposed eg qualified on the basis of material misstatement to score the mark.

Another weakness in answers provided here was to use out-of-date accounting standards to produce an answer. The examinable documents for Strategic Business Reporting are also examinable for this examination.

Part (b) was less well answered. Candidates were presented with two ethical issues for eight marks and often were unable to describe how the threats arose. In particular, other than the common mistake of not adequately explaining the threats to objectivity that were present specific to the scenario, candidates appeared unable to differentiate between a loan from any audit client and a loan on normal commercial terms from a client that happened to be a financial institution. Similarly, candidates did not appear to be able to differentiate between the safeguards appropriate for a non-listed client and one which was.

Marking guide	Marks

(a) (i) Generally up to 2 marks for full discussion of each matter and impact on opinion

Lease of testing equipment

- Lease at largest site is material to SOFP at 2.2% of total assets; leases at other two sites are also material at 2.8% of total assets (max 1 mark)
- General requirement of IFRS 16 to capitalise all leases on SOFP as right-of-use assets at PV of lease payments from commencement date (ie date asset is available for use)
- IFRS 16 exemption (optional) for short-term leases of less than 12 months with no purchase option hence if client elects, no need to recognise lease on SOFP (NB: no P/L effect yet as commencement date at year end)
- Short-term lease exemption must be made by class of underlying asset, hence treatment across three sites must be consistent
- To discuss exemption with FD at meeting: if elects not to take exemption across the three sites, assets and liabilities are materially understated; hence the proposed adjustment is correct and a right-of-use asset and lease liability of £475,000 should be recognised
- Alternatively, if client does elect to take exemption across all three sites, then assets and liabilities are materially overstated and right-of-use assets and lease liabilities of £625,000 should be derecognised

Impact on audit opinion:

- If client makes no adjustment, the statement of financial position is materially misstated and the audit opinion should be qualified on this basis

7

(ii) Generally up to 2 marks for full discussion of each matter and impact on opinion.

Asset impairment

- Impairment of £85,000 is not material in isolation to either SOFP or P/L (max 1 mark)
- New competitor is significant change in site's market and therefore impairment indicator; site is CGU (per intro to question) and therefore appropriate to conduct impairment test at this level
- Recoverable amount is higher of value in use and fair value less selling costs; fair value less costs of disposal is £3,515,000 and therefore asset is impaired by £85,000 (client appears to have incorrectly excluded cost of removing assets from calculation but correctly excluded the costs of business reorganisation)

Impact on audit opinion:

- Assets and profits are both (immaterially) overstated; hence if no adjustment made, there will be no impact on the audit opinion in relation to this issue in isolation

5

(b) **Turner Ltd**

Ethical and professional issues and actions to be taken by audit firm

Generally up to 1 mark for each issue and action.

Marking guide	Marks

Loan to member of the audit team

Issues:

- Potential self-interest and intimidation threats to auditor independence
- Key issue is whether 'the very best deal which the bank can offer' is made under normal lending procedures, terms and conditions
- If not, self-interest threat created would be so significant that no safeguards could reduce it to acceptable level and Janette should be told not to take loan
- If it is made under bank's normal lending procedures, terms and conditions, the loan does not create a threat to auditor's independence and Janette may accept the loan

Actions:

- Discuss terms and conditions of loan with Janette and business manager
- Inform audit engagement partner, who is responsible for ethical compliance
- Obtain draft loan documents and review details in order to establish whether under normal lending procedures, terms and conditions
- Advise Janette on outcome of review and whether she can accept loan and advise business manager of decision explaining rationale/ethical rules

Taverner Ltd

Actuarial valuation service

Issues:

- Potential self-review threat and management threat to auditor independence
- Must not assume management responsibilities, and must ensure that there is 'informed management' at Taverner Ltd
- Valuations must not be material to the financial statements

Actions:

- Ensure that management accepts responsibility for all judgements and assumptions
- Use of separate teams to mitigate the self-review threat

	8

Professional marks

Analysis and evaluation

- Appropriate use of the information to support discussion, draw appropriate conclusions and design appropriate responses
- Appropriate assessment of the ethical and professional issues relating to the assignment, using examples where relevant to support overall comments
- Balanced assessment of the information to determine the appropriate audit opinion in the circumstances

Professional scepticism and judgement

- Effective challenge of information, evidence and assumptions supplied and, techniques carried out to support key facts and/or decisions
- Appropriate application of professional judgement to draw conclusions and make informed decisions about the actions which are appropriate in the context and stage of the engagement.

Maximum	5
Total	25

(a) (i) Matters to be discussed with management in relation to the audit supervisor's proposed adjustments

Lease of testing equipment

The lease at Clark Ltd's largest site is material to the statement of financial position at 2.2% of total assets. The leases at the other two sites are also material at 2.8% of total assets.

The general recognition and measurement requirements of IFRS 16 *Leases* require lessees to recognise a right-of-use asset and a lease liability at the commencement date of the lease at the present value of the lease payments. The standard defines the commencement date as the date the asset is available for use by the lessee. Given that the commencement date is 31 May 20X8 therefore, it is appropriate on this basis to recognise the lease on the statement of financial position as at this date.

It is significant, however, that IFRS 16 also contains an optional exemption for short-term leases of less than 12 months' duration with no purchase option. If Clark Ltd elects to apply this exemption, it does not recognise the leased assets or lease liabilities on the statement of financial position but rather, it recognises the lease payments associated with those leases as an expense in the statement of profit or loss for the year on either a straight-line basis over the lease term or another systematic basis. However, IFRS 16 also requires that if this exemption is taken, it must be applied consistently by each class of underlying asset. Hence in this case, the client must either capitalise the leases across all three of the sites or apply the exemption consistently and not capitalise the leases across any of the sites. On either of these bases, as the commencement date of the lease coincides with the reporting date, there would not yet be any impact on Clark Ltd's statement of profit or loss for the year.

The audit manager should discuss the option of taking the short-term lease exemption with the finance director at tomorrow's meeting:

- If the client elects not to take the exemption across the three sites, assets and liabilities will be materially understated. Hence the audit supervisor's proposed adjustment is correct and a right-of-use asset and lease liability of £475,000 should be recognised on the statement of financial position.
- Alternatively, if the client does elect to take the exemption across all three sites, then assets and liabilities are materially overstated and right-of-use assets and lease liabilities of £625,000 should be derecognised on the statement of financial position.

Impact on audit opinion:

If the client does not make any adjustment to the financial statements, the statement of financial position is materially misstated on the basis of misapplication of an accounting standard and the audit opinion should be qualified.

(ii) **Asset impairment**

The asset impairment of £85,000 is not material in isolation to either the statement of financial position (0.4% of total assets) or the statement of profit or loss for the period (3.7% of profit before taxation).

According to IAS 36 *Impairment of Assets*, an entity should assess at the end of each reporting period whether there is any indication that an asset or a cash generating unit may be impaired. If any such indication exists, the entity shall estimate the recoverable amount of the asset. The standard states that potential impairment indicators include external sources of information such as significant changes in the market in which the entity operates. As each of Clark Ltd's sites is considered a cash generating unit for impairment review purposes, it seems appropriate therefore for the company to have conducted an impairment review at this site.

IAS 36 states that an asset or cash generating unit is impaired when the carrying amount exceeds the recoverable amount and it defines recoverable amount as the higher of the fair value less costs of disposal and the value in use. In the case of Clark Ltd, the auditor has agreed figures for carrying value and value in use and the key issue is the correct calculation of fair value less costs of disposal. Following IAS 36, the costs of disposal should include legal costs, transaction taxes and the costs of removing the assets but should exclude the costs associated with reorganising a business. The correct amount for fair value less costs of disposal is therefore £3,515,000 (£3.9 million – £126,000 – £174,000 – £85,000). Given that this is higher than the value in use of £2.9 million, the recoverable amount of the assets is also £3,515,000 and therefore the assets are impaired by £85,000 (£3.6 million – £3,515,000). The client appears to have incorrectly omitted the costs of removing the assets from its calculation of fair value less costs of disposal and as a result the statement of financial position and the statement of profit or loss for the year are both overstated by £85,000.

The audit supervisor's proposed adjustment is therefore correct and the finance director should be advised of this error at tomorrow's meeting. Even though the amount is immaterial to both the statement of financial position and statement of profit or loss for the year, it is appropriate to request that the adjustment is made to the financial statements.

Impact on audit opinion:

Given that assets and profits are both immaterially overstated, if no adjustment is made to the financial statements, it follows that there will be no impact on the audit opinion in relation to this matter in isolation.

(b) **Turner Ltd**

Ethical and professional issues and actions to be taken by the audit firm

Loan to member of the audit team

According to the FRC *Ethical Standard*, a loan to a member of the audit team may create a threat to the auditor's independence. If the loan is not made under normal lending procedures and terms and conditions, a self-interest threat would be created as a result of Janette Stott's financial interest in the audit client. The self-interest threat arises because of the potential personal benefit derived which may motivate the audit team member to behave in a manner aimed at protecting that benefit. In addition, an intimidation threat to objectivity may arise where a loan is made from the audit client to a member of the audit team. The threat arises because of a fear that the audit client may, for example, change the terms of the loan or recall the loan, thus influencing the behaviour of the auditor.

These threats to objectivity are normally considered to be so significant that no safeguards could reduce the threat to an acceptable level. It follows therefore that in most cases the audit team member should not accept such a loan or guarantee.

However, the *Ethical Standard* also states that a loan from an audit client which is a bank or similar institution to a member of the audit team which is made under normal business terms and conditions is acceptable. Examples of such loans include home mortgages, car loans and credit card balances.

It is possible therefore that the secured loan may be ethically acceptable, and the key issue is whether 'the very best terms which the bank can offer' fall within Turner Ltd's normal business terms and conditions. The bank's standard lending terms and conditions should be obtained and reviewed alongside the documentation for Janette Stott's loan. Ultimately, the audit engagement partner is responsible for ensuring that ethical principles are not breached, so the partner should be involved with the discussions. The matter should be discussed with Janette and the client's business manager in order to establish whether the loan is to be made under the bank's normal lending procedures. Janette should be advised of the outcome of this review and Turner Ltd's business manager should be advised of this decision, explaining the rationale and ethical rules behind it.

Actuarial valuation service

The FRC *Ethical Standard* states that an actuarial valuation service, as a type of valuation service, may threaten the integrity, objectivity and independence of the firm by creating a self-review threat and a management threat.

Taverner Ltd is not a public company and therefore is not listed. The *Ethical Standard* provides that such a service may be provided to an unlisted entity where:

- All significant judgements (including assumptions) are made by informed management
- The valuation has no material effect on the financial statements

The firm must therefore take and document steps to determine whether Taverner Ltd's management is sufficiently 'informed' about the judgements and assumptions involved in making the valuation so that these would be understood to have been made by management, and not by the firm.

It is also key that a determination is made regarding the materiality of the valuations to the financial statements.

If either of these criteria are not met then the service cannot be provided alongside the audit, and Coram & Co will need either to decline to provide the service or to withdraw from the audit.

If the above criteria are met, then it may be possible to provide the valuation service subject to the application of safeguards. These could include ensuring that management understands and acknowledges its responsibility for the valuations (mitigating the management threat), and the use of a separate engagement team for the valuation service and the audit (mitigating the self-review threat).

54 James & Co

Workbook references

Chapters 2, 4, 6, 7 and 9.

Top tips

This question is set at the review stage, requiring you to think critically about the quality of the audit work that has been performed.

It is a good idea here to make reference to the technical guidance that is available on quality management (namely ISA (UK) 220 (Revised), and ISQMs (UK) 1 and 2) where this is relevant. Although it is the case that many of the marks at this level are going to come out of the scenario, the examining team has commented time and again on the relative lack of knowledge displayed by candidates when it comes to auditing standards.

The question itself was probably of average difficulty for AAA. Candidates tend to enjoy criticising the performance of an audit, but the key to doing well here was to make this criticism as incisive as possible, referring to technical standards where possible in order to highlight the gap between what *has* happened and what *should have* happened.

Easy marks

The were some fairly easy points to be made in relation to the laws and regulations in part (c).

ACCA examining team's comments

This 25-mark question is set at the post-issuance, quality review stage in the audit process and tests several ethical and professional issues which have been identified as part of the review of the Bond Group (the Group) audit. While the context is that of a Group audit, many of the issues in the question are similar to those which would arise in individual company audits.

In this question, candidates are provided with the quality reviewer's findings from the perspective of the performance of the Group audit. The scenario acknowledges that audit quality has been poor and requires candidates to evaluate why something demonstrates that a poor-quality audit has been performed, and what specifically should be done better to address the issues.

This type of question is typically poorly answered by candidates in comparison to questions set at the planning or completion stage. Candidates often appear to lack the skills to apply the rules and principles learnt to practical scenarios and often provide unapplied answers as a result.

Unfortunately, many candidates for each issue simply stated 'audit quality is poor' or 'planning was not performed well', which does not demonstrate a candidate's understanding of what should have taken place and why. It is important to remember that the AAA exam is predominantly application, and such general comments will not obtain credit as a response to each individual planning or quality failing – often these comments will be restricted to a single concluding mark across the full question and as such candidates cannot obtain additional marks for repeating the same conclusion.

Similarly, recommendations need to be specific and again an answer which simply states 'better planning is needed' or 'more training is needed' is too generic to score marks at this level.

Another reason many candidates score low marks on these questions arises from a failure to appreciate that these reviews are occurring after the audit has been completed and the auditor's report issued. This means answers which recommend a long list of additional audit procedures, repeatedly saying that something will need to be resolved before issuing the auditor's report, or the firm needs to modify the audit opinion, are not appropriate in the circumstances and therefore cannot gain marks. As with many questions in the AAA exam, candidates will be better prepared to provide relevant responses if they are able to appreciate where in the audit cycle the question is set. Candidates should make sure that they consider this when they are planning their answer.

Marking guide

	Marks
(a) Generally, up to 2 marks for each well explained point	
Cameron Co	
• Internal audit – self-review threat and lack of professional scepticism (1 mark)	
• Internal audit – insufficient audit work on internal controls including no understanding or evaluation of year-end controls obtained	
• Internal audit – threat of assuming management responsibility and general risk that ethical code has not been followed by Carrey Associates	
• Timing and reliance on controls testing	
• Group audit firm has not evaluated Carrey Associates or obtained understanding of the firm	
• No audit work performed by Group audit team on Cameron Co's different accounting policies – Group consolidation could be misstated	
• Implications of former partner joining the component audit firm – familiarity and over reliance (1 mark)	
• Possible lack of competence of the Group audit partner (1 mark)	
Maximum	8
(b) Generally, up to 2 marks for each well explained point	
Dean Ltd	
• Lack of application of professional scepticism regarding valuation of financial asset	
• Asset likely to be overvalued – could have material impact on Dean Ltd's financial statements	
• Inappropriate application of Group materiality at component level	
Maximum	5

Marking guide	Marks
(c) Generally, up to 2 marks for each well explained point	
Horner Ltd	
• Auditor is incorrect and laws and regulations do impact the audit and financial statements	
• Auditor needs to gain understanding of applicable laws and regulations	
• Further evidence should be obtained, and the matter discussed with Group management	
• Provisions for fines and penalties have not been considered	
• Auditor may have a legal duty to disclose, or consider disclosing in the public interest	
• The audit firm may wish to seek legal advice regarding the situation (1 mark)	
Maximum	7
Professional marks	
Analysis and evaluation	
• Effective appraisal of the information to make suitable recommendations for appropriate courses of action	
• Appropriate assessment of the ethical and professional issues relating to the assignment, using examples where relevant to support overall comments	
Professional scepticism and professional judgment	
• Effective challenge and critical assessment of the conduct and extent of the audit work and evidence obtained with appropriate conclusions.	
• Demonstration of the ability to probe into the reasons for quality issues including the identification of missing information or additional information which would be required	
• Appropriate application of professional judgement to draw conclusions and make informed decisions about the actions which are appropriate in the context and stage of the engagement.	
Commercial acumen	
• Appropriate recognition of the potential impact of breaches of laws and regulations on the Group as a whole or the legal implications for James & Co	
• Assessment of the conclusions from the quality review on the audit engagement and any potential impact on the reputation of James & Co	
Maximum	5
Total	25

(a) **Cameron Co**

There are problems indicated by the review in relation to both the audit of Cameron Co's individual financial statements by Carrey Associates, and in the way the Group auditor has dealt with the issue of there being a new component auditor involved in the Group.

Internal audit

First, it is not appropriate that Carrey Associates has relied on the work performed by the internal audit team. A significant self-review threat to the objectivity of Carrey Associates arises from the firm providing both internal and external audit services to Cameron Co. The IESBA *International Code of Ethics for Professional Accountants* suggests that providing an audit client with an internal audit service creates a significant self-review threat because in subsequent audits the audit team will use the internal audit work performed, leading to potential over-reliance. Under the FRC *Revised Ethical Standard*, auditors are now prohibited from also acting as internal auditor to the same client. There is therefore a risk that the audit has not been performed with sufficient objectivity and professional scepticism. In addition, it is not clear whether appropriate safeguards are in place to reduce the threats to an acceptable level, for example by ensuring that the two services were provided by separate teams.

There is a risk that insufficient audit evidence has been obtained over internal controls. This is a breach of ISA (UK) 315 (Revised) *Identifying and Assessing the Risk of Material Misstatement*, which requires the auditor to obtain an understanding of the internal controls relevant to the audit, including an evaluation of the design and implementation of the internal controls. It appears that this audit work has not been performed at all, due to over-reliance on the internal audit work performed.

There is a further issue with the timing of when the internal controls had been tested, which took place in May 20X4. The financial year ended on 31 January 20X5, so it appears that the controls had not been evaluated for the last eight months of the financial year. ISA (UK) 330 The Auditor's Responses to Assessed Risks, states that if the auditor intends to rely on controls over a period of time the tests performed must be able to provide audit evidence that the control operated effectively over that period. This exacerbates the risk discussed above, as there could have been significant changes in internal controls during that period, which had not been identified by the external audit team.

This raises concerns over the quality of the audit which has been performed by Carrey Associates. Given that Cameron Co is material to the Group, any material misstatements which have not been detected by the component auditor could increase aggregation risk and have implications for the Group financial statements, which could also be materially misstated.

In addition to the self-review threat to objectivity, a threat of management responsibility arises, whereby the audit firm is making decisions and using judgment which is properly the responsibility of management. An audit firm should not assume management responsibility. This raises concern over Carrey Associates general approach to ethical issues, and whether the ethical threats raised have been properly evaluated by the firm.

Group auditor evaluation of Carrey Associates

The comment made in the Group audit working papers indicates that there has been no understanding obtained by the Group auditor in relation to the component auditors. This is a significant quality management problem and a breach of ISA (UK) 600 (Revised) *Special Considerations – Audits of Group Financial Statements (Including the Work of Component Auditors)* which requires that the group audit team obtain an understanding of the component auditor and be involved with the component auditor's risk assessment to identify risks of material misstatement. This is especially the case given that Cameron Co is a new component of the group, and this is James & Co's first experience of working with Carrey Associates.

The fact that an audit partner has left James & Co to work as an audit partner at Carrey Associates has no bearing on whether James & Co should have obtained an appropriate understanding of Carrey Associates. An understanding of whether Carrey Associates follow the same ethical framework as the rest of the Group and an understanding of their competence is required. It appears that the Group audit has been conducted without this necessary understanding being obtained and without adequate two-way dialogue between James & Co and Carrey Associates, which is a breach of ISA (UK) 600 (Revised).

In addition, a familiarity threat to objectivity arises because of the connection that the Group audit team will have with the audit partner now working for Carrey Associates and who worked on the audit of Cameron Co. The familiarity threat means that the Group audit team may have over-relied on the work of the component auditor and failed to apply appropriate professional scepticism.

Use of local accounting rules

Cameron Co uses local accounting rules in its individual financial statements, which is acceptable. However, for the purpose of consolidation, the same accounting policies must be applied across all Group companies, as required by IFRS 3 *Business Combinations*. The fact that the Group audit partner has concluded that no work is needed in relation to the accounting policies indicates poor quality audit work and insufficient audit evidence has been obtained to address potential aggregation risk present. Adjustments may have been necessary to Cameron Co's balances and transactions prior to consolidation; with no audit work being performed to assess whether this is the case there is a risk of material misstatement in the Group financial statements.

The fact that it is the Group audit partner who reached this conclusion indicates a lack of competence and raises concerns over the quality of the audit as a whole.

(b) **Dean Ltd**

Insufficient audit evidence has been obtained in relation to the financial asset. The audit team should not just have accepted management's valuation of £68,000, which could be based on inappropriate assumptions. An offer of £68,000 may have been received, but this has also not been verified by the audit team. As there is no active market for the shares, fair value should be based on an exit price at the measurement date and should reflect assumptions which market participants would use including risk. Even if the offer was genuinely received, this is not an appropriate basis for valuation of shares, especially given that the offer was made nine months before the year end. An appropriate level of professional scepticism has not been used in the audit of the financial asset.

Fair values should be determined close to the financial year end, and the £68,000 might reflect out-of-date perceptions of the value of Corden Ltd. From the information provided, it seems that the financial asset could be impaired and is likely to be overstated in value. Dean Ltd's 2% shareholding is recognised at £68,000; however, 2% of the net assets of Corden Ltd at 31 January 20X5 amounts to only £11,000. If the financial asset is overvalued, then any necessary adjustment would have a profit implication, and this is not mentioned in the audit working papers.

Using Group materiality in the audit of a subsidiary is not appropriate. The value of the financial asset is less than Group materiality, but it might be material to Dean Ltd's individual financial statements. It is not clear that the individual audit team determined an appropriate level of materiality as part of their planning of the individual company audit. The Group audit team should determine component materiality to be used by component auditors in their audit of subsidiary balances and transactions, and component materiality should be lower than materiality for the Group financial statements as a whole. Therefore, it seems likely that the Group audit team has not communicated an appropriate level of component materiality to the team auditing Dean Ltd.

While the possible adjustments in relation to the financial asset are not material to the Group, they could be material to Dean Ltd's individual financial statements, and there is a risk that an inappropriate audit opinion has been issued in relation to this subsidiary's individual financial statements.

(c) **Horner Ltd**

There has been a breach of relevant law and regulations. The audit team should have considered the requirements of ISA (UK) 250 Section A *Consideration of Laws and Regulations in an Audit of Financial Statements*. ISA (UK) 250 A states that while it is management's responsibility to ensure that the entity's operations are conducted in accordance with the provisions of laws and regulations, the auditor does have some responsibility in relation to compliance with laws and regulations, especially where a non-compliance has an impact on the financial statements.

The auditor is required by ISA (UK) 315 (Revised 2019) to gain an understanding of the legal and regulatory framework in which the audited entity operates. This will help the auditor to identify non-compliance and to assess the implications of non-compliance. Therefore, the auditor should ensure that a full knowledge and understanding of the relevant data protection laws and regulations is obtained in order to evaluate the implications of non-compliance.

ISA (UK) 250 A requires that when non-compliance is identified or suspected, the auditor shall obtain an understanding of the nature of the act and the circumstances in which it has occurred, and further information to evaluate the possible effect on the financial statements. Therefore, procedures should have been performed to obtain evidence about the suspected non-compliance, for example, to discuss the breach with management to understand how it happened, whether due to deliberate action or unintentional mistake, and who was responsible. In addition, the audit team should have performed further procedures, for example discussion with the company's legal advisors to understand the legal consequences of the breach.

From the information provided it seems that the audit team failed to obtain more information or evidence due to their belief that the situation had little to do with the audit. The audit has therefore not been performed appropriately, as the requirements of ISA (UK) 250 A have not been followed.

The matter could be immaterial in monetary terms, but without further investigation, it is not possible for the audit team to reach this conclusion. However, in many jurisdictions fines and penalties associated with data protection breaches are often significant. Also, the matter could be material by nature, so regardless of the monetary amounts involved, further work should have been performed.

ISA (UK) 250 A requires the matter to be discussed with management and where appropriate with those charged with governance. It appears that some discussion was held, as the audit manager is aware that the employee has been dismissed. However, the discussions should have been fully documented and raised to the level of Group management, as the matter could impact on the Group and not just on Horner Ltd.

The audit team should have considered the potential implications for the financial statements. The non-compliance could lead to regulatory authorities imposing fines or penalties on the Group, which may need to be provided for in both the individual and Group financial statements. Audit procedures should have been performed to determine the amount, materiality and probability of payment of any such fine or penalty imposed. The individual and Group financial statements could be materially misstated and given that an unmodified audit opinion has already been issued, this is a significant issue for James & Co to now consider.

In terms of reporting non-compliance to the relevant regulatory authorities, ISA (UK) 250 A requires the auditor to determine whether they have a responsibility to report the identified or suspected non-compliance to parties outside the entity. In the event that management or those charged with governance of the company or the Group fail to make the necessary disclosures to the regulatory authorities, James & Co should consider whether they should make the disclosure. This will depend on matters including whether there is a legal duty to disclose or whether it is considered to be in the public interest to do so. It seems that this has not been considered so far, but the audit firm can still make any necessary disclosures.

The *Code* requires auditors to comply with the principle of confidentiality, and if disclosure were to be made by the auditor, it would be advisable to seek legal advice on the matter. Further advice on disclosure in the public interest is given in the *Code*, which gives examples of situations where disclosure might be appropriate. These examples include references to an entity being involved in bribery and breaches of regulation which might impact adversely on public health and safety.

The *Code* also clarifies that in exceptional circumstances where the auditor believes there may be an imminent breach of a law or regulation, they may need to disclose the matter immediately to an appropriate authority. The decision to disclose will always be a matter for the auditor's judgement and where the disclosure is made in good faith, it will not constitute a breach of the duty of confidentiality.

> **Tutorial note.** Credit will also be awarded for discussion of relevant ethical threats to objectivity which may arise in relation to the non-compliance, including intimidation and self-interest threats.

55 Lifeson

Workbook references

Chapters 7, 8 and 11.

Top tips

It may be helpful to think about at which stage of the audit process a question is set. Question One is set at the planning stage; this question is set at the review stage, after fieldwork is complete but before the audit report has been signed. Part (b) of the question then moves on to just before the signing of the report.

Part (a) comprises two issues – a sale and leaseback and an impairment review of a non-current asset. The accounting knowledge required here was towards the top end for AAA. The first issue should have been reasonable for you, and although the second was trickier, you should have been able to gain enough marks to pass (ie 3–4 on this sub-part) by working through methodically and focusing on the easy marks.

Part (b) covered the auditor's report, and although the technical content here should have been straightforward, it did depend on you having taken the right track in part (a) of the question. That being said, if you are not sure of the answer to a question like this, there are likely to be marks available for setting out the matters to consider when modifying the opinion, and the details of the report that would be issued – perhaps in the different circumstances of a qualified or an adverse opinion.

Easy marks

The marks available for audit evidence tend to be easier to get, as long as you explain the evidence fully together with the reasons why you would expect to see it.

ACCA examining team's comments

Question Two was set at the completion stage of an audit and proved difficult for many candidates.

Very few candidates appeared to understand the concept of control underpinning the sale and lease back – often candidates performed the appropriate test of considering the proportion of the life of the property that would be leased back but then incorrectly concluded that renting the property for one fifth of its life was effectively still owning the property. What was more concerning was that a significant minority of candidates were still discussing the concept of operating and finance leases and applying outdated accounting standards to a topic that has been examinable under IFRS16 *Leases* for several sessions.

With regards to the impairment reversal, candidate performance was mixed. Many candidates realised that the reversal would be restricted and were able to obtain credit even if they didn't appreciate that the reversal was not restricted to the previous impairment charge but should be restricted to the written down value the asset would have had, had it not been impaired in the first place. Beyond that however many candidates suggested that the excess value of that amount could be recognised within Other Comprehensive Income which is not the case unless the company is using a revaluation model rather than a cost model for properties.

Many candidates were able to identify relevant audit procedures for the above accounting issues. In some instances this was the case even where they did not appear to fully understand the accounting issues themselves.

Part (b) required candidates to consider the effect of the reversal of the impairment on the auditor's report. Here candidates often assessed the significance of the misstatement by reference to the entire asset value rather than the error amount, resulting in the conclusion that an immaterial misstatement would result in an adverse opinion. It was also common here that where a candidate calculated that the error was immaterial, they would go on to conclude that it was in fact material. It is vital that candidates appreciate the concept of materiality and are able to correctly apply it at this level.

As noted in previous sessions, there was a significant minority of candidates who concluded that the immaterial misstatement should be disclosed in an emphasis of matter paragraph, again demonstrating a lack of understanding of the concept of materiality and when the use of an emphasis of matter paragraph is appropriate.

Marking guide **Marks**

(a) (i) **Matters and evidence**

Generally up to 1 mark for each matter explained and each piece of evidence recommended (unless otherwise stated).

Sale and leaseback transaction

Matters

- Consider treatment of sale and leaseback transaction as required by IFRS 16
- Assess whether control of asset has transferred to buyer
- Whether asset transfer is sale in line with IFRS 15
- IFRS 15 criteria based on transfer of control; ability to direct, use and obtain substantially all remaining benefits of asset
- Derecognise property and recognise right-of-use asset based on proportion of asset retained
- Recognise financial liability based on PV of lease payments
- Recognise gain/loss on transaction in P/L for year
- Reasoned conclusion that treatment appears to be correct on basis of information available

Evidence

- Copy of sale and leaseback agreement to confirm key details, eg rights of lessee and lessor to control asset; also: proceeds, rental amounts and timings, lease term, interest rate implicit in lease
- Discussions with management about transfer of control and correct treatment of sale and leaseback arrangement
- Board minutes for evidence of discussion of sale and leaseback transaction
- Review of local property market including trade journals, press articles, official statistics to confirm high demand for retail leases
- Review of surveyor reports on building to confirm expected life
- Agreement of carrying amount of property to non-current asset register
- Agreement of sale proceeds to cash book/bank statement
- Copy of client working papers for present value of lease payments
- Recalculation of PV of lease payments by auditor
- Review of financial statements to confirm that details of sale and leaseback transaction disclosed in line with IFRS 16 requirements

8

(ii) **Shopping mall – asset impairment**

Matters

- Materiality
- Whether client's calculation of recoverable amount based on value in use is in line with requirements of IAS 36
- Discussion of whether client has used appropriate discount factor for calculating value in use
- Whether NRV of shopping mall exceeds its value in use (at both dates)

- Reversal of impairment loss should be capped to depreciated historic cost had no impairment loss been recognised
- Resulting error: overstatement of profit and assets by £300,000

Evidence

- Agreement of opening balances for property to non-current asset register
- Physical inspection of shopping mall to confirm condition, occupancy level and reasonableness of depreciation policy and of management's cash flow forecasts
- Copy of client working papers for impairment review giving details of NRV of mall and value in use calculations
- Copy of client cash flow forecasts and budgets supporting value in use calculations
- Notes of discussions with management and assessment of reasonableness of assumptions used in forecasts and appropriateness of discount factor used in value in use calculations
- Management representations attesting to the reasonableness of assumptions and other related management judgements
- Recalculation of value in use by auditor
- Sensitivity analyses on forecasts and value in use calculations
- External confirmation of the shopping mall's net realisable value by an appropriately qualified, independent expert
- Notes of discussions with management in relation to incorrect recording of impairment reversal and need to include error in auditor's schedule of uncorrected misstatements

7

(b) **Auditor's report re shopping mall**

- Material misstatement due to inappropriate application of IAS 36
- Matter is not pervasive
- Qualified audit opinion
- Basis for qualified opinion paragraph

5

Professional marks

Analysis and evaluation

- Appropriate use of the information to support discussion, draw appropriate conclusions and design appropriate responses
- Identification of omissions from the analysis or further analysis which could be carried out
- Balanced assessment of the information to determine the appropriate audit opinion in the circumstances

Professional scepticism and judgement

- Effective challenge of information, evidence and assumptions supplied and, techniques carried out to support key facts and/or decisions
- Appropriate application of professional judgement to draw conclusions and make informed decisions about the actions which are appropriate in the context and stage of the engagement.

Maximum 5

Total 25

(a) (i) **Sale and leaseback transaction**

Matters

Transfer of control

The auditor needs to consider the correct treatment of the sale and leaseback transaction as required by IFRS 16 *Leases* which requires that an assessment should be performed based on the criteria specified in IFRS 15 *Revenue from Contracts with Customers* as to whether control of the asset has been retained by the seller or whether it has passed to the buyer. Control of an asset is defined by IFRS 15 as the ability to direct the use of and obtain substantially all of the remaining benefits from the asset. This includes the ability to prevent others from directing the use of and obtaining the benefits from the asset. The benefits related to the asset are the potential cash flows which may be obtained directly or indirectly.

Right-of-use asset

In this case, the lease term of ten years appears short compared to the asset's remaining life which is expected to exceed 50 years and given the demand for retail properties for rent in the area, it seems likely that Clive Ltd will direct the use of and obtain substantially all of the remaining benefits from the asset including the potential cash flows in the future. On the basis of the information available, therefore, the proposed derecognition of the property in Lifeson Ltd's financial statements and the recording of the transaction as a sale in accordance with IFRS 15 appears to be correct. Lifeson Ltd should therefore derecognise the property and recognise a right-of-use asset based on the proportion of the previous carrying amount of the asset effectively retained under the terms of the lease. In addition, it should recognise a financial liability based on the present value of the lease payments and any gain or loss arising on the transaction should be recognised in profit or loss for the year. In this case, therefore, the asset has been correctly derecognised but the auditor should investigate whether the company has recognised the right-of-use asset at the correct amount.

Evidence expected to be on file:

- A copy of the sale and leaseback agreement reviewed to confirm the key details including in particular the rights of the lessee and the lessor to control the asset.
- A working paper detailing all key aspects of the agreement required to identify the detailed accounting treatment including the sale proceeds, rental amounts and timings, the lease term and the interest rate implicit in the lease.
- Agreement of the sale proceeds as per the sale agreement to the cash book and/or bank statement to confirm the correct calculation of the gain or loss on disposal.
- Notes of discussions with management in relation to the transfer of control to confirm whether the correct treatment of the sale and leaseback arrangement has been determined.
- A copy of any client working papers in relation to the calculation of the right-of-use asset to identify whether the client has recognised the right-of-use asset at the correct amount.
- A review of the board minutes for evidence of management's discussion of the sale and leaseback transaction and any evidence in relation to the transfer of control.
- A review of the local property market including trade journals, press articles, official statistics to confirm high demand for retail leases.
- A review of surveyor reports on the property to confirm the expected remaining life of the property.

- A copy of the client's working papers for the calculation of the present value of the lease payments and a recalculation of the present value of the lease payments by the auditor in order to form a basis for confirming the detailed accounting treatment of the lease.
- Agreement of the carrying amount of the property to the non-current asset register to determine whether the correct amount has been derecognised and whether the gain or loss on disposal has been recorded correctly.
- A schedule calculating any gain or loss on the transaction, recalculated by the audit team and confirming that it only represents the gain or loss on rights transferred to Clive Ltd.
- Review of the draft financial statements to confirm that details of the sale and leaseback transaction, such as the gain or loss arising on the transaction, have been disclosed in line with the requirements of IFRS 16.

(ii) **Asset impairment**

Matters

Materiality

The carrying amount of the shopping mall represents 64.1% (£8.85 million/£13.8 million) of Lifeson Ltd's total assets at the reporting date and is therefore highly material to the company's financial statements.

Value in use

The auditor should consider whether the client's calculation of the shopping mall's recoverable amount based on value in use is in line with the requirements of IAS 36 *Impairment of Assets*. This should include an assessment of whether the client has used an appropriate discount factor for calculating value in use based on the rate which reflects current market assessments of the time value of money and the risks specific to the asset. In line with IAS 36's definition of recoverable amount as the higher of its fair value less costs to sell and its value in use, the auditor should also consider whether the fair value less selling costs of the shopping mall exceeds its value in use.

Reversal of impairment loss

IAS 36 requires that the increased carrying amount of an asset, such as property, attributable to a reversal of an impairment loss should not exceed the carrying amount which would have been determined, net of depreciation, had no impairment loss been recognised for the asset in prior years. In this case, therefore, recognition of the reversal of the impairment loss should be calculated as follows:

	£ million	£ million
Carrying amount as at 31 March 20X5 prior to recognition of impairment reversal (£8.25m × 18/19)		7.816
Recoverable amount based on impairment review as at 31 March 20X5	8.850	
Capped to £9.5m × 18/20	8.550	8.550
Impairment reversal to be recognised		**0.734**

As a result of Lifeson Ltd's failure to limit the impairment reversal to £0.734 million, profit and assets are overstated by £300,000 (1.034m – 0.734m).

Evidence expected to be on file:

- Agreement of the opening balances for the property to the non-current asset register as at 1 April 20X4 to confirm the correct amount has been brought forward in the client's working papers.
- Physical inspection of the shopping mall property to confirm its condition, occupancy level and to assess the reasonableness of the depreciation policy and forecast cash flows for the value in use calculation.

- Copy of the client working papers for impairment review giving evidence of the client's basis for assessing the fair value less selling costs of the mall and detailed calculations of its value in use.
- Copy of the client's cash flow forecasts and budgets supporting the value in use calculations.
- Notes of discussions with management in relation to the bases for the calculation of recoverable amount including an assessment of the reasonableness of the assumptions used by management in its forecasts and calculations and the appropriateness of the discount factor used in the value in use calculations.
- Written representations attesting to the reasonableness of its assumptions and other related management judgements.
- A recalculation of the value in use of the shopping mall by the auditor in order to confirm the accuracy of the client's calculation.
- Sensitivity analyses on the forecasts and the value in use calculations in order to assess the impact of any changes in the key assumptions.
- External confirmation of the shopping mall's net realisable value by an appropriately qualified, independent expert in order to ensure the recoverable amount has been correctly determined.
- Notes of discussions with management in relation to the incorrect recording of the impairment reversal and the need to include the error in the auditor's schedule of uncorrected misstatements.

(b) **Implications for the auditor's report**

Based on the analysis and discussion above, there is a misstatement in the financial statements in relation to the shopping mall which may have implications for this year's auditor's report.

Lifeson Ltd has incorrectly recognised the full impairment reversal of £1.034 million in profit for the year. As per IAS 36, the reversal of an impairment loss should not exceed the carrying amount which would have been determined had no impairment loss been recognised. Based on depreciation over a 20-year useful life, the carrying amount of the asset should be capped at £8.550 million and the reversal of the impairment to be recognised at £0.734 million (£8.550 million – £7.816 million). Assets and profit are currently overstated by £300,000 representing 2.2% of total assets and 14% of profit before tax which is material to both the statement of financial position and statement of profit or loss.

Overall impact on the auditor's report

The misstatement in relation to the shopping mall is individually material and if management fails to amend the financial statements, the auditor's opinion should be modified due to the material, but not pervasive, misstatement of the shopping mall in relation to both the statement of financial position and the statement of profit or loss for the year. A qualified opinion should therefore be given.

The auditor's report should include a qualified opinion paragraph at the start of report. This paragraph should be followed immediately by a basis for qualified opinion paragraph which should explain the reasons for the qualified auditor's opinion and which should quantify the impact of the matters identified on the financial statements.

56 Newman

Workbook references

Chapters 5, 10 and 15.

Top tips

This area has not been examined very frequently in recent years, but the fact that it was examined here is a warning against trying to question-spot. You must be ready to answer questions on any area of the syllabus. You should also note that explicit reference to sustainability information and reporting is referred to explicitly by the AAA syllabus, meaning that it could form part of questions set in this area.

Part (a) may have been intimidating if you had not revised this area thoroughly, but actually a lot of the points in the marking scheme are applicable to most kinds of engagement. You could have thought of general points, and then applied them to the situation given in the question. Note the examining team's comment about application below; AAA tutors never tire of telling students to apply their knowledge to the question.

Part (b) should have been straightforward, but just as in part (a) you need to make sure you applied yourself to the actual question, in part (b) you needed to be as specific as possible in coming up with realistic ways of verifying the KPIs.

Part (c) should also have been straightforward, provided you knew the answer! There is no substitute for knowledge here, especially as this is not a difficult area of the syllabus.

Easy marks

The first few marks in part (b)(i) and (ii) were easy, as you should have been able to think of at least a few procedures without much effort.

ACCA examining team's comments

Candidates responded reasonably well to parts of this question, though many answers did not reach their full potential by not being applied to the question scenario.

Some answers to part (a) were much too brief for the 11 marks available, amounting to little more than a bullet point list of matters to be considered but with no application to the scenario. Without application it was not possible to pass this requirement.

A fair proportion of answers to requirement (b) were sound, with precise procedures designed. But many recommended procedures relied too much on observation and enquiry, and ignored the fact that the client was a global company with 300,000 employees which led to some bizarre and meaningless procedures being given, such as 'observe a serious accident', 'inspect the location of a serious accident', 'ask how much is spent on training', and 'look at the training room to see how many chairs are there'. None of these could verify the KPIs and are pointless.

Requirement (c) was inadequately attempted overall. Answers were usually extremely brief, and it was clear that most candidates did not know the requirements of ISA (UK) 720. Most answers took a guess that the matter would need to be discussed with management, and that if unresolved there would be some kind of impact on the auditor's report (a qualified opinion was the usual recommendation). But few could say more than this about the issue. Some candidates assumed that some kind of money laundering was taking place, leading to irrelevant discussions of reporting the situation to outside authorities. Very few candidates recognised that if uncorrected, the issue should be included in the 'Other information' section of the auditor's report, as required by ISA (UK) 720. This could imply a lack of knowledge, or that some candidates are studying from out-of-date learning materials.

Marking guide | **Marks**

(a) **Matters**

Identify and explain acceptance matters.

0.5 mark for each matter identified (to max 4 marks) and up to 1½ further marks for explanation:

- Objectivity (up to 3 marks allowed)
- Client's specific requirements

- Competence
- Large scale engagement
- Fee level and profitability
- Time pressure
- Global engagement
- Risk
- Commercial considerations

11

(b) (i) **Procedures on number of serious accidents**

1 mark per specific procedure:

- HR records review
- Accident book review
- Determine criteria for serious accident
- Review legal correspondence
- Review board minutes
- Review documentation of health and safety inspections
- Ascertain any convictions for breach of health and safety rules

3

(ii) **Procedures on average training spend**

1 mark per specific procedure:

- Review approved training budget
- Review components of total spend for misclassified items
- Agree sample of invoices/contracts with training providers
- Agree sample to cash book/bank statement (0.5 only)
- Recalculate average

3

(c) **Action by Newman & Co**

1 mark per comment:

- Review audit work on charitable donations
- Discuss inconsistency with management/those charged with governance
- If refuse to change the figure, reconsider reliance on management representations
- Implication for auditor's report

3

Professional marks

Analysis and evaluation

- Appropriate use of the information to support discussion, draw appropriate conclusions and design appropriate responses
- Appropriate assessment of the ethical and professional issues relating to the assignment, using examples where relevant to support overall comments
- Balanced assessment of the information to determine the appropriate audit opinion in the circumstances

Professional scepticism and judgement

- Effective challenge of information, evidence and assumptions supplied and, techniques carried out to support key facts and/or decisions

- Appropriate application of professional judgement to draw conclusions and make informed decisions about the actions which are appropriate in the context and stage of the engagement | 5

Total | 25

(a) **Matters to consider include the following**

Ethical issues

In accordance with both the IESBA *Code of Ethics for Professional Accountants* and the FRC's *Ethical Standard* (section B5), a non-audit service must only be provided to an audit client after careful consideration of whether the firm's independence and objectivity in respect of the audit may be impaired, and of whether safeguards could be put in place to reduce this threat to an acceptable level or to eliminate it entirely. If such safeguards cannot be put in place, then the audit firm should not accept the non-audit engagement or should withdraw from it. It would appear that Eastwood is a public interest client, which means the list of approved non-audit work that an auditor can perform according to Appendix B of the FRC *Ethical Standard* is very short, and it is unlikely that this engagement would be found on that list.

This assignment would appear to carry particular threats in relation to fee dependence and advocacy. It is also a listed entity which can affect acceptance decisions.

Fees

Eastwood is a 'major client' of Newman & Co, and there is a risk that the provision of further, non-audit, services to Eastwood could lead to a breach in the acceptable level of recurring fees receivable from one audit client. In the case of a public interest client such as Eastwood, the IESBA *Code* states that the public may perceive an auditor's independence to be impaired where recurring fees start to make up 15% of total fees.

Advocacy

Newman & Co has been engaged by the client partly in response to the client receiving requests for a Sustainability Report from shareholders and pressure groups. This is a potentially risky context in which to provide such a report, as the report is likely to be scrutinised closely. Furthermore, Newman & Co may be perceived as management's advocate, which would be particularly damaging in the event of any dispute.

Newman & Co's independence would be strengthened by the fact that assurance work would be carried out by a separate team from the audit team.

Level of assurance

Assurance reports may be provided giving varying levels of assurance. It will be necessary to obtain clarification from Eastwood of the level of assurance that it requires, and whether it requires different levels of assurance for different KPIs. Clearly, the level of assurance required would affect the level of evidence required and hence the amount of work that needs to be done, which would in turn affect the fees charged. This should be clarified before accepting the engagement, and a form and wording for the proposed report should be agreed with Eastwood.

Competence

It is possible that Newman & Co may not have staff with the requisite experience available to undertake this engagement. The fundamental principle of professional competence and due care requires that members of an engagement team both possess and apply sufficient skill and knowledge to be able to perform the assignment.

If Newman & Co does not have staff with this skill and experience then it could contract an expert to do some of the work, but this would be likely to increase the costs associated with the engagement.

Resources

A total of 75 KPIs would be reported on, which means that this is likely to be a relatively large engagement. A large number of staff would probably be required to work on the engagement.

It is promising that Newman & Co has a dedicated sustainability reporting assurance team, which should put it in a good position to undertake the work. However, the fact that the team is new means that careful consideration must be given to whether it is capable of doing the work required.

Time pressure

It would be very difficult to gather sufficient evidence to provide an assurance report within the four weeks left until the annual report is published. This may cause staff to be working under significant time pressure, which increases the risk of mistakes being made. Newman & Co must clarify when Eastwood intends for the assurance report to be published.

Profitability

This is a large assignment, probably requiring the team to travel from Oldtown to Fartown to perform the work. This would clearly involve incurring significant costs and should be reflected in the level of fees charged.

The amount of work that would need to be done, and the short time frame in which to do it, mean that a high fee could be commanded here.

Travel

It is likely that members of the assurance department would need to travel to Fartown, and for the engagement to be accepted they must be willing to do so. It is not clear whether there are any language barriers to working in Fartown, and whether these might be overcome.

Risk

The context of the assignment indicates the presence of risks relating to the degree of scrutiny to which the assurance report would be likely to be subjected. In addition to the presence of interested pressure group and shareholders, Eastwood is listed on two stock exchanges and is thus fairly high profile. This may increase the level of evidence that Newman & Co would seek to obtain, which would in turn affect the level of fee charged.

Moreover, the inconsistency that has already come to light in respect of the charitable donations figure may indicate management manipulation of the KPIs, which adds to the risk associated with the assignment.

(b) (i)

- Review HR records of the number and type of accidents in the workplace.
- Review accident log books from a sample of locations.
- Discuss the definition of a 'serious' accident and establish the criteria applied to an accident to determine whether it is serious.
- Review correspondence with legal advisors which may indicate any legal action being taken against Eastwood.
- Review minutes of board meetings for discussions of serious accidents and repercussions for the company.
- Discussion with management/legal advisors, of whether Eastwood has any convictions for health and safety offences during the year.
- Enquire whether the company has received any health and safety visits. Review documentation from any of these for evidence of serious accidents.
- Talk to employees to identify any accidents not recorded in the accident book.

(ii)

- Review Eastwood's training budget in comparison with previous years to ascertain the overall level of planned spending on training.
- Obtain breakdown of the total training spend and review for any items misclassified as training costs.

- Agree significant components of the total training spend to supporting documentation, eg contracts and invoices from training providers.
- Agree the total amount spent on significant training programmes to cash book and/or bank statements.
- Using data on total number of employees provided by the payroll department, recalculate the annual training spend per employee.

(c) **Briefing notes**

To: Trainee Accountant

Subject: Other information – auditor's responsibilities

Introduction

These notes explain the responsibility of the auditor in relation to other information published with the financial statements, in the context of Eastwood plc's charitable donations.

Eastwood's Integrated Report contains a material inconsistency with the financial statements; charitable donations are stated as £10.5m in the Integrated Report and £9m in the financial statements.

Audit evidence has been obtained which supports the £9m figure in the financial statements. This evidence should be reviewed to ensure that it is sufficient and appropriate.

The matter should be discussed with management, who should be asked to change the figure in the Integrated Report. If management refuses to make this change, then the auditor's report should describe the misstatement of in the Other Information section of the auditor's report which should describe the inconsistency. The matter should also be communicated to those charged with governance.

The directors' report should be reviewed for any reference to charitable donations, as UK auditors are required to report under the Companies Act 2006 whether the information given in the directors' report is consistent with the information in the accounts. Any inconsistency would therefore be highlighted in the auditor's report.

Eastwood is listed on several stock exchanges, so Newman & Co should consider whether it has any other responsibilities in relation to all applicable Listing Rules.

Finally, if management refuses to change the Integrated Report, then this may indicate a lack of integrity on its part. Any reliance placed on management representations should be reconsidered in this light.

Conclusion

Newman & Co needs to consider carefully how it will meet its responsibilities in relation to Eastwood's other information.

57 Marr

Workbook references

Chapters 11 and 16.

Top tips

Part (a) was an enjoyable question (!). It featured a draft auditor's report which contained several errors, your approach to which should just be to work through the errors systematically. The material on ISA (UK) 701 was probably the most difficult and provided you with a good test in this area.

Part (b) was a difficult discussion of a current issue, but this is something that you do need to be aware of. Passing this question did not require an in-depth knowledge of data analytics.

Easy marks

There were easy marks in part (a) for recognising that an inappropriate opinion had been expressed.

ACCA examining team's comments

Part (a) was for 15 marks and asked for a critical appraisal of a proposed auditor's report. The report contained many errors of fact and of judgement, and well-prepared candidates scored highly here. There were some quite obvious matters that most candidates discussed, for example that the structure of the report was not correct, the wording was not professional, the basis for opinion paragraph lacked sufficient detail, and the nature of the modification was wrong in the circumstances described in the scenario. Most candidates also commented on the incorrect use of the Emphasis of Matter paragraph and correctly determined the materiality of the two issues described in the scenario. Overall, however, **answers to this requirement were often too short for the marks available**, and while most issues had been identified, they were **not always well explained**.

Note. The requirement for UK listed companies to disclose climate-related matters under the Task Force on Climate-Related Financial Disclosures (TCFD) was not in force when this question was originally set in 2014, so there are no examining team comments for this part of the question.

Marking guide	Marks
(a) **Evaluation of draft auditor's report**	
In general up to 1.5 marks for each relevant point of evaluation:	
• Incorrect presentation and combining of Opinion and Basis for Opinion paragraphs	
• Wording regarding 'proven conclusively' is inappropriate	
• Description of material misstatement should include quantification and impact on financial statements	
• The relevant financial reporting standard should be referred to	
• Unprofessional wording regarding the finance director	
• Inappropriate opinion given – should be modified due to material misstatement not due to disclaimer of opinion	
• Level of modification incorrect – it is material but not pervasive	
• Key audit matters (KAMs) – no introductory paragraph	
• Appears to give multiple opinions	
• Description needed for why the matter is a KAM	
• Description needed for how the KAM was addressed	
• Description is insufficiently detailed	
• Court case not fundamental so not appropriate to include in Emphasis of Matter paragraph	
• Emphasis of Matter should only be used for matters appropriately accounted for which is not the case (award up to 3 marks if both the £50,000 provision and the TCFD disclosure issue are adequately discussed)	
	15
(b) **Data analytics**	
In general up to 2 marks for each relevant discussion point:	
• Definitions	
• Manipulate complete data set	
• Importance of visual representations of data trends	
• Effect on ISAs – fundamental change v fundamental continuity	
	5

ANSWERS

Marking guide	Marks

Professional marks

Analysis and evaluation

- Appropriate use of the information to support discussion, draw appropriate conclusions and design appropriate responses
- Identification of omissions from the analysis or further analysis which could be carried out
- Balanced assessment of the information to determine the appropriate audit opinion in the circumstances

Professional scepticism and judgement

- Effective challenge of the information given in the draft auditor's report
- Appropriate application of professional judgement to draw conclusions and make informed decisions about the actions which are appropriate in the context and stage of the engagement.

Commercial acumen

- Appropriate recognition of the implications of data analytics for the auditing profession.

Maximum	5
Total	25

(a) There are several problems with the draft auditor's report.

Layout

The draft report contains a paragraph entitled 'Basis for opinion and disclaimer of opinion'. ISAs (UK) require two separate sections here, headed 'Basis for Opinion' and 'Opinion'.

The 'Basis for Opinion' section should be placed immediately after the 'Opinion' section, and its heading reflects the type of opinion being given – hence 'Basis for Qualified Opinion', 'Basis for Adverse Opinion', and so on.

Wording of report

The paragraph states that 'procedures have proven conclusively that trade receivables are materially misstated'. This is misleading. Audit procedures provide reasonable assurance, which is less than the absolute assurance implied by the words 'proven conclusively'.

The basis for modification paragraph should state the amount of the potential adjustment to receivables, along with its financial impact, referring to the relevant financial reporting standard.

The paragraph names the finance director, which is unnecessary and unprofessional. The statement that she 'refused to make an adjustment' is inflammatory and may leave the auditor open to legal action.

Opinion

An inappropriate auditor's opinion has been given here. At 23% of profit, any write-off of the receivable would be material. The draft report is therefore correct inasmuch as an unmodified opinion would be inappropriate because a material amount of the balance should be written-off.

However, the receivable is unlikely to be judged as pervasive to the financial statements, so the level of modification is wrong. Further, there has been no inability to obtain sufficient appropriate audit evidence, as would be implied by a disclaimer of opinion – as the draft report states, this is a material misstatement.

The opinion should be Qualified due to a material misstatement.

Key audit matters (KAMs)

ISA (UK) 701 *Communicating Key Audit Matters in the Independent Auditor's report* requires the auditor to include specified introductory language at the start of the KAMs section of the report (ISA (UK) 701: para. 11). This has not been included here, which constitutes a failure to apply ISA (UK) 701. The auditor's responsibilities section of the report would also discuss KAMs; we do not know whether this has been included correctly as this section has not been extracted.

This introduction should have stated that the auditor does 'not provide a separate opinion on these matters'. Instead of this, the draft report states that 'in our opinion revenue is presented fairly', which comes very close to expressing a separate opinion in relation to revenue. It is important that the auditor's opinion relates to the financial statements as a whole, and that KAMs are simply explanations of the matters of most significance to that audit.

ISA (UK) 701 requires the description of each KAM to include:

- Why the matter was considered to be a KAM
- How the matter was addressed (ISA (UK) 701: para. 13)

The draft report does attempt to describe why the matter was considered to be a KAM, but the description is insufficiently detailed, and could be construed to be a complaint about the complexity of Marr plc's policies. The description should have stated the factors that led the auditor to conclude that revenue recognition would require significant auditor attention, and it should have discussed the risks of material misstatement in this area.

The draft report fails to describe how the matter was addressed in the audit. It could have described how the auditor addressed the assessed risks of material misstatement, perhaps providing an overview of the procedures performed.

Emphasis of Matter (EoM)

The use of an EoM paragraph is inappropriate. An EoM is used to refer to a matter which is already correctly disclosed in the financial statements, but which is in need of extra emphasis by the auditor. By contrast, here the EoM refers to a provision not included in the financial statements. In reality this is a misstatement.

The £50,000 is not material, so the draft report is correct not to modify the opinion in this respect. The correct course of action would be to ask Marr plc to provide for this amount, and if they do not then keep track of it as an uncorrected misstatement. Although it is immaterial on its own, it may become material alongside other uncorrected misstatements.

Finally, using an EoM paragraph to point out the absence of any disclosure on Marr plc's compliance or otherwise with the requirements of the Task Force on Climate-Related Financial Disclosure (TCFD) is also inappropriate. Since 2022, all UK listed entities have been required under the Financial Conduct Authority (FCA) listing rules to either state in their annual report that their climate-related disclosures are consistent with the TCFD recommendations or explain why not. Any non-disclosure is a breach of these FCA requirements which the auditor is responsible for communicating in the auditor's report.

The means of communicating this non-disclosure depends on the location of the TCFD disclosure – should it only form part of the 'other information' in the annual report, it will be subject to the auditor's responsibilities for this under ISA (UK) 720. However, (as seems likely for a public company such as Marr plc) if it is expected to be included in the directors' report or strategic report, it will be considered statutory information which the auditor needs to assess for compliance with laws and regulations, and any non-compliance with the applicable legal requirements needs to be reported in the section of the auditor's report that covers 'Opinions on other matters prescribed by the Companies Act 2006'.

(b) Data analytics is the examination of data to try to identify patterns, trends or correlations. As the quantity of data has increased, it has become more necessary to evolve ways of processing and making sense of it. Data analytics is thus part of the 'Big data' movement, namely the qualitative shift in the amount of data that can be held and analysed by modern computers.

Recent advances in IT make it increasingly possible for auditors to examine and to manipulate a complete data set, ie 100% of the transactions. This has the potential to change the way audit testing works; rather than eg performing controls testing on a sample of items, it is possible to perform risk analysis on a whole population.

In an audit environment so saturated with data about a client, one of the key challenges for auditors is knowing how to make the best use of the data. To help avoid the phenomenon of 'drowning in data', audit data analytics tools allow auditors to visualise trends graphically, and to develop new ways of interrogating data to find trends and relationships.

Current auditing standards, such as ISAs (UK), are based on the technique of risk-based auditing which first became the norm in the 1970s, when it replaced the fully substantive approaches that had preceded it. It has been claimed in some quarters that these techniques will bring about changes of this magnitude to the profession. The sheer scale of the work that can be performed using data analytics techniques makes such a difference to auditors that new auditing standards are needed. Alternatively, others have claimed that auditing standards are fundamentally sound, but are in need of modernisation to reflect these techniques.

58 Sol & Co

Workbook references

Chapters 4, 7, 8, 10 and 11.

Top tips

Part (a) was the biggest part of this question and should have taken up the main chunk of your time (about 23 minutes).

The question itself may have looked intimidating, as it looks like the work has been done well, so there is not much for you to say. If this is the case, then do not be afraid of sometimes writing that you agree with what has been done. If you review the model answer, you will see that the first sentence under 'Inventory' is of this type ("The move to a just-in-time (JIT) inventory system is consistent with a fall in the inventory levels and inventory holding period."). This is merely a statement that what has been done by the auditor in the question is valid.

Take care, though: it is likely that there will not be marks on offer for simply repeating what has been given in the scenario, as this is something that weaker candidates tend to do. Perhaps there is a fine line between repetition of the scenario and affirmation of it, so you will need to make it clear to your marker that you are making a statement to the effect that what has happened is also what should have happened, and that it is correct.

Part (b) is a question format that we have seen several times in the AAA exam, namely the presentation of a schedule of uncorrected misstatements for you to examine. This being the case, there is a good chance that a question like this could be set in your exam. You've been warned!

This was probably easier than the first part of the question, with auditor's reports in particular being a popular area with candidates. The only thing really is that you might not have remembered IAS 20 in enough detail to deal with the misstatement; if this is the case then you will be aware of the need to revise your accounting standards before your exam.

Easy marks

The marks for materiality and for the auditor's report impact in (b) were among the easiest in the exam.

ACCA examining team's comments

This 25-mark question was set at the completion and reporting stage of an audit. As is typical of reporting questions, this is where the examining team see some of the strongest and some of the weakest demonstrations of auditing competence from candidates.

Stronger candidates often display strong **practical skills**, incorporating a good understanding of materiality and risk, a strong knowledge of the financial reporting which is needed to perform an audit, an ability to distinguish between auditor and client information and an understanding of the difference between financial statements, an auditor's report and an audit opinion.

Weaker candidates tend to lack the underlying knowledge of double entry accounting and are unable to distinguish between the client and the audit firm, between the financial statements and the auditor's report or demonstrate a good understanding of the concept of materiality.

In **part (b)**, the key things to note are:

- Information is auditor prepared not a client document.
- The year end was three months ago, and the main fieldwork stage of the audit is complete.

Candidates were expected to evaluate the information provided and to **identify inconsistencies between the results of testing and the auditor expectation**. Candidates were then asked for suitable procedures, relevant to the scenario, to enable the auditor to reach a conclusion ie, what else is needed to determine if the information in the financial statements is not materially misstated and suggest actions where appropriate. Candidates generally handled the evaluation of the subsequent events procedures well.

Most candidates were able identify the adjusting subsequent event where a major customer of the company had gone into liquidation. They were able to tie this back into the receivables analysis in the analytical procedures and recommend the action of requesting the write off the irrecoverable amounts and the procedure of obtaining confirmation from the liquidator.

Weaker candidates here appeared to think the client had calculated the ratios and the auditor needed to prove they were correct. Many wasted time trying to prove the inventory holding period calculations, rather than appreciating that the shorter than expected holding length combined with the increase in management's provision rate could suggest that obsolete inventory was a low risk, or an indicator inventory may be understated. Candidates often failed to distinguish between the management process of using a 'just in time' approach to inventory purchases and the accounting systems that feed into the financial statements. Many candidates still fail to distinguish between what is pre and post year end and many suggested the auditor go back to the inventory count and look for obsolete inventory despite it being three months in the past.

In **part (b)**, candidates were presented with a list of uncorrected misstatements compiled by the audit team. This is a relatively common format for completion questions, yet candidates often treat the points in the exhibit as a "matters and evidence" type question, giving the accounting rules and all the procedures which would have been expected to be on file.

Stronger candidates were able to identify the matters to be explained, giving an appropriate discussion of materiality, as well as describing the treatment of capital grants. They were able to identify that the material misstatement in respect to the grant would warrant a qualification on the basis of material misstatement, with the misstatement of receivables, which was immaterial, would have not impact, in isolation, on the audit opinion.

Weaker candidates stated that a provision should be made in respect of the repayment of the grant. There was no evidence that repayment was probable at the present time, therefore this did not meet the criteria for a provision. A possible repayment, which is one interpretation of the information in the scenario, would lead to a disclosure requirement only. These same candidates then tended to state that the overstated receivable was wrong and that the whole sale should be reversed and shown as an asset held for sale.

Marking guide	Marks
(a) **Arjan Ltd – evaluation of subsequent events and final analytical procedures**	
Generally, up to 1 mark for each valid comment of evaluation relation to:	
• Inventory holding	
• Inventory value	
• Inventory allowance	
• Receivables allowance	
Maximum	12

(b) **Barnaby Ltd – uncorrected misstatements and impact on audit opinion**

Generally, up to 1 mark per point explained:

- Encourage management to amend all misstatements
- Communicate the effect of all misstatements to those charged with governance
- Government grant
  - Inappropriate accounting treatment
  - Impact of the error
  - Materiality
  - Factual misstatement and adjustment required
  - Qualified opinion on basis of material misstatement
  - Not pervasive
  - Impact on basis for opinion paragraph
- Machine sale
  - Inappropriate accounting treatment
  - Impact of error
  - Materiality
  - No impact on auditor's opinion in isolation as not material

Maximum 8

Professional marks

Analysis and evaluation

- Effective appraisal of the evidence already obtained to identify inconsistencies that the auditor should seek to resolve in relation to Arjan Ltd
- Balanced assessment of the information to determine the appropriate audit opinion in the circumstances for Barnaby Ltd

Professional scepticism and professional judgement

- Effective challenge and critical assessment of information, evidence and assumptions supplied in relation to Arjan Co, and demonstration of professional judgement in identifying appropriate evidence to support conclusions for the audit engagement team.
- Appropriate application of professional scepticism and judgement to draw conclusions and make informed decisions which are appropriate at the completion phase of the Barnaby Co audit engagement.

Commercial acumen

- Appropriate recognition of the wider context of the information obtained during the audit regarding the uncorrected misstatements, and the need to obtain an understanding of management's reasons for not making any adjustments to the financial statements.

Maximum 5

Total 25

(a) **Arjan Ltd – evaluation of subsequent events and final analytical procedures**

Analytical procedures are performed as an overall review of the financial statements at the end of the audit to assess whether they are consistent with the auditor's understanding of the entity. Subsequent events procedures ensure that the sufficient and appropriate evidence in relation to events occurring up to the date of the auditor's report are appropriately reflected in the financial statements. Part of the final review process will include a review of the results of audit procedures to ensure that they support the findings and overall conclusions which have been drawn by the audit team.

Inventory

The move to a just-in-time (JIT) inventory system is consistent with a fall in the inventory levels and inventory holding period. Evidence to corroborate the year-end inventory balance has been primarily provided in the form of inventory count attendance for which no issues were identified. The extent of work performed at the inventory count is unclear from the documentation provided and it would be unusual that no further work was required on the existence and completeness of year-end inventory beyond inventory count attendance. It would be expected that the auditors perform a reconciliation of the inventory count data to the detailed analysis of the year-end inventory report during the audit to ensure that the report is accurately reflecting the inventory count data. It would also be expected that the accuracy of the cost of the inventory is tested with reference to purchase invoices and overhead absorption calculations for work in progress and finished goods on hand. As such, the evidence referred to in the final analytical procedures is insufficient to be able to conclude on the existence, completeness and accuracy of the inventory amounts held.

The increase in the write off for obsolete inventory as a percentage of inventory held is more unexpected. Even though this would still mean a smaller total amount of obsolete inventory held than in the previous year, it would not be expected that a higher obsolescence rate would be seen under a JIT system as, theoretically, inventory is only ordered to satisfy specific demand. As such, more evidence needs to be obtained in this regard, particularly as estimates such as these are susceptible to management manipulation and may be used to manipulate the profit of the company. Further discussions with management and production staff are needed to identify how this figure has been derived. It may be the case that the amount relates to specific items which should have already been written off, for example, if those goods are for a specific cancelled order. It could also be the case that this figure is based on a general percentage amount of inventory held at the year end. As inventory should be assessed on a line by line basis rather than as a general adjustment, the auditor would need to determine whether this would result in a material misstatement. The comment that the current allowance for obsolete inventory is immaterial and therefore no further work has been performed is inappropriate. A misstatement in this allowance could be material in conjunction with other misstatements and at present there is no evidence as to whether this value is under or overstated.

Trade receivables

The increase in the receivables collection period compared with the prior year appears to suggest trade receivables may be overstated due to an understatement of the allowance for irrecoverable trade receivables. The audit team has relied on direct confirmations from trade receivables as evidence of recoverability and this is inappropriate. While direct confirmation of balances can provide evidence over the existence and accuracy of balances, it does not provide sufficient evidence of recoverability and therefore the valuation of trade receivables.

In addition, the results of the subsequent events procedures contradict the assertion of the credit controller that Cami Ltd will settle their outstanding balance. The subsequent event identified for Arjan Ltd has been identified after the date of the financial statements but prior to the issue of the auditor's report. Given the late payments made by Cami Ltd to Arjan Ltd during the year ended 31 March 20X5 and the fact that Cami Ltd has entered liquidation so soon after the financial year end, it is likely this would be classed as an adjusting event under IAS® 10 *Events after the Reporting Period*, providing evidence of conditions existing at the end of the reporting period.

As with inventory, it is inappropriate to conclude that no further work is required because the reduction in the allowance is not material. It is possible that the allowance could be materially understated and further procedures should have been performed to confirm this is not the case.

(b) **Barnaby Ltd – uncorrected misstatements and impact on audit opinion**

During the completion stage of the audit, the effect of uncorrected misstatements must be evaluated by the auditor, as required by ISA (UK) 450 *Evaluation of Misstatements Identified*

During the Audit. This requires that the auditor obtains an understanding of management's reasons for not making recommended adjustments to the financial statements and that they take this into account when evaluating whether the financial statements as a whole are free from material misstatement.

In order to maintain accurate accounting records, management should be encouraged to adjust for all misstatements to ensure the risk of material misstatements in future periods is reduced due to the cumulative effect of immaterial uncorrected misstatements.

ISA (UK) 450 also requires that the auditor communicates with those charged with governance about uncorrected misstatements and the effect which they, individually or in aggregate, may have on the opinion in the auditor's report. Both matters included in the schedule of uncorrected misstatements will be discussed below and the impact on the auditor's opinion considered individually.

Government grant

In accordance with IAS 20 *Accounting for Government Grants and Disclosure of Government Assistance*, grants relating to assets may be presented in one of two ways: either as deferred income or by deducting the grant from the asset's carrying amount. The grant is then released to the statement of profit or loss in line with the use of the asset either as a release of the deferred income or through the lower depreciation charge arising where the asset cost has been reduced by the value of the grant.

The recognition of the grant in the profit for the year is incorrect. As the asset has not yet been purchased, the grant amount of £5 million should have been recognised as deferred income at the reporting date. As a result, profit is overstated, and liabilities are understated. As the grant represents 11.6% of profit before tax and 4.8% of total assets, this is material. This therefore represents a factual material misstatement and management should be asked to amend the financial statements.

If management does not amend the financial statements with respect to the government grant, then the auditor will issue a qualified opinion on the basis of a material misstatement. As the misstatement is confined to two specific elements and does not represent a substantial portion of the financial statements, this would not be considered pervasive.

A basis for qualified opinion paragraph would follow the qualified audit opinion which describes the matter giving rise to the qualification along with a quantification of the financial effects arising.

Machine sale

IFRS® 9 *Financial Instruments* requires receivables such as that arising on sale of the machine to be recognised initially at fair value and held on an amortised cost basis. The fair value of the receivable in this case is the amount due in one year, discounted back to the reporting date. Management recording the transaction at cash settlement value will result in an overstatement of receivables and an overstatement of profit on the disposal of the machine.

The amount of the overstatement is £1 million. This represents just under 1% of assets and 2.3% of profit before tax and therefore is unlikely to be considered material in isolation.

Management should be requested to make an adjustment for the misstatement. Even though it will not be material on its own, the adjustment will reduce the risk of cumulative uncorrected misstatements in future periods.

As the misstatement is not material, it will have no individual impact on the auditor's opinion.

> **Tutorial note.** Candidates will also be awarded credit for materiality assessed in a qualitative nature in respect of misapplication of an accounting policy.

59 Daley

Workbook references

Chapters 10 and 11.

Top tips

The scenario in parts (a) and (b) was eerily similar to some recent questions in this area, and you should have been well prepared for it. Going concern is a topical area as it has been a focal point for public criticism of auditors. Part (a) just asked you for going concern indicators; these should be familiar from your studies, but really the question is about thinking practically about the company's solvency and liquidity, and what could happen to it over the next 12 months.

Part (b) asked for audit evidence. In general, one mark is available for each well-explained point here, so what you want to avoid is producing a long list of poorly developed points, with each point scoring half a mark at best. Where possible, you need to explain why you would expect to see each piece of evidence.

Part (c) should really be a favourite area for students, as it is both relatively simple and examined regularly.

Easy marks

Part (c) was full of easy marks for your knowledge of the auditor's report.

ACCA examining team's comments

This was a 25-mark question covering the going concern assessment for a non-listed client and was set at the completion stage of the audit.

Requirement (a) asked candidates to evaluate matters which cast doubt on a client's ability to continue as a going concern (GC). Candidates were directed to perform analytical review of a cash flow forecast to aid in their evaluation and those who used the quantitative and discursive parts of the scenario to describe the GC risk indicators with an explanation of how that impacted on the company's future tended to score high marks on this question. Candidates who merely calculated ratios and stated the direction of movement or simply stated that an increase in the receivables collection period showed going concern issues attained very few marks. It is important that candidates demonstrate their knowledge of how each matter gives rise to an issue for trading as a going concern. For example, a fuller explanation would be that the increase in the receivables collection period may mean that there are irrecoverable debts which should be written off, increasing losses further, or that slow collection would decrease liquidity and therefore put pressure on the ability of the company to make payments as they fell due. A technique candidates could employ here would be to ask themselves 'why' as they get to the end of a sentence, allowing them to add a second sentence demonstrating their understanding. A minority of candidates appeared to lack focus on the question requirement and answered this as a RoMM discussion, covering risks of material misstatements in the forecast rather than relating the scenario to the GC issues required.

Part (b) requested an explanation of the audit evidence which would be needed with respect to the forecast and candidates scored best when they remembered this was future/prospective information, not historical, and where they related it specifically to the information given. For example, candidates who looked for specific assumptions in the information provided and devised sources of evidence to support each of those assumptions were able to attain far more marks than candidates who simply said evaluate the assumptions used by management in preparing the forecast. It is important that candidates appreciate that no two questions are the same and that the information given in the question should always be used to drive their answer.

Finally part (c) required candidates to explain why the directors may wish to exclude disclosures relating to going concern uncertainties in the notes to the financial statements and the possible implications on the auditor's report. Candidates were generally able to identify the reasons for non-disclosure but performed very poorly on the auditor's report implications.

Many candidates wrongly stated that the directors omitting a required disclosure would not constitute a material misstatement. Many therefore went on to conclude that the opinion would be unmodified but that going concern disclosures would be made in the auditor's report instead of in the notes to the financial statements. This is not the case and candidates should ensure they are familiar with the reporting requirements in ISA (UK) 570 *Going Concern*. Some candidates suggested including such disclosures in the Key Audit Matters section or to include an Emphasis of Matter paragraph, both of which would be inappropriate.

Marking guide **Marks**

(a) Going concern indicators

Up to 2 marks for each well-explained going concern indicator discussed.

Up to 3 marks for calculation of relevant ratios and trends.

Revenue and profitability

- Significant increase in revenue of 28.4% (potential overtrading indicator)
- Declining profit margins
- Increase in effective interest rate on long-term debt (lenders perceive as higher risk)
- Loss-making

Liquidity and working capital

- Declining liquidity
- Cash position has moved from positive to negative (overdraft) during year
- Poor working capital management

Gearing and finance

- Increased gearing
- Decline in interest cover
- Failure to replace non-current assets (7.5% decrease in year)

Legal claim

- Significant legal claim, company does not appear to have cash to settle it

Cash flow forecast

- Cash flow forecast indicates improving liquidity and working capital, however, this appears optimistic (eg growth rate, receivable days assumption)
- New competitor threatens to reduce market share
- Return to positive cash dependent on these assumptions and obtaining new bank finance which may not be forthcoming
- Company is dependent on obtaining new bank finance

Economic/political issues

- Impact of leaving EU on imports and being subject to currency exchange and other political and regulatory factor

9

(b) **Audit evidence on cash flow forecast**

Generally 1 mark for each well described source of audit evidence:

- Agreement of the opening cash position to cash book and bank reconciliation
- Accuracy check – recalculation
- Review of the results of any market research which has been conducted for next 12 months assessing impact of new competitor
- Discuss key assumptions made by management in preparation of forecast (including growth rate and receivables days) and assess consistency with

auditor's knowledge of the business and with management's intentions regarding the future of the company

- Agreement that the cash flow forecast is consistent with profit and other financial forecasts which have been prepared by management
- Comparison of the cash flow forecast for the period April–May 20X5 with management accounts for the same period
- Analytical review of the items included in the cash flow forecast, for example, categories of expenses, to look for items which may have been omitted
- Review legal correspondence in relation to legal claims and assess likelihood of losing actions, likely cost and likelihood of further actions in future
- If appropriate, ensure settlement of legal claims has been included in forecast
- Review correspondence with bank and supporting documentation for existing and proposed loan facilities
- Discuss with management likelihood of obtaining new finance
- Check calculation of finance cost and inclusion in forecast
- Ensure amount and timing of receipt of new finance is accurately reflected in forecast
- Inspect documentation in relation to new warehousing agreeing cost and check that cash outflow is included in forecast at correct amount and timing
- Review of board minutes re company's current trading position and ongoing negotiations with bankers
- Consideration of impact on cash flows and liquidity when company is incurring additional costs of compliance with all laws and regulations
- Obtain written representation

6

(c) **Directors' reasons for non-disclosure and implications for auditor's report**

Generally up to 1 mark for each point discussed:

Possible reasons for non-disclosure

- Desire to present company in positive light to investors and other third parties
- Particularly significant given current position of company, eg seeking to raise new finance; struggling to manage liquidity and working capital; need to maintain confidence with suppliers and customers especially with arrival of new competitor

Implications for auditor's report

- Auditor must assess whether absence of disclosure is material but not pervasive to financial statements or whether it is material and pervasive to financial statements

Material but not pervasive

- Qualified opinion due to material misstatement
- Basis for qualified opinion paragraph to be included giving details of going concern uncertainties and that financial statements do not adequately disclose these uncertainties

Material and pervasive

- Adverse opinion due to material misstatement where the financial statements 'do not present fairly'
- Basis for adverse opinion paragraph explaining grounds for adverse opinion
- Position of opinion and basis for (qualified/adverse) opinion paragraphs

- Well-reasoned conclusion on whether issue is pervasive —

5

Professional marks

Analysis and evaluation

- Appropriate use of the information to support discussion, draw appropriate conclusions and design appropriate responses
- Identification of omissions from the analysis or further analysis which could be carried out
- Balanced assessment of the information to determine the appropriate audit opinion in the circumstances

Professional scepticism and judgement

- Effective challenge of information, evidence and assumptions supplied and, techniques carried out to support key facts and/or decisions
- Appropriate application of professional judgement to draw conclusions and make informed decisions about the actions which are appropriate in the context and stage of the engagement

Commercial acumen

- Appreciation of the commercial context of the auditor's report and the effect on those charged with governance of the auditor modifying their report
- Appropriate consideration of the factors giving rise to the directors' possible motivations for not disclosing uncertainties in relation to going concern

Maximum	5
Total	25

(a) **Going concern indicators**

There is a range of matters which cast doubt on Daley Ltd's ability to continue as a going concern. In particular, the company appears to be exhibiting many of the indicators of a business which is overtrading.

Revenue and profitability

Daley Ltd has experienced a significant increase in revenue of 28.4% which may not be sustainable in the short to medium term without additional external sources of finance. The company is also experiencing a significant decline in its operating profit margin and net profit margin. It is notable that even after taking account of the provision, other operating expenses have increased by more than 4.3 times ((9.1 – 3.5)/1.3) resulting in an overall loss of £3.4 million in the current reporting period. It is possible that the company has had to reduce its selling prices in order to achieve the high level of sales growth and that this has resulted in a negative net profit margin this year of (30.1%).

Liquidity and working capital

Daley Ltd has also suffered a decline in liquidity as evidenced by a fall in its current ratio from 2.4 to 1.6 and in its acid test ratio from 1.1 to 0.6. A review of the company's working capital ratios indicates long and worsening inventory holding periods (481 days in 20X5 compared to 466 days in 20X4) and overall inventory has increased by 57% which may be indicative of problems in relation to the saleability of inventory which is in breach of domestic regulations. The company is currently taking on average 120 days to collect its trade debts (108 days in 20X4) and requires an average of 348 days in 20X5 (365 days in 20X4) to pay its trade payables. Although this is a fall in the average payment period compared to the prior year, it still appears to be a long period which may be related to ongoing payment disputes in relation to the regulatory breaches noted previously. Overall, trade payables have increased by 44.8% on the prior year and the company may struggle to settle this liability given its worsening cash position which may, in turn, result in a loss of goodwill with its suppliers and a refusal to supply or to withdraw credit in the future which would severely restrict the company's operations. The poor working capital management and declining liquidity have resulted in Daley Ltd's cash position deteriorating from a positive position of £0.6 million in 20X4 to an overdraft of £1.8 million in 20X5 which is significant at 7.8% of total assets.

Gearing and finance

In addition to problems with short-term finance and liquidity, Daley Ltd is also exhibiting a significant increase in gearing as evidenced by the increase in debt to equity from 2.3 in 20X4 to 6.4 in 20X5 and a fall in interest cover from 6.6 times to (1.5) times over the same period, indicating that the business is unable to service its current levels of finance. The company's finance costs as a percentage of long-term borrowings have increased from 5.6% in 20X4 to 13.4% in 20X5. This may be due at least in part to the interest on the overdraft proving to be an expensive way of financing the entity's operations and if the overdraft has not been agreed with the bank, the company may be incurring additional penalties and charges thereby putting additional strain on the company's cash flows. The increasing finance costs may also reflect lenders already perceiving Daley Ltd to be a high credit risk. It is also notable that non-current assets have decreased by 7.5% this year which suggests that the business is also struggling to replace and renew its existing capital expenditure levels. If this is the case, it may cast further doubt on the feasibility of the planned expansion of its operations.

Legal claim

Given Daley Ltd's current financial position, it seems unlikely that the business will be able to settle the legal claim of £3.5 million which threatens to place severe demands on the company's cash flow. Indeed, if there is a prospect of more claims arising in the future, the problems with the saleability of inventory and management of working capital as a result of the regulatory breaches discussed earlier may worsen further, leading to a greater deterioration in the company's cash flow position.

Cash flow forecast

Overall, Daley Ltd's ability to continue to trade appears to be dependent on obtaining the new bank finance which it has assumed in its cash flow forecast. The bank financing is needed to meet existing liabilities and it is doubtful whether sufficient funding will be available in order to finance the proposed expansion. Moreover, the forecast itself appears to be unrealistic in its other assumptions. In particular, the assumption that the business's revenue will grow by 25% seems optimistic given the arrival of a major competitor in its market place and the projected trade receivable collection period of 60 days may well be unachievable on the basis of the historic ratios identified above. A return to a positive cash position is dependent on these assumptions and obtaining the new bank finance which may not be forthcoming based on the bank's assessment of the business's current financial position and performance.

Economic and political issues

Given that the company's business model is importation of motor cars, its operations could be adversely impacted by changes in the economic and legal environment. For example, the fact that the UK is leaving the EU could mean that the company finds it more difficult or expensive to import vehicles, depending on their country of origin. The UK's exit from the EU also makes business planning difficult, as there are many uncertainties, for example, over changes in regulations, the imposition of tariffs and import duties, and possible impacts on the rate of exchange of foreign currency.

(b) **Audit evidence on the cash flow forecast**

The audit working papers should include sufficient evidence that appropriate audit procedures have been conducted in relation to the assumption that Daley Ltd is a going concern at the reporting date, including the following:

- Evidence of agreement of the opening cash position to the cash book and bank reconciliation.

- Reperformance by the audit team of the client's calculations in preparing the forecast in order to check its arithmetic accuracy.
- Details of a review of the results of any market research which has been conducted by Daley Ltd for the next 12 months in order to assess the potential impact of the new competitor.
- Notes from meetings with management detailing discussion of the key assumptions made by management in the preparation of the forecast (including the growth rate and receivables days) and an assessment of the consistency of the assumptions with the auditor's knowledge of the business and with management's intentions regarding the future of the company and corroborating evidence of assumptions.
- Evaluation by the audit team of previous profit and other financial forecasts and their outcome in order to assess the consistency of the cash flow forecast with other prospective information prepared by management.
- A comparison of the cash flow forecast for the period April to May 20X5 with management accounts for the same period in order to assess the accuracy of the forecast compared to actual data to date.
- Results of analytical review of the items included in the cash flow forecast including, for example, a detailed review of the breakdown of different categories of expenses in order to identify any items which may have been omitted.
- A review of correspondence with Daley Ltd's lawyers in relation to the legal claims in order to assess the likelihood of losing the actions, the likely cost and the possibility of further claims arising in the future.
- Based on the review of legal correspondence, confirmation that the settlement of the legal claims has been appropriately included in the cash flow forecast.
- A review of correspondence with Daley Ltd's bankers and supporting documentation for both the company's existing loan facilities and the proposed new loan.
- Minutes of discussions with management in relation to the likelihood of obtaining the new loan.
- Based on these reviews and discussions, a recalculation by the auditor of the finance cost and confirmation that the finance cost and the receipt of the loan have been accurately reflected in the cash flow forecast.
- Working paper detailing the review of the documentation in relation to the new warehousing agreeing the cost and checking that the cash outflow is included in the forecast at the correct amount and at the correct date.
- A review of board minutes in relation to the company's current trading position and the ongoing negotiations for the proposed new bank finance.
- A consideration of the impact on cash flows and liquidity when the company is incurring the additional costs of compliance with all laws and regulations.
- Obtain written representations from management confirming the reasonableness of the cash flow forecast.

(c) **Reasons for non-disclosure and implications for the auditor's report**

Motives for directors not wishing to make going concern disclosures

The directors' motives for non-disclosure of uncertainties in relation to going concern seem likely to reflect a desire to present the company in a positive light to investors and other third parties. This is a particularly sensitive issue at a time when the company is planning a major expansion and is seeking to raise significant new finance while struggling to manage its liquidity and working capital.

The disclosure of uncertainties in relation to going concern may well deter the bank from lending the new finance and may lead to a loss of confidence and goodwill with key suppliers and customers. Operational difficulties with suppliers and customers may prove to be particularly problematic with the arrival of the major new competitor in Daley Ltd's market in April 20X5.

Implications for the auditor's report

ISA (UK) 705 Modifications to the Opinion in the Independent Auditor's Report requires the auditor to modify the opinion in the auditor's report when they conclude that, based on the audit evidence obtained, the financial statements as a whole are not free from material misstatement. The failure to include disclosures in relation to material uncertainties in relation to going concern in Daley Ltd's financial statements represents a material omission which will therefore require a modification of the auditor's opinion. In this case, the auditor must exercise professional judgement and assess whether the absence of this disclosure is material but not pervasive to the financial statements or whether it is material and pervasive to the financial statements.

Material but not pervasive

If the auditor concludes that the omission of the required disclosures, such as the uncertainty over the bank loan and the possible outcome of the legal case, is material but not pervasive to the financial statements, a qualified audit opinion on the grounds of material misstatement is appropriate, as the directors have failed to include required disclosures. The auditor will include a 'Qualified Opinion' paragraph at the start of the auditor's report which will state that the financial statements are presented fairly in all material respects 'except for' the absence of this disclosure. The qualified opinion paragraph will be followed immediately by a 'Basis for Qualified Opinion' paragraph which will give details of the going concern uncertainties in relation to Daley Ltd and explain that the financial statements do not adequately disclose these uncertainties.

Material and pervasive

The auditor may conclude that the omission of the required disclosures as discussed above is material and pervasive to the financial statements, as in the auditor's opinion the lack of these disclosures will have a fundamental impact on the users' understanding of the financial statements. On this basis, an adverse audit opinion on the grounds of material misstatement is appropriate. The auditor will include an 'Adverse Opinion' paragraph at the start of the auditor's report which will state that the financial statements are not presented fairly in all material respects. The adverse opinion paragraph will be followed immediately by a 'Basis for Adverse Opinion' paragraph which will give details of the going concern uncertainties in relation to Daley Ltd and explain that in the opinion of the auditor, the omission of key disclosures in this respect are fundamental and pervasive to the financial statements and therefore require an adverse opinion.

Tutorial note. Key audit matters (KAM) disclosures are not relevant for Daley Ltd as a result of its unlisted status.

60 Basking

Workbook references

Chapters 7, 8, 10 and 11.

Top tips

Part (a) is a good example of the advantages to be conferred by reading ACCA's *Student Accountant*. The examining team has stated that topics featured in *Student Accountant* articles will be examined soon after the article, which is something that happened here.

This was a knowledge-based question and would have been very difficult for you if you were not familiar with ISA (UK) 450 *Evaluation of Misstatements Identified During the Audit*. The examining team has said in the past that candidates' knowledge of ISAs (UK) is sometimes poor, so if you struggled then this is something that you need to work on. It is a good idea, though, to focus your revision time on topics that appear in *Student Accountant* technical articles, as these are more likely to be examined.

Part (b) was a fair question on audit evidence. You are given the figures so that you can calculate materiality, so you should do so. The first matter, on depreciation, required you to extrapolate the error if you were to score well on the question. The question gave the information to do this (the carrying amount of the sample and the carrying amount of the whole balance), which you should take as a hint!

The second matter was a loan to a director that you should have recognised as a related party transaction. The third matter dealt with a judgement relating to an accounting estimate, and it should have been within your capabilities to pass this question part.

Easy marks

The marks available for calculating and evaluating materiality are easy, provided that you pick an appropriate benchmark (revenue, profit for the year or total assets). The marks for evaluating the effect on the audit opinion are also relatively easy.

Marking guide | **Marks**

(a) In general up to 1.5 mark for each relevant and adequate point of explanation. Award 0.5 mark for identification of a relevant matter and up to a further 1 mark for appropriate discussion. 0.5 mark should be awarded for relevant points which are either too brief or poorly explained:

Types of misstatement

- Identification and discussion of types of misstatement (max 1 mark)
- Impact on evaluation of impact on financial statements
- Subjectivity involved in judgemental matters
- Potential inaccuracy of projected misstatements

5

(b) In general up to 1 mark for each relevant and adequate point of explanation. 0.5 mark should be awarded for relevant points which are either too brief or poorly explained:

Depreciation

- Error in isolation immaterial (max 0.5 mark)
- Error also immaterial when projected to total population
- Client should be requested to amend the error
- Auditor should investigate revised non-current asset register
- If management refuses, there is still no material misstatement
- Unmodified opinion

Loan

- Related party transaction
- Material by nature
- Requires full disclosure in the financial statements
- Failure to adjust leads to a material but not pervasive misstatement
- Qualified opinion

Provision

- Calculation of potential provision values and value of adjustment
- Adjustment is material to statement of profit or loss
- Matter of judgement – must be reasoned and supported with evidence
- Potential for earnings management
- Request management to reinstate full provision
- Failure to adjust leads to a material but not pervasive misstatement
- Qualified opinion

15

Marking guide	**Marks**
Professional marks	
Analysis and evaluation	
• Appropriate use of the information to support discussion, draw appropriate conclusions and design appropriate responses	
• Identification of omissions from the analysis or further analysis which could be carried out	
• Balanced assessment of the information to determine the appropriate audit opinion in the circumstances	
Professional scepticism and judgement	
• Effective challenge of information, evidence and assumptions supplied and, techniques carried out to support key facts and/or decisions	
• Appropriate application of professional judgement to draw conclusions and make informed decisions about the actions which are appropriate in the context and stage of the engagement.	
Maximum	5
Total	25

(a) **Types of misstatement**

ISA (UK) 450 *Evaluation of Misstatements Identified During the Audit* identifies three types of misstatement:

(1) Factual misstatements

(2) Judgemental misstatements

(3) Projected misstatements

It is important for the auditor to consider the type of misstatement as the nature of an identified misstatement will have a significant impact on the auditor's evaluation of the misstatement and any consequent further actions necessary in response.

When the auditor discovers a factual misstatement, where there can be no doubt over the error, there is little room for discussion with management. Once a factual misstatement, such as a miscalculation of depreciation, has been established, management should be asked to correct it.

With regard to judgemental misstatements, the validity of the auditor's opinion and any consequent corrections recommended by the auditor are more open to debate. It is therefore vital that in such matters the auditor compiles sufficient evidence to justify why they believe management's judgement is inappropriate in a specific circumstance. Without this weight of evidence to support their position, it is unlikely that management will accept the auditor's view. Even with sufficient evidence, management may still disagree with the auditor's opinion and refuse to accept their judgement in a specific matter. This heightens the risk that the auditor makes an inappropriate conclusion and, ultimately, that they issue an incorrect auditor's report. If material matters of this nature are identified, it is vital that they are considered by a suitably senior member of the audit team.

Projected misstatements assume that an error identified in a sample may be repeated throughout the whole population. The smaller the size of the population originally tested, the lower the validity of this assumption. Clearly the auditor should not recommend the correction of a projected misstatement. These should be used by the audit team to determine the potential for a material misstatement in the wider population being tested and this should guide their decisions as to whether they need to extend their testing.

(b) (1) **Depreciation charge**

Matters

The error identified in the sample represents less than 0.001% of total assets and less than 0.02% of profits. In isolation the error is therefore immaterial.

The error is, however, limited to the sample audited, which represents only 3.6% of total vehicles. If the error is extrapolated to the whole population, it could potentially lead to a total error of £9.7million (0.35m/4.5m × 125m). This represents 0.03% of total assets and 0.4% of profits; and it would seem that the potential error is therefore also not material to the financial statements. The auditor should ensure that they understand how the error has occurred and if the error is isolated, for example, to a certain category of asset, as there is scope for the error to be greater depending on how the miscalculation has occurred.

Regardless of the immateriality of the projected misstatement, there is still a factual, known error in the financial statements. Management should be asked to correct the error in relation to the depreciation of newly acquired assets.

Management should be requested to make the corrected non-current asset register available to the audit team so that they are able to audit the revised register to determine its accuracy.

Furthermore, the auditor should seek evidence that, as well as correcting the error in the financial statements, the relevant system has been corrected to ensure that all new non-current asset purchases are correctly depreciated in the future so that it does not affect subsequent periods.

Opinion

If management refuses to amend the valuation of motor vehicles, then assets and depreciation will both be misstated by an immaterial amount.

As long as the auditor is satisfied that the source of the error has been corrected and this is not an ongoing issue which will affect subsequent periods, the auditor would issue a standard, unmodified audit opinion, stating that the financial statements are fairly presented in all material respects.

(2) **Loan**

Matters

The loan represents a related party transaction as it is between the company and one of its key management personnel.

The value of the loan may be trivial; it certainly is not material to the financial statements by value. Regardless, related party transactions are material by nature. In these circumstances, the directors of the company may be abusing their position and power for their own personal gain and it is likely that the loan is being provided to Mrs Angel on favourable or non-commercial terms.

For this reason, details relating to the loan must be disclosed in the financial statements, including the amount of the loan, who the loan has been made to and the amount outstanding at the end of the year.

The auditor in this circumstance will disagree with the judgement applied by management in their application of IAS 24 *Related Party Transactions* and the auditor should request that the additional disclosures are added to the financial statements.

Opinion

If management refuses to make the recommended adjustments to the financial statements, then the auditor will conclude that the financial statements are materially misstated due to a lack of appropriate disclosure. While the adjustment is material by nature, a lack of disclosure is unlikely to be considered to be pervasive to the financial statements as a whole.

In these circumstances the auditor should issue a qualified opinion, stating that 'except for' the matters identified the financial statements are fairly presented.

(3) **Provision**

A provision for 7% of one month's sales would total £328 million (£56,360m/12 × 7%). Reducing it to 4% would create a provision of £188 million (£56,360m/12 × 4%). As a result of the change in calculation, the amount of the provision would be reduced by £140 million.

As well as reducing the provision recognised on the statement of financial position, the release of the provision would also increase the profit reported by £140 million. At 5.5% of profit and 0.37% of total assets, the adjustment is material to the statement of profit or loss but not to the statement of financial position.

This is clearly a matter of judgement. The change must, however, be reasonable and supported by evidence that it is more appropriate to the circumstances of the business. The audit team has found no evidence to support the change made by management.

The risk associated with this is heightened because the release of provisions is a known earnings management technique and Basking plc has suffered a reduction in profits this year. The auditor must apply professional scepticism in these circumstances and be aware that management may be using this as a device to restore profits to help achieve their annual targets.

In these circumstances, it would be appropriate to ask the management team of Basking plc for some form of evidence that the change to their system will lead to a lower rate of refunds. In the absence of any evidence the auditor should explain that the change is purely speculative and, as it appears to be unjustified at the present time, that Basking plc should revert back to the original provision until there is evidence of improved effectiveness.

Opinion

If management refuses to amend the provision, it is likely that the auditor will conclude that the financial statements are materially misstated. In isolation it is unlikely that the auditor will conclude that this is a pervasive matter as it has limited impact on the financial statements as a whole.

In these circumstances the auditor should issue a qualified opinion, stating that 'except for' the matters identified the financial statements are fairly presented.

61 Hopper

Workbook references

Chapters 4, 9, 10 and 11.

Top tips

Part (a) required you to criticise an extract from an auditor's report. The way this question is set out might give you the impression that you're only supposed to be criticising the drafting of the report, not the judgements made by the auditor. If you did think this, then notice that there are quite a lot of marks available for eg discussing the actual opinion expressed.

You could think of this question as being about two things: (i) what the auditor has done in response to the issue (in this case, express an adverse opinion and include an emphasis of matter paragraph), and (ii) how the report has been written and presented.

It is clearly wrong to express an adverse opinion and include an emphasis of matter paragraph in relation to the same issue, so you should spend time saying why this is wrong and what the auditor should have done instead, ie made a judgement based on the materiality and the pervasiveness of the issue, and then either done nothing, qualified the opinion, or issued an adverse opinion.

The report is vague and waffly, so marks were available for pointing out where it should have been tightened up. Auditor's reports should not contain words like 'feel', which in this example is used because the audit senior is not sure of his/her ground. What the auditor needs are firm statements and relevant facts to back them up with.

In part (b), the bottom line is whether the issue is material to the group, and in this case it clearly isn't. There are effectively three marks in the marking scheme for this issue, ie for calculating and stating materiality, and for stating that there is no effect on the group auditor's report. That's 50% of the marks for this part of the question!

Other than that, you really just have to discuss the need for the group auditor to understand the issue by communicating both with the component auditor and with the entity. This is quite a difficult question in a way, because there is not that much more to say!

In part (c) you needed to discuss the quality management procedures. This hinged on realising both that this was a listed company (line two of the scenario) and that listed company audits must have engagement quality reviews. Even if you didn't know this you probably could have guessed, as an engagement quality review is your go-to quality management technique for these kinds of question.

Easy marks

The marks for calculating materiality in part (b).

ACCA examining team's comments

This question examined audit reporting, group audits and quality reviews. Candidates were required to critically appraise a draft audit report. This approach to an audit report question has been seen many times in the past and answers were generally good in this area. A minority of candidates, however, incorrectly spent time discussing the accounting treatment for contingent liabilities rather than contingent consideration in an acquisition context. This often led to the conclusion that there was no requirement to qualify the audit opinion therefore the shortcomings of the report were overlooked.

The second part of this question examined the impact of a qualification in a subsidiary audit report on the group audit report. In this case, stronger candidates identified that the limitation in scope as described in the question was immaterial and was unlikely to have an impact on the group audit report in isolation. Weaker candidates spent time considering the assessment of extent of reliance on component auditors or suggested that the error be corrected in the group financial statements reflecting inattention to the scenario which was clear that lack of evidence was the issue rather than an error to be adjusted. A significant proportion of candidates still propose adding other matter or emphasis of matter paragraphs into the audit report to draw attention to immaterial items that need not be disclosed.

Finally candidates were asked to describe quality management procedures which would be required for this listed client prior to the audit report being issued. This was particularly poorly answered with many candidates listing either general characteristics of quality management across the audit cycle or describing the general completion process tasks such as analytical review and disclosure check lists. The requirement to focus on the quality review required for listed clients and in particular this client, with a modified audit report was often missed or only mentioned briefly as perform a "hot" review. Some candidates suggested a cold review which would be performed after not prior to the issuance of the audit report.

Marking guide

Marks

(a) **Critical appraisal of auditor's report**

Generally up to 1.5 marks for each relevant point of appraisal:

- Heading of 'basis for paragraph' (1 max)
- Vagueness of description of subsidiary
- Quantification of contingent consideration
- Identification of note in financial statements
- Vagueness in relation to correct accounting treatment
- Quantification of the effects on the financial statements
- Vague reference to 'relevant accounting standard' (1 max)
- Opinion paragraph heading and positioning (1 max)
- Reference to materiality
- Pervasiveness of the matter

Marking guide	Marks
• Appropriate opinion qualified or unmodified	
• Use of emphasis of matter paragraph	
	10
(b) **Audit of component**	
Generally up to 1 mark for each action and each implication for the Hopper Group explained:	
• Consideration of significance to group	
• Discuss matter with component auditor	
• Discuss matter with management of Seurat Sweeteners Ltd or the Hopper Group	
• Sufficiency of audit evidence	
• Calculation of materiality	
• Materiality to the Hopper Group	
• No modification to the Hopper Group auditor's report	
• Potential communication to those charged with governance	
	6
(c) **Quality management procedures**	
Up to 1 mark for each procedure explained:	
• Appointment of reviewer for listed entities	
• Discuss lack of evidence in subsidiary	
• Discuss contingent consideration including review of working papers	
• Review draft auditor's report wording	
• Review of working papers to support judgements in opinion	
• Signing/dating of report after review complete	
	4
Professional marks	
Analysis and evaluation	
• Appropriate use of the information to support discussion, draw appropriate conclusions and design appropriate responses	
• Identification of omissions from the analysis or further analysis which could be carried out	
• Balanced assessment of the information to determine the effects on the auditor's report in the circumstances	
Professional scepticism and judgement	
• Effective challenge of information, evidence and assumptions supplied and, techniques carried out to support key facts and/or decisions	
• Appropriate application of professional judgement to draw conclusions and make informed decisions about the actions which are appropriate in the context and stage of the engagement.	
Maximum	5
Total	25

(a) **Critical appraisal of the draft auditor's report**

Type of opinion

When an auditor issues an opinion expressing that the financial statements 'do not give a true and fair view', this represents an adverse opinion. The paragraph explaining the modification should, therefore, be titled 'Basis for Adverse Opinion' rather than simply 'Basis for Modified Opinion'.

An adverse opinion means that the auditor considers the misstatement to be material and pervasive to the financial statements of the Hopper Group. According to ISA (UK) 705 *Modifications to Opinions in the Independent Auditor's Report*, pervasive matters are those which affect a substantial proportion of the financial statements or fundamentally affect the users' understanding of the financial statements. It is unlikely that the failure to recognise contingent consideration is pervasive; the main effect would be to understate goodwill and liabilities. This would not be considered a substantial proportion of the financial statements, neither would it be fundamental to understanding the Hopper Group's performance and position.

However, there is also some uncertainty as to whether the matter is even material. If the matter is determined to be material but not pervasive, then a qualified opinion would be appropriate on the basis of a material misstatement. If the matter is not material, then no modification would be necessary to the audit opinion.

Wording of opinion/report

The auditor's reference to 'the acquisition of the new subsidiary' is too vague; the Hopper Group may have purchased a number of subsidiaries which this phrase could relate to. It is important that the auditor provides adequate description of the event and in these circumstances, it would be appropriate to name the subsidiary referred to.

The auditor has not quantified the amount of the contingent element of the consideration. For the users to understand the potential implications of any necessary adjustments, they need to know how much the contingent consideration will be if it becomes payable. It is a requirement of ISA (UK) 705 that the auditor quantifies the financial effects of any misstatements, unless it is impracticable to do so.

In addition, the auditor should provide more description of the financial effects of the misstatement, including full quantification of the effect of the required adjustment to the assets, liabilities, incomes, revenues and equity of the Hopper Group.

The auditor should identify the note to the financial statements relevant to the contingent liability disclosure rather than just stating 'in the note'. This will improve the understandability and usefulness of the contents of the auditor's report.

The use of the term 'we do not feel that the treatment is correct' is too vague and not professional. While there may be some interpretation necessary when trying to apply financial reporting standards to unique circumstances, the expression used is ambiguous and may be interpreted as some form of disclaimer by the auditor with regard to the correct accounting treatment.

The auditor should clearly explain how the treatment applied in the financial statements has departed from the requirements of the relevant standard.

> **Tutorial note.** As an illustration to the above point, an appropriate wording would be: 'Management has not recognised the acquisition-date fair value of contingent consideration as part of the consideration transferred in exchange for the acquiree, which constitutes a departure from International Financial Reporting Standards.'

The ambiguity is compounded by the use of the phrase 'if this is the case, it would be appropriate to adjust the financial statements'. This once again suggests that the correct treatment is uncertain and perhaps open to interpretation.

If the auditor wishes to refer to a specific accounting standard, they should refer to its full title. Therefore instead of referring to 'the relevant standard' they should refer to IFRS 3 *Business Combinations*.

The opinion paragraph requires an appropriate heading. In this case the auditors have issued an adverse opinion and the paragraph should be headed 'Adverse Opinion'. The 'Averse opinion' paragraph should be placed before the 'Basis for adverse opinion' paragraph.

As with the basis paragraph, the opinion paragraph lacks authority; suggesting that the required adjustments 'may' materially affect the financial statements implies that there is a degree of uncertainty. This is not the case; the amount of the contingent consideration will be disclosed in the relevant purchase agreement, so the auditor should be able to determine whether the required adjustments are material or not. Regardless, the sentence discussing whether the balance is material or not is not required in the auditor's report as to warrant inclusion in the report the matter must be considered material. The disclosure of the nature and financial effect of the misstatement in the basis paragraph is sufficient.

Finally, the emphasis of matter paragraph should not be included in the auditor's report. According to ISA (UK) 706 *Emphasis of Matter Paragraphs and Other Matter Paragraphs in the Independent Auditor's Report*, an emphasis of matter paragraph is only used to draw attention to an uncertainty/matter of fundamental importance which is correctly accounted for and disclosed in the financial statements. An emphasis of matter is not required in this case for the following reasons:

- Emphasis of matter is only required to highlight matters which the auditor believes are fundamental to the users' understanding of the business. An example may be where a contingent liability exists which is so significant it could lead to the closure of the reporting entity (but without giving rise to a significant doubt over going concern, which would be dealt with differently). That is not the case with the Hopper Group; the contingent liability does not appear to be fundamental.
- Emphasis of matter is only used for matters where the auditor has obtained sufficient appropriate evidence that the matter is not materially misstated in the financial statements. If the financial statements are materially misstated, in this regard the matter would be fully disclosed by the auditor in the basis for qualified/adverse opinion paragraph and no emphasis of matter is necessary.

Tutorial note. Credit will be awarded where candidates refer to relevant FRC pronouncements in relation to auditor's reports, such as the latest Bulletin containing illustrative auditor's reports.

(b) **Communication from the component auditor**

The qualified opinion due to insufficient evidence may be a significant matter for the Hopper Group audit. While the possible adjustments relating to the current year may not be material to the Hopper Group, the inability to obtain sufficient appropriate evidence with regard to a material matter in Seurat Sweeteners Ltd's financial statements may indicate a control deficiency which the auditor was not aware of at the planning stage and it could indicate potential problems with regard to the integrity of management, which could also indicate a potential fraud. It could also indicate an unwillingness of management to provide information, which could create problems for future audits, particularly if research and development costs increase in future years. If the Group auditor suspects that any of these possibilities are true, they may need to reconsider their risk assessment and whether the audit procedures performed are still appropriate.

If the detail provided in the communication from the component auditor is insufficient, the Group auditor should first discuss the matter with the component auditor to see whether any further information can be provided. The Group auditor can request further working papers from the component auditor if this is necessary. However, if Seurat Sweeteners Ltd has not been able to provide sufficient appropriate evidence, it is unlikely that this will be effective.

If the discussions with the component auditor do not provide satisfactory responses to evaluate the potential impact on the Hopper Group, the Group auditor may need to communicate with either the management of Seurat Sweeteners Ltd or the Hopper Group to obtain necessary clarification with regard to the matter.

Following these procedures, the Group auditor needs to determine whether they have sufficient appropriate evidence to draw reasonable conclusions on the Hopper Group's financial statements. If they believe the lack of information presents a risk of material misstatement in the group financial statements, they can request that further audit procedures be performed, either by the component auditor or by themselves.

Ultimately the Group audit engagement partner has to evaluate the effect of the inability to obtain sufficient appropriate evidence on the audit opinion of the Hopper Group. The matter relates to research expenses totalling £1.2m, which represents 0.2% of the profit for the year and 0.03% of the total assets of the Hopper Group. It is therefore not material to the Hopper Group's financial statements. For this reason no modification to the auditor's report of the Hopper Group would be required as this does not represent a lack of sufficient appropriate evidence with regard to a matter which is material to the Group financial statements.

Although this may not have an impact on the Hopper Group audit opinion, this may be something the Group auditor wishes to bring to the attention of those charged with governance. This would be particularly likely if the Group auditor believed that this could indicate some form of fraud in Seurat Sweeteners Ltd, a serious deficiency in financial reporting controls or if this could create problems for accepting future audits due to management's unwillingness to provide access to accounting records.

A discussion with the Group audit committee, or those charged with governance of the Group would be an appropriate course of action.

(c) **Quality management procedures prior to issuing the auditor's report**

Both ISA (UK) 220 (Revised) *Quality Management for an Audit of Financial Statements* and ISQM (UK) 1 *Quality Management for Firms that Perform Audits or Reviews of Historical Financial Information, or Other Assurance or Related Services Agreements* require that an engagement quality reviewer shall be appointed for audits of financial statements of listed entities where ISQM 2 *Engagement Quality Reviews* should then be followed and the review performed in line with ISQM (UK) 2 *Engagement quality reviews*. The audit engagement partner then discusses significant matters arising during the audit engagement with the engagement quality reviewer.

The engagement quality reviewer and the engagement partner should discuss the failure to recognise the contingent consideration and its impact on the auditor's report. The engagement quality reviewer must review the financial statements and the proposed auditor's report, in particular focusing on the judgements made and conclusions reached in formulating the auditor's report and consideration of whether the proposed auditor's opinion is appropriate. The audit documentation relating to the acquisition of Seurat Sweeteners Ltd will be carefully reviewed, and the reviewer is likely to consider whether procedures performed in relation to these balances were appropriate.

Given the listed status of the Hopper Group, any modification to the auditor's report will be scrutinised, and the firm must be sure of any decision to modify the report, and the type of modification made. Once the engagement quality reviewer has considered the necessity of a modification, they should consider whether a qualified or an adverse opinion is appropriate in the circumstances. This is an important issue, given that it requires judgement as to whether the matters would be material or pervasive to the financial statements.

The engagement quality reviewer should ensure that there is adequate documentation regarding the judgements used in forming the final audit opinion, and that all necessary matters have been brought to the attention of those charged with governance.

The auditor's report must not be signed and dated until the completion of the engagement quality review.

> **Tutorial note.** In the case of the Hopper Group's audit, the lack of evidence in respect of research costs is unlikely to be discussed unless the audit engagement partner believes that the matter could be significant, for example, if they suspected the lack of evidence is being used to cover up a financial statement fraud.

62 Kilmister

> **Workbook references**
>
> Chapters 2, 10 and 11.

Top tips

This question split itself into two discrete parts on different aspects of completion.

Part (a) was a typical requirement to critically appraise a draft auditor's report, in this case one dealing with going concern difficulties. This is an area that has been flagged in recent examining teams' comments, so it is not surprising that it has been tested here.

The question itself should not contain any nasty surprises, but it does require you to have detailed knowledge of the auditor's report. There are marks available for points of detail, such as the order of the paragraphs or the missing reference to an ethical code.

Part (b) tested the report to those charged with governance, sometimes called a 'management letter'. If you were unsure of what this report is, then you may need to revisit your learning materials; it is important that you understand its basic purpose and contents.

Easy marks

are available for pointing out the incorrect paragraph order in part (a).

ACCA examining team's comments

This question was a 25-mark question which focused on completion and reporting and was in two sections.

With requirement (a), the majority of responses were extremely disappointing and generally reflects weak knowledge of auditor reporting requirements. There remain a number of candidates who continue to show a lack of understanding of basic ISA (UK) requirements such as incorrectly suggesting that an unmodified opinion should have 'unmodified' in the title of the opinion or that a material uncertainty related to going concern should be included within an emphasis of matter paragraph.

Many candidates suggested that the use of 'we believe' in the auditor's report is not appropriate wording, or that the use of 'in our opinion' suggests that the auditor is not independent from the client and therefore a familiarity threat is present. This demonstrates a significant lack of understanding of auditor's reports and ISA 700 (UK) *Forming an Opinion and Reporting on Financial Statements*.

Candidates were not expected to discuss what would or would not be present in a full report. Where candidates discussed, for example, 'the signature of the partner is missing' or 'responsibilities of the auditor are missing', this was not relevant to the requirement, which asked candidates to specifically critique the extract as presented. Discussion of given extracts of auditor's reports, again, should follow a structured approach and practising questions of this nature should allow candidates to score strong marks in these requirements.

Requirement (b) required candidates to discuss, along with reasons for discussion, specific matters raised in the scenario which should be reported to those charged with governance. Generally, candidates identified the 'matters to be included' and used an approach of calculating the materiality of the issue, discussing the relevant accounting standard and how the matter had been dealt with incorrectly. However, candidates were vague on why matters should be included within a report to those charged with governance and continued to answer the question as if it were asking about the impact on the audit opinion. This demonstrates a lack of understanding of the question requirement by a number of candidates.

Marking guide | **Marks**

(a) **Kilmister plc Critical appraisal of extract from draft auditor's report**

Up to 1 mark per issue explained.

- Addressee should be shareholders or members only (not directors)
- Incorrect order – opinion paragraph should be before basis for opinion
- Lack of specific reference to ethical code

Material uncertainty re going concern:

- Modification due to material misstatement re absence of disclosure qualified or adverse, depending on auditor's professional judgement re level of impact on financial statements
- Incorrect use of 'material uncertainty regarding going concern' paragraph this paragraph should be used when adequate disclosure has been made by directors in financial statements
- Details of uncertainty re going concerns should be given in basis for qualified/adverse opinion paragraph

Long-term contracts:

- Incorrect use of 'other information' paragraph should be used to describe auditor's responsibilities for 'other information' (eg rest of the annual report, including management report) and outcome of fulfilling those responsibilities
- Issue is area of significant auditor judgement which should be considered for inclusion as KAM which, as a listed company, Kilmister plc should disclose in separate KAM section of audit report
- KAM section should include explanation of what is a KAM
- KAM section should explain why matter is considered to be KAM
- KAM section should also explain how KAM was addressed by audit process

8

(b) **Taylor plc Report to those charged with governance**

Generally up to 1 mark for each matter identified and explained.

Revaluation of property portfolio

- Significant findings from audit should be reported to TCWG
- These include significant changes in accounting policy and material misstatements
- Revaluation of PPE should be consistent across a class of assets (IAS 16), four properties still carried at depreciated historic cost
- Four properties are material to SOFP (2.1% assets)
- Significant findings from audit also include significant difficulties encountered during audit such as information delays
- Delay makes audit less efficient and may result in increase in audit fee

Renovation of car parking facilities

- Taylor plc has derived economic benefits from expenditure, should be capitalised
- Material to SOFP (2.5% of assets)
- Incorrect application of IAS 16 and potential material misstatement should be included in report to TCWG as significant finding from audit
- Lack of authorisation indicates lack of management oversight and serious weakness in control which could allow fraud to occur
- Lack of integrity shown by management going ahead with renovation works without the necessary permission is example of management override and could be tone set throughout organisation
- Therefore this is a high-risk matter and they may wish to implement controls and procedures to prevent further breaches
- Report to TCWG should include recommendations to management to reduce business risk

Long association of audit partner

- Long association creates familiarity and self-interest threatsMatters to be communicated to TCWG include ethical issues in relation to auditor independence
- Audit partner in listed entity should be rotated at least every five years per FRC *Ethical Standard*
- FRC *Ethical Standard* does, however, allow for an additional two years if required, to safeguard audit quality
- Safeguards should be applied including independent internal or external review of engagement (as per scenario) -

12

Professional marks

Analysis and evaluation

- Appropriate use of the information to support discussion, draw appropriate conclusions and design appropriate responses
- Identification of the matters that should be communicated with those charged with the governance of Taylor
- Balanced assessment of the information to determine the appropriate audit opinion in the circumstances

Professional scepticism and judgement

- Effective challenge of information, evidence and assumptions supplied and, techniques carried out to support key facts and/or decisions
- Appropriate application of professional judgement to draw conclusions and make informed decisions about the actions which are appropriate in the context and stage of the engagement

Maximum	5
Total	25

(a) **Kilmister plc Critical appraisal of extract from draft auditor's report**

Presentation and structure of auditor's report extract

The structure and format of the auditor's report is prescribed by ISA (UK) 700 *Forming an Opinion and Reporting on Financial Statements*. In the UK, for entities incorporated under the Companies Act, the auditor is required to report to the company's members because the audit is undertaken on their behalf. Such auditor's reports are, therefore, typically addressed to either the members or the shareholders of the company. The title should not include any reference to the directors of Kilmister plc. In addition, the first two paragraphs are presented in the incorrect order, the opinion paragraph should precede the basis for opinion paragraph.

Reference to ethical code

ISA (UK) 700 requires that in the Basis for Opinion paragraph, the auditor should identify the relevant ethical requirements, naming the FRC *Ethical Standard* or IESBA *International Code of Ethics for Professional Accountants*. The draft auditor's report does not specifically refer to the ethical code which has been applied during the audit and is therefore not in compliance with the requirements of ISA (UK) 700.

Material uncertainty regarding going concern

ISA (UK) 570 *Going Concern* provides guidance on how an auditor should report uncertainties regarding going concern in the auditor's report. According to ISA (UK) 570, if adequate disclosure about the material uncertainty is not made in the financial statements, the auditor should express a qualified opinion or adverse opinion as appropriate.

The use of a 'material uncertainty regarding going concern' paragraph in the draft auditor's report extract is therefore incorrect. This paragraph should only be used when adequate disclosure has been made by the directors in the financial statements and would include a cross reference to this disclosure. Given that this disclosure has not been made, this is therefore not appropriate in this case.

In this case, therefore, the absence of any disclosure in the financial statements in relation to the uncertainties regarding going concern is grounds for a modification of the auditor's opinion. The modification is due to a material misstatement in relation to the absence of this key disclosure. If, in the auditor's professional judgement, the impact of this non-disclosure on the financial statements is material but not pervasive, a qualified opinion should be issued. In this case, the opinion paragraph should be headed 'qualified opinion' and this should be followed immediately by a 'basis for qualified opinion' paragraph. If, on the other hand, the auditor believes that the impact on the financial statements of the non-disclosure is both material and pervasive, an adverse opinion should be given. The opinion paragraph should then be headed 'adverse opinion' and should be followed immediately by a 'basis for adverse opinion' paragraph.

In addition, details of the uncertainty regarding going concern should be given in the basis for qualified or adverse opinion paragraph.

Long-term contracts

The use of the 'other information' section in this context is inappropriate. This section should be used to describe the auditor's responsibilities for 'other information' (eg the rest of the annual report, including the management report) and the outcome of fulfilling those responsibilities.

The disclosure regarding long-term contracts is more in line with the requirements of ISA (UK) 701 *Communicating Key Audit Matters in the Independent Auditor's Report*, where key audit matters are those which in the auditor's professional judgement were of most significance to the audit. In determining which matters to report, the auditor should take into account areas of significant auditor attention in performing the audit, including:

- Areas of higher assessed risk of material misstatement, or significant risks identified in accordance with ISA (UK) 315 (Revised) *Identifying and Assessing the Risks of Material Misstatement*.
- Significant auditor judgements relating to areas in the financial statements which involved significant management judgement, including accounting estimates which have been identified as having high estimation uncertainty.
- The effect on the audit of significant events or transactions which occurred during the period.

The extract from the draft auditor's report states that significant judgement is applied in assessing the percentage of completeness of material long-term contracts and that this percentage is then applied in calculating the revenue for the year. This is a matter of high risk requiring significant auditor attention and given that Kilmister plc is a listed entity, it would be appropriate for this to be disclosed in the KAM section of the auditor's report. The KAM section of the auditor's report should begin with an introductory paragraph explaining what a KAM is. The KAM section should then explain why this matter is considered to be a KAM due to the significant judgement involved in assessing the percentage completeness of the long-term contracts and the high risk of material misstatement associated with this judgement process. The KAM section should also include an explanation of how the KAM was addressed by the audit process and was influenced by the auditor's application of materiality. In this case, this might include, for example, an evaluation of the controls designed and implemented by Kilmister plc to monitor the progress of and the amounts owing on service and construction contracts; a review of the financial performance of key contracts against budgets and historical trends; and challenging management's estimates and judgements in respect of the progress to date on the contracts.

(b) **Taylor plc Report to those charged with governance**

A report to those charged with governance is produced to communicate matters relating to the external audit to those who are ultimately responsible for the financial statements. ISA (UK) 260 *Communication With Those Charged With Governance* requires the auditor to communicate many matters including independence and other ethical issues and the significant findings from the audit. In the case of Taylor plc, the matters to be communicated would include the following:

Revaluation of property portfolio

According to ISA (UK) 260, the significant findings from the audit include the auditor's views about significant qualitative aspects of the entity's accounting practices including accounting policies and any circumstances which affect the form and content of the auditor's report. In the case of Taylor plc, therefore, the significant findings from the audit would relate to the changes in the accounting policy in relation to the revaluation of property and related material misstatements and the following matters should be communicated:

IAS 16 *Property, Plant and Equipment* states the revaluation policy should be consistent across a class of assets. However, four properties, which are material to the statement of financial position at 2.1% of total assets, are still carried at depreciated historic cost. This therefore represents a breach of IAS 16 and a material misstatement, which will impact on the form and content of the auditor's report.

According to ISA (UK) 260, the significant findings from the audit also include significant difficulties encountered during the audit such as information delays. The independent external valuation reports requested by Eddie & Co at the planning stage were not available when requested by the auditor and it took three weeks before they were received by the audit team. The auditor should report this delay to those charged with governance, detailing its impact on the efficiency of the audit process together with any resulting increase in the audit fee.

Renovation of car parking facilities

The renovation expenditure on the car parking facilities at Taylor plc's properties should be recognised as an asset according to IAS 16 if it is probable that future economic benefits associated with the item will flow to the entity and the cost of the item can be measured reliably. In Taylor plc's case, the cost has been quantified as £13.2 million and it has already derived economic benefits in the form of a significant increase in customer numbers and revenue at each of these locations. The expenditure should therefore be capitalised and its inclusion in operating expenses is not in compliance with IAS 16. The amount of £13.2 million is also material to the statement of financial position at 2.5% of total assets. The incorrect application of IAS 16 and the material misstatement should be included in the report to those charged with governance as a significant finding from the audit which will impact on the form and content of the auditor's report.

ISA (UK) 265 *Communicating Deficiencies in Internal Control to Those Charged With Governance and Management* requires the auditor to communicate appropriately to those charged with governance deficiencies in internal control which the auditor has identified during the audit and which, in the auditor's professional judgement, are of sufficient importance to merit their respective attentions. The audit working papers include minutes of discussions with management which confirm that authorisation had not been gained for this expenditure. The lack of authorisation indicates a lack of management oversight and a serious weakness in control which could allow fraud to occur. Furthermore, the lack of integrity shown by management in going ahead with the renovation works without the necessary permission is an example of management override and could be indicative of the tone set throughout the organisation. This therefore represents a high-risk matter and they may wish to implement controls and procedures to prevent further breaches. The report to those charged with governance should include full details on this significant deficiency in internal control and should include recommendations to management in order to reduce the associated business risk.

Long association of audit partner

ISA (UK) 260 requires that for audits of financial statements of public interest entities, the auditor shall:

- Confirm annually in writing to the audit committee that the firm and partners, senior managers and managers conducting the audit are independent from the audited entity; and

- Discuss with the audit committee the threats to the auditor's independence and the safeguards applied to mitigate those threats.

Part of the communication on auditor independence must include a discussion relating to the audit engagement partner. Bryony Robertson has acted as audit engagement partner for Taylor plc for six consecutive years.

According to the FRC *Ethical Standard*, her long association with the audit client creates both familiarity and self-interest threats to auditor independence. The familiarity threat arises due to the long and potentially close relationship which she has with the staff of Taylor plc leading to her being too sympathetic to their interests or too accepting of their work. This in turn gives rise to a self-interest threat in that her long association and close relationship with the client create a personal interest which may inappropriately influence her professional judgement or behaviour.

In order to address these risks, the FRC *Ethical Standard* requires that an audit partner in a listed entity should be rotated every five years and therefore her six-year tenure as the audit partner of Taylor plc appears to be in clear breach of this provision. However, the FRC *Ethical Standard* does allow for an engagement partner to serve for an additional two years if the client's audit committee decides that a degree of flexibility over the timing of rotation is necessary to safeguard the quality of the audit. This could arise where the audit firm has no other partners with the necessary knowledge and experience who are able to take over as engagement partner, in this case due to the illness of Phillip Campbell. In these circumstances, safeguards should be applied such as the independent review of the engagement which is being performed.

63 Chester & Co

Workbook reference

Chapters 2, 5 and 11.

Top tips

Your approach to ethics questions such as this should be to work through the scenario with pen in hand, noting the threats as you go. It is important that you try to identify the threats to independence, taking care not to just list the threats that you think might be present. You then need to say why such a threat is present and suggest safeguards to reduce the threat to an appropriate level. It is a good idea to try to evaluate the seriousness of the threat, and to give a conclusion to each mini scenario, such as 'if these safeguards cannot be implemented then the auditor must decline to tender for this engagement'.

Practical professional and commercial considerations usually score well. The most straightforward example of this being that the audit firm should consider which of either the non-audit services or the audit will be most profitable for it to continue with.

Be very wary about writing about the risk of % fee thresholds being breached, as the examining team considers these to be general points that indicate a lack of application to the scenario at hand. It is not relevant to any of the mini scenarios in this question, for example, and you should only mention it in an answer if the scenario specifically hints that this might be problem.

The first requirement in part (c) was a normal AAA reporting requirement, while the second might have confused you as there was nothing wrong as such – except for the absence of an Emphasis of Matter paragraph. This might have led you to try to criticise the statement in the scenario that going concern was not an issue. With a question such as this, it is important to learn to distinguish between when the examining team is trying to tell you not to write about something (as here), and when a statement is there in the scenario for you to criticise it.

Easy marks

Easy marks were available for calculating materiality in part (c), as in almost all auditor reporting questions.

ACCA examining team's comments

In parts (a) and (b), two short scenarios were provided, describing a range of situations giving rise to ethical threats and other issues, with the requirement to identify and discuss the ethical and other professional issues raised, and to recommend any actions to be taken by the audit firm for each of the scenarios given. This is a fairly standard type of question for AAA, and many candidates performed well, obviously having practised some past exam questions.

Requirement (a) described a potential new audit client, a small owner-managed company providing financial services. There were several issues that candidates should have spotted in the scenario including a potential lack of integrity of the company's managing director, potential self-interest and self-review threats arising from the provision of non-audit services, threats arising from non-compliance with the regulatory body, and a potential for audit pre-conditions not to be met. The majority of candidates picked up on most of these issues and explained the ethical threats well. There has been a definite improvement in the way that candidates tackle this type of question, and in many cases close to the maximum marks were awarded.

Requirement (b) outlined the situation of an existing client facing going concern problems. The audit engagement partner had been asked to accompany the managing director to a meeting with the bank where additional finance would be sought, and there were intimidation threats in that the client had threatened to put the audit out for tender, and there were also outstanding fees. Again, candidates generally did well on this requirement, identifying and explaining the correct ethical threats, and on the whole recommending appropriate courses of action. The only problem in some scripts was a focus on the lack of integrity of the managing director, rather than discussing specific ethical threats raised.

Part (c) of the question described two issues and candidates were required to discuss the implications for the auditor's report. Unfortunately many candidates deviated from the requirement and spent time discussing the accounting treatment and audit procedures for an area where there was a limitation on the scope the audit. Candidates also lost time discussing audit procedures on going concern, which was flagged as already satisfactorily covered. The understanding of auditor's reports and their usage continues to be a weak area for many candidates despite it being a core part of the syllabus.

Marking guide **Marks**

(a) Generally 1 mark for each point identified and discussed:

Tetbury Ltd

- Customer due diligence/know your client procedures to be performed
- Audit firm's competence to audit a financial services client
- Acceptance decision should also include consideration of ethical threats
- Management integrity threatened by past investigation by financial services authority
- Integrity also threatened by possible inappropriate financial reporting
- Management may have intimidated the previous auditor
- Contact previous auditor for further information
- Controls appear weak leading to high audit risk
- Responses to high risk should be considered, eg use of experienced audit team
- Confirm client's intention to improve controls
- Threats to objectivity arise from giving business advice – perceived as assuming management responsibility
- Self-review and self-interest threats created
- Management threat created by giving business advice

ANSWERS

Marking guide	Marks
• Safeguards to be put in place, eg management acknowledge responsibility for business decisions	-
	7
(b) Generally 1 mark for each point identified and discussed:	
Stratford Ltd	
• Advocacy threat created by attending meeting	
• Management threat exists	
• Legal proximity may be created by attending meeting	
• Intimidation threat from threat of removal from office	
• Consider appropriate safeguards	
• Integrity of the managing director questionable	
• Overdue fees may represent self-interest threat	
• But amount may be insignificant and not long overdue	
• Audit engagement partner should discuss matter with ethics partner	
• Advocacy threat created by attending meeting	-
	5
(c) **Implications for the auditor's report and further actions**	
In general up to 1 mark for each well explained point and action point recommended:	
Military research	
• Expenses are material (must include relevant calculation)	
• Management imposed limitation on scope	
• Auditor should request that management removes the limitation	
• Communication of potential impact to those charged with governance	
• Impact on continuation of audit engagement	
• If limitation is not removed, audit opinion will be modified	
• Matter is material but, currently, not pervasive; qualified opinion	
• Basis for qualified opinion paragraph	
Fire	
• No modification of the audit opinion necessary	
• The major catastrophe will have a significant impact on results and make their interpretation difficult	
• Disclosures by management are of fundamental importance to users	
• Emphasis of matter paragraph required	-
	8

Professional marks

Analysis and evaluation

- Appropriate assessment of the ethical and professional issues raised, using examples where relevant to support overall comments
- Effective appraisal of the information to make suitable recommendations for appropriate courses of action
- Balanced assessment of the information to determine the appropriate audit opinion in each situation

Marking guide	Marks
Professional scepticism and judgement	
• Effective challenge of information, evidence and assumptions supplied and, techniques carried out to support key facts and/or decisions	
• Appropriate application of professional judgement to draw conclusions and make informed decisions about the actions which are appropriate in the context and stage of the engagement.	
Maximum	5
Total	25

(a) **Tetbury Ltd**

Professional competence

Tetbury operates in the highly regulated, complex environment of financial services. There is therefore a threat to Chester & Co's ability to conduct an audit in this area in line with the principle of professional competence and due care. This is a self-interest threat as a result of the prospective audit fee.

Customer due diligence

Given the complex and therefore risky nature of Tetbury's business environment, it is of paramount importance that Chester & Co conducts customer due diligence procedures before accepting such a client. The risk of Tetbury being involved in laundering money should be assessed carefully.

Previous auditors

The fact that the previous auditors resigned suggests that Tetbury's management may lack integrity. There is a risk that the problems which led to the previous auditors resigning may persist during the tenure of Chester & Co.

Chester & Co should ask Tetbury for permission to contact the previous auditors regarding the reasons for their resignation. They should be asked whether there are any matters of which Chester & Co should be made aware of in deciding whether to take on the audit. This is a self-interest threat to professional competence and due care, because Chester & Co may fail to exercise due care in order to secure the audit fee.

If Tetbury refuses permission to contact the previous auditors, then Chester & Co should withdraw from the tender process.

Controls

The fact that the reason given for the previous auditors' resignation points to a poor control environment at Tetbury. This is particularly worrisome given that it is an owner-managed business, in which the risk of management override of controls is perennially present. Bearing in mind also the increased need for robust internal controls in as highly-regulated an area as financial services, the Tetbury audit would surely be considered high-risk.

As a high-risk audit, Chester & Co would likely need to perform more audit procedures in order to reduce audit risk to an appropriate level. This would be costly and would need to be reflected in a high audit fee. The threat to Chester & Co's professional competence is in this light particularly acute. Chester & Co would need to consider carefully whether the Tetbury audit would be worth such a high risk.

Financial Conduct Authority investigation

The investigation suggests either a lack of integrity or a poor control environment, or both. In any event Chester & Co ought to find out more about this, for example by contacting the authority for further details.

Business development advice

There is a self-interest threat here in relation to the fee – if, for example, the total fee income from Tetbury is expected to represent a high proportion of Chester & Co's income. There may also be a self-review threat as it is possible that the advice may need to be audited, for example as part of the assessment of the going concern assumption.

The self-review threat can be mitigated by using separate engagement teams, separated by information barriers, or by an independent review of the audit work by a professional accountant.

It is important that Chester & Co avoids taking on management responsibilities, because were they to do so the tender must be declined as a result of what the FRC's *Ethical Standard* (FRC ES) describes as a management threat (in Part B5 *Non-audit Services Provided to Audited Entities*). Chester & Co must consider whether management is capable of making independent judgements and decisions on the basis of information provided. The threat can be avoided by obtaining written confirmation from Tetbury that it acknowledges responsibility for any decisions taken.

> **Tutorial note.** As Tetbury operates in the financial services industry, it is possible that it could be considered as a public interest entity. It was not considered to be one by the ACCA when this question was set, but it would not be unreasonable to think Tetbury a public interest entity and thus make business development advice ethically unacceptable.

(b) **Stratford Ltd**

Meeting

The request to attend the meeting with the bank suggests an advocacy threat, as the audit partner may be put in the position of supporting the view that the client will continue as a going concern, and that the bank should therefore offer it a loan.

There is also a management threat (FRC ES) if Chester & Co finds itself making judgements and decisions which are really management's responsibility.

Legally, there is a risk of creating proximity between Chester & Co and Stratford which could result in the bank taking legal action against the auditor in the event of Stratford defaulting on its loan.

In addition, the financial statements being presented at the meeting are only draft versions and have not been audited. It is crucial that Chester & Co does not allow Stratford to give the bank the impression that these financial statements come with any assurance.

It would probably not be possible to mitigate the advocacy threat with the audit engagement partner attending the meeting. It may be possible for another partner to attend, however, if it was made clear that they were not the audit partner and that no assurance was provided in respect of the draft financial statements.

Threat

The managing director's threat to put the audit out to tender is an intimidation threat. The managing director's overbearing behaviour, exploiting the audit firm's fear of losing the audit engagement, risks compromising the objectivity of the audit partner and the rest of the audit team.

This places a question mark over the managing director's integrity. Chester & Co should communicate with those charged with governance on this matter, for example with any other board members or with the audit committee. Chester & Co should consider resigning from the audit if the threat does not abate.

Fees

Overdue fees represent a self-interest threat per the IESBA *Code of Ethics* and the FRC ES (Part B4 *Fees, remuneration and evaluation policies, litigation, gifts and hospitality*), as the desire to recover the overdue fees may cause the auditors to issue an inappropriate audit opinion. There is also a risk that this may be perceived to be a loan made to Stratford.

In this case the fee relates to a debt that is likely to be only four months old, which reduces the seriousness of the problem. The severity of the threat would depend on the significance of the amount outstanding.

There is a risk that Stratford may not be able to pay the fees as a result of its problems with going concern. The FRC ES notes that the engagement partner should consider whether the resulting self-interest threat is outweighed by the benefit to the public of continuing to act as auditor to a firm which might find it difficult to find a successor auditor were it to resign.

Chester & Co should request that the audit fee be paid and should communicate the matter to those charged with governance. It may also wish to review the efficacy of its own system for credit control.

(c) **Military research project**

The research expenses represent 10.8% of profit for the year so they are material to the financial statements.

Chester & Co is unable to obtain sufficient appropriate evidence relating to the research expenses. Given the limitation imposed by management, the auditor will be unable to form a conclusion about the occurrence, completeness, accuracy or classification of the associated expenses.

ISA (UK) 705 *Modifications to the Opinion in the Independent Auditor's Report* requires that when management imposes a limitation on the scope of the audit, the auditor should request that they remove the limitation. If management refuses, the auditor should communicate the matter to those charged with governance, explaining the implications of the matter and the impact on this year's audit opinion. In addition, as this is a matter which is likely to arise again in future audits, the auditor should stress that the compound effect of this and the likelihood that there may be development cost implications to consider in the future may give rise to both a material and pervasive matter, which would give rise to a disclaimer of opinion.

As well as the implications on the auditor's report, those charged with governance should be informed that in accordance with ISA (UK) 210 *Agreeing the Terms of Audit Engagements*, the auditor may not be able to accept the audit engagement in the future if management continues to impose the limitation on the scope of the auditor's work and the auditor believes that it may result in them disclaiming their opinion.

In the current year under these circumstances, it will be necessary to issue a modified opinion. Given the claimed value of the expenses, it is likely that the matter will be considered material but not pervasive to the financial statements and a qualified opinion will be issued.

A Basis for Qualified Opinion section should be included immediately after the Auditor's Opinion section, and it should describe the matter giving rise to the modification.

Fire

Audit procedures have confirmed that the matter has been satisfactorily reflected in the financial statements. There are therefore no misstatements relevant to this matter and no modification to the audit opinion is necessary.

However, the accident caused the temporary suspension of operations for a number of months, with a significant impact on the results for the year. Overall, the associated reduction in sales and the expenses relating to the repairs have contributed to a £46 million reduction in profits. This may make interpretation of the current year's results difficult. Crow Ltd is still unable to operate at full capacity, so the matter will continue to affect performance in the following year.

This represents a major catastrophe which has had and continues to have a significant effect on the company's financial position. The disclosures provided by management in relation to this constitute a matter of fundamental importance to users, and they should be referred to in an emphasis of matter paragraph by Chester & Co, as described in ISA (UK) 706 *Emphasis of Matter Paragraphs and Other Matter Paragraphs in the Independent Auditor's Report.*

The auditor should include the paragraph immediately after the 'Basis for opinion' section, with an appropriate heading which includes the term 'emphasis of matter'. It may be appropriate for the paragraph to be entitled 'Emphasis of matter – effects of a fire'. The paragraph should clearly reference the matter being emphasised including a reference to where the full description of the matter may be found in the financial statements. The paragraph should make it clear that the audit opinion is not modified in respect of this matter.

64 Gillan

Workbook references

Chapters 8, 9 and 11.

Top tips

Part (a) required you to criticise a draft auditor's report, which should have been a straightforward requirement for you.

Parts (b) and (c) shifted the focus to another audit client, this time at the review stage, and tested disclosure issues and intra-group transactions, which is an area that the examining team feels has been answered poorly by candidates in recent sittings. This is therefore an examinable area, so if you struggled here then you may need to brush up your knowledge.

Easy marks

The marks for pointing out the inappropriate use of an emphasis of matter paragraph, in the auditor's report in (a), were not difficult to get.

ACCA examining team's comments

The first requirement was to critically appraise an extract from an auditor's report, which had been incorrectly prepared and needed amendment. Good candidates were able to explain when an issue should be included as a key audit matter or if the issue would result in a modification and hence needed to be part of the basis for opinion paragraph. Other candidates correctly commented that it would be inappropriate to include an emphasis of matter paragraph but that the report should include a section headed material uncertainty related to going concern.

The second part of this question was centred on the review of a Group of companies and required candidates to consider the matters outlined and to explain what audit evidence would be required. The first scenario included a foreign subsidiary that used local GAAP rather than IFRS. The subsidiary had forward commodity options with a fair value of £6.1m that had been disclosed at the year end rather than included on the statement of financial position. Stronger candidates were able to recognise that on consolidation, the subsidiary accounts should be aligned with IFRS and the derivatives recognised on the consolidated statement of financial position at fair value with the associated gains or losses being recognised in the consolidated statement of profit or loss. Further credit was then available for considering the evidence required to support the value of the derivatives. A number of weaker candidates disappointingly discussed the need to translate the year-end financial statements of the subsidiary, although the question had specifically stated that the subsidiary had the same functional and presentational currency as the parent.

The final scenario concerned the sale between a subsidiary and parent company that took place near to the year end with the sale recognised by the subsidiary before the year end but the goods not received by the parent until after the year end. This was a straightforward situation and the parent should have recorded the goods in transit in its individual financial statements. The fact that this had not been done indicated that there was a control weakness in the recognition and treatment of intra-group balances. Candidates were able to earn marks for discussing the need to eliminate intra group balances on consolidation and for obtaining evidence such as sales invoices, goods despatched notes at the subsidiary and purchase invoices, goods received notes at the parent to confirm dates and amounts. Better candidates were able to discuss the need to confirm the profit element of the transaction and ensure that this was also adjusted for by including a provision for unrealised profit.

Marking guide	Marks

(a) In general up to 1 mark for each well explained point:

KAM section

- KAM section should include introductory paragraph explaining what KAMs are
- Auditor not forming separate opinion on KAM

Customer liquidation

- Material to profit and assets (with calculation)
- Details of material misstatement should not be included in KAM section at all but should be given in basis for qualified opinion paragraph and should be clearly cross referenced to opinion paragraph
- Wording refers to reducing profit before tax when it should refer to increasing the loss before tax

Opinion paragraph

- Incorrectly positioned; should now be at start of auditor's report and should be clearly cross referenced to basis of opinion paragraph below which details the material misstatement
- Incorrect title; it should be headed simply 'Qualified Opinion'
- Qualified opinion appropriate on grounds of material misstatement

Going concern

- Following ISA (UK) 570 (Revised), use of an EoM paragraph no longer appropriate
- Auditor's report should now include section headed 'Material Uncertainty Related to Going Concern'
- Section should be immediately after basis for qualified opinion but before KAM section
- Should cross reference clearly to disclosure note where directors have given details of uncertainty
- If not adequately disclosed by directors, opinion should be a qualified opinion due to lack of disclosure

8

(b) **Willis Ltd**

Generally up to 1.5 marks for each matter and up to 1 mark for each evidence point explained.

Matters

- Materiality
- Group accounting policies should be consistent
- Treatment is acceptable in individual entity financial statements but not for Group accounts
- IFRS 9 requires recognition of derivatives on SOFP at fair value with gains and losses in profit or loss for period
- Fair value of derivatives is material to group profit (with supporting calculation)
- Directors may not have expertise required for valuation of the options
- Need for external independent evidence of fair value at reporting date

Evidence

- Fair value based on market prices or, if not available, independent expert valuation
- Audit documentation of review of derivative contracts and confirmation of terms and maturity dates

- Copy of the adjusting journal required to reflect the correct treatment in the financial statementsNotes of discussion with management in relation to the basis of their valuation and the accounting treatment

Knott Ltd

Generally up to 1.5 marks for each matter and up to 1 mark for each evidence point explained.

Matters

- Materiality
- Consolidated accounts are prepared from group perspective, inter-company transactions and balances must be eliminated on consolidation
- Details of the transactions need to be verified for individual entity financial statements
- Sales value of £77 million is material to group revenue and assets
- Unrealised profit of £7.7 million is material to group profit before tax
- Group receivables, revenue and profit therefore materially overstated
- Goods in transit: group inventory will be understated by £69.3 million (material to group assets)
- Group retained earnings will be overstated by £6.16 million and NCI by £1.54 million

Evidence

- Transaction agreed to underlying documents – sales invoices, goods despatch notes at Knott Ltd and goods received notes, purchase invoices at its parent company
- Cost of inventory confirmed to production records
- Confirmation of goods received note at parent dated 2 May 20X8 confirming details of inventory in transit
- Workings for the unrealised profit in stock calculation
- Sales invoice traced to sales ledger and details of sales value, etc agreed
- Copy of adjusting journal noted on errors schedule

12

Professional marks

Analysis and evaluation

- Appropriate use of the information to support discussion, draw appropriate conclusions and design appropriate responses
- Identification of omissions from the analysis or further analysis which could be carried out
- Balanced assessment of the information to determine the effect on the auditor's report in the circumstances

Professional scepticism and judgement

- Effective challenge of information, evidence and assumptions supplied and, techniques carried out to support key facts and/or decisions, particularly in relation to the extract of an auditor's report
- Appropriate application of professional judgement to draw conclusions and make informed decisions about the actions which are appropriate in the context and stage of the engagement.

Maximum	5
Total	25

(a) There are a number of issues to consider in critically appraising the auditor's report extract which has been drafted by the audit senior. These include the following:

Key audit matters (KAM)

The section should include an introductory paragraph explaining the concept of KAM in order for users of the auditor's report to understand its importance and significance. The introduction should also clearly state that the auditor is not forming a separate opinion on the items identified as KAM.

Customer liquidation

The amount owed by the customer of £287,253 is material to the loss before tax at 13.1% and to assets at 2%. The qualified opinion on the grounds of material misstatement is therefore appropriate. However, the details of the material misstatement should not be included in the KAM section at all but should be given in the basis for qualified opinion paragraph. This should also be clearly cross-referenced within the opinion paragraph itself. Furthermore, the wording of the report currently references reducing the profit before tax when it should refer to increasing the loss before tax.

Opinion paragraph

This is incorrectly positioned and incorrectly titled. It should be at the start of the auditor's report and should simply be titled 'Qualified Opinion'. The opinion paragraph should be clearly cross-referenced to the 'Basis for Qualified Opinion' paragraph which should be placed immediately below the opinion paragraph and should clearly describe the issue which has given rise to the qualified opinion. As above, the qualified opinion on the grounds of materiality is appropriate.

Going concern – Emphasis of matter

Following ISA (UK) 570 *Going Concern*, the use of an emphasis of matter paragraph to refer to uncertainties in relation to going concern disclosures in the financial statements is not appropriate. The auditor's report should now include a specific section headed 'Material Uncertainty Related to Going Concern' immediately after the basis for qualified opinion paragraph and before the KAM section. The material uncertainty related to going concern should be cross-referenced clearly to the disclosure note where the directors have given details of the uncertainty. If the matter has not been adequately disclosed by the directors in the financial statements, the auditor should give full details of the uncertainties in relation to going concern and the audit opinion should be qualified due to the material misstatement in relation to this lack of disclosure.

(b) **Willis Ltd**

Matters

The fair value of the derivatives of £6.1 million is material to consolidated profit before tax at 11.1% but in isolation, it is immaterial to consolidated assets at 0.4%.

IFRS 9 *Financial Instruments* requires the recognition of derivatives on the statement of financial position at fair value with the associated gains and losses being recognised in profit or loss for the period. The fair value of £6.1 million should therefore be included in current assets on the Group's consolidated statement of financial position and given that the options were entered into in the last three months of the period at no initial net investment, a fair value gain of £6.1 million should also be recorded in the Group's consolidated statement of profit or loss for the year. The treatment of the derivatives under local GAAP is acceptable in Willis Ltd's individual entity financial statements. For group purposes, however, accounting policies must be consistent and the profit before tax in the draft consolidated financial statements is materially understated.

The auditor must also exercise professional scepticism with regard to whether the directors have the required expertise to value the derivatives and should consider the need for independent, external evidence of the fair value of the options at the reporting date.

Evidence

- Details of the fair value of the options based on prices derived from an active market or, if this is not available, an independent expert valuation.

- Audit documentation of the review of derivative contracts and confirmation of the terms and maturity dates.
- Notes of a discussion with management in relation to the basis of their valuation and the accounting treatment required in the consolidated financial statements.

Knott Ltd

Matters

Consolidated financial statements are prepared from the group perspective and intra-group transactions and balances must be eliminated on consolidation. The sales value of £77 million is material to consolidated revenue at 1% and to consolidated assets at 4.9%. The unrealised profit of £7.7 million (£77m × 10%) is also material to consolidated profit before tax for the year at 14% (£7.7m/£55m). Group revenue, receivables and profit before tax are therefore materially overstated. The transactions should be verified in the accounting records of the individual entities to confirm that Knott Ltd has included the sale in its financial statements and that the parent company has not included the purchase in its financial statements. However, given that the goods are still in transit at the reporting date, group inventory will be understated by £69.3 million (£77m × 90%) which is also material to group assets at 4.4%. Consolidated retained earnings will be overstated by £6.16 million (£7.7 million × 80%) and non-controlling interests will be overstated by £1.54 million (£7.7 million × 20%). The accounting for the transaction within the individual entity financial statements will also be misstated.

The failure to identify and adjust for the intra-group trading transaction indicates a deficiency in internal control within the group and therefore increased control risk for the audit of the consolidated financial statements.

> **Tutorial note.** Credit will also be given to candidates who discuss the impact of the inter-company transactions on the financial statements of the individual entities.

Evidence

- Agreement of the transaction details to underlying documents such as sales invoices, goods despatch notes at Knott Ltd and goods received notes, purchase invoices at its parent company.
- The cost of the inventory in transit should have been confirmed to production records at Knott Ltd to confirm the 10% profit margin.
- A copy of the goods received note dated 2 April 20X8 raised by the parent company confirming details of the inventory in transit and the transaction being recorded in inventory and the purchase ledger after the year end.
- A copy of the sales invoice traced to Knott Ltd's sales ledger agreeing details of the sales value.
- The adjustments required to eliminate the transaction should be noted on a schedule of uncorrected misstatements for discussion with the client.

Part F: Other assignments

65 Leopard

Workbook references

Chapters 2 and 12.

Top tips

Part (a) covered due diligence and had a slightly unusual requirement that asked you to explain why each matter required further investigation. It is clearly important that your answer is focused on this specific requirement. In spite of this, however, your answer to this question would have covered much of the same material as a normal 'matters to consider' requirement.

The two issues themselves are relatively clear, but a few points can be noted. Firstly, your answer must focus on the issues from the point of view of valuing the business, rather than from a normal auditing or financial reporting perspective. Thus inventory valuation, for example, arises as a matter to consider; this is not from the perspective of IAS 2 *Inventories*, however, but for the purpose of determining the value of Zebra Ltd's assets.

Secondly, there are many points in the scenario that are not resolved. Much of the model answer consists of speculation about what might happen, which is important because the due diligence is focused on the possible value of the business in the future. This entails a different perspective from that of an external auditor.

Finally, it should be clear from the requirement that no marks are available for general theoretical discussions of the nature of due diligence.

Part (b) was altogether more difficult. This type of situation has been examined before, and you should be able to point out the advocacy and intimidation threats. The point about not assuming a management responsibility is important too, however, as is the self-review threat in relation to the loan application.

Easy marks

There are no particular easy marks in this question, with the possible exception of those available for stating what the ethical threat to independence is, and then explaining why this is a threat.

ACCA examining team's comments

This question focused on due diligence where a separate team from the firm were working on due diligence at an audit client. Here two issues had been identified and candidates had to explain why they warranted further investigation and what procedures they would perform. Stronger candidates here were able to see the future implication for the valuation of the target company from both the loss of a major customer and a new entrant into the market, and from the ownership of land with restricted use.

Candidates should try to remain focused on the future value of the company in such questions and not dwell on the financial reporting aspects. Here there was a piece of land recorded in the accounts at its historical cost of zero as it had been gifted. A significant portion of candidates spent time on this fact and stated that it was in breach of accounting rules not to revalue PPE. This is not the case – a revaluation model may be adopted by companies but is not required. The market value of the land was important in valuing the company but its carrying amount was not for the purposes of this question.

Part (b) of this question addressed ethical issues which would arise if the firm was to attend a meeting with the bank regarding financing for this acquisition and this requirement was well answered with well-prepared candidates being able to recognise advocacy and intimidation threats.

Candidates often missed the point that a separate team was already preparing the due diligence, as detailed in the scenario and incorrectly recognised the use of separate teams as a safeguard, which was not relevant.

It should be noted that to attract credit for ethical threats candidates should not simply state the name of the threat, they should explain what it means and relate it to the scenario. Simply listing the name of ethical threats does not attract credit. An example of wording required to attract the full credit for advocacy is below:

'The client's request for the auditor to attend the meeting with the bank would create an advocacy threat to objectivity, as the auditor would be perceived to be representing the client to the bank, and therefore the bank may take assurance from the auditors' response regarding the suitability of providing finance.'

Marking guide — **Marks**

(a) (i) **Due diligence investigation**

Generally up to 1.5 marks for each matter discussed. Award 0.5 mark for identification of a relevant point and up to a further 1 mark for appropriate discussion of the relevance of this point to the specific case.

Termination of contract:

- Impact on forecast revenues, costs and cash flows
- Wider implications of a new, cheaper supplier entering the market
- Potential impairment of assets employed specifically for the client

Gifted land:

- Possible restriction on sale to Cheetah Ltd
- Possible restriction on how land is used if purchased
- Uncertainty regarding how to value the land

6

(ii) **Procedures**

Up to 1 mark for each adequately explained procedure. Award 0.5 mark for relevant procedures which are poorly explained:

- Analytically review historic sales to customer
- Enquire of management about further repercussions
- Analytically review sales by customer to identify other major ones
- Review trade contracts/agreements with other major customers
- Inspect correspondence with major customers
- Identify inventories produced specifically for customer
- Inspect forecasts to ensure adequate adjustment made
- Inspect terms of gifted land
- Enquire of legal adviser re impact of restrictions
- Seek a valuation from an expert
- Identify potential options for land
- Prepare revised forecast excluding land

6

(b) **Meeting and forecast**

Up to 1 mark for each appropriately explained matter and recommended response. Award 0.5 mark for relevant matters/responses which are poorly explained:

- Advocacy threat

Marking guide	Marks
• Management threat	
• Self-review: loan transaction	
• Intimidation threat	
• Purpose/scope of meeting	
• Ascertain purpose of attending meeting	
• Obtain written representation	
• Obtain acknowledgement that 'informed management' exists	
• Have second partner to review the situation	
• Politely decline to attend	
• Explain that you are unable to review interim engagement progress	-
	8
Professional marks	
Analysis and evaluation	
• Appropriate use of the information to support discussion, draw appropriate conclusions and design appropriate responses	
• Appropriate assessment of the ethical and professional issues raised, using examples where relevant to support overall comments	
• Effective appraisal of the information to make suitable recommendations for appropriate courses of action	
Professional scepticism and judgement	
• Effective challenge of information, evidence and assumptions supplied and, techniques carried out to support key facts and/or decisions in relation to the due diligence review	
• Appropriate application of professional judgement to draw conclusions and make informed decisions about the actions which are appropriate in the context and stage of the engagement	
Maximum	5
Total	25

(a) (i) **Why the matters require further investigation**

Termination of contract

Impact on forecasts

The loss of the customer may lead to a reduction in forecast revenue by as much as 5% per year. This may also lead to a reduction in costs specifically relevant to servicing the customer. For example, sales staff specifically allocated to servicing this client.

This is significant because the forecast future cash flows of Zebra Ltd will be critical in determining the value of the company and the price offered by Cheetah Ltd. It is therefore vital to establish all of the potential revenue and cost implications of the loss of the customer to ascertain the impact on the purchase price.

Wider implications of new competitor

The customer referred to has switched to a new, cheaper supplier. This may have wider implications if the new supplier is directly targeting the customers of Zebra Ltd. It is possible that other customers may switch to the new supplier in the future, which would have further implications on future revenue and cost forecasts.

It may not be possible to determine the potential impact of the new supplier at this point, which increases the level of uncertainty associated with the potential acquisition.

Cheetah Ltd may be able to use this uncertainty as a tool for bargaining with the owners of Zebra Ltd over the final agreed price.

Possible impairment of other assets

The loss of a major customer may be an indication of impairment of the assets of Zebra Ltd. This will be particularly relevant if Zebra Ltd holds specific assets for manufacturing the unique furniture products made for this client.

As well as production assets, Zebra Ltd may also be holding inventories which are specifically relevant to the customer which cannot be re-used elsewhere or sold to other customers. If this is the case, these inventories will almost certainly be impaired.

If not performed at the year end, it may now be appropriate to conduct an impairment review to ensure that the valuation of the assets, as presented in the financial statements, is still appropriate in the circumstances.

Gifted land

Possible restriction on sale

The restriction on the sale of the land may mean that Zebra Ltd is prohibited from including the land as part of the acquisition by Cheetah Ltd. It is likely that following acquisition, Cheetah Ltd will not be able to initiate a sale of the land to an external company or develop or change its current use. This may act as a deal breaker if Cheetah Ltd is not able to obtain complete control over the land surrounding the entrance to the production facilities.

If Zebra Ltd is not permitted to include the land as part of the deal with Cheetah Ltd, then this may also have an impact on the purchase price as the owners of Zebra Ltd may have attributed some value to the land in their expectation of the price which they can achieve. If so, it will be important to ascertain the value attributed to the land by the owners to negotiate the reduction of the purchase price.

Possible limitation on future usage

If the land can be included as part of the acquisition deal, the restrictions may also mean that Cheetah Ltd is not able to use the land for their intended purpose, such as the future expansion of production facilities, resulting in the acquisition of Zebra Ltd not being an appropriate strategic fit for Cheetah Ltd if one of the key aims is future expansion. If this is the case, then this will severely limit the value of the land to the company.

If the land can be acquired but cannot be developed, it is likely that there will be ongoing maintenance costs and potentially other requirements and conditions regarding the upkeep of the nature reserve set out by the local authority, which need to be understood as part of the review. The cost of maintenance may result in a net annual cost to the business and this needs to be quantified as part of the due diligence work.

It will be vital to ascertain what restrictions are in place and whether the directors of Cheetah Ltd believe they can extract any value from the use of the land.

Based upon this, the directors of Cheetah Ltd may wish to try and negotiate the purchase of Zebra Ltd without the associated land or they may wish to negotiate a lower price based on the restricted usage.

Uncertainty regarding valuation

It may be difficult to accurately value the piece of land. The value attributed to it in the financial statements is zero, so this may not provide an appropriate basis for estimating the resale value. A land valuation expert may be able to provide an estimation of the current market value of the land without restriction on its use, but they may find it difficult to accurately value how much it is worth with the local authority restrictions. It may also be difficult to value the land based on the future cash flows attributable to it if it is not currently in use and its future usage is uncertain.

As a result, the valuation of the land may become a point of significant negotiation between the directors of Cheetah Ltd and Zebra Ltd. This may also become a deal breaker if the two parties are unable to reach agreement on the matter.

(ii) **Procedures**

Termination of contract

Analytically review the total historic value of revenue earned from the customer to help determine an appropriate estimate for the potential loss of future revenues and cash inflows.

Enquire of management whether the loss of the customer will have any other repercussions, such as the sale of specific assets or the redundancy of staff and the costs associated with this if such action was required.

Perform an analytical review to identify other major customers by value of revenue contributions to the business. For all major customers identified, review any supply agreements/contracts in place to determine when they expire.

If any contracts with major customers are due to expire within the next few years, enquire of management whether any discussions have taken place with those customers in relation to renegotiating the terms.

Obtain any correspondence available with the identified major customers to identify whether there is any indication that they may attempt to either renegotiate the terms of their agreements or switch them to a new supplier.

Enquire of a relevant manager, such as a production manager or sales manager, whether there is any specific inventory which has been produced in relation to the customer who is not renewing their agreement. If this is the case, obtain a breakdown of the total inventories produced for this client and discuss with management whether they will be able to sell this inventory at full price given the notice to terminate the contract.

Inspect the forecasts prepared by management to ensure that the changes to the revenue and cost streams identified above have been appropriately incorporated.

Gifted land

Review the terms supplied when the land was originally gifted to Zebra Ltd. Identify the specific restrictions in relation to how the land may be used and who the land may be sold to in the future.

Enquire of a legal adviser whether this will have any impact in relation to the sale of the land to Cheetah Ltd and their consequent usage of it.

Engage a land valuation expert to provide a valuation of the land. Ask them to consider the implications of the restrictions imposed upon the land in the valuation.

If Zebra Ltd is not permitted to sell the land, or the restrictions imposed on the usage of the land are too restrictive, seek legal advice in relation to the potential options, including whether the land can be gifted back to the local authority prior to the acquisition.

Inspect the forecasts prepared by the management of Zebra Ltd to identify the specific forecast costs and revenues associated with the usage of the land. Prepare a revised version of the forecasts which excludes these revenues and costs to identify the potential implications on the forecasts if the deal is conducted excluding the gifted land.

(b) **Ethical and other professional issues**

Advocacy threat

Accompanying the client to a meeting with their bankers will create an advocacy threat to objectivity as Leopard & Co may be perceived to be representatives of Cheetah Ltd. It also creates a management threat, whereby Leopard & Co is perceived to be taking responsibility in relation to decisions made in respect of the acquisition of Zebra Ltd and the associated financial arrangements.

The potential acquisition of Zebra Ltd falls under the scope of restructuring as defined by the FRC *Ethical Standard*. In relation to restructuring, to avoid undertaking an advocacy role on behalf of the entity, the audit firm should take particular care not to assume (or seen to be assuming) responsibility for the entity's proposals or being regarded as negotiating on behalf of the entity or advocating the appropriateness of the proposals such that its independence

ANSWERS

would be compromised. The Ethical Standard notes that this is particularly important when the audit firm attends meetings with the entity's bank or other interested parties.

According to the Ethical Standard, if the audit firm undertakes a management role or acts as advocate for the entity, the threats to integrity, objectivity and independence are such that no safeguards can reduce the threat to a level where independence is not compromised.

This is particularly relevant as the bank may wish to establish a number of facts relating to the suitability of providing finance to Cheetah Ltd. For example, they may ask for representations that the company will continue as a going concern and that any forecast cash flows presented are accurate. As Cheetah Ltd's auditor, these questions may be directed at the firm's representatives and the bank may take any response provided to their questions as assurance over these matters.

Self-review threat – loan transaction

Providing assistance in raising finance could fall under the scope of providing a corporate finance service, which according to the Ethical Standard includes situations where the audit firm is asked to advise the entity on how to fund its financing requirements. Even though it is not clear that Leopard & Co has been asked for advice on the financial arrangements, by attending the meeting with the client and supporting the acquisition of Zebra Ltd, the audit firm may give that impression. A self-review threat arises where the outcome or consequences of a corporate finance service provided by the audit firm may be material to the financial statements which will be subject to an engagement by the same firm.

This is a particular problem as the transaction will directly affect the financial statements, which the audit team will be responsible for auditing in consequent financial periods and therefore the audit team is likely to be more accepting of information provided or may not investigate issues as thoroughly, as the team may feel that much of this has been done via the due diligence.

> **Tutorial note.** The question does not state whether the client is listed, but if they are listed (and are thus a public interest entity), then providing corporate finance advice to that creates a self-review threat is prohibited under *Code* (*Code of Ethics*: para. R610.8).

Intimidation threat

The Ethical Standard defines the intimidation threat as arising when the conduct of the audit firm is influenced by fear or threats. The request by Cheetah Ltd to ensure that the interim review does not impede the application for a loan may be perceived as intimidation by the client. It appears as though they are putting pressure on Leopard & Co to finish the work based on the deadlines imposed by the bank, rather than those originally agreed with the client. This may force the auditor into changing their approach to any remaining procedures which would be considered to be undue influence of the client over the procedures performed.

This appears to be supported by a further threat relating to the upcoming tender for the audit. The management team of Cheetah Ltd appears to be suggesting that failing to ensure the interim review is completed on time for the loan decision may have an adverse impact on any consequent tender bid.

Purpose of meeting

It is not clear why representatives of Leopard & Co have been invited to attend the meeting with the bank. The purpose of both the due diligence service and the interim review is to report to the directors and owners of Cheetah Ltd, respectively. The firm has no responsibility to report to any third party, including potential lenders.

There may be an expectation for Leopard & Co to provide assurances to the bank in relation to the accuracy of forecasts presented or the financial position of Cheetah Ltd. If this is the case, it is outside the scope of any of the current engagements and Leopard & Co would not be in a position to provide this assurance.

Actions

The firm should ascertain the purpose of attending the meeting with the bank; if there is any expectation that it will provide assurances to the bank, then the request should be declined, explaining to Cheetah Ltd that the firm's responsibilities extend to reporting to the management and the owners of the company and not to any third parties.

If there is no expectation to provide any assurances and the firm is expected to attend the meeting solely in regard to your role of providing due diligence services to Cheetah Ltd and assisting them in determining a purchase price, then it may be possible for representatives of Leopard & Co to attend. It must be made clear, however, that no members of the audit team/interim audit team will be able to attend, and the firm will not be permitted to make any representations to the bank. A written representation should be obtained from management clarifying these points. The representation should also state that Cheetah Ltd possesses 'informed management' capable of making decisions regarding the acquisition of Zebra Ltd and the associated financial arrangements. This will help to reduce the advocacy and management threats to an acceptable level.

Should Leopard & Co provide a service to Cheetah Ltd which falls under the scope of a corporate finance service, then the audit committee of Cheetah Ltd must be informed. Additionally, safeguards should be put in place, including that any advice provided is reviewed by an independent corporate finance partner within the audit firm and that external independent advice on the corporate finance work is obtained.

On balance, Leopard & Co may consider that the threats, both real and perceived, are too great and it would be most prudent not to attend the meeting. If this is the case, Leopard & Co should politely decline the invitation, explaining the reasons why it is inappropriate. Leopard & Co should communicate with the directors of Cheetah Ltd explaining that the firm is unable to be involved in the interim review or to review any of the working papers. Leopard & Co should explain the reasons to the client. The firm should also explain that, if the client has any concerns, they should communicate with the interim review engagement partner to ascertain a reasonable timeframe for conclusion of this engagement.

Tutorial note. Credit will be awarded where candidates answer with reference to the IESBA *Code of Ethics for Professional Accountants*.

66 Beyer

Workbook references

Chapters 3, 5 and 14.

Top tips

In part (a) there are plenty of issues to be discussed in the 16 minutes available for this question part. As usual, every sentence of the scenario is there for a reason. It was crucial here that you read the first part of the scenario carefully, noticing that Beyer Co is not a client of your firm, and that therefore issues of auditor independence are not relevant here.

Part (b) should have been a nice question part. Procedures to quantify a loss are standard fare for forensics questions in AAA, and the second sub-part was almost reminiscent of an AA-level question.

Easy marks

Part (b)(i) features a fair number of marks for straightforward forensics procedures.

ACCA examining team's comments

This question was set in the context of a non-audit assignment for a non-audit client. Candidates were asked to consider acceptance criteria for an investigative forensic appointment in response to a fraud at a manufacturing company. The scenario detailed a fraud where inventory was stolen, and the assignment was to quantify the fraud for an insurance claim. Most candidates demonstrated the ability to apply acceptance criteria with reference to the specific question. A minority of candidates discussed irrelevant considerations that appeared to have been learnt from a previous question set in a similar context. Whilst the criteria for assessment were similar, some of those points were not relevant in this case and candidates wasted time in the exam discussing issues that would only be relevant to an existing audit client.

Part (b)(i) of this question asked candidates to suggest the steps or procedures that could be used to quantify the fraud and answers here tended to be either very good or very poor. Good answers methodically went through the process of identifying the fictitious customer, extracting data on cancelled orders and matching that to missing inventory through an inventory count. Weaker candidates were those who approached this by listing pre-learned procedures or without taking in to account the assignment and scenario. Such candidates often suggested tests that were based on samples as would be relevant to an audit rather than trying to definitively quantify the loss.

Other mistakes made here were focusing on sale price rather than cost or trying to trace the stolen inventory with reference to sales invoices despite the goods stolen not being invoiced. There was evidence of candidates listing procedures from a previous forensic investigation question that were not relevant to the scenario described and therefore could not be awarded credit.

Part (b)(ii) required candidates to identify and explain the deficiencies in controls that allowed the fraud to occur and recommend improvements. Candidates were often able to score maximum credit in this area by giving detailed explanations. Weaker candidates tended to identify the deficiency from the scenario but were unable to describe how it resulted in the fraud or made unspecific recommendations eg improve segregation of duties or someone should approve cancellations – to obtain full credit more detail was required such as who should approve a process or how duties should be segregated.

Marking guide **Marks**

(a) **Acceptance considerations**

Up to 2 marks for each issue explained.

- Scope of assignment
- Interaction with criminal investigation
- Form and contents of reports/audience
- Confidentiality (max 1 mark)
- Competence
- Resource availability (including technology and the ability to make deadlines)
- Customer due diligence requirements/reputational risks (award up to 1 additional mark for specific examples of information required as part of the customer due diligence)

8

(b) (i) **Procedures to quantify the loss**

1 mark for each relevant procedure described.

- Meet with audit committee/management to understand and document what they know about the fraud and who might be involved
- Discuss with the company's legal team what is known about the fraud at present and the source of the information
- If possible, interview the whistle-blower to identify the potential staff involved and the timescales over which the fraud has been perpetrated
- Obtain the prior year report to management from the auditor and inspect auditor's reports to identify any deficiencies or discrepancies in inventories identified by the auditors
- Obtain/prepare a reconciliation of all orders placed including cancelled orders to all invoices raised to identify the total of all orders placed but not invoiced to establish the maximum potential value of the theft

- Arrange to conduct a full inventory count to identify discrepancies between the inventory records and physical inventory
- Investigate records of inventory written off to identify possible attempts to disguise the missing items
- Interview sales, warehouse, and accounting staff to identify the system in place for creating a sales order and for setting up customers within the sales and inventory systems
- Use CAATs/data analytics to identify the total of cancelled orders within the inventory records system and any addresses which are associated with large volumes of cancellations
- Identify which cancelled orders are assigned to the sales representative identified by the whistle-blower
- Identify which customers those orders are assigned to and verify their existence within the invoicing system and, where possible, their registered business address to ensure they are genuine customers
- From this, identify fictitious customers and reconcile their cancelled orders to the inventory discrepancies identified
- Assess if the amounts ordered by the fictitious customers agree to the total discrepancies or if there is a further difference to be investigated
- Obtain inventory listing to identify the cost of the parts stolen and calculate the cost of the inventory identified as relating to the fictitious customer orders
- Using CAATs/data analytics identify any other sales staff with unusual levels of cancelled sales dispatches to see if this is a wider issue

6

(ii) **Control deficiencies and contribution to fraud**

Up to 2 marks for each point explained with up to 1 mark per recommendation.

- Lack of segregation of duties and monitoring
  - lack of integration of systems
  - lack of monitoring of order cancellations
- Lack of segregation of duties in warehouse counts
- Additional implications
- Recommendations

6

Professional marks

Analysis and evaluation

- Appropriate assessment of the ethical and professional issues raised, using examples where relevant to support overall comments
- Effective appraisal of the information to make suitable recommendations for appropriate courses of action

Professional scepticism and judgement

- Effective challenge of information, evidence and assumptions supplied and, techniques carried out to support key facts and/or decisions
- Appropriate application of professional judgement to draw conclusions and make informed decisions about the actions which are appropriate in the context and stage of the engagement

Marking guide	Marks
Commercial acumen	
• Inclusion of appropriate recommendations regarding the acceptance procedures in relation to forensic investigation for Beyer	
• Appropriate recognition of the wider implications on the engagement, the audit firm and the company	
Maximum	5
Total	25

(a) **Beyer Ltd**

Scope of the investigation

Kaffe & Co should establish the specific work which Beyer Ltd expects them to perform. It is likely that the quantification of the loss represents an agreed upon procedures engagement and these would need to be confirmed with Beyer Ltd in advance.

The identification and recommendation on controls issues is more likely to be of a consulting nature and the process and outcomes agreed with the client. The assignment may require specific competencies, such as the use of specialists in the use of computer-assisted audit/data analytics techniques and this should be identified prior to acceptance of the engagement.

Kaffe & Co would also need to establish the time period Beyer Ltd would like them to investigate. This will all have an impact on the total fee charged.

Establishing how Kaffe & Co's investigation relates to the criminal investigation

If the quantification of the loss were to become a criminal investigation, then the relevant authorities would take the lead. It is not clear whether the authorities would require additional, professional support in their investigation and, if so, what sort of assistance they would require. For example, it is possible that they would gather their own evidence, but they may require the use of an expert witness to verify their findings in court.

It is therefore vital that, before any terms are agreed or engagement contracts are signed, Kaffe & Co speaks to the authorities to ascertain whether there will be any criminal investigation and, if so, what their role might be in the investigation, and how they might interact with any other experts appointed by the authority to assist in the investigation.

Confidentiality

Firms providing professional services must always ensure that information relating to clients is not given to third parties without the permission of the client. In preparing the report for the insurance company, Kaffe & Co will need permission from Beyer Ltd to disclose the information to the insurance company. In an investigation such as this, it is highly likely that all of the evidence collected will have to be submitted to the authorities to assist with their criminal investigation. It is therefore vital that before Kaffe & Co accepts the assignment, they obtain permission to do so from the board of Beyer Ltd.

The types of reports and prospective users

The firm must confirm with Beyer Ltd what types of report they would expect as a result of the engagement and whom the reports would be distributed to. In forensic engagements, the procedures to be performed would normally be agreed and then the results of those procedures would be reported. It may be that the insurance company expects an opinion to be given on the results of the investigation and if this is the case, then the assurance issued would be limited to negative assurance. Kaffe & Co would usually expressly state that the report is not intended for use by third parties.

In this investigation, it is possible that the relevant authorities would want to use the results of the procedures to compile evidence for their case. It would, if this were the case, be important to establish if additional reports would be required for this.

Management also wants additional reports relating to the deficiencies identified in the control environment and systems recommendations on how to strengthen controls in this area. The form and content of such a report must be agreed upon in advance of accepting the assignment.

Professional competence

Before they can accept the role, Kaffe & Co must be certain that they have staff with the requisite competencies to be able to conduct the investigation effectively.

If this were conducted as a criminal investigation, it is also vital that the staff used have sufficient experience in relation to the gathering and safeguarding of evidence. Any failure to follow the relevant protocol may render the evidence useless to the legal case.

Time pressure, deadlines and resource availability

As well as having access to appropriate technology and staff with the requisite competencies to conduct the engagement, it is also vital that those resources are available to allow the investigation to be conducted in the time frame suggested. The insurance company is likely to set the time frame for any initial investigation. If the relevant authorities conduct an additional criminal investigation, Kaffe & Co must consider the extent of the possible investigation and whether they are able to commit the necessary resources without adversely affecting their other client commitments.

Client due diligence

As Beyer Ltd is a new client, Kaffe & Co may be required to perform client identification procedures as part of anti-money laundering regulations. The firm must explain the need to obtain information about the company and its directors before Beyer Ltd can be accepted as a client. If Beyer Ltd is unable, or refuses, to do this, then Kaffe & Co would not be able to take on Beyer Ltd as a client or proceed with the engagement.

(b) (i) **Procedures to be performed to quantify the inventory loss**

- Meet with the audit committee and members of management to understand and document what they know about the fraud and who might be involved.
- Discuss with the company's legal team what is known about the fraud at present and the source of the information.
- If possible, interview the whistle-blower to identify the potential staff involved and the timescales over which the fraud has been perpetrated.
- Obtain the prior year report to management from the auditor and inspect auditor's reports to identify any deficiencies or discrepancies in inventories identified by the auditors.
- Obtain/prepare a reconciliation of all orders placed including cancelled orders to all invoices raised to identify the total of all orders placed but not invoiced to establish the maximum potential value of the theft.
- Arrange to conduct a full inventory count to identify discrepancies between the inventory records and physical inventory.
- Investigate records of inventory written off to identify possible attempts to disguise the missing items.
- Interview sales, warehouse and accounting staff to identify the system in place for creating a sales order and for setting up customers within the sales and inventory systems.
- Use CAATs or other data analytics tools to identify the total of cancelled orders within the inventory records system and any addresses which are associated with large volumes of cancellations.
- Identify which cancelled orders are assigned to the sales representative identified by the whistle-blower.
- Identify which customers those orders are assigned to and verify their existence within the invoicing system and, where possible, their registered business address to ensure they are genuine customers.

ANSWERS

- From this, identify fictitious customers and reconcile their cancelled orders to the inventory discrepancies identified.
- Assess if the amounts ordered by the fictitious customers agree to the total discrepancies or if there is a further difference to be investigated.
- Obtain inventory listing to identify the cost of the parts stolen and calculate the cost of the inventory identified as relating to the fictitious customer orders.
- Using CAATs or other data analytics tools, identify any other sales staff with unusual levels of cancelled sales dispatches to see if this is a wider issue.

(ii) **Control deficiencies and recommendations**

Lack of segregation of duties and monitoring of order cancellations

There is a lack of internal control over the warehouse team, particularly in relation to authorisation and approval of transactions. The warehouse manager having the ability to create new customers on the system without authorisation has allowed fictitious customers to be created.

The ability of the sales representative to cancel orders and the ability of the warehouse manager to reverse dispatches without authorisation gives rise to a lack of segregation of duties. These processes should require authorisation from a senior member of staff, for instance, sales cancellations should be approved by the sales manager and reversed goods dispatches by the operations manager.

Additionally, the lack of reconciliation of the sales orders to the amounts invoiced allowed the cancellation of deliveries to avoid detection from any invoicing process. The consistent cancellation of dispatches relating to one customer from one sales representative may have drawn attention within the sales system had the transaction made it that far.

The existence of the inventory system in isolation from the invoicing and accounting system allowed for incomplete information to be relayed further up within the business. While this in itself is not an issue, it did mean that any management review of accounting and invoicing reports does not act as a means of review of the inventory management and dispatch system. In many businesses, a system which linked the inventory movements with the accounting and management information system would allow reports to be generated to monitor for unusual levels of returns and cancellations. In the absence of the ability to merge the two systems, it may be possible for additional reporting functions to be added to the inventory system to allow reports of returns and cancellations to be generated for review at a higher level than the warehouse manager to provide oversight of this area.

A proper monitoring system would have flagged that one sales representative in particular had higher than usual cancellation levels which could have been investigated and monitored by management.

It would also be possible to implement a system where all cancelled orders and reversed dispatches are processed outside of the sales and warehouse team, for example, by the accounts department.

Lack of segregation of duties in the warehouse counts

The lack of segregation of duties between warehouse staff and inventory count staff allowed the fictitious sales orders to pass unnoticed as the inventory discrepancy which would have flagged the issue was ineffective. An independent inventory count process using an external company or using staff from outside the warehouse to perform counts and reconcile the inventory amounts to inventory records would have identified missing inventory sooner.

Additional implications of the fraud

In addition to the value of the inventory stolen by the warehouse manager and sales representative, the business is not holding accurate records of its inventory, meaning that it may be in breach of the requirement to keep proper records of assets and liabilities and its assets are overstated. This may or may not be a material amount.

There is also a business risk arising from inaccurate inventory in that inventory believed to be on hand to satisfy genuine orders may not exist, causing delays and disruption to the ability of Beyer Ltd to satisfy customer orders in a timely manner causing customer satisfaction issues and potential loss of customers if the delays become unacceptable.

Recommendations

- Integration of the sales order and invoicing systems into the management information system.
- New customers should be created by the accounts department not the sales/dispatch teams.
- Authorisation process for cancelled orders/returns.
- Creation and regular review of exception reports and unusual trends including cancellation reports by higher level management to identify irregular or suspicious patterns.
- Regular inventory counts to be performed by staff independent of the warehouse and sales staff.

67 Mizzen

Workbook reference

Chapter 12.

Top tips

In part (a) it is crucial that you give only three benefits of due diligence, as any further benefits are unlikely to be marked. Another thing to avoid doing is writing about what a due diligence review is – this is not asked for in the requirement, and again receives no marks, serving only to eat into your time.

Although part (a) could be approached as a simply knowledge-based requirement, there are actually several clues in the scenario which you may have picked up on in your answer. For example, the fact that 'Baltimore Ltd has not previously acquired another company' suggests that it 'lacks the necessary skills' not just to set up a website, but to do a due diligence too.

Do not overlook the requirement in part (b) to recommend additional information needed. As long as you state not just what you need but also why you need it, you can pick up a lot of marks here with relatively little effort.

It is also worth noting that although this question features an embedded style of requirement, there are no professional marks available.

Easy marks

There were many easy marks for additional information in part (b).

ACCA examining team's report

This question focused on due diligence, a topic that had appeared in examinations several times previous to this sitting. The scenario described a due diligence assignment to be performed on the target company Mizzen Co, at the request of Baltimore Co. The history and activities of the target company was described in some detail, and some financial information provided for the last four years. For Baltimore Co, this would be their first acquisition and was being considered as a means to diversify the company's operations.

Requirement (a) asked candidates to discuss three benefits to Baltimore Ltd of a due diligence review being performed on Mizzen Ltd. While some reasonable answers were given, possibly by candidates who had practiced the past exam question containing a similar requirement, on the whole answers were unsatisfactory. The following factors contributed to inadequate performance in relation to this requirement:

- Writing answers that were much too brief for the marks available – it was common to see three sentences given as an answer to this requirement, which cannot be enough for a 6-mark requirement.
- At the other extreme, some very lengthy answers were given that usually failed to answer the question requirement and instead either simply wrote in detail on how a due diligence assignment should be performed, or suggested in some detail the operational benefits to Baltimore Ltd of acquiring Mizzen Ltd.
- Many answers failed to limit to three benefits and instead provided a bullet point list of benefits that were not discussed at all.

Requirement (b) was the main part of the question, and asked candidates, for 14 marks, to identify and explain the matters that the due diligence review would focus on, and to recommend the additional information needed. The answers provided to this requirement were extremely mixed in quality. There were some exceptionally sound answers, explaining relevant matters in sufficient depth, and using the financial information provided to come up with reasonable points. These answers also provided relevant requests for additional information.

However, the majority of answers were unsatisfactory. Most candidates picked up at least a few marks by identifying some of the matters that the review would focus on, but as in Question One, many candidates let themselves down by failing to explain the matters that they had identified in any real depth. It was common for answers to simply contain a list of bullet points with very little explanation at all, and only a limited amount of marks can be awarded to answers of this type.

Some points were better dealt with, including the following:

- Most answers picked up on the fact that Mizzen Ltd used premises owned by the venture capitalist company, and the fact that this arrangement would probably cease on the acquisition.
- Many candidates realised that the two founders of Mizzen Ltd were crucial to the company's success and that without them the acquisition would probably be pointless.
- Many candidates used the financial information to some extent, though sometimes only in a very limited way, but most picked up on the fact that Mizzen Ltd was paying finance charges, and so information would be needed to understand what those charges relate to.
- Many answers considered that revenue recognition would be a matter to focus on due to the relatively complex nature of the company's revenue streams.
- Some answers performed a little analytical review on the financial information to reveal that expenses were not increasing in line with revenue, and that this would need to be investigated.

The answers that were unsatisfactory, as well as containing inadequately explained points as mentioned above, also tended to focus too much on financial reporting matters, for example giving very lengthy discussions on the calculation of goodwill. While the accounting treatment of some items certainly was relevant to the answer, just focusing on these matters meant that candidates did not provide a broad enough range of comments to score well.

Another factor leading to poor marks for this requirement was that many candidates simply failed to recommend any additional information at all that would be needed in the review. Many candidates missed out on marks here, for example for recommending that a statement of financial position, management accounts and cash flow forecasts would be needed.

Some candidates supplied a lengthy discussion of matters relating to the acceptance of the due diligence assignment, such as agreeing fees and clarifying deadlines, which was not asked for.

Marking guide | **Marks**

(a) **Benefit of due diligence**

Up to 2 marks for each benefit discussed:

- Identification of assets and liabilities

- Review of operational issues
- Examination of financial position and performance
- Added credibility and expertise
- Added value for negotiation of purchase price
- Other advice can be given, eg on obtaining finance

6

(b) **Areas to focus on and additional information**

Generally up to 1.5 marks for each explanation of area to focus on:

- Equity owners of Mizzen Ltd and involvement of BizGrow
- Key skills and expertise
- Internally generated intangible assets
- Premises
- Other intangible assets
- Accounting policy on revenue recognition
- Sustainability and relevance of revenue streams
- Operating expenses
- Finance charges
- Cash management

1 mark for each specific additional information recommended:

- Contract or legal documentation dealing with BizGrow's investment in Mizzen Ltd
- A register of shareholders showing all shareholders of Mizzen Ltd
- An organisational structure
- A list of employees and their role within the company, obligations and compensation
- A list of freelance web designers used by Mizzen Ltd, and a description of the work they perform
- The key terms of contracts or agreements with freelance web designers
- A list of all IT innovations which have been created and developed by Mizzen Ltd, and details of any patent or copyright agreements relating to them
- Agreements with employees regarding assignment of intellectual property and confidentiality
- Copies of the customer databases
- A list of companies which have contracts with Mizzen Ltd for website development and maintenance
- A copy of all contracts with customers for review of the period for maintenance
- A breakdown of the revenue that has been generated from making each database available to other companies, and the dates when they were made available
- A summary of the controls which are in place to ensure that the database details are regularly updated
- A copy of the premises rental agreement with BizGrow
- Non-current asset register showing descriptions and values of all assets used in the business
- Copies of any lease agreements

- Mizzen Ltd's stated accounting policy on revenue recognition
- Systems and controls documentation over the processing of revenue receipts
- Analysis of expenses included in operating expenses for each year and copies of documentation relating to ongoing expenses such as salaries and other overheads
- Copies of management accounts to agree expenses in the audited accounts are in line and to perform more detailed analytical review
- The full set of financial statements and auditor's reports
- Any agreements with banks or other external providers of finance

14

Professional marks

Analysis and evaluation

- Appropriate use of the information to support discussion, draw appropriate conclusions and design appropriate responses
- Identification of omissions from the analysis or further analysis which could be carried out
- Balanced assessment of the information to determine the additional information that would be required to conduct the review

Professional scepticism and judgement

- Appropriate application of professional judgement to draw conclusions and make informed decisions about the actions which are appropriate in the context and stage of the engagement.

Commercial acumen

- Appropriate consideration of the benefits and drawbacks of due diligence in the commercial context of a company wishing to make an acquisition

Maximum	5
Total	25

(a) **Identifying assets**

The review would aim to identify and value the assets and liabilities of the target company. This would include items not recognised on Mizzen Ltd's financial statements. For example, it is possible that Mizzen may have intangible assets that are not recognised separately, but which may be valued. These could become part of any goodwill acquired on acquisition.

The review would also seek to discover previously hidden liabilities, such as contingent liabilities, which could potentially be very significant to Baltimore Ltd.

Operational issues

The review would focus on operational issues. This might include, for example, an examination of Mizzen's different revenue streams with a view to assessing how Baltimore might seek to benefit from them after the acquisition. The review may also focus on the strategic fit between Baltimore and Mizzen, attempting to determine the extent to which Mizzen meets Baltimore's needs.

This could involve a review of Mizzen's financial position and performance, focusing in particular on its potential for future growth or profitability.

Credibility

Obtaining an external due diligence review would allow Baltimore's management to focus on its own operational matters and yet still receive a timely review. Such a review would be conducted by an independent expert, with experience and knowledge in this area which Baltimore's management lacks, since it has not previously acquired another company. The review would give the benefit of a sharp, fresh pair of eyes which might spot things that Baltimore's management may have missed.

It is for this reason that an externally provided review would be more credible than an internal one, something which may help persuade Baltimore's bank to lend it the money which it believes itself to need.

(b) **Equity owners**

It is crucial to determine the identity of Mizzen's majority shareholder. It appears likely that this is BizGrow, but further information is needed.

This is important because if BizGrow does own the shares then it is with BizGrow that Baltimore would need to negotiate the purchase of Mizzen. If BizGrow does not want to sell its shares, then Mizzen cannot be bought. However, it is unclear how Baltimore came to identify Mizzen as an acquisition target in the first place, and it is possible that BizGrow may have had something to do with this.

Funding

It is noted that Vic and Lou secured funds from BizGrow. The nature of any agreement that was made needs to be ascertained, as it is possible that Mizzen may owe BizGrow a substantial amount of money. This would be material to any decision Baltimore might make about the acquisition.

The precise nature of the ongoing relationship between Mizzen and BizGrow is unclear. It is possible that BizGrow is involved with Mizzen at an operational level. Any agreements between the two parties should be obtained and scrutinised.

Examination of the statement of profit or loss reveals a finance cost of £250,000 which appears to be fixed. It is unlikely that this is interest on a loan because loan interest would change as the balance is repaid. It is therefore possible that this is a management charge from BizGrow, which would be indicative of ongoing involvement. We would need to understand the nature of any liabilities Mizzen may have in relation to this charge.

Reputation

Mizzen's good reputation, and its having won awards for website design, is key evidence for its expertise in this area. This should be verified to external evidence. Customer satisfaction could be gauged by obtaining the results of any customer satisfaction surveys that may have been conducted.

Vic and Lou

Vic and Lou appear to be crucial to the success of Mizzen, so Baltimore would want them to be involved in future. It is not certain, however, that they would want to be involved with Baltimore and its website, and they may wish to concentrate on their own more innovative work. The acquisition would be much less attractive to Baltimore were they to leave.

Vic and Lou's intentions post-acquisition should be determined. It may be possible to structure any future deal in such a way that Vic and Lou would be required to continue working at Mizzen for a set period after the acquisition.

Staff

Mizzen is a business with few tangible assets, which relies heavily on the expertise of its staff, who may leave after any acquisition – particularly if Vic and Lou were to leave. It would make little sense to acquire Mizzen for its staff only to find that they leave on acquisition.

An organisational structure should be obtained in order to identify management and key personnel within Mizzen.

It is also possible that Baltimore may wish to restructure Mizzen after acquisition. In this case it is likely that redundancy payments would need to be made to staff members losing their jobs. The amount of any possible liability in this eventuality should be estimated as part of the review.

Freelancers

Mizzen has been using freelancers recently, which may result in a drop in the quality of work done by comparison with established staff. This should be investigated as it may affect Mizzen's ostensibly impeccable reputation.

Intangible assets

Mizzen has few assets but is likely to have important intangible assets which would form part of any goodwill paid on acquisition. Vic and Lou have developed new website interfaces, and it should be determined whether any resulting intellectual property belongs to them personally or to Mizzen. Valuing these assets is likely to be difficult.

Customer databases should also be valued, which again is likely to be difficult owing to the absence of any active market for assets of this kind.

Premises

It is apparent that the £1,000 nominal rent paid to BizGrow would increase after the acquisition, so it should be determined what an equivalent market rent might be for the premises. Alternatively, the premises may no longer be available, in which case the rent should be ascertained for premises meeting Mizzen's needs. It may be possible for Mizzen to operate from Baltimore's premises, in which case any opportunity costs should be considered.

Tangible assets

Mizzen's tangible assets need to be valued, and it should be determined whether they are owned or held under lease, as it is possible that Mizzen may be liable for any future lease payments.

Revenue recognition

The first revenue stream should be split into two components, with the revenue relating to maintenance being recognised as deferred income and spread over the contract period. There is a risk that revenue is recognised too early, inflating Mizzen's profit in the short term.

Relevance of revenue

Baltimore needs Mizzen to develop a website for it, and it should be asked whether Baltimore might be better off simply paying Mizzen £10,000 to develop a website rather than acquiring the whole company.

It is clear that Mizzen would have the expertise to do this because it operates its own subscription-based website. It should therefore be able to create something of a similar nature for Baltimore.

The third revenue stream in particular does not appear relevant to Baltimore, and it should be considered how this revenue stream would be managed after the acquisition.

Revenue increase

Revenue rose 23.7% from 20X2 to 20X3, which is an impressive increase although it is lower than the 60.4% increase from 20X1 to 20X2. The question is whether such a growth rate might feasibly be achieved in the future. It will therefore be necessary to scrutinise Mizzen's forecasts and plans for future growth.

Operating expenses

Operating expenses in 20X2 were 58.3% of revenue, but only 49.6% in 20X3. This is unusual and may be indicative of efficiencies being achieved as Mizzen grows. It does not, however, tally with the fact that freelancers have been used this year, which would be expected to increase operating expenses in relation to revenue.

A detailed review needs to be performed on operating expenses to ensure that expenses are complete and are recorded accurately.

Cash

Mizzen's cash position should be confirmed to its bank statement. Although the company is not lacking cash, from its statements of profit or loss one would expect it to be in a better cash position than it is in. It is possible that cash has been paid out in dividends to shareholders.

Further information

- Copy of Mizzen's register of shareholders, to determine the identity of the majority shareholder
- Copy of any agreement between BizGrow and Vic and Lou, to help understand their ongoing relationship as well as BizGrow's planned exit route
- Agreements of any loans received by Mizzen
- Full audited financial statements of Mizzen
- Details of awards won for website design, including press reports, trade journals, for evidence of Mizzen's good reputation
- Details of any customer satisfaction surveys conducted by Mizzen
- Copies of contracts with Vic and Lou
- Copy of organisational structure
- Copies of contracts with key employees containing details of any redundancy payments that might be due in the future, along with other employee benefits and entitlements that are due to them
- List of freelance designers used by Mizzen, together with copies of contracts
- Details of any copyrights or patents owned by Vic and Lou or Mizzen
- Copy of rental agreement with BizGrow, to be scrutinised for details of possible rental payments after acquisition
- Details of tangible non-current assets owned or operated by Mizzen
- Copies of any lease agreements for non-current assets such as computers or fixtures and fittings
- Copies of projected financial information for the next year
- Detailed management accounts, including breakdown of operating expenses to ascertain reasons for rising operating margin
- Details of any dividend payments made over the last three years

68 Jacob

Workbook references

Chapters 12 and 13.

Top tips

Part (a) was of around average difficulty. You should have been able to pass this part of the question by explaining each of your points well.

Part (b) should have been simpler than part (a). It was important here that you didn't go over your time limit, but that you wrote enough (in terms of quality, not quantity!) to gain marks for each thing you say. The key to actually getting marks is to be specific about what information you are asking for and making sure that everything you say is relevant to the scenario. It is a waste of time asking for information that is relevant to due diligence in general, but not to Locke Ltd in particular. Also, it is no good just stating what information you need, you have to make sure that you say why you need it.

You might have enjoyed part (c) (relatively speaking), as there was plenty to criticise in the assurance report – it can feel good to be in command of your knowledge. This question part was largely a mark gathering exercise, which meant you should have been careful not to go over your time on it.

Easy marks

There were plenty of easy marks in part (b), for example, saying that more information needs to be obtained regarding the court case against Locke Ltd.

ACCA examining team's comments

Requirement (a), for five marks, required an explanation of three benefits of an externally provided due diligence review to the audit client. This was reasonably well answered, though many answers were not made very specific to the scenario and tended to discuss the benefits of any due diligence review rather than an externally provided one.

Requirement (b) asked for additional information to be made available for the firm's due diligence review. Answers were satisfactory, and the majority of candidates did not struggle to apply their knowledge to the scenario, usually providing some very focused answers dealing well with the specifics of the question scenario.

Part (c) involved reviewing a non-audit assurance report which had been prepared in conjunction with seeking a bank loan. Good answers highlighted that the report had been poorly written (in that it was not correctly addressed, provided positive assurance, was not time-bound and was self-contradictory) and explained how each of these should be remedied. Poorer answers only concentrated on omissions, such as the lack of a date on the report.

Marking guide	Marks
(a) **Benefits of due diligence**	
Up to 2 marks for each benefit explained:	
• Identify and value assets and liabilities to be acquired	
• Identify and allow planning for operational issues	
• Provision by external experts – technically competent and time efficient	
• Assessment of potential impact of court case	
• Evaluation of the liquidity position of Locke Ltd	
• Enhanced credibility provided by an independent review	
	5
(b) **Information required**	
Generally 0.5 mark for identification and up to 1 further mark for explanation (maximum 3 marks for identification):	
• Service contracts of directors	
• Organisational structure	
• Lease/arrangement regarding head office	
• Details of land purchased	
• Planning permission for new head office	
• Prior year accounts and management accounts	
• Forecasts and budgets	
• Loan agreement	
• Overdraft facility details	
• Legal correspondence	
• Customer satisfaction surveys	
• Details of warranty agreements	
• Outsourcing agreement	
	9

Marking guide	Marks
(c) **Critique of assurance report**	
• Addressee inappropriate	
• Type of forecast reviewed	
• Period covered by the forecast	
• Document forecast is included in and page references	
• Assurance standards complied with	
• Responsibility for preparation	
• Reference to assumptions	
• Negative statement of assurance	
• International Financial Reporting Standards	
• Inappropriate caveat	
• Reference to purpose and distribution of the report	
	6

Professional marks

Analysis and evaluation

- Appropriate use of the information to support discussion, draw appropriate conclusions and design appropriate responses
- Balanced assessment of the information to determine the additional information that would be required to conduct the review

Professional scepticism and judgement

- Appropriate application of professional judgement to draw conclusions and make informed decisions about the actions which are appropriate in the context and stage of the engagement.
- Critical assessment of the proposed assurance report, including awareness of information not taken into account by the extract

Commercial acumen

- Appropriate consideration of the benefits of due diligence in the commercial context of a company wishing to make an acquisition

Maximum	5
Total	25

(a) One benefit of due diligence here is that it will help in assigning a valuation to Locke Ltd. The review would seek to identify all of Locke Ltd' s potential assets and liabilities and provide a value for them. This valuation may include amounts not included within the financial statements, for example any contingent assets or liabilities that are not required to be recognised or disclosed by IAS 37. Armed with this valuation, management would be in a better position to negotiate a price for the business.

A second benefit is that the review should obtain further information about the company's operations. For example, it may be able to obtain further information about the extent of Locke Ltd' s possible liability relating to its court case. It may also be able to provide an indication of the extent to which Locke Ltd' s reputation may be tarnished by the court case.

A third benefit is that since the due diligence review is prepared externally, the directors' time is freed up to concentrate on operational matters. The review will be prepared time-efficiently, and the independence of the firm providing the review helps contribute to the good governance of Jacob Ltd.

> **Tutorial note.** The answer above includes three benefits. Credit will be awarded for explanation of any benefits which are specific to the scenario.

(b) Further information should include:

Employment contracts

Contracts for directors and other key personnel should be obtained. It may be that Jacob will seek to terminate the employment of directors after the acquisition. The contracts should be inspected for any amounts payable on termination.

Organisational structure

It may be that Jacob will want to keep hold of key personnel. In order to identify them, an organisational structure should be obtained.

Lease agreements re building

Jacob may wish to relocate away from the building owned by the family estate, in which case the signed lease agreements should be inspected for any penalty clauses for early termination.

New head office – purchase documentation

Documents relating to the land purchase should be obtained to ascertain its value should Jacob wish to sell it, or to see whether it might be put to an alternative use. Alternatively, it may be possible for the land not to be included in the acquisition.

Details should be obtained of any other commitments made in relation to the new head office. For example, construction contracts may have been entered into; these should be obtained, along with details of any possible penalties for termination.

Audited financial statements

Audited financial statements should be obtained in order to verify that Locke has indeed grown rapidly in the last three years.

These will also provide information helpful for the valuation of assets, the existence of contingent liabilities, etc.

Finally, they will allow an assessment to be made of Locke's liquidity, which may be particularly important in view of its use of an overdraft facility during the winter months.

Management accounts and forecasts

These should be obtained for future periods in order to assess Locke's possible future profitability.

Asset valuations

Any significant non-current assets should be assessed for their market value, if they are held in the accounts at historical cost.

Signed bank loan agreement

This should be obtained in order to ascertain the repayment terms, the interest rate, as well as any charges held as security over the company and/or its assets.

The amount of the loan may be significant, as purchasing a company with high financial gearing may affect Jacob's own exposure to risk.

Overdraft details

Details such as the maximum facility available to Locke, the interest rate, and when it is due for renewal.

It is possible that Locke may be a significant drain on Jacob's cash resources during the winter months, so Jacob will need to assess its own ability to take on such a possible commitment.

Information from legal counsel

This should be obtained regarding the court case with the famous actor. This should ascertain the extent of Locke's probably liability, along with the timescale for the case.

Information on bad publicity

The bad publicity from the legal case may affect Locke's ability to generate revenue in future, so information about the extent of the possible brand damage should be sought.

Information on Locke's 'good reputation'

This claim should be substantiated as far as possible, for example by reference to industry journals, customer satisfaction surveys, levels of customer complaints, etc.

Contract with Austin Ltd

This should be examined in order to understand exactly what services Austin provides, and what the cost of these services is. Jacob may wish to bring some of these activities back in-house.

(c) **Assurance report on examination of forecast**

Addressee

The report is currently addressed to the shareholders of Tulip Ltd which is not appropriate. The intended users for the report are more likely to be the board of directors, who wishes to use it in conjunction with a loan application, and the report should be addressed as such.

Type of forecast

The report fails to specify what forecast the assurance relates to. Companies can forecast various elements of financial performance, position and cash flow. It is vital to identify specifically which forecast, and which elements of the forecast, are covered by the assurance report.

Period covered

The assurance report fails to specify the period covered by the forecast. This is important because it is plausible that only part of the forecast is covered by the assurance report, particularly if it is a long range forecast.

Specific document and page reference

The assurance report simply refers to the forecast 'contained in the loan proposal'. This is not specific enough. This increases the risk that the same forecast can be reissued with the assurance report in other loan proposals. The assurance report should state the title of the document the forecast is included in and the page numbers upon which assurance is being provided.

Relevant standards

The report simply refers to 'relevant standards'; it should state which standards have been followed during the engagement. Given the nature of the assignment the report should state that it has been conducted in accordance with ISAE 3400 *The Examination of Prospective Financial Information.*

Responsibility for preparation

The content of the report in relation to setting out the respective responsibilities of the practitioner and the responsible party are not in line with the relevant standards. Rather than stating that the practitioner is not responsible for the preparation of the forecast, ISAE 3400 specifies that the assurance report should state that management is responsible for the information provided and the assumptions upon which it is based.

Detail regarding the relevant assumptions

The assurance report should make it clear what assumptions the forecast is based upon and what assumptions the assurance report relates to. To this end the report should refer to the note in the forecast where the underlying assumptions are presented.

Negative statement of assurance needed

The assurance provided in the draft assurance report is worded positively; ISAE 3400 requires that for an examination of prospective financial information a statement of negative assurance is provided.

For an unmodified report, such as that presented in the draft, the wording used should state that 'based upon our examination of the evidence supporting the assumptions, nothing has come to our attention which causes us to believe...'

IFRS

The report should refer to 'International Financial Reporting Standards' rather than 'IFRS'.

Inappropriate caveat

The caveat at the end of the report should be reworded as it somewhat undermines the credibility of the forecast and the assurance provided by stating that the forecast is unlikely to be accurate.

A more appropriate statement would refer to the uncertainty in relation to the nature of a forecast and that the actual results may vary from those anticipated.

Reference to the purpose and distribution of the report

It is common practice for a report on prospective financial information to include a reference to the purpose of the information and on its distribution. Thyme & Co should consider including this reference as a means of limiting the distribution of the report to the intended parties.

69 Crocus

Workbook reference

Chapter 14.

Top tips

This question looks at the topic of forensic audits. Many of the points were covered in an article published by the examining team in *Student Accountant* shortly before the exam, and you would have scored well if you had read this article. It is vital that you keep up to date with relevant articles in *Student Accountant* to do well in this exam.

Easy marks

These are available in parts (a) and (c) of this question as they are both knowledge-based.

ACCA examining team's comments

Requirement (b) was the core of the question. Unfortunately, two common problems detracted from the quality of many answers for this requirement. Firstly, providing tactless and unnecessary comments regarding whether the assignment should be accepted. Such comments show that candidates had failed to read and understand the scenario. Secondly, the procedures suggested were often too vague, or not even procedures at all.

Requirement (c) was not often well answered. This requirement asked for the application of the fundamental ethical principles to the provision of a forensic investigation service. Many answers were just not applied in any way, making little or no reference to forensics.

Marking guide	**Marks**
(a) Up to 1.5 marks per comment:	
• Consider whether firm has skills	
• Staff availability	
• No independence issues	
• Commercial considerations	
	4

(b) Up to 1.5 marks per comment:

- Aim – clarify fraud taken place
- Aim – discover the perpetrator(s)
- Aim – prosecute the perpetrator(s)
- Aim – quantify losses
- Method – consider type of fraud – ghost employee
- Method – understand how it could have taken place – controls override
- Method – collect evidence – suffice and relevant – allow up to 3 extra marks here if examples given of procedures that could be performed
- Method – interview suspect
- Method – produce reports
- Expert witness
- Advice and recommendations to prevent another fraud

11

(c) **Professional ethics – application of fundamental principles**

Up to 1.5 marks per comment:

- Integrity (max 1 mark)
- Objectivity
- Professional competence and due care
- Confidentiality
- Professional behaviour

1 mark for recognition that principles apply to all professional engagements

5

Professional marks

Analysis and evaluation

- Appropriate assessment of the ethical and professional issues raised, using examples where relevant to support overall comments
- Effective appraisal of the information to make suitable recommendations for appropriate courses of action

Professional scepticism and judgement

- Effective challenge of information, evidence and assumptions supplied and, techniques carried out to support key facts and/or decisions
- Appropriate application of professional judgement to draw conclusions and make informed decisions about the actions which are appropriate in the context and stage of the engagement.

Commercial acumen

- Recognition of the appropriate commercial considerations of the audit firm

Maximum	5
Total	25

(a) The audit firm should first consider whether it has the required skills and experience to perform the work if the engagement were accepted. Forensic investigations are specialist assignments, requiring a detailed knowledge of fraud investigation techniques and the legal framework; they cannot simply be performed by an external auditor. Investigators must have received training in interview and interrogation techniques, and in maintaining the safe custody of evidence gathered.

The firm does have a dedicated forensic investigation department, which suggests that it does have this expertise. Practical arrangements will therefore need to be made to ensure that the requisite staff are available to perform the investigation.

The fact that Crocus Ltd is not an audit client means that there are no independence issues to consider before acceptance.

Finally, commercial considerations are important. The negotiated fee should be sufficiently high to compensate for the specialist nature of the work, and the likely involvement of senior and experienced members of the firm in the investigation.

(b) **Objectives of a forensic investigation**

When investigating an alleged fraud, such as at Crocus Ltd, the first objective of a forensic investigation would be to **prove that deliberate fraudulent activity has actually occurred**. The employees may have been left on the payroll in error, rather than a deliberate attempt to misappropriate cash.

Once it has been established that a fraud has taken place, a forensic investigation would then aim to **identify the perpetrator or perpetrators** of the fraud. Evidence would be gathered for use in any potential court proceedings, for example, an interview with the suspected fraudster(s).

Finally, the forensic investigation may try to **quantify the financial loss** suffered as a result of the fraud. Legally, no crime has been committed unless Crocus Ltd has suffered a financial loss.

Steps involved in a forensic investigation into the payroll fraud

Establishing the type of fraud that has taken place

At Crocus Ltd, redundant employees have not been removed from the payroll. Payments to these fictitious employees (known as 'ghost employees') are now being made to the fraudster.

Determining for how long the fraud has been operating

It is likely that the fraud started on the date of the factory closure, but this will need to be confirmed.

Identifying how the fraud operated and was concealed

The forensic investigation team will determine how the fraud was conducted at Crocus Ltd and how the perpetrator concealed their actions. It appears there was a problem with internal controls over amendments to payroll data. Somehow an employee has been able to make changes to the payroll data without being detected until after payments have taken place. A control should have been in place to ensure that all amendments to payroll data are approved by a more senior member of staff before any payments are made.

Gathering evidence

Evidence will be collected by the forensic investigation team and must be sufficient to prove the following:

- That a fraud has taken place
- Who has committed the fraud and how
- The amount of financial loss suffered by Crocus Ltd

The evidence must also be relevant to the alleged case. It is important to use a skilled team to collect the evidence and keep a clear trail of its custody so that it cannot be challenged in court.

At Crocus Ltd, evidence could be obtained by the following methods:

- Reviewing and testing the authorisation procedures for the monthly payroll
- Using computer assisted audit techniques (CAATs) to look for alteration of payroll details
- Using CAATs to search for employees with no contact details, employees who have not taken holiday or sick pay, and bank account details which are the same for more than one employee
- Reconciling employees' details in the payroll database with human resources records

- Interviewing the suspect and ideally acquiring a confession. This interview is generally delayed until there is enough evidence to extract a confession and will form a key part of evidence to be presented in court.

Reporting

Once all the evidence has been collected, the forensic investigator will produce a report for the client. This report will summarise all evidence, detail the amount of financial loss suffered as a result of the fraud, and identify the suspected fraudster. It is likely that this report will be used as evidence in court.

The report may also include advice to the client to help prevent a reoccurrence of the fraud. Advice given is often in the form of suggested improvements to internal controls and systems.

Court proceedings

The forensic investigation team is likely to be called as an expert witness in any resulting court case. Team members will be asked questions about the investigation and to explain the evidence presented.

(c) **Application of fundamental principles of the IESBA's *Code of Ethics for Professional Accountants* to a forensic investigation**

The fundamental principles of the IESBA's *Code of Ethics* apply to all professional assignments.

Integrity

Forensic accountants are often, by definition, working in an environment dealing with individuals who are dishonest and lack integrity. If there is any risk that their own integrity will be compromised, they should decline or withdraw from the assignment.

Objectivity

The report produced by the forensic investigator will be used as evidence in court and must apply an opinion which is independent. A useful test of independence is that the investigator would express the same opinion if given the same instructions by the opposing party. Investigators should not take it upon themselves to promote the point of view of the party instructing them or engage in the role of advocates. Any perceived threats to objectivity will undermine the credibility of the accountant's opinion.

A perceived threat to objectivity may occur when an audit firm asks its auditors to conduct a forensic investigation. In this case there would be three threats to the firm's objectivity:

- **Advocacy.** The audit firm may feel compelled to promote the view of the client in court as they are concerned about losing an audit client and the resulting fees.
- **Management involvement.** The audit firm may be seen as making management decisions about the implication of the fraud.
- **Self-review.** A forensic investigation will require any loss suffered to be quantified. If this amount is material to the financial statements, the audit firm may end up auditing their own estimation.

The IESBA *Code* states that appropriate safeguards should be put in place to minimise these threats. If safeguards cannot reduce the threat to an acceptable level, then the firm cannot provide both services.

Professional competence and due care

Forensic investigations may require very specialised skills which require training. Examples of these skills would include:

- Evidence gathering that requires specific IT skills
- An understanding of the legal framework
- Knowledge of evidence gathering methods and the safe custody of evidence

A firm should consider very carefully whether they have adequate skills and resources before accepting the assignment. Evidence presented in court could be discredited if the team is thought to be incompetent.

Confidentiality

Forensic accountants will often be working for one party to a dispute and have access to very sensitive information. Subject, of course, to legal rules of disclosures in court cases, it is clearly essential to maintain the strictest confidentiality.

Professional behaviour

Fraud cases and other situations such as takeover disputes can be very much in the public eye. Any lapse in the professionalism of, say, an expert witness could do serious damage to the reputation of the profession as a whole.

70 Prosperitas

> **Workbook reference**
>
> Chapter 15.
>
> **Top tips**
>
> Notice that the email asks you to 'explain' the grounds. This means that you must say what they are, and then give as much further information as you can. For example, what does 'just and equitable' mean? How does a court decide that a company cannot pay its debts – how much does it have to owe?
>
> It is important to be clear about what you are being asked. In the second part of the question, do not confuse members' and creditors' (payables') winding up on one hand, with compulsory and voluntary winding up on the other.
>
> **Easy marks**
>
> In questions like this which are very technical, marks are available for just stating the law and require little application. You should be able to pass the question by repeating book knowledge.
>
> **ACCA examining team's comments**
>
> This is a preparation question which has not been examined, hence there are no comments.

Marking guide	Marks
(a) Generally 1 mark for each valid point made	
• Context of compulsory winding up	
• Unable to pay debts (2 marks max.)	
• Just and equitable ground (3 marks max.)	
	5
(b) Generally 1 mark for each valid point made	
• Instigation	
• Creditors' meeting (3 marks max.)	
• Liquidator (2 marks max.)	
• Statement of affairs	
	6
(c) Generally 1 mark for each valid point made	
• Compulsory winding up (3 marks max.)	
• Commencement	
• Specific effects (3 marks max.)	
• Retrospective effect (3 marks max.)	
	9

Marking guide	Marks
Professional marks	
Analysis and evaluation	
• Appropriate use of the information in the email to draw appropriate conclusions	
• Identification and prioritisation of key issues and stakeholders from scenario	
Professional scepticism and judgement	
• Application of professional judgement to tailor the solution to the circumstances of Prosperitas	
Commercial acumen	
• Appropriate recognition of wider issues for future of Prosperitas	
• Accurate evaluation of the implications of the proposed actions on all concerned with the company	
Maximum	5
Total	25

Briefing Notes

For: Sue Dixon

By: Khalid Huq

Subject: Prosperitas Ltd

These briefing notes identify and explain the main grounds for winding up a company; explain the distinguishing features of a creditors' voluntary winding up; and explain the immediate legal effect of a court order for compulsory winding up.

(a) **Compulsory winding-up**

A compulsory winding-up is one ordered by the court under s.122 of the Insolvency Act 1986, on one or more of seven specified grounds. The two most important of these grounds are:

- That the company is unable to pay its debts
- That it is just and equitable to wind up the company

Unable to pay its debts

Where a creditor is owed more than £750 and makes a written demand for payment and the company fails to pay the debt, or offer reasonable security for it, within three weeks, the company is deemed unable to pay its debts. The creditor may persuade the court of the company's inability to settle its debts in other ways, for example by proving that the company's assets are less than its liabilities.

Just and equitable ground

The just and equitable ground is usually relied on by a member who is dissatisfied with the directors' or controlling shareholders' management of the company, provided they can show that no other remedy is available and satisfactory.

A member who is dissatisfied with the directors or controlling shareholders over the management of the company may petition the court for a winding up on the basis that to do so is just and equitable. Such winding up orders have been made where the substratum (the only main object) of the company no longer exists (*Re German Date Coffee Co* 1882), where the company was formed for an illegal or fraudulent purpose, where there is a complete deadlock in the management of the company's affairs (*Re Yenidje Tobacco Co Ltd* 1916) and where the trust and confidence between both directors and shareholders in a small company have broken down (*Ebrahimi v Westbourne Galleries Ltd* 1973).

ANSWERS

(b) **Creditors' voluntary winding-up**

The winding up is instigated by a special resolution of the company in a general meeting, by which the company states that it cannot continue to trade because of its liabilities. Private companies may pass a written resolution with a three quarters majority.

Creditors' meeting

The company must call a meeting of creditors for a day not later than the 14th day after the day on which the special resolution was passed. The creditors must receive at least seven days notice of the meeting.

The notice must state either:

- The name and address of an insolvency practitioner who will furnish creditors free of charge with such information as they reasonably require, or
- A place in the locality where on the two business days before the meeting of creditors is held, a list of the names and addresses of the company's creditors will be available for inspection free of charge.

Notice of the creditors' meeting must be advertised in the Gazette and in at least two newspapers circulating in the locality in which the company's principal place of business was situated.

Liquidator

During the period before the creditors' meeting but after the resolution for winding-up the members' nominee will act as provisional liquidator. They will have restricted powers to act during this period, subject to application to the court. This restriction is necessitated to avoid the practice of 'centrebinding', whereby the assets are fraudulently disposed of before the creditors' meeting.

At the creditors' meeting the creditors may appoint their own nominee to act as liquidator. The creditors' choice will prevail over the members' choice if there is a conflict; usually there is not.

Statement of affairs

The directors of the company must prepare and lay before the creditors' meeting a statement of affairs of the company but, importantly, they do not have to make a statutory declaration of solvency.

(c) **Compulsory winding-up**

The statutory provisions on **compulsory winding up** are in the Insolvency Act 1986, to which all section references in this question refer.

The two **general effects** of compulsory liquidation are:

- That the management of the company passes to a liquidator and the **directors' powers cease**
- **Dispositions** of the company's **property** or **shares**, and **actions** against the company, are **restrained**

There is **no** automatic cancellation of company contracts, but many commercial contracts provide for cancellation at the option of the other party if the company goes into liquidation.

Commencement

Compulsory winding up is deemed to commence from the date on which the petition was presented, unless the company was then already in voluntary liquidation. In effect the order for compulsory liquidation is retrospective.

Specific effects

The more **specific effects** of compulsory liquidation are as follows.

- The **Official Receiver** becomes **liquidator** from the making of the order, and they continue until some other liquidator, who must be an insolvency practitioner, is appointed: s 136.
- The **powers of the directors are terminated** and they are **dismissed**.

- Any **disposition of the company's property** from the commencement of the liquidation **is void** unless approved by the court.

Retrospective effect

The court may give approval with **retrospective effect** but it is safer to apply for it in advance, when the petition has been represented. The court will only give its approval if it considers that it is in the interests of the company and its creditors that the company should continue to carry on its business pending a decision on the petition.

- Any **transfer of the company's shares is void** unless approved by the court: s 127.
- **No creditor may commence or continue legal action** against the company except with the leave of the court: s 126.
- The **employment of the company's staffceases** unless the liquidator retains them to carry on the business.
- **Floating charges crystallise.**

71 Jansen

Workbook references

Chapters 4, 10 and 13.

Top tips

This question is made up of two unrelated scenarios; one scenario features a non-audit engagement on prospective financial information (PFI); the other scenario is an insolvency scenario.

Part (a) was quite neat in the sense that the first sub-part (a)(i) focused on the first few paragraphs of the scenario, while the next sub-part (a)(ii) focused on the remaining information.

Part (a)(i) tested the matters to consider before accepting the appointment for the PFI engagement. This was partly a test of knowledge – the IESBA *Code of ethics* suggests the advocacy threat and the self-review threat – but could also have been answered simply by picking up cues from the scenario.

The next sub-part (ii) might have felt more familiar to you, dealing as it did in examination procedures. Your starting point should have been the notes, which gave you some assumptions that you should have tried to pick holes in.

One important point is that marks were available in this question for actually performing basic analytical procedures using the figures provided. This is unusual, given that the requirement did not ask you to do this – and indeed, asks for procedures to be only 'recommended', not actually performed – but you should bear this in mind when working on similar questions in the future.

Part (b) tested your knowledge of insolvency, a UK-specific syllabus area. The requirement here had two parts, the first of which was knowledge-based and second of which required some application skills. This second part was unusual for AAA because you were asked for the implications for the directors, ie not for the going concern review itself, but for the directors personally.

The distinction between fraudulent and wrongful trading is fairly straightforward, and hinges on the question of intent. However in order to score well here you would have needed to know more than just this, so if you struggled in this area then you will need to refresh your knowledge. Insolvency is an important part of the UK syllabus.

Easy marks

The mark for testing the arithmetic accuracy of the forecast in (a)(ii) was among the easiest on the exam.

ACCA examining team's comments

Part (a) asked for the considerations for an audit firm when deciding whether it could provide assurance on prospective financial information. Candidates could score well on this requirement if they had prepared by reviewing similar past requirements, the specimen exam or if they were aware of the content of ISAE 3400 *The Examination of Prospective Financial Information*. The main weaknesses in answers on this requirement was where candidates did not tailor their answer to an existing client and hence lost time giving detail on customer due diligence, or where candidates did not give detail on the ethical threats arising. This is a common area where candidates lose marks. Another area of this requirement where candidates limited their capacity to score well was by focusing on post-acceptance issues such as the production of an engagement letter rather than the pre-acceptance decision issues.

Candidates were then asked to describe procedures to be performed on the profit forecast. The majority of candidates scored well on this section and a large number of answers provided a much clearer description of audit procedures than that seen in previous sessions. A minority of candidates made bland comments about agreeing opening balances and loan covenants which were not relevant to the statement of profit or loss.

Marking guide | **Marks**

(a) **Narley Ltd**

(i) **Matters to be considered before acceptance of engagement**

Up to 2 marks for each matter explained:

- Auditor independence including potentially significant advocacy threat and possible self-review and self-interest threats
- Intended use of report, eg solely for bank or wider distribution
- Nature of assumptions and time period covered (in this case two years)
- Availability of experienced, competent staff and time frame for assurance work
- Appropriate safeguards to reduce risks to acceptable level
- Details of PFI to be given to bank, eg forecast P/Lnly?

5

(ii) **Examination procedures to be performed**

Generally up to 1 mark for each described procedure. Also allow 1 mark for each relevant analytical procedure used to max of 3 marks:

- Check arithmetic accuracy of forecast
- Agree accounting policies consistent with financial statements and comply with IFRS Standards
- Discuss key assumptions with management and assess reasonableness
- Review market research documentation and discuss with management
- Obtain and review customer contracts for new customers to confirm projected growth in revenue
- Obtain written representations from management on reasonableness and completeness of assumptions
- Assess competence and experience of client staff preparing forecasts including accuracy of PFI prepared in previous periods and reasons for any significant variances
- Perform analytical review of key trends; up to 3 marks for analysis of key trends by candidates including:

  - Growth in revenue
  - Cost of sales as % of revenue
  - Declining trend in admin expenses
  - Increase in net profit margin
- Review of capex forecasts and agreement to invoices/supplier quotations
- Recalculate depreciation and ensure correct inclusion of depreciation on new HGVs and warehousing facilities
- Obtain and review breakdown of operating expenses; ensure all items appropriately included, eg advertising/marketing costs; additional staff costs for new drivers including recruitment expenses; any trading tariffs with overseas market and any forex implications
- Inspect recent utility bills and assess reasonableness of forecast utility overheads
- Obtain and review documentation for existing loan agreements with bank and draft documentation for new loan and recalculate finance costs

7

(b) **Krupt Ltd**

Generally up to 1 mark for each point explained.

Fraudulent trading:

- Definition: carrying on business of insolvent company with intent to defraud creditors
- Can apply to any person knowingly a party to fraudulent trading
- Burden of proof: beyond reasonable doubt (criminal offence)
- Penalties and liability (0.5 mark each):
  - Imprisonment up to 10 years
  - Personal (civil) liability for debts of company
  - Disqualification as company director for up to 15 years

Wrongful trading:

- Definition: carrying on business of insolvent company when ought to have concluded/realised that no reasonable prospect of avoiding insolvent liquidation (and that creditors would therefore suffer losses)
- Only applies to company directors (including shadow directors)
- Burden of proof: balance of probabilities (civil wrong)
- Penalties and liability (0.5 mark each):
  - Personal (civil) liability for debts of company
  - Disqualification as company director for up to 15 years

Implications for Krupt Ltd:

- Mr and Mrs Krupt appear to have bought substantial quantity of goods on credit in order to ensure that bank will have sufficient secured assets to cover its debt without having to call in the personal guarantee on the directors' house; transaction will effectively transfer losses on to unsecured creditors; amounts look suspicious in that there is now sufficient inventory to cover the secured loan from the bank, ie £750,000 + £500,000 = £1,250,000 compared to a loan of £1,200,000 (up to 2 marks for this analysis if clearly stated and developed)

Marking guide	Marks
• If court concludes beyond reasonable doubt that this was intentional, imprisonment/personal liability/ disqualification will all be possible penalties	
• If court concludes insufficient evidence of fraudulent trading, it seems likely that wrongful trading will apply: Mr and Mrs Krupt are directors of company, clear evidence based on audit supervisor's findings that ought to have realised creditors would suffer losses	
• Hence liquidator will be able to seize Mr and Mrs Krupt's house (and other assets) to swell pool of assets available to distribute to all creditors of company (including unsecured)	
	8
Professional marks	
Analysis and evaluation	
• Appropriate use of the information to support discussion, draw appropriate conclusions and design appropriate responses	
• Identification of omissions from the analysis or further analysis which could be carried out	
Professional scepticism and judgement	
• Appropriate application of professional judgement to draw conclusions and make informed decisions about the actions which are appropriate in the context and stage of the engagement.	
Commercial acumen	
• Inclusion of appropriate recommendations regarding the quality management issues present	
• Appropriate recognition of the wider implications on the engagement, the audit firm and the company.	
Maximum	5
Total	25

(a) **Narley Ltd**

(i) **Matters to be considered before acceptance of engagement**

When considering acceptance of the engagement to review Narley Ltd's prospective financial information (PFI), Jansen & Co must consider whether it is ethically acceptable to perform the review. The review of the PFI represents a non-assurance service and providing this service in addition to the audit may create an advocacy threat. An advocacy threat arises when the auditor is asked to promote or represent their client in some way. In this situation there is a risk of the auditor being seen to promote the interests of the client with a third party such as a bank. As a result, there is a danger that the auditor will be biased in favour of the client and therefore cannot be fully objective. Accepting the assignment may also create a self-interest threat as a result of the auditor being perceived to have an interest in the outcome of negotiations with a third party and which may motivate the auditor to behave in order to protect that interest. A self-review threat may also arise because the negotiations may result in facts and amounts which will form part of the audited financial statements. As a result, the auditor will be auditing financial statements which in part at least represent work which they themselves have performed. It follows that there is a risk that the auditor will not be sufficiently objective in performing the audit and may fail to identify any shortcomings in their own work.

In the case of Narley Ltd, the advocacy threat appears to be particularly significant as the audit firm could be seen to be promoting the interests of the audit client to the bank. The auditor should therefore only accept the engagement if adequate safeguards can be put in place to manage the threat to independence to an acceptable level. Potential safeguards might include the following:

- The use of separate teams of suitably experienced staff for the audit and the review of the PFI
- Independent senior review of the PFI working papers
- Discussion of the potential ethical issues and threats to auditor independence with those charged with governance at Narley Ltd

It should be noted, however, that it would not be possible to manage a significant advocacy threat through such safeguards and in such a case the appointment should not be accepted.

Jansen & Co should also consider the following matters in making their acceptance decision:

- The intended use of the information – for example, whether it will be used solely for the purpose of the proposed loan finance
- Whether the information will be for general or limited distribution – the auditor needs to consider who will receive the report and potentially rely upon it
- The nature of the assumptions, that is, whether they are best-estimate or hypothetical assumptions – in this case it seems likely that they will be best estimate assumptions as Narley Ltd expects to obtain finance in order to fund its planned expansion
- The elements to be included in the information – Jansen & Co needs to clarify the exact content of the PFI which they are being asked to report on, for example, whether it only includes the forecast statements of profit or loss or whether it also includes forecast statements of financial position and forecast cash flow statements
- The period covered by the information – shorter term forecasts are likely to be more reliable than projections over a longer period

Jansen & Co must also consider whether the firm has sufficient staff available with the appropriate skills and experience to perform the review engagement in line with the client's required reporting deadlines.

Overall, the auditor must assess the risks associated with the review engagement and should not accept an engagement when the assumptions are clearly unrealistic or when the auditor believes that the prospective financial information will be inappropriate for its intended use.

(ii) **Examination procedures to be performed**

The examination procedures which should be performed in respect of Narley Ltd's forecast statements of profit or loss include the following:

- The arithmetic accuracy of the forecast statements of profit or loss should be confirmed
- Confirmation that the accounting policies used in the forecast statements are consistent with those used in the audited financial statements and that they comply with IFRS Standards
- Discuss the key assumptions which have been made by the client in the preparation of the forecast statements with management assessing their reasonableness and consistency with the audit firm's cumulative knowledge and understanding of the client
- Review of market research documentation in Narley Ltd's existing markets and the new market and discuss it with management to assess whether the growth patterns being forecast represent reasonable and realistic expectations
- Obtain copies of any new customer contracts for existing and new markets to confirm the reasonableness of the projected growth in revenue
- Obtain a written representation from management confirming the reasonableness and completeness of the assumptions they have made in preparing the forecasts
- The competence and experience of4 the client staff who have prepared the forecasts should be assessed; the assessment should include the accuracy of PFI which has

ANSWERS

been prepared in previous periods and the reasons for any significant variances compared to actual outcomes

- Recalculation of depreciation to ensure the correct inclusion of depreciation on the new HGVs and warehousing facilities within the forecast statements
- Obtain and review a breakdown of operating expenses in order to ensure that all items have been appropriately included, for example: advertising and marketing costs; additional staff costs for the new drivers including recruitment expenses; any trading tariffs relevant to operating in the new market and any foreign currency and exchange implications
- Recent utility bills should be inspected and an assessment of the reasonableness of forecast utility overheads should be performed
- Obtain and review the supporting documentation for Narley Ltd's existing loan agreements with the bank as well as the draft documentation for the new loan; the forecast finance costs should be recalculated and agreed to the forecast statements
- Perform analytical review, followed by discussion with management to seek corroborating evidence of key trends and ratios including:
  - Growth in revenue (26% from 20X8 to 20X9; 29% from 20X9 to 20Y0)
  - Cost of sales as a percentage of revenue (75.5% in 20X8; 71.3% in 20X9; 69.7% in 20Y0)
  - The declining trend in administrative expenses (decrease of 4.2% from 20X8 to 20X9; 5.6% from 20X9 to 20Y0)
  - The increase in the net profit margin (6.9% in 20X8; 15.2% in 20X9; 20.4% in 20Y0).

(b) **Krupt Ltd**

Potential liability and penalties as a result of actions for fraudulent and wrongful trading

Fraudulent trading:

Fraudulent trading is defined by the Insolvency Act 1986 (IA 1986) as carrying on the business of an insolvent company with the intent to defraud the company's creditors. Actions for fraudulent trading can be brought against any person who is knowingly a party to the fraudulent trading.

Fraudulent trading is a criminal offence and, as such, the burden of proof in a court action requires the prosecution's evidence to have established its case beyond reasonable doubt. In this regard, it is key to a successful action that the prosecution has established that intent was present in the defendant's actions.

The penalties and liability which may result from a successful action for fraudulent trading are imprisonment for up to 10 years, personal (civil) liability for the debts of company and disqualification from being a company director for up to 15 years.

Wrongful trading:

Wrongful trading is defined by IA 1986 as carrying on the business of an insolvent company when it ought to have been concluded that there was no reasonable prospect of the company avoiding insolvent liquidation and that the creditors of the company would therefore suffer losses. In contrast to fraudulent trading, it is not necessary to establish intent and wrongful trading is a civil wrong rather than a criminal offence. It is also significant that an action for wrongful trading can only be brought against company directors (including shadow directors).

As a civil wrong, the burden of proof for wrongful trading is the weaker test of the balance of probabilities. The penalties and liability which may result from a successful action for wrongful trading are personal (civil) liability of the directors for the debts of the company and disqualification from being a company director for up to 15 years.

Implications for Krupt Ltd:

Mr and Mrs Krupt appear to have bought a substantial quantity of goods on credit in order to ensure that the bank will have sufficient secured assets to cover its debt without having to call in the personal guarantee on the directors' house. The amounts involved in this transaction may be grounds for additional suspicion that the directors' actions were intended to defraud creditors – the inventory balance is now £1,250,000 (£750,000 + £500,000) which is just enough to cover the bank's secured loan. The transaction will thereby effectively transfer the losses which the directors would otherwise suffer under their personal guarantees to the bank onto the company's unsecured creditors. If the transaction has been intentionally designed to achieve this outcome, the actions of Mr and Mrs Krupt would constitute fraudulent trading. The key issue in proving this would therefore be whether the evidence establishes this intent beyond reasonable doubt. If a court were to conclude beyond reasonable doubt that it was intentional, imprisonment for up to 10 years, personal liability for the debts of the company and disqualification from being a company director for up to 15 years will all be possible penalties which the court may impose on Mr and Mrs Krupt.

Alternatively, if there is insufficient evidence of fraudulent trading, it may still be possible for creditors to bring a successful action for wrongful trading as a result of the weaker evidence test of the balance of probabilities and the fact that there is no need to establish intent. Moreover, it seems likely that an action for wrongful trading would succeed against Mr and Mrs Krupt.

They are both directors of the company and there appears to be clear evidence based on the audit supervisor's findings that they ought to have realised that the creditors of the company would suffer losses. As a result of a successful action for wrongful trading, it follows that the liquidator will be able to seize Mr and Mrs Krupt's domestic residence and other assets in order to swell the pool of assets available to distribute to all of the creditors of the company (including the unsecured creditors).

Mock Exams

ACCA

Advanced Audit and Assurance – UK (AAA – UK)

Mock Exam 1

March 2020 Exam (amended)

Questions	
Time allowed	3 hours 15 minutes
ALL THREE questions are compulsory and MUST be attempted	

DO NOT OPEN THIS EXAM UNTIL YOU ARE READY TO START UNDER EXAMINATION CONDITIONS

Section A

1 Rick Group

It is 1 July 20X5. You are a manager in the audit department of Atlanta & Co, a firm of Chartered Certified Accountants. You are working on the audit of the Rick Group (the Group), which has a financial year ending 30 September 20X5. The Group, a listed entity, offers an internet television network, with over 10 million subscription members in eight countries.

You are provided with the following exhibits:

(1) An email which you have received from the Group audit engagement partner.

(2) Background information and matters relevant to audit planning.

(3) Selected financial information from the Group management accounts.

(4) An extract from the audit strategy document prepared by Neegan Associates, the component auditor which audits one of the Group's subsidiaries.

(5) Details of the planned acquisition of a new foreign subsidiary, Michonne Co, and a possible joint audit arrangement.

Required

Respond to the instructions in the email from the audit engagement partner.

Note. The split of the mark allocation is shown in the partner's email (Exhibit 1). **(40 marks)**

Professional marks will be awarded for the demonstration of skill in communication, analysis and evaluation, professional scepticism and judgement and commercial acumen in your answer. **(10 marks)**

(Total = 50 marks)

Exhibit 1: Email from audit engagement partner

To: Audit manager

From: Carol Morgan, Audit engagement partner

Date: Audit planning for the Rick Group

Subject: 1 July 20X5

I have provided you with some information in the form of a number of exhibits which you should use to help you with planning the audit of the Rick Group (the Group) for the financial year ending 30 September 20X5. Based on the analysis I have done on this industry, it is appropriate for overall materiality to be based on the profitability of the group as this is a key focus for investors.

I require you to prepare briefing notes for my own use, in which you:

(a) Using the information in **all exhibits**, evaluate and prioritise the significant audit risks to be considered in planning the Group audit. **(21 marks)**

(b) Using the information provided in Exhibit 4:

(i) Evaluate the extract from the component auditor's strategy, commenting on the audit strategy responses and ethical matters relating to the issues identified; and **(7 marks)**

(ii) Design the principal audit procedures which you will instruct the component auditor to perform on the sale of property to the Group chief executive officer. **(6 marks)**

(c) Using Exhibit 5, discuss whether it is appropriate for a joint audit to be performed on Michonne Co, commenting on the advantages and disadvantages of a joint audit arrangement. **(6 marks)**

Thank you

Exhibit 2: Background information

The Group started to offer an internet streaming service for films and TV programmes ten years ago. The Group's business model is to acquire licences for films and TV programmes and customers pay a monthly subscription fee to access them and watch online.

The Group has a subsidiary in each country in which it offers its subscription service. Atlanta & Co audits all of the subsidiaries with the exception of Daryl Co, one of the Group's foreign subsidiaries, which is audited by a local firm called Neegan Associates. All companies within the Group have the same financial year end, and with the exception of Daryl Co, which reports under local accounting standards, the Group companies all use IFRS® Standards as their financial reporting framework.

Matters relevant to audit planning

Following a discussion between the Group audit engagement partner and a representative of the Group audit committee, several matters were noted as being relevant to the audit planning:

Legal case

In January 20X5, a legal case was initiated against the Group by Glenn Ltd, a film production company. Glenn Ltd claims that the Group has infringed copyright by streaming a film in specific countries for which a licence has not been acquired. The Group insists that the film is covered by a general licence which was acquired several years ago. The Group finance director is not willing to recognise the legal claim within the financial statements as he is confident that the claim against the Group will not be successful, and he does not want to discuss it further with the audit team, emphasising that there is no relevant documentation available for evaluation at this time.

Daryl Co

Neegan Associates provides the audit service to Daryl Co, one of the Group's foreign subsidiaries. Daryl Co is one of the Group's larger subsidiaries, it is a listed company in its home jurisdiction, with total assets of £140 million. Due to internet service issues where Daryl Co is based, a significant number of customers have cancelled their subscriptions, and the company is projected to make a loss this year.

Daryl Co is the only subsidiary which does not follow IFRS Standards, as in its local jurisdiction companies must follow local accounting rules. It uses the same currency as the rest of the Group.

Daryl Co was acquired several years ago, and goodwill of £38 million is recognised in the Group financial statements in respect of the company.

Exhibit 3: Selected financial information

	Note	*Projected to 30 September 20X5*	*Actual to 30 September 20X4*
		£ million	£ million
Group revenue	1	980	780
Operating profit		78.4	70.2
Profit before tax		60.1	58.7
Total assets		780	600
Included in total assets:			
Intangible assets – licences	2	580	420
Intangible assets – goodwill	3	135	135
Number of subscription customers		**10,500,000**	**8,070,000**

Notes.

1 The Group's main source of revenue is from monthly membership fees. Members are billed in advance of the start of their monthly membership and revenue is recognised when the bill is sent to the customer, all of whom pay by credit card. The price of a regular subscription has remained at £8·20 per month throughout 20X4 and 20X5. Occasionally, the Group offers a free trial period to new customers. This year, the Group also introduced a new premium subscription package, which allows customers to add two family members to their subscription for an additional fee of £5 per month.

2 The Group acquires content licences per title in order to stream film and TV content to its subscribers. The content licences are each for a fixed time period, varying between three and five years. The Group capitalises the cost per title as an intangible asset. Group policy is to amortise licences over a five-year period, the finance director justifies this as being 'the most prudent' accounting treatment.

3 Goodwill arising on business combinations is tested annually for impairment in accordance with IAS® 36 *Impairment of Assets*. Due to the strong performance of the Group, no impairment of goodwill has been recognised in recent years.

Exhibit 4: Extract from component auditor strategy document

The points below are an extract from the audit strategy prepared by Neegan Associates in relation to their audit of Daryl Co. Other sections of the audit strategy, including the audit risk assessment, have been reviewed by the Group audit team and are considered satisfactory so you do not need to consider them. Materiality has been set by Neegan Associates, in agreement with Atlanta & Co, at £1.4million.

Issue identified by Neegan Associates	Audit strategy response by Neegan Associates
Payroll	**Planned audit procedures:**
From 1 October 20X4, payroll accounting services are provided to Daryl Co by Neegan Associates as an additional non-audit engagement.	• Agree the total payroll figure, estimated to be £6 million, from the statement of profit or loss to the payroll reports generated by Neegan Associates. • No further audit procedures are considered necessary.
Sale of property	**Planned audit procedures:**
Daryl Co sold a small, unused building located on the coast to the Group's chief executive officer (CEO) in February 20X5, for £50,000. The amount is still outstanding for payment. The Group CEO is planning to use the property as a holiday home.	• Confirm £50,000 is included in receivables within current assets. • No further audit procedures are considered necessary because the transaction is not material to the financial statements, and local accounting rules do not require disclosure of the transaction.

Exhibit 5: Potential new subsidiary

The Group is planning the acquisition of a new foreign subsidiary, Michonne Co, which is located in Farland. The negotiations are at an advanced stage, and it is likely that the acquisition will take place in October 20X5.

The Group's audit committee has suggested that if the acquisition goes ahead, due to the distant location of the company and the fact that Atlanta & Co has no offices in Farland, a joint audit could be performed with Michonne Co's current auditors, Lucille Associates, a small local firm of Chartered Certified Accountants.

Section B

2 Saul

It is 1 July 20X5. You work in the audit department of Saul & Co. The Goodman Group (the Group) is an audit client of your firm and the audit for the financial year ended 31 December 20X4 is in the completion stage. The Group, which is not listed, installs and maintains security systems for businesses and residential customers.

Materiality for the audit of the Group financial statements has been determined to be £400,000. You are reviewing the audit working papers, and have gathered the following information:

Fraud

The Group finance director has informed the audit team that during the year, a fraud was carried out by a manager, Mike Trout, in one of the Group's procurement departments. The manager had raised fictitious supplier invoices and paid the invoiced amounts into his personal bank account. When questioned by the Group's finance director, Mike Trout confessed that he had stolen £40,000 from the Group. The finance director asked the audit team not to perform any procedures in relation to the fraud, as the amount is immaterial. He also stated that the financial statements would not be adjusted in relation to the fraud.

The only audit evidence on file is a written representation from management acknowledging the existence of the fraud, and a list of the fictitious invoices which had been raised by the manager, provided by the finance director. The audit working papers conclude that the fraud is immaterial and no further work is needed.

Development costs

In August 20X4, the Group commenced development of a new security system, and incurred expenditure of £600,000 up to the financial year end, which has been capitalised as an intangible non-current asset. The only audit evidence obtained in relation to this balance is as follows:

- Agreement of a sample of the costs included in the £600,000 capitalised to supporting documentation such as supplier invoices.
- Cash flow projection for the project, which indicates that a positive cash flow will be generated by 20X8. The projection has been arithmetically checked.
- A written representation from management stating that 'management considers that the development of this new product will be successful'.

You are aware that when the Group finance director was asked about the cash flow projection which he had prepared, he was reluctant to answer questions, simply saying that 'the assumptions underlying the projection have been agreed to assumptions contained in the Group's business plan'. He provided a spreadsheet showing the projection, but the underlying information could not be accessed as the file was password protected and the Group finance director would not provide the password to the audit team.

Trade receivables

Trade receivables recognised in the Group's current assets includes a balance of £500,000 relating to a specific customer, Hamlyn Ltd. As at 31 December 20X4, the balance was more than six months overdue for payment. The Group credit controller states that they are confident that the debt will be recovered in full, however as of 1 July 20X5, the debt had not been repaid.

Required

(a) (i) Discuss the implications of the fraud for the completion of the audit, and the actions to be taken by the auditor. **(6 marks)**

(ii) In respect of the development costs ONLY:

- Comment on the sufficiency and appropriateness of the audit evidence obtained
- Recommend the actions to be taken by the auditor, including the further evidence which should be obtained

(6 marks)

(b) The audit work is now complete, and the Group auditor's report is due to be issued in the next few days. Materiality for the audit of the Group financial statements has continued to be determined to be £400,000. You have been tasked with reviewing the draft auditor's report and the following supplementary information which has been prepared at the end of the audit:

- The audit partner has concluded that the fraud is immaterial and that all necessary work has been performed by the audit team.
- Further audit procedures were successfully performed on the development costs, and a conclusion was reached by the audit team that the recognition of the £600,000 as an intangible asset is appropriate.
- A letter was received from Hamlyn Ltd's administrators on 29 July 20X5, stating that Hamlyn Ltd is in liquidation, and that its creditors will receive a payment of 10% of outstanding balances. The audit team has concluded that £50,000 can remain recognised as a trade receivable, and that £450,000 should be written off as irrecoverable. However, the Group refuses to make any adjustment, and the full £500,000 remains recognised as a trade receivable in the final Group financial statements.

Draft auditor's report

Based on the above conclusions, the audit supervisor has drafted the auditor's report which includes the following extract:

Basis for opinion and opinion

Audit procedures indicate that trade receivables are overstated by £500,000. For this reason we consider that the Group financial statements are likely to be materially misstated and do not fairly present the financial position and performance of the Group for the year ended 31 December 20X4.

Emphasis of matter

There are two matters to which we draw your attention:

(1) A fraud was discovered, as a result of which we have determined that £40,000 was stolen from the Group. This does not impact the financial statements but we wish to highlight the illegal activity which took place during the year.

(2) The Group finance director obstructed our audit by refusing to allow access to audit evidence. He has also refused to adjust the financial statements in relation to the material misstatement of trade receivables, which led to the qualified audit opinion being issued. For this reason, we wish to resign as auditor with immediate effect.

Required

Critically appraise the extract from the proposed auditor's report of the Goodman Group for the year ended 31 December 20X4.

Note. You are NOT required to re-draft the extracts from the auditor's report. **(8 marks)**

Professional marks will be awarded for the demonstration of skill in analysis and evaluation, professional scepticism and judgement and commercial acumen in your answer. **(5 marks)**

(Total = 25 marks)

3 Moritz

(a) It is 1 July 20X5. You are a manager in Moritz & Co, a firm of Chartered Certified Accountants which offers a range of services to audit and non-audit clients. Your firm has been asked to consider a potential engagement to review and provide an assurance report on prospective financial information (PFI) for Lavenza Ltd, which is not an audit client of your firm. Moritz & Co has already conducted specific client identification procedures in line with money laundering regulations with satisfactory results.

Lavenza Ltd has approached your firm in order to obtain an independent assurance opinion on a cash flow forecast which is being prepared for its bankers in support of an application for an increase in its existing overdraft facility. The following cash flow forecast has been prepared by the finance director of Lavenza Ltd for the 12 months to 30 June 20X6:

Lavenza Ltd cash flow forecast for the 12 months ending 30 June 20X6

	3 months to 30 September 20X5	*3 months to 31 December 20X5*	*3 months to 31 March 20X6*	*3 months to 30 June 20X5 20X6*
	£'000	£'000	£'000	£'000
Operating cash receipts				
Cash sales – high street shops	4,343	4,690	5,065	5,471
Cash sales – online	6,782	7,053	7,335	7,628
Receipts from credit sales – online	11,987	12,346	12,717	13,099
	23,112	24,089	25,117	26,198
Operating cash payments				
Purchases of inventory	(10,846)	(11,388)	(11,730)	(12,316)
Salaries	(7,254)	(7,109)	(7,180)	(7,384)
Overheads	(6,459)	(6,265)	(6,391)	(6,659)
	(24,559)	(24,762)	(25,301)	(26,359)
Other cash flows				
Initial costs of new high street shops	(2,143)	(1,128)		
Online marketing campaign	(624)	(431)	(386)	(278)
	(2,767)	(1,559)	(386)	(278)
Cash flow for the period	(4,214)	(2,232)	(570)	(439)
Opening cash	(9,193)	(13,407)	(15,639)	(16,209)
Closing cash	(13,407)	(15,639)	(16,209)	(16,648)

The following information is also relevant:

(1) Lavenza Ltd is a retailer of academic textbooks which it sells through its own network of book shops and online through its website. The revenue from the website includes both cash sales and sales on credit to educational institutions. The company has provided historical analysis from its trade receivables ledger indicating that for sales made on credit, 10% pay in the month of the sale, 62% after 30 days, 16% after 60 days, 8% after 90 days and the remainder are irrecoverable debts.

(2) The company already has an established presence in large cities with universities but has seen a decline in its core operations in recent years which has led to a decrease in revenue and a fall in liquidity. In order to reverse these trends, the company is planning to extend its operations by opening new shops in small cities with universities and large colleges.

(3) Lavenza Ltd's management is planning an online marketing campaign targeted at the university sector which they believe will increase the company's market share by approximately 3%.

(4) The company has an existing overdraft facility of £12 million with its bankers and has requested an increase in the facility to £17 million.

Required

(i) Explain the matters to be considered by Moritz & Co before accepting the engagement to review and report on Lavenza Ltd's prospective financial information; and

(6 marks)

(ii) Assuming Moritz & Co accepts the engagement, recommend the examination procedures to be performed in respect of Lavenza Ltd's cash flow forecast. **(7 marks)**

(b) You have also been asked to advise the directors of a different audit client, Alucard Ltd, in relation to potential insolvency procedures and their implications for the directors.

You have been the manager responsible for the audit of Alucard Ltd for the last three years. Alucard Ltd manufactures pet foods which it sells to wholesale and retail customers both in the UK and internationally. The company has experienced a decrease in profitability in recent years as a result of increased trading tariffs making its products more expensive for its international customers. Alucard Ltd has experienced a significant fall in demand for its products and five months ago, the company's largest international customer, Holden Co, cancelled its contract with Alucard Ltd. Historically, Holden Co has represented approximately 45% of Alucard Ltd's total sales revenue.

The company's managing director, Bella Lugosi, remains confident that the company will be able to replace the lost sales and has insisted on maintaining existing operating levels. As a result, Alucard Ltd's payables payment period has increased from 45 days to 73 days over the last five months and the company's cash position has deteriorated to the point where it is unable to pay its creditors as they fall due. A review of the client's records has also identified that the company has three months of arrears of unpaid taxes including PAYE and NIC and has received penalty notices in relation to its failure to file its last audited financial statements with Companies House. The company's management accounts have shown a negative cash balance in excess of its overdraft facility and a net liabilities position for the last three months.

The directors of Alucard Ltd have approached you in relation to their concerns about the company's current financial difficulties and potential insolvency. They have also heard that if directors are found to have conducted fraudulent or wrongful trading, there can be significant consequences including personal liability to the company's creditors. They have asked you to prepare information to be presented at next week's board meeting in order to advise them on:

(1) The key features of the administration process; and

(2) Whether based on the information provided, they might be personally liable to Alucard Ltd's creditors.

Required

Respond to the request made by the directors of Alucard Ltd.

(7 marks)

Professional marks will be awarded for the demonstration of skill in analysis and evaluation, professional scepticism and judgement and commercial acumen in your answer. **(5 marks)**

(Total = 25 marks)

Answers

DO NOT TURN THIS PAGE UNTIL YOU HAVE COMPLETED THE MOCK EXAM

A plan of attack

If this had been the real Advanced Audit and Assurance exam and you had been told to start the exam, what would have been going through your mind?

An important thing to say (while there is still time) is that it is vital to have a good breadth of knowledge of the syllabus because the question requirements for each question will relate to different areas of the AAA syllabus. However, don't panic. Below we provide guidance on how to approach the exam.

Approaching the answer

It is vital that you attempt all the questions in the exam to increase your chances of passing. The best way to do this is to make sure you stick to the time allocation for each question – both in total and for each of the question parts. The worst thing you can do is run over time in one question and then find that you don't have enough time for the remaining questions, leading you to miss out on some of the easier marks in those questions.

Section A consists of one long case-study style question set at the planning stage of the audit. This may contain detailed information such as extracts from financial statements and audit working papers. A range of requirements will be set for this question but will mainly cover areas from syllabus areas A to D inclusive.

Question 1 is for 50 marks, all set at the planning stage in the context of a single scenario, here dealing with the audit of a large group. As it is a very long question, it is important that you break it down into its component parts as this will make it easier to manage – and enable you to allocate your time to each of them.

Section B contains two more compulsory questions and may be set on any area of the AAA syllabus.

Question 2, for 25 marks, featured a review of audit evidence and a requirement to critique an auditor's report.

Question 3 offers 25 marks that were made up of two mini scenarios, one dealing with an engagement to review prospective financial information, and the other featuring a requirement in relation to the insolvency process.

Forget about it!

And don't worry if you found the exam difficult. More than likely other candidates did too. If this were the real thing, you would need to forget the exam the minute you finished it and think about the next one. Or, if it is the last one, celebrate!

Section A

1 Rick Group

Workbook references

Chapters 6, 7 and 9.

Top tips

Your general approach should be to read the requirement carefully, and then to work through the question noting down issues (audit risks) as they occur to you.

Part (a) was the standard requirement to 'evaluate and prioritise significant' risks – in this case audit risks, which means that points regarding the audit itself (detection risk) are valid. It is very important that you do not limit yourself to just a few exhibits – the question tells you to cover all of them, and you must do this if you are to pass this part. It is also noteworthy that AAA requirements in Question One tend to ask you to prioritise risks in addition to evaluating them. This does not mean that you need to eg, rank the risks in order, but rather that your discussion of the risks needs to include a consideration of their significance for the audit. You will not score well in this question part if you merely list all of the risks but without writing about their relative importance for the audit.

ANSWERS

Part (b) focused on the component auditor's strategy document. This is a novel requirement for AAA and requires you to think about the appropriateness of the component auditor's strategy from the point of view of the group auditor.

Joint audits, in part (c), are an area that have been examined before and which remain topical.

The examiner's comments here are substantial, but they are worth reading because they give you an insight into what candidates actually did when this question came up in their exam, and they offer some information about how to score marks and how to avoid common pitfalls.

Easy marks

The presentation marks here are valuable and are well worth the time it takes to get them.

ACCA examiner's comments

This question was a compulsory 50-mark case study consisting of four parts and focused on the planning phase of the group audit of an existing client. The group was a listed entity and offered a subscription-based internet streaming service for films and TV programmes.

It should be noted that only a brief introduction is required, and time should not be spent writing a half-page introduction or a lengthy conclusion. For a structured, well-presented answer, simple headed paragraphs are enough to score these marks. Candidates need not be concerned with spending time underlining or numbering headings, so long as it is clear which question is being attempted. For clarity marks, the marker will consider whether they understood the candidate's response and the discussion satisfied the question requirement. Candidates will not be penalised for poor spelling or grammar.

With **requirement (a)**, candidates generally performed well on this section of the question, yet it was disappointing to see candidates focus on what appeared to be rote learnt risks and points which were not relevant to the question.

A number of candidates discussed the risk of the foreign subsidiaries having different year ends to the group, yet the question clearly stated all companies within the group had the same year end, and no marks were awarded.

General consolidation risks, intra-group eliminations, disclosures required for listed entities were all deemed speculative risks and did not receive credit. There was no evidence within the question that the group companies traded with each other or that the group was recently listed and therefore may not adhere to stock market listing requirements or corporate governance requirements, for example. Candidates are advised to use the detail of the specific scenario given and discuss the risks accordingly to demonstrate application of audit knowledge to a given scenario.

A further area that demonstrated a lack of application to the scenario surrounded the impairment of goodwill performed by the group on an annual basis. A number of candidates discussed the general treatment of goodwill, that it is to be tested for impairment on an annual basis and that management had not tested impairment and therefore concluding on the financial statement impact that goodwill would be overstated. The question clearly referred to the group correctly performing the annual impairment review but had not recognised impairment due to strong performance. The key issue here was the indicator of impairment within the foreign subsidiary and the impact this would have on the impairment review performed.

Some other common issues noted in candidate answers for Audit Risk included:

- Discussing audit procedures to be performed which did not meet the question requirement and therefore no credit was awarded. If required, this will normally form a separate requirement within the question and should be answered where applicable.
- Several candidates discussed the annual incentive and suggested it was a share-based payment which was incorrect and showed that many candidates had not read the question carefully enough.
- Several candidates appear to only possess a brief overview of the accounting standards without sufficient knowledge of the underlying principles. It is disappointing to see, for example, the accounting rule for IAS 37 *Provisions, Contingent Liabilities and Contingent*

Assets not described sufficiently considering it is one of the easier accounting standards for candidates to apply.

Overall, candidates would be advised to read the requirement carefully to ensure the answer given is relevant and not too generic to avoid losing marks, that would be easily achievable.

Candidates that demonstrated good technique in calculating materiality, identifying the audit risk in the scenario, discussing the relevant accounting treatment and finally the impact the error will have on the financial statements scored well.

Requirement (b) (i), for seven marks asked candidates to evaluate an extract from the component auditor's strategy for two issues and to also comment on the ethical issues arising from the issues identified.

Generally, the responses to the evaluation of the component auditor's strategy were disappointing. The question stated that **only** the three points within the extract were to be reviewed and that other sections of the strategy, including risk assessment had been reviewed already by the group audit team and considered satisfactory. A number of candidates continued to comment that due to the lack of other detail, the component auditors were not competent and should not be relied upon.

The question was testing the candidates' knowledge of understanding the difference between the component audit for the individual subsidiary financial statements compared to that of the group. There is a significant gap in candidates' learning relating to this.

A number of candidates showed a lack of understanding regarding materiality and stated that materiality thresholds are stated within the ISA (International Standards of Auditing), when this is not correct as there are no set rules as to how the level of materiality should be arrived at, rather a percentage is applied to a chosen benchmark as a starting point. Many candidates did not mention the importance of auditor judgement in relation to materiality. Where candidates referred to the auditor being in breach of the auditing standard in the calculation of materiality, marks could not be awarded without further development.

A number of candidates were unable to appreciate the difference between the component financial statements and the group financial statements. A number of candidates referred to the related party transaction to the group CEO requiring disclosure in the notes to the financial statements. The key issue here is that the related party transaction is required to be disclosed in the consolidated financial statements from the group perspective and therefore needed to be specifically addressed as part of the group audit.

Requirement (b)(ii), for six marks asked candidates to design the principal audit procedures which would be instructed to the component auditor to perform on the sale of the property to the Group CEO. Overall candidates scored well here, yet there were instances that were disappointing to note such as significant numbers suggesting procedures to check physical existence of the property (that had been sold before the year end), or to verify the asset was remaining in the fixed asset register, again despite the asset being sold to the CEO prior to the year end.

Candidates that applied good technique to procedures questions, such as stating what procedure they would perform along with the purpose of the procedures will score well.

Requirement (c) for six marks asked candidates to discuss the appropriateness of a joint audit in relation to a planned acquisition of a new foreign subsidiary and to state advantages and disadvantages of a joint audit. This requirement should have scored well, as it was an easier requirement and was answered well by students who had learnt the topic area.

However, a number of students appeared to confuse a joint audit with a group and component audit situations and therefore marks would not be awarded for discussions of discussing competence of the component auditor and ethical requirements as these were not relevant to the requirement.

(a) **Audit risk evaluation**

In addition, 0.5 mark for relevant trends or calculations which form part of the evaluation of audit risk (max 2 marks).

Appropriate materiality calculations (max 2 marks) and justified materiality level should be awarded to a maximum of 1 mark.

- Analytical review
- Reliance on component auditor (2 marks)
- Daryl Co – possible impairment
- Trends in revenue and revenue recognition (2 marks)
- Amortisation of licences
- Legal case
- Group finance director's attitude (2 marks)
- Daryl Co – local accounting rules (2 marks)
- Post year-end acquisition of Michonne Co

Maximum — 21

(b) (i) **Evaluation of Neegan Associates' audit strategy**

Up to 1 mark for each issue evaluated:

Payroll

- Further procedures necessary given the materiality of the payroll
- Requirement of ISA (UK) 600 (Revised) that same ethical guidelines should be applied
- Self-review threat from Neegan Associates providing the service – explained
- The service should not have been provided due to Daryl Co's listed status

Sale of property

- Transaction should be disclosed in Group accounts and is material by nature
- No consideration of whether the profit on disposal has been properly determined
- Risk that the transaction is subject to bias given that company is loss making
- Property might not even have been sold, could be window dressing
- No procedures to confirm asset has been removed from the financial statements or on the recoverability of the amount outstanding
- Conclusion on audit quality

Maximum — 7

(ii) **Audit procedures on sale of property**

- Review board minutes to see if the property sale has been discussed and formally approved by the company's board
- Agree the £50,000 sale price to the legal documentation relating to the sale of the property to the Group CEO
- Confirm the book value of the property at the date of disposal to underlying accounting records and non-current asset register
- Confirm that the asset has been removed from the company accounts at the date of disposal
- Obtain management's determination of profit or loss on disposal, re-perform the calculation based on supporting evidence, and agree the profit or loss is recognised appropriately in the company statement of

Obtain an estimate of the fair value of the property, for example, by comparison to the current market price of similar propertiesprofit or loss

- Obtain written representations from company management that all matters related to this related party transaction have been disclosed to the Group management and to the Group audit team
- Obtain written representation from the Group CEO regarding the transaction, to confirm the amount which is outstanding, and the likely timescale for payment
- Review cash receipts after the reporting date to confirm whether or not the £50,000 has been received from the Group CEO

Maximum 6

(c) **Joint audit**

Up to 1 mark for each relevant point discussed:

Justification in favour of joint audit

- Retain local auditors' knowledge of company
- Local auditors' knowledge of local regulations
- Atlanta & Co can provide additional skills and resources
- Cost effective – reduce travel expenses, local firm likely to be cheaper
- Enhanced audit quality

Possible disadvantages of joint audit

- Employing two audit firms could be more expensive
- Problems in allocating work and determining responsibilities
- Auditor liability issues
- Recommendation

Maximum 6

Professional marks

Communication

- Briefing note format and structure - use of headings/sub-headings and an introduction
- Style, language and clarity - appropriate layout and tone of briefing notes, presentation of materiality and relevant calculations, appropriate use of the CBE tools, easy to follow and understand
- Effectiveness and clarity of communication - answer is relevant and tailored to the scenario
- Adherence to the specific requests made by the audit engagement partner

Analysis and Evaluation

- Appropriate use of the information to determine and apply suitable calculations
- Appropriate use of the information relating to the sale of the property to design appropriate audit procedures
- Effective prioritisation of the results of the audit risk evaluation to demonstrate the likelihood and magnitude of risks and to facilitate the allocation of appropriate responses
- Balanced discussion of the professional and practical issues when evaluating working with component auditors in a Group engagement.

Professional scepticism and judgement

- Appropriate application of professional judgement to draw conclusions and make informed decisions following recognition of unusual or unexpected movements, missing/incomplete information or challenging presented information as part of the risk evaluation

- Determination and justification of a suitable materiality level, appropriately and consistently applied
- Identification of possible management bias and consideration of the impact on the financial statements and the possible reasons for management's preference for certain accounting treatments
- Effective application of technical and ethical guidance to effectively challenge and critically assess how management has responded to the legal claim and the adequacy of any provision or disclosure requirements.

Commercial acumen

- Use of effective examples and/or calculations from the scenario to illustrate points or recommendations
- Appropriate recognition of the wider implications when considering entering into a joint audit engagement. 10

Total 50

Word Processor

Briefing notes

To: Audit engagement partner

From: Audit manager

Subject: Rick Group – Audit planning

Introduction

These briefing notes are prepared to assist with planning the audit of the Rick Group (the Group) for the financial year ending 30 September 20X5. The notes contain an evaluation of the audit risks, which should be considered in planning the Group audit. The notes also evaluate the audit strategy, which has been prepared by Neegan Associates for the audit of Daryl Co and recommend further audit procedures to be performed by the component auditors. Finally, the briefing notes address the issue of a potential joint audit, should a new subsidiary be acquired in Farland next year.

Note. Remember, you can access the ACCA's Practice Platform to learn how to attempt AAA questions using the CBE software.

(a) **Audit risk evaluation**

Materiality

For the purposes of these briefing notes, the following overall materiality level will be used to assess the significance of identified risks and as requested, this has been based on the profitability of the company.

Benchmarks

5-10% of profit before tax = range of £3,005,000-£6,010,000.

This benchmark is only a starting point for determining planning materiality and therefore professional judgment will need to be applied when determining a final level to be applied during the course of the audit. This is an existing client, and no significant control issues have been noted at the planning stage or in previous audits. Therefore, the overall risk assessment is deemed to be low so the materiality benchmark of £6million has been set as an appropriate level at the planning stage. This materiality may need to be revisited during the audit or at a later stage if information or testing (control or substantive) indicates potential issues.

Financial analysis

Balances which are subject to judgment should be considered carefully when assessing audit risks of the Group. Licences are significant as they are intangible assets representing 74.4% of total Group assets. The audit work will need to ensure that the valuation and that of the goodwill of Daryl Co, which has seen significant trading issues during the year.

The financial information shows that total revenue is projected to increase by 25·6% this financial year. This is a significant increase and it could indicate that revenue is overstated. However, the number of subscription members is projected to increase by 30·1%, so possibly the increase in revenue is simply as a result of the Group attracting more customers – but this is a very significant increase and will need to be substantiated.

The audit risks for these areas are considered further in these briefing notes.

Reliance on component auditors

As group auditor, we should exercise professional judgement in determining the components at which audit work will be performed. Daryl Co's assets equate to 17·9% of the Group's total projected assets and so Daryl Co is certainly material to the group.

Given the materiality of Daryl Co, the Group audit team needs to consider the extent of reliance which can be placed on the audit of the company conducted by Neegan Associates. The independence and competence of Neegan Associates will need to be evaluated by the Group audit team, though presumably as the audit firm already has experience of Neegan Associates from previous years' audits, this evaluation will already have been performed. However, independence is threatened by the fact that Neegan Associates has been engaged in providing a non-audit service to Daryl Co since 1 October 20X4. This matter is discussed further in the section of the briefing notes dealing with the component auditor's strategy. Any material misstatements which may remain uncorrected in Daryl Co will impact on the consolidated financial statements, leading to increased aggregation risk and therefore increased audit risk at the Group level.

Daryl Co – possible impairment

The goodwill of £38million in relation to Daryl Co is material to the Group financial statements based on the threshold of £6million.

According to IAS 36 *Impairment of Assets*, goodwill should be tested for impairment annually, which is the Group's accounting policy. The audit strategy prepared by Neegan Associates indicates that Daryl Co is loss making this year, which is an indication of impairment. Therefore, management will need to factor this into their impairment review. As the Group's performance in the past has been strong, no goodwill impairment has been recognised, and management may lack experience in dealing with a loss-making subsidiary as part of their impairment testing. There is also an incentive for impairment losses not to be recognised, due to the annual incentive scheme which is based on profit.

For these reasons, there is an audit risk that goodwill could be overstated, and expenses understated, if any necessary impairment loss is not correctly determined and recognised.

Trend in revenue

The financial information shows that total revenue is projected to increase by 25·6% this financial year. However, when looking at revenue per customer per year, this is projected to fall from £96·65 in 20X4 to £93·33 in 20X5. Revenue per customer per month is therefore projected to fall from £8·05 in 20X4 to £7·78 in 20X5. These trends seem to contradict the introduction of the new premium subscription package, which should bring in additional revenue per customer. Possibly the premium subscription has not been taken up by many customers. It is, however, unusual to see a downwards trend in revenue per customer per month, given that the price of a regular subscription has remained the same as in the previous year, at £8·20 per month. Possibly the figures are impacted by the free trial period offered to new customers. These trends will need to be investigated to ensure that revenue is being measured appropriately and recognised at the correct point in time.

There is also a risk arising from the Group invoicing customers in advance, with revenue recognised when the bill is sent to the customer. Possibly this could lead to early recognition of revenue, i.e. recognising prior to the Group providing a service to its customers. IFRS 15 *Revenue from Contracts with Customers* requires that revenue is recognised when a performance obligation is satisfied by transferring a promised good or service to a customer, and when providing a service over time, it can be difficult to determine how much service has been provided and therefore the amount of revenue which can be recognised at a particular point in time. There is therefore a risk of overstatement of revenue if the requirements of IFRS 15 are not adhered to.

Amortisation of licences

The licences recognised as intangible assets are highly material to the Group. Given that each licence is for a fixed period, it is appropriate to amortise the cost of each licence over that fixed period in accordance with IAS 38 *Intangible Assets*, which requires that the cost of an intangible asset with a finite useful life should be amortised on a systematic basis over its life.

Therefore, the Group's accounting policy to amortise all licences over a five-year period may be too simplistic, especially given the significance of the balance to the Group financial statements. Some of the licences have a shorter life, and some may be longer, indicating that the determination of amortisation for the class of assets as a whole may not be accurate, leading to over or undervaluation of intangible assets and over or understatement of profit.

The finance director's assertion that the accounting policy is 'the most prudent' is not appropriate. The accounting policy should be based on the specific, relevant IAS 38 requirements. It could be a means of earnings management, i.e. to minimise the amortisation charge and maximise profits.

The auditor should also consider whether this issue has arisen in previous years' audits. The Group may have changed its estimation technique with regard to amortisation of intangible assets; if this is the case, the rationale for the change must be understood.

Legal case

In January 20X5, a legal case was brought against the Group. From the information provided, it is not possible to determine if it is material, however, there should be appropriate consideration as to whether the court case gives rise to an obligation at the reporting date.

According to IAS® 37 *Provisions, Contingent Liabilities and Contingent Assets*, a provision should be recognised as a liability if there is a present obligation as a result of past events which gives rise to a probable outflow of economic benefit which can be reliably measured. There is therefore an audit risk that if any necessary provision is not recognised, liabilities and expenses will be understated.

If there is a possible obligation at the reporting date, then disclosure of the contingent liability should be made in the notes to the financial statements. There is a risk of inadequate disclosure if the Group finance director refuses to make appropriate disclosure in the notes – this is an audit risk whether the situation gives rise to a provision or a contingent liability, as provisions also have disclosure requirements which may not be complied with.

Group finance director's attitude

There may be a further issue related to the legal case regarding the attitude of the Group finance director, who appears to have dismissed the accounting implications of the legal case and is reluctant to discuss the matter with the audit team. This could indicate that the Group finance director is deliberately obstructing the work of the audit team, and perhaps has something to hide. This indicates a potential wider issue, that the Group finance director is imposing a limitation on the scope of the audit. The Group audit strategy should consider this issue, and the audit engagement partner may wish to discuss the issue with the Group audit committee as a matter of urgency.

This increases the risk that the legal claim will not be recognised appropriately in the financial statements, and the audit team must approach this issue with a heightened degree of professional scepticism.

There may be other areas in which professional scepticism should be applied, for instance, in respect of the amortisation of intangible assets, which will be discussed later in the briefing notes, and where the Group finance director appears to be using inappropriate justifications for the Group's accounting treatment of licence fees.

Daryl Co – local accounting rules

This company is the only component of the Group which does not use IFRS® Standards as its financial reporting framework. Daryl Co's financial statements will be prepared under local accounting rules and audited by Neegan Associates on that basis. In accordance with IFRS® 3 *Business Combinations*, for the purpose of consolidation the Group's accounting policies must be applied to all balances and transactions which form part of the consolidated financial statements. There is an audit risk that the Group's policies are not applied correctly, meaning that the amounts consolidated in respect of Daryl Co are not recognised, measured or disclosed appropriately.

Post year-end acquisition of Michonne Co

The acquisition of Michonne Co is planned to take place within a month of the reporting date. It is therefore a significant event which is taking place after the year end and as such, it falls under the scope of IAS 10 *Events After the Reporting Period*. According to IAS 10, a non-adjusting event is an event which is indicative of a condition which arose after the end of the reporting period, and which should be disclosed if they are of such importance that non-disclosure would affect the ability of users to make proper evaluations and decisions. The required disclosure includes the nature of the event and an estimate of its financial effect or a statement that a reasonable estimate of the effect cannot be made. In addition, IFRS 3 requires disclosure of information about a business combination whose acquisition date is after the end of the reporting period but before the financial statements are authorised for issue.

There is therefore an audit risk that the disclosure in relation to the acquisition of Michonne Co is not complete or accurate.

(b) (i) **Evaluation of component auditor's audit strategy**

Audit of payroll

The audit work planned on payroll appears to be limited due to the audit firm, Neegan Associates, having performed a payroll service for Daryl Co since 1 October 20X4. This is not appropriate and will not provide sufficient and appropriate audit evidence regarding the £6 million payroll expense. Given that payroll is material to the company's financial statements, based on Neegan Associates' own materiality threshold of £1·4 million, further testing will be required.

An ethical threat to auditor's independence is raised by the provision of the payroll service to the client. There is a significant self-review threat which means that Neegan Associates is over-relying on the work they have performed on payroll as a non-audit engagement and are not planning to audit the £6 million at all.

Providing this type of non-audit service might be allowed in the jurisdiction where Neegan Associates operates. However, according to ISA (UK) 600 (Revised) *Special Considerations – Audits of Group Financial Statements (Including the Work of Component Auditors)*, when performing work on the financial information of a component for a group audit, the component auditor is subject to ethical requirements which are relevant to the group audit. Such requirements may be different or in addition to those applying to the component auditor when performing a statutory audit in the component auditor's jurisdiction.

Therefore, the IESBA *International Code of Ethics for Professional Accountants (the Code)* should be applied. The Code states that for a listed company, a firm shall not provide accounting or bookkeeping services, including payroll services, which results in financial information which forms the basis of financial statements on which the firm will provide an opinion. Therefore, as Daryl Co is listed, the service should not have been provided.

ANSWERS

There also needs to be discussion of the situation with Neegan Associates and the management of Daryl Co and the Group, with the objective of ensuring that an alternative provider is found for the payroll accounting services.

Sale of property

In the individual financial statements of Daryl Co, under local accounting rules the sale of property to the Group chief executive officer (CEO) does not need to be disclosed. However, from the Group perspective, it meets the definition of a related party transaction under IAS 24 *Related Party Disclosures* and will need to be disclosed in the consolidated financial statements. As the transaction would also be considered to be material by nature, the Group audit team must therefore provide instructions to Neegan Associates on the additional audit work to be performed which will enable sufficient and appropriate evidence to be obtained in respect of the transaction and disclosure. These procedures will be outlined in the next section of these briefing notes.

The cash proceeds arising on the sale of the property are well below the materiality level determined by Neegan Associates, so this might justify the minimal audit procedures which have been planned in relation to the individual financial statements. However, the procedures do not consider how the profit or loss being made on the disposal is determined or whether the asset has been properly removed from the accounting records. The carrying amount of the asset itself may be material to the financial statements of the company.

There may be an incentive to recognise a higher profit than is appropriate on this transaction due to trading difficulties encountered by the company during the year, so the transaction may be at risk of material misstatement with the objective of maximising the profit recognised.

There is no evidence that the transaction is *bona fide* – the CEO has not yet paid for the property and the whole transaction could be an attempt to window dress the financial statements. Overall, this evaluation has indicated that there are problems in how Neegan Associates has planned the audit of Daryl Co. The audit work, which is planned will not provide sufficient, appropriate audit evidence in relation to the issues identified.

Therefore, the Group audit team will need to consider the overall planning of the audit of Daryl Co and the level of testing they subsequently request that Neegan Associates carries out to satisfy themselves of the accuracy of the figures presented in Daryl Co's financial statements for inclusion in the consolidated financial statements.

(ii) **Audit procedures on sale of property**

- Review board minutes to see if the property sale has been deliberated, i.e. has the rationale for the transaction been discussed, and formally approved by the company's board.
- Agree the £50,000 sale price to the legal documentation relating to the sale of the property to the Group CEO.
- Confirm the carrying amount of the property at the date of disposal to underlying accounting records and the non-current asset register.
- Confirm that the asset has been removed from the company accounts at the date of disposal.
- Obtain management's determination of profit or loss on disposal, re-perform the calculation based on supporting evidence, and agree the profit or loss is recognised appropriately in the company statement of profit or loss.
- Obtain an estimate of the fair value of the property, for example, by comparison to the current market price of similar properties and consider the reasonableness of the transaction and sale price.
- Obtain written representations from company management that all matters related to this related party transaction have been disclosed to the Group management and to the Group audit team.

- Obtain written representation from the Group CEO regarding the transaction, to confirm the amount which is outstanding, and the likely timescale for payment.
- Review cash receipts after the reporting date to confirm whether or not the £50,000 has been received from the Group CEO.

(c) **Discussion and justification for a joint audit of Michonne Co**

In a joint audit, two or more audit firms are responsible for conducting the audit and for issuing the audit opinion. The main advantage of a joint audit of Michonne Co is that the local audit firm's understanding and experience will be retained, and that will be a valuable input to the audit. At the same time, Atlanta & Co can provide additional skills and resources if necessary.

Farland may have different regulations to the rest of the Group, for example, there may be a different financial reporting framework. It therefore makes sense for Lucille Associates, the local auditors, to retain some input to the audit as they will have detailed knowledge of such regulations.

The fact that the company is located in a distant location means that from a practical point of view it may be difficult for Atlanta & Co to provide staff to perform the majority of the audit work. It will be more cost effective for this to be carried out by local auditors.

Two audit firms can also stand together against aggressive accounting treatments. In this way, a joint audit can enhance the quality of the audit. The benchmarking which takes place between the two firms raises the level of service quality.

Disadvantages of a joint audit of Michonne Co

The main disadvantage is that for the Group, having a joint audit is likely to be more expensive than appointing just one audit firm. However, the costs are likely to be less than if Atlanta & Co took sole responsibility, as having the current auditors retain an involvement will at least cut down on travel expenses. Due to the size of the respective firms, Lucille Associates will probably offer a cheaper audit service than Atlanta & Co.

For the audit firms, there may be problems in deciding on responsibilities, allocating work, and they will need to work very closely together to ensure that no duties go underperformed, and that the quality of the audit is maintained. There is a risk that the two firms will not agree on a range of matters, for example, audit methodology, resources needed and review procedures, which would make the working relationship difficult to manage.

Problems could arise in terms of liability because both firms have provided the audit opinion; in the event of litigation, both firms would be jointly liable. While both of the firms would be insured, they could blame each other for any negligence which was discovered, making the litigation process more complex than if a single audit firm had provided the audit opinion.

Recommendation

On balance, the merits of performing a joint audit outweigh the possible disadvantages, especially if the two audit firms can agree on the division of work and pool their expertise and resources to provide a high-quality audit.

Conclusion

The briefing notes indicate that there are several significant audit risks to be addressed, in particular, there are risks relating to the foreign subsidiary and relating to the revenue and the accounting treatment applied to intangible assets. The valuation of the licences (adequacy of the amortisation policy) and the potential impairment of the goodwill of Daryl Co may materially affect the profitability forecast for the year. The audit team need to ensure adequate evidence and question assumptions when considering whether the valuation of these balances is appropriate. Ensuring the appropriate disclosures and accounting treatment in respect of the legal claim is also a material item due to the nature and the apparent reluctance by the finance director to provide details about the nature or size of the claim. In respect of the component audit firm, there are some concerns over the adequacy of their audit planning, which will need further consideration in developing the Group audit strategy. Finally, performing a joint audit on Michonne Co appears to be a good way to perform a high-quality audit on this new subsidiary.

Section B

2 Saul

Workbook references

Chapters 4, 7, 8 and 11.

Top tips

This question is set at the review stage, requiring you to think critically about audit evidence that has been obtained already.

Part (a)(i) covered a fraud and may have been tough going. There are plenty of points in the model answer, however, this question provided a good test of your ability to apply professional scepticism to this area.

Part (a)(ii) looked at audit evidence and was a relatively standard requirement. This is typical of what you could see in your exam, and at this stage in your studies you should have been able to score reasonably well on this requirement

Part (b) was the audit report requirement for this exam. Criticising an auditor's report may be satisfying, but only eight marks are available for it so you needed to ensure that you did not go over your allotted time for this question part.

Easy marks

The marks for audit evidence should have been easy to get, provided that what you wrote was specific enough for the marker to give you the mark. There were also some fairly easy points to be made in relation to the auditor's report in part (b).

ACCA examiner's comments

This question was a 25-mark compulsory question which focused on completion and reporting and was in two sections.

Requirement (a)(i) for six marks, required candidates to discuss the implications of a fraud which had occurred during the year for the completion of the audit and any actions to be taken by the auditor. Generally, candidates performed poorly on this requirement with a significant number of candidates believing that an immaterial fraud would result in the audit opinion being qualified, which is disappointing.

Several candidates discussed the fraud and inferred an internal control issue within the procurement department, but only a minority went on to consider an overall internal control issue and that internal controls should be reassessed, or substantive testing should be performed.

A number of candidates suggested a list of controls that should be recommended for the procurement department, which did not meet the question requirement and therefore scored no marks.

Requirement (a)(ii) asked candidates to comment on the sufficiency and appropriateness of audit evidence obtained in respect of development costs capitalised.

Again, the **requirement (a)(ii)** was generally poorly answered by candidates. A number of candidates' comments that a sample of invoices selected for testing was not appropriate and that 100% of invoices should be tested.

A significant number of candidates correctly identified that the evidence on file for the development costs was not sufficient but missed the point that it could include research costs and went along the angle of approval of the costs to be capitalised in general.

A significant number of candidates stated the accounting standard rules for capitalisation of development costs, yet the requirement was not a 'matters to consider and evidence expected to be on file' requirement and therefore was not relevant to the question and did not receive credit.

Requirement (b) for eight marks asked candidates to critically appraise an extract from the auditor's report, which had been incorrectly prepared and required amendment.

This requirement was a roll forward from the requirement in part (a), and not a standalone critique style question. A number of candidates missed the narrative that two of the three issues had been resolved, being the audit partner concluding the fraud was immaterial and all necessary work had now been performed, and that further procedures surrounding the development costs had been performed and that is was deemed appropriate that the costs were capitalised correctly. Candidates that did not focus on the narrative did not realise these two issues should not have been included within the report and continued to appraise them incorrectly.

The majority of candidates were able to correctly identify the format issues within the report such as the incorrect structure. The wording of the extract suggested an adverse opinion was being given, and many candidates identified this was incorrect, it being more likely a qualified opinion was appropriate in the circumstances.

Candidates were not expected to discuss what would or would not be present in a full report. Where candidates discussed, for example, 'the signature of the partner is missing' or 'responsibilities of the auditor are missing', this was not relevant to the requirement, which asked candidates to specifically critique the extract as presented. Discussion of given extracts of auditor's reports, again, should follow a structured approach and practicing questions of this nature should allow candidates to score strong marks in these requirements.

Candidates would benefit from a more detailed knowledge of ISA (UK) 700 *Forming an Opinion and Reporting on Financial Statements*, in particular to review the appendices which show real examples of the auditor's report and typical wording which is appropriate.

Marking guide

Marks

(a) (i) Generally, up to 1 mark for each relevant point of discussion/action or further evidence:

Fraud

- Cannot determine whether fraud is immaterial without obtaining further evidence
- Insufficient to rely on a conversation between Group finance director and the alleged fraudster as a source of evidence
- Group finance director could be involved and attempting to conceal the true extent of the fraud
- Audit team needs to use professional scepticism in relation to assertions made about the fraud
- Financial statements could be materially misstated/Group finance director refusing to adjust
- Auditor should consider reporting responsibilities to management/those charged with governance (TCWG)
- Potential to report externally after taking legal advice
- Consideration of client confidentiality

Maximum — 6

(ii) **Development costs**

- Development costs are material and the audit work performed is insufficient to determine whether research costs have been inappropriately capitalised
- Intangible assets could be materially overstated and profit overstated
- Agreeing amounts to invoices does not confirm the nature of the expenditure

ANSWERS

- Arithmetically checking the spreadsheet does not provide assurance on the assumptions which underpin the projections
- The Group finance director refusing to allow full access to the spreadsheet increases risk and the audit team should apply professional scepticism
- Attitude and actions of the Group finance director should be discussed with TCWG
- Reliance on a written representation is not appropriate
- Further evidence (1 mark for each evidence point explained)

Maximum 6

(b) **Critique of draft auditor's report**

Generally, up to 1 mark for each point explained:

- Combination of opinion and basis for opinion paragraphs not appropriate
- Headings not correct – should be qualified opinion and basis for qualified opinion
- Qualified opinion paragraph wording is ambiguous and needs clarification
- Basis for qualified opinion paragraph should contain further details on the rationale for the auditor's opinion
- Explanation of proper use of emphasis of matter paragraph
- Fraud is immaterial and not fundamental to users' understanding
- Not professional to mention fraud in the auditor's report
- Difficulties in the audit should be reported to TCWG, not to the shareholders in the auditor's report
- Unprofessional and possible libellous wording used in relation to the Group finance director
- Not appropriate to mention resignation in the auditor's report – should be discussed with TCWG

Maximum 8

Professional marks

Analysis and evaluation

- Effectively analysis and identification of issues and omissions in the draft auditor's report
- Appropriate use of the information to support discussion, draw appropriate conclusions and design appropriate responses
- Appropriate recommendations in relation to necessary actions which reflect the stage of engagement

Professional scepticism and judgement

- Effective challenge and critical assessment of the conduct and extent of the audit work and evidence obtained with appropriate conclusions.
- Appropriate application of professional judgement to draw conclusions and make informed decisions about the actions which are appropriate in the context and stage of the engagement.
- Demonstration of the ability to probe for further information

Commercial acumen

- Inclusion of appropriate recommendations regarding how Those Charged with Governance and the audit firm should respond to the situation

Maximum 5

Total 25

(a) (i) **Fraud**

If the full extent of the fraud is £40,000, then the audit team is correct to determine that the fraud is immaterial to the financial statements. However, without performing further procedures it is not possible to reach that conclusion. There is no auditor-generated evidence to support the assertion that £40,000 is the total amount of stolen funds. Relying solely on a conversation between the Group finance director and the manager who carried out the fraud and a list of invoices provided by the Group finance director is not acceptable as this evidence is not sufficiently reliable.

Indeed, the Group finance director could be involved with the fraud and is attempting to deceive the auditor and minimise the suspected scale of the fraud in order to deter further procedures being carried out, or investigation or actions being taken. The auditor should approach the comments made by the Group finance director with an attitude of professional scepticism, especially given that he has asked the audit team not to investigate further, which raises suspicion that he may be covering up the fact that the fraud was on a larger scale than has been made known to the auditor.

There are two courses of action for the auditor. First, further independent investigations should be carried out in order for the auditor to obtain sufficient and appropriate evidence relating to the amount of the fraud. This is particularly important given that the Group finance director seems unwilling to make any adjustment to the financial statements. If the fraud is actually more financially significant, the financial statements could be materially misstated, but without further audit evidence, the auditor cannot determine whether this is the case.

Second, the auditor should consider whether reporting is necessary. ISA (UK) 240 *The Auditor's Responsibilities Relating to Fraud in an Audit of Financial Statements* requires that when fraud has taken place, auditors shall communicate these matters on a timely basis to the appropriate level of management in order to inform those with primary responsibility for the prevention and detection of fraud of matters relevant to their responsibilities. Given that the Group finance director alerted the auditor to the fraud, it seems likely that management and those charged with governance are already aware of the fraud. However, the auditor should consider whether a formal, written communication is needed.

In addition to reporting to management and those charged with governance, ISA (UK) 240 requires that the auditor shall determine whether there is a responsibility to report the occurrence or suspicion to a party outside the entity. The auditor's duty to maintain the confidentiality of client information makes such reporting potentially difficult, and the auditor may wish to take legal advice before reporting externally.

> **Tutorial note.** Anti-money laundering legislation is likely to impose a duty on auditors to report suspected money laundering activity. Suspicions relating to fraud are likely to be required to be reported under this legislation. Therefore, credit will be awarded for relevant consideration of whether Saul & Co should report the fraud on this basis.

(ii) **Development costs**

Given that the development costs are material to the Group financial statements, more audit work should have been carried out to determine whether it is acceptable that all, or some, of the £600,000 should have been capitalised. There is a risk that research costs, which must be expensed, have not been distinguished from development costs, which can only be capitalised when certain criteria have been met. Currently, there is not sufficient, appropriate audit evidence to conclude that the accounting treatment is appropriate, and intangible assets could be materially misstated.

Agreement of amounts to invoice provides evidence of the value of expenditure, but does not provide sufficient, appropriate evidence as to the nature of the expenditure, i.e. the procedure is not necessarily an evaluation of whether it is capital or revenue expenditure.

Performing an arithmetic check on a spreadsheet does provide some evidence over the accuracy of the calculations but does not provide sufficient, appropriate evidence on the validity of the projections, and in particular, there is no evidence that the assumptions are sound. Given that the Group finance director has not allowed the audit team access to information supporting the spreadsheet and has refused to answer questions, he may have something to hide, and the audit of the projection should be approached with a high degree of professional scepticism. The assumptions may not be sound and may contradict other audit evidence.

The attitude and actions of the Group finance director, which indicate a lack of integrity, should be discussed with the audit committee, as the committee should be in a position to discuss the situation with him, with the objective of making all necessary information available to the audit team.

Finally, there appears to be over-reliance on a written representation from management. ISA (UK) 580 *Written Representations* states that written representations should be used to support other audit evidence and are not sufficient evidence on their own. In this situation, it appears that the representation is the only evidence which has been sought in regard to the likely success of the new product development which is inappropriate.

Further evidence should be obtained to distinguish between research costs and development costs, and to support whether the development costs meet the recognition criteria in IAS 38 *Intangible Assets*, and to confirm whether all of the £600,000 should be capitalised. Further evidence should be obtained, including:

- A discussion with the project manager to obtain their view on the likely launch date for the new product, anticipated level of demand, any problems foreseen with completion of the project.
- A further review of a sample of the costs included in the £600,000, including evaluation of whether the costs are capital or revenue in nature.
- For the sample of costs, review purchase invoices and ensure they are in the name of the company to confirm the rights and obligations assertion of the capitalised costs.
- Results of any market research to support the assertion that the new product will generate future economic benefit.
- A discussion with management to identify how they have incurred development costs without carrying out any research first.
- Assuming that the Group finance director makes the supporting documentation, including assumptions, available to the audit team, the assumptions should be reviewed for reasonableness, with the auditor considering whether they are in line with business understanding and with other audit evidence obtained.

(b)

Word Processor

Critique of auditor's report – headings and structure

The report should not have the opinion and basis for opinion combined in one paragraph. The report should start with the opinion paragraph, which is then followed by the basis for opinion.

In addition to separating out the paragraphs, they should be given appropriate headings. According to ISA (UK) 705 *Modifications to the Opinion in the Independent Auditor's Report*, when the opinion is modified, the heading should be used to denote the type of modification which is being made to the opinion – in this case the title 'Qualified opinion' seems most appropriate. The basis for opinion paragraph should be headed 'Basis for qualified opinion'.

Qualified opinion

The qualified opinion paragraph should be worded differently. According to ISA (UK) 705, when the opinion is modified the following wording should be used: 'Except for the effects of the matter(s) described in the Basis for Qualified Opinion section, the accompanying financial statements present fairly, in all material respects (or give a true and fair view of) [...]'

The draft opinion paragraph uses different wording – in particular, using the phrase, 'The financial statements are likely to be materially misstated' does not indicate that a firm conclusion has been reached and could give users of the report some doubt as to the credibility of the auditor's opinion.

Basis for qualified opinion

This paragraph should contain further information on the reasons for the modification, including a description and quantification of the financial effects of the material misstatement. In this case, the paragraph should refer to the overstatement of trade receivables of £450,000 and the overstatement of profit by the same amount. Currently, the paragraph refers to an overstatement of £500,000, which contradicts the conclusion based on audit evidence.

Emphasis of matter paragraph

According to ISA (UK) 706 *Emphasis of Matter Paragraphs and Other Matter Paragraphs in the Independent Auditor's Report*, an emphasis of matter (EOM) paragraph is used when the auditor considers it necessary to draw users' attention to a matter that is of such importance that it is fundamental to users' understanding of the financial statements. The matter discussed in the EOM paragraph must be properly presented and disclosed in the financial statements.

The draft auditor's report includes an EOM that is being used to discuss two matters, neither of which are appropriate for inclusion in an EOM. First, the EOM describes the fraud that has taken place during the year. This matter is immaterial in monetary terms and therefore is not likely to be considered to be fundamental to users' understanding of the financial statements.

In addition, it is not professional to highlight illegal activity in this way, and it could increase the risk of litigation from the Group, as this amounts to a breach of confidentiality.

Second, the EOM refers to the difficulties encountered in the audit of trade receivables due to the Group finance director refusing to allow full access to necessary sources of evidence. This matter should not be reported to shareholders in the auditor's report. The appropriate method of reporting is to those charged with governance of the Group, as required by ISA (UK) 260 *Communication With Those Charged With Governance*. ISA (UK) 260 requires the auditor to communicate to those charged with governance regarding a range of matters, including significant difficulties, if any, encountered during the audit.

Related to this, stating that it is the Group finance director personally who is responsible for the material misstatement and hence the modification of the auditor's opinion is not professional and could raise further legal problems. For example, the Group finance director could accuse the audit firm of making false statements or defamation of character.

In addition, referring to the potential resignation of the audit firm anywhere in the auditor's report is not appropriate. This matter should be discussed with those charged with governance who will then take the matter up with the Group's shareholders.

3 Moritz

Workbook reference

Chapters 5, 13 and 15.

Top tips

This may have been the easiest question in exam, so those who left themselves with enough time to finish it properly would have benefitted from their prudence.

Part (a) covered the review of cash flow forecast. Part (i) on acceptance issues was straightforward in the sense that if you knew the material here then you could have scored well. Part (ii), on the procedures themselves, was again straightforward. The approach here is essentially to think about what might have gone wrong with the forecast, and to come up with procedures to address these points. Your starting point should therefore have been the information given in the scenario – rather than, for example, any calculations that you might have made on the basis of the figures.

Part (b) covered the topic of insolvency. The requirement here contained a number of marks for knowledge which you should really have, together with a requirement to determine whether the directors were personally liable. Insolvency is perhaps not the most examinable area of AAA UK, but it does come up regularly so you will need to be able to answer questions of this nature.

Easy marks

Part (a)(iii) contained some fairly easy marks for your knowledge of a PFI report.

ACCA examiner's comments

This question was a 25-mark compulsory question which focused on acceptance of an engagement to review a report on prospective financial information (PFI) and procedures to be performed on the cash flow statement.

Requirement (a)(i) for six marks, required candidates to explain the matters to be considered before accepting the PFI engagement. This was a requirement where candidates would be expected to score highly, and overall did achieve good marks. The only noticeable point from candidate answers related to considerations of client due diligence to be considered as the question clearly stated this had already been performed, therefore where discussed as a consideration credit would not be available.

Requirement (a)(ii) for nine marks required candidates to recommend procedures to be performed in respect of the cash flow statement. Overall, candidates made a good attempt at the requirement and scored well. It was disappointing to see a small number of candidates answer the requirement using only analytical procedures ie calculating trends and ratios as this alone did not answer the requirement and therefore scored minimal credit.

The quality of answers for Question three was generally of a good standard and candidates were able to demonstrate application of their knowledge to the scenario.

Marking guide | **Marks**

(a) (i) **Lavenza Co**

Matters to consider before accepting the review engagement

Up to 2 marks for each matter explained:

- Intended use of the cash flow forecast
- Distribution of the information
- Period covered by the cash flow forecast and key assumptions used
- Scope of the work
- Resources and skills

- Client integrity
- Ethical matters

Maximum 6

(ii) **Examination procedures on cash flow forecast**

Generally, 1 mark for each specific procedure described:

- Cast the forecast to confirm accuracy
- Confirm consistency of accounting policies with those used in last audited financial statements
- Agree opening cash position to cash book and bank statement
- Discuss key assumptions underlying forecast with management
- Analytically review cash flow trends comparing with historical data
- Agree average collection and payment periods to recent sales and purchase ledgers
- Recalculate patterns of cash flows based on management's assumptions
- Perform sensitivity analyses varying key assumptions
- Agree salaries to latest payroll records
- Obtain and review breakdown of overhead costs
- For sample of overhead costs, review supporting documentation
- Obtain and review budgets and analyses of costs to date for new shops and marketing campaign
- Review board minutes for discussion of new shops and marketing campaign
- Review outcomes of previous management forecasts
- Discuss possible cost omissions with preparer, eg finance costs, capital expenditure, tax payments
- Obtain written representations from management (with justification)
- Request confirmation from the bank of potential terms of additional finance to confirm the interest rate
- Consider whether finance charge in forecast cash flow appears reasonable

Maximum 7

(b) **Alucard Ltd**

Key features of administration

Generally up to 1 mark for each point explained:

- Explanation/definition of administration
- Key features of administration (up to 2 marks)
- Explanation of key feature or implication of fraudulent trading:
  - Intent to defraud must be proven
  - Action can be taken against anyone aware of the fraudulent trading
  - Criminal offence, proof must be beyond reasonable doubt
  - Penalties include imprisonment, personal liability for company debts, disqualification as a director
- Explanation of key feature or implication of wrongful trading:
  - No intent to defraud – the offence is continuing to trade when directors should have known that creditors are likely to suffer losses
  - Action can only be taken against directors

ANSWERS

- Discussion of indicators from scenario – 1 mark for each valid pointCivil offence, a lower level of proof is needed
- Penalties include personal liability for company debts and disqualification as a director

- Reasoned conclusion on whether Alucard Ltd's directors will incur personal liability

Maximum	7

Professional marks

Analysis and evaluation

- Appropriate use of the information to support discussions and draw appropriate conclusions
- Appropriate assessment of the ethical and professional issues raised, using examples where relevant, to support overall comments
- Balanced discussion of the issues connected to a non-assurance engagement, resulting in a justified conclusion and proposed course of action.

Professional scepticism and judgement

- Effective challenge and critical assessment of the assumptions used by management in preparing the cash flow forecast
- Demonstration of the ability to probe for further information in order to make an assessment of the completeness of the cash flow forecast.
- Appropriate recommendations and justification of the assurance procedures to be undertaken in respect of the cash flow forecast

Commercial acumen

- Demonstration of commercial awareness by recognizing wider issues which may affect the forecast and the assumptions by management

Maximum	5
Total	25

(a) **Lavenza Ltd**

(i) **Matters to consider before accepting the review engagement**

Before accepting the review engagement to review and provide an assurance report on Lavenza Ltd's cash flow forecast, ISAE 3400 *The Examination of Prospective Financial Information* identifies a number of matters which need to be considered:

The intended use of the information

Moritz & Co must consider, for example, whether the cash flow forecast and assurance report will be used solely for the purpose of the increase in Lavenza Ltd's overdraft facility. If Lavenza Ltd is planning to use the assurance report for purposes other than an extension to its current overdraft, for example, to arrange new loan finance from the company's bank, this must be made clear to Moritz & Co.

Whether the information will be for general or limited distribution

Moritz & Co needs to consider who will receive the report and potentially rely upon it as this will impact on the firm's assessment of the risk associated with the engagement. If the cash flow forecast is intended for general distribution, this will increase the level of risk for Moritz & Co as a larger audience will rely on it. In this case, if the information will be used solely in support of the application to the bank and will not be made available to other parties, this should be confirmed before accepting the engagement and will reduce the risk of the assignment.

The period covered by the cash flow forecast and the key assumptions used

Moritz & Co must also consider the period covered by the cash flow forecast and the key assumptions which have been used in its preparation. Short-term forecasts are likely to be easier to verify and provide assurance on than longer term projections. ISAE 3400 states that a prospective financial information (PFI) engagement should not be accepted when the assumptions used in its preparation are clearly unrealistic or when the practitioner believes that the PFI will be inappropriate for its intended use. In the case of Lavenza Ltd, although the forecast is only for 12 months, the growth rates assumed in relation to its operating cash receipts may, for example, be judged to be unrealistic given recent trends in its business and the requested overdraft facility of £17 million for the next six months may prove to be insufficient.

The scope of the work

Moritz & Co will need to consider the specific terms of the engagement, the level of assurance being sought by Lavenza Ltd and the form of the report required by the bank. Moritz & Co will need to clearly identify the elements which it is being asked to report on – for example, is it being asked to report on the cash flow forecast only or is the firm also being asked to report on accompanying narrative or other PFI. Due to the uncertainty of forecasts and the inevitable subjectivity involved in their preparation, Moritz & Co will need to confirm that it is only being asked to provide negative assurance as to whether management's assumptions provide a reasonable basis for the cash flow forecast and to give an opinion as to whether it is properly prepared on the basis of these assumptions.

Resources and skills

The firm needs to consider whether it has sufficient staff available with the appropriate skills and experience needed to perform the PFI engagement for Lavenza Ltd. Moritz & Co should also consider whether it can meet the deadline for completing the work and whether it will have access to all relevant information and client staff. Given the company's predicted need for cash in the next six months, presumably the extended overdraft facility will need to be provided very soon and this may lead to Moritz & Co being under pressure to meet a tight reporting deadline.

Client integrity

ISQM (UK)1 *Quality Management for Firms that Perform Audits or Reviews of Financial Statements, or Other Assurance or Related Services Engagements* requires Moritz & Co to consider the integrity of Lavenza Ltd's management in relation to the acceptance decision. In particular, the firm should consider management's reasons for appointing a different firm from its auditors and the potential for management bias in the preparation of a cash flow forecast in support of its required overdraft facility.

In addition to the matters identified by ISAE 3400 and ISQM (UK) 1, Moritz & Co should also consider the following ethical matters before accepting the review engagement:

Ethical matters

Given that Moritz & Co are not the auditors, the firm's independence from Lavenza Ltd will not have been previously considered. In this regard, it is important to ensure that there are no threats to the firm's objectivity which might prevent it from accepting the appointment. If the firm is not independent and its objectivity is compromised, the reliability of the assurance report will be undermined.

Moritz & Co should also consider why the auditors have not been asked to provide the assurance report on Lavenza Ltd's cash flow forecast. In order to provide an assurance report on PFI, a good understanding of the client and its business is required, and the incumbent audit firm will usually have the requisite knowledge and understanding. Moritz & Co should therefore consider whether the use of a different firm creates a risk that the client may be hoping that the firm may not be in a position to effectively challenge the key assumptions underlying the preparation of the forecast. When a professional accountant is asked to perform work for a non-audit client, they should be given permission by the client to contact its auditors in order to obtain relevant information. If this permission is not given, the appointment should be declined.

Overall, Moritz & Co must assess the risks associated with the review engagement and should not accept an engagement when the assumptions are clearly unrealistic or when the firm believes that the prospective financial information will be inappropriate for its intended use.

(ii) **Examination procedures on cash flow forecast**

- Cast the cash flow forecast to confirm its mathematical accuracy.
- Confirm the consistency of the accounting policies used in the preparation of the forecast financial statements with those used in the last audited financial statements.
- Agree the opening cash position of £9,193,000 to the cash book and the bank statement.
- Discuss the key assumptions underlying the preparation of the forecast with management, including:
  - the predicted growth rates in operating cash receipts of 13·4% over the year compared to an equivalent growth rate of only 7·3% in operating cash payments.
  - the stated collection and payment periods in relation to receivables and payables.
  - confirm that the assumptions appear reasonable and are consistent with the firm's knowledge and understanding of the client.
- Analytically review the forecast trends in cash flows comparing with them with historical cash flow statements and other forecast data which is available for the sector and local economy.
- Agree the predicted collection and payment periods to the most recent sales ledgers and purchase ledgers.
- Recalculate the patterns of cash flows based on management's historical analysis of credit sales to confirm that the forecast has been properly prepared on the basis of these assumptions.
- Perform sensitivity analyses on the cash flow forecast by varying the key assumptions (in particular, in relation to growth rates and payment periods) and assessing the impact of these variations on the company's forecast cash position.
- Agree the salary payments to the latest payroll records and cash book payments analyses.
- Obtain and review a breakdown of the forecast overhead payments and compare it to historical management accounts and current budgets. Review the schedule to ensure that non-cash items such as depreciation, amortisation and bad debts have not been included.
- For a sample of overhead costs, review the supporting documentation such as invoices and utility bills and agree the amount paid each month to the cash book.
- Obtain and review budgets and analyses of costs to date for the new shops and the online marketing campaign ensuring that the forecast includes all of the budgeted costs and does not include any costs which have already been incurred. Agree a sample of costs to supporting documentation such as invoices, quotations and lease agreements.
- Review board minutes for discussion of the new shops and the marketing campaign.
- Review the outcomes of previous management forecasts and assess their accuracy compared to actual data.
- Discuss possible cost omissions with the preparer of the forecast, for example, Lavenza Ltd's cash flow forecast does not include finance costs, tax payments and does not include any capital expenditure other than the new shops.
- Obtain written representations from management confirming the reasonableness of their assumptions and that all relevant information has been provided to Moritz & Co.
- Request confirmation from the bank of the potential terms of the additional finance being negotiated, to confirm the interest rate.
- Consider whether the finance charge in the forecast cash flow appears reasonable.

Tutorial note. Credit will be awarded for relevant numerical analysis of the cash flow forecast applied appropriately within the answer.

(b)

Word Processor

Paragraph

Alucard Ltd

Key features of the administration process

Alucard Ltd's inability to pay its creditors as they fall due and the net liabilities position shown by the company's management accounts over the last three months indicate that the company is insolvent.

The aim of administration is to save the company, if possible. A licensed insolvency practitioner (IP) is appointed to act as administrator and effectively takes control of the company in an attempt to rescue it as a going concern. Once the process has been initiated, there is a moratorium on creditors' actions which protects the company while a restructuring plan is prepared. This is important for Alucard Ltd, which is struggling to manage its cash position. In the light of its payment period, some of the creditors' balances may be long overdue and the creditors may already be considering actions to recover the amounts owed.

Administration can commence without a court order. The directors themselves may be able to appoint an administrator, though this depends on the company's articles of association. Alternatively, the company (a majority of shareholders) or qualifying floating charge holders can apply for administration without going through the court. If the directors or the company commence appointing an administrator, notice must be given to any qualifying floating charge holders who are entitled to appoint an administrator. Alternatively, administration proceedings can involve a court order. The company (a majority of shareholders), the directors, one or more creditors or, in rare cases, the Justice and Chief Executive of the Magistrates' Court, can apply to the court for an administration order. The court will consider the application and will grant the administration order if it appears that the company is unable to pay its debts.

Whichever method of appointment of an administrator is employed, the advantage for the company is that the moratorium would allow Alucard Ltd some much needed breathing space and time to resolve its cash-flow problems. The directors will, however, lose control of the company and all operational decisions will be made by the administrator, who also has the power to remove or appoint directors. The administrator will prepare a proposal regarding the future of the company, which will be sent to all shareholders and creditors, and a creditors' meeting will be held at which the proposal will be accepted or rejected. Administration can normally last for up to 12 months and, if at any point the administrator believes that the company cannot be saved, they will recommend that a liquidator should be appointed and the company will be wound up.

Personal liability for the company's debts

The directors of Alucard Ltd may incur personal liability for the company's debts where they have provided personal guarantees or been involved in either fraudulent or wrongful trading. The main difference between the two is intent. Directors who take part in fraudulent trading have a clear intent to deceive and defraud their creditors and customers.

Fraudulent trading:

Fraudulent trading is defined by the Insolvency Act 1986 (IA 1986) as carrying on the business of an insolvent company with the intent to defraud the company's creditors. Actions for fraudulent trading can be brought against any person who is knowingly a party to the fraudulent trading.

Fraudulent trading is a criminal offence and as such, the burden of proof in a court action requires the prosecution's evidence to have established its case beyond reasonable doubt. In this regard, it is key to a successful action that the prosecution has established that intent was present in the defendant's actions.

The penalties and liability which may result from a successful action for fraudulent trading are imprisonment for up to 10 years, personal (civil) liability for the debts of company, and disqualification from being a company director for up to 15 years.

Wrongful trading:

Wrongful trading is defined by IA 1986 as carrying on the business of an insolvent company when it ought to have concluded that there was no reasonable prospect of the company avoiding insolvent liquidation, and that the creditors of the company would therefore suffer losses. In contrast to fraudulent trading, it is not necessary to establish intent and wrongful trading is a civil wrong rather than a criminal offence. It is also significant that an action for wrongful trading can only be brought against company directors (including shadow directors).

As a civil wrong, the burden of proof for wrongful trading is the weaker test of the balance of probabilities. The penalties and liability which may result from a successful action for wrongful trading are personal (civil) liability of the directors for the debts of the company and disqualification from being a company director for up to 15 years.

Potential issues for the directors of Alucard Ltd

The contract with Holden Co, which represented approximately 45% of the company's total sales revenue, was cancelled five months ago. The company's payment period has increased from 45 days to 73 days over this five-month period and the company's cash position has deteriorated to the point where it is unable to pay its creditors as they fall due. The company's management accounts have shown a negative cash balance in excess of its overdraft facility and a net liabilities position for the last three months. In addition, Alucard Ltd has three months of arrears of unpaid PAYE and NIC, and it has received penalty notices in relation to its failure to file its last audited financial statements with Companies House. This provides further evidence that the company cannot pay its liabilities as they fall due and that it is failing to make statutory information available to its creditors. It would appear therefore that there have been clear indicators that the company was potentially insolvent, which the directors should have identified and acted upon. Instead of this, however, they have continued to trade at existing operational levels and to make purchases on credit from the company's suppliers. If it can be established that these actions were made with the intention of defrauding creditors, then they will be guilty of fraudulent trading. Alternatively, if they have carried on the business of the company when they ought to have realised that creditors would suffer losses, then they will have been a party to wrongful trading. In either case, they will incur personal liability to the company's creditors.

ACCA

Advanced Audit and Assurance – UK (AAA – UK)

Mock Exam 2

ACCA Specimen Exam

Questions	
Time allowed	3 hours 15 minutes
ALL THREE questions are compulsory and MUST be attempted	

DO NOT OPEN THIS EXAM UNTIL YOU ARE READY TO START UNDER EXAMINATION CONDITIONS

Section A

1 Pegasus & Co

It is 1 July 20X5. You are a manager in the audit department of Pegasus & Co, a firm of Chartered Certified Accountants. You are assigned to the audit of the Crux Group (the Group), which has a financial year ending 30 September 20X5, and is a listed entity.

Pegasus & Co was appointed auditor to the Group in January 20X5.

The Group operates in the travel industry, offering a selection of worldwide itineraries and has a fleet of 20 cruises ships. The Group operates three brands which provide different types of cruise experience.

The following **exhibits**, available on the left-hand side of the screen, provide information relevant to the question:

(1) Partner's email – an email which you have received from Norma Star, the Group audit engagement partner.

(2) Background information – information and matters relevant to audit planning.

(3) Selected financial information – extracts from the Group management accounts.

(4) Audit team meeting notes – extracts from meeting notes taken at a recent audit team meeting.

This information should be used to answer the question **requirement** within your choses **response option(s)**.

Required

Respond to the instructions in the email from the audit engagement partner.

Note. The split of the mark allocation is shown in Exhibit 1 – Partner's email. **(40 marks)**

Professional marks will be awarded for the demonstration of skill in communication, analysis and evaluation, professional scepticism and judgement, and commercial acumen in your answer.

(10 marks)

(Total = 50 marks)

Exhibit 1: Email from audit engagement partner

To: Audit manager

From: Norma Star, Audit engagement partner

Date: 1 July 20X5

Subject: Audit planning for the Crux Group

Hello

I have provided you with some information which you should use to help you with planning the audit of our new client, the Crux Group (the Group), for the financial year ending 30 September 20X5. Based on the analysis I have done on this industry, it is appropriate for overall materiality to be based on the profitability of the Group as this is a key focus for investors and providers of finance.

I require you to prepare briefing notes for my own use, in which you:

(a) Using the information in all exhibits, evaluate and prioritise the significant audit risks to be considered in planning the Group audit.

Note

You are NOT required to consider audit risks relating to foreign exchange transactions and balances, as this will be planned separately. **(25 marks)**

(b) Design the principal audit procedures to be performed on the segmental information relating to the Group's revenue. **(5 marks)**

(c) Using the information in Exhibit 4:

Evaluate the matters to be considered in deciding whether Pegasus & Co should accept the engagement to provide advice on the Group's social and environmental information. **(10 marks)**

Thank you

Exhibit 2: Group operations

The Group operates cruises under three brands which offer passengers a variety of cruise itineraries with a wide choice of destinations. Cruises typically last for two weeks, though some last for up to six weeks.

The brands are internally generated and therefore are not recognised as intangible assets within the Group financial statements.

Information about the three brands operated by the Group is as follows:

Sunseeker Cruises – Cruises which visit beach destinations in the Caribbean, Europe and North America.

Explorer Cruises – Cruises which focus on visiting cities and landmarks around the world.

Pioneer Cruises – Cruises which take in areas of natural beauty including the Antarctic and Alaska.

Business developments in the year

Sunseeker Cruises

In this financial year, the Group will spend £75 million on upgrading and maintenance of the Sunseeker Cruise ships. These luxury ships have to adhere to a very high standard, so the Group regularly incurs high expenditure on their maintenance. As well as refurbishment, several ships have been enhanced by the installation of new entertainment facilities including cinemas and gyms. Equipment in the gyms will need to be replaced on average every three years.

Explorer Cruises

The Explorer Cruise ships, while still luxurious, are the oldest ships in the fleet, and the Group is gradually replacing these with new ships. During this financial year, two new ships with a total cost of £110 million will come into use. The ships took three years to build, and were constructed by Vela Shipbuilders Ltd, a company which is not owned by the Group. However, the chairman of the Group, Max Draco, is also the chairman of Vela Shipbuilders Ltd, and his son is the company's chief executive officer. The purchase of the ships was financed through a £110 million loan with a fixed interest rate of 6% per annum. A further three ships are currently under construction by Vela Shipbuilders Ltd. The Group has taken out a loan of £180 million with a 6·5% fixed interest rate to finance this capital expenditure.

Pioneer Cruises

These cruises are for more adventurous travellers and are growing in popularity. In order to visit certain destinations on these specialist cruises, the Group has to acquire operating licences from the local governments. The cost of licence acquisition is capitalised as an intangible asset.

Exhibit 3: Crux Group – Extracts from the Group management accounts

	Note	*Projected to 30 September 20X5*	*Actual to 30 September 20X4*
		£ million	*£ million*
Group revenue	1	764	670
Operating profit		145	101

	Note	Projected to 30 September 20X5 £ million	Actual to 30 September 20X4 £ million
Profit before tax		**81**	**65**
Total assets		**1,800**	**1,780**
Included in total assets:			
Intangible assets – operating licences	2	56	57
Property, plant and equipment	3	1,520	1,510

Notes.

1 Revenue includes passenger ticket sales, which accounts for approximately 85% of revenue. When customers book a cruise, they are required to pay a refundable 20% deposit, which is initially recognised as deferred revenue. The balance of 80% is paid at least six weeks before the cruise commences and at that point it is also recognised as a deferred revenue. The full amount of the ticket price is transferred to revenue when the cruise starts irrespective of the duration of the cruise.

The remaining 15% of revenue is derived from on-board sales of food, drinks, entertainment and other items to passengers. Management monitors this revenue stream closely as it achieves a high gross profit margin, and staff are encouraged to maximise these sales to customers.

Revenue is presented on a segmental basis in the notes to the financial statements, with segments based on the three brands of the Group:

Revenue per operating segment	*Projected to 30 September 20X5* £ million	*Actual to 30 September 20X4* £ million
Sunseeker Cruises	320	288
Explorer Cruises	180	190
Pioneer Cruises	264	192
Total	**764**	**670**

2 Operating licences are required for the Pioneer Cruise ships to visit certain destinations. Licences are amortised over the specific period to which each licence relates.

3 Property, plant and equipment is comprised as follows:

Property, plant and equipment	*Projected to 30 September 20X5* *£ million*	*Actual to 30 September 20X4* *£ million*
Ships in use	2,041	2,010
Ships under construction	83	62
Other property, plant and equipment	180	173
	2,034	**2,245**
Accumulated depreciation	(784)	(735)

Property, plant and equipment	*Projected to 30 September 20X5*	*Actual to 30 September 20X4*
	£ million	£ million
Carrying amount	**1,520**	**1,510**

Exhibit 4: Audit team meeting notes

A meeting took place yesterday in which the audit engagement partner discussed several issues:

Recent development affecting Pioneer Cruises

Last week, the governments of several countries which form a major part of the Pioneer Cruise itineraries withdrew their operating licences with immediate effect. The governments have stated that this is likely to be a temporary measure being put in place to limit the number of tourists visiting areas of natural beauty, but they will not confirm when the Group can resume operations in these countries.

Cybersecurity attack

Last month, the Group suffered a cybersecurity attack in which the personal information of 1,400 customers, including their credit card details, were stolen. According to a representative of the Group audit committee, the Group's internal audit team had not properly assessed the risks relating to cybersecurity, which is a requirement of recently introduced data protection legislation in the jurisdiction in which the Group operates. The issue which led to the cybersecurity attack has now been resolved.

Social and environmental information

The Group audit committee has enquired whether Pegasus & Co can provide an additional service, to advise management on how to measure certain social and environmental information which is to be published on the Group's website and is required by new regulations in the industry and is required to be submitted to regulatory authorities. The social and environmental information relates to matters such as water efficiency, energy consumption, charitable donations and initiatives which support diversity in the workplace. In recognition that this work is quite urgent, as the deadline for submission to the regulatory authorities falls within the next month, the Group audit committee has stated it is willing to pay an 'enhanced fee' for this service.

Section B

2 Welford & Co

It is 1 July 20X5. You are an audit manager in Welford & Co, a firm of Chartered Certified Accountants. Your role includes performing post-issuance audit quality reviews, and you have been asked to review the audit work performed on Rivers plc for the financial year ended 31 January 20X5.

The following **exhibits**, available on the left-hand side of the screen, provide information relevant to the question:

(1) Team and fees – information regarding the audit team composition, the time spent on the audit and fees charged to the client.

(2) Going concern – details some matters you have identified during your review of the going concern section of the audit file.

This information should be used to answer the question **requirement** within the **response option** provided.

Required

Evaluate the quality of the planning and performance of the audit of Rivers plc, discussing the quality management, ethical and other professional issues raised and recommending appropriate actions to be taken. **(20 marks)**

Professional marks will be awarded for the demonstration of skill in analysis and evaluation, professional scepticism and judgement and commercial acumen in your answer. **(5 marks)**

(Total = 25 marks)

Exhibit 1: Team and fees

Rivers plc is a listed company operating in the construction industry. The company complies with corporate governance regulations and has an audit committee. Rivers plc has been an audit client of Welford & Co for eight years, and Bob Newbold has been the audit engagement partner during this time.

Rivers plc's auditor's report was signed by Bob Newbold and issued last week. The report contained an unmodified opinion.

Welford & Co requires its staff to record each hour they spend working on each client in the firm's time management system. From reviewing the time records relating to the audit of Rivers plc, you are aware that Bob and the other audit team members recorded the following amount of time on the audit:

Bob Newbold – audit engagement partner	2 hours
Pat Canley – senior audit manager	6 hours
Anesa Kineton – audit manager	35 hours
Six audit assistants	130 hours
Total time spent on audit	173 hours

It is apparent from your review that almost all of the detailed review of the audit working papers was completed by Anesa Kineton, who has evidenced her review by stating 'final review' on each page of the audit file. She has recently been promoted to audit manager.

You are also aware that Bob Newbold booked a total of 40 hours to Rivers plc in respect of non-audit work performed. The only information you can find in the documentation is that the non-audit work related to a 'special investigation', and that Bob confirms that it does not create a threat to auditor objectivity.

The total fee charged for the audit was £250,000 and the fee for the 'special investigation' was £890,000.

Exhibit 2: Going concern

From reviewing the audit working papers, you are aware that going concern was identified as a significant audit risk at the planning stage of the audit due to low profit margins or losses being made on many of the company's construction contracts and increasing economic uncertainty. The company typically has 20 contracts ongoing at any time.

Most of the audit work on going concern was performed by Mary Loxley, an audit assistant who has just taken her last professional exam and is not yet qualified. The majority of the audit work performed on going concern focused on a review of five major contracts to determine their profitability. The management of Rivers plc identified the major contracts for review and provided Mary with forecasts indicating that the contracts would all make a small profit. Mary confirmed that the assumptions used in the forecasts agreed to assumptions used in previous years. Mary also used the firm's data analytics tool to confirm the mathematical accuracy of the forecasts and that the assumptions set out by management had been appropriately reflected in the forecasts. Following this work, Mary concluded that the contracts which she had reviewed support the going concern status of the company.

Having reviewed these major contracts, Mary completed the conclusion on going concern, stating that there is no significant uncertainty over going concern.

Mary commented that due to the effectiveness of the data analytics tool, she only had to record eight hours in relation to the work she had performed on going concern.

3 Myron plc

It is 1 July 20X5. You are the manager responsible for the audit of Myron plc. a listed company and you are in the process of completing the audit of the financial statements for the year ended 31 March 20X5. The auditor's report is due to be signed in the next few weeks. The company's principal operating activity is the publication of trade and scientific journals.

The draft financial statements recognise revenue of £108 million (20X4: £102 million), profit before tax of £9.3 million (20X4: £8.2 million) and total assets of £150 million (20X4: £149 million). Materiality has been set at £0.5 million.

The following **exhibits**, available on the left-hand side of the screen, provide information relevant to the question:

(1) Completion matters – details regarding an issue you have discovered during your review of the audit working papers.

(2) Chairman's statement – management has provided you with an extract from the chairman's statement which they intend to publish in the annual report.

This information should be used to answer the question **requirements** within the **response option** provided.

Required

(a) **Using the information contained in Exhibit 1:**

(1) Comment on the completion matters to be considered in relation to the issue described and recommend the further actions necessary before the auditor's report can be signed; and

(2) Evaluate the implications for the auditor's report if no adjustments are made to the financial statements.

(10 marks)

(b) **Using the information contained in Exhibit 2:**

Required

(i) Described the auditor's responsibilities in relation to the other information presented with audited financial statements and evaluate the matters arising from the extract from the chairman's statement; and **(5 marks)**

(ii) Assuming no changes are made to the chairman's statement, evaluate the implications for the completion of the audit and the auditor's report. **(5 marks)**

Professional marks will be awarded for the demonstration of skill in analysis and evaluation, and professional scepticism and judgement in your answer. **(5 marks)**

(Total = 25 marks)

Exhibit 1: Completion matters

You are in the process of reviewing the audit working papers and have identified the following potential issue:

Sale of division

Myron plc is at the advanced stage of negotiations to sell its scientific publishing division to a competitor. This division contributed revenue of £13 million and profit before tax of £1·4 million during the year to 31 March 20X5. The draft sale agreement which is due to be finalised by 1 August 20X5 shows an agreed sale price after costs of disposal of £42 million. The division is a separate cash generating unit of Myron plc. None of the assets of the division are held under a revaluation policy and depreciation is charged on a straight-line basis over the determined useful life of the assets.

The finance director of Myron plc has not made any disclosures with respect to the upcoming sale in the financial statements for the year ended 31 March 20X5 as he considers it to be part of next year's accounting transactions. However, the division has been written down from its current carrying amount of £45 million to its estimated value in use of £41 million in the financial statements for the year ended 31 March 20X5.

Exhibit 2: Chairman's statement

As part of your review of Myron plc, you have also been presented with an extract from the draft Chairman's statement which will be published in the annual report alongside the financial statements for the year.

Extract from Chairman's statement

The company's results for the year are extremely positive. Our year-on-year revenue growth is 5·9% and our profit growth is even stronger at 13·4%. All our revenue streams have performed well, especially the scientific publishing division, and we are looking forward to exciting and sustained growth levels again next year. As you can see from our auditor's report, the auditors agree that our results are strong and a sound basis for taking the company to an even greater place next year.

We have also made significant progress with our social and environmental aims of reducing our carbon footprint and encouraging re-use and recycling across our divisions. We are proud to announce that we have now moved all our printed products to recycled paper.

To help with your review of the information, you also have the following analysis of the results for the year.

	Year ended 31 March 20X5			*Year ended 31 March 20X4*		
	Other divisions	*Scientific publishing division*	*Total*	*Other divisions*	*Scientific publishing division*	*Total*
	£million	£million	£million	£million	£million	£million
Revenue	95	13	108	93	9	102

	Year ended 31 March 20X5			Year ended 31 March 20X4		
	Other divisions	*Scientific publishing division*	*Total*	*Other divisions*	*Scientific publishing division*	*Total*
	£million	£million	£million	£million	£million	£million
Profit before tax	7.9	1.4	9.3	7.5	0.7	8.2

A file note from the audit supervisor states that at least three of the publications Myron plc sells are not prepared on recycled paper.

A) MARE, Materiality, Acc Standars, Risk, Evidence/Action

Answers

DO NOT TURN THIS PAGE UNTIL YOU HAVE COMPLETED THE MOCK EXAM

A plan of attack

If this had been the real Advanced Audit and Assurance exam and you had been told to start the exam, what would have been going through your mind?

An important thing to say (while there is still time) is that it is vital to have a good breadth of knowledge of the syllabus because the question requirements for each question will relate to different areas of the AAA syllabus. However, don't panic. Below we provide guidance on how to approach the exam.

Approaching the answer

It is vital that you attempt all the questions in the exam to increase your chances of passing. The best way to do this is to make sure you stick to the time allocation for each question – both in total and for each of the question parts. The worst thing you can do is run over time in one question and then find that you don't have enough time for the remaining questions, leading you to miss out on some of the easier marks in those questions.

Section A consists of one long case-study style question set at the planning stage of the audit. This may contain detailed information such as extracts from financial statements and audit working papers. A range of requirements will be set for this question but will mainly cover areas from syllabus areas A to D inclusive.

Question 1 is for 50 marks, all set at the planning stage in the context of a single scenario, here dealing with the audit of a group. As it is a very long question, it is important that you break it down into its component parts as this will make it easier to manage – and enable you to allocate your time to each of them.

Section B contains two more compulsory questions and may be set on any area of the AAA syllabus.

Question 2, for 25 marks, featured a review of a completed audit and touched on many different aspects of the management of the audit process (quality management, ethics and other professional issues).

Question 3 offers 25 marks set in the completion phase, covering matters around the auditor's report and other information.

Forget about it!

And don't worry if you found the exam difficult. More than likely other candidates did too. If this were the real thing, you would need to forget the exam the minute you finished it and think about the next one. Or, if it is the last one, celebrate!

Section A

1 Pegasus & Co

Workbook references

Chapters 5, 6, 7, 9 and 15.

Top tips

Your general approach should be to read the requirement carefully, and then to work through the question noting down issues (audit risks) as they occur to you.

Part (a) asked for audit risks, as was expected. It is crucial that you make an effort to prioritise risks, instead of simply listing them. You can do this most simply by stating in your conclusion the risks that are the most important (and since this is the ACCA Specimen exam, the conclusion given here can serve as a model for yours). One pitfall to avoid would be simply stating that every risk you identify is important; you can avoid this by only stating that the most important risks are significant and, where you encounter a risk that does exist but which is not significant, state this.

It is important that you heed the warning not to consider risks from forex transactions as there will be no marks available here for these. The key to scoring well here is to make sure that your answer is the right length – enough to pass this question part, but without writing so much that you go over your time allocation. You should look to develop each point you make thoroughly, trying to connect together points where this is possible.

Part (b) was on procedures on segmental information. This is not an area that is tested often, so its inclusion here should serve as a warning against revising only those topics that you think are more examinable.

Part (c) related to the acceptance of a non-audit engagement. You may have found this to be particularly challenging; if this was the case then the key would be to focus on trying to pass this part of the question. You only need to score five marks here to do this.

Easy marks

The presentation marks here are valuable and are well worth the time it takes to get them.

Marking guide **Marks**

(a) **Audit risk evaluation**

Up to 3 marks for each significant audit risk, (unless indicated otherwise). Marks may be awarded for other, relevant audit risks not included in the marking guide.

In addition, 0.5 mark for relevant trends or calculations which form part of the evaluation of audit risk (max 3 marks).

Appropriate materiality calculations and justified materiality level should be awarded to a maximum of 2 marks.

- New audit client (2 marks)
- Revenue recognition
- Upgrade and maintenance costs
- Component depreciation
- Cybersecurity breach (control risk, corporate governance weakness, data corruption, financial statement implications – max 5 marks)
- Related party transaction disclosure
- Operating licences
- Borrowing costs
- Revenue and profit trends
- On-board sales

Maximum 25

(b) **Audit procedures on segmental reporting**

Up to 1 mark for each relevant audit procedure. Examples are provided below, and marks will be awarded for other relevant points.

- Review the financial reports sent to the highest level of management to confirm the basis of segmental information which is reported internally
- Review the Group's organisational structure to confirm identify of the chief operating decision maker
- Discuss with management the means by which segmental information is reviewed by the chief operating decision maker
- Review board minutes to see that segmental information is subject to regular review
- Discuss with management whether the on-board sales should be reported separately

• Obtain a breakdown of the revenue to confirm that revenue has been appropriately allocated between the reportable segments	
• Perform analytical procedures to determine trends for each segment and discuss unusual patterns with management.	
• Recalculate the revenue totals from the breakdown provided to confirm that they are reportable segments	-
Maximum	5
(c) **Additional service to provide advice on social and environmental information**	
Up to 1 mark for each relevant answer point explained:	
• Assuming management responsibility identified and fully explained	
• Assuming management responsibility is prohibited	
• Self-review threat identified and fully explained	
• Self-review threat increased if the social/environmental information included in annual report	
• Self-interest threat identified and fully explained	
• Pressure to perform work quickly	
• Appropriate safeguards recommended (1 mark each to max 3 marks)	
• Group audit committee to approve non-audit work	
• It may be prohibited in the jurisdiction of the Group	
• Scope of the work, and specific requirements from the regulators	
• Level of assurance which may be required and who is going to provide this	
• Skill and competence to perform work	-
Maximum	10

Professional marks

Communication

- Briefing notes format and structure – use of headings/sub-headings and an introduction
- Style, language and clarity – appropriate layout and tone of briefing notes, presentation of materiality and relevant calculations, appropriate use of the CBE tools, easy to follow and understand
- Effectiveness and clarity of communication – answer is relevant and tailored to the scenario
- Adherence to the specific requests made by the audit engagement partner

Analysis and evaluation

- Appropriate use of the information to determine suitable calculations
- Appropriate use of the information to support discussions and draw appropriate conclusions
- Assimilation of all relevant information to ensure that the risk evaluation performed considers the impact of contradictory or unusual movements
- Effective prioritisation of the results of the risk evaluation to demonstrate the likelihood and magnitude of risks and to facilitate the allocation of appropriate responses
- Balanced discussion of the information to objectively make a recommendation or decision

Professional scepticism and judgement

- Effective challenge of information supplied, and techniques carried out to support key facts and/or decisions
- Determination and justification of a suitable materiality level, appropriately and consistently applied

Marking guide | **Marks**

- Appropriate application of professional judgement to draw conclusions and make informed decisions about the courses of action which are appropriate in the context of the audit engagement

Commercial acumen

- Audit procedures are practical and plausible in the context of the Crux Group
- Use of effective examples and/or calculations from the scenario to illustrate points or recommendations
- Recognition of the appropriate commercial considerations of the audit firm

Maximum	10
Total	50

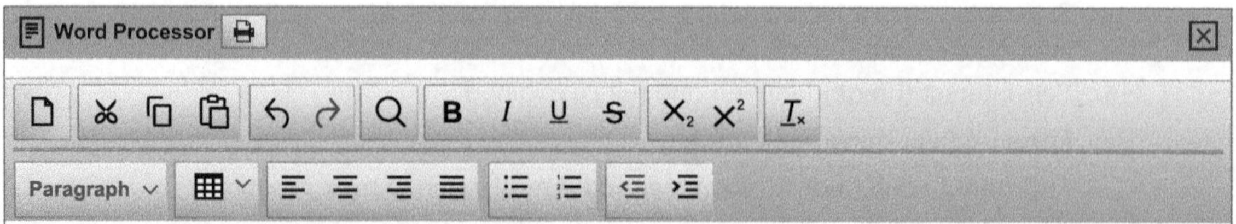

Briefing Notes

To: **Audit engagement partner**

From: **Audit manager**

Subject: **Crux Group – Audit Planning**

Introduction

These briefing notes are prepared to assist with planning the audit of the Crux Group (the Group) for the financial year ending 30 September 20X5. The notes contain an evaluation of the significant audit risks that should be considered in planning the Group audit, which has been structured to prioritise the risks in terms of the likelihood and magnitude of misstatement in relation to each risk. The notes also recommend the audit procedures to be performed on the Group's segmental disclosure of revenue. Finally, there is a discussion of the matters to be considered by Pegasus & Co in relation to a proposed additional engagement to advise management on the Group's social and environmental information.

Note. Remember, you can access the ACCA's Practice Platform to learn how to attempt AAA questions using the CBE software.

(a) **Evaluation of audit risk**

Materiality

For the purposes of these briefing notes the following overall materiality level will be used to assess the significance of identified risks and as requested this has been based on the profitability of the Group.

Benchmarks

Using profit before tax or operating profit as a suggested benchmark, see spreadsheet for detailed calculations, results in a suggested range of £4.05 million to £14.5 million.

These benchmarks are only a starting point for determining materiality and professional judgement will need to be applied in determining a final level to be used during the course of the audit. As this is a new client and therefore an initial audit engagement, due to the increased detection risk, materiality should be set at the lower level of the range at £4 million.

New audit client

The Group is a new client, our firm having been appointed six months ago. This gives rise to detection risk, as our firm does not have experience with the client, making it more difficult for us to detect material misstatements. However, this risk can be mitigated through rigorous audit planning, including obtaining a thorough understanding of the business of the Group.

In addition, there is a risk that opening balances and comparative information may not be correct. As the prior year figures were not audited by Pegasus & Co, if any misstatements existed in relation to the opening balances this would have a significant impact on our ability to gather sufficient and appropriate evidence over closing balances. As such we should plan to audit the opening balances carefully, in accordance with ISA (UK) 510 *Initial Audit Engagements – Opening Balances*, to ensure that opening balances and comparative information are both free from material misstatement.

Revenue recognition

An audit risk arises in relation to the timing of revenue recognition. Given the requirement of ISA (UK) 240 *The Auditor's Responsibilities Relating to Fraud in an Audit of Financial Statements*, that when assessing audit risks the auditor shall presume there are risks of fraud in relation to revenue recognition this could be a significant area of concern. It is appropriate that customer deposits are recognised as deferred revenue when they are received. This is in line with IFRS® 15 *Revenue from Contracts with Customers* which requires that revenue is recognised when a performance obligation is satisfied, and therefore any amounts paid to the Group by customers before a cruise begins are not revenue and should be deferred. However, the policy of recognising all of the revenue from a ticket sale when the cruise starts may not be in line with the principles of IFRS 15 because the Group is performing its obligations over time, which may be as long as a six-week period for some cruises. This is a problem of cut-off, meaning that recognition of all revenue at the start of a cruise could result in overstated revenue and understated liabilities.

Upgrade and maintenance costs

The Group incurs high costs in relation to upgrade and maintenance of its fleet of ships. For the Sunseeker ships, £75 million is being spent this year. Based on initial materiality calculations, this amount is material to the financial statements and represents 92.6% of profit before tax and is therefore extremely significant. There is an audit risk that costs are not appropriately distinguished between capital expenditure and operating expenditure. Upgrade costs, including costs relating to new facilities such as gyms, should be capitalised, but maintenance costs should be expensed. There is a risk that assets are overstated, and expenses understated, if operating expenses have been inappropriately capitalised. A further risk relates to depreciation expenses, which will be overstated if capital expenditure is overstated.

Component depreciation

IAS® 16 *Property, Plant and Equipment* requires that each part of an item of property, plant, and equipment (PPE) with a cost which is significant in relation to the total cost of the item must be depreciated separately. There is a risk that ships in use are not broken down into component parts for the purpose of determining the individual cost, useful life, and residual value of each part. For example, if significant, the gym equipment should be depreciated over three years and therefore requires separate consideration from other assets such as ship exterior, engine, etc. There is an audit risk that depreciation is not correctly determined on this component basis, meaning that the assets and their associated depreciation expense could be over or understated in value. This risk is also heightened due to the unusual movement in relation to the accumulated depreciation figure, which has only increased by £49 million in the year. Information is not given on the Group's depreciation policy, however compared to the total cost of PPE at the financial year end of £2,304 million, this equates to only 2.1%, which appears quite low, suggesting understatement.

Cybersecurity attack

The recent cybersecurity attack could highlight that internal controls are deficient within the Group. Even though this particular problem has now been rectified, if the Group internal audit team had not properly identified or responded to these cybersecurity risks, there could be other areas, including controls over financial reporting, which are deficient, leading to control risk. The situation could also indicate wider weaknesses in the Group's corporate governance arrangements, for example, if the audit committee is not appropriately discharging its responsibilities with regards to internal audit.

> **Tutorial note.** Based on best practice the audit committee should review and approve the annual internal audit plan and monitor and review the effectiveness of internal audit work. The audit committee should ensure that the internal audit plan is aligned to the key risks of the business. Credit will be awarded for discussion of these issues in the context of the cybersecurity attack.

In addition, the cybersecurity attack could have resulted in corrupted data or loss of data relating to the sales system, if the customer details were integrated with the accounting system. There is an audit risk that reported revenue figures are inaccurate, incomplete, or invalid. Though the issue could be confined to the sales system, it is possible that other figures could also be affected.

Finally, the cybersecurity incident is likely to result in some fines or penalties being levied against the Group as it seems the risk was not properly dealt with, leaving customer information vulnerable to attack. It may be necessary for the Group to recognise a provision or disclose a contingent liability depending on the likelihood of a cash payment being made, and the materiality of any such payment, in accordance with IAS 37 *Provisions, Contingent Liabilities and Contingent Assets*. The related audit risk is understated liabilities and understated expenses or incomplete disclosures if any necessary liability is not recognised or disclosure not made in the notes to the financial statements.

Related party transaction

It appears that Vela Shipbuilders Ltd, which is building new Explorer Cruise ships for the Group, is a related party of the Group. This is because Max Draco is the chairman of both the Group and Vela Shipbuilders Ltd. According to IAS 24 *Related Party Disclosures*, a related party relationship exists where a person has control or joint control, significant influence, or is a member of the key management personnel of two reporting entities. The fact that Max Draco's son is the chief executive officer of Vela Shipbuilders Ltd also indicates a related party relationship between the Group and the company.

IAS 24 requires that where there have been transactions between related parties, there should be disclosure of the nature of the related party relationship as well as information about the transactions and outstanding balances necessary for an understanding of the potential effect of the relationship on the financial statements. There is an audit risk that the necessary disclosures regarding the Group's purchases of ships from Vela Shipbuilders Ltd are not made in the Group financial statements.

The related party transactions are material by their nature, but they are also likely to be material by monetary value. The information provided does not specify how much has been paid in cash from the Group to Vela Shipbuilders Ltd during the year, but the amount could be significant given that the Group has presumably paid any final instalments on the ships which have come into use during the year, as well as initial instalments on the new ships starting construction this year.

Operating licences

The Group's operating licences of £56 million are material to the financial statements. It is appropriate that the licences are recognised as intangible assets and that they are amortised according to their specific useful life. However, an audit risk arises due to the possible impairment of some or all of these licences, which arises from the governments having withdrawn the licenses in some countries where the Group operates their Pioneer cruises. While the licence withdrawal is apparently temporary in nature, the withdrawal is an indicator of impairment and it is possible that the operating licences are worth nothing, so should be written off in full. Management should conduct an impairment review in accordance with IAS 36 *Impairment of Assets* to determine the recoverable amount of the licences and if this is less than the carrying amount, recognise an impairment loss accordingly. If this does not take place, the intangible assets are likely to be overstated, and profit overstated.

> **Tutorial note.** Credit will also be awarded for discussion regarding de-recognition of the operating licences as well as their reduction in value, and for considering whether the Pioneer Cruise ships also need to be reviewed for impairment.

Borrowing costs

The ships being constructed fall under the definition of a qualifying asset under IAS 23 *Borrowing Costs*, which defines a qualifying asset as an asset that takes a substantial period of time to get ready for its intended use or sale. This includes property, plant, and equipment during the relevant construction period, which for the ships is three years. IAS 23 requires that borrowing costs which are directly attributable to the acquisition, construction or production of a qualifying asset should be capitalised. The audit risk is that interest costs have not been appropriately capitalised and instead have been treated as finance costs, which would understate assets and understate profit for the year.

The amounts involved appear to be material. The information does not state precisely when the loans were taken out and when construction of the ships commenced or when they come into use by the Group on completion, so it is not possible to determine exactly when capitalisation of finance costs should commence and cease. However, looking at the loan of £180 million taken out for the ships currently under construction, the interest for the year would be £11.7 million, which is a material amount.

Revenue and profit trends

Overall Group revenue is projected to increase by 14% in the year. The segmental information shows that this overall increase is comprised of different movements across the three brands (see spreadsheet for detailed calculations) and there are some potential risks associated with these movements.

The different trends for each segment could be explained by business reasons, however there is a potential risk that revenue has been misclassified between the segments, eg revenue from Explorer Cruises could be understated while revenue from Pioneer Cruises is overstated.

In particular, the projected revenue for Pioneer Cruises could be impacted by the recent withdrawal of operating licenses which affects the operation of these cruise itineraries. Management may not have factored this into their projections, and there is a risk that this segment's revenue is overstated.

Operating profit is projected to increase by 43.6% in the year, and profit before tax is projected to increase by 24.6% in the year. While the increased margins could be due to economies of scale, the increase in profit appears out of line with the increase in revenue and could indicate that expenses are understated or misclassified.

On-board sales

On-board sales of food, drink, and entertainment account for approximately 15% of revenue. There is a risk that this is a reportable operating segment, but the projected operating segment information does not disclose this revenue separately. According to IFRS 8 *Operating Segments*, an operating segment is a component of an entity which engages in business activities from which it may earn revenues and incur expenses, whose operating results are reviewed regularly by the entity's chief operating decision maker and for which discrete financial information is available which seems to be the case in this instance.

A reportable segment exists where the segment's revenue is 10% or more of the combined revenue of all operating segments. There is a risk of incomplete disclosure of revenue by reportable segments if on-board sales meet the definition of an operating segment and it is not disclosed in the notes to the financial statements as such.

(b) **Principal audit procedures to be performed on the segmental information**

- Review the financial reports sent to the highest level of management to confirm the basis of segmental information which is reported internally and confirm that this basis is used in the notes to the published financial statements.
- Review the Group's organisational structure to confirm the identity of the chief operating decision maker.

- Discuss with management the means by which segmental information is reviewed by the chief operating decision maker, eg through monthly financial reports and discussion at board meetings.
- Review board minutes to confirm that the segments as disclosed are used as the basis for monitoring financial performance.
- Discuss with management whether the on-board sales should be reported separately given that it appears to constitute a reportable segment contributing more than 10% of total Group sales and is actively monitored.
- Obtain a breakdown of the revenue, eg by cruise line or individual ship, to confirm that revenue has been appropriately allocated between the reportable segments.
- Perform analytical procedures to determine trends for each segment and discuss unusual patterns with management.
- Recalculate the revenue totals from the breakdown provided to confirm that they are reportable segments, ie that they each contribute more than 10% of revenue.

(c) **Additional service to advise management on measurement of social and environmental information**

The Group's request for Pegasus & Co to advise management on its social and environmental reporting creates an ethical threat to objectivity. Providing additional, non-audit services to an audit client can create several threats to the objectivity and independence of the auditor.

The IESBA *International Code of Ethics for Professional Accountants* (the Code) does not specifically discuss this type of additional engagement, so the audit firm should apply the general framework to consider whether it is appropriate to provide the service. This means that the firm should evaluate the significance of the threats to independence and consider whether safeguards can reduce the threats to an acceptable level.

Perhaps the most significant ethical issue, is that providing advice to management, which would involve determining how social and environmental information is measured and published could be perceived as taking on management responsibilities, which is prohibited by the Code. To avoid taking on management responsibilities, the audit firm must be satisfied that client management makes all judgements and decisions that are the proper responsibility of management. Measures to achieve this could include:

- Ensuring that a member of the Group's management with appropriate skill, knowledge and experience is designated to be responsible for the client's decisions and to oversee the service,
- Management oversees the work performed and evaluates the results, and
- Management accepts responsibility for any actions arising as a result of the service provided.

A self-review threat could also arise if Pegasus & Co provides the service to the Group. Some of the social and environmental information could be related to transactions or balances within the financial statements which will be subject to audit, for example the value of charitable donations. The self-review threat means that less scrutiny may be used in performing procedures due to over-reliance on work previously performed by the audit firm. This potentially impacts on the level of professional scepticism applied during the audit and the quality of work carried out.

There could be a further self-review threat depending on whether the social and environmental information will form part of the Group's annual report. If this is the case, the audit team is required by ISA (UK) 720 *The Auditor's Responsibilities Relating to Other Information*, to read the other information included in the annual report and to consider whether there is a material inconsistency between the other information and the financial statements and to also consider whether there is a material inconsistency between the other information and the auditor's knowledge obtained in the audit. This requirement creates a self-review threat if members of the audit team have been involved with the additional service to provide advice on measurement of the social and environmental information.

A self-interest threat can also be created by the provision of non-audit services where the fee is significant enough to create actual or perceived economic dependence on the audit client. The Group is willing to pay an 'enhanced fee' for this service due to its urgent nature, and while this does not necessarily create fee-dependency there could be a perception that the audit firm has secured a lucrative fee income in addition to the income from providing the audit.

The Group needs the work to be carried out to a tight deadline, which could impact on the scope and extent of the procedures which the firm can carry out, also impacting on the quality of work and the risk of the engagement. This pressure to perform work quickly within the next month could be viewed as intimidation by the client.

All of these threats are heightened by the fact that the Group is a listed entity, therefore a public interest entity in the terminology of the *Code.*

Other safeguards could possibly be used to reduce the threats identified to an acceptable level. These may include having a team separate from the audit team, including a separate partner, perform the work on the social and environmental information; and conducting a review of both the audit and additional service by the engagement quality reviewer.

The audit firm should discuss the request with the Group audit committee, who ultimately will need to approve that the firm can perform the service. The corporate governance code under which the Group operates may restrict or prohibit the provision of non-audit services by the audit firm in the case of listed entities, so the audit committee should consider if any such restrictions exist.

Discussions should also be held regarding the new regulatory requirements. The audit firm should be clear on the reliance which will be placed on the report by the regulatory authorities and matters such as whether an assurance report is required, and if so, who will be performing this work. In addition, there may be specific requirements which impact on the scope of the work, for example whether any specific KPIs are required to be published.

Finally, even if the ethical issues can be overcome, the firm should consider whether it has the skills and competencies to provide the advice to management. This can be quite specialised work and it is not necessarily the case that the firm will have staff with the appropriate skills available to carry out the work, especially if the work is to be carried out to a tight deadline.

In conclusion in terms of providing advice to management on social and environmental information, this will be difficult to do without breaching ethical principles and should be further discussed with the Group audit committee.

Conclusion

These briefing notes highlight a number of significant audit risks, including those relating to property, plant and equipment, revenue recognition and disclosure requirements. A number of audit procedures have been recommended in relation to the audit of segmental information provided in relation to revenue. As mentioned, the provision of the additional service should be further discussed with the Group audit committee.

Section B

2 Welford & Co

Workbook references

Chapters 2, 4, and 5.

Top tips

Question two of this exam was divided into two mini scenarios, one covering a completed audit and the other an audit yet to take place.

The question required you essentially to criticise the conduct of the completed audit. There were 20 marks available here, so your answer to this part would have needed to be substantial. This makes it important to set everything out as clearly as you possibly can, so that the marker can follow everything and award you as many marks as possible!

It was important here not to overlook the requirement to recommend appropriate actions to be taken. The audit is now complete, so these actions cannot be just the actions that should have been taken at the time, but rather what the auditor will need to do now that everything has already happened.

Easy marks

There were some clear difficulties with the audit that should have given rise to some easy points for you to make.

Marking guide **Marks**

Rivers plc

Generally, up to 1 mark for each well explained point:

- Long association of audit partner breaches the IESBA Code 7-year maximum period allowed
- Self-interest threat identified and explained
- Familiarity threat identified and explained
- Recommend replace Bob with a new audit partner as soon as possible
- Firm's monitoring of the length of time partners act for clients seems deficient
- Audit partner should have spent more time on the audit and in particular on the final review
- The total amount of time spent on the audit appears low for the audit of a listed company – implications for audit quality
- Inappropriate delegation of tasks, the junior audit manager lacks experience
- There may not be sufficient, appropriate evidence to support the audit opinion
- Welford & Co may have provided a prohibited non-audit service to Rivers plc, a listed company
- The size of fee for the non-audit service creates a self-interest threat
- Bob's involvement with the non-audit service creates familiarity threats to audit objectivity
- Lack of documentation could indicate that no work has been performed – possibly a bribe from the client
- Welford & Co to review policies, procedures and documentation on engagement acceptance
- Apparent lack of Engagement Quality Review being carried out before the audit opinion was issued.

Marking guide	Marks
• Inappropriate delegation of work on going concern to an inexperienced audit assistant	
• Sample of contracts reviewed is too small – insufficient evidence obtained	
• Management selection of contracts is likely to be subject to bias – the auditor should select which contracts should be reviewed	
• Over-reliance on and misunderstanding of use of data analytics tools	
• Insufficient work on going concern – assumptions should be challenged not agreed to prior year	
• Data analytics could have been used to carry out specific going concern testing such as sensitivity analysis	
• Lack of time spent on going concern testing due to over-reliance on data analytics	
• Additional training required	
• Client audit committee – should have identified the ethical and audit quality issues	
• Overall conclusion relating to the quality of the engagement	
Maximum	20
Professional marks	
Analysis and evaluation	
• Appropriate assessment of the ethical and professional issues raised, using examples where relevant to support overall comments	
• Effective appraisal of the information to make suitable recommendations for appropriate courses of action	
Professional scepticism and judgement	
• Effective challenge and critical assessment of the evidence supplied with appropriate conclusions	
• Demonstration of the ability to probe into the reasons for quality issues including the identification of missing information or additional information which would be required	
• Appropriate application of professional judgement to draw conclusions and make informed comments regarding the quality of the work carried out.	
Commercial acumen	
• Inclusion of appropriate recommendations regarding the additional quality management procedures required by the firm	
• Appropriate recognition of the wider implications on the engagement, the audit firm and the company.	
Maximum	5
Total	25

Rivers plc

A review of the information relating to the audit of Rivers plc indicates many problems with how the audit has been planned and performed which imply that the audit has not been conducted in accordance with ISA (UK) 220 (Revised) *Quality Management for an Audit of Financial Statements*, ISQM (UK) 1 *Quality Management for Firms that Perform Audits or Reviews of Financial Statements, or other Assurance and Related Services Engagements*, and the IESBA *International Code of Ethics for Professional Accountants (the Code).*

ANSWERS

Audit partner rotation

Bob Newbold has been acting as audit engagement partner for eight years. As Rivers plc is a listed company this goes against the requirements of the Code which requires that an individual shall not act as the engagement partner for more than seven years. The problem is that long association of the engagement partner with the client leads to a self-interest threat to auditor objectivity, whereby the audit firm's judgement is affected by concern over losing the long-standing client. There may also be a familiarity threat due to close relationships between the audit engagement partner and management of Rivers plc, meaning that the partner ceases to exercise sufficient professional scepticism, impacting on audit quality. This is especially the case given that Bob Newbold is performing additional non-audit services for the client, which will be discussed further below. Bob Newbold should be replaced as soon as possible by another audit engagement partner.

The fact that Bob has been allowed to continue as audit partner for longer than the period allowed by the Code indicates that Welford & Co does not have appropriate policies and procedures designed to provide it with reasonable assurance that the firm and its personnel comply with relevant ethical requirements, as required by ISQM (UK)1. The firm should review whether its monitoring of the length of time that audit engagement partners act for clients is operating effectively and make any necessary improvements to internal controls to ensure compliance with ISQM (UK) 1.

> **Tutorial note.** The Code does allow a key audit partner to serve an additional year in situations where continuity is especially important to audit quality, as long as the threat to independence can be eliminated or reduced to an acceptable level. Credit will be awarded for appropriate discussion on this issue. Credit will also be awarded for reference to the (5+2) = 7-year possible tenure under the FRC *Revised Ethical Standard.*

Supervision and review

Bob Newbold has booked only two hours for audit work performed on Rivers plc. This is not sufficient time for the audit partner to perform their duties adequately. The audit partner is required to take overall responsibility for the supervision and performance of the audit. He should have spent an appropriate amount of time performing a review of the audit working papers in order to be satisfied that sufficient appropriate audit evidence had been obtained; this is a requirement of ISA (UK) 220 (Revised). Instead it appears that most of the final review was performed by a newly promoted audit manager who would not have the necessary experience to perform this review. It is possible that there is insufficient evidence to support the audit opinion which has been issued, or that inappropriate evidence has been obtained.

There is also a related issue regarding the delegation of work. Possibly some of the detailed review of the working papers could have been delegated to someone other than the audit partner, in which case the senior audit manager Pat Canley would be the appropriate person to perform this work. However, Pat only recorded six hours of work on the audit. Thus, confirming that too much of the review has been delegated to the junior audit manager, especially given that going concern was identified as a significant audit risk, meaning that the partner has even more reason for involvement in the final review of audit work.

There is also an issue around the overall amount of time which has been recorded for the audit work performed on this client. A total of 173 hours does not seem sufficient for the audit of a listed company, suggesting that audit quality could have been impacted by inadequate time spent in planning and performing the audit work.

Special investigation

Bob Newbold's focus appears to have been on the special investigation performed for Rivers plc, to which he booked 40 hours of time.

There is insufficient documentation as to the nature of this non-audit work, and it could relate to the provision of a non-audit service which is not allowed for a public interest entity. Rivers plc is a listed company, and the Code prohibits the audit firm from providing certain non-audit services, for example certain internal audit services, valuation services and tax services. The lack of documentation means that Welford & Co could have provided a prohibited service and therefore be in breach of the Code.

The fact that £890,000 was charged for this special investigation indicates that it was a substantial engagement and just the matter of inadequate documentation is a cause for concern. There is also a possibility that in actual fact no work has been performed, and the firm has accepted this money from the client but provided no service. This would be a very serious issue, could be perceived as a bribe, and it should be investigated with urgency.

However, there are also possible threats to auditor objectivity including a self-interest threat due to the monetary value of the service provided meaning that Bob Newbold's attention seems to have been focused on the special investigation rather than the audit, leading to the problems of inappropriate delegation of this work as discussed above. His additional involvement with Rivers plc by providing this work compounds the familiarity threat also discussed previously. Depending on the nature of the work performed for the client there may also be other threats to objectivity including self-review and advocacy.

A self-interest threat is created as the value of the services provided is substantial compared to the audit fee. The fact the non-audit fees are so high would create a proportionately bigger intimidation threat because they would form a larger part of the firm's income and the audit firm may not be objective for fear of losing the client.

Welford & Co should ensure that its policies and documentation on engagement acceptance, especially in relation to additional services for existing audit clients, are reviewed and made more robust if necessary.

Engagement Quality Review

As this is a listed audit client, an Engagement Quality Review should have been performed. It is not clear whether this took place or not, but no time has been recorded for this review. If a pre-issuance review was carried out, then it should have picked up these problems prior to the audit opinion being issued.

Audit of going concern

The audit work on going concern has been inappropriately delegated to an audit assistant who would not have the necessary skill or experience. This is especially concerning given that going concern was identified as a significant audit risk, and that the work involves using judgement to evaluate information relating to contract performance. The work should have been performed by a more senior member of the team, probably one of the audit managers, who is more able to exercise professional scepticism and to challenge management where necessary on the assumptions underpinning the forecasts. Mary certainly should not have documented the conclusion on going concern, the conclusion should be reached by a more experienced auditor having reviewed all of the evidence obtained.

It is concerning that the audit work appears to have been based on a review of contracts which were selected by management. First, only five contracts were reviewed but the company is typically working on 20 contracts at one time. So, it is likely that the coverage of the audit work was insufficient, and more contracts should have been subject to review. Given the risk attached to going concern perhaps all of the contracts currently being carried out should have been reviewed, or the sample selected based on the auditor's evaluation of the risk associated with each contract and their materiality.

Second, management may have selected the better performing contracts for Mary to review. This would create a false impression of the performance of the company as a whole, leading to an inappropriate conclusion on going concern being reached. Mary, or one of the more senior members of the audit team, should have challenged management on the selection of these contracts.

Finally, the work performed by Mary on this small selection of contracts appears insufficient and inappropriate. The audit assistant also appears to have placed too much reliance on the firm's data analytics tool and demonstrates a lack of understanding of how the data analytics tools should be used to obtain audit evidence. By simply using the data analytics tool to agree the mathematical accuracy of the forecasts and the assumptions, insufficient testing has been carried out in relation to these key documents. Assumptions should not just be agreed as consistent with the previous year, especially in a situation of increasing economic uncertainty as applies in this case. Assumptions should be challenged, and other work performed as required by ISA (UK) 570 *Going Concern*. The data analytics tool could have been used more appropriately, eg to perform sensitivity analysis which would have allowed for identification of areas of concern or requiring further investigation.

The lack of further audit procedures means that the audit evidence is not likely to be sufficiently robust in this significant area. This is further demonstrated by the fact that Mary only spent eight hours on this critical area of the audit work and has commented that this was due to the evidence generated by the data analytics tool. This again demonstrates the over-reliance placed on this tool, raising a concern that staff require further training in the use of and interpretation of evidence generated in this way.

Audit Committee

It is concerning that the audit committee of Rivers plc does not appear to have raised concerns about the issues discussed, especially the provision of the non-audit service and the length of time which Bob Newbold has served as audit engagement partner. One of the roles of the audit committee is to oversee ethical issues relating to the external auditor and to be involved with the engagement of external providers. Welford & Co should ensure that these matters are discussed with the audit committee so that further ethical issues do not arise in the future.

Conclusion

From the discussion above it can be seen that there are many problems with the audit of Rivers plc. Bob Newbold appears to have ignored his responsibilities as audit engagement partner, and the audit firm needs to discuss this with him, consider further training or possibly taking disciplinary action against him. Welford & Co needs to implement procedures to ensure all work is carried out at the appropriate level of personnel with the appropriate experience, and that training is given to staff to ensure they understand the client does not pick or specify the audit work to be carried out in any area – it is to be selected by the audit team in accordance with the audit firms methodology and sampling tools. Training may also need to be provided in the appropriate use of audit data analytics tools as a basis for obtaining audit evidence.

3 Myron plc

Workbook reference

Chapters 8, 10 and 11.

Top tips

This question covered two separate issues related to a single audit client.

Part (a) may have appeared intimidating but if you had found a way to keep your cool then there were marks on offer. You needed to calculate materiality for each issue, taking care to choose the most appropriate benchmark and to conclude on whether the issue is material. Then you should work through the accounting treatments given and recommend the actions that should be taken.

It is key not to overlook the auditor's report implications, as the marks available for correctly stating these were among the easiest on the exam.

Part (b) covered other information and featured a relatively large number of marks for simple knowledge (in (i)). This should have been a strong part of the exam for you, but notice its positioning at the very end of the paper; time management is a key professional skill, so you need to make use of this if you are going to get these (relatively) easy marks.

Easy marks

Part (a) contained easy marks for correctly calculating (and evaluating) materiality where this was possible.

Marking guide	Marks
(a) **Matters, further actions and auditor's report implications**	
Up to 1 mark for each point unless otherwise stated	
Matters	
• Assessment of finance director's approach	
• Assessment of materiality	
• Disclosure rules re held for sale/discontinued operations	
• Application to the scenario to conclude asset is held for sale (HFS)	
• Material misstatement of classification and disclosure	
• Accounting rule on valuation of held for sale assets	
• Rule that depreciation should cease when asset meets criteria of HFS	
• Application to the scenario to derive correct value	
• Materiality of the error in valuation	
Further actions	
• Request adjustment from management to recognise the discontinued operation and to separately disclose the assets held for sale	
• Request management to amend the carrying amount of the assets to the recoverable amount of £42 million	
• If management refuse escalate to Those Charged with Governance (TCWG)	
• If still refuse obtain written representation confirming intent to proceed	
Auditor's report implications	
• Qualified on basis of material misstatement	
• Justification of whether pervasive and possible adverse impact due to lack of significant disclosures	
• Basis of opinion paragraph position and content	
Maximum	10
(b) (i) **Auditor's responsibilities in relation to other information presented with the financial statements**	
Assessment of ISA (UK) requirements including:	
• Auditor must read other information for inconsistency with financial statements or understanding of the business	
• Consider the source of the inconsistency	
- A material misstatement of the other information exists;	
- A material misstatement of the financial statements exists; or	
- The auditor's understanding of the entity and its environment needs to be updated.	
• Auditor does not give opinion on the other information	
Matters arising from Chairman's statement	
• Growth discussion ignores discontinued operation	
• Calculations to support the ongoing growth	

Marking guide | **Marks**

- Statement obscures actual growth hence misleading/material misstatement in other information
- Inappropriate reference to the content of the auditor's report
- Misstatement of fact regarding recycled paper usage
- Judgement as to whether it is material misstatement of other information

Maximum 5

(ii) **Implications for the completion of the audit**

- Seek further information to confirm understanding
- Request management to correct
- Escalate to TCWG
- Impact on assessment of management integrity and written representations
- Notify TCWG effect on auditor's report
- Consider resigning

Implications for the auditor's report arising from the draft Chairman's statement

- Addressed in other information paragraph to draw attention to issue covering
  - Statement other information not audited
  - Responsibilities of auditor regarding other information
  - Description of uncorrected misstatements
- Auditor's opinion is not modified.

Maximum 5

Professional marks

Analysis and evaluation

- Appropriate use of the information to support discussion, draw appropriate conclusions and design appropriate responses
- Identification of omissions from the analysis or further analysis which could be carried out
- Balanced assessment of the information to determine the appropriate audit opinion in the circumstances

Professional scepticism and judgement

- Effective challenge of information, evidence and assumptions supplied and, techniques carried out to support key facts and/or decisions
- Appropriate application of professional judgement to draw conclusions and make informed decisions about the actions which are appropriate in the context and stage of the engagement.

Maximum 5

Total 25

(a) **Matters, further actions and auditor's report implications**

Matters

The company is at an advanced stage of negotiations with a competitor to sell its scientific publishing division. Currently the finance director has not included any reference to the sale in the financial statements for the year ended 31 March 20X5 and there is no appropriate justification for this. The finance director's assessment that the sale only affects next year's financial statements is incorrect.

Materiality

The revenue of the scientific publishing division of £13 million and the profit of the division of £1.4 million are both material. The assets of the division are also significant, as they represent 27.3% of the company's total assets, based on their value in use which is recognised in the financial statements.

Discontinued operation and classification of assets held for sale

IFRS 5 *Non-Current Assets Held for Sale and Discontinued Operations* defines a discontinued operation as a component of an entity which either has been disposed of or is classified as held for sale, and:

- represents either a separate major line of business or a geographical area of operations; and
- is part of a single co-ordinated plan to dispose of a separate major line of business or geographical area of operation.

IFRS 5 requires specific disclosures in relation to assets held for sale and discontinued operations, including that the assets are recognised as current assets and the results of the discontinued operation are presented separately in the statement of profit or loss and the statement of cash flows.

According to IFRS 5, a disposal group of assets should be classified as held for sale where management plans to sell the assets, and the sale is highly probable. Conditions which indicate that a sale is highly probable are:

- management is committed to a plan to sell
- the asset is available for immediate sale
- an active programme to locate a buyer is initiated
- the sale is highly probable, within 12 months of classification as held for sale (subject to limited exceptions)
- the asset is being actively marketed for sale at a sales price reasonable in relation to its fair value
- actions required to complete the plan indicate that it is unlikely that plan will be significantly changed or withdrawn.

In respect of the scientific publishing division, management has decided to sell the division and a buyer has been found. The advanced stage of negotiations would suggest the sale is highly probable.

As a result, important disclosures are currently missing from the financial statements which could mislead users with respect to the future revenue, profits, assets and cash flows of the company. Failing to provide information about the sale of the division could be seen as a significant omission from the financial statements, especially given the materiality of the assets of the division to the company's assets as a whole.

There is therefore a material misstatement as the scientific publishing division has not been classified as held for sale and its profit presented as a discontinued operation and the necessary disclosures have not been made in the financial statements.

Held for sale – valuation

IFRS 5 provides further guidance regarding the valuation of the assets held for sale. Prior to classification as held for sale, the disposal group should be reviewed for impairment in accordance with IAS® 36 Impairment of Assets. This impairment review would require the asset to be held at the lower of carrying amount and recoverable amount where the recoverable amount is the higher of value in use or fair value less costs of disposal.

In this case the recoverable amount would be £42 million representing the fair value less costs of disposal. Management has valued the disposal group based on its value in use at £41 million which means that assets and profit are currently understated by £1 million. This represents 10.7% of profit before tax and is material to the profit for the year.

ANSWERS

After classification as held for sale, non-current assets or disposal groups are measured at the lower of carrying amount and fair value less costs which would continue to be £42 million. Depreciation ceases to be charged when an asset is classified as held for sale.

Further actions

- The auditor should request that management adjusts the financial statements to recognise the discontinued operation and to separately disclose the assets held for sale in accordance with IFRS 5.
- In addition, the client should be requested to amend the carrying amount of the assets to the recoverable amount of £42 million in line with IFRS 5 requirements.
- If management refuses to adjust the financial statements, the auditor should communicate the misstatements to those charged with governance. They should repeat the request and inform them of the modifications which would be made to the auditor's report if the adjustments are not made.
- If management still refuses to amend the financial statements, the auditor should request a written representation from management confirming their intent to proceed without amending the financial statements and that they are aware of the potential repercussions.

Word Processor

Auditor's report implications

If the adjustments are not made, then there is a material misstatement in the financial statements. The matter has resulted in an understatement of assets and profits by £1 million, which in isolation is unlikely to be pervasive as limited components of the financial statements are affected. This would result in a qualified audit opinion in which the auditor's report would state that 'except for' the material misstatement in relation to the valuation of the assets held for sale, the financial statements are fairly stated.

However, there are also several important disclosures omitted that would be required for users to understand both the current financial position of the company and its ability to generate future revenue and profits. As such, it would be a matter of judgement as to whether the lack of disclosures, in conjunction with the material misstatement mentioned above, have a pervasive impact on the financial statements. Depending on the auditor's judgement on this issue, this may give rise to an adverse opinion if the auditor considered the impact of these issues to result in the financial statements being wholly misleading.

Depending on the opinion provided, a basis for qualified or adverse opinion paragraph would be added underneath the opinion paragraph to describe and quantify the effects of the misstatements.

(b) (i) **Auditor's responsibility for other information presented with the financial statements**

ISA (UK) 720 *The Auditor's Responsibilities Relating to Other Information* requires the auditor to read other information, defined as financial or non-financial information (other than financial statements and the auditor's report thereon), included in an entity's annual report.

The purpose of reading the other information is to consider whether there is a material inconsistency between the other information and the financial statements or between the other information and the auditor's knowledge obtained during the course of the audit. If the auditor identifies that a material inconsistency appears to exist, or becomes aware that the other information appears to be materially misstated, the auditor should discuss the matter with management and, if necessary, perform other procedures to conclude whether:

(1) A material misstatement of the other information exists;

(2) A material misstatement of the financial statements exists; or

(3) The auditor's understanding of the entity and its environment needs to be updated.

The auditor does not audit the other information and does not express an opinion covering the other information.

Matters identified from the chairman's statement

In this case, the chairman's statement refers to strong growth in the year, in particular the scientific publishing division and suggests that the growth will continue. In the current year, the scientific publishing division represented 12% of revenue and 15% of profit before tax and is a material component of the company. As the scientific publishing division will be disposed of early in the next financial period, it will not continue to form part of the basis for revenue or growth, and the chairman's statement could be considered misleading. Further, because of the disposal, on a like for like basis it is more likely that the financial statements for the year ended 31 March 20X6 will include a reduction in revenue rather than growth.

In addition, the remainder of the business has experienced a lower level of growth in revenue and profits in the period than the scientific publishing division. Revenue growth of continuing business is 2% compared to 44% in the scientific publishing division. Profit growth of the ongoing business is 5% compared to 100% for the scientific publishing division.

ISA (UK) 720 states that a misstatement of the other information exists when the other information is incorrectly stated or otherwise misleading, including because it omits or obscures information necessary for a proper understanding of a matter disclosed in the other information. In the case of the chairman's statement regarding growth of the company, it could be argued that the way the information is presented obscures the understanding of the growth and profitability of the ongoing business. As mentioned above, this would be considered very misleading.

The chairman has also made an inappropriate reference to the view of the auditor, implying that the auditor's report validates this assertion. The statement also appears to inappropriately pre-empt that the auditor's report will provide an unmodified opinion which based on the assessment above may not be the case given the material misstatement and lack of disclosures. This is inappropriate and all reference to the auditor's report should be removed.

In addition, there is also an issue arising with respect to the use of recycled paper. The chairman's statement in this case is inconsistent with the knowledge obtained during the audit. Whether the auditor considers this to be material would be a matter of judgement, depending on how many publications there are in total and the proportion using non-recycled paper and whether the issue may be material by nature rather than by size. This could be the case if it is perceived that there is a deliberate misrepresentation of facts which may be misleading to the users of the financial statements.

(ii) **Implications for completion of the audit**

The auditor should discuss with management and the chairman the information in the statement which appears to be inaccurate or inconsistent. In particular, this should focus on a discussion of the misleading growth analysis given that the scientific publishing division will not be contributing to company performance once it is sold.

In the case of the incorrect disclosure relating to the use of recycled paper, the auditor should seek further information to support the file note regarding publications not using recycled paper. The names of those publications should be obtained, and a discussion held with the production manager to confirm the auditor's understanding.

Following these investigations and discussions, the auditor should then request that any information which is inaccurate, inappropriate, or inconsistent is removed or amended in the chairman's report.

If management refuse to make the changes, then the auditor's request should be escalated to those charged with governance. The auditor should also consider the effect of this situation on their assessment of management integrity and whether it effects the reliance which can be placed on written representations from management. If the issue remains unresolved then the auditor should take appropriate action, including:

- Considering the implications for the auditor's report and communicating with those charged with governance about how the auditor plans to address the issues in the auditor's report; or
- Withdrawing from the engagement, where withdrawal is possible under applicable law or regulation.

Implications for the auditor's report

If the other information remains uncorrected the auditor would use the Other Information section of the auditor's report to draw the users' attention to the misstatements in the chairman's statement. This paragraph would include:

- A statement that management is responsible for the other information;
- A statement that the auditor's opinion does not cover the other information and, accordingly, that the auditor does not express (or will not express) an audit opinion or any form of assurance conclusion thereon;
- A description of the auditor's responsibilities relating to reading, considering and reporting on other information as required by this ISA; and
- A statement that describes the uncorrected material misstatement of the other information.
- As the inconsistency is in the chairman's statement rather than the audited financial statement the audit opinion is not modified as a result.

ACCA

Advanced Audit and Assurance – UK (AAA – UK)

Mock Exam 3

March/June 2022 Hybrid Exam (amended)

Questions	
Time allowed	3 hours 15 minutes
ALL THREE questions are compulsory and MUST be attempted	

DO NOT OPEN THIS EXAM UNTIL YOU ARE READY TO START UNDER EXAMINATION CONDITIONS

Section A

1 Pascal & Co

It is 1 July 20X5. You are a manager in Pascal & Co, a firm of Chartered Certified Accountants, and you are responsible for the audit of The Infinite Ltd, a new audit client with a financial year ending 30 September 20X5. The Infinite Ltd is an owner managed family business. The company owns and operates a theme park, The Infinite Park, which includes theme park rides, arcade style games and food and drink outlets. Brian Fox, the audit engagement partner, met with the company's finance director yesterday to discuss recent developments and financial performance.

In addition, Brian has also requested that you review the client acceptance procedures, which were carried out on another new client, Meadow Ltd, which operates a similar business to The Infinite Ltd.

The following exhibits, available on the left-hand side of the screen, provide information relevant to the question:

(1) Partner's email - an email which you have received from Brian Fox, the audit engagement partner in relation to The Infinite Ltd and Meadow Ltd.

(2) Background information - information from The Infinite Ltd website giving background information about the company and its operations.

(3) Meeting notes - notes from a meeting between Brian Fox and the finance director of The Infinite Ltd.

(4) Preliminary analytical procedures - summary of key issues arising from preliminary analytical procedures, performed by the audit team, on The Infinite Ltd projected financial statements.

(5) Meadow Ltd - a copy of the client acceptance assessment performed on Meadow Ltd prior to audit acceptance.

This information should be used to answer the question requirement within your chosen response option(s).

Required

Respond to the instructions in the email from the audit engagement partner.

Note. The split of the mark allocation is shown in the partner's email (Exhibit 1). **(40 marks)**

Professional marks will be awarded for the demonstration of skill in communication, analysis and evaluation, professional scepticism and judgement, and commercial acumen in your answer. **(10 marks)**

(Total = 50 marks)

Exhibit 1: Partner's email

To: Audit Manager

From: Brian Fox, Audit engagement partner

Subject: Audit planning for The Infinite Ltd, and acceptance procedures for Meadow Ltd

Date: 1 July 20X5

Hello

You need to start planning The Infinite Ltd audit, and to help with this I have provided you with some relevant information. I met with the finance director yesterday to discuss a number of matters including some recent business developments. The finance director has been with the company since it was founded but is not a member of the family who own the company.

Using the information provided in Exhibits 2, 3 and 4, I require you to prepare briefing notes for my own use, in which you:

(a) Evaluate and prioritise the significant risks of material misstatement to be considered in planning the audit for The Infinite Ltd for the financial year ending 30 September 20X5. **(24 marks)**

(b) As you are probably aware, the theme park industry has recently experienced some bad publicity relating to another one of our new audit clients, Meadow Ltd, whereby newspapers alleged the company was under investigation for money laundering. Meadow Ltd operates a similar business to The Infinite Ltd. As a result of this, in your briefing notes you should also:

Discuss the responsibility of auditors with respect to money laundering and evaluate whether there are any indicators of money laundering activities by either The Infinite Ltd or its staff. **(8 marks)**

(c) Using Exhibit 5, conduct a review of the information contained in the Meadow Ltd client acceptance assessment to evaluate weaknesses in Pascal & Co's acceptance procedures and recommend improvements which should be implemented. **(8 marks)**

Thank you.

Exhibit 2: Background information

The Infinite Park opened for business more than 40 years ago and today is one of the most popular theme parks in the UK. The Infinite Park started out with a handful of simple theme park rides and has expanded to become a 50-acre park with many different attractions. The theme park is split into two zones, each with its own unique attractions and each providing high-quality food, drink, and shopping experiences:

The 'Speed Zone' offers some of the biggest and best rides for those who like adventure.

The 'Family Zone' offers smaller rides for children.

Recent business developments relating to both zones are described in Exhibit 3.

The Infinite Park accepts cash, all major credit cards and electronic payments. Tickets for large theme park rides are sold separately at the ticket station in the Speed Zone.

Exhibit 3: Meeting notes

Operating licences

The company operates the theme park under two licences issued by the relevant UK government authority. One of these covers the operation and maintenance of the theme park rides, and the other is the licence to sell food and drinks. The theme park is subject to an annual visit by a government inspector.

Theme-park rides

The latest external safety inspection was carried out in June 20X5 and, while the report has not been officially received, the inspector has raised several specific action points. These highlighted inadequate maintenance, concern over ageing rides, and lack of modern safety features. The official report from the inspector is expected to be received by 31 July 20X5. There will then be a second inspection in October 20X5 to confirm that all issues have been addressed, after which the inspector will either approve or withhold the renewal of the operating licence in respect of the theme park rides. The finance director is confident that the licence will be renewed.

In April 20X5, the ticket station in the Speed Zone was upgraded to enable it to take electronic payments only. Prior to this, only cash payments could be accepted. As the amounts of cash handled there were often high, the managing director's sons were the only people allowed to sell tickets to reduce the risk of theft by employees. Now that payments are only electronic, staff are assigned to the ticket station through the normal park rota system. The finance noted that unexpectedly this has resulted in a fall in ticket sales compared to the equivalent months last year.

Employees

The theme park staff comprise a small number of permanent staff supplemented with a large number of temporary seasonal staff in the summer months when the theme park is busy. Some of these staff are paid in cash. The company does not make deductions for payroll taxes for these temporary staff members as they are deemed to earn under the thresholds for paying tax. The company is 100% owned by the managing director and both of his sons are employed as permanent members of staff at the park.

Food and drink

The sales of food and drink are generally equally split between cash and electronic payments. Sales in all the food outlets has been growing this year, however, the main restaurant has seen a fall in sales and margins over the last two months. This may be as a result of two cases of food poisoning which occurred in January and March and led to some negative publicity in a local newspaper. Several of the food poisoning victims are suing the company. The Infinite Ltd's legal adviser, who is a friend of the managing director, has suggested that the customers are unlikely to win the case, as they may have contracted the food poisoning elsewhere.

Gift shop sales

Recently, the theme park started employing staff to dress as famous children's animation characters and walk around the Family Zone to pose for photographs with children. Since the introduction of this practice, gift shop revenue has doubled. The gift shops sell merchandise created specifically for the theme park. However, there have been complaints about the quality of the products with customers complaining that they break easily.

The finance director mentioned that all the shops in the Family Zone have seen an increase in sales, but they are particularly impressed with the performance of one of the gift shops where sales and margins are far higher than any other outlet in the theme park. In addition, as most of the sales are in cash, there are no fees to pay to the credit card company. The finance director also mentioned that one of the managing director's sons was recently transferred to this shop.

Sale and leaseback

The managing director wishes to release some funds from the business and, as such, has been negotiating a sale and leaseback arrangement with a national bank. The arrangement is expected to be in place before the financial year end. Under the terms of the arrangement, the company would sell the theme park buildings to the bank in exchange for a payment of £1 million, which is their current market value. The buildings would be leased back over 20 years at an annual rental of £75,000. This would incorporate an interest rate of 5%, which is the current market rate, and the resulting net present value of the lease rental payments would be £934,666. The finance director intends to account for the sale as a disposal and the lease payments as rental expenses. The audit engagement partner, Brian Fox, has already reviewed the draft agreement and has concluded that the arrangement meets the criteria to be recognised as a sale.

Previous auditors

The finance director expressed his desire for a good auditor–client relationship and is hoping that we do not impose too many 'pointless rules' on the company like the previous auditors. He says that the managing director likes to be left uninterrupted to run his business without being bothered. The only two people with access to the accounting system are the finance director and the managing director, who sometimes makes money transfers to an international bank account which is held in his name.

Exhibit 4: Preliminary analytical procedures

A summary of the key financial information and findings from the preliminary analytical procedures of The Infinite Ltd projected financial statements are detailed below:

Revenue	**£13·2 million (20X4 £11·9 million)**
Profit before tax	**£2·3 million (20X4 £2·5 million)**
Total assets	**£9·5 million (20X4 £9·6 million)**

Tax

The effective tax rate has fallen to 10% of profit before tax (PBT) (20X4 15% of PBT).

Property, plant and equipment

	£000	£000
Land	6,000	6,000
Buildings	854	821
Theme-park rides	1,431	1,530
Other	75	76
	8,360	**8,427**

Land is held without depreciation under a revaluation model. The last valuation was performed seven years ago.

All other assets are held with a useful life of 30 years.

Inventory

Inventory levels have risen to £0·35 million (20X4: £0·25 million). The increase is due to bulk ordering of the new merchandise for shops to take advantage of discounts offered by suppliers.

Provisions

Current liabilities include a general provision of £0·25 million (20X4: £0·13 million) which represent amounts set aside to cover unexpected costs.

Director's loan

Long-term liabilities include a £3 million (20X4: £3 million) loan from the managing director to the company.

Exhibit 5: Meadow Ltd

Details of the audit acceptance assessment performed on Meadow Ltd prior to audit acceptance is detailed below:

Pascal & Co **Client acceptance checklist**	
Company name:	Meadow Ltd
Financial documents obtained:	Financial statements for last four years
References:	To be obtained
Previous auditor:	Doomsday & Co
Professional clearance obtained and reviewed:	Verbal - no issues
Intended users of financial statements:	Owner managers only
High/unusual risks - do any of the following apply? • **Public held shares** • **High-risk industry** • **Developing business** • **Significant recent changes in management** • **Poor financial condition**	None

• Other	
Firm independence confirmed?	Yes
Firm competence confirmed?	Yes
Firm resources confirmed?	Yes
Fees agreed?	Yes
Money laundering procedures:	
• **Client identity confirmed**	Passport of owner and his wife
• **Company identity confirmed**	Certificate of incorporation obtained
• **Politically exposed persons at company**	None
• **Money laundering risk assessment**	Low risk
Proposed partner:	To be confirmed
Signature of partner and date:	

No other paperwork appears to be filed with this document.

Section B

2 Marr & Co

It is 1 July 20X5. You are a manager in Marr & Co, a firm of Chartered Certified Accountants and you are currently carrying out work for Morrissey Ltd.

Marr & Co is a relatively small firm, with annual practice income of £15 million, of which approximately half is generated from providing tax, corporate finance and accounting services to its clients. Marr & Co also has a number of audit clients, all of which are manufacturing companies, and a dedicated team of staff work on these audit clients.

The following exhibits, available on the left-hand side of the screen, provide information relevant to the question:

(1) Background information - details about Morrissey Ltd and a due diligence assignment relating to Brodie Ltd.

(2) Brodie Ltd - information on Brodie Ltd's intangible assets and financing arrangements.

(3) Email from finance director - an email you received from Morrissey Ltd's finance director.

This information should be used to answer the question requirements within the response option provided.

Required

(a) Using the information in Exhibits 1 and 2:

(i) Explain the specific enquiries you should make of Brodie Ltd's management relevant to the company's intangible assets. **(7 marks)**

(ii) Recommend, with reasons, the principal additional information which should be made available by Brodie Ltd's management in relation to the company's financing arrangements. **(5 marks)**

(b) It is now 1 December 20X5. Prior to the acquisition of Brodie Ltd, Marr & Co was appointed to provide corporate finance advice to Morrissey Ltd in relation to raising finance of approximately £35 million to fund the acquisition. You have now received an email from the finance director of Morrissey Ltd.

Required

Using the information in Exhibit 3:

Comment on the ethical and professional issues to be considered by Marr & Co in relation to the request from the finance director. **(8 marks)**

Professional marks will be awarded for the demonstration of skill in analysis and evaluation, professional scepticism and judgement, and commercial acumen in your answer. **(5 marks)**

(Total = 25 marks)

Exhibit 1: Background information

Marr & Co has been appointed by Morrissey Ltd, a textile manufacturer and not currently an audit client of Marr & Co, to carry out a due diligence assignment. Marr & Co conducted all necessary client acceptance procedures prior to agreeing to perform the due diligence assignment, which you will assist the partner in planning.

Morrissey Ltd has identified Brodie Ltd for potential acquisition. Brodie Ltd is also a textile manufacturer, and the company has grown rapidly in the last five years, its growth based on the success of its organic textiles, which it sells to clothing manufacturers.

The terms of the due diligence assignment include that Marr & Co should focus part of its investigation on the intangible assets of Brodie Ltd, in particular the valuation of these assets and their operational significance, and also on the company's financing arrangements.

Exhibit 2: Brodie Ltd

From a discussion with the finance director of Morrissey Ltd, you have the following information about the intangible assets of the target company, Brodie Ltd:

Brodie Ltd imports some of the dyes used in its manufacturing process, for which an import licence is necessary. The three-year import licence costs £1·5 million and is recognised as an intangible asset in the financial statements, amortised over three years.

The company's textiles are manufactured using the unique 'PureFab' manufacturing process, which was developed to increase the durability of its organic textiles. The 'PureFab' manufacturing process is protected by a patent, which was secured seven years ago and which prevents other manufacturers from using the same process or describing products as 'PureFab' textiles. The cost of the patent was £1 million, and this is recognised as an intangible asset in the company's financial statements, amortised over 10 years, which is the life of the patent.

You have also gathered the following information about Brodie Ltd's current financing arrangements:

Source of finance	£'000	Further comments
Equity shares	6,800	This is the value of the company's issued equity shares
Bank loan	2,400	Secured on the company's property, plant and equipment

Exhibit 3: Email from finance director

To: Audit engagement partner

From: Paul Hook, Finance director, Morrissey Ltd

Subject: Appointment as auditor

Date: 1 December 20X5

Hello

Following the successful acquisition of Brodie Ltd, we would like to appoint your firm as auditor. The appointment would include the audit of Morrissey Ltd, Brodie Ltd, and the consolidated financial statements of the new Group, for the financial year ending 31 December 20X5.

With this being the first acquisition made by Morrissey Ltd, our accountants have little experience with Group accounting, and I qualified a long time ago, so we are also expecting your firm to prepare the consolidated financial statements from the individual financial statements of Morrissey Ltd and Brodie Ltd, which I will provide to you. We don't think the consolidated financial statements will really be used, so to save time we will not publish notes to the Group financial statements – the individual accounts provide all of the information which users might need.

We have notified our existing audit provider, Butler Associates, that we wish to remove them from office. We are in a dispute with Butler Associates regarding fees – having negotiated a reduction in audit fee compared to the previous year, an invoice they sent to us in respect of last year's audit contains an unexpected additional amount. When we queried this with Butler Associates, they justified the amount as relating to additional work performed on payroll, which they felt was necessary due to a number of errors they had found in payroll processing. We have also informed the management of Brodie Ltd that we intend to replace their audit provider with Marr & Co.

Assuming that your firm accepts appointment as auditor, we will invite the partner and manager assigned to the audit to attend a textile industry conference. I think this will help you to obtain a better understanding of the industry, as well as giving you the opportunity to meet some other textile manufacturers. You could do some networking and perhaps meet new potential clients. We will pay for all of your conference expenses and for the flights; the conference is being held in a top hotel in Hawaii.

I look forward to hearing from you.

Paul

3 Wheeler & Co

It is 1 July 20X5. You are an audit manager in Wheeler & Co, a firm of Chartered Certified Accountants. The audit fieldwork of one of your clients, Byres Ltd, for the year ended 31 March 20X5 is nearly complete. Byres Ltd is an unlisted, family-owned business which produces innovative cleaning equipment.

The following exhibit, available on the left-hand side of the screen, provides information relevant to the question:

(1) Audit matters – Summary of the key issues the audit supervisor has flagged for your attention.

This information should be used to answer the question requirements within the response option provided.

Required

(a) Using the information in the Exhibit, comment on the matters to be considered, and explain the audit evidence you should expect to find during your review of the audit working papers.

Note. The following mark allocation is provided as guidance for this question:

(i) New product **(7 marks)**

(ii) Warranty provision **(8 marks)**

(b) It is now 1 September 20X5 and the auditor's report on Byres Ltd's financial statements for the year ended 31 March 20X5 is due to be issued in the next few days. The audit team has gathered sufficient and appropriate audit evidence in relation to the new product costs, and appropriate adjustments have been made in respect of the associated research and development costs. However, management has indicated that they are not willing to make any further adjustments in relation to the warranty provision. Following further testing, the audit team has concluded that the warranty provision should have been determined using the same estimation method as in previous years, based on a percentage of sales.

Required

Discuss the implications for the auditor's report on the basis that no further adjustments have been made to the financial statements in relation to the warranty provision. **(5 marks)**

Professional marks will be awarded for the demonstration of skill in analysis and evaluation and professional scepticism, and judgement in your answer. **(5 marks)**

(Total = 25 marks)

Exhibit: Audit matters

The draft financial statements recognise revenue of £55·5 million (20X4: £50 million), profit before taxation for the year of £6·3 million (20X4: £5·4 million) and total assets of £31·6 million (20X4: £30·2 million).

New product

Byres Ltd has started development of a new smart vacuum cleaner which is operated by an application on a user's mobile phone. A working prototype of this product has been developed which generated significant interest at trade exhibitions. However, the current cost of production is £2,000 per unit after problems in product development caused the project costs to go over budget. The audit team held discussions with the product design director, who informed them that he is sceptical as to whether there will be a sufficient market for this new product at a profitable selling price. The audit team has been provided with market research reports, which suggest that a maximum selling price of £1,000 is achievable. The owner and chief executive officer (CEO), William Byres, has assured the audit team that the total costs which have been incurred on the new product, totalling £250,000, meet the relevant recognition criteria and as such have been capitalised as an intangible asset in the financial statements. Commercial production of the new product has not yet commenced.

Warranty provision

Byres Ltd has an established standard warranty scheme in place for its retail customers where the company will refund retail customers for any reason within a 12-month period of the date of sale. This is a standard warranty, offered to all customers of Byres Ltd at no extra cost. Byres Ltd does not operate an extended warranty scheme. At any point in time, there is a significant amount of uncertainty in relation to the measurement of the warranty provision, but the finance director and finance department has previously estimated the provision at the year end based on a percentage of total sales. In previous years, the audit team has concluded that this has been a reasonable basis for the provision.

However, this year the CEO has also been involved in estimating the value of the year-end warranty provision. For the year ended 31 March 20X5, the warranty provision is £2·1 million, based on the CEO's estimate (20X4: £4·3 million). During discussions with the sales director, the audit team noted that neither the range of customers nor the nature of the warranties had changed significantly compared to the prior year. Discussions with the customer services manager have not indicated any unusual levels of complaints or faults with the products during the year which would justify a change in how the warranty provision should be estimated.

Answers

DO NOT TURN THIS PAGE UNTIL YOU HAVE COMPLETED THE MOCK EXAM

A plan of attack

If this had been the real Advanced Audit and Assurance exam and you had been told to start the exam, what would have been going through your mind?

An important thing to say (while there is still time) is that it is vital to have a good breadth of knowledge of the syllabus because the question requirements for each question will relate to different areas of the AAA syllabus. However, don't panic. Below we provide guidance on how to approach the exam.

Approaching the answer

It is vital that you attempt all the questions in the exam to increase your chances of passing. The best way to do this is to make sure you stick to the time allocation for each question – both in total and for each of the question parts. The worst thing you can do is run over time in one question and then find that you don't have enough time for the remaining questions, leading you to miss out on some of the easier marks in those questions.

Section A consists of one long case-study style question set at the planning stage of the audit. This may contain detailed information such as extracts from financial statements and audit working papers. A range of requirements will be set for this question but will only cover areas from syllabus areas A to D inclusive.

Question 1 is for 50 marks, all set at the planning stage in the context of a single scenario, here dealing with the audit of a new audit client that operates a theme park. It is a long question and so it is important that you break it down into its component parts as this will make it easier to manage – and enable you to allocate your time to each of them.

Section B contains two more compulsory questions, and may be set on any area of the AAA syllabus.

Question 2, for 25 marks, featured a trio of audits to review for quality management and other professional issues.

Question 3 offers 25 marks that were set in a developing scenario, asking first for the required audit evidence, and then for an evaluation of a draft auditor's report.

Forget about it!

And don't worry if you found the exam difficult. More than likely other candidates did too. If this were the real thing, you would need to forget the exam the minute you finished it and think about the next one. Or, if it is the last one, celebrate!

Section A

1 Pascal & Co

Workbook references

Chapters 1, 3, 5 and 6.

Top tips

This is a long question which contained lots of information. The best way to score good marks in relation to part (a) (evaluating and prioritising significant risks of material misstatement) was to work your way through the information in Exhibit 3. Remember that to score marks you need to **evaluate** rather than just identify issues that may lead to ROMM. You should also analyse the financial information provided and perform calculations relating to material where relevant.

In part (b), you should have recognised that cash-based businesses are more susceptible to money laundering and, even though family members tend to work in the areas where cash is more heavily used, it simply isn't possible to eliminate this risk.

A good place to start for part (c) was the client acceptance checklist in Exhibit 5, which highlighted several areas where little work had been performed.

Easy marks

There were several easy marks in part (a) provided that you explained how this impacted the ROMM. For example, land had not been revalued for seven years and so the carrying amount in the statement of financial position is likely to be materially misstated (undervalued), assuming prices have increased.

ACCA examining team's comments

This question was a typical Section A question set at the planning stage, with requirements focusing on matters specific to the planning stage of an initial audit engagement, an evaluation of the significant risks of material misstatement, responsibilities regarding money laundering along with evaluation of indicators specific to the scenario, and a review of an acceptance assessment.

This requirement is typical in volume and nature to many planning questions and examines a major area of the syllabus – risk. It is important to notice that the requirement asked for an **evaluation**, not simply a list of risks, or a strategy or procedures to address those risks. The examining team is testing whether candidates can understand how and why a risk arises and the implications that this has on the financial statements or the audit itself. It is looking for an assessment of materiality, a demonstration of knowledge of the underlying accounting rules, and the application of that to the scenario to identify the potential impact on the financial statements. A well evaluated risk has in-depth analysis. Candidates writing only a sentence or two are unlikely to attain many of the marks available for each risk. Candidates are reminded that there are useful technical and exam guidance articles on the ACCA website which will provide additional support in approaching and answering questions on risk.

An issue that arises repeatedly is that candidates are attempting to find 12 risks for a 24-mark question and conducting little or no in-depth analysis of any of them. This will not attain a pass mark. This means some of the risks stated in these candidate answers will be speculative or not significant and, therefore, will not obtain credit. Each risk generally has a minimum of three marks attached to it. **More complex risks carry additional credit. Materiality and calculation marks are over and above the marks available for the discussion of a risk.** The marking guide published for this question has 13 areas of risks, some of which are deemed more basic financial accounting issues that carry lower marks and therefore should be more easily obtained by candidates.

Overall, this requirement was answered reasonably well by many candidates, but more candidates than expected failed to identify the easier risks in the scenario and demonstrated a weaker than expected level of more basic accounting treatment. This resulted in many candidates failing to obtain what should have been easier marks.

The requirement for part (b) was focused on the responsibility that auditors have regarding money laundering and an evaluation of the indicators detailed in the scenario with respect to money laundering. Additional credit was awarded if a candidate successfully linked the scenario-specific indicator to the stage of money laundering. Generally, the requirement was well answered in response to candidates evaluating the indicators within the question suggesting there was a risk of money laundering.

The most alarming issue highlighted in a significant number of candidate responses was where candidates stated that a suspicion of money laundering should be disclosed to those charged with governance, the audit committee (even though in the present scenario the company didn't have one), and a minority of candidates stated it should be disclosed in the notes to the financial statements or the audit report in the public interest.

This action would amount to the auditor committing a criminal offence of tipping off the client, and it is disappointing to see the number of candidates who failed to understand the difference between money laundering and fraud.

The final requirement was focused on reviewing the acceptance assessment procedures performed by the auditors on a different company, Meadow Co, and discussing the weaknesses in the procedures performed, and recommending improvements the firm should implement.

There was a mixed response here, which candidates either answered well and were able to evaluate the weaknesses or stated general acceptance procedures to be performed and failed to respond specifically to the requirement.

It was noted that a number of candidates discussed the need to communicate with the previous auditor, which is correct for a requirement for general consideration at acceptance. In the context of this scenario, however, the extract of the acceptance assessment stated that verbal clearance had been obtained, hence the previous auditor had been contacted. A number of candidates failed to recognise that the issue in this weakness was that only a verbal confirmation had been received and that this should have been obtained in writing. Where candidates discussed the weaknesses specific to the scenario, marks were awarded, however, generic comments regarding communication with the previous auditors did not meet the requirement and demonstrated candidates failed to successfully understand the requirement.

Marking guide — **Marks**

(a) **Risk of material misstatement evaluation**

In relation to the matters listed below:

Up to 3 marks for each risk of material misstatement evaluated unless otherwise indicated.

In addition, 0.5 mark for relevant ratios and 0.5 mark for relevant trends to a maximum of 3 marks.

Relevant materiality calculations will be awarded to a maximum of 3 marks.

- Going concern – potential operating licence withdrawal
- Valuation of land – lack of recent valuation
- Valuation of rides – impairment
- Inventory valuation (2 marks)
- Revenue, risk of overstatement (2 marks)
- Revenue, risk of understatement
- Sale and leaseback (up to a max of 5 marks)
- Legal case – contingent liability (2 marks)
- General provisions
- Related party transactions (2 marks)
- Tax
- Payroll costs – cash based
- Management override/lack of segregation of duties (2 marks)

24

(b) **Money laundering**

Generally, 1 mark for each relevant point of discussion/explanation:

- Definition of money laundering
- Customer due diligence
- Reporting channels
- Recordkeeping
- Training
- Cash-based business/placement
- Unexpected trends in ride sales/shop sales and margins
- Use of family
- Money transfers

8

ANSWERS

(c) **Acceptance procedures**

Generally, 1 mark for each relevant point of discussion/explanation:

- General requirement for customer due diligence (CDD) before acceptance
- Level of CDD depends on the level of risk at client
- Form too brief
- Form lacks supporting evidence
- No justification of CDD level required
- Insufficient identification of beneficial owners and directors
- Money laundering flags not all considered
- References outstanding
- Professional clearance should be in writing and reviewed
- Risk assessment appears incorrect/insufficient
- Company identity does not prove current directors and address
- No partner assigned/approval

8

Professional marks

Communication

- Briefing notes format and structure – use of headings/sub-headings and an introduction
- Style, language and clarity – appropriate layout and tone of briefing notes, presentation of materiality and relevant calculations, appropriate use of the CBE tools, easy to follow and understand
- Effectiveness and clarity of communication – answer is relevant and tailored to the scenario, and risks of material misstatement are prioritised
- Adherence to the specific requests made by the audit engagement partner

Analysis and evaluation

- Appropriate use of the information to determine suitable calculations
- Appropriate use of the information to support discussions and draw appropriate conclusions
- Effective prioritisation of the results of the risk evaluation to demonstrate the likelihood and magnitude of risks and to facilitate the allocation of appropriate responses
- Evaluation of related issues, for example, holistic consideration of several issues to determine the risk of material misstatement relating to going concern
- Balanced discussion of the information to objectively make a recommendation or decision

Professional scepticism and judgement

- Effective challenge of information supplied, and techniques carried out to complete client acceptance documentation
- Determination and justification of a suitable materiality level, appropriately and consistently applied
- Appropriate application of professional judgement to draw conclusions and make informed decisions about the courses of action that are appropriate in the context of the audit engagement

Commercial acumen

- Use of effective examples and/or calculations from the scenario to illustrate points, such as insufficient consideration of the risks of money laundering

Marking guide	Marks
• Recognition of the potential impact on the audit firm's reputation of having clients that operate within an industry that has experienced bad publicity	
Maximum	10
Total	50

Word Processor

Briefing notes

To: Brian Fox, Audit engagement partner

From: Audit manager

Subject: Audit planning in relation to The Infinite Ltd and assessment of client acceptance performed on Meadow Ltd

Introduction

These briefing notes have been prepared to assist in planning the audit of The Infinite Ltd for the year ending 30 September 20X5. The notes begin with an evaluation and prioritisation of the significant risks of material misstatement which should be considered in planning the audit. The notes then discuss risk factors relating to money laundering arising from The Infinite Ltd's operations and our responsibility as auditors with respect to money laundering. Finally, the notes evaluate the weaknesses in Pascal & Co's client acceptance of the client Meadow Ltd and recommend improvements to the firm's client acceptance procedures.

Note. Remember, you can access the ACCA's Practice Platform to learn how to attempt AAA questions using the CBE software.

(a) **Evaluation of risks of material misstatement**

Licence/going concern

The company is dependent on licences for its ability to operate. There is a risk that these licences are revoked if breaches in regulations occur. The company will then not be allowed to offer the products and services covered by the licence, affecting the company's ability to operate as a going concern. In particular, the licence to operate the theme park rides may be revoked due to health and safety breaches. Although this is not the sole activity at the park, it does form a major part of the offering on which other areas rely to attract customers, and, as such, the potential loss of the operating licence may require disclosures to be made in the notes to the accounts describing the uncertainty arising. Such disclosures are material to the users' understanding of the financial statements and there is a risk that these disclosures are not included within the financial statements.

Valuation of land

The company holds land representing 63% of the company's total assets. This is highly material. The company is correct not to depreciate the land held. The use of a revaluation model is permitted by IAS® 16 Property, Plant and Equipment, however, where this is used, the valuation must be kept up to date. The most recent valuation was carried out seven years ago and this is likely to require updating for 20X5. Any gain or loss on revaluation, which is not a result of impairment, should be shown within other comprehensive income and recognised in equity. As such values require specialist knowledge to calculate, it is likely that an expert will be required to value the land.

There is a risk of inaccurate valuation of land if the valuation is not up to date or if the valuer is not appropriately independent and qualified. This is likely to result in either an over or understatement of the land and equity.

Valuation of rides

The rides represent 15·1% of total assets and are material to the financial statements. According to IAS 36 *Impairment of Assets*, an entity should assess at the end of each reporting period whether there is any indication that an asset or a cash generating unit may be impaired. If any such indication exists, the entity shall estimate the recoverable amount of the asset. The standard states that potential impairment indicators include obsolescence and physical damage. The findings of the government inspector suggesting that the assets are aging, lack modern safety features and are not properly maintained are all indicators of impairment and as such management should prepare an impairment review of the park's rides.

IAS 36 states that an asset or cash generating unit is impaired when the carrying amount exceeds the recoverable amount and it defines recoverable amount as the higher of the fair value less costs of disposal and the value in use.

There is a risk that management does not conduct an impairment review or that the review does not take into account the inspector's findings resulting in the overvaluation of property, plant and equipment and understatement of costs.

Revenue

The Infinite Ltd operates a business where a large amount of revenue is received in cash. In a company where a substantial proportion of revenue is generated through cash sales, there is a high risk of unrecorded sales arising from the theft of cash received from customers. This risk is increased through the use of so many casual workers. Management appears to try to reduce this risk via the use of management's family in areas where cash accepted is unusually high. However, it is not possible for family members to accept all cash sales. If this is the case, then revenues and cash may be understated.

There is also a risk of revenue overstatement within the park. As The Infinite Ltd's business is cash-based, it provides an ideal environment for cash acquired through illegal activities to be legitimised by adding it to the cash paid genuinely by customers and posting it through the accounts. This is discussed further later in these notes.

Inventory

The company holds inventory in the form of food, drinks and merchandise. Inventories represent 3·7% of assets and are material. The food and drinks are of a perishable nature and as such have a short life span. The merchandise appears to be

low quality with frequent breakages and a health and safety risk. IAS 2 *Inventories* requires inventory to be held at the lower of cost and net realisable value. It is possible that defective items or goods past their sell by date have not been written off appropriately. If this is the case, then inventories are overstated, and cost of sales understated.

Sale and leaseback

The company is entering into a sale and leaseback with regard to the park buildings. The value of the buildings in the projected statement of financial position is £854,000. This represents 9% of total assets and is material.

Under IFRS® 16 *Leases*, where a sale has occurred, The Infinite Ltd should recognise a right-of-use asset for the buildings replacing the previously held building asset. This would be measured at the proportion of the previous carrying amount which is retained for use by The Infinite Ltd.

The present value of the lease in this case is £934,666. This represents 93·5% (£934,666/£1,000,000) of the market value of the buildings. The proportion of the previous carrying amount which is retained for use by the company is therefore 93·5% of the carrying amount of £854,000, which equates to £798,205.

The Infinite Ltd should therefore recognise a right of use asset of £798,205 and a lease liability at present value of the future cash payments of £934,666. It will recognise a cash receipt of £1,000,000 and derecognise property, plant and equipment of £854,000. The remaining difference is the gain on disposal of the buildings which is recognised in the statement of profit or loss.

Example:

Dr Cash		£1,000,000
Dr Right-of-use asset		£798,205
	Cr Property, plant and equipment	£854,000
	Cr Lease liability	£934,666
	Cr Gain on disposal	£9,539

The finance director intends to account for the sale as a simple disposal and then recognise a rental expense each year. This would result in a gain of £146,000 being recognised on the disposal, overstating profit on disposal. In addition, both assets and liabilities would be understated as the right-of-use asset and the present value of lease payments would not be included in the statement of financial position. Failure to unwind the discount on the lease liability would result in an understatement of finance costs and the rentals charged against profit would overstate expenses.

Legal cases – food poisoning

There is currently outstanding litigation against the company. The amounts of the claims are not yet known. Management is not planning on making disclosures in the financial statements regarding the case as this may prejudice the outcome of the case. IAS 37 *Provisions, Contingent Liabilities and Contingent Assets* requires that contingent liabilities are disclosed in the notes to the financial statements, hence there is a risk of insufficient disclosure which could be material by nature.

General provisions

The projected statement of financial position shows a general provision of £250,000, representing 2·6% of assets which is material to the statement of financial position. The increase in the general provision in the year of £120,000 represents 5·2% of profit before tax (PBT) and is material to the profit for the year.

IAS 37 states that an entity must recognise a provision if, and only if:

- a present obligation (legal or constructive) has arisen as a result of a past event (the obligating event),
- payment is probable ('more likely than not'), and
- the amount can be estimated reliably.

The general provision does not appear to relate to a present obligation and, as such, is not permitted. This could be a means by which the company reduces profits in order to reduce the tax payable or a means of profit smoothing. As a result, it is likely that if this provision remains, then liabilities are overstated and expenses overstated.

Related party disclosures

The managing director has a director's loan outstanding which does not appear to have changed in value over the year. There are also international money transfers made to an account in the managing director's name which implies that he may be taking money from the company without it being an official salary payment. IAS 24 *Related Party Disclosures* defines a related party transaction as a transfer of resources, services, or obligations between related parties, regardless of whether a price is charged. Related party transactions are material by nature. As the managing director is a related party, this means that transactions between himself and the company will need to be disclosed in the notes to the financial statements. There is a risk that appropriate disclosures are not made for all related party transactions.

Tax

The projected tax expense for the year is material at 10% PBT. This figure represents an effective tax rate of 10% compared to 15% in the previous year. This appears low. The use of general provisions may result in an incorrect profit figure on which to calculate company tax liabilities. This would result in understated tax expense in the statement of profit or loss and understated liabilities.

Payroll

The payment of wages in cash creates a risk that not all wages payments are recorded in the financial statements and therefore wages paid out of cash sales are unrecorded as well as the associated cash sales; there is therefore a risk both revenue and expenses are understated.

In addition, there is a risk with employees paid in cash that incomplete deductions have been made for employee taxes including PAYE and National Insurance Contributions. This may give rise to further compliance risks and liabilities for unpaid employee tax.

Management override

The owner manager and his family appear to take a very active role in the business and may fail to make a distinction between the business as a separate entity and themselves. There is evidence that management bypasses controls within the business through direct access to the company funds and accounts. There is a lack of segregation of duties and given that the management appears to have a disregard for certain laws and regulations, this is likely to mean that the control environment is weak and there is a resulting higher risk of fraud and error in the financial statements.

(b) **Money laundering**

Money laundering is defined as the process by which criminals attempt to conceal the origin and ownership of the proceeds of their criminal activity, allowing them to maintain control over the proceeds and, ultimately, providing a legitimate cover for the sources of their income.

Auditors are required to:

- perform customer due diligence, ie procedures designed to acquire knowledge about the firm's clients and prospective clients and to verify their identity as well as monitor business relationships and transactions
- create channels within the audit firm for internal reporting including appointment of a money laundering reporting officer (MLRO) to receive the money laundering reports to which personnel report suspicions or knowledge of money laundering activities
- keep records, including details of customer due diligence and supporting evidence for business relationships, which need to be kept for five years after the end of a relationship and records of transactions, which also need to be kept for five years
- take measures to make relevant employees aware of the law relating to money laundering and terrorist finance, and to train those employees in how to recognise and deal with transactions which may be related to money laundering or terrorist financing
- put in place ongoing monitoring procedures to ensure that policies are up to date and being followed

The MLRO will be responsible for reporting incidents to the relevant authorities. Auditors must be careful to avoid tipping off any party suspected of money laundering.

The Infinite Ltd's business is cash-based, making it an ideal environment for cash acquired through illegal activities to be legitimised by adding it to the cash paid genuinely by customers and posting it through the financial statements. This is known as placement.

There are a lot of cash transactions, and it would be possible to incorporate funds to be laundered with the funds from customers. The ticket sales for rides would be an ideal place for this to occur as there is no monitoring of the number of people actually taking part in the ride, so actual sales would be hard to prove. The fact that ride sales have fallen since the introduction of electronic payments and at the same time the gift shop run by the owner's son has seen increased volumes of cash sales and higher margins suggests that this may have been the case previously and that the shop may now be used for money laundering.

The use of family members for areas of high cash transactions and the managing director making transfers to his international account outside of the normal accounting for the business further increases the risk that money laundering may be occurring. It may be that the staffing choice is for the valid business purpose of reducing risk of theft from staff and that the transactions are properly accounted for and valid, however, it is not clear in this case.

The fact that the managing director likes to be left in peace and the finance director does not query transactions could also represent a red flag.

(c) **Acceptance procedures**

Auditors are required, prior to establishing a client relationship or accepting an engagement, to have controls in place to address the risks arising from it. The risk profile of the business should show where particular risks are likely to arise, and so where certain procedures will be needed to tackle them. These procedures should be easy to understand and easy to use for all relevant employees who will need them. Sufficient flexibility should be built in to allow the procedures to identify, and adapt to, unusual situations.

Different clients will have different levels of risk and the level of risk should dictate the level of client due diligence performed.

Criticisms of the content of the client acceptance documentation

Overall, the acceptance document appears too brief and there is a lack of information to support the conclusions within the document. Where a conclusion is given in the acceptance form, the evidence to support that conclusion should be filed with it.

There is no section evidencing and justifying the type of customer due diligence required. Depending on the nature of the client and the risks, either standard, simplified or enhanced due diligence will be required. The form of due diligence to be used and the basis for that decision should be included within the acceptance documentation. Part of this would include an assessment of client integrity, which does not appear to be considered anywhere on the form, even though it is a requirement of ISQM (UK) 1 *Quality Management For Firms That Perform Audits or Reviews of Financial Statements, or Other Assurance or Related Services Engagements*.

ISQM (UK) 1 also requires the firm to consider whether it is competent to perform the engagement and has the capabilities, including time and resources, to do so and whether it can comply with relevant ethical requirements. None of these issues appear to have been considered.

There is no reference to the beneficial owners and the control structure of the company. The auditor should seek to prove the identity of the company and key individuals including all directors and shareholders with more than 25% of the shares or voting rights of the company. There should also be a section for the source of wealth and funds of the business.

The money laundering risk assessment is too brief. This should identify whether there are any potential areas of high risk for money laundering. Such things include unusual or unexplained transactions, a cash intensive business, and unusual or complicated corporate structures.

Specific criticisms of the information gathered for Meadow Ltd

The first thing to note is that the documentation does not state what its objective is, so that the person completing it is obtaining the information with its objective in mind, for example, the following could be included at the beginning of the assessment:

Objective

To obtain appropriate evidence regarding the organisation and the identity of its owners in order to comply with the money laundering regulations.

The assessment should also document:

- whether full understanding has been gained regarding the ownership structure of the organisation

- evidence which has been obtained regarding the organisation's activity and how it has been established and agreed as *bona fide*

No references have been received prior to acceptance of the client which means that the firm's client due diligence procedures have not been properly adhered to.

The professional clearance from the predecessor auditor should be received in writing prior to acceptance and this should be reviewed for potential issues and filed with the form on the permanent file. Where this is not received, the firm should document the reasons why and whether they have reported this to their regulatory body.

Client risk assessment states that the company has no high/unusual risk. A cash-based business is likely to give rise to risks and the fact that Meadow Ltd is being investigated with respect to money laundering suggests that risks existed which were not considered on the acceptance form.

The money laundering section appears too brief, client identity would involve more people than just the owner and his wife. This should be extended to shareholders who ultimately own or control more than 25% of the shares along with other directors of the company. If the business is deemed to be sufficiently high risk that enhanced due diligence is required, then a second document such as a driving licence would also be required.

For confirming the company identity, a certificate of incorporation alone is not sufficient to confirm the principal trading address, current directors, and major shareholders. A Companies House search should have been performed to confirm these details, and the results of the search retained.

The checklist does not state whether it has been confirmed that the person the firm is dealing with is properly authorised to do so by the client. It should document the appropriate steps taken to be satisfied that the person the firm dealing with is properly authorised by the client.

There has been no partner assigned to the client prior to acceptance and no signature of a partner to approve the client acceptance. This is a failure in the firm's control procedures as it should not be possible to accept new clients without partner level approval and evidence that the risk assessment has been reviewed.

Section B

2 Marr & Co

Workbook references

Chapters 2 and 12.

Top Tips

The first part of this question was set in the context of conducting due diligence work for an existing client. There was a lot of information in Exhibit 2, which should have enabled you to understand that Brodie Ltd owned both an import licence and a patent, and you needed to discuss the enquiries you would make to Brodie Co's management to determine their importance to the business, their valuation, and whether they are protected in any way. Additionally Exhibit 2 explained that Brodie Ltd is funded via a bank loan and you were asked for additional information you would need about this. Here, you should have discussed information such as whether the loans contain covenants and whether any of these have been breached, as well as considerations as to whether Brodie Co can afford the cost of having this finance.

The second part of the question was a typical requirement asking you to comment on the ethical and professional issues to be considered in relation to taking on the audit of both Morrissey and Brodie. Exhibit 3 provided lots of ideas to build on here.

Easy marks

In part (b), there were relatively straightforward marks to be gained by considering the ethical threats associated with auditing Morrissey, such as the self-review threat from having performed the due diligence work. Other straightforward points included professional considerations concerning the integrity of Morrissey's management and whether the preconditions for an audit were satisfied.

ACCA examining team's comments

In part (a)(i) the requirement asked candidates to discuss specific enquiries that should be made with the management team regarding the intangible assets which consisted of the licence and the patent. The assignment is a due diligence assignment, not an audit, and therefore detailed substantive procedures would not be performed.

Strong candidates made a reasonable attempt at evaluating discussions to be made to the client concerning the assets, such as:

- When the licence was acquired, and the term of the licence to determine when the renewal of the licence is required
- The terms and conditions of the licence to assist the auditor in determining any restrictions on the licence
- Any likely issues associated with re-acquiring the licence in the future
- The terms of the patent and whether the patent can be renewed at the expiration date

A well-attempted answer tailored the response to consider why we would make specific enquiries as part of the due diligence assignment for the acquirer to have detailed information regarding the target company to assist in their decision-making process. Generally, the depth of answers fell short of that expected from a professional-level candidate.

Part (a)(ii) required candidates to recommend the additional information that would be required and made available to them regarding the target company's financial arrangements (equity shares and a bank loan). Generally, the requirement was poorly answered with the main issue noted being the lack of understanding by the candidates on the difference between performing audit procedures and discussing additional information required relating to specific items.

Additional information is required by the auditor to enable them to gain a better understanding surrounding a certain issue/area, and it does not necessarily need to be in the form of documentary evidence. The information can also be obtained from making enquiries with management alongside reviewing documentation. Strong candidates evaluated the additional information required and also evaluated why we would need it. Weaker candidates merely stated substantive procedures to address risk around the sources of finance, which did not meet the question requirement.

Requirement (b) was a standard ethics and professional issues requirement. AAA candidates should expect ethics to be examinable, and this requirement should achieve high marks based on brought forward knowledge from previous ACCA examinations, including detailed knowledge from AA.

Strong candidates used Exhibit 3 and successfully identified the threats and linked them to the specific detail in the scenario, along with an explanation of how the threat will impact the auditor and the fundamental principles that we are required to adhere to. Safeguards and actions were also considered in order to bring the threat down to an acceptable level.

Overall, a mixed response.

Marking guide **Marks**

(a) (i) **Specific enquiries relating to Brodie Ltd's intangible asset**

Up to 1 mark for each enquiry recommended and adequately explained.

In relation to the import licence:

- Acquisition date of the import licence, and confirm that the licence lasts for three years. This indicates to Morrissey Ltd when the next licence will need to be acquired
- Obtain evidence (original invoice, contract, details of the terms and conditions regarding the import licence) regarding the initial cost and expected period which the patent will be valid for to assess whether the current amount in the financial statements (cost and amortisation) is accurate
- The terms of the licence, including the specific goods covered by the licence and whether the licence applies to goods imported only from certain countries
- Value of purchases of dye made during the financial year under the import licence – this will indicate how important the licence is to the operations of the company
- Any problem foreseen with the import licence being reacquired at the end of the three-year period, any potential problems with reacquiring the licence could disrupt the company's procurement and manufacturing process
- Any plans to source the dye from an alternative supplier, perhaps a supplier for which an import licence would not be necessary, saving on the cost of reacquiring a licence
- Enquire with management whether there have been any breaches of the import licence, such as fines, which could affect the likelihood of Brodie Co obtaining a new import licence once the three years are complete

In relation to the patent:

- Obtain evidence (original invoice, contract, details of the terms and conditions regarding the patent) regarding the initial cost and expected period which the patent will be valid for to assess whether the current amount in the financial statements (cost and amortisation) is accurate
- The terms of the patent, to obtain an understanding of matters including: the specific manufacturing process to which it relates, whether the

patent applies to all of the company's manufacturing, and if the patent applies just in the country in which it was issued, or does it apply in other countries

- Whether the patent can be renewed when it expires, and if so, whether an additional fee is payable to the patent authority
- Whether there have been any infringements or any competitors developing a similar manufacturing process, indicating increased competition
- Discuss with management whether there are any factors which may affect the carrying amount of the patent in the financial statements
- The value of sales made under the 'PureFab' label, to confirm that there is economic benefit being generated from the patented manufacturing process
- Request permission that the Intellectual Property Office send a certified copy of the register entry. This will include details of the owner of the patent and the time period for the patent

7

(ii) **Additional information relating to financing arrangements**

Up to 1 mark for each piece of information recommended and adequately explained.

- The number of equity shares in issue, the value per share, and the voting rights attached to each share, to consider how many shares to acquire in order to gain control
- The company's authorised share capital, to provide understanding as to whether Morrissey Ltd's shareholding will be a fresh share issue or whether existing shareholders will need to be bought out of their shareholding
- The rate of interest payable on the bank loan, whether interest is fixed or variable rate for forecasting the relevant cash flows
- The redemption dates of the bank loan, and whether a premium is payable on the redemption of any debt, for forecasting the relevant cash flows
- Whether any loan covenants exist, in relation to the bank loan, and the terms of such covenants; the acquisition itself could trigger a breach of covenant
- Whether any covenants have been breached in the past, this indicates management's capability of managing the company's finance
- Bank loan details on the charge over company property, plant and equipment, whether it is a fixed charge over certain assets
- Details of any other sources of finance used by the company, to ensure that all sources of finance have been identified
- Enquire if management has any plans for alternative arrangements should current facilities not be extended, this will give an idea of how the company will overcome any difficulties encountered as a result of not being able to renegotiate current facilities

5

(b) **Ethical and other professional matters**

Up to 2 marks for each relevant and well explained point and 1 mark for each relevant and appropriate safeguard.

Marking guide	Marks
• Ethical issue – self-review threat regarding having previously performed due diligence and corporate finance work	
• Safeguards: separate team for audit	
• Ethical issue – self-review threat regarding preparation of consolidated financial statements (management threat)	
• No safeguard appropriate – management to prepare the consolidated financial statements – not 'routine or mechanical in nature'	
• Ethical issue – self-interest threat from providing range of services, fee dependency	
• Ethical issue – self-interest and familiarity threats re gifts and hospitality	
• Low fee and impact on audit quality	
• Non-reappointment of previous audit firm – intimidation/dispute over fees	
• Audit preconditions – ISA (UK) 210 requirements and management responsibility to prepare complete financial statements	
• Competence of management and quality of financial reporting	
• Competence and resources	
	8

Professional marks

Analysis and evaluation

- Appropriate consideration of how important the import licence is to Brodie Ltd's business
- Appropriate consideration of the impact any non-renewal of the import licence will have on Brodie Ltd's ability to continue trading
- Discussion of the extent of protection the patent provides to Brodie Ltd from competitors
- Appropriate consideration as to whether Brodie Ltd has breached any funding covenants and the impact of this on the ability to retain current funding and raise finance in the future

Professional scepticism and judgement

- Effective consideration of the reasons provided by Morrissey Ltd for changing auditors
- Effective consideration of the ethical threats to Marr & Co of taking on the audit of Morrissey Ltd
- Application of professional judgement over the value and lifespan of the intangibles held by Brodie Ltd

Commercial acumen

- Consideration of the perceived threat to Marr & Co's independence if it becomes reliant on Morrissey Ltd for a considerable proportion of the gross practice income
- Consideration of whether a fair audit fee can be obtained for the audit of Morrissey given the amount of work required and the pressure placed on its existing auditors to reduce audit fees

Maximum	5
Total	25

(a) (i) **Specific enquiries relating to Brodie Ltd's intangible asset**

In relation to the import licence:

- Enquire with management to ascertain the acquisition date of the import licence and confirm that the licence lasts for three years. This indicates to Morrissey Ltd when the next licence will need to be acquired.

- Obtain evidence (original invoice, contract, details of the terms and conditions regarding the import licence) regarding the initial cost and expected period which the licence will be valid for to assess whether the current amount in the financial statements (cost and amortisation) is accurate.
- To obtain understanding of the nature and scope of the licence, discuss and confirm the terms with management, including the specific goods covered by the licence and whether the licence applies to goods imported only from certain countries.
- Ask management to provide information to show the value of purchases of dye made during the financial year under the import licence – this will indicate how important the licence is to the operations of the company and whether it is essential that the licence is reacquired once it expires.
- Enquire with management whether they envisage any problem with the import licence being re-acquired at the end of the three-year period, for example, if there were political sanctions against the country from which the dye is imported. Any potential problems with reacquiring the licence could disrupt the company's procurement and manufacturing process.
- Enquire with management whether there have been any breaches of the import licence, such as fines, which could affect the likelihood of Brodie Co obtaining a new import licence once the three years are complete.
- Discuss with management whether there are any plans to source the dye from an alternative supplier, perhaps a supplier for which an import licence would not be necessary, saving on the cost of reacquiring a licence.

In relation to the patent:

- Obtain evidence (original invoice, contract, details of the terms and conditions regarding the patent) regarding the initial cost and expected period which the patent will be valid for to assess whether the current amount in the financial statements (cost and amortisation) is accurate.
- Discuss the terms of the patent, to obtain an understanding of matters including:
  - The specific manufacturing process to which it relates,
  - Whether the patent applies to all of the company's manufacturing, or just part of it,
  - If the patent applies just in the country in which it was issued, or does it apply in other countries.
- Discuss whether the patent can be renewed when it expires, and if so, whether an additional fee is payable to the patent authority. This will help Morrissey Ltd to understand the period over which the manufacturing process can be protected in the future.
- Enquire with management as to whether there have been any infringements of the patent by competitors, or whether management is aware of any competitors developing a similar manufacturing process. This could indicate that when the patent expires in three years, and if it cannot be renewed, the company will face increased competition should other manufacturers develop a similar production process.
- Assess whether there is any impairment of the patent, caused by a new process superseding the one attached to the patent.

- Discuss with management whether there are any factors which may affect the carrying amount of the patent in the financial statements.
- Ask management to provide information showing the value of sales made under the 'PureFab' label, to confirm that there is economic benefit being generated from the patented manufacturing process.
- Request permission that the Intellectual Property Office send Marr & Co a certified copy of the register entry. This will include details of the owner of the patent and the time period for the patent.

(ii) **Additional information to be made available in relation to the company's financing arrangements**

- In relation to the equity shares, the number of equity shares in issue, the value per share, and the voting rights attached to each share. This is essential information for Morrissey Ltd to consider how many shares to acquire in order to gain control of Brodie Ltd.
- The company's authorised share capital, to ascertain the capacity of Brodie Ltd to issue further shares. This will help form an understanding as to whether Morrissey Ltd's shareholding will result from a fresh share issue or whether existing shareholders will need to be bought out of their shareholding.
- The rate of interest payable on the bank loan, whether interest is fixed or variable rate for forecasting the relevant cash flows.
- The redemption dates of the bank loan, and whether a premium is payable on the redemption of any debt, for forecasting the relevant cash flows.
- Whether any loan covenants exist in relation to the bank loan, and the terms of such covenants. The acquisition itself could trigger a breach of covenant or lead to changes in payment terms.
- Management should also be asked to confirm whether any covenants have been breached in the past, this indicates their capability of managing the company's finances.
- In relation to the bank loan, details of the charge over company property, plant and equipment, in particular whether it is a fixed charge over certain assets, for example, does it apply specifically to the company's head office, or manufacturing plant.
- Details of any other sources of finance used by the company, for example, lease arrangements, debt factoring, directors' loans to the company. This is to ensure that all sources of finance have been identified and that Morrissey Ltd has complete understanding of Brodie Ltd's financing arrangements.
- Enquire if management has any plans for alternative arrangements should current facilities not be extended, this will give an idea of how the company will overcome any difficulties encountered as a result of not being able to renegotiate current facilities.

(b) **Ethical and professional issues**

Ethical issues

On the acceptance of client relationships and audit engagements, ISA (UK) 220 (Revised) *Quality Management for an Audit of Financial Statements* requires the audit firm to determine whether the firm and the engagement team can comply with relevant ethical requirements. This involves consideration of many factors, for example, whether there are any existing relationships between the audit firm and potential client, which could create threats to auditor objectivity.

In this case, a significant self-review threat arises should Marr & Co accept the appointment as auditor. The threat arises because Marr & Co, having performed the due diligence assignment on Brodie Ltd, and having helped Morrissey Ltd with the financial arrangements relating to the acquisition, will have been involved with many aspects of the individual and Group financial statements. This means that the audit firm may not approach elements of the audit of the financial statements with appropriate professional scepticism, not properly evaluating the results of previous judgements made, and over-relying on the work previously performed by the audit firm.

Marr & Co will need to evaluate the significance of this threat, based on matters such as the materiality of the balances and transactions involved, for example, the intangible assets of Brodie Ltd, and the level of subjectivity involved. It may be possible for Marr & Co to safeguard against the threat, for example, by using staff on the audit who had not previously worked on the due diligence or corporate finance engagements.

A related self-review threat relates to the finance director's request for Marr & Co to produce the Group financial statements. The FRC *Ethical Standard* states that providing an audit client with accounting services, such as preparing accounting records or financial statements, might create self-review (explained earlier) and management threats to objectivity when the firm subsequently audits the financial statements. The management threat arises where the auditor is taking on responsibilities properly belonging to management, in this case, the preparation of the Group financial statements.

The significance of the self-review and management threats depend on the nature and extent of the accounting services provided to the audit client and the level of public interest in the entity.

The *Ethical Standard* requires that the audit firm shall not provide services related to the preparation of accounting records and financial statements to an audit client unless the services are of a routine and mechanical nature. In addition, accounting services may not be provided where the accounting services would involve the firm undertaking part of the role of management or initiating transactions. Preparing the Group accounts would not be routine and mechanical – it would involve the auditor making judgements and taking responsibility for the whole of the consolidated financial statements. This would also be perceived as taking on significant management responsibility, and Marr & Co should not provide this service.

There is also a possible self-interest threat arising from the range of services provided to Morrissey Ltd. This could give rise to fee dependency, meaning that the audit firm is reluctant to act in a way which could jeopardise the relationship between audit firm and client, for fear of losing the fee income. The potential level of fee income should be estimated and compared to Marr & Co's total practice income, to see if fee dependency could be an issue.

A further ethical issue arises from the invitation from Morrissey Ltd to attend the industry conference in Hawaii. The offer by the client to pay for the audit partner and manager to attend this event constitutes an offer of gifts and hospitality, which can give rise to familiarity, self-interest and intimidation threats to objectivity.

The familiarity threat means that close relationships between the client and audit firm lead to the auditor being too sympathetic or accepting of the client's work, resulting in a loss of professional scepticism. The self-interest and intimidation threats arise due to the financial benefit of the gifts and hospitality, which could be seen as a bribe, and impact on the perceptions of the auditor's objectivity. The audit firm is likely to act in a way to keep the client happy, for example, overlooking accounting errors such as those indicated in the payroll system, in order to secure the trip to Hawaii.

The *Ethical Standard* states that the auditor shall not accept gifts or favours, including hospitality, from an audit client, unless an objective, reasonable and informed third party would consider the value thereof as trivial or inconsequential.

The offer of the trip to Hawaii should be declined as its value is likely to be more than trivial or inconsequential. The finance director may not realise that his offer puts the audit firm in a difficult position, and the problem raised by his offer should be explained, and the offer turned down. There is an additional issue in that the trip to Hawaii could be seen as a bribe.

ISA (UK) 220 (Revised) contains a specific requirement that the auditor shall include in the audit documentation all significant threats to the firm's independence as well as the safeguards applied to mitigate those threats. The matters outlined above and the auditor's responses should be appropriately documented in accordance with ISA (UK) 220.

Other professional issues

Client integrity

ISQM (UK) 1 *Quality Management for Firms that Perform Audits or Reviews of Financial Statements, or Other Assurance or Related Services Engagements* suggests that the reasons for the proposed appointment of the firm and removal of the previous firm should be considered when evaluating client integrity. According to ISQM (UK) 1, one of the matters, which impacts on integrity, is whether the client is aggressively concerned with maintaining the audit fee as low as possible. The comment made by the finance director regarding the reason for dismissal of Butler Associates could indicate that Morrissey Ltd has an expectation of low fees, which can impact on the quality of the audit and can increase detection risk if too few resources are allocated to the audit in an attempt to reduce the audit firm's costs.

The removal of the previous audit firm could also indicate that Morrissey Ltd may be difficult to deal with, possibly confrontational and aggressive in their attitude to the audit firm, though the invite to attend the industry event in Hawaii could indicate that management is keen to establish a good relationship with the audit firm. Their concerns regarding the previous audit firm's invoice may also be legitimate.

Audit preconditions

ISA (UK) 210 *Agreeing the Terms of Audit Engagements* requires an audit firm to establish whether the preconditions for an audit are present and if certain preconditions are not present, the audit engagement should not be accepted.

In this case, the finance director has stated that he does not want to provide notes to the consolidated financial statements, on the grounds that they are not useful. Failing to disclose notes to the consolidated financial statements would mean that the accounts are not prepared in accordance with IFRS® Standards, as IAS 1 *Presentation of Financial Statements* requires notes, comprising a summary of significant accounting policies and other explanatory notes, to be presented in order for the financial statements to be complete.

This matter will need to be discussed, and if the audit firm believes that management will not accept that they have a responsibility to prepare consolidated financial statements in accordance with IFRS Standards, then the appointment should not be accepted.

Internal control and quality of financial reporting

There is evidence that the internal control environment may not be strong due to the errors found by Butler Associates in payroll processing. In addition, the request by the finance director also raises an issue relating to the competence of the client. A finance director would be expected to have the necessary knowledge and skill to be able to prepare consolidated financial statements, and the fact that he has asked for assistance could indicate that there will be a high inherent risk of material misstatement in the financial statements. While these issues do not mean that the audit should be declined, they indicate that Marr & Co would need to approach the audit as high risk.

Competence and resources

Marr & Co should consider whether audit staff have experience in the textile industry and whether there will be enough staff available at the time when the audit needs to be performed. Manufacturing is not particularly unusual or challenging for an audit firm, so competence is unlikely to present a problem, especially as Marr & Co already has several audit clients who are manufacturers.

It is important to note that Marr & Co is a relatively small audit firm, and especially with the year end being less than a month away, there may be pressure on resources if the firm's other audit clients have the same year end, meaning that audit staff are already busy with other work. The firm should therefore confirm that it is able to complete the audit engagement within the

3 Wheeler & Co

Workbook references

Chapters 8, 10 and 11.

Top Tips

This question is a typical question set at the completion stage of the audit process. There are two matters outstanding – one relates to development costs which have been capitalised despite concern that the product is not commercially viable, and the other relates to the basis on which a warranty provision has been calculated compared to previous years.

Both areas are quite straightforward from a financial reporting perspective, however, in order to gain good marks you needed to both explain your concerns **and** explain the audit evidence you would need to see when you reviewed the working papers.

Part (b) continued with the warranty provision, which appears to be materially understated, and requires you to discuss the implications for the auditor's report if no adjustments are made to the financial statements in relation to the warranty provision. Technical accuracy here was key.

Easy marks

In part (b) the implications for the auditor's report were relatively straightforward. There was a material misstatement which, if left unchanged, would lead to a qualified audit opinion. This area is tested frequently, and you need to be confident in your understanding of how the auditor's report will change depending on what is being tested.

ACCA examining team's comments

This question was set at the completion and reporting stage of an audit. As is typical of reporting questions, this is where the examining team sees some of the strongest and some of the weakest demonstrations of auditing competence from candidates.

Overall, the majority of candidates performed well in part (a).

Successful candidates identified that the new product capitalised as development costs was unlikely to meet the criteria in IAS 38 *Intangible Assets*, as the selling price is noted to be less than the cost incurred and therefore would be loss making. To answer the requirement successfully, the candidate should:

- Calculate materiality of the issue
- Identify the incorrect accounting treatment by the client – linked to the scenario
- State the relevant accounting rule – how it should be dealt with
- Note the impact on the financial statements

The new product is recognised as development costs under IAS 38, and it was disappointing to note candidates who made reference to 'PIRATE' criteria. Whilst this is used as an acronym for candidates to assist them in retaining the knowledge of the criteria of IAS 38, marks will not be awarded unless a candidate demonstrates they have the knowledge of the criteria by listing them out specifically.

A number of candidates incorrectly stated that 4% of profit before tax was material, whereas it is below the benchmark of 5% and, therefore, not material. Calculating materiality incorrectly in a Section B question will ultimately affect how candidates answer the impact on the audit opinion. This latter requirement is normally examined separately, resulting in marks lost due to suggesting an incorrect impact on the audit opinion.

The warranty provision had declined in comparison with the prior year by over 50%. Materiality was generally successfully calculated correctly for this matter, and most candidates were awarded the additional trend marks available. The main issue here was that there was a reduction in the warranty provision, yet revenue had increased. This appears inconsistent, as there is an expectation the warranty provision would increase in line with increasing revenue. Candidates were required to identify this as being a potential management manipulation of the figures and that the auditors should adopt an increased level of professional scepticism.

In part (b) candidates were asked to assess the implication on the audit report if the adjustment to the warranty provision is not corrected. Stronger candidates correctly calculated the materiality of the understated liability and fully evaluated that the misstatement was material. For candidates to score maximum marks, the term 'not pervasive' must be explained – for example, it is isolated to one issue and the financial statements as a whole are not impacted.

Candidates should then indicate the correct opinion to be given – in this instance, a qualified opinion due to a material misstatement. Candidates should evaluate the impact on the report, in that the basis for opinion paragraph, which is situated below the opinion paragraph, is used to explain the reason for the modification. It is disappointing to note the number of candidates who continue to discuss the use of an Emphasis of Matter paragraph in response to this issue, which is wholly irrelevant, along with a number of candidates referring to the need for a Key Audit Matter paragraph, even though the scenario clearly stated the client is not listed.

Candidates are continuing to show a lack of knowledge regarding the content of auditor's reports and audit opinions issued.

Marking guide | **Marks**

(a) (i) **Matters and evidence in relation to the new product**

Matters

- Materiality
- Discussion of whether meets classification requirements
- Risk
- Accounting treatment

Evidence

- Review of board minutes for discussions relating to the commercial feasibility of the smart vacuum cleaners
- A schedule itemising the individual costs capitalised to date in the production of the smart vacuum cleaner prototype to ensure there are no research elements
- Notes of a discussion with management regarding the accounting treatment of the research costs and confirmation that they were written off
- Review of the results of tests performed on the products to demonstrate that the prototype is fully working
- Analysis of Byres Ltd's budgets for the development of the prototype against actual expenditure to determine if the product costs have deviated significantly from original budgets
- Market research of any similar existing products to determine if a price point over £2,000 per unit would be commercially viable
- Details of discussions with the product design director of any difficulties in the development of this product which have caused it to run over budget
- Written representation from management detailing their intention to complete the project, including a commitment of resources and the ability to fund the future cash requirements to bring the product to market

7

(ii) **Matters and evidence in relation to the warranty provision**

Matters

- Materiality
- Discussion of estimates
- Risk
- Accounting treatment

- Influence of CEO

Evidence

- A copy of management's calculation of the £2·1 million warranty provision, with all components agreed to underlying documentation, and arithmetically checked
- Notes of a meeting with management, at which the reasons for the reduction in the warranty provision were discussed, including the key assumptions used by management
- Analysis of total sales in terms of product mix against prior years with investigation into differences and a quantification of the effect this might have on the warranty provision
- A copy of any quality control reports, disaggregated by product, reviewed for any indications that certain product lines have fewer warranty claims than in previous years
- Notes of the meeting with the customer services manager where the levels of customer complaints and product faults were discussed
- A comparison of the prior year's calculation with actual warranties claimed post year end to determine the accuracy
- An evaluation of all key assumptions, considering consistency with the auditor's knowledge of the business, and a conclusion on their validity
- An independent estimate prepared by the audit team, compared to management's estimate, and with significant variances discussed with management
- A schedule obtained from management showing the movement in the provision in the accounting period, checked for arithmetic accuracy, and with opening and closing figures agreed to the draft financial statements and general ledger
- Evaluation by the audit team, and a conclusion on the appropriateness of the accounting entries used, especially in relation to the profit impact of the entries
- A file note documenting that the auditor has requested an adjustment requiring the warranty provision to be increased by £2·7 million

8

(b) **Auditor's report**

- Material misstatement due to inappropriate accounting estimates
- Calculation of possible misstatement
- Matter is not pervasive
- Qualified audit opinion
- Basis for qualified audit opinion

5

Professional marks

Analysis and evaluation

- Appropriate use of the information to determine the misstatements relating to capitalised development expenditure and the warranty provision including an assessment of their materiality.
- Appropriate consideration of the materiality of the misstatements relating to warranty provision in order to determine the impact on the auditor's report

Marking guide	Marks

- Detailed assessment of the information in the Exhibit to determine the matters that should be considered and the nature and extent of audit evidence which was still required

Professional scepticism and judgement

- Effective challenge of information supplied in relation to the sales value of the smart vacuum cleaner that places doubt over the commercial viability of the project and therefore the capitalisation of development expenditure
- Effective challenge of the inconsistent basis on which the warranty provision has been calculated in the current year
- Determination and justification of a suitable materiality level, appropriately and consistently applied
- Appropriate application of professional judgement to draw conclusions and make informed decisions about the impact on the auditor's report

Maximum	5
Total	25

(a) (i) **Matters and evidence in relation to the new product**

Matters

The carrying amount of the capitalised development costs in relation to the new product are immaterial as they amount to 0·8% of assets and immaterial to profit before tax at 4·0%.

There is a significant risk that the requirements of IAS 38 *Intangible Assets* have not been followed. Research costs must be expensed, and strict criteria must be applied to development expenditure to determine whether it should be capitalised and recognised as an intangible asset. Development costs are capitalised only after technical and commercial feasibility of the asset for sale or use have been established, and Byres Ltd must demonstrate an intention and ability to complete the development and that it will generate future economic benefits. Additionally, Byres Ltd must demonstrate the existence of a market, which given the product design director's comments appears uncertain.

There is a risk that research costs have been inappropriately classified as development costs and then capitalised, overstating assets and understating expenses. The product design director is uncertain as to whether the new product will generate sufficient economic benefits due to the sale price being unlikely to exceed the production costs per unit. It is therefore unlikely that the costs in relation to this product development continue to meet the criteria for capitalisation, so there is a risk that they have not been written off, overstating assets and profit.

Evidence expected to be on file:

- Review of board minutes for discussions relating to the commercial feasibility of the smart vacuum cleaners.
- Notes of a discussion with management regarding the accounting treatment of the research costs and confirmation that they were written off.
- A schedule itemising the individual costs capitalised to date in the production of the smart vacuum cleaner prototype to ensure there are no research elements.
- Review of the results of tests performed on the products to demonstrate that the prototype is fully operational.
- Analysis of Byres Ltd's budgets for the development of the prototype against actual expenditure to determine if the product costs have deviated significantly from original budgets.

- Alternative market research of any similar existing products to determine if a price point over £2,000 per unit would be commercially viable.
- Details of discussions with the product design director of any difficulties in the development of this product which have caused it to run over budget.
- Written representation from management detailing their intention to complete the project, including a commitment of resources and the ability to fund the future cash requirements to bring the product to market.

(ii) **Matters and evidence in relation to the warranty provision**

Matters

The warranty provision is material as it amounts to 6·6% of total assets and 33·3% of profit before tax respectively. The provision has changed in value over the year, declining by £2·2 million which is a significant reduction of 51·2%. This is despite revenue increasing during the year by £5·5 million which is a significant increase of 11·0% and the provision has historically and effectively been based on a percentage of total sales in prior years.

Based on the information provided, in 20X4, the warranty provision was 8·6% of revenue (4·3/50m). In 20X5, the warranty provision is only 3·8% (2·1/55·5m) of revenue. Therefore, since the chief executive officer's (CEO) involvement with estimating the warranty provision, the value of the provision has reduced significantly compared to the value which would normally be expected.

According to ISA (UK) 540 *Auditing Accounting Estimates including Fair Value Accounting Estimates and Related Disclosures*, the audit team should have tested how management made the accounting estimate, and the data on which it is based. The audit team should also have tested the operating effectiveness of any relevant controls and developed their own point estimate or range in order to evaluate management's estimate.

The value of the warranty provision would normally be expected to increase in line with revenue, particularly as the sales director has indicated neither the range of customers nor the nature of the warranty have changed significantly compared to the prior year. There has also not been any change in the level of customer complaints or faulty items which, if present, may indicate problems with the quality of the company's products. The audit team must fully understand the reasons for the reduction in the warranty provision. There could be valid reasons, for example, the sales mix between products could be different which failed to trigger a similar level of warranty provision, but the change in value should be fully investigated by the team.

Consideration should be given to the accounting entries which have been made to effect the change in the value of the provision. The validity of any credit entry to profit as a result of the reduction in value of the provision should have been scrutinised as this could indicate creative accountancy and earnings management. In the event that the provision has been underestimated in the current year, then future accounting periods would require higher expenses charged to the statement of profit or loss.

In previous years, the finance director and finance department had dealt with the judgement when estimating the warranty provision, however, this year the CEO has had significant input. There is therefore an increased risk of management bias in the estimation techniques. The audit team should approach this issue with professional scepticism and consider the motivation of the CEO in involving himself in accounting issues which had previously been left to the finance director.

Evidence expected to be on file:

- A copy of management's calculation of the £2·1 million warranty provision, with all components agreed to underlying documentation, and arithmetically checked.
- Notes of a meeting with management, at which the reasons for the reduction in the warranty provision were discussed, including the key assumptions used by management.

- Analysis of total sales in terms of product mix against prior years with investigation into differences and a quantification of the effect this might have on the warranty provision.
- A copy of any quality control reports, disaggregated by product, reviewed for any indications that certain product lines have fewer warranty claims than in previous years.
- Notes of the meeting with the customer services manager where the levels of customer complaints and product faults were discussed.
- A comparison of the prior year's calculation with actual warranties claimed post year end to determine the accuracy.
- An evaluation of all key assumptions, considering consistency with the auditor's knowledge of the business, and a conclusion on their validity.
- An independent estimate prepared by the audit team, compared to management's estimate, and with significant variances discussed with management.
- A schedule obtained from management showing the movement in the provision in the accounting period, checked for arithmetic accuracy, and with opening and closing figures agreed to the draft financial statements and general ledger.
- Evaluation by the audit team, and a conclusion on the appropriateness of the accounting entries used, especially in relation to the profit impact of the entries.
- A file note documenting that the auditor has requested an adjustment requiring the warranty provision to be increased by £2·7million.

(b) Word Processor

Paragraph

Implications for the auditor's report

Warranty provision

Accounting estimates are always difficult to determine with any degree of certainty, however, the work carried out by the audit team suggests that the value of the warranty provision has been suppressed. Assuming that the provision should have increased consistently with increase in revenue of 11%, it would be expected that the year-end warranty provision should be around £4·8 million. The actual provision recorded in Byres Ltd's financial statements is only £2·1 million, therefore, the liability appears to be understated by £2·7 million. At 8·5% of total assets, the likely error in the provision is highly material to the statement of financial position.

Overall impact on the auditor's report

The misstatement in relation to the warranty provision is individually material and, if management fails to amend the financial statements, the auditor's opinion should be modified due to the material, but not pervasive, misstatement. The misstatement of the warranty provision is confined to specific accounts in the financial statements and does not represent a substantial proportion of the financial statements. A **qualified opinion** should therefore be given.

The auditor's report should include a qualified opinion paragraph at the start of the report. This paragraph should be followed immediately by a **basis for qualified opinion paragraph,** which should explain the reasons for the qualified auditor's opinion and should quantify the impact of the matters identified on the financial statements.

ACCA

Advanced Audit and Assurance – UK (AAA – UK)

Mock Exam 4

September 2022 Exam

Questions	
Time allowed	3 hours 15 minutes
All THREE questions are compulsory and MUST be attempted	

DO NOT OPEN THIS EXAM UNTIL YOU ARE READY TO START UNDER EXAMINATION CONDITIONS

Section A

1 Winberry plc

It is 1 July 20X5. You are a manager in the audit department of Quince & Co, a firm of Chartered Certified Accountants, and you are responsible for the audit of Winberry plc, a listed entity and an existing client of your firm. The company has a financial year ending 30 September 20X5, and you are about to start planning this year's audit.

The following exhibits, available on the left-hand side of the screen, provide information relevant to the question:

(1) Partner's email – an email which you have received from Olivia Fig, the audit engagement partner.

(2) Meeting notes – notes of a meeting which Olivia Fig recently attended with the audit committee of Winberry plc focusing on understanding the current operation and future strategy of the business.

(3) Financial information – selected financial information from Winberry plc's management accounts.

(4) Internet search – the headline results from an internet search performed by the audit team about the business and industry.

This information should be used to answer the question requirement within your chosen response option(s).

Required

Respond to the instructions in the email from the audit engagement partner.

Note. The split of the mark allocation is shown in Exhibit 1 – Partner's email. **(40 marks)**

Professional marks will be awarded for the demonstration of skill in communication, analysis and evaluation, professional scepticism and judgement, and commercial acumen in your answer. **(10 marks)**

(Total = 50 marks)

Exhibit 1: Partner's email

To: Audit manager

From: Olivia Fig, Audit engagement partner

Subject: Winberry plc audit planning

Date: 1 July 20X5

Hello

I attended a planning meeting last week with the finance director and a representative of the audit committee of Winberry plc, at which we discussed business developments during the year and plans for the future. I have provided you with my notes from this meeting, as well as some background information about the company from the permanent audit file. Based on the analysis I have done on this industry, it is appropriate for overall materiality to be based on profit before tax as this is a key focus for investors and providers of finance.

Using the information provided in all the exhibits, I require you to prepare briefing notes for my own use, in which you:

(a) Evaluate the significant business risks facing the company. **(10 marks)**

(b) Evaluate and prioritise the significant risks of material misstatement to be considered in planning the audit for the financial year ending 30 September 20X5. **(16 marks)**

Note: You should refer to ALL exhibits when carrying out the requested risk evaluations.

(c)	Design the principal audit procedures to be performed in respect of the classification of the investment in Luxury Pet Supplies (LPS) Ltd. **(7 marks)**
(d)	With reference to the data protection issue referred to in Exhibit 2, discuss Quince & Co's responsibilities in relation to Winberry plc's compliance with laws and regulations. **(7 marks)**

Thank you

Exhibit 2: Meeting notes

Winberry plc is a listed company operating as a retailer in the online grocery market with coverage of 75% of the UK. The company has a loyal and growing customer base who place orders via either the company's website or an application (app) which can be installed on a customer's mobile phone. Winberry plc fulfils grocery orders, delivering to customers' homes via a fleet of company-owned refrigerated delivery vehicles. Winberry plc prides itself on having a market-leading inventory system which ensures that customers can only order groceries which are currently available. This helps Winberry plc's customers avoid the inconvenience of ordering unavailable items.

A significant proportion of the groceries supplied by Winberry plc are perishable products, the sale and storage of which is highly regulated through food safety regulations. Winberry plc employs experienced food and product technology professionals to ensure that the company complies with all food safety legislation.

The directors of Winberry plc are pursuing ambitious expansion plans in order to establish a strong position in the home delivery grocery market and to explore business partnerships in associated markets.

International expansion

Winberry plc is planning to expand into the foreign country of Farland by setting up operations similar to its existing business. Farland uses the same currency as Winberry plc's existing operations. The investment is expected to cost £125 million. Winberry plc does not currently have the funds for this expansion but is in advanced negotiations with its current bankers, who are keen to provide loan financing on the same basis and covenant as the existing loan finance. The expansion is expected to occur in 20X6.

Data protection issue

Two months ago, Winberry plc suffered a cybersecurity attack in which the personal information of 2,500 customers, including their credit card details, was stolen. According to a representative of the audit committee, the company's internal audit team had not properly assessed the risks relating to cybersecurity, which is a requirement of data protection legislation in the UK. The issue which led to the cybersecurity attack has now been resolved. Winberry plc did not make any reports of the breach to regulators.

Exhibit 3: Financial information

	Note	Projected to 30 September 20X5 £ million	Actual to 30 September 20X4 £ million
Revenue			
Groceries	**1**	587	358
Pet goods (from LPS Ltd)	**2**	10	-
Total revenue		**597**	**358**
Operating profit		172	110

	Note	Projected to 30 September 20X5 £ million	Actual to 30 September 20X4 £ million
Profit before tax		53	31
Total assets		**957**	**884**
Included in total assets:			
Net assets as consolidated relating to the subsidiary, LPS Ltd	**2**	60	-
Property, plant and equipment – relating to fire damaged warehouse	**3**	67	70
Long-term borrowing	**4**	33	5
Number of premium delivery pass costumers		**146,250**	-

Notes.

1 Groceries revenue includes revenue earned for a new initiative launched during the year by Winberry plc. This guarantees a weekly delivery slot for customers who sign up for a premium delivery pass. The premium delivery pass is an annual membership with a fee of £60. This fee is invoiced in advance and the revenue is recognised in full at the time of invoicing.

2 Winberry plc has entered into a joint venture agreement with Durian Ltd and is investing £30 million in a newly formed company, Luxury Pet Supplies Ltd (LPS Ltd), representing 50% of the share capital of the company. The remaining 50% shareholding is owned by Durian Ltd, a leading national chain of vets and pet goods suppliers. The contract behind this investment states that Winberry plc and Durian Ltd will work together to develop the supply of a range of pet supplies, food, toys and accessories. This joint venture agreement utilises the established online presence of Winberry plc and their distribution network, and Durian Ltd's existing knowledge of the pet goods supplies market. Both parties will have equal voting rights and equal rights to the net assets of LPS Ltd with profits to be shared equally. The investment is expected to take place in August 20X5.

The finance director of Winberry plc plans to consolidate the results of LPS Ltd as a subsidiary; the share of the results attributable to Durian Ltd is shown as a non-controlling interest. 100% of LPS Ltd's revenue from incorporation is shown separately in the financial information above owing to Winberry plc's full compliance with IFRS 8 Operating Segments. The finance director believes that despite Winberry plc and Durian Ltd each owning 50% of LPS Ltd, and having equal representation on the board of directors, Winberry plc's contribution of knowledge to the joint venture is greater and therefore Winberry plc should consolidate the investment.

3 In January 20X5, there was a fire in one of Winberry plc's five warehouses which completely destroyed the premises, but fortunately no staff were injured. The warehouse serviced the northern region of Winberry plc's customer base. The finance director has not written down the carrying amount of the warehouse in property, plant and equipment as he is confident that the company's insurance policy will cover all costs. The insurance company has confirmed that they will repay Winberry plc for the inventory lost during the fire, however, the

claim for the warehouse building and machinery is still on-going. Winberry plc was able to utilise their remaining four warehouses to provide coverage to the northern region customers.

4 Long-term borrowing comprises a bank loan taken out by Winberry plc to fund the joint venture of LPS Ltd with Durian Ltd and the purchase of electric delivery vehicles. The bank issued the loan on the same terms as their existing loan which has a covenant that interest cover is maintained at 3.

Exhibit 4: Internet search

Search results for Winberry plc

3 November 20X4

Keeping up with demand, Winberry plc ahead in home delivery grocery revolution

The groceries trade journal, Perishables Planet, reports that demand for online groceries delivery has reached an all-time high and shows no sign of slowing down. Traditional supermarkets cannot keep up with the demand, leaving opportunities for gains in market share for online operators.

15 January 20X5

Local residents to bring legal action against Winberry plc

A group of 30 local residents who claim their health was affected by toxic fumes from the huge fire at Winberry plc's northern warehouse are bringing action to claim for compensation. The local residents' legal representative confirmed that they had served a claim against Winberry plc as they believe there were health and safety breaches due to failings in the sprinkler systems to bring the fire under control quickly. Winberry plc's health and safety department has launched an investigation which concluded warehouse staff had manually overridden the automatic sprinkler system to prevent water damage to goods.

18 February 20X5

Eco-friendly vans cause delivery disruption for Winberry plc

A new fleet of 80 electric vehicles, costing £50,000 each, has caused delivery chaos to Winberry plc's loyal customers. The vehicles can only travel for 100 miles without requiring recharging, which has left customers experiencing delays of up to four hours for their groceries. The eco-friendly vans were initially selected for purchase by management based on a suitable delivery range, however, at the request of Winberry plc, the manufacturer of the vans added refrigeration units to each vehicle which has significantly reduced the distance the vans can travel on a single battery charge.

Section B

2 Forsythia Group ((amended))

It is 1 July 20X5. You are an audit manager in Magnolia & Co, and you are currently conducting an Engagement Quality Review on the audit of the Forsythia Group (the Group), which is a listed entity. Your firm is appointed to audit the consolidated financial statements and the individual financial statements of all Group companies.

The following exhibit, available on the left-hand side of the screen, provides information relevant to the question:

(1) Forsythia Group – summary of comments made by the audit team regarding the performance of the audit.

This information should be used to answer the question requirement within the response option provided.

Required

Evaluate the quality management and other professional matters identified during your review in respect of the planning and performance of the Forsythia Group audit, and recommend appropriate actions to be taken. **(20 marks)**

Professional marks will be awarded for the demonstration of skill in analysis and evaluation, professional scepticism and judgement, and commercial acumen in your answer. **(5 marks)**

(Total = 25 marks)

Exhibit: Forsythia Group

The audit of the Forsythia Group (the Group) for the year ended 31 March 20X5 is in the completion stage and the auditor's report is due to be issued next week.

The Group has diverse operations, focusing on manufacturing, but is also involved with activities in some other areas, such as agriculture. The draft consolidated financial statements include revenue of £129 million (20X4: £113 million), profit before tax of £18·6 million (20X4: £23·2 million) and total assets of £465 million (20X4: £460 million).

You have discussed the Group audit with a junior member of the audit team, who made the following comments about how it was planned and carried out:

'On 10 June 20X5, the Group acquired another subsidiary, Robin Ltd, which is forecast to increase the Group's total revenue by around 20%. This meant that the Group chief finance officer (CFO) had little time to discuss matters with the audit team. The acquisition has taken place quickly, and so did not form part of the audit planning, which took place in January 20X5. The audit engagement partner said that we did not need to perform audit work on any aspect of the acquisition as, according to the CFO, it will all be accounted for in next year's financial statements.

'Due to pressure to reduce the costs of the audit, the audit manager arranged for the audit procedures on revenue recognised by several material subsidiaries, including a subsidiary in the agricultural industry, to be delegated to Camelia Associates, an unconnected firm. The audit manager said that we can rely on the evidence obtained by Camelia Associates as they are a firm of qualified accountants.

'I also audited the Group's intangible assets, which involved evaluating the assumptions relating to the appropriateness of capitalisation of £1·2 million of development costs in the year. I could not discuss this with the CFO and no one else was available, so I agreed the assumptions, for example, relating to technical feasibility and commercial viability, to the Group's business plan and concluded that they were consistent. This is the first year that development costs have been recognised as an intangible asset in the Group financial statements.

'Yew Ltd, which operates in the agricultural industry, is a subsidiary of the Group. At the audit planning stage, in line with the previous year's audit, it was not considered likely to increase aggregation risk. However, due to the specialist nature of the operations of the company, a consultant should have been used to provide input on some technical matters, as stated in the audit strategy and audit plan. Due to cost implications, the consultant was not engaged, and the section of the audit strategy and audit plan containing instructions relating to the consultant was deleted from the audit files.'

Following your conversation with the audit assistant, you reviewed the audit working papers and found the following:

- The audit evidence obtained by Camelia Associates has not been reviewed by the audit manager or partner.
- No further evidence has been obtained relating to the development expenditure.
- Yew Ltd has total assets of £60·5 million (20X4: £83 million) and revenue of £6·5 million (20X4: £6·4 million).

3 Geller Ltd

It is 1 July 20X5. You are an audit manager in Bing & Co, working on the audit of Geller Ltd, a UK-based book and magazine publisher.

Geller Ltd has a financial year ended 31 March 20X5 and you are reviewing the work performed on going concern.

The following exhibits, available on the left-hand side of the screen, provide information relevant to the question:

(1) Audit file notes – a summary of audit working papers relevant to going concern.

(2) Cash flow forecast – a cash flow forecast covering the period to 31 March 20X7 prepared by management.

This information should be used to answer the question requirements within your chosen response option(s).

Required

Using the information in Exhibits 1 and 2:

(a) Evaluate the assumptions used by management and the completeness of the cash flow forecast prepared, explaining why particular assumptions should be challenged and approached with professional scepticism. **(10 marks)**

(b) Explain the audit evidence in respect of the CASH RECEIPTS included in the cash flow which you would expect to find in your review of the audit working papers on going concern. **(5 marks)**

(c) It is now 1 August 20X5 and you have not been able to obtain sufficient, appropriate audit evidence to support the assumptions used to prepare the cash flow forecast. In particular, there is no arrangement in place to sell the Happy Travels publishing range in January 20X6. The audit assistant proposes to issue an unmodified audit opinion but to include a Material Uncertainty Related to Going Concern section within the auditor's report to highlight the problems facing the company.

Required

Discuss the appropriateness of the audit assistant's proposal for the auditor's report. **(5 marks)**

Professional marks will be awarded for the demonstration of skill in analysis and evaluation, professional scepticism and judgement, and commercial acumen in your answer. **(5 marks)**

(Total = 25 marks)

Exhibit 1: Audit file notes

Audit working paper

Prepared by: An Auditor

Subject: Going concern issues highlighted for audit manager and proposal for auditor's report

Date: 29 June 20X5

Our audit work indicates that there are significant operating and financial problems facing the company. Management has prepared a cash flow forecast which they believe should provide evidence that Geller Ltd is a going concern.

Operating problems noted during the audit of going concern

Geller Ltd's business is significantly impacted by an industry-wide deterioration in demand for printed books and magazines. The company has recently acquired a digital publishing business at a cost of £25 million, and management is confident that Geller Ltd will soon be able to offer a broad range of digital books and magazines. However, authors of printed books will need to give consent for their books to be converted to a digital format. This consent must be obtained prior to the books being made available for sale on digital platforms.

Authors are paid royalties based on sales of their books, typically around 5% of the revenue generated from their titles. There is concern that due to the company's cash position, there may be delays in making royalty payments to some authors.

In addition, the rapid growth of online retailers has impacted negatively on the company's sales, as Geller Ltd has not, until recently, devoted marketing resources to engagement with online retailers. Analytical procedures show that revenue has declined by 20% this year, accelerating the trend seen in previous years. In the financial years ended 31 March 20X3 and 31 March 20X4, revenue fell by 10% and 12% respectively.

One of the company's recent successes is contracting a very popular author to write a series of three children's books. The author, Chandler Muriel, who has sold millions of books worldwide, has delivered the first book in the series, which was published in January 20X5. Sales of the book since its publication have been disappointing, at only £135,000. Management explains that this is due to a rival company publishing a similar book in December 20X4. Chandler Muriel's second book is due to be published in August 20X5, and the third in January 20X6.

Financial issues

Geller Ltd faces a liquidity problem, having only £78,000 of cash at 31 March 20X5. The company has an overdraft facility of £250,000 and in addition, agreed undrawn borrowing facilities of £1 million. There is an existing £5 million unsecured bank loan which is due for repayment on 30 September 20X5.

Disclosure relating to going concern

Management has confirmed that they will provide full details of the going concern problems facing Geller Ltd in the notes to the financial statements.

Happy Travels publishing range

Geller Ltd has made the decision to sell its popular Happy Travels range. This is a range of books aimed at the student traveller and include maps as well as suggested hostels and activities. Geller Ltd anticipates significant interest in the range, with a sale expected in January 20X6.

Exhibit 2: Cash flow forecast

Cash flow forecast for the two years ended 31 March 20X7

Six-month periods to:					
		30 September 20X5	31 March 20X6	30 September 20X6	31 March 20X7

Six-month periods to:					
	Note	$'000	$'000	$'000	$'000
Cash receipts from customers	1	10,000.00	10,200.00	10,404.00	10,924.20
Cash receipt from sale of Happy Travels range	2		6,000.00		
Cash outflows relating to operating expenses	3	(10,400.00)	(10,504.00)	(10,609.04)	(10,715.13)
Interest payments and other finance costs		(125.00)	(125.00)	(125.00)	0.00
Loan repayment	4	-	-	(5,000.00)	-
Net cash flow		**(525.00)**	**5,571.00**	**(5,330.04)**	**209.07**
Opening cash		78.00	(447.00)	5,124.00	(206.04)
Closing cash		**(447.00)**	**5,124.00**	**(206.04)**	**3.03**

Notes and key assumptions

(1) Monthly sales are based on management's forecasts which predict sales growth of 2% in each six-month period. The sales growth is anticipated based on several assumptions, including that a full range of digital book and magazine titles will be available from 1 August 20X5 and that closer connections with online retailers will drive an increase in sales. In addition, management assumes that sales from Chandler Muriel's books will generate income of approximately $250,000 per six-month period.

(2) Management has recently decided to sell the Happy Travels range of books. The estimated sales value of the range is based on a multiple of the annual sales generated by the range. This is the company's standard basis of calculating expected sales prices, which Geller Co has used in recent years when it has sold other ranges of books. Management is confident that a buyer will be found and that the sale will go ahead in January 20X6.

(3) Operating expenses, including royalties, are forecast to increase by 1% per six-month period, in line with general costs of inflation.

(4) Geller Ltd has a $5 million loan which is due for repayment on 30 September 20X5. Management has started the process of renegotiating the repayment terms of this loan and is confident that the bank will agree to extend the repayment date to 30 September 20X6.

Answers

DO NOT TURN THIS PAGE UNTIL YOU HAVE COMPLETED THE MOCK EXAM

A plan of attack

If this had been the real Advanced Audit and Assurance exam and you had been told to start the exam, what would have been going through your mind?

An important thing to say (while there is still time) is that it is vital to have a good breadth of knowledge of the syllabus because the question requirements for each question will relate to different areas of the AAA syllabus. However, don't panic. Below we provide guidance on how to approach the exam.

Approaching the answer

It is vital that you attempt all the questions in the exam to increase your chances of passing. The best way to do this is to make sure you stick to the time allocation for each question – both in total and for each of the question parts. The worst thing you can do is run over time in one question and then find that you don't have enough time for the remaining questions, leading you to miss out on some of the easier marks in those questions.

Section A consists of one long case-study style question set at the planning stage of the audit. This may contain detailed information such as extracts from financial statements and audit working papers. A range of requirements will be set for this question but will only cover areas from syllabus areas A to D inclusive.

Question 1 is for 50 marks, all set at the planning stage in the context of a single scenario, here dealing with the audit of a listed entity which entered into a joint venture agreement two months before the end of the reporting period. The entity also suffered a significant warehouse fire during the year and is seeking to finance plans to expand overseas in the next accounting period. It is a very long question and so it is important that you break it down into its component parts as this will make it easier to manage – and enable you to allocate your time to each of them.

Section B contains two more compulsory questions and may be set on any area of the AAA syllabus.

Question 2, for 25 marks, featured an Engagement Quality Review relating to a listed group where the Group Chief Finance Officer did not have sufficient time to give to the audit team and where some key IFRS Accounting Standards had not been adhered to.

Question 3 offers 25 marks testing the audit of the cash flow forecast where there is significant concern relating to the entity's ability to continue as a going concern and asks you to consider the appropriateness of the planned auditor's opinion.

Forget about it!

And don't worry if you found the exam difficult. More than likely other candidates did too. If this were the real thing, you would need to forget the exam the minute you finished it and think about the next one. Or, if it is the last one, celebrate!

Section A

1 Winberry plc

Workbook references

Chapters 1, 6, 7 and 9.

Top Tips

This is a long question which contained lots of information. The best way to score good marks in relation to part (a) (evaluate the significant business risk) was to pull together the information in exhibits 2, 3 and 4 where the same risks were discussed more than once. Similarly, exhibits 2 and 3 would have been particularly helpful for part (b) (evaluating and prioritising significant risks of material misstatement). Remember though, to score marks in both part (a) and part (b) you need to evaluate rather than just identify issues which may lead to business risks/RoMM. For part (a), you should also analyse the financial information provided and perform calculations relating to material where relevant.

In part (c), you should have focussed on the documentation that surrounds the acquisition of an investment, as well as evidence concerning how LPS Ltd would be managed in order to design audit procedures in respect of the classification of the investment in LPS.

A good place to start for part (d) was your knowledge of the auditor's responsibilities in relation to the consideration of laws and regulations.

Easy marks

There were several easy marks in part (b) provided that you explained how this impacted the RoMM. For example, management had not conducted an impairment review following the warehouse fire and so the carrying amount in the statement of financial position is likely to be materially misstated (over-valued), as the insurance claim should be considered separately.

ACCA examining team's comments

This question was a typical Section A question set at the planning stage, with requirements focusing on matters specific to the planning stage of an audit engagement, an evaluation of the significant business risks, an evaluation and prioritisation of the significant RoMM, designing specific audit procedures in relation to the classification of a joint venture, and discussing the audit firm's responsibilities in relation to a breach of laws and regulations. Professional skills marks were available for all four of the professional skills associated with the syllabus.

Part (a) tested the evaluation of significant business risks. In the AAA exam, significant risks are considered to be those which would have a significant impact on the client business and where there is a significant probability of these risks occurring, after any mitigations stated in the information provided. Risks that are of a remote likelihood of occurring, already mitigated against, or will have an insignificant impact are not considered to be 'significant risks'. Candidates are required to identify what is significant in the context of the specific scenario, demonstrating good professional judgement and an ability to disseminate the important information whilst assessing the risks that may affect the audit. Many candidates were able to identify the risk that the insurance claim for damaged property (Exhibit 3) might not be successful and were able to describe the impact on the company cashflows for the initial credit. Stronger candidates then went on to assess that this risk in the light of the deliberate deactivation of the sprinkler system, may mean that the insurance claim is unsuccessful. These candidates not only provided a well-thought-out evaluation for the purpose of scoring technical marks, but they were also demonstrating the skill of **professional scepticism** in recognising the insurance claim might not be successful. Credit was also available for the demonstration of **commercial acumen** in appreciating the claim was less likely to be successful given that the fire safety systems had been overridden as this contributed to the levels of damage incurred at the warehouse.

Weaker candidates often discussed the implication of the risk without attempting to evaluate the scale of the risk. Typical responses by candidates who did not score sufficient credit to pass the exam would simply state that something which had occurred in the scenario, such as 'there might be a fire in the warehouse', whilst failing to assess the implication on the business.

A well-evaluated risk has in depth analysis. Candidates writing only a sentence or two are unlikely to attain many of the marks available for each risk.

Some candidates described risks which were not considered significant for credit. The most common ones seen by the examining team were currency risks arising in a proposed expansion overseas, despite being told that the two countries use the same currency. Other weaker responses suggested that food safety breaches may occur, even though candidates were told that this risk was mitigated using food safety specialists. Other candidates remarked that going concern was a risk because the company might lose its licence to operate, even though no information was provided in the scenario to suggest a licence was required to operate.

Overall in this section, many candidates were able to identify sufficient risks to pass the requirement. Fewer candidates identified the risks of the company's decision to diversify into a new industry through a joint venture, or the cost implications relating to the poor performance of the electric vehicles. These were topics less frequently seen in past questions and served as a differentiator between stronger candidates who were able to identify the risks from the scenario and demonstrate their professional skills of analysis and evaluation of the evidence provided.

In part (b), candidates are expected to perform relevant analysis to support an evaluation of risks of material misstatement (RoMMs). Candidates often achieved strong marks in this section for the identification of the RoMMs but fewer obtained the marks for the evaluation of those risks. Many candidates are continuing to rely on basic or generic explanations, which fail to refer to the information in the scenario. Candidates who refer to the specific information provide more in-depth answers and are also able to assess the scale of the risk in the context of the specific audit client.

Materiality: specific marks were available in this requirement for the calculation and application of materiality in line with the new syllabus guidance and for the prioritisation of the risks identified. Whilst a significant number of candidates appeared prepared for the new syllabus and followed the new materiality guidance, very few attempted to prioritise risks and were unable to access the professional skills marks for this skill.

Candidates are expected to initially determine a materiality threshold for the audit, as would be used in practice. Three technical marks are available for the materiality determination. Candidates are expected to demonstrate a knowledge of the appropriate percentage range for the benchmark instructed by the audit partner – in this question, profit before tax was to be utilised with candidates expected to use 5-10% as their range – and calculate the monetary amount in respect of the range. Candidates must then use their professional judgement to select an appropriate materiality threshold given the risk levels which exist in the audit and provide a brief justification for their choice. Each of these steps examines a different aspect of understanding or skills required of an auditor.

It was disappointing to note that some candidates calculated a range appropriately, then failed to justify a materiality threshold for the audit. The examining team will give credit for any reasonable explanation of the chosen materiality threshold, as the mark is to recognise that there is the application of professional judgement and that a candidate can justify their response. It is not required that candidates select the identical percentage or figure, or that they provide a justification identical to that shown in the model answer. For example, in this question, some candidates stated the higher end of the range was justified because this was an existing client and some stated the lower end was more appropriate due to the accounting errors that the finance director was making. Alternative answers which were awarded credit included those that suggested that an amount in the middle of the range was appropriate, because whilst this was an existing client, the expansion into a new market increased the risk. All of these obtained the mark for justifying the chosen materiality threshold.

An issue that arises repeatedly is candidates attempting to find eight risks for a 16-mark question and conducting little or no in-depth analysis of any of them. This will not be sufficient to attain a pass mark.

The scenario contained information which gave rise to six significant risks, of which most candidates were able to identify at least four. These were asset impairments of warehouse, misclassification of an investment, provisions, revenue recognition, impairment of electric vehicles, and control risks over data. Each of these could be evaluated in the context of the scenario using the information provided, ensuring that the underlying accounting treatment was correct. The majority of marks available in AAA will be for the application of the financial reporting knowledge to the specific audit scenario, not simply for the knowledge itself.

It was disappointing to see that very few candidates attempted any prioritisation of the risks as specifically stated in the requirement. Professional skill marks were available to the candidates who attempted this requirement. Candidates were expected to identify the most significant risks, and then provide a brief justification for their choice. Again, credit was awarded for candidates who offered a reasonable explanation, and therefore, a range of possible explanations are valid. Candidates should be aware this mark is for the act of justifying the reason not for the actual justification used. Candidates can obtain these marks by either ordering their answer in priority order and stating this is the case or by summarising in a conclusion which risk, or risks, are the most significant. Where candidates use this latter method, if a candidate does not state which one or two risks are the most significant but simply lists some or all their identified risks, this will not be sufficient for credit.

The requirement in part (c) is typical of a section A question and requires candidates to design audit procedures to address a specific risk arising in the question. In this question, the procedures were to determine the correct classification of an investment which has been treated as a subsidiary by the client but which is more likely to be a joint venture.

Candidates were generally able to pass this requirement, with stronger candidates attaining maximum marks. These supplied procedures which identified sources of information available to the auditor who can then determine whether the company has control over LPS Ltd, or whether it meets the criteria of a joint venture.

Weaker candidates who did not pay attention to the wording of the requirement and focused on the significant risk of classification instead gave procedures covering lower-risk assertions, such as cost and acquisition date, or asked for a management representation stating this was a subsidiary, which would not be an appropriate form of evidence to justify the incorrect classification.

Professional skills marks available for this requirement focused on communication skills demonstrated through the ability of candidates to follow the specific instructions provided by the audit partner to focus on classification.

For part (d), candidates needed to have sufficient knowledge of auditing standards ISA (UK) 250A *Consideration of Laws and Regulations in an Audit of Financial Statements* and ISA (UK) 315 (Revised) *Identifying and Assessing the Risks of Material Misstatement*. These standards require the auditor to understand the risks of non-compliance of management with laws and regulations, and to describe how auditors should respond to non-compliance by management. This technical auditing knowledge is required to be applied to the specific scenario to achieve a pass mark for this requirement. Candidates were provided with specific information on the relevant legal requirements and how the client had breached those requirements. In general, candidates who applied their knowledge to the scenario scored high or full marks, and those who simply stated the auditor responsibilities in more general terms scored poorly.

Stronger candidates who discussed the lack of integrity displayed through management's reluctance to self-report, and who then evaluated the impact of this behaviour in the context of the wider audit, were awarded additional professional scepticism and judgement marks. It was pleasing to see some candidates linking the requirements of assessing client continuation procedures with the introduction of ISQM (UK) 1.

Marking guide

		Marks
(a)	Up to 2 marks for each business risk (unless indicated otherwise). Marks may be awarded for other, relevant business risks not included in the marking guide. In addition, 0.5 mark for relevant trends or calculations which form part of the evaluation of business risk (max 3 marks across the whole question). • Damage to operations – warehouse fire • International expansion • Investment in Luxury Pet Supplies Ltd • Loan finance • Eco-friendly delivery vans • Legal case • Cyberattack • Perishable products	
	Maximum	10
(b)	Up to 3 marks for each risk of material misstatement (unless indicated otherwise). Marks may be awarded for other, relevant risks not included in the marking guide. Appropriate materiality calculations and justified materiality level should be awarded to a maximum of 3 marks.	

- Warehouse fire
- Revenue recognition – annual membership
- Investment in LPS Ltd
- Corporate governance (max 2 marks)
- Eco-friendly delivery vans
- Legal provision
- Pressure on results (max 2 marks)

Maximum 16

(c)
- Obtain the legal documentation supporting the investment and agree the details of the investment including:
- The rights and obligations of the investing parties
- The date of the investment and the voting rights attached to the shares to assist in the understanding of the control of the venture
- Number of shares purchased and the voting rights attached to the shares
- The nature of the profit-sharing arrangement between Winberry Plc and Durian Ltd
- The nature of access to LPS Ltd's assets under the terms of the agreement
- Confirmation that there is no restriction of the company's shared control of LPS Ltd
- Review board minutes to understand the business rationale for the investment
- Review minutes of relevant meetings between the company and Durian Co to confirm that control is shared between the two investors and to understand the nature of the relationship and the decision-making process, particularly if any party holds the right to veto decisions
- Obtain documentation such as LPS Ltd's organisational structure to confirm that the company has successfully appointed members to the board of the company and that those members have equal power to the members appointed by Durian Ltd

Maximum 7

(d) Generally, 1 mark for each explained or applied point:

- Management responsibility for laws and regulations, specifically data protection
- Auditor responsibility re non-compliance with law and regulations
- Auditor required to understand legal framework as part of understanding the business
- Evidence required to understand and evaluate the impact on FS
- Must perform procedures in this regard
- Reporting requirements (up to 3 marks)
- Confidentiality

Maximum 7

Professional marks

Communication

- Briefing note format and structure – use of headings/sub-headings and an introduction
- Style, language and clarity – appropriate layout and tone of briefing notes, presentation of materiality and relevant calculations, appropriate use of the CBE tools, easy to follow and

Marking guide	Marks
understand	
• Effectiveness and clarity of communication – answer is relevant and tailored to the scenario	
• Adherence to the specific requests made by the audit engagement partner	
Analysis and evaluation	
• Appropriate use of the information to determine and apply suitable specific calculations which are relevant to the scenario	
• Risk evaluation (RoMMs) is effectively prioritised, focusing on significance and only taking account of risks which would result in material misstatements	
• Balanced discussion of the issues connected to the auditor's responsibilities in relation to laws and regulations, resulting in a justified conclusion	
Professional scepticism and professional judgement	
• Displays scepticism by questioning and challenging management's treatment of specific accounting issues or the identification of unusual or unexpected movements, missing/incomplete information or challenging presented information	
• Determination and justification of suitable materiality level appropriately and consistently applied	
• Identification and recognition of indicators of possible management bias. Consideration of the impact on the financial statements and the possible reasons for management's preference for certain accounting treatments	
• Recognition of need to establish the audit status of the joint venture and make professional contact with the auditors of the joint venture	
• Effective application of technical and ethical guidance to effectively challenge and critically assess how management has responded to the data breach in the question	
Commercial acumen	
• Use of effective examples and/or calculations from the scenario to illustrate points or recommendations	
• Appropriate use of the industry information to evaluate business risks	
Maximum	10
Total	50

Briefing notes

To: Olivia Fig, audit engagement partner

From: Audit manager

Subject: Audit planning in relation to Winberry plc

Date: 1 July 20X5

Introduction

These briefing notes have been prepared to assist in planning the audit of Winberry plc. The notes begin with an evaluation of the significant business risks facing the company and continue with an evaluation of the significant risks of material misstatement which should be considered in planning the audit. The risks of material misstatement have been structured to prioritise the risks in terms of the likelihood and magnitude of misstatement in relation to each risk. The notes also include the recommended principal audit procedures which have been designed in respect of the investment in Luxury Pet Supplies Ltd (LPS Ltd). Finally, the notes consider the audit implications of a cybersecurity attack which took place during the year.

(a) **Evaluation of significant business risks**

Damage to operations caused by the warehouse fire

The fire has caused the destruction of the warehouse servicing Winberry plc's northern customer base. Winberry plc will certainly incur higher costs to increase capacity at the existing warehouses and, more significantly, incur greater transport costs by using alternative warehouses to supply this region. If there is disruption to services due to an interruption of grocery service, then this will cause a detrimental effect to Winberry plc's reputation which is likely to result in a fall in sales and profit. The damage to Winberry plc's business could be amplified by the fact that online grocery delivery is a growing market and a failure to adequately service new customers to the sector could restrict this growth opportunity.

International expansion

The expansion into Farland introduces a business risk in that the company will be managing operations in a foreign country for the first time. Farland may have different laws and regulations compared to the UK, so there is a heightened risk of non-compliance. The types of groceries typically bought by consumers in Farland may be different from in the UK and management may not have experience in their procurement, distribution and sale. There are also risks associated with Winberry plc's ability to set up an overseas distribution network, including the warehouses, delivery vehicles and suitably qualified staff and to comply with foreign legislation. All of these issues create a risk that the international expansion may not be successful, and at the same time will represent a drain on management's time and resources. Operations in the UK may suffer as a result.

Investment in LPS Ltd

The joint venture represents a new method of expansion for Winberry plc and introduces a possible reputational risk if they are unable to replicate their own high standards in the joint venture. Any quality issues with products or delivery problems with LPS Ltd could have repercussions for Winberry plc's reputation and this may, consequently, lead to a reduction in sales. There is also the possibility of a clash in management styles and techniques of the two different partners in the joint venture leading to conflict, which may affect the business strategy, management focus and consequently impact financial performance. Management may struggle to deal with the increased number of operations which they need to monitor and control, or they may focus so much on ensuring the success of the new joint venture that existing activities are neglected. These issues heighten the risk of the joint venture failing to be successful and produce a satisfactory return on the £30 million initial investment.

Loan finance

The £125 million expansion into Farland is to be funded by loan finance. The additional debt financing will increase Winberry plc's gearing and result in a higher business risk to ensure that the international expansion is successful and that the interest-bearing loan is covered without detriment to the cash flow of the existing business. Winberry plc's existing bank loans have the covenant that interest cover must remain above 3. The expansion and additional proposed loan will therefore make it more difficult to maintain the required interest cover level and if the international expansion fails, Winberry plc is at risk of defaulting on the bank covenant and the bank recalling the loan.

Due to the recent joint venture, rapid growth in sales and the planned expansion into Farland, Winberry plc is at risk from overtrading. The current management team may not be able to adequately control the high level of growth and may neglect Winberry plc's core business, causing loss of market share. This is particularly heightened as the home delivery grocery market is noted as experiencing high levels of growth and will attract strong competition.

Eco-friendly delivery vans

The eco-friendly delivery vans have been noted as causing delays of up to four hours, which will cause inconvenience to Winberry plc's customers and reputational damage. Winberry plc's customers value the convenience of grocery delivery, and a four-hour delay would severely negate this perceived benefit. Winberry plc would be likely to lose customers if the delivery delays continue and therefore sales and profits would suffer, as well as the company having to bear the cost of any compensation or refunds which could be claimed by customers for the delays to their deliveries.

Legal case

The legal case being brought against Winberry plc by local residents regarding the warehouse which was destroyed by fire will first cause reputational damage when the media report on the case and Winberry plc is associated with toxic fumes and damage to public health. The result of the internet search demonstrates that the case is already reported in the public domain and therefore some reputational damage is likely, thereby reducing sales and profits. There is also the business risk that the legal case will require defending or settlement and therefore legal fees or compensation payments will be incurred, with a further risk of having to pay damages and fines if Winberry plc is found liable of damaging public health through toxic fumes from the warehouse fire. The information provided regarding Winberry plc's staff circumventing safety controls increases the likelihood that Winberry plc will be found negligent and possibly lose the legal case.

Cyberattack

The internet search, if accurate, states that the company had not fulfilled the requirements of the data protection legislation and corporate governance principles. This may result in reputational damage to the firm as well as the possible requirement to pay fines or penalties which both could result in cash outflows from Winberry plc, whether it is by cash payments or reduced sales. The risk of a fine or penalty is increased due to the fact that the directors of Winberry plc have not reported the breach to the regulator. The apparent concealment of the data breach, by management not reporting the issue to regulators, may also indicate a lack of integrity or a lack of understanding by management, of law and regulations. The audit team should also consider the impact on the reliance on corporate governance matters concerning the business.

> **Tutorial note.** Credit will be given to candidates who refer to the potential corporate governance issues due to Winberry plc being a listed company.

Perishable products

The nature of Winberry plc's grocery delivery is that a large proportion of inventory is perishable and therefore has a limited shelf-life. The perishable nature of the goods results in any delays to delivery, such caused by the breakdown of the eco-friendly delivery vans, having a greater impact to the profits of Winberry plc than if the goods were not perishable. This means that there is a significant risk to the business of wastage and any inefficiency in storage or distribution will increase spoilage of inventory and result in a loss of profit for Winberry plc. In addition, the joint venture of LPS Ltd will introduce a new range of perishable products which will have different storage requirements.

(b) **Evaluation of significant risks of material misstatement**

Materiality

For the purposes of these briefing notes, the following overall materiality level will be used to assess the significance of identified risks and as requested this has been based on the profitability of the company.

Benchmarks

5–10% of profit before tax = range of £2·65 million–£5·3 million

This benchmark is only a starting point for determining planning materiality and professional judgement will need to be applied in determining a final level to be applied during the course of the audit. This is an existing client, and we have cumulative knowledge and experience of Winberry plc, however, the changes to the company's operations in the year increase the level of risk in the current year. Therefore, materiality has been based on 7·5% of profit before tax at £3·975 million and has been set at £4 million.

Financial analysis

Revenue is projected to increase by 66·8%, operating profit by 56·4% and profit before tax by 71%, all of which are broadly consistent with each other. During the year, Winberry plc has a new premium delivery pass revenue stream; however, this is not sufficient to explain the projected increase in revenue.

Total assets are forecast to increase by 8·3% which may seem overly optimistic given that a large warehouse has been destroyed by fire during the year without being written down, and Winberry plc is accounting for the assets of the new joint venture in LPS Ltd in their entirety by incorrectly consolidating LPS Ltd as a subsidiary. There is a risk that assets are overstated.

Warehouse fire

The most significant identified risk would be the assessment of the carrying amount of the fire damaged warehouse which is clearly above the materiality threshold of £4 million. The damage to the warehouse should have triggered an impairment review, as required by IAS® 36 *Impairment of Assets*. However, the finance director has wrongly assumed that the insurance cover on the warehouse relieves Winberry plc of the requirement to properly assess the impairment of the warehouse and perform the calculations in accordance with IAS 36. Impairment is measured by comparing the carrying amount of an asset with its recoverable amount. The recoverable amount is the higher of value in use and fair value less costs to sell the asset. The significance of the warehouse fire is not simply a quantitative one, but also an indicator of potential management bias and the impact of their judgement on the financial statements. The risks of material misstatement regarding this issue are, therefore, of high significance to the audit team.

As the warehouse has been destroyed by the fire, it is likely that the value in use is nil and the fair value less costs to sell would also have to consider the warehouse in its current condition as the warehouse is badly damaged and the machinery needs to be completely replaced. According to IAS 36, the cash flow projections which are used to determine the value in use of the impaired asset should relate to the asset in its current condition – expenditures to improve or enhance the asset's performance should not be anticipated, however, the finance director has not carried out an impairment review as he is confident the company's insurance policy will cover the cost of reinstating it to its previous condition. This is against the criteria of IAS 36 and there is a risk that property, plant and equipment is overstated and the impairment cost is understated.

In addition, it is important that any amount claimed through the insurance policy is recognised separately from the warehouse. It is important that the current status of the insurance claim is verified during the audit process and, if necessary, prior to the completion of the audit. This will determine to what extent the warehouse should be impaired in the financial statements.

Investment in LPS Ltd

The financial information shows that LPS Ltd revenue is projected to reach £10 million this year. The investment is expected to occur in August 20X5, so based on these projections the £10 million revenue is for a maximum of two months, which is clearly above the determined materiality threshold. Winberry plc is also recognising the total assets of the joint venture of £60 million which is also in excess of the materiality threshold.

From the information provided in the extract from the management accounts, it seems that the investment is a joint venture, with control of LPS Ltd shared between Winberry plc and Durian Ltd. IFRS® 11 *Joint Arrangements* defines a joint venture as a joint arrangement whereby the parties who have joint control of the arrangement have rights to the net assets of the arrangement. IFRS 11 requires that a joint venturer recognises its interest in a joint venture as an investment and shall account for that investment using the equity method in accordance with IAS 28 *Investments in Associates and Joint Ventures*. The finance director

ANSWERS

has stated that he intends to consolidate the results of LPS Ltd; the share of the results attributable to Durian Ltd is shown as a non-controlling interest. The finance director believes that despite Winberry plc and Durian Ltd each owning 50% of LPS Ltd and having equal representation on the board of directors, Winberry plc's contribution of knowledge to the joint venture is greater and therefore Winberry plc should consolidate the investment as a subsidiary. This treatment is contrary to IFRS 11, whereby the control is considered to be joint if the investors in the venture have equal shareholdings and equal representation on the board of directors. There is no evidence that Winberry plc holds a right to veto decisions, which is a possible way the finance director could justify that Winberry plc holds overall control and would be entitled to consolidate LPS Ltd.

The impact of the full consolidation of LPS Ltd by Winberry plc as a subsidiary would not have a net effect of overstating Winberry plc's retained profit or net assets. This is because the non-controlling interest of Durian Ltd would be represented on the statement of profit or loss and statement of financial position. The attributable profit and equity of non-controlling interests belonging to Durian Ltd would be shown in the proportion agreed of 50%, however, the gross totals of all areas in Winberry plc's statement of financial position and profit or loss would be inflated by LPS Ltd being incorrectly consolidated as a subsidiary undertaking. The consolidation of the full results of LPS Ltd would, however, increase Winberry plc's revenue, operating profit and total assets which may be the motivation for the finance director to claim that Winberry plc controls LPS Ltd and is entitled to fully consolidate the results.

Revenue recognition – premium delivery pass

There is a risk arising from Winberry plc recognising revenue for customers in advance of the satisfaction of the performance obligation for the annual premium delivery pass, with revenue recognised when the invoice is sent to the customer. This is leading to early recognition of revenue, i.e. recognising prior to the company providing a service to its customers. IFRS 15 *Revenue from Contracts with Customers* requires that revenue is recognised when a performance obligation is satisfied by transferring a promised good or service to a customer. As the premium delivery pass covers 12 months and the company is providing the service over time, it can be difficult to determine how much service has been provided and therefore the amount of revenue which can be recognised at a particular point in time. It does not appear that the requirements of IFRS 15 are being adhered to and there is a risk that revenue is being overstated and the associated contract obligation is understated.

Winberry plc also has a further revenue recognition risk that revenue from orders is recognised at the point of order rather than at the time of delivery. As previously stated, IFRS 15 states that revenue is recognised when a performance obligation is satisfied and in Winberry plc's case, this would be when the goods are delivered to the customer. There is a risk that revenue is being overstated and the associated contract obligation is understated.

Corporate governance

The recent cybersecurity attack could highlight that internal controls are deficient within the company. Even though this particular problem has now been rectified, if Winberry plc had not properly identified or responded to these cybersecurity risks, there remains the possibility that there could be other areas which are deficient, leading to control risk. The issue also indicates that the audit committee is not appropriately fulfilling its responsibilities with regards to internal audit in accordance with the UK Corporate Governance Code, which could indicate wider weaknesses in the company's corporate governance arrangements and resulting in increasing risk of material misstatement.

Legal provision

The internet search results show that a legal case was brought against Winberry plc in January 20X5. From the information provided, it is not possible to determine if the amount involved is material, however, there should be appropriate consideration as to whether the court case gives rise to an obligation at the reporting date. According to IAS 37 *Provisions, Contingent Liabilities and Contingent Assets*, a provision should be recognised as a liability if there is a present obligation as a result of past events which gives rise to a probable outflow of economic benefit which can be reliably measured. The warehouse fire is a known event, so if there has been harm brought about to people in the local area as result of this, then it is feasible that there is a liability as a result of a past event. A risk of material misstatement therefore arises that if any necessary provision is not recognised, liabilities and expenses will be understated. If there is a possible obligation at the reporting date, then disclosure of the contingent liability should be made in the notes to the financial statements. There is a risk of inadequate disclosure; this is a risk whether the situation gives rise to a provision or a contingent liability, as provisions also have disclosure requirements which may not be complied with.

A further risk is that any legal fees associated with the claim have not been accrued within the financial statements. As the claim has arisen during the year, the expense must be included in this year's profit or loss account, even if the claim is still on-going at the year end.

The fact that the legal claim was not discussed at the meeting with the audit partner may cast doubts on the overall integrity of senior management, and on the credibility of the financial statements. Management representations should be approached with a degree of professional scepticism during the audit.

Pressure on results

The company is a listed entity and the shareholders will be looking for a return on their investment in the form of a dividend payment and there will be pressure for the company to show good financial performance; this is compounded by the company's ambitious international expansion plans and the requirement to maintain adequate interest cover to continue to meet the bank's covenant. Pressure to return a better performance creates an incentive for management bias which means that management may use earnings management techniques, or other methods of creative accounting, to create a healthier picture of financial performance than is actually the case. This creates an inherent risk of material misstatement, at the financial statement level. Management bias could also have led to some of the accounting treatments suggested by the finance director, such as the early recognition of revenue from the premium delivery pass, which works to improve the company's profit and total assets for the year.

Eco-friendly delivery vans

The eco-friendly delivery vans noted in the internet search total £4 million (80 x £50,000) and this meets the threshold of materiality. There is a risk, however, that the eco-friendly delivery vans are impaired as the ability of the vans to make deliveries in line with Winberry plc's delivery schedules appears to be reduced. Impairment is measured by comparing the carrying amount of an asset with its recoverable amount. The recoverable amount is the higher of value in use and fair value less costs to sell the asset. There is a risk that the value in use is lowered due to the reduced ability of the eco-friendly vans to deliver goods efficiently and effectively. The fair value less costs to sell of the assets may also be impacted by the delivery range of the vans. There is a risk that the carrying amount of the eco-friendly vans is overstated and the impairment expense is understated.

Conclusion

The risks of material misstatement have been ordered with regard to the estimated magnitude of any misstatement and the likelihood of such a misstatement occurring. For example, the warehouse fire is the highest quantitative area which is deemed to be at risk of material misstatement, is newly occurring in the year and there is a significant risk of management bias in the measurement of the impairment. Similarly, the joint venture with Durian Ltd is quantitatively material and a fundamental change in both operation and accounting for Winberry plc, so deemed high risk. In contrast, the eco-friendly delivery vans are borderline to the stated threshold of materiality and therefore at lower risk of material misstatement than the other risks as outlined above.

In conclusion, Winberry plc has a significant number of audit and business risks which could result in material misstatement in the financial statements. Quince & Co should reassess their assessed level of planning materiality to ensure that the risk profile of the company is adequately reflected in the level of testing planned. The audit should be planned to assign highly competent staff for the high risk, judgemental areas of the audit such as the impairment of the fire damaged warehouse.

Tutorial note. Credit can be awarded where the candidate assumes that the delivery pass revenue does not accrue evenly.

(c) **Audit procedures**

Principal audit procedures in respect of the classification of the investment in LPS Ltd

- Obtain the legal documentation supporting the investment and agree the details of the investment including:
  - The rights and obligations of the investing parties to understand the implications for the reporting by Winberry plc in the financial statements
  - The date of the investment
  - Number of shares purchased and the voting rights attached to the shares to assist in the understanding of the control of the venture
  - The nature of the profit-sharing arrangement between Winberry plc and Durian Ltd
  - The nature of access to LPS Ltd's assets under the terms of the agreement
  - Contact and communication with the auditors of the joint venture if not Quince & Co
  - Confirmation that there is no restriction of the company's shared control of LPS Ltd.
- Review board minutes to understand the business rationale for the investment and to assess the amount of control/existence of joint control of the venture.
- Review minutes of relevant meetings between the company and Durian Ltd to confirm that control is shared between the two investors and to understand the nature of the relationship and the decision-making process, particularly if any party holds the right to veto decisions.
- Obtain documentation such as LPS Ltd's organisational structure to confirm that the company has successfully appointed members to the board of the company and that those members have equal power to the members appointed by Durian Ltd.

(d) **Auditor's responsibilities in relation to an audit client's compliance with laws and regulations**

Winberry plc appears to be in breach of relevant law and regulations regarding the protection of customer data. ISA (UK) 250A *Consideration of Laws and Regulations in an Audit of Financial Statements* states that while it is management's responsibility to ensure the entity's operations are conducted in accordance with the provisions of laws and regulations, the auditor is responsible for obtaining sufficient and appropriate audit evidence regarding compliance with laws and regulations. Auditors need to assess the evidence especially where non-compliance has an impact on the financial statements or where any non-compliance will affect the entity's ability to continue its operations.

The auditor is required by ISA (UK) 315 (Revised) *Identifying and Assessing the Risks of Material Misstatement* to gain an understanding of the legal and regulatory framework in which the audited entity operates. This will help the auditor to identify non-compliance and to assess the implications of non-compliance. Therefore, the auditor should ensure they have a full knowledge and understanding of the UK data protection regulations in order to evaluate the implications of non-compliance by Winberry plc.

ISA (UK) 250A requires when non-compliance is identified or suspected, the auditor shall obtain an understanding of the nature of the act and the circumstances in which it has occurred, and further information to evaluate the possible effect on the financial statements. Procedures must be performed to obtain evidence about the instances of non-compliance in relation to the data protection breach, for example, discussions with management to understand how the data breach occurred.

In addition, the audit team should perform further procedures, for example, discussion with Winberry plc's legal advisers to understand the legal and operational consequences of the breach including likely fines and exposure to litigation and assess the materiality of such exposure.

ISA (UK) 250A requires the auditor to determine whether they have a responsibility to report the identified or suspected non-compliance to parties outside the entity. In the event that management or those charged with governance of Winberry plc fail to make the necessary disclosures to the regulatory authorities, Quince & Co should consider whether they should make the disclosure. This will depend on matters including whether there is a legal duty to disclose or whether it is considered to be in the public interest to do so. As Winberry plc has not yet notified the regulator or the affected users, Quince & Co should initially encourage the directors to report the issue themselves before making disclosures they deem are required under the auditor's obligations described above.

Auditors should comply with the fundamental principle of confidentiality, and if disclosure were to be made by the auditor, it would be advisable to seek legal advice on the matter.

Section B

2 Forsythia Group

Workbook references

Chapters 2, 4 and 9.

Top Tips

To score well on this question you needed to be familiar with the new suite of standards issued in relation to quality management. However, knowledge alone would not have been sufficient to gain you a pass on this question. Rather you needed to take this knowledge and apply it to the scenario provided and discuss, for example, how the lack of CFO time given to the audit team and the use of junior audit staff to audit intangibles contributed to quality management issues on the audit.

Easy marks

Easy marks were available for recognising that the acquisition of Robin Co should have been disclosed as a material non-adjusting event after the reporting period, and also for highlighting that a junior member of the audit team should not be auditing intangibles, particularly as this was the first year that development costs had been recognised and the matter could not be discussed with the CFO.

ACCA examining team's comments

Forsythia was a quality management question with a single requirement to evaluate quality management issues in relation to a group audit. Professional skill marks were available for analysis and evaluation, professional scepticism and judgement, and commercial acumen. It is the first quality management question under the new suite of quality management standards and candidates were provided with an article ahead of the session highlighting the main changes. Within the question, topics such as identification of increased aggregation risk, outsourcing of audit work, and ethical threats such as intimidation and self-interest were also examined.

Answers to this question were mixed. Candidates who answered the question from a practical approach, applying the principles of quality management to the scenario scored well. The majority of answers, however, were generic and unapplied, failing to demonstrate an understanding of how the principles of quality management were potentially breached in the scenario.

The question covered four specific situations which had been identified by the engagement quality reviewer through a review of the audit file. Further information regarding the audit process was obtained through discussion with the audit junior about their experience on the audit.

The first issue related to an acquisition made after the year end. This impacted the time the group chief finance officer (CFO) had available to engage with the audit team during the audit. In addition to the lack of the availability of the CFO, the acquisition had only been determined after the audit planning stage and was, therefore, not included in the audit plan. The audit plan had not been updated as a result of this new information and the CFO had dismissed the acquisition as not being a relevant matter for the current audit. The audit engagement partner agreed with the client position. As this would have formed a material subsequent event requiring disclosure, this was incorrect. Actions that were relevant here, in the pre issuance stage of the audit cycle, were to obtain the evidence that would be required to support the disclosures before the report is issued. Candidates who then went on to identify that the acceptance of the client's position on this, suggesting that the partner is either incompetent or too trusting of the client, were able to obtain professional marks for scepticism and acumen. It was pleasing to see that the majority of candidates were able to identify that the acquisition was relevant to the audit and why this was a significant issue. However, fewer candidates expanded on this conclusion to suggest further appropriate actions or why the situation might have arisen.

The second issue related to the outsourcing of revenue recognition in several subsidiaries to another audit firm, Camellia Associates, without checking the competence and objectivity of the firm beforehand. Most candidates identified that Camelia Associates should be assessed for these criteria and its work reviewed. Fewer candidates questioned the appropriateness of outsourcing such a material risk area, in particular, when one of the subsidiaries operated in a specialist industry. The main motivator for the outsourcing was to keep costs low and candidates were able to obtain professional skills marks for questioning why the costs needed to be minimised and whether there was a self-interest threat at play as a result of quoting an inappropriately low fee.

The third issue was the delegation of audit work on intangible assets to a junior member of the audit team. The majority of candidates were able to say that this was inappropriate due to the complexity of the area, and that the junior was likely to lack sufficient knowledge or experience. Fewer candidates explained why the intangible assets contained difficult judgements or why this was a higher risk this year (due to this being the first year in which development costs had been capitalised). Additional credit was available for those candidates who questioned whether the junior team member had been intimidated by having to approach the busy CFO for the information, or for assessing that the evidence obtained did not cover all the assertions relating to development costs and that all the evidence was internally generated.

The final issue in the question was centred around a subsidiary operating in the agriculture sector. Several issues arose with respect to this subsidiary, which potentially increased aggregation risk, and should have been subject to more detailed audit procedures. Many candidates were able to identify that this may increase aggregation risk. Stronger candidates correctly identified that it was likely to increase aggregation risk for qualitative reasons and that it increased aggregation risk quantitively in the previous year, which suggested failures in the previous audit too.

Surprisingly few candidates identified the serious breach in quality arising from the deletion of a section of the audit plan to cut costs. Those who did highlight this issue appropriately questioned the integrity of the person who deleted this and linked this back to the inappropriately low fee and the implication that profits were being prioritised over audit quality. Professional skill marks were available for candidates who demonstrated this professional scepticism.

Candidates were then able to score marks for a conclusion based on their analysis and were awarded professional skills marks for analysing the specific details in the scenario to demonstrate an understanding of the quality issues. This was achieved by explaining why there was an issue, not simply that there was an issue. Credit was also available for questioning why the issues arose and for recommending actions appropriate to the stage of the audit process, with stronger candidates stating that the auditor's report should not be issued until the issues were resolved and that sufficient appropriate evidence on which to base the audit opinion had been obtained.

Marking guide | **Marks**

1 mark for each well explained point and 0.5 mark for relevant trends to a maximum of 2 marks.

General

- Introduction/reason for EQR review as listed (ISQM (UK) 1)
- Additional procedures – examples

Robin Co

- Acquisition of Robin Co is a non-adjusting subsequent event
- Audit partner ignoring the event indicates lack of knowledge or desire to minimise audit costs

- Budget constraints are impediments to professional scepticism
- Audit planning should be revisited when new information come to attention of auditor
- Lack of competence/deliberate omission of information increases risk of material misstatement
- Audit procedures should be performed on this issue as a matter of urgency
- Implication for auditor's opinion if necessary, disclosures not made
- Discussion with the Group audit committee to discuss the disclosures to be made in the financial statements

Camelia Associates

- Should have been a review of work performed – further audit evidence is required
- Camelia Associates may not have sufficient knowledge/understanding of Group
- Increase in revenue and unusual activities increase the risk of inappropriate evidence
- Revenue contains risk of fraud so problematical to delegate this high-risk area of the audit
- The work performed should be subject to urgent review and further procedures may need to be performed

Development expenditure

- Possibility of inappropriate accounting treatment to increase profit
- Insufficient audit evidence obtained over assumptions, additional procedures should be performed

Yew Ltd

- Likely to increase aggregation risk (max 3 marks)
- If not identified as increasing aggregation risk, necessary audit procedures not performed
- Not engaging the consultant to save costs is not appropriate as ISQM (UK) 1 requires audit firms to allocate the resources on the engagement to ensure a quality engagement
- Possible that some risks have not been identified
- Audit strategy and audit plan should not be changed without justification and documentation
- Possible issue of integrity due to deleting audit working papers
- Overall conclusion on quality of work performed

Maximum	20

Professional marks

Analysis and evaluation

- Appropriate assessment of the issues raised in relation to audit quality, using examples where relevant to support overall comments
- Effective appraisal of the information to make suitable recommendations for courses of action which are appropriate for the stage of the audit process

Professional scepticism and professional judgement

- Effective challenge and critical assessment of how the audit was performed with appropriate conclusions
- Demonstration of the ability to probe into the reasons for quality issues including the identification of missing information or additional information which would be required

Commercial acumen

- Demonstrates commercial awareness regarding the impact of inherent issues on the quality of the engagement 5

Total 25

Forsythia Group – evaluation of audit quality

As the Forsythia Group is a listed entity, it is appropriate that an engagement quality review (EQR) is taking place. This is accordance *with International Standard on Quality Management* (UK) 1, which requires an EQR to be performed on the audit of listed entities.

Acquisition of Robin Ltd

The acquisition of a subsidiary after the financial year end should not be ignored by the audit team. This is an example of a subsequent event which, according to ISA (UK) 560 *Subsequent Events*, needs to be considered by the audit team because the event may need to be recognised or disclosed in the Group financial statements. In this case, the acquisition of a subsidiary after the year end is a significant non-adjusting event in respect of which no adjustment is needed to the financial statements, but disclosure should be made in the notes.

The audit engagement partner is therefore incorrect to agree with the chief finance officer's (CFO) assertion that the matter will only be recognised in next year's financial statements. Given that the subsidiary is forecast to increase Group revenue by 20%, it appears that the acquisition is material to the financial statements and audit procedures should be performed to determine and conclude on the disclosures necessary. The audit engagement partner's statement could indicate a concerning lack of knowledge or could be due to the apparent cost constraints on the audit, encouraging the partner to cut back on necessary audit work. ISA (UK) 220 (Revised) *Quality Management for an Audit of Financial Statements* includes budgets constraints as one of the key impediments to the exercise of professional scepticism on an engagement. Due to this cost pressure, the audit engagement partner could be failing to apply an appropriate level of professional scepticism by agreeing with the CFO and failing to challenge this assertion.

The leadership team of Magnolia & Co is responsible and accountable for firm-wide audit quality. As it is an audit partner who is at fault here, this suggests potentially wider quality risks within the audit firm, with implications for the quality of other audits performed by this audit partner and possibly other audit partners.

Audit planning should be revisited as the audit progresses. According to ISA (UK) 300 *Planning an Audit of Financial Statements*, the auditor shall update and change the overall audit strategy and the audit plan as necessary during the course of the audit. This may be the case when information comes to the auditor's attention which differs significantly from the information available when the auditor planned the audit procedures. Given the speed at which the acquisition of Robin Ltd has occurred, it is understandable why this acquisition was not known at the time of planning, but the audit engagement partner should have reacted to the acquisition of Robin Ltd by modifying the planned audit procedures as necessary. Audit procedures need to be performed as a matter of urgency to ensure that the audit team has sufficient and appropriate audit evidence with regard to the acquisition.

If the Group CFO is planning not to disclose information about the acquisition in this year's financial statements, this could indicate a lack of competence, or a deliberate intention to omit the necessary disclosures which would indicate a lack of integrity. In either case, this increases the level of audit risk, and further audit work may be needed with regard to other areas of the financial statements, for example, more specific procedures to look for significant subsequent events, such as reviewing the minutes of board meetings or correspondence with legal advisers.

If the necessary disclosures are not made in the Group financial statements, a material misstatement would exist, with implications for the auditor's opinion on the Group financial statements. The issue should be discussed with the Group audit committee once relevant audit procedures have been performed to determine the nature and extent of the disclosure to be made in the financial statements.

Delegation of audit work to Camelia Associates

It is not prohibited for audit work to be delegated to other audit firms. However, the evidence obtained should not just be accepted without proper review and the audit work of Camelia Associates cannot simply be relied upon, as suggested by the audit manager. ISA (UK) 220 (Revised) requires that the engagement partner shall determine, through review of audit documentation and discussion with the engagement team, that sufficient, appropriate audit evidence has been obtained to support the conclusions reached and for the auditor's report to be issued. Without review, the audit engagement partner cannot consider whether the evidence obtained has been performed in accordance with the audit plan or whether it is sufficient and appropriate to support the audit opinion.

Delegating the audit of revenue is particularly problematical given that the Group's revenue has increased significantly, by 14·2% this year. Camelia Associates has performed audit work on the revenue of material subsidiaries and they may not have appropriate knowledge and understanding of the Group to perform good quality audit work on this significant area of the audit, in particular in relation to the revenue generated by the subsidiary which operates in the agricultural industry. They may also not have sufficient resources to have performed the work to a good quality.

Camelia Associates is a firm of accountants – this does not necessarily mean that they are a registered audit firm and they may not be competent to conduct audit work. Even if Camelia Associates is a firm of auditors, they may not necessarily have experience of group audits including specialised activities such as agriculture, which increases the level of concern over the quality of audit evidence which has been obtained in respect of the Group's revenue. Further assessment of the competency and qualifications should be undertaken of Camelia Associates and to ensure that they are a registered firm of auditors.

Finally, ISA (UK) 240 *The Auditor's Responsibilities Relating to Fraud in an Audit of Financial Statements* requires the auditor to work on the presumption that there are risks of fraud in revenue recognition. Therefore, revenue is usually approached as a high-risk area of the audit, so the delegation of audit work in respect of revenue is likely to be inappropriate.

The work which has been performed by Camelia Associates should be fully reviewed in order to determine whether sufficient and appropriate audit evidence has been obtained in relation to revenue. Further audit procedures, such as analytical procedures on the revenue figures of the subsidiaries, may need to be performed by the audit team if the work of Camelia Associates cannot be relied upon or is insufficient.

Development expenditure

The accounting treatment of the capitalised development costs is also significant as this could indicate deliberate misapplication of the requirements of the relevant financial reporting standards in order to boost the profit reported by the Group during the year, as profit before tax has decreased by nearly 20% on the prior year. The fact that this is the first year in which development costs have been capitalised increases the risk that the accounting treatment is inappropriate.

Insufficient audit evidence has been obtained relating to the capitalised development expenditure. Confirming that a set of management assumptions agrees to the assumptions from another source does not provide evidence on the validity of the assumptions themselves. Further audit procedures need to be performed in order for the auditor to conclude on the appropriateness of the accounting treatment applied, for example, checking that the criteria for classification as development costs set out in IAS 38 *Intangible Assets* have been met.

ISQM (UK) 1 requires that individuals are assigned to perform activities within the system of quality management who have appropriate competence and capabilities, including sufficient time, to perform such activities. In this situation, assigning the audit of development expenditure to a junior member of the audit team is not appropriate. This issue should have been dealt with by a more senior member of the audit team, who could have been in a better position to discuss the matter with the Group CFO and would understand that further evidence is necessary before concluding on the appropriateness of the accounting treatment.

Yew Ltd

The audit engagement partner has suggested that Yew Ltd does not increase aggregation risk. Aggregation risk is the probability that the aggregate of uncorrected and undetected misstatements exceeds the materiality for the financial statements for the group as a whole. Based on the draft financial statements, Yew Ltd represents 13% of Group assets and 5% of Group revenue and based on the prior year financial statements, Yew Ltd represented 18% of Group assets and 5·7% of Group revenue in the previous year. Furthermore, the reduction in the value of its assets of 27·1% is unusual and significant.

Additionally, the operations of Yew Ltd are in the agricultural industry. This is a specialised industry and different from the main operations of the Group. This creates a significant risk of material misstatement which requires special audit consideration. Therefore, due to its operations differing from the rest of the Group, it is even more likely that Yew Ltd increases aggregation risk.

The audit quality risk raised is that Yew Ltd has not been identified as increasing aggregation risk at the planning stage of the audit either this year or in the prior year, and therefore some of the requirements of ISA (UK) 600 (Revised) in relation to aggregation risk are likely not to have been adhered to, for example, an inappropriate materiality level may have been used.

It is concerning that Yew Ltd was not identified as increasing aggregation risk in the previous year, when based on monetary values alone its assets made it significant to the Group. The rationale behind this needs to be investigated and additional audit work may need to be performed on Yew Ltd, including the engagement of the consultant to provide advice on the specialist aspects of Yew Ltd's operations. The cost involved should not be regarded as a deterrent.

It is also concerning that the consultant was not engaged due to cost pressure. ISA (UK) 220 (Revised) requires that the audit engagement partner shall take responsibility for consultation on difficult and contentious matters and deciding not to follow the audit strategy for the reason of saving costs is not appropriate. A lack of input and insight from the consultant could mean that audit risks specific to Yew Ltd have not been identified and that inappropriate and insufficient audit evidence has been obtained, with implications for both the individual financial statements of the company and the consolidated Group financial statements.

ISA (UK) 300 requires that any significant changes to the audit strategy or audit plan, including reasons for the changes, should be fully documented, and it appears that this has not happened. Sections of the audit strategy and audit plan should not be deleted, even if there are valid reasons for changes to them. There could be an integrity issue given that audit working papers have been deleted, perhaps in an attempt to conceal the fact that planned audit procedures have not been performed.

Conclusion

There are many concerns raised regarding the management of engagement quality, at least on the engagement of the Forsythia Group. Audits should be conducted with adherence to ISA (UK) 220 and it seems that this has not happened in relation to the audit of the Group. It appears that due to cost constraints, important elements of the audit plan have not been followed, and the audit has not been appropriately directed, supervised or reviewed. In accordance with ISQM (UK) 1, remedial actions in response to the identified deficiencies in audit quality should be designed and implemented.

Further work should be performed as necessary, and these issues resolved prior to the issuance of the auditor's report. The additional procedures to be performed could take some time, and it would be advisable to discuss with the client whether it is possible to extend the deadline for completion of the audit.

3 Geller Ltd

Workbook references

Chapters 10, 11 and 13.

Top Tips

Use the information in Exhibits 1 and 2 to inform your answers to parts (a) and (b) making sure that you consider the reasonableness and consistency of the assumptions used to produce the cash flow forecast.

Make sure you are technically precise in part (c) in terms of how the auditor's report may need to be modified.

Easy marks

There were easy marks available in part (a), for example, questioning the likelihood and timing of the Happy Travels range when the decision to sell the range has only just been made and assuming that the loan repayment date can be renegotiated.

ACCA examining team's comments

This was a completion question centred around the going concern assessment of an audit client in a declining market. Going concern and audit reporting are two areas most crucial for an auditor to understand but are two of the areas where overall candidate performance is disappointing. Candidates often do not demonstrate professional scepticism when auditing client information involving the future and often are unable to devise ways to assess the prospective financial information rather than the more historical information, which is examined at AA. This is compounded by a reluctance to evaluate opinion options rather than replicating a knowledge of the types of audit opinion that is examined already at AA.

Candidates who performed well on part (a) were able to link the assumptions to the specific business environment, demonstrating professional scepticism when questioning the basis of the judgements made by management. These stronger candidates gained credit for both technical marks for the specific evaluation points as well as professional skills marks for the demonstration of professional scepticism by challenging managements' assumptions with specific explanations. Marks were also available for the demonstration of commercial acumen when making this challenge. Examples of commercial acumen seen in candidates' answers included questioning whether the bank would agree to extend a repayment date given the current performance of the company, whether a higher interest rate might be charged by the bank on any extension of repayment due to the higher default risk the loan would carry or questioning management's assertion that books two and three in a series would sell more than book one, given that people generally would read book one in a series before moving onto a sequel.

Part (b) was either answered very well or very poorly. Those candidates who appreciated they needed to support the assumptions in the forecast with regard to future cash receipts did very well, with any valid procedure being awarded credit. Areas which attracted credit included verifying typical payment patterns for existing customers, quantifying the progress on obtaining digital publication rights from authors, identifying whether any potential buyers had expressed an interest in purchasing the Happy Travels range of books, and obtaining any contracts signed with digital outlets. Candidates were also credited for assessing the reliability of the first period of the forecast with the actual results to date during the forecast period.

A particularly useful approach by candidates was to take each of the assumptions in the cash flow being assessed and describing a procedure to assess whether it was reasonable. Weaker candidates who provided generic procedures not tailored to the scenario obtained little credit – for example, reference to a written management representation supporting the information or generic reviews of board minutes.

It is also important to note that some superficially similar procedures have very different levels of validity in this situation. For example, comparing customer payment patterns to historical payment trends and credit terms to help assess whether the pattern of receipts from customers settling sales invoices is valid. Comparing forecast sales receipts to historical sales levels is not appropriate, as we are told that the market and sales levels have been declining year on year, yet management are predicting growth this year. This means last year's sales are not indicative of the forecast sales, so the comparison is not appropriate.

It was disappointing to note that candidates performed poorly on part (c). Candidates were told that sufficient audit evidence had not been obtained to allow the auditor to conclude on the appropriateness of preparing the financial statements on a going concern basis. The audit assistant had proposed using a material uncertainty relating to going concern paragraph

(MURGC) as the client management had agreed full disclosure of the going concern uncertainties in the financial statements (Exhibit 1):

Candidates should have explained that the MURGC paragraph is used when the audit opinion is unmodified, and the client has made adequate disclosure of the uncertainty.

Candidates were expected to assess whether it was appropriate to propose the unmodified opinion, using the information in the scenario to make the determination: The information stated that the auditor could not obtain sufficient appropriate audit evidence to support the assumptions in the cash flow. When the auditor has not been able to obtain sufficient appropriate audit evidence over a material aspect of the financial statements, there are two options for the opinion:

(1) A qualified opinion on the basis of the inability to obtain sufficient appropriate audit evidence where the issue is material and not pervasive

(2) The auditor may provide a disclaimer where no opinion is issued if the matter is material and pervasive

Stronger candidates received credit for assessing and justifying whether this matter is pervasive to the financial statements. As it related to the going concern of the company, this would generally be considered pervasive, however, this is a matter of judgement. Candidates obtained credit for the act of making that judgement and the explanations given, and this was followed through to the audit opinion marks.

As with the rest of the exam, candidates could only pass this requirement when the answer was applied to the specific scenario in the question. A knowledge of different types of audit reports alone would not gain sufficient credit to pass this requirement. Professional skills marks associated with this part of question were awarded for analysis and evaluation in the context of the scenario and the use of judgement to determine an appropriate audit opinion.

Marking guide

Marks

(a) Generally, up to 1 mark for each relevant point of evaluation:

- Cash receipts from customers:
  - Creation of digital publishing division
  - Relationships with online retailers
  - Authors' permission for online versions of products
  - Sales from Chandler Muriel's books
- Sale of Happy Travels
- Operating expenses including advances to authors, royalties, marketing expenses for new Chandler Muriel books, digital book costs (licences, administration, software)
- Interest payments
- Loan repayment
- Missing tax expense
- Dividends
- Conclusion

Maximum — 10

(b)
- Notes of a discussion with appropriate personnel, e.g. sales director and commissioning editors, to obtain understanding of how management justify a 2% growth rate per six-month period given the company's recent declining revenues, including specific evidence relating to the company's plans to develop closer relations with online retailers
- Copies of any signed customer contracts, e.g. from physical or online retailers, and copies of market research performed on the company's product ranges to corroborate the forecast sales figures. This evidence should be both

ANSWERS

general in nature and also specific to the range of books to be published by Chandler Muriel, to justify the specific sales forecast in respect of this book series

- A copy of the signed contract between Geller Ltd and Chandler Muriel to confirm the expected publication dates of the books and the amounts of any advances and royalty payments due
- Relating to the plans to launch a full range of digital books and magazines:
  - Notes of a discussion with management regarding the process which has been made and confirmation that the author agreements have been obtained and the readiness of the digital platform
  - For a sample of authors, a copy of their agreement to allow Geller Ltd to create and publish digital versions of their books
- Notes of a discussion with management regarding the plans to sell the Happy Travels range, specifically to confirm:
  - whether any buyers have yet expressed an interest, and if so, the stage of any negotiations
  - understanding of the rationale used by management in using the multiple of annual sales model to estimate the potential sales value of Happy Travels
- Confirmation, from a review of board minutes, that the sale of the Happy Travels range has been discussed and approved by management
- Confirmation that the assumptions in relation to cash receipts underpinning the cash flow forecast are consistent with the audit team's knowledge of the business and the environment in which Geller Co is operating
- Sensitivity analysis performed on cash receipts by varying the key assumptions and an assessment of the impact of these variations on the company's forecast cash position
- Written representations from management confirming the reasonableness of their assumptions relating to cash receipts and that all relevant information has been provided to Bing & Co
- A review of the cash book from 1 April 20X5 to the date of the auditor's report, identifying any significant cash receipts which do not appear to have been included in the forecasts

Maximum 5

(c) Auditor's report

Up to 1 mark for each relevant point explained:

- If sufficient and appropriate evidence obtained, the assistant's suggestion would be appropriate
- But lack of evidence means that the opinion should be modified
- Likely to be both material and pervasive, so a disclaimer of opinion is appropriate **OR** Justification of a qualified opinion where the issue is deemed to be material and not pervasive
- Basis for Disclaimer of Opinion section to be provided (if deemed to be pervasive); **OR** Basis for Qualified Opinion section to be provided
- Other impacts on auditor's report (max 2 marks)

Tutorial note: Candidates must explain their rationale regarding the pervasiveness of the issue to gain the credit. A conclusion is required, and credit is awarded for justification and the correct impact on the auditor's report using that judgement.

Maximum 5

Marking guide	Marks
Professional marks	
Analysis and evaluation	
• Appropriate assessment of the issues raised in relation to Geller Ltd's going concern situation, using examples where relevant to support overall comments	
• Identification of omissions from the analysis with an effective appraisal of the information to make suitable recommendations for appropriate courses of action	
Professional scepticism and professional judgement	
• Effective challenge and critical assessment of how management has prepared the cash flow forecast, with appropriate conclusions	
• Balanced assessment and use of professional judgement of the information to conclude upon the appropriate audit opinion in the circumstances	
Commercial acumen	
• Appropriate recognition of the wider implications on the engagement, the audit firm and the company	
Maximum	5
Total	25

(a) **Evaluation of the assumptions used by management in preparing the cash flow forecast**

Cash receipts from customers

Management has assumed growth of 2% in each six-month period, which appears optimistic given that this year revenue has decreased by 20%, which is a continuation and worsening of a longer-term trend.

The assumptions underpinning management's expectation of a reversal in this downward trend in revenue both appear to be flawed for a number of reasons:

- First, the assumption that a full range of digital book and magazine titles will be available in August 20X5 seems extremely optimistic. The digital publishing acquisition is a recent event, and there is no indication from the information provided by management as to how a full digital offering will be created by August 20X5, which is only one month away.
- The cash flow forecast contains no specific expenditure relating to the creation of this digital portfolio, so it is unclear how this business development is supported given the apparent lack of resources being devoted to it.
- There are also no specific cash flows included in the forecast relating to forging closer connections with online retailers, so it is difficult to see how this assumption is supported.
- In addition, not all authors may give permission for their books to be converted into digital format, so the company may not be able to offer a full range, as is suggested.
- If the sale of the Happy Travels range goes ahead, the company will lose the cash receipts from sales of those titles.

Second, the assumption that Chandler Muriel's books will generate £250,000 each six-month period should be challenged, for the following reasons:

- The first book has apparently not sold well, so there is a question over whether this book, and the others in the series which are due to be published in the next two years, will generate this level of income.
- It may also be overly optimistic to assume that Chandler Muriel will be able to deliver the books for publication in quick succession, in time to meet the publication deadlines set by Geller Ltd.

- In addition, it seems odd that the income assumed to be generated is £250,000 per six months – this round sum figure should be challenged.
- With the publication of additional books in the series, it would be expected that the income stream would increase rather than remain static.

The final point in relation to the cash receipts from customers included in the forecast is that the 2% sales growth has not been applied consistently. The final six-month period, to 31 March 20X7, is based on a 5% increase in cash receipts. The reason for this should be challenged – it could be a genuine mistake, or it could be a deliberate manipulation. Without a 5% increase in the final six-month period, the cash position is negative, a motive for management bias in the calculations.

Cash receipt from sale of Happy Travels range

The decision to sell this range of books has only recently been made, and it may be optimistic to assume that the sale will actually go ahead, especially given the industry-wide deterioration in demand for printed books. Even if a buyer is found, the sale may not go ahead in January 20X6, which is only six months away.

In addition, the estimated cash receipt on sale should be challenged. Just because other ranges of books have successfully sold in the past, with a sale price based on a multiple of annual sales, it does not mean that the same model can be used for this particular range of books.

Management has an incentive to include an estimated sales receipt which will cover the bank loan repayment which is due to be paid, according to the forecast and presuming the repayment date is successfully extended, in September 20X6. This is a significant motivation for overestimating the amount to be raised on the sale of Happy Travels.

Operating expenses

It is overly simplistic to assume an increase in operating expenses of 1% per six-month period based on inflation. This may be an attempt to understate operating expenses and improve the appearance of the cash flow forecast. Some operating expenses may be missing, e.g. as mentioned above, any specific operating expenses required to create the digital range of books and magazines, and marketing expenses related to promoting sales using online retailers.

Operating expenses are likely to include advances paid to authors and royalty payments relating to the volume of sales of their books. If sales are expected to increase by 2% per six-month period, then royalty payments would be also expected to increase, but this does not appear to have been factored into the operating cash outflows.

In addition, there are no specific cash outflows in relation to the recently acquired digital publishing division, yet it is likely that significant costs and cash outflows are likely to be incurred in merging this into the existing business and preparing the digital books and magazines which are due to be launched next month.

Interest payments and other finance costs

This cash outflow is static at £125,000 until the point at which the forecast assumes that the loan will be repaid. This should be challenged, because the company is clearly using an overdraft for many months and will also need to utilise the undrawn borrowing facilities once the overdraft limit of £250,000 is breached – this is forecast to happen in the six-month period to 30 September 20X5. The finance costs should therefore increase and fluctuate, depending on the utilisation of the overdraft and borrowing facility which takes place.

In addition, assuming no finance costs in the final six-month period should be challenged – the company has a negative cash position forecast at 30 September 20X6, so there presumably will be some overdraft interest payments which will need to be made.

Loan repayment

It is not certain that the bank will agree to renegotiate the loan repayment date to 30 September 20X6, which is the date assumed in the cash flow forecast. This assumption may be over-optimistic and an attempt to move the timing of the significant cash outflow on the loan repayment to after the company has received the cash on disposal of Happy Travels (which itself is uncertain).

If the bank does not agree to change the repayment date, or if the sale of Happy Travels is delayed or does not take place, or does not raise at least £5 million, then it will not be possible for Geller Ltd to repay the bank loan. This would cause serious going concern problems, and therefore creates significant pressure on the company's management to manipulate the timing and the amount of the cash flows.

Tax expenses

There does not appear to be any cash flows relating to tax payments included in the forecast. If management is claiming that there will be no tax payments during the period covered by the forecast, this assertion needs to be approached with professional scepticism as it is unlikely that no tax payments at all will occur during this time. These payments may be deliberately omitted to improve the cash flow position as shown in the forecast.

Dividends

No dividend payments are included in the cash flow forecast, which could be a genuine situation if shareholders are not expecting to receive any dividend payment in the next few years. However, the omission of dividend payments could be a way for management to improve the cash flow forecast.

Conclusion

There is a significant risk that the assumptions used in preparation of the cash flow forecast are not realistic and have been applied to make the cash flow forecast look positive in an attempt to present a much more favourable impression of the company's going concern position to the audit team.

(b) **Evidence expected on cash receipts**

- Notes of a discussion with appropriate personnel, e.g. sales director and commissioning editors, to obtain understanding of how management justify a 2% growth rate per six-month period given the company's recent declining revenues, including specific evidence relating to the company's plans to develop closer relations with online retailers.
- Copies of any signed customer contracts, e.g. from physical or online retailers, and copies of market research performed on the company's product ranges to corroborate the forecast sales figures. This evidence should be both general in nature and also specific to the range of books to be published by Chandler Muriel, to justify the specific sales forecast in respect of this book series.
- A copy of the signed contract between Geller Ltd and Chandler Muriel to confirm the expected publication dates of the books and the amounts of any advances and royalty payments due.
- Relating to the plans to launch a full range of digital books and magazines:
  - Notes of a discussion with management regarding the process which has been made and confirmation that the author agreements have been obtained and the readiness of the digital platform.
  - For a sample of authors, a copy of their agreement to allow Geller Ltd to create and publish digital versions of their books.
- Notes of a discussion with management regarding the plans to sell the Happy Travels range, specifically to confirm:
  - Whether any buyers have yet expressed an interest, and if so, the stage of any negotiations; and
  - An understanding of the rationale used by management in using the multiple of annual sales model to estimate the potential sales value of Happy Travels.
- Confirmation, from a review of board minutes, that the sale of the Happy Travels range has been discussed and approved by management.

- Confirmation that the assumptions in relation to cash receipts underpinning the cash flow forecast are consistent with the audit team's knowledge of the business and the environment in which Geller Ltd is operating.
- Sensitivity analysis performed on cash receipts by varying the key assumptions and an assessment of the impact of these variations on the company's forecast cash position.
- Written representations from management confirming the reasonableness of their assumptions relating to cash receipts and that all relevant information has been provided to Bing & Co.
- A review of the cash book from 1 April 20X5 to the date of the auditor's report, identifying any significant cash receipts which do not appear to have been included in the forecasts.

(c) **Auditor's report**

The audit assistant is correct to identify that there is a significant going concern issue facing Geller Ltd due to the uncertainty over the sale of the Happy Travels publishing range, and as a consequence, the company may be unable to repay its borrowings. If sufficient evidence were available to support the use of the going concern basis of accounting in the financial statements and to confirm the adequacy of relevant notes to the financial statements, an unmodified opinion could be issued, and the auditor's report would include a Material Uncertainty Related to Going Concern section to highlight the issue for users of the auditor's report.

However, the lack of evidence over the assumptions used in the cash flow forecast and in particular in relation to the sale of the Happy Travels range means that the auditor should consider modifying the audit opinion in accordance with ISA (UK) 705 *Modifications to the Opinion in the Independent Auditor's Report*. ISA (UK) 705 requires that the auditor shall disclaim an opinion when the auditor is unable to obtain sufficient, appropriate audit evidence on which to base the opinion, and the auditor concludes that the possible effects on the financial statements of undetected misstatements, if any, could be both material and pervasive.

The seriousness of the going concern problems facing Geller Ltd, particularly whether the company will be able to use the sales proceeds from the sale of the Happy Travels range to repay its borrowings, should be considered both material and pervasive as it impacts on the survival of the company.

When the auditor disclaims an opinion due to an inability to obtain sufficient, appropriate audit evidence, ISA (UK) 705 requires that the auditor shall:

- State that the auditor does not express an opinion on the financial statements;
- State that, because of the significance of the matter(s) described in the Basis for Disclaimer of Opinion section, the auditor has not been able to obtain sufficient, appropriate audit evidence to provide a basis for an audit opinion on the financial statements; and
- Instead of stating the financial statements have been audited, state that the auditor was engaged to audit the financial statements.

A Basis for Disclaimer of Opinion section should be included in the auditor's report to explain the reasons for the inability to obtain sufficient, appropriate evidence.

> **Tutorial note.** Credit is awarded where candidates assess and **justify** that the impact on the financial statements is not pervasive. Credit is awarded for concluding, based on this justification, that a qualified audit opinion is appropriate, as the issue of the inability to obtain sufficient, appropriate evidence is material but not pervasive.

Tell us what you think

Got comments or feedback on this book? Let us know.
Use your QR code reader:

Or, visit:
https://bppgroup.fra1.qualtrics.com/jfe/form/SV_9TrxTtw8jSvO7Pv

Need to get in touch with customer service?

www.bpp.com/request-support

Spotted an error?

www.bpp.com/learningmedia/Errata